Education State Rankings
2008–2009

Other titles in the State Fact Finder series

City Crime Rankings

Crime State Rankings

Health Care State Rankings

State Rankings

State Trends

Education State Rankings
2008–2009

PreK–12 Education in the 50 United States

Seventh Edition

Kathleen O'Leary Morgan
and
Scott Morgan

Editors

CQ PRESS

A Division of SAGE

Washington, D.C.

CQ Press
2300 N Street, NW, Suite 800
Washington, DC 20037

Phone: 202-729-1900; toll-free, 1-866-4CQ-PRESS (1-866-427-7737)

Web: www.cqpress.com

Cover design: Silverander Communications
Cover photo: "Science Student" from iStock

♾The paper used in this publication exceeds the requirements of the American
National Standard for Information Sciences—Permanence of Paper for Printed
Library Materials, ANSI Z39.48-1992.

Printed and bound in the United States of America

12 11 10 09 08   1 2 3 4 5

ISBN 978-0-87289-931-5

Contents

Detailed Table of Contents

III. GRADUATES AND ACHIEVEMENT

IV. SAFETY AND DISCIPLINE

V. SPECIAL EDUCATION

Preface

How much are teachers paid in your state? What portion of state education funds are used for classroom instruction? How much funding does the federal government contribute for elementary and secondary education? How safe are public schools? What are the average reading and math scores for students in your state? Discover the answers to these and hundreds of other questions in this newly updated edition of *Education State Rankings*.

Although the federal No Child Left Behind Act has been in effect since 2002, the debate continues about whether the law has brought positive change to America's public schools. Policymakers and administrators at all levels of government still cannot agree on how best to achieve excellence in public education. Given these differences of opinion, access to straightforward, unbiased, and reliable state elementary and secondary education information is more important than ever. *Education State Rankings 2008–2009* provides just that, offering a large collection of user-friendly state statistics on school districts and facilities, finance, graduation and achievement, test scores, school safety, special education, teachers and staff, enrollment, and much more.

Notes for *Education State Rankings 2008–2009*

Our goal in publishing *Education State Rankings* is to translate the thousands of education statistics available through federal and state governments and education interest groups into instantly understandable and meaningful state comparisons.

We have made every effort to ensure that this seventh edition of *Education State Rankings* offers readers a collection of reliable, well-organized statistics. Data are presented in alphabetical and rank order, so readers can easily locate information for a particular state and just as quickly learn where that state ranks among the others. Sources and other important information are clearly shown at the bottom of each page, and national totals, rates, and percentages are prominently displayed at the top of each table. Alternating lines of the tables are shaded in gray for easier reading. In addition, we provide numerous information-finding tools: a thorough table of contents, table listings at the beginning of each chapter, a detailed index, and a glossary of key terms. We have also included a roster of sources and their addresses, phone numbers, and Web sites.

The statistics in *Education State Rankings 2008–2009* require no additional calculations. All states are ranked from highest to lowest: for ties within a given ranking, the states are listed alphabetically. Negative numbers appear in parentheses. In tables with national totals (as opposed to rates, per capita data, and the like), a separate column shows the percentage of the national total represented by each state. This column—headed by "% of USA"—is particularly interesting when compared with a state's share of the nation's population.

Among the more interesting tables in *Education State Rankings* are those in which we have combined data from various sources. These are tables sourced as "CQ Press using data from . . ." Estimated graduation rates, special education, pupil–teacher ratios, and public education expenditures for salaries, wages, and benefits per teacher are just a few examples of these editor-generated statistical comparisons.

For those researchers who are interested in focusing on elementary and secondary education in just one state, we offer our *Education State Perspective* series. These twenty-page, comb-bound reports feature data and ranking information for a single state pulled from *Education State Rankings 2008–2009*. (For example, *Connecticut Education in Perspective* contains preK–12 education information for Connecticut only.) *Education State Rankings* is also available electronically, on CD-ROM. For more information, please contact CQ Press customer service at 1-866-427-7737.

Which Is the Smartest State?

We take great pride in presenting straightforward and unbiased statistics. Each year, we also conduct an analysis of the numbers in an effort to determine which state is "smartest." The results of this analysis—based on twenty factors that reflect excellence in the classroom, a strong commitment to students and teachers, and efficient public schools—appear on page xvii.

Exciting Changes for Morgan Quitno Press

Since May 2007, Morgan Quitno's reference books have been published by CQ Press of Washington, D.C. A division of SAGE, CQ Press is the premier publisher of books, directories, periodicals, and electronic products on American government and politics.

Although our publishing structure has changed, our commitment to bringing the highest-quality publications to our customers has not. *Education State Rankings* is one of six titles in our series of easy-to-use, affordable reference publications.

We owe a huge "thank you" to the numerous education experts, librarians, and government officials who helped us navigate the world of education statistics. Many thanks as well to you, our readers, for offering invaluable feedback to help us continue to improve our books. We appreciate your support and look forward to providing you with top-quality reference titles for many years to come.

Kathleen O'Leary Morgan and Scott Morgan
Editors

Smartest State Award

Massachusetts is back! It has been three years since the Bay State last earned the coveted title of America's Smartest State. Vermont held first place honors in 2005, 2006, and 2007, but this year, it could not beat Massachusetts's long-standing dedication to education.

The seventh annual Smartest State Award is based on twenty factors chosen from *Education State Rankings 2008–2009*. These key education indicators include expenditures for instruction, pupil–teacher ratios, high school graduation rates, student attendance, and proficiency in reading, writing, science, and math. Our goal is to measure states based on student achievement, spending that goes directly to the classroom, and personal attention from teachers.

Massachusetts excels in a number of important areas. The percentage of the state's students who are proficient in reading and math is the highest of any state. Massachusetts also ranks among the top three states in science and writing proficiency. In addition, the state boasts the lowest pupil–teacher ratio for its special education programs.

Joining Massachusetts at the top of the state rankings list are Vermont, New Jersey, Connecticut, and Wisconsin. At the opposite end of the rankings scale—unchanged from last year's rankings—Mississippi holds on to last place and is preceded by Nevada, Arizona, New Mexico, and Louisiana.

Methodology

To calculate the Smartest State Award rankings, we divided the twenty factors into two groups: those that are negative, for which a high ranking would be considered bad, and those that are positive, for which a high ranking would be considered good. The factors in this year's rankings are the same as those used last year.

We then processed rates for each of the twenty factors through a formula that measures how a state compares to the national average for a given category; the formula takes the positive and negative nature of each factor into account. Once these computations were complete, we assigned equal weights to each factor. Finally, we added these weighted scores to determine each state's final score.

The farther a state scores above the national average, the higher (and smarter) it ranks. The farther it scores below the national average, the lower (and less smart) it ranks. This same methodology is used for our annual Healthiest State, Safest and Most Dangerous State, and Safest and Most Dangerous City Awards.

Congratulations to the very smart students and teachers of Massachusetts!

Editors

Smartest State Award

2008–09	State	2007–08	Score	2008–09	State	2007–08	Score
1	Massachusetts	2	23.73	26	Florida	31	(1.23)
2	Vermont	1	22.94	27	Kentucky	32	(1.53)
3	New Jersey	4	19.98	28	Illinois	35	(1.92)
4	Connecticut	3	13.53	29	Delaware	30	(2.11)
5	Wisconsin	6	13.04	30	Colorado	23	(2.22)
6	Virginia	5	12.67	31	North Carolina	28	(2.38)
7	Montana	8	10.77	32	South Carolina	33	(2.44)
8	Maine	7	10.61	33	Utah	34	(2.99)
9	New Hampshire	12	10.33	34	Tennessee	36	(3.69)
10	Pennsylvania	9	10.11	35	Texas	29	(3.85)
11	Iowa	11	7.87	36	Arkansas	37	(4.52)
12	Minnesota	10	6.67	37	Georgia	40	(5.43)
13	New York	16	5.25	38	Oklahoma	39	(6.43)
14	Rhode Island	13	5.22	39	Alabama	42	(6.84)
15	Nebraska	15	4.99	40	Michigan	26	(7.29)
16	Maryland	17	4.76	41	Oregon	38	(7.38)
17	Idaho	14	4.70	42	West Virginia	41	(8.74)
18	Kansas	21	3.82	43	Hawaii	43	(8.94)
19	Indiana	22	3.15	44	Alaska	44	(12.01)
20	Missouri	18	3.04	45	California	45	(13.07)
21	Wyoming	20	2.88	46	Louisiana	46	(14.66)
22	North Dakota	19	2.63	47	New Mexico	47	(15.14)
23	Washington	27	0.77	48	Arizona	48	(15.65)
24	South Dakota	24	(0.67)	49	Nevada	49	(19.50)
25	Ohio	25	(1.14)	50	Mississippi	50	(20.24)

POSITIVE (+) AND NEGATIVE (-) FACTORS CONSIDERED:

Public Elementary and Secondary School Revenue per $1,000 Personal Income (Table 54) +

Percent of Public Elementary and Secondary School Current Expenditures Used for Instruction (Table 136) +

Percent of Population Graduated from High School (Table 181) +

Average Freshman Graduation Rate for Public High Schools (Table 181) +

Percent of Public School Fourth Graders Proficient or Better in Reading (Table 213) +

Percent of Public School Eighth Graders Proficient or Better in Reading (Table 226) +

Percent of Public School Fourth Graders Proficient or Better in Mathematics (Table 239) +

Percent of Public School Eighth Graders Proficient or Better in Mathematics (Table 252) +

Percent of Public School Fourth Graders Proficient or Better in Science (Table 265) +

Percent of Public School Eighth Graders Proficient or Better in Science (Table 273) +

Percent of Public School Fourth Graders Proficient or Better in Writing (Table 281) +

Percent of Public School Eighth Graders Proficient or Better in Writing (Table 289) +

Average Teacher Salary as a Percent of Average Annual Pay of All Workers (Table 393) +

Percent of School-Age Population in Public Schools (Table 413) +

Average Daily Attendance as a Percent of Fall Enrollment in Public Elementary and Secondary Schools (Table 428) +

Public High School Dropout Rate (Table 197) -

Special Education Pupil–Teacher Ratio (Table 366) -

Percent of Public Elementary and Secondary School Staff Who Are School District Administrators (Table 401) -

Public Elementary School Pupil–Teacher Ratio (Table 423) -

Public Secondary School Pupil–Teacher Ratio (Table 424) -

Previous Smart State Rankings

	'08–'09	'07–'08	'06–'07	'05–'06	'04–'05	'03–'04	'02–'03
Alabama	39	42	45	43	44	46	41
Alaska	44	44	46	44	45	23	25
Arizona	48	48	50	50	48	45	44
Arkansas	36	37	32	37	36	38	38
California	45	45	47	46	43	44	29
Colorado	30	23	27	23	21	35	27
Connecticut	4	3	3	2	2	3	1
Delaware	29	30	28	25	27	19	43
Florida	26	31	29	36	39	40	47
Georgia	37	40	41	40	38	36	40
Hawaii	43	43	42	42	42	43	45
Idaho	17	14	20	28	29	30	22
Illinois	28	35	35	32	24	27	33
Indiana	19	22	24	26	17	13	9
Iowa	11	11	9	14	8	8	11
Kansas	18	21	15	13	15	15	14
Kentucky	27	32	31	35	37	37	28
Louisiana	46	46	44	45	46	47	49
Maine	8	7	5	5	11	6	5
Maryland	16	17	18	19	18	18	30
Massachusetts	1	2	2	3	1	1	7
Michigan	40	26	39	27	31	20	20
Minnesota	12	10	13	6	7	12	12
Mississippi	50	50	48	49	47	48	48
Missouri	20	18	22	21	26	28	31
Montana	7	8	7	9	10	4	3
Nebraska	15	15	11	12	13	11	13
Nevada	49	49	49	47	49	49	46
New Hampshire	9	12	12	15	14	26	19
New Jersey	3	4	4	4	4	5	4
New Mexico	47	47	43	48	50	50	50
New York	13	16	16	10	6	10	26
North Carolina	31	28	23	22	25	21	24
North Dakota	22	19	21	20	19	24	21
Ohio	25	25	34	31	20	22	41
Oklahoma	38	39	36	39	40	39	32
Oregon	41	38	40	38	35	32	23
Pennsylvania	10	9	10	11	9	7	15
Rhode Island	14	13	14	16	23	16	10
South Carolina	32	33	26	29	32	41	36
South Dakota	24	24	17	18	22	31	34
Tennessee	34	36	30	41	41	42	39
Texas	35	29	25	24	33	34	16
Utah	33	34	38	33	28	25	17
Vermont	2	1	1	1	3	2	2
Virginia	6	5	6	7	12	17	37
Washington	23	27	33	30	30	33	35
West Virginia	42	41	37	34	33	29	18
Wisconsin	5	6	8	8	5	8	6
Wyoming	21	20	19	17	16	14	8

I. Districts and Facilities

Special Note for Districts and Facilities Chapter
At the time that *Education State Rankings* went to print, the National Center for Education Statistics (NCES) was delayed in issuing updated district and facility data for the 2006–2007 school year. Accordingly, statistics for the 2005–2006 school year are the most recent available and are provided in this chapter.

Once the new statistics are available, they will be posted on NCES' Common Core of Data Web site: http://nces.ed.gov/ccd.

Public Elementary and Secondary Education Agencies in 2006

National Total = 17,721 Agencies*

ALPHA ORDER

RANK	STATE	AGENCIES	% of USA
34	Alabama	165	0.9%
45	Alaska	54	0.3%
9	Arizona	601	3.4%
23	Arkansas	291	1.6%
2	California	1,128	6.4%
30	Colorado	201	1.1%
31	Connecticut	196	1.1%
47	Delaware	35	0.2%
42	Florida	74	0.4%
29	Georgia	204	1.2%
50	Hawaii	1	0.0%
37	Idaho	123	0.7%
3	Illinois	1,084	6.1%
18	Indiana	364	2.1%
17	Iowa	377	2.1%
21	Kansas	312	1.8%
31	Kentucky	196	1.1%
40	Louisiana	88	0.5%
20	Maine	329	1.9%
48	Maryland	25	0.1%
15	Massachusetts	495	2.8%
5	Michigan	831	4.7%
11	Minnesota	561	3.2%
35	Mississippi	163	0.9%
12	Missouri	532	3.0%
14	Montana	509	2.9%
13	Nebraska	514	2.9%
49	Nevada	18	0.1%
24	New Hampshire	264	1.5%
8	New Jersey	669	3.8%
39	New Mexico	89	0.5%
6	New York	819	4.6%
28	North Carolina	216	1.2%
25	North Dakota	245	1.4%
4	Ohio	1,044	5.9%
10	Oklahoma	600	3.4%
27	Oregon	221	1.2%
7	Pennsylvania	730	4.1%
46	Rhode Island	50	0.3%
38	South Carolina	102	0.6%
33	South Dakota	188	1.1%
36	Tennessee	136	0.8%
1	Texas	1,268	7.2%
41	Utah	82	0.5%
19	Vermont	363	2.0%
26	Virginia	226	1.3%
22	Washington	306	1.7%
44	West Virginia	57	0.3%
16	Wisconsin	460	2.6%
43	Wyoming	62	0.3%

RANK ORDER

RANK	STATE	AGENCIES	% of USA
1	Texas	1,268	7.2%
2	California	1,128	6.4%
3	Illinois	1,084	6.1%
4	Ohio	1,044	5.9%
5	Michigan	831	4.7%
6	New York	819	4.6%
7	Pennsylvania	730	4.1%
8	New Jersey	669	3.8%
9	Arizona	601	3.4%
10	Oklahoma	600	3.4%
11	Minnesota	561	3.2%
12	Missouri	532	3.0%
13	Nebraska	514	2.9%
14	Montana	509	2.9%
15	Massachusetts	495	2.8%
16	Wisconsin	460	2.6%
17	Iowa	377	2.1%
18	Indiana	364	2.1%
19	Vermont	363	2.0%
20	Maine	329	1.9%
21	Kansas	312	1.8%
22	Washington	306	1.7%
23	Arkansas	291	1.6%
24	New Hampshire	264	1.5%
25	North Dakota	245	1.4%
26	Virginia	226	1.3%
27	Oregon	221	1.2%
28	North Carolina	216	1.2%
29	Georgia	204	1.2%
30	Colorado	201	1.1%
31	Connecticut	196	1.1%
31	Kentucky	196	1.1%
33	South Dakota	188	1.1%
34	Alabama	165	0.9%
35	Mississippi	163	0.9%
36	Tennessee	136	0.8%
37	Idaho	123	0.7%
38	South Carolina	102	0.6%
39	New Mexico	89	0.5%
40	Louisiana	88	0.5%
41	Utah	82	0.5%
42	Florida	74	0.4%
43	Wyoming	62	0.3%
44	West Virginia	57	0.3%
45	Alaska	54	0.3%
46	Rhode Island	50	0.3%
47	Delaware	35	0.2%
48	Maryland	25	0.1%
49	Nevada	18	0.1%
50	Hawaii	1	0.0%
	District of Columbia	53	0.3%

Source: U.S. Department of Education, National Center for Education Statistics
   "2007 Digest of Education Statistics" (http://nces.ed.gov/programs/digest/index.asp)
*For school year 2005-2006. Agencies include regular school districts, regional education service agencies, state operated
agencies, federally operated agencies, and "other" agencies. Some states include each charter school as a separate agency.

Regular Public Elementary and Secondary School Districts in 2006

National Total = 14,166 Districts*

ALPHA ORDER

RANK	STATE	DISTRICTS	% of USA
32	Alabama	165	1.2%
43	Alaska	54	0.4%
23	Arizona	218	1.5%
22	Arkansas	253	1.8%
2	California	987	7.0%
27	Colorado	179	1.3%
31	Connecticut	166	1.2%
48	Delaware	19	0.1%
41	Florida	67	0.5%
26	Georgia	180	1.3%
50	Hawaii	1	0.0%
36	Idaho	122	0.9%
3	Illinois	875	6.2%
20	Indiana	294	2.1%
14	Iowa	365	2.6%
18	Kansas	300	2.1%
29	Kentucky	176	1.2%
40	Louisiana	68	0.5%
21	Maine	285	2.0%
47	Maryland	24	0.2%
15	Massachusetts	350	2.5%
7	Michigan	552	3.9%
16	Minnesota	343	2.4%
33	Mississippi	152	1.1%
9	Missouri	524	3.7%
13	Montana	430	3.0%
11	Nebraska	474	3.3%
49	Nevada	17	0.1%
27	New Hampshire	179	1.3%
5	New Jersey	615	4.3%
38	New Mexico	89	0.6%
4	New York	697	4.9%
37	North Carolina	115	0.8%
24	North Dakota	204	1.4%
6	Ohio	614	4.3%
8	Oklahoma	540	3.8%
25	Oregon	200	1.4%
10	Pennsylvania	501	3.5%
46	Rhode Island	32	0.2%
39	South Carolina	85	0.6%
30	South Dakota	168	1.2%
34	Tennessee	136	1.0%
1	Texas	1,035	7.3%
45	Utah	40	0.3%
17	Vermont	302	2.1%
35	Virginia	134	0.9%
19	Washington	296	2.1%
42	West Virginia	55	0.4%
12	Wisconsin	440	3.1%
44	Wyoming	48	0.3%

RANK ORDER

RANK	STATE	DISTRICTS	% of USA
1	Texas	1,035	7.3%
2	California	987	7.0%
3	Illinois	875	6.2%
4	New York	697	4.9%
5	New Jersey	615	4.3%
6	Ohio	614	4.3%
7	Michigan	552	3.9%
8	Oklahoma	540	3.8%
9	Missouri	524	3.7%
10	Pennsylvania	501	3.5%
11	Nebraska	474	3.3%
12	Wisconsin	440	3.1%
13	Montana	430	3.0%
14	Iowa	365	2.6%
15	Massachusetts	350	2.5%
16	Minnesota	343	2.4%
17	Vermont	302	2.1%
18	Kansas	300	2.1%
19	Washington	296	2.1%
20	Indiana	294	2.1%
21	Maine	285	2.0%
22	Arkansas	253	1.8%
23	Arizona	218	1.5%
24	North Dakota	204	1.4%
25	Oregon	200	1.4%
26	Georgia	180	1.3%
27	Colorado	179	1.3%
27	New Hampshire	179	1.3%
29	Kentucky	176	1.2%
30	South Dakota	168	1.2%
31	Connecticut	166	1.2%
32	Alabama	165	1.2%
33	Mississippi	152	1.1%
34	Tennessee	136	1.0%
35	Virginia	134	0.9%
36	Idaho	122	0.9%
37	North Carolina	115	0.8%
38	New Mexico	89	0.6%
39	South Carolina	85	0.6%
40	Louisiana	68	0.5%
41	Florida	67	0.5%
42	West Virginia	55	0.4%
43	Alaska	54	0.4%
44	Wyoming	48	0.3%
45	Utah	40	0.3%
46	Rhode Island	32	0.2%
47	Maryland	24	0.2%
48	Delaware	19	0.1%
49	Nevada	17	0.1%
50	Hawaii	1	0.0%
	District of Columbia	1	0.0%

Source: U.S. Department of Education, National Center for Education Statistics
"2007 Digest of Education Statistics" (http://nces.ed.gov/programs/digest/index.asp)
*For school year 2005-2006. Regular school districts are agencies responsible for providing free public education for school-age children residing within their jurisdiction. Included in these figures are districts that reported having no students. This can occur when a small district has no pupils or contracts with another district to educate the students under its jurisdiction.

Regular Public School Districts Providing Pre-Kindergarten to 12th Grade Education in 2006
National Total = 10,622 Districts*

ALPHA ORDER

RANK	STATE	DISTRICTS	% of USA
27	Alabama	147	1.4%
41	Alaska	53	0.5%
34	Arizona	98	0.9%
16	Arkansas	252	2.4%
8	California	394	3.7%
19	Colorado	179	1.7%
29	Connecticut	121	1.1%
48	Delaware	16	0.2%
38	Florida	67	0.6%
21	Georgia	177	1.7%
50	Hawaii	1	0.0%
33	Idaho	111	1.0%
9	Illinois	389	3.7%
14	Indiana	291	2.7%
11	Iowa	342	3.2%
13	Kansas	299	2.8%
23	Kentucky	171	1.6%
37	Louisiana	68	0.6%
32	Maine	114	1.1%
47	Maryland	24	0.2%
22	Massachusetts	176	1.7%
4	Michigan	524	4.9%
12	Minnesota	328	3.1%
26	Mississippi	148	1.4%
6	Missouri	449	4.2%
42	Montana	52	0.5%
15	Nebraska	254	2.4%
48	Nevada	16	0.2%
39	New Hampshire	65	0.6%
18	New Jersey	223	2.1%
35	New Mexico	89	0.8%
2	New York	677	6.4%
31	North Carolina	115	1.1%
25	North Dakota	154	1.4%
3	Ohio	612	5.8%
7	Oklahoma	429	4.0%
19	Oregon	179	1.7%
5	Pennsylvania	498	4.7%
46	Rhode Island	28	0.3%
36	South Carolina	85	0.8%
24	South Dakota	161	1.5%
29	Tennessee	121	1.1%
1	Texas	995	9.4%
44	Utah	40	0.4%
45	Vermont	35	0.3%
28	Virginia	134	1.3%
17	Washington	248	2.3%
40	West Virginia	55	0.5%
10	Wisconsin	369	3.5%
43	Wyoming	48	0.5%

RANK ORDER

RANK	STATE	DISTRICTS	% of USA
1	Texas	995	9.4%
2	New York	677	6.4%
3	Ohio	612	5.8%
4	Michigan	524	4.9%
5	Pennsylvania	498	4.7%
6	Missouri	449	4.2%
7	Oklahoma	429	4.0%
8	California	394	3.7%
9	Illinois	389	3.7%
10	Wisconsin	369	3.5%
11	Iowa	342	3.2%
12	Minnesota	328	3.1%
13	Kansas	299	2.8%
14	Indiana	291	2.7%
15	Nebraska	254	2.4%
16	Arkansas	252	2.4%
17	Washington	248	2.3%
18	New Jersey	223	2.1%
19	Colorado	179	1.7%
19	Oregon	179	1.7%
21	Georgia	177	1.7%
22	Massachusetts	176	1.7%
23	Kentucky	171	1.6%
24	South Dakota	161	1.5%
25	North Dakota	154	1.4%
26	Mississippi	148	1.4%
27	Alabama	147	1.4%
28	Virginia	134	1.3%
29	Connecticut	121	1.1%
29	Tennessee	121	1.1%
31	North Carolina	115	1.1%
32	Maine	114	1.1%
33	Idaho	111	1.0%
34	Arizona	98	0.9%
35	New Mexico	89	0.8%
36	South Carolina	85	0.8%
37	Louisiana	68	0.6%
38	Florida	67	0.6%
39	New Hampshire	65	0.6%
40	West Virginia	55	0.5%
41	Alaska	53	0.5%
42	Montana	52	0.5%
43	Wyoming	48	0.5%
44	Utah	40	0.4%
45	Vermont	35	0.3%
46	Rhode Island	28	0.3%
47	Maryland	24	0.2%
48	Delaware	16	0.2%
48	Nevada	16	0.2%
50	Hawaii	1	0.0%
	District of Columbia	1	0.0%

Source: U.S. Department of Education, National Center for Education Statistics
"Common Core of Data (CCD) Database" (http://nces.ed.gov/ccd/)
*For school year 2005-2006. Includes districts with beginning ranges of pre-kindergarten, kindergarten, or first grade and completion of 12th grade.

Percent of Regular Public Elementary and Secondary School Districts Providing Pre-Kindergarten to 12th Grade Education: 2006
National Percent = 74.8%*

RANK	STATE	PERCENT
31	Alabama	89.1
19	Alaska	98.1
43	Arizona	45.0
15	Arkansas	99.6
46	California	39.9
1	Colorado	100.0
40	Connecticut	72.9
35	Delaware	84.2
1	Florida	100.0
18	Georgia	98.3
1	Hawaii	100.0
29	Idaho	91.0
44	Illinois	44.5
17	Indiana	99.0
27	Iowa	93.7
13	Kansas	99.7
21	Kentucky	97.2
1	Louisiana	100.0
45	Maine	40.0
1	Maryland	100.0
42	Massachusetts	50.3
25	Michigan	94.9
24	Minnesota	95.6
20	Mississippi	97.4
34	Missouri	85.7
49	Montana	12.1
41	Nebraska	53.6
26	Nevada	94.1
47	New Hampshire	36.3
47	New Jersey	36.3
1	New Mexico	100.0
28	New York	92.7
1	North Carolina	100.0
39	North Dakota	75.5
13	Ohio	99.7
38	Oklahoma	79.4
30	Oregon	89.5
16	Pennsylvania	99.4
33	Rhode Island	87.5
1	South Carolina	100.0
23	South Dakota	95.8
32	Tennessee	89.0
22	Texas	96.1
1	Utah	100.0
50	Vermont	11.6
1	Virginia	100.0
37	Washington	83.8
1	West Virginia	100.0
36	Wisconsin	83.9
1	Wyoming	100.0

RANK	STATE	PERCENT
1	Colorado	100.0
1	Florida	100.0
1	Hawaii	100.0
1	Louisiana	100.0
1	Maryland	100.0
1	New Mexico	100.0
1	North Carolina	100.0
1	South Carolina	100.0
1	Utah	100.0
1	Virginia	100.0
1	West Virginia	100.0
1	Wyoming	100.0
13	Kansas	99.7
13	Ohio	99.7
15	Arkansas	99.6
16	Pennsylvania	99.4
17	Indiana	99.0
18	Georgia	98.3
19	Alaska	98.1
20	Mississippi	97.4
21	Kentucky	97.2
22	Texas	96.1
23	South Dakota	95.8
24	Minnesota	95.6
25	Michigan	94.9
26	Nevada	94.1
27	Iowa	93.7
28	New York	92.7
29	Idaho	91.0
30	Oregon	89.5
31	Alabama	89.1
32	Tennessee	89.0
33	Rhode Island	87.5
34	Missouri	85.7
35	Delaware	84.2
36	Wisconsin	83.9
37	Washington	83.8
38	Oklahoma	79.4
39	North Dakota	75.5
40	Connecticut	72.9
41	Nebraska	53.6
42	Massachusetts	50.3
43	Arizona	45.0
44	Illinois	44.5
45	Maine	40.0
46	California	39.9
47	New Hampshire	36.3
47	New Jersey	36.3
49	Montana	12.1
50	Vermont	11.6

| | District of Columbia | 100.0 |

Source: CQ Press using data from U.S. Department of Education, National Center for Education Statistics
  "Common Core of Data (CCD) Database" (http://nces.ed.gov/ccd/)
*For school year 2005-2006. Regular school districts are agencies responsible for providing free public education for school-age children residing within their jurisdiction. Included in these figures are 367 districts that reported having no students. This can occur when a small district has no pupils or contracts with another district to educate the students under its jurisdiction.

Public Elementary and Secondary Schools in 2006

National Total = 97,382 Schools*

<table>
<tr><td colspan="4">ALPHA ORDER</td><td colspan="4">RANK ORDER</td></tr>
<tr><th>RANK</th><th>STATE</th><th>SCHOOLS</th><th>% of USA</th><th>RANK</th><th>STATE</th><th>SCHOOLS</th><th>% of USA</th></tr>
<tr><td>23</td><td>Alabama</td><td>1,585</td><td>1.6%</td><td>1</td><td>California</td><td>9,650</td><td>9.9%</td></tr>
<tr><td>44</td><td>Alaska</td><td>502</td><td>0.5%</td><td>2</td><td>Texas</td><td>8,517</td><td>8.7%</td></tr>
<tr><td>17</td><td>Arizona</td><td>2,078</td><td>2.1%</td><td>3</td><td>New York</td><td>4,669</td><td>4.8%</td></tr>
<tr><td>32</td><td>Arkansas</td><td>1,138</td><td>1.2%</td><td>4</td><td>Illinois</td><td>4,401</td><td>4.5%</td></tr>
<tr><td>1</td><td>California</td><td>9,650</td><td>9.9%</td><td>5</td><td>Michigan</td><td>4,090</td><td>4.2%</td></tr>
<tr><td>21</td><td>Colorado</td><td>1,707</td><td>1.8%</td><td>6</td><td>Ohio</td><td>4,007</td><td>4.1%</td></tr>
<tr><td>33</td><td>Connecticut</td><td>1,111</td><td>1.1%</td><td>7</td><td>Florida</td><td>3,723</td><td>3.8%</td></tr>
<tr><td>50</td><td>Delaware</td><td>222</td><td>0.2%</td><td>8</td><td>Pennsylvania</td><td>3,250</td><td>3.3%</td></tr>
<tr><td>7</td><td>Florida</td><td>3,723</td><td>3.8%</td><td>9</td><td>Minnesota</td><td>2,644</td><td>2.7%</td></tr>
<tr><td>11</td><td>Georgia</td><td>2,389</td><td>2.5%</td><td>10</td><td>New Jersey</td><td>2,474</td><td>2.5%</td></tr>
<tr><td>49</td><td>Hawaii</td><td>285</td><td>0.3%</td><td>11</td><td>Georgia</td><td>2,389</td><td>2.5%</td></tr>
<tr><td>40</td><td>Idaho</td><td>706</td><td>0.7%</td><td>12</td><td>Missouri</td><td>2,361</td><td>2.4%</td></tr>
<tr><td>4</td><td>Illinois</td><td>4,401</td><td>4.5%</td><td>13</td><td>North Carolina</td><td>2,347</td><td>2.4%</td></tr>
<tr><td>18</td><td>Indiana</td><td>1,977</td><td>2.0%</td><td>14</td><td>Washington</td><td>2,269</td><td>2.3%</td></tr>
<tr><td>24</td><td>Iowa</td><td>1,512</td><td>1.6%</td><td>15</td><td>Wisconsin</td><td>2,246</td><td>2.3%</td></tr>
<tr><td>27</td><td>Kansas</td><td>1,407</td><td>1.4%</td><td>16</td><td>Virginia</td><td>2,079</td><td>2.1%</td></tr>
<tr><td>26</td><td>Kentucky</td><td>1,409</td><td>1.4%</td><td>17</td><td>Arizona</td><td>2,078</td><td>2.1%</td></tr>
<tr><td>28</td><td>Louisiana</td><td>1,390</td><td>1.4%</td><td>18</td><td>Indiana</td><td>1,977</td><td>2.0%</td></tr>
<tr><td>41</td><td>Maine</td><td>679</td><td>0.7%</td><td>19</td><td>Massachusetts</td><td>1,879</td><td>1.9%</td></tr>
<tr><td>25</td><td>Maryland</td><td>1,430</td><td>1.5%</td><td>20</td><td>Oklahoma</td><td>1,788</td><td>1.8%</td></tr>
<tr><td>19</td><td>Massachusetts</td><td>1,879</td><td>1.9%</td><td>21</td><td>Colorado</td><td>1,707</td><td>1.8%</td></tr>
<tr><td>5</td><td>Michigan</td><td>4,090</td><td>4.2%</td><td>22</td><td>Tennessee</td><td>1,700</td><td>1.7%</td></tr>
<tr><td>9</td><td>Minnesota</td><td>2,644</td><td>2.7%</td><td>23</td><td>Alabama</td><td>1,585</td><td>1.6%</td></tr>
<tr><td>34</td><td>Mississippi</td><td>1,051</td><td>1.1%</td><td>24</td><td>Iowa</td><td>1,512</td><td>1.6%</td></tr>
<tr><td>12</td><td>Missouri</td><td>2,361</td><td>2.4%</td><td>25</td><td>Maryland</td><td>1,430</td><td>1.5%</td></tr>
<tr><td>37</td><td>Montana</td><td>840</td><td>0.9%</td><td>26</td><td>Kentucky</td><td>1,409</td><td>1.4%</td></tr>
<tr><td>30</td><td>Nebraska</td><td>1,225</td><td>1.3%</td><td>27</td><td>Kansas</td><td>1,407</td><td>1.4%</td></tr>
<tr><td>42</td><td>Nevada</td><td>557</td><td>0.6%</td><td>28</td><td>Louisiana</td><td>1,390</td><td>1.4%</td></tr>
<tr><td>45</td><td>New Hampshire</td><td>480</td><td>0.5%</td><td>29</td><td>Oregon</td><td>1,260</td><td>1.3%</td></tr>
<tr><td>10</td><td>New Jersey</td><td>2,474</td><td>2.5%</td><td>30</td><td>Nebraska</td><td>1,225</td><td>1.3%</td></tr>
<tr><td>36</td><td>New Mexico</td><td>854</td><td>0.9%</td><td>31</td><td>South Carolina</td><td>1,152</td><td>1.2%</td></tr>
<tr><td>3</td><td>New York</td><td>4,669</td><td>4.8%</td><td>32</td><td>Arkansas</td><td>1,138</td><td>1.2%</td></tr>
<tr><td>13</td><td>North Carolina</td><td>2,347</td><td>2.4%</td><td>33</td><td>Connecticut</td><td>1,111</td><td>1.1%</td></tr>
<tr><td>43</td><td>North Dakota</td><td>539</td><td>0.6%</td><td>34</td><td>Mississippi</td><td>1,051</td><td>1.1%</td></tr>
<tr><td>6</td><td>Ohio</td><td>4,007</td><td>4.1%</td><td>35</td><td>Utah</td><td>956</td><td>1.0%</td></tr>
<tr><td>20</td><td>Oklahoma</td><td>1,788</td><td>1.8%</td><td>36</td><td>New Mexico</td><td>854</td><td>0.9%</td></tr>
<tr><td>29</td><td>Oregon</td><td>1,260</td><td>1.3%</td><td>37</td><td>Montana</td><td>840</td><td>0.9%</td></tr>
<tr><td>8</td><td>Pennsylvania</td><td>3,250</td><td>3.3%</td><td>38</td><td>West Virginia</td><td>784</td><td>0.8%</td></tr>
<tr><td>48</td><td>Rhode Island</td><td>338</td><td>0.3%</td><td>39</td><td>South Dakota</td><td>725</td><td>0.7%</td></tr>
<tr><td>31</td><td>South Carolina</td><td>1,152</td><td>1.2%</td><td>40</td><td>Idaho</td><td>706</td><td>0.7%</td></tr>
<tr><td>39</td><td>South Dakota</td><td>725</td><td>0.7%</td><td>41</td><td>Maine</td><td>679</td><td>0.7%</td></tr>
<tr><td>22</td><td>Tennessee</td><td>1,700</td><td>1.7%</td><td>42</td><td>Nevada</td><td>557</td><td>0.6%</td></tr>
<tr><td>2</td><td>Texas</td><td>8,517</td><td>8.7%</td><td>43</td><td>North Dakota</td><td>539</td><td>0.6%</td></tr>
<tr><td>35</td><td>Utah</td><td>956</td><td>1.0%</td><td>44</td><td>Alaska</td><td>502</td><td>0.5%</td></tr>
<tr><td>46</td><td>Vermont</td><td>392</td><td>0.4%</td><td>45</td><td>New Hampshire</td><td>480</td><td>0.5%</td></tr>
<tr><td>16</td><td>Virginia</td><td>2,079</td><td>2.1%</td><td>46</td><td>Vermont</td><td>392</td><td>0.4%</td></tr>
<tr><td>14</td><td>Washington</td><td>2,269</td><td>2.3%</td><td>47</td><td>Wyoming</td><td>379</td><td>0.4%</td></tr>
<tr><td>38</td><td>West Virginia</td><td>784</td><td>0.8%</td><td>48</td><td>Rhode Island</td><td>338</td><td>0.3%</td></tr>
<tr><td>15</td><td>Wisconsin</td><td>2,246</td><td>2.3%</td><td>49</td><td>Hawaii</td><td>285</td><td>0.3%</td></tr>
<tr><td>47</td><td>Wyoming</td><td>379</td><td>0.4%</td><td>50</td><td>Delaware</td><td>222</td><td>0.2%</td></tr>
<tr><td></td><td></td><td></td><td></td><td></td><td>District of Columbia</td><td>229</td><td>0.2%</td></tr>
</table>

Source: U.S. Department of Education, National Center for Education Statistics
 "Common Core of Data (CCD) Database" (http://nces.ed.gov/ccd/)
*For school year 2005-2006. Includes 2,579 schools without membership and 958 schools whose membership is reported for some other school.

Regular Public Elementary and Secondary Schools in 2006

National Total = 87,585 Schools*

ALPHA ORDER				RANK ORDER			
RANK	STATE	SCHOOLS	% of USA	RANK	STATE	SCHOOLS	% of USA
25	Alabama	1,352	1.5%	1	California	8,234	9.4%
45	Alaska	447	0.5%	2	Texas	7,240	8.3%
14	Arizona	1,877	2.1%	3	New York	4,374	5.0%
31	Arkansas	1,102	1.3%	4	Illinois	3,909	4.5%
1	California	8,234	9.4%	4	Ohio	3,909	4.5%
22	Colorado	1,613	1.8%	6	Michigan	3,578	4.1%
33	Connecticut	1,022	1.2%	7	Pennsylvania	3,141	3.6%
50	Delaware	173	0.2%	8	Florida	3,043	3.5%
8	Florida	3,043	3.5%	9	New Jersey	2,337	2.7%
13	Georgia	2,121	2.4%	10	North Carolina	2,245	2.6%
49	Hawaii	281	0.3%	11	Missouri	2,199	2.5%
41	Idaho	608	0.7%	12	Wisconsin	2,168	2.5%
4	Illinois	3,909	4.5%	13	Georgia	2,121	2.4%
15	Indiana	1,869	2.1%	14	Arizona	1,877	2.1%
23	Iowa	1,427	1.6%	15	Indiana	1,869	2.1%
24	Kansas	1,406	1.6%	16	Washington	1,867	2.1%
27	Kentucky	1,242	1.4%	17	Virginia	1,854	2.1%
28	Louisiana	1,232	1.4%	18	Massachusetts	1,818	2.1%
40	Maine	648	0.7%	19	Oklahoma	1,788	2.0%
26	Maryland	1,282	1.5%	20	Minnesota	1,650	1.9%
18	Massachusetts	1,818	2.1%	21	Tennessee	1,634	1.9%
6	Michigan	3,578	4.1%	22	Colorado	1,613	1.8%
20	Minnesota	1,650	1.9%	23	Iowa	1,427	1.6%
34	Mississippi	900	1.0%	24	Kansas	1,406	1.6%
11	Missouri	2,199	2.5%	25	Alabama	1,352	1.5%
35	Montana	834	1.0%	26	Maryland	1,282	1.5%
30	Nebraska	1,186	1.4%	27	Kentucky	1,242	1.4%
42	Nevada	524	0.6%	28	Louisiana	1,232	1.4%
44	New Hampshire	480	0.5%	29	Oregon	1,222	1.4%
9	New Jersey	2,337	2.7%	30	Nebraska	1,186	1.4%
37	New Mexico	784	0.9%	31	Arkansas	1,102	1.3%
3	New York	4,374	5.0%	32	South Carolina	1,092	1.2%
10	North Carolina	2,245	2.6%	33	Connecticut	1,022	1.2%
43	North Dakota	501	0.6%	34	Mississippi	900	1.0%
4	Ohio	3,909	4.5%	35	Montana	834	1.0%
19	Oklahoma	1,788	2.0%	36	Utah	788	0.9%
29	Oregon	1,222	1.4%	37	New Mexico	784	0.9%
7	Pennsylvania	3,141	3.6%	38	West Virginia	713	0.8%
48	Rhode Island	310	0.4%	39	South Dakota	695	0.8%
32	South Carolina	1,092	1.2%	40	Maine	648	0.7%
39	South Dakota	695	0.8%	41	Idaho	608	0.7%
21	Tennessee	1,634	1.9%	42	Nevada	524	0.6%
2	Texas	7,240	8.3%	43	North Dakota	501	0.6%
36	Utah	788	0.9%	44	New Hampshire	480	0.5%
47	Vermont	316	0.4%	45	Alaska	447	0.5%
17	Virginia	1,854	2.1%	46	Wyoming	347	0.4%
16	Washington	1,867	2.1%	47	Vermont	316	0.4%
38	West Virginia	713	0.8%	48	Rhode Island	310	0.4%
12	Wisconsin	2,168	2.5%	49	Hawaii	281	0.3%
46	Wyoming	347	0.4%	50	Delaware	173	0.2%
					District of Columbia	203	0.2%

Source: U.S. Department of Education, National Center for Education Statistics
"Common Core of Data (CCD) Database" (http://nces.ed.gov/ccd/)
*For school year 2005-2006. Includes 769 schools without membership. Excludes schools solely for special education, vocational education, or alternative education.

Title I Eligible Public Elementary and Secondary Schools in 2006

National Total = 53,820 Schools*

ALPHA ORDER

RANK	STATE	SCHOOLS	% of USA
24	Alabama	868	1.6%
41	Alaska	278	0.5%
18	Arizona	998	1.9%
25	Arkansas	838	1.6%
1	California	5,536	10.3%
20	Colorado	918	1.7%
35	Connecticut	490	0.9%
49	Delaware	100	0.2%
9	Florida	1,398	2.6%
14	Georgia	1,156	2.1%
46	Hawaii	201	0.4%
33	Idaho	502	0.9%
5	Illinois	2,312	4.3%
7	Indiana	1,781	3.3%
29	Iowa	669	1.2%
27	Kansas	682	1.3%
22	Kentucky	886	1.6%
23	Louisiana	874	1.6%
34	Maine	500	0.9%
37	Maryland	386	0.7%
17	Massachusetts	1,054	2.0%
16	Michigan	1,106	2.1%
19	Minnesota	950	1.8%
30	Mississippi	667	1.2%
13	Missouri	1,164	2.2%
27	Montana	682	1.3%
36	Nebraska	461	0.9%
48	Nevada	120	0.2%
43	New Hampshire	227	0.4%
NA	New Jersey**	NA	NA
31	New Mexico	576	1.1%
3	New York	3,188	5.9%
15	North Carolina	1,121	2.1%
39	North Dakota	347	0.6%
4	Ohio	2,755	5.1%
10	Oklahoma	1,316	2.4%
11	Oregon	1,254	2.3%
6	Pennsylvania	2,198	4.1%
47	Rhode Island	146	0.3%
32	South Carolina	517	1.0%
40	South Dakota	342	0.6%
21	Tennessee	907	1.7%
2	Texas	5,341	9.9%
42	Utah	237	0.4%
44	Vermont	220	0.4%
26	Virginia	771	1.4%
12	Washington	1,229	2.3%
38	West Virginia	358	0.7%
8	Wisconsin	1,428	2.7%
45	Wyoming	214	0.4%

RANK ORDER

RANK	STATE	SCHOOLS	% of USA
1	California	5,536	10.3%
2	Texas	5,341	9.9%
3	New York	3,188	5.9%
4	Ohio	2,755	5.1%
5	Illinois	2,312	4.3%
6	Pennsylvania	2,198	4.1%
7	Indiana	1,781	3.3%
8	Wisconsin	1,428	2.7%
9	Florida	1,398	2.6%
10	Oklahoma	1,316	2.4%
11	Oregon	1,254	2.3%
12	Washington	1,229	2.3%
13	Missouri	1,164	2.2%
14	Georgia	1,156	2.1%
15	North Carolina	1,121	2.1%
16	Michigan	1,106	2.1%
17	Massachusetts	1,054	2.0%
18	Arizona	998	1.9%
19	Minnesota	950	1.8%
20	Colorado	918	1.7%
21	Tennessee	907	1.7%
22	Kentucky	886	1.6%
23	Louisiana	874	1.6%
24	Alabama	868	1.6%
25	Arkansas	838	1.6%
26	Virginia	771	1.4%
27	Kansas	682	1.3%
27	Montana	682	1.3%
29	Iowa	669	1.2%
30	Mississippi	667	1.2%
31	New Mexico	576	1.1%
32	South Carolina	517	1.0%
33	Idaho	502	0.9%
34	Maine	500	0.9%
35	Connecticut	490	0.9%
36	Nebraska	461	0.9%
37	Maryland	386	0.7%
38	West Virginia	358	0.7%
39	North Dakota	347	0.6%
40	South Dakota	342	0.6%
41	Alaska	278	0.5%
42	Utah	237	0.4%
43	New Hampshire	227	0.4%
44	Vermont	220	0.4%
45	Wyoming	214	0.4%
46	Hawaii	201	0.4%
47	Rhode Island	146	0.3%
48	Nevada	120	0.2%
49	Delaware	100	0.2%
NA	New Jersey**	NA	NA
	District of Columbia	193	0.4%

Source: U.S. Department of Education, National Center for Education Statistics
   "Common Core of Data (CCD) Database" (http://nces.ed.gov/ccd/)
*For school year 2005-2006. National total excludes states shown as not reporting. Title I schools are eligible for Title I federal funding to assist disadvantaged students. Includes schools with and without school-wide Title I programs.
**Not available.

Percent of Public Elementary and Secondary Schools
That are Title I Eligible: 2006
National Percent = 55.3%*

RANK	STATE	PERCENT
24	Alabama	54.8
23	Alaska	55.4
32	Arizona	48.0
4	Arkansas	73.6
19	California	57.4
26	Colorado	53.8
40	Connecticut	44.1
37	Delaware	45.0
42	Florida	37.6
31	Georgia	48.4
8	Hawaii	70.5
7	Idaho	71.1
28	Illinois	52.5
2	Indiana	90.1
39	Iowa	44.2
30	Kansas	48.5
16	Kentucky	62.9
16	Louisiana	62.9
4	Maine	73.6
46	Maryland	27.0
21	Massachusetts	56.1
46	Michigan	27.0
45	Minnesota	35.9
15	Mississippi	63.5
29	Missouri	49.3
3	Montana	81.2
42	Nebraska	37.6
49	Nevada	21.5
34	New Hampshire	47.3
NA	New Jersey**	NA
12	New Mexico	67.4
10	New York	68.3
33	North Carolina	47.8
13	North Dakota	64.4
9	Ohio	68.8
4	Oklahoma	73.6
1	Oregon	99.5
11	Pennsylvania	67.6
41	Rhode Island	43.2
38	South Carolina	44.9
35	South Dakota	47.2
27	Tennessee	53.4
18	Texas	62.7
48	Utah	24.8
21	Vermont	56.1
44	Virginia	37.1
25	Washington	54.2
36	West Virginia	45.7
14	Wisconsin	63.6
20	Wyoming	56.5

RANK	STATE	PERCENT
1	Oregon	99.5
2	Indiana	90.1
3	Montana	81.2
4	Arkansas	73.6
4	Maine	73.6
4	Oklahoma	73.6
7	Idaho	71.1
8	Hawaii	70.5
9	Ohio	68.8
10	New York	68.3
11	Pennsylvania	67.6
12	New Mexico	67.4
13	North Dakota	64.4
14	Wisconsin	63.6
15	Mississippi	63.5
16	Kentucky	62.9
16	Louisiana	62.9
18	Texas	62.7
19	California	57.4
20	Wyoming	56.5
21	Massachusetts	56.1
21	Vermont	56.1
23	Alaska	55.4
24	Alabama	54.8
25	Washington	54.2
26	Colorado	53.8
27	Tennessee	53.4
28	Illinois	52.5
29	Missouri	49.3
30	Kansas	48.5
31	Georgia	48.4
32	Arizona	48.0
33	North Carolina	47.8
34	New Hampshire	47.3
35	South Dakota	47.2
36	West Virginia	45.7
37	Delaware	45.0
38	South Carolina	44.9
39	Iowa	44.2
40	Connecticut	44.1
41	Rhode Island	43.2
42	Florida	37.6
42	Nebraska	37.6
44	Virginia	37.1
45	Minnesota	35.9
46	Maryland	27.0
46	Michigan	27.0
48	Utah	24.8
49	Nevada	21.5
NA	New Jersey**	NA

| | District of Columbia | 84.3 |

Source: CQ Press using data from U.S. Department of Education, National Center for Education Statistics
"Common Core of Data (CCD) Database" (http://nces.ed.gov/ccd/)

*For school year 2005-2006. National percent excludes states shown as not reporting. Title I schools are eligible for Title I federal funding to assist disadvantaged students. Includes schools with and without school-wide Title I programs.
**Not available.

Title I School-Wide Public Elementary and Secondary Schools in 2006

National Total = 30,582 Schools*

ALPHA ORDER

RANK	STATE	SCHOOLS	% of USA
15	Alabama	735	2.4%
41	Alaska	114	0.4%
19	Arizona	570	1.9%
18	Arkansas	607	2.0%
2	California	3,445	11.3%
25	Colorado	374	1.2%
38	Connecticut	140	0.5%
46	Delaware	68	0.2%
4	Florida	1,355	4.4%
8	Georgia	954	3.1%
36	Hawaii	163	0.5%
42	Idaho	96	0.3%
9	Illinois	943	3.1%
34	Indiana	172	0.6%
39	Iowa	135	0.4%
29	Kansas	279	0.9%
11	Kentucky	788	2.6%
12	Louisiana	771	2.5%
48	Maine	48	0.2%
28	Maryland	327	1.1%
22	Massachusetts	481	1.6%
5	Michigan	1,106	3.6%
30	Minnesota	274	0.9%
16	Mississippi	630	2.1%
24	Missouri	424	1.4%
35	Montana	165	0.5%
32	Nebraska	205	0.7%
40	Nevada	120	0.4%
49	New Hampshire	34	0.1%
NA	New Jersey**	NA	NA
23	New Mexico	452	1.5%
3	New York	1,425	4.7%
10	North Carolina	920	3.0%
45	North Dakota	70	0.2%
7	Ohio	984	3.2%
6	Oklahoma	999	3.3%
27	Oregon	332	1.1%
17	Pennsylvania	612	2.0%
47	Rhode Island	64	0.2%
21	South Carolina	488	1.6%
37	South Dakota	151	0.5%
14	Tennessee	767	2.5%
1	Texas	4,972	16.3%
33	Utah	191	0.6%
43	Vermont	95	0.3%
12	Virginia	771	2.5%
20	Washington	519	1.7%
31	West Virginia	273	0.9%
26	Wisconsin	342	1.1%
44	Wyoming	72	0.2%

RANK ORDER

RANK	STATE	SCHOOLS	% of USA
1	Texas	4,972	16.3%
2	California	3,445	11.3%
3	New York	1,425	4.7%
4	Florida	1,355	4.4%
5	Michigan	1,106	3.6%
6	Oklahoma	999	3.3%
7	Ohio	984	3.2%
8	Georgia	954	3.1%
9	Illinois	943	3.1%
10	North Carolina	920	3.0%
11	Kentucky	788	2.6%
12	Louisiana	771	2.5%
12	Virginia	771	2.5%
14	Tennessee	767	2.5%
15	Alabama	735	2.4%
16	Mississippi	630	2.1%
17	Pennsylvania	612	2.0%
18	Arkansas	607	2.0%
19	Arizona	570	1.9%
20	Washington	519	1.7%
21	South Carolina	488	1.6%
22	Massachusetts	481	1.6%
23	New Mexico	452	1.5%
24	Missouri	424	1.4%
25	Colorado	374	1.2%
26	Wisconsin	342	1.1%
27	Oregon	332	1.1%
28	Maryland	327	1.1%
29	Kansas	279	0.9%
30	Minnesota	274	0.9%
31	West Virginia	273	0.9%
32	Nebraska	205	0.7%
33	Utah	191	0.6%
34	Indiana	172	0.6%
35	Montana	165	0.5%
36	Hawaii	163	0.5%
37	South Dakota	151	0.5%
38	Connecticut	140	0.5%
39	Iowa	135	0.4%
40	Nevada	120	0.4%
41	Alaska	114	0.4%
42	Idaho	96	0.3%
43	Vermont	95	0.3%
44	Wyoming	72	0.2%
45	North Dakota	70	0.2%
46	Delaware	68	0.2%
47	Rhode Island	64	0.2%
48	Maine	48	0.2%
49	New Hampshire	34	0.1%
NA	New Jersey**	NA	NA
	District of Columbia	185	0.6%

Source: U.S. Department of Education, National Center for Education Statistics
"Common Core of Data (CCD) Database" (http://nces.ed.gov/ccd/)
*For school year 2005-2006. National total excludes states shown as not reporting. Title I school-wide schools are those in which all of the pupils enrolled are eligible for Title I federal funding, which assists disadvantaged students.
**Not available.

Percent of Public Elementary and Secondary Schools
That are Title I School-Wide Schools: 2006
National Percent = 31.4%*

ALPHA ORDER

RANK	STATE	PERCENT
9	Alabama	46.4
28	Alaska	22.7
20	Arizona	27.4
7	Arkansas	53.3
16	California	35.7
29	Colorado	21.9
44	Connecticut	12.6
18	Delaware	30.6
15	Florida	36.4
12	Georgia	39.9
3	Hawaii	57.2
42	Idaho	13.6
31	Illinois	21.4
47	Indiana	8.7
46	Iowa	8.9
34	Kansas	19.8
4	Kentucky	55.9
6	Louisiana	55.5
48	Maine	7.1
26	Maryland	22.9
23	Massachusetts	25.6
21	Michigan	27.0
45	Minnesota	10.4
1	Mississippi	59.9
39	Missouri	18.0
35	Montana	19.6
40	Nebraska	16.7
30	Nevada	21.5
48	New Hampshire	7.1
NA	New Jersey**	NA
8	New Mexico	52.9
19	New York	30.5
13	North Carolina	39.2
43	North Dakota	13.0
24	Ohio	24.6
4	Oklahoma	55.9
22	Oregon	26.3
38	Pennsylvania	18.8
37	Rhode Island	18.9
11	South Carolina	42.4
32	South Dakota	20.8
10	Tennessee	45.1
2	Texas	58.4
33	Utah	20.0
25	Vermont	24.2
14	Virginia	37.1
26	Washington	22.9
17	West Virginia	34.8
41	Wisconsin	15.2
36	Wyoming	19.0

RANK ORDER

RANK	STATE	PERCENT
1	Mississippi	59.9
2	Texas	58.4
3	Hawaii	57.2
4	Kentucky	55.9
4	Oklahoma	55.9
6	Louisiana	55.5
7	Arkansas	53.3
8	New Mexico	52.9
9	Alabama	46.4
10	Tennessee	45.1
11	South Carolina	42.4
12	Georgia	39.9
13	North Carolina	39.2
14	Virginia	37.1
15	Florida	36.4
16	California	35.7
17	West Virginia	34.8
18	Delaware	30.6
19	New York	30.5
20	Arizona	27.4
21	Michigan	27.0
22	Oregon	26.3
23	Massachusetts	25.6
24	Ohio	24.6
25	Vermont	24.2
26	Maryland	22.9
26	Washington	22.9
28	Alaska	22.7
29	Colorado	21.9
30	Nevada	21.5
31	Illinois	21.4
32	South Dakota	20.8
33	Utah	20.0
34	Kansas	19.8
35	Montana	19.6
36	Wyoming	19.0
37	Rhode Island	18.9
38	Pennsylvania	18.8
39	Missouri	18.0
40	Nebraska	16.7
41	Wisconsin	15.2
42	Idaho	13.6
43	North Dakota	13.0
44	Connecticut	12.6
45	Minnesota	10.4
46	Iowa	8.9
47	Indiana	8.7
48	Maine	7.1
48	New Hampshire	7.1
NA	New Jersey**	NA

District of Columbia	80.8

Source: CQ Press using data from U.S. Department of Education, National Center for Education Statistics
     "Common Core of Data (CCD) Database" (http://nces.ed.gov/ccd/)
*For school year 2005-2006. National percent excludes states shown as not reporting. Title I school-wide schools are those in which all of the pupils enrolled are eligible for Title I federal funding, which assists disadvantaged students.
**Not available.

Special Education Public Elementary and Secondary Schools in 2006

National Total = 2,128 Schools*

ALPHA ORDER

RANK	STATE	SCHOOLS	% of USA
9	Alabama	65	3.1%
39	Alaska	3	0.1%
28	Arizona	11	0.5%
36	Arkansas	5	0.2%
6	California	128	6.0%
27	Colorado	12	0.6%
18	Connecticut	37	1.7%
23	Delaware	15	0.7%
5	Florida	133	6.3%
11	Georgia	54	2.5%
39	Hawaii	3	0.1%
29	Idaho	10	0.5%
2	Illinois	275	12.9%
14	Indiana	50	2.3%
31	Iowa	9	0.4%
45	Kansas	0	0.0%
29	Kentucky	10	0.5%
16	Louisiana	43	2.0%
38	Maine	4	0.2%
15	Maryland	49	2.3%
36	Massachusetts	5	0.2%
3	Michigan	181	8.5%
1	Minnesota	288	13.5%
45	Mississippi	0	0.0%
20	Missouri	23	1.1%
42	Montana	2	0.1%
17	Nebraska	39	1.8%
44	Nevada	1	0.0%
45	New Hampshire	0	0.0%
8	New Jersey	81	3.8%
24	New Mexico	14	0.7%
4	New York	153	7.2%
21	North Carolina	22	1.0%
19	North Dakota	31	1.5%
26	Ohio	13	0.6%
45	Oklahoma	0	0.0%
42	Oregon	2	0.1%
24	Pennsylvania	14	0.7%
39	Rhode Island	3	0.1%
31	South Carolina	9	0.4%
35	South Dakota	7	0.3%
22	Tennessee	16	0.8%
45	Texas	0	0.0%
11	Utah	54	2.5%
10	Vermont	59	2.8%
13	Virginia	52	2.4%
7	Washington	112	5.3%
33	West Virginia	8	0.4%
33	Wisconsin	8	0.4%
45	Wyoming	0	0.0%

RANK ORDER

RANK	STATE	SCHOOLS	% of USA
1	Minnesota	288	13.5%
2	Illinois	275	12.9%
3	Michigan	181	8.5%
4	New York	153	7.2%
5	Florida	133	6.3%
6	California	128	6.0%
7	Washington	112	5.3%
8	New Jersey	81	3.8%
9	Alabama	65	3.1%
10	Vermont	59	2.8%
11	Georgia	54	2.5%
11	Utah	54	2.5%
13	Virginia	52	2.4%
14	Indiana	50	2.3%
15	Maryland	49	2.3%
16	Louisiana	43	2.0%
17	Nebraska	39	1.8%
18	Connecticut	37	1.7%
19	North Dakota	31	1.5%
20	Missouri	23	1.1%
21	North Carolina	22	1.0%
22	Tennessee	16	0.8%
23	Delaware	15	0.7%
24	New Mexico	14	0.7%
24	Pennsylvania	14	0.7%
26	Ohio	13	0.6%
27	Colorado	12	0.6%
28	Arizona	11	0.5%
29	Idaho	10	0.5%
29	Kentucky	10	0.5%
31	Iowa	9	0.4%
31	South Carolina	9	0.4%
33	West Virginia	8	0.4%
33	Wisconsin	8	0.4%
35	South Dakota	7	0.3%
36	Arkansas	5	0.2%
36	Massachusetts	5	0.2%
38	Maine	4	0.2%
39	Alaska	3	0.1%
39	Hawaii	3	0.1%
39	Rhode Island	3	0.1%
42	Montana	2	0.1%
42	Oregon	2	0.1%
44	Nevada	1	0.0%
45	Kansas	0	0.0%
45	Mississippi	0	0.0%
45	New Hampshire	0	0.0%
45	Oklahoma	0	0.0%
45	Texas	0	0.0%
45	Wyoming	0	0.0%
	District of Columbia	15	0.7%

Source: U.S. Department of Education, National Center for Education Statistics
"Common Core of Data (CCD) Database" (http://nces.ed.gov/ccd/)
*For school year 2005-2006.

Percent of Public Elementary and Secondary Schools
That are Special Education Schools: 2006
National Percent = 2.2%*

ALPHA ORDER

RANK	STATE	PERCENT
9	Alabama	4.1
33	Alaska	0.6
36	Arizona	0.5
37	Arkansas	0.4
22	California	1.3
31	Colorado	0.7
12	Connecticut	3.3
3	Delaware	6.8
10	Florida	3.6
19	Georgia	2.3
23	Hawaii	1.1
21	Idaho	1.4
4	Illinois	6.2
17	Indiana	2.5
33	Iowa	0.6
45	Kansas	0.0
31	Kentucky	0.7
16	Louisiana	3.1
33	Maine	0.6
11	Maryland	3.4
40	Massachusetts	0.3
8	Michigan	4.4
2	Minnesota	10.9
45	Mississippi	0.0
24	Missouri	1.0
42	Montana	0.2
15	Nebraska	3.2
42	Nevada	0.2
45	New Hampshire	0.0
12	New Jersey	3.3
20	New Mexico	1.6
12	New York	3.3
27	North Carolina	0.9
5	North Dakota	5.8
40	Ohio	0.3
45	Oklahoma	0.0
42	Oregon	0.2
37	Pennsylvania	0.4
27	Rhode Island	0.9
30	South Carolina	0.8
24	South Dakota	1.0
27	Tennessee	0.9
45	Texas	0.0
6	Utah	5.6
1	Vermont	15.1
17	Virginia	2.5
7	Washington	4.9
24	West Virginia	1.0
37	Wisconsin	0.4
45	Wyoming	0.0

RANK ORDER

RANK	STATE	PERCENT
1	Vermont	15.1
2	Minnesota	10.9
3	Delaware	6.8
4	Illinois	6.2
5	North Dakota	5.8
6	Utah	5.6
7	Washington	4.9
8	Michigan	4.4
9	Alabama	4.1
10	Florida	3.6
11	Maryland	3.4
12	Connecticut	3.3
12	New Jersey	3.3
12	New York	3.3
15	Nebraska	3.2
16	Louisiana	3.1
17	Indiana	2.5
17	Virginia	2.5
19	Georgia	2.3
20	New Mexico	1.6
21	Idaho	1.4
22	California	1.3
23	Hawaii	1.1
24	Missouri	1.0
24	South Dakota	1.0
24	West Virginia	1.0
27	North Carolina	0.9
27	Rhode Island	0.9
27	Tennessee	0.9
30	South Carolina	0.8
31	Colorado	0.7
31	Kentucky	0.7
33	Alaska	0.6
33	Iowa	0.6
33	Maine	0.6
36	Arizona	0.5
37	Arkansas	0.4
37	Pennsylvania	0.4
37	Wisconsin	0.4
40	Massachusetts	0.3
40	Ohio	0.3
42	Montana	0.2
42	Nevada	0.2
42	Oregon	0.2
45	Kansas	0.0
45	Mississippi	0.0
45	New Hampshire	0.0
45	Oklahoma	0.0
45	Texas	0.0
45	Wyoming	0.0

District of Columbia	6.6

Source: CQ Press using data from U.S. Department of Education, National Center for Education Statistics
    "Common Core of Data (CCD) Database" (http://nces.ed.gov/ccd/)
*For school year 2005-2006.

Vocational Public Elementary and Secondary Schools in 2006

National Total = 1,221 Schools*

ALPHA ORDER

RANK	STATE	SCHOOLS	% of USA
6	Alabama	75	6.1%
37	Alaska	2	0.2%
1	Arizona	121	9.9%
19	Arkansas	24	2.0%
4	California	76	6.2%
32	Colorado	5	0.4%
22	Connecticut	17	1.4%
32	Delaware	5	0.4%
14	Florida	34	2.8%
39	Georgia	0	0.0%
39	Hawaii	0	0.0%
26	Idaho	11	0.9%
10	Illinois	50	4.1%
17	Indiana	28	2.3%
39	Iowa	0	0.0%
39	Kansas	0	0.0%
28	Kentucky	9	0.7%
30	Louisiana	7	0.6%
18	Maine	27	2.2%
19	Maryland	24	2.0%
12	Massachusetts	39	3.2%
11	Michigan	47	3.8%
24	Minnesota	13	1.1%
2	Mississippi	89	7.3%
7	Missouri	60	4.9%
39	Montana	0	0.0%
39	Nebraska	0	0.0%
38	Nevada	1	0.1%
39	New Hampshire	0	0.0%
8	New Jersey	56	4.6%
34	New Mexico	3	0.2%
16	New York	30	2.5%
28	North Carolina	9	0.7%
30	North Dakota	7	0.6%
4	Ohio	76	6.2%
39	Oklahoma	0	0.0%
39	Oregon	0	0.0%
3	Pennsylvania	85	7.0%
25	Rhode Island	12	1.0%
12	South Carolina	39	3.2%
39	South Dakota	0	0.0%
21	Tennessee	23	1.9%
39	Texas	0	0.0%
34	Utah	3	0.2%
23	Vermont	15	1.2%
9	Virginia	51	4.2%
26	Washington	11	0.9%
15	West Virginia	33	2.7%
34	Wisconsin	3	0.2%
39	Wyoming	0	0.0%

RANK ORDER

RANK	STATE	SCHOOLS	% of USA
1	Arizona	121	9.9%
2	Mississippi	89	7.3%
3	Pennsylvania	85	7.0%
4	California	76	6.2%
4	Ohio	76	6.2%
6	Alabama	75	6.1%
7	Missouri	60	4.9%
8	New Jersey	56	4.6%
9	Virginia	51	4.2%
10	Illinois	50	4.1%
11	Michigan	47	3.8%
12	Massachusetts	39	3.2%
12	South Carolina	39	3.2%
14	Florida	34	2.8%
15	West Virginia	33	2.7%
16	New York	30	2.5%
17	Indiana	28	2.3%
18	Maine	27	2.2%
19	Arkansas	24	2.0%
19	Maryland	24	2.0%
21	Tennessee	23	1.9%
22	Connecticut	17	1.4%
23	Vermont	15	1.2%
24	Minnesota	13	1.1%
25	Rhode Island	12	1.0%
26	Idaho	11	0.9%
26	Washington	11	0.9%
28	Kentucky	9	0.7%
28	North Carolina	9	0.7%
30	Louisiana	7	0.6%
30	North Dakota	7	0.6%
32	Colorado	5	0.4%
32	Delaware	5	0.4%
34	New Mexico	3	0.2%
34	Utah	3	0.2%
34	Wisconsin	3	0.2%
37	Alaska	2	0.2%
38	Nevada	1	0.1%
39	Georgia	0	0.0%
39	Hawaii	0	0.0%
39	Iowa	0	0.0%
39	Kansas	0	0.0%
39	Montana	0	0.0%
39	Nebraska	0	0.0%
39	New Hampshire	0	0.0%
39	Oklahoma	0	0.0%
39	Oregon	0	0.0%
39	South Dakota	0	0.0%
39	Texas	0	0.0%
39	Wyoming	0	0.0%
	District of Columbia	1	0.1%

Source: U.S. Department of Education, National Center for Education Statistics
"Common Core of Data (CCD) Database" (http://nces.ed.gov/ccd/)
*For school year 2005-2006.

Percent of Public Elementary and Secondary Schools
That are Vocational Schools: 2006
National Percent = 1.3%*

ALPHA ORDER

ALPHA ORDER

RANK ORDER

RANK	STATE	PERCENT
3	Alabama	4.7
32	Alaska	0.4
2	Arizona	5.8
14	Arkansas	2.1
26	California	0.8
35	Colorado	0.3
19	Connecticut	1.5
12	Delaware	2.3
25	Florida	0.9
39	Georgia	0.0
39	Hawaii	0.0
18	Idaho	1.6
23	Illinois	1.1
20	Indiana	1.4
39	Iowa	0.0
39	Kansas	0.0
27	Kentucky	0.6
29	Louisiana	0.5
5	Maine	4.0
17	Maryland	1.7
14	Massachusetts	2.1
23	Michigan	1.1
29	Minnesota	0.5
1	Mississippi	8.5
10	Missouri	2.5
39	Montana	0.0
39	Nebraska	0.0
37	Nevada	0.2
39	New Hampshire	0.0
12	New Jersey	2.3
32	New Mexico	0.4
27	New York	0.6
32	North Carolina	0.4
22	North Dakota	1.3
16	Ohio	1.9
39	Oklahoma	0.0
39	Oregon	0.0
9	Pennsylvania	2.6
7	Rhode Island	3.6
8	South Carolina	3.4
39	South Dakota	0.0
20	Tennessee	1.4
39	Texas	0.0
35	Utah	0.3
6	Vermont	3.8
10	Virginia	2.5
29	Washington	0.5
4	West Virginia	4.2
38	Wisconsin	0.1
39	Wyoming	0.0

RANK	STATE	PERCENT
1	Mississippi	8.5
2	Arizona	5.8
3	Alabama	4.7
4	West Virginia	4.2
5	Maine	4.0
6	Vermont	3.8
7	Rhode Island	3.6
8	South Carolina	3.4
9	Pennsylvania	2.6
10	Missouri	2.5
10	Virginia	2.5
12	Delaware	2.3
12	New Jersey	2.3
14	Arkansas	2.1
14	Massachusetts	2.1
16	Ohio	1.9
17	Maryland	1.7
18	Idaho	1.6
19	Connecticut	1.5
20	Indiana	1.4
20	Tennessee	1.4
22	North Dakota	1.3
23	Illinois	1.1
23	Michigan	1.1
25	Florida	0.9
26	California	0.8
27	Kentucky	0.6
27	New York	0.6
29	Louisiana	0.5
29	Minnesota	0.5
29	Washington	0.5
32	Alaska	0.4
32	New Mexico	0.4
32	North Carolina	0.4
35	Colorado	0.3
35	Utah	0.3
37	Nevada	0.2
38	Wisconsin	0.1
39	Georgia	0.0
39	Hawaii	0.0
39	Iowa	0.0
39	Kansas	0.0
39	Montana	0.0
39	Nebraska	0.0
39	New Hampshire	0.0
39	Oklahoma	0.0
39	Oregon	0.0
39	South Dakota	0.0
39	Texas	0.0
39	Wyoming	0.0

District of Columbia 0.4

Source: CQ Press using data from U.S. Department of Education, National Center for Education Statistics
    "Common Core of Data (CCD) Database" (http://nces.ed.gov/ccd/)
*For school year 2005-2006.

Alternative Education Public Elementary and Secondary Schools in 2006

National Total = 6,448 Schools*

ALPHA ORDER

RANK	STATE	SCHOOLS	% of USA
14	Alabama	93	1.4%
25	Alaska	50	0.8%
21	Arizona	69	1.1%
40	Arkansas	7	0.1%
2	California	1,212	18.8%
16	Colorado	77	1.2%
27	Connecticut	35	0.5%
32	Delaware	29	0.4%
4	Florida	513	8.0%
7	Georgia	214	3.3%
43	Hawaii	1	0.0%
16	Idaho	77	1.2%
8	Illinois	167	2.6%
30	Indiana	30	0.5%
18	Iowa	76	1.2%
43	Kansas	1	0.0%
9	Kentucky	148	2.3%
13	Louisiana	108	1.7%
45	Maine	0	0.0%
19	Maryland	75	1.2%
35	Massachusetts	17	0.3%
5	Michigan	284	4.4%
3	Minnesota	693	10.7%
23	Mississippi	62	1.0%
15	Missouri	79	1.2%
41	Montana	4	0.1%
45	Nebraska	0	0.0%
29	Nevada	31	0.5%
45	New Hampshire	0	0.0%
45	New Jersey	0	0.0%
24	New Mexico	53	0.8%
11	New York	112	1.7%
20	North Carolina	71	1.1%
45	North Dakota	0	0.0%
39	Ohio	9	0.1%
45	Oklahoma	0	0.0%
26	Oregon	36	0.6%
38	Pennsylvania	10	0.2%
36	Rhode Island	13	0.2%
37	South Carolina	12	0.2%
34	South Dakota	23	0.4%
33	Tennessee	27	0.4%
1	Texas	1,277	19.8%
12	Utah	111	1.7%
42	Vermont	2	0.0%
10	Virginia	122	1.9%
6	Washington	279	4.3%
30	West Virginia	30	0.5%
22	Wisconsin	67	1.0%
28	Wyoming	32	0.5%

RANK ORDER

RANK	STATE	SCHOOLS	% of USA
1	Texas	1,277	19.8%
2	California	1,212	18.8%
3	Minnesota	693	10.7%
4	Florida	513	8.0%
5	Michigan	284	4.4%
6	Washington	279	4.3%
7	Georgia	214	3.3%
8	Illinois	167	2.6%
9	Kentucky	148	2.3%
10	Virginia	122	1.9%
11	New York	112	1.7%
12	Utah	111	1.7%
13	Louisiana	108	1.7%
14	Alabama	93	1.4%
15	Missouri	79	1.2%
16	Colorado	77	1.2%
16	Idaho	77	1.2%
18	Iowa	76	1.2%
19	Maryland	75	1.2%
20	North Carolina	71	1.1%
21	Arizona	69	1.1%
22	Wisconsin	67	1.0%
23	Mississippi	62	1.0%
24	New Mexico	53	0.8%
25	Alaska	50	0.8%
26	Oregon	36	0.6%
27	Connecticut	35	0.5%
28	Wyoming	32	0.5%
29	Nevada	31	0.5%
30	Indiana	30	0.5%
30	West Virginia	30	0.5%
32	Delaware	29	0.4%
33	Tennessee	27	0.4%
34	South Dakota	23	0.4%
35	Massachusetts	17	0.3%
36	Rhode Island	13	0.2%
37	South Carolina	12	0.2%
38	Pennsylvania	10	0.2%
39	Ohio	9	0.1%
40	Arkansas	7	0.1%
41	Montana	4	0.1%
42	Vermont	2	0.0%
43	Hawaii	1	0.0%
43	Kansas	1	0.0%
45	Maine	0	0.0%
45	Nebraska	0	0.0%
45	New Hampshire	0	0.0%
45	New Jersey	0	0.0%
45	North Dakota	0	0.0%
45	Oklahoma	0	0.0%
	District of Columbia	10	0.2%

Source: U.S. Department of Education, National Center for Education Statistics
   "Common Core of Data (CCD) Database" (http://nces.ed.gov/ccd/)
*For school year 2005-2006.

Percent of Public Elementary and Secondary Schools
That are Alternative Education Schools: 2006
National Percent = 6.6%*

ALPHA ORDER

RANK	STATE	PERCENT
16	Alabama	5.9
10	Alaska	10.0
26	Arizona	3.3
38	Arkansas	0.6
5	California	12.6
22	Colorado	4.5
28	Connecticut	3.2
4	Delaware	13.1
3	Florida	13.8
11	Georgia	9.0
41	Hawaii	0.4
8	Idaho	10.9
23	Illinois	3.8
35	Indiana	1.5
21	Iowa	5.0
44	Kansas	0.1
9	Kentucky	10.5
13	Louisiana	7.8
45	Maine	0.0
20	Maryland	5.2
37	Massachusetts	0.9
14	Michigan	6.9
1	Minnesota	26.2
16	Mississippi	5.9
26	Missouri	3.3
39	Montana	0.5
45	Nebraska	0.0
19	Nevada	5.6
45	New Hampshire	0.0
45	New Jersey	0.0
15	New Mexico	6.2
33	New York	2.4
30	North Carolina	3.0
45	North Dakota	0.0
43	Ohio	0.2
45	Oklahoma	0.0
32	Oregon	2.9
42	Pennsylvania	0.3
23	Rhode Island	3.8
36	South Carolina	1.0
28	South Dakota	3.2
34	Tennessee	1.6
2	Texas	15.0
7	Utah	11.6
39	Vermont	0.5
16	Virginia	5.9
6	Washington	12.3
23	West Virginia	3.8
30	Wisconsin	3.0
12	Wyoming	8.4

RANK ORDER

RANK	STATE	PERCENT
1	Minnesota	26.2
2	Texas	15.0
3	Florida	13.8
4	Delaware	13.1
5	California	12.6
6	Washington	12.3
7	Utah	11.6
8	Idaho	10.9
9	Kentucky	10.5
10	Alaska	10.0
11	Georgia	9.0
12	Wyoming	8.4
13	Louisiana	7.8
14	Michigan	6.9
15	New Mexico	6.2
16	Alabama	5.9
16	Mississippi	5.9
16	Virginia	5.9
19	Nevada	5.6
20	Maryland	5.2
21	Iowa	5.0
22	Colorado	4.5
23	Illinois	3.8
23	Rhode Island	3.8
23	West Virginia	3.8
26	Arizona	3.3
26	Missouri	3.3
28	Connecticut	3.2
28	South Dakota	3.2
30	North Carolina	3.0
30	Wisconsin	3.0
32	Oregon	2.9
33	New York	2.4
34	Tennessee	1.6
35	Indiana	1.5
36	South Carolina	1.0
37	Massachusetts	0.9
38	Arkansas	0.6
39	Montana	0.5
39	Vermont	0.5
41	Hawaii	0.4
42	Pennsylvania	0.3
43	Ohio	0.2
44	Kansas	0.1
45	Maine	0.0
45	Nebraska	0.0
45	New Hampshire	0.0
45	New Jersey	0.0
45	North Dakota	0.0
45	Oklahoma	0.0
	District of Columbia	4.4

Source: CQ Press using data from U.S. Department of Education, National Center for Education Statistics
  "Common Core of Data (CCD) Database" (http://nces.ed.gov/ccd/)
*For school year 2005-2006.

Public Elementary and Secondary Magnet Schools in 2006

Reporting States Total = 2,736 Schools*

ALPHA ORDER

RANK	STATE	SCHOOLS	% of USA
15	Alabama	35	1.3%
20	Alaska	17	0.6%
7	Arizona	100	3.7%
22	Arkansas	12	0.4%
1	California	519	19.0%
24	Colorado	10	0.4%
14	Connecticut	43	1.6%
28	Delaware	2	0.1%
NA	Florida**	NA	NA
10	Georgia	62	2.3%
NA	Hawaii**	NA	NA
NA	Idaho**	NA	NA
3	Illinois	347	12.7%
17	Indiana	26	1.0%
NA	Iowa**	NA	NA
19	Kansas	25	0.9%
11	Kentucky	46	1.7%
8	Louisiana	68	2.5%
29	Maine	1	0.0%
NA	Maryland**	NA	NA
26	Massachusetts	3	0.1%
2	Michigan	402	14.7%
9	Minnesota	65	2.4%
20	Mississippi	17	0.6%
12	Missouri	44	1.6%
NA	Montana**	NA	NA
NA	Nebraska**	NA	NA
NA	Nevada**	NA	NA
NA	New Hampshire**	NA	NA
NA	New Jersey**	NA	NA
26	New Mexico	3	0.1%
4	New York	181	6.6%
6	North Carolina	144	5.3%
NA	North Dakota**	NA	NA
NA	Ohio**	NA	NA
NA	Oklahoma**	NA	NA
NA	Oregon**	NA	NA
12	Pennsylvania	44	1.6%
NA	Rhode Island**	NA	NA
17	South Carolina	26	1.0%
NA	South Dakota**	NA	NA
16	Tennessee	32	1.2%
NA	Texas**	NA	NA
23	Utah	11	0.4%
NA	Vermont**	NA	NA
5	Virginia	176	6.4%
NA	Washington**	NA	NA
NA	West Virginia**	NA	NA
25	Wisconsin	5	0.2%
NA	Wyoming**	NA	NA

RANK ORDER

RANK	STATE	SCHOOLS	% of USA
1	California	519	19.0%
2	Michigan	402	14.7%
3	Illinois	347	12.7%
4	New York	181	6.6%
5	Virginia	176	6.4%
6	North Carolina	144	5.3%
7	Arizona	100	3.7%
8	Louisiana	68	2.5%
9	Minnesota	65	2.4%
10	Georgia	62	2.3%
11	Kentucky	46	1.7%
12	Missouri	44	1.6%
12	Pennsylvania	44	1.6%
14	Connecticut	43	1.6%
15	Alabama	35	1.3%
16	Tennessee	32	1.2%
17	Indiana	26	1.0%
17	South Carolina	26	1.0%
19	Kansas	25	0.9%
20	Alaska	17	0.6%
20	Mississippi	17	0.6%
22	Arkansas	12	0.4%
23	Utah	11	0.4%
24	Colorado	10	0.4%
25	Wisconsin	5	0.2%
26	Massachusetts	3	0.1%
26	New Mexico	3	0.1%
28	Delaware	2	0.1%
29	Maine	1	0.0%
NA	Florida**	NA	NA
NA	Hawaii**	NA	NA
NA	Idaho**	NA	NA
NA	Iowa**	NA	NA
NA	Maryland**	NA	NA
NA	Montana**	NA	NA
NA	Nebraska**	NA	NA
NA	Nevada**	NA	NA
NA	New Hampshire**	NA	NA
NA	New Jersey**	NA	NA
NA	North Dakota**	NA	NA
NA	Ohio**	NA	NA
NA	Oklahoma**	NA	NA
NA	Oregon**	NA	NA
NA	Rhode Island**	NA	NA
NA	South Dakota**	NA	NA
NA	Texas**	NA	NA
NA	Vermont**	NA	NA
NA	Washington**	NA	NA
NA	West Virginia**	NA	NA
NA	Wyoming**	NA	NA
	District of Columbia	3	0.1%

Source: U.S. Department of Education, National Center for Education Statistics
   "Common Core of Data (CCD) Database" (http://nces.ed.gov/ccd/)
*For school year 2005-2006. National total is only for reporting states. Magnet schools are those designed to attract students of different racial/ethnic backgrounds for the purpose of reducing racial isolation, or to provide an academic or social focus on a specific theme (e.g., performing arts).
**Not available or not applicable.

Percent of Public Elementary and Secondary
That are Magnet Schools: 2006
Reporting States Percent = 4.3%*

ALPHA ORDER

RANK	STATE	PERCENT
15	Alabama	2.2
10	Alaska	3.4
7	Arizona	4.8
23	Arkansas	1.1
5	California	5.4
25	Colorado	0.6
8	Connecticut	3.9
24	Delaware	0.9
NA	Florida**	NA
12	Georgia	2.6
NA	Hawaii**	NA
NA	Idaho**	NA
3	Illinois	7.9
21	Indiana	1.3
NA	Iowa**	NA
18	Kansas	1.8
11	Kentucky	3.3
6	Louisiana	4.9
29	Maine	0.1
NA	Maryland**	NA
27	Massachusetts	0.2
1	Michigan	9.8
13	Minnesota	2.5
19	Mississippi	1.6
16	Missouri	1.9
NA	Montana**	NA
NA	Nebraska**	NA
NA	Nevada**	NA
NA	New Hampshire**	NA
NA	New Jersey**	NA
26	New Mexico	0.4
8	New York	3.9
4	North Carolina	6.1
NA	North Dakota**	NA
NA	Ohio**	NA
NA	Oklahoma**	NA
NA	Oregon**	NA
20	Pennsylvania	1.4
NA	Rhode Island**	NA
14	South Carolina	2.3
NA	South Dakota**	NA
16	Tennessee	1.9
NA	Texas**	NA
22	Utah	1.2
NA	Vermont**	NA
2	Virginia	8.5
NA	Washington**	NA
NA	West Virginia**	NA
27	Wisconsin	0.2
NA	Wyoming**	NA

RANK ORDER

RANK	STATE	PERCENT
1	Michigan	9.8
2	Virginia	8.5
3	Illinois	7.9
4	North Carolina	6.1
5	California	5.4
6	Louisiana	4.9
7	Arizona	4.8
8	Connecticut	3.9
8	New York	3.9
10	Alaska	3.4
11	Kentucky	3.3
12	Georgia	2.6
13	Minnesota	2.5
14	South Carolina	2.3
15	Alabama	2.2
16	Missouri	1.9
16	Tennessee	1.9
18	Kansas	1.8
19	Mississippi	1.6
20	Pennsylvania	1.4
21	Indiana	1.3
22	Utah	1.2
23	Arkansas	1.1
24	Delaware	0.9
25	Colorado	0.6
26	New Mexico	0.4
27	Massachusetts	0.2
27	Wisconsin	0.2
29	Maine	0.1
NA	Florida**	NA
NA	Hawaii**	NA
NA	Idaho**	NA
NA	Iowa**	NA
NA	Maryland**	NA
NA	Montana**	NA
NA	Nebraska**	NA
NA	Nevada**	NA
NA	New Hampshire**	NA
NA	New Jersey**	NA
NA	North Dakota**	NA
NA	Ohio**	NA
NA	Oklahoma**	NA
NA	Oregon**	NA
NA	Rhode Island**	NA
NA	South Dakota**	NA
NA	Texas**	NA
NA	Vermont**	NA
NA	Washington**	NA
NA	West Virginia**	NA
NA	Wyoming**	NA

District of Columbia	1.3

Source: CQ Press using data from U.S. Department of Education, National Center for Education Statistics
"Common Core of Data (CCD) Database" (http://nces.ed.gov/ccd/)

*For school year 2005-2006. National percent is only for reporting states. Magnet schools are those designed to attract students of different racial/ethnic backgrounds for the purpose of reducing racial isolation, or to provide an academic or social focus on a specific theme (e.g., performing arts).

**Not available or not applicable.

Public Elementary and Secondary Charter Schools in 2006

National Total = 3,780 Schools*

ALPHA ORDER

RANK	STATE	SCHOOLS	% of USA
NA	Alabama**	NA	NA
26	Alaska	23	0.6%
2	Arizona	501	13.3%
28	Arkansas	19	0.5%
1	California	543	14.4%
9	Colorado	121	3.2%
31	Connecticut	14	0.4%
33	Delaware	13	0.3%
3	Florida	342	9.0%
14	Georgia	58	1.5%
21	Hawaii	27	0.7%
23	Idaho	26	0.7%
19	Illinois	29	0.8%
19	Indiana	29	0.8%
36	Iowa	6	0.2%
23	Kansas	26	0.7%
NA	Kentucky**	NA	NA
23	Louisiana	26	0.7%
NA	Maine**	NA	NA
30	Maryland	15	0.4%
13	Massachusetts	59	1.6%
6	Michigan	264	7.0%
8	Minnesota	161	4.3%
40	Mississippi	1	0.0%
26	Missouri	23	0.6%
NA	Montana**	NA	NA
NA	Nebraska**	NA	NA
28	Nevada	19	0.5%
36	New Hampshire	6	0.2%
15	New Jersey	54	1.4%
17	New Mexico	53	1.4%
12	New York	79	2.1%
11	North Carolina	99	2.6%
NA	North Dakota**	NA	NA
5	Ohio	316	8.4%
31	Oklahoma	14	0.4%
15	Oregon	54	1.4%
10	Pennsylvania	116	3.1%
35	Rhode Island	11	0.3%
21	South Carolina	27	0.7%
NA	South Dakota**	NA	NA
34	Tennessee	12	0.3%
4	Texas	319	8.4%
18	Utah	36	1.0%
NA	Vermont**	NA	NA
38	Virginia	3	0.1%
NA	Washington**	NA	NA
NA	West Virginia**	NA	NA
7	Wisconsin	181	4.8%
38	Wyoming	3	0.1%

RANK ORDER

RANK	STATE	SCHOOLS	% of USA
1	California	543	14.4%
2	Arizona	501	13.3%
3	Florida	342	9.0%
4	Texas	319	8.4%
5	Ohio	316	8.4%
6	Michigan	264	7.0%
7	Wisconsin	181	4.8%
8	Minnesota	161	4.3%
9	Colorado	121	3.2%
10	Pennsylvania	116	3.1%
11	North Carolina	99	2.6%
12	New York	79	2.1%
13	Massachusetts	59	1.6%
14	Georgia	58	1.5%
15	New Jersey	54	1.4%
15	Oregon	54	1.4%
17	New Mexico	53	1.4%
18	Utah	36	1.0%
19	Illinois	29	0.8%
19	Indiana	29	0.8%
21	Hawaii	27	0.7%
21	South Carolina	27	0.7%
23	Idaho	26	0.7%
23	Kansas	26	0.7%
23	Louisiana	26	0.7%
26	Alaska	23	0.6%
26	Missouri	23	0.6%
28	Arkansas	19	0.5%
28	Nevada	19	0.5%
30	Maryland	15	0.4%
31	Connecticut	14	0.4%
31	Oklahoma	14	0.4%
33	Delaware	13	0.3%
34	Tennessee	12	0.3%
35	Rhode Island	11	0.3%
36	Iowa	6	0.2%
36	New Hampshire	6	0.2%
38	Virginia	3	0.1%
38	Wyoming	3	0.1%
40	Mississippi	1	0.0%
NA	Alabama**	NA	NA
NA	Kentucky**	NA	NA
NA	Maine**	NA	NA
NA	Montana**	NA	NA
NA	Nebraska**	NA	NA
NA	North Dakota**	NA	NA
NA	South Dakota**	NA	NA
NA	Vermont**	NA	NA
NA	Washington**	NA	NA
NA	West Virginia**	NA	NA
	District of Columbia	52	1.4%

Source: U.S. Department of Education, National Center for Education Statistics
   "Common Core of Data (CCD) Database" (http://nces.ed.gov/ccd/)
*For school year 2005-2006. Charter schools provide free public elementary/secondary education under a charter granted by the state legislature or other appropriate authority.
**Not available or not applicable.

Percent of Public Elementary and Secondary
That are Charter Schools: 2006
National Percent = 3.9%*

ALPHA ORDER

RANK	STATE	PERCENT
NA	Alabama**	NA
12	Alaska	4.6
1	Arizona	24.1
27	Arkansas	1.7
11	California	5.6
6	Colorado	7.1
30	Connecticut	1.3
10	Delaware	5.9
3	Florida	9.2
22	Georgia	2.4
2	Hawaii	9.5
16	Idaho	3.7
36	Illinois	0.7
29	Indiana	1.5
38	Iowa	0.4
26	Kansas	1.8
NA	Kentucky**	NA
25	Louisiana	1.9
NA	Maine**	NA
32	Maryland	1.0
21	Massachusetts	3.1
7	Michigan	6.5
9	Minnesota	6.1
39	Mississippi	0.1
32	Missouri	1.0
NA	Montana**	NA
NA	Nebraska**	NA
19	Nevada	3.4
30	New Hampshire	1.3
24	New Jersey	2.2
8	New Mexico	6.2
27	New York	1.7
14	North Carolina	4.2
NA	North Dakota**	NA
5	Ohio	7.9
34	Oklahoma	0.8
13	Oregon	4.3
18	Pennsylvania	3.6
20	Rhode Island	3.3
23	South Carolina	2.3
NA	South Dakota**	NA
36	Tennessee	0.7
16	Texas	3.7
15	Utah	3.8
NA	Vermont**	NA
39	Virginia	0.1
NA	Washington**	NA
NA	West Virginia**	NA
4	Wisconsin	8.1
34	Wyoming	0.8

RANK ORDER

RANK	STATE	PERCENT
1	Arizona	24.1
2	Hawaii	9.5
3	Florida	9.2
4	Wisconsin	8.1
5	Ohio	7.9
6	Colorado	7.1
7	Michigan	6.5
8	New Mexico	6.2
9	Minnesota	6.1
10	Delaware	5.9
11	California	5.6
12	Alaska	4.6
13	Oregon	4.3
14	North Carolina	4.2
15	Utah	3.8
16	Idaho	3.7
16	Texas	3.7
18	Pennsylvania	3.6
19	Nevada	3.4
20	Rhode Island	3.3
21	Massachusetts	3.1
22	Georgia	2.4
23	South Carolina	2.3
24	New Jersey	2.2
25	Louisiana	1.9
26	Kansas	1.8
27	Arkansas	1.7
27	New York	1.7
29	Indiana	1.5
30	Connecticut	1.3
30	New Hampshire	1.3
32	Maryland	1.0
32	Missouri	1.0
34	Oklahoma	0.8
34	Wyoming	0.8
36	Illinois	0.7
36	Tennessee	0.7
38	Iowa	0.4
39	Mississippi	0.1
39	Virginia	0.1
NA	Alabama**	NA
NA	Kentucky**	NA
NA	Maine**	NA
NA	Montana**	NA
NA	Nebraska**	NA
NA	North Dakota**	NA
NA	South Dakota**	NA
NA	Vermont**	NA
NA	Washington**	NA
NA	West Virginia**	NA

District of Columbia	22.7

Source: CQ Press using data from U.S. Department of Education, National Center for Education Statistics
   "Common Core of Data (CCD) Database" (http://nces.ed.gov/ccd/)
*For school year 2005-2006. Charter schools provide free public elementary/secondary education under a charter granted by the state legislature or other appropriate authority.
**Not available or not applicable.

Average Size of Public Elementary and Secondary Schools in 2006

National Average = 552.6 Students*

ALPHA ORDER

RANK	STATE	STUDENTS
21	Alabama	549.8
45	Alaska	269.9
19	Arizona	551.7
33	Arkansas	430.6
4	California	744.8
31	Colorado	474.9
20	Connecticut	550.5
8	Delaware	648.9
1	Florida	868.2
3	Georgia	769.9
5	Hawaii	659.3
35	Idaho	426.3
23	Illinois	532.6
17	Indiana	552.9
41	Iowa	335.1
42	Kansas	331.6
24	Kentucky	523.3
25	Louisiana	519.3
43	Maine	302.5
7	Maryland	650.8
26	Massachusetts	514.9
28	Michigan	482.2
27	Minnesota	495.8
18	Mississippi	552.4
36	Missouri	416.4
50	Montana	174.2
46	Nebraska	251.8
2	Nevada	785.4
34	New Hampshire	428.7
14	New Jersey	584.6
37	New Mexico	408.4
13	New York	626.4
12	North Carolina	628.6
48	North Dakota	197.4
29	Ohio	477.0
40	Oklahoma	355.0
32	Oregon	441.4
16	Pennsylvania	571.5
30	Rhode Island	476.2
10	South Carolina	637.8
49	South Dakota	175.6
15	Tennessee	581.9
11	Texas	632.6
9	Utah	644.1
44	Vermont	299.5
6	Virginia	658.8
22	Washington	532.8
39	West Virginia	391.9
38	Wisconsin	404.2
47	Wyoming	240.0

RANK ORDER

RANK	STATE	STUDENTS
1	Florida	868.2
2	Nevada	785.4
3	Georgia	769.9
4	California	744.8
5	Hawaii	659.3
6	Virginia	658.8
7	Maryland	650.8
8	Delaware	648.9
9	Utah	644.1
10	South Carolina	637.8
11	Texas	632.6
12	North Carolina	628.6
13	New York	626.4
14	New Jersey	584.6
15	Tennessee	581.9
16	Pennsylvania	571.5
17	Indiana	552.9
18	Mississippi	552.4
19	Arizona	551.7
20	Connecticut	550.5
21	Alabama	549.8
22	Washington	532.8
23	Illinois	532.6
24	Kentucky	523.3
25	Louisiana	519.3
26	Massachusetts	514.9
27	Minnesota	495.8
28	Michigan	482.2
29	Ohio	477.0
30	Rhode Island	476.2
31	Colorado	474.9
32	Oregon	441.4
33	Arkansas	430.6
34	New Hampshire	428.7
35	Idaho	426.3
36	Missouri	416.4
37	New Mexico	408.4
38	Wisconsin	404.2
39	West Virginia	391.9
40	Oklahoma	355.0
41	Iowa	335.1
42	Kansas	331.6
43	Maine	302.5
44	Vermont	299.5
45	Alaska	269.9
46	Nebraska	251.8
47	Wyoming	240.0
48	North Dakota	197.4
49	South Dakota	175.6
50	Montana	174.2
	District of Columbia	352.7

Source: U.S. Department of Education, National Center for Education Statistics
   "Common Core of Data (CCD) Database" (http://nces.ed.gov/ccd/)
*For school year 2005-2006. Includes primary, middle, high, and other schools.

Membership Size of Largest Public Elementary and Secondary Schools in 2006

National Average = 3,059 Students*

ALPHA ORDER				RANK ORDER		
RANK	STATE	STUDENTS		RANK	STATE	STUDENTS
32	Alabama	2,464		1	Ohio	6,245
38	Alaska	2,249		2	Illinois	5,452
18	Arizona	3,198		3	California	5,336
33	Arkansas	2,422		4	New Jersey	5,216
3	California	5,336		5	Florida	5,060
12	Colorado	3,678		6	Texas	4,872
28	Connecticut	2,568		7	New York	4,538
34	Delaware	2,331		8	Pennsylvania	4,399
5	Florida	5,060		9	Massachusetts	4,282
13	Georgia	3,581		10	Virginia	4,163
27	Hawaii	2,579		11	Indiana	3,916
42	Idaho	2,173		12	Colorado	3,678
2	Illinois	5,452		13	Georgia	3,581
11	Indiana	3,916		14	New Hampshire	3,392
44	Iowa	2,141		15	Nevada	3,311
37	Kansas	2,300		16	Minnesota	3,267
41	Kentucky	2,209		17	South Carolina	3,203
35	Louisiana	2,309		18	Arizona	3,198
49	Maine	1,496		19	Maryland	3,057
19	Maryland	3,057		20	Washington	2,997
9	Massachusetts	4,282		21	North Carolina	2,992
23	Michigan	2,869		22	New Mexico	2,954
16	Minnesota	3,267		23	Michigan	2,869
46	Mississippi	1,924		24	Missouri	2,806
24	Missouri	2,806		25	Oregon	2,767
43	Montana	2,143		26	Tennessee	2,706
29	Nebraska	2,557		27	Hawaii	2,579
15	Nevada	3,311		28	Connecticut	2,568
14	New Hampshire	3,392		29	Nebraska	2,557
4	New Jersey	5,216		30	Utah	2,491
22	New Mexico	2,954		31	Wisconsin	2,477
7	New York	4,538		32	Alabama	2,464
21	North Carolina	2,992		33	Arkansas	2,422
47	North Dakota	1,623		34	Delaware	2,331
1	Ohio	6,245		35	Louisiana	2,309
40	Oklahoma	2,220		36	West Virginia	2,302
25	Oregon	2,767		37	Kansas	2,300
8	Pennsylvania	4,399		38	Alaska	2,249
45	Rhode Island	2,029		39	South Dakota	2,227
17	South Carolina	3,203		40	Oklahoma	2,220
39	South Dakota	2,227		41	Kentucky	2,209
26	Tennessee	2,706		42	Idaho	2,173
6	Texas	4,872		43	Montana	2,143
30	Utah	2,491		44	Iowa	2,141
48	Vermont	1,533		45	Rhode Island	2,029
10	Virginia	4,163		46	Mississippi	1,924
20	Washington	2,997		47	North Dakota	1,623
36	West Virginia	2,302		48	Vermont	1,533
31	Wisconsin	2,477		49	Maine	1,496
50	Wyoming	1,491		50	Wyoming	1,491
					District of Columbia	3,514

Source: U.S. Department of Education, National Center for Education Statistics
    "Common Core of Data (CCD) Database" (http://nces.ed.gov/ccd/)
*For school year 2005-2006. Includes primary, middle, high, and other schools.

Membership Size of Smallest Public Elementary and Secondary Schools in 2006

National Average = 11 Students*

<table>
<tr><td colspan="3">ALPHA ORDER</td><td colspan="3">RANK ORDER</td></tr>
<tr><th>RANK</th><th>STATE</th><th>STUDENTS</th><th>RANK</th><th>STATE</th><th>STUDENTS</th></tr>
<tr><td>3</td><td>Alabama</td><td>50</td><td>1</td><td>Louisiana</td><td>71</td></tr>
<tr><td>20</td><td>Alaska</td><td>5</td><td>2</td><td>Kentucky</td><td>54</td></tr>
<tr><td>28</td><td>Arizona</td><td>3</td><td>3</td><td>Alabama</td><td>50</td></tr>
<tr><td>10</td><td>Arkansas</td><td>15</td><td>4</td><td>Delaware</td><td>47</td></tr>
<tr><td>40</td><td>California</td><td>1</td><td>5</td><td>Hawaii</td><td>34</td></tr>
<tr><td>40</td><td>Colorado</td><td>1</td><td>6</td><td>Illinois</td><td>33</td></tr>
<tr><td>34</td><td>Connecticut</td><td>2</td><td>7</td><td>West Virginia</td><td>26</td></tr>
<tr><td>4</td><td>Delaware</td><td>47</td><td>8</td><td>Georgia</td><td>23</td></tr>
<tr><td>34</td><td>Florida</td><td>2</td><td>9</td><td>Virginia</td><td>22</td></tr>
<tr><td>8</td><td>Georgia</td><td>23</td><td>10</td><td>Arkansas</td><td>15</td></tr>
<tr><td>5</td><td>Hawaii</td><td>34</td><td>10</td><td>Pennsylvania</td><td>15</td></tr>
<tr><td>22</td><td>Idaho</td><td>4</td><td>12</td><td>South Carolina</td><td>14</td></tr>
<tr><td>6</td><td>Illinois</td><td>33</td><td>13</td><td>New Jersey</td><td>11</td></tr>
<tr><td>15</td><td>Indiana</td><td>8</td><td>14</td><td>Mississippi</td><td>10</td></tr>
<tr><td>34</td><td>Iowa</td><td>2</td><td>15</td><td>Indiana</td><td>8</td></tr>
<tr><td>28</td><td>Kansas</td><td>3</td><td>15</td><td>Nevada</td><td>8</td></tr>
<tr><td>2</td><td>Kentucky</td><td>54</td><td>17</td><td>Maryland</td><td>7</td></tr>
<tr><td>1</td><td>Louisiana</td><td>71</td><td>18</td><td>Oklahoma</td><td>6</td></tr>
<tr><td>34</td><td>Maine</td><td>2</td><td>18</td><td>Vermont</td><td>6</td></tr>
<tr><td>17</td><td>Maryland</td><td>7</td><td>20</td><td>Alaska</td><td>5</td></tr>
<tr><td>34</td><td>Massachusetts</td><td>2</td><td>20</td><td>New York</td><td>5</td></tr>
<tr><td>34</td><td>Michigan</td><td>2</td><td>22</td><td>Idaho</td><td>4</td></tr>
<tr><td>40</td><td>Minnesota</td><td>1</td><td>22</td><td>Missouri</td><td>4</td></tr>
<tr><td>14</td><td>Mississippi</td><td>10</td><td>22</td><td>North Dakota</td><td>4</td></tr>
<tr><td>22</td><td>Missouri</td><td>4</td><td>22</td><td>Rhode Island</td><td>4</td></tr>
<tr><td>40</td><td>Montana</td><td>1</td><td>22</td><td>Utah</td><td>4</td></tr>
<tr><td>40</td><td>Nebraska</td><td>1</td><td>22</td><td>Washington</td><td>4</td></tr>
<tr><td>15</td><td>Nevada</td><td>8</td><td>28</td><td>Arizona</td><td>3</td></tr>
<tr><td>28</td><td>New Hampshire</td><td>3</td><td>28</td><td>Kansas</td><td>3</td></tr>
<tr><td>13</td><td>New Jersey</td><td>11</td><td>28</td><td>New Hampshire</td><td>3</td></tr>
<tr><td>40</td><td>New Mexico</td><td>1</td><td>28</td><td>North Carolina</td><td>3</td></tr>
<tr><td>20</td><td>New York</td><td>5</td><td>28</td><td>South Dakota</td><td>3</td></tr>
<tr><td>28</td><td>North Carolina</td><td>3</td><td>28</td><td>Tennessee</td><td>3</td></tr>
<tr><td>22</td><td>North Dakota</td><td>4</td><td>34</td><td>Connecticut</td><td>2</td></tr>
<tr><td>40</td><td>Ohio</td><td>1</td><td>34</td><td>Florida</td><td>2</td></tr>
<tr><td>18</td><td>Oklahoma</td><td>6</td><td>34</td><td>Iowa</td><td>2</td></tr>
<tr><td>40</td><td>Oregon</td><td>1</td><td>34</td><td>Maine</td><td>2</td></tr>
<tr><td>10</td><td>Pennsylvania</td><td>15</td><td>34</td><td>Massachusetts</td><td>2</td></tr>
<tr><td>22</td><td>Rhode Island</td><td>4</td><td>34</td><td>Michigan</td><td>2</td></tr>
<tr><td>12</td><td>South Carolina</td><td>14</td><td>40</td><td>California</td><td>1</td></tr>
<tr><td>28</td><td>South Dakota</td><td>3</td><td>40</td><td>Colorado</td><td>1</td></tr>
<tr><td>28</td><td>Tennessee</td><td>3</td><td>40</td><td>Minnesota</td><td>1</td></tr>
<tr><td>40</td><td>Texas</td><td>1</td><td>40</td><td>Montana</td><td>1</td></tr>
<tr><td>22</td><td>Utah</td><td>4</td><td>40</td><td>Nebraska</td><td>1</td></tr>
<tr><td>18</td><td>Vermont</td><td>6</td><td>40</td><td>New Mexico</td><td>1</td></tr>
<tr><td>9</td><td>Virginia</td><td>22</td><td>40</td><td>Ohio</td><td>1</td></tr>
<tr><td>22</td><td>Washington</td><td>4</td><td>40</td><td>Oregon</td><td>1</td></tr>
<tr><td>7</td><td>West Virginia</td><td>26</td><td>40</td><td>Texas</td><td>1</td></tr>
<tr><td>40</td><td>Wisconsin</td><td>1</td><td>40</td><td>Wisconsin</td><td>1</td></tr>
<tr><td>40</td><td>Wyoming</td><td>1</td><td>40</td><td>Wyoming</td><td>1</td></tr>
<tr><td></td><td></td><td></td><td></td><td>District of Columbia</td><td>22</td></tr>
</table>

Source: U.S. Department of Education, National Center for Education Statistics
"Common Core of Data (CCD) Database" (http://nces.ed.gov/ccd/)
*For school year 2005-2006. Includes primary, middle, high, and other schools.

Public Primary Schools in 2006

National Total = 51,972 Schools*

ALPHA ORDER

RANK	STATE	SCHOOLS	% of USA		RANK	STATE	SCHOOLS	% of USA
28	Alabama	709	1.4%		1	California	5,583	10.7%
49	Alaska	169	0.3%		2	Texas	4,029	7.8%
18	Arizona	1,083	2.1%		3	New York	2,499	4.8%
32	Arkansas	562	1.1%		4	Illinois	2,476	4.8%
1	California	5,583	10.7%		5	Ohio	2,151	4.1%
19	Colorado	989	1.9%		6	Michigan	2,042	3.9%
33	Connecticut	551	1.1%		7	Florida	1,909	3.7%
50	Delaware	107	0.2%		8	Pennsylvania	1,905	3.7%
7	Florida	1,909	3.7%		9	New Jersey	1,528	2.9%
11	Georgia	1,244	2.4%		10	North Carolina	1,355	2.6%
48	Hawaii	180	0.3%		11	Georgia	1,244	2.4%
41	Idaho	343	0.7%		12	Wisconsin	1,234	2.4%
4	Illinois	2,476	4.8%		13	Missouri	1,231	2.4%
16	Indiana	1,144	2.2%		14	Virginia	1,180	2.3%
25	Iowa	773	1.5%		15	Massachusetts	1,167	2.2%
24	Kansas	780	1.5%		16	Indiana	1,144	2.2%
26	Kentucky	741	1.4%		17	Washington	1,128	2.2%
29	Louisiana	698	1.3%		18	Arizona	1,083	2.1%
39	Maine	404	0.8%		19	Colorado	989	1.9%
23	Maryland	858	1.7%		20	Tennessee	979	1.9%
15	Massachusetts	1,167	2.2%		21	Oklahoma	967	1.9%
6	Michigan	2,042	3.9%		22	Minnesota	925	1.8%
22	Minnesota	925	1.8%		23	Maryland	858	1.7%
37	Mississippi	448	0.9%		24	Kansas	780	1.5%
13	Missouri	1,231	2.4%		25	Iowa	773	1.5%
38	Montana	431	0.8%		26	Kentucky	741	1.4%
27	Nebraska	734	1.4%		27	Nebraska	734	1.4%
42	Nevada	335	0.6%		28	Alabama	709	1.4%
43	New Hampshire	299	0.6%		29	Louisiana	698	1.3%
9	New Jersey	1,528	2.9%		30	Oregon	651	1.3%
36	New Mexico	458	0.9%		31	South Carolina	630	1.2%
3	New York	2,499	4.8%		32	Arkansas	562	1.1%
10	North Carolina	1,355	2.6%		33	Connecticut	551	1.1%
44	North Dakota	287	0.6%		34	Utah	501	1.0%
5	Ohio	2,151	4.1%		35	West Virginia	466	0.9%
21	Oklahoma	967	1.9%		36	New Mexico	458	0.9%
30	Oregon	651	1.3%		37	Mississippi	448	0.9%
8	Pennsylvania	1,905	3.7%		38	Montana	431	0.8%
46	Rhode Island	206	0.4%		39	Maine	404	0.8%
31	South Carolina	630	1.2%		40	South Dakota	348	0.7%
40	South Dakota	348	0.7%		41	Idaho	343	0.7%
20	Tennessee	979	1.9%		42	Nevada	335	0.6%
2	Texas	4,029	7.8%		43	New Hampshire	299	0.6%
34	Utah	501	1.0%		44	North Dakota	287	0.6%
45	Vermont	223	0.4%		45	Vermont	223	0.4%
14	Virginia	1,180	2.3%		46	Rhode Island	206	0.4%
17	Washington	1,128	2.2%		47	Wyoming	200	0.4%
35	West Virginia	466	0.9%		48	Hawaii	180	0.3%
12	Wisconsin	1,234	2.4%		49	Alaska	169	0.3%
47	Wyoming	200	0.4%		50	Delaware	107	0.2%
						District of Columbia	132	0.3%

Source: U.S. Department of Education, National Center for Education Statistics
"Common Core of Data (CCD) Database" (http://nces.ed.gov/ccd/)
*Estimate for school year 2005-2006. Primary grades are determined by states and range from a low of pre-kindergarten to a high of 8th grade.

Average Size of Public Primary Schools in 2006

National Average = 445.2 Students*

ALPHA ORDER			RANK ORDER		
RANK	STATE	STUDENTS	RANK	STATE	STUDENTS
17	Alabama	460.6	1	Florida	665.0
38	Alaska	319.1	2	Georgia	617.4
8	Arizona	514.7	3	Nevada	600.6
27	Arkansas	391.6	4	California	548.5
4	California	548.5	5	Texas	545.8
28	Colorado	386.6	6	Utah	532.4
18	Connecticut	456.0	7	South Carolina	528.4
11	Delaware	499.5	8	Arizona	514.7
1	Florida	665.0	9	New York	512.1
2	Georgia	617.4	10	Hawaii	512.0
10	Hawaii	512.0	11	Delaware	499.5
32	Idaho	351.5	12	North Carolina	498.2
21	Illinois	439.1	13	Mississippi	489.6
22	Indiana	428.1	14	Virginia	483.2
43	Iowa	281.4	15	Tennessee	471.2
41	Kansas	290.9	16	Maryland	462.6
25	Kentucky	414.2	17	Alabama	460.6
19	Louisiana	450.4	18	Connecticut	456.0
44	Maine	217.2	19	Louisiana	450.4
16	Maryland	462.6	20	New Jersey	440.9
30	Massachusetts	385.5	21	Illinois	439.1
31	Michigan	373.4	22	Indiana	428.1
26	Minnesota	403.8	23	Pennsylvania	427.1
13	Mississippi	489.6	24	Washington	416.5
35	Missouri	344.5	25	Kentucky	414.2
50	Montana	157.5	26	Minnesota	403.8
46	Nebraska	191.8	27	Arkansas	391.6
3	Nevada	600.6	28	Colorado	386.6
40	New Hampshire	300.9	29	Ohio	386.5
20	New Jersey	440.9	30	Massachusetts	385.5
36	New Mexico	336.6	31	Michigan	373.4
9	New York	512.1	32	Idaho	351.5
12	North Carolina	498.2	33	Oklahoma	345.2
48	North Dakota	165.1	34	Oregon	344.9
29	Ohio	386.5	35	Missouri	344.5
33	Oklahoma	345.2	36	New Mexico	336.6
34	Oregon	344.9	37	Wisconsin	329.1
23	Pennsylvania	427.1	38	Alaska	319.1
39	Rhode Island	316.8	39	Rhode Island	316.8
7	South Carolina	528.4	40	New Hampshire	300.9
49	South Dakota	163.1	41	Kansas	290.9
15	Tennessee	471.2	42	West Virginia	289.8
5	Texas	545.8	43	Iowa	281.4
6	Utah	532.4	44	Maine	217.2
45	Vermont	216.2	45	Vermont	216.2
14	Virginia	483.2	46	Nebraska	191.8
24	Washington	416.5	46	Wyoming	191.8
42	West Virginia	289.8	48	North Dakota	165.1
37	Wisconsin	329.1	49	South Dakota	163.1
46	Wyoming	191.8	50	Montana	157.5

District of Columbia	293.5

Source: U.S. Department of Education, National Center for Education Statistics
    "Common Core of Data (CCD) Database" (http://nces.ed.gov/ccd/)
*Estimate for school year 2005-2006. Primary grades are determined by states and range from a low of pre-kindergarten to a high of 8th grade.

Percent of Public Schools that are Primary Schools in 2006

National Percent = 59.9%*

ALPHA ORDER

RANK	STATE	PERCENT
45	Alabama	52.8
50	Alaska	37.8
27	Arizona	58.7
47	Arkansas	51.1
2	California	67.9
19	Colorado	61.3
42	Connecticut	54.3
17	Delaware	61.8
14	Florida	63.4
24	Georgia	60.2
10	Hawaii	64.3
35	Idaho	56.9
13	Illinois	63.5
18	Indiana	61.4
41	Iowa	54.4
40	Kansas	55.5
20	Kentucky	61.1
36	Louisiana	56.7
15	Maine	62.5
3	Maryland	66.9
11	Massachusetts	64.2
26	Michigan	59.3
36	Minnesota	56.7
49	Mississippi	50.0
38	Missouri	56.2
46	Montana	51.7
7	Nebraska	64.9
9	Nevada	64.5
16	New Hampshire	62.3
5	New Jersey	65.5
28	New Mexico	58.4
34	New York	57.1
23	North Carolina	60.5
31	North Dakota	57.6
39	Ohio	55.9
43	Oklahoma	54.1
43	Oregon	54.1
21	Pennsylvania	60.6
4	Rhode Island	66.5
30	South Carolina	57.7
48	South Dakota	50.5
25	Tennessee	60.1
32	Texas	57.3
8	Utah	64.8
1	Vermont	70.6
11	Virginia	64.2
21	Washington	60.6
6	West Virginia	65.4
32	Wisconsin	57.3
29	Wyoming	57.8

RANK ORDER

RANK	STATE	PERCENT
1	Vermont	70.6
2	California	67.9
3	Maryland	66.9
4	Rhode Island	66.5
5	New Jersey	65.5
6	West Virginia	65.4
7	Nebraska	64.9
8	Utah	64.8
9	Nevada	64.5
10	Hawaii	64.3
11	Massachusetts	64.2
11	Virginia	64.2
13	Illinois	63.5
14	Florida	63.4
15	Maine	62.5
16	New Hampshire	62.3
17	Delaware	61.8
18	Indiana	61.4
19	Colorado	61.3
20	Kentucky	61.1
21	Pennsylvania	60.6
21	Washington	60.6
23	North Carolina	60.5
24	Georgia	60.2
25	Tennessee	60.1
26	Michigan	59.3
27	Arizona	58.7
28	New Mexico	58.4
29	Wyoming	57.8
30	South Carolina	57.7
31	North Dakota	57.6
32	Texas	57.3
32	Wisconsin	57.3
34	New York	57.1
35	Idaho	56.9
36	Louisiana	56.7
36	Minnesota	56.7
38	Missouri	56.2
39	Ohio	55.9
40	Kansas	55.5
41	Iowa	54.4
42	Connecticut	54.3
43	Oklahoma	54.1
43	Oregon	54.1
45	Alabama	52.8
46	Montana	51.7
47	Arkansas	51.1
48	South Dakota	50.5
49	Mississippi	50.0
50	Alaska	37.8

District of Columbia 65.0

Source: CQ Press using data from U.S. Department of Education, National Center for Education Statistics
"Common Core of Data (CCD) Database" (http://nces.ed.gov/ccd/)
*Estimated percent of regular public schools for school year 2005-2006. Primary grades are determined by states and range from a low of pre-kindergarten to a high of 8th grade.

Public Middle Schools in 2006

National Total = 16,121 Schools*

ALPHA ORDER

RANK ORDER

RANK	STATE	SCHOOLS	% of USA
23	Alabama	254	1.6%
49	Alaska	34	0.2%
25	Arizona	249	1.5%
31	Arkansas	212	1.3%
2	California	1,340	8.3%
20	Colorado	290	1.8%
36	Connecticut	160	1.0%
46	Delaware	39	0.2%
8	Florida	548	3.4%
11	Georgia	450	2.8%
47	Hawaii	37	0.2%
40	Idaho	113	0.7%
4	Illinois	739	4.6%
16	Indiana	341	2.1%
21	Iowa	285	1.8%
22	Kansas	255	1.6%
28	Kentucky	238	1.5%
27	Louisiana	242	1.5%
39	Maine	115	0.7%
29	Maryland	234	1.5%
15	Massachusetts	342	2.1%
6	Michigan	642	4.0%
26	Minnesota	245	1.5%
33	Mississippi	182	1.1%
12	Missouri	377	2.3%
30	Montana	232	1.4%
41	Nebraska	108	0.7%
43	Nevada	88	0.5%
42	New Hampshire	99	0.6%
10	New Jersey	453	2.8%
34	New Mexico	173	1.1%
3	New York	834	5.2%
9	North Carolina	467	2.9%
48	North Dakota	36	0.2%
5	Ohio	734	4.6%
18	Oklahoma	333	2.1%
32	Oregon	188	1.2%
7	Pennsylvania	559	3.5%
45	Rhode Island	57	0.4%
23	South Carolina	254	1.6%
35	South Dakota	170	1.1%
19	Tennessee	313	1.9%
1	Texas	1,605	10.0%
37	Utah	132	0.8%
50	Vermont	27	0.2%
16	Virginia	341	2.1%
14	Washington	351	2.2%
38	West Virginia	125	0.8%
13	Wisconsin	373	2.3%
44	Wyoming	77	0.5%

RANK	STATE	SCHOOLS	% of USA
1	Texas	1,605	10.0%
2	California	1,340	8.3%
3	New York	834	5.2%
4	Illinois	739	4.6%
5	Ohio	734	4.6%
6	Michigan	642	4.0%
7	Pennsylvania	559	3.5%
8	Florida	548	3.4%
9	North Carolina	467	2.9%
10	New Jersey	453	2.8%
11	Georgia	450	2.8%
12	Missouri	377	2.3%
13	Wisconsin	373	2.3%
14	Washington	351	2.2%
15	Massachusetts	342	2.1%
16	Indiana	341	2.1%
16	Virginia	341	2.1%
18	Oklahoma	333	2.1%
19	Tennessee	313	1.9%
20	Colorado	290	1.8%
21	Iowa	285	1.8%
22	Kansas	255	1.6%
23	Alabama	254	1.6%
23	South Carolina	254	1.6%
25	Arizona	249	1.5%
26	Minnesota	245	1.5%
27	Louisiana	242	1.5%
28	Kentucky	238	1.5%
29	Maryland	234	1.5%
30	Montana	232	1.4%
31	Arkansas	212	1.3%
32	Oregon	188	1.2%
33	Mississippi	182	1.1%
34	New Mexico	173	1.1%
35	South Dakota	170	1.1%
36	Connecticut	160	1.0%
37	Utah	132	0.8%
38	West Virginia	125	0.8%
39	Maine	115	0.7%
40	Idaho	113	0.7%
41	Nebraska	108	0.7%
42	New Hampshire	99	0.6%
43	Nevada	88	0.5%
44	Wyoming	77	0.5%
45	Rhode Island	57	0.4%
46	Delaware	39	0.2%
47	Hawaii	37	0.2%
48	North Dakota	36	0.2%
49	Alaska	34	0.2%
50	Vermont	27	0.2%
	District of Columbia	29	0.2%

Source: U.S. Department of Education, National Center for Education Statistics
"Common Core of Data (CCD) Database" (http://nces.ed.gov/ccd/)
*Estimate for school year 2005-2006. Middle school grades are determined by states and range from a low of 4th grade to a high of 9th grade.

Average Size of Public Middle Schools in 2006

National Average = 603.4 Students*

ALPHA ORDER				RANK ORDER		
RANK	STATE	STUDENTS		RANK	STATE	STUDENTS
24	Alabama	575.4		1	Nevada	1,030.6
34	Alaska	493.1		2	Florida	974.5
15	Arizona	627.2		3	California	882.0
37	Arkansas	473.7		4	Georgia	812.7
3	California	882.0		5	Hawaii	811.5
29	Colorado	513.1		6	Maryland	780.2
22	Connecticut	602.3		7	Virginia	763.1
9	Delaware	732.0		8	Utah	753.9
2	Florida	974.5		9	Delaware	732.0
4	Georgia	812.7		10	North Carolina	673.3
5	Hawaii	811.5		11	New York	672.0
30	Idaho	505.6		12	Pennsylvania	638.7
36	Illinois	487.2		13	Rhode Island	633.4
21	Indiana	602.4		14	South Carolina	630.8
46	Iowa	337.5		15	Arizona	627.2
45	Kansas	352.3		16	New Jersey	625.3
26	Kentucky	567.4		17	Texas	621.9
28	Louisiana	522.5		18	Minnesota	617.6
44	Maine	375.0		19	Tennessee	609.1
6	Maryland	780.2		20	Massachusetts	603.0
20	Massachusetts	603.0		21	Indiana	602.4
27	Michigan	538.6		22	Connecticut	602.3
18	Minnesota	617.6		23	Washington	586.6
25	Mississippi	568.5		24	Alabama	575.4
32	Missouri	497.4		25	Mississippi	568.5
50	Montana	126.6		26	Kentucky	567.4
40	Nebraska	408.3		27	Michigan	538.6
1	Nevada	1,030.6		28	Louisiana	522.5
35	New Hampshire	489.3		29	Colorado	513.1
16	New Jersey	625.3		30	Idaho	505.6
41	New Mexico	402.6		31	Oregon	504.6
11	New York	672.0		32	Missouri	497.4
10	North Carolina	673.3		33	Ohio	494.2
42	North Dakota	400.6		34	Alaska	493.1
33	Ohio	494.2		35	New Hampshire	489.3
43	Oklahoma	379.0		36	Illinois	487.2
31	Oregon	504.6		37	Arkansas	473.7
12	Pennsylvania	638.7		38	West Virginia	468.9
13	Rhode Island	633.4		39	Wisconsin	434.7
14	South Carolina	630.8		40	Nebraska	408.3
49	South Dakota	153.1		41	New Mexico	402.6
19	Tennessee	609.1		42	North Dakota	400.6
17	Texas	621.9		43	Oklahoma	379.0
8	Utah	753.9		44	Maine	375.0
47	Vermont	330.3		45	Kansas	352.3
7	Virginia	763.1		46	Iowa	337.5
23	Washington	586.6		47	Vermont	330.3
38	West Virginia	468.9		48	Wyoming	264.1
39	Wisconsin	434.7		49	South Dakota	153.1
48	Wyoming	264.1		50	Montana	126.6
					District of Columbia	363.4

Source: U.S. Department of Education, National Center for Education Statistics
    "Common Core of Data (CCD) Database" (http://nces.ed.gov/ccd/)
*Estimate for school year 2005-2006. Middle school grades are determined by states and range from a low of 4th grade to a high of 9th grade.

Percent of Public Schools That are Middle Schools in 2006

National Percent = 18.6%*

ALPHA ORDER				RANK ORDER		
RANK	STATE	PERCENT		RANK	STATE	PERCENT
21	Alabama	18.9		1	Montana	27.8
49	Alaska	7.6		2	South Dakota	24.7
45	Arizona	13.5		3	South Carolina	23.3
16	Arkansas	19.3		4	Texas	22.8
41	California	16.3		5	Delaware	22.5
33	Colorado	18.0		6	Wyoming	22.3
42	Connecticut	15.8		7	New Mexico	22.1
5	Delaware	22.5		8	Georgia	21.8
31	Florida	18.2		9	North Carolina	20.8
8	Georgia	21.8		10	New Hampshire	20.6
46	Hawaii	13.2		11	Mississippi	20.3
24	Idaho	18.7		12	Iowa	20.1
20	Illinois	19.0		13	Louisiana	19.7
29	Indiana	18.3		14	Kentucky	19.6
12	Iowa	20.1		15	New Jersey	19.4
32	Kansas	18.1		16	Arkansas	19.3
14	Kentucky	19.6		17	Tennessee	19.2
13	Louisiana	19.7		18	New York	19.1
34	Maine	17.8		18	Ohio	19.1
29	Maryland	18.3		20	Illinois	19.0
23	Massachusetts	18.8		21	Alabama	18.9
25	Michigan	18.6		21	Washington	18.9
44	Minnesota	15.0		23	Massachusetts	18.8
11	Mississippi	20.3		24	Idaho	18.7
38	Missouri	17.2		25	Michigan	18.6
1	Montana	27.8		25	Oklahoma	18.6
47	Nebraska	9.5		25	Virginia	18.6
40	Nevada	17.0		28	Rhode Island	18.4
10	New Hampshire	20.6		29	Indiana	18.3
15	New Jersey	19.4		29	Maryland	18.3
7	New Mexico	22.1		31	Florida	18.2
18	New York	19.1		32	Kansas	18.1
9	North Carolina	20.8		33	Colorado	18.0
50	North Dakota	7.2		34	Maine	17.8
18	Ohio	19.1		34	Pennsylvania	17.8
25	Oklahoma	18.6		36	West Virginia	17.5
43	Oregon	15.6		37	Wisconsin	17.3
34	Pennsylvania	17.8		38	Missouri	17.2
28	Rhode Island	18.4		39	Utah	17.1
3	South Carolina	23.3		40	Nevada	17.0
2	South Dakota	24.7		41	California	16.3
17	Tennessee	19.2		42	Connecticut	15.8
4	Texas	22.8		43	Oregon	15.6
39	Utah	17.1		44	Minnesota	15.0
48	Vermont	8.5		45	Arizona	13.5
25	Virginia	18.6		46	Hawaii	13.2
21	Washington	18.9		47	Nebraska	9.5
36	West Virginia	17.5		48	Vermont	8.5
37	Wisconsin	17.3		49	Alaska	7.6
6	Wyoming	22.3		50	North Dakota	7.2

District of Columbia   14.3

Source: CQ Press using data from U.S. Department of Education, National Center for Education Statistics
"Common Core of Data (CCD) Database" (http://nces.ed.gov/ccd/)
*Estimated percent of regular public schools for school year 2005-2006. Middle school grades are determined by states and range from a low of 4th grade to a high of 9th grade.

Public High Schools in 2006

National Total = 15,409 Schools*

<table>
<tr><th colspan="4">ALPHA ORDER</th><th colspan="4">RANK ORDER</th></tr>
<tr><th>RANK</th><th>STATE</th><th>SCHOOLS</th><th>% of USA</th><th>RANK</th><th>STATE</th><th>SCHOOLS</th><th>% of USA</th></tr>
<tr><td>26</td><td>Alabama</td><td>275</td><td>1.8%</td><td>1</td><td>Texas</td><td>1,109</td><td>7.2%</td></tr>
<tr><td>46</td><td>Alaska</td><td>51</td><td>0.3%</td><td>2</td><td>California</td><td>1,062</td><td>6.9%</td></tr>
<tr><td>13</td><td>Arizona</td><td>385</td><td>2.5%</td><td>3</td><td>Ohio</td><td>770</td><td>5.0%</td></tr>
<tr><td>22</td><td>Arkansas</td><td>297</td><td>1.9%</td><td>4</td><td>New York</td><td>764</td><td>5.0%</td></tr>
<tr><td>2</td><td>California</td><td>1,062</td><td>6.9%</td><td>5</td><td>Illinois</td><td>620</td><td>4.0%</td></tr>
<tr><td>25</td><td>Colorado</td><td>278</td><td>1.8%</td><td>6</td><td>Michigan</td><td>600</td><td>3.9%</td></tr>
<tr><td>37</td><td>Connecticut</td><td>148</td><td>1.0%</td><td>7</td><td>Pennsylvania</td><td>599</td><td>3.9%</td></tr>
<tr><td>50</td><td>Delaware</td><td>25</td><td>0.2%</td><td>8</td><td>Missouri</td><td>491</td><td>3.2%</td></tr>
<tr><td>11</td><td>Florida</td><td>417</td><td>2.7%</td><td>9</td><td>Wisconsin</td><td>471</td><td>3.1%</td></tr>
<tr><td>16</td><td>Georgia</td><td>341</td><td>2.2%</td><td>10</td><td>Oklahoma</td><td>466</td><td>3.0%</td></tr>
<tr><td>49</td><td>Hawaii</td><td>42</td><td>0.3%</td><td>11</td><td>Florida</td><td>417</td><td>2.7%</td></tr>
<tr><td>39</td><td>Idaho</td><td>117</td><td>0.8%</td><td>11</td><td>Minnesota</td><td>417</td><td>2.7%</td></tr>
<tr><td>5</td><td>Illinois</td><td>620</td><td>4.0%</td><td>13</td><td>Arizona</td><td>385</td><td>2.5%</td></tr>
<tr><td>17</td><td>Indiana</td><td>329</td><td>2.1%</td><td>14</td><td>North Carolina</td><td>362</td><td>2.3%</td></tr>
<tr><td>18</td><td>Iowa</td><td>327</td><td>2.1%</td><td>15</td><td>Kansas</td><td>347</td><td>2.3%</td></tr>
<tr><td>15</td><td>Kansas</td><td>347</td><td>2.3%</td><td>16</td><td>Georgia</td><td>341</td><td>2.2%</td></tr>
<tr><td>28</td><td>Kentucky</td><td>221</td><td>1.4%</td><td>17</td><td>Indiana</td><td>329</td><td>2.1%</td></tr>
<tr><td>30</td><td>Louisiana</td><td>211</td><td>1.4%</td><td>18</td><td>Iowa</td><td>327</td><td>2.1%</td></tr>
<tr><td>42</td><td>Maine</td><td>111</td><td>0.7%</td><td>19</td><td>New Jersey</td><td>325</td><td>2.1%</td></tr>
<tr><td>33</td><td>Maryland</td><td>177</td><td>1.1%</td><td>20</td><td>Washington</td><td>305</td><td>2.0%</td></tr>
<tr><td>27</td><td>Massachusetts</td><td>260</td><td>1.7%</td><td>21</td><td>Virginia</td><td>298</td><td>1.9%</td></tr>
<tr><td>6</td><td>Michigan</td><td>600</td><td>3.9%</td><td>22</td><td>Arkansas</td><td>297</td><td>1.9%</td></tr>
<tr><td>11</td><td>Minnesota</td><td>417</td><td>2.7%</td><td>23</td><td>Tennessee</td><td>289</td><td>1.9%</td></tr>
<tr><td>32</td><td>Mississippi</td><td>190</td><td>1.2%</td><td>24</td><td>Nebraska</td><td>287</td><td>1.9%</td></tr>
<tr><td>8</td><td>Missouri</td><td>491</td><td>3.2%</td><td>25</td><td>Colorado</td><td>278</td><td>1.8%</td></tr>
<tr><td>35</td><td>Montana</td><td>169</td><td>1.1%</td><td>26</td><td>Alabama</td><td>275</td><td>1.8%</td></tr>
<tr><td>24</td><td>Nebraska</td><td>287</td><td>1.9%</td><td>27</td><td>Massachusetts</td><td>260</td><td>1.7%</td></tr>
<tr><td>44</td><td>Nevada</td><td>78</td><td>0.5%</td><td>28</td><td>Kentucky</td><td>221</td><td>1.4%</td></tr>
<tr><td>43</td><td>New Hampshire</td><td>79</td><td>0.5%</td><td>29</td><td>Oregon</td><td>217</td><td>1.4%</td></tr>
<tr><td>19</td><td>New Jersey</td><td>325</td><td>2.1%</td><td>30</td><td>Louisiana</td><td>211</td><td>1.4%</td></tr>
<tr><td>38</td><td>New Mexico</td><td>136</td><td>0.9%</td><td>31</td><td>South Carolina</td><td>194</td><td>1.3%</td></tr>
<tr><td>4</td><td>New York</td><td>764</td><td>5.0%</td><td>32</td><td>Mississippi</td><td>190</td><td>1.2%</td></tr>
<tr><td>14</td><td>North Carolina</td><td>362</td><td>2.3%</td><td>33</td><td>Maryland</td><td>177</td><td>1.1%</td></tr>
<tr><td>34</td><td>North Dakota</td><td>172</td><td>1.1%</td><td>34</td><td>North Dakota</td><td>172</td><td>1.1%</td></tr>
<tr><td>3</td><td>Ohio</td><td>770</td><td>5.0%</td><td>35</td><td>Montana</td><td>169</td><td>1.1%</td></tr>
<tr><td>10</td><td>Oklahoma</td><td>466</td><td>3.0%</td><td>36</td><td>South Dakota</td><td>165</td><td>1.1%</td></tr>
<tr><td>29</td><td>Oregon</td><td>217</td><td>1.4%</td><td>37</td><td>Connecticut</td><td>148</td><td>1.0%</td></tr>
<tr><td>7</td><td>Pennsylvania</td><td>599</td><td>3.9%</td><td>38</td><td>New Mexico</td><td>136</td><td>0.9%</td></tr>
<tr><td>48</td><td>Rhode Island</td><td>44</td><td>0.3%</td><td>39</td><td>Idaho</td><td>117</td><td>0.8%</td></tr>
<tr><td>31</td><td>South Carolina</td><td>194</td><td>1.3%</td><td>39</td><td>Utah</td><td>117</td><td>0.8%</td></tr>
<tr><td>36</td><td>South Dakota</td><td>165</td><td>1.1%</td><td>41</td><td>West Virginia</td><td>114</td><td>0.7%</td></tr>
<tr><td>23</td><td>Tennessee</td><td>289</td><td>1.9%</td><td>42</td><td>Maine</td><td>111</td><td>0.7%</td></tr>
<tr><td>1</td><td>Texas</td><td>1,109</td><td>7.2%</td><td>43</td><td>New Hampshire</td><td>79</td><td>0.5%</td></tr>
<tr><td>39</td><td>Utah</td><td>117</td><td>0.8%</td><td>44</td><td>Nevada</td><td>78</td><td>0.5%</td></tr>
<tr><td>47</td><td>Vermont</td><td>48</td><td>0.3%</td><td>45</td><td>Wyoming</td><td>64</td><td>0.4%</td></tr>
<tr><td>21</td><td>Virginia</td><td>298</td><td>1.9%</td><td>46</td><td>Alaska</td><td>51</td><td>0.3%</td></tr>
<tr><td>20</td><td>Washington</td><td>305</td><td>2.0%</td><td>47</td><td>Vermont</td><td>48</td><td>0.3%</td></tr>
<tr><td>41</td><td>West Virginia</td><td>114</td><td>0.7%</td><td>48</td><td>Rhode Island</td><td>44</td><td>0.3%</td></tr>
<tr><td>9</td><td>Wisconsin</td><td>471</td><td>3.1%</td><td>49</td><td>Hawaii</td><td>42</td><td>0.3%</td></tr>
<tr><td>45</td><td>Wyoming</td><td>64</td><td>0.4%</td><td>50</td><td>Delaware</td><td>25</td><td>0.2%</td></tr>
<tr><td></td><td></td><td></td><td></td><td></td><td>District of Columbia</td><td>28</td><td>0.2%</td></tr>
</table>

Source: U.S. Department of Education, National Center for Education Statistics
   "Common Core of Data (CCD) Database" (http://nces.ed.gov/ccd/)
*Estimate for school year 2005-2006. High school grades are determined by states and range from a low of 7th grade to a high of 12th grade.

Average Size of Public High Schools in 2006

National Average = 886.9 Students*

ALPHA ORDER				RANK ORDER		
RANK	STATE	STUDENTS		RANK	STATE	STUDENTS
32	Alabama	714.4		1	Florida	1,745.4
37	Alaska	634.8		2	California	1,643.4
31	Arizona	715.7		3	Maryland	1,413.6
43	Arkansas	441.1		4	Nevada	1,408.2
2	California	1,643.4		5	Hawaii	1,335.1
27	Colorado	757.1		6	Georgia	1,296.6
24	Connecticut	832.1		7	Virginia	1,233.1
9	Delaware	1,180.6		8	New Jersey	1,208.0
1	Florida	1,745.4		9	Delaware	1,180.6
6	Georgia	1,296.6		10	North Carolina	1,097.1
5	Hawaii	1,335.1		11	Rhode Island	1,037.9
39	Idaho	581.8		12	New York	1,024.6
16	Illinois	961.8		13	Texas	1,021.4
21	Indiana	925.0		14	South Carolina	1,011.7
42	Iowa	463.5		15	Utah	997.8
44	Kansas	418.4		16	Illinois	961.8
23	Kentucky	844.9		17	Pennsylvania	951.8
26	Louisiana	774.4		18	Massachusetts	944.0
41	Maine	553.5		19	Washington	942.9
3	Maryland	1,413.6		20	Tennessee	934.0
18	Massachusetts	944.0		21	Indiana	925.0
25	Michigan	828.3		22	New Hampshire	850.8
36	Minnesota	641.2		23	Kentucky	844.9
33	Mississippi	688.1		24	Connecticut	832.1
40	Missouri	566.0		25	Michigan	828.3
48	Montana	278.2		26	Louisiana	774.4
46	Nebraska	348.0		27	Colorado	757.1
4	Nevada	1,408.2		28	Ohio	732.9
22	New Hampshire	850.8		29	West Virginia	725.4
8	New Jersey	1,208.0		30	Oregon	720.6
35	New Mexico	647.7		31	Arizona	715.7
12	New York	1,024.6		32	Alabama	714.4
10	North Carolina	1,097.1		33	Mississippi	688.1
50	North Dakota	199.7		34	Vermont	664.5
28	Ohio	732.9		35	New Mexico	647.7
47	Oklahoma	341.7		36	Minnesota	641.2
30	Oregon	720.6		37	Alaska	634.8
17	Pennsylvania	951.8		38	Wisconsin	592.4
11	Rhode Island	1,037.9		39	Idaho	581.8
14	South Carolina	1,011.7		40	Missouri	566.0
49	South Dakota	209.2		41	Maine	553.5
20	Tennessee	934.0		42	Iowa	463.5
13	Texas	1,021.4		43	Arkansas	441.1
15	Utah	997.8		44	Kansas	418.4
34	Vermont	664.5		45	Wyoming	365.5
7	Virginia	1,233.1		46	Nebraska	348.0
19	Washington	942.9		47	Oklahoma	341.7
29	West Virginia	725.4		48	Montana	278.2
38	Wisconsin	592.4		49	South Dakota	209.2
45	Wyoming	365.5		50	North Dakota	199.7
					District of Columbia	493.5

Source: U.S. Department of Education, National Center for Education Statistics
"Common Core of Data (CCD) Database" (http://nces.ed.gov/ccd/)
*Estimate for school year 2005-2006. High school grades are determined by states and range from a low of 7th grade to a high of 12th grade.

Percent of Public Schools That are High Schools in 2006

National Percent = 17.8%*

RANK	STATE	PERCENT
13	Alabama	20.5
50	Alaska	11.4
12	Arizona	20.9
2	Arkansas	27.0
49	California	12.9
27	Colorado	17.2
42	Connecticut	14.6
43	Delaware	14.5
47	Florida	13.8
30	Georgia	16.5
40	Hawaii	15.0
16	Idaho	19.4
36	Illinois	15.9
23	Indiana	17.7
8	Iowa	23.0
6	Kansas	24.7
19	Kentucky	18.2
29	Louisiana	17.1
27	Maine	17.2
47	Maryland	13.8
44	Massachusetts	14.3
25	Michigan	17.4
4	Minnesota	25.6
11	Mississippi	21.2
9	Missouri	22.4
14	Montana	20.3
5	Nebraska	25.4
40	Nevada	15.0
30	New Hampshire	16.5
46	New Jersey	13.9
26	New Mexico	17.3
24	New York	17.5
33	North Carolina	16.2
1	North Dakota	34.5
15	Ohio	20.0
3	Oklahoma	26.1
20	Oregon	18.0
17	Pennsylvania	19.1
45	Rhode Island	14.2
21	South Carolina	17.8
7	South Dakota	23.9
21	Tennessee	17.8
37	Texas	15.8
39	Utah	15.1
38	Vermont	15.2
33	Virginia	16.2
32	Washington	16.4
35	West Virginia	16.0
10	Wisconsin	21.9
18	Wyoming	18.5

RANK	STATE	PERCENT
1	North Dakota	34.5
2	Arkansas	27.0
3	Oklahoma	26.1
4	Minnesota	25.6
5	Nebraska	25.4
6	Kansas	24.7
7	South Dakota	23.9
8	Iowa	23.0
9	Missouri	22.4
10	Wisconsin	21.9
11	Mississippi	21.2
12	Arizona	20.9
13	Alabama	20.5
14	Montana	20.3
15	Ohio	20.0
16	Idaho	19.4
17	Pennsylvania	19.1
18	Wyoming	18.5
19	Kentucky	18.2
20	Oregon	18.0
21	South Carolina	17.8
21	Tennessee	17.8
23	Indiana	17.7
24	New York	17.5
25	Michigan	17.4
26	New Mexico	17.3
27	Colorado	17.2
27	Maine	17.2
29	Louisiana	17.1
30	Georgia	16.5
30	New Hampshire	16.5
32	Washington	16.4
33	North Carolina	16.2
33	Virginia	16.2
35	West Virginia	16.0
36	Illinois	15.9
37	Texas	15.8
38	Vermont	15.2
39	Utah	15.1
40	Hawaii	15.0
40	Nevada	15.0
42	Connecticut	14.6
43	Delaware	14.5
44	Massachusetts	14.3
45	Rhode Island	14.2
46	New Jersey	13.9
47	Florida	13.8
47	Maryland	13.8
49	California	12.9
50	Alaska	11.4
	District of Columbia	13.8

Source: CQ Press using data from U.S. Department of Education, National Center for Education Statistics
"Common Core of Data (CCD) Database" (http://nces.ed.gov/ccd/)
*Estimated percent of regular public schools for school year 2005-2006. High school grades are determined by states and range from a low of 7th grade to a high of 12th grade.

"Other" Public Schools in 2006

National Total = 3,290 Schools*

ALPHA ORDER

RANK	STATE	SCHOOLS	% of USA
11	Alabama	106	3.2%
4	Alaska	193	5.9%
10	Arizona	129	3.9%
28	Arkansas	28	0.9%
3	California	239	7.3%
20	Colorado	56	1.7%
7	Connecticut	156	4.7%
48	Delaware	2	0.1%
9	Florida	137	4.2%
26	Georgia	32	1.0%
33	Hawaii	21	0.6%
27	Idaho	30	0.9%
18	Illinois	64	1.9%
21	Indiana	50	1.5%
25	Iowa	36	1.1%
30	Kansas	24	0.7%
41	Kentucky	12	0.4%
13	Louisiana	80	2.4%
38	Maine	16	0.5%
39	Maryland	13	0.4%
22	Massachusetts	49	1.5%
6	Michigan	160	4.9%
24	Minnesota	44	1.3%
16	Mississippi	76	2.3%
12	Missouri	91	2.8%
48	Montana	2	0.1%
48	Nebraska	2	0.1%
35	Nevada	18	0.5%
45	New Hampshire	3	0.1%
29	New Jersey	26	0.8%
37	New Mexico	17	0.5%
2	New York	277	8.4%
19	North Carolina	57	1.7%
45	North Dakota	3	0.1%
5	Ohio	191	5.8%
32	Oklahoma	22	0.7%
8	Oregon	148	4.5%
14	Pennsylvania	78	2.4%
45	Rhode Island	3	0.1%
39	South Carolina	13	0.4%
43	South Dakota	6	0.2%
23	Tennessee	47	1.4%
1	Texas	293	8.9%
31	Utah	23	0.7%
35	Vermont	18	0.5%
34	Virginia	19	0.6%
15	Washington	77	2.3%
42	West Virginia	8	0.2%
16	Wisconsin	76	2.3%
44	Wyoming	5	0.2%

RANK ORDER

RANK	STATE	SCHOOLS	% of USA
1	Texas	293	8.9%
2	New York	277	8.4%
3	California	239	7.3%
4	Alaska	193	5.9%
5	Ohio	191	5.8%
6	Michigan	160	4.9%
7	Connecticut	156	4.7%
8	Oregon	148	4.5%
9	Florida	137	4.2%
10	Arizona	129	3.9%
11	Alabama	106	3.2%
12	Missouri	91	2.8%
13	Louisiana	80	2.4%
14	Pennsylvania	78	2.4%
15	Washington	77	2.3%
16	Mississippi	76	2.3%
16	Wisconsin	76	2.3%
18	Illinois	64	1.9%
19	North Carolina	57	1.7%
20	Colorado	56	1.7%
21	Indiana	50	1.5%
22	Massachusetts	49	1.5%
23	Tennessee	47	1.4%
24	Minnesota	44	1.3%
25	Iowa	36	1.1%
26	Georgia	32	1.0%
27	Idaho	30	0.9%
28	Arkansas	28	0.9%
29	New Jersey	26	0.8%
30	Kansas	24	0.7%
31	Utah	23	0.7%
32	Oklahoma	22	0.7%
33	Hawaii	21	0.6%
34	Virginia	19	0.6%
35	Nevada	18	0.5%
35	Vermont	18	0.5%
37	New Mexico	17	0.5%
38	Maine	16	0.5%
39	Maryland	13	0.4%
39	South Carolina	13	0.4%
41	Kentucky	12	0.4%
42	West Virginia	8	0.2%
43	South Dakota	6	0.2%
44	Wyoming	5	0.2%
45	New Hampshire	3	0.1%
45	North Dakota	3	0.1%
45	Rhode Island	3	0.1%
48	Delaware	2	0.1%
48	Montana	2	0.1%
48	Nebraska	2	0.1%
	District of Columbia	14	0.4%

Source: U.S. Department of Education, National Center for Education Statistics
   "Common Core of Data (CCD) Database" (http://nces.ed.gov/ccd/)
*Estimate for school year 2005-2006. "Other" schools are all schools not falling within primary, middle, or high school categories.
This includes ungraded schools.

Percent of Public Schools That are "Other" Schools in 2006

National Percent = 3.8%*

RANK	STATE	PERCENT
5	Alabama	7.9
1	Alaska	43.2
7	Arizona	7.0
27	Arkansas	2.5
22	California	2.9
18	Colorado	3.5
2	Connecticut	15.4
37	Delaware	1.2
14	Florida	4.5
35	Georgia	1.5
6	Hawaii	7.5
11	Idaho	5.0
34	Illinois	1.6
24	Indiana	2.7
27	Iowa	2.5
33	Kansas	1.7
42	Kentucky	1.0
8	Louisiana	6.5
27	Maine	2.5
42	Maryland	1.0
24	Massachusetts	2.7
13	Michigan	4.6
24	Minnesota	2.7
4	Mississippi	8.5
15	Missouri	4.2
49	Montana	0.2
49	Nebraska	0.2
18	Nevada	3.5
47	New Hampshire	0.6
40	New Jersey	1.1
32	New Mexico	2.2
9	New York	6.3
27	North Carolina	2.5
47	North Dakota	0.6
11	Ohio	5.0
37	Oklahoma	1.2
3	Oregon	12.3
27	Pennsylvania	2.5
42	Rhode Island	1.0
37	South Carolina	1.2
46	South Dakota	0.9
22	Tennessee	2.9
15	Texas	4.2
21	Utah	3.0
10	Vermont	5.7
42	Virginia	1.0
17	Washington	4.1
40	West Virginia	1.1
18	Wisconsin	3.5
36	Wyoming	1.4

RANK	STATE	PERCENT
1	Alaska	43.2
2	Connecticut	15.4
3	Oregon	12.3
4	Mississippi	8.5
5	Alabama	7.9
6	Hawaii	7.5
7	Arizona	7.0
8	Louisiana	6.5
9	New York	6.3
10	Vermont	5.7
11	Idaho	5.0
11	Ohio	5.0
13	Michigan	4.6
14	Florida	4.5
15	Missouri	4.2
15	Texas	4.2
17	Washington	4.1
18	Colorado	3.5
18	Nevada	3.5
18	Wisconsin	3.5
21	Utah	3.0
22	California	2.9
22	Tennessee	2.9
24	Indiana	2.7
24	Massachusetts	2.7
24	Minnesota	2.7
27	Arkansas	2.5
27	Iowa	2.5
27	Maine	2.5
27	North Carolina	2.5
27	Pennsylvania	2.5
32	New Mexico	2.2
33	Kansas	1.7
34	Illinois	1.6
35	Georgia	1.5
36	Wyoming	1.4
37	Delaware	1.2
37	Oklahoma	1.2
37	South Carolina	1.2
40	New Jersey	1.1
40	West Virginia	1.1
42	Kentucky	1.0
42	Maryland	1.0
42	Rhode Island	1.0
42	Virginia	1.0
46	South Dakota	0.9
47	New Hampshire	0.6
47	North Dakota	0.6
49	Montana	0.2
49	Nebraska	0.2

	District of Columbia	6.9

Source: CQ Press using data from U.S. Department of Education, National Center for Education Statistics
"Common Core of Data (CCD) Database" (http://nces.ed.gov/ccd/)
*Estimated percent of regular public schools for school year 2005-2006. "Other" schools are all schools not falling within primary, middle, or high school categories. This includes ungraded schools.

Private Elementary and Secondary Schools in 2006

National Total = 28,996 Schools*

ALPHA ORDER				RANK ORDER			
RANK	STATE	SCHOOLS	% of USA	RANK	STATE	SCHOOLS	% of USA
21	Alabama	435	1.5%	1	California	3,352	11.6%
47	Alaska**	86	0.3%	2	New York	1,970	6.8%
30	Arizona	287	1.0%	3	Pennsylvania	1,969	6.8%
35	Arkansas	217	0.7%	4	Florida	1,872	6.5%
1	California	3,352	11.6%	5	Illinois	1,413	4.9%
27	Colorado	333	1.1%	6	Texas	1,373	4.7%
26	Connecticut	356	1.2%	7	New Jersey	962	3.3%
45	Delaware	110	0.4%	8	Wisconsin	948	3.3%
4	Florida	1,872	6.5%	9	Ohio	939	3.2%
14	Georgia	715	2.5%	10	Michigan	856	3.0%
44	Hawaii	115	0.4%	11	Indiana	795	2.7%
41	Idaho	123	0.4%	12	Virginia	738	2.5%
5	Illinois	1,413	4.9%	13	Massachusetts	720	2.5%
11	Indiana	795	2.7%	14	Georgia	715	2.5%
31	Iowa	278	1.0%	15	Missouri	659	2.3%
25	Kansas**	405	1.4%	16	Maryland	656	2.3%
21	Kentucky**	435	1.5%	17	North Carolina	624	2.2%
24	Louisiana	422	1.5%	17	Washington	624	2.2%
38	Maine	148	0.5%	19	Tennessee	565	1.9%
16	Maryland	656	2.3%	20	Minnesota	555	1.9%
13	Massachusetts	720	2.5%	21	Alabama	435	1.5%
10	Michigan	856	3.0%	21	Kentucky**	435	1.5%
20	Minnesota	555	1.9%	23	Oregon	431	1.5%
29	Mississippi	298	1.0%	24	Louisiana	422	1.5%
15	Missouri	659	2.3%	25	Kansas**	405	1.4%
32	Montana**	239	0.8%	26	Connecticut	356	1.2%
34	Nebraska	223	0.8%	27	Colorado	333	1.1%
42	Nevada	117	0.4%	28	South Carolina	307	1.1%
37	New Hampshire	173	0.6%	29	Mississippi	298	1.0%
7	New Jersey	962	3.3%	30	Arizona	287	1.0%
36	New Mexico	183	0.6%	31	Iowa	278	1.0%
2	New York	1,970	6.8%	32	Montana**	239	0.8%
17	North Carolina	624	2.2%	33	Oklahoma**	232	0.8%
49	North Dakota	45	0.2%	34	Nebraska	223	0.8%
9	Ohio	939	3.2%	35	Arkansas	217	0.7%
33	Oklahoma**	232	0.8%	36	New Mexico	183	0.6%
23	Oregon	431	1.5%	37	New Hampshire	173	0.6%
3	Pennsylvania	1,969	6.8%	38	Maine	148	0.5%
40	Rhode Island	132	0.5%	39	West Virginia	145	0.5%
28	South Carolina	307	1.1%	40	Rhode Island	132	0.5%
48	South Dakota	83	0.3%	41	Idaho	123	0.4%
19	Tennessee	565	1.9%	42	Nevada	117	0.4%
6	Texas	1,373	4.7%	42	Vermont	117	0.4%
46	Utah	100	0.3%	44	Hawaii	115	0.4%
42	Vermont	117	0.4%	45	Delaware	110	0.4%
12	Virginia	738	2.5%	46	Utah	100	0.3%
17	Washington	624	2.2%	47	Alaska**	86	0.3%
39	West Virginia	145	0.5%	48	South Dakota	83	0.3%
8	Wisconsin	948	3.3%	49	North Dakota	45	0.2%
50	Wyoming	34	0.1%	50	Wyoming	34	0.1%
					District of Columbia	83	0.3%

Source: U.S. Department of Education, Institute of Education Sciences
    "Characteristics of Private Schools in the United States" (http://nces.ed.gov/pubs2008/2008315.pdf)
*For school year 2005-2006.
**Interpret data for these states with caution.

II. Finance

Estimated Public Elementary and Secondary School Revenue in 2007

National Total = $530,340,144,000*

ALPHA ORDER			
RANK	STATE	REVENUE	% of USA
26	Alabama	$6,139,024,000	1.2%
48	Alaska	1,346,246,000	0.3%
20	Arizona	8,430,531,000	1.6%
32	Arkansas	4,308,417,000	0.8%
1	California	67,460,001,000	12.7%
22	Colorado	7,427,625,000	1.4%
21	Connecticut	8,330,662,000	1.6%
43	Delaware	1,676,156,000	0.3%
4	Florida	27,556,082,000	5.2%
10	Georgia	16,777,376,000	3.2%
38	Hawaii	2,801,364,000	0.5%
42	Idaho	1,963,215,000	0.4%
6	Illinois	21,566,352,000	4.1%
14	Indiana	10,947,708,000	2.1%
31	Iowa	4,813,747,000	0.9%
30	Kansas	4,922,503,000	0.9%
27	Kentucky	6,061,203,000	1.1%
24	Louisiana	7,114,886,000	1.3%
40	Maine	2,424,997,000	0.5%
15	Maryland	10,523,272,000	2.0%
11	Massachusetts	14,584,811,000	2.8%
9	Michigan	19,579,507,000	3.7%
18	Minnesota	9,429,235,000	1.8%
33	Mississippi	3,933,100,000	0.7%
19	Missouri	9,241,660,000	1.7%
47	Montana	1,372,063,000	0.3%
39	Nebraska	2,619,990,000	0.5%
36	Nevada	3,104,334,000	0.6%
41	New Hampshire	2,401,022,000	0.5%
8	New Jersey	21,167,006,000	4.0%
35	New Mexico	3,277,222,000	0.6%
3	New York	43,032,887,000	8.1%
13	North Carolina	11,280,769,000	2.1%
50	North Dakota	967,345,000	0.2%
7	Ohio	21,509,807,000	4.1%
29	Oklahoma	5,053,779,000	1.0%
28	Oregon	5,742,139,000	1.1%
5	Pennsylvania	23,870,782,000	4.5%
44	Rhode Island	1,635,754,000	0.3%
25	South Carolina	6,870,445,000	1.3%
49	South Dakota	1,144,465,000	0.2%
23	Tennessee	7,421,887,000	1.4%
2	Texas	44,266,715,000	8.3%
34	Utah	3,470,425,000	0.7%
46	Vermont	1,397,078,000	0.3%
12	Virginia	13,444,882,000	2.5%
16	Washington	10,394,671,000	2.0%
37	West Virginia	3,042,217,000	0.6%
17	Wisconsin	10,130,078,000	1.9%
45	Wyoming	1,481,158,000	0.3%

RANK ORDER			
RANK	STATE	REVENUE	% of USA
1	California	$67,460,001,000	12.7%
2	Texas	44,266,715,000	8.3%
3	New York	43,032,887,000	8.1%
4	Florida	27,556,082,000	5.2%
5	Pennsylvania	23,870,782,000	4.5%
6	Illinois	21,566,352,000	4.1%
7	Ohio	21,509,807,000	4.1%
8	New Jersey	21,167,006,000	4.0%
9	Michigan	19,579,507,000	3.7%
10	Georgia	16,777,376,000	3.2%
11	Massachusetts	14,584,811,000	2.8%
12	Virginia	13,444,882,000	2.5%
13	North Carolina	11,280,769,000	2.1%
14	Indiana	10,947,708,000	2.1%
15	Maryland	10,523,272,000	2.0%
16	Washington	10,394,671,000	2.0%
17	Wisconsin	10,130,078,000	1.9%
18	Minnesota	9,429,235,000	1.8%
19	Missouri	9,241,660,000	1.7%
20	Arizona	8,430,531,000	1.6%
21	Connecticut	8,330,662,000	1.6%
22	Colorado	7,427,625,000	1.4%
23	Tennessee	7,421,887,000	1.4%
24	Louisiana	7,114,886,000	1.3%
25	South Carolina	6,870,445,000	1.3%
26	Alabama	6,139,024,000	1.2%
27	Kentucky	6,061,203,000	1.1%
28	Oregon	5,742,139,000	1.1%
29	Oklahoma	5,053,779,000	1.0%
30	Kansas	4,922,503,000	0.9%
31	Iowa	4,813,747,000	0.9%
32	Arkansas	4,308,417,000	0.8%
33	Mississippi	3,933,100,000	0.7%
34	Utah	3,470,425,000	0.7%
35	New Mexico	3,277,222,000	0.6%
36	Nevada	3,104,334,000	0.6%
37	West Virginia	3,042,217,000	0.6%
38	Hawaii	2,801,364,000	0.5%
39	Nebraska	2,619,990,000	0.5%
40	Maine	2,424,997,000	0.5%
41	New Hampshire	2,401,022,000	0.5%
42	Idaho	1,963,215,000	0.4%
43	Delaware	1,676,156,000	0.3%
44	Rhode Island	1,635,754,000	0.3%
45	Wyoming	1,481,158,000	0.3%
46	Vermont	1,397,078,000	0.3%
47	Montana	1,372,063,000	0.3%
48	Alaska	1,346,246,000	0.3%
49	South Dakota	1,144,465,000	0.2%
50	North Dakota	967,345,000	0.2%
	District of Columbia	881,544,000	0.2%

Source: National Education Association, Washington, D.C.
   "Rankings & Estimates" (Copyright © 2007, NEA, used with permission, http://www.nea.org/edstats/index.html)
*Estimates for school year 2006-2007.

Estimated Per Capita Public Elementary and Secondary School Revenue in 2007
National Per Capita = $1,758*

ALPHA ORDER

RANK	STATE	PER CAPITA
45	Alabama	$1,327
8	Alaska	1,970
44	Arizona	1,330
35	Arkansas	1,520
15	California	1,846
34	Colorado	1,528
3	Connecticut	2,379
10	Delaware	1,938
37	Florida	1,510
21	Georgia	1,758
7	Hawaii	2,183
47	Idaho	1,309
25	Illinois	1,678
23	Indiana	1,725
28	Iowa	1,611
20	Kansas	1,773
41	Kentucky	1,429
27	Louisiana	1,657
16	Maine	1,841
13	Maryland	1,873
4	Massachusetts	2,261
9	Michigan	1,944
18	Minnesota	1,814
43	Mississippi	1,348
30	Missouri	1,572
40	Montana	1,432
38	Nebraska	1,476
49	Nevada	1,210
17	New Hampshire	1,825
2	New Jersey	2,437
26	New Mexico	1,664
6	New York	2,230
48	North Carolina	1,245
36	North Dakota	1,512
12	Ohio	1,876
42	Oklahoma	1,397
33	Oregon	1,532
11	Pennsylvania	1,920
32	Rhode Island	1,546
31	South Carolina	1,559
39	South Dakota	1,437
50	Tennessee	1,205
14	Texas	1,852
46	Utah	1,312
5	Vermont	2,249
22	Virginia	1,743
29	Washington	1,607
24	West Virginia	1,679
19	Wisconsin	1,808
1	Wyoming	2,833

RANK ORDER

RANK	STATE	PER CAPITA
1	Wyoming	$2,833
2	New Jersey	2,437
3	Connecticut	2,379
4	Massachusetts	2,261
5	Vermont	2,249
6	New York	2,230
7	Hawaii	2,183
8	Alaska	1,970
9	Michigan	1,944
10	Delaware	1,938
11	Pennsylvania	1,920
12	Ohio	1,876
13	Maryland	1,873
14	Texas	1,852
15	California	1,846
16	Maine	1,841
17	New Hampshire	1,825
18	Minnesota	1,814
19	Wisconsin	1,808
20	Kansas	1,773
21	Georgia	1,758
22	Virginia	1,743
23	Indiana	1,725
24	West Virginia	1,679
25	Illinois	1,678
26	New Mexico	1,664
27	Louisiana	1,657
28	Iowa	1,611
29	Washington	1,607
30	Missouri	1,572
31	South Carolina	1,559
32	Rhode Island	1,546
33	Oregon	1,532
34	Colorado	1,528
35	Arkansas	1,520
36	North Dakota	1,512
37	Florida	1,510
38	Nebraska	1,476
39	South Dakota	1,437
40	Montana	1,432
41	Kentucky	1,429
42	Oklahoma	1,397
43	Mississippi	1,348
44	Arizona	1,330
45	Alabama	1,327
46	Utah	1,312
47	Idaho	1,309
48	North Carolina	1,245
49	Nevada	1,210
50	Tennessee	1,205
	District of Columbia	1,498

Source: CQ Press using data from National Education Association, Washington, D.C.
"Rankings & Estimates" (Copyright © 2007, NEA, used with permission, http://www.nea.org/edstats/index.html)
*Estimates for school year 2006-2007. Per capita calculated with 2007 population.

Estimated Per Pupil Public Elementary and Secondary School Revenue in 2007

National Per Pupil = $10,847*

ALPHA ORDER			RANK ORDER		
RANK	STATE	PER PUPIL	RANK	STATE	PER PUPIL
42	Alabama	$8,301	1	Wyoming	$17,506
28	Alaska	10,134	2	Hawaii	15,501
43	Arizona	8,156	3	New York	15,316
38	Arkansas	9,473	4	New Jersey	15,244
19	California	10,735	5	Vermont	15,092
40	Colorado	9,354	6	Massachusetts	15,065
7	Connecticut	14,519	7	Connecticut	14,519
8	Delaware	13,709	8	Delaware	13,709
23	Florida	10,345	9	Pennsylvania	13,106
24	Georgia	10,298	10	Maine	12,385
2	Hawaii	15,501	11	Maryland	12,364
48	Idaho	7,338	12	New Hampshire	11,663
27	Illinois	10,181	13	Wisconsin	11,555
20	Indiana	10,574	14	Ohio	11,530
33	Iowa	9,964	15	Minnesota	11,380
22	Kansas	10,451	16	Michigan	11,290
39	Kentucky	9,375	17	Virginia	10,933
21	Louisiana	10,527	18	West Virginia	10,815
10	Maine	12,385	19	California	10,735
11	Maryland	12,364	20	Indiana	10,574
6	Massachusetts	15,065	21	Louisiana	10,527
16	Michigan	11,290	22	Kansas	10,451
15	Minnesota	11,380	23	Florida	10,345
45	Mississippi	7,960	24	Georgia	10,298
25	Missouri	10,287	25	Missouri	10,287
37	Montana	9,501	26	Oregon	10,202
41	Nebraska	9,124	27	Illinois	10,181
49	Nevada	7,280	28	Alaska	10,134
12	New Hampshire	11,663	29	North Dakota	10,119
4	New Jersey	15,244	30	Washington	10,108
32	New Mexico	9,974	31	Rhode Island	10,081
3	New York	15,316	32	New Mexico	9,974
44	North Carolina	8,039	33	Iowa	9,964
29	North Dakota	10,119	34	South Carolina	9,962
14	Ohio	11,530	35	Texas	9,672
46	Oklahoma	7,909	36	South Dakota	9,515
26	Oregon	10,202	37	Montana	9,501
9	Pennsylvania	13,106	38	Arkansas	9,473
31	Rhode Island	10,081	39	Kentucky	9,375
34	South Carolina	9,962	40	Colorado	9,354
36	South Dakota	9,515	41	Nebraska	9,124
47	Tennessee	7,808	42	Alabama	8,301
35	Texas	9,672	43	Arizona	8,156
50	Utah	7,143	44	North Carolina	8,039
5	Vermont	15,092	45	Mississippi	7,960
17	Virginia	10,933	46	Oklahoma	7,909
30	Washington	10,108	47	Tennessee	7,808
18	West Virginia	10,815	48	Idaho	7,338
13	Wisconsin	11,555	49	Nevada	7,280
1	Wyoming	17,506	50	Utah	7,143
				District of Columbia	14,884

Source: CQ Press using data from National Education Association, Washington, D.C.
    "Rankings & Estimates" (Copyright © 2007, NEA, used with permission, http://www.nea.org/edstats/index.html)
*Estimates for school year 2006-2007. Based on student membership.

Estimated Public Elementary and Secondary School
Current Expenditures in 2007
National Total = $467,266,787,000*

ALPHA ORDER				RANK ORDER			
RANK	STATE	EXPENDITURES	% of USA	RANK	STATE	EXPENDITURES	% of USA
26	Alabama	$5,673,616,000	1.2%	1	California	$55,511,744,000	11.9%
45	Alaska	1,380,530,000	0.3%	2	New York	39,914,079,000	8.5%
24	Arizona	5,888,332,000	1.3%	3	Texas	36,836,951,000	7.9%
31	Arkansas	4,050,028,000	0.9%	4	Florida	22,624,018,000	4.8%
1	California	55,511,744,000	11.9%	5	Illinois	22,037,871,000	4.7%
21	Colorado	7,063,139,000	1.5%	6	Pennsylvania	20,588,194,000	4.4%
19	Connecticut	7,461,678,000	1.6%	7	New Jersey	20,377,229,000	4.4%
44	Delaware	1,536,293,000	0.3%	8	Ohio	19,705,080,000	4.2%
4	Florida	22,624,018,000	4.8%	9	Michigan	17,704,565,000	3.8%
10	Georgia	14,335,118,000	3.1%	10	Georgia	14,335,118,000	3.1%
42	Hawaii	1,885,019,000	0.4%	11	Massachusetts	12,870,218,000	2.8%
41	Idaho	1,919,802,000	0.4%	12	Virginia	12,033,240,000	2.6%
5	Illinois	22,037,871,000	4.7%	13	North Carolina	11,225,216,000	2.4%
14	Indiana	9,659,508,000	2.1%	14	Indiana	9,659,508,000	2.1%
32	Iowa	3,933,003,000	0.8%	15	Wisconsin	9,145,695,000	2.0%
30	Kansas	4,146,612,000	0.9%	16	Washington	8,977,812,000	1.9%
27	Kentucky	5,469,063,000	1.2%	17	Maryland	8,764,940,000	1.9%
25	Louisiana	5,851,062,000	1.3%	18	Minnesota	8,404,587,000	1.8%
39	Maine	2,361,939,000	0.5%	19	Connecticut	7,461,678,000	1.6%
17	Maryland	8,764,940,000	1.9%	20	Missouri	7,339,896,000	1.6%
11	Massachusetts	12,870,218,000	2.8%	21	Colorado	7,063,139,000	1.5%
9	Michigan	17,704,565,000	3.8%	22	Tennessee	6,896,413,000	1.5%
18	Minnesota	8,404,587,000	1.8%	23	South Carolina	6,396,072,000	1.4%
33	Mississippi	3,392,666,000	0.7%	24	Arizona	5,888,332,000	1.3%
20	Missouri	7,339,896,000	1.6%	25	Louisiana	5,851,062,000	1.3%
46	Montana	1,253,854,000	0.3%	26	Alabama	5,673,616,000	1.2%
38	Nebraska	2,385,974,000	0.5%	27	Kentucky	5,469,063,000	1.2%
34	Nevada	2,969,158,000	0.6%	28	Oregon	5,059,393,000	1.1%
40	New Hampshire	2,221,731,000	0.5%	29	Oklahoma	4,526,694,000	1.0%
7	New Jersey	20,377,229,000	4.4%	30	Kansas	4,146,612,000	0.9%
35	New Mexico	2,968,830,000	0.6%	31	Arkansas	4,050,028,000	0.9%
2	New York	39,914,079,000	8.5%	32	Iowa	3,933,003,000	0.8%
13	North Carolina	11,225,216,000	2.4%	33	Mississippi	3,392,666,000	0.7%
50	North Dakota	786,605,000	0.2%	34	Nevada	2,969,158,000	0.6%
8	Ohio	19,705,080,000	4.2%	35	New Mexico	2,968,830,000	0.6%
29	Oklahoma	4,526,694,000	1.0%	36	West Virginia	2,832,919,000	0.6%
28	Oregon	5,059,393,000	1.1%	37	Utah	2,696,707,000	0.6%
6	Pennsylvania	20,588,194,000	4.4%	38	Nebraska	2,385,974,000	0.5%
43	Rhode Island	1,866,520,000	0.4%	39	Maine	2,361,939,000	0.5%
23	South Carolina	6,396,072,000	1.4%	40	New Hampshire	2,221,731,000	0.5%
49	South Dakota	990,783,000	0.2%	41	Idaho	1,919,802,000	0.4%
22	Tennessee	6,896,413,000	1.5%	42	Hawaii	1,885,019,000	0.4%
3	Texas	36,836,951,000	7.9%	43	Rhode Island	1,866,520,000	0.4%
37	Utah	2,696,707,000	0.6%	44	Delaware	1,536,293,000	0.3%
47	Vermont	1,239,093,000	0.3%	45	Alaska	1,380,530,000	0.3%
12	Virginia	12,033,240,000	2.6%	46	Montana	1,253,854,000	0.3%
16	Washington	8,977,812,000	1.9%	47	Vermont	1,239,093,000	0.3%
36	West Virginia	2,832,919,000	0.6%	48	Wyoming	1,127,688,000	0.2%
15	Wisconsin	9,145,695,000	2.0%	49	South Dakota	990,783,000	0.2%
48	Wyoming	1,127,688,000	0.2%	50	North Dakota	786,605,000	0.2%
					District of Columbia	979,612,000	0.2%

Source: National Education Association, Washington, D.C.
   "Rankings & Estimates" (Copyright © 2007, NEA, used with permission, http://www.nea.org/edstats/index.html)
*Estimates for school year 2006-2007.

Estimated Per Capita Public Elementary and Secondary School Current Expenditures in 2007
National Per Capita = $1,549*

ALPHA ORDER

RANK	STATE	PER CAPITA
45	Alabama	$1,226
5	Alaska	2,020
50	Arizona	929
30	Arkansas	1,429
23	California	1,519
28	Colorado	1,453
3	Connecticut	2,131
9	Delaware	1,777
42	Florida	1,240
25	Georgia	1,502
27	Hawaii	1,469
38	Idaho	1,280
13	Illinois	1,715
22	Indiana	1,522
35	Iowa	1,316
26	Kansas	1,494
37	Kentucky	1,289
32	Louisiana	1,363
8	Maine	1,793
19	Maryland	1,560
6	Massachusetts	1,995
11	Michigan	1,758
17	Minnesota	1,617
46	Mississippi	1,162
40	Missouri	1,249
36	Montana	1,309
34	Nebraska	1,345
47	Nevada	1,157
14	New Hampshire	1,688
1	New Jersey	2,346
24	New Mexico	1,507
4	New York	2,068
43	North Carolina	1,239
44	North Dakota	1,230
12	Ohio	1,718
39	Oklahoma	1,251
33	Oregon	1,350
15	Pennsylvania	1,656
10	Rhode Island	1,764
29	South Carolina	1,451
41	South Dakota	1,244
48	Tennessee	1,120
21	Texas	1,541
49	Utah	1,019
6	Vermont	1,995
19	Virginia	1,560
31	Washington	1,388
18	West Virginia	1,563
16	Wisconsin	1,633
2	Wyoming	2,157

RANK ORDER

RANK	STATE	PER CAPITA
1	New Jersey	$2,346
2	Wyoming	2,157
3	Connecticut	2,131
4	New York	2,068
5	Alaska	2,020
6	Massachusetts	1,995
6	Vermont	1,995
8	Maine	1,793
9	Delaware	1,777
10	Rhode Island	1,764
11	Michigan	1,758
12	Ohio	1,718
13	Illinois	1,715
14	New Hampshire	1,688
15	Pennsylvania	1,656
16	Wisconsin	1,633
17	Minnesota	1,617
18	West Virginia	1,563
19	Maryland	1,560
19	Virginia	1,560
21	Texas	1,541
22	Indiana	1,522
23	California	1,519
24	New Mexico	1,507
25	Georgia	1,502
26	Kansas	1,494
27	Hawaii	1,469
28	Colorado	1,453
29	South Carolina	1,451
30	Arkansas	1,429
31	Washington	1,388
32	Louisiana	1,363
33	Oregon	1,350
34	Nebraska	1,345
35	Iowa	1,316
36	Montana	1,309
37	Kentucky	1,289
38	Idaho	1,280
39	Oklahoma	1,251
40	Missouri	1,249
41	South Dakota	1,244
42	Florida	1,240
43	North Carolina	1,239
44	North Dakota	1,230
45	Alabama	1,226
46	Mississippi	1,162
47	Nevada	1,157
48	Tennessee	1,120
49	Utah	1,019
50	Arizona	929
	District of Columbia	1,665

Source: CQ Press using data from National Education Association, Washington, D.C.
"Rankings & Estimates" (Copyright © 2007, NEA, used with permission, http://www.nea.org/edstats/index.html)
*Estimates for school year 2006-2007. Per capita calculated with 2007 population.

Estimated Per Pupil Public Elementary and Secondary School Current Expenditures in 2007
National Per Pupil = $9,557*

ALPHA ORDER

RANK	STATE	PER PUPIL
43	Alabama	$7,672
16	Alaska	10,392
49	Arizona	5,696
26	Arkansas	8,905
28	California	8,834
27	Colorado	8,895
6	Connecticut	13,005
7	Delaware	12,565
34	Florida	8,493
30	Georgia	8,799
14	Hawaii	10,431
45	Idaho	7,176
15	Illinois	10,404
22	Indiana	9,330
40	Iowa	8,141
29	Kansas	8,804
35	Kentucky	8,459
33	Louisiana	8,657
8	Maine	12,063
17	Maryland	10,298
5	Massachusetts	13,294
18	Michigan	10,209
19	Minnesota	10,143
48	Mississippi	6,866
39	Missouri	8,170
32	Montana	8,682
36	Nebraska	8,309
47	Nevada	6,963
11	New Hampshire	10,792
1	New Jersey	14,675
24	New Mexico	9,036
2	New York	14,206
42	North Carolina	8,000
38	North Dakota	8,228
12	Ohio	10,563
46	Oklahoma	7,084
25	Oregon	8,989
10	Pennsylvania	11,304
9	Rhode Island	11,503
23	South Carolina	9,274
37	South Dakota	8,237
44	Tennessee	7,255
41	Texas	8,048
50	Utah	5,551
3	Vermont	13,385
21	Virginia	9,785
31	Washington	8,730
20	West Virginia	10,071
13	Wisconsin	10,432
4	Wyoming	13,328

RANK ORDER

RANK	STATE	PER PUPIL
1	New Jersey	$14,675
2	New York	14,206
3	Vermont	13,385
4	Wyoming	13,328
5	Massachusetts	13,294
6	Connecticut	13,005
7	Delaware	12,565
8	Maine	12,063
9	Rhode Island	11,503
10	Pennsylvania	11,304
11	New Hampshire	10,792
12	Ohio	10,563
13	Wisconsin	10,432
14	Hawaii	10,431
15	Illinois	10,404
16	Alaska	10,392
17	Maryland	10,298
18	Michigan	10,209
19	Minnesota	10,143
20	West Virginia	10,071
21	Virginia	9,785
22	Indiana	9,330
23	South Carolina	9,274
24	New Mexico	9,036
25	Oregon	8,989
26	Arkansas	8,905
27	Colorado	8,895
28	California	8,834
29	Kansas	8,804
30	Georgia	8,799
31	Washington	8,730
32	Montana	8,682
33	Louisiana	8,657
34	Florida	8,493
35	Kentucky	8,459
36	Nebraska	8,309
37	South Dakota	8,237
38	North Dakota	8,228
39	Missouri	8,170
40	Iowa	8,141
41	Texas	8,048
42	North Carolina	8,000
43	Alabama	7,672
44	Tennessee	7,255
45	Idaho	7,176
46	Oklahoma	7,084
47	Nevada	6,963
48	Mississippi	6,866
49	Arizona	5,696
50	Utah	5,551
	District of Columbia	16,540

Source: National Education Association, Washington, D.C.
    "Rankings & Estimates" (Copyright © 2007, NEA, used with permission, http://www.nea.org/edstats/index.html)
*Estimates for school year 2006-2007. Based on student membership.

U.S. Department of Education Grants for State Assessments in 2008

National Total = $408,732,480*

ALPHA ORDER

RANK	STATE	GRANTS	% of USA
23	Alabama	$6,627,911	1.6%
47	Alaska	3,582,506	0.9%
13	Arizona	8,207,500	2.0%
33	Arkansas	5,231,827	1.3%
1	California	32,918,202	8.1%
22	Colorado	6,750,164	1.7%
29	Connecticut	5,710,938	1.4%
45	Delaware	3,653,124	0.9%
4	Florida	15,883,630	3.9%
9	Georgia	10,983,721	2.7%
42	Hawaii	3,885,522	1.0%
38	Idaho	4,286,349	1.0%
5	Illinois	13,269,377	3.2%
14	Indiana	8,112,893	2.0%
32	Iowa	5,293,799	1.3%
34	Kansas	5,224,636	1.3%
26	Kentucky	6,228,945	1.5%
24	Louisiana	6,477,064	1.6%
41	Maine	3,928,770	1.0%
19	Maryland	7,369,906	1.8%
17	Massachusetts	7,698,993	1.9%
8	Michigan	11,071,168	2.7%
21	Minnesota	7,033,188	1.7%
31	Mississippi	5,444,802	1.3%
18	Missouri	7,590,619	1.9%
44	Montana	3,713,659	0.9%
37	Nebraska	4,407,681	1.1%
35	Nevada	5,070,705	1.2%
40	New Hampshire	3,992,570	1.0%
11	New Jersey	9,706,321	2.4%
36	New Mexico	4,581,141	1.1%
3	New York	17,313,693	4.2%
10	North Carolina	10,030,709	2.5%
48	North Dakota	3,457,530	0.8%
7	Ohio	11,968,326	2.9%
27	Oklahoma	5,840,560	1.4%
28	Oregon	5,787,861	1.4%
6	Pennsylvania	12,151,657	3.0%
43	Rhode Island	3,764,106	0.9%
25	South Carolina	6,397,912	1.6%
46	South Dakota	3,624,926	0.9%
16	Tennessee	7,725,238	1.9%
2	Texas	23,621,959	5.8%
30	Utah	5,496,829	1.3%
49	Vermont	3,440,162	0.8%
12	Virginia	8,819,272	2.2%
15	Washington	7,953,805	1.9%
39	West Virginia	4,258,969	1.0%
20	Wisconsin	7,293,993	1.8%
50	Wyoming	3,398,143	0.8%

RANK ORDER

RANK	STATE	GRANTS	% of USA
1	California	$32,918,202	8.1%
2	Texas	23,621,959	5.8%
3	New York	17,313,693	4.2%
4	Florida	15,883,630	3.9%
5	Illinois	13,269,377	3.2%
6	Pennsylvania	12,151,657	3.0%
7	Ohio	11,968,326	2.9%
8	Michigan	11,071,168	2.7%
9	Georgia	10,983,721	2.7%
10	North Carolina	10,030,709	2.5%
11	New Jersey	9,706,321	2.4%
12	Virginia	8,819,272	2.2%
13	Arizona	8,207,500	2.0%
14	Indiana	8,112,893	2.0%
15	Washington	7,953,805	1.9%
16	Tennessee	7,725,238	1.9%
17	Massachusetts	7,698,993	1.9%
18	Missouri	7,590,619	1.9%
19	Maryland	7,369,906	1.8%
20	Wisconsin	7,293,993	1.8%
21	Minnesota	7,033,188	1.7%
22	Colorado	6,750,164	1.7%
23	Alabama	6,627,911	1.6%
24	Louisiana	6,477,064	1.6%
25	South Carolina	6,397,912	1.6%
26	Kentucky	6,228,945	1.5%
27	Oklahoma	5,840,560	1.4%
28	Oregon	5,787,861	1.4%
29	Connecticut	5,710,938	1.4%
30	Utah	5,496,829	1.3%
31	Mississippi	5,444,802	1.3%
32	Iowa	5,293,799	1.3%
33	Arkansas	5,231,827	1.3%
34	Kansas	5,224,636	1.3%
35	Nevada	5,070,705	1.2%
36	New Mexico	4,581,141	1.1%
37	Nebraska	4,407,681	1.1%
38	Idaho	4,286,349	1.0%
39	West Virginia	4,258,969	1.0%
40	New Hampshire	3,992,570	1.0%
41	Maine	3,928,770	1.0%
42	Hawaii	3,885,522	1.0%
43	Rhode Island	3,764,106	0.9%
44	Montana	3,713,659	0.9%
45	Delaware	3,653,124	0.9%
46	South Dakota	3,624,926	0.9%
47	Alaska	3,582,506	0.9%
48	North Dakota	3,457,530	0.8%
49	Vermont	3,440,162	0.8%
50	Wyoming	3,398,143	0.8%
	District of Columbia	3,344,879	0.8%

Source: U.S. Department of Education, Budget Office
  "FY 2001-2009 State Tables" (http://www.ed.gov/about/overview/budget/statetables/index.html)
*Estimates for fiscal year 2008 appropriation. Includes $19,104,320 in grants to U.S. territories and Indian tribe set-aside.

U.S. Department of Education Title I Grants to
Local Educational Agencies in 2008
National Total = $13,898,874,505*

ALPHA ORDER

RANK	STATE	GRANTS	% of USA
19	Alabama	$215,312,266	1.5%
45	Alaska	38,846,247	0.3%
13	Arizona	274,873,780	2.0%
27	Arkansas	144,216,120	1.0%
1	California	1,698,413,216	12.2%
29	Colorado	135,346,909	1.0%
31	Connecticut	115,597,198	0.8%
46	Delaware	38,379,903	0.3%
4	Florida	656,163,113	4.7%
9	Georgia	446,095,296	3.2%
42	Hawaii	44,323,337	0.3%
41	Idaho	46,678,787	0.3%
5	Illinois	593,810,555	4.3%
14	Indiana	247,041,955	1.8%
36	Iowa	72,687,658	0.5%
34	Kansas	95,429,987	0.7%
20	Kentucky	208,483,651	1.5%
11	Louisiana	294,758,296	2.1%
40	Maine	51,551,262	0.4%
23	Maryland	192,323,996	1.4%
16	Massachusetts	233,710,793	1.7%
7	Michigan	527,085,755	3.8%
30	Minnesota	126,897,284	0.9%
25	Mississippi	187,418,162	1.3%
18	Missouri	225,118,411	1.6%
43	Montana	43,550,783	0.3%
37	Nebraska	60,224,064	0.4%
35	Nevada	80,811,629	0.6%
47	New Hampshire	38,197,944	0.3%
12	New Jersey	286,905,787	2.1%
32	New Mexico	113,123,860	0.8%
3	New York	1,227,204,670	8.8%
10	North Carolina	358,528,632	2.6%
48	North Dakota	33,741,847	0.2%
8	Ohio	511,651,899	3.7%
26	Oklahoma	148,495,113	1.1%
28	Oregon	139,925,962	1.0%
6	Pennsylvania	565,477,754	4.1%
39	Rhode Island	52,997,967	0.4%
21	South Carolina	205,528,923	1.5%
44	South Dakota	41,538,517	0.3%
15	Tennessee	239,239,539	1.7%
2	Texas	1,299,288,079	9.3%
38	Utah	60,051,773	0.4%
49	Vermont	32,862,030	0.2%
17	Virginia	226,015,948	1.6%
24	Washington	191,798,261	1.4%
33	West Virginia	99,572,757	0.7%
22	Wisconsin	198,986,480	1.4%
50	Wyoming	31,515,708	0.2%

RANK ORDER

RANK	STATE	GRANTS	% of USA
1	California	$1,698,413,216	12.2%
2	Texas	1,299,288,079	9.3%
3	New York	1,227,204,670	8.8%
4	Florida	656,163,113	4.7%
5	Illinois	593,810,555	4.3%
6	Pennsylvania	565,477,754	4.1%
7	Michigan	527,085,755	3.8%
8	Ohio	511,651,899	3.7%
9	Georgia	446,095,296	3.2%
10	North Carolina	358,528,632	2.6%
11	Louisiana	294,758,296	2.1%
12	New Jersey	286,905,787	2.1%
13	Arizona	274,873,780	2.0%
14	Indiana	247,041,955	1.8%
15	Tennessee	239,239,539	1.7%
16	Massachusetts	233,710,793	1.7%
17	Virginia	226,015,948	1.6%
18	Missouri	225,118,411	1.6%
19	Alabama	215,312,266	1.5%
20	Kentucky	208,483,651	1.5%
21	South Carolina	205,528,923	1.5%
22	Wisconsin	198,986,480	1.4%
23	Maryland	192,323,996	1.4%
24	Washington	191,798,261	1.4%
25	Mississippi	187,418,162	1.3%
26	Oklahoma	148,495,113	1.1%
27	Arkansas	144,216,120	1.0%
28	Oregon	139,925,962	1.0%
29	Colorado	135,346,909	1.0%
30	Minnesota	126,897,284	0.9%
31	Connecticut	115,597,198	0.8%
32	New Mexico	113,123,860	0.8%
33	West Virginia	99,572,757	0.7%
34	Kansas	95,429,987	0.7%
35	Nevada	80,811,629	0.6%
36	Iowa	72,687,658	0.5%
37	Nebraska	60,224,064	0.4%
38	Utah	60,051,773	0.4%
39	Rhode Island	52,997,967	0.4%
40	Maine	51,551,262	0.4%
41	Idaho	46,678,787	0.3%
42	Hawaii	44,323,337	0.3%
43	Montana	43,550,783	0.3%
44	South Dakota	41,538,517	0.3%
45	Alaska	38,846,247	0.3%
46	Delaware	38,379,903	0.3%
47	New Hampshire	38,197,944	0.3%
48	North Dakota	33,741,847	0.2%
49	Vermont	32,862,030	0.2%
50	Wyoming	31,515,708	0.2%
	District of Columbia	47,307,729	0.3%

Source: U.S. Department of Education, Budget Office
"FY 2001-2009 State Tables" (http://www.ed.gov/about/overview/budget/statetables/index.html)
*Estimates for fiscal year 2008 appropriation. Includes $653,766,913 in grants to U.S. territories and Indian tribe set-aside. Title I schools are eligible for Title I federal funding to assist disadvantaged students.

U.S. Department of Education Title I Reading First State Grants in 2008

National Total = $393,012,000*

ALPHA ORDER					RANK ORDER			

RANK	STATE	GRANTS	% of USA		RANK	STATE	GRANTS	% of USA
14	Alabama	$7,308,254	1.9%		1	California	$50,837,601	12.9%
44	Alaska	935,641	0.2%		2	Texas	41,747,494	10.6%
12	Arizona	8,707,881	2.2%		3	New York	25,219,857	6.4%
26	Arkansas	4,595,240	1.2%		4	Florida	20,135,397	5.1%
1	California	50,837,601	12.9%		5	Illinois	14,504,845	3.7%
27	Colorado	4,320,985	1.1%		6	Ohio	13,698,801	3.5%
33	Connecticut	2,635,389	0.7%		7	Michigan	13,098,894	3.3%
44	Delaware	935,641	0.2%		8	Pennsylvania	12,963,676	3.3%
4	Florida	20,135,397	5.1%		9	Georgia	12,911,473	3.3%
9	Georgia	12,911,473	3.3%		10	North Carolina	12,218,578	3.1%
43	Hawaii	1,007,088	0.3%		11	Louisiana	9,360,627	2.4%
38	Idaho	1,659,707	0.4%		12	Arizona	8,707,881	2.2%
5	Illinois	14,504,845	3.7%		13	Tennessee	8,244,338	2.1%
16	Indiana	7,054,328	1.8%		14	Alabama	7,308,254	1.9%
36	Iowa	2,438,207	0.6%		15	Missouri	7,233,515	1.8%
34	Kansas	2,555,090	0.7%		16	Indiana	7,054,328	1.8%
21	Kentucky	6,213,567	1.6%		17	New Jersey	7,005,733	1.8%
11	Louisiana	9,360,627	2.4%		18	Virginia	6,511,802	1.7%
40	Maine	1,225,024	0.3%		19	South Carolina	6,400,393	1.6%
29	Maryland	4,176,515	1.1%		20	Mississippi	6,309,399	1.6%
23	Massachusetts	5,482,686	1.4%		21	Kentucky	6,213,567	1.6%
7	Michigan	13,098,894	3.3%		22	Washington	6,169,598	1.6%
30	Minnesota	3,721,969	0.9%		23	Massachusetts	5,482,686	1.4%
20	Mississippi	6,309,399	1.6%		24	Oklahoma	5,127,496	1.3%
15	Missouri	7,233,515	1.8%		25	Wisconsin	4,870,302	1.2%
42	Montana	1,128,258	0.3%		26	Arkansas	4,595,240	1.2%
39	Nebraska	1,639,802	0.4%		27	Colorado	4,320,985	1.1%
35	Nevada	2,490,749	0.6%		28	Oregon	4,221,290	1.1%
44	New Hampshire	935,641	0.2%		29	Maryland	4,176,515	1.1%
17	New Jersey	7,005,733	1.8%		30	Minnesota	3,721,969	0.9%
31	New Mexico	3,506,920	0.9%		31	New Mexico	3,506,920	0.9%
3	New York	25,219,857	6.4%		32	West Virginia	2,726,340	0.7%
10	North Carolina	12,218,578	3.1%		33	Connecticut	2,635,389	0.7%
44	North Dakota	935,641	0.2%		34	Kansas	2,555,090	0.7%
6	Ohio	13,698,801	3.5%		35	Nevada	2,490,749	0.6%
24	Oklahoma	5,127,496	1.3%		36	Iowa	2,438,207	0.6%
28	Oregon	4,221,290	1.1%		37	Utah	2,186,445	0.6%
8	Pennsylvania	12,963,676	3.3%		38	Idaho	1,659,707	0.4%
41	Rhode Island	1,199,899	0.3%		39	Nebraska	1,639,802	0.4%
19	South Carolina	6,400,393	1.6%		40	Maine	1,225,024	0.3%
44	South Dakota	935,641	0.2%		41	Rhode Island	1,199,899	0.3%
13	Tennessee	8,244,338	2.1%		42	Montana	1,128,258	0.3%
2	Texas	41,747,494	10.6%		43	Hawaii	1,007,088	0.3%
37	Utah	2,186,445	0.6%		44	Alaska	935,641	0.2%
44	Vermont	935,641	0.2%		44	Delaware	935,641	0.2%
18	Virginia	6,511,802	1.7%		44	New Hampshire	935,641	0.2%
22	Washington	6,169,598	1.6%		44	North Dakota	935,641	0.2%
32	West Virginia	2,726,340	0.7%		44	South Dakota	935,641	0.2%
25	Wisconsin	4,870,302	1.2%		44	Vermont	935,641	0.2%
44	Wyoming	935,641	0.2%		44	Wyoming	935,641	0.2%
						District of Columbia	935,641	0.2%

Source: U.S. Department of Education, Budget Office
   "FY 2001-2009 State Tables" (http://www.ed.gov/about/overview/budget/statetables/index.html)
*Estimates for fiscal year 2008 appropriation. Includes $18,755,420 in grants to U.S. territories and Indian tribe set-aside.
Funds are dedicated to help states and local school districts eliminate the reading deficit by establishing high-quality,
comprehensive reading instruction in kindergarten through the third grade.

U.S. Department of Education Grants for Improving Teacher Quality in 2008

National Total = $2,935,248,441*

ALPHA ORDER

RANK	STATE	GRANTS	% of USA
20	Alabama	$47,018,200	1.6%
39	Alaska	13,987,032	0.5%
18	Arizona	48,635,038	1.7%
30	Arkansas	28,692,584	1.0%
1	California	332,854,904	11.3%
28	Colorado	32,975,388	1.1%
31	Connecticut	26,679,875	0.9%
39	Delaware	13,987,032	0.5%
4	Florida	133,957,142	4.6%
9	Georgia	79,401,753	2.7%
39	Hawaii	13,987,032	0.5%
39	Idaho	13,987,032	0.5%
5	Illinois	117,680,290	4.0%
17	Indiana	50,368,699	1.7%
35	Iowa	22,318,054	0.8%
34	Kansas	22,705,842	0.8%
22	Kentucky	45,107,765	1.5%
12	Louisiana	65,226,437	2.2%
39	Maine	13,987,032	0.5%
24	Maryland	41,357,474	1.4%
14	Massachusetts	51,793,550	1.8%
7	Michigan	112,109,766	3.8%
25	Minnesota	38,482,785	1.3%
23	Mississippi	42,781,932	1.5%
16	Missouri	50,977,867	1.7%
39	Montana	13,987,032	0.5%
38	Nebraska	14,263,975	0.5%
37	Nevada	15,524,495	0.5%
39	New Hampshire	13,987,032	0.5%
11	New Jersey	65,311,095	2.2%
33	New Mexico	23,044,481	0.8%
3	New York	227,484,226	7.8%
10	North Carolina	68,094,000	2.3%
39	North Dakota	13,987,032	0.5%
8	Ohio	107,784,210	3.7%
27	Oklahoma	33,969,928	1.2%
29	Oregon	28,900,179	1.0%
6	Pennsylvania	115,223,435	3.9%
39	Rhode Island	13,987,032	0.5%
26	South Carolina	37,978,750	1.3%
39	South Dakota	13,987,032	0.5%
15	Tennessee	51,217,243	1.7%
2	Texas	247,415,976	8.4%
36	Utah	19,074,503	0.6%
39	Vermont	13,987,032	0.5%
13	Virginia	52,503,196	1.8%
19	Washington	48,000,430	1.6%
32	West Virginia	23,713,215	0.8%
21	Wisconsin	46,372,266	1.6%
39	Wyoming	13,987,032	0.5%

RANK ORDER

RANK	STATE	GRANTS	% of USA
1	California	$332,854,904	11.3%
2	Texas	247,415,976	8.4%
3	New York	227,484,226	7.8%
4	Florida	133,957,142	4.6%
5	Illinois	117,680,290	4.0%
6	Pennsylvania	115,223,435	3.9%
7	Michigan	112,109,766	3.8%
8	Ohio	107,784,210	3.7%
9	Georgia	79,401,753	2.7%
10	North Carolina	68,094,000	2.3%
11	New Jersey	65,311,095	2.2%
12	Louisiana	65,226,437	2.2%
13	Virginia	52,503,196	1.8%
14	Massachusetts	51,793,550	1.8%
15	Tennessee	51,217,243	1.7%
16	Missouri	50,977,867	1.7%
17	Indiana	50,368,699	1.7%
18	Arizona	48,635,038	1.7%
19	Washington	48,000,430	1.6%
20	Alabama	47,018,200	1.6%
21	Wisconsin	46,372,266	1.6%
22	Kentucky	45,107,765	1.5%
23	Mississippi	42,781,932	1.5%
24	Maryland	41,357,474	1.4%
25	Minnesota	38,482,785	1.3%
26	South Carolina	37,978,750	1.3%
27	Oklahoma	33,969,928	1.2%
28	Colorado	32,975,388	1.1%
29	Oregon	28,900,179	1.0%
30	Arkansas	28,692,584	1.0%
31	Connecticut	26,679,875	0.9%
32	West Virginia	23,713,215	0.8%
33	New Mexico	23,044,481	0.8%
34	Kansas	22,705,842	0.8%
35	Iowa	22,318,054	0.8%
36	Utah	19,074,503	0.6%
37	Nevada	15,524,495	0.5%
38	Nebraska	14,263,975	0.5%
39	Alaska	13,987,032	0.5%
39	Delaware	13,987,032	0.5%
39	Hawaii	13,987,032	0.5%
39	Idaho	13,987,032	0.5%
39	Maine	13,987,032	0.5%
39	Montana	13,987,032	0.5%
39	New Hampshire	13,987,032	0.5%
39	North Dakota	13,987,032	0.5%
39	Rhode Island	13,987,032	0.5%
39	South Dakota	13,987,032	0.5%
39	Vermont	13,987,032	0.5%
39	Wyoming	13,987,032	0.5%
	District of Columbia	13,987,032	0.5%

Source: U.S. Department of Education, Budget Office
    "FY 2001-2009 State Tables" (http://www.ed.gov/about/overview/budget/statetables/index.html)
*Estimates for fiscal year 2008 appropriation. Includes $136,416,077 in grants to U.S. territories and Indian tribe set-aside. The purpose of these grants is to help increase the academic achievement of all students by helping schools and school districts ensure that all teachers are highly qualified to teach. State and local educational agencies receive funds on a formula basis, as does the state agency for higher education.

Public Elementary and Secondary School Revenue in 2006

National Total = $521,116,397,000*

<table>
<tr><td colspan="4">ALPHA ORDER</td><td colspan="4">RANK ORDER</td></tr>
<tr><td>RANK</td><td>STATE</td><td>REVENUE</td><td>% of USA</td><td>RANK</td><td>STATE</td><td>REVENUE</td><td>% of USA</td></tr>
<tr><td>26</td><td>Alabama</td><td>$6,362,217,000</td><td>1.2%</td><td>1</td><td>California</td><td>$64,206,902,000</td><td>12.3%</td></tr>
<tr><td>44</td><td>Alaska</td><td>1,625,138,000</td><td>0.3%</td><td>2</td><td>New York</td><td>46,826,867,000</td><td>9.0%</td></tr>
<tr><td>21</td><td>Arizona</td><td>8,061,138,000</td><td>1.5%</td><td>3</td><td>Texas</td><td>40,988,805,000</td><td>7.9%</td></tr>
<tr><td>33</td><td>Arkansas</td><td>4,234,383,000</td><td>0.8%</td><td>4</td><td>Florida</td><td>25,418,734,000</td><td>4.9%</td></tr>
<tr><td>1</td><td>California</td><td>64,206,902,000</td><td>12.3%</td><td>5</td><td>New Jersey</td><td>23,107,783,000</td><td>4.4%</td></tr>
<tr><td>22</td><td>Colorado</td><td>7,237,022,000</td><td>1.4%</td><td>6</td><td>Pennsylvania</td><td>22,772,190,000</td><td>4.4%</td></tr>
<tr><td>20</td><td>Connecticut</td><td>8,287,208,000</td><td>1.6%</td><td>7</td><td>Illinois</td><td>22,093,022,000</td><td>4.2%</td></tr>
<tr><td>45</td><td>Delaware</td><td>1,503,177,000</td><td>0.3%</td><td>8</td><td>Ohio</td><td>20,534,909,000</td><td>3.9%</td></tr>
<tr><td>4</td><td>Florida</td><td>25,418,734,000</td><td>4.9%</td><td>9</td><td>Michigan</td><td>18,845,848,000</td><td>3.6%</td></tr>
<tr><td>10</td><td>Georgia</td><td>16,157,870,000</td><td>3.1%</td><td>10</td><td>Georgia</td><td>16,157,870,000</td><td>3.1%</td></tr>
<tr><td>39</td><td>Hawaii</td><td>2,705,532,000</td><td>0.5%</td><td>11</td><td>Massachusetts</td><td>14,042,262,000</td><td>2.7%</td></tr>
<tr><td>43</td><td>Idaho</td><td>1,874,662,000</td><td>0.4%</td><td>12</td><td>Virginia</td><td>12,952,183,000</td><td>2.5%</td></tr>
<tr><td>7</td><td>Illinois</td><td>22,093,022,000</td><td>4.2%</td><td>13</td><td>North Carolina</td><td>11,708,667,000</td><td>2.2%</td></tr>
<tr><td>14</td><td>Indiana</td><td>11,317,028,000</td><td>2.2%</td><td>14</td><td>Indiana</td><td>11,317,028,000</td><td>2.2%</td></tr>
<tr><td>30</td><td>Iowa</td><td>4,724,109,000</td><td>0.9%</td><td>15</td><td>Maryland</td><td>10,689,764,000</td><td>2.1%</td></tr>
<tr><td>31</td><td>Kansas</td><td>4,646,910,000</td><td>0.9%</td><td>16</td><td>Wisconsin</td><td>9,704,331,000</td><td>1.9%</td></tr>
<tr><td>27</td><td>Kentucky</td><td>5,999,705,000</td><td>1.2%</td><td>17</td><td>Washington</td><td>9,655,800,000</td><td>1.9%</td></tr>
<tr><td>24</td><td>Louisiana</td><td>6,778,539,000</td><td>1.3%</td><td>18</td><td>Minnesota</td><td>9,006,444,000</td><td>1.7%</td></tr>
<tr><td>41</td><td>Maine</td><td>2,285,272,000</td><td>0.4%</td><td>19</td><td>Missouri</td><td>8,778,294,000</td><td>1.7%</td></tr>
<tr><td>15</td><td>Maryland</td><td>10,689,764,000</td><td>2.1%</td><td>20</td><td>Connecticut</td><td>8,287,208,000</td><td>1.6%</td></tr>
<tr><td>11</td><td>Massachusetts</td><td>14,042,262,000</td><td>2.7%</td><td>21</td><td>Arizona</td><td>8,061,138,000</td><td>1.5%</td></tr>
<tr><td>9</td><td>Michigan</td><td>18,845,848,000</td><td>3.6%</td><td>22</td><td>Colorado</td><td>7,237,022,000</td><td>1.4%</td></tr>
<tr><td>18</td><td>Minnesota</td><td>9,006,444,000</td><td>1.7%</td><td>23</td><td>Tennessee</td><td>7,164,914,000</td><td>1.4%</td></tr>
<tr><td>32</td><td>Mississippi</td><td>4,269,711,000</td><td>0.8%</td><td>24</td><td>Louisiana</td><td>6,778,539,000</td><td>1.3%</td></tr>
<tr><td>19</td><td>Missouri</td><td>8,778,294,000</td><td>1.7%</td><td>25</td><td>South Carolina</td><td>6,741,029,000</td><td>1.3%</td></tr>
<tr><td>46</td><td>Montana</td><td>1,365,225,000</td><td>0.3%</td><td>26</td><td>Alabama</td><td>6,362,217,000</td><td>1.2%</td></tr>
<tr><td>37</td><td>Nebraska</td><td>3,016,840,000</td><td>0.6%</td><td>27</td><td>Kentucky</td><td>5,999,705,000</td><td>1.2%</td></tr>
<tr><td>34</td><td>Nevada</td><td>3,688,834,000</td><td>0.7%</td><td>28</td><td>Oregon</td><td>5,382,038,000</td><td>1.0%</td></tr>
<tr><td>40</td><td>New Hampshire</td><td>2,362,887,000</td><td>0.5%</td><td>29</td><td>Oklahoma</td><td>5,119,239,000</td><td>1.0%</td></tr>
<tr><td>5</td><td>New Jersey</td><td>23,107,783,000</td><td>4.4%</td><td>30</td><td>Iowa</td><td>4,724,109,000</td><td>0.9%</td></tr>
<tr><td>36</td><td>New Mexico</td><td>3,083,986,000</td><td>0.6%</td><td>31</td><td>Kansas</td><td>4,646,910,000</td><td>0.9%</td></tr>
<tr><td>2</td><td>New York</td><td>46,826,867,000</td><td>9.0%</td><td>32</td><td>Mississippi</td><td>4,269,711,000</td><td>0.8%</td></tr>
<tr><td>13</td><td>North Carolina</td><td>11,708,667,000</td><td>2.2%</td><td>33</td><td>Arkansas</td><td>4,234,383,000</td><td>0.8%</td></tr>
<tr><td>50</td><td>North Dakota</td><td>963,559,000</td><td>0.2%</td><td>34</td><td>Nevada</td><td>3,688,834,000</td><td>0.7%</td></tr>
<tr><td>8</td><td>Ohio</td><td>20,534,909,000</td><td>3.9%</td><td>35</td><td>Utah</td><td>3,377,212,000</td><td>0.6%</td></tr>
<tr><td>29</td><td>Oklahoma</td><td>5,119,239,000</td><td>1.0%</td><td>36</td><td>New Mexico</td><td>3,083,986,000</td><td>0.6%</td></tr>
<tr><td>28</td><td>Oregon</td><td>5,382,038,000</td><td>1.0%</td><td>37</td><td>Nebraska</td><td>3,016,840,000</td><td>0.6%</td></tr>
<tr><td>6</td><td>Pennsylvania</td><td>22,772,190,000</td><td>4.4%</td><td>38</td><td>West Virginia</td><td>2,806,752,000</td><td>0.5%</td></tr>
<tr><td>42</td><td>Rhode Island</td><td>1,993,380,000</td><td>0.4%</td><td>39</td><td>Hawaii</td><td>2,705,532,000</td><td>0.5%</td></tr>
<tr><td>25</td><td>South Carolina</td><td>6,741,029,000</td><td>1.3%</td><td>40</td><td>New Hampshire</td><td>2,362,887,000</td><td>0.5%</td></tr>
<tr><td>49</td><td>South Dakota</td><td>1,083,723,000</td><td>0.2%</td><td>41</td><td>Maine</td><td>2,285,272,000</td><td>0.4%</td></tr>
<tr><td>23</td><td>Tennessee</td><td>7,164,914,000</td><td>1.4%</td><td>42</td><td>Rhode Island</td><td>1,993,380,000</td><td>0.4%</td></tr>
<tr><td>3</td><td>Texas</td><td>40,988,805,000</td><td>7.9%</td><td>43</td><td>Idaho</td><td>1,874,662,000</td><td>0.4%</td></tr>
<tr><td>35</td><td>Utah</td><td>3,377,212,000</td><td>0.6%</td><td>44</td><td>Alaska</td><td>1,625,138,000</td><td>0.3%</td></tr>
<tr><td>47</td><td>Vermont</td><td>1,323,136,000</td><td>0.3%</td><td>45</td><td>Delaware</td><td>1,503,177,000</td><td>0.3%</td></tr>
<tr><td>12</td><td>Virginia</td><td>12,952,183,000</td><td>2.5%</td><td>46</td><td>Montana</td><td>1,365,225,000</td><td>0.3%</td></tr>
<tr><td>17</td><td>Washington</td><td>9,655,800,000</td><td>1.9%</td><td>47</td><td>Vermont</td><td>1,323,136,000</td><td>0.3%</td></tr>
<tr><td>38</td><td>West Virginia</td><td>2,806,752,000</td><td>0.5%</td><td>48</td><td>Wyoming</td><td>1,148,354,000</td><td>0.2%</td></tr>
<tr><td>16</td><td>Wisconsin</td><td>9,704,331,000</td><td>1.9%</td><td>49</td><td>South Dakota</td><td>1,083,723,000</td><td>0.2%</td></tr>
<tr><td>48</td><td>Wyoming</td><td>1,148,354,000</td><td>0.2%</td><td>50</td><td>North Dakota</td><td>963,559,000</td><td>0.2%</td></tr>
<tr><td></td><td></td><td></td><td></td><td></td><td>District of Columbia</td><td>1,092,863,000</td><td>0.2%</td></tr>
</table>

Source: U.S. Bureau of the Census, Governments Division
   "Public Education Finances: 2006" (http://www.census.gov/govs/www/school06.html)
*Revenue includes all money received by a school system from external sources (net of refunds) other than from issuance of debt or liquidation of investments. Does not include noncash transactions such as receipt of services, commodities, or other "receipts in-kind." Excludes duplicative interschool system transactions.

Per Capita Public Elementary and Secondary School Revenue in 2006

National Per Capita = $1,744*

ALPHA ORDER

RANK ORDER

RANK	STATE	PER CAPITA		RANK	STATE	PER CAPITA
44	Alabama	$1,386		1	New Jersey	$2,666
3	Alaska	2,399		2	New York	2,429
48	Arizona	1,307		3	Alaska	2,399
35	Arkansas	1,507		4	Connecticut	2,371
16	California	1,771		5	Wyoming	2,240
32	Colorado	1,518		6	Massachusetts	2,182
4	Connecticut	2,371		7	Vermont	2,131
17	Delaware	1,763		8	Hawaii	2,116
43	Florida	1,408		9	Maryland	1,908
22	Georgia	1,730		10	Rhode Island	1,878
8	Hawaii	2,116		11	Michigan	1,865
49	Idaho	1,281		12	Pennsylvania	1,836
23	Illinois	1,729		13	New Hampshire	1,801
14	Indiana	1,796		14	Indiana	1,796
28	Iowa	1,589		15	Ohio	1,791
26	Kansas	1,686		16	California	1,771
42	Kentucky	1,427		17	Delaware	1,763
27	Louisiana	1,597		18	Texas	1,751
21	Maine	1,738		19	Minnesota	1,747
9	Maryland	1,908		20	Wisconsin	1,741
6	Massachusetts	2,182		21	Maine	1,738
11	Michigan	1,865		22	Georgia	1,730
19	Minnesota	1,747		23	Illinois	1,729
38	Mississippi	1,473		24	Nebraska	1,710
36	Missouri	1,504		25	Virginia	1,695
40	Montana	1,442		26	Kansas	1,686
24	Nebraska	1,710		27	Louisiana	1,597
37	Nevada	1,480		28	Iowa	1,589
13	New Hampshire	1,801		29	New Mexico	1,588
1	New Jersey	2,666		30	South Carolina	1,557
29	New Mexico	1,588		31	West Virginia	1,552
2	New York	2,429		32	Colorado	1,518
46	North Carolina	1,320		33	Washington	1,515
34	North Dakota	1,512		34	North Dakota	1,512
15	Ohio	1,791		35	Arkansas	1,507
41	Oklahoma	1,431		36	Missouri	1,504
39	Oregon	1,458		37	Nevada	1,480
12	Pennsylvania	1,836		38	Mississippi	1,473
10	Rhode Island	1,878		39	Oregon	1,458
30	South Carolina	1,557		40	Montana	1,442
45	South Dakota	1,374		41	Oklahoma	1,431
50	Tennessee	1,179		42	Kentucky	1,427
18	Texas	1,751		43	Florida	1,408
47	Utah	1,309		44	Alabama	1,386
7	Vermont	2,131		45	South Dakota	1,374
25	Virginia	1,695		46	North Carolina	1,320
33	Washington	1,515		47	Utah	1,309
31	West Virginia	1,552		48	Arizona	1,307
20	Wisconsin	1,741		49	Idaho	1,281
5	Wyoming	2,240		50	Tennessee	1,179
					District of Columbia	1,867

Source: CQ Press using data from U.S. Bureau of the Census, Governments Division
"Public Education Finances: 2006" (http://www.census.gov/govs/www/school06.html)
*Revenue includes all money received by a school system from external sources (net of refunds) other than from issuance of debt or liquidation of investments. Does not include noncash transactions such as receipt of services, commodities, or other "receipts in-kind." Excludes duplicative interschool system transactions.

Public Elementary and Secondary School Revenue per
$1,000 Personal Income in 2006
National Ratio = $50.67*

ALPHA ORDER

RANK	STATE	RATIO
34	Alabama	$47.81
1	Alaska	66.88
43	Arizona	44.57
14	Arkansas	56.58
35	California	47.63
48	Colorado	41.16
28	Connecticut	49.63
31	Delaware	48.16
47	Florida	41.21
13	Georgia	56.91
4	Hawaii	61.03
40	Idaho	46.39
36	Illinois	47.60
9	Indiana	58.48
25	Iowa	50.61
23	Kansas	51.76
24	Kentucky	50.72
6	Louisiana	60.69
15	Maine	56.24
41	Maryland	45.99
26	Massachusetts	50.06
12	Michigan	57.02
38	Minnesota	47.27
10	Mississippi	57.67
29	Missouri	48.25
27	Montana	49.98
21	Nebraska	52.26
49	Nevada	40.87
30	New Hampshire	48.24
3	New Jersey	61.29
11	New Mexico	57.10
7	New York	59.25
45	North Carolina	43.86
37	North Dakota	47.37
16	Ohio	56.21
33	Oklahoma	48.07
39	Oregon	46.94
20	Pennsylvania	52.73
22	Rhode Island	51.93
17	South Carolina	55.84
44	South Dakota	43.96
50	Tennessee	38.81
18	Texas	53.91
32	Utah	48.13
2	Vermont	65.10
42	Virginia	45.09
46	Washington	42.95
8	West Virginia	58.53
19	Wisconsin	53.33
5	Wyoming	60.74

RANK ORDER

RANK	STATE	RATIO
1	Alaska	$66.88
2	Vermont	65.10
3	New Jersey	61.29
4	Hawaii	61.03
5	Wyoming	60.74
6	Louisiana	60.69
7	New York	59.25
8	West Virginia	58.53
9	Indiana	58.48
10	Mississippi	57.67
11	New Mexico	57.10
12	Michigan	57.02
13	Georgia	56.91
14	Arkansas	56.58
15	Maine	56.24
16	Ohio	56.21
17	South Carolina	55.84
18	Texas	53.91
19	Wisconsin	53.33
20	Pennsylvania	52.73
21	Nebraska	52.26
22	Rhode Island	51.93
23	Kansas	51.76
24	Kentucky	50.72
25	Iowa	50.61
26	Massachusetts	50.06
27	Montana	49.98
28	Connecticut	49.63
29	Missouri	48.25
30	New Hampshire	48.24
31	Delaware	48.16
32	Utah	48.13
33	Oklahoma	48.07
34	Alabama	47.81
35	California	47.63
36	Illinois	47.60
37	North Dakota	47.37
38	Minnesota	47.27
39	Oregon	46.94
40	Idaho	46.39
41	Maryland	45.99
42	Virginia	45.09
43	Arizona	44.57
44	South Dakota	43.96
45	North Carolina	43.86
46	Washington	42.95
47	Florida	41.21
48	Colorado	41.16
49	Nevada	40.87
50	Tennessee	38.81
	District of Columbia	35.03

Source: U.S. Bureau of the Census, Governments Division
"Public Education Finances: 2006" (http://www.census.gov/govs/www/school06.html)
*Revenue includes all money received by a school system from external sources (net of refunds) other than from issuance of debt or liquidation of investments. Does not include noncash transactions such as receipt of services, commodities, or other "receipts in-kind."

Per Pupil Public Elementary and Secondary School Revenue in 2006

National Per Pupil = $10,771*

ALPHA ORDER

RANK	STATE	PER PUPIL
44	Alabama	$8,560
12	Alaska	12,229
47	Arizona	8,025
39	Arkansas	8,960
24	California	10,264
37	Colorado	9,285
3	Connecticut	14,893
9	Delaware	13,143
33	Florida	9,542
25	Georgia	10,113
4	Hawaii	14,799
49	Idaho	7,257
22	Illinois	10,506
17	Indiana	11,028
29	Iowa	9,771
27	Kansas	9,973
42	Kentucky	8,828
23	Louisiana	10,456
14	Maine	11,709
11	Maryland	12,430
5	Massachusetts	14,782
19	Michigan	10,900
18	Minnesota	11,010
43	Mississippi	8,644
32	Missouri	9,585
35	Montana	9,399
21	Nebraska	10,543
40	Nevada	8,937
13	New Hampshire	11,753
2	New Jersey	16,743
34	New Mexico	9,438
1	New York	16,800
45	North Carolina	8,434
28	North Dakota	9,815
15	Ohio	11,606
46	Oklahoma	8,069
30	Oregon	9,668
10	Pennsylvania	12,942
8	Rhode Island	13,279
31	South Carolina	9,643
41	South Dakota	8,904
48	Tennessee	7,512
38	Texas	9,210
50	Utah	6,802
6	Vermont	14,329
20	Virginia	10,672
36	Washington	9,359
26	West Virginia	10,032
16	Wisconsin	11,160
7	Wyoming	13,329

RANK ORDER

RANK	STATE	PER PUPIL
1	New York	$16,800
2	New Jersey	16,743
3	Connecticut	14,893
4	Hawaii	14,799
5	Massachusetts	14,782
6	Vermont	14,329
7	Wyoming	13,329
8	Rhode Island	13,279
9	Delaware	13,143
10	Pennsylvania	12,942
11	Maryland	12,430
12	Alaska	12,229
13	New Hampshire	11,753
14	Maine	11,709
15	Ohio	11,606
16	Wisconsin	11,160
17	Indiana	11,028
18	Minnesota	11,010
19	Michigan	10,900
20	Virginia	10,672
21	Nebraska	10,543
22	Illinois	10,506
23	Louisiana	10,456
24	California	10,264
25	Georgia	10,113
26	West Virginia	10,032
27	Kansas	9,973
28	North Dakota	9,815
29	Iowa	9,771
30	Oregon	9,668
31	South Carolina	9,643
32	Missouri	9,585
33	Florida	9,542
34	New Mexico	9,438
35	Montana	9,399
36	Washington	9,359
37	Colorado	9,285
38	Texas	9,210
39	Arkansas	8,960
40	Nevada	8,937
41	South Dakota	8,904
42	Kentucky	8,828
43	Mississippi	8,644
44	Alabama	8,560
45	North Carolina	8,434
46	Oklahoma	8,069
47	Arizona	8,025
48	Tennessee	7,512
49	Idaho	7,257
50	Utah	6,802
	District of Columbia	18,332

Source: U.S. Bureau of the Census, Governments Division
"Public Education Finances: 2006" (http://www.census.gov/govs/www/school06.html)
*Based on student membership. Revenue includes all money received by a school system from external sources (net of refunds) other than from issuance of debt or liquidation of investments. Does not include noncash transactions such as receipt of services, commodities, or other "receipts in-kind."

Public Elementary and Secondary School Revenue from Federal Sources in 2006
National Total = $47,100,781,000*

ALPHA ORDER

RANK	STATE	REVENUE	% of USA
21	Alabama	$730,112,000	1.6%
38	Alaska	289,855,000	0.6%
13	Arizona	963,600,000	2.0%
30	Arkansas	482,038,000	1.0%
1	California	7,421,482,000	15.8%
28	Colorado	520,673,000	1.1%
33	Connecticut	388,080,000	0.8%
49	Delaware	109,044,000	0.2%
4	Florida	2,460,004,000	5.2%
9	Georgia	1,455,212,000	3.1%
40	Hawaii	225,393,000	0.5%
42	Idaho	201,040,000	0.4%
5	Illinois	1,886,721,000	4.0%
20	Indiana	740,036,000	1.6%
32	Iowa	397,290,000	0.8%
36	Kansas	340,728,000	0.7%
22	Kentucky	680,251,000	1.4%
10	Louisiana	1,276,913,000	2.7%
41	Maine	201,447,000	0.4%
24	Maryland	663,284,000	1.4%
18	Massachusetts	749,362,000	1.6%
7	Michigan	1,524,718,000	3.2%
27	Minnesota	558,287,000	1.2%
15	Mississippi	856,762,000	1.8%
19	Missouri	740,742,000	1.6%
43	Montana	190,226,000	0.4%
37	Nebraska	301,764,000	0.6%
39	Nevada	258,814,000	0.5%
47	New Hampshire	130,088,000	0.3%
12	New Jersey	982,557,000	2.1%
31	New Mexico	446,994,000	0.9%
3	New York	3,340,216,000	7.1%
11	North Carolina	1,184,622,000	2.5%
45	North Dakota	151,248,000	0.3%
8	Ohio	1,479,925,000	3.1%
25	Oklahoma	654,807,000	1.4%
29	Oregon	516,962,000	1.1%
6	Pennsylvania	1,794,419,000	3.8%
46	Rhode Island	149,493,000	0.3%
23	South Carolina	664,113,000	1.4%
44	South Dakota	177,452,000	0.4%
17	Tennessee	793,477,000	1.7%
2	Texas	4,735,208,000	10.1%
35	Utah	342,862,000	0.7%
50	Vermont	102,791,000	0.2%
14	Virginia	866,982,000	1.8%
16	Washington	801,941,000	1.7%
34	West Virginia	346,628,000	0.7%
26	Wisconsin	580,810,000	1.2%
48	Wyoming	115,937,000	0.2%

RANK ORDER

RANK	STATE	REVENUE	% of USA
1	California	$7,421,482,000	15.8%
2	Texas	4,735,208,000	10.1%
3	New York	3,340,216,000	7.1%
4	Florida	2,460,004,000	5.2%
5	Illinois	1,886,721,000	4.0%
6	Pennsylvania	1,794,419,000	3.8%
7	Michigan	1,524,718,000	3.2%
8	Ohio	1,479,925,000	3.1%
9	Georgia	1,455,212,000	3.1%
10	Louisiana	1,276,913,000	2.7%
11	North Carolina	1,184,622,000	2.5%
12	New Jersey	982,557,000	2.1%
13	Arizona	963,600,000	2.0%
14	Virginia	866,982,000	1.8%
15	Mississippi	856,762,000	1.8%
16	Washington	801,941,000	1.7%
17	Tennessee	793,477,000	1.7%
18	Massachusetts	749,362,000	1.6%
19	Missouri	740,742,000	1.6%
20	Indiana	740,036,000	1.6%
21	Alabama	730,112,000	1.6%
22	Kentucky	680,251,000	1.4%
23	South Carolina	664,113,000	1.4%
24	Maryland	663,284,000	1.4%
25	Oklahoma	654,807,000	1.4%
26	Wisconsin	580,810,000	1.2%
27	Minnesota	558,287,000	1.2%
28	Colorado	520,673,000	1.1%
29	Oregon	516,962,000	1.1%
30	Arkansas	482,038,000	1.0%
31	New Mexico	446,994,000	0.9%
32	Iowa	397,290,000	0.8%
33	Connecticut	388,080,000	0.8%
34	West Virginia	346,628,000	0.7%
35	Utah	342,862,000	0.7%
36	Kansas	340,728,000	0.7%
37	Nebraska	301,764,000	0.6%
38	Alaska	289,855,000	0.6%
39	Nevada	258,814,000	0.5%
40	Hawaii	225,393,000	0.5%
41	Maine	201,447,000	0.4%
42	Idaho	201,040,000	0.4%
43	Montana	190,226,000	0.4%
44	South Dakota	177,452,000	0.4%
45	North Dakota	151,248,000	0.3%
46	Rhode Island	149,493,000	0.3%
47	New Hampshire	130,088,000	0.3%
48	Wyoming	115,937,000	0.2%
49	Delaware	109,044,000	0.2%
50	Vermont	102,791,000	0.2%
	District of Columbia	127,371,000	0.3%

Source: U.S. Bureau of the Census, Governments Division
"Public Education Finances: 2006" (http://www.census.gov/govs/www/school06.html)
*Includes federal revenue passed through state governments as well as federal outlays directly received. Includes all such revenue received by a school system from federal sources (net of refunds) other than from issuance of debt or liquidation of investments. Does not include noncash transactions such as receipt of services, commodities, or other "receipts in-kind."

Per Capita Public Elementary and Secondary School Revenue from Federal Sources in 2006
National Per Capita = $158*

ALPHA ORDER

RANK	STATE	PER CAPITA
19	Alabama	$159
1	Alaska	428
20	Arizona	156
15	Arkansas	172
8	California	205
46	Colorado	109
45	Connecticut	111
36	Delaware	128
30	Florida	136
20	Georgia	156
13	Hawaii	176
29	Idaho	137
25	Illinois	148
41	Indiana	117
31	Iowa	134
39	Kansas	124
18	Kentucky	162
2	Louisiana	301
22	Maine	153
40	Maryland	118
42	Massachusetts	116
24	Michigan	151
47	Minnesota	108
3	Mississippi	296
37	Missouri	127
10	Montana	201
16	Nebraska	171
48	Nevada	104
50	New Hampshire	99
43	New Jersey	113
5	New Mexico	230
14	New York	173
31	North Carolina	134
4	North Dakota	237
35	Ohio	129
12	Oklahoma	183
28	Oregon	140
26	Pennsylvania	145
27	Rhode Island	141
22	South Carolina	153
7	South Dakota	225
34	Tennessee	131
9	Texas	202
33	Utah	133
17	Vermont	166
43	Virginia	113
38	Washington	126
11	West Virginia	192
48	Wisconsin	104
6	Wyoming	226

RANK ORDER

RANK	STATE	PER CAPITA
1	Alaska	$428
2	Louisiana	301
3	Mississippi	296
4	North Dakota	237
5	New Mexico	230
6	Wyoming	226
7	South Dakota	225
8	California	205
9	Texas	202
10	Montana	201
11	West Virginia	192
12	Oklahoma	183
13	Hawaii	176
14	New York	173
15	Arkansas	172
16	Nebraska	171
17	Vermont	166
18	Kentucky	162
19	Alabama	159
20	Arizona	156
20	Georgia	156
22	Maine	153
22	South Carolina	153
24	Michigan	151
25	Illinois	148
26	Pennsylvania	145
27	Rhode Island	141
28	Oregon	140
29	Idaho	137
30	Florida	136
31	Iowa	134
31	North Carolina	134
33	Utah	133
34	Tennessee	131
35	Ohio	129
36	Delaware	128
37	Missouri	127
38	Washington	126
39	Kansas	124
40	Maryland	118
41	Indiana	117
42	Massachusetts	116
43	New Jersey	113
43	Virginia	113
45	Connecticut	111
46	Colorado	109
47	Minnesota	108
48	Nevada	104
48	Wisconsin	104
50	New Hampshire	99

| District of Columbia | | 218 |

Source: CQ Press using data from U.S. Bureau of the Census, Governments Division
"Public Education Finances: 2006" (http://www.census.gov/govs/www/school06.html)
*Includes federal revenue passed through state governments as well as federal outlays directly received. Includes all such revenue received by a school system from federal sources (net of refunds) other than from issuance of debt or liquidation of investments. Does not include noncash transactions such as receipt of services, commodities, or other "receipts in-kind."

Public Elementary and Secondary School Revenue from Federal Sources per $1,000 Personal Income in 2006
National Ratio = $4.58*

ALPHA ORDER

RANK	STATE	RATIO
16	Alabama	$5.49
1	Alaska	11.93
17	Arizona	5.33
9	Arkansas	6.44
14	California	5.51
43	Colorado	2.96
50	Connecticut	2.32
40	Delaware	3.49
35	Florida	3.99
19	Georgia	5.13
20	Hawaii	5.08
22	Idaho	4.97
33	Illinois	4.06
37	Indiana	3.82
29	Iowa	4.26
38	Kansas	3.80
13	Kentucky	5.75
3	Louisiana	11.43
23	Maine	4.96
46	Maryland	2.85
47	Massachusetts	2.67
25	Michigan	4.61
44	Minnesota	2.93
2	Mississippi	11.57
32	Missouri	4.07
8	Montana	6.96
18	Nebraska	5.23
45	Nevada	2.87
48	New Hampshire	2.66
49	New Jersey	2.61
4	New Mexico	8.28
30	New York	4.23
27	North Carolina	4.44
5	North Dakota	7.44
34	Ohio	4.05
11	Oklahoma	6.15
26	Oregon	4.51
31	Pennsylvania	4.16
36	Rhode Island	3.89
15	South Carolina	5.50
7	South Dakota	7.20
28	Tennessee	4.30
10	Texas	6.23
24	Utah	4.89
21	Vermont	5.06
42	Virginia	3.02
39	Washington	3.57
6	West Virginia	7.23
41	Wisconsin	3.19
12	Wyoming	6.13

RANK ORDER

RANK	STATE	RATIO
1	Alaska	$11.93
2	Mississippi	11.57
3	Louisiana	11.43
4	New Mexico	8.28
5	North Dakota	7.44
6	West Virginia	7.23
7	South Dakota	7.20
8	Montana	6.96
9	Arkansas	6.44
10	Texas	6.23
11	Oklahoma	6.15
12	Wyoming	6.13
13	Kentucky	5.75
14	California	5.51
15	South Carolina	5.50
16	Alabama	5.49
17	Arizona	5.33
18	Nebraska	5.23
19	Georgia	5.13
20	Hawaii	5.08
21	Vermont	5.06
22	Idaho	4.97
23	Maine	4.96
24	Utah	4.89
25	Michigan	4.61
26	Oregon	4.51
27	North Carolina	4.44
28	Tennessee	4.30
29	Iowa	4.26
30	New York	4.23
31	Pennsylvania	4.16
32	Missouri	4.07
33	Illinois	4.06
34	Ohio	4.05
35	Florida	3.99
36	Rhode Island	3.89
37	Indiana	3.82
38	Kansas	3.80
39	Washington	3.57
40	Delaware	3.49
41	Wisconsin	3.19
42	Virginia	3.02
43	Colorado	2.96
44	Minnesota	2.93
45	Nevada	2.87
46	Maryland	2.85
47	Massachusetts	2.67
48	New Hampshire	2.66
49	New Jersey	2.61
50	Connecticut	2.32
	District of Columbia	4.08

Source: U.S. Bureau of the Census, Governments Division
    "Public Education Finances: 2006" (http://www.census.gov/govs/www/school06.html)
*Includes federal revenue passed through state governments as well as federal outlays directly received. Includes all such revenue received by a school system from federal sources (net of refunds) other than from issuance of debt or liquidation of investments. Does not include noncash transactions.

Per Pupil Public Elementary and Secondary School
Revenue from Federal Sources in 2006
National Per Pupil = $974*

ALPHA ORDER

RANK	STATE	PER PUPIL
22	Alabama	$982
1	Alaska	2,181
23	Arizona	959
18	Arkansas	1,020
12	California	1,186
47	Colorado	668
44	Connecticut	697
24	Delaware	953
27	Florida	923
28	Georgia	911
10	Hawaii	1,233
37	Idaho	778
29	Illinois	897
41	Indiana	721
34	Iowa	822
40	Kansas	731
20	Kentucky	1,001
2	Louisiana	1,970
16	Maine	1,032
39	Maryland	771
36	Massachusetts	789
30	Michigan	882
46	Minnesota	682
3	Mississippi	1,735
35	Missouri	809
8	Montana	1,310
15	Nebraska	1,055
50	Nevada	627
49	New Hampshire	647
43	New Jersey	712
6	New Mexico	1,368
11	New York	1,198
31	North Carolina	853
4	North Dakota	1,541
32	Ohio	836
16	Oklahoma	1,032
26	Oregon	929
18	Pennsylvania	1,020
21	Rhode Island	996
25	South Carolina	950
5	South Dakota	1,458
33	Tennessee	832
14	Texas	1,064
45	Utah	691
13	Vermont	1,113
42	Virginia	714
38	Washington	777
9	West Virginia	1,239
47	Wisconsin	668
7	Wyoming	1,346

RANK ORDER

RANK	STATE	PER PUPIL
1	Alaska	$2,181
2	Louisiana	1,970
3	Mississippi	1,735
4	North Dakota	1,541
5	South Dakota	1,458
6	New Mexico	1,368
7	Wyoming	1,346
8	Montana	1,310
9	West Virginia	1,239
10	Hawaii	1,233
11	New York	1,198
12	California	1,186
13	Vermont	1,113
14	Texas	1,064
15	Nebraska	1,055
16	Maine	1,032
16	Oklahoma	1,032
18	Arkansas	1,020
18	Pennsylvania	1,020
20	Kentucky	1,001
21	Rhode Island	996
22	Alabama	982
23	Arizona	959
24	Delaware	953
25	South Carolina	950
26	Oregon	929
27	Florida	923
28	Georgia	911
29	Illinois	897
30	Michigan	882
31	North Carolina	853
32	Ohio	836
33	Tennessee	832
34	Iowa	822
35	Missouri	809
36	Massachusetts	789
37	Idaho	778
38	Washington	777
39	Maryland	771
40	Kansas	731
41	Indiana	721
42	Virginia	714
43	New Jersey	712
44	Connecticut	697
45	Utah	691
46	Minnesota	682
47	Colorado	668
47	Wisconsin	668
49	New Hampshire	647
50	Nevada	627
	District of Columbia	2,137

Source: U.S. Bureau of the Census, Governments Division
   "Public Education Finances: 2006" (http://www.census.gov/govs/www/school06.html)
*Based on student membership. Includes federal revenue passed through state governments as well as federal outlays directly received. Includes all such revenue received by a school system from federal sources (net of refunds) other than from issuance of debt or liquidation of investments. Does not include noncash transactions such as receipt of services, commodities, or other "receipts in-kind."

Percent of Public Elementary and Secondary School Revenue from Federal Sources in 2006
National Percent = 9.0%*

ALPHA ORDER

RANK	STATE	PERCENT
13	Alabama	11.5
3	Alaska	17.8
10	Arizona	12.0
14	Arkansas	11.4
11	California	11.6
38	Colorado	7.2
49	Connecticut	4.7
36	Delaware	7.3
23	Florida	9.7
25	Georgia	9.0
30	Hawaii	8.3
17	Idaho	10.7
27	Illinois	8.5
43	Indiana	6.5
28	Iowa	8.4
36	Kansas	7.3
15	Kentucky	11.3
2	Louisiana	18.8
26	Maine	8.8
44	Maryland	6.2
48	Massachusetts	5.3
32	Michigan	8.1
44	Minnesota	6.2
1	Mississippi	20.1
28	Missouri	8.4
7	Montana	13.9
21	Nebraska	10.0
41	Nevada	7.0
47	New Hampshire	5.5
50	New Jersey	4.3
6	New Mexico	14.5
40	New York	7.1
19	North Carolina	10.1
5	North Dakota	15.7
38	Ohio	7.2
8	Oklahoma	12.8
24	Oregon	9.6
33	Pennsylvania	7.9
35	Rhode Island	7.5
22	South Carolina	9.9
4	South Dakota	16.4
16	Tennessee	11.1
11	Texas	11.6
18	Utah	10.2
34	Vermont	7.8
42	Virginia	6.7
30	Washington	8.3
9	West Virginia	12.3
46	Wisconsin	6.0
19	Wyoming	10.1

RANK ORDER

RANK	STATE	PERCENT
1	Mississippi	20.1
2	Louisiana	18.8
3	Alaska	17.8
4	South Dakota	16.4
5	North Dakota	15.7
6	New Mexico	14.5
7	Montana	13.9
8	Oklahoma	12.8
9	West Virginia	12.3
10	Arizona	12.0
11	California	11.6
11	Texas	11.6
13	Alabama	11.5
14	Arkansas	11.4
15	Kentucky	11.3
16	Tennessee	11.1
17	Idaho	10.7
18	Utah	10.2
19	North Carolina	10.1
19	Wyoming	10.1
21	Nebraska	10.0
22	South Carolina	9.9
23	Florida	9.7
24	Oregon	9.6
25	Georgia	9.0
26	Maine	8.8
27	Illinois	8.5
28	Iowa	8.4
28	Missouri	8.4
30	Hawaii	8.3
30	Washington	8.3
32	Michigan	8.1
33	Pennsylvania	7.9
34	Vermont	7.8
35	Rhode Island	7.5
36	Delaware	7.3
36	Kansas	7.3
38	Colorado	7.2
38	Ohio	7.2
40	New York	7.1
41	Nevada	7.0
42	Virginia	6.7
43	Indiana	6.5
44	Maryland	6.2
44	Minnesota	6.2
46	Wisconsin	6.0
47	New Hampshire	5.5
48	Massachusetts	5.3
49	Connecticut	4.7
50	New Jersey	4.3

	District of Columbia	11.7

Source: U.S. Bureau of the Census, Governments Division
    "Public Education Finances: 2006" (http://www.census.gov/govs/www/school06.html)
*Includes federal revenue passed through state governments as well as federal outlays directly received. Includes all such revenue received by a school system from federal sources (net of refunds) other than from issuance of debt or liquidation of investments. Does not include noncash transactions such as receipt of services, commodities, or other "receipts in-kind."

Public Elementary and Secondary School
Federal Government Revenue for Child Nutrition Programs in 2006
National Total = $8,913,237,000*

ALPHA ORDER				RANK ORDER			
RANK	STATE	REVENUE	% of USA	RANK	STATE	REVENUE	% of USA
13	Alabama	$177,851,000	2.0%	1	California	$1,223,054,000	13.7%
42	Alaska	25,559,000	0.3%	2	Texas	1,100,875,000	12.4%
15	Arizona	174,097,000	2.0%	3	Florida	519,260,000	5.8%
26	Arkansas	116,432,000	1.3%	4	New York	478,459,000	5.4%
1	California	1,223,054,000	13.7%	5	Georgia	392,267,000	4.4%
30	Colorado	90,139,000	1.0%	6	Illinois	345,197,000	3.9%
35	Connecticut	68,525,000	0.8%	7	North Carolina	329,298,000	3.7%
45	Delaware	19,522,000	0.2%	8	Pennsylvania	281,372,000	3.2%
3	Florida	519,260,000	5.8%	9	Ohio	235,117,000	2.6%
5	Georgia	392,267,000	4.4%	10	Michigan	227,489,000	2.6%
40	Hawaii	29,600,000	0.3%	11	Tennessee	207,903,000	2.3%
38	Idaho	45,682,000	0.5%	12	Louisiana	184,590,000	2.1%
6	Illinois	345,197,000	3.9%	13	Alabama	177,851,000	2.0%
18	Indiana	167,710,000	1.9%	14	New Jersey	175,270,000	2.0%
34	Iowa	72,759,000	0.8%	15	Arizona	174,097,000	2.0%
31	Kansas	83,284,000	0.9%	16	South Carolina	173,221,000	1.9%
20	Kentucky	163,243,000	1.8%	17	Virginia	172,312,000	1.9%
12	Louisiana	184,590,000	2.1%	18	Indiana	167,710,000	1.9%
41	Maine	26,043,000	0.3%	19	Missouri	166,400,000	1.9%
24	Maryland	119,469,000	1.3%	20	Kentucky	163,243,000	1.8%
25	Massachusetts	117,677,000	1.3%	21	Mississippi	162,475,000	1.8%
10	Michigan	227,489,000	2.6%	22	Washington	145,914,000	1.6%
27	Minnesota	106,988,000	1.2%	23	Oklahoma	140,680,000	1.6%
21	Mississippi	162,475,000	1.8%	24	Maryland	119,469,000	1.3%
19	Missouri	166,400,000	1.9%	25	Massachusetts	117,677,000	1.3%
44	Montana	20,197,000	0.2%	26	Arkansas	116,432,000	1.3%
39	Nebraska	45,082,000	0.5%	27	Minnesota	106,988,000	1.2%
37	Nevada	58,308,000	0.7%	28	Wisconsin	106,171,000	1.2%
47	New Hampshire	16,962,000	0.2%	29	Oregon	92,022,000	1.0%
14	New Jersey	175,270,000	2.0%	30	Colorado	90,139,000	1.0%
33	New Mexico	76,259,000	0.9%	31	Kansas	83,284,000	0.9%
4	New York	478,459,000	5.4%	32	Utah	77,694,000	0.9%
7	North Carolina	329,298,000	3.7%	33	New Mexico	76,259,000	0.9%
48	North Dakota	12,590,000	0.1%	34	Iowa	72,759,000	0.8%
9	Ohio	235,117,000	2.6%	35	Connecticut	68,525,000	0.8%
23	Oklahoma	140,680,000	1.6%	36	West Virginia	63,683,000	0.7%
29	Oregon	92,022,000	1.0%	37	Nevada	58,308,000	0.7%
8	Pennsylvania	281,372,000	3.2%	38	Idaho	45,682,000	0.5%
43	Rhode Island	23,587,000	0.3%	39	Nebraska	45,082,000	0.5%
16	South Carolina	173,221,000	1.9%	40	Hawaii	29,600,000	0.3%
46	South Dakota	17,907,000	0.2%	41	Maine	26,043,000	0.3%
11	Tennessee	207,903,000	2.3%	42	Alaska	25,559,000	0.3%
2	Texas	1,100,875,000	12.4%	43	Rhode Island	23,587,000	0.3%
32	Utah	77,694,000	0.9%	44	Montana	20,197,000	0.2%
50	Vermont	10,635,000	0.1%	45	Delaware	19,522,000	0.2%
17	Virginia	172,312,000	1.9%	46	South Dakota	17,907,000	0.2%
22	Washington	145,914,000	1.6%	47	New Hampshire	16,962,000	0.2%
36	West Virginia	63,683,000	0.7%	48	North Dakota	12,590,000	0.1%
28	Wisconsin	106,171,000	1.2%	49	Wyoming	10,961,000	0.1%
49	Wyoming	10,961,000	0.1%	50	Vermont	10,635,000	0.1%
					District of Columbia	15,446,000	0.2%

Source: U.S. Bureau of the Census, Governments Division
  "Public Education Finances: 2006" (http://www.census.gov/govs/www/school06.html)
*Federal revenue passed through state governments. Includes payments by the Department of Agriculture for the National School Lunch, Special Milk, School Breakfast, and Ala Carte Programs. Excludes the value of donated commodities.

Percent of Public Elementary and Secondary School Federal Revenue Used for Child Nutrition Programs in 2006
National Percent = 18.9%*

ALPHA ORDER

RANK	STATE	PERCENT
5	Alabama	24.4
49	Alaska	8.8
25	Arizona	18.1
7	Arkansas	24.2
33	California	16.5
31	Colorado	17.3
30	Connecticut	17.7
27	Delaware	17.9
16	Florida	21.1
2	Georgia	27.0
42	Hawaii	13.1
10	Idaho	22.7
21	Illinois	18.3
10	Indiana	22.7
21	Iowa	18.3
5	Kansas	24.4
8	Kentucky	24.0
40	Louisiana	14.5
44	Maine	12.9
26	Maryland	18.0
36	Massachusetts	15.7
38	Michigan	14.9
18	Minnesota	19.2
19	Mississippi	19.0
13	Missouri	22.5
45	Montana	10.6
38	Nebraska	14.9
13	Nevada	22.5
43	New Hampshire	13.0
28	New Jersey	17.8
32	New Mexico	17.1
41	New York	14.3
1	North Carolina	27.8
50	North Dakota	8.3
34	Ohio	15.9
15	Oklahoma	21.5
28	Oregon	17.8
36	Pennsylvania	15.7
35	Rhode Island	15.8
4	South Carolina	26.1
47	South Dakota	10.1
3	Tennessee	26.2
9	Texas	23.2
10	Utah	22.7
46	Vermont	10.3
17	Virginia	19.9
24	Washington	18.2
20	West Virginia	18.4
21	Wisconsin	18.3
48	Wyoming	9.5

RANK ORDER

RANK	STATE	PERCENT
1	North Carolina	27.8
2	Georgia	27.0
3	Tennessee	26.2
4	South Carolina	26.1
5	Alabama	24.4
5	Kansas	24.4
7	Arkansas	24.2
8	Kentucky	24.0
9	Texas	23.2
10	Idaho	22.7
10	Indiana	22.7
10	Utah	22.7
13	Missouri	22.5
13	Nevada	22.5
15	Oklahoma	21.5
16	Florida	21.1
17	Virginia	19.9
18	Minnesota	19.2
19	Mississippi	19.0
20	West Virginia	18.4
21	Illinois	18.3
21	Iowa	18.3
21	Wisconsin	18.3
24	Washington	18.2
25	Arizona	18.1
26	Maryland	18.0
27	Delaware	17.9
28	New Jersey	17.8
28	Oregon	17.8
30	Connecticut	17.7
31	Colorado	17.3
32	New Mexico	17.1
33	California	16.5
34	Ohio	15.9
35	Rhode Island	15.8
36	Massachusetts	15.7
36	Pennsylvania	15.7
38	Michigan	14.9
38	Nebraska	14.9
40	Louisiana	14.5
41	New York	14.3
42	Hawaii	13.1
43	New Hampshire	13.0
44	Maine	12.9
45	Montana	10.6
46	Vermont	10.3
47	South Dakota	10.1
48	Wyoming	9.5
49	Alaska	8.8
50	North Dakota	8.3

| | District of Columbia | 12.1 |

Source: CQ Press using data from U.S. Bureau of the Census, Governments Division
"Public Education Finances: 2006" (http://www.census.gov/govs/www/school06.html)
*Federal revenue passed through state governments. Includes payments by the Department of Agriculture for the National School Lunch, Special Milk, School Breakfast, and Ala Carte Programs. Excludes the value of donated commodities. Figured as a percent of all federal revenue whether passed through state governments or received directly.

Federal Government Revenue for Public Elementary and Secondary School Compensatory (Title I) Programs in 2006
National Total = $11,371,494,000*

ALPHA ORDER

RANK	STATE	REVENUE	% of USA
12	Alabama	$220,121,000	1.9%
40	Alaska	42,170,000	0.4%
9	Arizona	255,591,000	2.2%
25	Arkansas	118,160,000	1.0%
1	California	2,174,622,000	19.1%
24	Colorado	144,180,000	1.3%
26	Connecticut	112,581,000	1.0%
43	Delaware	32,026,000	0.3%
4	Florida	612,907,000	5.4%
NA	Georgia**	NA	NA
38	Hawaii	46,525,000	0.4%
35	Idaho	48,064,000	0.4%
5	Illinois	542,370,000	4.8%
17	Indiana	176,490,000	1.6%
32	Iowa	64,242,000	0.6%
30	Kansas	88,184,000	0.8%
NA	Kentucky**	NA	NA
10	Louisiana	228,160,000	2.0%
37	Maine	47,553,000	0.4%
22	Maryland	161,911,000	1.4%
13	Massachusetts	215,796,000	1.9%
7	Michigan	403,851,000	3.6%
29	Minnesota	95,681,000	0.8%
18	Mississippi	176,021,000	1.5%
15	Missouri	191,847,000	1.7%
39	Montana	45,111,000	0.4%
33	Nebraska	62,694,000	0.6%
31	Nevada	71,280,000	0.6%
46	New Hampshire	29,550,000	0.3%
8	New Jersey	259,350,000	2.3%
28	New Mexico	99,778,000	0.9%
2	New York	1,271,939,000	11.2%
NA	North Carolina**	NA	NA
41	North Dakota	38,167,000	0.3%
NA	Ohio**	NA	NA
21	Oklahoma	166,410,000	1.5%
23	Oregon	160,451,000	1.4%
6	Pennsylvania	482,505,000	4.2%
36	Rhode Island	47,642,000	0.4%
19	South Carolina	169,383,000	1.5%
42	South Dakota	37,311,000	0.3%
16	Tennessee	190,906,000	1.7%
3	Texas	1,157,764,000	10.2%
34	Utah	53,245,000	0.5%
45	Vermont	29,714,000	0.3%
11	Virginia	220,177,000	1.9%
14	Washington	205,066,000	1.8%
27	West Virginia	110,808,000	1.0%
20	Wisconsin	168,729,000	1.5%
44	Wyoming	30,213,000	0.3%

RANK ORDER

RANK	STATE	REVENUE	% of USA
1	California	$2,174,622,000	19.1%
2	New York	1,271,939,000	11.2%
3	Texas	1,157,764,000	10.2%
4	Florida	612,907,000	5.4%
5	Illinois	542,370,000	4.8%
6	Pennsylvania	482,505,000	4.2%
7	Michigan	403,851,000	3.6%
8	New Jersey	259,350,000	2.3%
9	Arizona	255,591,000	2.2%
10	Louisiana	228,160,000	2.0%
11	Virginia	220,177,000	1.9%
12	Alabama	220,121,000	1.9%
13	Massachusetts	215,796,000	1.9%
14	Washington	205,066,000	1.8%
15	Missouri	191,847,000	1.7%
16	Tennessee	190,906,000	1.7%
17	Indiana	176,490,000	1.6%
18	Mississippi	176,021,000	1.5%
19	South Carolina	169,383,000	1.5%
20	Wisconsin	168,729,000	1.5%
21	Oklahoma	166,410,000	1.5%
22	Maryland	161,911,000	1.4%
23	Oregon	160,451,000	1.4%
24	Colorado	144,180,000	1.3%
25	Arkansas	118,160,000	1.0%
26	Connecticut	112,581,000	1.0%
27	West Virginia	110,808,000	1.0%
28	New Mexico	99,778,000	0.9%
29	Minnesota	95,681,000	0.8%
30	Kansas	88,184,000	0.8%
31	Nevada	71,280,000	0.6%
32	Iowa	64,242,000	0.6%
33	Nebraska	62,694,000	0.6%
34	Utah	53,245,000	0.5%
35	Idaho	48,064,000	0.4%
36	Rhode Island	47,642,000	0.4%
37	Maine	47,553,000	0.4%
38	Hawaii	46,525,000	0.4%
39	Montana	45,111,000	0.4%
40	Alaska	42,170,000	0.4%
41	North Dakota	38,167,000	0.3%
42	South Dakota	37,311,000	0.3%
43	Delaware	32,026,000	0.3%
44	Wyoming	30,213,000	0.3%
45	Vermont	29,714,000	0.3%
46	New Hampshire	29,550,000	0.3%
NA	Georgia**	NA	NA
NA	Kentucky**	NA	NA
NA	North Carolina**	NA	NA
NA	Ohio**	NA	NA
	District of Columbia	64,248,000	0.6%

Source: U.S. Bureau of the Census, Governments Division
    "Public Education Finances: 2006" (http://www.census.gov/govs/www/school06.html)
*National total is only for states shown separately. This is federal revenue passed through state governments. Revenue authorized by Title I of the Elementary-Secondary Education Act. Includes basic, concentration, and migratory education grants.
**Not available.

Percent of Public Elementary and Secondary School Federal Revenue Used for Compensatory (Title I) Programs in 2006
National Percent = 24.1%*

ALPHA ORDER

RANK	STATE	PERCENT
5	Alabama	30.1
46	Alaska	14.5
16	Arizona	26.5
28	Arkansas	24.5
7	California	29.3
13	Colorado	27.7
9	Connecticut	29.0
6	Delaware	29.4
27	Florida	24.9
NA	Georgia**	NA
40	Hawaii	20.6
32	Idaho	23.9
12	Illinois	28.7
33	Indiana	23.8
44	Iowa	16.2
20	Kansas	25.9
NA	Kentucky**	NA
42	Louisiana	17.9
35	Maine	23.6
30	Maryland	24.4
11	Massachusetts	28.8
16	Michigan	26.5
43	Minnesota	17.1
41	Mississippi	20.5
20	Missouri	25.9
34	Montana	23.7
39	Nebraska	20.8
14	Nevada	27.5
36	New Hampshire	22.7
18	New Jersey	26.4
37	New Mexico	22.3
1	New York	38.1
NA	North Carolina**	NA
26	North Dakota	25.2
NA	Ohio**	NA
24	Oklahoma	25.4
4	Oregon	31.0
15	Pennsylvania	26.9
3	Rhode Island	31.9
23	South Carolina	25.5
38	South Dakota	21.0
31	Tennessee	24.1
28	Texas	24.5
45	Utah	15.5
10	Vermont	28.9
24	Virginia	25.4
22	Washington	25.6
2	West Virginia	32.0
8	Wisconsin	29.1
19	Wyoming	26.1

RANK ORDER

RANK	STATE	PERCENT
1	New York	38.1
2	West Virginia	32.0
3	Rhode Island	31.9
4	Oregon	31.0
5	Alabama	30.1
6	Delaware	29.4
7	California	29.3
8	Wisconsin	29.1
9	Connecticut	29.0
10	Vermont	28.9
11	Massachusetts	28.8
12	Illinois	28.7
13	Colorado	27.7
14	Nevada	27.5
15	Pennsylvania	26.9
16	Arizona	26.5
16	Michigan	26.5
18	New Jersey	26.4
19	Wyoming	26.1
20	Kansas	25.9
20	Missouri	25.9
22	Washington	25.6
23	South Carolina	25.5
24	Oklahoma	25.4
24	Virginia	25.4
26	North Dakota	25.2
27	Florida	24.9
28	Arkansas	24.5
28	Texas	24.5
30	Maryland	24.4
31	Tennessee	24.1
32	Idaho	23.9
33	Indiana	23.8
34	Montana	23.7
35	Maine	23.6
36	New Hampshire	22.7
37	New Mexico	22.3
38	South Dakota	21.0
39	Nebraska	20.8
40	Hawaii	20.6
41	Mississippi	20.5
42	Louisiana	17.9
43	Minnesota	17.1
44	Iowa	16.2
45	Utah	15.5
46	Alaska	14.5
NA	Georgia**	NA
NA	Kentucky**	NA
NA	North Carolina**	NA
NA	Ohio**	NA

| | District of Columbia | 50.4 |

Source: CQ Press using data from U.S. Bureau of the Census, Governments Division
"Public Education Finances: 2006" (http://www.census.gov/govs/www/school06.html)
*National percent is only for states shown separately. This is federal revenue passed through state governments. Revenue authorized by Title I of the Elementary-Secondary Education Act. Includes basic, concentration, and migratory education grants.
**Not available.

Federal Government Revenue for Public Elementary and Secondary School Vocational Programs in 2006
National Total = $642,236,000*

ALPHA ORDER

RANK	STATE	REVENUE	% of USA
11	Alabama	$19,195,000	3.0%
38	Alaska	3,099,000	0.5%
12	Arizona	18,224,000	2.8%
18	Arkansas	11,427,000	1.8%
1	California	71,578,000	11.1%
26	Colorado	6,561,000	1.0%
24	Connecticut	7,622,000	1.2%
33	Delaware	4,133,000	0.6%
3	Florida	41,549,000	6.5%
NA	Georgia**	NA	NA
41	Hawaii	2,416,000	0.4%
35	Idaho	3,501,000	0.5%
8	Illinois	25,043,000	3.9%
17	Indiana	12,012,000	1.9%
25	Iowa	6,985,000	1.1%
45	Kansas	1,605,000	0.2%
NA	Kentucky**	NA	NA
20	Louisiana	10,296,000	1.6%
42	Maine	2,322,000	0.4%
19	Maryland	11,271,000	1.8%
16	Massachusetts	13,005,000	2.0%
10	Michigan	23,010,000	3.6%
44	Minnesota	1,685,000	0.3%
27	Mississippi	6,170,000	1.0%
14	Missouri	14,086,000	2.2%
37	Montana	3,291,000	0.5%
36	Nebraska	3,372,000	0.5%
30	Nevada	5,281,000	0.8%
34	New Hampshire	3,696,000	0.6%
21	New Jersey	8,848,000	1.4%
28	New Mexico	5,895,000	0.9%
4	New York	41,231,000	6.4%
NA	North Carolina**	NA	NA
39	North Dakota	2,589,000	0.4%
5	Ohio	38,994,000	6.1%
6	Oklahoma	32,854,000	5.1%
22	Oregon	8,488,000	1.3%
7	Pennsylvania	32,729,000	5.1%
32	Rhode Island	4,197,000	0.7%
15	South Carolina	13,176,000	2.1%
46	South Dakota	954,000	0.1%
9	Tennessee	23,988,000	3.7%
2	Texas	48,700,000	7.6%
29	Utah	5,859,000	0.9%
43	Vermont	2,271,000	0.4%
13	Virginia	17,599,000	2.7%
23	Washington	7,879,000	1.2%
NA	West Virginia**	NA	NA
31	Wisconsin	5,092,000	0.8%
40	Wyoming	2,498,000	0.4%

RANK ORDER

RANK	STATE	REVENUE	% of USA
1	California	$71,578,000	11.1%
2	Texas	48,700,000	7.6%
3	Florida	41,549,000	6.5%
4	New York	41,231,000	6.4%
5	Ohio	38,994,000	6.1%
6	Oklahoma	32,854,000	5.1%
7	Pennsylvania	32,729,000	5.1%
8	Illinois	25,043,000	3.9%
9	Tennessee	23,988,000	3.7%
10	Michigan	23,010,000	3.6%
11	Alabama	19,195,000	3.0%
12	Arizona	18,224,000	2.8%
13	Virginia	17,599,000	2.7%
14	Missouri	14,086,000	2.2%
15	South Carolina	13,176,000	2.1%
16	Massachusetts	13,005,000	2.0%
17	Indiana	12,012,000	1.9%
18	Arkansas	11,427,000	1.8%
19	Maryland	11,271,000	1.8%
20	Louisiana	10,296,000	1.6%
21	New Jersey	8,848,000	1.4%
22	Oregon	8,488,000	1.3%
23	Washington	7,879,000	1.2%
24	Connecticut	7,622,000	1.2%
25	Iowa	6,985,000	1.1%
26	Colorado	6,561,000	1.0%
27	Mississippi	6,170,000	1.0%
28	New Mexico	5,895,000	0.9%
29	Utah	5,859,000	0.9%
30	Nevada	5,281,000	0.8%
31	Wisconsin	5,092,000	0.8%
32	Rhode Island	4,197,000	0.7%
33	Delaware	4,133,000	0.6%
34	New Hampshire	3,696,000	0.6%
35	Idaho	3,501,000	0.5%
36	Nebraska	3,372,000	0.5%
37	Montana	3,291,000	0.5%
38	Alaska	3,099,000	0.5%
39	North Dakota	2,589,000	0.4%
40	Wyoming	2,498,000	0.4%
41	Hawaii	2,416,000	0.4%
42	Maine	2,322,000	0.4%
43	Vermont	2,271,000	0.4%
44	Minnesota	1,685,000	0.3%
45	Kansas	1,605,000	0.2%
46	South Dakota	954,000	0.1%
NA	Georgia**	NA	NA
NA	Kentucky**	NA	NA
NA	North Carolina**	NA	NA
NA	West Virginia**	NA	NA
	District of Columbia	5,960,000	0.9%

Source: U.S. Bureau of the Census, Governments Division
  "Public Education Finances: 2006" (http://www.census.gov/govs/www/school06.html)
*National total is only for states shown separately. This is federal revenue passed through state governments. Revenue from the Carl Perkins Vocational Education Act. Includes revenue from Title II (Basic Grants) and Title III-E (Tech-Prep Education).
**Not available.

Percent of Public Elementary and Secondary School Federal Revenue Used for Vocational Programs in 2006
National Percent = 1.4%*

ALPHA ORDER

RANK	STATE	PERCENT
6	Alabama	2.6
34	Alaska	1.1
15	Arizona	1.9
8	Arkansas	2.4
37	California	1.0
29	Colorado	1.3
11	Connecticut	2.0
2	Delaware	3.8
19	Florida	1.7
NA	Georgia**	NA
34	Hawaii	1.1
19	Idaho	1.7
29	Illinois	1.3
26	Indiana	1.6
17	Iowa	1.8
44	Kansas	0.5
NA	Kentucky**	NA
42	Louisiana	0.8
32	Maine	1.2
19	Maryland	1.7
19	Massachusetts	1.7
28	Michigan	1.5
46	Minnesota	0.3
43	Mississippi	0.7
15	Missouri	1.9
19	Montana	1.7
34	Nebraska	1.1
11	Nevada	2.0
4	New Hampshire	2.8
40	New Jersey	0.9
29	New Mexico	1.3
32	New York	1.2
NA	North Carolina**	NA
19	North Dakota	1.7
6	Ohio	2.6
1	Oklahoma	5.0
26	Oregon	1.6
17	Pennsylvania	1.8
4	Rhode Island	2.8
11	South Carolina	2.0
44	South Dakota	0.5
3	Tennessee	3.0
37	Texas	1.0
19	Utah	1.7
9	Vermont	2.2
11	Virginia	2.0
37	Washington	1.0
NA	West Virginia**	NA
40	Wisconsin	0.9
9	Wyoming	2.2

RANK ORDER

RANK	STATE	PERCENT
1	Oklahoma	5.0
2	Delaware	3.8
3	Tennessee	3.0
4	New Hampshire	2.8
4	Rhode Island	2.8
6	Alabama	2.6
6	Ohio	2.6
8	Arkansas	2.4
9	Vermont	2.2
9	Wyoming	2.2
11	Connecticut	2.0
11	Nevada	2.0
11	South Carolina	2.0
11	Virginia	2.0
15	Arizona	1.9
15	Missouri	1.9
17	Iowa	1.8
17	Pennsylvania	1.8
19	Florida	1.7
19	Idaho	1.7
19	Maryland	1.7
19	Massachusetts	1.7
19	Montana	1.7
19	North Dakota	1.7
19	Utah	1.7
26	Indiana	1.6
26	Oregon	1.6
28	Michigan	1.5
29	Colorado	1.3
29	Illinois	1.3
29	New Mexico	1.3
32	Maine	1.2
32	New York	1.2
34	Alaska	1.1
34	Hawaii	1.1
34	Nebraska	1.1
37	California	1.0
37	Texas	1.0
37	Washington	1.0
40	New Jersey	0.9
40	Wisconsin	0.9
42	Louisiana	0.8
43	Mississippi	0.7
44	Kansas	0.5
44	South Dakota	0.5
46	Minnesota	0.3
NA	Georgia**	NA
NA	Kentucky**	NA
NA	North Carolina**	NA
NA	West Virginia**	NA

District of Columbia   4.7

Source: CQ Press using data from U.S. Bureau of the Census, Governments Division
"Public Education Finances: 2006" (http://www.census.gov/govs/www/school06.html)
*National percent is only for states shown separately. This is federal revenue passed through state governments. Revenue from the Carl Perkins Vocational Education Act. Includes revenue from Title II (Basic Grants) and Title III-E (Tech-Prep Education).
**Not available.

Percent of Public Elementary and Secondary School Federal Revenue Distributed Through States in 2006
National Percent = 92.4%*

ALPHA ORDER

RANK	STATE	PERCENT
27	Alabama	92.1
50	Alaska	48.9
43	Arizona	83.5
21	Arkansas	93.3
19	California	93.5
36	Colorado	89.6
37	Connecticut	89.4
1	Delaware	100.0
20	Florida	93.4
21	Georgia	93.3
45	Hawaii	80.5
33	Idaho	90.8
12	Illinois	94.9
6	Indiana	98.0
35	Iowa	90.0
15	Kansas	94.0
23	Kentucky	93.1
27	Louisiana	92.1
10	Maine	96.0
32	Maryland	91.1
16	Massachusetts	93.9
34	Michigan	90.2
31	Minnesota	91.6
11	Mississippi	95.5
26	Missouri	92.2
46	Montana	69.6
44	Nebraska	81.6
16	Nevada	93.9
14	New Hampshire	94.1
4	New Jersey	98.5
48	New Mexico	66.8
2	New York	99.3
5	North Carolina	98.4
47	North Dakota	67.2
13	Ohio	94.2
42	Oklahoma	86.1
24	Oregon	92.6
29	Pennsylvania	92.0
9	Rhode Island	96.1
3	South Carolina	99.0
49	South Dakota	65.1
8	Tennessee	96.4
29	Texas	92.0
25	Utah	92.4
37	Vermont	89.4
40	Virginia	87.1
41	Washington	86.9
7	West Virginia	96.7
18	Wisconsin	93.7
39	Wyoming	87.3

RANK ORDER

RANK	STATE	PERCENT
1	Delaware	100.0
2	New York	99.3
3	South Carolina	99.0
4	New Jersey	98.5
5	North Carolina	98.4
6	Indiana	98.0
7	West Virginia	96.7
8	Tennessee	96.4
9	Rhode Island	96.1
10	Maine	96.0
11	Mississippi	95.5
12	Illinois	94.9
13	Ohio	94.2
14	New Hampshire	94.1
15	Kansas	94.0
16	Massachusetts	93.9
16	Nevada	93.9
18	Wisconsin	93.7
19	California	93.5
20	Florida	93.4
21	Arkansas	93.3
21	Georgia	93.3
23	Kentucky	93.1
24	Oregon	92.6
25	Utah	92.4
26	Missouri	92.2
27	Alabama	92.1
27	Louisiana	92.1
29	Pennsylvania	92.0
29	Texas	92.0
31	Minnesota	91.6
32	Maryland	91.1
33	Idaho	90.8
34	Michigan	90.2
35	Iowa	90.0
36	Colorado	89.6
37	Connecticut	89.4
37	Vermont	89.4
39	Wyoming	87.3
40	Virginia	87.1
41	Washington	86.9
42	Oklahoma	86.1
43	Arizona	83.5
44	Nebraska	81.6
45	Hawaii	80.5
46	Montana	69.6
47	North Dakota	67.2
48	New Mexico	66.8
49	South Dakota	65.1
50	Alaska	48.9

District of Columbia — 98.8

Source: CQ Press using data from U.S. Bureau of the Census, Governments Division
"Public Education Finances: 2006" (http://www.census.gov/govs/www/school06.html)
*Includes all such revenue received by a school system from federal sources (net of refunds) other than from issuance of debt or liquidation of investments. Does not include noncash transactions such as receipt of services, commodities, or other "receipts in-kind."

Public Elementary and Secondary School
Revenue from State Sources in 2006
National Total = $242,785,457,000*

RANK	STATE	REVENUE	% of USA		RANK	STATE	REVENUE	% of USA
21	Alabama	$3,540,436,000	1.5%		1	California	$37,439,651,000	15.4%
45	Alaska	918,976,000	0.4%		2	New York	20,183,518,000	8.3%
20	Arizona	3,635,388,000	1.5%		3	Texas	13,503,141,000	5.6%
24	Arkansas	3,108,910,000	1.3%		4	Michigan	11,172,247,000	4.6%
1	California	37,439,651,000	15.4%		5	Florida	10,215,772,000	4.2%
26	Colorado	3,087,795,000	1.3%		6	New Jersey	9,540,387,000	3.9%
23	Connecticut	3,148,507,000	1.3%		7	Ohio	8,695,982,000	3.6%
41	Delaware	969,809,000	0.4%		8	Pennsylvania	7,973,651,000	3.3%
5	Florida	10,215,772,000	4.2%		9	Illinois	7,144,629,000	2.9%
10	Georgia	7,136,011,000	2.9%		10	Georgia	7,136,011,000	2.9%
32	Hawaii	2,431,735,000	1.0%		11	North Carolina	6,846,954,000	2.8%
40	Idaho	1,046,128,000	0.4%		12	Minnesota	6,368,364,000	2.6%
9	Illinois	7,144,629,000	2.9%		13	Massachusetts	6,175,593,000	2.5%
15	Indiana	5,380,185,000	2.2%		14	Washington	5,899,155,000	2.4%
34	Iowa	2,158,255,000	0.9%		15	Indiana	5,380,185,000	2.2%
30	Kansas	2,640,757,000	1.1%		16	Virginia	5,126,114,000	2.1%
22	Kentucky	3,439,085,000	1.4%		17	Wisconsin	5,066,552,000	2.1%
28	Louisiana	2,814,302,000	1.2%		18	Maryland	4,189,334,000	1.7%
43	Maine	947,857,000	0.4%		19	Missouri	3,830,104,000	1.6%
18	Maryland	4,189,334,000	1.7%		20	Arizona	3,635,388,000	1.5%
13	Massachusetts	6,175,593,000	2.5%		21	Alabama	3,540,436,000	1.5%
4	Michigan	11,172,247,000	4.6%		22	Kentucky	3,439,085,000	1.4%
12	Minnesota	6,368,364,000	2.6%		23	Connecticut	3,148,507,000	1.3%
36	Mississippi	2,108,733,000	0.9%		24	Arkansas	3,108,910,000	1.3%
19	Missouri	3,830,104,000	1.6%		25	Tennessee	3,097,824,000	1.3%
47	Montana	626,958,000	0.3%		26	Colorado	3,087,795,000	1.3%
42	Nebraska	948,001,000	0.4%		27	South Carolina	3,023,114,000	1.2%
35	Nevada	2,137,351,000	0.9%		28	Louisiana	2,814,302,000	1.2%
44	New Hampshire	925,677,000	0.4%		29	Oregon	2,737,088,000	1.1%
6	New Jersey	9,540,387,000	3.9%		30	Kansas	2,640,757,000	1.1%
33	New Mexico	2,197,044,000	0.9%		31	Oklahoma	2,570,987,000	1.1%
2	New York	20,183,518,000	8.3%		32	Hawaii	2,431,735,000	1.0%
11	North Carolina	6,846,954,000	2.8%		33	New Mexico	2,197,044,000	0.9%
50	North Dakota	348,475,000	0.1%		34	Iowa	2,158,255,000	0.9%
7	Ohio	8,695,982,000	3.6%		35	Nevada	2,137,351,000	0.9%
31	Oklahoma	2,570,987,000	1.1%		36	Mississippi	2,108,733,000	0.9%
29	Oregon	2,737,088,000	1.1%		37	Utah	1,825,910,000	0.8%
8	Pennsylvania	7,973,651,000	3.3%		38	West Virginia	1,649,661,000	0.7%
46	Rhode Island	797,349,000	0.3%		39	Vermont	1,153,104,000	0.5%
27	South Carolina	3,023,114,000	1.2%		40	Idaho	1,046,128,000	0.4%
49	South Dakota	355,719,000	0.1%		41	Delaware	969,809,000	0.4%
25	Tennessee	3,097,824,000	1.3%		42	Nebraska	948,001,000	0.4%
3	Texas	13,503,141,000	5.6%		43	Maine	947,857,000	0.4%
37	Utah	1,825,910,000	0.8%		44	New Hampshire	925,677,000	0.4%
39	Vermont	1,153,104,000	0.5%		45	Alaska	918,976,000	0.4%
16	Virginia	5,126,114,000	2.1%		46	Rhode Island	797,349,000	0.3%
14	Washington	5,899,155,000	2.4%		47	Montana	626,958,000	0.3%
38	West Virginia	1,649,661,000	0.7%		48	Wyoming	507,178,000	0.2%
17	Wisconsin	5,066,552,000	2.1%		49	South Dakota	355,719,000	0.1%
48	Wyoming	507,178,000	0.2%		50	North Dakota	348,475,000	0.1%

ALPHA ORDER — RANK ORDER

District of Columbia**   NA   NA

Source: U.S. Bureau of the Census, Governments Division
    "Public Education Finances: 2006" (http://www.census.gov/govs/www/school06.html)
*Consists only of revenue originating from state governments. Includes all such revenue received by a school system (net of refunds) other than from issuance of debt or liquidation of investments. Does not include noncash transactions such as receipt of services, commodities, or other "receipts in-kind."
**Not applicable.

Per Capita Public Elementary and Secondary School Revenue from State Sources in 2006
National Per Capita = $813*

ALPHA ORDER

RANK	STATE	PER CAPITA
23	Alabama	$771
3	Alaska	1,357
43	Arizona	590
7	Arkansas	1,107
11	California	1,033
41	Colorado	648
18	Connecticut	901
5	Delaware	1,137
45	Florida	566
24	Georgia	764
1	Hawaii	1,902
33	Idaho	715
46	Illinois	559
20	Indiana	854
30	Iowa	726
14	Kansas	958
21	Kentucky	818
38	Louisiana	663
31	Maine	721
27	Maryland	748
13	Massachusetts	960
8	Michigan	1,106
4	Minnesota	1,235
29	Mississippi	727
40	Missouri	656
39	Montana	662
48	Nebraska	537
19	Nevada	858
35	New Hampshire	706
9	New Jersey	1,101
6	New Mexico	1,131
10	New York	1,047
22	North Carolina	772
47	North Dakota	547
25	Ohio	759
32	Oklahoma	719
28	Oregon	742
42	Pennsylvania	643
26	Rhode Island	751
36	South Carolina	698
50	South Dakota	451
49	Tennessee	510
44	Texas	577
34	Utah	708
2	Vermont	1,858
37	Virginia	671
15	Washington	925
16	West Virginia	912
17	Wisconsin	909
12	Wyoming	989

RANK ORDER

RANK	STATE	PER CAPITA
1	Hawaii	$1,902
2	Vermont	1,858
3	Alaska	1,357
4	Minnesota	1,235
5	Delaware	1,137
6	New Mexico	1,131
7	Arkansas	1,107
8	Michigan	1,106
9	New Jersey	1,101
10	New York	1,047
11	California	1,033
12	Wyoming	989
13	Massachusetts	960
14	Kansas	958
15	Washington	925
16	West Virginia	912
17	Wisconsin	909
18	Connecticut	901
19	Nevada	858
20	Indiana	854
21	Kentucky	818
22	North Carolina	772
23	Alabama	771
24	Georgia	764
25	Ohio	759
26	Rhode Island	751
27	Maryland	748
28	Oregon	742
29	Mississippi	727
30	Iowa	726
31	Maine	721
32	Oklahoma	719
33	Idaho	715
34	Utah	708
35	New Hampshire	706
36	South Carolina	698
37	Virginia	671
38	Louisiana	663
39	Montana	662
40	Missouri	656
41	Colorado	648
42	Pennsylvania	643
43	Arizona	590
44	Texas	577
45	Florida	566
46	Illinois	559
47	North Dakota	547
48	Nebraska	537
49	Tennessee	510
50	South Dakota	451

District of Columbia**   NA

Source: CQ Press using data from U.S. Bureau of the Census, Governments Division
   "Public Education Finances: 2006" (http://www.census.gov/govs/www/school06.html)
*Consists only of revenue originating from state governments. Includes all such revenue received by a school system (net of refunds) other than from issuance of debt or liquidation of investments. Does not include noncash transactions such as receipt of services, commodities, or other "receipts in-kind."
**Not applicable.

Public Elementary and Secondary School Revenue from State Sources per $1,000 Personal Income in 2006
National Ratio = $23.61*

ALPHA ORDER			RANK ORDER		
RANK	STATE	RATIO	RANK	STATE	RATIO
17	Alabama	$26.61	1	Vermont	$56.74
5	Alaska	37.82	2	Hawaii	54.85
37	Arizona	20.10	3	Arkansas	41.54
3	Arkansas	41.54	4	New Mexico	40.68
15	California	27.78	5	Alaska	37.82
44	Colorado	17.56	6	West Virginia	34.40
39	Connecticut	18.85	7	Michigan	33.81
9	Delaware	31.07	8	Minnesota	33.42
47	Florida	16.56	9	Delaware	31.07
25	Georgia	25.13	10	Kansas	29.42
2	Hawaii	54.85	11	Kentucky	29.07
20	Idaho	25.89	12	Mississippi	28.48
49	Illinois	15.39	13	Wisconsin	27.84
14	Indiana	27.80	14	Indiana	27.80
32	Iowa	23.12	15	California	27.78
10	Kansas	29.42	16	Wyoming	26.82
11	Kentucky	29.07	17	Alabama	26.61
24	Louisiana	25.20	18	Washington	26.24
31	Maine	23.33	19	Utah	26.02
41	Maryland	18.02	20	Idaho	25.89
34	Massachusetts	22.02	21	North Carolina	25.65
7	Michigan	33.81	22	New York	25.54
8	Minnesota	33.42	23	New Jersey	25.31
12	Mississippi	28.48	24	Louisiana	25.20
35	Missouri	21.05	25	Georgia	25.13
33	Montana	22.95	26	South Carolina	25.04
48	Nebraska	16.42	27	Oklahoma	24.14
30	Nevada	23.68	28	Oregon	23.87
38	New Hampshire	18.90	29	Ohio	23.80
23	New Jersey	25.31	30	Nevada	23.68
4	New Mexico	40.68	31	Maine	23.33
22	New York	25.54	32	Iowa	23.12
21	North Carolina	25.65	33	Montana	22.95
45	North Dakota	17.13	34	Massachusetts	22.02
29	Ohio	23.80	35	Missouri	21.05
27	Oklahoma	24.14	36	Rhode Island	20.77
28	Oregon	23.87	37	Arizona	20.10
40	Pennsylvania	18.46	38	New Hampshire	18.90
36	Rhode Island	20.77	39	Connecticut	18.85
26	South Carolina	25.04	40	Pennsylvania	18.46
50	South Dakota	14.43	41	Maryland	18.02
46	Tennessee	16.78	42	Virginia	17.85
43	Texas	17.76	43	Texas	17.76
19	Utah	26.02	44	Colorado	17.56
1	Vermont	56.74	45	North Dakota	17.13
42	Virginia	17.85	46	Tennessee	16.78
18	Washington	26.24	47	Florida	16.56
6	West Virginia	34.40	48	Nebraska	16.42
13	Wisconsin	27.84	49	Illinois	15.39
16	Wyoming	26.82	50	South Dakota	14.43
				District of Columbia**	NA

Source: U.S. Bureau of the Census, Governments Division
"Public Education Finances: 2006" (http://www.census.gov/govs/www/school06.html)
*Consists only of revenue originating from state governments. Includes all such revenue received by a school system (net of refunds) other than from issuance of debt or liquidation of investments. Does not include noncash transactions such as receipt of services, commodities, or other "receipts in-kind."
**Not applicable.

Per Pupil Public Elementary and Secondary School Revenue from State Sources in 2006
National Per Pupil = $5,018*

ALPHA ORDER

RANK	STATE	PER PUPIL
28	Alabama	$4,763
6	Alaska	6,915
44	Arizona	3,619
9	Arkansas	6,578
12	California	5,985
41	Colorado	3,962
18	Connecticut	5,658
3	Delaware	8,480
42	Florida	3,835
31	Georgia	4,466
1	Hawaii	13,301
40	Idaho	4,050
46	Illinois	3,398
20	Indiana	5,243
32	Iowa	4,464
17	Kansas	5,668
22	Kentucky	5,060
33	Louisiana	4,341
27	Maine	4,856
26	Maryland	4,871
10	Massachusetts	6,501
11	Michigan	6,462
4	Minnesota	7,785
36	Mississippi	4,269
38	Missouri	4,182
35	Montana	4,316
47	Nebraska	3,313
21	Nevada	5,178
29	New Hampshire	4,604
7	New Jersey	6,913
8	New Mexico	6,724
5	New York	7,241
23	North Carolina	4,932
45	North Dakota	3,550
25	Ohio	4,915
39	Oklahoma	4,052
24	Oregon	4,917
30	Pennsylvania	4,532
19	Rhode Island	5,312
34	South Carolina	4,325
50	South Dakota	2,922
48	Tennessee	3,248
49	Texas	3,034
43	Utah	3,678
2	Vermont	12,488
37	Virginia	4,224
16	Washington	5,718
13	West Virginia	5,896
15	Wisconsin	5,826
14	Wyoming	5,887

RANK ORDER

RANK	STATE	PER PUPIL
1	Hawaii	$13,301
2	Vermont	12,488
3	Delaware	8,480
4	Minnesota	7,785
5	New York	7,241
6	Alaska	6,915
7	New Jersey	6,913
8	New Mexico	6,724
9	Arkansas	6,578
10	Massachusetts	6,501
11	Michigan	6,462
12	California	5,985
13	West Virginia	5,896
14	Wyoming	5,887
15	Wisconsin	5,826
16	Washington	5,718
17	Kansas	5,668
18	Connecticut	5,658
19	Rhode Island	5,312
20	Indiana	5,243
21	Nevada	5,178
22	Kentucky	5,060
23	North Carolina	4,932
24	Oregon	4,917
25	Ohio	4,915
26	Maryland	4,871
27	Maine	4,856
28	Alabama	4,763
29	New Hampshire	4,604
30	Pennsylvania	4,532
31	Georgia	4,466
32	Iowa	4,464
33	Louisiana	4,341
34	South Carolina	4,325
35	Montana	4,316
36	Mississippi	4,269
37	Virginia	4,224
38	Missouri	4,182
39	Oklahoma	4,052
40	Idaho	4,050
41	Colorado	3,962
42	Florida	3,835
43	Utah	3,678
44	Arizona	3,619
45	North Dakota	3,550
46	Illinois	3,398
47	Nebraska	3,313
48	Tennessee	3,248
49	Texas	3,034
50	South Dakota	2,922

District of Columbia**   NA

Source: U.S. Bureau of the Census, Governments Division
    "Public Education Finances: 2006" (http://www.census.gov/govs/www/school06.html)
*Based on student membership. Consists only of revenue originating from state governments. Includes all such revenue received by a school system (net of refunds) other than from issuance of debt or liquidation of investments. Does not include noncash transactions such as receipt of services, commodities, or other "receipts in-kind."
**Not applicable.

Percent of Public Elementary and Secondary School
Revenue from State Sources in 2006
National Percent = 46.6%*

RANK	STATE	PERCENT
17	Alabama	55.6
15	Alaska	56.5
26	Arizona	45.1
3	Arkansas	73.4
11	California	58.3
34	Colorado	42.7
44	Connecticut	38.0
6	Delaware	64.5
39	Florida	40.2
28	Georgia	44.2
1	Hawaii	89.9
16	Idaho	55.8
49	Illinois	32.3
23	Indiana	47.5
25	Iowa	45.7
14	Kansas	56.8
13	Kentucky	57.3
36	Louisiana	41.5
36	Maine	41.5
42	Maryland	39.2
30	Massachusetts	44.0
8	Michigan	59.3
5	Minnesota	70.7
22	Mississippi	49.4
31	Missouri	43.6
24	Montana	45.9
50	Nebraska	31.4
12	Nevada	57.9
42	New Hampshire	39.2
38	New Jersey	41.3
4	New Mexico	71.2
33	New York	43.1
10	North Carolina	58.5
45	North Dakota	36.2
35	Ohio	42.3
21	Oklahoma	50.2
20	Oregon	50.9
46	Pennsylvania	35.0
40	Rhode Island	40.0
27	South Carolina	44.8
48	South Dakota	32.8
32	Tennessee	43.2
47	Texas	32.9
18	Utah	54.1
2	Vermont	87.1
41	Virginia	39.6
7	Washington	61.1
9	West Virginia	58.8
19	Wisconsin	52.2
28	Wyoming	44.2

RANK	STATE	PERCENT
1	Hawaii	89.9
2	Vermont	87.1
3	Arkansas	73.4
4	New Mexico	71.2
5	Minnesota	70.7
6	Delaware	64.5
7	Washington	61.1
8	Michigan	59.3
9	West Virginia	58.8
10	North Carolina	58.5
11	California	58.3
12	Nevada	57.9
13	Kentucky	57.3
14	Kansas	56.8
15	Alaska	56.5
16	Idaho	55.8
17	Alabama	55.6
18	Utah	54.1
19	Wisconsin	52.2
20	Oregon	50.9
21	Oklahoma	50.2
22	Mississippi	49.4
23	Indiana	47.5
24	Montana	45.9
25	Iowa	45.7
26	Arizona	45.1
27	South Carolina	44.8
28	Georgia	44.2
28	Wyoming	44.2
30	Massachusetts	44.0
31	Missouri	43.6
32	Tennessee	43.2
33	New York	43.1
34	Colorado	42.7
35	Ohio	42.3
36	Louisiana	41.5
36	Maine	41.5
38	New Jersey	41.3
39	Florida	40.2
40	Rhode Island	40.0
41	Virginia	39.6
42	Maryland	39.2
42	New Hampshire	39.2
44	Connecticut	38.0
45	North Dakota	36.2
46	Pennsylvania	35.0
47	Texas	32.9
48	South Dakota	32.8
49	Illinois	32.3
50	Nebraska	31.4

	District of Columbia**	NA

Source: U.S. Bureau of the Census, Governments Division
   "Public Education Finances: 2006" (http://www.census.gov/govs/www/school06.html)
*Consists only of revenue originating from state governments. Includes all such revenue received by a school system (net of refunds) other than from issuance of debt or liquidation of investments. Does not include noncash transactions such as receipt of services, commodities, or other "receipts in-kind."
**Not applicable.

State Government Revenue for Public Elementary and Secondary School Formula Assistance Programs in 2006
National Total = $163,966,447,000*

ALPHA ORDER

RANK	STATE	REVENUE	% of USA
19	Alabama	$3,002,656,000	1.8%
40	Alaska	806,528,000	0.5%
18	Arizona	3,088,192,000	1.9%
31	Arkansas	1,845,142,000	1.1%
1	California	21,725,719,000	13.3%
21	Colorado	2,863,724,000	1.7%
34	Connecticut	1,299,908,000	0.8%
44	Delaware	675,138,000	0.4%
15	Florida	3,641,892,000	2.2%
7	Georgia	6,037,690,000	3.7%
33	Hawaii	1,731,951,000	1.1%
41	Idaho	784,598,000	0.5%
12	Illinois	4,396,295,000	2.7%
8	Indiana	4,590,335,000	2.8%
30	Iowa	1,963,621,000	1.2%
26	Kansas	2,138,537,000	1.3%
27	Kentucky	2,134,242,000	1.3%
22	Louisiana	2,611,707,000	1.6%
42	Maine	783,928,000	0.5%
24	Maryland	2,338,037,000	1.4%
17	Massachusetts	3,288,347,000	2.0%
4	Michigan	9,678,807,000	5.9%
9	Minnesota	4,579,138,000	2.8%
28	Mississippi	1,987,587,000	1.2%
25	Missouri	2,199,108,000	1.3%
47	Montana	500,927,000	0.3%
43	Nebraska	724,228,000	0.4%
46	Nevada	634,046,000	0.4%
39	New Hampshire	835,968,000	0.5%
16	New Jersey	3,414,612,000	2.1%
29	New Mexico	1,964,755,000	1.2%
2	New York	11,872,833,000	7.2%
6	North Carolina	6,592,349,000	4.0%
50	North Dakota	268,464,000	0.2%
5	Ohio	7,105,000,000	4.3%
32	Oklahoma	1,826,731,000	1.1%
23	Oregon	2,551,302,000	1.6%
10	Pennsylvania	4,498,991,000	2.7%
45	Rhode Island	665,736,000	0.4%
38	South Carolina	863,080,000	0.5%
49	South Dakota	297,230,000	0.2%
20	Tennessee	2,928,545,000	1.8%
3	Texas	10,297,734,000	6.3%
37	Utah	900,689,000	0.5%
35	Vermont	981,200,000	0.6%
14	Virginia	3,971,593,000	2.4%
13	Washington	4,276,702,000	2.6%
36	West Virginia	963,636,000	0.6%
11	Wisconsin	4,458,875,000	2.7%
48	Wyoming	378,394,000	0.2%

RANK ORDER

RANK	STATE	REVENUE	% of USA
1	California	$21,725,719,000	13.3%
2	New York	11,872,833,000	7.2%
3	Texas	10,297,734,000	6.3%
4	Michigan	9,678,807,000	5.9%
5	Ohio	7,105,000,000	4.3%
6	North Carolina	6,592,349,000	4.0%
7	Georgia	6,037,690,000	3.7%
8	Indiana	4,590,335,000	2.8%
9	Minnesota	4,579,138,000	2.8%
10	Pennsylvania	4,498,991,000	2.7%
11	Wisconsin	4,458,875,000	2.7%
12	Illinois	4,396,295,000	2.7%
13	Washington	4,276,702,000	2.6%
14	Virginia	3,971,593,000	2.4%
15	Florida	3,641,892,000	2.2%
16	New Jersey	3,414,612,000	2.1%
17	Massachusetts	3,288,347,000	2.0%
18	Arizona	3,088,192,000	1.9%
19	Alabama	3,002,656,000	1.8%
20	Tennessee	2,928,545,000	1.8%
21	Colorado	2,863,724,000	1.7%
22	Louisiana	2,611,707,000	1.6%
23	Oregon	2,551,302,000	1.6%
24	Maryland	2,338,037,000	1.4%
25	Missouri	2,199,108,000	1.3%
26	Kansas	2,138,537,000	1.3%
27	Kentucky	2,134,242,000	1.3%
28	Mississippi	1,987,587,000	1.2%
29	New Mexico	1,964,755,000	1.2%
30	Iowa	1,963,621,000	1.2%
31	Arkansas	1,845,142,000	1.1%
32	Oklahoma	1,826,731,000	1.1%
33	Hawaii	1,731,951,000	1.1%
34	Connecticut	1,299,908,000	0.8%
35	Vermont	981,200,000	0.6%
36	West Virginia	963,636,000	0.6%
37	Utah	900,689,000	0.5%
38	South Carolina	863,080,000	0.5%
39	New Hampshire	835,968,000	0.5%
40	Alaska	806,528,000	0.5%
41	Idaho	784,598,000	0.5%
42	Maine	783,928,000	0.5%
43	Nebraska	724,228,000	0.4%
44	Delaware	675,138,000	0.4%
45	Rhode Island	665,736,000	0.4%
46	Nevada	634,046,000	0.4%
47	Montana	500,927,000	0.3%
48	Wyoming	378,394,000	0.2%
49	South Dakota	297,230,000	0.2%
50	North Dakota	268,464,000	0.2%
	District of Columbia**	NA	NA

Source: U.S. Bureau of the Census, Governments Division
"Public Education Finances: 2006" (http://www.census.gov/govs/www/school06.html)
*Revenue from general noncategorical state assistance programs such as foundation, minimum or basic formula support, apportionment, equalization, flat or block grants, and state public school fund distributions. This category also includes revenue dedicated from major state taxes, such as income and sales taxes.
**Not applicable.

Percent of Public Elementary and Secondary School
State Government Revenue Used for Formula Assistance Programs in 2006
National Percent = 67.5%*

ALPHA ORDER

ALPHA ORDER

RANK ORDER

RANK	STATE	PERCENT		RANK	STATE	PERCENT
16	Alabama	84.8		1	North Carolina	96.3
11	Alaska	87.8		2	Tennessee	94.5
15	Arizona	84.9		3	Mississippi	94.3
37	Arkansas	59.4		4	Oregon	93.2
40	California	58.0		5	Louisiana	92.8
6	Colorado	92.7		6	Colorado	92.7
46	Connecticut	41.3		7	Iowa	91.0
34	Delaware	69.6		8	New Hampshire	90.3
48	Florida	35.6		9	New Mexico	89.4
17	Georgia	84.6		10	Wisconsin	88.0
32	Hawaii	71.2		11	Alaska	87.8
28	Idaho	75.0		12	Michigan	86.6
36	Illinois	61.5		13	Indiana	85.3
13	Indiana	85.3		14	Vermont	85.1
7	Iowa	91.0		15	Arizona	84.9
22	Kansas	81.0		16	Alabama	84.8
35	Kentucky	62.1		17	Georgia	84.6
5	Louisiana	92.8		18	South Dakota	83.6
20	Maine	82.7		19	Rhode Island	83.5
43	Maryland	55.8		20	Maine	82.7
44	Massachusetts	53.2		21	Ohio	81.7
12	Michigan	86.6		22	Kansas	81.0
31	Minnesota	71.9		23	Montana	79.9
3	Mississippi	94.3		24	Virginia	77.5
41	Missouri	57.4		25	North Dakota	77.0
23	Montana	79.9		26	Nebraska	76.4
26	Nebraska	76.4		27	Texas	76.3
49	Nevada	29.7		28	Idaho	75.0
8	New Hampshire	90.3		29	Wyoming	74.6
47	New Jersey	35.8		30	Washington	72.5
9	New Mexico	89.4		31	Minnesota	71.9
38	New York	58.8		32	Hawaii	71.2
1	North Carolina	96.3		33	Oklahoma	71.1
25	North Dakota	77.0		34	Delaware	69.6
21	Ohio	81.7		35	Kentucky	62.1
33	Oklahoma	71.1		36	Illinois	61.5
4	Oregon	93.2		37	Arkansas	59.4
42	Pennsylvania	56.4		38	New York	58.8
19	Rhode Island	83.5		39	West Virginia	58.4
50	South Carolina	28.5		40	California	58.0
18	South Dakota	83.6		41	Missouri	57.4
2	Tennessee	94.5		42	Pennsylvania	56.4
27	Texas	76.3		43	Maryland	55.8
45	Utah	49.3		44	Massachusetts	53.2
14	Vermont	85.1		45	Utah	49.3
24	Virginia	77.5		46	Connecticut	41.3
30	Washington	72.5		47	New Jersey	35.8
39	West Virginia	58.4		48	Florida	35.6
10	Wisconsin	88.0		49	Nevada	29.7
29	Wyoming	74.6		50	South Carolina	28.5

District of Columbia**   NA

Source: CQ Press using data from U.S. Bureau of the Census, Governments Division
   "Public Education Finances: 2006" (http://www.census.gov/govs/www/school06.html)
*Revenue from general noncategorical state assistance programs such as foundation, minimum or basic formula support, apportionment, equalization, flat or block grants, and state public school fund distributions. This category also includes revenue dedicated from major state taxes, such as income and sales taxes.
**Not applicable.

State Government Revenue for Public Elementary and Secondary School Compensatory Programs in 2006
National Total = $5,873,442,000*

ALPHA ORDER

RANK	STATE	REVENUE	% of USA
11	Alabama	$66,482,000	1.1%
25	Alaska	0	0.0%
16	Arizona	20,477,000	0.3%
9	Arkansas	153,384,000	2.6%
2	California	1,248,953,000	21.3%
25	Colorado	0	0.0%
15	Connecticut	25,322,000	0.4%
25	Delaware	0	0.0%
25	Florida	0	0.0%
25	Georgia	0	0.0%
18	Hawaii	13,194,000	0.2%
25	Idaho	0	0.0%
21	Illinois	6,517,000	0.1%
19	Indiana	12,822,000	0.2%
20	Iowa	9,628,000	0.2%
25	Kansas	0	0.0%
25	Kentucky	0	0.0%
25	Louisiana	0	0.0%
25	Maine	0	0.0%
3	Maryland	605,113,000	10.3%
25	Massachusetts	0	0.0%
5	Michigan	295,103,000	5.0%
6	Minnesota	289,479,000	4.9%
13	Mississippi	29,364,000	0.5%
25	Missouri	0	0.0%
25	Montana	0	0.0%
25	Nebraska	0	0.0%
23	Nevada	2,585,000	0.0%
25	New Hampshire	0	0.0%
1	New Jersey	2,177,110,000	37.1%
24	New Mexico	2,347,000	0.0%
25	New York	0	0.0%
25	North Carolina	0	0.0%
25	North Dakota	0	0.0%
4	Ohio	328,131,000	5.6%
17	Oklahoma	18,920,000	0.3%
25	Oregon	0	0.0%
12	Pennsylvania	54,802,000	0.9%
25	Rhode Island	0	0.0%
8	South Carolina	170,868,000	2.9%
25	South Dakota	0	0.0%
25	Tennessee	0	0.0%
25	Texas	0	0.0%
14	Utah	25,742,000	0.4%
25	Vermont	0	0.0%
7	Virginia	217,074,000	3.7%
10	Washington	97,161,000	1.7%
22	West Virginia	2,864,000	0.0%
25	Wisconsin	0	0.0%
25	Wyoming	0	0.0%

RANK ORDER

RANK	STATE	REVENUE	% of USA
1	New Jersey	$2,177,110,000	37.1%
2	California	1,248,953,000	21.3%
3	Maryland	605,113,000	10.3%
4	Ohio	328,131,000	5.6%
5	Michigan	295,103,000	5.0%
6	Minnesota	289,479,000	4.9%
7	Virginia	217,074,000	3.7%
8	South Carolina	170,868,000	2.9%
9	Arkansas	153,384,000	2.6%
10	Washington	97,161,000	1.7%
11	Alabama	66,482,000	1.1%
12	Pennsylvania	54,802,000	0.9%
13	Mississippi	29,364,000	0.5%
14	Utah	25,742,000	0.4%
15	Connecticut	25,322,000	0.4%
16	Arizona	20,477,000	0.3%
17	Oklahoma	18,920,000	0.3%
18	Hawaii	13,194,000	0.2%
19	Indiana	12,822,000	0.2%
20	Iowa	9,628,000	0.2%
21	Illinois	6,517,000	0.1%
22	West Virginia	2,864,000	0.0%
23	Nevada	2,585,000	0.0%
24	New Mexico	2,347,000	0.0%
25	Alaska	0	0.0%
25	Colorado	0	0.0%
25	Delaware	0	0.0%
25	Florida	0	0.0%
25	Georgia	0	0.0%
25	Idaho	0	0.0%
25	Kansas	0	0.0%
25	Kentucky	0	0.0%
25	Louisiana	0	0.0%
25	Maine	0	0.0%
25	Massachusetts	0	0.0%
25	Missouri	0	0.0%
25	Montana	0	0.0%
25	Nebraska	0	0.0%
25	New Hampshire	0	0.0%
25	New York	0	0.0%
25	North Carolina	0	0.0%
25	North Dakota	0	0.0%
25	Oregon	0	0.0%
25	Rhode Island	0	0.0%
25	South Dakota	0	0.0%
25	Tennessee	0	0.0%
25	Texas	0	0.0%
25	Vermont	0	0.0%
25	Wisconsin	0	0.0%
25	Wyoming	0	0.0%
	District of Columbia**	NA	NA

Source: U.S. Bureau of the Census, Governments Division
   "Public Education Finances: 2006" (http://www.census.gov/govs/www/school06.html)
*Revenue for "at risk" or other economically disadvantaged students including migratory children. Also includes monies from state programs directed toward the attainment of basic skills and categorical education excellence and quality education programs that provide more than staff enhancements--such as materials and resource centers.
**Not applicable.

Percent of Public Elementary and Secondary School
State Government Revenue Used for Compensatory Programs in 2006
National Percent = 2.4%*

ALPHA ORDER

RANK ORDER

RANK	STATE	PERCENT	RANK	STATE	PERCENT
10	Alabama	1.9	1	New Jersey	22.8
25	Alaska	0.0	2	Maryland	14.4
17	Arizona	0.6	3	South Carolina	5.7
4	Arkansas	4.9	4	Arkansas	4.9
8	California	3.3	5	Minnesota	4.5
25	Colorado	0.0	6	Virginia	4.2
14	Connecticut	0.8	7	Ohio	3.8
25	Delaware	0.0	8	California	3.3
25	Florida	0.0	9	Michigan	2.6
25	Georgia	0.0	10	Alabama	1.9
18	Hawaii	0.5	11	Washington	1.6
25	Idaho	0.0	12	Mississippi	1.4
22	Illinois	0.1	12	Utah	1.4
20	Indiana	0.2	14	Connecticut	0.8
19	Iowa	0.4	15	Oklahoma	0.7
25	Kansas	0.0	15	Pennsylvania	0.7
25	Kentucky	0.0	17	Arizona	0.6
25	Louisiana	0.0	18	Hawaii	0.5
25	Maine	0.0	19	Iowa	0.4
2	Maryland	14.4	20	Indiana	0.2
25	Massachusetts	0.0	20	West Virginia	0.2
9	Michigan	2.6	22	Illinois	0.1
5	Minnesota	4.5	22	Nevada	0.1
12	Mississippi	1.4	22	New Mexico	0.1
25	Missouri	0.0	25	Alaska	0.0
25	Montana	0.0	25	Colorado	0.0
25	Nebraska	0.0	25	Delaware	0.0
22	Nevada	0.1	25	Florida	0.0
25	New Hampshire	0.0	25	Georgia	0.0
1	New Jersey	22.8	25	Idaho	0.0
22	New Mexico	0.1	25	Kansas	0.0
25	New York	0.0	25	Kentucky	0.0
25	North Carolina	0.0	25	Louisiana	0.0
25	North Dakota	0.0	25	Maine	0.0
7	Ohio	3.8	25	Massachusetts	0.0
15	Oklahoma	0.7	25	Missouri	0.0
25	Oregon	0.0	25	Montana	0.0
15	Pennsylvania	0.7	25	Nebraska	0.0
25	Rhode Island	0.0	25	New Hampshire	0.0
3	South Carolina	5.7	25	New York	0.0
25	South Dakota	0.0	25	North Carolina	0.0
25	Tennessee	0.0	25	North Dakota	0.0
25	Texas	0.0	25	Oregon	0.0
12	Utah	1.4	25	Rhode Island	0.0
25	Vermont	0.0	25	South Dakota	0.0
6	Virginia	4.2	25	Tennessee	0.0
11	Washington	1.6	25	Texas	0.0
20	West Virginia	0.2	25	Vermont	0.0
25	Wisconsin	0.0	25	Wisconsin	0.0
25	Wyoming	0.0	25	Wyoming	0.0

District of Columbia**   NA

Source: CQ Press using data from U.S. Bureau of the Census, Governments Division
    "Public Education Finances: 2006" (http://www.census.gov/govs/www/school06.html)
*Revenue for "at risk" or other economically disadvantaged students including migratory children. Also includes monies from
state programs directed toward the attainment of basic skills and categorical education excellence and quality education programs
that provide more than staff enhancements--such as materials and resource centers.
**Not applicable.

State Government Revenue for Public Elementary and Secondary School Special Education Programs in 2006
National Total = $15,248,466,000*

ALPHA ORDER

RANK	STATE	REVENUE	% of USA
33	Alabama	$880,000	0.0%
38	Alaska	0	0.0%
34	Arizona	404,000	0.0%
18	Arkansas	187,645,000	1.2%
1	California	2,918,603,000	19.1%
22	Colorado	109,960,000	0.7%
11	Connecticut	410,932,000	2.7%
35	Delaware	316,000	0.0%
3	Florida	1,328,532,000	8.7%
38	Georgia	0	0.0%
12	Hawaii	394,819,000	2.6%
31	Idaho	2,724,000	0.0%
8	Illinois	536,429,000	3.5%
25	Indiana	36,157,000	0.2%
32	Iowa	1,470,000	0.0%
17	Kansas	285,709,000	1.9%
38	Kentucky	0	0.0%
26	Louisiana	26,476,000	0.2%
36	Maine	62,000	0.0%
16	Maryland	288,731,000	1.9%
38	Massachusetts	0	0.0%
6	Michigan	883,029,000	5.8%
7	Minnesota	627,432,000	4.1%
30	Mississippi	3,523,000	0.0%
15	Missouri	288,952,000	1.9%
29	Montana	4,464,000	0.0%
20	Nebraska	164,872,000	1.1%
23	Nevada	93,639,000	0.6%
38	New Hampshire	0	0.0%
4	New Jersey	976,882,000	6.4%
38	New Mexico	0	0.0%
2	New York	2,816,073,000	18.5%
38	North Carolina	0	0.0%
27	North Dakota	23,126,000	0.2%
38	Ohio	0	0.0%
37	Oklahoma	31,000	0.0%
38	Oregon	0	0.0%
5	Pennsylvania	955,347,000	6.3%
38	Rhode Island	0	0.0%
14	South Carolina	315,239,000	2.1%
24	South Dakota	42,228,000	0.3%
38	Tennessee	0	0.0%
38	Texas	0	0.0%
19	Utah	172,313,000	1.1%
21	Vermont	118,819,000	0.8%
10	Virginia	423,609,000	2.8%
9	Washington	482,764,000	3.2%
28	West Virginia	7,149,000	0.0%
13	Wisconsin	319,126,000	2.1%
38	Wyoming	0	0.0%

RANK ORDER

RANK	STATE	REVENUE	% of USA
1	California	$2,918,603,000	19.1%
2	New York	2,816,073,000	18.5%
3	Florida	1,328,532,000	8.7%
4	New Jersey	976,882,000	6.4%
5	Pennsylvania	955,347,000	6.3%
6	Michigan	883,029,000	5.8%
7	Minnesota	627,432,000	4.1%
8	Illinois	536,429,000	3.5%
9	Washington	482,764,000	3.2%
10	Virginia	423,609,000	2.8%
11	Connecticut	410,932,000	2.7%
12	Hawaii	394,819,000	2.6%
13	Wisconsin	319,126,000	2.1%
14	South Carolina	315,239,000	2.1%
15	Missouri	288,952,000	1.9%
16	Maryland	288,731,000	1.9%
17	Kansas	285,709,000	1.9%
18	Arkansas	187,645,000	1.2%
19	Utah	172,313,000	1.1%
20	Nebraska	164,872,000	1.1%
21	Vermont	118,819,000	0.8%
22	Colorado	109,960,000	0.7%
23	Nevada	93,639,000	0.6%
24	South Dakota	42,228,000	0.3%
25	Indiana	36,157,000	0.2%
26	Louisiana	26,476,000	0.2%
27	North Dakota	23,126,000	0.2%
28	West Virginia	7,149,000	0.0%
29	Montana	4,464,000	0.0%
30	Mississippi	3,523,000	0.0%
31	Idaho	2,724,000	0.0%
32	Iowa	1,470,000	0.0%
33	Alabama	880,000	0.0%
34	Arizona	404,000	0.0%
35	Delaware	316,000	0.0%
36	Maine	62,000	0.0%
37	Oklahoma	31,000	0.0%
38	Alaska	0	0.0%
38	Georgia	0	0.0%
38	Kentucky	0	0.0%
38	Massachusetts	0	0.0%
38	New Hampshire	0	0.0%
38	New Mexico	0	0.0%
38	North Carolina	0	0.0%
38	Ohio	0	0.0%
38	Oregon	0	0.0%
38	Rhode Island	0	0.0%
38	Tennessee	0	0.0%
38	Texas	0	0.0%
38	Wyoming	0	0.0%
	District of Columbia**	NA	NA

Source: U.S. Bureau of the Census, Governments Division
    "Public Education Finances: 2006" (http://www.census.gov/govs/www/school06.html)
*Revenue for the education of students with special needs, such as those with physical and mental handicaps.
**Not applicable.

Percent of Public Elementary and Secondary School
State Government Revenue Used for Special Education Programs in 2006
National Percent = 6.3%*

RANK	STATE	PERCENT
33	Alabama	0.0
33	Alaska	0.0
33	Arizona	0.0
23	Arkansas	6.0
17	California	7.8
25	Colorado	3.6
4	Connecticut	13.1
33	Delaware	0.0
5	Florida	13.0
33	Georgia	0.0
2	Hawaii	16.2
30	Idaho	0.3
18	Illinois	7.5
27	Indiana	0.7
32	Iowa	0.1
8	Kansas	10.8
33	Kentucky	0.0
26	Louisiana	0.9
33	Maine	0.0
20	Maryland	6.9
33	Massachusetts	0.0
16	Michigan	7.9
12	Minnesota	9.9
31	Mississippi	0.2
18	Missouri	7.5
27	Montana	0.7
1	Nebraska	17.4
24	Nevada	4.4
33	New Hampshire	0.0
11	New Jersey	10.2
33	New Mexico	0.0
3	New York	14.0
33	North Carolina	0.0
21	North Dakota	6.6
33	Ohio	0.0
33	Oklahoma	0.0
33	Oregon	0.0
6	Pennsylvania	12.0
33	Rhode Island	0.0
9	South Carolina	10.4
7	South Dakota	11.9
33	Tennessee	0.0
33	Texas	0.0
13	Utah	9.4
10	Vermont	10.3
14	Virginia	8.3
15	Washington	8.2
29	West Virginia	0.4
22	Wisconsin	6.3
33	Wyoming	0.0

RANK	STATE	PERCENT
1	Nebraska	17.4
2	Hawaii	16.2
3	New York	14.0
4	Connecticut	13.1
5	Florida	13.0
6	Pennsylvania	12.0
7	South Dakota	11.9
8	Kansas	10.8
9	South Carolina	10.4
10	Vermont	10.3
11	New Jersey	10.2
12	Minnesota	9.9
13	Utah	9.4
14	Virginia	8.3
15	Washington	8.2
16	Michigan	7.9
17	California	7.8
18	Illinois	7.5
18	Missouri	7.5
20	Maryland	6.9
21	North Dakota	6.6
22	Wisconsin	6.3
23	Arkansas	6.0
24	Nevada	4.4
25	Colorado	3.6
26	Louisiana	0.9
27	Indiana	0.7
27	Montana	0.7
29	West Virginia	0.4
30	Idaho	0.3
31	Mississippi	0.2
32	Iowa	0.1
33	Alabama	0.0
33	Alaska	0.0
33	Arizona	0.0
33	Delaware	0.0
33	Georgia	0.0
33	Kentucky	0.0
33	Maine	0.0
33	Massachusetts	0.0
33	New Hampshire	0.0
33	New Mexico	0.0
33	North Carolina	0.0
33	Ohio	0.0
33	Oklahoma	0.0
33	Oregon	0.0
33	Rhode Island	0.0
33	Tennessee	0.0
33	Texas	0.0
33	Wyoming	0.0

District of Columbia**	NA

Source: CQ Press using data from U.S. Bureau of the Census, Governments Division
   "Public Education Finances: 2006" (http://www.census.gov/govs/www/school06.html)
*Revenue for the education of students with special needs, such as those with physical and mental handicaps.
**Not applicable.

State Government Revenue for Public Elementary and Secondary School Vocational Programs in 2006
National Total = $923,305,000*

RANK	STATE	REVENUE	% of USA
33	Alabama	$0	0.0%
33	Alaska	0	0.0%
14	Arizona	12,840,000	1.4%
13	Arkansas	17,246,000	1.9%
20	California	4,801,000	0.5%
12	Colorado	19,919,000	2.2%
26	Connecticut	2,703,000	0.3%
33	Delaware	0	0.0%
2	Florida	189,003,000	20.5%
33	Georgia	0	0.0%
18	Hawaii	7,415,000	0.8%
16	Idaho	8,436,000	0.9%
7	Illinois	38,693,000	4.2%
27	Indiana	2,521,000	0.3%
25	Iowa	3,009,000	0.3%
33	Kansas	0	0.0%
24	Kentucky	3,069,000	0.3%
33	Louisiana	0	0.0%
33	Maine	0	0.0%
33	Maryland	0	0.0%
31	Massachusetts	193,000	0.0%
9	Michigan	34,348,000	3.7%
15	Minnesota	8,965,000	1.0%
8	Mississippi	35,961,000	3.9%
10	Missouri	28,200,000	3.1%
28	Montana	884,000	0.1%
33	Nebraska	0	0.0%
29	Nevada	818,000	0.1%
19	New Hampshire	6,314,000	0.7%
6	New Jersey	39,106,000	4.2%
32	New Mexico	64,000	0.0%
33	New York	0	0.0%
33	North Carolina	0	0.0%
21	North Dakota	4,258,000	0.5%
23	Ohio	3,528,000	0.4%
11	Oklahoma	23,634,000	2.6%
33	Oregon	0	0.0%
4	Pennsylvania	60,143,000	6.5%
33	Rhode Island	0	0.0%
1	South Carolina	237,297,000	25.7%
33	South Dakota	0	0.0%
30	Tennessee	392,000	0.0%
33	Texas	0	0.0%
5	Utah	52,828,000	5.7%
17	Vermont	7,986,000	0.9%
3	Virginia	64,483,000	7.0%
33	Washington	0	0.0%
22	West Virginia	4,248,000	0.5%
33	Wisconsin	0	0.0%
33	Wyoming	0	0.0%

RANK	STATE	REVENUE	% of USA
1	South Carolina	$237,297,000	25.7%
2	Florida	189,003,000	20.5%
3	Virginia	64,483,000	7.0%
4	Pennsylvania	60,143,000	6.5%
5	Utah	52,828,000	5.7%
6	New Jersey	39,106,000	4.2%
7	Illinois	38,693,000	4.2%
8	Mississippi	35,961,000	3.9%
9	Michigan	34,348,000	3.7%
10	Missouri	28,200,000	3.1%
11	Oklahoma	23,634,000	2.6%
12	Colorado	19,919,000	2.2%
13	Arkansas	17,246,000	1.9%
14	Arizona	12,840,000	1.4%
15	Minnesota	8,965,000	1.0%
16	Idaho	8,436,000	0.9%
17	Vermont	7,986,000	0.9%
18	Hawaii	7,415,000	0.8%
19	New Hampshire	6,314,000	0.7%
20	California	4,801,000	0.5%
21	North Dakota	4,258,000	0.5%
22	West Virginia	4,248,000	0.5%
23	Ohio	3,528,000	0.4%
24	Kentucky	3,069,000	0.3%
25	Iowa	3,009,000	0.3%
26	Connecticut	2,703,000	0.3%
27	Indiana	2,521,000	0.3%
28	Montana	884,000	0.1%
29	Nevada	818,000	0.1%
30	Tennessee	392,000	0.0%
31	Massachusetts	193,000	0.0%
32	New Mexico	64,000	0.0%
33	Alabama	0	0.0%
33	Alaska	0	0.0%
33	Delaware	0	0.0%
33	Georgia	0	0.0%
33	Kansas	0	0.0%
33	Louisiana	0	0.0%
33	Maine	0	0.0%
33	Maryland	0	0.0%
33	Nebraska	0	0.0%
33	New York	0	0.0%
33	North Carolina	0	0.0%
33	Oregon	0	0.0%
33	Rhode Island	0	0.0%
33	South Dakota	0	0.0%
33	Texas	0	0.0%
33	Washington	0	0.0%
33	Wisconsin	0	0.0%
33	Wyoming	0	0.0%
	District of Columbia**	NA	NA

Source: U.S. Bureau of the Census, Governments Division
    "Public Education Finances: 2006" (http://www.census.gov/govs/www/school06.html)
*Revenue for state vocational education assistance programs including career education programs.
**Not applicable.

Percent of Public Elementary and Secondary School State Government Revenue Used for Vocational Programs in 2006
National Percent = 0.4%*

ALPHA ORDER

RANK	STATE	PERCENT
26	Alabama	0.0
26	Alaska	0.0
16	Arizona	0.4
13	Arkansas	0.6
26	California	0.0
13	Colorado	0.6
21	Connecticut	0.1
26	Delaware	0.0
3	Florida	1.9
26	Georgia	0.0
18	Hawaii	0.3
8	Idaho	0.8
15	Illinois	0.5
26	Indiana	0.0
21	Iowa	0.1
26	Kansas	0.0
21	Kentucky	0.1
26	Louisiana	0.0
26	Maine	0.0
26	Maryland	0.0
26	Massachusetts	0.0
18	Michigan	0.3
21	Minnesota	0.1
4	Mississippi	1.7
10	Missouri	0.7
21	Montana	0.1
26	Nebraska	0.0
26	Nevada	0.0
10	New Hampshire	0.7
16	New Jersey	0.4
26	New Mexico	0.0
26	New York	0.0
26	North Carolina	0.0
6	North Dakota	1.2
26	Ohio	0.0
7	Oklahoma	0.9
26	Oregon	0.0
8	Pennsylvania	0.8
26	Rhode Island	0.0
1	South Carolina	7.8
26	South Dakota	0.0
26	Tennessee	0.0
26	Texas	0.0
2	Utah	2.9
10	Vermont	0.7
5	Virginia	1.3
26	Washington	0.0
18	West Virginia	0.3
26	Wisconsin	0.0
26	Wyoming	0.0

RANK ORDER

RANK	STATE	PERCENT
1	South Carolina	7.8
2	Utah	2.9
3	Florida	1.9
4	Mississippi	1.7
5	Virginia	1.3
6	North Dakota	1.2
7	Oklahoma	0.9
8	Idaho	0.8
8	Pennsylvania	0.8
10	Missouri	0.7
10	New Hampshire	0.7
10	Vermont	0.7
13	Arkansas	0.6
13	Colorado	0.6
15	Illinois	0.5
16	Arizona	0.4
16	New Jersey	0.4
18	Hawaii	0.3
18	Michigan	0.3
18	West Virginia	0.3
21	Connecticut	0.1
21	Iowa	0.1
21	Kentucky	0.1
21	Minnesota	0.1
21	Montana	0.1
26	Alabama	0.0
26	Alaska	0.0
26	California	0.0
26	Delaware	0.0
26	Georgia	0.0
26	Indiana	0.0
26	Kansas	0.0
26	Louisiana	0.0
26	Maine	0.0
26	Maryland	0.0
26	Massachusetts	0.0
26	Nebraska	0.0
26	Nevada	0.0
26	New Mexico	0.0
26	New York	0.0
26	North Carolina	0.0
26	Ohio	0.0
26	Oregon	0.0
26	Rhode Island	0.0
26	South Dakota	0.0
26	Tennessee	0.0
26	Texas	0.0
26	Washington	0.0
26	Wisconsin	0.0
26	Wyoming	0.0

District of Columbia**   NA

Source: CQ Press using data from U.S. Bureau of the Census, Governments Division
   "Public Education Finances: 2006" (http://www.census.gov/govs/www/school06.html)
*Revenue for state vocational education assistance programs including career education programs.
**Not applicable.

State Government Revenue for Public Elementary and Secondary School Transportation Programs in 2006
National Total = $4,079,894,000*

ALPHA ORDER

RANK	STATE	REVENUE	% of USA
6	Alabama	$264,366,000	6.5%
17	Alaska	54,370,000	1.3%
31	Arizona	0	0.0%
31	Arkansas	0	0.0%
2	California	556,282,000	13.6%
19	Colorado	40,944,000	1.0%
16	Connecticut	55,942,000	1.4%
12	Delaware	61,939,000	1.5%
3	Florida	451,432,000	11.1%
31	Georgia	0	0.0%
20	Hawaii	23,505,000	0.6%
14	Idaho	60,476,000	1.5%
4	Illinois	404,010,000	9.9%
30	Indiana	13,000	0.0%
26	Iowa	7,994,000	0.2%
31	Kansas	0	0.0%
28	Kentucky	611,000	0.0%
31	Louisiana	0	0.0%
31	Maine	0	0.0%
9	Maryland	187,505,000	4.6%
8	Massachusetts	228,355,000	5.6%
31	Michigan	0	0.0%
13	Minnesota	61,155,000	1.5%
31	Mississippi	0	0.0%
10	Missouri	155,888,000	3.8%
25	Montana	12,177,000	0.3%
29	Nebraska	28,000	0.0%
31	Nevada	0	0.0%
31	New Hampshire	0	0.0%
5	New Jersey	284,037,000	7.0%
11	New Mexico	103,905,000	2.5%
31	New York	0	0.0%
31	North Carolina	0	0.0%
23	North Dakota	16,583,000	0.4%
31	Ohio	0	0.0%
31	Oklahoma	0	0.0%
22	Oregon	16,933,000	0.4%
1	Pennsylvania	643,963,000	15.8%
31	Rhode Island	0	0.0%
18	South Carolina	42,845,000	1.1%
31	South Dakota	0	0.0%
31	Tennessee	0	0.0%
31	Texas	0	0.0%
15	Utah	57,038,000	1.4%
27	Vermont	927,000	0.0%
31	Virginia	0	0.0%
7	Washington	250,646,000	6.1%
24	West Virginia	15,082,000	0.4%
21	Wisconsin	20,943,000	0.5%
31	Wyoming	0	0.0%

RANK ORDER

RANK	STATE	REVENUE	% of USA
1	Pennsylvania	$643,963,000	15.8%
2	California	556,282,000	13.6%
3	Florida	451,432,000	11.1%
4	Illinois	404,010,000	9.9%
5	New Jersey	284,037,000	7.0%
6	Alabama	264,366,000	6.5%
7	Washington	250,646,000	6.1%
8	Massachusetts	228,355,000	5.6%
9	Maryland	187,505,000	4.6%
10	Missouri	155,888,000	3.8%
11	New Mexico	103,905,000	2.5%
12	Delaware	61,939,000	1.5%
13	Minnesota	61,155,000	1.5%
14	Idaho	60,476,000	1.5%
15	Utah	57,038,000	1.4%
16	Connecticut	55,942,000	1.4%
17	Alaska	54,370,000	1.3%
18	South Carolina	42,845,000	1.1%
19	Colorado	40,944,000	1.0%
20	Hawaii	23,505,000	0.6%
21	Wisconsin	20,943,000	0.5%
22	Oregon	16,933,000	0.4%
23	North Dakota	16,583,000	0.4%
24	West Virginia	15,082,000	0.4%
25	Montana	12,177,000	0.3%
26	Iowa	7,994,000	0.2%
27	Vermont	927,000	0.0%
28	Kentucky	611,000	0.0%
29	Nebraska	28,000	0.0%
30	Indiana	13,000	0.0%
31	Arizona	0	0.0%
31	Arkansas	0	0.0%
31	Georgia	0	0.0%
31	Kansas	0	0.0%
31	Louisiana	0	0.0%
31	Maine	0	0.0%
31	Michigan	0	0.0%
31	Mississippi	0	0.0%
31	Nevada	0	0.0%
31	New Hampshire	0	0.0%
31	New York	0	0.0%
31	North Carolina	0	0.0%
31	Ohio	0	0.0%
31	Oklahoma	0	0.0%
31	Rhode Island	0	0.0%
31	South Dakota	0	0.0%
31	Tennessee	0	0.0%
31	Texas	0	0.0%
31	Virginia	0	0.0%
31	Wyoming	0	0.0%
	District of Columbia**	NA	NA

Source: U.S. Bureau of the Census, Governments Division
   "Public Education Finances: 2006" (http://www.census.gov/govs/www/school06.html)
*Payments for various state transportation aid programs such as those that compensate the school system for part of its transportation expense and those that provide reimbursement for transportation salaries or school bus purchase.
**Not applicable.

Percent of Public Elementary and Secondary School
State Government Revenue Used for Transportation Programs in 2006
National Percent = 1.7%*

ALPHA ORDER

RANK	STATE	PERCENT
2	Alabama	7.5
4	Alaska	5.9
28	Arizona	0.0
28	Arkansas	0.0
18	California	1.5
20	Colorado	1.3
17	Connecticut	1.8
3	Delaware	6.4
10	Florida	4.4
28	Georgia	0.0
21	Hawaii	1.0
5	Idaho	5.8
6	Illinois	5.7
28	Indiana	0.0
25	Iowa	0.4
28	Kansas	0.0
28	Kentucky	0.0
28	Louisiana	0.0
28	Maine	0.0
9	Maryland	4.5
13	Massachusetts	3.7
28	Michigan	0.0
21	Minnesota	1.0
28	Mississippi	0.0
12	Missouri	4.1
16	Montana	1.9
28	Nebraska	0.0
28	Nevada	0.0
28	New Hampshire	0.0
15	New Jersey	3.0
8	New Mexico	4.7
28	New York	0.0
28	North Carolina	0.0
7	North Dakota	4.8
28	Ohio	0.0
28	Oklahoma	0.0
24	Oregon	0.6
1	Pennsylvania	8.1
28	Rhode Island	0.0
19	South Carolina	1.4
28	South Dakota	0.0
28	Tennessee	0.0
28	Texas	0.0
14	Utah	3.1
27	Vermont	0.1
28	Virginia	0.0
11	Washington	4.2
23	West Virginia	0.9
25	Wisconsin	0.4
28	Wyoming	0.0

RANK ORDER

RANK	STATE	PERCENT
1	Pennsylvania	8.1
2	Alabama	7.5
3	Delaware	6.4
4	Alaska	5.9
5	Idaho	5.8
6	Illinois	5.7
7	North Dakota	4.8
8	New Mexico	4.7
9	Maryland	4.5
10	Florida	4.4
11	Washington	4.2
12	Missouri	4.1
13	Massachusetts	3.7
14	Utah	3.1
15	New Jersey	3.0
16	Montana	1.9
17	Connecticut	1.8
18	California	1.5
19	South Carolina	1.4
20	Colorado	1.3
21	Hawaii	1.0
21	Minnesota	1.0
23	West Virginia	0.9
24	Oregon	0.6
25	Iowa	0.4
25	Wisconsin	0.4
27	Vermont	0.1
28	Arizona	0.0
28	Arkansas	0.0
28	Georgia	0.0
28	Indiana	0.0
28	Kansas	0.0
28	Kentucky	0.0
28	Louisiana	0.0
28	Maine	0.0
28	Michigan	0.0
28	Mississippi	0.0
28	Nebraska	0.0
28	Nevada	0.0
28	New Hampshire	0.0
28	New York	0.0
28	North Carolina	0.0
28	Ohio	0.0
28	Oklahoma	0.0
28	Rhode Island	0.0
28	South Dakota	0.0
28	Tennessee	0.0
28	Texas	0.0
28	Virginia	0.0
28	Wyoming	0.0

District of Columbia**   NA

Source: CQ Press using data from U.S. Bureau of the Census, Governments Division
   "Public Education Finances: 2006" (http://www.census.gov/govs/www/school06.html)
*Payments for various state transportation aid programs such as those that compensate the school system for part of its transportation expense and those that provide reimbursement for transportation salaries or school bus purchase.
**Not applicable.

Public Elementary and Secondary School
Revenue from Local Sources in 2006
National Total = $231,230,159,000*

ALPHA ORDER

RANK	STATE	REVENUE	% of USA
27	Alabama	$2,091,669,000	0.9%
48	Alaska	416,307,000	0.2%
20	Arizona	3,462,150,000	1.5%
40	Arkansas	643,435,000	0.3%
3	California	19,345,769,000	8.4%
19	Colorado	3,628,554,000	1.6%
15	Connecticut	4,750,621,000	2.1%
47	Delaware	424,324,000	0.2%
6	Florida	12,742,958,000	5.5%
9	Georgia	7,566,647,000	3.3%
50	Hawaii	48,404,000	0.0%
41	Idaho	627,494,000	0.3%
4	Illinois	13,061,672,000	5.6%
14	Indiana	5,196,807,000	2.2%
25	Iowa	2,168,564,000	0.9%
32	Kansas	1,665,425,000	0.7%
30	Kentucky	1,880,369,000	0.8%
24	Louisiana	2,687,324,000	1.2%
37	Maine	1,135,968,000	0.5%
13	Maryland	5,837,146,000	2.5%
10	Massachusetts	7,117,307,000	3.1%
12	Michigan	6,148,883,000	2.7%
28	Minnesota	2,079,793,000	0.9%
34	Mississippi	1,304,216,000	0.6%
16	Missouri	4,207,448,000	1.8%
43	Montana	548,041,000	0.2%
31	Nebraska	1,767,075,000	0.8%
35	Nevada	1,292,669,000	0.6%
33	New Hampshire	1,307,122,000	0.6%
7	New Jersey	12,584,839,000	5.4%
46	New Mexico	439,948,000	0.2%
1	New York	23,303,133,000	10.1%
18	North Carolina	3,677,091,000	1.6%
45	North Dakota	463,836,000	0.2%
8	Ohio	10,359,002,000	4.5%
29	Oklahoma	1,893,445,000	0.8%
26	Oregon	2,127,988,000	0.9%
5	Pennsylvania	13,004,120,000	5.6%
38	Rhode Island	1,046,538,000	0.5%
22	South Carolina	3,053,802,000	1.3%
42	South Dakota	550,552,000	0.2%
21	Tennessee	3,273,613,000	1.4%
2	Texas	22,750,456,000	9.8%
36	Utah	1,208,440,000	0.5%
49	Vermont	67,241,000	0.0%
11	Virginia	6,959,087,000	3.0%
23	Washington	2,954,704,000	1.3%
39	West Virginia	810,463,000	0.4%
17	Wisconsin	4,056,969,000	1.8%
44	Wyoming	525,239,000	0.2%

RANK ORDER

RANK	STATE	REVENUE	% of USA
1	New York	$23,303,133,000	10.1%
2	Texas	22,750,456,000	9.8%
3	California	19,345,769,000	8.4%
4	Illinois	13,061,672,000	5.6%
5	Pennsylvania	13,004,120,000	5.6%
6	Florida	12,742,958,000	5.5%
7	New Jersey	12,584,839,000	5.4%
8	Ohio	10,359,002,000	4.5%
9	Georgia	7,566,647,000	3.3%
10	Massachusetts	7,117,307,000	3.1%
11	Virginia	6,959,087,000	3.0%
12	Michigan	6,148,883,000	2.7%
13	Maryland	5,837,146,000	2.5%
14	Indiana	5,196,807,000	2.2%
15	Connecticut	4,750,621,000	2.1%
16	Missouri	4,207,448,000	1.8%
17	Wisconsin	4,056,969,000	1.8%
18	North Carolina	3,677,091,000	1.6%
19	Colorado	3,628,554,000	1.6%
20	Arizona	3,462,150,000	1.5%
21	Tennessee	3,273,613,000	1.4%
22	South Carolina	3,053,802,000	1.3%
23	Washington	2,954,704,000	1.3%
24	Louisiana	2,687,324,000	1.2%
25	Iowa	2,168,564,000	0.9%
26	Oregon	2,127,988,000	0.9%
27	Alabama	2,091,669,000	0.9%
28	Minnesota	2,079,793,000	0.9%
29	Oklahoma	1,893,445,000	0.8%
30	Kentucky	1,880,369,000	0.8%
31	Nebraska	1,767,075,000	0.8%
32	Kansas	1,665,425,000	0.7%
33	New Hampshire	1,307,122,000	0.6%
34	Mississippi	1,304,216,000	0.6%
35	Nevada	1,292,669,000	0.6%
36	Utah	1,208,440,000	0.5%
37	Maine	1,135,968,000	0.5%
38	Rhode Island	1,046,538,000	0.5%
39	West Virginia	810,463,000	0.4%
40	Arkansas	643,435,000	0.3%
41	Idaho	627,494,000	0.3%
42	South Dakota	550,552,000	0.2%
43	Montana	548,041,000	0.2%
44	Wyoming	525,239,000	0.2%
45	North Dakota	463,836,000	0.2%
46	New Mexico	439,948,000	0.2%
47	Delaware	424,324,000	0.2%
48	Alaska	416,307,000	0.2%
49	Vermont	67,241,000	0.0%
50	Hawaii	48,404,000	0.0%
	District of Columbia	965,492,000	0.4%

Source: U.S. Bureau of the Census, Governments Division
   "Public Education Finances: 2006" (http://www.census.gov/govs/www/school06.html)
*Revenue raised locally including taxes and charges. Includes all such revenue received by a school system from local sources (net of refunds) other than from issuance of debt or liquidation of investments. Does not include noncash transactions such as receipt of services, commodities, or other "receipts in-kind."

Per Capita Elementary and Secondary School Revenue from Local Sources in 2006
National Per Capita = $774*

ALPHA ORDER

RANK	STATE	PER CAPITA
40	Alabama	$456
27	Alaska	615
32	Arizona	562
47	Arkansas	229
34	California	534
18	Colorado	761
2	Connecticut	1,359
37	Delaware	498
23	Florida	706
17	Georgia	810
50	Hawaii	38
44	Idaho	429
8	Illinois	1,022
16	Indiana	825
19	Iowa	730
29	Kansas	604
43	Kentucky	447
26	Louisiana	633
15	Maine	864
6	Maryland	1,042
4	Massachusetts	1,106
28	Michigan	609
46	Minnesota	403
41	Mississippi	450
22	Missouri	721
30	Montana	579
9	Nebraska	1,002
36	Nevada	519
10	New Hampshire	996
1	New Jersey	1,452
48	New Mexico	227
3	New York	1,209
45	North Carolina	415
20	North Dakota	728
14	Ohio	904
35	Oklahoma	529
31	Oregon	577
5	Pennsylvania	1,048
11	Rhode Island	986
24	South Carolina	705
25	South Dakota	698
33	Tennessee	539
12	Texas	972
38	Utah	468
49	Vermont	108
13	Virginia	911
39	Washington	463
42	West Virginia	448
20	Wisconsin	728
7	Wyoming	1,024

RANK ORDER

RANK	STATE	PER CAPITA
1	New Jersey	$1,452
2	Connecticut	1,359
3	New York	1,209
4	Massachusetts	1,106
5	Pennsylvania	1,048
6	Maryland	1,042
7	Wyoming	1,024
8	Illinois	1,022
9	Nebraska	1,002
10	New Hampshire	996
11	Rhode Island	986
12	Texas	972
13	Virginia	911
14	Ohio	904
15	Maine	864
16	Indiana	825
17	Georgia	810
18	Colorado	761
19	Iowa	730
20	North Dakota	728
20	Wisconsin	728
22	Missouri	721
23	Florida	706
24	South Carolina	705
25	South Dakota	698
26	Louisiana	633
27	Alaska	615
28	Michigan	609
29	Kansas	604
30	Montana	579
31	Oregon	577
32	Arizona	562
33	Tennessee	539
34	California	534
35	Oklahoma	529
36	Nevada	519
37	Delaware	498
38	Utah	468
39	Washington	463
40	Alabama	456
41	Mississippi	450
42	West Virginia	448
43	Kentucky	447
44	Idaho	429
45	North Carolina	415
46	Minnesota	403
47	Arkansas	229
48	New Mexico	227
49	Vermont	108
50	Hawaii	38

District of Columbia 1,649

Source: CQ Press using data from U.S. Bureau of the Census, Governments Division
"Public Education Finances: 2006" (http://www.census.gov/govs/www/school06.html)
*Revenue raised locally including taxes and charges. Includes all such revenue received by a school system from local sources (net of refunds) other than from issuance of debt or liquidation of investments. Does not include noncash transactions such as receipt of services, commodities, or other "receipts in-kind."

Public Elementary and Secondary School Revenue from Local Sources per $1,000 Personal Income in 2006
National Ratio = $22.48*

ALPHA ORDER

RANK	STATE	RATIO
39	Alabama	$15.72
36	Alaska	17.13
28	Arizona	19.14
47	Arkansas	8.60
41	California	14.35
26	Colorado	20.64
6	Connecticut	28.45
44	Delaware	13.60
25	Florida	20.66
14	Georgia	26.65
50	Hawaii	1.09
40	Idaho	15.53
8	Illinois	28.14
12	Indiana	26.85
20	Iowa	23.23
31	Kansas	18.55
38	Kentucky	15.89
19	Louisiana	24.06
9	Maine	27.96
17	Maryland	25.11
15	Massachusetts	25.37
29	Michigan	18.61
46	Minnesota	10.92
34	Mississippi	17.62
21	Missouri	23.13
27	Montana	20.07
2	Nebraska	30.61
42	Nevada	14.32
13	New Hampshire	26.69
1	New Jersey	33.38
48	New Mexico	8.15
5	New York	29.49
43	North Carolina	13.77
22	North Dakota	22.80
7	Ohio	28.36
32	Oklahoma	17.78
30	Oregon	18.56
3	Pennsylvania	30.11
11	Rhode Island	27.26
16	South Carolina	25.29
23	South Dakota	22.33
33	Tennessee	17.73
4	Texas	29.92
35	Utah	17.22
49	Vermont	3.31
18	Virginia	24.23
45	Washington	13.14
37	West Virginia	16.90
24	Wisconsin	22.29
10	Wyoming	27.78

RANK ORDER

RANK	STATE	RATIO
1	New Jersey	$33.38
2	Nebraska	30.61
3	Pennsylvania	30.11
4	Texas	29.92
5	New York	29.49
6	Connecticut	28.45
7	Ohio	28.36
8	Illinois	28.14
9	Maine	27.96
10	Wyoming	27.78
11	Rhode Island	27.26
12	Indiana	26.85
13	New Hampshire	26.69
14	Georgia	26.65
15	Massachusetts	25.37
16	South Carolina	25.29
17	Maryland	25.11
18	Virginia	24.23
19	Louisiana	24.06
20	Iowa	23.23
21	Missouri	23.13
22	North Dakota	22.80
23	South Dakota	22.33
24	Wisconsin	22.29
25	Florida	20.66
26	Colorado	20.64
27	Montana	20.07
28	Arizona	19.14
29	Michigan	18.61
30	Oregon	18.56
31	Kansas	18.55
32	Oklahoma	17.78
33	Tennessee	17.73
34	Mississippi	17.62
35	Utah	17.22
36	Alaska	17.13
37	West Virginia	16.90
38	Kentucky	15.89
39	Alabama	15.72
40	Idaho	15.53
41	California	14.35
42	Nevada	14.32
43	North Carolina	13.77
44	Delaware	13.60
45	Washington	13.14
46	Minnesota	10.92
47	Arkansas	8.60
48	New Mexico	8.15
49	Vermont	3.31
50	Hawaii	1.09

District of Columbia   30.95

Source: U.S. Bureau of the Census, Governments Division
   "Public Education Finances: 2006" (http://www.census.gov/govs/www/school06.html)
*Revenue raised locally including taxes and charges. Includes all such revenue received by a school system from local sources (net of refunds) other than from issuance of debt or liquidation of investments. Does not include noncash transactions such as receipt of services, commodities, or other "receipts in-kind."

Per Pupil Elementary and Secondary School Revenue from Local Sources in 2006
National Per Pupil = $4,779*

ALPHA ORDER

RANK	STATE	PER PUPIL
40	Alabama	$2,814
34	Alaska	3,133
32	Arizona	3,447
47	Arkansas	1,361
36	California	3,092
21	Colorado	4,655
2	Connecticut	8,537
29	Delaware	3,710
17	Florida	4,783
18	Georgia	4,736
50	Hawaii	265
46	Idaho	2,429
9	Illinois	6,211
16	Indiana	5,064
24	Iowa	4,485
30	Kansas	3,574
41	Kentucky	2,767
26	Louisiana	4,145
13	Maine	5,820
7	Maryland	6,787
4	Massachusetts	7,492
31	Michigan	3,556
44	Minnesota	2,542
43	Mississippi	2,640
22	Missouri	4,594
28	Montana	3,773
10	Nebraska	6,175
35	Nevada	3,132
8	New Hampshire	6,502
1	New Jersey	9,119
48	New Mexico	1,346
3	New York	8,360
42	North Carolina	2,649
19	North Dakota	4,725
12	Ohio	5,855
37	Oklahoma	2,984
27	Oregon	3,823
5	Pennsylvania	7,391
6	Rhode Island	6,972
25	South Carolina	4,369
23	South Dakota	4,523
33	Tennessee	3,432
15	Texas	5,112
45	Utah	2,434
49	Vermont	728
14	Virginia	5,734
39	Washington	2,864
38	West Virginia	2,897
20	Wisconsin	4,665
11	Wyoming	6,096

RANK ORDER

RANK	STATE	PER PUPIL
1	New Jersey	$9,119
2	Connecticut	8,537
3	New York	8,360
4	Massachusetts	7,492
5	Pennsylvania	7,391
6	Rhode Island	6,972
7	Maryland	6,787
8	New Hampshire	6,502
9	Illinois	6,211
10	Nebraska	6,175
11	Wyoming	6,096
12	Ohio	5,855
13	Maine	5,820
14	Virginia	5,734
15	Texas	5,112
16	Indiana	5,064
17	Florida	4,783
18	Georgia	4,736
19	North Dakota	4,725
20	Wisconsin	4,665
21	Colorado	4,655
22	Missouri	4,594
23	South Dakota	4,523
24	Iowa	4,485
25	South Carolina	4,369
26	Louisiana	4,145
27	Oregon	3,823
28	Montana	3,773
29	Delaware	3,710
30	Kansas	3,574
31	Michigan	3,556
32	Arizona	3,447
33	Tennessee	3,432
34	Alaska	3,133
35	Nevada	3,132
36	California	3,092
37	Oklahoma	2,984
38	West Virginia	2,897
39	Washington	2,864
40	Alabama	2,814
41	Kentucky	2,767
42	North Carolina	2,649
43	Mississippi	2,640
44	Minnesota	2,542
45	Utah	2,434
46	Idaho	2,429
47	Arkansas	1,361
48	New Mexico	1,346
49	Vermont	728
50	Hawaii	265

District of Columbia   16,195

Source: U.S. Bureau of the Census, Governments Division
   "Public Education Finances: 2006" (http://www.census.gov/govs/www/school06.html)
*Based on student membership. Revenue raised locally including taxes and charges. Includes all such revenue received by a school system from local sources (net of refunds) other than from issuance of debt or liquidation of investments. Does not include noncash transactions such as receipt of services, commodities, or other "receipts in-kind."

Percent of Public Elementary and Secondary School
Revenue from Local Sources in 2006
National Percent = 44.4%*

ALPHA ORDER

RANK	STATE	PERCENT
36	Alabama	32.9
45	Alaska	25.6
26	Arizona	42.9
47	Arkansas	15.2
42	California	30.1
14	Colorado	50.1
3	Connecticut	57.3
44	Delaware	28.2
14	Florida	50.1
20	Georgia	46.8
50	Hawaii	1.8
35	Idaho	33.5
1	Illinois	59.1
21	Indiana	45.9
21	Iowa	45.9
32	Kansas	35.8
39	Kentucky	31.3
29	Louisiana	39.6
17	Maine	49.7
7	Maryland	54.6
12	Massachusetts	50.7
37	Michigan	32.6
46	Minnesota	23.1
41	Mississippi	30.5
19	Missouri	47.9
28	Montana	40.1
2	Nebraska	58.6
34	Nevada	35.0
6	New Hampshire	55.3
8	New Jersey	54.5
48	New Mexico	14.3
16	New York	49.8
38	North Carolina	31.4
18	North Dakota	48.1
13	Ohio	50.4
31	Oklahoma	37.0
30	Oregon	39.5
4	Pennsylvania	57.1
10	Rhode Island	52.5
25	South Carolina	45.3
11	South Dakota	50.8
23	Tennessee	45.7
5	Texas	55.5
32	Utah	35.8
49	Vermont	5.1
9	Virginia	53.7
40	Washington	30.6
43	West Virginia	28.9
27	Wisconsin	41.8
23	Wyoming	45.7

RANK ORDER

RANK	STATE	PERCENT
1	Illinois	59.1
2	Nebraska	58.6
3	Connecticut	57.3
4	Pennsylvania	57.1
5	Texas	55.5
6	New Hampshire	55.3
7	Maryland	54.6
8	New Jersey	54.5
9	Virginia	53.7
10	Rhode Island	52.5
11	South Dakota	50.8
12	Massachusetts	50.7
13	Ohio	50.4
14	Colorado	50.1
14	Florida	50.1
16	New York	49.8
17	Maine	49.7
18	North Dakota	48.1
19	Missouri	47.9
20	Georgia	46.8
21	Indiana	45.9
21	Iowa	45.9
23	Tennessee	45.7
23	Wyoming	45.7
25	South Carolina	45.3
26	Arizona	42.9
27	Wisconsin	41.8
28	Montana	40.1
29	Louisiana	39.6
30	Oregon	39.5
31	Oklahoma	37.0
32	Kansas	35.8
32	Utah	35.8
34	Nevada	35.0
35	Idaho	33.5
36	Alabama	32.9
37	Michigan	32.6
38	North Carolina	31.4
39	Kentucky	31.3
40	Washington	30.6
41	Mississippi	30.5
42	California	30.1
43	West Virginia	28.9
44	Delaware	28.2
45	Alaska	25.6
46	Minnesota	23.1
47	Arkansas	15.2
48	New Mexico	14.3
49	Vermont	5.1
50	Hawaii	1.8
	District of Columbia	88.3

Source: U.S. Bureau of the Census, Governments Division
"Public Education Finances: 2006" (http://www.census.gov/govs/www/school06.html)
*Revenue raised locally including taxes and charges. Includes all such revenue received by a school system from local sources (net of refunds) other than from issuance of debt or liquidation of investments. Does not include noncash transactions such as receipt of services, commodities, or other "receipts in-kind."

Public Elementary and Secondary School Local Source Revenue
From Property Taxes in 2006
National Total = $147,249,385,000*

ALPHA ORDER

RANK	STATE	REVENUE	% of USA
30	Alabama	$837,724,000	0.6%
43	Alaska	0	0.0%
15	Arizona	2,609,602,000	1.8%
35	Arkansas	379,614,000	0.3%
3	California	13,116,202,000	8.9%
14	Colorado	2,884,385,000	2.0%
43	Connecticut	0	0.0%
37	Delaware	355,449,000	0.2%
7	Florida	9,983,242,000	6.8%
10	Georgia	4,904,129,000	3.3%
43	Hawaii	0	0.0%
32	Idaho	547,833,000	0.4%
4	Illinois	11,761,703,000	8.0%
11	Indiana	4,102,602,000	2.8%
19	Iowa	1,479,265,000	1.0%
22	Kansas	1,264,566,000	0.9%
23	Kentucky	1,227,599,000	0.8%
29	Louisiana	885,964,000	0.6%
33	Maine	461,554,000	0.3%
43	Maryland	0	0.0%
43	Massachusetts	0	0.0%
9	Michigan	5,108,114,000	3.5%
24	Minnesota	1,052,864,000	0.7%
28	Mississippi	911,013,000	0.6%
13	Missouri	3,193,470,000	2.2%
39	Montana	342,290,000	0.2%
20	Nebraska	1,355,753,000	0.9%
25	Nevada	1,047,562,000	0.7%
26	New Hampshire	1,020,850,000	0.7%
5	New Jersey	10,260,962,000	7.0%
40	New Mexico	324,429,000	0.2%
2	New York	13,338,139,000	9.1%
43	North Carolina	0	0.0%
36	North Dakota	368,693,000	0.3%
8	Ohio	8,359,083,000	5.7%
21	Oklahoma	1,334,587,000	0.9%
18	Oregon	1,542,337,000	1.0%
6	Pennsylvania	10,009,710,000	6.8%
41	Rhode Island	86,741,000	0.1%
16	South Carolina	2,325,040,000	1.6%
34	South Dakota	460,891,000	0.3%
43	Tennessee	0	0.0%
1	Texas	20,089,419,000	13.6%
27	Utah	1,003,844,000	0.7%
42	Vermont	1,410,000	0.0%
43	Virginia	0	0.0%
17	Washington	2,263,611,000	1.5%
31	West Virginia	708,741,000	0.5%
12	Wisconsin	3,588,734,000	2.4%
38	Wyoming	349,665,000	0.2%

RANK ORDER

RANK	STATE	REVENUE	% of USA
1	Texas	$20,089,419,000	13.6%
2	New York	13,338,139,000	9.1%
3	California	13,116,202,000	8.9%
4	Illinois	11,761,703,000	8.0%
5	New Jersey	10,260,962,000	7.0%
6	Pennsylvania	10,009,710,000	6.8%
7	Florida	9,983,242,000	6.8%
8	Ohio	8,359,083,000	5.7%
9	Michigan	5,108,114,000	3.5%
10	Georgia	4,904,129,000	3.3%
11	Indiana	4,102,602,000	2.8%
12	Wisconsin	3,588,734,000	2.4%
13	Missouri	3,193,470,000	2.2%
14	Colorado	2,884,385,000	2.0%
15	Arizona	2,609,602,000	1.8%
16	South Carolina	2,325,040,000	1.6%
17	Washington	2,263,611,000	1.5%
18	Oregon	1,542,337,000	1.0%
19	Iowa	1,479,265,000	1.0%
20	Nebraska	1,355,753,000	0.9%
21	Oklahoma	1,334,587,000	0.9%
22	Kansas	1,264,566,000	0.9%
23	Kentucky	1,227,599,000	0.8%
24	Minnesota	1,052,864,000	0.7%
25	Nevada	1,047,562,000	0.7%
26	New Hampshire	1,020,850,000	0.7%
27	Utah	1,003,844,000	0.7%
28	Mississippi	911,013,000	0.6%
29	Louisiana	885,964,000	0.6%
30	Alabama	837,724,000	0.6%
31	West Virginia	708,741,000	0.5%
32	Idaho	547,833,000	0.4%
33	Maine	461,554,000	0.3%
34	South Dakota	460,891,000	0.3%
35	Arkansas	379,614,000	0.3%
36	North Dakota	368,693,000	0.3%
37	Delaware	355,449,000	0.2%
38	Wyoming	349,665,000	0.2%
39	Montana	342,290,000	0.2%
40	New Mexico	324,429,000	0.2%
41	Rhode Island	86,741,000	0.1%
42	Vermont	1,410,000	0.0%
43	Alaska	0	0.0%
43	Connecticut	0	0.0%
43	Hawaii	0	0.0%
43	Maryland	0	0.0%
43	Massachusetts	0	0.0%
43	North Carolina	0	0.0%
43	Tennessee	0	0.0%
43	Virginia	0	0.0%
	District of Columbia	0	0.0%

Source: U.S. Bureau of the Census, Governments Division
   "Public Education Finances: 2006" (http://www.census.gov/govs/www/school06.html)
*Revenue from taxes based on ownership of property and measured by its value. Includes general property taxes relating to property as a whole, real and personal, tangible or intangible, whether taxed at a single rate or at classified rates, and taxes on selected types of property, such as motor vehicles or certain or all intangibles.

Percent of Public Elementary and Secondary School Local Source Revenue From Property Taxes in 2006
National Percent = 63.7%*

ALPHA ORDER

ALPHA ORDER

RANK	STATE	PERCENT
39	Alabama	40.1
43	Alaska	0.0
24	Arizona	75.4
35	Arkansas	59.0
30	California	67.8
13	Colorado	79.5
43	Connecticut	0.0
6	Delaware	83.8
16	Florida	78.3
33	Georgia	64.8
43	Hawaii	0.0
5	Idaho	87.3
1	Illinois	90.0
15	Indiana	78.9
29	Iowa	68.2
22	Kansas	75.9
32	Kentucky	65.3
40	Louisiana	33.0
38	Maine	40.6
43	Maryland	0.0
43	Massachusetts	0.0
8	Michigan	83.1
37	Minnesota	50.6
28	Mississippi	69.9
22	Missouri	75.9
34	Montana	62.5
19	Nebraska	76.7
11	Nevada	81.0
17	New Hampshire	78.1
10	New Jersey	81.5
25	New Mexico	73.7
36	New York	57.2
43	North Carolina	0.0
13	North Dakota	79.5
12	Ohio	80.7
27	Oklahoma	70.5
26	Oregon	72.5
18	Pennsylvania	77.0
41	Rhode Island	8.3
21	South Carolina	76.1
7	South Dakota	83.7
43	Tennessee	0.0
3	Texas	88.3
8	Utah	83.1
42	Vermont	2.1
43	Virginia	0.0
20	Washington	76.6
4	West Virginia	87.4
2	Wisconsin	88.5
31	Wyoming	66.6

RANK ORDER

RANK	STATE	PERCENT
1	Illinois	90.0
2	Wisconsin	88.5
3	Texas	88.3
4	West Virginia	87.4
5	Idaho	87.3
6	Delaware	83.8
7	South Dakota	83.7
8	Michigan	83.1
8	Utah	83.1
10	New Jersey	81.5
11	Nevada	81.0
12	Ohio	80.7
13	Colorado	79.5
13	North Dakota	79.5
15	Indiana	78.9
16	Florida	78.3
17	New Hampshire	78.1
18	Pennsylvania	77.0
19	Nebraska	76.7
20	Washington	76.6
21	South Carolina	76.1
22	Kansas	75.9
22	Missouri	75.9
24	Arizona	75.4
25	New Mexico	73.7
26	Oregon	72.5
27	Oklahoma	70.5
28	Mississippi	69.9
29	Iowa	68.2
30	California	67.8
31	Wyoming	66.6
32	Kentucky	65.3
33	Georgia	64.8
34	Montana	62.5
35	Arkansas	59.0
36	New York	57.2
37	Minnesota	50.6
38	Maine	40.6
39	Alabama	40.1
40	Louisiana	33.0
41	Rhode Island	8.3
42	Vermont	2.1
43	Alaska	0.0
43	Connecticut	0.0
43	Hawaii	0.0
43	Maryland	0.0
43	Massachusetts	0.0
43	North Carolina	0.0
43	Tennessee	0.0
43	Virginia	0.0
	District of Columbia	0.0

Source: CQ Press using data from U.S. Bureau of the Census, Governments Division
  "Public Education Finances: 2006" (http://www.census.gov/govs/www/school06.html)
*Revenue from taxes based on ownership of property and measured by its value. Includes general property taxes relating to property as a whole, real and personal, tangible or intangible, whether taxed at a single rate or at classified rates, and taxes on selected types of property, such as motor vehicles or certain or all intangibles.

Public Elementary and Secondary School Local Source Revenue From Other Local Taxes in 2006
National Total = $6,421,947,000*

ALPHA ORDER

RANK	STATE	REVENUE	% of USA
12	Alabama	$33,853,000	0.5%
23	Alaska	0	0.0%
23	Arizona	0	0.0%
21	Arkansas	744,000	0.0%
6	California	305,493,000	4.8%
10	Colorado	46,009,000	0.7%
23	Connecticut	0	0.0%
23	Delaware	0	0.0%
23	Florida	0	0.0%
2	Georgia	1,520,282,000	23.7%
23	Hawaii	0	0.0%
23	Idaho	0	0.0%
23	Illinois	0	0.0%
16	Indiana	8,217,000	0.1%
4	Iowa	404,159,000	6.3%
23	Kansas	0	0.0%
5	Kentucky	343,635,000	5.4%
3	Louisiana	1,442,906,000	22.5%
23	Maine	0	0.0%
23	Maryland	0	0.0%
23	Massachusetts	0	0.0%
23	Michigan	0	0.0%
23	Minnesota	0	0.0%
15	Mississippi	14,880,000	0.2%
8	Missouri	155,082,000	2.4%
23	Montana	0	0.0%
9	Nebraska	139,988,000	2.2%
19	Nevada	4,020,000	0.1%
23	New Hampshire	0	0.0%
23	New Jersey	0	0.0%
23	New Mexico	0	0.0%
11	New York	39,442,000	0.6%
23	North Carolina	0	0.0%
23	North Dakota	0	0.0%
7	Ohio	238,842,000	3.7%
23	Oklahoma	0	0.0%
23	Oregon	0	0.0%
1	Pennsylvania	1,666,180,000	25.9%
23	Rhode Island	0	0.0%
13	South Carolina	28,894,000	0.4%
14	South Dakota	15,939,000	0.2%
23	Tennessee	0	0.0%
23	Texas	0	0.0%
23	Utah	0	0.0%
18	Vermont	4,554,000	0.1%
23	Virginia	0	0.0%
20	Washington	1,848,000	0.0%
22	West Virginia	60,000	0.0%
23	Wisconsin	0	0.0%
17	Wyoming	6,920,000	0.1%

RANK ORDER

RANK	STATE	REVENUE	% of USA
1	Pennsylvania	$1,666,180,000	25.9%
2	Georgia	1,520,282,000	23.7%
3	Louisiana	1,442,906,000	22.5%
4	Iowa	404,159,000	6.3%
5	Kentucky	343,635,000	5.4%
6	California	305,493,000	4.8%
7	Ohio	238,842,000	3.7%
8	Missouri	155,082,000	2.4%
9	Nebraska	139,988,000	2.2%
10	Colorado	46,009,000	0.7%
11	New York	39,442,000	0.6%
12	Alabama	33,853,000	0.5%
13	South Carolina	28,894,000	0.4%
14	South Dakota	15,939,000	0.2%
15	Mississippi	14,880,000	0.2%
16	Indiana	8,217,000	0.1%
17	Wyoming	6,920,000	0.1%
18	Vermont	4,554,000	0.1%
19	Nevada	4,020,000	0.1%
20	Washington	1,848,000	0.0%
21	Arkansas	744,000	0.0%
22	West Virginia	60,000	0.0%
23	Alaska	0	0.0%
23	Arizona	0	0.0%
23	Connecticut	0	0.0%
23	Delaware	0	0.0%
23	Florida	0	0.0%
23	Hawaii	0	0.0%
23	Idaho	0	0.0%
23	Illinois	0	0.0%
23	Kansas	0	0.0%
23	Maine	0	0.0%
23	Maryland	0	0.0%
23	Massachusetts	0	0.0%
23	Michigan	0	0.0%
23	Minnesota	0	0.0%
23	Montana	0	0.0%
23	New Hampshire	0	0.0%
23	New Jersey	0	0.0%
23	New Mexico	0	0.0%
23	North Carolina	0	0.0%
23	North Dakota	0	0.0%
23	Oklahoma	0	0.0%
23	Oregon	0	0.0%
23	Rhode Island	0	0.0%
23	Tennessee	0	0.0%
23	Texas	0	0.0%
23	Utah	0	0.0%
23	Virginia	0	0.0%
23	Wisconsin	0	0.0%
	District of Columbia	0	0.0%

Source: U.S. Bureau of the Census, Governments Division
"Public Education Finances: 2006" (http://www.census.gov/govs/www/school06.html)
*Revenue from taxes other than property taxes.

Percent of Public Elementary and Secondary School Local Source Revenue From Other Local Taxes in 2006
National Percent = 2.8%*

ALPHA ORDER

RANK	STATE	PERCENT
11	Alabama	1.6
22	Alaska	0.0
22	Arizona	0.0
20	Arkansas	0.1
11	California	1.6
13	Colorado	1.3
22	Connecticut	0.0
22	Delaware	0.0
22	Florida	0.0
2	Georgia	20.1
22	Hawaii	0.0
22	Idaho	0.0
22	Illinois	0.0
18	Indiana	0.2
3	Iowa	18.6
22	Kansas	0.0
4	Kentucky	18.3
1	Louisiana	53.7
22	Maine	0.0
22	Maryland	0.0
22	Massachusetts	0.0
22	Michigan	0.0
22	Minnesota	0.0
15	Mississippi	1.1
8	Missouri	3.7
22	Montana	0.0
6	Nebraska	7.9
17	Nevada	0.3
22	New Hampshire	0.0
22	New Jersey	0.0
22	New Mexico	0.0
18	New York	0.2
22	North Carolina	0.0
22	North Dakota	0.0
10	Ohio	2.3
22	Oklahoma	0.0
22	Oregon	0.0
5	Pennsylvania	12.8
22	Rhode Island	0.0
16	South Carolina	0.9
9	South Dakota	2.9
22	Tennessee	0.0
22	Texas	0.0
22	Utah	0.0
7	Vermont	6.8
22	Virginia	0.0
20	Washington	0.1
22	West Virginia	0.0
22	Wisconsin	0.0
13	Wyoming	1.3

RANK ORDER

RANK	STATE	PERCENT
1	Louisiana	53.7
2	Georgia	20.1
3	Iowa	18.6
4	Kentucky	18.3
5	Pennsylvania	12.8
6	Nebraska	7.9
7	Vermont	6.8
8	Missouri	3.7
9	South Dakota	2.9
10	Ohio	2.3
11	Alabama	1.6
11	California	1.6
13	Colorado	1.3
13	Wyoming	1.3
15	Mississippi	1.1
16	South Carolina	0.9
17	Nevada	0.3
18	Indiana	0.2
18	New York	0.2
20	Arkansas	0.1
20	Washington	0.1
22	Alaska	0.0
22	Arizona	0.0
22	Connecticut	0.0
22	Delaware	0.0
22	Florida	0.0
22	Hawaii	0.0
22	Idaho	0.0
22	Illinois	0.0
22	Kansas	0.0
22	Maine	0.0
22	Maryland	0.0
22	Massachusetts	0.0
22	Michigan	0.0
22	Minnesota	0.0
22	Montana	0.0
22	New Hampshire	0.0
22	New Jersey	0.0
22	New Mexico	0.0
22	North Carolina	0.0
22	North Dakota	0.0
22	Oklahoma	0.0
22	Oregon	0.0
22	Rhode Island	0.0
22	Tennessee	0.0
22	Texas	0.0
22	Utah	0.0
22	Virginia	0.0
22	West Virginia	0.0
22	Wisconsin	0.0
	District of Columbia	0.0

Source: CQ Press using data from U.S. Bureau of the Census, Governments Division
    "Public Education Finances: 2006" (http://www.census.gov/govs/www/school06.html)
*Revenue from taxes other than property taxes.

Public Elementary and Secondary School Local Source Revenue From Parent Government Contributions in 2006
National Total = $39,188,880,000*

ALPHA ORDER

RANK	STATE	REVENUE	% of USA
17	Alabama	$0	0.0%
12	Alaska	350,142,000	0.9%
16	Arizona	2,587,000	0.0%
17	Arkansas	0	0.0%
10	California	706,002,000	1.8%
17	Colorado	0	0.0%
5	Connecticut	4,280,037,000	10.9%
17	Delaware	0	0.0%
17	Florida	0	0.0%
17	Georgia	0	0.0%
17	Hawaii	0	0.0%
17	Idaho	0	0.0%
17	Illinois	0	0.0%
17	Indiana	0	0.0%
17	Iowa	0	0.0%
17	Kansas	0	0.0%
17	Kentucky	0	0.0%
17	Louisiana	0	0.0%
11	Maine	604,483,000	1.5%
4	Maryland	5,279,999,000	13.5%
3	Massachusetts	5,652,164,000	14.4%
17	Michigan	0	0.0%
17	Minnesota	0	0.0%
15	Mississippi	2,915,000	0.0%
17	Missouri	0	0.0%
17	Montana	0	0.0%
17	Nebraska	0	0.0%
17	Nevada	0	0.0%
13	New Hampshire	194,783,000	0.5%
9	New Jersey	783,373,000	2.0%
17	New Mexico	0	0.0%
1	New York	7,892,380,000	20.1%
6	North Carolina	3,100,342,000	7.9%
17	North Dakota	0	0.0%
17	Ohio	0	0.0%
17	Oklahoma	0	0.0%
17	Oregon	0	0.0%
17	Pennsylvania	0	0.0%
8	Rhode Island	925,251,000	2.4%
17	South Carolina	0	0.0%
17	South Dakota	0	0.0%
7	Tennessee	2,160,619,000	5.5%
17	Texas	0	0.0%
17	Utah	0	0.0%
17	Vermont	0	0.0%
2	Virginia	6,300,366,000	16.1%
17	Washington	0	0.0%
17	West Virginia	0	0.0%
14	Wisconsin	15,144,000	0.0%
17	Wyoming	0	0.0%

RANK ORDER

RANK	STATE	REVENUE	% of USA
1	New York	$7,892,380,000	20.1%
2	Virginia	6,300,366,000	16.1%
3	Massachusetts	5,652,164,000	14.4%
4	Maryland	5,279,999,000	13.5%
5	Connecticut	4,280,037,000	10.9%
6	North Carolina	3,100,342,000	7.9%
7	Tennessee	2,160,619,000	5.5%
8	Rhode Island	925,251,000	2.4%
9	New Jersey	783,373,000	2.0%
10	California	706,002,000	1.8%
11	Maine	604,483,000	1.5%
12	Alaska	350,142,000	0.9%
13	New Hampshire	194,783,000	0.5%
14	Wisconsin	15,144,000	0.0%
15	Mississippi	2,915,000	0.0%
16	Arizona	2,587,000	0.0%
17	Alabama	0	0.0%
17	Arkansas	0	0.0%
17	Colorado	0	0.0%
17	Delaware	0	0.0%
17	Florida	0	0.0%
17	Georgia	0	0.0%
17	Hawaii	0	0.0%
17	Idaho	0	0.0%
17	Illinois	0	0.0%
17	Indiana	0	0.0%
17	Iowa	0	0.0%
17	Kansas	0	0.0%
17	Kentucky	0	0.0%
17	Louisiana	0	0.0%
17	Michigan	0	0.0%
17	Minnesota	0	0.0%
17	Missouri	0	0.0%
17	Montana	0	0.0%
17	Nebraska	0	0.0%
17	Nevada	0	0.0%
17	New Mexico	0	0.0%
17	North Dakota	0	0.0%
17	Ohio	0	0.0%
17	Oklahoma	0	0.0%
17	Oregon	0	0.0%
17	Pennsylvania	0	0.0%
17	South Carolina	0	0.0%
17	South Dakota	0	0.0%
17	Texas	0	0.0%
17	Utah	0	0.0%
17	Vermont	0	0.0%
17	Washington	0	0.0%
17	West Virginia	0	0.0%
17	Wyoming	0	0.0%
	District of Columbia	938,293,000	2.4%

Source: U.S. Bureau of the Census, Governments Division
"Public Education Finances: 2006" (http://www.census.gov/govs/www/school06.html)
*Tax receipts and other amounts appropriated by a parent government and transferred to its dependent school system. Although most of this revenue comes from property tax collections, the exact amounts derived from taxes or other revenue sources available to parent governments for their school systems frequently cannot be determined from state education agency accounting records and are therefore shown as parent government contributions.

Percent of Public Elementary and Secondary School Local Source Revenue From Parent Government Contributions in 2006
National Percent = 16.9%*

ALPHA ORDER

RANK ORDER

RANK	STATE	PERCENT		RANK	STATE	PERCENT
17	Alabama	0.0		1	Maryland	90.5
6	Alaska	84.1		1	Virginia	90.5
16	Arizona	0.1		3	Connecticut	90.1
17	Arkansas	0.0		4	Rhode Island	88.4
13	California	3.6		5	North Carolina	84.3
17	Colorado	0.0		6	Alaska	84.1
3	Connecticut	90.1		7	Massachusetts	79.4
17	Delaware	0.0		8	Tennessee	66.0
17	Florida	0.0		9	Maine	53.2
17	Georgia	0.0		10	New York	33.9
17	Hawaii	0.0		11	New Hampshire	14.9
17	Idaho	0.0		12	New Jersey	6.2
17	Illinois	0.0		13	California	3.6
17	Indiana	0.0		14	Wisconsin	0.4
17	Iowa	0.0		15	Mississippi	0.2
17	Kansas	0.0		16	Arizona	0.1
17	Kentucky	0.0		17	Alabama	0.0
17	Louisiana	0.0		17	Arkansas	0.0
9	Maine	53.2		17	Colorado	0.0
1	Maryland	90.5		17	Delaware	0.0
7	Massachusetts	79.4		17	Florida	0.0
17	Michigan	0.0		17	Georgia	0.0
17	Minnesota	0.0		17	Hawaii	0.0
15	Mississippi	0.2		17	Idaho	0.0
17	Missouri	0.0		17	Illinois	0.0
17	Montana	0.0		17	Indiana	0.0
17	Nebraska	0.0		17	Iowa	0.0
17	Nevada	0.0		17	Kansas	0.0
11	New Hampshire	14.9		17	Kentucky	0.0
12	New Jersey	6.2		17	Louisiana	0.0
17	New Mexico	0.0		17	Michigan	0.0
10	New York	33.9		17	Minnesota	0.0
5	North Carolina	84.3		17	Missouri	0.0
17	North Dakota	0.0		17	Montana	0.0
17	Ohio	0.0		17	Nebraska	0.0
17	Oklahoma	0.0		17	Nevada	0.0
17	Oregon	0.0		17	New Mexico	0.0
17	Pennsylvania	0.0		17	North Dakota	0.0
4	Rhode Island	88.4		17	Ohio	0.0
17	South Carolina	0.0		17	Oklahoma	0.0
17	South Dakota	0.0		17	Oregon	0.0
8	Tennessee	66.0		17	Pennsylvania	0.0
17	Texas	0.0		17	South Carolina	0.0
17	Utah	0.0		17	South Dakota	0.0
17	Vermont	0.0		17	Texas	0.0
1	Virginia	90.5		17	Utah	0.0
17	Washington	0.0		17	Vermont	0.0
17	West Virginia	0.0		17	Washington	0.0
14	Wisconsin	0.4		17	West Virginia	0.0
17	Wyoming	0.0		17	Wyoming	0.0

District of Columbia   97.2

Source: CQ Press using data from U.S. Bureau of the Census, Governments Division
"Public Education Finances: 2006" (http://www.census.gov/govs/www/school06.html)

*Tax receipts and other amounts appropriated by a parent government and transferred to its dependent school system. Although most of this revenue comes from property tax collections, the exact amounts derived from taxes or other revenue sources available to parent governments for their school systems frequently cannot be determined from state education agency accounting records and are therefore shown as parent government contributions.

Public Elementary and Secondary School Local Source Revenue
From Nonschool Local Government in 2006
National Total = $5,296,542,000*

ALPHA ORDER

RANK	STATE	REVENUE	% of USA
2	Alabama	$653,140,000	12.3%
43	Alaska	0	0.0%
5	Arizona	255,390,000	4.8%
35	Arkansas	4,611,000	0.1%
7	California	241,003,000	4.6%
28	Colorado	19,392,000	0.4%
4	Connecticut	339,818,000	6.4%
43	Delaware	0	0.0%
43	Florida	0	0.0%
8	Georgia	206,927,000	3.9%
37	Hawaii	1,818,000	0.0%
42	Idaho	79,000	0.0%
22	Illinois	64,188,000	1.2%
20	Indiana	69,678,000	1.3%
33	Iowa	5,168,000	0.1%
17	Kansas	111,495,000	2.1%
25	Kentucky	22,614,000	0.4%
24	Louisiana	26,488,000	0.5%
34	Maine	5,048,000	0.1%
43	Maryland	0	0.0%
1	Massachusetts	868,035,000	16.4%
26	Michigan	20,801,000	0.4%
16	Minnesota	118,979,000	2.2%
30	Mississippi	14,442,000	0.3%
12	Missouri	140,081,000	2.6%
18	Montana	111,246,000	2.1%
27	Nebraska	19,472,000	0.4%
40	Nevada	251,000	0.0%
41	New Hampshire	186,000	0.0%
9	New Jersey	198,724,000	3.8%
43	New Mexico	0	0.0%
6	New York	241,854,000	4.6%
43	North Carolina	0	0.0%
29	North Dakota	14,581,000	0.3%
19	Ohio	95,721,000	1.8%
13	Oklahoma	136,496,000	2.6%
10	Oregon	173,124,000	3.3%
11	Pennsylvania	152,957,000	2.9%
43	Rhode Island	0	0.0%
14	South Carolina	128,421,000	2.4%
36	South Dakota	2,894,000	0.1%
3	Tennessee	564,165,000	10.7%
23	Texas	55,308,000	1.0%
39	Utah	531,000	0.0%
38	Vermont	712,000	0.0%
43	Virginia	0	0.0%
31	Washington	10,710,000	0.2%
32	West Virginia	9,805,000	0.2%
21	Wisconsin	67,497,000	1.3%
15	Wyoming	122,692,000	2.3%

RANK ORDER

RANK	STATE	REVENUE	% of USA
1	Massachusetts	$868,035,000	16.4%
2	Alabama	653,140,000	12.3%
3	Tennessee	564,165,000	10.7%
4	Connecticut	339,818,000	6.4%
5	Arizona	255,390,000	4.8%
6	New York	241,854,000	4.6%
7	California	241,003,000	4.6%
8	Georgia	206,927,000	3.9%
9	New Jersey	198,724,000	3.8%
10	Oregon	173,124,000	3.3%
11	Pennsylvania	152,957,000	2.9%
12	Missouri	140,081,000	2.6%
13	Oklahoma	136,496,000	2.6%
14	South Carolina	128,421,000	2.4%
15	Wyoming	122,692,000	2.3%
16	Minnesota	118,979,000	2.2%
17	Kansas	111,495,000	2.1%
18	Montana	111,246,000	2.1%
19	Ohio	95,721,000	1.8%
20	Indiana	69,678,000	1.3%
21	Wisconsin	67,497,000	1.3%
22	Illinois	64,188,000	1.2%
23	Texas	55,308,000	1.0%
24	Louisiana	26,488,000	0.5%
25	Kentucky	22,614,000	0.4%
26	Michigan	20,801,000	0.4%
27	Nebraska	19,472,000	0.4%
28	Colorado	19,392,000	0.4%
29	North Dakota	14,581,000	0.3%
30	Mississippi	14,442,000	0.3%
31	Washington	10,710,000	0.2%
32	West Virginia	9,805,000	0.2%
33	Iowa	5,168,000	0.1%
34	Maine	5,048,000	0.1%
35	Arkansas	4,611,000	0.1%
36	South Dakota	2,894,000	0.1%
37	Hawaii	1,818,000	0.0%
38	Vermont	712,000	0.0%
39	Utah	531,000	0.0%
40	Nevada	251,000	0.0%
41	New Hampshire	186,000	0.0%
42	Idaho	79,000	0.0%
43	Alaska	0	0.0%
43	Delaware	0	0.0%
43	Florida	0	0.0%
43	Maryland	0	0.0%
43	New Mexico	0	0.0%
43	North Carolina	0	0.0%
43	Rhode Island	0	0.0%
43	Virginia	0	0.0%
	District of Columbia	0	0.0%

Source: U.S. Bureau of the Census, Governments Division
   "Public Education Finances: 2006" (http://www.census.gov/govs/www/school06.html)
*Revenue from local governments other than a parent government.

Percent of Public Elementary and Secondary School Local Source Revenue From Nonschool Local Government in 2006
National Percent = 2.3%*

ALPHA ORDER

RANK	STATE	PERCENT
1	Alabama	31.2
39	Alaska	0.0
7	Arizona	7.4
30	Arkansas	0.7
20	California	1.2
31	Colorado	0.5
8	Connecticut	7.2
39	Delaware	0.0
39	Florida	0.0
16	Georgia	2.7
13	Hawaii	3.8
39	Idaho	0.0
31	Illinois	0.5
19	Indiana	1.3
37	Iowa	0.2
10	Kansas	6.7
20	Kentucky	1.2
27	Louisiana	1.0
34	Maine	0.4
39	Maryland	0.0
5	Massachusetts	12.2
36	Michigan	0.3
11	Minnesota	5.7
24	Mississippi	1.1
14	Missouri	3.3
3	Montana	20.3
24	Nebraska	1.1
39	Nevada	0.0
39	New Hampshire	0.0
18	New Jersey	1.6
39	New Mexico	0.0
27	New York	1.0
39	North Carolina	0.0
15	North Dakota	3.1
29	Ohio	0.9
8	Oklahoma	7.2
6	Oregon	8.1
20	Pennsylvania	1.2
39	Rhode Island	0.0
12	South Carolina	4.2
31	South Dakota	0.5
4	Tennessee	17.2
37	Texas	0.2
39	Utah	0.0
24	Vermont	1.1
39	Virginia	0.0
34	Washington	0.4
20	West Virginia	1.2
17	Wisconsin	1.7
2	Wyoming	23.4

RANK ORDER

RANK	STATE	PERCENT
1	Alabama	31.2
2	Wyoming	23.4
3	Montana	20.3
4	Tennessee	17.2
5	Massachusetts	12.2
6	Oregon	8.1
7	Arizona	7.4
8	Connecticut	7.2
8	Oklahoma	7.2
10	Kansas	6.7
11	Minnesota	5.7
12	South Carolina	4.2
13	Hawaii	3.8
14	Missouri	3.3
15	North Dakota	3.1
16	Georgia	2.7
17	Wisconsin	1.7
18	New Jersey	1.6
19	Indiana	1.3
20	California	1.2
20	Kentucky	1.2
20	Pennsylvania	1.2
20	West Virginia	1.2
24	Mississippi	1.1
24	Nebraska	1.1
24	Vermont	1.1
27	Louisiana	1.0
27	New York	1.0
29	Ohio	0.9
30	Arkansas	0.7
31	Colorado	0.5
31	Illinois	0.5
31	South Dakota	0.5
34	Maine	0.4
34	Washington	0.4
36	Michigan	0.3
37	Iowa	0.2
37	Texas	0.2
39	Alaska	0.0
39	Delaware	0.0
39	Florida	0.0
39	Idaho	0.0
39	Maryland	0.0
39	Nevada	0.0
39	New Hampshire	0.0
39	New Mexico	0.0
39	North Carolina	0.0
39	Rhode Island	0.0
39	Utah	0.0
39	Virginia	0.0
	District of Columbia	0.0

Source: CQ Press using data from U.S. Bureau of the Census, Governments Division
"Public Education Finances: 2006" (http://www.census.gov/govs/www/school06.html)
*Revenue from local governments other than a parent government.

Public Elementary and Secondary School Local Source Revenue
From School Lunch Charges in 2006
National Total = $6,769,271,000*

ALPHA ORDER

RANK	STATE	REVENUE	% of USA
18	Alabama	$129,463,000	1.9%
50	Alaska	12,185,000	0.2%
23	Arizona	111,501,000	1.6%
33	Arkansas	54,366,000	0.8%
2	California	573,622,000	8.5%
26	Colorado	94,636,000	1.4%
22	Connecticut	116,503,000	1.7%
48	Delaware	16,242,000	0.2%
3	Florida	360,922,000	5.3%
12	Georgia	214,256,000	3.2%
45	Hawaii	20,564,000	0.3%
39	Idaho	28,781,000	0.4%
8	Illinois	259,561,000	3.8%
13	Indiana	198,660,000	2.9%
25	Iowa	102,540,000	1.5%
28	Kansas	85,280,000	1.3%
24	Kentucky	104,756,000	1.5%
36	Louisiana	40,866,000	0.6%
38	Maine	36,965,000	0.5%
20	Maryland	124,089,000	1.8%
15	Massachusetts	169,259,000	2.5%
10	Michigan	233,420,000	3.4%
14	Minnesota	187,857,000	2.8%
34	Mississippi	46,456,000	0.7%
17	Missouri	147,368,000	2.2%
47	Montana	17,131,000	0.3%
30	Nebraska	57,316,000	0.8%
37	Nevada	37,996,000	0.6%
35	New Hampshire	42,215,000	0.6%
7	New Jersey	293,539,000	4.3%
42	New Mexico	22,678,000	0.3%
6	New York	300,069,000	4.4%
9	North Carolina	252,644,000	3.7%
44	North Dakota	20,571,000	0.3%
5	Ohio	305,589,000	4.5%
29	Oklahoma	73,694,000	1.1%
31	Oregon	56,470,000	0.8%
4	Pennsylvania	327,045,000	4.8%
43	Rhode Island	21,116,000	0.3%
27	South Carolina	89,615,000	1.3%
41	South Dakota	24,065,000	0.4%
19	Tennessee	125,417,000	1.9%
1	Texas	600,312,000	8.9%
32	Utah	56,218,000	0.8%
46	Vermont	18,132,000	0.3%
11	Virginia	229,940,000	3.4%
21	Washington	119,315,000	1.8%
40	West Virginia	24,421,000	0.4%
16	Wisconsin	168,368,000	2.5%
49	Wyoming	14,288,000	0.2%

RANK ORDER

RANK	STATE	REVENUE	% of USA
1	Texas	$600,312,000	8.9%
2	California	573,622,000	8.5%
3	Florida	360,922,000	5.3%
4	Pennsylvania	327,045,000	4.8%
5	Ohio	305,589,000	4.5%
6	New York	300,069,000	4.4%
7	New Jersey	293,539,000	4.3%
8	Illinois	259,561,000	3.8%
9	North Carolina	252,644,000	3.7%
10	Michigan	233,420,000	3.4%
11	Virginia	229,940,000	3.4%
12	Georgia	214,256,000	3.2%
13	Indiana	198,660,000	2.9%
14	Minnesota	187,857,000	2.8%
15	Massachusetts	169,259,000	2.5%
16	Wisconsin	168,368,000	2.5%
17	Missouri	147,368,000	2.2%
18	Alabama	129,463,000	1.9%
19	Tennessee	125,417,000	1.9%
20	Maryland	124,089,000	1.8%
21	Washington	119,315,000	1.8%
22	Connecticut	116,503,000	1.7%
23	Arizona	111,501,000	1.6%
24	Kentucky	104,756,000	1.5%
25	Iowa	102,540,000	1.5%
26	Colorado	94,636,000	1.4%
27	South Carolina	89,615,000	1.3%
28	Kansas	85,280,000	1.3%
29	Oklahoma	73,694,000	1.1%
30	Nebraska	57,316,000	0.8%
31	Oregon	56,470,000	0.8%
32	Utah	56,218,000	0.8%
33	Arkansas	54,366,000	0.8%
34	Mississippi	46,456,000	0.7%
35	New Hampshire	42,215,000	0.6%
36	Louisiana	40,866,000	0.6%
37	Nevada	37,996,000	0.6%
38	Maine	36,965,000	0.5%
39	Idaho	28,781,000	0.4%
40	West Virginia	24,421,000	0.4%
41	South Dakota	24,065,000	0.4%
42	New Mexico	22,678,000	0.3%
43	Rhode Island	21,116,000	0.3%
44	North Dakota	20,571,000	0.3%
45	Hawaii	20,564,000	0.3%
46	Vermont	18,132,000	0.3%
47	Montana	17,131,000	0.3%
48	Delaware	16,242,000	0.2%
49	Wyoming	14,288,000	0.2%
50	Alaska	12,185,000	0.2%
	District of Columbia	989,000	0.0%

Source: U.S. Bureau of the Census, Governments Division
   "Public Education Finances: 2006" (http://www.census.gov/govs/www/school06.html)
*Gross collections from cafeteria sales to children and adults.

Percent of Public Elementary and Secondary School Local Source Revenue From School Lunch Charges in 2006
National Percent = 2.9%*

ALPHA ORDER

ALPHA ORDER

RANK	STATE	PERCENT
6	Alabama	6.2
32	Alaska	2.9
26	Arizona	3.2
4	Arkansas	8.4
30	California	3.0
40	Colorado	2.6
42	Connecticut	2.5
18	Delaware	3.8
36	Florida	2.8
36	Georgia	2.8
1	Hawaii	42.5
12	Idaho	4.6
47	Illinois	2.0
18	Indiana	3.8
10	Iowa	4.7
9	Kansas	5.1
7	Kentucky	5.6
49	Louisiana	1.5
24	Maine	3.3
46	Maryland	2.1
44	Massachusetts	2.4
18	Michigan	3.8
3	Minnesota	9.0
22	Mississippi	3.6
23	Missouri	3.5
29	Montana	3.1
26	Nebraska	3.2
32	Nevada	2.9
26	New Hampshire	3.2
45	New Jersey	2.3
8	New Mexico	5.2
50	New York	1.3
5	North Carolina	6.9
13	North Dakota	4.4
32	Ohio	2.9
17	Oklahoma	3.9
38	Oregon	2.7
42	Pennsylvania	2.5
47	Rhode Island	2.0
32	South Carolina	2.9
13	South Dakota	4.4
18	Tennessee	3.8
40	Texas	2.6
10	Utah	4.7
2	Vermont	27.0
24	Virginia	3.3
16	Washington	4.0
30	West Virginia	3.0
15	Wisconsin	4.2
38	Wyoming	2.7

RANK ORDER

RANK	STATE	PERCENT
1	Hawaii	42.5
2	Vermont	27.0
3	Minnesota	9.0
4	Arkansas	8.4
5	North Carolina	6.9
6	Alabama	6.2
7	Kentucky	5.6
8	New Mexico	5.2
9	Kansas	5.1
10	Iowa	4.7
10	Utah	4.7
12	Idaho	4.6
13	North Dakota	4.4
13	South Dakota	4.4
15	Wisconsin	4.2
16	Washington	4.0
17	Oklahoma	3.9
18	Delaware	3.8
18	Indiana	3.8
18	Michigan	3.8
18	Tennessee	3.8
22	Mississippi	3.6
23	Missouri	3.5
24	Maine	3.3
24	Virginia	3.3
26	Arizona	3.2
26	Nebraska	3.2
26	New Hampshire	3.2
29	Montana	3.1
30	California	3.0
30	West Virginia	3.0
32	Alaska	2.9
32	Nevada	2.9
32	Ohio	2.9
32	South Carolina	2.9
36	Florida	2.8
36	Georgia	2.8
38	Oregon	2.7
38	Wyoming	2.7
40	Colorado	2.6
40	Texas	2.6
42	Connecticut	2.5
42	Pennsylvania	2.5
44	Massachusetts	2.4
45	New Jersey	2.3
46	Maryland	2.1
47	Illinois	2.0
47	Rhode Island	2.0
49	Louisiana	1.5
50	New York	1.3
	District of Columbia	0.1

Source: CQ Press using data from U.S. Bureau of the Census, Governments Division
"Public Education Finances: 2006" (http://www.census.gov/govs/www/school06.html)
*Gross collections from cafeteria sales to children and adults.

Public Elementary and Secondary School Local Source Revenue
From Tuition and Transportation Fees in 2006
National Total = $1,091,354,000*

ALPHA ORDER

RANK	STATE	REVENUE	% of USA
38	Alabama	$3,535,000	0.3%
48	Alaska	7,000	0.0%
44	Arizona	1,112,000	0.1%
32	Arkansas	5,213,000	0.5%
8	California	54,801,000	5.0%
6	Colorado	60,103,000	5.5%
39	Connecticut	3,343,000	0.3%
49	Delaware	0	0.0%
23	Florida	10,451,000	1.0%
15	Georgia	27,160,000	2.5%
49	Hawaii	0	0.0%
41	Idaho	2,386,000	0.2%
13	Illinois	40,923,000	3.7%
19	Indiana	14,757,000	1.4%
21	Iowa	12,912,000	1.2%
22	Kansas	11,553,000	1.1%
27	Kentucky	9,131,000	0.8%
26	Louisiana	9,201,000	0.8%
30	Maine	6,265,000	0.6%
18	Maryland	19,090,000	1.7%
1	Massachusetts	88,965,000	8.2%
10	Michigan	45,156,000	4.1%
4	Minnesota	76,331,000	7.0%
31	Mississippi	5,516,000	0.5%
16	Missouri	23,394,000	2.1%
37	Montana	3,619,000	0.3%
35	Nebraska	4,150,000	0.4%
33	Nevada	4,634,000	0.4%
28	New Hampshire	6,942,000	0.6%
11	New Jersey	44,648,000	4.1%
40	New Mexico	2,726,000	0.2%
14	New York	39,162,000	3.6%
24	North Carolina	9,999,000	0.9%
46	North Dakota	862,000	0.1%
3	Ohio	76,824,000	7.0%
12	Oklahoma	41,219,000	3.8%
17	Oregon	20,023,000	1.8%
5	Pennsylvania	76,061,000	7.0%
45	Rhode Island	900,000	0.1%
25	South Carolina	9,249,000	0.8%
42	South Dakota	1,834,000	0.2%
29	Tennessee	6,672,000	0.6%
2	Texas	81,919,000	7.5%
20	Utah	13,098,000	1.2%
43	Vermont	1,795,000	0.2%
9	Virginia	45,347,000	4.2%
7	Washington	59,408,000	5.4%
36	West Virginia	3,624,000	0.3%
34	Wisconsin	4,543,000	0.4%
47	Wyoming	233,000	0.0%

RANK ORDER

RANK	STATE	REVENUE	% of USA
1	Massachusetts	$88,965,000	8.2%
2	Texas	81,919,000	7.5%
3	Ohio	76,824,000	7.0%
4	Minnesota	76,331,000	7.0%
5	Pennsylvania	76,061,000	7.0%
6	Colorado	60,103,000	5.5%
7	Washington	59,408,000	5.4%
8	California	54,801,000	5.0%
9	Virginia	45,347,000	4.2%
10	Michigan	45,156,000	4.1%
11	New Jersey	44,648,000	4.1%
12	Oklahoma	41,219,000	3.8%
13	Illinois	40,923,000	3.7%
14	New York	39,162,000	3.6%
15	Georgia	27,160,000	2.5%
16	Missouri	23,394,000	2.1%
17	Oregon	20,023,000	1.8%
18	Maryland	19,090,000	1.7%
19	Indiana	14,757,000	1.4%
20	Utah	13,098,000	1.2%
21	Iowa	12,912,000	1.2%
22	Kansas	11,553,000	1.1%
23	Florida	10,451,000	1.0%
24	North Carolina	9,999,000	0.9%
25	South Carolina	9,249,000	0.8%
26	Louisiana	9,201,000	0.8%
27	Kentucky	9,131,000	0.8%
28	New Hampshire	6,942,000	0.6%
29	Tennessee	6,672,000	0.6%
30	Maine	6,265,000	0.6%
31	Mississippi	5,516,000	0.5%
32	Arkansas	5,213,000	0.5%
33	Nevada	4,634,000	0.4%
34	Wisconsin	4,543,000	0.4%
35	Nebraska	4,150,000	0.4%
36	West Virginia	3,624,000	0.3%
37	Montana	3,619,000	0.3%
38	Alabama	3,535,000	0.3%
39	Connecticut	3,343,000	0.3%
40	New Mexico	2,726,000	0.2%
41	Idaho	2,386,000	0.2%
42	South Dakota	1,834,000	0.2%
43	Vermont	1,795,000	0.2%
44	Arizona	1,112,000	0.1%
45	Rhode Island	900,000	0.1%
46	North Dakota	862,000	0.1%
47	Wyoming	233,000	0.0%
48	Alaska	7,000	0.0%
49	Delaware	0	0.0%
49	Hawaii	0	0.0%
	District of Columbia	558,000	0.1%

Source: U.S. Bureau of the Census, Governments Division
   "Public Education Finances: 2006" (http://www.census.gov/govs/www/school06.html)
*Current charges for tuition and transportation fees paid by individuals.

Percent of Public Elementary and Secondary School Local Source Revenue From Tuition and Transportation Fees in 2006
National Percent = 0.5%*

ALPHA ORDER

RANK	STATE	PERCENT
37	Alabama	0.2
46	Alaska	0.0
46	Arizona	0.0
9	Arkansas	0.8
29	California	0.3
5	Colorado	1.7
42	Connecticut	0.1
46	Delaware	0.0
42	Florida	0.1
22	Georgia	0.4
46	Hawaii	0.0
22	Idaho	0.4
29	Illinois	0.3
29	Indiana	0.3
15	Iowa	0.6
10	Kansas	0.7
20	Kentucky	0.5
29	Louisiana	0.3
15	Maine	0.6
29	Maryland	0.3
6	Massachusetts	1.2
10	Michigan	0.7
1	Minnesota	3.7
22	Mississippi	0.4
15	Missouri	0.6
10	Montana	0.7
37	Nebraska	0.2
22	Nevada	0.4
20	New Hampshire	0.5
22	New Jersey	0.4
15	New Mexico	0.6
37	New York	0.2
29	North Carolina	0.3
37	North Dakota	0.2
10	Ohio	0.7
3	Oklahoma	2.2
8	Oregon	0.9
15	Pennsylvania	0.6
42	Rhode Island	0.1
29	South Carolina	0.3
29	South Dakota	0.3
37	Tennessee	0.2
22	Texas	0.4
7	Utah	1.1
2	Vermont	2.7
10	Virginia	0.7
4	Washington	2.0
22	West Virginia	0.4
42	Wisconsin	0.1
46	Wyoming	0.0

RANK ORDER

RANK	STATE	PERCENT
1	Minnesota	3.7
2	Vermont	2.7
3	Oklahoma	2.2
4	Washington	2.0
5	Colorado	1.7
6	Massachusetts	1.2
7	Utah	1.1
8	Oregon	0.9
9	Arkansas	0.8
10	Kansas	0.7
10	Michigan	0.7
10	Montana	0.7
10	Ohio	0.7
10	Virginia	0.7
15	Iowa	0.6
15	Maine	0.6
15	Missouri	0.6
15	New Mexico	0.6
15	Pennsylvania	0.6
20	Kentucky	0.5
20	New Hampshire	0.5
22	Georgia	0.4
22	Idaho	0.4
22	Mississippi	0.4
22	Nevada	0.4
22	New Jersey	0.4
22	Texas	0.4
22	West Virginia	0.4
29	California	0.3
29	Illinois	0.3
29	Indiana	0.3
29	Louisiana	0.3
29	Maryland	0.3
29	North Carolina	0.3
29	South Carolina	0.3
29	South Dakota	0.3
37	Alabama	0.2
37	Nebraska	0.2
37	New York	0.2
37	North Dakota	0.2
37	Tennessee	0.2
42	Connecticut	0.1
42	Florida	0.1
42	Rhode Island	0.1
42	Wisconsin	0.1
46	Alaska	0.0
46	Arizona	0.0
46	Delaware	0.0
46	Hawaii	0.0
46	Wyoming	0.0
	District of Columbia	0.1

Source: CQ Press using data from U.S. Bureau of the Census, Governments Division
"Public Education Finances: 2006" (http://www.census.gov/govs/www/school06.html)
*Current charges for tuition and transportation fees paid by individuals.

Public Elementary and Secondary School Local Source Revenue From Other Charges in 2006
National Total = $5,876,210,000*

<table>
<tr><td colspan="4">ALPHA ORDER</td><td colspan="4">RANK ORDER</td></tr>
<tr><td>RANK</td><td>STATE</td><td>REVENUE</td><td>% of USA</td><td>RANK</td><td>STATE</td><td>REVENUE</td><td>% of USA</td></tr>
<tr><td>11</td><td>Alabama</td><td>$197,643,000</td><td>3.4%</td><td>1</td><td>Florida</td><td>$638,442,000</td><td>10.9%</td></tr>
<tr><td>36</td><td>Alaska</td><td>15,145,000</td><td>0.3%</td><td>2</td><td>Ohio</td><td>558,230,000</td><td>9.5%</td></tr>
<tr><td>19</td><td>Arizona</td><td>113,627,000</td><td>1.9%</td><td>3</td><td>California</td><td>437,295,000</td><td>7.4%</td></tr>
<tr><td>23</td><td>Arkansas</td><td>87,877,000</td><td>1.5%</td><td>4</td><td>Tennessee</td><td>309,321,000</td><td>5.3%</td></tr>
<tr><td>3</td><td>California</td><td>437,295,000</td><td>7.4%</td><td>5</td><td>Georgia</td><td>278,326,000</td><td>4.7%</td></tr>
<tr><td>10</td><td>Colorado</td><td>208,497,000</td><td>3.5%</td><td>6</td><td>Michigan</td><td>276,560,000</td><td>4.7%</td></tr>
<tr><td>45</td><td>Connecticut</td><td>2,792,000</td><td>0.0%</td><td>7</td><td>Texas</td><td>265,050,000</td><td>4.5%</td></tr>
<tr><td>49</td><td>Delaware</td><td>793,000</td><td>0.0%</td><td>8</td><td>Missouri</td><td>215,181,000</td><td>3.7%</td></tr>
<tr><td>1</td><td>Florida</td><td>638,442,000</td><td>10.9%</td><td>9</td><td>Illinois</td><td>209,555,000</td><td>3.6%</td></tr>
<tr><td>5</td><td>Georgia</td><td>278,326,000</td><td>4.7%</td><td>10</td><td>Colorado</td><td>208,497,000</td><td>3.5%</td></tr>
<tr><td>50</td><td>Hawaii</td><td>751,000</td><td>0.0%</td><td>11</td><td>Alabama</td><td>197,643,000</td><td>3.4%</td></tr>
<tr><td>42</td><td>Idaho</td><td>5,011,000</td><td>0.1%</td><td>12</td><td>New Jersey</td><td>195,938,000</td><td>3.3%</td></tr>
<tr><td>9</td><td>Illinois</td><td>209,555,000</td><td>3.6%</td><td>13</td><td>Oklahoma</td><td>184,063,000</td><td>3.1%</td></tr>
<tr><td>16</td><td>Indiana</td><td>159,639,000</td><td>2.7%</td><td>14</td><td>Maryland</td><td>177,993,000</td><td>3.0%</td></tr>
<tr><td>29</td><td>Iowa</td><td>40,633,000</td><td>0.7%</td><td>15</td><td>Minnesota</td><td>172,274,000</td><td>2.9%</td></tr>
<tr><td>33</td><td>Kansas</td><td>23,798,000</td><td>0.4%</td><td>16</td><td>Indiana</td><td>159,639,000</td><td>2.7%</td></tr>
<tr><td>41</td><td>Kentucky</td><td>5,034,000</td><td>0.1%</td><td>17</td><td>Washington</td><td>148,570,000</td><td>2.5%</td></tr>
<tr><td>40</td><td>Louisiana</td><td>5,304,000</td><td>0.1%</td><td>18</td><td>South Carolina</td><td>138,781,000</td><td>2.4%</td></tr>
<tr><td>48</td><td>Maine</td><td>2,223,000</td><td>0.0%</td><td>19</td><td>Arizona</td><td>113,627,000</td><td>1.9%</td></tr>
<tr><td>14</td><td>Maryland</td><td>177,993,000</td><td>3.0%</td><td>20</td><td>New York</td><td>98,452,000</td><td>1.7%</td></tr>
<tr><td>31</td><td>Massachusetts</td><td>32,295,000</td><td>0.5%</td><td>21</td><td>Oregon</td><td>96,254,000</td><td>1.6%</td></tr>
<tr><td>6</td><td>Michigan</td><td>276,560,000</td><td>4.7%</td><td>22</td><td>Mississippi</td><td>95,912,000</td><td>1.6%</td></tr>
<tr><td>15</td><td>Minnesota</td><td>172,274,000</td><td>2.9%</td><td>23</td><td>Arkansas</td><td>87,877,000</td><td>1.5%</td></tr>
<tr><td>22</td><td>Mississippi</td><td>95,912,000</td><td>1.6%</td><td>24</td><td>Wisconsin</td><td>82,396,000</td><td>1.4%</td></tr>
<tr><td>8</td><td>Missouri</td><td>215,181,000</td><td>3.7%</td><td>25</td><td>Nevada</td><td>80,406,000</td><td>1.4%</td></tr>
<tr><td>30</td><td>Montana</td><td>34,827,000</td><td>0.6%</td><td>26</td><td>Nebraska</td><td>65,068,000</td><td>1.1%</td></tr>
<tr><td>26</td><td>Nebraska</td><td>65,068,000</td><td>1.1%</td><td>27</td><td>North Carolina</td><td>60,386,000</td><td>1.0%</td></tr>
<tr><td>25</td><td>Nevada</td><td>80,406,000</td><td>1.4%</td><td>28</td><td>Pennsylvania</td><td>43,425,000</td><td>0.7%</td></tr>
<tr><td>44</td><td>New Hampshire</td><td>3,863,000</td><td>0.1%</td><td>29</td><td>Iowa</td><td>40,633,000</td><td>0.7%</td></tr>
<tr><td>12</td><td>New Jersey</td><td>195,938,000</td><td>3.3%</td><td>30</td><td>Montana</td><td>34,827,000</td><td>0.6%</td></tr>
<tr><td>32</td><td>New Mexico</td><td>27,991,000</td><td>0.5%</td><td>31</td><td>Massachusetts</td><td>32,295,000</td><td>0.5%</td></tr>
<tr><td>20</td><td>New York</td><td>98,452,000</td><td>1.7%</td><td>32</td><td>New Mexico</td><td>27,991,000</td><td>0.5%</td></tr>
<tr><td>27</td><td>North Carolina</td><td>60,386,000</td><td>1.0%</td><td>33</td><td>Kansas</td><td>23,798,000</td><td>0.4%</td></tr>
<tr><td>34</td><td>North Dakota</td><td>23,413,000</td><td>0.4%</td><td>34</td><td>North Dakota</td><td>23,413,000</td><td>0.4%</td></tr>
<tr><td>2</td><td>Ohio</td><td>558,230,000</td><td>9.5%</td><td>35</td><td>Virginia</td><td>15,890,000</td><td>0.3%</td></tr>
<tr><td>13</td><td>Oklahoma</td><td>184,063,000</td><td>3.1%</td><td>36</td><td>Alaska</td><td>15,145,000</td><td>0.3%</td></tr>
<tr><td>21</td><td>Oregon</td><td>96,254,000</td><td>1.6%</td><td>37</td><td>Utah</td><td>8,522,000</td><td>0.1%</td></tr>
<tr><td>28</td><td>Pennsylvania</td><td>43,425,000</td><td>0.7%</td><td>38</td><td>South Dakota</td><td>8,234,000</td><td>0.1%</td></tr>
<tr><td>46</td><td>Rhode Island</td><td>2,539,000</td><td>0.0%</td><td>39</td><td>West Virginia</td><td>6,675,000</td><td>0.1%</td></tr>
<tr><td>18</td><td>South Carolina</td><td>138,781,000</td><td>2.4%</td><td>40</td><td>Louisiana</td><td>5,304,000</td><td>0.1%</td></tr>
<tr><td>38</td><td>South Dakota</td><td>8,234,000</td><td>0.1%</td><td>41</td><td>Kentucky</td><td>5,034,000</td><td>0.1%</td></tr>
<tr><td>4</td><td>Tennessee</td><td>309,321,000</td><td>5.3%</td><td>42</td><td>Idaho</td><td>5,011,000</td><td>0.1%</td></tr>
<tr><td>7</td><td>Texas</td><td>265,050,000</td><td>4.5%</td><td>43</td><td>Vermont</td><td>4,146,000</td><td>0.1%</td></tr>
<tr><td>37</td><td>Utah</td><td>8,522,000</td><td>0.1%</td><td>44</td><td>New Hampshire</td><td>3,863,000</td><td>0.1%</td></tr>
<tr><td>43</td><td>Vermont</td><td>4,146,000</td><td>0.1%</td><td>45</td><td>Connecticut</td><td>2,792,000</td><td>0.0%</td></tr>
<tr><td>35</td><td>Virginia</td><td>15,890,000</td><td>0.3%</td><td>46</td><td>Rhode Island</td><td>2,539,000</td><td>0.0%</td></tr>
<tr><td>17</td><td>Washington</td><td>148,570,000</td><td>2.5%</td><td>47</td><td>Wyoming</td><td>2,311,000</td><td>0.0%</td></tr>
<tr><td>39</td><td>West Virginia</td><td>6,675,000</td><td>0.1%</td><td>48</td><td>Maine</td><td>2,223,000</td><td>0.0%</td></tr>
<tr><td>24</td><td>Wisconsin</td><td>82,396,000</td><td>1.4%</td><td>49</td><td>Delaware</td><td>793,000</td><td>0.0%</td></tr>
<tr><td>47</td><td>Wyoming</td><td>2,311,000</td><td>0.0%</td><td>50</td><td>Hawaii</td><td>751,000</td><td>0.0%</td></tr>
<tr><td></td><td></td><td></td><td></td><td colspan="2">District of Columbia</td><td>8,859,000</td><td>0.2%</td></tr>
</table>

Source: U.S. Bureau of the Census, Governments Division
  "Public Education Finances: 2006" (http://www.census.gov/govs/www/school06.html)
*Amounts received from the public for performance of specific services benefiting the person charged and sales of commodities and services. Excludes school lunch sales, tuition, and transportation fees (shown separately). Includes revenue from the sale and rental of textbooks and receipts from centrally administered student activity funds.

Percent of Public Elementary and Secondary School Local Source Revenue From Other Charges in 2006
National Percent = 2.5%*

ALPHA ORDER

RANK	STATE	PERCENT
3	Alabama	9.4
22	Alaska	3.6
23	Arizona	3.3
1	Arkansas	13.7
26	California	2.3
11	Colorado	5.7
50	Connecticut	0.1
45	Delaware	0.2
14	Florida	5.0
20	Georgia	3.7
29	Hawaii	1.6
36	Idaho	0.8
29	Illinois	1.6
24	Indiana	3.1
28	Iowa	1.9
34	Kansas	1.4
42	Kentucky	0.3
45	Louisiana	0.2
45	Maine	0.2
25	Maryland	3.0
39	Massachusetts	0.5
17	Michigan	4.5
5	Minnesota	8.3
6	Mississippi	7.4
13	Missouri	5.1
7	Montana	6.4
20	Nebraska	3.7
9	Nevada	6.2
42	New Hampshire	0.3
29	New Jersey	1.6
7	New Mexico	6.4
40	New York	0.4
29	North Carolina	1.6
14	North Dakota	5.0
12	Ohio	5.4
2	Oklahoma	9.7
17	Oregon	4.5
42	Pennsylvania	0.3
45	Rhode Island	0.2
17	South Carolina	4.5
33	South Dakota	1.5
3	Tennessee	9.4
35	Texas	1.2
38	Utah	0.7
9	Vermont	6.2
45	Virginia	0.2
14	Washington	5.0
36	West Virginia	0.8
27	Wisconsin	2.0
40	Wyoming	0.4

RANK ORDER

RANK	STATE	PERCENT
1	Arkansas	13.7
2	Oklahoma	9.7
3	Alabama	9.4
3	Tennessee	9.4
5	Minnesota	8.3
6	Mississippi	7.4
7	Montana	6.4
7	New Mexico	6.4
9	Nevada	6.2
9	Vermont	6.2
11	Colorado	5.7
12	Ohio	5.4
13	Missouri	5.1
14	Florida	5.0
14	North Dakota	5.0
14	Washington	5.0
17	Michigan	4.5
17	Oregon	4.5
17	South Carolina	4.5
20	Georgia	3.7
20	Nebraska	3.7
22	Alaska	3.6
23	Arizona	3.3
24	Indiana	3.1
25	Maryland	3.0
26	California	2.3
27	Wisconsin	2.0
28	Iowa	1.9
29	Hawaii	1.6
29	Illinois	1.6
29	New Jersey	1.6
29	North Carolina	1.6
33	South Dakota	1.5
34	Kansas	1.4
35	Texas	1.2
36	Idaho	0.8
36	West Virginia	0.8
38	Utah	0.7
39	Massachusetts	0.5
40	New York	0.4
40	Wyoming	0.4
42	Kentucky	0.3
42	New Hampshire	0.3
42	Pennsylvania	0.3
45	Delaware	0.2
45	Louisiana	0.2
45	Maine	0.2
45	Rhode Island	0.2
45	Virginia	0.2
50	Connecticut	0.1
	District of Columbia	0.9

Source: CQ Press using data from U.S. Bureau of the Census, Governments Division
    "Public Education Finances: 2006" (http://www.census.gov/govs/www/school06.html)
*Amounts received from the public for performance of specific services benefiting the person charged and sales of commodities and services. Excludes school lunch sales, tuition, and transportation fees (shown separately). Includes revenue from the sale and rental of textbooks and receipts from centrally administered student activity funds.

Public Elementary and Secondary School Total Expenditures in 2006

National Total = $526,648,505,000*

ALPHA ORDER

RANK	STATE	EXPENDITURES	% of USA
25	Alabama	$6,587,255,000	1.3%
44	Alaska	1,817,656,000	0.3%
20	Arizona	7,934,177,000	1.5%
32	Arkansas	4,325,928,000	0.8%
1	California	66,195,456,000	12.6%
22	Colorado	7,736,560,000	1.5%
21	Connecticut	7,802,111,000	1.5%
45	Delaware	1,595,475,000	0.3%
4	Florida	26,609,155,000	5.1%
10	Georgia	15,826,406,000	3.0%
42	Hawaii	1,939,968,000	0.4%
43	Idaho	1,903,720,000	0.4%
7	Illinois	22,052,355,000	4.2%
14	Indiana	11,014,853,000	2.1%
30	Iowa	4,737,932,000	0.9%
31	Kansas	4,428,164,000	0.8%
26	Kentucky	6,111,751,000	1.2%
27	Louisiana	6,027,414,000	1.1%
40	Maine	2,301,201,000	0.4%
15	Maryland	10,357,637,000	2.0%
12	Massachusetts	13,205,176,000	2.5%
9	Michigan	19,628,328,000	3.7%
18	Minnesota	9,352,122,000	1.8%
33	Mississippi	4,066,036,000	0.8%
19	Missouri	8,558,380,000	1.6%
46	Montana	1,365,051,000	0.3%
38	Nebraska	2,841,874,000	0.5%
34	Nevada	4,019,425,000	0.8%
39	New Hampshire	2,341,854,000	0.4%
5	New Jersey	23,511,377,000	4.5%
36	New Mexico	3,091,482,000	0.6%
2	New York	47,878,872,000	9.1%
13	North Carolina	11,725,031,000	2.2%
50	North Dakota	957,143,000	0.2%
8	Ohio	20,435,243,000	3.9%
29	Oklahoma	5,088,830,000	1.0%
28	Oregon	5,372,927,000	1.0%
6	Pennsylvania	22,603,956,000	4.3%
41	Rhode Island	1,951,295,000	0.4%
24	South Carolina	7,132,059,000	1.4%
49	South Dakota	1,042,874,000	0.2%
23	Tennessee	7,363,845,000	1.4%
3	Texas	43,259,307,000	8.2%
35	Utah	3,369,265,000	0.6%
47	Vermont	1,285,458,000	0.2%
11	Virginia	13,310,530,000	2.5%
16	Washington	9,886,380,000	1.9%
37	West Virginia	2,851,589,000	0.5%
17	Wisconsin	9,628,719,000	1.8%
48	Wyoming	1,139,972,000	0.2%

RANK ORDER

RANK	STATE	EXPENDITURES	% of USA
1	California	$66,195,456,000	12.6%
2	New York	47,878,872,000	9.1%
3	Texas	43,259,307,000	8.2%
4	Florida	26,609,155,000	5.1%
5	New Jersey	23,511,377,000	4.5%
6	Pennsylvania	22,603,956,000	4.3%
7	Illinois	22,052,355,000	4.2%
8	Ohio	20,435,243,000	3.9%
9	Michigan	19,628,328,000	3.7%
10	Georgia	15,826,406,000	3.0%
11	Virginia	13,310,530,000	2.5%
12	Massachusetts	13,205,176,000	2.5%
13	North Carolina	11,725,031,000	2.2%
14	Indiana	11,014,853,000	2.1%
15	Maryland	10,357,637,000	2.0%
16	Washington	9,886,380,000	1.9%
17	Wisconsin	9,628,719,000	1.8%
18	Minnesota	9,352,122,000	1.8%
19	Missouri	8,558,380,000	1.6%
20	Arizona	7,934,177,000	1.5%
21	Connecticut	7,802,111,000	1.5%
22	Colorado	7,736,560,000	1.5%
23	Tennessee	7,363,845,000	1.4%
24	South Carolina	7,132,059,000	1.4%
25	Alabama	6,587,255,000	1.3%
26	Kentucky	6,111,751,000	1.2%
27	Louisiana	6,027,414,000	1.1%
28	Oregon	5,372,927,000	1.0%
29	Oklahoma	5,088,830,000	1.0%
30	Iowa	4,737,932,000	0.9%
31	Kansas	4,428,164,000	0.8%
32	Arkansas	4,325,928,000	0.8%
33	Mississippi	4,066,036,000	0.8%
34	Nevada	4,019,425,000	0.8%
35	Utah	3,369,265,000	0.6%
36	New Mexico	3,091,482,000	0.6%
37	West Virginia	2,851,589,000	0.5%
38	Nebraska	2,841,874,000	0.5%
39	New Hampshire	2,341,854,000	0.4%
40	Maine	2,301,201,000	0.4%
41	Rhode Island	1,951,295,000	0.4%
42	Hawaii	1,939,968,000	0.4%
43	Idaho	1,903,720,000	0.4%
44	Alaska	1,817,656,000	0.3%
45	Delaware	1,595,475,000	0.3%
46	Montana	1,365,051,000	0.3%
47	Vermont	1,285,458,000	0.2%
48	Wyoming	1,139,972,000	0.2%
49	South Dakota	1,042,874,000	0.2%
50	North Dakota	957,143,000	0.2%
	District of Columbia	1,078,931,000	0.2%

Source: U.S. Bureau of the Census, Governments Division
   "Public Education Finances: 2006" (http://www.census.gov/govs/www/school06.html)
*Includes current spending (including salaries, benefits, services, and supplies), capital outlay, and "other." "Other" includes
payments to state and local governments and interest on school system indebtedness.

Per Capita Public Elementary and Secondary School Total Expenditures in 2006
National Per Capita = $1,763*

ALPHA ORDER

RANK	STATE	PER CAPITA
41	Alabama	$1,435
2	Alaska	2,683
49	Arizona	1,287
33	Arkansas	1,540
13	California	1,826
25	Colorado	1,623
4	Connecticut	2,232
9	Delaware	1,871
36	Florida	1,474
23	Georgia	1,694
34	Hawaii	1,517
48	Idaho	1,300
22	Illinois	1,726
19	Indiana	1,748
29	Iowa	1,594
28	Kansas	1,607
39	Kentucky	1,454
43	Louisiana	1,420
18	Maine	1,750
10	Maryland	1,849
7	Massachusetts	2,052
8	Michigan	1,943
15	Minnesota	1,814
44	Mississippi	1,403
37	Missouri	1,466
40	Montana	1,442
27	Nebraska	1,611
26	Nevada	1,613
16	New Hampshire	1,785
1	New Jersey	2,713
30	New Mexico	1,592
3	New York	2,483
46	North Carolina	1,322
35	North Dakota	1,501
17	Ohio	1,783
42	Oklahoma	1,422
38	Oregon	1,456
14	Pennsylvania	1,822
12	Rhode Island	1,838
24	South Carolina	1,647
45	South Dakota	1,323
50	Tennessee	1,212
11	Texas	1,848
47	Utah	1,306
6	Vermont	2,071
20	Virginia	1,742
32	Washington	1,551
31	West Virginia	1,577
21	Wisconsin	1,728
5	Wyoming	2,223

RANK ORDER

RANK	STATE	PER CAPITA
1	New Jersey	$2,713
2	Alaska	2,683
3	New York	2,483
4	Connecticut	2,232
5	Wyoming	2,223
6	Vermont	2,071
7	Massachusetts	2,052
8	Michigan	1,943
9	Delaware	1,871
10	Maryland	1,849
11	Texas	1,848
12	Rhode Island	1,838
13	California	1,826
14	Pennsylvania	1,822
15	Minnesota	1,814
16	New Hampshire	1,785
17	Ohio	1,783
18	Maine	1,750
19	Indiana	1,748
20	Virginia	1,742
21	Wisconsin	1,728
22	Illinois	1,726
23	Georgia	1,694
24	South Carolina	1,647
25	Colorado	1,623
26	Nevada	1,613
27	Nebraska	1,611
28	Kansas	1,607
29	Iowa	1,594
30	New Mexico	1,592
31	West Virginia	1,577
32	Washington	1,551
33	Arkansas	1,540
34	Hawaii	1,517
35	North Dakota	1,501
36	Florida	1,474
37	Missouri	1,466
38	Oregon	1,456
39	Kentucky	1,454
40	Montana	1,442
41	Alabama	1,435
42	Oklahoma	1,422
43	Louisiana	1,420
44	Mississippi	1,403
45	South Dakota	1,323
46	North Carolina	1,322
47	Utah	1,306
48	Idaho	1,300
49	Arizona	1,287
50	Tennessee	1,212

| | District of Columbia | 1,843 |

Source: CQ Press using data from U.S. Bureau of the Census, Governments Division
"Public Education Finances: 2006" (http://www.census.gov/govs/www/school06.html)
*Includes current spending (including salaries, benefits, services, and supplies), capital outlay, and "other." "Other" includes payments to state and local governments and interest on school system indebtedness.

Per Pupil Elementary and Secondary School
Total Expenditures in 2006
National Per Pupil = $10,886

ALPHA ORDER

RANK	STATE	PER PUPIL
42	Alabama	$8,863
7	Alaska	13,678
47	Arizona	7,899
40	Arkansas	9,153
21	California	10,581
27	Colorado	9,926
3	Connecticut	14,021
4	Delaware	13,950
25	Florida	9,989
28	Georgia	9,906
20	Hawaii	10,611
49	Idaho	7,370
22	Illinois	10,487
19	Indiana	10,734
29	Iowa	9,800
35	Kansas	9,504
41	Kentucky	8,993
39	Louisiana	9,297
12	Maine	11,791
11	Maryland	12,043
6	Massachusetts	13,901
16	Michigan	11,352
15	Minnesota	11,432
45	Mississippi	8,232
38	Missouri	9,345
37	Montana	9,397
26	Nebraska	9,931
31	Nevada	9,738
13	New Hampshire	11,648
2	New Jersey	17,036
36	New Mexico	9,461
1	New York	17,177
44	North Carolina	8,446
30	North Dakota	9,750
14	Ohio	11,550
46	Oklahoma	8,021
33	Oregon	9,652
10	Pennsylvania	12,847
9	Rhode Island	12,999
23	South Carolina	10,203
43	South Dakota	8,568
48	Tennessee	7,721
32	Texas	9,721
50	Utah	6,786
5	Vermont	13,921
18	Virginia	10,968
34	Washington	9,583
24	West Virginia	10,192
17	Wisconsin	11,073
8	Wyoming	13,232

RANK ORDER

RANK	STATE	PER PUPIL
1	New York	$17,177
2	New Jersey	17,036
3	Connecticut	14,021
4	Delaware	13,950
5	Vermont	13,921
6	Massachusetts	13,901
7	Alaska	13,678
8	Wyoming	13,232
9	Rhode Island	12,999
10	Pennsylvania	12,847
11	Maryland	12,043
12	Maine	11,791
13	New Hampshire	11,648
14	Ohio	11,550
15	Minnesota	11,432
16	Michigan	11,352
17	Wisconsin	11,073
18	Virginia	10,968
19	Indiana	10,734
20	Hawaii	10,611
21	California	10,581
22	Illinois	10,487
23	South Carolina	10,203
24	West Virginia	10,192
25	Florida	9,989
26	Nebraska	9,931
27	Colorado	9,926
28	Georgia	9,906
29	Iowa	9,800
30	North Dakota	9,750
31	Nevada	9,738
32	Texas	9,721
33	Oregon	9,652
34	Washington	9,583
35	Kansas	9,504
36	New Mexico	9,461
37	Montana	9,397
38	Missouri	9,345
39	Louisiana	9,297
40	Arkansas	9,153
41	Kentucky	8,993
42	Alabama	8,863
43	South Dakota	8,568
44	North Carolina	8,446
45	Mississippi	8,232
46	Oklahoma	8,021
47	Arizona	7,899
48	Tennessee	7,721
49	Idaho	7,370
50	Utah	6,786
	District of Columbia	18,098

Source: CQ Press using data from U.S. Bureau of the Census, Governments Division
"Public Education Finances: 2006" (http://www.census.gov/govs/www/school06.html)
*Based on student membership. Includes current spending (including salaries, benefits, services, and supplies), capital outlay, and "other." "Other" includes payments to state and local governments and interest on school system indebtedness.

Public Elementary and Secondary School Current Expenditures in 2006

National Total = $451,487,812,000*

ALPHA ORDER

RANK	STATE	EXPENDITURES	% of USA
24	Alabama	$5,796,074,000	1.3%
44	Alaska	1,530,668,000	0.3%
22	Arizona	6,563,231,000	1.5%
32	Arkansas	3,774,479,000	0.8%
1	California	54,726,269,000	12.1%
23	Colorado	6,379,835,000	1.4%
20	Connecticut	7,052,667,000	1.6%
45	Delaware	1,349,940,000	0.3%
4	Florida	21,140,944,000	4.7%
10	Georgia	13,724,657,000	3.0%
42	Hawaii	1,864,980,000	0.4%
43	Idaho	1,667,833,000	0.4%
7	Illinois	19,388,389,000	4.3%
15	Indiana	9,085,817,000	2.0%
30	Iowa	4,069,015,000	0.9%
31	Kansas	3,915,746,000	0.9%
27	Kentucky	5,269,627,000	1.2%
26	Louisiana	5,468,389,000	1.2%
39	Maine	2,138,662,000	0.5%
14	Maryland	9,201,229,000	2.0%
11	Massachusetts	12,016,989,000	2.7%
9	Michigan	16,901,610,000	3.7%
18	Minnesota	7,833,177,000	1.7%
33	Mississippi	3,583,253,000	0.8%
19	Missouri	7,570,400,000	1.7%
46	Montana	1,252,968,000	0.3%
38	Nebraska	2,505,038,000	0.6%
34	Nevada	3,048,568,000	0.7%
40	New Hampshire	2,097,051,000	0.5%
5	New Jersey	21,039,298,000	4.7%
36	New Mexico	2,670,455,000	0.6%
2	New York	42,752,878,000	9.5%
13	North Carolina	10,305,665,000	2.3%
50	North Dakota	850,874,000	0.2%
8	Ohio	17,697,739,000	3.9%
29	Oklahoma	4,607,769,000	1.0%
28	Oregon	4,827,479,000	1.1%
6	Pennsylvania	19,667,803,000	4.4%
41	Rhode Island	1,891,260,000	0.4%
25	South Carolina	5,748,625,000	1.3%
49	South Dakota	935,925,000	0.2%
21	Tennessee	6,639,211,000	1.5%
3	Texas	33,952,123,000	7.5%
35	Utah	2,785,974,000	0.6%
47	Vermont	1,212,060,000	0.3%
12	Virginia	11,537,088,000	2.6%
17	Washington	8,120,022,000	1.8%
37	West Virginia	2,651,879,000	0.6%
16	Wisconsin	8,755,812,000	1.9%
48	Wyoming	968,244,000	0.2%

RANK ORDER

RANK	STATE	EXPENDITURES	% of USA
1	California	$54,726,269,000	12.1%
2	New York	42,752,878,000	9.5%
3	Texas	33,952,123,000	7.5%
4	Florida	21,140,944,000	4.7%
5	New Jersey	21,039,298,000	4.7%
6	Pennsylvania	19,667,803,000	4.4%
7	Illinois	19,388,389,000	4.3%
8	Ohio	17,697,739,000	3.9%
9	Michigan	16,901,610,000	3.7%
10	Georgia	13,724,657,000	3.0%
11	Massachusetts	12,016,989,000	2.7%
12	Virginia	11,537,088,000	2.6%
13	North Carolina	10,305,665,000	2.3%
14	Maryland	9,201,229,000	2.0%
15	Indiana	9,085,817,000	2.0%
16	Wisconsin	8,755,812,000	1.9%
17	Washington	8,120,022,000	1.8%
18	Minnesota	7,833,177,000	1.7%
19	Missouri	7,570,400,000	1.7%
20	Connecticut	7,052,667,000	1.6%
21	Tennessee	6,639,211,000	1.5%
22	Arizona	6,563,231,000	1.5%
23	Colorado	6,379,835,000	1.4%
24	Alabama	5,796,074,000	1.3%
25	South Carolina	5,748,625,000	1.3%
26	Louisiana	5,468,389,000	1.2%
27	Kentucky	5,269,627,000	1.2%
28	Oregon	4,827,479,000	1.1%
29	Oklahoma	4,607,769,000	1.0%
30	Iowa	4,069,015,000	0.9%
31	Kansas	3,915,746,000	0.9%
32	Arkansas	3,774,479,000	0.8%
33	Mississippi	3,583,253,000	0.8%
34	Nevada	3,048,568,000	0.7%
35	Utah	2,785,974,000	0.6%
36	New Mexico	2,670,455,000	0.6%
37	West Virginia	2,651,879,000	0.6%
38	Nebraska	2,505,038,000	0.6%
39	Maine	2,138,662,000	0.5%
40	New Hampshire	2,097,051,000	0.5%
41	Rhode Island	1,891,260,000	0.4%
42	Hawaii	1,864,980,000	0.4%
43	Idaho	1,667,833,000	0.4%
44	Alaska	1,530,668,000	0.3%
45	Delaware	1,349,940,000	0.3%
46	Montana	1,252,968,000	0.3%
47	Vermont	1,212,060,000	0.3%
48	Wyoming	968,244,000	0.2%
49	South Dakota	935,925,000	0.2%
50	North Dakota	850,874,000	0.2%
	District of Columbia	952,124,000	0.2%

Source: U.S. Bureau of the Census, Governments Division
    "Public Education Finances: 2006" (http://www.census.gov/govs/www/school06.html)
*Includes salaries, benefits, services, and supplies. Census expanded its usual "current expenditures" concept for education
finance reports to include all current public elementary and secondary education outlays regardless of the specific unit of
government that actually makes the expenditure.

Per Capita Public Elementary and Secondary School
Current Expenditures in 2006
National Per Capita = $1,511*

ALPHA ORDER

RANK	STATE	PER CAPITA
40	Alabama	$1,263
2	Alaska	2,259
50	Arizona	1,064
30	Arkansas	1,344
19	California	1,510
31	Colorado	1,339
4	Connecticut	2,017
14	Delaware	1,583
45	Florida	1,171
21	Georgia	1,469
23	Hawaii	1,459
47	Idaho	1,139
18	Illinois	1,517
25	Indiana	1,442
29	Iowa	1,369
26	Kansas	1,421
41	Kentucky	1,253
37	Louisiana	1,289
11	Maine	1,626
10	Maryland	1,642
7	Massachusetts	1,868
9	Michigan	1,673
17	Minnesota	1,520
42	Mississippi	1,236
36	Missouri	1,297
34	Montana	1,323
27	Nebraska	1,420
43	Nevada	1,223
12	New Hampshire	1,599
1	New Jersey	2,428
28	New Mexico	1,375
3	New York	2,217
46	North Carolina	1,162
32	North Dakota	1,335
16	Ohio	1,544
38	Oklahoma	1,288
35	Oregon	1,308
13	Pennsylvania	1,586
8	Rhode Island	1,781
33	South Carolina	1,328
44	South Dakota	1,187
48	Tennessee	1,093
24	Texas	1,450
49	Utah	1,080
5	Vermont	1,952
19	Virginia	1,510
39	Washington	1,274
22	West Virginia	1,466
15	Wisconsin	1,571
6	Wyoming	1,888

RANK ORDER

RANK	STATE	PER CAPITA
1	New Jersey	$2,428
2	Alaska	2,259
3	New York	2,217
4	Connecticut	2,017
5	Vermont	1,952
6	Wyoming	1,888
7	Massachusetts	1,868
8	Rhode Island	1,781
9	Michigan	1,673
10	Maryland	1,642
11	Maine	1,626
12	New Hampshire	1,599
13	Pennsylvania	1,586
14	Delaware	1,583
15	Wisconsin	1,571
16	Ohio	1,544
17	Minnesota	1,520
18	Illinois	1,517
19	California	1,510
19	Virginia	1,510
21	Georgia	1,469
22	West Virginia	1,466
23	Hawaii	1,459
24	Texas	1,450
25	Indiana	1,442
26	Kansas	1,421
27	Nebraska	1,420
28	New Mexico	1,375
29	Iowa	1,369
30	Arkansas	1,344
31	Colorado	1,339
32	North Dakota	1,335
33	South Carolina	1,328
34	Montana	1,323
35	Oregon	1,308
36	Missouri	1,297
37	Louisiana	1,289
38	Oklahoma	1,288
39	Washington	1,274
40	Alabama	1,263
41	Kentucky	1,253
42	Mississippi	1,236
43	Nevada	1,223
44	South Dakota	1,187
45	Florida	1,171
46	North Carolina	1,162
47	Idaho	1,139
48	Tennessee	1,093
49	Utah	1,080
50	Arizona	1,064
	District of Columbia	1,626

Source: CQ Press using data from U.S. Bureau of the Census, Governments Division
"Public Education Finances: 2006" (http://www.census.gov/govs/www/school06.html)
*Includes salaries, benefits, services, and supplies. Census expanded its usual "current expenditures" concept for education finance reports to include all current public elementary and secondary education outlays regardless of the specific unit of government that actually makes the expenditure.

Public Elementary and Secondary School Current Expenditures per $1,000 Personal Income in 2006
National Ratio = $43.34*

ALPHA ORDER

RANK	STATE	RATIO
27	Alabama	$42.75
1	Alaska	62.68
45	Arizona	35.94
8	Arkansas	50.10
39	California	39.62
47	Colorado	35.76
30	Connecticut	42.00
26	Delaware	42.83
50	Florida	33.51
13	Georgia	48.21
37	Hawaii	40.73
35	Idaho	41.17
34	Illinois	41.45
18	Indiana	46.63
24	Iowa	43.30
23	Kansas	43.57
22	Kentucky	44.02
11	Louisiana	48.77
6	Maine	52.03
40	Maryland	39.48
29	Massachusetts	42.63
9	Michigan	50.08
41	Minnesota	39.23
14	Mississippi	48.18
36	Missouri	40.81
19	Montana	45.64
24	Nebraska	43.30
49	Nevada	33.58
28	New Hampshire	42.69
3	New Jersey	55.31
10	New Mexico	48.92
5	New York	53.66
43	North Carolina	38.42
32	North Dakota	41.52
15	Ohio	47.72
33	Oklahoma	41.47
31	Oregon	41.94
20	Pennsylvania	45.03
12	Rhode Island	48.41
17	South Carolina	47.07
44	South Dakota	37.79
48	Tennessee	35.55
21	Texas	44.26
42	Utah	38.47
2	Vermont	59.44
38	Virginia	39.93
46	Washington	35.93
4	West Virginia	54.56
16	Wisconsin	47.64
7	Wyoming	51.02

RANK ORDER

RANK	STATE	RATIO
1	Alaska	$62.68
2	Vermont	59.44
3	New Jersey	55.31
4	West Virginia	54.56
5	New York	53.66
6	Maine	52.03
7	Wyoming	51.02
8	Arkansas	50.10
9	Michigan	50.08
10	New Mexico	48.92
11	Louisiana	48.77
12	Rhode Island	48.41
13	Georgia	48.21
14	Mississippi	48.18
15	Ohio	47.72
16	Wisconsin	47.64
17	South Carolina	47.07
18	Indiana	46.63
19	Montana	45.64
20	Pennsylvania	45.03
21	Texas	44.26
22	Kentucky	44.02
23	Kansas	43.57
24	Iowa	43.30
24	Nebraska	43.30
26	Delaware	42.83
27	Alabama	42.75
28	New Hampshire	42.69
29	Massachusetts	42.63
30	Connecticut	42.00
31	Oregon	41.94
32	North Dakota	41.52
33	Oklahoma	41.47
34	Illinois	41.45
35	Idaho	41.17
36	Missouri	40.81
37	Hawaii	40.73
38	Virginia	39.93
39	California	39.62
40	Maryland	39.48
41	Minnesota	39.23
42	Utah	38.47
43	North Carolina	38.42
44	South Dakota	37.79
45	Arizona	35.94
46	Washington	35.93
47	Colorado	35.76
48	Tennessee	35.55
49	Nevada	33.58
50	Florida	33.51
	District of Columbia	30.09

Source: U.S. Bureau of the Census, Governments Division

"Public Education Finances: 2006" (http://www.census.gov/govs/www/school06.html)

*Includes salaries, benefits, services, and supplies. Census expanded its usual "current expenditures" concept for education finance reports to include all current public elementary and secondary education outlays regardless of the specific unit of government that actually makes the expenditure.

Per Pupil Public Elementary and Secondary School Current Expenditures in 2006
National Per Pupil = $9,138*

ALPHA ORDER

RANK	STATE	PER PUPIL
41	Alabama	$7,646
8	Alaska	11,460
48	Arizona	6,472
36	Arkansas	7,927
28	California	8,486
35	Colorado	8,057
4	Connecticut	12,323
7	Delaware	11,633
38	Florida	7,759
26	Georgia	8,565
15	Hawaii	9,876
49	Idaho	6,440
20	Illinois	9,149
22	Indiana	8,793
31	Iowa	8,360
30	Kansas	8,392
39	Kentucky	7,662
29	Louisiana	8,402
12	Maine	10,586
11	Maryland	10,670
5	Massachusetts	11,981
17	Michigan	9,572
21	Minnesota	9,138
45	Mississippi	7,221
32	Missouri	8,107
25	Montana	8,581
23	Nebraska	8,736
44	Nevada	7,345
13	New Hampshire	10,079
2	New Jersey	14,630
34	New Mexico	8,086
1	New York	14,884
43	North Carolina	7,388
24	North Dakota	8,603
16	Ohio	9,598
46	Oklahoma	6,961
27	Oregon	8,545
10	Pennsylvania	11,028
6	Rhode Island	11,769
33	South Carolina	8,091
40	South Dakota	7,651
47	Tennessee	6,883
42	Texas	7,561
50	Utah	5,437
3	Vermont	12,614
18	Virginia	9,447
37	Washington	7,830
19	West Virginia	9,352
14	Wisconsin	9,970
9	Wyoming	11,197

RANK ORDER

RANK	STATE	PER PUPIL
1	New York	$14,884
2	New Jersey	14,630
3	Vermont	12,614
4	Connecticut	12,323
5	Massachusetts	11,981
6	Rhode Island	11,769
7	Delaware	11,633
8	Alaska	11,460
9	Wyoming	11,197
10	Pennsylvania	11,028
11	Maryland	10,670
12	Maine	10,586
13	New Hampshire	10,079
14	Wisconsin	9,970
15	Hawaii	9,876
16	Ohio	9,598
17	Michigan	9,572
18	Virginia	9,447
19	West Virginia	9,352
20	Illinois	9,149
21	Minnesota	9,138
22	Indiana	8,793
23	Nebraska	8,736
24	North Dakota	8,603
25	Montana	8,581
26	Georgia	8,565
27	Oregon	8,545
28	California	8,486
29	Louisiana	8,402
30	Kansas	8,392
31	Iowa	8,360
32	Missouri	8,107
33	South Carolina	8,091
34	New Mexico	8,086
35	Colorado	8,057
36	Arkansas	7,927
37	Washington	7,830
38	Florida	7,759
39	Kentucky	7,662
40	South Dakota	7,651
41	Alabama	7,646
42	Texas	7,561
43	North Carolina	7,388
44	Nevada	7,345
45	Mississippi	7,221
46	Oklahoma	6,961
47	Tennessee	6,883
48	Arizona	6,472
49	Idaho	6,440
50	Utah	5,437
	District of Columbia	13,446

Source: U.S. Bureau of the Census, Governments Division
"Public Education Finances: 2006" (http://www.census.gov/govs/www/school06.html)
*Based on student membership. Includes salaries, benefits, services, and supplies. For this per pupil calculation, Census has excluded expenditures for adult education, community services, and other nonelementary-secondary programs.

Percent Change in Per Pupil Public Elementary and Secondary School Current Expenditures: 2002 to 2006 (Adjusted for Inflation)
National Percent Change = 5.8% Increase*

ALPHA ORDER

RANK	STATE	PERCENT CHANGE
17	Alabama	11.5
26	Alaska	6.6
32	Arizona	4.5
5	Arkansas	15.5
44	California	0.7
33	Colorado	4.3
19	Connecticut	9.9
15	Delaware	11.9
10	Florida	14.2
34	Georgia	4.0
1	Hawaii	21.4
50	Idaho	(3.1)
41	Illinois	1.7
36	Indiana	3.4
40	Iowa	2.0
27	Kansas	6.1
30	Kentucky	5.2
7	Louisiana	14.9
13	Maine	13.0
16	Maryland	11.8
23	Massachusetts	8.4
45	Michigan	0.5
28	Minnesota	5.9
2	Mississippi	19.6
38	Missouri	3.0
21	Montana	8.9
31	Nebraska	5.0
22	Nevada	8.5
4	New Hampshire	15.9
11	New Jersey	14.0
20	New Mexico	9.1
7	New York	14.9
43	North Carolina	1.2
11	North Dakota	14.0
29	Ohio	5.6
48	Oklahoma	(0.8)
46	Oregon	0.0
18	Pennsylvania	11.2
9	Rhode Island	14.3
37	South Carolina	3.3
24	South Dakota	7.9
39	Tennessee	2.5
47	Texas	(0.1)
49	Utah	(0.9)
3	Vermont	16.2
14	Virginia	12.3
42	Washington	1.3
25	West Virginia	7.6
35	Wisconsin	3.7
6	Wyoming	15.2

RANK ORDER

RANK	STATE	PERCENT CHANGE
1	Hawaii	21.4
2	Mississippi	19.6
3	Vermont	16.2
4	New Hampshire	15.9
5	Arkansas	15.5
6	Wyoming	15.2
7	Louisiana	14.9
7	New York	14.9
9	Rhode Island	14.3
10	Florida	14.2
11	New Jersey	14.0
11	North Dakota	14.0
13	Maine	13.0
14	Virginia	12.3
15	Delaware	11.9
16	Maryland	11.8
17	Alabama	11.5
18	Pennsylvania	11.2
19	Connecticut	9.9
20	New Mexico	9.1
21	Montana	8.9
22	Nevada	8.5
23	Massachusetts	8.4
24	South Dakota	7.9
25	West Virginia	7.6
26	Alaska	6.6
27	Kansas	6.1
28	Minnesota	5.9
29	Ohio	5.6
30	Kentucky	5.2
31	Nebraska	5.0
32	Arizona	4.5
33	Colorado	4.3
34	Georgia	4.0
35	Wisconsin	3.7
36	Indiana	3.4
37	South Carolina	3.3
38	Missouri	3.0
39	Tennessee	2.5
40	Iowa	2.0
41	Illinois	1.7
42	Washington	1.3
43	North Carolina	1.2
44	California	0.7
45	Michigan	0.5
46	Oregon	0.0
47	Texas	(0.1)
48	Oklahoma	(0.8)
49	Utah	(0.9)
50	Idaho	(3.1)
	District of Columbia	(9.1)

Source: CQ Press using data from U.S. Bureau of the Census, Governments Division
   "Public Education Finances: 2006 and 2002" (http://www.census.gov/govs/www/school.html)
*School years 2005-2006 and 2001-2002. Adjusted for inflation to 2006 dollars using 1982-1984 as the index base period.

Percent Change in Per Pupil Public Elementary and Secondary School Current Expenditures: 1997 to 2006 (Adjusted for Inflation)
National Percent Change = 23.6% Increase*

ALPHA ORDER

RANK	STATE	PERCENT CHANGE
12	Alabama	32.9
49	Alaska	11.0
35	Arizona	18.8
9	Arkansas	37.1
18	California	28.4
30	Colorado	22.0
29	Connecticut	22.5
16	Delaware	30.7
36	Florida	18.3
20	Georgia	27.3
11	Hawaii	36.0
42	Idaho	16.0
24	Illinois	24.3
41	Indiana	16.2
40	Iowa	16.5
33	Kansas	20.1
37	Kentucky	18.0
3	Louisiana	44.8
13	Maine	32.5
22	Maryland	25.8
13	Massachusetts	32.5
48	Michigan	11.4
43	Minnesota	15.9
5	Mississippi	42.3
26	Missouri	23.3
23	Montana	25.2
31	Nebraska	21.4
44	Nevada	15.1
10	New Hampshire	36.8
27	New Jersey	23.0
7	New Mexico	38.7
6	New York	39.8
34	North Carolina	19.2
4	North Dakota	42.5
17	Ohio	29.5
39	Oklahoma	16.7
47	Oregon	12.1
28	Pennsylvania	22.6
21	Rhode Island	26.8
19	South Carolina	28.1
8	South Dakota	38.6
32	Tennessee	21.1
45	Texas	14.2
46	Utah	13.5
1	Vermont	49.7
15	Virginia	31.5
50	Washington	8.2
25	West Virginia	23.6
38	Wisconsin	17.7
2	Wyoming	49.3

RANK ORDER

RANK	STATE	PERCENT CHANGE
1	Vermont	49.7
2	Wyoming	49.3
3	Louisiana	44.8
4	North Dakota	42.5
5	Mississippi	42.3
6	New York	39.8
7	New Mexico	38.7
8	South Dakota	38.6
9	Arkansas	37.1
10	New Hampshire	36.8
11	Hawaii	36.0
12	Alabama	32.9
13	Maine	32.5
13	Massachusetts	32.5
15	Virginia	31.5
16	Delaware	30.7
17	Ohio	29.5
18	California	28.4
19	South Carolina	28.1
20	Georgia	27.3
21	Rhode Island	26.8
22	Maryland	25.8
23	Montana	25.2
24	Illinois	24.3
25	West Virginia	23.6
26	Missouri	23.3
27	New Jersey	23.0
28	Pennsylvania	22.6
29	Connecticut	22.5
30	Colorado	22.0
31	Nebraska	21.4
32	Tennessee	21.1
33	Kansas	20.1
34	North Carolina	19.2
35	Arizona	18.8
36	Florida	18.3
37	Kentucky	18.0
38	Wisconsin	17.7
39	Oklahoma	16.7
40	Iowa	16.5
41	Indiana	16.2
42	Idaho	16.0
43	Minnesota	15.9
44	Nevada	15.1
45	Texas	14.2
46	Utah	13.5
47	Oregon	12.1
48	Michigan	11.4
49	Alaska	11.0
50	Washington	8.2

	District of Columbia	32.9

Source: CQ Press using data from U.S. Bureau of the Census, Governments Division
"Public Education Finances: 2006 and 1997" (http://www.census.gov/govs/www/school.html)
*School years 2005-2006 and 1996-1997. Adjusted for inflation to 2006 dollars using 1982-1984 as the index base period.

Public Elementary and Secondary School
Current Expenditures as a Percent of Total Expenditures in 2006
National Percent = 85.7%*

ALPHA ORDER

RANK	STATE	PERCENT
24	Alabama	88.0
39	Alaska	84.2
41	Arizona	82.7
28	Arkansas	87.3
41	California	82.7
44	Colorado	82.5
11	Connecticut	90.4
38	Delaware	84.6
48	Florida	79.4
30	Georgia	86.7
2	Hawaii	96.1
27	Idaho	87.6
25	Illinois	87.9
44	Indiana	82.5
36	Iowa	85.9
21	Kansas	88.4
34	Kentucky	86.2
9	Louisiana	90.7
5	Maine	92.9
19	Maryland	88.8
7	Massachusetts	91.0
35	Michigan	86.1
40	Minnesota	83.8
22	Mississippi	88.1
20	Missouri	88.5
6	Montana	91.8
22	Nebraska	88.1
50	Nevada	75.8
15	New Hampshire	89.5
15	New Jersey	89.5
33	New Mexico	86.4
17	New York	89.3
25	North Carolina	87.9
18	North Dakota	88.9
32	Ohio	86.6
10	Oklahoma	90.5
13	Oregon	89.8
29	Pennsylvania	87.0
1	Rhode Island	96.9
47	South Carolina	80.6
14	South Dakota	89.7
12	Tennessee	90.2
49	Texas	78.5
41	Utah	82.7
3	Vermont	94.3
30	Virginia	86.7
46	Washington	82.1
4	West Virginia	93.0
8	Wisconsin	90.9
37	Wyoming	84.9

RANK ORDER

RANK	STATE	PERCENT
1	Rhode Island	96.9
2	Hawaii	96.1
3	Vermont	94.3
4	West Virginia	93.0
5	Maine	92.9
6	Montana	91.8
7	Massachusetts	91.0
8	Wisconsin	90.9
9	Louisiana	90.7
10	Oklahoma	90.5
11	Connecticut	90.4
12	Tennessee	90.2
13	Oregon	89.8
14	South Dakota	89.7
15	New Hampshire	89.5
15	New Jersey	89.5
17	New York	89.3
18	North Dakota	88.9
19	Maryland	88.8
20	Missouri	88.5
21	Kansas	88.4
22	Mississippi	88.1
22	Nebraska	88.1
24	Alabama	88.0
25	Illinois	87.9
25	North Carolina	87.9
27	Idaho	87.6
28	Arkansas	87.3
29	Pennsylvania	87.0
30	Georgia	86.7
30	Virginia	86.7
32	Ohio	86.6
33	New Mexico	86.4
34	Kentucky	86.2
35	Michigan	86.1
36	Iowa	85.9
37	Wyoming	84.9
38	Delaware	84.6
39	Alaska	84.2
40	Minnesota	83.8
41	Arizona	82.7
41	California	82.7
41	Utah	82.7
44	Colorado	82.5
44	Indiana	82.5
46	Washington	82.1
47	South Carolina	80.6
48	Florida	79.4
49	Texas	78.5
50	Nevada	75.8

	District of Columbia	88.2

Source: CQ Press using data from U.S. Bureau of the Census, Governments Division
"Public Education Finances: 2006" (http://www.census.gov/govs/www/school06.html)
*Includes salaries, benefits, services, and supplies. Census expanded its usual "current expenditures" concept for education finance reports to include all current public elementary and secondary education outlays regardless of the specific unit of government that actually makes the expenditure.

Public Elementary and Secondary School Capital Expenditures in 2006

National Total = $58,808,961,000*

ALPHA ORDER

RANK	STATE	EXPENDITURES	% of USA
24	Alabama	$666,550,000	1.1%
38	Alaska	236,931,000	0.4%
13	Arizona	1,143,569,000	1.9%
31	Arkansas	449,548,000	0.8%
1	California	10,047,331,000	17.1%
18	Colorado	1,024,225,000	1.7%
25	Connecticut	603,391,000	1.0%
39	Delaware	227,679,000	0.4%
3	Florida	4,860,930,000	8.3%
9	Georgia	1,930,006,000	3.3%
48	Hawaii	74,988,000	0.1%
41	Idaho	189,807,000	0.3%
7	Illinois	2,021,097,000	3.4%
19	Indiana	985,099,000	1.7%
26	Iowa	592,789,000	1.0%
35	Kansas	358,866,000	0.6%
23	Kentucky	686,124,000	1.2%
30	Louisiana	454,736,000	0.8%
44	Maine	115,871,000	0.2%
17	Maryland	1,037,525,000	1.8%
20	Massachusetts	904,979,000	1.5%
10	Michigan	1,842,154,000	3.1%
15	Minnesota	1,063,443,000	1.8%
33	Mississippi	413,302,000	0.7%
22	Missouri	758,141,000	1.3%
45	Montana	97,873,000	0.2%
37	Nebraska	280,954,000	0.5%
21	Nevada	760,380,000	1.3%
40	New Hampshire	201,565,000	0.3%
6	New Jersey	2,033,738,000	3.5%
34	New Mexico	385,590,000	0.7%
4	New York	3,970,683,000	6.8%
16	North Carolina	1,052,527,000	1.8%
46	North Dakota	92,963,000	0.2%
5	Ohio	2,177,340,000	3.7%
32	Oklahoma	436,567,000	0.7%
36	Oregon	319,231,000	0.5%
8	Pennsylvania	2,009,924,000	3.4%
50	Rhode Island	28,706,000	0.0%
14	South Carolina	1,128,702,000	1.9%
47	South Dakota	86,227,000	0.1%
27	Tennessee	573,015,000	1.0%
2	Texas	6,170,544,000	10.5%
29	Utah	504,723,000	0.9%
49	Vermont	59,192,000	0.1%
12	Virginia	1,298,749,000	2.2%
11	Washington	1,422,488,000	2.4%
42	West Virginia	187,462,000	0.3%
28	Wisconsin	545,716,000	0.9%
43	Wyoming	168,214,000	0.3%

RANK ORDER

RANK	STATE	EXPENDITURES	% of USA
1	California	$10,047,331,000	17.1%
2	Texas	6,170,544,000	10.5%
3	Florida	4,860,930,000	8.3%
4	New York	3,970,683,000	6.8%
5	Ohio	2,177,340,000	3.7%
6	New Jersey	2,033,738,000	3.5%
7	Illinois	2,021,097,000	3.4%
8	Pennsylvania	2,009,924,000	3.4%
9	Georgia	1,930,006,000	3.3%
10	Michigan	1,842,154,000	3.1%
11	Washington	1,422,488,000	2.4%
12	Virginia	1,298,749,000	2.2%
13	Arizona	1,143,569,000	1.9%
14	South Carolina	1,128,702,000	1.9%
15	Minnesota	1,063,443,000	1.8%
16	North Carolina	1,052,527,000	1.8%
17	Maryland	1,037,525,000	1.8%
18	Colorado	1,024,225,000	1.7%
19	Indiana	985,099,000	1.7%
20	Massachusetts	904,979,000	1.5%
21	Nevada	760,380,000	1.3%
22	Missouri	758,141,000	1.3%
23	Kentucky	686,124,000	1.2%
24	Alabama	666,550,000	1.1%
25	Connecticut	603,391,000	1.0%
26	Iowa	592,789,000	1.0%
27	Tennessee	573,015,000	1.0%
28	Wisconsin	545,716,000	0.9%
29	Utah	504,723,000	0.9%
30	Louisiana	454,736,000	0.8%
31	Arkansas	449,548,000	0.8%
32	Oklahoma	436,567,000	0.7%
33	Mississippi	413,302,000	0.7%
34	New Mexico	385,590,000	0.7%
35	Kansas	358,866,000	0.6%
36	Oregon	319,231,000	0.5%
37	Nebraska	280,954,000	0.5%
38	Alaska	236,931,000	0.4%
39	Delaware	227,679,000	0.4%
40	New Hampshire	201,565,000	0.3%
41	Idaho	189,807,000	0.3%
42	West Virginia	187,462,000	0.3%
43	Wyoming	168,214,000	0.3%
44	Maine	115,871,000	0.2%
45	Montana	97,873,000	0.2%
46	North Dakota	92,963,000	0.2%
47	South Dakota	86,227,000	0.1%
48	Hawaii	74,988,000	0.1%
49	Vermont	59,192,000	0.1%
50	Rhode Island	28,706,000	0.0%
	District of Columbia	126,807,000	0.2%

Source: U.S. Bureau of the Census, Governments Division
  "Public Education Finances: 2006" (http://www.census.gov/govs/www/school06.html)
*Includes expenditures for construction of buildings, roads and other improvements, purchases of equipment, land, structures, and payments for capital leases. Includes amounts for additions, replacements, and major alterations to structures, however, maintenance and repairs to such structures are considered current operation expenditures.

Per Capita Public Elementary and Secondary School Capital Expenditures in 2006
National Per Capita = $197*

ALPHA ORDER

RANK	STATE	PER CAPITA
32	Alabama	$145
1	Alaska	350
19	Arizona	185
26	Arkansas	160
4	California	277
11	Colorado	215
22	Connecticut	173
6	Delaware	267
5	Florida	269
12	Georgia	207
49	Hawaii	59
35	Idaho	130
28	Illinois	158
29	Indiana	156
15	Iowa	199
35	Kansas	130
24	Kentucky	163
41	Louisiana	107
47	Maine	88
19	Maryland	185
34	Massachusetts	141
21	Michigan	182
13	Minnesota	206
33	Mississippi	143
35	Missouri	130
43	Montana	103
27	Nebraska	159
3	Nevada	305
30	New Hampshire	154
9	New Jersey	235
15	New Mexico	199
13	New York	206
39	North Carolina	119
31	North Dakota	146
18	Ohio	190
38	Oklahoma	122
48	Oregon	86
25	Pennsylvania	162
50	Rhode Island	27
8	South Carolina	261
40	South Dakota	109
46	Tennessee	94
7	Texas	264
17	Utah	196
45	Vermont	95
23	Virginia	170
10	Washington	223
42	West Virginia	104
44	Wisconsin	98
2	Wyoming	328

RANK ORDER

RANK	STATE	PER CAPITA
1	Alaska	$350
2	Wyoming	328
3	Nevada	305
4	California	277
5	Florida	269
6	Delaware	267
7	Texas	264
8	South Carolina	261
9	New Jersey	235
10	Washington	223
11	Colorado	215
12	Georgia	207
13	Minnesota	206
13	New York	206
15	Iowa	199
15	New Mexico	199
17	Utah	196
18	Ohio	190
19	Arizona	185
19	Maryland	185
21	Michigan	182
22	Connecticut	173
23	Virginia	170
24	Kentucky	163
25	Pennsylvania	162
26	Arkansas	160
27	Nebraska	159
28	Illinois	158
29	Indiana	156
30	New Hampshire	154
31	North Dakota	146
32	Alabama	145
33	Mississippi	143
34	Massachusetts	141
35	Idaho	130
35	Kansas	130
35	Missouri	130
38	Oklahoma	122
39	North Carolina	119
40	South Dakota	109
41	Louisiana	107
42	West Virginia	104
43	Montana	103
44	Wisconsin	98
45	Vermont	95
46	Tennessee	94
47	Maine	88
48	Oregon	86
49	Hawaii	59
50	Rhode Island	27

District of Columbia — 217

Source: CQ Press using data from U.S. Bureau of the Census, Governments Division
"Public Education Finances: 2006" (http://www.census.gov/govs/www/school06.html)
*Includes expenditures for construction of buildings, roads and other improvements, purchases of equipment, land, structures, and payments for capital leases. Includes amounts for additions, replacements, and major alterations to structures, however, maintenance and repairs to such structures are considered current operation expenditures.

Per Pupil Elementary and Secondary School
Capital Expenditures in 2006
National Per Pupil = 1,216*

ALPHA ORDER

RANK	STATE	PER PUPIL
33	Alabama	$897
5	Alaska	1,783
20	Arizona	1,139
31	Arkansas	951
7	California	1,606
12	Colorado	1,314
21	Connecticut	1,084
1	Delaware	1,991
4	Florida	1,825
16	Georgia	1,208
49	Hawaii	410
38	Idaho	735
28	Illinois	961
29	Indiana	960
15	Iowa	1,226
36	Kansas	770
25	Kentucky	1,010
40	Louisiana	701
47	Maine	594
17	Maryland	1,206
30	Massachusetts	953
23	Michigan	1,065
13	Minnesota	1,300
34	Mississippi	837
35	Missouri	828
42	Montana	674
27	Nebraska	982
3	Nevada	1,842
26	New Hampshire	1,003
8	New Jersey	1,474
18	New Mexico	1,180
9	New York	1,425
37	North Carolina	758
32	North Dakota	947
14	Ohio	1,231
41	Oklahoma	688
48	Oregon	573
19	Pennsylvania	1,142
50	Rhode Island	191
6	South Carolina	1,615
39	South Dakota	708
46	Tennessee	601
10	Texas	1,387
24	Utah	1,017
44	Vermont	641
22	Virginia	1,070
11	Washington	1,379
43	West Virginia	670
45	Wisconsin	628
2	Wyoming	1,952

RANK ORDER

RANK	STATE	PER PUPIL
1	Delaware	$1,991
2	Wyoming	1,952
3	Nevada	1,842
4	Florida	1,825
5	Alaska	1,783
6	South Carolina	1,615
7	California	1,606
8	New Jersey	1,474
9	New York	1,425
10	Texas	1,387
11	Washington	1,379
12	Colorado	1,314
13	Minnesota	1,300
14	Ohio	1,231
15	Iowa	1,226
16	Georgia	1,208
17	Maryland	1,206
18	New Mexico	1,180
19	Pennsylvania	1,142
20	Arizona	1,139
21	Connecticut	1,084
22	Virginia	1,070
23	Michigan	1,065
24	Utah	1,017
25	Kentucky	1,010
26	New Hampshire	1,003
27	Nebraska	982
28	Illinois	961
29	Indiana	960
30	Massachusetts	953
31	Arkansas	951
32	North Dakota	947
33	Alabama	897
34	Mississippi	837
35	Missouri	828
36	Kansas	770
37	North Carolina	758
38	Idaho	735
39	South Dakota	708
40	Louisiana	701
41	Oklahoma	688
42	Montana	674
43	West Virginia	670
44	Vermont	641
45	Wisconsin	628
46	Tennessee	601
47	Maine	594
48	Oregon	573
49	Hawaii	410
50	Rhode Island	191

| | District of Columbia | 2,127 |

Source: CQ Press using data from U.S. Bureau of the Census, Governments Division
  "Public Education Finances: 2006" (http://www.census.gov/govs/www/school06.html)
*Based on student membership. Includes expenditures for construction of buildings, roads and other improvements, purchases of equipment, land, structures, and payments for capital leases. Includes amounts for additions, replacements, and major alterations to structures, however, maintenance and repairs to such structures are considered current operation expenditures.

Public Elementary and Secondary School
Capital Expenditures as a Percent of Total Expenditures in 2006
National Percent = 11.2%*

ALPHA ORDER

RANK	STATE	PERCENT
21	Alabama	10.1
12	Alaska	13.0
7	Arizona	14.4
19	Arkansas	10.4
4	California	15.2
11	Colorado	13.2
40	Connecticut	7.7
9	Delaware	14.3
2	Florida	18.3
15	Georgia	12.2
49	Hawaii	3.9
22	Idaho	10.0
28	Illinois	9.2
30	Indiana	8.9
13	Iowa	12.5
38	Kansas	8.1
17	Kentucky	11.2
41	Louisiana	7.5
47	Maine	5.0
22	Maryland	10.0
43	Massachusetts	6.9
27	Michigan	9.4
16	Minnesota	11.4
20	Mississippi	10.2
30	Missouri	8.9
42	Montana	7.2
24	Nebraska	9.9
1	Nevada	18.9
34	New Hampshire	8.6
33	New Jersey	8.7
13	New Mexico	12.5
36	New York	8.3
29	North Carolina	9.0
26	North Dakota	9.7
18	Ohio	10.7
34	Oklahoma	8.6
45	Oregon	5.9
30	Pennsylvania	8.9
50	Rhode Island	1.5
3	South Carolina	15.8
36	South Dakota	8.3
39	Tennessee	7.8
9	Texas	14.3
5	Utah	15.0
48	Vermont	4.6
25	Virginia	9.8
7	Washington	14.4
44	West Virginia	6.6
46	Wisconsin	5.7
6	Wyoming	14.8

RANK ORDER

RANK	STATE	PERCENT
1	Nevada	18.9
2	Florida	18.3
3	South Carolina	15.8
4	California	15.2
5	Utah	15.0
6	Wyoming	14.8
7	Arizona	14.4
7	Washington	14.4
9	Delaware	14.3
9	Texas	14.3
11	Colorado	13.2
12	Alaska	13.0
13	Iowa	12.5
13	New Mexico	12.5
15	Georgia	12.2
16	Minnesota	11.4
17	Kentucky	11.2
18	Ohio	10.7
19	Arkansas	10.4
20	Mississippi	10.2
21	Alabama	10.1
22	Idaho	10.0
22	Maryland	10.0
24	Nebraska	9.9
25	Virginia	9.8
26	North Dakota	9.7
27	Michigan	9.4
28	Illinois	9.2
29	North Carolina	9.0
30	Indiana	8.9
30	Missouri	8.9
30	Pennsylvania	8.9
33	New Jersey	8.7
34	New Hampshire	8.6
34	Oklahoma	8.6
36	New York	8.3
36	South Dakota	8.3
38	Kansas	8.1
39	Tennessee	7.8
40	Connecticut	7.7
41	Louisiana	7.5
42	Montana	7.2
43	Massachusetts	6.9
44	West Virginia	6.6
45	Oregon	5.9
46	Wisconsin	5.7
47	Maine	5.0
48	Vermont	4.6
49	Hawaii	3.9
50	Rhode Island	1.5
	District of Columbia	11.8

Source: CQ Press using data from U.S. Bureau of the Census, Governments Division
"Public Education Finances: 2006" (http://www.census.gov/govs/www/school06.html)
*Includes expenditures for construction of buildings, roads and other improvements, purchases of equipment, land, structures, and payments for capital leases. Includes amounts for additions, replacements, and major alterations to structures, however, maintenance and repairs to such structures are considered current operation expenditures.

Public Elementary and Secondary School "Other" Expenditures in 2006

National Total = $16,351,732,000*

ALPHA ORDER

RANK	STATE	EXPENDITURES	% of USA
28	Alabama	$124,631,000	0.8%
36	Alaska	50,057,000	0.3%
20	Arizona	227,377,000	1.4%
31	Arkansas	101,901,000	0.6%
2	California	1,421,856,000	8.7%
15	Colorado	332,500,000	2.0%
27	Connecticut	146,053,000	0.9%
44	Delaware	17,856,000	0.1%
8	Florida	607,281,000	3.7%
23	Georgia	171,743,000	1.1%
50	Hawaii	0	0.0%
38	Idaho	46,080,000	0.3%
7	Illinois	642,869,000	3.9%
4	Indiana	943,937,000	5.8%
33	Iowa	76,128,000	0.5%
25	Kansas	153,552,000	0.9%
24	Kentucky	156,000,000	1.0%
30	Louisiana	104,289,000	0.6%
37	Maine	46,668,000	0.3%
29	Maryland	118,883,000	0.7%
17	Massachusetts	283,208,000	1.7%
6	Michigan	884,564,000	5.4%
11	Minnesota	455,502,000	2.8%
34	Mississippi	69,481,000	0.4%
19	Missouri	229,839,000	1.4%
45	Montana	14,210,000	0.1%
35	Nebraska	55,882,000	0.3%
22	Nevada	210,477,000	1.3%
40	New Hampshire	43,238,000	0.3%
12	New Jersey	438,341,000	2.7%
41	New Mexico	35,437,000	0.2%
3	New York	1,155,311,000	7.1%
13	North Carolina	366,839,000	2.2%
47	North Dakota	13,306,000	0.1%
9	Ohio	560,164,000	3.4%
39	Oklahoma	44,494,000	0.3%
21	Oregon	226,217,000	1.4%
5	Pennsylvania	926,229,000	5.7%
42	Rhode Island	31,329,000	0.2%
18	South Carolina	254,732,000	1.6%
43	South Dakota	20,722,000	0.1%
26	Tennessee	151,619,000	0.9%
1	Texas	3,136,640,000	19.2%
32	Utah	78,568,000	0.5%
46	Vermont	14,206,000	0.1%
10	Virginia	474,693,000	2.9%
14	Washington	343,870,000	2.1%
48	West Virginia	12,248,000	0.1%
16	Wisconsin	327,191,000	2.0%
49	Wyoming	3,514,000	0.0%

RANK ORDER

RANK	STATE	EXPENDITURES	% of USA
1	Texas	$3,136,640,000	19.2%
2	California	1,421,856,000	8.7%
3	New York	1,155,311,000	7.1%
4	Indiana	943,937,000	5.8%
5	Pennsylvania	926,229,000	5.7%
6	Michigan	884,564,000	5.4%
7	Illinois	642,869,000	3.9%
8	Florida	607,281,000	3.7%
9	Ohio	560,164,000	3.4%
10	Virginia	474,693,000	2.9%
11	Minnesota	455,502,000	2.8%
12	New Jersey	438,341,000	2.7%
13	North Carolina	366,839,000	2.2%
14	Washington	343,870,000	2.1%
15	Colorado	332,500,000	2.0%
16	Wisconsin	327,191,000	2.0%
17	Massachusetts	283,208,000	1.7%
18	South Carolina	254,732,000	1.6%
19	Missouri	229,839,000	1.4%
20	Arizona	227,377,000	1.4%
21	Oregon	226,217,000	1.4%
22	Nevada	210,477,000	1.3%
23	Georgia	171,743,000	1.1%
24	Kentucky	156,000,000	1.0%
25	Kansas	153,552,000	0.9%
26	Tennessee	151,619,000	0.9%
27	Connecticut	146,053,000	0.9%
28	Alabama	124,631,000	0.8%
29	Maryland	118,883,000	0.7%
30	Louisiana	104,289,000	0.6%
31	Arkansas	101,901,000	0.6%
32	Utah	78,568,000	0.5%
33	Iowa	76,128,000	0.5%
34	Mississippi	69,481,000	0.4%
35	Nebraska	55,882,000	0.3%
36	Alaska	50,057,000	0.3%
37	Maine	46,668,000	0.3%
38	Idaho	46,080,000	0.3%
39	Oklahoma	44,494,000	0.3%
40	New Hampshire	43,238,000	0.3%
41	New Mexico	35,437,000	0.2%
42	Rhode Island	31,329,000	0.2%
43	South Dakota	20,722,000	0.1%
44	Delaware	17,856,000	0.1%
45	Montana	14,210,000	0.1%
46	Vermont	14,206,000	0.1%
47	North Dakota	13,306,000	0.1%
48	West Virginia	12,248,000	0.1%
49	Wyoming	3,514,000	0.0%
50	Hawaii	0	0.0%
	District of Columbia	0	0.0%

Source: U.S. Bureau of the Census, Governments Division
   "Public Education Finances: 2006" (http://www.census.gov/govs/www/school06.html)
*Current spending for other than elementary-secondary education instruction and support services activities. This includes food services, enterprise operations, community services (e.g. swimming pools and libraries), and adult education.

Per Capita Public Elementary and Secondary School "Other" Expenditures in 2006
National Per Capita = $54.73*

ALPHA ORDER

RANK	STATE	PER CAPITA
34	Alabama	$27.15
7	Alaska	73.89
25	Arizona	36.88
26	Arkansas	36.28
23	California	39.22
8	Colorado	69.76
20	Connecticut	41.78
42	Delaware	20.94
28	Florida	33.63
44	Georgia	18.38
50	Hawaii	0.00
31	Idaho	31.48
17	Illinois	50.31
1	Indiana	149.77
36	Iowa	25.61
14	Kansas	55.72
24	Kentucky	37.10
38	Louisiana	24.58
27	Maine	35.49
41	Maryland	21.22
19	Massachusetts	44.01
4	Michigan	87.56
3	Minnesota	88.37
39	Mississippi	23.97
22	Missouri	39.37
46	Montana	15.01
30	Nebraska	31.68
5	Nevada	84.45
29	New Hampshire	32.96
16	New Jersey	50.58
45	New Mexico	18.24
11	New York	59.92
21	North Carolina	41.36
43	North Dakota	20.87
18	Ohio	48.86
47	Oklahoma	12.44
10	Oregon	61.29
6	Pennsylvania	74.68
33	Rhode Island	29.51
12	South Carolina	58.83
35	South Dakota	26.28
37	Tennessee	24.96
2	Texas	134.00
32	Utah	30.46
40	Vermont	22.88
9	Virginia	62.13
15	Washington	53.94
49	West Virginia	6.77
13	Wisconsin	58.71
48	Wyoming	6.85

RANK ORDER

RANK	STATE	PER CAPITA
1	Indiana	$149.77
2	Texas	134.00
3	Minnesota	88.37
4	Michigan	87.56
5	Nevada	84.45
6	Pennsylvania	74.68
7	Alaska	73.89
8	Colorado	69.76
9	Virginia	62.13
10	Oregon	61.29
11	New York	59.92
12	South Carolina	58.83
13	Wisconsin	58.71
14	Kansas	55.72
15	Washington	53.94
16	New Jersey	50.58
17	Illinois	50.31
18	Ohio	48.86
19	Massachusetts	44.01
20	Connecticut	41.78
21	North Carolina	41.36
22	Missouri	39.37
23	California	39.22
24	Kentucky	37.10
25	Arizona	36.88
26	Arkansas	36.28
27	Maine	35.49
28	Florida	33.63
29	New Hampshire	32.96
30	Nebraska	31.68
31	Idaho	31.48
32	Utah	30.46
33	Rhode Island	29.51
34	Alabama	27.15
35	South Dakota	26.28
36	Iowa	25.61
37	Tennessee	24.96
38	Louisiana	24.58
39	Mississippi	23.97
40	Vermont	22.88
41	Maryland	21.22
42	Delaware	20.94
43	North Dakota	20.87
44	Georgia	18.38
45	New Mexico	18.24
46	Montana	15.01
47	Oklahoma	12.44
48	Wyoming	6.85
49	West Virginia	6.77
50	Hawaii	0.00
	District of Columbia	0.00

Source: CQ Press using data from U.S. Bureau of the Census, Governments Division
  "Public Education Finances: 2006" (http://www.census.gov/govs/www/school06.html)
*Current spending for other than elementary-secondary education instruction and support services activities. This includes food services, enterprise operations, community services (e.g. swimming pools and libraries), and adult education.

Per Pupil Elementary and Secondary School
"Other" Expenditures in 2006
National Per Pupil = $338*

ALPHA ORDER

RANK	STATE	PER PUPIL
34	Alabama	$168
11	Alaska	377
27	Arizona	226
28	Arkansas	216
26	California	227
7	Colorado	427
21	Connecticut	262
39	Delaware	156
25	Florida	228
45	Georgia	107
50	Hawaii	0
32	Idaho	178
18	Illinois	306
1	Indiana	920
38	Iowa	157
15	Kansas	330
24	Kentucky	230
35	Louisiana	161
23	Maine	239
42	Maryland	138
19	Massachusetts	298
5	Michigan	512
3	Minnesota	557
41	Mississippi	141
22	Missouri	251
46	Montana	98
31	Nebraska	195
6	Nevada	510
29	New Hampshire	215
16	New Jersey	318
44	New Mexico	108
8	New York	414
20	North Carolina	264
43	North Dakota	136
17	Ohio	317
47	Oklahoma	70
9	Oregon	406
4	Pennsylvania	526
30	Rhode Island	209
13	South Carolina	364
33	South Dakota	170
36	Tennessee	159
2	Texas	705
37	Utah	158
40	Vermont	154
10	Virginia	391
14	Washington	333
48	West Virginia	44
12	Wisconsin	376
49	Wyoming	41

RANK ORDER

RANK	STATE	PER PUPIL
1	Indiana	$920
2	Texas	705
3	Minnesota	557
4	Pennsylvania	526
5	Michigan	512
6	Nevada	510
7	Colorado	427
8	New York	414
9	Oregon	406
10	Virginia	391
11	Alaska	377
12	Wisconsin	376
13	South Carolina	364
14	Washington	333
15	Kansas	330
16	New Jersey	318
17	Ohio	317
18	Illinois	306
19	Massachusetts	298
20	North Carolina	264
21	Connecticut	262
22	Missouri	251
23	Maine	239
24	Kentucky	230
25	Florida	228
26	California	227
27	Arizona	226
28	Arkansas	216
29	New Hampshire	215
30	Rhode Island	209
31	Nebraska	195
32	Idaho	178
33	South Dakota	170
34	Alabama	168
35	Louisiana	161
36	Tennessee	159
37	Utah	158
38	Iowa	157
39	Delaware	156
40	Vermont	154
41	Mississippi	141
42	Maryland	138
43	North Dakota	136
44	New Mexico	108
45	Georgia	107
46	Montana	98
47	Oklahoma	70
48	West Virginia	44
49	Wyoming	41
50	Hawaii	0
	District of Columbia	0

Source: CQ Press using data from U.S. Bureau of the Census, Governments Division
"Public Education Finances: 2006" (http://www.census.gov/govs/www/school06.html)
*Based on student membership. Current spending for other than elementary-secondary education instruction and support services activities. This includes food services, enterprise operations, community services (e.g. swimming pools and libraries), and adult education.

Public Elementary and Secondary School
"Other" Expenditures as a Percent of Total Expenditures in 2006
National Percent = 3.1%*

ALPHA ORDER

RANK	STATE	PERCENT
32	Alabama	1.9
17	Alaska	2.8
15	Arizona	2.9
21	Arkansas	2.4
26	California	2.1
6	Colorado	4.3
32	Connecticut	1.9
41	Delaware	1.1
24	Florida	2.3
41	Georgia	1.1
50	Hawaii	0.0
21	Idaho	2.4
15	Illinois	2.9
1	Indiana	8.6
38	Iowa	1.6
11	Kansas	3.5
20	Kentucky	2.6
36	Louisiana	1.7
29	Maine	2.0
41	Maryland	1.1
26	Massachusetts	2.1
5	Michigan	4.5
4	Minnesota	4.9
36	Mississippi	1.7
18	Missouri	2.7
46	Montana	1.0
29	Nebraska	2.0
3	Nevada	5.2
35	New Hampshire	1.8
32	New Jersey	1.9
41	New Mexico	1.1
21	New York	2.4
14	North Carolina	3.1
40	North Dakota	1.4
18	Ohio	2.7
47	Oklahoma	0.9
7	Oregon	4.2
8	Pennsylvania	4.1
38	Rhode Island	1.6
9	South Carolina	3.6
29	South Dakota	2.0
26	Tennessee	2.1
2	Texas	7.3
24	Utah	2.3
41	Vermont	1.1
9	Virginia	3.6
11	Washington	3.5
48	West Virginia	0.4
13	Wisconsin	3.4
49	Wyoming	0.3

RANK ORDER

RANK	STATE	PERCENT
1	Indiana	8.6
2	Texas	7.3
3	Nevada	5.2
4	Minnesota	4.9
5	Michigan	4.5
6	Colorado	4.3
7	Oregon	4.2
8	Pennsylvania	4.1
9	South Carolina	3.6
9	Virginia	3.6
11	Kansas	3.5
11	Washington	3.5
13	Wisconsin	3.4
14	North Carolina	3.1
15	Arizona	2.9
15	Illinois	2.9
17	Alaska	2.8
18	Missouri	2.7
18	Ohio	2.7
20	Kentucky	2.6
21	Arkansas	2.4
21	Idaho	2.4
21	New York	2.4
24	Florida	2.3
24	Utah	2.3
26	California	2.1
26	Massachusetts	2.1
26	Tennessee	2.1
29	Maine	2.0
29	Nebraska	2.0
29	South Dakota	2.0
32	Alabama	1.9
32	Connecticut	1.9
32	New Jersey	1.9
35	New Hampshire	1.8
36	Louisiana	1.7
36	Mississippi	1.7
38	Iowa	1.6
38	Rhode Island	1.6
40	North Dakota	1.4
41	Delaware	1.1
41	Georgia	1.1
41	Maryland	1.1
41	New Mexico	1.1
41	Vermont	1.1
46	Montana	1.0
47	Oklahoma	0.9
48	West Virginia	0.4
49	Wyoming	0.3
50	Hawaii	0.0
	District of Columbia	0.0

Source: CQ Press using data from U.S. Bureau of the Census, Governments Division
"Public Education Finances: 2006" (http://www.census.gov/govs/www/school06.html)
*Current spending for other than elementary-secondary education instruction and support services activities. This includes food services, enterprise operations, community services (e.g. swimming pools and libraries), and adult education.

Public Elementary and Secondary School Current Expenditures for Salaries, Wages, and Benefits in 2006
National Total = $360,804,839,000*

ALPHA ORDER

ALPHA ORDER

RANK	STATE	EXPENDITURES	% of USA
24	Alabama	$4,548,541,000	1.3%
44	Alaska	1,187,108,000	0.3%
22	Arizona	5,171,074,000	1.4%
32	Arkansas	2,938,498,000	0.8%
1	California	44,230,248,000	12.3%
23	Colorado	4,821,649,000	1.3%
20	Connecticut	5,782,403,000	1.6%
45	Delaware	1,068,017,000	0.3%
5	Florida	16,203,110,000	4.5%
10	Georgia	11,433,821,000	3.2%
42	Hawaii	1,459,620,000	0.4%
43	Idaho	1,382,906,000	0.4%
6	Illinois	15,412,755,000	4.3%
15	Indiana	7,633,755,000	2.1%
29	Iowa	3,391,104,000	0.9%
31	Kansas	2,988,560,000	0.8%
26	Kentucky	4,457,850,000	1.2%
27	Louisiana	4,336,438,000	1.2%
39	Maine	1,709,773,000	0.5%
14	Maryland	7,693,136,000	2.1%
12	Massachusetts	9,603,951,000	2.7%
9	Michigan	13,623,927,000	3.8%
18	Minnesota	6,241,649,000	1.7%
33	Mississippi	2,811,647,000	0.8%
19	Missouri	6,008,296,000	1.7%
46	Montana	943,716,000	0.3%
38	Nebraska	1,960,411,000	0.5%
34	Nevada	2,394,643,000	0.7%
40	New Hampshire	1,627,068,000	0.5%
4	New Jersey	16,406,913,000	4.5%
37	New Mexico	2,126,660,000	0.6%
2	New York	34,574,740,000	9.6%
13	North Carolina	8,484,426,000	2.4%
50	North Dakota	671,104,000	0.2%
8	Ohio	14,169,831,000	3.9%
30	Oklahoma	3,250,843,000	0.9%
28	Oregon	3,809,836,000	1.1%
7	Pennsylvania	15,170,350,000	4.2%
41	Rhode Island	1,520,395,000	0.4%
25	South Carolina	4,541,639,000	1.3%
49	South Dakota	707,764,000	0.2%
21	Tennessee	5,304,747,000	1.5%
3	Texas	26,487,327,000	7.3%
35	Utah	2,295,395,000	0.6%
47	Vermont	936,415,000	0.3%
11	Virginia	9,851,733,000	2.7%
17	Washington	6,692,875,000	1.9%
36	West Virginia	2,238,318,000	0.6%
16	Wisconsin	7,116,651,000	2.0%
48	Wyoming	788,948,000	0.2%

RANK ORDER

RANK	STATE	EXPENDITURES	% of USA
1	California	$44,230,248,000	12.3%
2	New York	34,574,740,000	9.6%
3	Texas	26,487,327,000	7.3%
4	New Jersey	16,406,913,000	4.5%
5	Florida	16,203,110,000	4.5%
6	Illinois	15,412,755,000	4.3%
7	Pennsylvania	15,170,350,000	4.2%
8	Ohio	14,169,831,000	3.9%
9	Michigan	13,623,927,000	3.8%
10	Georgia	11,433,821,000	3.2%
11	Virginia	9,851,733,000	2.7%
12	Massachusetts	9,603,951,000	2.7%
13	North Carolina	8,484,426,000	2.4%
14	Maryland	7,693,136,000	2.1%
15	Indiana	7,633,755,000	2.1%
16	Wisconsin	7,116,651,000	2.0%
17	Washington	6,692,875,000	1.9%
18	Minnesota	6,241,649,000	1.7%
19	Missouri	6,008,296,000	1.7%
20	Connecticut	5,782,403,000	1.6%
21	Tennessee	5,304,747,000	1.5%
22	Arizona	5,171,074,000	1.4%
23	Colorado	4,821,649,000	1.3%
24	Alabama	4,548,541,000	1.3%
25	South Carolina	4,541,639,000	1.3%
26	Kentucky	4,457,850,000	1.2%
27	Louisiana	4,336,438,000	1.2%
28	Oregon	3,809,836,000	1.1%
29	Iowa	3,391,104,000	0.9%
30	Oklahoma	3,250,843,000	0.9%
31	Kansas	2,988,560,000	0.8%
32	Arkansas	2,938,498,000	0.8%
33	Mississippi	2,811,647,000	0.8%
34	Nevada	2,394,643,000	0.7%
35	Utah	2,295,395,000	0.6%
36	West Virginia	2,238,318,000	0.6%
37	New Mexico	2,126,660,000	0.6%
38	Nebraska	1,960,411,000	0.5%
39	Maine	1,709,773,000	0.5%
40	New Hampshire	1,627,068,000	0.5%
41	Rhode Island	1,520,395,000	0.4%
42	Hawaii	1,459,620,000	0.4%
43	Idaho	1,382,906,000	0.4%
44	Alaska	1,187,108,000	0.3%
45	Delaware	1,068,017,000	0.3%
46	Montana	943,716,000	0.3%
47	Vermont	936,415,000	0.3%
48	Wyoming	788,948,000	0.2%
49	South Dakota	707,764,000	0.2%
50	North Dakota	671,104,000	0.2%
	District of Columbia	592,255,000	0.2%

Source: CQ Press using data from U.S. Bureau of the Census, Governments Division
"Public Education Finances: 2006" (http://www.census.gov/govs/www/school06.html)
*Current spending for compensation of school system officers and employees. Consists of gross compensation before deductions for withheld taxes, retirement contributions, or other purposes. Also includes benefits such as contributions on behalf of employees for retirement coverage, social security, group health and life insurance, tuition reimbursement, worker's compensation, and unemployment compensation.

Per Capita Public Elementary and Secondary School Current Expenditures for Salaries, Wages, and Benefits in 2006
National Per Capita = $1,208*

ALPHA ORDER

RANK	STATE	PER CAPITA
40	Alabama	$991
3	Alaska	1,752
50	Arizona	839
34	Arkansas	1,046
20	California	1,220
38	Colorado	1,012
4	Connecticut	1,654
14	Delaware	1,252
47	Florida	897
18	Georgia	1,224
24	Hawaii	1,142
44	Idaho	945
23	Illinois	1,206
21	Indiana	1,211
25	Iowa	1,141
29	Kansas	1,084
30	Kentucky	1,060
37	Louisiana	1,022
11	Maine	1,300
9	Maryland	1,373
7	Massachusetts	1,493
10	Michigan	1,349
21	Minnesota	1,211
41	Mississippi	970
36	Missouri	1,029
39	Montana	997
27	Nebraska	1,111
42	Nevada	961
15	New Hampshire	1,240
1	New Jersey	1,893
28	New Mexico	1,095
2	New York	1,793
43	North Carolina	957
31	North Dakota	1,053
17	Ohio	1,236
45	Oklahoma	909
35	Oregon	1,032
19	Pennsylvania	1,223
8	Rhode Island	1,432
33	South Carolina	1,049
46	South Dakota	898
49	Tennessee	873
26	Texas	1,132
48	Utah	890
6	Vermont	1,508
12	Virginia	1,289
32	Washington	1,050
16	West Virginia	1,238
13	Wisconsin	1,277
5	Wyoming	1,539

RANK ORDER

RANK	STATE	PER CAPITA
1	New Jersey	$1,893
2	New York	1,793
3	Alaska	1,752
4	Connecticut	1,654
5	Wyoming	1,539
6	Vermont	1,508
7	Massachusetts	1,493
8	Rhode Island	1,432
9	Maryland	1,373
10	Michigan	1,349
11	Maine	1,300
12	Virginia	1,289
13	Wisconsin	1,277
14	Delaware	1,252
15	New Hampshire	1,240
16	West Virginia	1,238
17	Ohio	1,236
18	Georgia	1,224
19	Pennsylvania	1,223
20	California	1,220
21	Indiana	1,211
21	Minnesota	1,211
23	Illinois	1,206
24	Hawaii	1,142
25	Iowa	1,141
26	Texas	1,132
27	Nebraska	1,111
28	New Mexico	1,095
29	Kansas	1,084
30	Kentucky	1,060
31	North Dakota	1,053
32	Washington	1,050
33	South Carolina	1,049
34	Arkansas	1,046
35	Oregon	1,032
36	Missouri	1,029
37	Louisiana	1,022
38	Colorado	1,012
39	Montana	997
40	Alabama	991
41	Mississippi	970
42	Nevada	961
43	North Carolina	957
44	Idaho	945
45	Oklahoma	909
46	South Dakota	898
47	Florida	897
48	Utah	890
49	Tennessee	873
50	Arizona	839

| | District of Columbia | 1,012 |

Source: CQ Press using data from U.S. Bureau of the Census, Governments Division
  "Public Education Finances: 2006" (http://www.census.gov/govs/www/school06.html)
*Current spending for compensation of school system officers and employees. Consists of gross compensation before deductions for withheld taxes, retirement contributions, or other purposes. Also includes benefits such as contributions on behalf of employees for retirement coverage, social security, group health and life insurance, tuition reimbursement, worker's compensation, and unemployment compensation.

Per Pupil Public Elementary and Secondary School Current Expenditures for Salaries, Wages, and Benefits in 2006
National Per Pupil = $7,458*

ALPHA ORDER

RANK	STATE	PER PUPIL
39	Alabama	$6,120
10	Alaska	8,933
48	Arizona	5,148
37	Arkansas	6,218
24	California	7,070
38	Colorado	6,186
3	Connecticut	10,392
7	Delaware	9,338
41	Florida	6,082
23	Georgia	7,157
18	Hawaii	7,984
47	Idaho	5,354
22	Illinois	7,329
21	Indiana	7,439
25	Iowa	7,014
36	Kansas	6,414
31	Kentucky	6,559
29	Louisiana	6,689
11	Maine	8,760
9	Maryland	8,945
6	Massachusetts	10,110
19	Michigan	7,879
20	Minnesota	7,630
45	Mississippi	5,692
30	Missouri	6,560
33	Montana	6,497
26	Nebraska	6,851
44	Nevada	5,802
15	New Hampshire	8,093
2	New Jersey	11,888
32	New Mexico	6,508
1	New York	12,404
40	North Carolina	6,112
28	North Dakota	6,836
16	Ohio	8,009
49	Oklahoma	5,124
27	Oregon	6,844
12	Pennsylvania	8,622
5	Rhode Island	10,128
33	South Carolina	6,497
43	South Dakota	5,815
46	Tennessee	5,562
42	Texas	5,952
50	Utah	4,623
4	Vermont	10,141
14	Virginia	8,118
35	Washington	6,487
17	West Virginia	8,000
13	Wisconsin	8,184
8	Wyoming	9,157

RANK ORDER

RANK	STATE	PER PUPIL
1	New York	$12,404
2	New Jersey	11,888
3	Connecticut	10,392
4	Vermont	10,141
5	Rhode Island	10,128
6	Massachusetts	10,110
7	Delaware	9,338
8	Wyoming	9,157
9	Maryland	8,945
10	Alaska	8,933
11	Maine	8,760
12	Pennsylvania	8,622
13	Wisconsin	8,184
14	Virginia	8,118
15	New Hampshire	8,093
16	Ohio	8,009
17	West Virginia	8,000
18	Hawaii	7,984
19	Michigan	7,879
20	Minnesota	7,630
21	Indiana	7,439
22	Illinois	7,329
23	Georgia	7,157
24	California	7,070
25	Iowa	7,014
26	Nebraska	6,851
27	Oregon	6,844
28	North Dakota	6,836
29	Louisiana	6,689
30	Missouri	6,560
31	Kentucky	6,559
32	New Mexico	6,508
33	Montana	6,497
33	South Carolina	6,497
35	Washington	6,487
36	Kansas	6,414
37	Arkansas	6,218
38	Colorado	6,186
39	Alabama	6,120
40	North Carolina	6,112
41	Florida	6,082
42	Texas	5,952
43	South Dakota	5,815
44	Nevada	5,802
45	Mississippi	5,692
46	Tennessee	5,562
47	Idaho	5,354
48	Arizona	5,148
49	Oklahoma	5,124
50	Utah	4,623

District of Columbia	9,934

Source: CQ Press using data from U.S. Bureau of the Census, Governments Division
"Public Education Finances: 2006" (http://www.census.gov/govs/www/school06.html)
*Based on student membership. Current spending for compensation of school system officers and employees. Consists of gross compensation before deductions for withheld taxes, retirement contributions, or other purposes. Also includes benefits such as contributions on behalf of employees for retirement coverage, social security, group health and life insurance, tuition reimbursement, worker's compensation, and unemployment compensation.

Percent of Public Elementary and Secondary School Current Expenditures Used for Salaries, Wages, and Benefits in 2006
National Percent = 79.9%*

ALPHA ORDER

RANK ORDER

RANK	STATE	PERCENT		RANK	STATE	PERCENT
33	Alabama	78.5		1	Virginia	85.4
41	Alaska	77.6		2	Kentucky	84.6
32	Arizona	78.8		3	West Virginia	84.4
40	Arkansas	77.9		4	Indiana	84.0
16	California	80.8		5	Maryland	83.6
47	Colorado	75.6		6	Georgia	83.3
12	Connecticut	82.0		6	Iowa	83.3
28	Delaware	79.1		8	Idaho	82.9
45	Florida	76.6		9	Utah	82.4
6	Georgia	83.3		9	Washington	82.4
36	Hawaii	78.3		11	North Carolina	82.3
8	Idaho	82.9		12	Connecticut	82.0
25	Illinois	79.5		13	Wyoming	81.5
4	Indiana	84.0		14	Wisconsin	81.3
6	Iowa	83.3		15	New York	80.9
46	Kansas	76.3		16	California	80.8
2	Kentucky	84.6		17	Michigan	80.6
27	Louisiana	79.3		18	Rhode Island	80.4
20	Maine	79.9		19	Ohio	80.1
5	Maryland	83.6		20	Maine	79.9
20	Massachusetts	79.9		20	Massachusetts	79.9
17	Michigan	80.6		20	Tennessee	79.9
23	Minnesota	79.7		23	Minnesota	79.7
33	Mississippi	78.5		24	New Mexico	79.6
26	Missouri	79.4		25	Illinois	79.5
49	Montana	75.3		26	Missouri	79.4
36	Nebraska	78.3		27	Louisiana	79.3
33	Nevada	78.5		28	Delaware	79.1
41	New Hampshire	77.6		29	South Carolina	79.0
38	New Jersey	78.0		30	North Dakota	78.9
24	New Mexico	79.6		30	Oregon	78.9
15	New York	80.9		32	Arizona	78.8
11	North Carolina	82.3		33	Alabama	78.5
30	North Dakota	78.9		33	Mississippi	78.5
19	Ohio	80.1		33	Nevada	78.5
50	Oklahoma	70.6		36	Hawaii	78.3
30	Oregon	78.9		36	Nebraska	78.3
44	Pennsylvania	77.1		38	New Jersey	78.0
18	Rhode Island	80.4		38	Texas	78.0
29	South Carolina	79.0		40	Arkansas	77.9
47	South Dakota	75.6		41	Alaska	77.6
20	Tennessee	79.9		41	New Hampshire	77.6
38	Texas	78.0		43	Vermont	77.3
9	Utah	82.4		44	Pennsylvania	77.1
43	Vermont	77.3		45	Florida	76.6
1	Virginia	85.4		46	Kansas	76.3
9	Washington	82.4		47	Colorado	75.6
3	West Virginia	84.4		47	South Dakota	75.6
14	Wisconsin	81.3		49	Montana	75.3
13	Wyoming	81.5		50	Oklahoma	70.6

District of Columbia   62.2

Source: CQ Press using data from U.S. Bureau of the Census, Governments Division
   "Public Education Finances: 2006" (http://www.census.gov/govs/www/school06.html)
*Current spending for compensation of school system officers and employees. Consists of gross compensation before deductions for withheld taxes, retirement contributions, or other purposes. Also includes benefits such as contributions on behalf of employees for retirement coverage, social security, group health and life insurance, tuition reimbursement, worker's compensation, and unemployment compensation.

Public Elementary and Secondary School Current Expenditures for Salaries and Wages in 2006
National Total = $272,653,877,000*

ALPHA ORDER

RANK	STATE	EXPENDITURES	% of USA
26	Alabama	$3,290,656,000	1.2%
44	Alaska	840,229,000	0.3%
22	Arizona	4,116,291,000	1.5%
32	Arkansas	2,336,251,000	0.9%
1	California	33,256,468,000	12.2%
23	Colorado	3,927,684,000	1.4%
20	Connecticut	4,243,043,000	1.6%
45	Delaware	747,295,000	0.3%
4	Florida	12,574,129,000	4.6%
10	Georgia	8,852,138,000	3.2%
42	Hawaii	1,076,075,000	0.4%
43	Idaho	1,040,843,000	0.4%
6	Illinois	12,011,814,000	4.4%
16	Indiana	5,128,483,000	1.9%
28	Iowa	2,604,236,000	1.0%
31	Kansas	2,421,179,000	0.9%
25	Kentucky	3,365,386,000	1.2%
27	Louisiana	3,149,963,000	1.2%
39	Maine	1,260,496,000	0.5%
14	Maryland	5,697,389,000	2.1%
12	Massachusetts	6,892,111,000	2.5%
9	Michigan	9,299,015,000	3.4%
17	Minnesota	4,835,780,000	1.8%
33	Mississippi	2,171,136,000	0.8%
18	Missouri	4,804,250,000	1.8%
46	Montana	731,141,000	0.3%
37	Nebraska	1,483,342,000	0.5%
34	Nevada	1,790,812,000	0.7%
40	New Hampshire	1,211,004,000	0.4%
5	New Jersey	12,107,948,000	4.4%
35	New Mexico	1,647,784,000	0.6%
2	New York	25,062,886,000	9.2%
13	North Carolina	6,870,203,000	2.5%
50	North Dakota	526,678,000	0.2%
8	Ohio	10,542,050,000	3.9%
30	Oklahoma	2,556,444,000	0.9%
29	Oregon	2,590,425,000	1.0%
7	Pennsylvania	11,170,842,000	4.1%
41	Rhode Island	1,090,901,000	0.4%
24	South Carolina	3,548,280,000	1.3%
49	South Dakota	559,080,000	0.2%
21	Tennessee	4,158,103,000	1.5%
3	Texas	22,668,110,000	8.3%
36	Utah	1,629,750,000	0.6%
47	Vermont	701,947,000	0.3%
11	Virginia	7,563,916,000	2.8%
15	Washington	5,199,661,000	1.9%
38	West Virginia	1,468,323,000	0.5%
19	Wisconsin	4,726,984,000	1.7%
48	Wyoming	579,660,000	0.2%

RANK ORDER

RANK	STATE	EXPENDITURES	% of USA
1	California	$33,256,468,000	12.2%
2	New York	25,062,886,000	9.2%
3	Texas	22,668,110,000	8.3%
4	Florida	12,574,129,000	4.6%
5	New Jersey	12,107,948,000	4.4%
6	Illinois	12,011,814,000	4.4%
7	Pennsylvania	11,170,842,000	4.1%
8	Ohio	10,542,050,000	3.9%
9	Michigan	9,299,015,000	3.4%
10	Georgia	8,852,138,000	3.2%
11	Virginia	7,563,916,000	2.8%
12	Massachusetts	6,892,111,000	2.5%
13	North Carolina	6,870,203,000	2.5%
14	Maryland	5,697,389,000	2.1%
15	Washington	5,199,661,000	1.9%
16	Indiana	5,128,483,000	1.9%
17	Minnesota	4,835,780,000	1.8%
18	Missouri	4,804,250,000	1.8%
19	Wisconsin	4,726,984,000	1.7%
20	Connecticut	4,243,043,000	1.6%
21	Tennessee	4,158,103,000	1.5%
22	Arizona	4,116,291,000	1.5%
23	Colorado	3,927,684,000	1.4%
24	South Carolina	3,548,280,000	1.3%
25	Kentucky	3,365,386,000	1.2%
26	Alabama	3,290,656,000	1.2%
27	Louisiana	3,149,963,000	1.2%
28	Iowa	2,604,236,000	1.0%
29	Oregon	2,590,425,000	1.0%
30	Oklahoma	2,556,444,000	0.9%
31	Kansas	2,421,179,000	0.9%
32	Arkansas	2,336,251,000	0.9%
33	Mississippi	2,171,136,000	0.8%
34	Nevada	1,790,812,000	0.7%
35	New Mexico	1,647,784,000	0.6%
36	Utah	1,629,750,000	0.6%
37	Nebraska	1,483,342,000	0.5%
38	West Virginia	1,468,323,000	0.5%
39	Maine	1,260,496,000	0.5%
40	New Hampshire	1,211,004,000	0.4%
41	Rhode Island	1,090,901,000	0.4%
42	Hawaii	1,076,075,000	0.4%
43	Idaho	1,040,843,000	0.4%
44	Alaska	840,229,000	0.3%
45	Delaware	747,295,000	0.3%
46	Montana	731,141,000	0.3%
47	Vermont	701,947,000	0.3%
48	Wyoming	579,660,000	0.2%
49	South Dakota	559,080,000	0.2%
50	North Dakota	526,678,000	0.2%
	District of Columbia	525,263,000	0.2%

Source: U.S. Bureau of the Census, Governments Division
"Public Education Finances: 2006" (http://www.census.gov/govs/www/school06.html)
*Current spending for compensation of school system officers and employees. Consists of gross compensation before deductions for withheld taxes, retirement contributions, or other purposes.

Per Capita Public Elementary and Secondary School Current Expenditures for Salaries and Wages in 2006
National Per Capita = $913*

ALPHA ORDER

RANK	STATE	PER CAPITA
42	Alabama	$717
3	Alaska	1,240
49	Arizona	668
28	Arkansas	832
19	California	917
30	Colorado	824
4	Connecticut	1,214
22	Delaware	876
47	Florida	696
13	Georgia	948
26	Hawaii	842
44	Idaho	711
14	Illinois	940
34	Indiana	814
22	Iowa	876
21	Kansas	879
36	Kentucky	800
40	Louisiana	742
12	Maine	959
9	Maryland	1,017
7	Massachusetts	1,071
17	Michigan	920
15	Minnesota	938
39	Mississippi	749
31	Missouri	823
38	Montana	772
27	Nebraska	841
41	Nevada	719
16	New Hampshire	923
1	New Jersey	1,397
24	New Mexico	848
2	New York	1,300
37	North Carolina	775
29	North Dakota	826
17	Ohio	920
43	Oklahoma	715
46	Oregon	702
20	Pennsylvania	901
8	Rhode Island	1,028
32	South Carolina	819
45	South Dakota	709
48	Tennessee	684
11	Texas	968
50	Utah	632
5	Vermont	1,131
10	Virginia	990
33	Washington	816
35	West Virginia	812
24	Wisconsin	848
6	Wyoming	1,130

RANK ORDER

RANK	STATE	PER CAPITA
1	New Jersey	$1,397
2	New York	1,300
3	Alaska	1,240
4	Connecticut	1,214
5	Vermont	1,131
6	Wyoming	1,130
7	Massachusetts	1,071
8	Rhode Island	1,028
9	Maryland	1,017
10	Virginia	990
11	Texas	968
12	Maine	959
13	Georgia	948
14	Illinois	940
15	Minnesota	938
16	New Hampshire	923
17	Michigan	920
17	Ohio	920
19	California	917
20	Pennsylvania	901
21	Kansas	879
22	Delaware	876
22	Iowa	876
24	New Mexico	848
24	Wisconsin	848
26	Hawaii	842
27	Nebraska	841
28	Arkansas	832
29	North Dakota	826
30	Colorado	824
31	Missouri	823
32	South Carolina	819
33	Washington	816
34	Indiana	814
35	West Virginia	812
36	Kentucky	800
37	North Carolina	775
38	Montana	772
39	Mississippi	749
40	Louisiana	742
41	Nevada	719
42	Alabama	717
43	Oklahoma	715
44	Idaho	711
45	South Dakota	709
46	Oregon	702
47	Florida	696
48	Tennessee	684
49	Arizona	668
50	Utah	632

District of Columbia	897

Source: CQ Press using data from U.S. Bureau of the Census, Governments Division
  "Public Education Finances: 2006" (http://www.census.gov/govs/www/school06.html)
*Current spending for compensation of school system officers and employees. Consists of gross compensation before deductions for withheld taxes, retirement contributions, or other purposes.

Per Pupil Elementary and Secondary School Current Expenditures for Salaries and Wages in 2006
National Per Pupil = $5,636*

ALPHA ORDER

RANK	STATE	PER PUPIL
43	Alabama	$4,427
12	Alaska	6,323
47	Arizona	4,098
38	Arkansas	4,943
24	California	5,316
33	Colorado	5,039
3	Connecticut	7,625
9	Delaware	6,534
40	Florida	4,720
19	Georgia	5,541
17	Hawaii	5,886
48	Idaho	4,029
18	Illinois	5,712
35	Indiana	4,998
21	Iowa	5,386
27	Kansas	5,196
36	Kentucky	4,952
39	Louisiana	4,859
10	Maine	6,458
8	Maryland	6,625
6	Massachusetts	7,255
22	Michigan	5,378
16	Minnesota	5,911
44	Mississippi	4,395
26	Missouri	5,246
34	Montana	5,033
28	Nebraska	5,184
46	Nevada	4,339
14	New Hampshire	6,024
2	New Jersey	8,773
31	New Mexico	5,043
1	New York	8,992
37	North Carolina	4,949
23	North Dakota	5,365
15	Ohio	5,958
48	Oklahoma	4,029
41	Oregon	4,654
11	Pennsylvania	6,349
5	Rhode Island	7,267
30	South Carolina	5,076
42	South Dakota	4,593
45	Tennessee	4,360
29	Texas	5,094
50	Utah	3,282
4	Vermont	7,602
13	Virginia	6,233
32	Washington	5,040
25	West Virginia	5,248
20	Wisconsin	5,436
7	Wyoming	6,728

RANK ORDER

RANK	STATE	PER PUPIL
1	New York	$8,992
2	New Jersey	8,773
3	Connecticut	7,625
4	Vermont	7,602
5	Rhode Island	7,267
6	Massachusetts	7,255
7	Wyoming	6,728
8	Maryland	6,625
9	Delaware	6,534
10	Maine	6,458
11	Pennsylvania	6,349
12	Alaska	6,323
13	Virginia	6,233
14	New Hampshire	6,024
15	Ohio	5,958
16	Minnesota	5,911
17	Hawaii	5,886
18	Illinois	5,712
19	Georgia	5,541
20	Wisconsin	5,436
21	Iowa	5,386
22	Michigan	5,378
23	North Dakota	5,365
24	California	5,316
25	West Virginia	5,248
26	Missouri	5,246
27	Kansas	5,196
28	Nebraska	5,184
29	Texas	5,094
30	South Carolina	5,076
31	New Mexico	5,043
32	Washington	5,040
33	Colorado	5,039
34	Montana	5,033
35	Indiana	4,998
36	Kentucky	4,952
37	North Carolina	4,949
38	Arkansas	4,943
39	Louisiana	4,859
40	Florida	4,720
41	Oregon	4,654
42	South Dakota	4,593
43	Alabama	4,427
44	Mississippi	4,395
45	Tennessee	4,360
46	Nevada	4,339
47	Arizona	4,098
48	Idaho	4,029
48	Oklahoma	4,029
50	Utah	3,282

District of Columbia 8,811

Source: U.S. Bureau of the Census, Governments Division
"Public Education Finances: 2006" (http://www.census.gov/govs/www/school06.html)
*Based on student membership. For this per pupil calculation, Census has excluded expenditures for salaries and wages for adult education, community services, and other nonelementary-secondary programs.

Percent of Public Elementary and Secondary School Current Expenditures Used for Salaries and Wages in 2006
National Percent = 60.4%*

ALPHA ORDER

RANK	STATE	PERCENT
41	Alabama	56.8
48	Alaska	54.9
9	Arizona	62.7
13	Arkansas	61.9
21	California	60.8
20	Colorado	61.6
23	Connecticut	60.2
45	Delaware	55.4
27	Florida	59.5
4	Georgia	64.5
35	Hawaii	57.7
11	Idaho	62.4
12	Illinois	62.0
43	Indiana	56.4
5	Iowa	64.0
16	Kansas	61.8
7	Kentucky	63.9
38	Louisiana	57.6
29	Maine	58.9
13	Maryland	61.9
40	Massachusetts	57.4
47	Michigan	55.0
17	Minnesota	61.7
22	Mississippi	60.6
8	Missouri	63.5
33	Montana	58.4
28	Nebraska	59.2
30	Nevada	58.7
35	New Hampshire	57.7
39	New Jersey	57.5
17	New Mexico	61.7
31	New York	58.6
2	North Carolina	66.7
13	North Dakota	61.9
26	Ohio	59.6
44	Oklahoma	55.5
50	Oregon	53.7
41	Pennsylvania	56.8
35	Rhode Island	57.7
17	South Carolina	61.7
25	South Dakota	59.7
10	Tennessee	62.6
1	Texas	66.8
32	Utah	58.5
34	Vermont	57.9
3	Virginia	65.6
5	Washington	64.0
45	West Virginia	55.4
49	Wisconsin	54.0
24	Wyoming	59.9

RANK ORDER

RANK	STATE	PERCENT
1	Texas	66.8
2	North Carolina	66.7
3	Virginia	65.6
4	Georgia	64.5
5	Iowa	64.0
5	Washington	64.0
7	Kentucky	63.9
8	Missouri	63.5
9	Arizona	62.7
10	Tennessee	62.6
11	Idaho	62.4
12	Illinois	62.0
13	Arkansas	61.9
13	Maryland	61.9
13	North Dakota	61.9
16	Kansas	61.8
17	Minnesota	61.7
17	New Mexico	61.7
17	South Carolina	61.7
20	Colorado	61.6
21	California	60.8
22	Mississippi	60.6
23	Connecticut	60.2
24	Wyoming	59.9
25	South Dakota	59.7
26	Ohio	59.6
27	Florida	59.5
28	Nebraska	59.2
29	Maine	58.9
30	Nevada	58.7
31	New York	58.6
32	Utah	58.5
33	Montana	58.4
34	Vermont	57.9
35	Hawaii	57.7
35	New Hampshire	57.7
35	Rhode Island	57.7
38	Louisiana	57.6
39	New Jersey	57.5
40	Massachusetts	57.4
41	Alabama	56.8
41	Pennsylvania	56.8
43	Indiana	56.4
44	Oklahoma	55.5
45	Delaware	55.4
45	West Virginia	55.4
47	Michigan	55.0
48	Alaska	54.9
49	Wisconsin	54.0
50	Oregon	53.7
	District of Columbia	55.2

Source: CQ Press using data from U.S. Bureau of the Census, Governments Division
"Public Education Finances: 2006" (http://www.census.gov/govs/www/school06.html)
*Current spending for compensation of school system officers and employees. Consists of gross compensation before deductions for withheld taxes, retirement contributions, or other purposes.

Public Elementary and Secondary School Current Expenditures for Employee Benefits in 2006
National Total = $88,150,962,000*

ALPHA ORDER

RANK	STATE	EXPENDITURES	% of USA
20	Alabama	$1,257,885,000	1.4%
43	Alaska	346,879,000	0.4%
26	Arizona	1,054,783,000	1.2%
35	Arkansas	602,247,000	0.7%
1	California	10,973,780,000	12.4%
28	Colorado	893,965,000	1.0%
17	Connecticut	1,539,360,000	1.7%
45	Delaware	320,722,000	0.4%
7	Florida	3,628,981,000	4.1%
11	Georgia	2,581,683,000	2.9%
42	Hawaii	383,545,000	0.4%
44	Idaho	342,063,000	0.4%
9	Illinois	3,400,941,000	3.9%
12	Indiana	2,505,272,000	2.8%
29	Iowa	786,868,000	0.9%
36	Kansas	567,381,000	0.6%
25	Kentucky	1,092,464,000	1.2%
23	Louisiana	1,186,475,000	1.3%
39	Maine	449,277,000	0.5%
15	Maryland	1,995,747,000	2.3%
10	Massachusetts	2,711,840,000	3.1%
3	Michigan	4,324,912,000	4.9%
19	Minnesota	1,405,869,000	1.6%
33	Mississippi	640,511,000	0.7%
22	Missouri	1,204,046,000	1.4%
47	Montana	212,575,000	0.2%
38	Nebraska	477,069,000	0.5%
34	Nevada	603,831,000	0.7%
41	New Hampshire	416,064,000	0.5%
4	New Jersey	4,298,965,000	4.9%
37	New Mexico	478,876,000	0.5%
2	New York	9,511,854,000	10.8%
16	North Carolina	1,614,223,000	1.8%
50	North Dakota	144,426,000	0.2%
8	Ohio	3,627,781,000	4.1%
31	Oklahoma	694,399,000	0.8%
21	Oregon	1,219,411,000	1.4%
5	Pennsylvania	3,999,508,000	4.5%
40	Rhode Island	429,494,000	0.5%
27	South Carolina	993,359,000	1.1%
49	South Dakota	148,684,000	0.2%
24	Tennessee	1,146,644,000	1.3%
6	Texas	3,819,217,000	4.3%
32	Utah	665,645,000	0.8%
46	Vermont	234,468,000	0.3%
14	Virginia	2,287,817,000	2.6%
18	Washington	1,493,214,000	1.7%
30	West Virginia	769,995,000	0.9%
13	Wisconsin	2,389,667,000	2.7%
48	Wyoming	209,288,000	0.2%

RANK ORDER

RANK	STATE	EXPENDITURES	% of USA
1	California	$10,973,780,000	12.4%
2	New York	9,511,854,000	10.8%
3	Michigan	4,324,912,000	4.9%
4	New Jersey	4,298,965,000	4.9%
5	Pennsylvania	3,999,508,000	4.5%
6	Texas	3,819,217,000	4.3%
7	Florida	3,628,981,000	4.1%
8	Ohio	3,627,781,000	4.1%
9	Illinois	3,400,941,000	3.9%
10	Massachusetts	2,711,840,000	3.1%
11	Georgia	2,581,683,000	2.9%
12	Indiana	2,505,272,000	2.8%
13	Wisconsin	2,389,667,000	2.7%
14	Virginia	2,287,817,000	2.6%
15	Maryland	1,995,747,000	2.3%
16	North Carolina	1,614,223,000	1.8%
17	Connecticut	1,539,360,000	1.7%
18	Washington	1,493,214,000	1.7%
19	Minnesota	1,405,869,000	1.6%
20	Alabama	1,257,885,000	1.4%
21	Oregon	1,219,411,000	1.4%
22	Missouri	1,204,046,000	1.4%
23	Louisiana	1,186,475,000	1.3%
24	Tennessee	1,146,644,000	1.3%
25	Kentucky	1,092,464,000	1.2%
26	Arizona	1,054,783,000	1.2%
27	South Carolina	993,359,000	1.1%
28	Colorado	893,965,000	1.0%
29	Iowa	786,868,000	0.9%
30	West Virginia	769,995,000	0.9%
31	Oklahoma	694,399,000	0.8%
32	Utah	665,645,000	0.8%
33	Mississippi	640,511,000	0.7%
34	Nevada	603,831,000	0.7%
35	Arkansas	602,247,000	0.7%
36	Kansas	567,381,000	0.6%
37	New Mexico	478,876,000	0.5%
38	Nebraska	477,069,000	0.5%
39	Maine	449,277,000	0.5%
40	Rhode Island	429,494,000	0.5%
41	New Hampshire	416,064,000	0.5%
42	Hawaii	383,545,000	0.4%
43	Alaska	346,879,000	0.4%
44	Idaho	342,063,000	0.4%
45	Delaware	320,722,000	0.4%
46	Vermont	234,468,000	0.3%
47	Montana	212,575,000	0.2%
48	Wyoming	209,288,000	0.2%
49	South Dakota	148,684,000	0.2%
50	North Dakota	144,426,000	0.2%
	District of Columbia	66,992,000	0.1%

Source: U.S. Bureau of the Census, Governments Division
   "Public Education Finances: 2006" (http://www.census.gov/govs/www/school06.html)
*Amounts paid by the school system for fringe benefits. These amounts are not included in salaries and wages paid directly to employees. Includes contributions on behalf of employees for retirement coverage, social security, group health and life insurance, tuition reimbursement, worker's compensation, and unemployment compensation.

Per Capita Public Elementary and Secondary School Current Expenditures for Employee Benefits in 2006
National Per Capita = $295*

ALPHA ORDER

RANK	STATE	PER CAPITA
25	Alabama	$274
1	Alaska	512
49	Arizona	171
40	Arkansas	214
20	California	303
47	Colorado	188
4	Connecticut	440
13	Delaware	376
43	Florida	201
24	Georgia	276
21	Hawaii	300
34	Idaho	234
28	Illinois	266
11	Indiana	397
29	Iowa	265
41	Kansas	206
30	Kentucky	260
23	Louisiana	280
15	Maine	342
14	Maryland	356
8	Massachusetts	421
6	Michigan	428
26	Minnesota	273
39	Mississippi	221
41	Missouri	206
38	Montana	225
27	Nebraska	270
33	Nevada	242
18	New Hampshire	317
2	New Jersey	496
32	New Mexico	247
3	New York	493
48	North Carolina	182
37	North Dakota	227
19	Ohio	316
44	Oklahoma	194
16	Oregon	330
17	Pennsylvania	322
10	Rhode Island	405
36	South Carolina	229
45	South Dakota	189
45	Tennessee	189
50	Texas	163
31	Utah	258
12	Vermont	378
22	Virginia	299
34	Washington	234
7	West Virginia	426
5	Wisconsin	429
9	Wyoming	408

RANK ORDER

RANK	STATE	PER CAPITA
1	Alaska	$512
2	New Jersey	496
3	New York	493
4	Connecticut	440
5	Wisconsin	429
6	Michigan	428
7	West Virginia	426
8	Massachusetts	421
9	Wyoming	408
10	Rhode Island	405
11	Indiana	397
12	Vermont	378
13	Delaware	376
14	Maryland	356
15	Maine	342
16	Oregon	330
17	Pennsylvania	322
18	New Hampshire	317
19	Ohio	316
20	California	303
21	Hawaii	300
22	Virginia	299
23	Louisiana	280
24	Georgia	276
25	Alabama	274
26	Minnesota	273
27	Nebraska	270
28	Illinois	266
29	Iowa	265
30	Kentucky	260
31	Utah	258
32	New Mexico	247
33	Nevada	242
34	Idaho	234
34	Washington	234
36	South Carolina	229
37	North Dakota	227
38	Montana	225
39	Mississippi	221
40	Arkansas	214
41	Kansas	206
41	Missouri	206
43	Florida	201
44	Oklahoma	194
45	South Dakota	189
45	Tennessee	189
47	Colorado	188
48	North Carolina	182
49	Arizona	171
50	Texas	163
	District of Columbia	114

Source: CQ Press using data from U.S. Bureau of the Census, Governments Division
   "Public Education Finances: 2006" (http://www.census.gov/govs/www/school06.html)
*Amounts paid by the school system for fringe benefits. These amounts are not included in salaries and wages paid directly to employees. Includes contributions on behalf of employees for retirement coverage, social security, group health and life insurance, tuition reimbursement, worker's compensation, and unemployment compensation.

Per Pupil Public Elementary and Secondary School Current Expenditures for Employee Benefits in 2006
National Per Pupil = $1,822*

ALPHA ORDER

RANK	STATE	PER PUPIL
25	Alabama	$1,692
9	Alaska	2,610
49	Arizona	1,050
42	Arkansas	1,274
23	California	1,754
47	Colorado	1,147
6	Connecticut	2,766
5	Delaware	2,804
37	Florida	1,362
29	Georgia	1,616
18	Hawaii	2,098
39	Idaho	1,324
28	Illinois	1,617
12	Indiana	2,441
27	Iowa	1,628
44	Kansas	1,218
30	Kentucky	1,607
22	Louisiana	1,830
15	Maine	2,302
14	Maryland	2,321
4	Massachusetts	2,855
11	Michigan	2,501
24	Minnesota	1,719
41	Mississippi	1,297
40	Missouri	1,315
33	Montana	1,463
26	Nebraska	1,667
33	Nevada	1,463
19	New Hampshire	2,070
2	New Jersey	3,115
32	New Mexico	1,466
1	New York	3,412
46	North Carolina	1,163
31	North Dakota	1,471
20	Ohio	2,050
48	Oklahoma	1,094
17	Oregon	2,191
16	Pennsylvania	2,273
3	Rhode Island	2,861
36	South Carolina	1,421
43	South Dakota	1,222
45	Tennessee	1,202
50	Texas	858
38	Utah	1,341
10	Vermont	2,539
21	Virginia	1,885
35	Washington	1,447
7	West Virginia	2,752
8	Wisconsin	2,748
13	Wyoming	2,429

RANK ORDER

RANK	STATE	PER PUPIL
1	New York	$3,412
2	New Jersey	3,115
3	Rhode Island	2,861
4	Massachusetts	2,855
5	Delaware	2,804
6	Connecticut	2,766
7	West Virginia	2,752
8	Wisconsin	2,748
9	Alaska	2,610
10	Vermont	2,539
11	Michigan	2,501
12	Indiana	2,441
13	Wyoming	2,429
14	Maryland	2,321
15	Maine	2,302
16	Pennsylvania	2,273
17	Oregon	2,191
18	Hawaii	2,098
19	New Hampshire	2,070
20	Ohio	2,050
21	Virginia	1,885
22	Louisiana	1,830
23	California	1,754
24	Minnesota	1,719
25	Alabama	1,692
26	Nebraska	1,667
27	Iowa	1,628
28	Illinois	1,617
29	Georgia	1,616
30	Kentucky	1,607
31	North Dakota	1,471
32	New Mexico	1,466
33	Montana	1,463
33	Nevada	1,463
35	Washington	1,447
36	South Carolina	1,421
37	Florida	1,362
38	Utah	1,341
39	Idaho	1,324
40	Missouri	1,315
41	Mississippi	1,297
42	Arkansas	1,274
43	South Dakota	1,222
44	Kansas	1,218
45	Tennessee	1,202
46	North Carolina	1,163
47	Colorado	1,147
48	Oklahoma	1,094
49	Arizona	1,050
50	Texas	858
	District of Columbia	1,124

Source: U.S. Bureau of the Census, Governments Division
   "Public Education Finances: 2006" (http://www.census.gov/govs/www/school06.html)
*Based on student membership. For this per pupil calculation, Census has excluded expenditures for employee benefits for adult education, community services, and other nonelementary-secondary programs.

Percent of Public Elementary and Secondary School Current Expenditures Used for Employee Benefits in 2006
National Percent = 19.5%*

ALPHA ORDER

RANK	STATE	PERCENT
13	Alabama	21.7
8	Alaska	22.7
42	Arizona	16.1
43	Arkansas	16.0
24	California	20.1
49	Colorado	14.0
12	Connecticut	21.8
7	Delaware	23.8
39	Florida	17.2
31	Georgia	18.8
19	Hawaii	20.6
20	Idaho	20.5
36	Illinois	17.5
2	Indiana	27.6
28	Iowa	19.3
48	Kansas	14.5
18	Kentucky	20.7
13	Louisiana	21.7
17	Maine	21.0
13	Maryland	21.7
10	Massachusetts	22.6
4	Michigan	25.6
33	Minnesota	17.9
33	Mississippi	17.9
44	Missouri	15.9
40	Montana	17.0
30	Nebraska	19.0
25	Nevada	19.8
25	New Hampshire	19.8
22	New Jersey	20.4
33	New Mexico	17.9
11	New York	22.2
46	North Carolina	15.7
40	North Dakota	17.0
20	Ohio	20.5
47	Oklahoma	15.1
5	Oregon	25.3
23	Pennsylvania	20.3
8	Rhode Island	22.7
37	South Carolina	17.3
44	South Dakota	15.9
37	Tennessee	17.3
50	Texas	11.2
6	Utah	23.9
28	Vermont	19.3
25	Virginia	19.8
32	Washington	18.4
1	West Virginia	29.0
3	Wisconsin	27.3
16	Wyoming	21.6

RANK ORDER

RANK	STATE	PERCENT
1	West Virginia	29.0
2	Indiana	27.6
3	Wisconsin	27.3
4	Michigan	25.6
5	Oregon	25.3
6	Utah	23.9
7	Delaware	23.8
8	Alaska	22.7
8	Rhode Island	22.7
10	Massachusetts	22.6
11	New York	22.2
12	Connecticut	21.8
13	Alabama	21.7
13	Louisiana	21.7
13	Maryland	21.7
16	Wyoming	21.6
17	Maine	21.0
18	Kentucky	20.7
19	Hawaii	20.6
20	Idaho	20.5
20	Ohio	20.5
22	New Jersey	20.4
23	Pennsylvania	20.3
24	California	20.1
25	Nevada	19.8
25	New Hampshire	19.8
25	Virginia	19.8
28	Iowa	19.3
28	Vermont	19.3
30	Nebraska	19.0
31	Georgia	18.8
32	Washington	18.4
33	Minnesota	17.9
33	Mississippi	17.9
33	New Mexico	17.9
36	Illinois	17.5
37	South Carolina	17.3
37	Tennessee	17.3
39	Florida	17.2
40	Montana	17.0
40	North Dakota	17.0
42	Arizona	16.1
43	Arkansas	16.0
44	Missouri	15.9
44	South Dakota	15.9
46	North Carolina	15.7
47	Oklahoma	15.1
48	Kansas	14.5
49	Colorado	14.0
50	Texas	11.2

District of Columbia 7.0

Source: CQ Press using data from U.S. Bureau of the Census, Governments Division
"Public Education Finances: 2006" (http://www.census.gov/govs/www/school06.html)
*Amounts paid by the school system for fringe benefits. These amounts are not included in salaries and wages paid directly to employees. Includes contributions on behalf of employees for retirement coverage, social security, group health and life insurance, tuition reimbursement, worker's compensation, and unemployment compensation.

Public Elementary and Secondary School Current Expenditures for Instruction in 2006
National Total = $271,842,769,000*

ALPHA ORDER

RANK	STATE	EXPENDITURES	% of USA
24	Alabama	$3,326,656,000	1.2%
44	Alaska	871,434,000	0.3%
22	Arizona	3,733,989,000	1.4%
32	Arkansas	2,265,821,000	0.8%
1	California	32,387,671,000	11.9%
23	Colorado	3,562,901,000	1.3%
20	Connecticut	4,406,855,000	1.6%
45	Delaware	817,872,000	0.3%
5	Florida	12,211,602,000	4.5%
10	Georgia	8,583,817,000	3.2%
42	Hawaii	1,077,351,000	0.4%
43	Idaho	1,027,985,000	0.4%
7	Illinois	11,327,481,000	4.2%
15	Indiana	5,348,450,000	2.0%
30	Iowa	2,425,326,000	0.9%
31	Kansas	2,378,494,000	0.9%
27	Kentucky	3,082,253,000	1.1%
26	Louisiana	3,167,501,000	1.2%
39	Maine	1,376,177,000	0.5%
14	Maryland	5,535,192,000	2.0%
11	Massachusetts	7,613,569,000	2.8%
9	Michigan	9,400,832,000	3.5%
18	Minnesota	4,818,788,000	1.8%
33	Mississippi	2,096,028,000	0.8%
19	Missouri	4,483,151,000	1.6%
47	Montana	753,664,000	0.3%
36	Nebraska	1,570,629,000	0.6%
34	Nevada	1,840,698,000	0.7%
40	New Hampshire	1,332,640,000	0.5%
4	New Jersey	12,309,954,000	4.5%
38	New Mexico	1,500,318,000	0.6%
2	New York	29,589,517,000	10.9%
13	North Carolina	6,342,589,000	2.3%
50	North Dakota	513,113,000	0.2%
8	Ohio	10,048,571,000	3.7%
29	Oklahoma	2,437,935,000	0.9%
28	Oregon	2,834,418,000	1.0%
6	Pennsylvania	11,675,380,000	4.3%
41	Rhode Island	1,120,778,000	0.4%
25	South Carolina	3,310,899,000	1.2%
49	South Dakota	552,199,000	0.2%
21	Tennessee	4,248,091,000	1.6%
3	Texas	20,299,749,000	7.5%
35	Utah	1,709,307,000	0.6%
46	Vermont	763,591,000	0.3%
12	Virginia	7,024,659,000	2.6%
17	Washington	4,826,779,000	1.8%
37	West Virginia	1,569,685,000	0.6%
16	Wisconsin	5,290,595,000	1.9%
48	Wyoming	571,127,000	0.2%

RANK ORDER

RANK	STATE	EXPENDITURES	% of USA
1	California	$32,387,671,000	11.9%
2	New York	29,589,517,000	10.9%
3	Texas	20,299,749,000	7.5%
4	New Jersey	12,309,954,000	4.5%
5	Florida	12,211,602,000	4.5%
6	Pennsylvania	11,675,380,000	4.3%
7	Illinois	11,327,481,000	4.2%
8	Ohio	10,048,571,000	3.7%
9	Michigan	9,400,832,000	3.5%
10	Georgia	8,583,817,000	3.2%
11	Massachusetts	7,613,569,000	2.8%
12	Virginia	7,024,659,000	2.6%
13	North Carolina	6,342,589,000	2.3%
14	Maryland	5,535,192,000	2.0%
15	Indiana	5,348,450,000	2.0%
16	Wisconsin	5,290,595,000	1.9%
17	Washington	4,826,779,000	1.8%
18	Minnesota	4,818,788,000	1.8%
19	Missouri	4,483,151,000	1.6%
20	Connecticut	4,406,855,000	1.6%
21	Tennessee	4,248,091,000	1.6%
22	Arizona	3,733,989,000	1.4%
23	Colorado	3,562,901,000	1.3%
24	Alabama	3,326,656,000	1.2%
25	South Carolina	3,310,899,000	1.2%
26	Louisiana	3,167,501,000	1.2%
27	Kentucky	3,082,253,000	1.1%
28	Oregon	2,834,418,000	1.0%
29	Oklahoma	2,437,935,000	0.9%
30	Iowa	2,425,326,000	0.9%
31	Kansas	2,378,494,000	0.9%
32	Arkansas	2,265,821,000	0.8%
33	Mississippi	2,096,028,000	0.8%
34	Nevada	1,840,698,000	0.7%
35	Utah	1,709,307,000	0.6%
36	Nebraska	1,570,629,000	0.6%
37	West Virginia	1,569,685,000	0.6%
38	New Mexico	1,500,318,000	0.6%
39	Maine	1,376,177,000	0.5%
40	New Hampshire	1,332,640,000	0.5%
41	Rhode Island	1,120,778,000	0.4%
42	Hawaii	1,077,351,000	0.4%
43	Idaho	1,027,985,000	0.4%
44	Alaska	871,434,000	0.3%
45	Delaware	817,872,000	0.3%
46	Vermont	763,591,000	0.3%
47	Montana	753,664,000	0.3%
48	Wyoming	571,127,000	0.2%
49	South Dakota	552,199,000	0.2%
50	North Dakota	513,113,000	0.2%
	District of Columbia	478,688,000	0.2%

Source: U.S. Bureau of the Census, Governments Division
"Public Education Finances: 2006" (http://www.census.gov/govs/www/school06.html)
*Includes payments for instruction for salaries, employee benefits, supplies, materials, and contractual services. Excludes capital outlay, debt service, and interfund transfers. Instruction covers regular, special, and vocational programs offered in both the academic year and summer school. Excluded are support services (e.g. instructional staff support and administration) and other support activities as well as adult education and community services.

Per Capita Public Elementary and Secondary School Current Expenditures for Instruction in 2006
National Per Capita = $910*

ALPHA ORDER

RANK	STATE	PER CAPITA
41	Alabama	$725
3	Alaska	1,286
50	Arizona	606
29	Arkansas	807
19	California	893
37	Colorado	748
4	Connecticut	1,261
12	Delaware	959
48	Florida	676
17	Georgia	919
27	Hawaii	843
44	Idaho	702
21	Illinois	887
26	Indiana	849
28	Iowa	816
25	Kansas	863
40	Kentucky	733
38	Louisiana	746
9	Maine	1,047
11	Maryland	988
6	Massachusetts	1,183
16	Michigan	931
15	Minnesota	935
42	Mississippi	723
33	Missouri	768
31	Montana	796
20	Nebraska	890
39	Nevada	739
10	New Hampshire	1,016
2	New Jersey	1,420
32	New Mexico	772
1	New York	1,535
43	North Carolina	715
30	North Dakota	805
22	Ohio	877
47	Oklahoma	681
33	Oregon	768
14	Pennsylvania	941
8	Rhode Island	1,056
35	South Carolina	765
45	South Dakota	700
46	Tennessee	699
24	Texas	867
49	Utah	663
5	Vermont	1,230
17	Virginia	919
36	Washington	757
23	West Virginia	868
13	Wisconsin	949
7	Wyoming	1,114

RANK ORDER

RANK	STATE	PER CAPITA
1	New York	$1,535
2	New Jersey	1,420
3	Alaska	1,286
4	Connecticut	1,261
5	Vermont	1,230
6	Massachusetts	1,183
7	Wyoming	1,114
8	Rhode Island	1,056
9	Maine	1,047
10	New Hampshire	1,016
11	Maryland	988
12	Delaware	959
13	Wisconsin	949
14	Pennsylvania	941
15	Minnesota	935
16	Michigan	931
17	Georgia	919
17	Virginia	919
19	California	893
20	Nebraska	890
21	Illinois	887
22	Ohio	877
23	West Virginia	868
24	Texas	867
25	Kansas	863
26	Indiana	849
27	Hawaii	843
28	Iowa	816
29	Arkansas	807
30	North Dakota	805
31	Montana	796
32	New Mexico	772
33	Missouri	768
33	Oregon	768
35	South Carolina	765
36	Washington	757
37	Colorado	748
38	Louisiana	746
39	Nevada	739
40	Kentucky	733
41	Alabama	725
42	Mississippi	723
43	North Carolina	715
44	Idaho	702
45	South Dakota	700
46	Tennessee	699
47	Oklahoma	681
48	Florida	676
49	Utah	663
50	Arizona	606

District of Columbia   818

Source: CQ Press using data from U.S. Bureau of the Census, Governments Division
"Public Education Finances: 2006" (http://www.census.gov/govs/www/school06.html)
*Includes payments for instruction for salaries, employee benefits, supplies, materials, and contractual services. Excludes capital outlay, debt service, and interfund transfers. Instruction covers regular, special, and vocational programs offered in both the academic year and summer school. Excluded are support services (e.g. instructional staff support and administration) and other support activities as well as adult education and community services.

Per Pupil Public Elementary and Secondary School Current Expenditures for Instruction in 2006
National Per Pupil = $5,543*

ALPHA ORDER

RANK	STATE	PER PUPIL
43	Alabama	$4,469
11	Alaska	6,557
49	Arizona	3,717
33	Arkansas	4,788
27	California	5,127
39	Colorado	4,563
4	Connecticut	7,637
6	Delaware	7,096
37	Florida	4,584
23	Georgia	5,369
15	Hawaii	5,893
47	Idaho	3,980
22	Illinois	5,387
25	Indiana	5,212
29	Iowa	5,016
28	Kansas	5,103
41	Kentucky	4,535
32	Louisiana	4,886
8	Maine	6,804
12	Maryland	6,436
5	Massachusetts	7,406
20	Michigan	5,437
16	Minnesota	5,891
46	Mississippi	4,243
31	Missouri	4,895
26	Montana	5,188
19	Nebraska	5,489
44	Nevada	4,460
13	New Hampshire	6,307
2	New Jersey	8,441
36	New Mexico	4,591
1	New York	10,285
38	North Carolina	4,569
24	North Dakota	5,227
21	Ohio	5,425
48	Oklahoma	3,842
30	Oregon	4,999
10	Pennsylvania	6,612
7	Rhode Island	6,856
34	South Carolina	4,698
41	South Dakota	4,535
45	Tennessee	4,454
40	Texas	4,561
50	Utah	3,443
3	Vermont	7,800
17	Virginia	5,785
35	Washington	4,679
18	West Virginia	5,610
14	Wisconsin	6,084
9	Wyoming	6,629

RANK ORDER

RANK	STATE	PER PUPIL
1	New York	$10,285
2	New Jersey	8,441
3	Vermont	7,800
4	Connecticut	7,637
5	Massachusetts	7,406
6	Delaware	7,096
7	Rhode Island	6,856
8	Maine	6,804
9	Wyoming	6,629
10	Pennsylvania	6,612
11	Alaska	6,557
12	Maryland	6,436
13	New Hampshire	6,307
14	Wisconsin	6,084
15	Hawaii	5,893
16	Minnesota	5,891
17	Virginia	5,785
18	West Virginia	5,610
19	Nebraska	5,489
20	Michigan	5,437
21	Ohio	5,425
22	Illinois	5,387
23	Georgia	5,369
24	North Dakota	5,227
25	Indiana	5,212
26	Montana	5,188
27	California	5,127
28	Kansas	5,103
29	Iowa	5,016
30	Oregon	4,999
31	Missouri	4,895
32	Louisiana	4,886
33	Arkansas	4,788
34	South Carolina	4,698
35	Washington	4,679
36	New Mexico	4,591
37	Florida	4,584
38	North Carolina	4,569
39	Colorado	4,563
40	Texas	4,561
41	Kentucky	4,535
41	South Dakota	4,535
43	Alabama	4,469
44	Nevada	4,460
45	Tennessee	4,454
46	Mississippi	4,243
47	Idaho	3,980
48	Oklahoma	3,842
49	Arizona	3,717
50	Utah	3,443
	District of Columbia	5,729

Source: U.S. Bureau of the Census, Governments Division
  "Public Education Finances: 2006" (http://www.census.gov/govs/www/school06.html)
*Based on student membership. Includes payments for instruction for salaries, employee benefits, supplies, materials, and contractual services. Excludes capital outlay, debt service, and interfund transfers. Instruction covers regular, special, and vocational programs offered in both the academic year and summer school. Excluded are support services and other support activities as well as adult education and community services.

Public Elementary and Secondary School Current Expenditures for Instruction per $1,000 Personal Income in 2006
National Ratio = $26.43*

ALPHA ORDER

RANK	STATE	RATIO
33	Alabama	$25.00
3	Alaska	35.86
47	Arizona	20.64
7	Arkansas	30.28
40	California	24.03
49	Colorado	20.27
26	Connecticut	26.39
27	Delaware	26.20
50	Florida	19.80
8	Georgia	30.23
39	Hawaii	24.30
30	Idaho	25.44
37	Illinois	24.40
16	Indiana	27.64
29	Iowa	25.99
25	Kansas	26.49
28	Kentucky	26.05
13	Louisiana	28.36
4	Maine	33.87
41	Maryland	23.81
22	Massachusetts	27.14
12	Michigan	28.45
31	Minnesota	25.29
14	Mississippi	28.31
35	Missouri	24.64
17	Montana	27.59
20	Nebraska	27.21
48	Nevada	20.39
20	New Hampshire	27.21
6	New Jersey	32.65
15	New Mexico	27.78
2	New York	37.44
42	North Carolina	23.76
32	North Dakota	25.23
18	Ohio	27.51
44	Oklahoma	22.89
34	Oregon	24.72
23	Pennsylvania	27.04
10	Rhode Island	29.20
19	South Carolina	27.42
45	South Dakota	22.40
43	Tennessee	23.01
24	Texas	26.70
38	Utah	24.36
1	Vermont	37.57
36	Virginia	24.45
46	Washington	21.47
5	West Virginia	32.73
11	Wisconsin	29.07
9	Wyoming	30.21

RANK ORDER

RANK	STATE	RATIO
1	Vermont	$37.57
2	New York	37.44
3	Alaska	35.86
4	Maine	33.87
5	West Virginia	32.73
6	New Jersey	32.65
7	Arkansas	30.28
8	Georgia	30.23
9	Wyoming	30.21
10	Rhode Island	29.20
11	Wisconsin	29.07
12	Michigan	28.45
13	Louisiana	28.36
14	Mississippi	28.31
15	New Mexico	27.78
16	Indiana	27.64
17	Montana	27.59
18	Ohio	27.51
19	South Carolina	27.42
20	Nebraska	27.21
20	New Hampshire	27.21
22	Massachusetts	27.14
23	Pennsylvania	27.04
24	Texas	26.70
25	Kansas	26.49
26	Connecticut	26.39
27	Delaware	26.20
28	Kentucky	26.05
29	Iowa	25.99
30	Idaho	25.44
31	Minnesota	25.29
32	North Dakota	25.23
33	Alabama	25.00
34	Oregon	24.72
35	Missouri	24.64
36	Virginia	24.45
37	Illinois	24.40
38	Utah	24.36
39	Hawaii	24.30
40	California	24.03
41	Maryland	23.81
42	North Carolina	23.76
43	Tennessee	23.01
44	Oklahoma	22.89
45	South Dakota	22.40
46	Washington	21.47
47	Arizona	20.64
48	Nevada	20.39
49	Colorado	20.27
50	Florida	19.80
	District of Columbia	15.35

Source: U.S. Bureau of the Census, Governments Division
"Public Education Finances: 2006" (http://www.census.gov/govs/www/school06.html)
*Includes payments for instruction for salaries, employee benefits, supplies, materials, and contractual services. Excludes capital outlay, debt service, and interfund transfers. Instruction covers regular, special, and vocational programs offered in both the academic year and summer school. Excluded are support services.

Percent of Public Elementary and Secondary School Current Expenditures Used for Instruction in 2006
National Percent = 60.2%*

ALPHA ORDER

RANK	STATE	PERCENT
43	Alabama	57.4
44	Alaska	56.9
44	Arizona	56.9
22	Arkansas	60.0
28	California	59.2
48	Colorado	55.8
8	Connecticut	62.5
16	Delaware	60.6
40	Florida	57.8
8	Georgia	62.5
40	Hawaii	57.8
10	Idaho	61.6
38	Illinois	58.4
33	Indiana	58.9
24	Iowa	59.6
15	Kansas	60.7
35	Kentucky	58.5
39	Louisiana	57.9
2	Maine	64.3
20	Maryland	60.2
5	Massachusetts	63.4
49	Michigan	55.6
11	Minnesota	61.5
35	Mississippi	58.5
28	Missouri	59.2
20	Montana	60.2
7	Nebraska	62.7
17	Nevada	60.4
4	New Hampshire	63.5
35	New Jersey	58.5
47	New Mexico	56.2
1	New York	69.2
11	North Carolina	61.5
19	North Dakota	60.3
46	Ohio	56.8
50	Oklahoma	52.9
34	Oregon	58.7
25	Pennsylvania	59.4
27	Rhode Island	59.3
42	South Carolina	57.6
31	South Dakota	59.0
3	Tennessee	64.0
23	Texas	59.8
13	Utah	61.4
6	Vermont	63.0
14	Virginia	60.9
25	Washington	59.4
28	West Virginia	59.2
17	Wisconsin	60.4
31	Wyoming	59.0

RANK ORDER

RANK	STATE	PERCENT
1	New York	69.2
2	Maine	64.3
3	Tennessee	64.0
4	New Hampshire	63.5
5	Massachusetts	63.4
6	Vermont	63.0
7	Nebraska	62.7
8	Connecticut	62.5
8	Georgia	62.5
10	Idaho	61.6
11	Minnesota	61.5
11	North Carolina	61.5
13	Utah	61.4
14	Virginia	60.9
15	Kansas	60.7
16	Delaware	60.6
17	Nevada	60.4
17	Wisconsin	60.4
19	North Dakota	60.3
20	Maryland	60.2
20	Montana	60.2
22	Arkansas	60.0
23	Texas	59.8
24	Iowa	59.6
25	Pennsylvania	59.4
25	Washington	59.4
27	Rhode Island	59.3
28	California	59.2
28	Missouri	59.2
28	West Virginia	59.2
31	South Dakota	59.0
31	Wyoming	59.0
33	Indiana	58.9
34	Oregon	58.7
35	Kentucky	58.5
35	Mississippi	58.5
35	New Jersey	58.5
38	Illinois	58.4
39	Louisiana	57.9
40	Florida	57.8
40	Hawaii	57.8
42	South Carolina	57.6
43	Alabama	57.4
44	Alaska	56.9
44	Arizona	56.9
46	Ohio	56.8
47	New Mexico	56.2
48	Colorado	55.8
49	Michigan	55.6
50	Oklahoma	52.9

	District of Columbia	50.3

Source: CQ Press using data from U.S. Bureau of the Census, Governments Division
"Public Education Finances: 2006" (http://www.census.gov/govs/www/school06.html)

*Includes payments for instruction for salaries, employee benefits, supplies, materials, and contractual services. Excludes capital outlay, debt service, and interfund transfers. Instruction covers regular, special, and vocational programs offered in both the academic year and summer school. Excluded are support services (e.g. instructional staff support and administration) and other support activities as well as adult education and community services.

Public Elementary and Secondary School Current Expenditures for Salaries, Wages, and Benefits for Instruction in 2006
National Total = $242,832,899,000*

ALPHA ORDER

RANK	STATE	EXPENDITURES	% of USA
25	Alabama	$2,957,557,000	1.2%
44	Alaska	772,585,000	0.3%
22	Arizona	3,387,670,000	1.4%
32	Arkansas	1,952,636,000	0.8%
1	California	28,546,003,000	11.8%
23	Colorado	3,115,890,000	1.3%
20	Connecticut	4,002,745,000	1.6%
45	Delaware	743,851,000	0.3%
7	Florida	10,135,781,000	4.2%
10	Georgia	7,862,044,000	3.2%
43	Hawaii	936,371,000	0.4%
42	Idaho	950,912,000	0.4%
6	Illinois	10,296,879,000	4.2%
15	Indiana	5,181,318,000	2.1%
29	Iowa	2,256,418,000	0.9%
31	Kansas	1,964,735,000	0.8%
26	Kentucky	2,914,574,000	1.2%
27	Louisiana	2,896,504,000	1.2%
39	Maine	1,214,525,000	0.5%
14	Maryland	5,197,711,000	2.1%
11	Massachusetts	6,690,379,000	2.8%
9	Michigan	8,711,383,000	3.6%
17	Minnesota	4,405,245,000	1.8%
33	Mississippi	1,887,179,000	0.8%
19	Missouri	4,041,575,000	1.7%
47	Montana	642,292,000	0.3%
38	Nebraska	1,365,215,000	0.6%
35	Nevada	1,558,300,000	0.6%
40	New Hampshire	1,189,387,000	0.5%
4	New Jersey	10,675,601,000	4.4%
37	New Mexico	1,365,806,000	0.6%
2	New York	26,404,221,000	10.9%
13	North Carolina	5,800,320,000	2.4%
50	North Dakota	468,880,000	0.2%
8	Ohio	8,896,308,000	3.7%
30	Oklahoma	2,151,219,000	0.9%
28	Oregon	2,496,059,000	1.0%
5	Pennsylvania	10,418,166,000	4.3%
41	Rhode Island	1,012,179,000	0.4%
24	South Carolina	2,999,500,000	1.2%
49	South Dakota	486,034,000	0.2%
21	Tennessee	3,730,340,000	1.5%
3	Texas	17,765,427,000	7.3%
34	Utah	1,588,744,000	0.7%
46	Vermont	655,578,000	0.3%
12	Virginia	6,520,217,000	2.7%
18	Washington	4,367,409,000	1.8%
36	West Virginia	1,455,360,000	0.6%
16	Wisconsin	4,977,941,000	2.0%
48	Wyoming	513,058,000	0.2%

RANK ORDER

RANK	STATE	EXPENDITURES	% of USA
1	California	$28,546,003,000	11.8%
2	New York	26,404,221,000	10.9%
3	Texas	17,765,427,000	7.3%
4	New Jersey	10,675,601,000	4.4%
5	Pennsylvania	10,418,166,000	4.3%
6	Illinois	10,296,879,000	4.2%
7	Florida	10,135,781,000	4.2%
8	Ohio	8,896,308,000	3.7%
9	Michigan	8,711,383,000	3.6%
10	Georgia	7,862,044,000	3.2%
11	Massachusetts	6,690,379,000	2.8%
12	Virginia	6,520,217,000	2.7%
13	North Carolina	5,800,320,000	2.4%
14	Maryland	5,197,711,000	2.1%
15	Indiana	5,181,318,000	2.1%
16	Wisconsin	4,977,941,000	2.0%
17	Minnesota	4,405,245,000	1.8%
18	Washington	4,367,409,000	1.8%
19	Missouri	4,041,575,000	1.7%
20	Connecticut	4,002,745,000	1.6%
21	Tennessee	3,730,340,000	1.5%
22	Arizona	3,387,670,000	1.4%
23	Colorado	3,115,890,000	1.3%
24	South Carolina	2,999,500,000	1.2%
25	Alabama	2,957,557,000	1.2%
26	Kentucky	2,914,574,000	1.2%
27	Louisiana	2,896,504,000	1.2%
28	Oregon	2,496,059,000	1.0%
29	Iowa	2,256,418,000	0.9%
30	Oklahoma	2,151,219,000	0.9%
31	Kansas	1,964,735,000	0.8%
32	Arkansas	1,952,636,000	0.8%
33	Mississippi	1,887,179,000	0.8%
34	Utah	1,588,744,000	0.7%
35	Nevada	1,558,300,000	0.6%
36	West Virginia	1,455,360,000	0.6%
37	New Mexico	1,365,806,000	0.6%
38	Nebraska	1,365,215,000	0.6%
39	Maine	1,214,525,000	0.5%
40	New Hampshire	1,189,387,000	0.5%
41	Rhode Island	1,012,179,000	0.4%
42	Idaho	950,912,000	0.4%
43	Hawaii	936,371,000	0.4%
44	Alaska	772,585,000	0.3%
45	Delaware	743,851,000	0.3%
46	Vermont	655,578,000	0.3%
47	Montana	642,292,000	0.3%
48	Wyoming	513,058,000	0.2%
49	South Dakota	486,034,000	0.2%
50	North Dakota	468,880,000	0.2%
	District of Columbia	306,868,000	0.1%

Source: CQ Press using data from U.S. Bureau of the Census, Governments Division
   "Public Education Finances: 2006" (http://www.census.gov/govs/www/school06.html)
*Current spending for instruction in regular, special, and vocational programs. Excludes support services. Consists of gross compensation before deductions for withheld taxes, retirement contributions, or other purposes. Also includes benefits such as contributions on behalf of employees for retirement coverage, social security, group health and life insurance, tuition reimbursement, worker's compensation, and unemployment compensation.

Per Capita Public Elementary and Secondary School Current Expenditures for Salaries, Wages, and Benefits for Instruction in 2006
National Per Capita = $813*

ALPHA ORDER

RANK	STATE	PER PUPIL
43	Alabama	$644
4	Alaska	1,140
50	Arizona	549
31	Arkansas	695
22	California	787
39	Colorado	654
3	Connecticut	1,145
13	Delaware	872
49	Florida	561
17	Georgia	842
28	Hawaii	732
42	Idaho	650
20	Illinois	806
19	Indiana	822
25	Iowa	759
29	Kansas	713
32	Kentucky	693
36	Louisiana	683
10	Maine	924
9	Maryland	928
6	Massachusetts	1,040
14	Michigan	862
15	Minnesota	855
41	Mississippi	651
34	Missouri	692
37	Montana	678
24	Nebraska	774
44	Nevada	625
11	New Hampshire	907
2	New Jersey	1,232
30	New Mexico	703
1	New York	1,369
39	North Carolina	654
27	North Dakota	736
23	Ohio	776
48	Oklahoma	601
38	Oregon	676
18	Pennsylvania	840
8	Rhode Island	953
32	South Carolina	693
45	South Dakota	616
47	Tennessee	614
25	Texas	759
45	Utah	616
5	Vermont	1,056
16	Virginia	853
35	Washington	685
21	West Virginia	805
12	Wisconsin	893
7	Wyoming	1,001

RANK ORDER

RANK	STATE	PER PUPIL
1	New York	$1,369
2	New Jersey	1,232
3	Connecticut	1,145
4	Alaska	1,140
5	Vermont	1,056
6	Massachusetts	1,040
7	Wyoming	1,001
8	Rhode Island	953
9	Maryland	928
10	Maine	924
11	New Hampshire	907
12	Wisconsin	893
13	Delaware	872
14	Michigan	862
15	Minnesota	855
16	Virginia	853
17	Georgia	842
18	Pennsylvania	840
19	Indiana	822
20	Illinois	806
21	West Virginia	805
22	California	787
23	Ohio	776
24	Nebraska	774
25	Iowa	759
25	Texas	759
27	North Dakota	736
28	Hawaii	732
29	Kansas	713
30	New Mexico	703
31	Arkansas	695
32	Kentucky	693
32	South Carolina	693
34	Missouri	692
35	Washington	685
36	Louisiana	683
37	Montana	678
38	Oregon	676
39	Colorado	654
39	North Carolina	654
41	Mississippi	651
42	Idaho	650
43	Alabama	644
44	Nevada	625
45	South Dakota	616
45	Utah	616
47	Tennessee	614
48	Oklahoma	601
49	Florida	561
50	Arizona	549

District of Columbia 524

Source: CQ Press using data from U.S. Bureau of the Census, Governments Division
"Public Education Finances: 2006" (http://www.census.gov/govs/www/school06.html)
*Current spending for instruction in regular, special, and vocational programs. Excludes support services. Consists of gross compensation before deductions for withheld taxes, retirement contributions, or other purposes. Also includes benefits such as contributions on behalf of employees for retirement coverage, social security, group health and life insurance, tuition reimbursement, worker's compensation, and unemployment compensation.

Per Pupil Public Elementary and Secondary School Current Expenditures for Salaries, Wages, and Benefits for Instruction in 2006
National Per Pupil = $5,019*

ALPHA ORDER

RANK	STATE	PER PUPIL
42	Alabama	$3,979
13	Alaska	5,814
49	Arizona	3,373
38	Arkansas	4,132
27	California	4,563
39	Colorado	3,998
3	Connecticut	7,193
7	Delaware	6,504
45	Florida	3,805
22	Georgia	4,921
18	Hawaii	5,122
47	Idaho	3,681
23	Illinois	4,897
19	Indiana	5,049
26	Iowa	4,667
35	Kansas	4,217
33	Kentucky	4,289
29	Louisiana	4,468
8	Maine	6,223
9	Maryland	6,044
5	Massachusetts	7,043
20	Michigan	5,038
15	Minnesota	5,385
44	Mississippi	3,821
31	Missouri	4,413
30	Montana	4,422
25	Nebraska	4,771
46	Nevada	3,775
12	New Hampshire	5,916
2	New Jersey	7,735
36	New Mexico	4,180
1	New York	9,473
37	North Carolina	4,178
24	North Dakota	4,776
21	Ohio	5,028
48	Oklahoma	3,391
28	Oregon	4,484
11	Pennsylvania	5,921
6	Rhode Island	6,743
32	South Carolina	4,291
40	South Dakota	3,993
43	Tennessee	3,911
41	Texas	3,992
50	Utah	3,200
4	Vermont	7,100
16	Virginia	5,373
34	Washington	4,233
17	West Virginia	5,202
14	Wisconsin	5,724
10	Wyoming	5,955

RANK ORDER

RANK	STATE	PER PUPIL
1	New York	$9,473
2	New Jersey	7,735
3	Connecticut	7,193
4	Vermont	7,100
5	Massachusetts	7,043
6	Rhode Island	6,743
7	Delaware	6,504
8	Maine	6,223
9	Maryland	6,044
10	Wyoming	5,955
11	Pennsylvania	5,921
12	New Hampshire	5,916
13	Alaska	5,814
14	Wisconsin	5,724
15	Minnesota	5,385
16	Virginia	5,373
17	West Virginia	5,202
18	Hawaii	5,122
19	Indiana	5,049
20	Michigan	5,038
21	Ohio	5,028
22	Georgia	4,921
23	Illinois	4,897
24	North Dakota	4,776
25	Nebraska	4,771
26	Iowa	4,667
27	California	4,563
28	Oregon	4,484
29	Louisiana	4,468
30	Montana	4,422
31	Missouri	4,413
32	South Carolina	4,291
33	Kentucky	4,289
34	Washington	4,233
35	Kansas	4,217
36	New Mexico	4,180
37	North Carolina	4,178
38	Arkansas	4,132
39	Colorado	3,998
40	South Dakota	3,993
41	Texas	3,992
42	Alabama	3,979
43	Tennessee	3,911
44	Mississippi	3,821
45	Florida	3,805
46	Nevada	3,775
47	Idaho	3,681
48	Oklahoma	3,391
49	Arizona	3,373
50	Utah	3,200
	District of Columbia	5,147

Source: CQ Press using data from U.S. Bureau of the Census, Governments Division
"Public Education Finances: 2006" (http://www.census.gov/govs/www/school06.html)
*Based on student membership. Current spending for instruction in regular, special, and vocational programs. Excludes support services. Consists of gross compensation before deductions for withheld taxes, retirement contributions, or other purposes. Includes benefits such as contributions on behalf of employees for retirement coverage, social security, group health and life insurance, tuition reimbursement, worker's compensation, and unemployment compensation.

Percent of Public Elementary and Secondary School Current Expenditures Used for Salaries, Wages, and Benefits for Instruction in 2006
National Percent = 53.8%*

ALPHA ORDER

RANK	STATE	PERCENT
42	Alabama	51.0
44	Alaska	50.5
37	Arizona	51.6
35	Arkansas	51.7
32	California	52.2
48	Colorado	48.8
7	Connecticut	56.8
18	Delaware	55.1
49	Florida	47.9
2	Georgia	57.3
46	Hawaii	50.2
3	Idaho	57.0
26	Illinois	53.1
3	Indiana	57.0
16	Iowa	55.5
46	Kansas	50.2
17	Kentucky	55.3
27	Louisiana	53.0
7	Maine	56.8
10	Maryland	56.5
15	Massachusetts	55.7
38	Michigan	51.5
13	Minnesota	56.2
30	Mississippi	52.7
25	Missouri	53.4
39	Montana	51.3
21	Nebraska	54.5
40	Nevada	51.1
9	New Hampshire	56.7
43	New Jersey	50.7
40	New Mexico	51.1
1	New York	61.8
12	North Carolina	56.3
18	North Dakota	55.1
45	Ohio	50.3
50	Oklahoma	46.7
35	Oregon	51.7
27	Pennsylvania	53.0
24	Rhode Island	53.5
32	South Carolina	52.2
34	South Dakota	51.9
13	Tennessee	56.2
31	Texas	52.3
3	Utah	57.0
22	Vermont	54.1
10	Virginia	56.5
23	Washington	53.8
20	West Virginia	54.9
6	Wisconsin	56.9
27	Wyoming	53.0

RANK ORDER

RANK	STATE	PERCENT
1	New York	61.8
2	Georgia	57.3
3	Idaho	57.0
3	Indiana	57.0
3	Utah	57.0
6	Wisconsin	56.9
7	Connecticut	56.8
7	Maine	56.8
9	New Hampshire	56.7
10	Maryland	56.5
10	Virginia	56.5
12	North Carolina	56.3
13	Minnesota	56.2
13	Tennessee	56.2
15	Massachusetts	55.7
16	Iowa	55.5
17	Kentucky	55.3
18	Delaware	55.1
18	North Dakota	55.1
20	West Virginia	54.9
21	Nebraska	54.5
22	Vermont	54.1
23	Washington	53.8
24	Rhode Island	53.5
25	Missouri	53.4
26	Illinois	53.1
27	Louisiana	53.0
27	Pennsylvania	53.0
27	Wyoming	53.0
30	Mississippi	52.7
31	Texas	52.3
32	California	52.2
32	South Carolina	52.2
34	South Dakota	51.9
35	Arkansas	51.7
35	Oregon	51.7
37	Arizona	51.6
38	Michigan	51.5
39	Montana	51.3
40	Nevada	51.1
40	New Mexico	51.1
42	Alabama	51.0
43	New Jersey	50.7
44	Alaska	50.5
45	Ohio	50.3
46	Hawaii	50.2
46	Kansas	50.2
48	Colorado	48.8
49	Florida	47.9
50	Oklahoma	46.7

	District of Columbia	32.2

Source: CQ Press using data from U.S. Bureau of the Census, Governments Division
   "Public Education Finances: 2006" (http://www.census.gov/govs/www/school06.html)
*Current spending for instruction in regular, special, and vocational programs. Excludes support services. Consists of gross compensation before deductions for withheld taxes, retirement contributions, or other purposes. Also includes benefits such as contributions on behalf of employees for retirement coverage, social security, group health and life insurance, tuition reimbursement, worker's compensation, and unemployment compensation.

Public Elementary and Secondary School Current Expenditures for Salaries, Wages, and Benefits for Instruction per FTE Teacher in 2006
National Per Teacher = $77,411*

ALPHA ORDER

RANK	STATE	PER TEACHER
50	Alabama	$51,207
3	Alaska	97,647
31	Arizona	65,939
44	Arkansas	59,176
6	California	92,344
29	Colorado	67,972
2	Connecticut	100,858
5	Delaware	93,005
36	Florida	63,762
24	Georgia	72,438
14	Hawaii	83,411
32	Idaho	65,485
17	Illinois	76,924
12	Indiana	85,512
34	Iowa	64,137
47	Kansas	58,460
28	Kentucky	68,719
33	Louisiana	64,857
23	Maine	72,796
7	Maryland	91,695
8	Massachusetts	90,907
10	Michigan	87,255
11	Minnesota	86,197
43	Mississippi	60,038
42	Missouri	60,254
40	Montana	61,943
35	Nebraska	63,918
25	Nevada	71,666
18	New Hampshire	76,557
4	New Jersey	94,749
39	New Mexico	62,023
1	New York	120,573
41	North Carolina	60,632
46	North Dakota	58,588
20	Ohio	75,404
49	Oklahoma	51,424
9	Oregon	88,337
13	Pennsylvania	85,118
26	Rhode Island	70,787
38	South Carolina	62,215
48	South Dakota	53,241
37	Tennessee	62,594
45	Texas	58,743
27	Utah	69,097
21	Vermont	74,068
30	Virginia	67,807
16	Washington	81,622
22	West Virginia	72,987
15	Wisconsin	82,790
19	Wyoming	76,507

RANK ORDER

RANK	STATE	PER TEACHER
1	New York	$120,573
2	Connecticut	100,858
3	Alaska	97,647
4	New Jersey	94,749
5	Delaware	93,005
6	California	92,344
7	Maryland	91,695
8	Massachusetts	90,907
9	Oregon	88,337
10	Michigan	87,255
11	Minnesota	86,197
12	Indiana	85,512
13	Pennsylvania	85,118
14	Hawaii	83,411
15	Wisconsin	82,790
16	Washington	81,622
17	Illinois	76,924
18	New Hampshire	76,557
19	Wyoming	76,507
20	Ohio	75,404
21	Vermont	74,068
22	West Virginia	72,987
23	Maine	72,796
24	Georgia	72,438
25	Nevada	71,666
26	Rhode Island	70,787
27	Utah	69,097
28	Kentucky	68,719
29	Colorado	67,972
30	Virginia	67,807
31	Arizona	65,939
32	Idaho	65,485
33	Louisiana	64,857
34	Iowa	64,137
35	Nebraska	63,918
36	Florida	63,762
37	Tennessee	62,594
38	South Carolina	62,215
39	New Mexico	62,023
40	Montana	61,943
41	North Carolina	60,632
42	Missouri	60,254
43	Mississippi	60,038
44	Arkansas	59,176
45	Texas	58,743
46	North Dakota	58,588
47	Kansas	58,460
48	South Dakota	53,241
49	Oklahoma	51,424
50	Alabama	51,207
	District of Columbia	55,988

Source: CQ Press using data from U.S. Bureau of the Census, Governments Division
"Public Education Finances: 2006" (http://www.census.gov/govs/www/school06.html) and
"Common Core of Data (CCD) Database" (http://nces.ed.gov/ccd/)
*Current spending for instruction in regular, special, and vocational programs divided by full-time equivalent teacher counts for 2005-2006 school year. Excludes support services. Consists of gross compensation before deductions for withheld taxes, retirement contributions, or other purposes. Also includes employee benefits.

Public Elementary and Secondary School Current Expenditures for Salaries and Wages for Instruction in 2006
National Total = $184,369,075,000*

ALPHA ORDER

RANK	STATE	EXPENDITURES	% of USA
26	Alabama	$2,172,915,000	1.2%
44	Alaska	550,187,000	0.3%
22	Arizona	2,711,755,000	1.5%
32	Arkansas	1,552,172,000	0.8%
1	California	21,766,519,000	11.8%
23	Colorado	2,546,175,000	1.4%
21	Connecticut	2,935,591,000	1.6%
45	Delaware	519,702,000	0.3%
6	Florida	7,938,812,000	4.3%
9	Georgia	6,105,879,000	3.3%
43	Hawaii	691,902,000	0.4%
42	Idaho	719,855,000	0.4%
4	Illinois	8,153,879,000	4.4%
15	Indiana	3,459,076,000	1.9%
28	Iowa	1,732,271,000	0.9%
31	Kansas	1,594,761,000	0.9%
25	Kentucky	2,206,156,000	1.2%
27	Louisiana	2,120,992,000	1.2%
39	Maine	891,483,000	0.5%
14	Maryland	3,847,723,000	2.1%
13	Massachusetts	4,695,321,000	2.5%
10	Michigan	5,967,918,000	3.2%
17	Minnesota	3,405,687,000	1.8%
33	Mississippi	1,470,674,000	0.8%
19	Missouri	3,254,005,000	1.8%
46	Montana	501,186,000	0.3%
37	Nebraska	1,026,620,000	0.6%
34	Nevada	1,160,547,000	0.6%
40	New Hampshire	884,469,000	0.5%
5	New Jersey	7,966,714,000	4.3%
36	New Mexico	1,057,734,000	0.6%
2	New York	18,951,182,000	10.3%
12	North Carolina	4,711,687,000	2.6%
50	North Dakota	367,452,000	0.2%
8	Ohio	6,732,006,000	3.7%
30	Oklahoma	1,687,604,000	0.9%
29	Oregon	1,718,190,000	0.9%
7	Pennsylvania	7,784,396,000	4.2%
41	Rhode Island	737,734,000	0.4%
24	South Carolina	2,356,146,000	1.3%
48	South Dakota	385,944,000	0.2%
20	Tennessee	2,937,132,000	1.6%
3	Texas	15,318,791,000	8.3%
35	Utah	1,127,350,000	0.6%
47	Vermont	491,618,000	0.3%
11	Virginia	5,024,003,000	2.7%
16	Washington	3,425,040,000	1.9%
38	West Virginia	959,696,000	0.5%
18	Wisconsin	3,384,681,000	1.8%
49	Wyoming	378,852,000	0.2%

RANK ORDER

RANK	STATE	EXPENDITURES	% of USA
1	California	$21,766,519,000	11.8%
2	New York	18,951,182,000	10.3%
3	Texas	15,318,791,000	8.3%
4	Illinois	8,153,879,000	4.4%
5	New Jersey	7,966,714,000	4.3%
6	Florida	7,938,812,000	4.3%
7	Pennsylvania	7,784,396,000	4.2%
8	Ohio	6,732,006,000	3.7%
9	Georgia	6,105,879,000	3.3%
10	Michigan	5,967,918,000	3.2%
11	Virginia	5,024,003,000	2.7%
12	North Carolina	4,711,687,000	2.6%
13	Massachusetts	4,695,321,000	2.5%
14	Maryland	3,847,723,000	2.1%
15	Indiana	3,459,076,000	1.9%
16	Washington	3,425,040,000	1.9%
17	Minnesota	3,405,687,000	1.8%
18	Wisconsin	3,384,681,000	1.8%
19	Missouri	3,254,005,000	1.8%
20	Tennessee	2,937,132,000	1.6%
21	Connecticut	2,935,591,000	1.6%
22	Arizona	2,711,755,000	1.5%
23	Colorado	2,546,175,000	1.4%
24	South Carolina	2,356,146,000	1.3%
25	Kentucky	2,206,156,000	1.2%
26	Alabama	2,172,915,000	1.2%
27	Louisiana	2,120,992,000	1.2%
28	Iowa	1,732,271,000	0.9%
29	Oregon	1,718,190,000	0.9%
30	Oklahoma	1,687,604,000	0.9%
31	Kansas	1,594,761,000	0.9%
32	Arkansas	1,552,172,000	0.8%
33	Mississippi	1,470,674,000	0.8%
34	Nevada	1,160,547,000	0.6%
35	Utah	1,127,350,000	0.6%
36	New Mexico	1,057,734,000	0.6%
37	Nebraska	1,026,620,000	0.6%
38	West Virginia	959,696,000	0.5%
39	Maine	891,483,000	0.5%
40	New Hampshire	884,469,000	0.5%
41	Rhode Island	737,734,000	0.4%
42	Idaho	719,855,000	0.4%
43	Hawaii	691,902,000	0.4%
44	Alaska	550,187,000	0.3%
45	Delaware	519,702,000	0.3%
46	Montana	501,186,000	0.3%
47	Vermont	491,618,000	0.3%
48	South Dakota	385,944,000	0.2%
49	Wyoming	378,852,000	0.2%
50	North Dakota	367,452,000	0.2%
	District of Columbia	280,891,000	0.2%

Source: U.S. Bureau of the Census, Governments Division
    "Public Education Finances: 2006" (http://www.census.gov/govs/www/school06.html)
*Includes payments from all funds for salaries for instruction. Excludes capital outlay, debt service, and interfund transfers. Instruction covers regular, special, and vocational programs offered in both the academic year and summer school. Excluded are support services (e.g. instructional staff support and administration) and other support activities as well as adult education and community services.

Percent of Public Elementary and Secondary School Current Expenditures Used for Salaries and Wages for Instruction in 2006
National Percent = 40.8%*

ALPHA ORDER

RANK	STATE	PERCENT
44	Alabama	37.5
48	Alaska	35.9
19	Arizona	41.3
21	Arkansas	41.1
30	California	39.8
29	Colorado	39.9
18	Connecticut	41.6
38	Delaware	38.5
43	Florida	37.6
3	Georgia	44.5
45	Hawaii	37.1
8	Idaho	43.2
14	Illinois	42.1
39	Indiana	38.1
11	Iowa	42.6
25	Kansas	40.7
15	Kentucky	41.9
36	Louisiana	38.8
17	Maine	41.7
16	Maryland	41.8
33	Massachusetts	39.1
50	Michigan	35.3
6	Minnesota	43.5
22	Mississippi	41.0
10	Missouri	43.0
28	Montana	40.0
22	Nebraska	41.0
39	Nevada	38.1
12	New Hampshire	42.2
42	New Jersey	37.9
31	New Mexico	39.6
4	New York	44.3
1	North Carolina	45.7
8	North Dakota	43.2
41	Ohio	38.0
46	Oklahoma	36.6
49	Oregon	35.6
31	Pennsylvania	39.6
35	Rhode Island	39.0
22	South Carolina	41.0
20	South Dakota	41.2
5	Tennessee	44.2
2	Texas	45.1
27	Utah	40.5
26	Vermont	40.6
6	Virginia	43.5
12	Washington	42.2
47	West Virginia	36.2
37	Wisconsin	38.7
33	Wyoming	39.1

RANK ORDER

RANK	STATE	PERCENT
1	North Carolina	45.7
2	Texas	45.1
3	Georgia	44.5
4	New York	44.3
5	Tennessee	44.2
6	Minnesota	43.5
6	Virginia	43.5
8	Idaho	43.2
8	North Dakota	43.2
10	Missouri	43.0
11	Iowa	42.6
12	New Hampshire	42.2
12	Washington	42.2
14	Illinois	42.1
15	Kentucky	41.9
16	Maryland	41.8
17	Maine	41.7
18	Connecticut	41.6
19	Arizona	41.3
20	South Dakota	41.2
21	Arkansas	41.1
22	Mississippi	41.0
22	Nebraska	41.0
22	South Carolina	41.0
25	Kansas	40.7
26	Vermont	40.6
27	Utah	40.5
28	Montana	40.0
29	Colorado	39.9
30	California	39.8
31	New Mexico	39.6
31	Pennsylvania	39.6
33	Massachusetts	39.1
33	Wyoming	39.1
35	Rhode Island	39.0
36	Louisiana	38.8
37	Wisconsin	38.7
38	Delaware	38.5
39	Indiana	38.1
39	Nevada	38.1
41	Ohio	38.0
42	New Jersey	37.9
43	Florida	37.6
44	Alabama	37.5
45	Hawaii	37.1
46	Oklahoma	36.6
47	West Virginia	36.2
48	Alaska	35.9
49	Oregon	35.6
50	Michigan	35.3

District of Columbia 29.5

Source: CQ Press using data from U.S. Bureau of the Census, Governments Division
"Public Education Finances: 2006" (http://www.census.gov/govs/www/school06.html)
*Includes payments from all funds for salaries for instruction. Excludes capital outlay, debt service, and interfund transfers.
Instruction covers regular, special, and vocational programs offered in both the academic year and summer school. Excluded are support services (e.g. instructional staff support and administration) and other support activities as well as adult education and community services.

Public Elementary and Secondary School Current Expenditures for Employee Benefits for Instruction in 2006
National Total = $58,463,824,000*

ALPHA ORDER

RANK	STATE	EXPENDITURES	% of USA
22	Alabama	$784,642,000	1.3%
45	Alaska	222,398,000	0.4%
26	Arizona	675,915,000	1.2%
34	Arkansas	400,464,000	0.7%
2	California	6,779,484,000	11.6%
28	Colorado	569,715,000	1.0%
17	Connecticut	1,067,154,000	1.8%
44	Delaware	224,149,000	0.4%
7	Florida	2,196,969,000	3.8%
11	Georgia	1,756,165,000	3.0%
42	Hawaii	244,469,000	0.4%
43	Idaho	231,057,000	0.4%
9	Illinois	2,143,000,000	3.7%
12	Indiana	1,722,242,000	2.9%
29	Iowa	524,147,000	0.9%
36	Kansas	369,974,000	0.6%
25	Kentucky	708,418,000	1.2%
24	Louisiana	775,512,000	1.3%
38	Maine	323,042,000	0.6%
15	Maryland	1,349,988,000	2.3%
10	Massachusetts	1,995,058,000	3.4%
3	Michigan	2,743,465,000	4.7%
18	Minnesota	999,558,000	1.7%
33	Mississippi	416,505,000	0.7%
21	Missouri	787,570,000	1.3%
47	Montana	141,106,000	0.2%
37	Nebraska	338,595,000	0.6%
35	Nevada	397,753,000	0.7%
40	New Hampshire	304,918,000	0.5%
4	New Jersey	2,708,887,000	4.6%
39	New Mexico	308,072,000	0.5%
1	New York	7,453,039,000	12.7%
16	North Carolina	1,088,633,000	1.9%
49	North Dakota	101,428,000	0.2%
8	Ohio	2,164,302,000	3.7%
31	Oklahoma	463,615,000	0.8%
23	Oregon	777,869,000	1.3%
5	Pennsylvania	2,633,770,000	4.5%
41	Rhode Island	274,445,000	0.5%
27	South Carolina	643,354,000	1.1%
50	South Dakota	100,090,000	0.2%
20	Tennessee	793,208,000	1.4%
6	Texas	2,446,636,000	4.2%
32	Utah	461,394,000	0.8%
46	Vermont	163,960,000	0.3%
14	Virginia	1,496,214,000	2.6%
19	Washington	942,369,000	1.6%
30	West Virginia	495,664,000	0.8%
13	Wisconsin	1,593,260,000	2.7%
48	Wyoming	134,206,000	0.2%

RANK ORDER

RANK	STATE	EXPENDITURES	% of USA
1	New York	$7,453,039,000	12.7%
2	California	6,779,484,000	11.6%
3	Michigan	2,743,465,000	4.7%
4	New Jersey	2,708,887,000	4.6%
5	Pennsylvania	2,633,770,000	4.5%
6	Texas	2,446,636,000	4.2%
7	Florida	2,196,969,000	3.8%
8	Ohio	2,164,302,000	3.7%
9	Illinois	2,143,000,000	3.7%
10	Massachusetts	1,995,058,000	3.4%
11	Georgia	1,756,165,000	3.0%
12	Indiana	1,722,242,000	2.9%
13	Wisconsin	1,593,260,000	2.7%
14	Virginia	1,496,214,000	2.6%
15	Maryland	1,349,988,000	2.3%
16	North Carolina	1,088,633,000	1.9%
17	Connecticut	1,067,154,000	1.8%
18	Minnesota	999,558,000	1.7%
19	Washington	942,369,000	1.6%
20	Tennessee	793,208,000	1.4%
21	Missouri	787,570,000	1.3%
22	Alabama	784,642,000	1.3%
23	Oregon	777,869,000	1.3%
24	Louisiana	775,512,000	1.3%
25	Kentucky	708,418,000	1.2%
26	Arizona	675,915,000	1.2%
27	South Carolina	643,354,000	1.1%
28	Colorado	569,715,000	1.0%
29	Iowa	524,147,000	0.9%
30	West Virginia	495,664,000	0.8%
31	Oklahoma	463,615,000	0.8%
32	Utah	461,394,000	0.8%
33	Mississippi	416,505,000	0.7%
34	Arkansas	400,464,000	0.7%
35	Nevada	397,753,000	0.7%
36	Kansas	369,974,000	0.6%
37	Nebraska	338,595,000	0.6%
38	Maine	323,042,000	0.6%
39	New Mexico	308,072,000	0.5%
40	New Hampshire	304,918,000	0.5%
41	Rhode Island	274,445,000	0.5%
42	Hawaii	244,469,000	0.4%
43	Idaho	231,057,000	0.4%
44	Delaware	224,149,000	0.4%
45	Alaska	222,398,000	0.4%
46	Vermont	163,960,000	0.3%
47	Montana	141,106,000	0.2%
48	Wyoming	134,206,000	0.2%
49	North Dakota	101,428,000	0.2%
50	South Dakota	100,090,000	0.2%
	District of Columbia	25,977,000	0.0%

Source: U.S. Bureau of the Census, Governments Division
    "Public Education Finances: 2006" (http://www.census.gov/govs/www/school06.html)
*Includes payments from all funds for employee benefits for instruction. Excludes capital outlay, debt service, and interfund transfers. Instruction covers regular, special, and vocational programs offered in both the academic school year and summer school. It excludes support services (e.g. instructional staff support and administration) and other support activities as well as adult education and community services.

Percent of Public Elementary and Secondary School Current Expenditures Used for Employee Benefits for Instruction in 2006
National Percent = 12.9%*

ALPHA ORDER

RANK	STATE	PERCENT
19	Alabama	13.5
13	Alaska	14.5
46	Arizona	10.3
42	Arkansas	10.6
31	California	12.4
49	Colorado	8.9
10	Connecticut	15.1
5	Delaware	16.6
44	Florida	10.4
29	Georgia	12.8
24	Hawaii	13.1
17	Idaho	13.9
40	Illinois	11.1
1	Indiana	19.0
27	Iowa	12.9
48	Kansas	9.4
22	Kentucky	13.4
16	Louisiana	14.2
10	Maine	15.1
12	Maryland	14.7
5	Massachusetts	16.6
8	Michigan	16.2
29	Minnesota	12.8
35	Mississippi	11.6
44	Missouri	10.4
38	Montana	11.3
19	Nebraska	13.5
25	Nevada	13.0
13	New Hampshire	14.5
27	New Jersey	12.9
37	New Mexico	11.5
4	New York	17.4
42	North Carolina	10.6
33	North Dakota	11.9
32	Ohio	12.2
47	Oklahoma	10.1
9	Oregon	16.1
22	Pennsylvania	13.4
13	Rhode Island	14.5
39	South Carolina	11.2
41	South Dakota	10.7
33	Tennessee	11.9
50	Texas	7.2
5	Utah	16.6
19	Vermont	13.5
25	Virginia	13.0
35	Washington	11.6
2	West Virginia	18.7
3	Wisconsin	18.2
17	Wyoming	13.9

RANK ORDER

RANK	STATE	PERCENT
1	Indiana	19.0
2	West Virginia	18.7
3	Wisconsin	18.2
4	New York	17.4
5	Delaware	16.6
5	Massachusetts	16.6
5	Utah	16.6
8	Michigan	16.2
9	Oregon	16.1
10	Connecticut	15.1
10	Maine	15.1
12	Maryland	14.7
13	Alaska	14.5
13	New Hampshire	14.5
13	Rhode Island	14.5
16	Louisiana	14.2
17	Idaho	13.9
17	Wyoming	13.9
19	Alabama	13.5
19	Nebraska	13.5
19	Vermont	13.5
22	Kentucky	13.4
22	Pennsylvania	13.4
24	Hawaii	13.1
25	Nevada	13.0
25	Virginia	13.0
27	Iowa	12.9
27	New Jersey	12.9
29	Georgia	12.8
29	Minnesota	12.8
31	California	12.4
32	Ohio	12.2
33	North Dakota	11.9
33	Tennessee	11.9
35	Mississippi	11.6
35	Washington	11.6
37	New Mexico	11.5
38	Montana	11.3
39	South Carolina	11.2
40	Illinois	11.1
41	South Dakota	10.7
42	Arkansas	10.6
42	North Carolina	10.6
44	Florida	10.4
44	Missouri	10.4
46	Arizona	10.3
47	Oklahoma	10.1
48	Kansas	9.4
49	Colorado	8.9
50	Texas	7.2

	District of Columbia	2.7

Source: CQ Press using data from U.S. Bureau of the Census, Governments Division
"Public Education Finances: 2006" (http://www.census.gov/govs/www/school06.html)
*Includes payments from all funds for employee benefits for instruction. Excludes capital outlay, debt service, and interfund transfers. Instruction covers regular, special, and vocational programs offered in both the academic school year and summer school. It excludes support services (e.g. instructional staff support and administration) and other support activities as well as adult education and community services.

Public Elementary and Secondary Current Expenditures for Support Services in 2006
National Total = $156,003,270,000*

ALPHA ORDER

RANK	STATE	EXPENDITURES	% of USA
25	Alabama	$1,983,482,000	1.3%
43	Alaska	601,197,000	0.4%
20	Arizona	2,436,340,000	1.6%
32	Arkansas	1,297,593,000	0.8%
1	California	19,079,354,000	12.2%
19	Colorado	2,518,038,000	1.6%
21	Connecticut	2,354,944,000	1.5%
45	Delaware	467,410,000	0.3%
5	Florida	7,492,039,000	4.8%
10	Georgia	4,432,252,000	2.8%
42	Hawaii	643,718,000	0.4%
44	Idaho	557,225,000	0.4%
6	Illinois	7,242,674,000	4.6%
14	Indiana	3,313,154,000	2.1%
30	Iowa	1,428,006,000	0.9%
31	Kansas	1,345,794,000	0.9%
27	Kentucky	1,830,653,000	1.2%
26	Louisiana	1,962,367,000	1.3%
41	Maine	660,506,000	0.4%
15	Maryland	3,217,615,000	2.1%
11	Massachusetts	3,989,906,000	2.6%
9	Michigan	6,627,833,000	4.2%
22	Minnesota	2,317,030,000	1.5%
33	Mississippi	1,244,115,000	0.8%
18	Missouri	2,619,786,000	1.7%
46	Montana	442,662,000	0.3%
38	Nebraska	805,633,000	0.5%
34	Nevada	1,088,646,000	0.7%
39	New Hampshire	696,005,000	0.4%
4	New Jersey	7,892,051,000	5.1%
35	New Mexico	1,016,791,000	0.7%
2	New York	11,898,562,000	7.6%
13	North Carolina	3,344,466,000	2.1%
50	North Dakota	269,235,000	0.2%
8	Ohio	6,796,495,000	4.4%
29	Oklahoma	1,677,749,000	1.1%
28	Oregon	1,803,634,000	1.2%
7	Pennsylvania	7,025,760,000	4.5%
40	Rhode Island	690,355,000	0.4%
23	South Carolina	2,071,441,000	1.3%
49	South Dakota	334,845,000	0.2%
24	Tennessee	1,995,464,000	1.3%
3	Texas	11,672,256,000	7.5%
37	Utah	821,539,000	0.5%
47	Vermont	410,862,000	0.3%
12	Virginia	3,974,403,000	2.5%
17	Washington	2,852,334,000	1.8%
36	West Virginia	897,874,000	0.6%
16	Wisconsin	3,064,437,000	2.0%
48	Wyoming	362,807,000	0.2%

RANK ORDER

RANK	STATE	EXPENDITURES	% of USA
1	California	$19,079,354,000	12.2%
2	New York	11,898,562,000	7.6%
3	Texas	11,672,256,000	7.5%
4	New Jersey	7,892,051,000	5.1%
5	Florida	7,492,039,000	4.8%
6	Illinois	7,242,674,000	4.6%
7	Pennsylvania	7,025,760,000	4.5%
8	Ohio	6,796,495,000	4.4%
9	Michigan	6,627,833,000	4.2%
10	Georgia	4,432,252,000	2.8%
11	Massachusetts	3,989,906,000	2.6%
12	Virginia	3,974,403,000	2.5%
13	North Carolina	3,344,466,000	2.1%
14	Indiana	3,313,154,000	2.1%
15	Maryland	3,217,615,000	2.1%
16	Wisconsin	3,064,437,000	2.0%
17	Washington	2,852,334,000	1.8%
18	Missouri	2,619,786,000	1.7%
19	Colorado	2,518,038,000	1.6%
20	Arizona	2,436,340,000	1.6%
21	Connecticut	2,354,944,000	1.5%
22	Minnesota	2,317,030,000	1.5%
23	South Carolina	2,071,441,000	1.3%
24	Tennessee	1,995,464,000	1.3%
25	Alabama	1,983,482,000	1.3%
26	Louisiana	1,962,367,000	1.3%
27	Kentucky	1,830,653,000	1.2%
28	Oregon	1,803,634,000	1.2%
29	Oklahoma	1,677,749,000	1.1%
30	Iowa	1,428,006,000	0.9%
31	Kansas	1,345,794,000	0.9%
32	Arkansas	1,297,593,000	0.8%
33	Mississippi	1,244,115,000	0.8%
34	Nevada	1,088,646,000	0.7%
35	New Mexico	1,016,791,000	0.7%
36	West Virginia	897,874,000	0.6%
37	Utah	821,539,000	0.5%
38	Nebraska	805,633,000	0.5%
39	New Hampshire	696,005,000	0.4%
40	Rhode Island	690,355,000	0.4%
41	Maine	660,506,000	0.4%
42	Hawaii	643,718,000	0.4%
43	Alaska	601,197,000	0.4%
44	Idaho	557,225,000	0.4%
45	Delaware	467,410,000	0.3%
46	Montana	442,662,000	0.3%
47	Vermont	410,862,000	0.3%
48	Wyoming	362,807,000	0.2%
49	South Dakota	334,845,000	0.2%
50	North Dakota	269,235,000	0.2%
	District of Columbia	433,933,000	0.3%

Source: U.S. Bureau of the Census, Governments Division
"Public Education Finances: 2006" (http://www.census.gov/govs/www/school06.html)
*Includes payments for support services for salaries, employee benefits, supplies, materials, and contractual services.
Excludes capital outlay, debt service, and interfund transfers. Support services cover regular, special, and vocational programs offered in both the academic school year and summer school. It excludes instruction services as well as adult education and community services.

Per Capita Elementary and Secondary School Current Expenditures for Support Services in 2006
National Per Capita = $522*

ALPHA ORDER

RANK	STATE	PER CAPITA
41	Alabama	$432
2	Alaska	887
46	Arizona	395
33	Arkansas	462
18	California	526
17	Colorado	528
4	Connecticut	674
15	Delaware	548
45	Florida	415
30	Georgia	474
22	Hawaii	503
47	Idaho	381
12	Illinois	567
18	Indiana	526
28	Iowa	480
27	Kansas	488
40	Kentucky	435
33	Louisiana	462
23	Maine	502
11	Maryland	574
8	Massachusetts	620
6	Michigan	656
36	Minnesota	450
42	Mississippi	429
37	Missouri	449
32	Montana	468
35	Nebraska	457
39	Nevada	437
16	New Hampshire	531
1	New Jersey	911
20	New Mexico	523
9	New York	617
48	North Carolina	377
44	North Dakota	422
10	Ohio	593
31	Oklahoma	469
26	Oregon	489
13	Pennsylvania	566
7	Rhode Island	650
29	South Carolina	478
43	South Dakota	425
49	Tennessee	328
24	Texas	499
50	Utah	318
5	Vermont	662
21	Virginia	520
38	Washington	447
25	West Virginia	496
14	Wisconsin	550
3	Wyoming	708

RANK ORDER

RANK	STATE	PER CAPITA
1	New Jersey	$911
2	Alaska	887
3	Wyoming	708
4	Connecticut	674
5	Vermont	662
6	Michigan	656
7	Rhode Island	650
8	Massachusetts	620
9	New York	617
10	Ohio	593
11	Maryland	574
12	Illinois	567
13	Pennsylvania	566
14	Wisconsin	550
15	Delaware	548
16	New Hampshire	531
17	Colorado	528
18	California	526
18	Indiana	526
20	New Mexico	523
21	Virginia	520
22	Hawaii	503
23	Maine	502
24	Texas	499
25	West Virginia	496
26	Oregon	489
27	Kansas	488
28	Iowa	480
29	South Carolina	478
30	Georgia	474
31	Oklahoma	469
32	Montana	468
33	Arkansas	462
33	Louisiana	462
35	Nebraska	457
36	Minnesota	450
37	Missouri	449
38	Washington	447
39	Nevada	437
40	Kentucky	435
41	Alabama	432
42	Mississippi	429
43	South Dakota	425
44	North Dakota	422
45	Florida	415
46	Arizona	395
47	Idaho	381
48	North Carolina	377
49	Tennessee	328
50	Utah	318
	District of Columbia	741

Source: CQ Press using data from U.S. Bureau of the Census, Governments Division
"Public Education Finances: 2006" (http://www.census.gov/govs/www/school06.html)
*Includes payments for support services for salaries, employee benefits, supplies, materials, and contractual services. Excludes capital outlay, debt service, and interfund transfers. Support services cover regular, special, and vocational programs offered in both the academic school year and summer school. It excludes instruction services as well as adult education and community services.

Per Pupil Public Elementary and Secondary School Current Expenditures for Support Services in 2006
National Per Pupil = $3,225*

ALPHA ORDER

RANK	STATE	PER PUPIL
41	Alabama	$2,669
3	Alaska	4,524
46	Arizona	2,426
38	Arkansas	2,746
25	California	3,050
21	Colorado	3,231
6	Connecticut	4,232
9	Delaware	4,087
34	Florida	2,812
35	Georgia	2,774
15	Hawaii	3,521
48	Idaho	2,157
17	Illinois	3,444
22	Indiana	3,229
29	Iowa	2,954
30	Kansas	2,888
40	Kentucky	2,694
27	Louisiana	3,027
18	Maine	3,384
13	Maryland	3,741
8	Massachusetts	4,200
12	Michigan	3,833
32	Minnesota	2,832
45	Mississippi	2,519
31	Missouri	2,860
26	Montana	3,047
33	Nebraska	2,815
43	Nevada	2,638
16	New Hampshire	3,462
1	New Jersey	5,718
24	New Mexico	3,112
5	New York	4,269
47	North Carolina	2,409
39	North Dakota	2,742
11	Ohio	3,841
42	Oklahoma	2,644
20	Oregon	3,240
10	Pennsylvania	3,993
2	Rhode Island	4,599
28	South Carolina	2,963
37	South Dakota	2,751
49	Tennessee	2,092
44	Texas	2,623
50	Utah	1,655
4	Vermont	4,449
19	Virginia	3,275
36	Washington	2,765
23	West Virginia	3,209
14	Wisconsin	3,524
7	Wyoming	4,211

RANK ORDER

RANK	STATE	PER PUPIL
1	New Jersey	$5,718
2	Rhode Island	4,599
3	Alaska	4,524
4	Vermont	4,449
5	New York	4,269
6	Connecticut	4,232
7	Wyoming	4,211
8	Massachusetts	4,200
9	Delaware	4,087
10	Pennsylvania	3,993
11	Ohio	3,841
12	Michigan	3,833
13	Maryland	3,741
14	Wisconsin	3,524
15	Hawaii	3,521
16	New Hampshire	3,462
17	Illinois	3,444
18	Maine	3,384
19	Virginia	3,275
20	Oregon	3,240
21	Colorado	3,231
22	Indiana	3,229
23	West Virginia	3,209
24	New Mexico	3,112
25	California	3,050
26	Montana	3,047
27	Louisiana	3,027
28	South Carolina	2,963
29	Iowa	2,954
30	Kansas	2,888
31	Missouri	2,860
32	Minnesota	2,832
33	Nebraska	2,815
34	Florida	2,812
35	Georgia	2,774
36	Washington	2,765
37	South Dakota	2,751
38	Arkansas	2,746
39	North Dakota	2,742
40	Kentucky	2,694
41	Alabama	2,669
42	Oklahoma	2,644
43	Nevada	2,638
44	Texas	2,623
45	Mississippi	2,519
46	Arizona	2,426
47	North Carolina	2,409
48	Idaho	2,157
49	Tennessee	2,092
50	Utah	1,655

| | District of Columbia | 7,279 |

Source: U.S. Bureau of the Census, Governments Division
    "Public Education Finances: 2006" (http://www.census.gov/govs/www/school06.html)

*Based on student membership. Includes payments for support services for salaries, employee benefits, supplies, materials, and contractual services. Excludes capital outlay, debt service, and interfund transfers. Support services cover regular, special, and vocational programs offered in both the academic year and summer school. Excluded are instruction services as well as adult education and community services.

Percent of Public Elementary and Secondary School Current Expenditures
Used for Support Services in 2006
National Percent = 34.6%*

ALPHA ORDER

RANK	STATE	PERCENT
35	Alabama	34.2
2	Alaska	39.3
10	Arizona	37.1
31	Arkansas	34.4
25	California	34.9
1	Colorado	39.5
38	Connecticut	33.4
28	Delaware	34.6
19	Florida	35.4
43	Georgia	32.3
30	Hawaii	34.5
38	Idaho	33.4
8	Illinois	37.4
11	Indiana	36.5
21	Iowa	35.1
31	Kansas	34.4
26	Kentucky	34.7
15	Louisiana	35.9
46	Maine	30.9
23	Maryland	35.0
40	Massachusetts	33.2
3	Michigan	39.2
48	Minnesota	29.6
26	Mississippi	34.7
28	Missouri	34.6
20	Montana	35.3
44	Nebraska	32.2
17	Nevada	35.7
40	New Hampshire	33.2
6	New Jersey	37.5
5	New Mexico	38.1
50	New York	27.8
42	North Carolina	32.5
45	North Dakota	31.6
4	Ohio	38.4
13	Oklahoma	36.4
8	Oregon	37.4
17	Pennsylvania	35.7
11	Rhode Island	36.5
14	South Carolina	36.0
16	South Dakota	35.8
47	Tennessee	30.1
31	Texas	34.4
49	Utah	29.5
36	Vermont	33.9
31	Virginia	34.4
21	Washington	35.1
36	West Virginia	33.9
23	Wisconsin	35.0
6	Wyoming	37.5

RANK ORDER

RANK	STATE	PERCENT
1	Colorado	39.5
2	Alaska	39.3
3	Michigan	39.2
4	Ohio	38.4
5	New Mexico	38.1
6	New Jersey	37.5
6	Wyoming	37.5
8	Illinois	37.4
8	Oregon	37.4
10	Arizona	37.1
11	Indiana	36.5
11	Rhode Island	36.5
13	Oklahoma	36.4
14	South Carolina	36.0
15	Louisiana	35.9
16	South Dakota	35.8
17	Nevada	35.7
17	Pennsylvania	35.7
19	Florida	35.4
20	Montana	35.3
21	Iowa	35.1
21	Washington	35.1
23	Maryland	35.0
23	Wisconsin	35.0
25	California	34.9
26	Kentucky	34.7
26	Mississippi	34.7
28	Delaware	34.6
28	Missouri	34.6
30	Hawaii	34.5
31	Arkansas	34.4
31	Kansas	34.4
31	Texas	34.4
31	Virginia	34.4
35	Alabama	34.2
36	Vermont	33.9
36	West Virginia	33.9
38	Connecticut	33.4
38	Idaho	33.4
40	Massachusetts	33.2
40	New Hampshire	33.2
42	North Carolina	32.5
43	Georgia	32.3
44	Nebraska	32.2
45	North Dakota	31.6
46	Maine	30.9
47	Tennessee	30.1
48	Minnesota	29.6
49	Utah	29.5
50	New York	27.8

District of Columbia 45.6

Source: CQ Press using data from U.S. Bureau of the Census, Governments Division
"Public Education Finances: 2006" (http://www.census.gov/govs/www/school06.html)
*Includes payments for support services for salaries, employee benefits, supplies, materials, and contractual services.
Excludes capital outlay, debt service, and interfund transfers. Support services cover regular, special, and vocational programs offered in both the academic school year and summer school. It excludes instruction services as well as adult education and community services.

Public Elementary and Secondary School Current Expenditures for Salaries and Wages for Support Services in 2006
National Total = $79,434,671,000*

<table>
<tr><td colspan="4">ALPHA ORDER</td><td colspan="4">RANK ORDER</td></tr>
<tr><td>RANK</td><td>STATE</td><td>EXPENDITURES</td><td>% of USA</td><td>RANK</td><td>STATE</td><td>EXPENDITURES</td><td>% of USA</td></tr>
<tr><td>26</td><td>Alabama</td><td>$960,179,000</td><td>1.2%</td><td>1</td><td>California</td><td>$10,037,540,000</td><td>12.6%</td></tr>
<tr><td>44</td><td>Alaska</td><td>270,082,000</td><td>0.3%</td><td>2</td><td>Texas</td><td>6,631,713,000</td><td>8.3%</td></tr>
<tr><td>18</td><td>Arizona</td><td>1,302,521,000</td><td>1.6%</td><td>3</td><td>New York</td><td>5,498,801,000</td><td>6.9%</td></tr>
<tr><td>32</td><td>Arkansas</td><td>695,263,000</td><td>0.9%</td><td>4</td><td>Florida</td><td>4,092,044,000</td><td>5.2%</td></tr>
<tr><td>1</td><td>California</td><td>10,037,540,000</td><td>12.6%</td><td>5</td><td>New Jersey</td><td>3,890,867,000</td><td>4.9%</td></tr>
<tr><td>20</td><td>Colorado</td><td>1,259,910,000</td><td>1.6%</td><td>6</td><td>Illinois</td><td>3,597,769,000</td><td>4.5%</td></tr>
<tr><td>21</td><td>Connecticut</td><td>1,107,020,000</td><td>1.4%</td><td>7</td><td>Ohio</td><td>3,480,098,000</td><td>4.4%</td></tr>
<tr><td>46</td><td>Delaware</td><td>206,856,000</td><td>0.3%</td><td>8</td><td>Michigan</td><td>3,185,199,000</td><td>4.0%</td></tr>
<tr><td>4</td><td>Florida</td><td>4,092,044,000</td><td>5.2%</td><td>9</td><td>Pennsylvania</td><td>3,084,613,000</td><td>3.9%</td></tr>
<tr><td>10</td><td>Georgia</td><td>2,474,326,000</td><td>3.1%</td><td>10</td><td>Georgia</td><td>2,474,326,000</td><td>3.1%</td></tr>
<tr><td>41</td><td>Hawaii</td><td>310,878,000</td><td>0.4%</td><td>11</td><td>Virginia</td><td>2,303,905,000</td><td>2.9%</td></tr>
<tr><td>43</td><td>Idaho</td><td>292,153,000</td><td>0.4%</td><td>12</td><td>Massachusetts</td><td>1,988,606,000</td><td>2.5%</td></tr>
<tr><td>6</td><td>Illinois</td><td>3,597,769,000</td><td>4.5%</td><td>13</td><td>North Carolina</td><td>1,954,803,000</td><td>2.5%</td></tr>
<tr><td>16</td><td>Indiana</td><td>1,479,795,000</td><td>1.9%</td><td>14</td><td>Maryland</td><td>1,750,783,000</td><td>2.2%</td></tr>
<tr><td>29</td><td>Iowa</td><td>789,317,000</td><td>1.0%</td><td>15</td><td>Washington</td><td>1,664,656,000</td><td>2.1%</td></tr>
<tr><td>31</td><td>Kansas</td><td>744,789,000</td><td>0.9%</td><td>16</td><td>Indiana</td><td>1,479,795,000</td><td>1.9%</td></tr>
<tr><td>25</td><td>Kentucky</td><td>1,007,053,000</td><td>1.3%</td><td>17</td><td>Missouri</td><td>1,359,591,000</td><td>1.7%</td></tr>
<tr><td>27</td><td>Louisiana</td><td>895,634,000</td><td>1.1%</td><td>18</td><td>Arizona</td><td>1,302,521,000</td><td>1.6%</td></tr>
<tr><td>40</td><td>Maine</td><td>323,129,000</td><td>0.4%</td><td>19</td><td>Wisconsin</td><td>1,260,079,000</td><td>1.6%</td></tr>
<tr><td>14</td><td>Maryland</td><td>1,750,783,000</td><td>2.2%</td><td>20</td><td>Colorado</td><td>1,259,910,000</td><td>1.6%</td></tr>
<tr><td>12</td><td>Massachusetts</td><td>1,988,606,000</td><td>2.5%</td><td>21</td><td>Connecticut</td><td>1,107,020,000</td><td>1.4%</td></tr>
<tr><td>8</td><td>Michigan</td><td>3,185,199,000</td><td>4.0%</td><td>22</td><td>Minnesota</td><td>1,075,643,000</td><td>1.4%</td></tr>
<tr><td>22</td><td>Minnesota</td><td>1,075,643,000</td><td>1.4%</td><td>23</td><td>South Carolina</td><td>1,055,953,000</td><td>1.3%</td></tr>
<tr><td>33</td><td>Mississippi</td><td>607,301,000</td><td>0.8%</td><td>24</td><td>Tennessee</td><td>1,040,259,000</td><td>1.3%</td></tr>
<tr><td>17</td><td>Missouri</td><td>1,359,591,000</td><td>1.7%</td><td>25</td><td>Kentucky</td><td>1,007,053,000</td><td>1.3%</td></tr>
<tr><td>45</td><td>Montana</td><td>214,017,000</td><td>0.3%</td><td>26</td><td>Alabama</td><td>960,179,000</td><td>1.2%</td></tr>
<tr><td>38</td><td>Nebraska</td><td>411,531,000</td><td>0.5%</td><td>27</td><td>Louisiana</td><td>895,634,000</td><td>1.1%</td></tr>
<tr><td>34</td><td>Nevada</td><td>584,344,000</td><td>0.7%</td><td>28</td><td>Oregon</td><td>829,869,000</td><td>1.0%</td></tr>
<tr><td>42</td><td>New Hampshire</td><td>300,674,000</td><td>0.4%</td><td>29</td><td>Iowa</td><td>789,317,000</td><td>1.0%</td></tr>
<tr><td>5</td><td>New Jersey</td><td>3,890,867,000</td><td>4.9%</td><td>30</td><td>Oklahoma</td><td>773,328,000</td><td>1.0%</td></tr>
<tr><td>35</td><td>New Mexico</td><td>508,790,000</td><td>0.6%</td><td>31</td><td>Kansas</td><td>744,789,000</td><td>0.9%</td></tr>
<tr><td>3</td><td>New York</td><td>5,498,801,000</td><td>6.9%</td><td>32</td><td>Arkansas</td><td>695,263,000</td><td>0.9%</td></tr>
<tr><td>13</td><td>North Carolina</td><td>1,954,803,000</td><td>2.5%</td><td>33</td><td>Mississippi</td><td>607,301,000</td><td>0.8%</td></tr>
<tr><td>50</td><td>North Dakota</td><td>138,486,000</td><td>0.2%</td><td>34</td><td>Nevada</td><td>584,344,000</td><td>0.7%</td></tr>
<tr><td>7</td><td>Ohio</td><td>3,480,098,000</td><td>4.4%</td><td>35</td><td>New Mexico</td><td>508,790,000</td><td>0.6%</td></tr>
<tr><td>30</td><td>Oklahoma</td><td>773,328,000</td><td>1.0%</td><td>36</td><td>Utah</td><td>451,463,000</td><td>0.6%</td></tr>
<tr><td>28</td><td>Oregon</td><td>829,869,000</td><td>1.0%</td><td>37</td><td>West Virginia</td><td>428,376,000</td><td>0.5%</td></tr>
<tr><td>9</td><td>Pennsylvania</td><td>3,084,613,000</td><td>3.9%</td><td>38</td><td>Nebraska</td><td>411,531,000</td><td>0.5%</td></tr>
<tr><td>39</td><td>Rhode Island</td><td>349,598,000</td><td>0.4%</td><td>39</td><td>Rhode Island</td><td>349,598,000</td><td>0.4%</td></tr>
<tr><td>23</td><td>South Carolina</td><td>1,055,953,000</td><td>1.3%</td><td>40</td><td>Maine</td><td>323,129,000</td><td>0.4%</td></tr>
<tr><td>49</td><td>South Dakota</td><td>155,110,000</td><td>0.2%</td><td>41</td><td>Hawaii</td><td>310,878,000</td><td>0.4%</td></tr>
<tr><td>24</td><td>Tennessee</td><td>1,040,259,000</td><td>1.3%</td><td>42</td><td>New Hampshire</td><td>300,674,000</td><td>0.4%</td></tr>
<tr><td>2</td><td>Texas</td><td>6,631,713,000</td><td>8.3%</td><td>43</td><td>Idaho</td><td>292,153,000</td><td>0.4%</td></tr>
<tr><td>36</td><td>Utah</td><td>451,463,000</td><td>0.6%</td><td>44</td><td>Alaska</td><td>270,082,000</td><td>0.3%</td></tr>
<tr><td>47</td><td>Vermont</td><td>197,722,000</td><td>0.2%</td><td>45</td><td>Montana</td><td>214,017,000</td><td>0.3%</td></tr>
<tr><td>11</td><td>Virginia</td><td>2,303,905,000</td><td>2.9%</td><td>46</td><td>Delaware</td><td>206,856,000</td><td>0.3%</td></tr>
<tr><td>15</td><td>Washington</td><td>1,664,656,000</td><td>2.1%</td><td>47</td><td>Vermont</td><td>197,722,000</td><td>0.2%</td></tr>
<tr><td>37</td><td>West Virginia</td><td>428,376,000</td><td>0.5%</td><td>48</td><td>Wyoming</td><td>188,192,000</td><td>0.2%</td></tr>
<tr><td>19</td><td>Wisconsin</td><td>1,260,079,000</td><td>1.6%</td><td>49</td><td>South Dakota</td><td>155,110,000</td><td>0.2%</td></tr>
<tr><td>48</td><td>Wyoming</td><td>188,192,000</td><td>0.2%</td><td>50</td><td>North Dakota</td><td>138,486,000</td><td>0.2%</td></tr>
<tr><td></td><td></td><td></td><td></td><td></td><td>District of Columbia</td><td>224,043,000</td><td>0.3%</td></tr>
</table>

Source: U.S. Bureau of the Census, Governments Division
"Public Education Finances: 2006" (http://www.census.gov/govs/www/school06.html)
*Includes payments for support services for salaries. Excludes capital outlay, debt service, and interfund transfers. Support services cover regular, special, and vocational programs offered in both the academic year and summer school. It excludes instruction services as well as adult education and community services.

Percent of Public Elementary and Secondary School Current Expenditures Used for Salaries and Wages for Support Services in 2006
National Percent = 17.6%*

ALPHA ORDER

RANK	STATE	PERCENT
32	Alabama	16.6
25	Alaska	17.6
3	Arizona	19.8
20	Arkansas	18.4
22	California	18.3
4	Colorado	19.7
42	Connecticut	15.7
45	Delaware	15.3
7	Florida	19.4
23	Georgia	18.0
31	Hawaii	16.7
26	Idaho	17.5
17	Illinois	18.6
37	Indiana	16.3
7	Iowa	19.4
13	Kansas	19.0
11	Kentucky	19.1
35	Louisiana	16.4
46	Maine	15.1
13	Maryland	19.0
34	Massachusetts	16.5
16	Michigan	18.8
49	Minnesota	13.7
29	Mississippi	16.9
23	Missouri	18.0
28	Montana	17.1
35	Nebraska	16.4
10	Nevada	19.2
48	New Hampshire	14.3
18	New Jersey	18.5
11	New Mexico	19.1
50	New York	12.9
13	North Carolina	19.0
37	North Dakota	16.3
4	Ohio	19.7
30	Oklahoma	16.8
27	Oregon	17.2
42	Pennsylvania	15.7
18	Rhode Island	18.5
20	South Carolina	18.4
32	South Dakota	16.6
42	Tennessee	15.7
6	Texas	19.5
40	Utah	16.2
37	Vermont	16.3
2	Virginia	20.0
1	Washington	20.5
40	West Virginia	16.2
47	Wisconsin	14.4
7	Wyoming	19.4

RANK ORDER

RANK	STATE	PERCENT
1	Washington	20.5
2	Virginia	20.0
3	Arizona	19.8
4	Colorado	19.7
4	Ohio	19.7
6	Texas	19.5
7	Florida	19.4
7	Iowa	19.4
7	Wyoming	19.4
10	Nevada	19.2
11	Kentucky	19.1
11	New Mexico	19.1
13	Kansas	19.0
13	Maryland	19.0
13	North Carolina	19.0
16	Michigan	18.8
17	Illinois	18.6
18	New Jersey	18.5
18	Rhode Island	18.5
20	Arkansas	18.4
20	South Carolina	18.4
22	California	18.3
23	Georgia	18.0
23	Missouri	18.0
25	Alaska	17.6
26	Idaho	17.5
27	Oregon	17.2
28	Montana	17.1
29	Mississippi	16.9
30	Oklahoma	16.8
31	Hawaii	16.7
32	Alabama	16.6
32	South Dakota	16.6
34	Massachusetts	16.5
35	Louisiana	16.4
35	Nebraska	16.4
37	Indiana	16.3
37	North Dakota	16.3
37	Vermont	16.3
40	Utah	16.2
40	West Virginia	16.2
42	Connecticut	15.7
42	Pennsylvania	15.7
42	Tennessee	15.7
45	Delaware	15.3
46	Maine	15.1
47	Wisconsin	14.4
48	New Hampshire	14.3
49	Minnesota	13.7
50	New York	12.9

District of Columbia 23.5

Source: CQ Press using data from U.S. Bureau of the Census, Governments Division
  "Public Education Finances: 2006" (http://www.census.gov/govs/www/school06.html)
*Includes payments for support services for salaries. Excludes capital outlay, debt service, and interfund transfers. Support services cover regular, special, and vocational programs offered in both the academic year and summer school. It excludes instruction services as well as adult education and community services.

Public Elementary and Secondary School Current Expenditures for Employee Benefits for Support Services in 2006
National Total = $26,520,549,000*

ALPHA ORDER

RANK	STATE	EXPENDITURES	% of USA
20	Alabama	$385,172,000	1.5%
40	Alaska	115,506,000	0.4%
22	Arizona	350,327,000	1.3%
35	Arkansas	177,313,000	0.7%
1	California	3,701,504,000	14.0%
28	Colorado	295,631,000	1.1%
19	Connecticut	412,103,000	1.6%
45	Delaware	90,862,000	0.3%
6	Florida	1,233,670,000	4.7%
10	Georgia	766,925,000	2.9%
41	Hawaii	114,782,000	0.4%
44	Idaho	98,449,000	0.4%
9	Illinois	1,110,861,000	4.2%
11	Indiana	732,768,000	2.8%
29	Iowa	238,776,000	0.9%
36	Kansas	176,141,000	0.7%
24	Kentucky	338,876,000	1.3%
23	Louisiana	350,307,000	1.3%
42	Maine	113,356,000	0.4%
15	Maryland	604,328,000	2.3%
14	Massachusetts	676,233,000	2.5%
3	Michigan	1,514,265,000	5.7%
25	Minnesota	320,058,000	1.2%
33	Mississippi	184,991,000	0.7%
21	Missouri	352,016,000	1.3%
48	Montana	65,102,000	0.2%
39	Nebraska	127,506,000	0.5%
32	Nevada	194,065,000	0.7%
43	New Hampshire	104,646,000	0.4%
4	New Jersey	1,362,772,000	5.1%
38	New Mexico	150,621,000	0.6%
2	New York	1,990,596,000	7.5%
17	North Carolina	460,656,000	1.7%
50	North Dakota	38,563,000	0.1%
5	Ohio	1,320,053,000	5.0%
31	Oklahoma	204,435,000	0.8%
18	Oregon	416,558,000	1.6%
8	Pennsylvania	1,122,268,000	4.2%
37	Rhode Island	153,348,000	0.6%
26	South Carolina	305,646,000	1.2%
49	South Dakota	43,223,000	0.2%
27	Tennessee	300,236,000	1.1%
7	Texas	1,172,015,000	4.4%
34	Utah	180,845,000	0.7%
47	Vermont	66,674,000	0.3%
13	Virginia	712,531,000	2.7%
16	Washington	503,466,000	1.9%
30	West Virginia	234,679,000	0.9%
12	Wisconsin	726,885,000	2.7%
46	Wyoming	69,835,000	0.3%

RANK ORDER

RANK	STATE	EXPENDITURES	% of USA
1	California	$3,701,504,000	14.0%
2	New York	1,990,596,000	7.5%
3	Michigan	1,514,265,000	5.7%
4	New Jersey	1,362,772,000	5.1%
5	Ohio	1,320,053,000	5.0%
6	Florida	1,233,670,000	4.7%
7	Texas	1,172,015,000	4.4%
8	Pennsylvania	1,122,268,000	4.2%
9	Illinois	1,110,861,000	4.2%
10	Georgia	766,925,000	2.9%
11	Indiana	732,768,000	2.8%
12	Wisconsin	726,885,000	2.7%
13	Virginia	712,531,000	2.7%
14	Massachusetts	676,233,000	2.5%
15	Maryland	604,328,000	2.3%
16	Washington	503,466,000	1.9%
17	North Carolina	460,656,000	1.7%
18	Oregon	416,558,000	1.6%
19	Connecticut	412,103,000	1.6%
20	Alabama	385,172,000	1.5%
21	Missouri	352,016,000	1.3%
22	Arizona	350,327,000	1.3%
23	Louisiana	350,307,000	1.3%
24	Kentucky	338,876,000	1.3%
25	Minnesota	320,058,000	1.2%
26	South Carolina	305,646,000	1.2%
27	Tennessee	300,236,000	1.1%
28	Colorado	295,631,000	1.1%
29	Iowa	238,776,000	0.9%
30	West Virginia	234,679,000	0.9%
31	Oklahoma	204,435,000	0.8%
32	Nevada	194,065,000	0.7%
33	Mississippi	184,991,000	0.7%
34	Utah	180,845,000	0.7%
35	Arkansas	177,313,000	0.7%
36	Kansas	176,141,000	0.7%
37	Rhode Island	153,348,000	0.6%
38	New Mexico	150,621,000	0.6%
39	Nebraska	127,506,000	0.5%
40	Alaska	115,506,000	0.4%
41	Hawaii	114,782,000	0.4%
42	Maine	113,356,000	0.4%
43	New Hampshire	104,646,000	0.4%
44	Idaho	98,449,000	0.4%
45	Delaware	90,862,000	0.3%
46	Wyoming	69,835,000	0.3%
47	Vermont	66,674,000	0.3%
48	Montana	65,102,000	0.2%
49	South Dakota	43,223,000	0.2%
50	North Dakota	38,563,000	0.1%
	District of Columbia	38,105,000	0.1%

Source: U.S. Bureau of the Census, Governments Division
"Public Education Finances: 2006" (http://www.census.gov/govs/www/school06.html)
*Includes payments for support services for employee benefits. Excludes capital outlay, debt service, and interfund transfers. Support services cover regular, special, and vocational programs offered in both the academic year and summer school. It excludes instruction services as well as adult education and community services.

Percent of Public Elementary and Secondary School Current Expenditures Used for Employee Benefits for Support Services in 2006
National Percent = 5.9%*

ALPHA ORDER

RANK	STATE	PERCENT
12	Alabama	6.6
7	Alaska	7.5
32	Arizona	5.3
39	Arkansas	4.7
10	California	6.8
41	Colorado	4.6
24	Connecticut	5.8
11	Delaware	6.7
24	Florida	5.8
28	Georgia	5.6
19	Hawaii	6.2
22	Idaho	5.9
26	Illinois	5.7
5	Indiana	8.1
22	Iowa	5.9
44	Kansas	4.5
16	Kentucky	6.4
16	Louisiana	6.4
32	Maine	5.3
12	Maryland	6.6
28	Massachusetts	5.6
1	Michigan	9.0
49	Minnesota	4.1
35	Mississippi	5.2
41	Missouri	4.6
35	Montana	5.2
37	Nebraska	5.1
16	Nevada	6.4
38	New Hampshire	5.0
14	New Jersey	6.5
28	New Mexico	5.6
39	New York	4.7
44	North Carolina	4.5
44	North Dakota	4.5
7	Ohio	7.5
48	Oklahoma	4.4
3	Oregon	8.6
26	Pennsylvania	5.7
5	Rhode Island	8.1
32	South Carolina	5.3
41	South Dakota	4.6
44	Tennessee	4.5
50	Texas	3.5
14	Utah	6.5
31	Vermont	5.5
19	Virginia	6.2
19	Washington	6.2
2	West Virginia	8.8
4	Wisconsin	8.3
9	Wyoming	7.2

RANK ORDER

RANK	STATE	PERCENT
1	Michigan	9.0
2	West Virginia	8.8
3	Oregon	8.6
4	Wisconsin	8.3
5	Indiana	8.1
5	Rhode Island	8.1
7	Alaska	7.5
7	Ohio	7.5
9	Wyoming	7.2
10	California	6.8
11	Delaware	6.7
12	Alabama	6.6
12	Maryland	6.6
14	New Jersey	6.5
14	Utah	6.5
16	Kentucky	6.4
16	Louisiana	6.4
16	Nevada	6.4
19	Hawaii	6.2
19	Virginia	6.2
19	Washington	6.2
22	Idaho	5.9
22	Iowa	5.9
24	Connecticut	5.8
24	Florida	5.8
26	Illinois	5.7
26	Pennsylvania	5.7
28	Georgia	5.6
28	Massachusetts	5.6
28	New Mexico	5.6
31	Vermont	5.5
32	Arizona	5.3
32	Maine	5.3
32	South Carolina	5.3
35	Mississippi	5.2
35	Montana	5.2
37	Nebraska	5.1
38	New Hampshire	5.0
39	Arkansas	4.7
39	New York	4.7
41	Colorado	4.6
41	Missouri	4.6
41	South Dakota	4.6
44	Kansas	4.5
44	North Carolina	4.5
44	North Dakota	4.5
44	Tennessee	4.5
48	Oklahoma	4.4
49	Minnesota	4.1
50	Texas	3.5
	District of Columbia	4.0

Source: CQ Press using data from U.S. Bureau of the Census, Governments Division
"Public Education Finances: 2006" (http://www.census.gov/govs/www/school06.html)
*Includes payments for support services for employee benefits. Excludes capital outlay, debt service, and interfund transfers.
Support services cover regular, special, and vocational programs offered in both the academic year and summer school. It
excludes instruction services as well as adult education and community services.

Public Elementary and Secondary School Current Expenditures
for Pupil Support Services in 2006
National Total = $23,303,366,000*

ALPHA ORDER

RANK	STATE	EXPENDITURES	% of USA
23	Alabama	$292,929,000	1.3%
42	Alaska	93,131,000	0.4%
16	Arizona	426,682,000	1.8%
35	Arkansas	170,169,000	0.7%
1	California	2,405,481,000	10.3%
25	Colorado	274,007,000	1.2%
15	Connecticut	427,486,000	1.8%
47	Delaware	64,609,000	0.3%
8	Florida	973,340,000	4.2%
11	Georgia	655,634,000	2.8%
31	Hawaii	216,531,000	0.9%
43	Idaho	90,825,000	0.4%
5	Illinois	1,210,235,000	5.2%
17	Indiana	406,939,000	1.7%
27	Iowa	239,188,000	1.0%
34	Kansas	180,592,000	0.8%
32	Kentucky	214,381,000	0.9%
28	Louisiana	223,345,000	1.0%
45	Maine	77,884,000	0.3%
18	Maryland	396,830,000	1.7%
10	Massachusetts	773,594,000	3.3%
6	Michigan	1,207,906,000	5.2%
33	Minnesota	202,564,000	0.9%
36	Mississippi	160,083,000	0.7%
21	Missouri	355,782,000	1.5%
46	Montana	67,159,000	0.3%
38	Nebraska	113,369,000	0.5%
39	Nevada	111,124,000	0.5%
37	New Hampshire	146,733,000	0.6%
2	New Jersey	2,027,893,000	8.7%
26	New Mexico	254,618,000	1.1%
4	New York	1,221,892,000	5.2%
12	North Carolina	596,650,000	2.6%
50	North Dakota	34,289,000	0.1%
7	Ohio	1,037,979,000	4.5%
24	Oklahoma	291,900,000	1.3%
22	Oregon	337,559,000	1.4%
9	Pennsylvania	966,727,000	4.1%
30	Rhode Island	218,584,000	0.9%
19	South Carolina	390,670,000	1.7%
49	South Dakota	49,436,000	0.2%
29	Tennessee	222,423,000	1.0%
3	Texas	1,627,523,000	7.0%
40	Utah	94,239,000	0.4%
44	Vermont	90,624,000	0.4%
13	Virginia	548,473,000	2.4%
14	Washington	524,783,000	2.3%
41	West Virginia	93,655,000	0.4%
20	Wisconsin	383,492,000	1.6%
48	Wyoming	56,758,000	0.2%

RANK ORDER

RANK	STATE	EXPENDITURES	% of USA
1	California	$2,405,481,000	10.3%
2	New Jersey	2,027,893,000	8.7%
3	Texas	1,627,523,000	7.0%
4	New York	1,221,892,000	5.2%
5	Illinois	1,210,235,000	5.2%
6	Michigan	1,207,906,000	5.2%
7	Ohio	1,037,979,000	4.5%
8	Florida	973,340,000	4.2%
9	Pennsylvania	966,727,000	4.1%
10	Massachusetts	773,594,000	3.3%
11	Georgia	655,634,000	2.8%
12	North Carolina	596,650,000	2.6%
13	Virginia	548,473,000	2.4%
14	Washington	524,783,000	2.3%
15	Connecticut	427,486,000	1.8%
16	Arizona	426,682,000	1.8%
17	Indiana	406,939,000	1.7%
18	Maryland	396,830,000	1.7%
19	South Carolina	390,670,000	1.7%
20	Wisconsin	383,492,000	1.6%
21	Missouri	355,782,000	1.5%
22	Oregon	337,559,000	1.4%
23	Alabama	292,929,000	1.3%
24	Oklahoma	291,900,000	1.3%
25	Colorado	274,007,000	1.2%
26	New Mexico	254,618,000	1.1%
27	Iowa	239,188,000	1.0%
28	Louisiana	223,345,000	1.0%
29	Tennessee	222,423,000	1.0%
30	Rhode Island	218,584,000	0.9%
31	Hawaii	216,531,000	0.9%
32	Kentucky	214,381,000	0.9%
33	Minnesota	202,564,000	0.9%
34	Kansas	180,592,000	0.8%
35	Arkansas	170,169,000	0.7%
36	Mississippi	160,083,000	0.7%
37	New Hampshire	146,733,000	0.6%
38	Nebraska	113,369,000	0.5%
39	Nevada	111,124,000	0.5%
40	Utah	94,239,000	0.4%
41	West Virginia	93,655,000	0.4%
42	Alaska	93,131,000	0.4%
43	Idaho	90,825,000	0.4%
44	Vermont	90,624,000	0.4%
45	Maine	77,884,000	0.3%
46	Montana	67,159,000	0.3%
47	Delaware	64,609,000	0.3%
48	Wyoming	56,758,000	0.2%
49	South Dakota	49,436,000	0.2%
50	North Dakota	34,289,000	0.1%
	District of Columbia	54,667,000	0.2%

Source: U.S. Bureau of the Census, Governments Division
"Public Education Finances: 2006" (http://www.census.gov/govs/www/school06.html)
*Pupil support services include social work, counseling, record maintenance, nursing, psychological, and speech services. Includes salaries, benefits, services, and supplies. Census expanded its usual "current expenditures" concept for education finance reports to include all current public elementary and secondary education outlays regardless of the specific unit of government that actually makes the expenditure.

Percent of Public Elementary and Secondary School Current Expenditures Used for Pupil Support Services in 2006
National Percent = 5.2%*

ALPHA ORDER

RANK	STATE	PERCENT
24	Alabama	5.1
15	Alaska	6.1
10	Arizona	6.5
33	Arkansas	4.5
37	California	4.4
39	Colorado	4.3
15	Connecticut	6.1
26	Delaware	4.8
31	Florida	4.6
26	Georgia	4.8
1	Hawaii	11.6
21	Idaho	5.4
14	Illinois	6.2
33	Indiana	4.5
17	Iowa	5.9
31	Kansas	4.6
41	Kentucky	4.1
41	Louisiana	4.1
44	Maine	3.6
39	Maryland	4.3
12	Massachusetts	6.4
6	Michigan	7.1
50	Minnesota	2.6
33	Mississippi	4.5
30	Missouri	4.7
21	Montana	5.4
33	Nebraska	4.5
44	Nevada	3.6
7	New Hampshire	7.0
3	New Jersey	9.6
4	New Mexico	9.5
49	New York	2.9
20	North Carolina	5.8
43	North Dakota	4.0
17	Ohio	5.9
13	Oklahoma	6.3
7	Oregon	7.0
25	Pennsylvania	4.9
1	Rhode Island	11.6
9	South Carolina	6.8
23	South Dakota	5.3
47	Tennessee	3.4
26	Texas	4.8
47	Utah	3.4
5	Vermont	7.5
26	Virginia	4.8
10	Washington	6.5
46	West Virginia	3.5
37	Wisconsin	4.4
17	Wyoming	5.9

RANK ORDER

RANK	STATE	PERCENT
1	Hawaii	11.6
1	Rhode Island	11.6
3	New Jersey	9.6
4	New Mexico	9.5
5	Vermont	7.5
6	Michigan	7.1
7	New Hampshire	7.0
7	Oregon	7.0
9	South Carolina	6.8
10	Arizona	6.5
10	Washington	6.5
12	Massachusetts	6.4
13	Oklahoma	6.3
14	Illinois	6.2
15	Alaska	6.1
15	Connecticut	6.1
17	Iowa	5.9
17	Ohio	5.9
17	Wyoming	5.9
20	North Carolina	5.8
21	Idaho	5.4
21	Montana	5.4
23	South Dakota	5.3
24	Alabama	5.1
25	Pennsylvania	4.9
26	Delaware	4.8
26	Georgia	4.8
26	Texas	4.8
26	Virginia	4.8
30	Missouri	4.7
31	Florida	4.6
31	Kansas	4.6
33	Arkansas	4.5
33	Indiana	4.5
33	Mississippi	4.5
33	Nebraska	4.5
37	California	4.4
37	Wisconsin	4.4
39	Colorado	4.3
39	Maryland	4.3
41	Kentucky	4.1
41	Louisiana	4.1
43	North Dakota	4.0
44	Maine	3.6
44	Nevada	3.6
46	West Virginia	3.5
47	Tennessee	3.4
47	Utah	3.4
49	New York	2.9
50	Minnesota	2.6

District of Columbia 5.7

Source: CQ Press using data from U.S. Bureau of the Census, Governments Division
"Public Education Finances: 2006" (http://www.census.gov/govs/www/school06.html)
*Pupil support services include social work, counseling, record maintenance, nursing, psychological, and speech services. Includes salaries, benefits, services, and supplies. Census expanded its usual "current expenditures" concept for education finance reports to include all current public elementary and secondary education outlays regardless of the specific unit of government that actually makes the expenditure.

Public Elementary and Secondary School Current Expenditures
for Instructional Staff Support Services in 2006
National Total = $21,678,363,000*

ALPHA ORDER

RANK	STATE	EXPENDITURES	% of USA
24	Alabama	$280,192,000	1.3%
40	Alaska	83,139,000	0.4%
31	Arizona	182,560,000	0.8%
26	Arkansas	239,092,000	1.1%
1	California	3,393,151,000	15.7%
21	Colorado	325,628,000	1.5%
27	Connecticut	228,978,000	1.1%
50	Delaware	17,413,000	0.1%
3	Florida	1,396,080,000	6.4%
8	Georgia	747,392,000	3.4%
43	Hawaii	65,864,000	0.3%
42	Idaho	70,713,000	0.3%
6	Illinois	891,915,000	4.1%
23	Indiana	287,631,000	1.3%
29	Iowa	191,857,000	0.9%
32	Kansas	170,255,000	0.8%
22	Kentucky	294,819,000	1.4%
25	Louisiana	272,151,000	1.3%
41	Maine	75,164,000	0.3%
13	Maryland	495,893,000	2.3%
12	Massachusetts	696,540,000	3.2%
7	Michigan	824,686,000	3.8%
18	Minnesota	347,882,000	1.6%
33	Mississippi	168,450,000	0.8%
19	Missouri	337,621,000	1.6%
46	Montana	49,665,000	0.2%
38	Nebraska	86,715,000	0.4%
39	Nevada	83,659,000	0.4%
44	New Hampshire	65,675,000	0.3%
11	New Jersey	717,190,000	3.3%
35	New Mexico	118,682,000	0.5%
4	New York	1,174,236,000	5.4%
15	North Carolina	393,932,000	1.8%
49	North Dakota	25,226,000	0.1%
5	Ohio	1,131,979,000	5.2%
28	Oklahoma	198,570,000	0.9%
30	Oregon	190,864,000	0.9%
9	Pennsylvania	735,808,000	3.4%
37	Rhode Island	87,808,000	0.4%
16	South Carolina	380,266,000	1.8%
48	South Dakota	43,900,000	0.2%
20	Tennessee	337,481,000	1.6%
2	Texas	1,850,867,000	8.5%
34	Utah	125,613,000	0.6%
47	Vermont	44,972,000	0.2%
10	Virginia	735,158,000	3.4%
17	Washington	366,053,000	1.7%
36	West Virginia	100,835,000	0.5%
14	Wisconsin	425,902,000	2.0%
45	Wyoming	52,536,000	0.2%

RANK ORDER

RANK	STATE	EXPENDITURES	% of USA
1	California	$3,393,151,000	15.7%
2	Texas	1,850,867,000	8.5%
3	Florida	1,396,080,000	6.4%
4	New York	1,174,236,000	5.4%
5	Ohio	1,131,979,000	5.2%
6	Illinois	891,915,000	4.1%
7	Michigan	824,686,000	3.8%
8	Georgia	747,392,000	3.4%
9	Pennsylvania	735,808,000	3.4%
10	Virginia	735,158,000	3.4%
11	New Jersey	717,190,000	3.3%
12	Massachusetts	696,540,000	3.2%
13	Maryland	495,893,000	2.3%
14	Wisconsin	425,902,000	2.0%
15	North Carolina	393,932,000	1.8%
16	South Carolina	380,266,000	1.8%
17	Washington	366,053,000	1.7%
18	Minnesota	347,882,000	1.6%
19	Missouri	337,621,000	1.6%
20	Tennessee	337,481,000	1.6%
21	Colorado	325,628,000	1.5%
22	Kentucky	294,819,000	1.4%
23	Indiana	287,631,000	1.3%
24	Alabama	280,192,000	1.3%
25	Louisiana	272,151,000	1.3%
26	Arkansas	239,092,000	1.1%
27	Connecticut	228,978,000	1.1%
28	Oklahoma	198,570,000	0.9%
29	Iowa	191,857,000	0.9%
30	Oregon	190,864,000	0.9%
31	Arizona	182,560,000	0.8%
32	Kansas	170,255,000	0.8%
33	Mississippi	168,450,000	0.8%
34	Utah	125,613,000	0.6%
35	New Mexico	118,682,000	0.5%
36	West Virginia	100,835,000	0.5%
37	Rhode Island	87,808,000	0.4%
38	Nebraska	86,715,000	0.4%
39	Nevada	83,659,000	0.4%
40	Alaska	83,139,000	0.4%
41	Maine	75,164,000	0.3%
42	Idaho	70,713,000	0.3%
43	Hawaii	65,864,000	0.3%
44	New Hampshire	65,675,000	0.3%
45	Wyoming	52,536,000	0.2%
46	Montana	49,665,000	0.2%
47	Vermont	44,972,000	0.2%
48	South Dakota	43,900,000	0.2%
49	North Dakota	25,226,000	0.1%
50	Delaware	17,413,000	0.1%
	District of Columbia	69,705,000	0.3%

Source: U.S. Bureau of the Census, Governments Division
"Public Education Finances: 2006" (http://www.census.gov/govs/www/school06.html)
*Staff support services include curriculum development, instructional staff training, and media, library, audiovisual, television, and computer-assisted services. Includes salaries, benefits, services, and supplies. Census expanded its usual "current expenditures" concept for education finance reports to include all current public elementary and secondary education outlays regardless of the specific unit of government that actually makes the expenditure.

Percent of Public Elementary and Secondary School Current Expenditures Used for Instructional Staff Support Services in 2006
National Percent = 4.8%*

RANK	STATE	PERCENT
19	Alabama	4.8
10	Alaska	5.4
47	Arizona	2.8
5	Arkansas	6.3
6	California	6.2
14	Colorado	5.1
43	Connecticut	3.2
50	Delaware	1.3
1	Florida	6.6
10	Georgia	5.4
39	Hawaii	3.5
32	Idaho	4.2
23	Illinois	4.6
43	Indiana	3.2
20	Iowa	4.7
30	Kansas	4.3
8	Kentucky	5.6
16	Louisiana	5.0
39	Maine	3.5
10	Maryland	5.4
7	Massachusetts	5.8
17	Michigan	4.9
28	Minnesota	4.4
20	Mississippi	4.7
25	Missouri	4.5
33	Montana	4.0
39	Nebraska	3.5
48	Nevada	2.7
45	New Hampshire	3.1
42	New Jersey	3.4
28	New Mexico	4.4
48	New York	2.7
35	North Carolina	3.8
46	North Dakota	3.0
3	Ohio	6.4
30	Oklahoma	4.3
33	Oregon	4.0
37	Pennsylvania	3.7
23	Rhode Island	4.6
1	South Carolina	6.6
20	South Dakota	4.7
14	Tennessee	5.1
9	Texas	5.5
25	Utah	4.5
37	Vermont	3.7
3	Virginia	6.4
25	Washington	4.5
35	West Virginia	3.8
17	Wisconsin	4.9
10	Wyoming	5.4

RANK	STATE	PERCENT
1	Florida	6.6
1	South Carolina	6.6
3	Ohio	6.4
3	Virginia	6.4
5	Arkansas	6.3
6	California	6.2
7	Massachusetts	5.8
8	Kentucky	5.6
9	Texas	5.5
10	Alaska	5.4
10	Georgia	5.4
10	Maryland	5.4
10	Wyoming	5.4
14	Colorado	5.1
14	Tennessee	5.1
16	Louisiana	5.0
17	Michigan	4.9
17	Wisconsin	4.9
19	Alabama	4.8
20	Iowa	4.7
20	Mississippi	4.7
20	South Dakota	4.7
23	Illinois	4.6
23	Rhode Island	4.6
25	Missouri	4.5
25	Utah	4.5
25	Washington	4.5
28	Minnesota	4.4
28	New Mexico	4.4
30	Kansas	4.3
30	Oklahoma	4.3
32	Idaho	4.2
33	Montana	4.0
33	Oregon	4.0
35	North Carolina	3.8
35	West Virginia	3.8
37	Pennsylvania	3.7
37	Vermont	3.7
39	Hawaii	3.5
39	Maine	3.5
39	Nebraska	3.5
42	New Jersey	3.4
43	Connecticut	3.2
43	Indiana	3.2
45	New Hampshire	3.1
46	North Dakota	3.0
47	Arizona	2.8
48	Nevada	2.7
48	New York	2.7
50	Delaware	1.3

District of Columbia 7.3

Source: CQ Press using data from U.S. Bureau of the Census, Governments Division
"Public Education Finances: 2006" (http://www.census.gov/govs/www/school06.html)
*Staff support services include curriculum development, instructional staff training, and media, library, audiovisual, television, and computer-assisted services. Includes salaries, benefits, services, and supplies. Census expanded its usual "current expenditures" concept for education finance reports to include all current public elementary and secondary education outlays regardless of the specific unit of government that actually makes the expenditure.

Public Elementary and Secondary School Current Expenditures
for General Administration in 2006
National Total = $8,429,874,000*

ALPHA ORDER

RANK	STATE	EXPENDITURES	% of USA
17	Alabama	$153,734,000	1.8%
46	Alaska	23,169,000	0.3%
32	Arizona	90,168,000	1.1%
26	Arkansas	108,671,000	1.3%
5	California	477,921,000	5.7%
30	Colorado	95,015,000	1.1%
19	Connecticut	140,489,000	1.7%
49	Delaware	14,793,000	0.2%
12	Florida	208,163,000	2.5%
13	Georgia	179,375,000	2.1%
50	Hawaii	13,835,000	0.2%
42	Idaho	35,970,000	0.4%
2	Illinois	654,833,000	7.8%
16	Indiana	166,446,000	2.0%
24	Iowa	112,630,000	1.3%
25	Kansas	112,131,000	1.3%
23	Kentucky	125,253,000	1.5%
22	Louisiana	129,903,000	1.5%
39	Maine	44,242,000	0.5%
29	Maryland	97,017,000	1.2%
18	Massachusetts	153,589,000	1.8%
8	Michigan	330,473,000	3.9%
11	Minnesota	222,432,000	2.6%
28	Mississippi	102,442,000	1.2%
10	Missouri	223,648,000	2.7%
41	Montana	37,559,000	0.4%
31	Nebraska	93,551,000	1.1%
38	Nevada	52,289,000	0.6%
33	New Hampshire	71,706,000	0.9%
6	New Jersey	474,706,000	5.6%
37	New Mexico	64,071,000	0.8%
1	New York	717,950,000	8.5%
15	North Carolina	171,095,000	2.0%
40	North Dakota	38,677,000	0.5%
7	Ohio	469,647,000	5.6%
21	Oklahoma	130,987,000	1.6%
36	Oregon	65,449,000	0.8%
3	Pennsylvania	582,396,000	6.9%
47	Rhode Island	21,613,000	0.3%
34	South Carolina	68,239,000	0.8%
43	South Dakota	32,314,000	0.4%
20	Tennessee	137,905,000	1.6%
4	Texas	508,981,000	6.0%
44	Utah	30,172,000	0.4%
45	Vermont	29,829,000	0.4%
14	Virginia	172,879,000	2.1%
27	Washington	106,552,000	1.3%
35	West Virginia	66,539,000	0.8%
9	Wisconsin	227,775,000	2.7%
48	Wyoming	21,379,000	0.3%

RANK ORDER

RANK	STATE	EXPENDITURES	% of USA
1	New York	$717,950,000	8.5%
2	Illinois	654,833,000	7.8%
3	Pennsylvania	582,396,000	6.9%
4	Texas	508,981,000	6.0%
5	California	477,921,000	5.7%
6	New Jersey	474,706,000	5.6%
7	Ohio	469,647,000	5.6%
8	Michigan	330,473,000	3.9%
9	Wisconsin	227,775,000	2.7%
10	Missouri	223,648,000	2.7%
11	Minnesota	222,432,000	2.6%
12	Florida	208,163,000	2.5%
13	Georgia	179,375,000	2.1%
14	Virginia	172,879,000	2.1%
15	North Carolina	171,095,000	2.0%
16	Indiana	166,446,000	2.0%
17	Alabama	153,734,000	1.8%
18	Massachusetts	153,589,000	1.8%
19	Connecticut	140,489,000	1.7%
20	Tennessee	137,905,000	1.6%
21	Oklahoma	130,987,000	1.6%
22	Louisiana	129,903,000	1.5%
23	Kentucky	125,253,000	1.5%
24	Iowa	112,630,000	1.3%
25	Kansas	112,131,000	1.3%
26	Arkansas	108,671,000	1.3%
27	Washington	106,552,000	1.3%
28	Mississippi	102,442,000	1.2%
29	Maryland	97,017,000	1.2%
30	Colorado	95,015,000	1.1%
31	Nebraska	93,551,000	1.1%
32	Arizona	90,168,000	1.1%
33	New Hampshire	71,706,000	0.9%
34	South Carolina	68,239,000	0.8%
35	West Virginia	66,539,000	0.8%
36	Oregon	65,449,000	0.8%
37	New Mexico	64,071,000	0.8%
38	Nevada	52,289,000	0.6%
39	Maine	44,242,000	0.5%
40	North Dakota	38,677,000	0.5%
41	Montana	37,559,000	0.4%
42	Idaho	35,970,000	0.4%
43	South Dakota	32,314,000	0.4%
44	Utah	30,172,000	0.4%
45	Vermont	29,829,000	0.4%
46	Alaska	23,169,000	0.3%
47	Rhode Island	21,613,000	0.3%
48	Wyoming	21,379,000	0.3%
49	Delaware	14,793,000	0.2%
50	Hawaii	13,835,000	0.2%
	District of Columbia	19,272,000	0.2%

Source: U.S. Bureau of the Census, Governments Division
   "Public Education Finances: 2006" (http://www.census.gov/govs/www/school06.html)
*General administration includes expenditures for board of education and office of the superintendent services. Includes salaries, benefits, services, and supplies. Census expanded its usual "current expenditures" concept for education finance reports to include all current public elementary and secondary education outlays regardless of the specific unit of government that actually makes the expenditure.

Per Pupil Public Elementary and Secondary School Current Expenditures for General Administration in 2006
National Per Pupil = $174*

ALPHA ORDER

RANK	STATE	PER PUPIL
22	Alabama	$207
29	Alaska	174
46	Arizona	90
20	Arkansas	230
48	California	76
39	Colorado	122
14	Connecticut	252
36	Delaware	129
47	Florida	78
43	Georgia	112
48	Hawaii	76
35	Idaho	139
7	Illinois	311
30	Indiana	162
19	Iowa	233
17	Kansas	241
28	Kentucky	184
25	Louisiana	200
21	Maine	227
42	Maryland	113
30	Massachusetts	162
27	Michigan	191
8	Minnesota	272
22	Mississippi	207
16	Missouri	244
12	Montana	259
5	Nebraska	327
37	Nevada	127
2	New Hampshire	357
3	New Jersey	344
26	New Mexico	196
13	New York	258
38	North Carolina	123
1	North Dakota	394
9	Ohio	265
24	Oklahoma	206
40	Oregon	118
4	Pennsylvania	331
33	Rhode Island	144
45	South Carolina	98
9	South Dakota	265
32	Tennessee	145
41	Texas	114
50	Utah	61
6	Vermont	323
34	Virginia	142
44	Washington	103
18	West Virginia	238
11	Wisconsin	262
15	Wyoming	248

RANK ORDER

RANK	STATE	PER PUPIL
1	North Dakota	$394
2	New Hampshire	357
3	New Jersey	344
4	Pennsylvania	331
5	Nebraska	327
6	Vermont	323
7	Illinois	311
8	Minnesota	272
9	Ohio	265
9	South Dakota	265
11	Wisconsin	262
12	Montana	259
13	New York	258
14	Connecticut	252
15	Wyoming	248
16	Missouri	244
17	Kansas	241
18	West Virginia	238
19	Iowa	233
20	Arkansas	230
21	Maine	227
22	Alabama	207
22	Mississippi	207
24	Oklahoma	206
25	Louisiana	200
26	New Mexico	196
27	Michigan	191
28	Kentucky	184
29	Alaska	174
30	Indiana	162
30	Massachusetts	162
32	Tennessee	145
33	Rhode Island	144
34	Virginia	142
35	Idaho	139
36	Delaware	129
37	Nevada	127
38	North Carolina	123
39	Colorado	122
40	Oregon	118
41	Texas	114
42	Maryland	113
43	Georgia	112
44	Washington	103
45	South Carolina	98
46	Arizona	90
47	Florida	78
48	California	76
48	Hawaii	76
50	Utah	61

| | District of Columbia | 323 |

Source: U.S. Bureau of the Census, Governments Division
   "Public Education Finances: 2006" (http://www.census.gov/govs/www/school06.html)
*Based on student membership. General administration includes expenditures for board of education and office of the superintendent services. For this per pupil calculation, Census has excluded current spending for adult education, community services, and other nonelementary-secondary programs.

Public Elementary and Secondary School Current Expenditures for General Administration per $1,000 Personal Income in 2006
National Ratio = $0.82*

ALPHA ORDER

RANK	STATE	RATIO
21	Alabama	$1.16
27	Alaska	0.95
43	Arizona	0.50
5	Arkansas	1.45
48	California	0.35
42	Colorado	0.54
31	Connecticut	0.84
44	Delaware	0.47
49	Florida	0.34
35	Georgia	0.63
50	Hawaii	0.31
29	Idaho	0.89
6	Illinois	1.41
30	Indiana	0.86
18	Iowa	1.21
14	Kansas	1.25
25	Kentucky	1.06
21	Louisiana	1.16
24	Maine	1.09
47	Maryland	0.42
41	Massachusetts	0.55
26	Michigan	1.00
20	Minnesota	1.17
8	Mississippi	1.38
16	Missouri	1.23
8	Montana	1.38
2	Nebraska	1.62
37	Nevada	0.58
4	New Hampshire	1.46
13	New Jersey	1.26
19	New Mexico	1.19
28	New York	0.91
34	North Carolina	0.64
1	North Dakota	1.90
12	Ohio	1.29
16	Oklahoma	1.23
38	Oregon	0.57
10	Pennsylvania	1.35
40	Rhode Island	0.56
38	South Carolina	0.57
11	South Dakota	1.31
32	Tennessee	0.75
33	Texas	0.67
46	Utah	0.43
3	Vermont	1.47
36	Virginia	0.60
44	Washington	0.47
7	West Virginia	1.39
14	Wisconsin	1.25
23	Wyoming	1.13

RANK ORDER

RANK	STATE	RATIO
1	North Dakota	$1.90
2	Nebraska	1.62
3	Vermont	1.47
4	New Hampshire	1.46
5	Arkansas	1.45
6	Illinois	1.41
7	West Virginia	1.39
8	Mississippi	1.38
8	Montana	1.38
10	Pennsylvania	1.35
11	South Dakota	1.31
12	Ohio	1.29
13	New Jersey	1.26
14	Kansas	1.25
14	Wisconsin	1.25
16	Missouri	1.23
16	Oklahoma	1.23
18	Iowa	1.21
19	New Mexico	1.19
20	Minnesota	1.17
21	Alabama	1.16
21	Louisiana	1.16
23	Wyoming	1.13
24	Maine	1.09
25	Kentucky	1.06
26	Michigan	1.00
27	Alaska	0.95
28	New York	0.91
29	Idaho	0.89
30	Indiana	0.86
31	Connecticut	0.84
32	Tennessee	0.75
33	Texas	0.67
34	North Carolina	0.64
35	Georgia	0.63
36	Virginia	0.60
37	Nevada	0.58
38	Oregon	0.57
38	South Carolina	0.57
40	Rhode Island	0.56
41	Massachusetts	0.55
42	Colorado	0.54
43	Arizona	0.50
44	Delaware	0.47
44	Washington	0.47
46	Utah	0.43
47	Maryland	0.42
48	California	0.35
49	Florida	0.34
50	Hawaii	0.31
	District of Columbia	0.62

Source: U.S. Bureau of the Census, Governments Division
"Public Education Finances: 2006" (http://www.census.gov/govs/www/school06.html)
*General administration includes expenditures for board of education and office of the superintendent services. Includes salaries, benefits, services, and supplies.

Percent of Public Elementary and Secondary School Current Expenditures Used for General Administration in 2006
National Percent = 1.9%*

ALPHA ORDER

RANK	STATE	PERCENT
15	Alabama	2.7
34	Alaska	1.5
38	Arizona	1.4
9	Arkansas	2.9
49	California	0.9
34	Colorado	1.5
28	Connecticut	2.0
44	Delaware	1.1
48	Florida	1.0
40	Georgia	1.3
50	Hawaii	0.7
24	Idaho	2.2
4	Illinois	3.4
30	Indiana	1.8
12	Iowa	2.8
9	Kansas	2.9
20	Kentucky	2.4
20	Louisiana	2.4
26	Maine	2.1
44	Maryland	1.1
40	Massachusetts	1.3
28	Michigan	2.0
12	Minnesota	2.8
9	Mississippi	2.9
6	Missouri	3.0
6	Montana	3.0
2	Nebraska	3.7
31	Nevada	1.7
4	New Hampshire	3.4
23	New Jersey	2.3
20	New Mexico	2.4
31	New York	1.7
31	North Carolina	1.7
1	North Dakota	4.5
15	Ohio	2.7
12	Oklahoma	2.8
38	Oregon	1.4
6	Pennsylvania	3.0
44	Rhode Island	1.1
43	South Carolina	1.2
3	South Dakota	3.5
26	Tennessee	2.1
34	Texas	1.5
44	Utah	1.1
18	Vermont	2.5
34	Virginia	1.5
40	Washington	1.3
18	West Virginia	2.5
17	Wisconsin	2.6
24	Wyoming	2.2

RANK ORDER

RANK	STATE	PERCENT
1	North Dakota	4.5
2	Nebraska	3.7
3	South Dakota	3.5
4	Illinois	3.4
4	New Hampshire	3.4
6	Missouri	3.0
6	Montana	3.0
6	Pennsylvania	3.0
9	Arkansas	2.9
9	Kansas	2.9
9	Mississippi	2.9
12	Iowa	2.8
12	Minnesota	2.8
12	Oklahoma	2.8
15	Alabama	2.7
15	Ohio	2.7
17	Wisconsin	2.6
18	Vermont	2.5
18	West Virginia	2.5
20	Kentucky	2.4
20	Louisiana	2.4
20	New Mexico	2.4
23	New Jersey	2.3
24	Idaho	2.2
24	Wyoming	2.2
26	Maine	2.1
26	Tennessee	2.1
28	Connecticut	2.0
28	Michigan	2.0
30	Indiana	1.8
31	Nevada	1.7
31	New York	1.7
31	North Carolina	1.7
34	Alaska	1.5
34	Colorado	1.5
34	Texas	1.5
34	Virginia	1.5
38	Arizona	1.4
38	Oregon	1.4
40	Georgia	1.3
40	Massachusetts	1.3
40	Washington	1.3
43	South Carolina	1.2
44	Delaware	1.1
44	Maryland	1.1
44	Rhode Island	1.1
44	Utah	1.1
48	Florida	1.0
49	California	0.9
50	Hawaii	0.7
	District of Columbia	2.0

Source: CQ Press using data from U.S. Bureau of the Census, Governments Division
"Public Education Finances: 2006" (http://www.census.gov/govs/www/school06.html)
*General administration includes expenditures for board of education and office of the superintendent services. Includes salaries, benefits, services, and supplies. Census expanded its usual "current expenditures" concept for education finance reports to include all current public elementary and secondary education outlays regardless of the specific unit of government that actually makes the expenditure.

Public Elementary and Secondary School Current Expenditures for School Administration in 2006
National Total = $24,521,915,000*

ALPHA ORDER

RANK	STATE	EXPENDITURES	% of USA
22	Alabama	$351,330,000	1.4%
44	Alaska	90,314,000	0.4%
23	Arizona	331,417,000	1.4%
33	Arkansas	200,557,000	0.8%
1	California	3,597,480,000	14.7%
19	Colorado	413,677,000	1.7%
20	Connecticut	399,648,000	1.6%
46	Delaware	75,510,000	0.3%
4	Florida	1,173,798,000	4.8%
9	Georgia	851,824,000	3.5%
39	Hawaii	121,151,000	0.5%
42	Idaho	95,380,000	0.4%
7	Illinois	980,464,000	4.0%
15	Indiana	513,220,000	2.1%
29	Iowa	239,962,000	1.0%
31	Kansas	232,284,000	0.9%
27	Kentucky	283,340,000	1.2%
28	Louisiana	281,017,000	1.1%
41	Maine	113,880,000	0.5%
13	Maryland	638,116,000	2.6%
14	Massachusetts	514,082,000	2.1%
6	Michigan	990,939,000	4.0%
25	Minnesota	315,319,000	1.3%
34	Mississippi	194,839,000	0.8%
18	Missouri	423,804,000	1.7%
47	Montana	68,709,000	0.3%
38	Nebraska	134,930,000	0.6%
32	Nevada	205,994,000	0.8%
40	New Hampshire	116,098,000	0.5%
5	New Jersey	1,001,322,000	4.1%
35	New Mexico	167,818,000	0.7%
3	New York	1,642,286,000	6.7%
12	North Carolina	665,354,000	2.7%
50	North Dakota	40,043,000	0.2%
8	Ohio	950,961,000	3.9%
30	Oklahoma	238,963,000	1.0%
26	Oregon	301,852,000	1.2%
10	Pennsylvania	809,678,000	3.3%
43	Rhode Island	91,981,000	0.4%
24	South Carolina	326,067,000	1.3%
49	South Dakota	44,645,000	0.2%
21	Tennessee	364,222,000	1.5%
2	Texas	1,838,278,000	7.5%
36	Utah	163,249,000	0.7%
45	Vermont	80,988,000	0.3%
11	Virginia	665,993,000	2.7%
16	Washington	489,466,000	2.0%
37	West Virginia	140,743,000	0.6%
17	Wisconsin	443,553,000	1.8%
48	Wyoming	53,895,000	0.2%

RANK ORDER

RANK	STATE	EXPENDITURES	% of USA
1	California	$3,597,480,000	14.7%
2	Texas	1,838,278,000	7.5%
3	New York	1,642,286,000	6.7%
4	Florida	1,173,798,000	4.8%
5	New Jersey	1,001,322,000	4.1%
6	Michigan	990,939,000	4.0%
7	Illinois	980,464,000	4.0%
8	Ohio	950,961,000	3.9%
9	Georgia	851,824,000	3.5%
10	Pennsylvania	809,678,000	3.3%
11	Virginia	665,993,000	2.7%
12	North Carolina	665,354,000	2.7%
13	Maryland	638,116,000	2.6%
14	Massachusetts	514,082,000	2.1%
15	Indiana	513,220,000	2.1%
16	Washington	489,466,000	2.0%
17	Wisconsin	443,553,000	1.8%
18	Missouri	423,804,000	1.7%
19	Colorado	413,677,000	1.7%
20	Connecticut	399,648,000	1.6%
21	Tennessee	364,222,000	1.5%
22	Alabama	351,330,000	1.4%
23	Arizona	331,417,000	1.4%
24	South Carolina	326,067,000	1.3%
25	Minnesota	315,319,000	1.3%
26	Oregon	301,852,000	1.2%
27	Kentucky	283,340,000	1.2%
28	Louisiana	281,017,000	1.1%
29	Iowa	239,962,000	1.0%
30	Oklahoma	238,963,000	1.0%
31	Kansas	232,284,000	0.9%
32	Nevada	205,994,000	0.8%
33	Arkansas	200,557,000	0.8%
34	Mississippi	194,839,000	0.8%
35	New Mexico	167,818,000	0.7%
36	Utah	163,249,000	0.7%
37	West Virginia	140,743,000	0.6%
38	Nebraska	134,930,000	0.6%
39	Hawaii	121,151,000	0.5%
40	New Hampshire	116,098,000	0.5%
41	Maine	113,880,000	0.5%
42	Idaho	95,380,000	0.4%
43	Rhode Island	91,981,000	0.4%
44	Alaska	90,314,000	0.4%
45	Vermont	80,988,000	0.3%
46	Delaware	75,510,000	0.3%
47	Montana	68,709,000	0.3%
48	Wyoming	53,895,000	0.2%
49	South Dakota	44,645,000	0.2%
50	North Dakota	40,043,000	0.2%
	District of Columbia	51,475,000	0.2%

Source: U.S. Bureau of the Census, Governments Division
   "Public Education Finances: 2006" (http://www.census.gov/govs/www/school06.html)
*School administration includes expenditures for the office of principal services. Includes salaries, benefits, services, and supplies. Census expanded its usual "current expenditures" concept for education finance reports to include all current public elementary and secondary education outlays regardless of the specific unit of government that actually makes the expenditure.

Per Pupil Public Elementary and Secondary School Current Expenditures
for School Administration in 2006
National Per Pupil = $507*

ALPHA ORDER

RANK	STATE	PER PUPIL
30	Alabama	$473
5	Alaska	680
49	Arizona	330
39	Arkansas	424
13	California	575
20	Colorado	531
4	Connecticut	718
7	Delaware	660
37	Florida	441
19	Georgia	533
6	Hawaii	663
47	Idaho	369
33	Illinois	466
24	Indiana	500
27	Iowa	496
25	Kansas	499
40	Kentucky	417
38	Louisiana	433
11	Maine	583
2	Maryland	742
17	Massachusetts	541
14	Michigan	573
44	Minnesota	385
43	Mississippi	394
35	Missouri	463
30	Montana	473
32	Nebraska	472
25	Nevada	499
12	New Hampshire	577
3	New Jersey	726
21	New Mexico	514
10	New York	589
28	North Carolina	479
42	North Dakota	408
18	Ohio	537
46	Oklahoma	377
16	Oregon	542
36	Pennsylvania	460
9	Rhode Island	613
33	South Carolina	466
48	South Dakota	367
45	Tennessee	382
41	Texas	413
50	Utah	329
1	Vermont	877
15	Virginia	549
29	Washington	474
23	West Virginia	503
22	Wisconsin	510
8	Wyoming	626

RANK ORDER

RANK	STATE	PER PUPIL
1	Vermont	$877
2	Maryland	742
3	New Jersey	726
4	Connecticut	718
5	Alaska	680
6	Hawaii	663
7	Delaware	660
8	Wyoming	626
9	Rhode Island	613
10	New York	589
11	Maine	583
12	New Hampshire	577
13	California	575
14	Michigan	573
15	Virginia	549
16	Oregon	542
17	Massachusetts	541
18	Ohio	537
19	Georgia	533
20	Colorado	531
21	New Mexico	514
22	Wisconsin	510
23	West Virginia	503
24	Indiana	500
25	Kansas	499
25	Nevada	499
27	Iowa	496
28	North Carolina	479
29	Washington	474
30	Alabama	473
30	Montana	473
32	Nebraska	472
33	Illinois	466
33	South Carolina	466
35	Missouri	463
36	Pennsylvania	460
37	Florida	441
38	Louisiana	433
39	Arkansas	424
40	Kentucky	417
41	Texas	413
42	North Dakota	408
43	Mississippi	394
44	Minnesota	385
45	Tennessee	382
46	Oklahoma	377
47	Idaho	369
48	South Dakota	367
49	Arizona	330
50	Utah	329
	District of Columbia	863

Source: U.S. Bureau of the Census, Governments Division
"Public Education Finances: 2006" (http://www.census.gov/govs/www/school06.html)
*Based on student membership. School administration includes expenditures for the office of principal services. For this per pupil calculation, Census has excluded current spending for adult education, community services, and other nonelementary-secondary programs.

Public Elementary and Secondary School Current Expenditures for School Administration per $1,000 Personal Income in 2006
National Ratio = $2.38*

ALPHA ORDER			RANK ORDER		
RANK	STATE	RATIO	RANK	STATE	RATIO
16	Alabama	$2.64	1	Vermont	$3.98
2	Alaska	3.72	2	Alaska	3.72
47	Arizona	1.83	3	New Mexico	3.11
12	Arkansas	2.68	4	Georgia	3.00
13	California	2.67	4	Michigan	3.00
33	Colorado	2.35	6	West Virginia	2.93
30	Connecticut	2.39	7	Wyoming	2.85
26	Delaware	2.42	8	Maine	2.80
45	Florida	1.90	9	Maryland	2.75
4	Georgia	3.00	10	Hawaii	2.73
10	Hawaii	2.73	11	South Carolina	2.70
32	Idaho	2.36	12	Arkansas	2.68
41	Illinois	2.11	13	California	2.67
15	Indiana	2.65	14	New Jersey	2.66
21	Iowa	2.57	15	Indiana	2.65
20	Kansas	2.59	16	Alabama	2.64
28	Kentucky	2.40	17	Mississippi	2.63
22	Louisiana	2.52	17	Oregon	2.63
8	Maine	2.80	19	Ohio	2.60
9	Maryland	2.75	20	Kansas	2.59
47	Massachusetts	1.83	21	Iowa	2.57
4	Michigan	3.00	22	Louisiana	2.52
50	Minnesota	1.65	22	Montana	2.52
17	Mississippi	2.63	24	North Carolina	2.49
35	Missouri	2.33	25	Wisconsin	2.44
22	Montana	2.52	26	Delaware	2.42
34	Nebraska	2.34	26	Texas	2.42
38	Nevada	2.28	28	Kentucky	2.40
31	New Hampshire	2.37	28	Rhode Island	2.40
14	New Jersey	2.66	30	Connecticut	2.39
3	New Mexico	3.11	31	New Hampshire	2.37
42	New York	2.08	32	Idaho	2.36
24	North Carolina	2.49	33	Colorado	2.35
43	North Dakota	1.97	34	Nebraska	2.34
19	Ohio	2.60	35	Missouri	2.33
39	Oklahoma	2.24	35	Utah	2.33
17	Oregon	2.63	37	Virginia	2.32
46	Pennsylvania	1.87	38	Nevada	2.28
28	Rhode Island	2.40	39	Oklahoma	2.24
11	South Carolina	2.70	40	Washington	2.18
49	South Dakota	1.81	41	Illinois	2.11
43	Tennessee	1.97	42	New York	2.08
26	Texas	2.42	43	North Dakota	1.97
35	Utah	2.33	43	Tennessee	1.97
1	Vermont	3.98	45	Florida	1.90
37	Virginia	2.32	46	Pennsylvania	1.87
40	Washington	2.18	47	Arizona	1.83
6	West Virginia	2.93	47	Massachusetts	1.83
25	Wisconsin	2.44	49	South Dakota	1.81
7	Wyoming	2.85	50	Minnesota	1.65
				District of Columbia	1.65

Source: U.S. Bureau of the Census, Governments Division
   "Public Education Finances: 2006" (http://www.census.gov/govs/www/school06.html)
*School administration includes expenditures for the office of principal services. Includes salaries, benefits, services, and supplies.

Percent of Public Elementary and Secondary School Current Expenditures Used for School Administration in 2006
National Percent = 5.4%*

ALPHA ORDER

RANK	STATE	PERCENT
11	Alabama	6.1
13	Alaska	5.9
42	Arizona	5.0
35	Arkansas	5.3
4	California	6.6
5	Colorado	6.5
19	Connecticut	5.7
22	Delaware	5.6
22	Florida	5.6
10	Georgia	6.2
5	Hawaii	6.5
19	Idaho	5.7
39	Illinois	5.1
22	Indiana	5.6
13	Iowa	5.9
13	Kansas	5.9
30	Kentucky	5.4
39	Louisiana	5.1
35	Maine	5.3
1	Maryland	6.9
47	Massachusetts	4.3
13	Michigan	5.9
49	Minnesota	4.0
30	Mississippi	5.4
22	Missouri	5.6
27	Montana	5.5
30	Nebraska	5.4
2	Nevada	6.8
27	New Hampshire	5.5
44	New Jersey	4.8
8	New Mexico	6.3
50	New York	3.8
5	North Carolina	6.5
46	North Dakota	4.7
30	Ohio	5.4
38	Oklahoma	5.2
8	Oregon	6.3
48	Pennsylvania	4.1
43	Rhode Island	4.9
19	South Carolina	5.7
44	South Dakota	4.8
27	Tennessee	5.5
30	Texas	5.4
13	Utah	5.9
3	Vermont	6.7
18	Virginia	5.8
12	Washington	6.0
35	West Virginia	5.3
39	Wisconsin	5.1
22	Wyoming	5.6

RANK ORDER

RANK	STATE	PERCENT
1	Maryland	6.9
2	Nevada	6.8
3	Vermont	6.7
4	California	6.6
5	Colorado	6.5
5	Hawaii	6.5
5	North Carolina	6.5
8	New Mexico	6.3
8	Oregon	6.3
10	Georgia	6.2
11	Alabama	6.1
12	Washington	6.0
13	Alaska	5.9
13	Iowa	5.9
13	Kansas	5.9
13	Michigan	5.9
13	Utah	5.9
18	Virginia	5.8
19	Connecticut	5.7
19	Idaho	5.7
19	South Carolina	5.7
22	Delaware	5.6
22	Florida	5.6
22	Indiana	5.6
22	Missouri	5.6
22	Wyoming	5.6
27	Montana	5.5
27	New Hampshire	5.5
27	Tennessee	5.5
30	Kentucky	5.4
30	Mississippi	5.4
30	Nebraska	5.4
30	Ohio	5.4
30	Texas	5.4
35	Arkansas	5.3
35	Maine	5.3
35	West Virginia	5.3
38	Oklahoma	5.2
39	Illinois	5.1
39	Louisiana	5.1
39	Wisconsin	5.1
42	Arizona	5.0
43	Rhode Island	4.9
44	New Jersey	4.8
44	South Dakota	4.8
46	North Dakota	4.7
47	Massachusetts	4.3
48	Pennsylvania	4.1
49	Minnesota	4.0
50	New York	3.8

District of Columbia 5.4

Source: CQ Press using data from U.S. Bureau of the Census, Governments Division
   "Public Education Finances: 2006" (http://www.census.gov/govs/www/school06.html)
*School administration includes expenditures for the office of principal services. Includes salaries, benefits, services, and supplies. Census expanded its usual "current expenditures" concept for education finance reports to include all current public elementary and secondary education outlays regardless of the specific unit of government that actually makes the expenditure.

Public Elementary and Secondary School Current Expenditures for Pupil Transportation in 2006
National Total = $19,309,197,000*

ALPHA ORDER

RANK	STATE	EXPENDITURES	% of USA
24	Alabama	$262,791,000	1.4%
45	Alaska	53,352,000	0.3%
23	Arizona	297,088,000	1.5%
35	Arkansas	136,316,000	0.7%
2	California	1,365,513,000	7.1%
29	Colorado	182,019,000	0.9%
19	Connecticut	336,387,000	1.7%
42	Delaware	78,129,000	0.4%
7	Florida	875,987,000	4.5%
10	Georgia	562,487,000	2.9%
49	Hawaii	34,786,000	0.2%
40	Idaho	80,888,000	0.4%
5	Illinois	955,243,000	4.9%
12	Indiana	518,630,000	2.7%
33	Iowa	146,193,000	0.8%
30	Kansas	159,712,000	0.8%
21	Kentucky	309,087,000	1.6%
22	Louisiana	301,498,000	1.6%
37	Maine	95,338,000	0.5%
13	Maryland	479,442,000	2.5%
14	Massachusetts	465,142,000	2.4%
9	Michigan	737,963,000	3.8%
15	Minnesota	413,709,000	2.1%
31	Mississippi	156,881,000	0.8%
17	Missouri	365,079,000	1.9%
44	Montana	58,031,000	0.3%
43	Nebraska	74,085,000	0.4%
34	Nevada	136,604,000	0.7%
39	New Hampshire	90,524,000	0.5%
3	New Jersey	1,116,755,000	5.8%
36	New Mexico	108,278,000	0.6%
1	New York	2,503,555,000	13.0%
16	North Carolina	397,519,000	2.1%
48	North Dakota	36,226,000	0.2%
8	Ohio	791,580,000	4.1%
32	Oklahoma	153,274,000	0.8%
26	Oregon	213,654,000	1.1%
4	Pennsylvania	1,085,816,000	5.6%
41	Rhode Island	80,616,000	0.4%
27	South Carolina	204,226,000	1.1%
50	South Dakota	32,269,000	0.2%
25	Tennessee	242,859,000	1.3%
6	Texas	927,000,000	4.8%
38	Utah	94,284,000	0.5%
47	Vermont	40,310,000	0.2%
11	Virginia	559,354,000	2.9%
20	Washington	335,594,000	1.7%
28	West Virginia	188,801,000	1.0%
18	Wisconsin	353,066,000	1.8%
46	Wyoming	42,132,000	0.2%

RANK ORDER

RANK	STATE	EXPENDITURES	% of USA
1	New York	$2,503,555,000	13.0%
2	California	1,365,513,000	7.1%
3	New Jersey	1,116,755,000	5.8%
4	Pennsylvania	1,085,816,000	5.6%
5	Illinois	955,243,000	4.9%
6	Texas	927,000,000	4.8%
7	Florida	875,987,000	4.5%
8	Ohio	791,580,000	4.1%
9	Michigan	737,963,000	3.8%
10	Georgia	562,487,000	2.9%
11	Virginia	559,354,000	2.9%
12	Indiana	518,630,000	2.7%
13	Maryland	479,442,000	2.5%
14	Massachusetts	465,142,000	2.4%
15	Minnesota	413,709,000	2.1%
16	North Carolina	397,519,000	2.1%
17	Missouri	365,079,000	1.9%
18	Wisconsin	353,066,000	1.8%
19	Connecticut	336,387,000	1.7%
20	Washington	335,594,000	1.7%
21	Kentucky	309,087,000	1.6%
22	Louisiana	301,498,000	1.6%
23	Arizona	297,088,000	1.5%
24	Alabama	262,791,000	1.4%
25	Tennessee	242,859,000	1.3%
26	Oregon	213,654,000	1.1%
27	South Carolina	204,226,000	1.1%
28	West Virginia	188,801,000	1.0%
29	Colorado	182,019,000	0.9%
30	Kansas	159,712,000	0.8%
31	Mississippi	156,881,000	0.8%
32	Oklahoma	153,274,000	0.8%
33	Iowa	146,193,000	0.8%
34	Nevada	136,604,000	0.7%
35	Arkansas	136,316,000	0.7%
36	New Mexico	108,278,000	0.6%
37	Maine	95,338,000	0.5%
38	Utah	94,284,000	0.5%
39	New Hampshire	90,524,000	0.5%
40	Idaho	80,888,000	0.4%
41	Rhode Island	80,616,000	0.4%
42	Delaware	78,129,000	0.4%
43	Nebraska	74,085,000	0.4%
44	Montana	58,031,000	0.3%
45	Alaska	53,352,000	0.3%
46	Wyoming	42,132,000	0.2%
47	Vermont	40,310,000	0.2%
48	North Dakota	36,226,000	0.2%
49	Hawaii	34,786,000	0.2%
50	South Dakota	32,269,000	0.2%
	District of Columbia	73,125,000	0.4%

Source: U.S. Bureau of the Census, Governments Division
   "Public Education Finances: 2006" (http://www.census.gov/govs/www/school06.html)
*Includes transportation of public school students including vehicle operation, monitoring riders, and vehicle servicing and maintenance. Includes salaries, benefits, services, and supplies. Census expanded its usual "current expenditures" concept for education finance reports to include all current public elementary and secondary education outlays regardless of the specific unit of government that actually makes the expenditure.

Percent of Public Elementary and Secondary School Current Expenditures Used for Pupil Transportation in 2006
National percent = 4.3%*

ALPHA ORDER

RANK	STATE	PERCENT
17	Alabama	4.5
41	Alaska	3.5
17	Arizona	4.5
38	Arkansas	3.6
49	California	2.5
47	Colorado	2.9
12	Connecticut	4.8
4	Delaware	5.8
29	Florida	4.1
29	Georgia	4.1
50	Hawaii	1.9
12	Idaho	4.8
11	Illinois	4.9
5	Indiana	5.7
38	Iowa	3.6
29	Kansas	4.1
2	Kentucky	5.9
6	Louisiana	5.5
17	Maine	4.5
10	Maryland	5.2
35	Massachusetts	3.9
22	Michigan	4.4
8	Minnesota	5.3
22	Mississippi	4.4
12	Missouri	4.8
16	Montana	4.6
46	Nebraska	3.0
17	Nevada	4.5
26	New Hampshire	4.3
8	New Jersey	5.3
29	New Mexico	4.1
2	New York	5.9
35	North Carolina	3.9
26	North Dakota	4.3
17	Ohio	4.5
44	Oklahoma	3.3
22	Oregon	4.4
6	Pennsylvania	5.5
26	Rhode Island	4.3
38	South Carolina	3.6
42	South Dakota	3.4
37	Tennessee	3.7
48	Texas	2.7
42	Utah	3.4
44	Vermont	3.3
12	Virginia	4.8
29	Washington	4.1
1	West Virginia	7.1
34	Wisconsin	4.0
22	Wyoming	4.4

RANK ORDER

RANK	STATE	PERCENT
1	West Virginia	7.1
2	Kentucky	5.9
2	New York	5.9
4	Delaware	5.8
5	Indiana	5.7
6	Louisiana	5.5
6	Pennsylvania	5.5
8	Minnesota	5.3
8	New Jersey	5.3
10	Maryland	5.2
11	Illinois	4.9
12	Connecticut	4.8
12	Idaho	4.8
12	Missouri	4.8
12	Virginia	4.8
16	Montana	4.6
17	Alabama	4.5
17	Arizona	4.5
17	Maine	4.5
17	Nevada	4.5
17	Ohio	4.5
22	Michigan	4.4
22	Mississippi	4.4
22	Oregon	4.4
22	Wyoming	4.4
26	New Hampshire	4.3
26	North Dakota	4.3
26	Rhode Island	4.3
29	Florida	4.1
29	Georgia	4.1
29	Kansas	4.1
29	New Mexico	4.1
29	Washington	4.1
34	Wisconsin	4.0
35	Massachusetts	3.9
35	North Carolina	3.9
37	Tennessee	3.7
38	Arkansas	3.6
38	Iowa	3.6
38	South Carolina	3.6
41	Alaska	3.5
42	South Dakota	3.4
42	Utah	3.4
44	Oklahoma	3.3
44	Vermont	3.3
46	Nebraska	3.0
47	Colorado	2.9
48	Texas	2.7
49	California	2.5
50	Hawaii	1.9

District of Columbia   7.7

Source: CQ Press using data from U.S. Bureau of the Census, Governments Division
"Public Education Finances: 2006" (http://www.census.gov/govs/www/school06.html)
*Includes transportation of public school students including vehicle operation, monitoring riders, and vehicle servicing and maintenance. Includes salaries, benefits, services, and supplies. Census expanded its usual "current expenditures" concept for education finance reports to include all current public elementary and secondary education outlays regardless of the specific unit of government that actually makes the expenditure.

Public Elementary and Secondary School Current Expenditures
for Operation and Maintenance of Facilities in 2006
National Total = $43,647,946,000*

ALPHA ORDER

RANK	STATE	EXPENDITURES	% of USA
26	Alabama	$528,412,000	1.2%
40	Alaska	201,223,000	0.5%
17	Arizona	785,212,000	1.8%
33	Arkansas	350,007,000	0.8%
1	California	5,203,292,000	11.9%
21	Colorado	657,657,000	1.5%
20	Connecticut	663,250,000	1.5%
46	Delaware	129,773,000	0.3%
4	Florida	2,325,103,000	5.3%
12	Georgia	1,020,931,000	2.3%
44	Hawaii	141,315,000	0.3%
42	Idaho	152,286,000	0.3%
7	Illinois	1,925,642,000	4.4%
13	Indiana	995,116,000	2.3%
32	Iowa	377,385,000	0.9%
30	Kansas	394,582,000	0.9%
28	Kentucky	483,582,000	1.1%
22	Louisiana	611,398,000	1.4%
39	Maine	216,341,000	0.5%
14	Maryland	851,747,000	2.0%
10	Massachusetts	1,118,159,000	2.6%
8	Michigan	1,788,804,000	4.1%
24	Minnesota	588,064,000	1.3%
31	Mississippi	391,063,000	0.9%
19	Missouri	759,203,000	1.7%
45	Montana	130,064,000	0.3%
38	Nebraska	232,170,000	0.5%
34	Nevada	303,030,000	0.7%
41	New Hampshire	185,314,000	0.4%
5	New Jersey	2,079,567,000	4.8%
35	New Mexico	264,897,000	0.6%
3	New York	3,622,727,000	8.3%
15	North Carolina	843,440,000	1.9%
50	North Dakota	73,709,000	0.2%
9	Ohio	1,623,587,000	3.7%
27	Oklahoma	525,904,000	1.2%
29	Oregon	401,950,000	0.9%
6	Pennsylvania	1,952,054,000	4.5%
43	Rhode Island	152,105,000	0.3%
25	South Carolina	532,029,000	1.2%
48	South Dakota	100,052,000	0.2%
23	Tennessee	594,414,000	1.4%
2	Texas	3,811,028,000	8.7%
37	Utah	256,358,000	0.6%
49	Vermont	96,845,000	0.2%
11	Virginia	1,116,048,000	2.6%
18	Washington	759,231,000	1.7%
36	West Virginia	264,823,000	0.6%
16	Wisconsin	841,035,000	1.9%
47	Wyoming	102,132,000	0.2%

RANK ORDER

RANK	STATE	EXPENDITURES	% of USA
1	California	$5,203,292,000	11.9%
2	Texas	3,811,028,000	8.7%
3	New York	3,622,727,000	8.3%
4	Florida	2,325,103,000	5.3%
5	New Jersey	2,079,567,000	4.8%
6	Pennsylvania	1,952,054,000	4.5%
7	Illinois	1,925,642,000	4.4%
8	Michigan	1,788,804,000	4.1%
9	Ohio	1,623,587,000	3.7%
10	Massachusetts	1,118,159,000	2.6%
11	Virginia	1,116,048,000	2.6%
12	Georgia	1,020,931,000	2.3%
13	Indiana	995,116,000	2.3%
14	Maryland	851,747,000	2.0%
15	North Carolina	843,440,000	1.9%
16	Wisconsin	841,035,000	1.9%
17	Arizona	785,212,000	1.8%
18	Washington	759,231,000	1.7%
19	Missouri	759,203,000	1.7%
20	Connecticut	663,250,000	1.5%
21	Colorado	657,657,000	1.5%
22	Louisiana	611,398,000	1.4%
23	Tennessee	594,414,000	1.4%
24	Minnesota	588,064,000	1.3%
25	South Carolina	532,029,000	1.2%
26	Alabama	528,412,000	1.2%
27	Oklahoma	525,904,000	1.2%
28	Kentucky	483,582,000	1.1%
29	Oregon	401,950,000	0.9%
30	Kansas	394,582,000	0.9%
31	Mississippi	391,063,000	0.9%
32	Iowa	377,385,000	0.9%
33	Arkansas	350,007,000	0.8%
34	Nevada	303,030,000	0.7%
35	New Mexico	264,897,000	0.6%
36	West Virginia	264,823,000	0.6%
37	Utah	256,358,000	0.6%
38	Nebraska	232,170,000	0.5%
39	Maine	216,341,000	0.5%
40	Alaska	201,223,000	0.5%
41	New Hampshire	185,314,000	0.4%
42	Idaho	152,286,000	0.3%
43	Rhode Island	152,105,000	0.3%
44	Hawaii	141,315,000	0.3%
45	Montana	130,064,000	0.3%
46	Delaware	129,773,000	0.3%
47	Wyoming	102,132,000	0.2%
48	South Dakota	100,052,000	0.2%
49	Vermont	96,845,000	0.2%
50	North Dakota	73,709,000	0.2%
	District of Columbia	123,886,000	0.3%

Source: U.S. Bureau of the Census, Governments Division
"Public Education Finances: 2006" (http://www.census.gov/govs/www/school06.html)
*Includes building services, care and upkeep of grounds and equipment, nonstudent transportation, vehicle maintenance, and security services. Includes salaries, benefits, services, and supplies. Census expanded its usual "current expenditures" concept for education finance reports to include all current public elementary and secondary education outlays regardless of the specific unit of government that actually makes the expenditure.

Percent of Public Elementary and Secondary School Current Expenditures Used for Operations and Maintenance of Facilities in 2006
National Percent = 9.7%*

RANK	STATE	PERCENT
38	Alabama	9.1
1	Alaska	13.1
2	Arizona	12.0
29	Arkansas	9.3
26	California	9.5
13	Colorado	10.3
27	Connecticut	9.4
24	Delaware	9.6
6	Florida	11.0
50	Georgia	7.4
48	Hawaii	7.6
38	Idaho	9.1
18	Illinois	9.9
6	Indiana	11.0
29	Iowa	9.3
14	Kansas	10.1
35	Kentucky	9.2
4	Louisiana	11.2
14	Maine	10.1
29	Maryland	9.3
29	Massachusetts	9.3
10	Michigan	10.6
49	Minnesota	7.5
8	Mississippi	10.9
16	Missouri	10.0
12	Montana	10.4
29	Nebraska	9.3
18	Nevada	9.9
41	New Hampshire	8.8
18	New Jersey	9.9
18	New Mexico	9.9
43	New York	8.5
45	North Carolina	8.2
42	North Dakota	8.7
35	Ohio	9.2
3	Oklahoma	11.4
44	Oregon	8.3
18	Pennsylvania	9.9
46	Rhode Island	8.0
29	South Carolina	9.3
9	South Dakota	10.7
40	Tennessee	9.0
4	Texas	11.2
35	Utah	9.2
46	Vermont	8.0
23	Virginia	9.7
27	Washington	9.4
16	West Virginia	10.0
24	Wisconsin	9.6
11	Wyoming	10.5

RANK	STATE	PERCENT
1	Alaska	13.1
2	Arizona	12.0
3	Oklahoma	11.4
4	Louisiana	11.2
4	Texas	11.2
6	Florida	11.0
6	Indiana	11.0
8	Mississippi	10.9
9	South Dakota	10.7
10	Michigan	10.6
11	Wyoming	10.5
12	Montana	10.4
13	Colorado	10.3
14	Kansas	10.1
14	Maine	10.1
16	Missouri	10.0
16	West Virginia	10.0
18	Illinois	9.9
18	Nevada	9.9
18	New Jersey	9.9
18	New Mexico	9.9
18	Pennsylvania	9.9
23	Virginia	9.7
24	Delaware	9.6
24	Wisconsin	9.6
26	California	9.5
27	Connecticut	9.4
27	Washington	9.4
29	Arkansas	9.3
29	Iowa	9.3
29	Maryland	9.3
29	Massachusetts	9.3
29	Nebraska	9.3
29	South Carolina	9.3
35	Kentucky	9.2
35	Ohio	9.2
35	Utah	9.2
38	Alabama	9.1
38	Idaho	9.1
40	Tennessee	9.0
41	New Hampshire	8.8
42	North Dakota	8.7
43	New York	8.5
44	Oregon	8.3
45	North Carolina	8.2
46	Rhode Island	8.0
46	Vermont	8.0
48	Hawaii	7.6
49	Minnesota	7.5
50	Georgia	7.4

	District of Columbia	13.0

Source: CQ Press using data from U.S. Bureau of the Census, Governments Division
"Public Education Finances: 2006" (http://www.census.gov/govs/www/school06.html)
*Includes building services, care and upkeep of grounds and equipment, nonstudent transportation, vehicle maintenance, and security services. Includes salaries, benefits, services, and supplies. Census expanded its usual "current expenditures" concept for education finance reports to include all current public elementary and secondary education outlays regardless of the specific unit of government that actually makes the expenditure.

State and Local Government Expenditures for Elementary and Secondary Education in 2006
National Total = $500,527,662,000*

ALPHA ORDER

RANK	STATE	EXPENDITURES	% of USA
25	Alabama	$6,552,215,000	1.3%
44	Alaska	1,797,278,000	0.4%
20	Arizona	7,737,742,000	1.5%
31	Arkansas	4,130,799,000	0.8%
1	California	64,120,762,000	12.8%
21	Colorado	7,418,124,000	1.5%
23	Connecticut	7,308,070,000	1.5%
45	Delaware	1,616,178,000	0.3%
4	Florida	26,022,019,000	5.2%
10	Georgia	15,405,290,000	3.1%
42	Hawaii	1,937,230,000	0.4%
43	Idaho	1,856,893,000	0.4%
7	Illinois	20,688,589,000	4.1%
14	Indiana	9,773,748,000	2.0%
30	Iowa	4,661,811,000	0.9%
32	Kansas	4,117,364,000	0.8%
27	Kentucky	5,183,328,000	1.0%
26	Louisiana	5,962,672,000	1.2%
40	Maine	2,129,772,000	0.4%
15	Maryland	9,722,594,000	1.9%
12	Massachusetts	11,608,055,000	2.3%
9	Michigan	17,232,992,000	3.4%
18	Minnesota	8,898,683,000	1.8%
33	Mississippi	3,996,588,000	0.8%
19	Missouri	8,330,413,000	1.7%
46	Montana	1,351,358,000	0.3%
37	Nebraska	2,724,220,000	0.5%
34	Nevada	3,808,948,000	0.8%
39	New Hampshire	2,286,783,000	0.5%
5	New Jersey	21,916,583,000	4.4%
36	New Mexico	3,056,165,000	0.6%
2	New York	45,450,507,000	9.1%
13	North Carolina	11,501,994,000	2.3%
50	North Dakota	949,027,000	0.2%
8	Ohio	19,875,665,000	4.0%
29	Oklahoma	5,018,183,000	1.0%
28	Oregon	5,146,735,000	1.0%
6	Pennsylvania	21,692,242,000	4.3%
41	Rhode Island	1,956,737,000	0.4%
24	South Carolina	6,938,614,000	1.4%
49	South Dakota	1,011,132,000	0.2%
22	Tennessee	7,392,710,000	1.5%
3	Texas	38,566,506,000	7.7%
35	Utah	3,290,697,000	0.7%
47	Vermont	1,244,749,000	0.2%
11	Virginia	13,151,802,000	2.6%
16	Washington	9,544,778,000	1.9%
38	West Virginia	2,603,707,000	0.5%
17	Wisconsin	9,336,693,000	1.9%
48	Wyoming	1,136,677,000	0.2%

RANK ORDER

RANK	STATE	EXPENDITURES	% of USA
1	California	$64,120,762,000	12.8%
2	New York	45,450,507,000	9.1%
3	Texas	38,566,506,000	7.7%
4	Florida	26,022,019,000	5.2%
5	New Jersey	21,916,583,000	4.4%
6	Pennsylvania	21,692,242,000	4.3%
7	Illinois	20,688,589,000	4.1%
8	Ohio	19,875,665,000	4.0%
9	Michigan	17,232,992,000	3.4%
10	Georgia	15,405,290,000	3.1%
11	Virginia	13,151,802,000	2.6%
12	Massachusetts	11,608,055,000	2.3%
13	North Carolina	11,501,994,000	2.3%
14	Indiana	9,773,748,000	2.0%
15	Maryland	9,722,594,000	1.9%
16	Washington	9,544,778,000	1.9%
17	Wisconsin	9,336,693,000	1.9%
18	Minnesota	8,898,683,000	1.8%
19	Missouri	8,330,413,000	1.7%
20	Arizona	7,737,742,000	1.5%
21	Colorado	7,418,124,000	1.5%
22	Tennessee	7,392,710,000	1.5%
23	Connecticut	7,308,070,000	1.5%
24	South Carolina	6,938,614,000	1.4%
25	Alabama	6,552,215,000	1.3%
26	Louisiana	5,962,672,000	1.2%
27	Kentucky	5,183,328,000	1.0%
28	Oregon	5,146,735,000	1.0%
29	Oklahoma	5,018,183,000	1.0%
30	Iowa	4,661,811,000	0.9%
31	Arkansas	4,130,799,000	0.8%
32	Kansas	4,117,364,000	0.8%
33	Mississippi	3,996,588,000	0.8%
34	Nevada	3,808,948,000	0.8%
35	Utah	3,290,697,000	0.7%
36	New Mexico	3,056,165,000	0.6%
37	Nebraska	2,724,220,000	0.5%
38	West Virginia	2,603,707,000	0.5%
39	New Hampshire	2,286,783,000	0.5%
40	Maine	2,129,772,000	0.4%
41	Rhode Island	1,956,737,000	0.4%
42	Hawaii	1,937,230,000	0.4%
43	Idaho	1,856,893,000	0.4%
44	Alaska	1,797,278,000	0.4%
45	Delaware	1,616,178,000	0.3%
46	Montana	1,351,358,000	0.3%
47	Vermont	1,244,749,000	0.2%
48	Wyoming	1,136,677,000	0.2%
49	South Dakota	1,011,132,000	0.2%
50	North Dakota	949,027,000	0.2%
	District of Columbia	1,365,241,000	0.3%

Source: U.S. Bureau of the Census, Governments Division
   "State and Local Government Finances 2005-2006" (http://www.census.gov/govs/www/estimate06.html)
*Direct general expenditures. Includes capital outlays.

Per Capita State and Local Government Expenditures for Elementary and Secondary Education in 2006
National Per Capita = $1,675*

ALPHA ORDER

RANK	STATE	PER CAPITA
37	Alabama	$1,427
1	Alaska	2,653
48	Arizona	1,255
34	Arkansas	1,471
10	California	1,769
26	Colorado	1,556
5	Connecticut	2,091
7	Delaware	1,895
35	Florida	1,441
19	Georgia	1,649
30	Hawaii	1,515
47	Idaho	1,268
22	Illinois	1,619
27	Indiana	1,551
25	Iowa	1,568
32	Kansas	1,494
49	Kentucky	1,233
40	Louisiana	1,405
21	Maine	1,620
13	Maryland	1,736
9	Massachusetts	1,804
17	Michigan	1,706
15	Minnesota	1,726
43	Mississippi	1,379
37	Missouri	1,427
37	Montana	1,427
28	Nebraska	1,545
29	Nevada	1,528
12	New Hampshire	1,743
2	New Jersey	2,529
24	New Mexico	1,573
3	New York	2,357
44	North Carolina	1,297
33	North Dakota	1,489
14	Ohio	1,734
41	Oklahoma	1,403
42	Oregon	1,394
11	Pennsylvania	1,749
8	Rhode Island	1,843
23	South Carolina	1,602
45	South Dakota	1,282
50	Tennessee	1,217
20	Texas	1,648
46	Utah	1,276
6	Vermont	2,005
16	Virginia	1,721
31	Washington	1,497
36	West Virginia	1,440
18	Wisconsin	1,675
4	Wyoming	2,217

RANK ORDER

RANK	STATE	PER CAPITA
1	Alaska	$2,653
2	New Jersey	2,529
3	New York	2,357
4	Wyoming	2,217
5	Connecticut	2,091
6	Vermont	2,005
7	Delaware	1,895
8	Rhode Island	1,843
9	Massachusetts	1,804
10	California	1,769
11	Pennsylvania	1,749
12	New Hampshire	1,743
13	Maryland	1,736
14	Ohio	1,734
15	Minnesota	1,726
16	Virginia	1,721
17	Michigan	1,706
18	Wisconsin	1,675
19	Georgia	1,649
20	Texas	1,648
21	Maine	1,620
22	Illinois	1,619
23	South Carolina	1,602
24	New Mexico	1,573
25	Iowa	1,568
26	Colorado	1,556
27	Indiana	1,551
28	Nebraska	1,545
29	Nevada	1,528
30	Hawaii	1,515
31	Washington	1,497
32	Kansas	1,494
33	North Dakota	1,489
34	Arkansas	1,471
35	Florida	1,441
36	West Virginia	1,440
37	Alabama	1,427
37	Missouri	1,427
37	Montana	1,427
40	Louisiana	1,405
41	Oklahoma	1,403
42	Oregon	1,394
43	Mississippi	1,379
44	North Carolina	1,297
45	South Dakota	1,282
46	Utah	1,276
47	Idaho	1,268
48	Arizona	1,255
49	Kentucky	1,233
50	Tennessee	1,217
	District of Columbia	2,332

Source: CQ Press using data from U.S. Bureau of the Census, Governments Division
   "State and Local Government Finances 2005-2006" (http://www.census.gov/govs/www/estimate06.html)
*Direct general expenditures. Includes capital outlays.

State and Local Government Expenditures for Elementary and Secondary Education as a Percent of All Education Expenditures in 2006
National Percent = 68.8%*

ALPHA ORDER

RANK	STATE	PERCENT
44	Alabama	60.1
6	Alaska	73.2
28	Arizona	65.6
32	Arkansas	64.7
13	California	69.4
20	Colorado	67.8
4	Connecticut	73.6
41	Delaware	61.1
4	Florida	73.6
8	Georgia	72.4
24	Hawaii	66.5
33	Idaho	64.6
11	Illinois	70.3
25	Indiana	65.7
45	Iowa	59.9
41	Kansas	61.1
46	Kentucky	59.6
30	Louisiana	65.3
10	Maine	71.0
22	Maryland	67.6
18	Massachusetts	68.2
29	Michigan	65.4
18	Minnesota	68.2
37	Mississippi	62.2
12	Missouri	69.8
35	Montana	62.5
34	Nebraska	62.6
3	Nevada	74.3
7	New Hampshire	72.9
2	New Jersey	78.9
47	New Mexico	58.6
1	New York	79.5
48	North Carolina	57.6
49	North Dakota	57.0
14	Ohio	69.1
35	Oklahoma	62.5
39	Oregon	61.7
15	Pennsylvania	69.0
9	Rhode Island	72.2
25	South Carolina	65.7
25	South Dakota	65.7
20	Tennessee	67.8
16	Texas	68.8
50	Utah	55.4
40	Vermont	61.3
17	Virginia	68.3
37	Washington	62.2
43	West Virginia	60.8
31	Wisconsin	65.1
23	Wyoming	67.1

RANK ORDER

RANK	STATE	PERCENT
1	New York	79.5
2	New Jersey	78.9
3	Nevada	74.3
4	Connecticut	73.6
4	Florida	73.6
6	Alaska	73.2
7	New Hampshire	72.9
8	Georgia	72.4
9	Rhode Island	72.2
10	Maine	71.0
11	Illinois	70.3
12	Missouri	69.8
13	California	69.4
14	Ohio	69.1
15	Pennsylvania	69.0
16	Texas	68.8
17	Virginia	68.3
18	Massachusetts	68.2
18	Minnesota	68.2
20	Colorado	67.8
20	Tennessee	67.8
22	Maryland	67.6
23	Wyoming	67.1
24	Hawaii	66.5
25	Indiana	65.7
25	South Carolina	65.7
25	South Dakota	65.7
28	Arizona	65.6
29	Michigan	65.4
30	Louisiana	65.3
31	Wisconsin	65.1
32	Arkansas	64.7
33	Idaho	64.6
34	Nebraska	62.6
35	Montana	62.5
35	Oklahoma	62.5
37	Mississippi	62.2
37	Washington	62.2
39	Oregon	61.7
40	Vermont	61.3
41	Delaware	61.1
41	Kansas	61.1
43	West Virginia	60.8
44	Alabama	60.1
45	Iowa	59.9
46	Kentucky	59.6
47	New Mexico	58.6
48	North Carolina	57.6
49	North Dakota	57.0
50	Utah	55.4

	District of Columbia	92.4

Source: CQ Press using data from U.S. Bureau of the Census, Governments Division
"State and Local Government Finances 2005-2006" (http://www.census.gov/govs/www/estimate06.html)
*Direct general expenditures. Includes capital outlays.

Expenditures for Elementary and Secondary Education as a Percent of All State and Local Government Expenditures in 2006
National Percent = 23.6%*

ALPHA ORDER

RANK	STATE	PERCENT
37	Alabama	21.3
50	Alaska	19.2
34	Arizona	21.6
9	Arkansas	24.9
30	California	21.8
15	Colorado	24.1
5	Connecticut	26.6
31	Delaware	21.7
38	Florida	21.2
2	Georgia	28.4
48	Hawaii	19.7
29	Idaho	22.0
11	Illinois	24.6
12	Indiana	24.5
27	Iowa	22.6
25	Kansas	22.8
46	Kentucky	20.5
49	Louisiana	19.6
36	Maine	21.4
10	Maryland	24.7
28	Massachusetts	22.1
7	Michigan	25.9
24	Minnesota	23.0
43	Mississippi	20.8
15	Missouri	24.1
31	Montana	21.7
22	Nebraska	23.3
19	Nevada	23.7
3	New Hampshire	28.1
1	New Jersey	30.8
44	New Mexico	20.6
22	New York	23.3
44	North Carolina	20.6
42	North Dakota	21.0
14	Ohio	24.2
15	Oklahoma	24.1
47	Oregon	20.3
13	Pennsylvania	24.3
19	Rhode Island	23.7
18	South Carolina	23.9
31	South Dakota	21.7
35	Tennessee	21.5
4	Texas	27.9
40	Utah	21.1
8	Vermont	25.3
6	Virginia	26.1
40	Washington	21.1
25	West Virginia	22.8
19	Wisconsin	23.7
38	Wyoming	21.2

RANK ORDER

RANK	STATE	PERCENT
1	New Jersey	30.8
2	Georgia	28.4
3	New Hampshire	28.1
4	Texas	27.9
5	Connecticut	26.6
6	Virginia	26.1
7	Michigan	25.9
8	Vermont	25.3
9	Arkansas	24.9
10	Maryland	24.7
11	Illinois	24.6
12	Indiana	24.5
13	Pennsylvania	24.3
14	Ohio	24.2
15	Colorado	24.1
15	Missouri	24.1
15	Oklahoma	24.1
18	South Carolina	23.9
19	Nevada	23.7
19	Rhode Island	23.7
19	Wisconsin	23.7
22	Nebraska	23.3
22	New York	23.3
24	Minnesota	23.0
25	Kansas	22.8
25	West Virginia	22.8
27	Iowa	22.6
28	Massachusetts	22.1
29	Idaho	22.0
30	California	21.8
31	Delaware	21.7
31	Montana	21.7
31	South Dakota	21.7
34	Arizona	21.6
35	Tennessee	21.5
36	Maine	21.4
37	Alabama	21.3
38	Florida	21.2
38	Wyoming	21.2
40	Utah	21.1
40	Washington	21.1
42	North Dakota	21.0
43	Mississippi	20.8
44	New Mexico	20.6
44	North Carolina	20.6
46	Kentucky	20.5
47	Oregon	20.3
48	Hawaii	19.7
49	Louisiana	19.6
50	Alaska	19.2

	District of Columbia	17.1

Source: CQ Press using data from U.S. Bureau of the Census, Governments Division
"State and Local Government Finances 2005-2006" (http://www.census.gov/govs/www/estimate06.html)
*Direct general expenditures. Includes capital outlays.

State Expenditures for Preschool in 2007

National Total = $3,724,382,129*

ALPHA ORDER

RANK	STATE	EXPENDITURES	% of USA
35	Alabama	$5,369,898	0.1%
39	Alaska	0	0.0%
30	Arizona	12,077,496	0.3%
17	Arkansas	58,775,935	1.6%
4	California	295,104,549	7.9%
24	Colorado	28,965,099	0.8%
16	Connecticut	65,755,670	1.8%
34	Delaware	5,685,800	0.2%
6	Florida	290,406,902	7.8%
3	Georgia	309,579,383	8.3%
39	Hawaii	0	0.0%
39	Idaho	0	0.0%
7	Illinois	283,020,000	7.6%
39	Indiana	0	0.0%
33	Iowa	6,800,000	0.2%
28	Kansas	15,500,000	0.4%
12	Kentucky	75,127,000	2.0%
14	Louisiana	74,719,738	2.0%
36	Maine	4,247,915	0.1%
13	Maryland	74,910,729	2.0%
15	Massachusetts	65,816,357	1.8%
9	Michigan	90,850,000	2.4%
26	Minnesota	19,100,000	0.5%
39	Mississippi	0	0.0%
29	Missouri	12,631,001	0.3%
39	Montana	0	0.0%
37	Nebraska	3,677,596	0.1%
38	Nevada	3,152,479	0.1%
39	New Hampshire	0	0.0%
2	New Jersey	477,466,737	12.8%
32	New Mexico	8,149,234	0.2%
5	New York	292,413,929	7.9%
10	North Carolina	84,635,709	2.3%
39	North Dakota	0	0.0%
27	Ohio	19,002,195	0.5%
8	Oklahoma	118,003,070	3.2%
25	Oregon	27,000,000	0.7%
18	Pennsylvania	55,648,261	1.5%
39	Rhode Island	0	0.0%
23	South Carolina	34,747,844	0.9%
39	South Dakota	0	0.0%
19	Tennessee	55,000,000	1.5%
1	Texas	532,687,148	14.3%
39	Utah	0	0.0%
31	Vermont	10,206,693	0.3%
21	Virginia	44,713,471	1.2%
22	Washington	35,083,000	0.9%
20	West Virginia	47,338,791	1.3%
11	Wisconsin	81,012,500	2.2%
39	Wyoming	0	0.0%

RANK ORDER

RANK	STATE	EXPENDITURES	% of USA
1	Texas	$532,687,148	14.3%
2	New Jersey	477,466,737	12.8%
3	Georgia	309,579,383	8.3%
4	California	295,104,549	7.9%
5	New York	292,413,929	7.9%
6	Florida	290,406,902	7.8%
7	Illinois	283,020,000	7.6%
8	Oklahoma	118,003,070	3.2%
9	Michigan	90,850,000	2.4%
10	North Carolina	84,635,709	2.3%
11	Wisconsin	81,012,500	2.2%
12	Kentucky	75,127,000	2.0%
13	Maryland	74,910,729	2.0%
14	Louisiana	74,719,738	2.0%
15	Massachusetts	65,816,357	1.8%
16	Connecticut	65,755,670	1.8%
17	Arkansas	58,775,935	1.6%
18	Pennsylvania	55,648,261	1.5%
19	Tennessee	55,000,000	1.5%
20	West Virginia	47,338,791	1.3%
21	Virginia	44,713,471	1.2%
22	Washington	35,083,000	0.9%
23	South Carolina	34,747,844	0.9%
24	Colorado	28,965,099	0.8%
25	Oregon	27,000,000	0.7%
26	Minnesota	19,100,000	0.5%
27	Ohio	19,002,195	0.5%
28	Kansas	15,500,000	0.4%
29	Missouri	12,631,001	0.3%
30	Arizona	12,077,496	0.3%
31	Vermont	10,206,693	0.3%
32	New Mexico	8,149,234	0.2%
33	Iowa	6,800,000	0.2%
34	Delaware	5,685,800	0.2%
35	Alabama	5,369,898	0.1%
36	Maine	4,247,915	0.1%
37	Nebraska	3,677,596	0.1%
38	Nevada	3,152,479	0.1%
39	Alaska	0	0.0%
39	Hawaii	0	0.0%
39	Idaho	0	0.0%
39	Indiana	0	0.0%
39	Mississippi	0	0.0%
39	Montana	0	0.0%
39	New Hampshire	0	0.0%
39	North Dakota	0	0.0%
39	Rhode Island	0	0.0%
39	South Dakota	0	0.0%
39	Utah	0	0.0%
39	Wyoming	0	0.0%
	District of Columbia**	NA	NA

Source: Rutgers, The State University of New Jersey, National Institute for Early Education Research
"The State of Preschool: 2007 State Preschool Yearbook" (http://nieer.org/yearbook/)
*School year 2006-2007. State spending figures do not include all money received from federal and local sources. They are not estimates of total costs. The state figures do include some flow-through money from federal sources.
**Not available.

Per Pupil State Expenditures for Preschool in 2007

National Per Pupil = $3,642*

ALPHA ORDER

RANK ORDER

RANK	STATE	PER PUPIL
9	Alabama	$5,056
39	Alaska	0
33	Arizona	2,379
12	Arkansas	4,316
18	California	3,486
36	Colorado	2,047
3	Connecticut	7,707
5	Delaware	6,745
34	Florida	2,335
15	Georgia	4,111
39	Hawaii	0
39	Idaho	0
22	Illinois	3,322
39	Indiana	0
26	Iowa	2,966
29	Kansas	2,596
19	Kentucky	3,474
8	Louisiana	5,138
37	Maine	1,877
27	Maryland	2,918
16	Massachusetts	3,681
14	Michigan	4,167
4	Minnesota	7,251
39	Mississippi	0
31	Missouri	2,540
39	Montana	0
35	Nebraska	2,273
22	Nevada	3,322
39	New Hampshire	0
1	New Jersey	10,494
25	New Mexico	2,975
20	New York	3,454
10	North Carolina	4,712
39	North Dakota	0
32	Ohio	2,515
21	Oklahoma	3,433
2	Oregon	7,853
7	Pennsylvania	5,519
39	Rhode Island	0
38	South Carolina	1,600
39	South Dakota	0
13	Tennessee	4,168
28	Texas	2,836
39	Utah	0
30	Vermont	2,577
17	Virginia	3,577
6	Washington	6,010
11	West Virginia	4,441
24	Wisconsin	3,178
39	Wyoming	0

RANK	STATE	PER PUPIL
1	New Jersey	$10,494
2	Oregon	7,853
3	Connecticut	7,707
4	Minnesota	7,251
5	Delaware	6,745
6	Washington	6,010
7	Pennsylvania	5,519
8	Louisiana	5,138
9	Alabama	5,056
10	North Carolina	4,712
11	West Virginia	4,441
12	Arkansas	4,316
13	Tennessee	4,168
14	Michigan	4,167
15	Georgia	4,111
16	Massachusetts	3,681
17	Virginia	3,577
18	California	3,486
19	Kentucky	3,474
20	New York	3,454
21	Oklahoma	3,433
22	Illinois	3,322
22	Nevada	3,322
24	Wisconsin	3,178
25	New Mexico	2,975
26	Iowa	2,966
27	Maryland	2,918
28	Texas	2,836
29	Kansas	2,596
30	Vermont	2,577
31	Missouri	2,540
32	Ohio	2,515
33	Arizona	2,379
34	Florida	2,335
35	Nebraska	2,273
36	Colorado	2,047
37	Maine	1,877
38	South Carolina	1,600
39	Alaska	0
39	Hawaii	0
39	Idaho	0
39	Indiana	0
39	Mississippi	0
39	Montana	0
39	New Hampshire	0
39	North Dakota	0
39	Rhode Island	0
39	South Dakota	0
39	Utah	0
39	Wyoming	0

District of Columbia**   NA

Source: Rutgers, The State University of New Jersey, National Institute for Early Education Research
"The State of Preschool: 2007 State Preschool Yearbook" (http://nieer.org/yearbook/)
*School year 2006-2007. State spending figures do not include all money received from federal and local sources. They are not estimates of total costs. The state figures do include some flow-through money from federal sources.
**Not available.

Federal Allocations for Head Start Program in 2007

National Total = $6,654,316,023*

ALPHA ORDER

RANK	STATE	ALLOCATIONS	% of USA
18	Alabama	$107,069,710	1.6%
49	Alaska	12,524,123	0.2%
19	Arizona	103,928,297	1.6%
29	Arkansas	64,793,182	1.0%
1	California	835,094,424	12.5%
28	Colorado	68,621,163	1.0%
32	Connecticut	52,112,641	0.8%
48	Delaware	13,290,490	0.2%
5	Florida	264,221,005	4.0%
9	Georgia	169,203,527	2.5%
40	Hawaii	22,980,561	0.3%
41	Idaho	22,907,992	0.3%
4	Illinois	271,880,496	4.1%
22	Indiana	96,596,956	1.5%
33	Iowa	51,762,241	0.8%
34	Kansas	51,136,866	0.8%
17	Kentucky	108,290,595	1.6%
11	Louisiana	146,504,237	2.2%
38	Maine	27,724,725	0.4%
26	Maryland	78,356,161	1.2%
16	Massachusetts	108,797,056	1.6%
7	Michigan	235,517,531	3.5%
27	Minnesota	72,300,453	1.1%
10	Mississippi	162,356,794	2.4%
15	Missouri	119,482,617	1.8%
43	Montana	21,035,544	0.3%
37	Nebraska	36,207,292	0.5%
39	Nevada	24,380,031	0.4%
47	New Hampshire	13,441,195	0.2%
13	New Jersey	129,545,483	1.9%
31	New Mexico	52,515,381	0.8%
3	New York	434,979,286	6.5%
12	North Carolina	141,857,656	2.1%
45	North Dakota	17,245,660	0.3%
6	Ohio	247,914,736	3.7%
25	Oklahoma	81,384,010	1.2%
30	Oregon	59,714,535	0.9%
8	Pennsylvania	229,113,424	3.4%
42	Rhode Island	22,105,950	0.3%
24	South Carolina	82,842,414	1.2%
44	South Dakota	18,902,974	0.3%
14	Tennessee	119,832,346	1.8%
2	Texas	480,685,049	7.2%
36	Utah	37,920,068	0.6%
46	Vermont	13,615,255	0.2%
21	Virginia	99,506,637	1.5%
20	Washington	100,776,184	1.5%
35	West Virginia	50,851,993	0.8%
23	Wisconsin	91,252,718	1.4%
50	Wyoming	12,422,337	0.2%

RANK ORDER

RANK	STATE	ALLOCATIONS	% of USA
1	California	$835,094,424	12.5%
2	Texas	480,685,049	7.2%
3	New York	434,979,286	6.5%
4	Illinois	271,880,496	4.1%
5	Florida	264,221,005	4.0%
6	Ohio	247,914,736	3.7%
7	Michigan	235,517,531	3.5%
8	Pennsylvania	229,113,424	3.4%
9	Georgia	169,203,527	2.5%
10	Mississippi	162,356,794	2.4%
11	Louisiana	146,504,237	2.2%
12	North Carolina	141,857,656	2.1%
13	New Jersey	129,545,483	1.9%
14	Tennessee	119,832,346	1.8%
15	Missouri	119,482,617	1.8%
16	Massachusetts	108,797,056	1.6%
17	Kentucky	108,290,595	1.6%
18	Alabama	107,069,710	1.6%
19	Arizona	103,928,297	1.6%
20	Washington	100,776,184	1.5%
21	Virginia	99,506,637	1.5%
22	Indiana	96,596,956	1.5%
23	Wisconsin	91,252,718	1.4%
24	South Carolina	82,842,414	1.2%
25	Oklahoma	81,384,010	1.2%
26	Maryland	78,356,161	1.2%
27	Minnesota	72,300,453	1.1%
28	Colorado	68,621,163	1.0%
29	Arkansas	64,793,182	1.0%
30	Oregon	59,714,535	0.9%
31	New Mexico	52,515,381	0.8%
32	Connecticut	52,112,641	0.8%
33	Iowa	51,762,241	0.8%
34	Kansas	51,136,866	0.8%
35	West Virginia	50,851,993	0.8%
36	Utah	37,920,068	0.6%
37	Nebraska	36,207,292	0.5%
38	Maine	27,724,725	0.4%
39	Nevada	24,380,031	0.4%
40	Hawaii	22,980,561	0.3%
41	Idaho	22,907,992	0.3%
42	Rhode Island	22,105,950	0.3%
43	Montana	21,035,544	0.3%
44	South Dakota	18,902,974	0.3%
45	North Dakota	17,245,660	0.3%
46	Vermont	13,615,255	0.2%
47	New Hampshire	13,441,195	0.2%
48	Delaware	13,290,490	0.2%
49	Alaska	12,524,123	0.2%
50	Wyoming	12,422,337	0.2%
	District of Columbia	25,211,331	0.4%

Source: U.S. Department of Health and Human Services, Administration for Children and Families
   "Head Start Fact Sheet" (http://www.acf.hhs.gov/programs/ohs/about/fy2008.html)
*For fiscal year 2007. National total includes $475,885,637 to Migrant and Native American programs and $265,717,054 to U.S. territories. Does not include $233,597,000 in "support activities" expenditures.

Per Child Federal Allocations for Head Start Program in 2007

National Per Child = $7,325*

<table>
<tr><td colspan="3">ALPHA ORDER</td><td colspan="3">RANK ORDER</td></tr>
<tr><td>RANK</td><td>STATE</td><td>PER CHILD</td><td>RANK</td><td>STATE</td><td>PER CHILD</td></tr>
<tr><td>43</td><td>Alabama</td><td>$6,539</td><td>1</td><td>Washington</td><td>$8,936</td></tr>
<tr><td>9</td><td>Alaska</td><td>7,912</td><td>2</td><td>New York</td><td>8,910</td></tr>
<tr><td>10</td><td>Arizona</td><td>7,888</td><td>3</td><td>Nevada</td><td>8,853</td></tr>
<tr><td>50</td><td>Arkansas</td><td>6,012</td><td>4</td><td>Vermont</td><td>8,773</td></tr>
<tr><td>7</td><td>California</td><td>8,491</td><td>5</td><td>New Jersey</td><td>8,721</td></tr>
<tr><td>29</td><td>Colorado</td><td>6,988</td><td>6</td><td>Massachusetts</td><td>8,495</td></tr>
<tr><td>16</td><td>Connecticut</td><td>7,365</td><td>7</td><td>California</td><td>8,491</td></tr>
<tr><td>46</td><td>Delaware</td><td>6,417</td><td>8</td><td>New Hampshire</td><td>8,236</td></tr>
<tr><td>15</td><td>Florida</td><td>7,452</td><td>9</td><td>Alaska</td><td>7,912</td></tr>
<tr><td>20</td><td>Georgia</td><td>7,220</td><td>10</td><td>Arizona</td><td>7,888</td></tr>
<tr><td>13</td><td>Hawaii</td><td>7,537</td><td>11</td><td>Idaho</td><td>7,784</td></tr>
<tr><td>11</td><td>Idaho</td><td>7,784</td><td>12</td><td>Maryland</td><td>7,573</td></tr>
<tr><td>30</td><td>Illinois</td><td>6,859</td><td>13</td><td>Hawaii</td><td>7,537</td></tr>
<tr><td>32</td><td>Indiana</td><td>6,796</td><td>14</td><td>North Carolina</td><td>7,481</td></tr>
<tr><td>40</td><td>Iowa</td><td>6,714</td><td>15</td><td>Florida</td><td>7,452</td></tr>
<tr><td>47</td><td>Kansas</td><td>6,253</td><td>16</td><td>Connecticut</td><td>7,365</td></tr>
<tr><td>38</td><td>Kentucky</td><td>6,739</td><td>17</td><td>Virginia</td><td>7,361</td></tr>
<tr><td>33</td><td>Louisiana</td><td>6,785</td><td>18</td><td>North Dakota</td><td>7,329</td></tr>
<tr><td>23</td><td>Maine</td><td>7,162</td><td>19</td><td>Tennessee</td><td>7,308</td></tr>
<tr><td>12</td><td>Maryland</td><td>7,573</td><td>20</td><td>Georgia</td><td>7,220</td></tr>
<tr><td>6</td><td>Massachusetts</td><td>8,495</td><td>21</td><td>New Mexico</td><td>7,215</td></tr>
<tr><td>39</td><td>Michigan</td><td>6,716</td><td>22</td><td>Montana</td><td>7,206</td></tr>
<tr><td>28</td><td>Minnesota</td><td>6,998</td><td>23</td><td>Maine</td><td>7,162</td></tr>
<tr><td>48</td><td>Mississippi</td><td>6,091</td><td>24</td><td>Nebraska</td><td>7,127</td></tr>
<tr><td>31</td><td>Missouri</td><td>6,845</td><td>25</td><td>Rhode Island</td><td>7,122</td></tr>
<tr><td>22</td><td>Montana</td><td>7,206</td><td>26</td><td>Texas</td><td>7,108</td></tr>
<tr><td>24</td><td>Nebraska</td><td>7,127</td><td>27</td><td>Utah</td><td>7,022</td></tr>
<tr><td>3</td><td>Nevada</td><td>8,853</td><td>28</td><td>Minnesota</td><td>6,998</td></tr>
<tr><td>8</td><td>New Hampshire</td><td>8,236</td><td>29</td><td>Colorado</td><td>6,988</td></tr>
<tr><td>5</td><td>New Jersey</td><td>8,721</td><td>30</td><td>Illinois</td><td>6,859</td></tr>
<tr><td>21</td><td>New Mexico</td><td>7,215</td><td>31</td><td>Missouri</td><td>6,845</td></tr>
<tr><td>2</td><td>New York</td><td>8,910</td><td>32</td><td>Indiana</td><td>6,796</td></tr>
<tr><td>14</td><td>North Carolina</td><td>7,481</td><td>33</td><td>Louisiana</td><td>6,785</td></tr>
<tr><td>18</td><td>North Dakota</td><td>7,329</td><td>34</td><td>Oregon</td><td>6,775</td></tr>
<tr><td>44</td><td>Ohio</td><td>6,534</td><td>35</td><td>South Carolina</td><td>6,764</td></tr>
<tr><td>49</td><td>Oklahoma</td><td>6,040</td><td>36</td><td>Wyoming</td><td>6,751</td></tr>
<tr><td>34</td><td>Oregon</td><td>6,775</td><td>37</td><td>Wisconsin</td><td>6,740</td></tr>
<tr><td>45</td><td>Pennsylvania</td><td>6,479</td><td>38</td><td>Kentucky</td><td>6,739</td></tr>
<tr><td>25</td><td>Rhode Island</td><td>7,122</td><td>39</td><td>Michigan</td><td>6,716</td></tr>
<tr><td>35</td><td>South Carolina</td><td>6,764</td><td>40</td><td>Iowa</td><td>6,714</td></tr>
<tr><td>41</td><td>South Dakota</td><td>6,687</td><td>41</td><td>South Dakota</td><td>6,687</td></tr>
<tr><td>19</td><td>Tennessee</td><td>7,308</td><td>42</td><td>West Virginia</td><td>6,620</td></tr>
<tr><td>26</td><td>Texas</td><td>7,108</td><td>43</td><td>Alabama</td><td>6,539</td></tr>
<tr><td>27</td><td>Utah</td><td>7,022</td><td>44</td><td>Ohio</td><td>6,534</td></tr>
<tr><td>4</td><td>Vermont</td><td>8,773</td><td>45</td><td>Pennsylvania</td><td>6,479</td></tr>
<tr><td>17</td><td>Virginia</td><td>7,361</td><td>46</td><td>Delaware</td><td>6,417</td></tr>
<tr><td>1</td><td>Washington</td><td>8,936</td><td>47</td><td>Kansas</td><td>6,253</td></tr>
<tr><td>42</td><td>West Virginia</td><td>6,620</td><td>48</td><td>Mississippi</td><td>6,091</td></tr>
<tr><td>37</td><td>Wisconsin</td><td>6,740</td><td>49</td><td>Oklahoma</td><td>6,040</td></tr>
<tr><td>36</td><td>Wyoming</td><td>6,751</td><td>50</td><td>Arkansas</td><td>6,012</td></tr>
<tr><td></td><td></td><td></td><td></td><td>District of Columbia</td><td>7,409</td></tr>
</table>

Source: CQ Press using data from U.S. Department of Health and Human Services, Administration for Children and Families
"Head Start Fact Sheet" (http://www.acf.hhs.gov/programs/ohs/about/fy2008.html)
*For fiscal year 2007. National rate includes enrollees in Migrant and Native American programs and in U.S. territories. Does not include "support activities" expenditures.

III. Graduates and Achievement

Percent of Population Graduated from High School in 2006

National Percent = 85.5%*

ALPHA ORDER

RANK	STATE	PERCENT
42	Alabama	82.1
2	Alaska	92.0
39	Arizona	83.1
41	Arkansas	82.5
46	California	80.8
13	Colorado	90.0
22	Connecticut	88.4
33	Delaware	86.0
30	Florida	86.7
36	Georgia	84.2
20	Hawaii	88.7
19	Idaho	88.9
25	Illinois	87.6
23	Indiana	88.2
11	Iowa	90.4
12	Kansas	90.2
48	Kentucky	79.9
49	Louisiana	79.7
18	Maine	89.3
28	Maryland	87.2
14	Massachusetts	89.9
16	Michigan	89.7
1	Minnesota	93.0
45	Mississippi	81.1
29	Missouri	87.1
4	Montana	91.4
9	Nebraska	91.0
34	Nevada	85.6
3	New Hampshire	91.6
30	New Jersey	86.7
43	New Mexico	81.8
35	New York	85.1
36	North Carolina	84.2
20	North Dakota	88.7
24	Ohio	88.1
26	Oklahoma	87.5
16	Oregon	89.7
26	Pennsylvania	87.5
38	Rhode Island	84.0
39	South Carolina	83.1
14	South Dakota	89.9
47	Tennessee	80.7
50	Texas	78.7
5	Utah	91.2
9	Vermont	91.0
32	Virginia	86.5
6	Washington	91.1
44	West Virginia	81.5
6	Wisconsin	91.1
6	Wyoming	91.1

RANK ORDER

RANK	STATE	PERCENT
1	Minnesota	93.0
2	Alaska	92.0
3	New Hampshire	91.6
4	Montana	91.4
5	Utah	91.2
6	Washington	91.1
6	Wisconsin	91.1
6	Wyoming	91.1
9	Nebraska	91.0
9	Vermont	91.0
11	Iowa	90.4
12	Kansas	90.2
13	Colorado	90.0
14	Massachusetts	89.9
14	South Dakota	89.9
16	Michigan	89.7
16	Oregon	89.7
18	Maine	89.3
19	Idaho	88.9
20	Hawaii	88.7
20	North Dakota	88.7
22	Connecticut	88.4
23	Indiana	88.2
24	Ohio	88.1
25	Illinois	87.6
26	Oklahoma	87.5
26	Pennsylvania	87.5
28	Maryland	87.2
29	Missouri	87.1
30	Florida	86.7
30	New Jersey	86.7
32	Virginia	86.5
33	Delaware	86.0
34	Nevada	85.6
35	New York	85.1
36	Georgia	84.2
36	North Carolina	84.2
38	Rhode Island	84.0
39	Arizona	83.1
39	South Carolina	83.1
41	Arkansas	82.5
42	Alabama	82.1
43	New Mexico	81.8
44	West Virginia	81.5
45	Mississippi	81.1
46	California	80.8
47	Tennessee	80.7
48	Kentucky	79.9
49	Louisiana	79.7
50	Texas	78.7

District of Columbia   83.3

Source: U.S. Bureau of the Census, American Community Survey
"Educational Attainment in the United States: 2006" (www.census.gov/population/www/socdemo/education/cps2006.html)
*Persons age 25 and older. Includes equivalency status.

Estimated Public High School Graduates in 2007

National Total = 2,904,641 Graduates*

<table>
<tr><td colspan="4">ALPHA ORDER</td><td colspan="4">RANK ORDER</td></tr>
<tr><th>RANK</th><th>STATE</th><th>GRADUATES</th><th>% of USA</th><th>RANK</th><th>STATE</th><th>GRADUATES</th><th>% of USA</th></tr>
<tr><td>25</td><td>Alabama</td><td>37,789</td><td>1.3%</td><td>1</td><td>California</td><td>361,206</td><td>12.4%</td></tr>
<tr><td>46</td><td>Alaska</td><td>7,886</td><td>0.3%</td><td>2</td><td>Texas</td><td>241,256</td><td>8.3%</td></tr>
<tr><td>13</td><td>Arizona</td><td>68,141</td><td>2.3%</td><td>3</td><td>New York</td><td>163,673</td><td>5.6%</td></tr>
<tr><td>32</td><td>Arkansas</td><td>28,965</td><td>1.0%</td><td>4</td><td>Florida</td><td>134,307</td><td>4.6%</td></tr>
<tr><td>1</td><td>California</td><td>361,206</td><td>12.4%</td><td>5</td><td>Pennsylvania</td><td>129,800</td><td>4.5%</td></tr>
<tr><td>22</td><td>Colorado</td><td>47,361</td><td>1.6%</td><td>6</td><td>Illinois</td><td>127,349</td><td>4.4%</td></tr>
<tr><td>27</td><td>Connecticut</td><td>36,222</td><td>1.2%</td><td>7</td><td>Ohio</td><td>117,541</td><td>4.0%</td></tr>
<tr><td>48</td><td>Delaware</td><td>7,392</td><td>0.3%</td><td>8</td><td>Michigan</td><td>103,708</td><td>3.6%</td></tr>
<tr><td>4</td><td>Florida</td><td>134,307</td><td>4.6%</td><td>9</td><td>New Jersey</td><td>89,858</td><td>3.1%</td></tr>
<tr><td>10</td><td>Georgia</td><td>85,939</td><td>3.0%</td><td>10</td><td>Georgia</td><td>85,939</td><td>3.0%</td></tr>
<tr><td>42</td><td>Hawaii</td><td>10,700</td><td>0.4%</td><td>11</td><td>North Carolina</td><td>79,248</td><td>2.7%</td></tr>
<tr><td>39</td><td>Idaho</td><td>15,901</td><td>0.5%</td><td>12</td><td>Virginia</td><td>78,548</td><td>2.7%</td></tr>
<tr><td>6</td><td>Illinois</td><td>127,349</td><td>4.4%</td><td>13</td><td>Arizona</td><td>68,141</td><td>2.3%</td></tr>
<tr><td>21</td><td>Indiana</td><td>55,829</td><td>1.9%</td><td>14</td><td>Wisconsin</td><td>64,345</td><td>2.2%</td></tr>
<tr><td>29</td><td>Iowa</td><td>33,912</td><td>1.2%</td><td>15</td><td>Massachusetts</td><td>63,900</td><td>2.2%</td></tr>
<tr><td>31</td><td>Kansas</td><td>29,800</td><td>1.0%</td><td>16</td><td>Minnesota</td><td>63,304</td><td>2.2%</td></tr>
<tr><td>24</td><td>Kentucky</td><td>38,769</td><td>1.3%</td><td>17</td><td>Missouri</td><td>60,351</td><td>2.1%</td></tr>
<tr><td>30</td><td>Louisiana</td><td>33,123</td><td>1.1%</td><td>18</td><td>Maryland</td><td>58,166</td><td>2.0%</td></tr>
<tr><td>41</td><td>Maine</td><td>14,216</td><td>0.5%</td><td>19</td><td>Washington</td><td>58,120</td><td>2.0%</td></tr>
<tr><td>18</td><td>Maryland</td><td>58,166</td><td>2.0%</td><td>20</td><td>Tennessee</td><td>56,630</td><td>1.9%</td></tr>
<tr><td>15</td><td>Massachusetts</td><td>63,900</td><td>2.2%</td><td>21</td><td>Indiana</td><td>55,829</td><td>1.9%</td></tr>
<tr><td>8</td><td>Michigan</td><td>103,708</td><td>3.6%</td><td>22</td><td>Colorado</td><td>47,361</td><td>1.6%</td></tr>
<tr><td>16</td><td>Minnesota</td><td>63,304</td><td>2.2%</td><td>23</td><td>South Carolina</td><td>39,107</td><td>1.3%</td></tr>
<tr><td>34</td><td>Mississippi</td><td>23,813</td><td>0.8%</td><td>24</td><td>Kentucky</td><td>38,769</td><td>1.3%</td></tr>
<tr><td>17</td><td>Missouri</td><td>60,351</td><td>2.1%</td><td>25</td><td>Alabama</td><td>37,789</td><td>1.3%</td></tr>
<tr><td>43</td><td>Montana</td><td>10,283</td><td>0.4%</td><td>26</td><td>Oklahoma</td><td>36,536</td><td>1.3%</td></tr>
<tr><td>36</td><td>Nebraska</td><td>19,870</td><td>0.7%</td><td>27</td><td>Connecticut</td><td>36,222</td><td>1.2%</td></tr>
<tr><td>35</td><td>Nevada</td><td>20,290</td><td>0.7%</td><td>28</td><td>Oregon</td><td>34,287</td><td>1.2%</td></tr>
<tr><td>40</td><td>New Hampshire</td><td>14,724</td><td>0.5%</td><td>29</td><td>Iowa</td><td>33,912</td><td>1.2%</td></tr>
<tr><td>9</td><td>New Jersey</td><td>89,858</td><td>3.1%</td><td>30</td><td>Louisiana</td><td>33,123</td><td>1.1%</td></tr>
<tr><td>37</td><td>New Mexico</td><td>17,472</td><td>0.6%</td><td>31</td><td>Kansas</td><td>29,800</td><td>1.0%</td></tr>
<tr><td>3</td><td>New York</td><td>163,673</td><td>5.6%</td><td>32</td><td>Arkansas</td><td>28,965</td><td>1.0%</td></tr>
<tr><td>11</td><td>North Carolina</td><td>79,248</td><td>2.7%</td><td>33</td><td>Utah</td><td>27,951</td><td>1.0%</td></tr>
<tr><td>49</td><td>North Dakota</td><td>7,013</td><td>0.2%</td><td>34</td><td>Mississippi</td><td>23,813</td><td>0.8%</td></tr>
<tr><td>7</td><td>Ohio</td><td>117,541</td><td>4.0%</td><td>35</td><td>Nevada</td><td>20,290</td><td>0.7%</td></tr>
<tr><td>26</td><td>Oklahoma</td><td>36,536</td><td>1.3%</td><td>36</td><td>Nebraska</td><td>19,870</td><td>0.7%</td></tr>
<tr><td>28</td><td>Oregon</td><td>34,287</td><td>1.2%</td><td>37</td><td>New Mexico</td><td>17,472</td><td>0.6%</td></tr>
<tr><td>5</td><td>Pennsylvania</td><td>129,800</td><td>4.5%</td><td>38</td><td>West Virginia</td><td>17,378</td><td>0.6%</td></tr>
<tr><td>44</td><td>Rhode Island</td><td>9,190</td><td>0.3%</td><td>39</td><td>Idaho</td><td>15,901</td><td>0.5%</td></tr>
<tr><td>23</td><td>South Carolina</td><td>39,107</td><td>1.3%</td><td>40</td><td>New Hampshire</td><td>14,724</td><td>0.5%</td></tr>
<tr><td>45</td><td>South Dakota</td><td>8,292</td><td>0.3%</td><td>41</td><td>Maine</td><td>14,216</td><td>0.5%</td></tr>
<tr><td>20</td><td>Tennessee</td><td>56,630</td><td>1.9%</td><td>42</td><td>Hawaii</td><td>10,700</td><td>0.4%</td></tr>
<tr><td>2</td><td>Texas</td><td>241,256</td><td>8.3%</td><td>43</td><td>Montana</td><td>10,283</td><td>0.4%</td></tr>
<tr><td>33</td><td>Utah</td><td>27,951</td><td>1.0%</td><td>44</td><td>Rhode Island</td><td>9,190</td><td>0.3%</td></tr>
<tr><td>47</td><td>Vermont</td><td>7,636</td><td>0.3%</td><td>45</td><td>South Dakota</td><td>8,292</td><td>0.3%</td></tr>
<tr><td>12</td><td>Virginia</td><td>78,548</td><td>2.7%</td><td>46</td><td>Alaska</td><td>7,886</td><td>0.3%</td></tr>
<tr><td>19</td><td>Washington</td><td>58,120</td><td>2.0%</td><td>47</td><td>Vermont</td><td>7,636</td><td>0.3%</td></tr>
<tr><td>38</td><td>West Virginia</td><td>17,378</td><td>0.6%</td><td>48</td><td>Delaware</td><td>7,392</td><td>0.3%</td></tr>
<tr><td>14</td><td>Wisconsin</td><td>64,345</td><td>2.2%</td><td>49</td><td>North Dakota</td><td>7,013</td><td>0.2%</td></tr>
<tr><td>50</td><td>Wyoming</td><td>5,525</td><td>0.2%</td><td>50</td><td>Wyoming</td><td>5,525</td><td>0.2%</td></tr>
<tr><td></td><td></td><td></td><td></td><td></td><td>District of Columbia</td><td>2,018</td><td>0.1%</td></tr>
</table>

Source: National Education Association, Washington, D.C.
"Rankings & Estimates" (Copyright © 2007, NEA, used with permission, http://www.nea.org/edstats/index.html)
*Estimates for school year 2006-2007.

Estimated Public High School Graduation Rate in 2007

National Rate = 69.3% Graduated*

ALPHA ORDER

RANK	STATE	RATE
44	Alabama	60.3
35	Alaska	66.8
14	Arizona	77.8
15	Arkansas	77.7
32	California	68.3
21	Colorado	74.8
22	Connecticut	74.5
34	Delaware	67.1
50	Florida	53.0
42	Georgia	63.6
38	Hawaii	65.0
18	Idaho	76.6
29	Illinois	73.0
36	Indiana	65.7
4	Iowa	83.8
17	Kansas	77.0
31	Kentucky	70.8
48	Louisiana	56.6
3	Maine	84.2
24	Maryland	73.9
19	Massachusetts	76.3
33	Michigan	67.5
1	Minnesota	90.8
45	Mississippi	60.2
13	Missouri	78.2
11	Montana	79.6
7	Nebraska	81.5
47	Nevada	58.3
8	New Hampshire	80.5
5	New Jersey	82.8
46	New Mexico	58.6
42	New York	63.6
40	North Carolina	64.7
12	North Dakota	78.3
28	Ohio	73.1
25	Oklahoma	73.8
23	Oregon	74.2
9	Pennsylvania	80.1
39	Rhode Island	64.8
49	South Carolina	56.3
10	South Dakota	79.9
30	Tennessee	71.5
41	Texas	63.8
16	Utah	77.6
2	Vermont	90.7
26	Virginia	73.4
37	Washington	65.4
27	West Virginia	73.3
6	Wisconsin	82.7
20	Wyoming	75.2

RANK ORDER

RANK	STATE	RATE
1	Minnesota	90.8
2	Vermont	90.7
3	Maine	84.2
4	Iowa	83.8
5	New Jersey	82.8
6	Wisconsin	82.7
7	Nebraska	81.5
8	New Hampshire	80.5
9	Pennsylvania	80.1
10	South Dakota	79.9
11	Montana	79.6
12	North Dakota	78.3
13	Missouri	78.2
14	Arizona	77.8
15	Arkansas	77.7
16	Utah	77.6
17	Kansas	77.0
18	Idaho	76.6
19	Massachusetts	76.3
20	Wyoming	75.2
21	Colorado	74.8
22	Connecticut	74.5
23	Oregon	74.2
24	Maryland	73.9
25	Oklahoma	73.8
26	Virginia	73.4
27	West Virginia	73.3
28	Ohio	73.1
29	Illinois	73.0
30	Tennessee	71.5
31	Kentucky	70.8
32	California	68.3
33	Michigan	67.5
34	Delaware	67.1
35	Alaska	66.8
36	Indiana	65.7
37	Washington	65.4
38	Hawaii	65.0
39	Rhode Island	64.8
40	North Carolina	64.7
41	Texas	63.8
42	Georgia	63.6
42	New York	63.6
44	Alabama	60.3
45	Mississippi	60.2
46	New Mexico	58.6
47	Nevada	58.3
48	Louisiana	56.6
49	South Carolina	56.3
50	Florida	53.0

District of Columbia 35.7

Source: CQ Press using data from National Education Association, Washington, D.C.
"Rankings & Estimates" (Copyright © 2007, NEA, used with permission, http://www.nea.org/edstats/index.html) and
U.S. Department of Education, National Center for Education Statistics
"Common Core of Data (CCD) Database" (http://nces.ed.gov/ccd/)
*Calculated by comparing estimated number of public high school graduates in 2007 with 9th grade enrollment in Fall 2003. Data
exclude ungraded pupils and have not been adjusted for interstate migration or switching to or from private schools.

Averaged Freshman Graduation Rate for Public High Schools in 2005

National Average = 74.7%*

ALPHA ORDER

RANK	STATE	PERCENT
41	Alabama	65.9
45	Alaska	64.1
8	Arizona	84.7
30	Arkansas	75.7
33	California	74.6
27	Colorado	76.7
14	Connecticut	80.9
37	Delaware	73.1
44	Florida	64.6
48	Georgia	61.7
31	Hawaii	75.1
13	Idaho	81.0
19	Illinois	79.4
36	Indiana	73.2
3	Iowa	86.6
21	Kansas	79.2
29	Kentucky	75.9
46	Louisiana	63.9
23	Maine	78.6
20	Maryland	79.3
22	Massachusetts	78.7
38	Michigan	73.0
6	Minnesota	85.9
47	Mississippi	63.3
15	Missouri	80.6
12	Montana	81.5
1	Nebraska	87.8
50	Nevada	55.8
17	New Hampshire	80.1
7	New Jersey	85.1
42	New Mexico	65.4
43	New York	65.3
39	North Carolina	72.6
5	North Dakota	86.3
16	Ohio	80.2
26	Oklahoma	76.9
34	Oregon	74.2
10	Pennsylvania	82.5
24	Rhode Island	78.4
49	South Carolina	60.1
11	South Dakota	82.3
40	Tennessee	68.5
35	Texas	74.0
9	Utah	84.4
4	Vermont	86.5
18	Virginia	79.6
32	Washington	75.0
25	West Virginia	77.3
2	Wisconsin	86.7
27	Wyoming	76.7

RANK ORDER

RANK	STATE	PERCENT
1	Nebraska	87.8
2	Wisconsin	86.7
3	Iowa	86.6
4	Vermont	86.5
5	North Dakota	86.3
6	Minnesota	85.9
7	New Jersey	85.1
8	Arizona	84.7
9	Utah	84.4
10	Pennsylvania	82.5
11	South Dakota	82.3
12	Montana	81.5
13	Idaho	81.0
14	Connecticut	80.9
15	Missouri	80.6
16	Ohio	80.2
17	New Hampshire	80.1
18	Virginia	79.6
19	Illinois	79.4
20	Maryland	79.3
21	Kansas	79.2
22	Massachusetts	78.7
23	Maine	78.6
24	Rhode Island	78.4
25	West Virginia	77.3
26	Oklahoma	76.9
27	Colorado	76.7
27	Wyoming	76.7
29	Kentucky	75.9
30	Arkansas	75.7
31	Hawaii	75.1
32	Washington	75.0
33	California	74.6
34	Oregon	74.2
35	Texas	74.0
36	Indiana	73.2
37	Delaware	73.1
38	Michigan	73.0
39	North Carolina	72.6
40	Tennessee	68.5
41	Alabama	65.9
42	New Mexico	65.4
43	New York	65.3
44	Florida	64.6
45	Alaska	64.1
46	Louisiana	63.9
47	Mississippi	63.3
48	Georgia	61.7
49	South Carolina	60.1
50	Nevada	55.8

	District of Columbia	68.8

Source: U.S. Department of Education, National Center for Education Statistics
  "Public Elementary and Secondary School Student Enrollment, High School Completions" (NCES 2007352)
    (http://nces.ed.gov/pubs2007/2007352.pdf)
*This rate is calculated by comparing the incoming freshman class enrollment of school year 2001-2002 with the number of graduates with regular diplomas four years later (2004-2005). The incoming class enrollment figure is an average of the eighth grade from five years earlier, the ninth grade four years earlier and the tenth grade from three years earlier.

Public High School Graduates in 2005

National Total = 2,799,250 Graduates*

ALPHA ORDER						RANK ORDER			
RANK	STATE	GRADUATES	% of USA			RANK	STATE	GRADUATES	% of USA
24	Alabama	37,453	1.3%			1	California	355,217	12.7%
49	Alaska	6,909	0.2%			2	Texas	239,717	8.6%
16	Arizona	59,498	2.1%			3	New York	153,203	5.5%
33	Arkansas	26,621	1.0%			4	Florida	133,318	4.8%
1	California	355,217	12.7%			5	Pennsylvania	124,758	4.5%
22	Colorado	44,532	1.6%			6	Illinois	123,615	4.4%
27	Connecticut	35,515	1.3%			7	Ohio	116,702	4.2%
48	Delaware	6,934	0.2%			8	Michigan	101,582	3.6%
4	Florida	133,318	4.8%			9	New Jersey	86,502	3.1%
12	Georgia	70,834	2.5%			10	North Carolina	75,010	2.7%
42	Hawaii	10,813	0.4%			11	Virginia	73,667	2.6%
38	Idaho	15,768	0.6%			12	Georgia	70,834	2.5%
6	Illinois	123,615	4.4%			13	Wisconsin	63,229	2.3%
19	Indiana	55,444	2.0%			14	Washington	61,094	2.2%
28	Iowa	33,547	1.2%			15	Massachusetts	59,665	2.1%
31	Kansas	30,355	1.1%			16	Arizona	59,498	2.1%
23	Kentucky	38,399	1.4%			17	Minnesota	58,391	2.1%
26	Louisiana	36,009	1.3%			18	Missouri	57,841	2.1%
41	Maine	13,077	0.5%			19	Indiana	55,444	2.0%
20	Maryland	54,170	1.9%			20	Maryland	54,170	1.9%
15	Massachusetts	59,665	2.1%			21	Tennessee	47,967	1.7%
8	Michigan	101,582	3.6%			22	Colorado	44,532	1.6%
17	Minnesota	58,391	2.1%			23	Kentucky	38,399	1.4%
34	Mississippi	23,523	0.8%			24	Alabama	37,453	1.3%
18	Missouri	57,841	2.1%			25	Oklahoma	36,227	1.3%
43	Montana	10,335	0.4%			26	Louisiana	36,009	1.3%
35	Nebraska	19,940	0.7%			27	Connecticut	35,515	1.3%
39	Nevada	15,740	0.6%			28	Iowa	33,547	1.2%
40	New Hampshire	13,775	0.5%			29	South Carolina	33,439	1.2%
9	New Jersey	86,502	3.1%			30	Oregon	32,602	1.2%
36	New Mexico	17,353	0.6%			31	Kansas	30,355	1.1%
3	New York	153,203	5.5%			32	Utah	30,253	1.1%
10	North Carolina	75,010	2.7%			33	Arkansas	26,621	1.0%
46	North Dakota	7,555	0.3%			34	Mississippi	23,523	0.8%
7	Ohio	116,702	4.2%			35	Nebraska	19,940	0.7%
25	Oklahoma	36,227	1.3%			36	New Mexico	17,353	0.6%
30	Oregon	32,602	1.2%			37	West Virginia	17,137	0.6%
5	Pennsylvania	124,758	4.5%			38	Idaho	15,768	0.6%
44	Rhode Island	9,881	0.4%			39	Nevada	15,740	0.6%
29	South Carolina	33,439	1.2%			40	New Hampshire	13,775	0.5%
45	South Dakota	8,585	0.3%			41	Maine	13,077	0.5%
21	Tennessee	47,967	1.7%			42	Hawaii	10,813	0.4%
2	Texas	239,717	8.6%			43	Montana	10,335	0.4%
32	Utah	30,253	1.1%			44	Rhode Island	9,881	0.4%
47	Vermont	7,152	0.3%			45	South Dakota	8,585	0.3%
11	Virginia	73,667	2.6%			46	North Dakota	7,555	0.3%
14	Washington	61,094	2.2%			47	Vermont	7,152	0.3%
37	West Virginia	17,137	0.6%			48	Delaware	6,934	0.2%
13	Wisconsin	63,229	2.3%			49	Alaska	6,909	0.2%
50	Wyoming	5,616	0.2%			50	Wyoming	5,616	0.2%
							District of Columbia	2,781	0.1%

Source: U.S. Department of Education, National Center for Education Statistics
    "Common Core of Data (CCD) Database" (http://nces.ed.gov/ccd/)
*For school year 2004-2005. Excludes persons receiving high school equivalency certificates and graduates of federal schools
for American Indians.

Percent Change in Public High School Graduates: 2001 to 2005

National Percent Change = 9.0% Increase*

ALPHA ORDER

RANK	STATE	PERCENT CHANGE
36	Alabama	1.0
34	Alaska	1.4
1	Arizona	27.3
41	Arkansas	(1.8)
10	California	12.7
8	Colorado	13.5
5	Connecticut	16.9
27	Delaware	4.8
2	Florida	20.0
9	Georgia	13.3
22	Hawaii	7.0
39	Idaho	(1.1)
12	Illinois	11.7
40	Indiana	(1.3)
37	Iowa	(0.7)
31	Kansas	3.4
30	Kentucky	3.9
47	Louisiana	(6.0)
32	Maine	3.3
17	Maryland	10.1
18	Massachusetts	9.7
25	Michigan	5.2
33	Minnesota	3.2
38	Mississippi	(0.9)
23	Missouri	6.8
43	Montana	(2.8)
34	Nebraska	1.4
29	Nevada	4.1
11	New Hampshire	12.0
7	New Jersey	13.6
46	New Mexico	(4.6)
21	New York	8.0
3	North Carolina	18.5
50	North Dakota	(10.5)
26	Ohio	4.9
44	Oklahoma	(3.3)
20	Oregon	8.9
19	Pennsylvania	9.0
6	Rhode Island	14.9
14	South Carolina	11.4
44	South Dakota	(3.3)
4	Tennessee	18.0
15	Texas	11.3
42	Utah	(2.5)
28	Vermont	4.3
13	Virginia	11.5
16	Washington	10.9
48	West Virginia	(7.1)
24	Wisconsin	6.6
49	Wyoming	(7.5)

RANK ORDER

RANK	STATE	PERCENT CHANGE
1	Arizona	27.3
2	Florida	20.0
3	North Carolina	18.5
4	Tennessee	18.0
5	Connecticut	16.9
6	Rhode Island	14.9
7	New Jersey	13.6
8	Colorado	13.5
9	Georgia	13.3
10	California	12.7
11	New Hampshire	12.0
12	Illinois	11.7
13	Virginia	11.5
14	South Carolina	11.4
15	Texas	11.3
16	Washington	10.9
17	Maryland	10.1
18	Massachusetts	9.7
19	Pennsylvania	9.0
20	Oregon	8.9
21	New York	8.0
22	Hawaii	7.0
23	Missouri	6.8
24	Wisconsin	6.6
25	Michigan	5.2
26	Ohio	4.9
27	Delaware	4.8
28	Vermont	4.3
29	Nevada	4.1
30	Kentucky	3.9
31	Kansas	3.4
32	Maine	3.3
33	Minnesota	3.2
34	Alaska	1.4
34	Nebraska	1.4
36	Alabama	1.0
37	Iowa	(0.7)
38	Mississippi	(0.9)
39	Idaho	(1.1)
40	Indiana	(1.3)
41	Arkansas	(1.8)
42	Utah	(2.5)
43	Montana	(2.8)
44	Oklahoma	(3.3)
44	South Dakota	(3.3)
46	New Mexico	(4.6)
47	Louisiana	(6.0)
48	West Virginia	(7.1)
49	Wyoming	(7.5)
50	North Dakota	(10.5)

District of Columbia   (1.0)

Source: CQ Press using data from U.S. Department of Education, National Center for Education Statistics
   "Common Core of Data (CCD) Database" (http://nces.ed.gov/ccd/)
*Based on school years 2004-2005 and 2000-2001. Excludes persons receiving high school equivalency certificates and
graduates of federal schools for American Indians.

Reported Public High School Equivalency Recipients in 2004

National Total = 184,885 Recipients*

ALPHA ORDER

RANK	STATE	RECIPIENTS	% of USA
15	Alabama	4,198	2.3%
42	Alaska	1,008	0.5%
23	Arizona	3,539	1.9%
24	Arkansas	3,386	1.8%
4	California	9,452	5.1%
17	Colorado	4,012	2.2%
40	Connecticut	1,140	0.6%
50	Delaware	155	0.1%
1	Florida	15,692	8.5%
5	Georgia	8,598	4.7%
43	Hawaii	790	0.4%
37	Idaho	1,615	0.9%
8	Illinois	5,858	3.2%
13	Indiana	4,589	2.5%
35	Iowa	1,716	0.9%
32	Kansas	2,055	1.1%
21	Kentucky	3,657	2.0%
16	Louisiana	4,179	2.3%
39	Maine	1,192	0.6%
27	Maryland	2,762	1.5%
18	Massachusetts	3,927	2.1%
14	Michigan	4,502	2.4%
28	Minnesota	2,574	1.4%
22	Mississippi	3,575	1.9%
19	Missouri	3,731	2.0%
38	Montana	1,256	0.7%
41	Nebraska	1,043	0.6%
34	Nevada	1,924	1.0%
44	New Hampshire	721	0.4%
29	New Jersey	2,562	1.4%
30	New Mexico	2,403	1.3%
3	New York	11,567	6.3%
12	North Carolina	4,697	2.5%
48	North Dakota	527	0.3%
11	Ohio	4,932	2.7%
25	Oklahoma	2,955	1.6%
20	Oregon	3,729	2.0%
6	Pennsylvania	6,023	3.3%
47	Rhode Island	582	0.3%
33	South Carolina	1,979	1.1%
46	South Dakota	672	0.4%
9	Tennessee	5,360	2.9%
2	Texas	14,706	8.0%
31	Utah	2,324	1.3%
49	Vermont	374	0.2%
7	Virginia	5,861	3.2%
10	Washington	5,336	2.9%
36	West Virginia	1,665	0.9%
26	Wisconsin	2,883	1.6%
45	Wyoming	703	0.4%

RANK ORDER

RANK	STATE	RECIPIENTS	% of USA
1	Florida	15,692	8.5%
2	Texas	14,706	8.0%
3	New York	11,567	6.3%
4	California	9,452	5.1%
5	Georgia	8,598	4.7%
6	Pennsylvania	6,023	3.3%
7	Virginia	5,861	3.2%
8	Illinois	5,858	3.2%
9	Tennessee	5,360	2.9%
10	Washington	5,336	2.9%
11	Ohio	4,932	2.7%
12	North Carolina	4,697	2.5%
13	Indiana	4,589	2.5%
14	Michigan	4,502	2.4%
15	Alabama	4,198	2.3%
16	Louisiana	4,179	2.3%
17	Colorado	4,012	2.2%
18	Massachusetts	3,927	2.1%
19	Missouri	3,731	2.0%
20	Oregon	3,729	2.0%
21	Kentucky	3,657	2.0%
22	Mississippi	3,575	1.9%
23	Arizona	3,539	1.9%
24	Arkansas	3,386	1.8%
25	Oklahoma	2,955	1.6%
26	Wisconsin	2,883	1.6%
27	Maryland	2,762	1.5%
28	Minnesota	2,574	1.4%
29	New Jersey	2,562	1.4%
30	New Mexico	2,403	1.3%
31	Utah	2,324	1.3%
32	Kansas	2,055	1.1%
33	South Carolina	1,979	1.1%
34	Nevada	1,924	1.0%
35	Iowa	1,716	0.9%
36	West Virginia	1,665	0.9%
37	Idaho	1,615	0.9%
38	Montana	1,256	0.7%
39	Maine	1,192	0.6%
40	Connecticut	1,140	0.6%
41	Nebraska	1,043	0.6%
42	Alaska	1,008	0.5%
43	Hawaii	790	0.4%
44	New Hampshire	721	0.4%
45	Wyoming	703	0.4%
46	South Dakota	672	0.4%
47	Rhode Island	582	0.3%
48	North Dakota	527	0.3%
49	Vermont	374	0.2%
50	Delaware	155	0.1%
	District of Columbia	199	0.1%

Source: U.S. Department of Education, National Center for Education Statistics
   "Common Core of Data (CCD) Database" (http://nces.ed.gov/ccd/)
*For school year 2003-2004. Includes recipients age 19 or younger.

Other Public High School Completers in 2005

National Total = 54,012 Students*

ALPHA ORDER

RANK	STATE	STUDENTS	% of USA
8	Alabama	2,537	4.7%
21	Alaska	327	0.6%
NA	Arizona**	NA	NA
30	Arkansas	77	0.1%
NA	California**	NA	NA
17	Colorado	526	1.0%
32	Connecticut	45	0.1%
24	Delaware	168	0.3%
1	Florida	8,550	15.8%
2	Georgia	8,294	15.4%
23	Hawaii	201	0.4%
28	Idaho	109	0.2%
NA	Illinois**	NA	NA
13	Indiana	1,577	2.9%
29	Iowa	94	0.2%
NA	Kansas**	NA	NA
19	Kentucky	383	0.7%
10	Louisiana	1,776	3.3%
20	Maine	330	0.6%
16	Maryland	580	1.1%
14	Massachusetts	988	1.8%
22	Michigan	253	0.5%
NA	Minnesota**	NA	NA
11	Mississippi	1,657	3.1%
NA	Missouri**	NA	NA
NA	Montana**	NA	NA
25	Nebraska	149	0.3%
9	Nevada	2,496	4.6%
31	New Hampshire	72	0.1%
NA	New Jersey**	NA	NA
18	New Mexico	484	0.9%
3	New York	5,677	10.5%
12	North Carolina	1,653	3.1%
NA	North Dakota**	NA	NA
NA	Ohio**	NA	NA
NA	Oklahoma**	NA	NA
4	Oregon	4,266	7.9%
NA	Pennsylvania**	NA	NA
35	Rhode Island	22	0.0%
7	South Carolina	2,753	5.1%
NA	South Dakota**	NA	NA
5	Tennessee	3,198	5.9%
NA	Texas**	NA	NA
26	Utah	146	0.3%
34	Vermont	27	0.0%
6	Virginia	3,193	5.9%
27	Washington	119	0.2%
NA	West Virginia**	NA	NA
15	Wisconsin	931	1.7%
33	Wyoming	37	0.1%

RANK ORDER

RANK	STATE	STUDENTS	% of USA
1	Florida	8,550	15.8%
2	Georgia	8,294	15.4%
3	New York	5,677	10.5%
4	Oregon	4,266	7.9%
5	Tennessee	3,198	5.9%
6	Virginia	3,193	5.9%
7	South Carolina	2,753	5.1%
8	Alabama	2,537	4.7%
9	Nevada	2,496	4.6%
10	Louisiana	1,776	3.3%
11	Mississippi	1,657	3.1%
12	North Carolina	1,653	3.1%
13	Indiana	1,577	2.9%
14	Massachusetts	988	1.8%
15	Wisconsin	931	1.7%
16	Maryland	580	1.1%
17	Colorado	526	1.0%
18	New Mexico	484	0.9%
19	Kentucky	383	0.7%
20	Maine	330	0.6%
21	Alaska	327	0.6%
22	Michigan	253	0.5%
23	Hawaii	201	0.4%
24	Delaware	168	0.3%
25	Nebraska	149	0.3%
26	Utah	146	0.3%
27	Washington	119	0.2%
28	Idaho	109	0.2%
29	Iowa	94	0.2%
30	Arkansas	77	0.1%
31	New Hampshire	72	0.1%
32	Connecticut	45	0.1%
33	Wyoming	37	0.1%
34	Vermont	27	0.0%
35	Rhode Island	22	0.0%
NA	Arizona**	NA	NA
NA	California**	NA	NA
NA	Illinois**	NA	NA
NA	Kansas**	NA	NA
NA	Minnesota**	NA	NA
NA	Missouri**	NA	NA
NA	Montana**	NA	NA
NA	New Jersey**	NA	NA
NA	North Dakota**	NA	NA
NA	Ohio**	NA	NA
NA	Oklahoma**	NA	NA
NA	Pennsylvania**	NA	NA
NA	South Dakota**	NA	NA
NA	Texas**	NA	NA
NA	West Virginia**	NA	NA
	District of Columbia	317	0.6%

Source: U.S. Department of Education, National Center for Education Statistics
      "Common Core of Data (CCD) Database" (http://nces.ed.gov/ccd/)
*For 2004-2005 school year. Includes students receiving a certificate of attendance or other certificate of completion in lieu of a diploma.
**Either no students in this category or data not available.

Estimated Public High School Graduation Rate in 2005

National Rate = 69.8% Graduated*

ALPHA ORDER

RANK	STATE	PERCENT
43	Alabama	61.4
46	Alaska	58.9
8	Arizona	81.7
22	Arkansas	74.2
31	California	71.1
32	Colorado	71.0
18	Connecticut	76.2
38	Delaware	65.4
48	Florida	53.6
47	Georgia	55.0
36	Hawaii	67.4
12	Idaho	79.1
21	Illinois	74.7
34	Indiana	70.2
5	Iowa	84.3
13	Kansas	78.6
30	Kentucky	71.7
41	Louisiana	63.0
14	Maine	78.4
24	Maryland	73.9
22	Massachusetts	74.2
35	Michigan	69.7
4	Minnesota	84.6
44	Mississippi	61.1
17	Missouri	77.0
11	Montana	79.5
6	Nebraska	83.6
50	Nevada	49.1
15	New Hampshire	78.1
1	New Jersey	87.6
45	New Mexico	60.2
42	New York	62.4
37	North Carolina	65.7
3	North Dakota	84.8
20	Ohio	74.9
24	Oklahoma	73.9
29	Oregon	72.3
16	Pennsylvania	78.0
28	Rhode Island	73.0
49	South Carolina	52.0
10	South Dakota	80.8
40	Tennessee	64.5
39	Texas	65.3
2	Utah	86.4
7	Vermont	83.2
27	Virginia	73.2
33	Washington	70.7
26	West Virginia	73.5
9	Wisconsin	81.3
19	Wyoming	75.5

RANK ORDER

RANK	STATE	PERCENT
1	New Jersey	87.6
2	Utah	86.4
3	North Dakota	84.8
4	Minnesota	84.6
5	Iowa	84.3
6	Nebraska	83.6
7	Vermont	83.2
8	Arizona	81.7
9	Wisconsin	81.3
10	South Dakota	80.8
11	Montana	79.5
12	Idaho	79.1
13	Kansas	78.6
14	Maine	78.4
15	New Hampshire	78.1
16	Pennsylvania	78.0
17	Missouri	77.0
18	Connecticut	76.2
19	Wyoming	75.5
20	Ohio	74.9
21	Illinois	74.7
22	Arkansas	74.2
22	Massachusetts	74.2
24	Maryland	73.9
24	Oklahoma	73.9
26	West Virginia	73.5
27	Virginia	73.2
28	Rhode Island	73.0
29	Oregon	72.3
30	Kentucky	71.7
31	California	71.1
32	Colorado	71.0
33	Washington	70.7
34	Indiana	70.2
35	Michigan	69.7
36	Hawaii	67.4
37	North Carolina	65.7
38	Delaware	65.4
39	Texas	65.3
40	Tennessee	64.5
41	Louisiana	63.0
42	New York	62.4
43	Alabama	61.4
44	Mississippi	61.1
45	New Mexico	60.2
46	Alaska	58.9
47	Georgia	55.0
48	Florida	53.6
49	South Carolina	52.0
50	Nevada	49.1

District of Columbia	69.3

Source: CQ Press using data from U.S. Department of Education, National Center for Education Statistics
   "Common Core of Data (CCD) Database" (http://nces.ed.gov/ccd/)
*Calculated by comparing reported number of public high school graduates in 2005 with 9th grade enrollment in Fall 2001. Data
exclude ungraded pupils and have not been adjusted for interstate migration or switching to private schools.

Estimated Public High School Graduation Rate for White Students in 2005

Reporting States Estimated Rate = 77.7% Graduated*

RANK	STATE	PERCENT
40	Alabama	66.9
41	Alaska	66.1
5	Arizona	88.4
30	Arkansas	75.5
18	California	79.2
19	Colorado	78.4
11	Connecticut	84.1
36	Delaware	71.3
45	Florida	60.3
44	Georgia	61.3
43	Hawaii	64.3
NA	Idaho**	NA
10	Illinois	84.8
31	Indiana	73.7
8	Iowa	85.8
14	Kansas	82.3
35	Kentucky	72.2
39	Louisiana	68.0
22	Maine	77.5
17	Maryland	79.8
16	Massachusetts	79.9
24	Michigan	76.9
6	Minnesota	88.0
42	Mississippi	65.0
15	Missouri	80.3
13	Montana	82.5
4	Nebraska	88.5
46	Nevada	56.9
NA	New Hampshire**	NA
1	New Jersey	92.6
38	New Mexico	70.0
20	New York	78.3
37	North Carolina	71.1
3	North Dakota	89.1
25	Ohio	76.8
29	Oklahoma	75.8
31	Oregon	73.7
12	Pennsylvania	83.6
26	Rhode Island	76.3
NA	South Carolina**	NA
9	South Dakota	85.4
NA	Tennessee**	NA
28	Texas	75.9
2	Utah	89.5
27	Vermont	76.2
23	Virginia	77.3
34	Washington	73.1
33	West Virginia	73.5
7	Wisconsin	87.5
21	Wyoming	77.7

RANK	STATE	PERCENT
1	New Jersey	92.6
2	Utah	89.5
3	North Dakota	89.1
4	Nebraska	88.5
5	Arizona	88.4
6	Minnesota	88.0
7	Wisconsin	87.5
8	Iowa	85.8
9	South Dakota	85.4
10	Illinois	84.8
11	Connecticut	84.1
12	Pennsylvania	83.6
13	Montana	82.5
14	Kansas	82.3
15	Missouri	80.3
16	Massachusetts	79.9
17	Maryland	79.8
18	California	79.2
19	Colorado	78.4
20	New York	78.3
21	Wyoming	77.7
22	Maine	77.5
23	Virginia	77.3
24	Michigan	76.9
25	Ohio	76.8
26	Rhode Island	76.3
27	Vermont	76.2
28	Texas	75.9
29	Oklahoma	75.8
30	Arkansas	75.5
31	Indiana	73.7
31	Oregon	73.7
33	West Virginia	73.5
34	Washington	73.1
35	Kentucky	72.2
36	Delaware	71.3
37	North Carolina	71.1
38	New Mexico	70.0
39	Louisiana	68.0
40	Alabama	66.9
41	Alaska	66.1
42	Mississippi	65.0
43	Hawaii	64.3
44	Georgia	61.3
45	Florida	60.3
46	Nevada	56.9
NA	Idaho**	NA
NA	New Hampshire**	NA
NA	South Carolina**	NA
NA	Tennessee**	NA

District of Columbia   92.0

Source: CQ Press using data from U.S. Department of Education, National Center for Education Statistics "Common Core of Data (CCD) Database" (http://nces.ed.gov/ccd/)

*Based on reporting states' totals and excludes students for whom race/ethnicity was not reported. Excludes white Hispanics. Calculated by comparing estimated number of public high school graduates in 2005 with 9th grade enrollment in Fall 2001. Data exclude ungraded pupils and have not been adjusted for interstate migration or switching to or from private schools. A state's rate can be higher than 100% due to such changes. **Not available.

Estimated Public High School Graduation Rate for Black Students in 2005

Reporting States Estimated Rate = 52.9% Graduated*

ALPHA ORDER			RANK ORDER		
RANK	STATE	PERCENT	RANK	STATE	PERCENT
35	Alabama	51.6	1	Maine	92.0
40	Alaska	47.4	2	North Dakota	86.1
3	Arizona	84.7	3	Arizona	84.7
9	Arkansas	67.1	4	Vermont	77.5
16	California	61.1	5	New Jersey	72.9
21	Colorado	60.1	5	Utah	72.9
23	Connecticut	59.6	7	South Dakota	72.2
34	Delaware	55.0	8	Rhode Island	67.4
45	Florida	40.2	9	Arkansas	67.1
42	Georgia	44.9	10	West Virginia	65.4
25	Hawaii	59.0	11	Kansas	64.2
NA	Idaho**	NA	11	Kentucky	64.2
37	Illinois	51.5	13	Maryland	63.9
39	Indiana	47.9	14	Iowa	62.3
14	Iowa	62.3	15	Oklahoma	62.0
11	Kansas	64.2	16	California	61.1
11	Kentucky	64.2	17	Missouri	60.9
33	Louisiana	56.2	18	New Mexico	60.7
1	Maine	92.0	19	Montana	60.6
13	Maryland	63.9	20	Virginia	60.3
24	Massachusetts	59.3	21	Colorado	60.1
41	Michigan	45.7	22	Minnesota	59.8
22	Minnesota	59.8	23	Connecticut	59.6
31	Mississippi	56.9	24	Massachusetts	59.3
17	Missouri	60.9	25	Hawaii	59.0
19	Montana	60.6	26	Oregon	58.7
38	Nebraska	51.4	27	Texas	58.6
46	Nevada	36.4	28	Washington	57.6
NA	New Hampshire**	NA	29	North Carolina	57.1
5	New Jersey	72.9	29	Wyoming	57.1
18	New Mexico	60.7	31	Mississippi	56.9
44	New York	42.3	32	Pennsylvania	56.8
29	North Carolina	57.1	33	Louisiana	56.2
2	North Dakota	86.1	34	Delaware	55.0
35	Ohio	51.6	35	Alabama	51.6
15	Oklahoma	62.0	35	Ohio	51.6
26	Oregon	58.7	37	Illinois	51.5
32	Pennsylvania	56.8	38	Nebraska	51.4
8	Rhode Island	67.4	39	Indiana	47.9
NA	South Carolina**	NA	40	Alaska	47.4
7	South Dakota	72.2	41	Michigan	45.7
NA	Tennessee**	NA	42	Georgia	44.9
27	Texas	58.6	43	Wisconsin	44.2
5	Utah	72.9	44	New York	42.3
4	Vermont	77.5	45	Florida	40.2
20	Virginia	60.3	46	Nevada	36.4
28	Washington	57.6	NA	Idaho**	NA
10	West Virginia	65.4	NA	New Hampshire**	NA
43	Wisconsin	44.2	NA	South Carolina**	NA
29	Wyoming	57.1	NA	Tennessee**	NA
				District of Columbia	72.2

Source: CQ Press using data from U.S. Department of Education, National Center for Education Statistics
   "Common Core of Data (CCD) Database" (http://nces.ed.gov/ccd/)
*Based on reporting states' totals and excludes students for whom race/ethnicity was not reported. Excludes black Hispanics.
Calculated by comparing estimated number of public high school graduates in 2005 with 9th grade enrollment in Fall 2001. Data
exclude ungraded pupils and have not been adjusted for interstate migration or switching to or from private schools. A state's rate
can be higher than 100% due to such changes. **Not available.

Estimated Public High School Graduation Rate for Hispanic Students in 2005

Reporting States Estimated Rate = 57.4% Graduated*

ALPHA ORDER				RANK ORDER		
RANK	STATE	PERCENT		RANK	STATE	PERCENT
36	Alabama	54.4		1	Vermont	109.4
46	Alaska	26.2		2	West Virginia	102.4
9	Arizona	71.6		3	Maine	100.0
7	Arkansas	80.5		4	Kentucky	83.7
26	California	60.8		5	Missouri	81.6
41	Colorado	50.7		6	Montana	80.8
38	Connecticut	53.2		7	Arkansas	80.5
37	Delaware	53.6		8	New Jersey	78.4
40	Florida	51.2		9	Arizona	71.6
43	Georgia	42.7		10	Maryland	70.5
22	Hawaii	63.3		11	South Dakota	70.0
NA	Idaho**	NA		12	Louisiana	69.9
25	Illinois	60.9		13	Nebraska	67.6
30	Indiana	59.0		14	Virginia	67.0
15	Iowa	66.2		15	Iowa	66.2
34	Kansas	55.5		16	North Dakota	65.5
4	Kentucky	83.7		17	Mississippi	64.4
12	Louisiana	69.9		18	Oklahoma	64.3
3	Maine	100.0		18	Wyoming	64.3
10	Maryland	70.5		20	Wisconsin	63.6
42	Massachusetts	48.8		21	Oregon	63.5
39	Michigan	51.3		22	Hawaii	63.3
23	Minnesota	62.3		23	Minnesota	62.3
17	Mississippi	64.4		24	Rhode Island	61.2
5	Missouri	81.6		25	Illinois	60.9
6	Montana	80.8		26	California	60.8
13	Nebraska	67.6		27	Ohio	60.7
45	Nevada	34.3		28	Utah	60.1
NA	New Hampshire**	NA		29	Pennsylvania	59.2
8	New Jersey	78.4		30	Indiana	59.0
35	New Mexico	55.0		31	North Carolina	55.9
44	New York	39.7		32	Texas	55.8
31	North Carolina	55.9		33	Washington	55.6
16	North Dakota	65.5		34	Kansas	55.5
27	Ohio	60.7		35	New Mexico	55.0
18	Oklahoma	64.3		36	Alabama	54.4
21	Oregon	63.5		37	Delaware	53.6
29	Pennsylvania	59.2		38	Connecticut	53.2
24	Rhode Island	61.2		39	Michigan	51.3
NA	South Carolina**	NA		40	Florida	51.2
11	South Dakota	70.0		41	Colorado	50.7
NA	Tennessee**	NA		42	Massachusetts	48.8
32	Texas	55.8		43	Georgia	42.7
28	Utah	60.1		44	New York	39.7
1	Vermont	109.4		45	Nevada	34.3
14	Virginia	67.0		46	Alaska	26.2
33	Washington	55.6		NA	Idaho**	NA
2	West Virginia	102.4		NA	New Hampshire**	NA
20	Wisconsin	63.6		NA	South Carolina**	NA
18	Wyoming	64.3		NA	Tennessee**	NA

District of Columbia   44.4

Source: CQ Press using data from U.S. Department of Education, National Center for Education Statistics
   "Common Core of Data (CCD) Database" (http://nces.ed.gov/ccd/)
*Based on reporting states' totals and excludes students for whom race/ethnicity was not reported. Calculated by comparing estimated number of public high school graduates in 2005 with 9th grade enrollment in Fall 2001. Data exclude ungraded pupils and have not been adjusted for interstate migration or switching to or from private schools. A state's rate can be higher than 100% due to such changes. **Not available.

Estimated Public High School Graduation Rate for Asian Students in 2005

Reporting States Estimated Rate = 86.9% Graduated*

ALPHA ORDER

RANK	STATE	PERCENT
34	Alabama	86.2
42	Alaska	73.5
3	Arizona	109.9
2	Arkansas	110.9
25	California	89.2
23	Colorado	90.5
18	Connecticut	95.6
7	Delaware	105.1
40	Florida	81.3
37	Georgia	83.2
46	Hawaii	68.8
NA	Idaho**	NA
13	Illinois	97.7
15	Indiana	96.8
11	Iowa	98.6
28	Kansas	88.4
5	Kentucky	107.3
29	Louisiana	87.6
1	Maine	113.9
17	Maryland	95.8
38	Massachusetts	82.2
27	Michigan	89.0
35	Minnesota	85.1
25	Mississippi	89.2
8	Missouri	103.4
21	Montana	92.3
12	Nebraska	98.0
45	Nevada	69.4
NA	New Hampshire**	NA
9	New Jersey	102.2
33	New Mexico	86.5
43	New York	70.9
36	North Carolina	84.5
41	North Dakota	80.5
10	Ohio	99.8
14	Oklahoma	97.2
20	Oregon	92.5
19	Pennsylvania	94.7
44	Rhode Island	69.9
NA	South Carolina**	NA
6	South Dakota	107.0
NA	Tennessee**	NA
22	Texas	90.7
32	Utah	86.8
23	Vermont	90.5
16	Virginia	96.1
39	Washington	82.1
4	West Virginia	107.4
31	Wisconsin	87.4
30	Wyoming	87.5

RANK ORDER

RANK	STATE	PERCENT
1	Maine	113.9
2	Arkansas	110.9
3	Arizona	109.9
4	West Virginia	107.4
5	Kentucky	107.3
6	South Dakota	107.0
7	Delaware	105.1
8	Missouri	103.4
9	New Jersey	102.2
10	Ohio	99.8
11	Iowa	98.6
12	Nebraska	98.0
13	Illinois	97.7
14	Oklahoma	97.2
15	Indiana	96.8
16	Virginia	96.1
17	Maryland	95.8
18	Connecticut	95.6
19	Pennsylvania	94.7
20	Oregon	92.5
21	Montana	92.3
22	Texas	90.7
23	Colorado	90.5
23	Vermont	90.5
25	California	89.2
25	Mississippi	89.2
27	Michigan	89.0
28	Kansas	88.4
29	Louisiana	87.6
30	Wyoming	87.5
31	Wisconsin	87.4
32	Utah	86.8
33	New Mexico	86.5
34	Alabama	86.2
35	Minnesota	85.1
36	North Carolina	84.5
37	Georgia	83.2
38	Massachusetts	82.2
39	Washington	82.1
40	Florida	81.3
41	North Dakota	80.5
42	Alaska	73.5
43	New York	70.9
44	Rhode Island	69.9
45	Nevada	69.4
46	Hawaii	68.8
NA	Idaho**	NA
NA	New Hampshire**	NA
NA	South Carolina**	NA
NA	Tennessee**	NA

District of Columbia	57.1

Source: CQ Press using data from U.S. Department of Education, National Center for Education Statistics
   "Common Core of Data (CCD) Database" (http://nces.ed.gov/ccd/)
*Based on reporting states' totals and excludes students for whom race/ethnicity was not reported. Includes Pacific Islander.
Calculated by comparing estimated number of public high school graduates in 2005 with 9th grade enrollment in Fall 2001. Data
exclude ungraded pupils and have not been adjusted for interstate migration or switching to or from private schools. A state's rate
can be higher than 100% due to such changes. **Not available.

Estimated Public High School Graduation Rate for American Indian Students in 2005
Reporting States Estimated Rate = 62.3% Graduated*

ALPHA ORDER

RANK	STATE	PERCENT
4	Alabama	84.0
41	Alaska	40.6
14	Arizona	71.7
2	Arkansas	92.7
18	California	63.6
28	Colorado	57.2
16	Connecticut	66.9
9	Delaware	76.9
5	Florida	83.9
39	Georgia	44.2
7	Hawaii	77.2
NA	Idaho**	NA
1	Illinois	100.0
26	Indiana	57.5
15	Iowa	71.6
12	Kansas	75.3
38	Kentucky	44.8
22	Louisiana	61.4
7	Maine	77.2
13	Maryland	72.4
44	Massachusetts	39.6
33	Michigan	50.6
27	Minnesota	57.4
24	Mississippi	60.4
3	Missouri	89.4
29	Montana	55.2
32	Nebraska	51.2
42	Nevada	40.1
NA	New Hampshire**	NA
NA	New Jersey**	NA
31	New Mexico	52.2
30	New York	54.3
40	North Carolina	44.0
35	North Dakota	49.9
25	Ohio	59.8
11	Oklahoma	76.1
20	Oregon	62.9
36	Pennsylvania	46.5
37	Rhode Island	45.2
NA	South Carolina**	NA
43	South Dakota	39.9
NA	Tennessee**	NA
10	Texas	76.2
17	Utah	65.8
21	Vermont	62.3
6	Virginia	78.8
34	Washington	50.2
18	West Virginia	63.6
23	Wisconsin	60.9
45	Wyoming	36.5

RANK ORDER

RANK	STATE	PERCENT
1	Illinois	100.0
2	Arkansas	92.7
3	Missouri	89.4
4	Alabama	84.0
5	Florida	83.9
6	Virginia	78.8
7	Hawaii	77.2
7	Maine	77.2
9	Delaware	76.9
10	Texas	76.2
11	Oklahoma	76.1
12	Kansas	75.3
13	Maryland	72.4
14	Arizona	71.7
15	Iowa	71.6
16	Connecticut	66.9
17	Utah	65.8
18	California	63.6
18	West Virginia	63.6
20	Oregon	62.9
21	Vermont	62.3
22	Louisiana	61.4
23	Wisconsin	60.9
24	Mississippi	60.4
25	Ohio	59.8
26	Indiana	57.5
27	Minnesota	57.4
28	Colorado	57.2
29	Montana	55.2
30	New York	54.3
31	New Mexico	52.2
32	Nebraska	51.2
33	Michigan	50.6
34	Washington	50.2
35	North Dakota	49.9
36	Pennsylvania	46.5
37	Rhode Island	45.2
38	Kentucky	44.8
39	Georgia	44.2
40	North Carolina	44.0
41	Alaska	40.6
42	Nevada	40.1
43	South Dakota	39.9
44	Massachusetts	39.6
45	Wyoming	36.5
NA	Idaho**	NA
NA	New Hampshire**	NA
NA	New Jersey**	NA
NA	South Carolina**	NA
NA	Tennessee**	NA
	District of Columbia**	NA

Source: CQ Press using data from U.S. Department of Education, National Center for Education Statistics
"Common Core of Data (CCD) Database" (http://nces.ed.gov/ccd/)
*Based on reporting states' totals and excludes students for whom race/ethnicity was not reported. Includes Alaska Native.
Calculated by comparing estimated number of public high school graduates in 2005 with 9th grade enrollment in Fall 2001. Data
exclude ungraded pupils and have not been adjusted for interstate migration or switching to or from private schools. A state's rate
can be higher than 100% due to such changes. **Not available.

Private High School Graduates in 2005

National Total = 307,249 Graduates*

ALPHA ORDER					RANK ORDER			
RANK	**STATE**	**GRADUATES**	**% of USA**		**RANK**	**STATE**	**GRADUATES**	**% of USA**
22	Alabama	5,191	1.7%		1	California	33,541	10.9%
49	Alaska	291	0.1%		2	New York	28,471	9.3%
32	Arizona	2,634	0.9%		3	Pennsylvania	17,980	5.9%
25	Arkansas**	3,919	1.3%		4	Florida	16,824	5.5%
1	California	33,541	10.9%		5	Illinois	14,352	4.7%
31	Colorado	2,843	0.9%		6	Ohio	13,070	4.3%
19	Connecticut	5,589	1.8%		7	New Jersey	12,826	4.2%
40	Delaware	1,663	0.5%		8	Texas	11,498	3.7%
4	Florida	16,824	5.5%		9	Massachusetts	10,942	3.6%
15	Georgia	7,302	2.4%		10	Montana**	9,228	3.0%
39	Hawaii	1,674	0.5%		11	Maryland	8,519	2.8%
46	Idaho	555	0.2%		12	Missouri	8,348	2.7%
5	Illinois	14,352	4.7%		13	Michigan	8,051	2.6%
21	Indiana	5,267	1.7%		14	Louisiana	7,956	2.6%
27	Iowa**	3,267	1.1%		15	Georgia	7,302	2.4%
36	Kansas	2,082	0.7%		16	Virginia	7,094	2.3%
26	Kentucky	3,718	1.2%		17	Tennessee	5,864	1.9%
14	Louisiana	7,956	2.6%		18	Wisconsin	5,665	1.8%
33	Maine	2,350	0.8%		19	Connecticut	5,589	1.8%
11	Maryland	8,519	2.8%		20	North Carolina	5,333	1.7%
9	Massachusetts	10,942	3.6%		21	Indiana	5,267	1.7%
13	Michigan	8,051	2.6%		22	Alabama	5,191	1.7%
24	Minnesota	4,272	1.4%		23	Washington	4,595	1.5%
28	Mississippi	3,146	1.0%		24	Minnesota	4,272	1.4%
12	Missouri	8,348	2.7%		25	Arkansas**	3,919	1.3%
10	Montana**	9,228	3.0%		26	Kentucky	3,718	1.2%
34	Nebraska	2,274	0.7%		27	Iowa**	3,267	1.1%
45	Nevada	662	0.2%		28	Mississippi	3,146	1.0%
35	New Hampshire	2,163	0.7%		29	South Carolina	2,950	1.0%
7	New Jersey	12,826	4.2%		30	Oregon	2,848	0.9%
41	New Mexico	1,400	0.5%		31	Colorado	2,843	0.9%
2	New York	28,471	9.3%		32	Arizona	2,634	0.9%
20	North Carolina	5,333	1.7%		33	Maine	2,350	0.8%
48	North Dakota	421	0.1%		34	Nebraska	2,274	0.7%
6	Ohio	13,070	4.3%		35	New Hampshire	2,163	0.7%
38	Oklahoma	1,780	0.6%		36	Kansas	2,082	0.7%
30	Oregon	2,848	0.9%		37	Rhode Island	1,807	0.6%
3	Pennsylvania	17,980	5.9%		38	Oklahoma	1,780	0.6%
37	Rhode Island	1,807	0.6%		39	Hawaii	1,674	0.5%
29	South Carolina	2,950	1.0%		40	Delaware	1,663	0.5%
47	South Dakota	508	0.2%		41	New Mexico	1,400	0.5%
17	Tennessee	5,864	1.9%		42	Vermont	1,150	0.4%
8	Texas	11,498	3.7%		43	Utah	1,088	0.4%
43	Utah	1,088	0.4%		44	West Virginia	796	0.3%
42	Vermont	1,150	0.4%		45	Nevada	662	0.2%
16	Virginia	7,094	2.3%		46	Idaho	555	0.2%
23	Washington	4,595	1.5%		47	South Dakota	508	0.2%
44	West Virginia	796	0.3%		48	North Dakota	421	0.1%
18	Wisconsin	5,665	1.8%		49	Alaska	291	0.1%
NA	Wyoming***	NA	NA		NA	Wyoming***	NA	NA
					District of Columbia		1,447	0.5%

Source: U.S. Department of Education, Institute of Education Sciences
"Characteristics of Private Schools in the United States" (http://nces.ed.gov/pubs2008/2008315.pdf)
*For school year 2004-2005.
**Interpret data for these states with caution.
***Not available.

Public High School Dropouts in 2005

National Total = 540,382 Dropouts*

ALPHA ORDER

RANK	STATE	DROPOUTS	% of USA
26	Alabama	5,925	1.1%
32	Alaska	3,349	0.6%
10	Arizona	19,980	3.7%
27	Arkansas	5,845	1.1%
1	California	60,524	11.2%
11	Colorado	17,497	3.2%
NA	Connecticut**	NA	NA
40	Delaware	1,883	0.3%
4	Florida	27,633	5.1%
6	Georgia	24,280	4.5%
35	Hawaii	2,547	0.5%
37	Idaho	2,363	0.4%
5	Illinois	27,380	5.1%
19	Indiana	7,580	1.4%
33	Iowa	3,302	0.6%
34	Kansas	3,113	0.6%
22	Kentucky	6,522	1.2%
14	Louisiana	14,210	2.6%
41	Maine	1,748	0.3%
16	Maryland	10,468	1.9%
15	Massachusetts	11,146	2.1%
8	Michigan	20,612	3.8%
NA	Minnesota**	NA	NA
30	Mississippi	3,650	0.7%
17	Missouri	10,270	1.9%
43	Montana	1,628	0.3%
36	Nebraska	2,431	0.4%
24	Nevada	6,436	1.2%
38	New Hampshire	2,306	0.4%
NA	New Jersey**	NA	NA
29	New Mexico	4,126	0.8%
2	New York	50,004	9.3%
7	North Carolina	20,998	3.9%
46	North Dakota	624	0.1%
9	Ohio	20,089	3.7%
25	Oklahoma	6,256	1.2%
NA	Oregon**	NA	NA
12	Pennsylvania	17,018	3.1%
39	Rhode Island	1,999	0.4%
23	South Carolina	6,477	1.2%
42	South Dakota	1,716	0.3%
20	Tennessee	7,311	1.4%
3	Texas	43,475	8.0%
28	Utah	5,518	1.0%
45	Vermont	839	0.2%
18	Virginia	8,989	1.7%
13	Washington	14,641	2.7%
31	West Virginia	3,377	0.6%
21	Wisconsin	6,847	1.3%
44	Wyoming	1,304	0.2%

RANK ORDER

RANK	STATE	DROPOUTS	% of USA
1	California	60,524	11.2%
2	New York	50,004	9.3%
3	Texas	43,475	8.0%
4	Florida	27,633	5.1%
5	Illinois	27,380	5.1%
6	Georgia	24,280	4.5%
7	North Carolina	20,998	3.9%
8	Michigan	20,612	3.8%
9	Ohio	20,089	3.7%
10	Arizona	19,980	3.7%
11	Colorado	17,497	3.2%
12	Pennsylvania	17,018	3.1%
13	Washington	14,641	2.7%
14	Louisiana	14,210	2.6%
15	Massachusetts	11,146	2.1%
16	Maryland	10,468	1.9%
17	Missouri	10,270	1.9%
18	Virginia	8,989	1.7%
19	Indiana	7,580	1.4%
20	Tennessee	7,311	1.4%
21	Wisconsin	6,847	1.3%
22	Kentucky	6,522	1.2%
23	South Carolina	6,477	1.2%
24	Nevada	6,436	1.2%
25	Oklahoma	6,256	1.2%
26	Alabama	5,925	1.1%
27	Arkansas	5,845	1.1%
28	Utah	5,518	1.0%
29	New Mexico	4,126	0.8%
30	Mississippi	3,650	0.7%
31	West Virginia	3,377	0.6%
32	Alaska	3,349	0.6%
33	Iowa	3,302	0.6%
34	Kansas	3,113	0.6%
35	Hawaii	2,547	0.5%
36	Nebraska	2,431	0.4%
37	Idaho	2,363	0.4%
38	New Hampshire	2,306	0.4%
39	Rhode Island	1,999	0.4%
40	Delaware	1,883	0.3%
41	Maine	1,748	0.3%
42	South Dakota	1,716	0.3%
43	Montana	1,628	0.3%
44	Wyoming	1,304	0.2%
45	Vermont	839	0.2%
46	North Dakota	624	0.1%
NA	Connecticut**	NA	NA
NA	Minnesota**	NA	NA
NA	New Jersey**	NA	NA
NA	Oregon**	NA	NA
	District of Columbia**	NA	NA

Source: U.S. Department of Education, National Center for Education Statistics
   "Numbers and Rates of Public High School Dropouts: School Year 2004-05" (NCES 2008-305, December 2007)
   (http://nces.ed.gov/pubsearch/pubsinfo.asp?pubid=2008305)
*"Event" dropout figures showing the number of 9th-12th grade dropouts. National total include figures for states not shown if the state reported dropouts for some grades but not all.
**Not available.

Public High School Dropout Rate in 2005

National Rate = 3.9%*

ALPHA ORDER

RANK	STATE	RATE
35	Alabama	2.8
1	Alaska	8.2
4	Arizona	6.2
15	Arkansas	4.3
32	California	3.1
2	Colorado	7.8
NA	Connecticut**	NA
8	Delaware	5.3
25	Florida	3.5
7	Georgia	5.6
11	Hawaii	4.7
33	Idaho	3.0
12	Illinois	4.5
41	Indiana	2.5
44	Iowa	2.2
45	Kansas	2.1
25	Kentucky	3.5
3	Louisiana	7.5
35	Maine	2.8
19	Maryland	3.9
21	Massachusetts	3.8
19	Michigan	3.9
NA	Minnesota**	NA
35	Mississippi	2.8
22	Missouri	3.7
30	Montana	3.4
38	Nebraska	2.7
5	Nevada	5.8
25	New Hampshire	3.5
NA	New Jersey**	NA
16	New Mexico	4.2
6	New York	5.7
9	North Carolina	5.2
46	North Dakota	1.9
25	Ohio	3.5
25	Oklahoma	3.5
NA	Oregon**	NA
34	Pennsylvania	2.9
17	Rhode Island	4.1
31	South Carolina	3.3
14	South Dakota	4.4
38	Tennessee	2.7
24	Texas	3.6
22	Utah	3.7
40	Vermont	2.6
41	Virginia	2.5
12	Washington	4.5
17	West Virginia	4.1
43	Wisconsin	2.4
10	Wyoming	4.8

RANK ORDER

RANK	STATE	RATE
1	Alaska	8.2
2	Colorado	7.8
3	Louisiana	7.5
4	Arizona	6.2
5	Nevada	5.8
6	New York	5.7
7	Georgia	5.6
8	Delaware	5.3
9	North Carolina	5.2
10	Wyoming	4.8
11	Hawaii	4.7
12	Illinois	4.5
12	Washington	4.5
14	South Dakota	4.4
15	Arkansas	4.3
16	New Mexico	4.2
17	Rhode Island	4.1
17	West Virginia	4.1
19	Maryland	3.9
19	Michigan	3.9
21	Massachusetts	3.8
22	Missouri	3.7
22	Utah	3.7
24	Texas	3.6
25	Florida	3.5
25	Kentucky	3.5
25	New Hampshire	3.5
25	Ohio	3.5
25	Oklahoma	3.5
30	Montana	3.4
31	South Carolina	3.3
32	California	3.1
33	Idaho	3.0
34	Pennsylvania	2.9
35	Alabama	2.8
35	Maine	2.8
35	Mississippi	2.8
38	Nebraska	2.7
38	Tennessee	2.7
40	Vermont	2.6
41	Indiana	2.5
41	Virginia	2.5
43	Wisconsin	2.4
44	Iowa	2.2
45	Kansas	2.1
46	North Dakota	1.9
NA	Connecticut**	NA
NA	Minnesota**	NA
NA	New Jersey**	NA
NA	Oregon**	NA
	District of Columbia**	NA

Source: U.S. Department of Education, National Center for Education Statistics
   "Numbers and Rates of Public High School Dropouts: School Year 2004-05" (NCES 2008-305, December 2007)
      (http://nces.ed.gov/pubsearch/pubsinfo.asp?pubid=2008305)
*"Event" dropout rates showing the number of 9th-12th grade dropouts divided by the number of students enrolled at the beginning of the school year in those grades. National rate is for reporting states.
**Not available.

White Public High School Dropout Rate in 2005

National Rate = 2.8%*

ALPHA ORDER

RANK	STATE	RATE
23	Alabama	2.7
1	Alaska	6.3
11	Arizona	3.8
NA	Arkansas**	NA
34	California	2.0
3	Colorado	5.2
NA	Connecticut**	NA
7	Delaware	4.3
18	Florida	2.8
5	Georgia	5.0
2	Hawaii	5.7
25	Idaho	2.6
30	Illinois	2.3
30	Indiana	2.3
37	Iowa	1.8
37	Kansas	1.8
13	Kentucky	3.2
3	Louisiana	5.2
23	Maine	2.7
28	Maryland	2.5
16	Massachusetts	3.0
18	Michigan	2.8
NA	Minnesota**	NA
30	Mississippi	2.3
13	Missouri	3.2
18	Montana	2.8
35	Nebraska	1.9
NA	Nevada**	NA
12	New Hampshire	3.4
NA	New Jersey**	NA
42	New Mexico	1.0
18	New York	2.8
6	North Carolina	4.6
41	North Dakota	1.4
28	Ohio	2.5
15	Oklahoma	3.1
NA	Oregon**	NA
35	Pennsylvania	1.9
NA	Rhode Island**	NA
18	South Carolina	2.8
25	South Dakota	2.6
NA	Tennessee**	NA
33	Texas	2.1
16	Utah	3.0
25	Vermont	2.6
37	Virginia	1.8
10	Washington	3.9
9	West Virginia	4.0
40	Wisconsin	1.5
8	Wyoming	4.2

RANK ORDER

RANK	STATE	RATE
1	Alaska	6.3
2	Hawaii	5.7
3	Colorado	5.2
3	Louisiana	5.2
5	Georgia	5.0
6	North Carolina	4.6
7	Delaware	4.3
8	Wyoming	4.2
9	West Virginia	4.0
10	Washington	3.9
11	Arizona	3.8
12	New Hampshire	3.4
13	Kentucky	3.2
13	Missouri	3.2
15	Oklahoma	3.1
16	Massachusetts	3.0
16	Utah	3.0
18	Florida	2.8
18	Michigan	2.8
18	Montana	2.8
18	New York	2.8
18	South Carolina	2.8
23	Alabama	2.7
23	Maine	2.7
25	Idaho	2.6
25	South Dakota	2.6
25	Vermont	2.6
28	Maryland	2.5
28	Ohio	2.5
30	Illinois	2.3
30	Indiana	2.3
30	Mississippi	2.3
33	Texas	2.1
34	California	2.0
35	Nebraska	1.9
35	Pennsylvania	1.9
37	Iowa	1.8
37	Kansas	1.8
37	Virginia	1.8
40	Wisconsin	1.5
41	North Dakota	1.4
42	New Mexico	1.0
NA	Arkansas**	NA
NA	Connecticut**	NA
NA	Minnesota**	NA
NA	Nevada**	NA
NA	New Jersey**	NA
NA	Oregon**	NA
NA	Rhode Island**	NA
NA	Tennessee**	NA
	District of Columbia**	NA

Source: U.S. Department of Education, National Center for Education Statistics
    "Numbers and Rates of Public High School Dropouts: School Year 2004-05" (NCES 2008-305, December 2007)
        (http://nces.ed.gov/pubsearch/pubsinfo.asp?pubid=2008305)

*"Event" dropout rates showing the number of 9th-12th grade dropouts divided by the number of students enrolled at the beginning of the school year in those grades. National rate is for reporting states. Does not include white Hispanics.
**Not available.

Black Public High School Dropout Rate in 2005

National Rate = 6.0%*

RANK	STATE	RATE
42	Alabama	3.2
1	Alaska	12.7
14	Arizona	7.0
26	Arkansas	5.8
30	California	5.5
2	Colorado	11.1
46	Connecticut	2.9
15	Delaware	6.6
33	Florida	4.8
22	Georgia	6.1
28	Hawaii	5.7
34	Idaho	4.7
5	Illinois	9.1
41	Indiana	3.3
21	Iowa	6.2
39	Kansas	3.7
29	Kentucky	5.6
3	Louisiana	10.2
37	Maine	4.0
24	Maryland	6.0
19	Massachusetts	6.3
10	Michigan	7.5
6	Minnesota	8.8
42	Mississippi	3.2
17	Missouri	6.4
47	Montana	2.2
19	Nebraska	6.3
NA	Nevada**	NA
22	New Hampshire	6.1
45	New Jersey	3.1
26	New Mexico	5.8
4	New York	9.6
24	North Carolina	6.0
32	North Dakota	5.0
7	Ohio	8.1
34	Oklahoma	4.7
NA	Oregon**	NA
17	Pennsylvania	6.4
13	Rhode Island	7.1
38	South Carolina	3.9
10	South Dakota	7.5
NA	Tennessee**	NA
36	Texas	4.2
12	Utah	7.4
40	Vermont	3.5
42	Virginia	3.2
16	Washington	6.5
31	West Virginia	5.4
9	Wisconsin	7.9
8	Wyoming	8.0

RANK ORDER

RANK	STATE	RATE
1	Alaska	12.7
2	Colorado	11.1
3	Louisiana	10.2
4	New York	9.6
5	Illinois	9.1
6	Minnesota	8.8
7	Ohio	8.1
8	Wyoming	8.0
9	Wisconsin	7.9
10	Michigan	7.5
10	South Dakota	7.5
12	Utah	7.4
13	Rhode Island	7.1
14	Arizona	7.0
15	Delaware	6.6
16	Washington	6.5
17	Missouri	6.4
17	Pennsylvania	6.4
19	Massachusetts	6.3
19	Nebraska	6.3
21	Iowa	6.2
22	Georgia	6.1
22	New Hampshire	6.1
24	Maryland	6.0
24	North Carolina	6.0
26	Arkansas	5.8
26	New Mexico	5.8
28	Hawaii	5.7
29	Kentucky	5.6
30	California	5.5
31	West Virginia	5.4
32	North Dakota	5.0
33	Florida	4.8
34	Idaho	4.7
34	Oklahoma	4.7
36	Texas	4.2
37	Maine	4.0
38	South Carolina	3.9
39	Kansas	3.7
40	Vermont	3.5
41	Indiana	3.3
42	Alabama	3.2
42	Mississippi	3.2
42	Virginia	3.2
45	New Jersey	3.1
46	Connecticut	2.9
47	Montana	2.2
NA	Nevada**	NA
NA	Oregon**	NA
NA	Tennessee**	NA
	District of Columbia**	NA

Source: U.S. Department of Education, National Center for Education Statistics
"Numbers and Rates of Public High School Dropouts: School Year 2004-05" (NCES 2008-305, December 2007)
(http://nces.ed.gov/pubsearch/pubsinfo.asp?pubid=2008305)
*"Event" dropout rates showing the number of 9th-12th grade dropouts divided by the number of students enrolled at the beginning of the school year in those grades. National rate is for reporting states. Does not include black Hispanics.
**Not available.

Hispanic Public High School Dropout Rate in 2005

National Rate = 5.8%*

ALPHA ORDER				RANK ORDER		
RANK	STATE	RATE		RANK	STATE	RATE
44	Alabama	3.3		1	Colorado	15.2
2	Alaska	11.2		2	Alaska	11.2
6	Arizona	9.5		3	New York	10.6
23	Arkansas	6.4		4	Delaware	10.4
39	California	4.0		5	South Dakota	9.8
1	Colorado	15.2		6	Arizona	9.5
39	Connecticut	4.0		7	Wyoming	9.3
4	Delaware	10.4		8	Massachusetts	9.1
37	Florida	4.2		9	North Carolina	8.7
11	Georgia	8.4		9	Utah	8.7
30	Hawaii	5.2		11	Georgia	8.4
22	Idaho	6.5		12	Illinois	8.1
12	Illinois	8.1		13	Michigan	8.0
37	Indiana	4.2		14	Rhode Island	7.9
24	Iowa	6.3		15	Washington	7.8
42	Kansas	3.7		16	Louisiana	7.7
41	Kentucky	3.8		17	Oklahoma	7.6
16	Louisiana	7.7		17	Pennsylvania	7.6
35	Maine	4.6		19	Ohio	7.1
31	Maryland	5.1		20	Nebraska	6.9
8	Massachusetts	9.1		21	Virginia	6.8
13	Michigan	8.0		22	Idaho	6.5
NA	Minnesota**	NA		23	Arkansas	6.4
46	Mississippi	2.5		24	Iowa	6.3
31	Missouri	5.1		25	New Mexico	6.2
36	Montana	4.5		26	New Hampshire	6.0
20	Nebraska	6.9		27	Wisconsin	5.7
NA	Nevada**	NA		28	West Virginia	5.5
26	New Hampshire	6.0		29	South Carolina	5.3
43	New Jersey	3.5		30	Hawaii	5.2
25	New Mexico	6.2		31	Maryland	5.1
3	New York	10.6		31	Missouri	5.1
9	North Carolina	8.7		31	Texas	5.1
34	North Dakota	4.8		34	North Dakota	4.8
19	Ohio	7.1		35	Maine	4.6
17	Oklahoma	7.6		36	Montana	4.5
NA	Oregon**	NA		37	Florida	4.2
17	Pennsylvania	7.6		37	Indiana	4.2
14	Rhode Island	7.9		39	California	4.0
29	South Carolina	5.3		39	Connecticut	4.0
5	South Dakota	9.8		41	Kentucky	3.8
NA	Tennessee**	NA		42	Kansas	3.7
31	Texas	5.1		43	New Jersey	3.5
9	Utah	8.7		44	Alabama	3.3
45	Vermont	2.7		45	Vermont	2.7
21	Virginia	6.8		46	Mississippi	2.5
15	Washington	7.8		NA	Minnesota**	NA
28	West Virginia	5.5		NA	Nevada**	NA
27	Wisconsin	5.7		NA	Oregon**	NA
7	Wyoming	9.3		NA	Tennessee**	NA
					District of Columbia**	NA

Source: U.S. Department of Education, National Center for Education Statistics
   "Numbers and Rates of Public High School Dropouts: School Year 2004-05" (NCES 2008-305, December 2007)
      (http://nces.ed.gov/pubsearch/pubsinfo.asp?pubid=2008305)
*"Event" dropout rates showing the number of 9th-12th grade dropouts divided by the number of students enrolled at the beginning
of the school year in those grades. National rate is for reporting states. Hispanics can be of any race.
**Not available.

Asian Public High School Dropout Rate in 2005

National Rate = 2.5%*

ALPHA ORDER				RANK ORDER		
RANK	STATE	RATE		RANK	STATE	RATE
43	Alabama	1.2		1	Alaska	7.5
1	Alaska	7.5		2	New York	5.2
24	Arizona	2.2		2	Rhode Island	5.2
10	Arkansas	3.2		2	South Dakota	5.2
32	California	1.6		5	Colorado	4.9
5	Colorado	4.9		6	Utah	4.8
NA	Connecticut**	NA		7	Hawaii	4.3
18	Delaware	2.5		8	Louisiana	3.9
32	Florida	1.6		8	Michigan	3.9
14	Georgia	2.6		10	Arkansas	3.2
7	Hawaii	4.3		10	New Mexico	3.2
24	Idaho	2.2		12	Washington	3.1
23	Illinois	2.3		13	North Dakota	2.9
44	Indiana	1.1		14	Georgia	2.6
28	Iowa	1.8		14	Maine	2.6
36	Kansas	1.4		14	Massachusetts	2.6
39	Kentucky	1.3		14	North Carolina	2.6
8	Louisiana	3.9		18	Delaware	2.5
14	Maine	2.6		18	New Hampshire	2.5
36	Maryland	1.4		18	Pennsylvania	2.5
14	Massachusetts	2.6		18	Wisconsin	2.5
8	Michigan	3.9		22	Nebraska	2.4
NA	Minnesota**	NA		23	Illinois	2.3
39	Mississippi	1.3		24	Arizona	2.2
32	Missouri	1.6		24	Idaho	2.2
24	Montana	2.2		24	Montana	2.2
22	Nebraska	2.4		27	Ohio	1.9
NA	Nevada**	NA		28	Iowa	1.8
18	New Hampshire	2.5		28	Oklahoma	1.8
NA	New Jersey**	NA		28	West Virginia	1.8
10	New Mexico	3.2		28	Wyoming	1.8
2	New York	5.2		32	California	1.6
14	North Carolina	2.6		32	Florida	1.6
13	North Dakota	2.9		32	Missouri	1.6
27	Ohio	1.9		32	Virginia	1.6
28	Oklahoma	1.8		36	Kansas	1.4
NA	Oregon**	NA		36	Maryland	1.4
18	Pennsylvania	2.5		36	Texas	1.4
2	Rhode Island	5.2		39	Kentucky	1.3
39	South Carolina	1.3		39	Mississippi	1.3
2	South Dakota	5.2		39	South Carolina	1.3
NA	Tennessee**	NA		39	Vermont	1.3
36	Texas	1.4		43	Alabama	1.2
6	Utah	4.8		44	Indiana	1.1
39	Vermont	1.3		NA	Connecticut**	NA
32	Virginia	1.6		NA	Minnesota**	NA
12	Washington	3.1		NA	Nevada**	NA
28	West Virginia	1.8		NA	New Jersey**	NA
18	Wisconsin	2.5		NA	Oregon**	NA
28	Wyoming	1.8		NA	Tennessee**	NA
					District of Columbia**	NA

Source: U.S. Department of Education, National Center for Education Statistics
   "Numbers and Rates of Public High School Dropouts: School Year 2004-05" (NCES 2008-305, December 2007)
      (http://nces.ed.gov/pubsearch/pubsinfo.asp?pubid=2008305)
*"Event" dropout rates showing the number of 9th-12th grade dropouts divided by the number of students enrolled at the beginning
of the school year in those grades. National rate is for reporting states. Includes Pacific Islanders.
**Not available.

American Indian Public High School Dropout Rate in 2005

National Rate = 6.7%*

ALPHA ORDER

RANK	STATE	RATE
43	Alabama	1.2
3	Alaska	11.2
5	Arizona	9.9
NA	Arkansas**	NA
31	California	4.3
2	Colorado	13.7
40	Connecticut	3.1
38	Delaware	3.2
34	Florida	3.5
17	Georgia	6.1
6	Hawaii	9.5
20	Idaho	5.8
32	Illinois	4.1
28	Indiana	4.9
20	Iowa	5.8
35	Kansas	3.4
44	Kentucky	0.0
4	Louisiana	10.1
14	Maine	7.6
36	Maryland	3.3
23	Massachusetts	5.4
20	Michigan	5.8
NA	Minnesota**	NA
38	Mississippi	3.2
26	Missouri	5.0
11	Montana	8.6
6	Nebraska	9.5
NA	Nevada**	NA
26	New Hampshire	5.0
NA	New Jersey**	NA
25	New Mexico	5.1
13	New York	8.1
8	North Carolina	9.2
16	North Dakota	6.5
9	Ohio	8.7
36	Oklahoma	3.3
NA	Oregon**	NA
42	Pennsylvania	2.1
14	Rhode Island	7.6
30	South Carolina	4.6
1	South Dakota	21.7
NA	Tennessee**	NA
32	Texas	4.1
18	Utah	6.0
23	Vermont	5.4
41	Virginia	3.0
12	Washington	8.3
29	West Virginia	4.8
19	Wisconsin	5.9
9	Wyoming	8.7

RANK ORDER

RANK	STATE	RATE
1	South Dakota	21.7
2	Colorado	13.7
3	Alaska	11.2
4	Louisiana	10.1
5	Arizona	9.9
6	Hawaii	9.5
6	Nebraska	9.5
8	North Carolina	9.2
9	Ohio	8.7
9	Wyoming	8.7
11	Montana	8.6
12	Washington	8.3
13	New York	8.1
14	Maine	7.6
14	Rhode Island	7.6
16	North Dakota	6.5
17	Georgia	6.1
18	Utah	6.0
19	Wisconsin	5.9
20	Idaho	5.8
20	Iowa	5.8
20	Michigan	5.8
23	Massachusetts	5.4
23	Vermont	5.4
25	New Mexico	5.1
26	Missouri	5.0
26	New Hampshire	5.0
28	Indiana	4.9
29	West Virginia	4.8
30	South Carolina	4.6
31	California	4.3
32	Illinois	4.1
32	Texas	4.1
34	Florida	3.5
35	Kansas	3.4
36	Maryland	3.3
36	Oklahoma	3.3
38	Delaware	3.2
38	Mississippi	3.2
40	Connecticut	3.1
41	Virginia	3.0
42	Pennsylvania	2.1
43	Alabama	1.2
44	Kentucky	0.0
NA	Arkansas**	NA
NA	Minnesota**	NA
NA	Nevada**	NA
NA	New Jersey**	NA
NA	Oregon**	NA
NA	Tennessee**	NA
	District of Columbia**	NA

Source: U.S. Department of Education, National Center for Education Statistics
   "Numbers and Rates of Public High School Dropouts: School Year 2004-05" (NCES 2008-305, December 2007)
      (http://nces.ed.gov/pubsearch/pubsinfo.asp?pubid=2008305)
*"Event" dropout rates showing the number of 9th-12th grade dropouts divided by the number of students enrolled at the beginning
of the school year in those grades. National rate is for reporting states.
**Not available.

ACT Average Composite Score in 2008

National Average = 21.1*

ALPHA ORDER

RANK	STATE	AVERAGE SCORE
44	Alabama	20.4
32	Alaska	21.2
21	Arizona	21.9
41	Arkansas	20.6
13	California	22.2
43	Colorado	20.5
2	Connecticut	23.3
9	Delaware	22.6
48	Florida	19.8
41	Georgia	20.6
26	Hawaii	21.6
29	Idaho	21.5
36	Illinois	20.7
16	Indiana	22.0
11	Iowa	22.4
16	Kansas	22.0
35	Kentucky	20.9
45	Louisiana	20.3
6	Maine	22.7
16	Maryland	22.0
1	Massachusetts	23.6
49	Michigan	19.6
9	Minnesota	22.6
50	Mississippi	18.9
26	Missouri	21.6
16	Montana	22.0
15	Nebraska	22.1
30	Nevada	21.3
3	New Hampshire	23.1
6	New Jersey	22.7
45	New Mexico	20.3
3	New York	23.1
30	North Carolina	21.3
26	North Dakota	21.6
25	Ohio	21.7
36	Oklahoma	20.7
32	Oregon	21.2
13	Pennsylvania	22.2
21	Rhode Island	21.9
47	South Carolina	19.9
16	South Dakota	22.0
36	Tennessee	20.7
36	Texas	20.7
23	Utah	21.8
6	Vermont	22.7
23	Virginia	21.8
3	Washington	23.1
36	West Virginia	20.7
12	Wisconsin	22.3
34	Wyoming	21.1

RANK ORDER

RANK	STATE	AVERAGE SCORE
1	Massachusetts	23.6
2	Connecticut	23.3
3	New Hampshire	23.1
3	New York	23.1
3	Washington	23.1
6	Maine	22.7
6	New Jersey	22.7
6	Vermont	22.7
9	Delaware	22.6
9	Minnesota	22.6
11	Iowa	22.4
12	Wisconsin	22.3
13	California	22.2
13	Pennsylvania	22.2
15	Nebraska	22.1
16	Indiana	22.0
16	Kansas	22.0
16	Maryland	22.0
16	Montana	22.0
16	South Dakota	22.0
21	Arizona	21.9
21	Rhode Island	21.9
23	Utah	21.8
23	Virginia	21.8
25	Ohio	21.7
26	Hawaii	21.6
26	Missouri	21.6
26	North Dakota	21.6
29	Idaho	21.5
30	Nevada	21.3
30	North Carolina	21.3
32	Alaska	21.2
32	Oregon	21.2
34	Wyoming	21.1
35	Kentucky	20.9
36	Illinois	20.7
36	Oklahoma	20.7
36	Tennessee	20.7
36	Texas	20.7
36	West Virginia	20.7
41	Arkansas	20.6
41	Georgia	20.6
43	Colorado	20.5
44	Alabama	20.4
45	Louisiana	20.3
45	New Mexico	20.3
47	South Carolina	19.9
48	Florida	19.8
49	Michigan	19.6
50	Mississippi	18.9

District of Columbia   19.1

Source: The American College Testing Program (Copyright © 2008)
"Average ACT Scores by State" (http://www.act.org/news/data/08/states-text.html)
*The ACT score range is 1 to 36. Approximately 1.42 million 2008 U.S. high school students took the test. Caution should be used in using ACT scores to compare states. The percentage of high school students taking the test varies greatly from one state to another. For example, all 11th grade students in Colorado and Michigan are required to take the test but, in Maine, only 9 percent of 11th grade students took the test.

ACT Average Math Score in 2008

National Average = 21.0*

RANK	STATE	AVERAGE SCORE		RANK	STATE	AVERAGE SCORE
48	Alabama	19.5		1	Massachusetts	23.9
31	Alaska	21.2		2	New York	23.5
16	Arizona	22.1		3	Connecticut	23.3
40	Arkansas	20.1		4	New Jersey	23.2
7	California	22.8		4	Washington	23.2
38	Colorado	20.3		6	New Hampshire	23.0
3	Connecticut	23.3		7	California	22.8
9	Delaware	22.5		8	Minnesota	22.6
42	Florida	20.0		9	Delaware	22.5
37	Georgia	20.6		9	Maine	22.5
12	Hawaii	22.3		11	Vermont	22.4
28	Idaho	21.4		12	Hawaii	22.3
36	Illinois	20.7		12	Pennsylvania	22.3
15	Indiana	22.2		12	Wisconsin	22.3
17	Iowa	22.0		15	Indiana	22.2
21	Kansas	21.8		16	Arizona	22.1
39	Kentucky	20.2		17	Iowa	22.0
46	Louisiana	19.7		17	Maryland	22.0
9	Maine	22.5		19	Rhode Island	21.9
17	Maryland	22.0		19	South Dakota	21.9
1	Massachusetts	23.9		21	Kansas	21.8
48	Michigan	19.5		21	Montana	21.8
8	Minnesota	22.6		21	Nebraska	21.8
50	Mississippi	18.2		21	North Carolina	21.8
34	Missouri	21.0		21	Virginia	21.8
21	Montana	21.8		26	North Dakota	21.6
21	Nebraska	21.8		27	Ohio	21.5
28	Nevada	21.4		28	Idaho	21.4
6	New Hampshire	23.0		28	Nevada	21.4
4	New Jersey	23.2		28	Oregon	21.4
44	New Mexico	19.8		31	Alaska	21.2
2	New York	23.5		31	Texas	21.2
21	North Carolina	21.8		33	Utah	21.1
26	North Dakota	21.6		34	Missouri	21.0
27	Ohio	21.5		35	Wyoming	20.8
44	Oklahoma	19.8		36	Illinois	20.7
28	Oregon	21.4		37	Georgia	20.6
12	Pennsylvania	22.3		38	Colorado	20.3
19	Rhode Island	21.9		39	Kentucky	20.2
40	South Carolina	20.1		40	Arkansas	20.1
19	South Dakota	21.9		40	South Carolina	20.1
43	Tennessee	19.9		42	Florida	20.0
31	Texas	21.2		43	Tennessee	19.9
33	Utah	21.1		44	New Mexico	19.8
11	Vermont	22.4		44	Oklahoma	19.8
21	Virginia	21.8		46	Louisiana	19.7
4	Washington	23.2		47	West Virginia	19.6
47	West Virginia	19.6		48	Alabama	19.5
12	Wisconsin	22.3		48	Michigan	19.5
35	Wyoming	20.8		50	Mississippi	18.2
					District of Columbia	19.2

Source: The American College Testing Program (Copyright © 2008)
  "Average ACT Scores by State" (http://www.act.org/news/data/08/states-text.html)
*The ACT score range is 1 to 36. Approximately 1.42 million 2008 U.S. high school students took the test. Caution should be used in using ACT scores to compare states. The percentage of high school students taking the test varies greatly from one state to another. For example, all 11th grade students in Colorado and Michigan are required to take the test but, in Maine, only 9 percent of 11th grade students took the test.

ACT Average Reading Score in 2008

National Average = 21.4*

AVERAGE SCORE

ALPHA ORDER

RANK	STATE	AVERAGE SCORE
43	Alabama	20.8
28	Alaska	21.8
20	Arizona	22.3
39	Arkansas	21.0
19	California	22.4
43	Colorado	20.8
4	Connecticut	23.6
8	Delaware	23.1
46	Florida	20.3
41	Georgia	20.9
34	Hawaii	21.6
24	Idaho	22.2
45	Illinois	20.6
15	Indiana	22.5
10	Iowa	22.9
13	Kansas	22.6
35	Kentucky	21.5
46	Louisiana	20.3
7	Maine	23.2
20	Maryland	22.3
1	Massachusetts	24.0
49	Michigan	19.8
9	Minnesota	23.0
50	Mississippi	19.1
27	Missouri	22.0
12	Montana	22.7
15	Nebraska	22.5
32	Nevada	21.7
2	New Hampshire	23.7
10	New Jersey	22.9
39	New Mexico	21.0
5	New York	23.3
32	North Carolina	21.7
28	North Dakota	21.8
26	Ohio	22.1
36	Oklahoma	21.4
28	Oregon	21.8
15	Pennsylvania	22.5
20	Rhode Island	22.3
48	South Carolina	20.0
20	South Dakota	22.3
38	Tennessee	21.1
41	Texas	20.9
15	Utah	22.5
5	Vermont	23.3
24	Virginia	22.2
2	Washington	23.7
36	West Virginia	21.4
13	Wisconsin	22.6
28	Wyoming	21.8

RANK ORDER

RANK	STATE	AVERAGE SCORE
1	Massachusetts	24.0
2	New Hampshire	23.7
2	Washington	23.7
4	Connecticut	23.6
5	New York	23.3
5	Vermont	23.3
7	Maine	23.2
8	Delaware	23.1
9	Minnesota	23.0
10	Iowa	22.9
10	New Jersey	22.9
12	Montana	22.7
13	Kansas	22.6
13	Wisconsin	22.6
15	Indiana	22.5
15	Nebraska	22.5
15	Pennsylvania	22.5
15	Utah	22.5
19	California	22.4
20	Arizona	22.3
20	Maryland	22.3
20	Rhode Island	22.3
20	South Dakota	22.3
24	Idaho	22.2
24	Virginia	22.2
26	Ohio	22.1
27	Missouri	22.0
28	Alaska	21.8
28	North Dakota	21.8
28	Oregon	21.8
28	Wyoming	21.8
32	Nevada	21.7
32	North Carolina	21.7
34	Hawaii	21.6
35	Kentucky	21.5
36	Oklahoma	21.4
36	West Virginia	21.4
38	Tennessee	21.1
39	Arkansas	21.0
39	New Mexico	21.0
41	Georgia	20.9
41	Texas	20.9
43	Alabama	20.8
43	Colorado	20.8
45	Illinois	20.6
46	Florida	20.3
46	Louisiana	20.3
48	South Carolina	20.0
49	Michigan	19.8
50	Mississippi	19.1

District of Columbia	19.6

Source: The American College Testing Program (Copyright © 2008)
"Average ACT Scores by State" (http://www.act.org/news/data/08/states-text.html)
*The ACT score range is 1 to 36. Approximately 1.42 million 2008 U.S. high school students took the test. Caution should be used in using ACT scores to compare states. The percentage of high school students taking the test varies greatly from one state to another. For example, all 11th grade students in Colorado and Michigan are required to take the test but, in Maine, only 9 percent of 11th grade students took the test.

Average Math SAT Score in 2007

National Average Score = 515*

RANK	STATE	AVERAGE SCORE		RANK	STATE	AVERAGE SCORE
18	Alabama	556		1	Iowa	613
31	Alaska	517		2	Illinois	611
27	Arizona	525		3	Minnesota	603
15	Arkansas	566		4	South Dakota	602
32	California	516		5	Wisconsin	598
16	Colorado	565		6	North Dakota	596
33	Connecticut	512		7	Missouri	594
46	Delaware	496		8	Kansas	590
46	Florida	496		9	Nebraska	585
49	Georgia	495		10	Michigan	579
40	Hawaii	506		11	Oklahoma	571
24	Idaho	539		11	Wyoming	571
2	Illinois	611		13	Tennessee	569
37	Indiana	507		14	Louisiana	567
1	Iowa	613		15	Arkansas	566
8	Kansas	590		16	Colorado	565
16	Kentucky	565		16	Kentucky	565
14	Louisiana	567		18	Alabama	556
50	Maine	465		18	Utah	556
43	Maryland	502		20	Mississippi	549
28	Massachusetts	522		21	New Mexico	546
10	Michigan	579		22	Montana	543
3	Minnesota	603		23	Ohio	542
20	Mississippi	549		24	Idaho	539
7	Missouri	594		25	Washington	531
22	Montana	543		26	Oregon	526
9	Nebraska	585		27	Arizona	525
40	Nevada	506		28	Massachusetts	522
29	New Hampshire	521		29	New Hampshire	521
35	New Jersey	510		30	Vermont	518
21	New Mexico	546		31	Alaska	517
42	New York	505		32	California	516
36	North Carolina	509		33	Connecticut	512
6	North Dakota	596		34	Virginia	511
23	Ohio	542		35	New Jersey	510
11	Oklahoma	571		36	North Carolina	509
26	Oregon	526		37	Indiana	507
44	Pennsylvania	499		37	Texas	507
45	Rhode Island	498		37	West Virginia	507
46	South Carolina	496		40	Hawaii	506
4	South Dakota	602		40	Nevada	506
13	Tennessee	569		42	New York	505
37	Texas	507		43	Maryland	502
18	Utah	556		44	Pennsylvania	499
30	Vermont	518		45	Rhode Island	498
34	Virginia	511		46	Delaware	496
25	Washington	531		46	Florida	496
37	West Virginia	507		46	South Carolina	496
5	Wisconsin	598		49	Georgia	495
11	Wyoming	571		50	Maine	465
					District of Columbia	462

Source: The College Board, New York, NY

    "2007 College-Bound Seniors" (http://www.collegeboard.com/about/news_info/cbsenior/yr2007/links.html)

*The SAT score range is 200 to 800. The College Board strongly cautions against comparing states based on SAT scores alone. The percentage of high school students taking the test varies greatly from one state to another. For example, three percent of graduating seniors in South Dakota took the test compared to 100 percent of such students in Maine. The SAT was formerly known as the Scholastic Aptitude Test.

Average Critical Reading SAT Score in 2007

National Average Score = 502*

<table>
<tr><td colspan="3">ALPHA ORDER</td><td colspan="3">RANK ORDER</td></tr>
<tr><td>RANK</td><td>STATE</td><td>AVERAGE SCORE</td><td>RANK</td><td>STATE</td><td>AVERAGE SCORE</td></tr>
<tr><td>18</td><td>Alabama</td><td>563</td><td>1</td><td>Iowa</td><td>608</td></tr>
<tr><td>28</td><td>Alaska</td><td>519</td><td>2</td><td>Minnesota</td><td>596</td></tr>
<tr><td>28</td><td>Arizona</td><td>519</td><td>3</td><td>Illinois</td><td>594</td></tr>
<tr><td>10</td><td>Arkansas</td><td>578</td><td>3</td><td>Missouri</td><td>594</td></tr>
<tr><td>37</td><td>California</td><td>499</td><td>5</td><td>South Dakota</td><td>589</td></tr>
<tr><td>19</td><td>Colorado</td><td>560</td><td>6</td><td>Wisconsin</td><td>587</td></tr>
<tr><td>34</td><td>Connecticut</td><td>510</td><td>7</td><td>North Dakota</td><td>584</td></tr>
<tr><td>38</td><td>Delaware</td><td>497</td><td>8</td><td>Kansas</td><td>583</td></tr>
<tr><td>38</td><td>Florida</td><td>497</td><td>9</td><td>Nebraska</td><td>579</td></tr>
<tr><td>44</td><td>Georgia</td><td>494</td><td>10</td><td>Arkansas</td><td>578</td></tr>
<tr><td>49</td><td>Hawaii</td><td>484</td><td>10</td><td>Oklahoma</td><td>578</td></tr>
<tr><td>22</td><td>Idaho</td><td>541</td><td>12</td><td>Tennessee</td><td>574</td></tr>
<tr><td>3</td><td>Illinois</td><td>594</td><td>13</td><td>Louisiana</td><td>569</td></tr>
<tr><td>38</td><td>Indiana</td><td>497</td><td>14</td><td>Michigan</td><td>568</td></tr>
<tr><td>1</td><td>Iowa</td><td>608</td><td>14</td><td>Mississippi</td><td>568</td></tr>
<tr><td>8</td><td>Kansas</td><td>583</td><td>16</td><td>Kentucky</td><td>567</td></tr>
<tr><td>16</td><td>Kentucky</td><td>567</td><td>17</td><td>Wyoming</td><td>565</td></tr>
<tr><td>13</td><td>Louisiana</td><td>569</td><td>18</td><td>Alabama</td><td>563</td></tr>
<tr><td>50</td><td>Maine</td><td>466</td><td>19</td><td>Colorado</td><td>560</td></tr>
<tr><td>35</td><td>Maryland</td><td>500</td><td>20</td><td>Utah</td><td>558</td></tr>
<tr><td>32</td><td>Massachusetts</td><td>513</td><td>21</td><td>New Mexico</td><td>555</td></tr>
<tr><td>14</td><td>Michigan</td><td>568</td><td>22</td><td>Idaho</td><td>541</td></tr>
<tr><td>2</td><td>Minnesota</td><td>596</td><td>23</td><td>Montana</td><td>538</td></tr>
<tr><td>14</td><td>Mississippi</td><td>568</td><td>24</td><td>Ohio</td><td>536</td></tr>
<tr><td>3</td><td>Missouri</td><td>594</td><td>25</td><td>Washington</td><td>526</td></tr>
<tr><td>23</td><td>Montana</td><td>538</td><td>26</td><td>Oregon</td><td>522</td></tr>
<tr><td>9</td><td>Nebraska</td><td>579</td><td>27</td><td>New Hampshire</td><td>521</td></tr>
<tr><td>35</td><td>Nevada</td><td>500</td><td>28</td><td>Alaska</td><td>519</td></tr>
<tr><td>27</td><td>New Hampshire</td><td>521</td><td>28</td><td>Arizona</td><td>519</td></tr>
<tr><td>42</td><td>New Jersey</td><td>495</td><td>30</td><td>Vermont</td><td>516</td></tr>
<tr><td>21</td><td>New Mexico</td><td>555</td><td>30</td><td>West Virginia</td><td>516</td></tr>
<tr><td>47</td><td>New York</td><td>491</td><td>32</td><td>Massachusetts</td><td>513</td></tr>
<tr><td>42</td><td>North Carolina</td><td>495</td><td>33</td><td>Virginia</td><td>511</td></tr>
<tr><td>7</td><td>North Dakota</td><td>584</td><td>34</td><td>Connecticut</td><td>510</td></tr>
<tr><td>24</td><td>Ohio</td><td>536</td><td>35</td><td>Maryland</td><td>500</td></tr>
<tr><td>10</td><td>Oklahoma</td><td>578</td><td>35</td><td>Nevada</td><td>500</td></tr>
<tr><td>26</td><td>Oregon</td><td>522</td><td>37</td><td>California</td><td>499</td></tr>
<tr><td>45</td><td>Pennsylvania</td><td>493</td><td>38</td><td>Delaware</td><td>497</td></tr>
<tr><td>41</td><td>Rhode Island</td><td>496</td><td>38</td><td>Florida</td><td>497</td></tr>
<tr><td>48</td><td>South Carolina</td><td>488</td><td>38</td><td>Indiana</td><td>497</td></tr>
<tr><td>5</td><td>South Dakota</td><td>589</td><td>41</td><td>Rhode Island</td><td>496</td></tr>
<tr><td>12</td><td>Tennessee</td><td>574</td><td>42</td><td>New Jersey</td><td>495</td></tr>
<tr><td>46</td><td>Texas</td><td>492</td><td>42</td><td>North Carolina</td><td>495</td></tr>
<tr><td>20</td><td>Utah</td><td>558</td><td>44</td><td>Georgia</td><td>494</td></tr>
<tr><td>30</td><td>Vermont</td><td>516</td><td>45</td><td>Pennsylvania</td><td>493</td></tr>
<tr><td>33</td><td>Virginia</td><td>511</td><td>46</td><td>Texas</td><td>492</td></tr>
<tr><td>25</td><td>Washington</td><td>526</td><td>47</td><td>New York</td><td>491</td></tr>
<tr><td>30</td><td>West Virginia</td><td>516</td><td>48</td><td>South Carolina</td><td>488</td></tr>
<tr><td>6</td><td>Wisconsin</td><td>587</td><td>49</td><td>Hawaii</td><td>484</td></tr>
<tr><td>17</td><td>Wyoming</td><td>565</td><td>50</td><td>Maine</td><td>466</td></tr>
<tr><td></td><td></td><td></td><td></td><td>District of Columbia</td><td>478</td></tr>
</table>

Source: The College Board, New York, NY

"2007 College-Bound Seniors" (http://www.collegeboard.com/about/news_info/cbsenior/yr2007/links.html)

*The SAT score range is 200 to 800. The College Board strongly cautions against comparing states based on SAT scores alone. The percentage of high school students taking the test varies greatly from one state to another. For example, three percent of graduating seniors in South Dakota took the test compared to 100 percent of such students in Maine. The SAT was formerly known as the Scholastic Aptitude Test.

Average Writing SAT Score in 2007

National Average Score = 494*

ALPHA ORDER

RANK	STATE	AVERAGE SCORE
15	Alabama	554
38	Alaska	491
31	Arizona	502
9	Arkansas	565
33	California	498
18	Colorado	549
26	Connecticut	511
39	Delaware	486
47	Florida	479
40	Georgia	483
49	Hawaii	473
24	Idaho	519
1	Illinois	588
40	Indiana	483
3	Iowa	586
6	Kansas	569
16	Kentucky	553
10	Louisiana	563
50	Maine	457
35	Maryland	496
26	Massachusetts	511
16	Michigan	553
4	Minnesota	577
13	Mississippi	560
2	Missouri	587
22	Montana	522
11	Nebraska	562
46	Nevada	480
25	New Hampshire	512
36	New Jersey	494
21	New Mexico	540
42	New York	482
42	North Carolina	482
11	North Dakota	562
22	Ohio	522
14	Oklahoma	559
31	Oregon	502
42	Pennsylvania	482
37	Rhode Island	492
48	South Carolina	475
8	South Dakota	567
7	Tennessee	568
42	Texas	482
19	Utah	544
29	Vermont	508
33	Virginia	498
28	Washington	510
30	West Virginia	505
5	Wisconsin	575
19	Wyoming	544

RANK ORDER

RANK	STATE	AVERAGE SCORE
1	Illinois	588
2	Missouri	587
3	Iowa	586
4	Minnesota	577
5	Wisconsin	575
6	Kansas	569
7	Tennessee	568
8	South Dakota	567
9	Arkansas	565
10	Louisiana	563
11	Nebraska	562
11	North Dakota	562
13	Mississippi	560
14	Oklahoma	559
15	Alabama	554
16	Kentucky	553
16	Michigan	553
18	Colorado	549
19	Utah	544
19	Wyoming	544
21	New Mexico	540
22	Montana	522
22	Ohio	522
24	Idaho	519
25	New Hampshire	512
26	Connecticut	511
26	Massachusetts	511
28	Washington	510
29	Vermont	508
30	West Virginia	505
31	Arizona	502
31	Oregon	502
33	California	498
33	Virginia	498
35	Maryland	496
36	New Jersey	494
37	Rhode Island	492
38	Alaska	491
39	Delaware	486
40	Georgia	483
40	Indiana	483
42	New York	482
42	North Carolina	482
42	Pennsylvania	482
42	Texas	482
46	Nevada	480
47	Florida	479
48	South Carolina	475
49	Hawaii	473
50	Maine	457
	District of Columbia	471

Source: The College Board, New York, NY
   "2007 College-Bound Seniors" (http://www.collegeboard.com/about/news_info/cbsenior/yr2007/links.html)
*The SAT score range is 200 to 800. The College Board strongly cautions against comparing states based on SAT scores alone.
The percentage of high school students taking the test varies greatly from one state to another. For example, three percent of
graduating seniors in South Dakota took the test compared to 100 percent of such students in Maine.   The SAT was formerly
known as the Scholastic Aptitude Test.

Average Reading Score for Public School Fourth Graders in 2007

National Average Score = 220*

ALPHA ORDER

RANK	STATE	AVERAGE SCORE
38	Alabama	216
42	Alaska	214
47	Arizona	210
36	Arkansas	217
48	California	209
18	Colorado	224
5	Connecticut	227
12	Delaware	225
18	Florida	224
32	Georgia	219
44	Hawaii	213
22	Idaho	223
32	Illinois	219
26	Indiana	222
12	Iowa	225
12	Kansas	225
26	Kentucky	222
50	Louisiana	207
8	Maine	226
12	Maryland	225
1	Massachusetts	236
30	Michigan	220
12	Minnesota	225
49	Mississippi	208
28	Missouri	221
5	Montana	227
22	Nebraska	223
46	Nevada	211
3	New Hampshire	229
2	New Jersey	231
45	New Mexico	212
18	New York	224
35	North Carolina	218
8	North Dakota	226
8	Ohio	226
36	Oklahoma	217
40	Oregon	215
8	Pennsylvania	226
32	Rhode Island	219
42	South Carolina	214
22	South Dakota	223
38	Tennessee	216
30	Texas	220
28	Utah	221
4	Vermont	228
5	Virginia	227
18	Washington	224
40	West Virginia	215
22	Wisconsin	223
12	Wyoming	225

RANK ORDER

RANK	STATE	AVERAGE SCORE
1	Massachusetts	236
2	New Jersey	231
3	New Hampshire	229
4	Vermont	228
5	Connecticut	227
5	Montana	227
5	Virginia	227
8	Maine	226
8	North Dakota	226
8	Ohio	226
8	Pennsylvania	226
12	Delaware	225
12	Iowa	225
12	Kansas	225
12	Maryland	225
12	Minnesota	225
12	Wyoming	225
18	Colorado	224
18	Florida	224
18	New York	224
18	Washington	224
22	Idaho	223
22	Nebraska	223
22	South Dakota	223
22	Wisconsin	223
26	Indiana	222
26	Kentucky	222
28	Missouri	221
28	Utah	221
30	Michigan	220
30	Texas	220
32	Georgia	219
32	Illinois	219
32	Rhode Island	219
35	North Carolina	218
36	Arkansas	217
36	Oklahoma	217
38	Alabama	216
38	Tennessee	216
40	Oregon	215
40	West Virginia	215
42	Alaska	214
42	South Carolina	214
44	Hawaii	213
45	New Mexico	212
46	Nevada	211
47	Arizona	210
48	California	209
49	Mississippi	208
50	Louisiana	207
	District of Columbia	197

Source: U.S. Department of Education, National Center for Education Statistics
   "The Nation's Report Card: Reading 2007" (http://nces.ed.gov/nationsreportcard/)
*These scores are from the National Assessment of Educational Progress (NAEP). Scale ranges from 0 to 500.

Average Reading Score for Public School Fourth Grade Males in 2007

National Average = 216*

<table>
<tr><td colspan="3">ALPHA ORDER</td><td colspan="3">RANK ORDER</td></tr>
<tr><th>RANK</th><th>STATE</th><th>AVERAGE SCORE</th><th>RANK</th><th>STATE</th><th>AVERAGE SCORE</th></tr>
<tr><td>37</td><td>Alabama</td><td>213</td><td>1</td><td>Massachusetts</td><td>233</td></tr>
<tr><td>42</td><td>Alaska</td><td>210</td><td>2</td><td>New Jersey</td><td>228</td></tr>
<tr><td>47</td><td>Arizona</td><td>206</td><td>3</td><td>New Hampshire</td><td>226</td></tr>
<tr><td>37</td><td>Arkansas</td><td>213</td><td>4</td><td>Montana</td><td>225</td></tr>
<tr><td>48</td><td>California</td><td>204</td><td>4</td><td>Vermont</td><td>225</td></tr>
<tr><td>17</td><td>Colorado</td><td>221</td><td>6</td><td>Connecticut</td><td>224</td></tr>
<tr><td>6</td><td>Connecticut</td><td>224</td><td>6</td><td>North Dakota</td><td>224</td></tr>
<tr><td>13</td><td>Delaware</td><td>222</td><td>6</td><td>Virginia</td><td>224</td></tr>
<tr><td>23</td><td>Florida</td><td>220</td><td>9</td><td>Maine</td><td>223</td></tr>
<tr><td>31</td><td>Georgia</td><td>216</td><td>9</td><td>Minnesota</td><td>223</td></tr>
<tr><td>45</td><td>Hawaii</td><td>208</td><td>9</td><td>Ohio</td><td>223</td></tr>
<tr><td>17</td><td>Idaho</td><td>221</td><td>9</td><td>Pennsylvania</td><td>223</td></tr>
<tr><td>28</td><td>Illinois</td><td>217</td><td>13</td><td>Delaware</td><td>222</td></tr>
<tr><td>26</td><td>Indiana</td><td>219</td><td>13</td><td>Iowa</td><td>222</td></tr>
<tr><td>13</td><td>Iowa</td><td>222</td><td>13</td><td>Wisconsin</td><td>222</td></tr>
<tr><td>17</td><td>Kansas</td><td>221</td><td>13</td><td>Wyoming</td><td>222</td></tr>
<tr><td>26</td><td>Kentucky</td><td>219</td><td>17</td><td>Colorado</td><td>221</td></tr>
<tr><td>50</td><td>Louisiana</td><td>203</td><td>17</td><td>Idaho</td><td>221</td></tr>
<tr><td>9</td><td>Maine</td><td>223</td><td>17</td><td>Kansas</td><td>221</td></tr>
<tr><td>17</td><td>Maryland</td><td>221</td><td>17</td><td>Maryland</td><td>221</td></tr>
<tr><td>1</td><td>Massachusetts</td><td>233</td><td>17</td><td>Nebraska</td><td>221</td></tr>
<tr><td>31</td><td>Michigan</td><td>216</td><td>17</td><td>Washington</td><td>221</td></tr>
<tr><td>9</td><td>Minnesota</td><td>223</td><td>23</td><td>Florida</td><td>220</td></tr>
<tr><td>48</td><td>Mississippi</td><td>204</td><td>23</td><td>New York</td><td>220</td></tr>
<tr><td>31</td><td>Missouri</td><td>216</td><td>23</td><td>South Dakota</td><td>220</td></tr>
<tr><td>4</td><td>Montana</td><td>225</td><td>26</td><td>Indiana</td><td>219</td></tr>
<tr><td>17</td><td>Nebraska</td><td>221</td><td>26</td><td>Kentucky</td><td>219</td></tr>
<tr><td>45</td><td>Nevada</td><td>208</td><td>28</td><td>Illinois</td><td>217</td></tr>
<tr><td>3</td><td>New Hampshire</td><td>226</td><td>28</td><td>Texas</td><td>217</td></tr>
<tr><td>2</td><td>New Jersey</td><td>228</td><td>28</td><td>Utah</td><td>217</td></tr>
<tr><td>42</td><td>New Mexico</td><td>210</td><td>31</td><td>Georgia</td><td>216</td></tr>
<tr><td>23</td><td>New York</td><td>220</td><td>31</td><td>Michigan</td><td>216</td></tr>
<tr><td>35</td><td>North Carolina</td><td>214</td><td>31</td><td>Missouri</td><td>216</td></tr>
<tr><td>6</td><td>North Dakota</td><td>224</td><td>34</td><td>Rhode Island</td><td>215</td></tr>
<tr><td>9</td><td>Ohio</td><td>223</td><td>35</td><td>North Carolina</td><td>214</td></tr>
<tr><td>35</td><td>Oklahoma</td><td>214</td><td>35</td><td>Oklahoma</td><td>214</td></tr>
<tr><td>40</td><td>Oregon</td><td>212</td><td>37</td><td>Alabama</td><td>213</td></tr>
<tr><td>9</td><td>Pennsylvania</td><td>223</td><td>37</td><td>Arkansas</td><td>213</td></tr>
<tr><td>34</td><td>Rhode Island</td><td>215</td><td>37</td><td>Tennessee</td><td>213</td></tr>
<tr><td>42</td><td>South Carolina</td><td>210</td><td>40</td><td>Oregon</td><td>212</td></tr>
<tr><td>23</td><td>South Dakota</td><td>220</td><td>41</td><td>West Virginia</td><td>211</td></tr>
<tr><td>37</td><td>Tennessee</td><td>213</td><td>42</td><td>Alaska</td><td>210</td></tr>
<tr><td>28</td><td>Texas</td><td>217</td><td>42</td><td>New Mexico</td><td>210</td></tr>
<tr><td>28</td><td>Utah</td><td>217</td><td>42</td><td>South Carolina</td><td>210</td></tr>
<tr><td>4</td><td>Vermont</td><td>225</td><td>45</td><td>Hawaii</td><td>208</td></tr>
<tr><td>6</td><td>Virginia</td><td>224</td><td>45</td><td>Nevada</td><td>208</td></tr>
<tr><td>17</td><td>Washington</td><td>221</td><td>47</td><td>Arizona</td><td>206</td></tr>
<tr><td>41</td><td>West Virginia</td><td>211</td><td>48</td><td>California</td><td>204</td></tr>
<tr><td>13</td><td>Wisconsin</td><td>222</td><td>48</td><td>Mississippi</td><td>204</td></tr>
<tr><td>13</td><td>Wyoming</td><td>222</td><td>50</td><td>Louisiana</td><td>203</td></tr>
<tr><td></td><td></td><td></td><td></td><td>District of Columbia</td><td>194</td></tr>
</table>

Source: U.S. Department of Education, National Center for Education Statistics
"The Nation's Report Card: Reading 2007" (http://nces.ed.gov/nationsreportcard/)
*These scores are from the National Assessment of Educational Progress (NAEP). Scale ranges from 0 to 500.

Average Reading Score for Public School Fourth Grade Females in 2007

National Average Score = 223*

ALPHA ORDER

RANK	STATE	AVERAGE SCORE
39	Alabama	219
39	Alaska	219
45	Arizona	214
36	Arkansas	221
47	California	213
22	Colorado	226
5	Connecticut	231
9	Delaware	228
17	Florida	227
33	Georgia	222
39	Hawaii	219
22	Idaho	226
33	Illinois	222
28	Indiana	224
9	Iowa	228
9	Kansas	228
22	Kentucky	226
49	Louisiana	212
9	Maine	228
9	Maryland	228
1	Massachusetts	238
28	Michigan	224
17	Minnesota	227
49	Mississippi	212
25	Missouri	225
9	Montana	228
25	Nebraska	225
45	Nevada	214
3	New Hampshire	232
2	New Jersey	234
47	New Mexico	213
17	New York	227
33	North Carolina	222
8	North Dakota	229
9	Ohio	228
37	Oklahoma	220
43	Oregon	218
6	Pennsylvania	230
31	Rhode Island	223
43	South Carolina	218
17	South Dakota	227
39	Tennessee	219
31	Texas	223
25	Utah	225
3	Vermont	232
6	Virginia	230
17	Washington	227
37	West Virginia	220
28	Wisconsin	224
9	Wyoming	228

RANK ORDER

RANK	STATE	AVERAGE SCORE
1	Massachusetts	238
2	New Jersey	234
3	New Hampshire	232
3	Vermont	232
5	Connecticut	231
6	Pennsylvania	230
6	Virginia	230
8	North Dakota	229
9	Delaware	228
9	Iowa	228
9	Kansas	228
9	Maine	228
9	Maryland	228
9	Montana	228
9	Ohio	228
9	Wyoming	228
17	Florida	227
17	Minnesota	227
17	New York	227
17	South Dakota	227
17	Washington	227
22	Colorado	226
22	Idaho	226
22	Kentucky	226
25	Missouri	225
25	Nebraska	225
25	Utah	225
28	Indiana	224
28	Michigan	224
28	Wisconsin	224
31	Rhode Island	223
31	Texas	223
33	Georgia	222
33	Illinois	222
33	North Carolina	222
36	Arkansas	221
37	Oklahoma	220
37	West Virginia	220
39	Alabama	219
39	Alaska	219
39	Hawaii	219
39	Tennessee	219
43	Oregon	218
43	South Carolina	218
45	Arizona	214
45	Nevada	214
47	California	213
47	New Mexico	213
49	Louisiana	212
49	Mississippi	212
	District of Columbia	200

Source: U.S. Department of Education, National Center for Education Statistics
"The Nation's Report Card: Reading 2007" (http://nces.ed.gov/nationsreportcard/)
*These scores are from the National Assessment of Educational Progress (NAEP). Scale ranges from 0 to 500.

Average Reading Score for Public School Fourth Graders Eligible for Free or Reduced Price Lunch Program in 2007
National Average Score = 205*

ALPHA ORDER			RANK ORDER		
RANK	STATE	AVERAGE SCORE	RANK	STATE	AVERAGE SCORE
37	Alabama	203	1	Montana	215
47	Alaska	197	1	North Dakota	215
49	Arizona	196	3	Delaware	214
32	Arkansas	205	3	Massachusetts	214
50	California	195	3	Wyoming	214
29	Colorado	206	6	Florida	213
42	Connecticut	201	6	Maine	213
3	Delaware	214	6	Virginia	213
6	Florida	213	9	Idaho	212
26	Georgia	207	9	Iowa	212
37	Hawaii	203	9	Kansas	212
9	Idaho	212	9	Kentucky	212
35	Illinois	204	9	New Hampshire	212
18	Indiana	209	9	Vermont	212
9	Iowa	212	15	Ohio	211
9	Kansas	212	16	New Jersey	210
9	Kentucky	212	16	Washington	210
44	Louisiana	200	18	Indiana	209
6	Maine	213	18	New York	209
26	Maryland	207	18	Oklahoma	209
3	Massachusetts	214	18	South Dakota	209
35	Michigan	204	18	Texas	209
29	Minnesota	206	23	Missouri	208
44	Mississippi	200	23	Nebraska	208
23	Missouri	208	23	Utah	208
1	Montana	215	26	Georgia	207
23	Nebraska	208	26	Maryland	207
47	Nevada	197	26	Pennsylvania	207
9	New Hampshire	212	29	Colorado	206
16	New Jersey	210	29	Minnesota	206
37	New Mexico	203	29	West Virginia	206
18	New York	209	32	Arkansas	205
32	North Carolina	205	32	North Carolina	205
1	North Dakota	215	32	Wisconsin	205
15	Ohio	211	35	Illinois	204
18	Oklahoma	209	35	Michigan	204
44	Oregon	200	37	Alabama	203
26	Pennsylvania	207	37	Hawaii	203
40	Rhode Island	202	37	New Mexico	203
42	South Carolina	201	40	Rhode Island	202
18	South Dakota	209	40	Tennessee	202
40	Tennessee	202	42	Connecticut	201
18	Texas	209	42	South Carolina	201
23	Utah	208	44	Louisiana	200
9	Vermont	212	44	Mississippi	200
6	Virginia	213	44	Oregon	200
16	Washington	210	47	Alaska	197
29	West Virginia	206	47	Nevada	197
32	Wisconsin	205	49	Arizona	196
3	Wyoming	214	50	California	195
				District of Columbia	188

Source: U.S. Department of Education, National Center for Education Statistics
"The Nation's Report Card: Reading 2007" (http://nces.ed.gov/nationsreportcard/)
*These scores are from the National Assessment of Educational Progress (NAEP). Scale ranges from 0 to 500.

Percent of Public School Fourth Graders
Proficient or Better in Reading in 2007
National Percent = 32%*

ALPHA ORDER

RANK	STATE	PERCENT
34	Alabama	29
34	Alaska	29
45	Arizona	24
34	Arkansas	29
48	California	23
10	Colorado	36
3	Connecticut	41
23	Delaware	34
23	Florida	34
38	Georgia	28
43	Hawaii	26
20	Idaho	35
29	Illinois	32
27	Indiana	33
10	Iowa	36
10	Kansas	36
27	Kentucky	33
49	Louisiana	20
10	Maine	36
10	Maryland	36
1	Massachusetts	49
29	Michigan	32
9	Minnesota	37
50	Mississippi	19
29	Missouri	32
7	Montana	39
20	Nebraska	35
45	Nevada	24
3	New Hampshire	41
2	New Jersey	43
45	New Mexico	24
10	New York	36
34	North Carolina	29
20	North Dakota	35
10	Ohio	36
41	Oklahoma	27
38	Oregon	28
6	Pennsylvania	40
32	Rhode Island	31
43	South Carolina	26
23	South Dakota	34
41	Tennessee	27
33	Texas	30
23	Utah	34
3	Vermont	41
8	Virginia	38
10	Washington	36
38	West Virginia	28
10	Wisconsin	36
10	Wyoming	36

RANK ORDER

RANK	STATE	PERCENT
1	Massachusetts	49
2	New Jersey	43
3	Connecticut	41
3	New Hampshire	41
3	Vermont	41
6	Pennsylvania	40
7	Montana	39
8	Virginia	38
9	Minnesota	37
10	Colorado	36
10	Iowa	36
10	Kansas	36
10	Maine	36
10	Maryland	36
10	New York	36
10	Ohio	36
10	Washington	36
10	Wisconsin	36
10	Wyoming	36
20	Idaho	35
20	Nebraska	35
20	North Dakota	35
23	Delaware	34
23	Florida	34
23	South Dakota	34
23	Utah	34
27	Indiana	33
27	Kentucky	33
29	Illinois	32
29	Michigan	32
29	Missouri	32
32	Rhode Island	31
33	Texas	30
34	Alabama	29
34	Alaska	29
34	Arkansas	29
34	North Carolina	29
38	Georgia	28
38	Oregon	28
38	West Virginia	28
41	Oklahoma	27
41	Tennessee	27
43	Hawaii	26
43	South Carolina	26
45	Arizona	24
45	Nevada	24
45	New Mexico	24
48	California	23
49	Louisiana	20
50	Mississippi	19

	District of Columbia	14

Source: U.S. Department of Education, National Center for Education Statistics
   "The Nation's Report Card: Reading 2007" (http://nces.ed.gov/nationsreportcard/)
*There are four achievement levels: Below Basic, Basic, Proficient, and Advanced. Proficient represents solid academic mastery for 4th graders. Students reaching this level have demonstrated competency over challenging subject matter, including subject matter knowledge, application of such knowledge to real-world situations, and analytical skills appropriate to the subject matter.

Percent of Public School Fourth Grade Males
Proficient or Better in Reading in 2007
National Percent = 29%*

ALPHA ORDER

RANK	STATE	PERCENT
31	Alabama	27
41	Alaska	24
46	Arizona	22
36	Arkansas	25
48	California	19
10	Colorado	34
3	Connecticut	37
29	Delaware	29
24	Florida	30
36	Georgia	25
46	Hawaii	22
19	Idaho	32
24	Illinois	30
23	Indiana	31
19	Iowa	32
14	Kansas	33
24	Kentucky	30
49	Louisiana	17
14	Maine	33
19	Maryland	32
1	Massachusetts	46
29	Michigan	29
8	Minnesota	35
50	Mississippi	16
31	Missouri	27
7	Montana	36
14	Nebraska	33
44	Nevada	23
3	New Hampshire	37
2	New Jersey	39
41	New Mexico	24
14	New York	33
35	North Carolina	26
19	North Dakota	32
14	Ohio	33
36	Oklahoma	25
36	Oregon	25
3	Pennsylvania	37
31	Rhode Island	27
44	South Carolina	23
24	South Dakota	30
36	Tennessee	25
31	Texas	27
24	Utah	30
3	Vermont	37
10	Virginia	34
10	Washington	34
41	West Virginia	24
8	Wisconsin	35
10	Wyoming	34

RANK ORDER

RANK	STATE	PERCENT
1	Massachusetts	46
2	New Jersey	39
3	Connecticut	37
3	New Hampshire	37
3	Pennsylvania	37
3	Vermont	37
7	Montana	36
8	Minnesota	35
8	Wisconsin	35
10	Colorado	34
10	Virginia	34
10	Washington	34
10	Wyoming	34
14	Kansas	33
14	Maine	33
14	Nebraska	33
14	New York	33
14	Ohio	33
19	Idaho	32
19	Iowa	32
19	Maryland	32
19	North Dakota	32
23	Indiana	31
24	Florida	30
24	Illinois	30
24	Kentucky	30
24	South Dakota	30
24	Utah	30
29	Delaware	29
29	Michigan	29
31	Alabama	27
31	Missouri	27
31	Rhode Island	27
31	Texas	27
35	North Carolina	26
36	Arkansas	25
36	Georgia	25
36	Oklahoma	25
36	Oregon	25
36	Tennessee	25
41	Alaska	24
41	New Mexico	24
41	West Virginia	24
44	Nevada	23
44	South Carolina	23
46	Arizona	22
46	Hawaii	22
48	California	19
49	Louisiana	17
50	Mississippi	16

	District of Columbia	12

Source: U.S. Department of Education, National Center for Education Statistics
   "The Nation's Report Card: Reading 2007" (http://nces.ed.gov/nationsreportcard/)
*There are four achievement levels: Below Basic, Basic, Proficient, and Advanced. Proficient represents solid academic
mastery for 4th graders. Students reaching this level have demonstrated competency over challenging subject matter, including
subject matter knowledge, application of such knowledge to real-world situations, and analytical skills appropriate to the subject
matter.

Percent of Public School Fourth Grade Females
Proficient or Better in Reading in 2007
National Percent = 35%*

ALPHA ORDER

ALPHA ORDER

RANK	STATE	PERCENT
39	Alabama	31
33	Alaska	33
45	Arizona	27
36	Arkansas	32
46	California	26
18	Colorado	38
3	Connecticut	46
18	Delaware	38
18	Florida	38
39	Georgia	31
41	Hawaii	29
18	Idaho	38
30	Illinois	35
30	Indiana	35
9	Iowa	40
9	Kansas	40
25	Kentucky	37
49	Louisiana	23
18	Maine	38
9	Maryland	40
1	Massachusetts	52
27	Michigan	36
12	Minnesota	39
50	Mississippi	22
25	Missouri	37
7	Montana	41
27	Nebraska	36
46	Nevada	26
3	New Hampshire	46
2	New Jersey	47
48	New Mexico	24
12	New York	39
33	North Carolina	33
12	North Dakota	39
12	Ohio	39
41	Oklahoma	29
36	Oregon	32
6	Pennsylvania	44
30	Rhode Island	35
41	South Carolina	29
18	South Dakota	38
41	Tennessee	29
33	Texas	33
18	Utah	38
5	Vermont	45
7	Virginia	41
12	Washington	39
36	West Virginia	32
27	Wisconsin	36
12	Wyoming	39

RANK ORDER

RANK	STATE	PERCENT
1	Massachusetts	52
2	New Jersey	47
3	Connecticut	46
3	New Hampshire	46
5	Vermont	45
6	Pennsylvania	44
7	Montana	41
7	Virginia	41
9	Iowa	40
9	Kansas	40
9	Maryland	40
12	Minnesota	39
12	New York	39
12	North Dakota	39
12	Ohio	39
12	Washington	39
12	Wyoming	39
18	Colorado	38
18	Delaware	38
18	Florida	38
18	Idaho	38
18	Maine	38
18	South Dakota	38
18	Utah	38
25	Kentucky	37
25	Missouri	37
27	Michigan	36
27	Nebraska	36
27	Wisconsin	36
30	Illinois	35
30	Indiana	35
30	Rhode Island	35
33	Alaska	33
33	North Carolina	33
33	Texas	33
36	Arkansas	32
36	Oregon	32
36	West Virginia	32
39	Alabama	31
39	Georgia	31
41	Hawaii	29
41	Oklahoma	29
41	South Carolina	29
41	Tennessee	29
45	Arizona	27
46	California	26
46	Nevada	26
48	New Mexico	24
49	Louisiana	23
50	Mississippi	22

	District of Columbia	16

Source: U.S. Department of Education, National Center for Education Statistics
    "The Nation's Report Card: Reading 2007" (http://nces.ed.gov/nationsreportcard/)
*There are four achievement levels: Below Basic, Basic, Proficient, and Advanced. Proficient represents solid academic mastery for 4th graders. Students reaching this level have demonstrated competency over challenging subject matter, including subject matter knowledge, application of such knowledge to real-world situations, and analytical skills appropriate to the subject matter.

Percent of Public School Fourth Graders Eligible for Free or Reduced Price Lunch Program Proficient or Better in Reading in 2007
National Percent = 17%*

ALPHA ORDER

RANK	STATE	PERCENT
37	Alabama	15
37	Alaska	15
46	Arizona	13
29	Arkansas	17
50	California	11
29	Colorado	17
46	Connecticut	13
19	Delaware	19
6	Florida	22
37	Georgia	15
32	Hawaii	16
3	Idaho	23
32	Illinois	16
19	Indiana	19
6	Iowa	22
9	Kansas	21
9	Kentucky	21
41	Louisiana	14
14	Maine	20
32	Maryland	16
6	Massachusetts	22
32	Michigan	16
19	Minnesota	19
49	Mississippi	12
27	Missouri	18
1	Montana	26
14	Nebraska	20
46	Nevada	13
9	New Hampshire	21
14	New Jersey	20
37	New Mexico	15
14	New York	20
32	North Carolina	16
3	North Dakota	23
19	Ohio	19
19	Oklahoma	19
41	Oregon	14
19	Pennsylvania	19
41	Rhode Island	14
41	South Carolina	14
19	South Dakota	19
41	Tennessee	14
29	Texas	17
3	Utah	23
9	Vermont	21
14	Virginia	20
9	Washington	21
19	West Virginia	19
27	Wisconsin	18
2	Wyoming	24

RANK ORDER

RANK	STATE	PERCENT
1	Montana	26
2	Wyoming	24
3	Idaho	23
3	North Dakota	23
3	Utah	23
6	Florida	22
6	Iowa	22
6	Massachusetts	22
9	Kansas	21
9	Kentucky	21
9	New Hampshire	21
9	Vermont	21
9	Washington	21
14	Maine	20
14	Nebraska	20
14	New Jersey	20
14	New York	20
14	Virginia	20
19	Delaware	19
19	Indiana	19
19	Minnesota	19
19	Ohio	19
19	Oklahoma	19
19	Pennsylvania	19
19	South Dakota	19
19	West Virginia	19
27	Missouri	18
27	Wisconsin	18
29	Arkansas	17
29	Colorado	17
29	Texas	17
32	Hawaii	16
32	Illinois	16
32	Maryland	16
32	Michigan	16
32	North Carolina	16
37	Alabama	15
37	Alaska	15
37	Georgia	15
37	New Mexico	15
41	Louisiana	14
41	Oregon	14
41	Rhode Island	14
41	South Carolina	14
41	Tennessee	14
46	Arizona	13
46	Connecticut	13
46	Nevada	13
49	Mississippi	12
50	California	11

	District of Columbia	6

Source: U.S. Department of Education, National Center for Education Statistics
   "The Nation's Report Card: Reading 2007" (http://nces.ed.gov/nationsreportcard/)
*There are four achievement levels: Below Basic, Basic, Proficient, and Advanced. Proficient represents solid academic mastery for 4th graders. Students reaching this level have demonstrated competency over challenging subject matter, including subject matter knowledge, application of such knowledge to real-world situations, and analytical skills appropriate to the subject matter.

Percent of White Public School Fourth Graders
Proficient or Better in Reading in 2007
National Percent = 42%*

ALPHA ORDER

RANK	STATE	PERCENT
27	Alabama	39
21	Alaska	40
39	Arizona	36
39	Arkansas	36
21	California	40
5	Colorado	47
2	Connecticut	52
9	Delaware	44
9	Florida	44
21	Georgia	40
21	Hawaii	40
27	Idaho	39
12	Illinois	42
36	Indiana	37
33	Iowa	38
17	Kansas	41
39	Kentucky	36
47	Louisiana	31
39	Maine	36
4	Maryland	49
1	Massachusetts	56
27	Michigan	39
12	Minnesota	42
47	Mississippi	31
36	Missouri	37
12	Montana	42
21	Nebraska	40
43	Nevada	35
12	New Hampshire	42
2	New Jersey	52
21	New Mexico	40
5	New York	47
27	North Carolina	39
33	North Dakota	38
12	Ohio	42
47	Oklahoma	31
45	Oregon	34
5	Pennsylvania	47
27	Rhode Island	39
43	South Carolina	35
36	South Dakota	37
45	Tennessee	34
9	Texas	44
33	Utah	38
17	Vermont	41
8	Virginia	46
17	Washington	41
50	West Virginia	28
17	Wisconsin	41
27	Wyoming	39

RANK ORDER

RANK	STATE	PERCENT
1	Massachusetts	56
2	Connecticut	52
2	New Jersey	52
4	Maryland	49
5	Colorado	47
5	New York	47
5	Pennsylvania	47
8	Virginia	46
9	Delaware	44
9	Florida	44
9	Texas	44
12	Illinois	42
12	Minnesota	42
12	Montana	42
12	New Hampshire	42
12	Ohio	42
17	Kansas	41
17	Vermont	41
17	Washington	41
17	Wisconsin	41
21	Alaska	40
21	California	40
21	Georgia	40
21	Hawaii	40
21	Nebraska	40
21	New Mexico	40
27	Alabama	39
27	Idaho	39
27	Michigan	39
27	North Carolina	39
27	Rhode Island	39
27	Wyoming	39
33	Iowa	38
33	North Dakota	38
33	Utah	38
36	Indiana	37
36	Missouri	37
36	South Dakota	37
39	Arizona	36
39	Arkansas	36
39	Kentucky	36
39	Maine	36
43	Nevada	35
43	South Carolina	35
45	Oregon	34
45	Tennessee	34
47	Louisiana	31
47	Mississippi	31
47	Oklahoma	31
50	West Virginia	28

District of Columbia	74

Source: U.S. Department of Education, National Center for Education Statistics
"The Nation's Report Card: Reading 2007" (http://nces.ed.gov/nationsreportcard/)
*There are four achievement levels: Below Basic, Basic, Proficient, and Advanced. Proficient represents solid academic mastery for 4th graders. Students reaching this level have demonstrated competency over challenging subject matter, including subject matter knowledge, application of such knowledge to real-world situations, and analytical skills appropriate to the subject matter.

Percent of Black Public School Fourth Graders
Proficient or Better in Reading in 2007
National Percent = 14%*

ALPHA ORDER

RANK	STATE	PERCENT
24	Alabama	13
5	Alaska	20
5	Arizona	20
39	Arkansas	9
24	California	13
9	Colorado	18
18	Connecticut	15
9	Delaware	18
15	Florida	16
20	Georgia	14
2	Hawaii	23
NA	Idaho**	NA
20	Illinois	14
28	Indiana	12
15	Iowa	16
9	Kansas	18
20	Kentucky	14
39	Louisiana	9
NA	Maine**	NA
12	Maryland	17
7	Massachusetts	19
28	Michigan	12
28	Minnesota	12
41	Mississippi	8
28	Missouri	12
NA	Montana**	NA
36	Nebraska	10
15	Nevada	16
1	New Hampshire	25
3	New Jersey	22
18	New Mexico	15
12	New York	17
28	North Carolina	12
NA	North Dakota**	NA
20	Ohio	14
34	Oklahoma	11
36	Oregon	10
24	Pennsylvania	13
36	Rhode Island	10
28	South Carolina	12
NA	South Dakota**	NA
41	Tennessee	8
12	Texas	17
NA	Utah**	NA
NA	Vermont**	NA
7	Virginia	19
4	Washington	21
24	West Virginia	13
34	Wisconsin	11
NA	Wyoming**	NA

RANK ORDER

RANK	STATE	PERCENT
1	New Hampshire	25
2	Hawaii	23
3	New Jersey	22
4	Washington	21
5	Alaska	20
5	Arizona	20
7	Massachusetts	19
7	Virginia	19
9	Colorado	18
9	Delaware	18
9	Kansas	18
12	Maryland	17
12	New York	17
12	Texas	17
15	Florida	16
15	Iowa	16
15	Nevada	16
18	Connecticut	15
18	New Mexico	15
20	Georgia	14
20	Illinois	14
20	Kentucky	14
20	Ohio	14
24	Alabama	13
24	California	13
24	Pennsylvania	13
24	West Virginia	13
28	Indiana	12
28	Michigan	12
28	Minnesota	12
28	Missouri	12
28	North Carolina	12
28	South Carolina	12
34	Oklahoma	11
34	Wisconsin	11
36	Nebraska	10
36	Oregon	10
36	Rhode Island	10
39	Arkansas	9
39	Louisiana	9
41	Mississippi	8
41	Tennessee	8
NA	Idaho**	NA
NA	Maine**	NA
NA	Montana**	NA
NA	North Dakota**	NA
NA	South Dakota**	NA
NA	Utah**	NA
NA	Vermont**	NA
NA	Wyoming**	NA

	District of Columbia	9

Source: U.S. Department of Education, National Center for Education Statistics
   "The Nation's Report Card: Reading 2007" (http://nces.ed.gov/nationsreportcard/)
*There are four achievement levels: Below Basic, Basic, Proficient, and Advanced. Proficient represents solid academic mastery for 4th graders. Students reaching this level have demonstrated competency over challenging subject matter, including subject matter knowledge, application of such knowledge to real-world situations, and analytical skills appropriate to the subject matter. **Sample size insufficient.

Percent of Hispanic Public School Fourth Graders
Proficient or Better in Reading in 2007
National Percent = 17%*

ALPHA ORDER

RANK	STATE	PERCENT
24	Alabama	17
24	Alaska	17
41	Arizona	13
29	Arkansas	16
43	California	11
34	Colorado	15
29	Connecticut	16
5	Delaware	24
2	Florida	28
8	Georgia	21
8	Hawaii	21
34	Idaho	15
18	Illinois	18
24	Indiana	17
18	Iowa	18
16	Kansas	19
NA	Kentucky**	NA
3	Louisiana	26
NA	Maine**	NA
8	Maryland	21
18	Massachusetts	18
16	Michigan	19
29	Minnesota	16
NA	Mississippi**	NA
7	Missouri	22
1	Montana	30
29	Nebraska	16
40	Nevada	14
14	New Hampshire	20
6	New Jersey	23
29	New Mexico	16
18	New York	18
18	North Carolina	18
NA	North Dakota**	NA
8	Ohio	21
34	Oklahoma	15
44	Oregon	10
34	Pennsylvania	15
42	Rhode Island	12
24	South Carolina	17
34	South Dakota	15
14	Tennessee	20
8	Texas	21
34	Utah	15
NA	Vermont**	NA
3	Virginia	26
18	Washington	18
NA	West Virginia**	NA
24	Wisconsin	17
8	Wyoming	21

RANK ORDER

RANK	STATE	PERCENT
1	Montana	30
2	Florida	28
3	Louisiana	26
3	Virginia	26
5	Delaware	24
6	New Jersey	23
7	Missouri	22
8	Georgia	21
8	Hawaii	21
8	Maryland	21
8	Ohio	21
8	Texas	21
8	Wyoming	21
14	New Hampshire	20
14	Tennessee	20
16	Kansas	19
16	Michigan	19
18	Illinois	18
18	Iowa	18
18	Massachusetts	18
18	New York	18
18	North Carolina	18
18	Washington	18
24	Alabama	17
24	Alaska	17
24	Indiana	17
24	South Carolina	17
24	Wisconsin	17
29	Arkansas	16
29	Connecticut	16
29	Minnesota	16
29	Nebraska	16
29	New Mexico	16
34	Colorado	15
34	Idaho	15
34	Oklahoma	15
34	Pennsylvania	15
34	South Dakota	15
34	Utah	15
40	Nevada	14
41	Arizona	13
42	Rhode Island	12
43	California	11
44	Oregon	10
NA	Kentucky**	NA
NA	Maine**	NA
NA	Mississippi**	NA
NA	North Dakota**	NA
NA	Vermont**	NA
NA	West Virginia**	NA

	District of Columbia	15

Source: U.S. Department of Education, National Center for Education Statistics
   "The Nation's Report Card: Reading 2007" (http://nces.ed.gov/nationsreportcard/)
*There are four achievement levels: Below Basic, Basic, Proficient, and Advanced. Proficient represents solid academic
mastery for 4th graders. Students reaching this level have demonstrated competency over challenging subject matter, including
subject matter knowledge, application of such knowledge to real-world situations, and analytical skills appropriate to the subject
matter. **Sample size insufficient.

Percent of Asian Public School Fourth Graders
Proficient or Better in Reading in 2007
National Percent = 45%*

ALPHA ORDER

RANK	STATE	PERCENT
NA	Alabama**	NA
28	Alaska	28
15	Arizona	46
NA	Arkansas**	NA
18	California	42
13	Colorado	47
3	Connecticut	59
1	Delaware	62
5	Florida	57
9	Georgia	49
30	Hawaii	22
NA	Idaho**	NA
7	Illinois	54
NA	Indiana**	NA
9	Iowa	49
18	Kansas	42
NA	Kentucky**	NA
NA	Louisiana**	NA
NA	Maine**	NA
5	Maryland	57
4	Massachusetts	58
16	Michigan	44
27	Minnesota	29
NA	Mississippi**	NA
NA	Missouri**	NA
NA	Montana**	NA
NA	Nebraska**	NA
25	Nevada	30
17	New Hampshire	43
2	New Jersey	60
NA	New Mexico**	NA
8	New York	50
20	North Carolina	41
NA	North Dakota**	NA
NA	Ohio**	NA
22	Oklahoma	36
24	Oregon	32
20	Pennsylvania	41
25	Rhode Island	30
NA	South Carolina**	NA
NA	South Dakota**	NA
NA	Tennessee**	NA
11	Texas	48
29	Utah	26
NA	Vermont**	NA
11	Virginia	48
13	Washington	47
NA	West Virginia**	NA
23	Wisconsin	33
NA	Wyoming**	NA

RANK ORDER

RANK	STATE	PERCENT
1	Delaware	62
2	New Jersey	60
3	Connecticut	59
4	Massachusetts	58
5	Florida	57
5	Maryland	57
7	Illinois	54
8	New York	50
9	Georgia	49
9	Iowa	49
11	Texas	48
11	Virginia	48
13	Colorado	47
13	Washington	47
15	Arizona	46
16	Michigan	44
17	New Hampshire	43
18	California	42
18	Kansas	42
20	North Carolina	41
20	Pennsylvania	41
22	Oklahoma	36
23	Wisconsin	33
24	Oregon	32
25	Nevada	30
25	Rhode Island	30
27	Minnesota	29
28	Alaska	28
29	Utah	26
30	Hawaii	22
NA	Alabama**	NA
NA	Arkansas**	NA
NA	Idaho**	NA
NA	Indiana**	NA
NA	Kentucky**	NA
NA	Louisiana**	NA
NA	Maine**	NA
NA	Mississippi**	NA
NA	Missouri**	NA
NA	Montana**	NA
NA	Nebraska**	NA
NA	New Mexico**	NA
NA	North Dakota**	NA
NA	Ohio**	NA
NA	South Carolina**	NA
NA	South Dakota**	NA
NA	Tennessee**	NA
NA	Vermont**	NA
NA	West Virginia**	NA
NA	Wyoming**	NA
	District of Columbia**	NA

Source: U.S. Department of Education, National Center for Education Statistics
   "The Nation's Report Card: Reading 2007" (http://nces.ed.gov/nationsreportcard/)
*There are four achievement levels: Below Basic, Basic, Proficient, and Advanced. Proficient represents solid academic mastery for 4th graders. Students reaching this level have demonstrated competency over challenging subject matter, including subject matter knowledge, application of such knowledge to real-world situations, and analytical skills appropriate to the subject matter. **Sample size insufficient.

Percent of Disabled Public School Fourth Graders
Proficient or Better in Reading in 2007
National Percent = 13%*

ALPHA ORDER

RANK	STATE	PERCENT
34	Alabama	11
37	Alaska	10
37	Arizona	10
34	Arkansas	11
44	California	8
21	Colorado	13
28	Connecticut	12
13	Delaware	16
28	Florida	12
7	Georgia	17
49	Hawaii	7
34	Idaho	11
16	Illinois	14
21	Indiana	13
50	Iowa	6
21	Kansas	13
5	Kentucky	18
44	Louisiana	8
16	Maine	14
14	Maryland	15
3	Massachusetts	23
16	Michigan	14
7	Minnesota	17
37	Mississippi	10
28	Missouri	12
21	Montana	13
7	Nebraska	17
4	Nevada	22
16	New Hampshire	14
5	New Jersey	18
21	New Mexico	13
44	New York	8
37	North Carolina	10
7	North Dakota	17
28	Ohio	12
44	Oklahoma	8
41	Oregon	9
14	Pennsylvania	15
28	Rhode Island	12
44	South Carolina	8
7	South Dakota	17
1	Tennessee	25
7	Texas	17
41	Utah	9
28	Vermont	12
2	Virginia	24
21	Washington	13
41	West Virginia	9
16	Wisconsin	14
21	Wyoming	13

RANK ORDER

RANK	STATE	PERCENT
1	Tennessee	25
2	Virginia	24
3	Massachusetts	23
4	Nevada	22
5	Kentucky	18
5	New Jersey	18
7	Georgia	17
7	Minnesota	17
7	Nebraska	17
7	North Dakota	17
7	South Dakota	17
7	Texas	17
13	Delaware	16
14	Maryland	15
14	Pennsylvania	15
16	Illinois	14
16	Maine	14
16	Michigan	14
16	New Hampshire	14
16	Wisconsin	14
21	Colorado	13
21	Indiana	13
21	Kansas	13
21	Montana	13
21	New Mexico	13
21	Washington	13
21	Wyoming	13
28	Connecticut	12
28	Florida	12
28	Missouri	12
28	Ohio	12
28	Rhode Island	12
28	Vermont	12
34	Alabama	11
34	Arkansas	11
34	Idaho	11
37	Alaska	10
37	Arizona	10
37	Mississippi	10
37	North Carolina	10
41	Oregon	9
41	Utah	9
41	West Virginia	9
44	California	8
44	Louisiana	8
44	New York	8
44	Oklahoma	8
44	South Carolina	8
49	Hawaii	7
50	Iowa	6
	District of Columbia	5

Source: U.S. Department of Education, National Center for Education Statistics
   "The Nation's Report Card: Reading 2007" (http://nces.ed.gov/nationsreportcard/)
*There are four achievement levels: Below Basic, Basic, Proficient, and Advanced. Proficient represents solid academic
mastery for 4th graders. Students reaching this level have demonstrated competency over challenging subject matter, including
subject matter knowledge, application of such knowledge to real-world situations, and analytical skills appropriate to the subject
matter. Based only on disabled students who were assessed.

Average Reading Score for Public School Eighth Graders in 2007

National Average Score = 261*

ALPHA ORDER

RANK	STATE	AVERAGE SCORE
45	Alabama	252
35	Alaska	259
42	Arizona	255
39	Arkansas	258
47	California	251
17	Colorado	266
12	Connecticut	267
20	Delaware	265
32	Florida	260
35	Georgia	259
47	Hawaii	251
20	Idaho	265
27	Illinois	263
24	Indiana	264
12	Iowa	267
12	Kansas	267
29	Kentucky	262
44	Louisiana	253
4	Maine	270
20	Maryland	265
1	Massachusetts	273
32	Michigan	260
8	Minnesota	268
50	Mississippi	250
27	Missouri	263
3	Montana	271
12	Nebraska	267
45	Nevada	252
4	New Hampshire	270
4	New Jersey	270
47	New Mexico	251
24	New York	264
35	North Carolina	259
8	North Dakota	268
8	Ohio	268
32	Oklahoma	260
17	Oregon	266
8	Pennsylvania	268
39	Rhode Island	258
41	South Carolina	257
4	South Dakota	270
35	Tennessee	259
31	Texas	261
29	Utah	262
1	Vermont	273
12	Virginia	267
20	Washington	265
42	West Virginia	255
24	Wisconsin	264
17	Wyoming	266

RANK ORDER

RANK	STATE	AVERAGE SCORE
1	Massachusetts	273
1	Vermont	273
3	Montana	271
4	Maine	270
4	New Hampshire	270
4	New Jersey	270
4	South Dakota	270
8	Minnesota	268
8	North Dakota	268
8	Ohio	268
8	Pennsylvania	268
12	Connecticut	267
12	Iowa	267
12	Kansas	267
12	Nebraska	267
12	Virginia	267
17	Colorado	266
17	Oregon	266
17	Wyoming	266
20	Delaware	265
20	Idaho	265
20	Maryland	265
20	Washington	265
24	Indiana	264
24	New York	264
24	Wisconsin	264
27	Illinois	263
27	Missouri	263
29	Kentucky	262
29	Utah	262
31	Texas	261
32	Florida	260
32	Michigan	260
32	Oklahoma	260
35	Alaska	259
35	Georgia	259
35	North Carolina	259
35	Tennessee	259
39	Arkansas	258
39	Rhode Island	258
41	South Carolina	257
42	Arizona	255
42	West Virginia	255
44	Louisiana	253
45	Alabama	252
45	Nevada	252
47	California	251
47	Hawaii	251
47	New Mexico	251
50	Mississippi	250

| | District of Columbia | 241 |

Source: U.S. Department of Education, National Center for Education Statistics
   "The Nation's Report Card: Reading 2007" (http://nces.ed.gov/nationsreportcard/)
*These scores are from the National Assessment of Educational Progress (NAEP). Scale ranges from 0 to 500.

Average Reading Score for Public School Eighth Grade Males in 2007

National Average Score = 256*

ALPHA ORDER

ALPHA ORDER

RANK	STATE	AVERAGE SCORE
45	Alabama	247
38	Alaska	253
42	Arizona	251
38	Arkansas	253
47	California	246
14	Colorado	262
14	Connecticut	262
19	Delaware	260
35	Florida	254
38	Georgia	253
50	Hawaii	244
19	Idaho	260
24	Illinois	259
24	Indiana	259
11	Iowa	263
11	Kansas	263
29	Kentucky	257
43	Louisiana	248
7	Maine	264
19	Maryland	260
1	Massachusetts	269
33	Michigan	255
11	Minnesota	263
47	Mississippi	246
24	Missouri	259
5	Montana	265
14	Nebraska	262
49	Nevada	245
7	New Hampshire	264
3	New Jersey	266
45	New Mexico	247
27	New York	258
35	North Carolina	254
7	North Dakota	264
7	Ohio	264
33	Oklahoma	255
19	Oregon	260
5	Pennsylvania	265
31	Rhode Island	256
38	South Carolina	253
3	South Dakota	266
35	Tennessee	254
31	Texas	256
27	Utah	258
2	Vermont	268
14	Virginia	262
19	Washington	260
43	West Virginia	248
29	Wisconsin	257
18	Wyoming	261

RANK ORDER

RANK	STATE	AVERAGE SCORE
1	Massachusetts	269
2	Vermont	268
3	New Jersey	266
3	South Dakota	266
5	Montana	265
5	Pennsylvania	265
7	Maine	264
7	New Hampshire	264
7	North Dakota	264
7	Ohio	264
11	Iowa	263
11	Kansas	263
11	Minnesota	263
14	Colorado	262
14	Connecticut	262
14	Nebraska	262
14	Virginia	262
18	Wyoming	261
19	Delaware	260
19	Idaho	260
19	Maryland	260
19	Oregon	260
19	Washington	260
24	Illinois	259
24	Indiana	259
24	Missouri	259
27	New York	258
27	Utah	258
29	Kentucky	257
29	Wisconsin	257
31	Rhode Island	256
31	Texas	256
33	Michigan	255
33	Oklahoma	255
35	Florida	254
35	North Carolina	254
35	Tennessee	254
38	Alaska	253
38	Arkansas	253
38	Georgia	253
38	South Carolina	253
42	Arizona	251
43	Louisiana	248
43	West Virginia	248
45	Alabama	247
45	New Mexico	247
47	California	246
47	Mississippi	246
49	Nevada	245
50	Hawaii	244
	District of Columbia	235

Source: U.S. Department of Education, National Center for Education Statistics
   "The Nation's Report Card: Reading 2007" (http://nces.ed.gov/nationsreportcard/)
*These scores are from the National Assessment of Educational Progress (NAEP). Scale ranges from 0 to 500.

Average Reading Score for Public School Eighth Grade Females in 2007

National Average Score = 266*

ALPHA ORDER

RANK	STATE	AVERAGE SCORE
47	Alabama	257
35	Alaska	264
43	Arizona	259
39	Arkansas	263
47	California	257
17	Colorado	271
9	Connecticut	272
25	Delaware	269
30	Florida	266
35	Georgia	264
43	Hawaii	259
20	Idaho	270
28	Illinois	267
20	Indiana	270
9	Iowa	272
9	Kansas	272
30	Kentucky	266
46	Louisiana	258
4	Maine	276
20	Maryland	270
1	Massachusetts	278
30	Michigan	266
6	Minnesota	274
49	Mississippi	255
27	Missouri	268
1	Montana	278
9	Nebraska	272
43	Nevada	259
5	New Hampshire	275
6	New Jersey	274
49	New Mexico	255
25	New York	269
34	North Carolina	265
9	North Dakota	272
9	Ohio	272
35	Oklahoma	264
17	Oregon	271
20	Pennsylvania	270
42	Rhode Island	261
40	South Carolina	262
6	South Dakota	274
35	Tennessee	264
30	Texas	266
28	Utah	267
1	Vermont	278
9	Virginia	272
20	Washington	270
40	West Virginia	262
9	Wisconsin	272
17	Wyoming	271

RANK ORDER

RANK	STATE	AVERAGE SCORE
1	Massachusetts	278
1	Montana	278
1	Vermont	278
4	Maine	276
5	New Hampshire	275
6	Minnesota	274
6	New Jersey	274
6	South Dakota	274
9	Connecticut	272
9	Iowa	272
9	Kansas	272
9	Nebraska	272
9	North Dakota	272
9	Ohio	272
9	Virginia	272
9	Wisconsin	272
17	Colorado	271
17	Oregon	271
17	Wyoming	271
20	Idaho	270
20	Indiana	270
20	Maryland	270
20	Pennsylvania	270
20	Washington	270
25	Delaware	269
25	New York	269
27	Missouri	268
28	Illinois	267
28	Utah	267
30	Florida	266
30	Kentucky	266
30	Michigan	266
30	Texas	266
34	North Carolina	265
35	Alaska	264
35	Georgia	264
35	Oklahoma	264
35	Tennessee	264
39	Arkansas	263
40	South Carolina	262
40	West Virginia	262
42	Rhode Island	261
43	Arizona	259
43	Hawaii	259
43	Nevada	259
46	Louisiana	258
47	Alabama	257
47	California	257
49	Mississippi	255
49	New Mexico	255
	District of Columbia	245

Source: U.S. Department of Education, National Center for Education Statistics
   "The Nation's Report Card: Reading 2007" (http://nces.ed.gov/nationsreportcard/)
*These scores are from the National Assessment of Educational Progress (NAEP). Scale ranges from 0 to 500.

Average Reading Score for Public School Eighth Graders
Eligible for Free or Reduced Price Lunch Program in 2007
National Average Score = 247*

ALPHA ORDER

RANK	STATE	AVERAGE SCORE
47	Alabama	241
40	Alaska	244
47	Arizona	241
32	Arkansas	247
50	California	239
22	Colorado	251
42	Connecticut	243
10	Delaware	254
29	Florida	249
32	Georgia	247
42	Hawaii	243
7	Idaho	256
29	Illinois	249
22	Indiana	251
13	Iowa	253
13	Kansas	253
17	Kentucky	252
38	Louisiana	245
1	Maine	261
22	Maryland	251
7	Massachusetts	256
40	Michigan	244
10	Minnesota	254
44	Mississippi	242
17	Missouri	252
2	Montana	260
10	Nebraska	254
49	Nevada	240
6	New Hampshire	257
22	New Jersey	251
44	New Mexico	242
28	New York	250
35	North Carolina	246
5	North Dakota	258
22	Ohio	251
17	Oklahoma	252
13	Oregon	253
13	Pennsylvania	253
44	Rhode Island	242
38	South Carolina	245
4	South Dakota	259
32	Tennessee	247
29	Texas	249
17	Utah	252
2	Vermont	260
17	Virginia	252
22	Washington	251
35	West Virginia	246
35	Wisconsin	246
9	Wyoming	255

RANK ORDER

RANK	STATE	AVERAGE SCORE
1	Maine	261
2	Montana	260
2	Vermont	260
4	South Dakota	259
5	North Dakota	258
6	New Hampshire	257
7	Idaho	256
7	Massachusetts	256
9	Wyoming	255
10	Delaware	254
10	Minnesota	254
10	Nebraska	254
13	Iowa	253
13	Kansas	253
13	Oregon	253
13	Pennsylvania	253
17	Kentucky	252
17	Missouri	252
17	Oklahoma	252
17	Utah	252
17	Virginia	252
22	Colorado	251
22	Indiana	251
22	Maryland	251
22	New Jersey	251
22	Ohio	251
22	Washington	251
28	New York	250
29	Florida	249
29	Illinois	249
29	Texas	249
32	Arkansas	247
32	Georgia	247
32	Tennessee	247
35	North Carolina	246
35	West Virginia	246
35	Wisconsin	246
38	Louisiana	245
38	South Carolina	245
40	Alaska	244
40	Michigan	244
42	Connecticut	243
42	Hawaii	243
44	Mississippi	242
44	New Mexico	242
44	Rhode Island	242
47	Alabama	241
47	Arizona	241
49	Nevada	240
50	California	239

District of Columbia	234

Source: U.S. Department of Education, National Center for Education Statistics
   "The Nation's Report Card: Reading 2007" (http://nces.ed.gov/nationsreportcard/)
*These scores are from the National Assessment of Educational Progress (NAEP). Scale ranges from 0 to 500.

Percent of Public School Eighth Graders
Proficient or Better in Reading in 2007
National Percent = 29%*

ALPHA ORDER

RANK	STATE	PERCENT
45	Alabama	21
35	Alaska	27
42	Arizona	24
40	Arkansas	25
45	California	21
13	Colorado	35
5	Connecticut	37
25	Delaware	31
30	Florida	28
37	Georgia	26
47	Hawaii	20
22	Idaho	32
28	Illinois	30
25	Indiana	31
10	Iowa	36
13	Kansas	35
30	Kentucky	28
48	Louisiana	19
5	Maine	37
19	Maryland	33
1	Massachusetts	43
30	Michigan	28
5	Minnesota	37
49	Mississippi	17
25	Missouri	31
3	Montana	39
13	Nebraska	35
44	Nevada	22
5	New Hampshire	37
3	New Jersey	39
49	New Mexico	17
22	New York	32
30	North Carolina	28
22	North Dakota	32
10	Ohio	36
37	Oklahoma	26
16	Oregon	34
10	Pennsylvania	36
35	Rhode Island	27
40	South Carolina	25
5	South Dakota	37
37	Tennessee	26
30	Texas	28
28	Utah	30
2	Vermont	42
16	Virginia	34
16	Washington	34
43	West Virginia	23
19	Wisconsin	33
19	Wyoming	33

RANK ORDER

RANK	STATE	PERCENT
1	Massachusetts	43
2	Vermont	42
3	Montana	39
3	New Jersey	39
5	Connecticut	37
5	Maine	37
5	Minnesota	37
5	New Hampshire	37
5	South Dakota	37
10	Iowa	36
10	Ohio	36
10	Pennsylvania	36
13	Colorado	35
13	Kansas	35
13	Nebraska	35
16	Oregon	34
16	Virginia	34
16	Washington	34
19	Maryland	33
19	Wisconsin	33
19	Wyoming	33
22	Idaho	32
22	New York	32
22	North Dakota	32
25	Delaware	31
25	Indiana	31
25	Missouri	31
28	Illinois	30
28	Utah	30
30	Florida	28
30	Kentucky	28
30	Michigan	28
30	North Carolina	28
30	Texas	28
35	Alaska	27
35	Rhode Island	27
37	Georgia	26
37	Oklahoma	26
37	Tennessee	26
40	Arkansas	25
40	South Carolina	25
42	Arizona	24
43	West Virginia	23
44	Nevada	22
45	Alabama	21
45	California	21
47	Hawaii	20
48	Louisiana	19
49	Mississippi	17
49	New Mexico	17
	District of Columbia	12

Source: U.S. Department of Education, National Center for Education Statistics
   "The Nation's Report Card: Reading 2007" (http://nces.ed.gov/nationsreportcard/)
*There are four achievement levels: Below Basic, Basic, Proficient, and Advanced. Proficient represents solid academic mastery for 8th graders. Students reaching this level have demonstrated competency over challenging subject matter, including subject matter knowledge, application of such knowledge to real-world situations, and analytical skills appropriate to the subject matter.

Percent of Public School Eighth Grade Males
Proficient or Better in Reading in 2007
National Percent = 24%*

<table>
<tr><td colspan="3">ALPHA ORDER</td><td colspan="3">RANK ORDER</td></tr>
<tr><td>RANK</td><td>STATE</td><td>PERCENT</td><td>RANK</td><td>STATE</td><td>PERCENT</td></tr>
<tr><td>44</td><td>Alabama</td><td>18</td><td>1</td><td>Massachusetts</td><td>37</td></tr>
<tr><td>35</td><td>Alaska</td><td>22</td><td>2</td><td>New Jersey</td><td>35</td></tr>
<tr><td>37</td><td>Arizona</td><td>21</td><td>2</td><td>Vermont</td><td>35</td></tr>
<tr><td>37</td><td>Arkansas</td><td>21</td><td>4</td><td>Pennsylvania</td><td>33</td></tr>
<tr><td>45</td><td>California</td><td>17</td><td>5</td><td>South Dakota</td><td>32</td></tr>
<tr><td>13</td><td>Colorado</td><td>29</td><td>6</td><td>Connecticut</td><td>31</td></tr>
<tr><td>6</td><td>Connecticut</td><td>31</td><td>6</td><td>Montana</td><td>31</td></tr>
<tr><td>23</td><td>Delaware</td><td>26</td><td>6</td><td>New Hampshire</td><td>31</td></tr>
<tr><td>35</td><td>Florida</td><td>22</td><td>6</td><td>Ohio</td><td>31</td></tr>
<tr><td>42</td><td>Georgia</td><td>20</td><td>10</td><td>Iowa</td><td>30</td></tr>
<tr><td>49</td><td>Hawaii</td><td>14</td><td>10</td><td>Kansas</td><td>30</td></tr>
<tr><td>20</td><td>Idaho</td><td>27</td><td>10</td><td>Minnesota</td><td>30</td></tr>
<tr><td>23</td><td>Illinois</td><td>26</td><td>13</td><td>Colorado</td><td>29</td></tr>
<tr><td>23</td><td>Indiana</td><td>26</td><td>13</td><td>Maine</td><td>29</td></tr>
<tr><td>10</td><td>Iowa</td><td>30</td><td>15</td><td>Maryland</td><td>28</td></tr>
<tr><td>10</td><td>Kansas</td><td>30</td><td>15</td><td>Nebraska</td><td>28</td></tr>
<tr><td>32</td><td>Kentucky</td><td>23</td><td>15</td><td>Oregon</td><td>28</td></tr>
<tr><td>46</td><td>Louisiana</td><td>16</td><td>15</td><td>Virginia</td><td>28</td></tr>
<tr><td>13</td><td>Maine</td><td>29</td><td>15</td><td>Washington</td><td>28</td></tr>
<tr><td>15</td><td>Maryland</td><td>28</td><td>20</td><td>Idaho</td><td>27</td></tr>
<tr><td>1</td><td>Massachusetts</td><td>37</td><td>20</td><td>Missouri</td><td>27</td></tr>
<tr><td>32</td><td>Michigan</td><td>23</td><td>20</td><td>Wyoming</td><td>27</td></tr>
<tr><td>10</td><td>Minnesota</td><td>30</td><td>23</td><td>Delaware</td><td>26</td></tr>
<tr><td>48</td><td>Mississippi</td><td>15</td><td>23</td><td>Illinois</td><td>26</td></tr>
<tr><td>20</td><td>Missouri</td><td>27</td><td>23</td><td>Indiana</td><td>26</td></tr>
<tr><td>6</td><td>Montana</td><td>31</td><td>23</td><td>New York</td><td>26</td></tr>
<tr><td>15</td><td>Nebraska</td><td>28</td><td>23</td><td>North Dakota</td><td>26</td></tr>
<tr><td>46</td><td>Nevada</td><td>16</td><td>23</td><td>Utah</td><td>26</td></tr>
<tr><td>6</td><td>New Hampshire</td><td>31</td><td>29</td><td>Wisconsin</td><td>25</td></tr>
<tr><td>2</td><td>New Jersey</td><td>35</td><td>30</td><td>North Carolina</td><td>24</td></tr>
<tr><td>49</td><td>New Mexico</td><td>14</td><td>30</td><td>Rhode Island</td><td>24</td></tr>
<tr><td>23</td><td>New York</td><td>26</td><td>32</td><td>Kentucky</td><td>23</td></tr>
<tr><td>30</td><td>North Carolina</td><td>24</td><td>32</td><td>Michigan</td><td>23</td></tr>
<tr><td>23</td><td>North Dakota</td><td>26</td><td>32</td><td>Texas</td><td>23</td></tr>
<tr><td>6</td><td>Ohio</td><td>31</td><td>35</td><td>Alaska</td><td>22</td></tr>
<tr><td>37</td><td>Oklahoma</td><td>21</td><td>35</td><td>Florida</td><td>22</td></tr>
<tr><td>15</td><td>Oregon</td><td>28</td><td>37</td><td>Arizona</td><td>21</td></tr>
<tr><td>4</td><td>Pennsylvania</td><td>33</td><td>37</td><td>Arkansas</td><td>21</td></tr>
<tr><td>30</td><td>Rhode Island</td><td>24</td><td>37</td><td>Oklahoma</td><td>21</td></tr>
<tr><td>37</td><td>South Carolina</td><td>21</td><td>37</td><td>South Carolina</td><td>21</td></tr>
<tr><td>5</td><td>South Dakota</td><td>32</td><td>37</td><td>Tennessee</td><td>21</td></tr>
<tr><td>37</td><td>Tennessee</td><td>21</td><td>42</td><td>Georgia</td><td>20</td></tr>
<tr><td>32</td><td>Texas</td><td>23</td><td>43</td><td>West Virginia</td><td>19</td></tr>
<tr><td>23</td><td>Utah</td><td>26</td><td>44</td><td>Alabama</td><td>18</td></tr>
<tr><td>2</td><td>Vermont</td><td>35</td><td>45</td><td>California</td><td>17</td></tr>
<tr><td>15</td><td>Virginia</td><td>28</td><td>46</td><td>Louisiana</td><td>16</td></tr>
<tr><td>15</td><td>Washington</td><td>28</td><td>46</td><td>Nevada</td><td>16</td></tr>
<tr><td>43</td><td>West Virginia</td><td>19</td><td>48</td><td>Mississippi</td><td>15</td></tr>
<tr><td>29</td><td>Wisconsin</td><td>25</td><td>49</td><td>Hawaii</td><td>14</td></tr>
<tr><td>20</td><td>Wyoming</td><td>27</td><td>49</td><td>New Mexico</td><td>14</td></tr>
<tr><td></td><td></td><td></td><td></td><td>District of Columbia</td><td>9</td></tr>
</table>

Source: U.S. Department of Education, National Center for Education Statistics
   "The Nation's Report Card: Reading 2007" (http://nces.ed.gov/nationsreportcard/)
*There are four achievement levels: Below Basic, Basic, Proficient, and Advanced. Proficient represents solid academic mastery for 8th graders. Students reaching this level have demonstrated competency over challenging subject matter, including subject matter knowledge, application of such knowledge to real-world situations, and analytical skills appropriate to the subject matter.

Percent of Public School Eighth Grade Females
Proficient or Better in Reading in 2007
National Percent = 34%*

ALPHA ORDER

RANK	STATE	PERCENT
47	Alabama	25
32	Alaska	33
41	Arizona	28
39	Arkansas	30
45	California	26
11	Colorado	41
7	Connecticut	43
26	Delaware	35
29	Florida	34
36	Georgia	31
45	Hawaii	26
24	Idaho	36
29	Illinois	34
24	Indiana	36
9	Iowa	42
11	Kansas	41
34	Kentucky	32
48	Louisiana	23
4	Maine	45
21	Maryland	38
1	Massachusetts	50
29	Michigan	34
5	Minnesota	44
50	Mississippi	20
26	Missouri	35
3	Montana	47
9	Nebraska	42
43	Nevada	27
5	New Hampshire	44
7	New Jersey	43
49	New Mexico	21
21	New York	38
32	North Carolina	33
21	North Dakota	38
15	Ohio	40
36	Oklahoma	31
15	Oregon	40
15	Pennsylvania	40
36	Rhode Island	31
41	South Carolina	28
11	South Dakota	41
39	Tennessee	30
34	Texas	32
26	Utah	35
2	Vermont	49
19	Virginia	39
15	Washington	40
43	West Virginia	27
11	Wisconsin	41
19	Wyoming	39

RANK ORDER

RANK	STATE	PERCENT
1	Massachusetts	50
2	Vermont	49
3	Montana	47
4	Maine	45
5	Minnesota	44
5	New Hampshire	44
7	Connecticut	43
7	New Jersey	43
9	Iowa	42
9	Nebraska	42
11	Colorado	41
11	Kansas	41
11	South Dakota	41
11	Wisconsin	41
15	Ohio	40
15	Oregon	40
15	Pennsylvania	40
15	Washington	40
19	Virginia	39
19	Wyoming	39
21	Maryland	38
21	New York	38
21	North Dakota	38
24	Idaho	36
24	Indiana	36
26	Delaware	35
26	Missouri	35
26	Utah	35
29	Florida	34
29	Illinois	34
29	Michigan	34
32	Alaska	33
32	North Carolina	33
34	Kentucky	32
34	Texas	32
36	Georgia	31
36	Oklahoma	31
36	Rhode Island	31
39	Arkansas	30
39	Tennessee	30
41	Arizona	28
41	South Carolina	28
43	Nevada	27
43	West Virginia	27
45	California	26
45	Hawaii	26
47	Alabama	25
48	Louisiana	23
49	New Mexico	21
50	Mississippi	20
	District of Columbia	15

Source: U.S. Department of Education, National Center for Education Statistics
   "The Nation's Report Card: Reading 2007" (http://nces.ed.gov/nationsreportcard/)
*There are four achievement levels: Below Basic, Basic, Proficient, and Advanced. Proficient represents solid academic mastery for 8th graders. Students reaching this level have demonstrated competency over challenging subject matter, including subject matter knowledge, application of such knowledge to real-world situations, and analytical skills appropriate to the subject matter.

Percent of Public School Eighth Graders Eligible for Free or Reduced Lunch Program Proficient or Better in Reading in 2007
National Percent = 15%*

ALPHA ORDER

RANK	STATE	PERCENT
45	Alabama	11
35	Alaska	14
45	Arizona	11
31	Arkansas	15
45	California	11
19	Colorado	18
35	Connecticut	14
19	Delaware	18
23	Florida	17
35	Georgia	14
40	Hawaii	13
6	Idaho	22
31	Illinois	15
26	Indiana	16
6	Iowa	22
13	Kansas	20
23	Kentucky	17
41	Louisiana	12
1	Maine	26
23	Maryland	17
13	Massachusetts	20
41	Michigan	12
9	Minnesota	21
49	Mississippi	10
19	Missouri	18
5	Montana	24
9	Nebraska	21
41	Nevada	12
2	New Hampshire	25
26	New Jersey	16
49	New Mexico	10
18	New York	19
35	North Carolina	14
13	North Dakota	20
26	Ohio	16
19	Oklahoma	18
9	Oregon	21
13	Pennsylvania	20
41	Rhode Island	12
45	South Carolina	11
2	South Dakota	25
35	Tennessee	14
31	Texas	15
9	Utah	21
2	Vermont	25
26	Virginia	16
13	Washington	20
31	West Virginia	15
26	Wisconsin	16
6	Wyoming	22

RANK ORDER

RANK	STATE	PERCENT
1	Maine	26
2	New Hampshire	25
2	South Dakota	25
2	Vermont	25
5	Montana	24
6	Idaho	22
6	Iowa	22
6	Wyoming	22
9	Minnesota	21
9	Nebraska	21
9	Oregon	21
9	Utah	21
13	Kansas	20
13	Massachusetts	20
13	North Dakota	20
13	Pennsylvania	20
13	Washington	20
18	New York	19
19	Colorado	18
19	Delaware	18
19	Missouri	18
19	Oklahoma	18
23	Florida	17
23	Kentucky	17
23	Maryland	17
26	Indiana	16
26	New Jersey	16
26	Ohio	16
26	Virginia	16
26	Wisconsin	16
31	Arkansas	15
31	Illinois	15
31	Texas	15
31	West Virginia	15
35	Alaska	14
35	Connecticut	14
35	Georgia	14
35	North Carolina	14
35	Tennessee	14
40	Hawaii	13
41	Louisiana	12
41	Michigan	12
41	Nevada	12
41	Rhode Island	12
45	Alabama	11
45	Arizona	11
45	California	11
45	South Carolina	11
49	Mississippi	10
49	New Mexico	10

District of Columbia	7

Source: U.S. Department of Education, National Center for Education Statistics
"The Nation's Report Card: Reading 2007" (http://nces.ed.gov/nationsreportcard/)
*There are four achievement levels: Below Basic, Basic, Proficient, and Advanced. Proficient represents solid academic mastery for 8th graders. Students reaching this level have demonstrated competency over challenging subject matter, including subject matter knowledge, application of such knowledge to real-world situations, and analytical skills appropriate to the subject matter.

Percent of White Public School Eighth Graders
Proficient or Better in Reading in 2007
National Percent = 38%*

ALPHA ORDER				RANK ORDER		
RANK	STATE	PERCENT		RANK	STATE	PERCENT
46	Alabama	29		1	Massachusetts	49
29	Alaska	36		2	New Jersey	48
25	Arizona	37		3	Connecticut	46
40	Arkansas	32		4	Maryland	45
35	California	34		5	Colorado	43
5	Colorado	43		5	New York	43
3	Connecticut	46		5	Texas	43
11	Delaware	41		8	Montana	42
29	Florida	36		8	Ohio	42
20	Georgia	38		8	Vermont	42
42	Hawaii	31		11	Delaware	41
35	Idaho	34		11	Minnesota	41
20	Illinois	38		11	Pennsylvania	41
32	Indiana	35		14	Kansas	40
20	Iowa	38		14	Virginia	40
14	Kansas	40		16	Nebraska	39
44	Kentucky	30		16	North Carolina	39
46	Louisiana	29		16	South Dakota	39
20	Maine	38		16	Washington	39
4	Maryland	45		20	Georgia	38
1	Massachusetts	49		20	Illinois	38
35	Michigan	34		20	Iowa	38
11	Minnesota	41		20	Maine	38
46	Mississippi	29		20	Wisconsin	38
25	Missouri	37		25	Arizona	37
8	Montana	42		25	Missouri	37
16	Nebraska	39		25	New Hampshire	37
44	Nevada	30		25	Oregon	37
25	New Hampshire	37		29	Alaska	36
2	New Jersey	48		29	Florida	36
46	New Mexico	29		29	Wyoming	36
5	New York	43		32	Indiana	35
16	North Carolina	39		32	Rhode Island	35
35	North Dakota	34		32	South Carolina	35
8	Ohio	42		35	California	34
42	Oklahoma	31		35	Idaho	34
25	Oregon	37		35	Michigan	34
11	Pennsylvania	41		35	North Dakota	34
32	Rhode Island	35		39	Utah	33
32	South Carolina	35		40	Arkansas	32
16	South Dakota	39		40	Tennessee	32
40	Tennessee	32		42	Hawaii	31
5	Texas	43		42	Oklahoma	31
39	Utah	33		44	Kentucky	30
8	Vermont	42		44	Nevada	30
14	Virginia	40		46	Alabama	29
16	Washington	39		46	Louisiana	29
50	West Virginia	23		46	Mississippi	29
20	Wisconsin	38		46	New Mexico	29
29	Wyoming	36		50	West Virginia	23
					District of Columbia**	NA

Source: U.S. Department of Education, National Center for Education Statistics
   "The Nation's Report Card: Reading 2007" (http://nces.ed.gov/nationsreportcard/)
*There are four achievement levels: Below Basic, Basic, Proficient, and Advanced. Proficient represents solid academic
mastery for 8th graders. Students reaching this level have demonstrated competency over challenging subject matter, including
subject matter knowledge, application of such knowledge to real-world situations, and analytical skills appropriate to the subject
matter. **Sample size insufficient.

Percent of Black Public School Eighth Graders
Proficient or Better in Reading in 2007
National Percent = 12%*

ALPHA ORDER

ALPHA ORDER

RANK	STATE	PERCENT
34	Alabama	9
5	Alaska	17
3	Arizona	19
36	Arkansas	8
28	California	10
4	Colorado	18
23	Connecticut	12
12	Delaware	14
18	Florida	13
18	Georgia	13
1	Hawaii	21
NA	Idaho**	NA
28	Illinois	10
28	Indiana	10
5	Iowa	17
23	Kansas	12
12	Kentucky	14
36	Louisiana	8
NA	Maine**	NA
12	Maryland	14
5	Massachusetts	17
40	Michigan	7
18	Minnesota	13
40	Mississippi	7
28	Missouri	10
NA	Montana**	NA
23	Nebraska	12
9	Nevada	16
NA	New Hampshire**	NA
5	New Jersey	17
18	New Mexico	13
12	New York	14
28	North Carolina	10
NA	North Dakota**	NA
23	Ohio	12
18	Oklahoma	13
1	Oregon	21
12	Pennsylvania	14
28	Rhode Island	10
34	South Carolina	9
NA	South Dakota**	NA
36	Tennessee	8
12	Texas	14
NA	Utah**	NA
NA	Vermont**	NA
9	Virginia	16
9	Washington	16
27	West Virginia	11
36	Wisconsin	8
NA	Wyoming**	NA

RANK ORDER

RANK	STATE	PERCENT
1	Hawaii	21
1	Oregon	21
3	Arizona	19
4	Colorado	18
5	Alaska	17
5	Iowa	17
5	Massachusetts	17
5	New Jersey	17
9	Nevada	16
9	Virginia	16
9	Washington	16
12	Delaware	14
12	Kentucky	14
12	Maryland	14
12	New York	14
12	Pennsylvania	14
12	Texas	14
18	Florida	13
18	Georgia	13
18	Minnesota	13
18	New Mexico	13
18	Oklahoma	13
23	Connecticut	12
23	Kansas	12
23	Nebraska	12
23	Ohio	12
27	West Virginia	11
28	California	10
28	Illinois	10
28	Indiana	10
28	Missouri	10
28	North Carolina	10
28	Rhode Island	10
34	Alabama	9
34	South Carolina	9
36	Arkansas	8
36	Louisiana	8
36	Tennessee	8
36	Wisconsin	8
40	Michigan	7
40	Mississippi	7
NA	Idaho**	NA
NA	Maine**	NA
NA	Montana**	NA
NA	New Hampshire**	NA
NA	North Dakota**	NA
NA	South Dakota**	NA
NA	Utah**	NA
NA	Vermont**	NA
NA	Wyoming**	NA
	District of Columbia	9

Source: U.S. Department of Education, National Center for Education Statistics
  "The Nation's Report Card: Reading 2007" (http://nces.ed.gov/nationsreportcard/)
*There are four achievement levels: Below Basic, Basic, Proficient, and Advanced. Proficient represents solid academic
mastery for 8th graders. Students reaching this level have demonstrated competency over challenging subject matter, including
subject matter knowledge, application of such knowledge to real-world situations, and analytical skills appropriate to the subject
matter. **Sample size insufficient.

Percent of Hispanic Public School Eighth Graders
Proficient or Better in Reading in 2007
National Percent = 14%*

<table>
<tr><td colspan="3">ALPHA ORDER</td><td colspan="3">RANK ORDER</td></tr>
<tr><td>RANK</td><td>STATE</td><td>PERCENT</td><td>RANK</td><td>STATE</td><td>PERCENT</td></tr>
<tr><td>11</td><td>Alabama</td><td>20</td><td>1</td><td>Ohio</td><td>31</td></tr>
<tr><td>3</td><td>Alaska</td><td>24</td><td>2</td><td>Virginia</td><td>25</td></tr>
<tr><td>37</td><td>Arizona</td><td>11</td><td>3</td><td>Alaska</td><td>24</td></tr>
<tr><td>25</td><td>Arkansas</td><td>15</td><td>3</td><td>Maryland</td><td>24</td></tr>
<tr><td>37</td><td>California</td><td>11</td><td>5</td><td>Florida</td><td>23</td></tr>
<tr><td>15</td><td>Colorado</td><td>17</td><td>6</td><td>New Jersey</td><td>22</td></tr>
<tr><td>28</td><td>Connecticut</td><td>14</td><td>7</td><td>Delaware</td><td>21</td></tr>
<tr><td>7</td><td>Delaware</td><td>21</td><td>7</td><td>Hawaii</td><td>21</td></tr>
<tr><td>5</td><td>Florida</td><td>23</td><td>7</td><td>Indiana</td><td>21</td></tr>
<tr><td>15</td><td>Georgia</td><td>17</td><td>7</td><td>Nebraska</td><td>21</td></tr>
<tr><td>7</td><td>Hawaii</td><td>21</td><td>11</td><td>Alabama</td><td>20</td></tr>
<tr><td>28</td><td>Idaho</td><td>14</td><td>11</td><td>New Hampshire</td><td>20</td></tr>
<tr><td>19</td><td>Illinois</td><td>16</td><td>13</td><td>Minnesota</td><td>19</td></tr>
<tr><td>7</td><td>Indiana</td><td>21</td><td>14</td><td>Tennessee</td><td>18</td></tr>
<tr><td>19</td><td>Iowa</td><td>16</td><td>15</td><td>Colorado</td><td>17</td></tr>
<tr><td>15</td><td>Kansas</td><td>17</td><td>15</td><td>Georgia</td><td>17</td></tr>
<tr><td>NA</td><td>Kentucky**</td><td>NA</td><td>15</td><td>Kansas</td><td>17</td></tr>
<tr><td>NA</td><td>Louisiana**</td><td>NA</td><td>15</td><td>Wisconsin</td><td>17</td></tr>
<tr><td>NA</td><td>Maine**</td><td>NA</td><td>19</td><td>Illinois</td><td>16</td></tr>
<tr><td>3</td><td>Maryland</td><td>24</td><td>19</td><td>Iowa</td><td>16</td></tr>
<tr><td>25</td><td>Massachusetts</td><td>15</td><td>19</td><td>New York</td><td>16</td></tr>
<tr><td>28</td><td>Michigan</td><td>14</td><td>19</td><td>North Carolina</td><td>16</td></tr>
<tr><td>13</td><td>Minnesota</td><td>19</td><td>19</td><td>Texas</td><td>16</td></tr>
<tr><td>NA</td><td>Mississippi**</td><td>NA</td><td>19</td><td>Washington</td><td>16</td></tr>
<tr><td>34</td><td>Missouri</td><td>12</td><td>25</td><td>Arkansas</td><td>15</td></tr>
<tr><td>NA</td><td>Montana**</td><td>NA</td><td>25</td><td>Massachusetts</td><td>15</td></tr>
<tr><td>7</td><td>Nebraska</td><td>21</td><td>25</td><td>South Carolina</td><td>15</td></tr>
<tr><td>37</td><td>Nevada</td><td>11</td><td>28</td><td>Connecticut</td><td>14</td></tr>
<tr><td>11</td><td>New Hampshire</td><td>20</td><td>28</td><td>Idaho</td><td>14</td></tr>
<tr><td>6</td><td>New Jersey</td><td>22</td><td>28</td><td>Michigan</td><td>14</td></tr>
<tr><td>34</td><td>New Mexico</td><td>12</td><td>28</td><td>Oregon</td><td>14</td></tr>
<tr><td>19</td><td>New York</td><td>16</td><td>28</td><td>Pennsylvania</td><td>14</td></tr>
<tr><td>19</td><td>North Carolina</td><td>16</td><td>33</td><td>Wyoming</td><td>13</td></tr>
<tr><td>NA</td><td>North Dakota**</td><td>NA</td><td>34</td><td>Missouri</td><td>12</td></tr>
<tr><td>1</td><td>Ohio</td><td>31</td><td>34</td><td>New Mexico</td><td>12</td></tr>
<tr><td>40</td><td>Oklahoma</td><td>9</td><td>34</td><td>Utah</td><td>12</td></tr>
<tr><td>28</td><td>Oregon</td><td>14</td><td>37</td><td>Arizona</td><td>11</td></tr>
<tr><td>28</td><td>Pennsylvania</td><td>14</td><td>37</td><td>California</td><td>11</td></tr>
<tr><td>41</td><td>Rhode Island</td><td>6</td><td>37</td><td>Nevada</td><td>11</td></tr>
<tr><td>25</td><td>South Carolina</td><td>15</td><td>40</td><td>Oklahoma</td><td>9</td></tr>
<tr><td>NA</td><td>South Dakota**</td><td>NA</td><td>41</td><td>Rhode Island</td><td>6</td></tr>
<tr><td>14</td><td>Tennessee</td><td>18</td><td>NA</td><td>Kentucky**</td><td>NA</td></tr>
<tr><td>19</td><td>Texas</td><td>16</td><td>NA</td><td>Louisiana**</td><td>NA</td></tr>
<tr><td>34</td><td>Utah</td><td>12</td><td>NA</td><td>Maine**</td><td>NA</td></tr>
<tr><td>NA</td><td>Vermont**</td><td>NA</td><td>NA</td><td>Mississippi**</td><td>NA</td></tr>
<tr><td>2</td><td>Virginia</td><td>25</td><td>NA</td><td>Montana**</td><td>NA</td></tr>
<tr><td>19</td><td>Washington</td><td>16</td><td>NA</td><td>North Dakota**</td><td>NA</td></tr>
<tr><td>NA</td><td>West Virginia**</td><td>NA</td><td>NA</td><td>South Dakota**</td><td>NA</td></tr>
<tr><td>15</td><td>Wisconsin</td><td>17</td><td>NA</td><td>Vermont**</td><td>NA</td></tr>
<tr><td>33</td><td>Wyoming</td><td>13</td><td>NA</td><td>West Virginia**</td><td>NA</td></tr>
<tr><td></td><td></td><td></td><td></td><td>District of Columbia</td><td>19</td></tr>
</table>

Source: U.S. Department of Education, National Center for Education Statistics
"The Nation's Report Card: Reading 2007" (http://nces.ed.gov/nationsreportcard/)
*There are four achievement levels: Below Basic, Basic, Proficient, and Advanced. Proficient represents solid academic mastery for 8th graders. Students reaching this level have demonstrated competency over challenging subject matter, including subject matter knowledge, application of such knowledge to real-world situations, and analytical skills appropriate to the subject matter. **Sample size insufficient.

Percent of Asian Public School Eighth Graders
Proficient or Better in Reading in 2007
National Percent = 40%*

ALPHA ORDER

RANK	STATE	PERCENT
NA	Alabama**	NA
19	Alaska	27
7	Arizona	48
NA	Arkansas**	NA
16	California	35
15	Colorado	36
11	Connecticut	45
8	Delaware	47
9	Florida	46
NA	Georgia**	NA
24	Hawaii	18
NA	Idaho**	NA
9	Illinois	46
NA	Indiana**	NA
NA	Iowa**	NA
NA	Kansas**	NA
NA	Kentucky**	NA
NA	Louisiana**	NA
NA	Maine**	NA
1	Maryland	62
4	Massachusetts	54
NA	Michigan**	NA
19	Minnesota	27
NA	Mississippi**	NA
NA	Missouri**	NA
NA	Montana**	NA
NA	Nebraska**	NA
23	Nevada	26
NA	New Hampshire**	NA
3	New Jersey	57
NA	New Mexico**	NA
13	New York	37
17	North Carolina	34
NA	North Dakota**	NA
NA	Ohio**	NA
NA	Oklahoma**	NA
12	Oregon	44
2	Pennsylvania	58
19	Rhode Island	27
NA	South Carolina**	NA
NA	South Dakota**	NA
NA	Tennessee**	NA
6	Texas	52
18	Utah	30
NA	Vermont**	NA
4	Virginia	54
13	Washington	37
NA	West Virginia**	NA
19	Wisconsin	27
NA	Wyoming**	NA

RANK ORDER

RANK	STATE	PERCENT
1	Maryland	62
2	Pennsylvania	58
3	New Jersey	57
4	Massachusetts	54
4	Virginia	54
6	Texas	52
7	Arizona	48
8	Delaware	47
9	Florida	46
9	Illinois	46
11	Connecticut	45
12	Oregon	44
13	New York	37
13	Washington	37
15	Colorado	36
16	California	35
17	North Carolina	34
18	Utah	30
19	Alaska	27
19	Minnesota	27
19	Rhode Island	27
19	Wisconsin	27
23	Nevada	26
24	Hawaii	18
NA	Alabama**	NA
NA	Arkansas**	NA
NA	Georgia**	NA
NA	Idaho**	NA
NA	Indiana**	NA
NA	Iowa**	NA
NA	Kansas**	NA
NA	Kentucky**	NA
NA	Louisiana**	NA
NA	Maine**	NA
NA	Michigan**	NA
NA	Mississippi**	NA
NA	Missouri**	NA
NA	Montana**	NA
NA	Nebraska**	NA
NA	New Hampshire**	NA
NA	New Mexico**	NA
NA	North Dakota**	NA
NA	Ohio**	NA
NA	Oklahoma**	NA
NA	South Carolina**	NA
NA	South Dakota**	NA
NA	Tennessee**	NA
NA	Vermont**	NA
NA	West Virginia**	NA
NA	Wyoming**	NA
	District of Columbia**	NA

Source: U.S. Department of Education, National Center for Education Statistics
    "The Nation's Report Card: Reading 2007" (http://nces.ed.gov/nationsreportcard/)
*There are four achievement levels: Below Basic, Basic, Proficient, and Advanced. Proficient represents solid academic
mastery for 8th graders. Students reaching this level have demonstrated competency over challenging subject matter, including
subject matter knowledge, application of such knowledge to real-world situations, and analytical skills appropriate to the subject
matter. **Sample size insufficient.

Percent of Disabled Public School Eighth Graders
Proficient or Better in Reading in 2007
National Percent = 7%*

ALPHA ORDER

RANK	STATE	PERCENT
50	Alabama	1
24	Alaska	6
37	Arizona	5
45	Arkansas	3
40	California	4
14	Colorado	8
14	Connecticut	8
6	Delaware	10
19	Florida	7
24	Georgia	6
40	Hawaii	4
24	Idaho	6
14	Illinois	8
37	Indiana	5
40	Iowa	4
24	Kansas	6
19	Kentucky	7
45	Louisiana	3
4	Maine	11
10	Maryland	9
3	Massachusetts	13
24	Michigan	6
6	Minnesota	10
49	Mississippi	2
24	Missouri	6
19	Montana	7
14	Nebraska	8
19	Nevada	7
4	New Hampshire	11
6	New Jersey	10
24	New Mexico	6
10	New York	9
19	North Carolina	7
14	North Dakota	8
10	Ohio	9
40	Oklahoma	4
24	Oregon	6
6	Pennsylvania	10
24	Rhode Island	6
24	South Carolina	6
24	South Dakota	6
2	Tennessee	15
37	Texas	5
40	Utah	4
1	Vermont	17
10	Virginia	9
24	Washington	6
45	West Virginia	3
45	Wisconsin	3
24	Wyoming	6

RANK ORDER

RANK	STATE	PERCENT
1	Vermont	17
2	Tennessee	15
3	Massachusetts	13
4	Maine	11
4	New Hampshire	11
6	Delaware	10
6	Minnesota	10
6	New Jersey	10
6	Pennsylvania	10
10	Maryland	9
10	New York	9
10	Ohio	9
10	Virginia	9
14	Colorado	8
14	Connecticut	8
14	Illinois	8
14	Nebraska	8
14	North Dakota	8
19	Florida	7
19	Kentucky	7
19	Montana	7
19	Nevada	7
19	North Carolina	7
24	Alaska	6
24	Georgia	6
24	Idaho	6
24	Kansas	6
24	Michigan	6
24	Missouri	6
24	New Mexico	6
24	Oregon	6
24	Rhode Island	6
24	South Carolina	6
24	South Dakota	6
24	Washington	6
24	Wyoming	6
37	Arizona	5
37	Indiana	5
37	Texas	5
40	California	4
40	Hawaii	4
40	Iowa	4
40	Oklahoma	4
40	Utah	4
45	Arkansas	3
45	Louisiana	3
45	West Virginia	3
45	Wisconsin	3
49	Mississippi	2
50	Alabama	1
	District of Columbia	4

Source: U.S. Department of Education, National Center for Education Statistics
   "The Nation's Report Card: Reading 2007" (http://nces.ed.gov/nationsreportcard/)
*There are four achievement levels: Below Basic, Basic, Proficient, and Advanced. Proficient represents solid academic
mastery for 8th graders. Students reaching this level have demonstrated competency over challenging subject matter, including
subject matter knowledge, application of such knowledge to real-world situations, and analytical skills appropriate to the subject
matter. Based only on disabled students who were assessed.

Average Public School Fourth Grade Mathematics Score in 2007

National Average Score = 239*

ALPHA ORDER

RANK	STATE	AVERAGE SCORE
48	Alabama	229
33	Alaska	237
44	Arizona	232
30	Arkansas	238
46	California	230
26	Colorado	240
15	Connecticut	243
19	Delaware	242
19	Florida	242
40	Georgia	235
42	Hawaii	234
24	Idaho	241
33	Illinois	237
7	Indiana	245
15	Iowa	243
4	Kansas	248
40	Kentucky	235
46	Louisiana	230
19	Maine	242
26	Maryland	240
1	Massachusetts	252
30	Michigan	238
5	Minnesota	247
49	Mississippi	228
28	Missouri	239
10	Montana	244
30	Nebraska	238
44	Nevada	232
2	New Hampshire	249
2	New Jersey	249
49	New Mexico	228
15	New York	243
19	North Carolina	242
7	North Dakota	245
7	Ohio	245
33	Oklahoma	237
37	Oregon	236
10	Pennsylvania	244
37	Rhode Island	236
33	South Carolina	237
24	South Dakota	241
43	Tennessee	233
19	Texas	242
28	Utah	239
6	Vermont	246
10	Virginia	244
15	Washington	243
37	West Virginia	236
10	Wisconsin	244
10	Wyoming	244

RANK ORDER

RANK	STATE	AVERAGE SCORE
1	Massachusetts	252
2	New Hampshire	249
2	New Jersey	249
4	Kansas	248
5	Minnesota	247
6	Vermont	246
7	Indiana	245
7	North Dakota	245
7	Ohio	245
10	Montana	244
10	Pennsylvania	244
10	Virginia	244
10	Wisconsin	244
10	Wyoming	244
15	Connecticut	243
15	Iowa	243
15	New York	243
15	Washington	243
19	Delaware	242
19	Florida	242
19	Maine	242
19	North Carolina	242
19	Texas	242
24	Idaho	241
24	South Dakota	241
26	Colorado	240
26	Maryland	240
28	Missouri	239
28	Utah	239
30	Arkansas	238
30	Michigan	238
30	Nebraska	238
33	Alaska	237
33	Illinois	237
33	Oklahoma	237
33	South Carolina	237
37	Oregon	236
37	Rhode Island	236
37	West Virginia	236
40	Georgia	235
40	Kentucky	235
42	Hawaii	234
43	Tennessee	233
44	Arizona	232
44	Nevada	232
46	California	230
46	Louisiana	230
48	Alabama	229
49	Mississippi	228
49	New Mexico	228

| | District of Columbia | 214 |

Source: U.S. Department of Education, National Center for Education Statistics
  "The Nation's Report Card: Mathematics 2007" (http://nces.ed.gov/nationsreportcard/)
*These scores are from the National Assessment of Educational Progress (NAEP). Scale ranges from 0 to 500.

Average Mathematics Score for Public School Fourth Grade Males in 2007

National Average Score = 240*

ALPHA ORDER				RANK ORDER		
RANK	STATE	AVERAGE SCORE		RANK	STATE	AVERAGE SCORE
48	Alabama	229		1	Massachusetts	254
32	Alaska	238		2	New Hampshire	250
43	Arizona	233		2	New Jersey	250
32	Arkansas	238		4	Kansas	249
46	California	231		4	Minnesota	249
23	Colorado	242		6	North Dakota	248
19	Connecticut	243		6	Vermont	248
23	Delaware	242		8	Indiana	246
19	Florida	243		8	Ohio	246
39	Georgia	236		10	Montana	245
43	Hawaii	233		10	Pennsylvania	245
23	Idaho	242		10	Virginia	245
31	Illinois	239		10	Wisconsin	245
8	Indiana	246		14	Iowa	244
14	Iowa	244		14	Maine	244
4	Kansas	249		14	New York	244
38	Kentucky	237		14	Washington	244
47	Louisiana	230		14	Wyoming	244
14	Maine	244		19	Connecticut	243
23	Maryland	242		19	Florida	243
1	Massachusetts	254		19	North Carolina	243
32	Michigan	238		19	Texas	243
4	Minnesota	249		23	Colorado	242
50	Mississippi	228		23	Delaware	242
29	Missouri	240		23	Idaho	242
10	Montana	245		23	Maryland	242
29	Nebraska	240		23	South Dakota	242
43	Nevada	233		28	Utah	241
2	New Hampshire	250		29	Missouri	240
2	New Jersey	250		29	Nebraska	240
48	New Mexico	229		31	Illinois	239
14	New York	244		32	Alaska	238
19	North Carolina	243		32	Arkansas	238
6	North Dakota	248		32	Michigan	238
8	Ohio	246		32	Oklahoma	238
32	Oklahoma	238		32	Oregon	238
32	Oregon	238		32	West Virginia	238
10	Pennsylvania	245		38	Kentucky	237
39	Rhode Island	236		39	Georgia	236
39	South Carolina	236		39	Rhode Island	236
23	South Dakota	242		39	South Carolina	236
42	Tennessee	234		42	Tennessee	234
19	Texas	243		43	Arizona	233
28	Utah	241		43	Hawaii	233
6	Vermont	248		43	Nevada	233
10	Virginia	245		46	California	231
14	Washington	244		47	Louisiana	230
32	West Virginia	238		48	Alabama	229
10	Wisconsin	245		48	New Mexico	229
14	Wyoming	244		50	Mississippi	228
					District of Columbia	213

Source: U.S. Department of Education, National Center for Education Statistics
   "The Nation's Report Card: Mathematics 2007" (http://nces.ed.gov/nationsreportcard/)
*These scores are from the National Assessment of Educational Progress (NAEP). Scale ranges from 0 to 500.

Average Mathematics Score for Public School Fourth Grade Females in 2007

National Average Score = 238*

<table>
<tr><td colspan="3">ALPHA ORDER</td><td colspan="3">RANK ORDER</td></tr>
<tr><td>RANK</td><td>STATE</td><td>AVERAGE SCORE</td><td>RANK</td><td>STATE</td><td>AVERAGE SCORE</td></tr>
<tr><td>48</td><td>Alabama</td><td>228</td><td>1</td><td>Massachusetts</td><td>251</td></tr>
<tr><td>31</td><td>Alaska</td><td>237</td><td>2</td><td>Kansas</td><td>247</td></tr>
<tr><td>44</td><td>Arizona</td><td>230</td><td>2</td><td>New Hampshire</td><td>247</td></tr>
<tr><td>31</td><td>Arkansas</td><td>237</td><td>2</td><td>New Jersey</td><td>247</td></tr>
<tr><td>47</td><td>California</td><td>229</td><td>5</td><td>Minnesota</td><td>245</td></tr>
<tr><td>26</td><td>Colorado</td><td>239</td><td>5</td><td>Vermont</td><td>245</td></tr>
<tr><td>13</td><td>Connecticut</td><td>242</td><td>7</td><td>Indiana</td><td>244</td></tr>
<tr><td>18</td><td>Delaware</td><td>241</td><td>8</td><td>North Dakota</td><td>243</td></tr>
<tr><td>18</td><td>Florida</td><td>241</td><td>8</td><td>Ohio</td><td>243</td></tr>
<tr><td>40</td><td>Georgia</td><td>234</td><td>8</td><td>Pennsylvania</td><td>243</td></tr>
<tr><td>34</td><td>Hawaii</td><td>236</td><td>8</td><td>Wisconsin</td><td>243</td></tr>
<tr><td>24</td><td>Idaho</td><td>240</td><td>8</td><td>Wyoming</td><td>243</td></tr>
<tr><td>37</td><td>Illinois</td><td>235</td><td>13</td><td>Connecticut</td><td>242</td></tr>
<tr><td>7</td><td>Indiana</td><td>244</td><td>13</td><td>Montana</td><td>242</td></tr>
<tr><td>18</td><td>Iowa</td><td>241</td><td>13</td><td>New York</td><td>242</td></tr>
<tr><td>2</td><td>Kansas</td><td>247</td><td>13</td><td>Texas</td><td>242</td></tr>
<tr><td>40</td><td>Kentucky</td><td>234</td><td>13</td><td>Virginia</td><td>242</td></tr>
<tr><td>44</td><td>Louisiana</td><td>230</td><td>18</td><td>Delaware</td><td>241</td></tr>
<tr><td>18</td><td>Maine</td><td>241</td><td>18</td><td>Florida</td><td>241</td></tr>
<tr><td>26</td><td>Maryland</td><td>239</td><td>18</td><td>Iowa</td><td>241</td></tr>
<tr><td>1</td><td>Massachusetts</td><td>251</td><td>18</td><td>Maine</td><td>241</td></tr>
<tr><td>31</td><td>Michigan</td><td>237</td><td>18</td><td>North Carolina</td><td>241</td></tr>
<tr><td>5</td><td>Minnesota</td><td>245</td><td>18</td><td>Washington</td><td>241</td></tr>
<tr><td>49</td><td>Mississippi</td><td>227</td><td>24</td><td>Idaho</td><td>240</td></tr>
<tr><td>28</td><td>Missouri</td><td>238</td><td>24</td><td>South Dakota</td><td>240</td></tr>
<tr><td>13</td><td>Montana</td><td>242</td><td>26</td><td>Colorado</td><td>239</td></tr>
<tr><td>34</td><td>Nebraska</td><td>236</td><td>26</td><td>Maryland</td><td>239</td></tr>
<tr><td>44</td><td>Nevada</td><td>230</td><td>28</td><td>Missouri</td><td>238</td></tr>
<tr><td>2</td><td>New Hampshire</td><td>247</td><td>28</td><td>South Carolina</td><td>238</td></tr>
<tr><td>2</td><td>New Jersey</td><td>247</td><td>28</td><td>Utah</td><td>238</td></tr>
<tr><td>49</td><td>New Mexico</td><td>227</td><td>31</td><td>Alaska</td><td>237</td></tr>
<tr><td>13</td><td>New York</td><td>242</td><td>31</td><td>Arkansas</td><td>237</td></tr>
<tr><td>18</td><td>North Carolina</td><td>241</td><td>31</td><td>Michigan</td><td>237</td></tr>
<tr><td>8</td><td>North Dakota</td><td>243</td><td>34</td><td>Hawaii</td><td>236</td></tr>
<tr><td>8</td><td>Ohio</td><td>243</td><td>34</td><td>Nebraska</td><td>236</td></tr>
<tr><td>34</td><td>Oklahoma</td><td>236</td><td>34</td><td>Oklahoma</td><td>236</td></tr>
<tr><td>40</td><td>Oregon</td><td>234</td><td>37</td><td>Illinois</td><td>235</td></tr>
<tr><td>8</td><td>Pennsylvania</td><td>243</td><td>37</td><td>Rhode Island</td><td>235</td></tr>
<tr><td>37</td><td>Rhode Island</td><td>235</td><td>37</td><td>West Virginia</td><td>235</td></tr>
<tr><td>28</td><td>South Carolina</td><td>238</td><td>40</td><td>Georgia</td><td>234</td></tr>
<tr><td>24</td><td>South Dakota</td><td>240</td><td>40</td><td>Kentucky</td><td>234</td></tr>
<tr><td>43</td><td>Tennessee</td><td>231</td><td>40</td><td>Oregon</td><td>234</td></tr>
<tr><td>13</td><td>Texas</td><td>242</td><td>43</td><td>Tennessee</td><td>231</td></tr>
<tr><td>28</td><td>Utah</td><td>238</td><td>44</td><td>Arizona</td><td>230</td></tr>
<tr><td>5</td><td>Vermont</td><td>245</td><td>44</td><td>Louisiana</td><td>230</td></tr>
<tr><td>13</td><td>Virginia</td><td>242</td><td>44</td><td>Nevada</td><td>230</td></tr>
<tr><td>18</td><td>Washington</td><td>241</td><td>47</td><td>California</td><td>229</td></tr>
<tr><td>37</td><td>West Virginia</td><td>235</td><td>48</td><td>Alabama</td><td>228</td></tr>
<tr><td>8</td><td>Wisconsin</td><td>243</td><td>49</td><td>Mississippi</td><td>227</td></tr>
<tr><td>8</td><td>Wyoming</td><td>243</td><td>49</td><td>New Mexico</td><td>227</td></tr>
<tr><td></td><td></td><td></td><td></td><td>District of Columbia</td><td>214</td></tr>
</table>

Source: U.S. Department of Education, National Center for Education Statistics
"The Nation's Report Card: Mathematics 2007" (http://nces.ed.gov/nationsreportcard/)
*These scores are from the National Assessment of Educational Progress (NAEP). Scale ranges from 0 to 500.

Average Mathematics Score for Public School Fourth Graders
Eligible for Free or Reduced Price Lunch Program in 2007
National Average Score = 227*

ALPHA ORDER

RANK	STATE	AVERAGE SCORE
50	Alabama	217
33	Alaska	225
48	Arizona	219
24	Arkansas	229
48	California	219
33	Colorado	225
43	Connecticut	222
13	Delaware	232
10	Florida	233
38	Georgia	224
38	Hawaii	224
13	Idaho	232
41	Illinois	223
5	Indiana	235
17	Iowa	231
1	Kansas	237
30	Kentucky	226
33	Louisiana	225
13	Maine	232
33	Maryland	225
1	Massachusetts	237
38	Michigan	224
13	Minnesota	232
43	Mississippi	222
27	Missouri	228
8	Montana	234
33	Nebraska	225
46	Nevada	221
3	New Hampshire	236
10	New Jersey	233
46	New Mexico	221
10	New York	233
17	North Carolina	231
5	North Dakota	235
19	Ohio	230
19	Oklahoma	230
30	Oregon	226
29	Pennsylvania	227
43	Rhode Island	222
30	South Carolina	226
19	South Dakota	230
41	Tennessee	223
5	Texas	235
24	Utah	229
8	Vermont	234
19	Virginia	230
19	Washington	230
24	West Virginia	229
27	Wisconsin	228
3	Wyoming	236

RANK ORDER

RANK	STATE	AVERAGE SCORE
1	Kansas	237
1	Massachusetts	237
3	New Hampshire	236
3	Wyoming	236
5	Indiana	235
5	North Dakota	235
5	Texas	235
8	Montana	234
8	Vermont	234
10	Florida	233
10	New Jersey	233
10	New York	233
13	Delaware	232
13	Idaho	232
13	Maine	232
13	Minnesota	232
17	Iowa	231
17	North Carolina	231
19	Ohio	230
19	Oklahoma	230
19	South Dakota	230
19	Virginia	230
19	Washington	230
24	Arkansas	229
24	Utah	229
24	West Virginia	229
27	Missouri	228
27	Wisconsin	228
29	Pennsylvania	227
30	Kentucky	226
30	Oregon	226
30	South Carolina	226
33	Alaska	225
33	Colorado	225
33	Louisiana	225
33	Maryland	225
33	Nebraska	225
38	Georgia	224
38	Hawaii	224
38	Michigan	224
41	Illinois	223
41	Tennessee	223
43	Connecticut	222
43	Mississippi	222
43	Rhode Island	222
46	Nevada	221
46	New Mexico	221
48	Arizona	219
48	California	219
50	Alabama	217
	District of Columbia	207

Source: U.S. Department of Education, National Center for Education Statistics
   "The Nation's Report Card: Mathematics 2007" (http://nces.ed.gov/nationsreportcard/)
*These scores are from the National Assessment of Educational Progress (NAEP). Scale ranges from 0 to 500.

Percent of Public School Fourth Graders Proficient or Better in Mathematics in 2007
National Percent = 39%*

ALPHA ORDER

RANK	STATE	PERCENT
47	Alabama	26
29	Alaska	38
42	Arizona	31
32	Arkansas	37
44	California	30
20	Colorado	41
12	Connecticut	45
23	Delaware	40
23	Florida	40
41	Georgia	32
38	Hawaii	33
23	Idaho	40
34	Illinois	36
9	Indiana	46
16	Iowa	43
4	Kansas	51
42	Kentucky	31
48	Louisiana	24
18	Maine	42
23	Maryland	40
1	Massachusetts	58
32	Michigan	37
4	Minnesota	51
50	Mississippi	21
29	Missouri	38
13	Montana	44
29	Nebraska	38
44	Nevada	30
2	New Hampshire	52
2	New Jersey	52
48	New Mexico	24
16	New York	43
20	North Carolina	41
9	North Dakota	46
9	Ohio	46
38	Oklahoma	33
36	Oregon	35
7	Pennsylvania	47
37	Rhode Island	34
34	South Carolina	36
20	South Dakota	41
46	Tennessee	29
23	Texas	40
28	Utah	39
6	Vermont	49
18	Virginia	42
13	Washington	44
38	West Virginia	33
7	Wisconsin	47
13	Wyoming	44

RANK ORDER

RANK	STATE	PERCENT
1	Massachusetts	58
2	New Hampshire	52
2	New Jersey	52
4	Kansas	51
4	Minnesota	51
6	Vermont	49
7	Pennsylvania	47
7	Wisconsin	47
9	Indiana	46
9	North Dakota	46
9	Ohio	46
12	Connecticut	45
13	Montana	44
13	Washington	44
13	Wyoming	44
16	Iowa	43
16	New York	43
18	Maine	42
18	Virginia	42
20	Colorado	41
20	North Carolina	41
20	South Dakota	41
23	Delaware	40
23	Florida	40
23	Idaho	40
23	Maryland	40
23	Texas	40
28	Utah	39
29	Alaska	38
29	Missouri	38
29	Nebraska	38
32	Arkansas	37
32	Michigan	37
34	Illinois	36
34	South Carolina	36
36	Oregon	35
37	Rhode Island	34
38	Hawaii	33
38	Oklahoma	33
38	West Virginia	33
41	Georgia	32
42	Arizona	31
42	Kentucky	31
44	California	30
44	Nevada	30
46	Tennessee	29
47	Alabama	26
48	Louisiana	24
48	New Mexico	24
50	Mississippi	21

District of Columbia	14

Source: U.S. Department of Education, National Center for Education Statistics
"The Nation's Report Card: Mathematics 2007" (http://nces.ed.gov/nationsreportcard/)
*There are four achievement levels: Below Basic, Basic, Proficient, and Advanced. Proficient represents solid academic mastery for 4th graders. Students reaching this level have demonstrated competency over challenging subject matter, including subject matter knowledge, application of such knowledge to real-world situations, and analytical skills appropriate to the subject matter.

Percent of Public School Fourth Grade Males
Proficient or Better in Mathematics in 2007
National Percent = 41%*

ALPHA ORDER

RANK	STATE	PERCENT
47	Alabama	27
33	Alaska	38
39	Arizona	34
33	Arkansas	38
45	California	31
18	Colorado	44
13	Connecticut	46
28	Delaware	40
20	Florida	43
41	Georgia	33
41	Hawaii	33
25	Idaho	42
28	Illinois	40
10	Indiana	48
13	Iowa	46
3	Kansas	54
41	Kentucky	33
49	Louisiana	25
20	Maine	43
20	Maryland	43
1	Massachusetts	60
32	Michigan	39
3	Minnesota	54
50	Mississippi	22
28	Missouri	40
12	Montana	47
28	Nebraska	40
41	Nevada	33
3	New Hampshire	54
2	New Jersey	55
48	New Mexico	26
17	New York	45
20	North Carolina	43
7	North Dakota	50
9	Ohio	49
39	Oklahoma	34
33	Oregon	38
7	Pennsylvania	50
36	Rhode Island	36
36	South Carolina	36
20	South Dakota	43
45	Tennessee	31
27	Texas	41
25	Utah	42
6	Vermont	51
18	Virginia	44
13	Washington	46
38	West Virginia	35
10	Wisconsin	48
13	Wyoming	46

RANK ORDER

RANK	STATE	PERCENT
1	Massachusetts	60
2	New Jersey	55
3	Kansas	54
3	Minnesota	54
3	New Hampshire	54
6	Vermont	51
7	North Dakota	50
7	Pennsylvania	50
9	Ohio	49
10	Indiana	48
10	Wisconsin	48
12	Montana	47
13	Connecticut	46
13	Iowa	46
13	Washington	46
13	Wyoming	46
17	New York	45
18	Colorado	44
18	Virginia	44
20	Florida	43
20	Maine	43
20	Maryland	43
20	North Carolina	43
20	South Dakota	43
25	Idaho	42
25	Utah	42
27	Texas	41
28	Delaware	40
28	Illinois	40
28	Missouri	40
28	Nebraska	40
32	Michigan	39
33	Alaska	38
33	Arkansas	38
33	Oregon	38
36	Rhode Island	36
36	South Carolina	36
38	West Virginia	35
39	Arizona	34
39	Oklahoma	34
41	Georgia	33
41	Hawaii	33
41	Kentucky	33
41	Nevada	33
45	California	31
45	Tennessee	31
47	Alabama	27
48	New Mexico	26
49	Louisiana	25
50	Mississippi	22

District of Columbia — 14

Source: U.S. Department of Education, National Center for Education Statistics
"The Nation's Report Card: Mathematics 2007" (http://nces.ed.gov/nationsreportcard/)
*There are four achievement levels: Below Basic, Basic, Proficient, and Advanced. Proficient represents solid academic mastery for 4th graders. Students reaching this level have demonstrated competency over challenging subject matter, including subject matter knowledge, application of such knowledge to real-world situations, and analytical skills appropriate to the subject matter.

Percent of Public School Fourth Grade Females
Proficient or Better in Mathematics in 2007
National Percent = 36%*

ALPHA ORDER

RANK	STATE	PERCENT
47	Alabama	25
27	Alaska	37
44	Arizona	27
32	Arkansas	35
43	California	28
23	Colorado	38
10	Connecticut	43
17	Delaware	40
23	Florida	38
40	Georgia	30
35	Hawaii	34
23	Idaho	38
36	Illinois	33
8	Indiana	45
17	Iowa	40
4	Kansas	48
42	Kentucky	29
48	Louisiana	24
17	Maine	40
27	Maryland	37
1	Massachusetts	55
32	Michigan	35
5	Minnesota	47
50	Mississippi	20
27	Missouri	37
13	Montana	42
32	Nebraska	35
44	Nevada	27
2	New Hampshire	49
2	New Jersey	49
49	New Mexico	23
13	New York	42
20	North Carolina	39
15	North Dakota	41
10	Ohio	43
39	Oklahoma	31
37	Oregon	32
9	Pennsylvania	44
37	Rhode Island	32
31	South Carolina	36
23	South Dakota	38
46	Tennessee	26
20	Texas	39
27	Utah	37
5	Vermont	47
20	Virginia	39
15	Washington	41
40	West Virginia	30
7	Wisconsin	46
10	Wyoming	43

RANK ORDER

RANK	STATE	PERCENT
1	Massachusetts	55
2	New Hampshire	49
2	New Jersey	49
4	Kansas	48
5	Minnesota	47
5	Vermont	47
7	Wisconsin	46
8	Indiana	45
9	Pennsylvania	44
10	Connecticut	43
10	Ohio	43
10	Wyoming	43
13	Montana	42
13	New York	42
15	North Dakota	41
15	Washington	41
17	Delaware	40
17	Iowa	40
17	Maine	40
20	North Carolina	39
20	Texas	39
20	Virginia	39
23	Colorado	38
23	Florida	38
23	Idaho	38
23	South Dakota	38
27	Alaska	37
27	Maryland	37
27	Missouri	37
27	Utah	37
31	South Carolina	36
32	Arkansas	35
32	Michigan	35
32	Nebraska	35
35	Hawaii	34
36	Illinois	33
37	Oregon	32
37	Rhode Island	32
39	Oklahoma	31
40	Georgia	30
40	West Virginia	30
42	Kentucky	29
43	California	28
44	Arizona	27
44	Nevada	27
46	Tennessee	26
47	Alabama	25
48	Louisiana	24
49	New Mexico	23
50	Mississippi	20

District of Columbia — 13

Source: U.S. Department of Education, National Center for Education Statistics
"The Nation's Report Card: Mathematics 2007" (http://nces.ed.gov/nationsreportcard/)
*There are four achievement levels: Below Basic, Basic, Proficient, and Advanced. Proficient represents solid academic mastery for 4th graders. Students reaching this level have demonstrated competency over challenging subject matter, including subject matter knowledge, application of such knowledge to real-world situations, and analytical skills appropriate to the subject matter.

Percent of Public School Fourth Graders Eligible for Free or Reduced Price Lunch Program Proficient or Better in Mathematics in 2007
National Percent = 22%

ALPHA ORDER

RANK	STATE	PERCENT
49	Alabama	13
23	Alaska	23
48	Arizona	15
21	Arkansas	24
43	California	16
30	Colorado	21
43	Connecticut	16
23	Delaware	23
17	Florida	25
43	Georgia	16
33	Hawaii	20
11	Idaho	27
40	Illinois	17
6	Indiana	30
14	Iowa	26
1	Kansas	34
38	Kentucky	18
40	Louisiana	17
11	Maine	27
37	Maryland	19
2	Massachusetts	32
33	Michigan	20
9	Minnesota	28
49	Mississippi	13
26	Missouri	22
6	Montana	30
30	Nebraska	21
43	Nevada	16
2	New Hampshire	32
14	New Jersey	26
43	New Mexico	16
9	New York	28
21	North Carolina	24
6	North Dakota	30
23	Ohio	23
26	Oklahoma	22
30	Oregon	21
26	Pennsylvania	22
38	Rhode Island	18
33	South Carolina	20
17	South Dakota	25
40	Tennessee	17
11	Texas	27
17	Utah	25
5	Vermont	31
33	Virginia	20
14	Washington	26
26	West Virginia	22
17	Wisconsin	25
2	Wyoming	32

RANK ORDER

RANK	STATE	PERCENT
1	Kansas	34
2	Massachusetts	32
2	New Hampshire	32
2	Wyoming	32
5	Vermont	31
6	Indiana	30
6	Montana	30
6	North Dakota	30
9	Minnesota	28
9	New York	28
11	Idaho	27
11	Maine	27
11	Texas	27
14	Iowa	26
14	New Jersey	26
14	Washington	26
17	Florida	25
17	South Dakota	25
17	Utah	25
17	Wisconsin	25
21	Arkansas	24
21	North Carolina	24
23	Alaska	23
23	Delaware	23
23	Ohio	23
26	Missouri	22
26	Oklahoma	22
26	Pennsylvania	22
26	West Virginia	22
30	Colorado	21
30	Nebraska	21
30	Oregon	21
33	Hawaii	20
33	Michigan	20
33	South Carolina	20
33	Virginia	20
37	Maryland	19
38	Kentucky	18
38	Rhode Island	18
40	Illinois	17
40	Louisiana	17
40	Tennessee	17
43	California	16
43	Connecticut	16
43	Georgia	16
43	Nevada	16
43	New Mexico	16
48	Arizona	15
49	Alabama	13
49	Mississippi	13
	District of Columbia	7

Source: U.S. Department of Education, National Center for Education Statistics
    "The Nation's Report Card: Mathematics 2007" (http://nces.ed.gov/nationsreportcard/)
*There are four achievement levels: Below Basic, Basic, Proficient, and Advanced. Proficient represents solid academic mastery for 4th graders. Students reaching this level have demonstrated competency over challenging subject matter, including subject matter knowledge, application of such knowledge to real-world situations, and analytical skills appropriate to the subject matter.

Percent of White Public School Fourth Graders Proficient or Better in Mathematics in 2007
National Percent = 51%*

ALPHA ORDER

RANK	STATE	PERCENT
46	Alabama	36
21	Alaska	50
27	Arizona	48
29	Arkansas	46
18	California	52
10	Colorado	54
6	Connecticut	57
13	Delaware	53
10	Florida	54
29	Georgia	46
29	Hawaii	46
34	Idaho	45
21	Illinois	50
18	Indiana	52
29	Iowa	46
4	Kansas	58
48	Kentucky	34
45	Louisiana	37
39	Maine	43
9	Maryland	55
1	Massachusetts	65
38	Michigan	44
4	Minnesota	58
48	Mississippi	34
34	Missouri	45
25	Montana	49
34	Nebraska	45
39	Nevada	43
13	New Hampshire	53
2	New Jersey	63
39	New Mexico	43
7	New York	56
7	North Carolina	56
25	North Dakota	49
13	Ohio	53
44	Oklahoma	39
43	Oregon	40
13	Pennsylvania	53
42	Rhode Island	41
21	South Carolina	50
29	South Dakota	46
46	Tennessee	36
3	Texas	59
34	Utah	45
21	Vermont	50
13	Virginia	53
20	Washington	51
50	West Virginia	33
10	Wisconsin	54
27	Wyoming	48

RANK ORDER

RANK	STATE	PERCENT
1	Massachusetts	65
2	New Jersey	63
3	Texas	59
4	Kansas	58
4	Minnesota	58
6	Connecticut	57
7	New York	56
7	North Carolina	56
9	Maryland	55
10	Colorado	54
10	Florida	54
10	Wisconsin	54
13	Delaware	53
13	New Hampshire	53
13	Ohio	53
13	Pennsylvania	53
13	Virginia	53
18	California	52
18	Indiana	52
20	Washington	51
21	Alaska	50
21	Illinois	50
21	South Carolina	50
21	Vermont	50
25	Montana	49
25	North Dakota	49
27	Arizona	48
27	Wyoming	48
29	Arkansas	46
29	Georgia	46
29	Hawaii	46
29	Iowa	46
29	South Dakota	46
34	Idaho	45
34	Missouri	45
34	Nebraska	45
34	Utah	45
38	Michigan	44
39	Maine	43
39	Nevada	43
39	New Mexico	43
42	Rhode Island	41
43	Oregon	40
44	Oklahoma	39
45	Louisiana	37
46	Alabama	36
46	Tennessee	36
48	Kentucky	34
48	Mississippi	34
50	West Virginia	33

District of Columbia	73

Source: U.S. Department of Education, National Center for Education Statistics
    "The Nation's Report Card: Mathematics 2007" (http://nces.ed.gov/nationsreportcard/)
*There are four achievement levels: Below Basic, Basic, Proficient, and Advanced. Proficient represents solid academic mastery for 4th graders. Students reaching this level have demonstrated competency over challenging subject matter, including subject matter knowledge, application of such knowledge to real-world situations, and analytical skills appropriate to the subject matter.

Percent of Black Public School Fourth Graders Proficient or Better in Mathematics in 2007
National Percent = 15%*

ALPHA ORDER

RANK	STATE	PERCENT
38	Alabama	10
5	Alaska	22
20	Arizona	16
33	Arkansas	12
25	California	15
8	Colorado	20
25	Connecticut	15
8	Delaware	20
25	Florida	15
32	Georgia	13
4	Hawaii	24
NA	Idaho**	NA
41	Illinois	9
30	Indiana	14
16	Iowa	17
6	Kansas	21
33	Kentucky	12
37	Louisiana	11
16	Maine	17
16	Maryland	17
1	Massachusetts	26
33	Michigan	12
20	Minnesota	16
41	Mississippi	9
33	Missouri	12
NA	Montana**	NA
41	Nebraska	9
20	Nevada	16
2	New Hampshire	25
2	New Jersey	25
11	New Mexico	18
11	New York	18
25	North Carolina	15
NA	North Dakota**	NA
11	Ohio	18
38	Oklahoma	10
20	Oregon	16
11	Pennsylvania	18
20	Rhode Island	16
30	South Carolina	14
25	South Dakota	15
41	Tennessee	9
6	Texas	21
NA	Utah**	NA
NA	Vermont**	NA
11	Virginia	18
16	Washington	17
10	West Virginia	19
38	Wisconsin	10
NA	Wyoming**	NA

RANK ORDER

RANK	STATE	PERCENT
1	Massachusetts	26
2	New Hampshire	25
2	New Jersey	25
4	Hawaii	24
5	Alaska	22
6	Kansas	21
6	Texas	21
8	Colorado	20
8	Delaware	20
10	West Virginia	19
11	New Mexico	18
11	New York	18
11	Ohio	18
11	Pennsylvania	18
11	Virginia	18
16	Iowa	17
16	Maine	17
16	Maryland	17
16	Washington	17
20	Arizona	16
20	Minnesota	16
20	Nevada	16
20	Oregon	16
20	Rhode Island	16
25	California	15
25	Connecticut	15
25	Florida	15
25	North Carolina	15
25	South Dakota	15
30	Indiana	14
30	South Carolina	14
32	Georgia	13
33	Arkansas	12
33	Kentucky	12
33	Michigan	12
33	Missouri	12
37	Louisiana	11
38	Alabama	10
38	Oklahoma	10
38	Wisconsin	10
41	Illinois	9
41	Mississippi	9
41	Nebraska	9
41	Tennessee	9
NA	Idaho**	NA
NA	Montana**	NA
NA	North Dakota**	NA
NA	Utah**	NA
NA	Vermont**	NA
NA	Wyoming**	NA

District of Columbia 8

Source: U.S. Department of Education, National Center for Education Statistics
"The Nation's Report Card: Mathematics 2007" (http://nces.ed.gov/nationsreportcard/)
*There are four achievement levels: Below Basic, Basic, Proficient, and Advanced. Proficient represents solid academic mastery for 4th graders. Students reaching this level have demonstrated competency over challenging subject matter, including subject matter knowledge, application of such knowledge to real-world situations, and analytical skills appropriate to the subject matter. **Sample size insufficient.

Percent of Hispanic Public School Fourth Graders Proficient or Better in Mathematics in 2007
National Percent = 22%*

ALPHA ORDER

RANK	STATE	PERCENT
36	Alabama	17
13	Alaska	26
39	Arizona	15
23	Arkansas	22
39	California	15
29	Colorado	19
33	Connecticut	18
17	Delaware	25
2	Florida	33
28	Georgia	20
29	Hawaii	19
33	Idaho	18
29	Illinois	19
13	Indiana	26
17	Iowa	25
5	Kansas	29
39	Kentucky	15
3	Louisiana	31
NA	Maine**	NA
7	Maryland	28
21	Massachusetts	23
13	Michigan	26
23	Minnesota	22
NA	Mississippi**	NA
13	Missouri	26
1	Montana	40
39	Nebraska	15
33	Nevada	18
11	New Hampshire	27
5	New Jersey	29
37	New Mexico	16
17	New York	25
7	North Carolina	28
NA	North Dakota**	NA
17	Ohio	25
23	Oklahoma	22
45	Oregon	12
7	Pennsylvania	28
39	Rhode Island	15
26	South Carolina	21
26	South Dakota	21
39	Tennessee	15
4	Texas	30
37	Utah	16
NA	Vermont**	NA
7	Virginia	28
29	Washington	19
NA	West Virginia**	NA
11	Wisconsin	27
21	Wyoming	23

RANK ORDER

RANK	STATE	PERCENT
1	Montana	40
2	Florida	33
3	Louisiana	31
4	Texas	30
5	Kansas	29
5	New Jersey	29
7	Maryland	28
7	North Carolina	28
7	Pennsylvania	28
7	Virginia	28
11	New Hampshire	27
11	Wisconsin	27
13	Alaska	26
13	Indiana	26
13	Michigan	26
13	Missouri	26
17	Delaware	25
17	Iowa	25
17	New York	25
17	Ohio	25
21	Massachusetts	23
21	Wyoming	23
23	Arkansas	22
23	Minnesota	22
23	Oklahoma	22
26	South Carolina	21
26	South Dakota	21
28	Georgia	20
29	Colorado	19
29	Hawaii	19
29	Illinois	19
29	Washington	19
33	Connecticut	18
33	Idaho	18
33	Nevada	18
36	Alabama	17
37	New Mexico	16
37	Utah	16
39	Arizona	15
39	California	15
39	Kentucky	15
39	Nebraska	15
39	Rhode Island	15
39	Tennessee	15
45	Oregon	12
NA	Maine**	NA
NA	Mississippi**	NA
NA	North Dakota**	NA
NA	Vermont**	NA
NA	West Virginia**	NA
	District of Columbia	19

Source: U.S. Department of Education, National Center for Education Statistics
"The Nation's Report Card: Mathematics 2007" (http://nces.ed.gov/nationsreportcard/)
*There are four achievement levels: Below Basic, Basic, Proficient, and Advanced. Proficient represents solid academic mastery for 4th graders. Students reaching this level have demonstrated competency over challenging subject matter, including subject matter knowledge, application of such knowledge to real-world situations, and analytical skills appropriate to the subject matter. **Sample size insufficient.

Percent of Asian Public School Fourth Graders Proficient or Better in Mathematics in 2007
National Percent = 59%*

ALPHA ORDER

RANK	STATE	PERCENT
NA	Alabama**	NA
29	Alaska	37
16	Arizona	59
27	Arkansas	41
18	California	56
20	Colorado	53
10	Connecticut	64
2	Delaware	70
16	Florida	59
12	Georgia	63
30	Hawaii	31
NA	Idaho**	NA
13	Illinois	62
NA	Indiana**	NA
NA	Iowa**	NA
7	Kansas	67
NA	Kentucky**	NA
NA	Louisiana**	NA
NA	Maine**	NA
6	Maryland	68
8	Massachusetts	66
4	Michigan	69
25	Minnesota	43
NA	Mississippi**	NA
NA	Missouri**	NA
NA	Montana**	NA
NA	Nebraska**	NA
25	Nevada	43
10	New Hampshire	64
1	New Jersey	78
NA	New Mexico**	NA
4	New York	69
14	North Carolina	60
NA	North Dakota**	NA
NA	Ohio**	NA
23	Oklahoma	48
20	Oregon	53
8	Pennsylvania	66
27	Rhode Island	41
NA	South Carolina**	NA
NA	South Dakota**	NA
NA	Tennessee**	NA
2	Texas	70
24	Utah	44
NA	Vermont**	NA
14	Virginia	60
19	Washington	54
NA	West Virginia**	NA
22	Wisconsin	50
NA	Wyoming**	NA

RANK ORDER

RANK	STATE	PERCENT
1	New Jersey	78
2	Delaware	70
2	Texas	70
4	Michigan	69
4	New York	69
6	Maryland	68
7	Kansas	67
8	Massachusetts	66
8	Pennsylvania	66
10	Connecticut	64
10	New Hampshire	64
12	Georgia	63
13	Illinois	62
14	North Carolina	60
14	Virginia	60
16	Arizona	59
16	Florida	59
18	California	56
19	Washington	54
20	Colorado	53
20	Oregon	53
22	Wisconsin	50
23	Oklahoma	48
24	Utah	44
25	Minnesota	43
25	Nevada	43
27	Arkansas	41
27	Rhode Island	41
29	Alaska	37
30	Hawaii	31
NA	Alabama**	NA
NA	Idaho**	NA
NA	Indiana**	NA
NA	Iowa**	NA
NA	Kentucky**	NA
NA	Louisiana**	NA
NA	Maine**	NA
NA	Mississippi**	NA
NA	Missouri**	NA
NA	Montana**	NA
NA	Nebraska**	NA
NA	New Mexico**	NA
NA	North Dakota**	NA
NA	Ohio**	NA
NA	South Carolina**	NA
NA	South Dakota**	NA
NA	Tennessee**	NA
NA	Vermont**	NA
NA	West Virginia**	NA
NA	Wyoming**	NA
	District of Columbia**	NA

Source: U.S. Department of Education, National Center for Education Statistics
   "The Nation's Report Card: Mathematics 2007" (http://nces.ed.gov/nationsreportcard/)
*There are four achievement levels: Below Basic, Basic, Proficient, and Advanced. Proficient represents solid academic mastery for 4th graders. Students reaching this level have demonstrated competency over challenging subject matter, including subject matter knowledge, application of such knowledge to real-world situations, and analytical skills appropriate to the subject matter. **Sample size insufficient.

Percent of Disabled Public School Fourth Graders Proficient or Better in Mathematics in 2007
National Percent = 19%*

ALPHA ORDER

RANK	STATE	PERCENT
49	Alabama	8
39	Alaska	14
45	Arizona	13
25	Arkansas	18
39	California	14
39	Colorado	14
45	Connecticut	13
13	Delaware	22
25	Florida	18
25	Georgia	18
49	Hawaii	8
39	Idaho	14
13	Illinois	22
5	Indiana	25
36	Iowa	15
10	Kansas	23
22	Kentucky	19
47	Louisiana	11
18	Maine	21
18	Maryland	21
1	Massachusetts	33
31	Michigan	16
5	Minnesota	25
39	Mississippi	14
10	Missouri	23
25	Montana	18
30	Nebraska	17
2	Nevada	26
5	New Hampshire	25
5	New Jersey	25
48	New Mexico	9
36	New York	15
13	North Carolina	22
9	North Dakota	24
13	Ohio	22
39	Oklahoma	14
31	Oregon	16
2	Pennsylvania	26
36	Rhode Island	15
31	South Carolina	16
13	South Dakota	22
22	Tennessee	19
10	Texas	23
31	Utah	16
31	Vermont	16
2	Virginia	26
18	Washington	21
25	West Virginia	18
18	Wisconsin	21
22	Wyoming	19

RANK ORDER

RANK	STATE	PERCENT
1	Massachusetts	33
2	Nevada	26
2	Pennsylvania	26
2	Virginia	26
5	Indiana	25
5	Minnesota	25
5	New Hampshire	25
5	New Jersey	25
9	North Dakota	24
10	Kansas	23
10	Missouri	23
10	Texas	23
13	Delaware	22
13	Illinois	22
13	North Carolina	22
13	Ohio	22
13	South Dakota	22
18	Maine	21
18	Maryland	21
18	Washington	21
18	Wisconsin	21
22	Kentucky	19
22	Tennessee	19
22	Wyoming	19
25	Arkansas	18
25	Florida	18
25	Georgia	18
25	Montana	18
25	West Virginia	18
30	Nebraska	17
31	Michigan	16
31	Oregon	16
31	South Carolina	16
31	Utah	16
31	Vermont	16
36	Iowa	15
36	New York	15
36	Rhode Island	15
39	Alaska	14
39	California	14
39	Colorado	14
39	Idaho	14
39	Mississippi	14
39	Oklahoma	14
45	Arizona	13
45	Connecticut	13
47	Louisiana	11
48	New Mexico	9
49	Alabama	8
49	Hawaii	8

| | District of Columbia | 3 |

Source: U.S. Department of Education, National Center for Education Statistics
"The Nation's Report Card: Mathematics 2007" (http://nces.ed.gov/nationsreportcard/)
*There are four achievement levels: Below Basic, Basic, Proficient, and Advanced. Proficient represents solid academic mastery for 4th graders. Students reaching this level have demonstrated competency over challenging subject matter, including subject matter knowledge, application of such knowledge to real-world situations, and analytical skills appropriate to the subject matter. Based only on disabled students who were assessed.

Average Public School Eighth Grade Mathematics Score in 2007

National Average Score = 280*

ALPHA ORDER

RANK	STATE	AVERAGE SCORE
49	Alabama	266
26	Alaska	283
37	Arizona	276
41	Arkansas	274
45	California	270
12	Colorado	286
28	Connecticut	282
26	Delaware	283
35	Florida	277
38	Georgia	275
47	Hawaii	269
22	Idaho	284
32	Illinois	280
18	Indiana	285
18	Iowa	285
5	Kansas	290
34	Kentucky	279
43	Louisiana	272
12	Maine	286
12	Maryland	286
1	Massachusetts	298
35	Michigan	277
2	Minnesota	292
50	Mississippi	265
30	Missouri	281
10	Montana	287
22	Nebraska	284
44	Nevada	271
7	New Hampshire	288
6	New Jersey	289
48	New Mexico	268
32	New York	280
22	North Carolina	284
2	North Dakota	292
18	Ohio	285
38	Oklahoma	275
22	Oregon	284
12	Pennsylvania	286
38	Rhode Island	275
28	South Carolina	282
7	South Dakota	288
41	Tennessee	274
12	Texas	286
30	Utah	281
4	Vermont	291
7	Virginia	288
18	Washington	285
45	West Virginia	270
12	Wisconsin	286
10	Wyoming	287

RANK ORDER

RANK	STATE	AVERAGE SCORE
1	Massachusetts	298
2	Minnesota	292
2	North Dakota	292
4	Vermont	291
5	Kansas	290
6	New Jersey	289
7	New Hampshire	288
7	South Dakota	288
7	Virginia	288
10	Montana	287
10	Wyoming	287
12	Colorado	286
12	Maine	286
12	Maryland	286
12	Pennsylvania	286
12	Texas	286
12	Wisconsin	286
18	Indiana	285
18	Iowa	285
18	Ohio	285
18	Washington	285
22	Idaho	284
22	Nebraska	284
22	North Carolina	284
22	Oregon	284
26	Alaska	283
26	Delaware	283
28	Connecticut	282
28	South Carolina	282
30	Missouri	281
30	Utah	281
32	Illinois	280
32	New York	280
34	Kentucky	279
35	Florida	277
35	Michigan	277
37	Arizona	276
38	Georgia	275
38	Oklahoma	275
38	Rhode Island	275
41	Arkansas	274
41	Tennessee	274
43	Louisiana	272
44	Nevada	271
45	California	270
45	West Virginia	270
47	Hawaii	269
48	New Mexico	268
49	Alabama	266
50	Mississippi	265

	District of Columbia	248

Source: U.S. Department of Education, National Center for Education Statistics
  "The Nation's Report Card: Mathematics 2007" (http://nces.ed.gov/nationsreportcard/)
*These scores are from the National Assessment of Educational Progress (NAEP). Scale ranges from 0 to 500.

Average Mathematics Score for Public School Eighth Grade Males in 2007

National Average Score = 281*

RANK	STATE	AVERAGE SCORE
48	Alabama	267
27	Alaska	282
37	Arizona	277
42	Arkansas	274
46	California	270
13	Colorado	287
27	Connecticut	282
21	Delaware	285
35	Florida	278
41	Georgia	275
48	Hawaii	267
21	Idaho	285
27	Illinois	282
19	Indiana	286
13	Iowa	287
5	Kansas	291
34	Kentucky	280
43	Louisiana	273
10	Maine	288
13	Maryland	287
1	Massachusetts	300
35	Michigan	278
3	Minnesota	292
50	Mississippi	266
27	Missouri	282
13	Montana	287
21	Nebraska	285
44	Nevada	271
10	New Hampshire	288
6	New Jersey	290
47	New Mexico	268
32	New York	281
21	North Carolina	285
2	North Dakota	293
19	Ohio	286
37	Oklahoma	277
21	Oregon	285
8	Pennsylvania	289
40	Rhode Island	276
32	South Carolina	281
6	South Dakota	290
37	Tennessee	277
13	Texas	287
27	Utah	282
3	Vermont	292
8	Virginia	289
21	Washington	285
44	West Virginia	271
13	Wisconsin	287
10	Wyoming	288

RANK	STATE	AVERAGE SCORE
1	Massachusetts	300
2	North Dakota	293
3	Minnesota	292
3	Vermont	292
5	Kansas	291
6	New Jersey	290
6	South Dakota	290
8	Pennsylvania	289
8	Virginia	289
10	Maine	288
10	New Hampshire	288
10	Wyoming	288
13	Colorado	287
13	Iowa	287
13	Maryland	287
13	Montana	287
13	Texas	287
13	Wisconsin	287
19	Indiana	286
19	Ohio	286
21	Delaware	285
21	Idaho	285
21	Nebraska	285
21	North Carolina	285
21	Oregon	285
21	Washington	285
27	Alaska	282
27	Connecticut	282
27	Illinois	282
27	Missouri	282
27	Utah	282
32	New York	281
32	South Carolina	281
34	Kentucky	280
35	Florida	278
35	Michigan	278
37	Arizona	277
37	Oklahoma	277
37	Tennessee	277
40	Rhode Island	276
41	Georgia	275
42	Arkansas	274
43	Louisiana	273
44	Nevada	271
44	West Virginia	271
46	California	270
47	New Mexico	268
48	Alabama	267
48	Hawaii	267
50	Mississippi	266

	District of Columbia	248

Source: U.S. Department of Education, National Center for Education Statistics
   "The Nation's Report Card: Mathematics 2007" (http://nces.ed.gov/nationsreportcard/)
*These scores are from the National Assessment of Educational Progress (NAEP). Scale ranges from 0 to 500.

Average Mathematics Score for Public School Eighth Grade Females in 2007

National Average Score = 279*

ALPHA ORDER

RANK	STATE	AVERAGE SCORE
49	Alabama	265
20	Alaska	283
38	Arizona	274
38	Arkansas	274
44	California	270
10	Colorado	286
20	Connecticut	283
29	Delaware	281
34	Florida	277
38	Georgia	274
44	Hawaii	270
26	Idaho	282
32	Illinois	279
16	Indiana	284
16	Iowa	284
5	Kansas	289
34	Kentucky	277
42	Louisiana	272
13	Maine	285
16	Maryland	284
1	Massachusetts	296
36	Michigan	275
2	Minnesota	292
50	Mississippi	264
32	Missouri	279
7	Montana	287
26	Nebraska	282
44	Nevada	270
7	New Hampshire	287
6	New Jersey	288
48	New Mexico	267
30	New York	280
20	North Carolina	283
3	North Dakota	290
20	Ohio	283
41	Oklahoma	273
20	Oregon	283
20	Pennsylvania	283
36	Rhode Island	275
26	South Carolina	282
7	South Dakota	287
43	Tennessee	271
13	Texas	285
30	Utah	280
3	Vermont	290
10	Virginia	286
13	Washington	285
47	West Virginia	269
16	Wisconsin	284
10	Wyoming	286

RANK ORDER

RANK	STATE	AVERAGE SCORE
1	Massachusetts	296
2	Minnesota	292
3	North Dakota	290
3	Vermont	290
5	Kansas	289
6	New Jersey	288
7	Montana	287
7	New Hampshire	287
7	South Dakota	287
10	Colorado	286
10	Virginia	286
10	Wyoming	286
13	Maine	285
13	Texas	285
13	Washington	285
16	Indiana	284
16	Iowa	284
16	Maryland	284
16	Wisconsin	284
20	Alaska	283
20	Connecticut	283
20	North Carolina	283
20	Ohio	283
20	Oregon	283
20	Pennsylvania	283
26	Idaho	282
26	Nebraska	282
26	South Carolina	282
29	Delaware	281
30	New York	280
30	Utah	280
32	Illinois	279
32	Missouri	279
34	Florida	277
34	Kentucky	277
36	Michigan	275
36	Rhode Island	275
38	Arizona	274
38	Arkansas	274
38	Georgia	274
41	Oklahoma	273
42	Louisiana	272
43	Tennessee	271
44	California	270
44	Hawaii	270
44	Nevada	270
47	West Virginia	269
48	New Mexico	267
49	Alabama	265
50	Mississippi	264

	District of Columbia	248

Source: U.S. Department of Education, National Center for Education Statistics
  "The Nation's Report Card: Mathematics 2007" (http://nces.ed.gov/nationsreportcard/)
*These scores are from the National Assessment of Educational Progress (NAEP). Scale ranges from 0 to 500.

Average Mathematics Score for Public School Eighth Graders Eligible for Free or Reduced Price Lunch Program in 2007
National Average Score = 265*

ALPHA ORDER			RANK ORDER		
RANK	STATE	AVERAGE SCORE	RANK	STATE	AVERAGE SCORE
50	Alabama	250	1	North Dakota	280
28	Alaska	266	2	Vermont	277
37	Arizona	262	3	Kansas	275
36	Arkansas	263	3	Maine	275
46	California	257	3	Massachusetts	275
24	Colorado	267	3	South Dakota	275
49	Connecticut	256	3	Texas	275
14	Delaware	270	3	Wyoming	275
32	Florida	265	9	Idaho	273
37	Georgia	262	9	Minnesota	273
44	Hawaii	258	11	Montana	272
9	Idaho	273	12	Indiana	271
37	Illinois	262	12	New Hampshire	271
12	Indiana	271	14	Delaware	270
14	Iowa	270	14	Iowa	270
3	Kansas	275	14	Oregon	270
24	Kentucky	267	17	South Carolina	269
34	Louisiana	264	18	Maryland	268
3	Maine	275	18	New York	268
18	Maryland	268	18	North Carolina	268
3	Massachusetts	275	18	Ohio	268
42	Michigan	259	18	Virginia	268
9	Minnesota	273	18	Washington	268
46	Mississippi	257	24	Colorado	267
28	Missouri	266	24	Kentucky	267
11	Montana	272	24	Pennsylvania	267
32	Nebraska	265	24	Utah	267
42	Nevada	259	28	Alaska	266
12	New Hampshire	271	28	Missouri	266
28	New Jersey	266	28	New Jersey	266
44	New Mexico	258	28	Wisconsin	266
18	New York	268	32	Florida	265
18	North Carolina	268	32	Nebraska	265
1	North Dakota	280	34	Louisiana	264
18	Ohio	268	34	Oklahoma	264
34	Oklahoma	264	36	Arkansas	263
14	Oregon	270	37	Arizona	262
24	Pennsylvania	267	37	Georgia	262
46	Rhode Island	257	37	Illinois	262
17	South Carolina	269	37	Tennessee	262
3	South Dakota	275	41	West Virginia	260
37	Tennessee	262	42	Michigan	259
3	Texas	275	42	Nevada	259
24	Utah	267	44	Hawaii	258
2	Vermont	277	44	New Mexico	258
18	Virginia	268	46	California	257
18	Washington	268	46	Mississippi	257
41	West Virginia	260	46	Rhode Island	257
28	Wisconsin	266	49	Connecticut	256
3	Wyoming	275	50	Alabama	250
				District of Columbia	243

Source: U.S. Department of Education, National Center for Education Statistics
"The Nation's Report Card: Mathematics 2007" (http://nces.ed.gov/nationsreportcard/)
*These scores are from the National Assessment of Educational Progress (NAEP). Scale ranges from 0 to 500.

Percent of Public School Eighth Graders Proficient or Better in Mathematics in 2007
National Percent = 31%*

ALPHA ORDER

RANK	STATE	PERCENT
48	Alabama	18
27	Alaska	32
38	Arizona	26
40	Arkansas	24
40	California	24
11	Colorado	37
17	Connecticut	35
30	Delaware	31
36	Florida	27
39	Georgia	25
44	Hawaii	21
24	Idaho	34
30	Illinois	31
17	Indiana	35
17	Iowa	35
5	Kansas	40
36	Kentucky	27
46	Louisiana	19
24	Maine	34
11	Maryland	37
1	Massachusetts	51
34	Michigan	29
2	Minnesota	43
50	Mississippi	14
32	Missouri	30
8	Montana	38
17	Nebraska	35
42	Nevada	23
8	New Hampshire	38
5	New Jersey	40
49	New Mexico	17
32	New York	30
24	North Carolina	34
3	North Dakota	41
17	Ohio	35
44	Oklahoma	21
17	Oregon	35
8	Pennsylvania	38
35	Rhode Island	28
27	South Carolina	32
7	South Dakota	39
42	Tennessee	23
17	Texas	35
27	Utah	32
3	Vermont	41
11	Virginia	37
15	Washington	36
46	West Virginia	19
11	Wisconsin	37
15	Wyoming	36

RANK ORDER

RANK	STATE	PERCENT
1	Massachusetts	51
2	Minnesota	43
3	North Dakota	41
3	Vermont	41
5	Kansas	40
5	New Jersey	40
7	South Dakota	39
8	Montana	38
8	New Hampshire	38
8	Pennsylvania	38
11	Colorado	37
11	Maryland	37
11	Virginia	37
11	Wisconsin	37
15	Washington	36
15	Wyoming	36
17	Connecticut	35
17	Indiana	35
17	Iowa	35
17	Nebraska	35
17	Ohio	35
17	Oregon	35
17	Texas	35
24	Idaho	34
24	Maine	34
24	North Carolina	34
27	Alaska	32
27	South Carolina	32
27	Utah	32
30	Delaware	31
30	Illinois	31
32	Missouri	30
32	New York	30
34	Michigan	29
35	Rhode Island	28
36	Florida	27
36	Kentucky	27
38	Arizona	26
39	Georgia	25
40	Arkansas	24
40	California	24
42	Nevada	23
42	Tennessee	23
44	Hawaii	21
44	Oklahoma	21
46	Louisiana	19
46	West Virginia	19
48	Alabama	18
49	New Mexico	17
50	Mississippi	14

	District of Columbia	8

Source: U.S. Department of Education, National Center for Education Statistics
"The Nation's Report Card: Mathematics 2007" (http://nces.ed.gov/nationsreportcard/)
*There are four achievement levels: Below Basic, Basic, Proficient, and Advanced. Proficient represents solid academic mastery for 8th graders. Students reaching this level have demonstrated competency over challenging subject matter, including subject matter knowledge, application of such knowledge to real-world situations, and analytical skills appropriate to the subject matter.

Percent of Public School Eighth Grade Males
Proficient or Better in Mathematics in 2007
National Percent = 33%*

ALPHA ORDER

RANK	STATE	PERCENT
45	Alabama	21
29	Alaska	33
34	Arizona	30
39	Arkansas	26
42	California	25
12	Colorado	38
26	Connecticut	35
27	Delaware	34
37	Florida	29
39	Georgia	26
47	Hawaii	20
24	Idaho	36
29	Illinois	33
16	Indiana	37
16	Iowa	37
7	Kansas	41
34	Kentucky	30
47	Louisiana	20
16	Maine	37
12	Maryland	38
1	Massachusetts	53
34	Michigan	30
2	Minnesota	44
50	Mississippi	16
32	Missouri	32
11	Montana	39
16	Nebraska	37
43	Nevada	24
12	New Hampshire	38
3	New Jersey	43
49	New Mexico	19
33	New York	31
24	North Carolina	36
3	North Dakota	43
12	Ohio	38
43	Oklahoma	24
16	Oregon	37
6	Pennsylvania	42
37	Rhode Island	29
29	South Carolina	33
7	South Dakota	41
39	Tennessee	26
16	Texas	37
27	Utah	34
3	Vermont	43
9	Virginia	40
16	Washington	37
45	West Virginia	21
9	Wisconsin	40
16	Wyoming	37

RANK ORDER

RANK	STATE	PERCENT
1	Massachusetts	53
2	Minnesota	44
3	New Jersey	43
3	North Dakota	43
3	Vermont	43
6	Pennsylvania	42
7	Kansas	41
7	South Dakota	41
9	Virginia	40
9	Wisconsin	40
11	Montana	39
12	Colorado	38
12	Maryland	38
12	New Hampshire	38
12	Ohio	38
16	Indiana	37
16	Iowa	37
16	Maine	37
16	Nebraska	37
16	Oregon	37
16	Texas	37
16	Washington	37
16	Wyoming	37
24	Idaho	36
24	North Carolina	36
26	Connecticut	35
27	Delaware	34
27	Utah	34
29	Alaska	33
29	Illinois	33
29	South Carolina	33
32	Missouri	32
33	New York	31
34	Arizona	30
34	Kentucky	30
34	Michigan	30
37	Florida	29
37	Rhode Island	29
39	Arkansas	26
39	Georgia	26
39	Tennessee	26
42	California	25
43	Nevada	24
43	Oklahoma	24
45	Alabama	21
45	West Virginia	21
47	Hawaii	20
47	Louisiana	20
49	New Mexico	19
50	Mississippi	16

District of Columbia   8

Source: U.S. Department of Education, National Center for Education Statistics
   "The Nation's Report Card: Mathematics 2007" (http://nces.ed.gov/nationsreportcard/)
*There are four achievement levels: Below Basic, Basic, Proficient, and Advanced.   Proficient represents solid academic mastery for 8th graders. Students reaching this level have demonstrated competency over challenging subject matter, including subject matter knowledge, application of such knowledge to real-world situations, and analytical skills appropriate to the subject matter.

Percent of Public School Eighth Grade Females
Proficient or Better in Mathematics in 2007
National Percent = 29%*

ALPHA ORDER

RANK	STATE	PERCENT
49	Alabama	15
23	Alaska	32
38	Arizona	23
41	Arkansas	22
38	California	23
8	Colorado	37
14	Connecticut	34
30	Delaware	29
36	Florida	26
38	Georgia	23
41	Hawaii	22
23	Idaho	32
30	Illinois	29
18	Indiana	33
18	Iowa	33
4	Kansas	39
37	Kentucky	24
45	Louisiana	18
23	Maine	32
11	Maryland	35
1	Massachusetts	48
34	Michigan	27
2	Minnesota	43
50	Mississippi	12
33	Missouri	28
10	Montana	36
23	Nebraska	32
41	Nevada	22
6	New Hampshire	38
6	New Jersey	38
47	New Mexico	16
30	New York	29
18	North Carolina	33
4	North Dakota	39
18	Ohio	33
45	Oklahoma	18
18	Oregon	33
11	Pennsylvania	35
34	Rhode Island	27
28	South Carolina	31
8	South Dakota	37
44	Tennessee	20
23	Texas	32
29	Utah	30
3	Vermont	40
14	Virginia	34
11	Washington	35
47	West Virginia	16
14	Wisconsin	34
14	Wyoming	34

RANK ORDER

RANK	STATE	PERCENT
1	Massachusetts	48
2	Minnesota	43
3	Vermont	40
4	Kansas	39
4	North Dakota	39
6	New Hampshire	38
6	New Jersey	38
8	Colorado	37
8	South Dakota	37
10	Montana	36
11	Maryland	35
11	Pennsylvania	35
11	Washington	35
14	Connecticut	34
14	Virginia	34
14	Wisconsin	34
14	Wyoming	34
18	Indiana	33
18	Iowa	33
18	North Carolina	33
18	Ohio	33
18	Oregon	33
23	Alaska	32
23	Idaho	32
23	Maine	32
23	Nebraska	32
23	Texas	32
28	South Carolina	31
29	Utah	30
30	Delaware	29
30	Illinois	29
30	New York	29
33	Missouri	28
34	Michigan	27
34	Rhode Island	27
36	Florida	26
37	Kentucky	24
38	Arizona	23
38	California	23
38	Georgia	23
41	Arkansas	22
41	Hawaii	22
41	Nevada	22
44	Tennessee	20
45	Louisiana	18
45	Oklahoma	18
47	New Mexico	16
47	West Virginia	16
49	Alabama	15
50	Mississippi	12

	District of Columbia	8

Source: U.S. Department of Education, National Center for Education Statistics
   "The Nation's Report Card: Mathematics 2007" (http://nces.ed.gov/nationsreportcard/)
*There are four achievement levels: Below Basic, Basic, Proficient, and Advanced. Proficient represents solid academic mastery for 8th graders. Students reaching this level have demonstrated competency over challenging subject matter, including subject matter knowledge, application of such knowledge to real-world situations, and analytical skills appropriate to the subject matter.

Percent of Public School Eighth Graders Eligible for Free or Reduced Price Lunch Program Proficient or Better in Mathematics in 2007
National Percent = 15%*

ALPHA ORDER

RANK	STATE	PERCENT
50	Alabama	6
22	Alaska	17
36	Arizona	13
34	Arkansas	14
41	California	12
22	Colorado	17
45	Connecticut	10
27	Delaware	16
27	Florida	16
41	Georgia	12
36	Hawaii	13
7	Idaho	22
36	Illinois	13
12	Indiana	20
12	Iowa	20
5	Kansas	23
31	Kentucky	15
44	Louisiana	11
10	Maine	21
31	Maryland	15
2	Massachusetts	25
34	Michigan	14
7	Minnesota	22
49	Mississippi	7
27	Missouri	16
7	Montana	22
22	Nebraska	17
36	Nevada	13
19	New Hampshire	18
22	New Jersey	17
48	New Mexico	9
15	New York	19
22	North Carolina	17
1	North Dakota	29
27	Ohio	16
36	Oklahoma	13
12	Oregon	20
15	Pennsylvania	19
45	Rhode Island	10
19	South Carolina	18
3	South Dakota	24
41	Tennessee	12
10	Texas	21
15	Utah	19
3	Vermont	24
31	Virginia	15
15	Washington	19
45	West Virginia	10
19	Wisconsin	18
5	Wyoming	23

RANK ORDER

RANK	STATE	PERCENT
1	North Dakota	29
2	Massachusetts	25
3	South Dakota	24
3	Vermont	24
5	Kansas	23
5	Wyoming	23
7	Idaho	22
7	Minnesota	22
7	Montana	22
10	Maine	21
10	Texas	21
12	Indiana	20
12	Iowa	20
12	Oregon	20
15	New York	19
15	Pennsylvania	19
15	Utah	19
15	Washington	19
19	New Hampshire	18
19	South Carolina	18
19	Wisconsin	18
22	Alaska	17
22	Colorado	17
22	Nebraska	17
22	New Jersey	17
22	North Carolina	17
27	Delaware	16
27	Florida	16
27	Missouri	16
27	Ohio	16
31	Kentucky	15
31	Maryland	15
31	Virginia	15
34	Arkansas	14
34	Michigan	14
36	Arizona	13
36	Hawaii	13
36	Illinois	13
36	Nevada	13
36	Oklahoma	13
41	California	12
41	Georgia	12
41	Tennessee	12
44	Louisiana	11
45	Connecticut	10
45	Rhode Island	10
45	West Virginia	10
48	New Mexico	9
49	Mississippi	7
50	Alabama	6

District of Columbia	4

Source: U.S. Department of Education, National Center for Education Statistics
"The Nation's Report Card: Mathematics 2007" (http://nces.ed.gov/nationsreportcard/)
*There are four achievement levels: Below Basic, Basic, Proficient, and Advanced. Proficient represents solid academic mastery for 8th graders. Students reaching this level have demonstrated competency over challenging subject matter, including subject matter knowledge, application of such knowledge to real-world situations, and analytical skills appropriate to the subject matter.

Percent of White Public School Eighth Graders Proficient or Better in Mathematics in 2007
National Percent = 41%*

ALPHA ORDER

RANK	STATE	PERCENT
47	Alabama	27
10	Alaska	44
24	Arizona	40
42	Arkansas	31
26	California	39
5	Colorado	48
10	Connecticut	44
15	Delaware	43
33	Florida	37
33	Georgia	37
45	Hawaii	28
31	Idaho	38
21	Illinois	41
24	Indiana	40
31	Iowa	38
8	Kansas	46
44	Kentucky	29
45	Louisiana	28
37	Maine	35
2	Maryland	53
1	Massachusetts	58
37	Michigan	35
5	Minnesota	48
49	Mississippi	24
35	Missouri	36
21	Montana	41
21	Nebraska	41
41	Nevada	32
26	New Hampshire	39
4	New Jersey	51
40	New Mexico	33
26	New York	39
8	North Carolina	46
10	North Dakota	44
17	Ohio	42
48	Oklahoma	25
26	Oregon	39
10	Pennsylvania	44
37	Rhode Island	35
10	South Carolina	44
15	South Dakota	43
43	Tennessee	30
2	Texas	53
35	Utah	36
17	Vermont	42
7	Virginia	47
17	Washington	42
50	West Virginia	19
17	Wisconsin	42
26	Wyoming	39

RANK ORDER

RANK	STATE	PERCENT
1	Massachusetts	58
2	Maryland	53
2	Texas	53
4	New Jersey	51
5	Colorado	48
5	Minnesota	48
7	Virginia	47
8	Kansas	46
8	North Carolina	46
10	Alaska	44
10	Connecticut	44
10	North Dakota	44
10	Pennsylvania	44
10	South Carolina	44
15	Delaware	43
15	South Dakota	43
17	Ohio	42
17	Vermont	42
17	Washington	42
17	Wisconsin	42
21	Illinois	41
21	Montana	41
21	Nebraska	41
24	Arizona	40
24	Indiana	40
26	California	39
26	New Hampshire	39
26	New York	39
26	Oregon	39
26	Wyoming	39
31	Idaho	38
31	Iowa	38
33	Florida	37
33	Georgia	37
35	Missouri	36
35	Utah	36
37	Maine	35
37	Michigan	35
37	Rhode Island	35
40	New Mexico	33
41	Nevada	32
42	Arkansas	31
43	Tennessee	30
44	Kentucky	29
45	Hawaii	28
45	Louisiana	28
47	Alabama	27
48	Oklahoma	25
49	Mississippi	24
50	West Virginia	19

District of Columbia**   NA

Source: U.S. Department of Education, National Center for Education Statistics
   "The Nation's Report Card: Mathematics 2007" (http://nces.ed.gov/nationsreportcard/)
*There are four achievement levels: Below Basic, Basic, Proficient, and Advanced. Proficient represents solid academic mastery for 8th graders. Students reaching this level have demonstrated competency over challenging subject matter, including subject matter knowledge, application of such knowledge to real-world situations, and analytical skills appropriate to the subject matter. **Sample size insufficient.

Percent of Black Public School Eighth Graders Proficient or Better in Mathematics in 2007
National Percent = 11%*

ALPHA ORDER

RANK	STATE	PERCENT
38	Alabama	4
6	Alaska	15
6	Arizona	15
25	Arkansas	9
22	California	10
2	Colorado	21
30	Connecticut	7
22	Delaware	10
18	Florida	11
18	Georgia	11
NA	Hawaii**	NA
NA	Idaho**	NA
30	Illinois	7
25	Indiana	9
18	Iowa	11
3	Kansas	16
18	Kentucky	11
30	Louisiana	7
NA	Maine**	NA
13	Maryland	13
13	Massachusetts	13
36	Michigan	5
10	Minnesota	14
38	Mississippi	4
34	Missouri	6
NA	Montana**	NA
36	Nebraska	5
16	Nevada	12
NA	New Hampshire**	NA
10	New Jersey	14
16	New Mexico	12
22	New York	10
10	North Carolina	14
NA	North Dakota**	NA
25	Ohio	9
25	Oklahoma	9
1	Oregon	28
13	Pennsylvania	13
25	Rhode Island	9
6	South Carolina	15
NA	South Dakota**	NA
30	Tennessee	7
3	Texas	16
NA	Utah**	NA
NA	Vermont**	NA
6	Virginia	15
3	Washington	16
38	West Virginia	4
34	Wisconsin	6
NA	Wyoming**	NA

RANK ORDER

RANK	STATE	PERCENT
1	Oregon	28
2	Colorado	21
3	Kansas	16
3	Texas	16
3	Washington	16
6	Alaska	15
6	Arizona	15
6	South Carolina	15
6	Virginia	15
10	Minnesota	14
10	New Jersey	14
10	North Carolina	14
13	Maryland	13
13	Massachusetts	13
13	Pennsylvania	13
16	Nevada	12
16	New Mexico	12
18	Florida	11
18	Georgia	11
18	Iowa	11
18	Kentucky	11
22	California	10
22	Delaware	10
22	New York	10
25	Arkansas	9
25	Indiana	9
25	Ohio	9
25	Oklahoma	9
25	Rhode Island	9
30	Connecticut	7
30	Illinois	7
30	Louisiana	7
30	Tennessee	7
34	Missouri	6
34	Wisconsin	6
36	Michigan	5
36	Nebraska	5
38	Alabama	4
38	Mississippi	4
38	West Virginia	4
NA	Hawaii**	NA
NA	Idaho**	NA
NA	Maine**	NA
NA	Montana**	NA
NA	New Hampshire**	NA
NA	North Dakota**	NA
NA	South Dakota**	NA
NA	Utah**	NA
NA	Vermont**	NA
NA	Wyoming**	NA

District of Columbia — 6

Source: U.S. Department of Education, National Center for Education Statistics
"The Nation's Report Card: Mathematics 2007" (http://nces.ed.gov/nationsreportcard/)
*There are four achievement levels: Below Basic, Basic, Proficient, and Advanced. Proficient represents solid academic mastery for 8th graders. Students reaching this level have demonstrated competency over challenging subject matter, including subject matter knowledge, application of such knowledge to real-world situations, and analytical skills appropriate to the subject matter. **Sample size insufficient.

Percent of Hispanic Public School Eighth Graders Proficient or Better in Mathematics in 2007
National Percent = 15%*

<table>
<tr><td colspan="3">ALPHA ORDER</td><td colspan="3">RANK ORDER</td></tr>
<tr><td>RANK</td><td>STATE</td><td>PERCENT</td><td>RANK</td><td>STATE</td><td>PERCENT</td></tr>
<tr><td>42</td><td>Alabama</td><td>3</td><td>1</td><td>Ohio</td><td>25</td></tr>
<tr><td>3</td><td>Alaska</td><td>23</td><td>2</td><td>Virginia</td><td>24</td></tr>
<tr><td>31</td><td>Arizona</td><td>12</td><td>3</td><td>Alaska</td><td>23</td></tr>
<tr><td>39</td><td>Arkansas</td><td>8</td><td>3</td><td>North Carolina</td><td>23</td></tr>
<tr><td>36</td><td>California</td><td>10</td><td>3</td><td>South Carolina</td><td>23</td></tr>
<tr><td>26</td><td>Colorado</td><td>13</td><td>3</td><td>Texas</td><td>23</td></tr>
<tr><td>36</td><td>Connecticut</td><td>10</td><td>7</td><td>Wyoming</td><td>22</td></tr>
<tr><td>16</td><td>Delaware</td><td>17</td><td>8</td><td>Florida</td><td>21</td></tr>
<tr><td>8</td><td>Florida</td><td>21</td><td>8</td><td>Maryland</td><td>21</td></tr>
<tr><td>19</td><td>Georgia</td><td>16</td><td>10</td><td>Indiana</td><td>20</td></tr>
<tr><td>22</td><td>Hawaii</td><td>15</td><td>10</td><td>New Jersey</td><td>20</td></tr>
<tr><td>19</td><td>Idaho</td><td>16</td><td>12</td><td>Massachusetts</td><td>19</td></tr>
<tr><td>26</td><td>Illinois</td><td>13</td><td>13</td><td>Minnesota</td><td>18</td></tr>
<tr><td>10</td><td>Indiana</td><td>20</td><td>13</td><td>South Dakota</td><td>18</td></tr>
<tr><td>26</td><td>Iowa</td><td>13</td><td>13</td><td>Wisconsin</td><td>18</td></tr>
<tr><td>19</td><td>Kansas</td><td>16</td><td>16</td><td>Delaware</td><td>17</td></tr>
<tr><td>NA</td><td>Kentucky**</td><td>NA</td><td>16</td><td>Missouri</td><td>17</td></tr>
<tr><td>NA</td><td>Louisiana**</td><td>NA</td><td>16</td><td>Pennsylvania</td><td>17</td></tr>
<tr><td>NA</td><td>Maine**</td><td>NA</td><td>19</td><td>Georgia</td><td>16</td></tr>
<tr><td>8</td><td>Maryland</td><td>21</td><td>19</td><td>Idaho</td><td>16</td></tr>
<tr><td>12</td><td>Massachusetts</td><td>19</td><td>19</td><td>Kansas</td><td>16</td></tr>
<tr><td>33</td><td>Michigan</td><td>11</td><td>22</td><td>Hawaii</td><td>15</td></tr>
<tr><td>13</td><td>Minnesota</td><td>18</td><td>22</td><td>New York</td><td>15</td></tr>
<tr><td>NA</td><td>Mississippi**</td><td>NA</td><td>24</td><td>New Hampshire</td><td>14</td></tr>
<tr><td>16</td><td>Missouri</td><td>17</td><td>24</td><td>Oregon</td><td>14</td></tr>
<tr><td>NA</td><td>Montana**</td><td>NA</td><td>26</td><td>Colorado</td><td>13</td></tr>
<tr><td>33</td><td>Nebraska</td><td>11</td><td>26</td><td>Illinois</td><td>13</td></tr>
<tr><td>33</td><td>Nevada</td><td>11</td><td>26</td><td>Iowa</td><td>13</td></tr>
<tr><td>24</td><td>New Hampshire</td><td>14</td><td>26</td><td>Tennessee</td><td>13</td></tr>
<tr><td>10</td><td>New Jersey</td><td>20</td><td>26</td><td>Washington</td><td>13</td></tr>
<tr><td>36</td><td>New Mexico</td><td>10</td><td>31</td><td>Arizona</td><td>12</td></tr>
<tr><td>22</td><td>New York</td><td>15</td><td>31</td><td>Utah</td><td>12</td></tr>
<tr><td>3</td><td>North Carolina</td><td>23</td><td>33</td><td>Michigan</td><td>11</td></tr>
<tr><td>NA</td><td>North Dakota**</td><td>NA</td><td>33</td><td>Nebraska</td><td>11</td></tr>
<tr><td>1</td><td>Ohio</td><td>25</td><td>33</td><td>Nevada</td><td>11</td></tr>
<tr><td>39</td><td>Oklahoma</td><td>8</td><td>36</td><td>California</td><td>10</td></tr>
<tr><td>24</td><td>Oregon</td><td>14</td><td>36</td><td>Connecticut</td><td>10</td></tr>
<tr><td>16</td><td>Pennsylvania</td><td>17</td><td>36</td><td>New Mexico</td><td>10</td></tr>
<tr><td>41</td><td>Rhode Island</td><td>7</td><td>39</td><td>Arkansas</td><td>8</td></tr>
<tr><td>3</td><td>South Carolina</td><td>23</td><td>39</td><td>Oklahoma</td><td>8</td></tr>
<tr><td>13</td><td>South Dakota</td><td>18</td><td>41</td><td>Rhode Island</td><td>7</td></tr>
<tr><td>26</td><td>Tennessee</td><td>13</td><td>42</td><td>Alabama</td><td>3</td></tr>
<tr><td>3</td><td>Texas</td><td>23</td><td>NA</td><td>Kentucky**</td><td>NA</td></tr>
<tr><td>31</td><td>Utah</td><td>12</td><td>NA</td><td>Louisiana**</td><td>NA</td></tr>
<tr><td>NA</td><td>Vermont**</td><td>NA</td><td>NA</td><td>Maine**</td><td>NA</td></tr>
<tr><td>2</td><td>Virginia</td><td>24</td><td>NA</td><td>Mississippi**</td><td>NA</td></tr>
<tr><td>26</td><td>Washington</td><td>13</td><td>NA</td><td>Montana**</td><td>NA</td></tr>
<tr><td>NA</td><td>West Virginia**</td><td>NA</td><td>NA</td><td>North Dakota**</td><td>NA</td></tr>
<tr><td>13</td><td>Wisconsin</td><td>18</td><td>NA</td><td>Vermont**</td><td>NA</td></tr>
<tr><td>7</td><td>Wyoming</td><td>22</td><td>NA</td><td>West Virginia**</td><td>NA</td></tr>
<tr><td></td><td></td><td></td><td></td><td>District of Columbia</td><td>9</td></tr>
</table>

Source: U.S. Department of Education, National Center for Education Statistics
"The Nation's Report Card: Mathematics 2007" (http://nces.ed.gov/nationsreportcard/)
*There are four achievement levels: Below Basic, Basic, Proficient, and Advanced. Proficient represents solid academic mastery for 8th graders. Students reaching this level have demonstrated competency over challenging subject matter, including subject matter knowledge, application of such knowledge to real-world situations, and analytical skills appropriate to the subject matter. **Sample size insufficient.

Percent of Asian Public School Eighth Graders Proficient or Better in Mathematics in 2007
National Percent = 49%*

ALPHA ORDER

RANK	STATE	PERCENT
NA	Alabama**	NA
22	Alaska	33
12	Arizona	52
NA	Arkansas**	NA
17	California	46
15	Colorado	48
7	Connecticut	61
6	Delaware	65
15	Florida	48
NA	Georgia**	NA
25	Hawaii	20
NA	Idaho**	NA
8	Illinois	55
NA	Indiana**	NA
NA	Iowa**	NA
12	Kansas	52
NA	Kentucky**	NA
NA	Louisiana**	NA
NA	Maine**	NA
4	Maryland	66
1	Massachusetts	74
NA	Michigan**	NA
21	Minnesota	34
NA	Mississippi**	NA
NA	Missouri**	NA
NA	Montana**	NA
NA	Nebraska**	NA
20	Nevada	36
NA	New Hampshire**	NA
2	New Jersey	69
NA	New Mexico**	NA
9	New York	53
14	North Carolina	50
NA	North Dakota**	NA
NA	Ohio**	NA
NA	Oklahoma**	NA
9	Oregon	53
4	Pennsylvania	66
24	Rhode Island	31
NA	South Carolina**	NA
NA	South Dakota**	NA
NA	Tennessee**	NA
3	Texas	67
23	Utah	32
NA	Vermont**	NA
9	Virginia	53
18	Washington	41
NA	West Virginia**	NA
19	Wisconsin	40
NA	Wyoming**	NA

RANK ORDER

RANK	STATE	PERCENT
1	Massachusetts	74
2	New Jersey	69
3	Texas	67
4	Maryland	66
4	Pennsylvania	66
6	Delaware	65
7	Connecticut	61
8	Illinois	55
9	New York	53
9	Oregon	53
9	Virginia	53
12	Arizona	52
12	Kansas	52
14	North Carolina	50
15	Colorado	48
15	Florida	48
17	California	46
18	Washington	41
19	Wisconsin	40
20	Nevada	36
21	Minnesota	34
22	Alaska	33
23	Utah	32
24	Rhode Island	31
25	Hawaii	20
NA	Alabama**	NA
NA	Arkansas**	NA
NA	Georgia**	NA
NA	Idaho**	NA
NA	Indiana**	NA
NA	Iowa**	NA
NA	Kentucky**	NA
NA	Louisiana**	NA
NA	Maine**	NA
NA	Michigan**	NA
NA	Mississippi**	NA
NA	Missouri**	NA
NA	Montana**	NA
NA	Nebraska**	NA
NA	New Hampshire**	NA
NA	New Mexico**	NA
NA	North Dakota**	NA
NA	Ohio**	NA
NA	Oklahoma**	NA
NA	South Carolina**	NA
NA	South Dakota**	NA
NA	Tennessee**	NA
NA	Vermont**	NA
NA	West Virginia**	NA
NA	Wyoming**	NA
	District of Columbia**	NA

Source: U.S. Department of Education, National Center for Education Statistics
"The Nation's Report Card: Mathematics 2007" (http://nces.ed.gov/nationsreportcard/)
*There are four achievement levels: Below Basic, Basic, Proficient, and Advanced. Proficient represents solid academic mastery for 8th graders. Students reaching this level have demonstrated competency over challenging subject matter, including subject matter knowledge, application of such knowledge to real-world situations, and analytical skills appropriate to the subject matter. **Sample size insufficient.

Percent of Disabled Public School Eighth Graders Proficient or Better in Mathematics in 2007
National Percent = 8%*

ALPHA ORDER

RANK	STATE	PERCENT
49	Alabama	1
25	Alaska	7
41	Arizona	4
45	Arkansas	3
37	California	5
9	Colorado	11
13	Connecticut	9
7	Delaware	12
20	Florida	8
32	Georgia	6
48	Hawaii	2
37	Idaho	5
25	Illinois	7
9	Indiana	11
32	Iowa	6
13	Kansas	9
25	Kentucky	7
41	Louisiana	4
9	Maine	11
2	Maryland	16
1	Massachusetts	18
41	Michigan	4
9	Minnesota	11
50	Mississippi	0
25	Missouri	7
37	Montana	5
20	Nebraska	8
13	Nevada	9
13	New Hampshire	9
13	New Jersey	9
32	New Mexico	6
32	New York	6
4	North Carolina	14
13	North Dakota	9
25	Ohio	7
45	Oklahoma	3
13	Oregon	9
4	Pennsylvania	14
37	Rhode Island	5
25	South Carolina	7
20	South Dakota	8
3	Tennessee	15
20	Texas	8
45	Utah	3
7	Vermont	12
6	Virginia	13
25	Washington	7
41	West Virginia	4
20	Wisconsin	8
32	Wyoming	6

RANK ORDER

RANK	STATE	PERCENT
1	Massachusetts	18
2	Maryland	16
3	Tennessee	15
4	North Carolina	14
4	Pennsylvania	14
6	Virginia	13
7	Delaware	12
7	Vermont	12
9	Colorado	11
9	Indiana	11
9	Maine	11
9	Minnesota	11
13	Connecticut	9
13	Kansas	9
13	Nevada	9
13	New Hampshire	9
13	New Jersey	9
13	North Dakota	9
13	Oregon	9
20	Florida	8
20	Nebraska	8
20	South Dakota	8
20	Texas	8
20	Wisconsin	8
25	Alaska	7
25	Illinois	7
25	Kentucky	7
25	Missouri	7
25	Ohio	7
25	South Carolina	7
25	Washington	7
32	Georgia	6
32	Iowa	6
32	New Mexico	6
32	New York	6
32	Wyoming	6
37	California	5
37	Idaho	5
37	Montana	5
37	Rhode Island	5
41	Arizona	4
41	Louisiana	4
41	Michigan	4
41	West Virginia	4
45	Arkansas	3
45	Oklahoma	3
45	Utah	3
48	Hawaii	2
49	Alabama	1
50	Mississippi	0
	District of Columbia	1

Source: U.S. Department of Education, National Center for Education Statistics
"The Nation's Report Card: Mathematics 2007" (http://nces.ed.gov/nationsreportcard/)
*There are four achievement levels: Below Basic, Basic, Proficient, and Advanced. Proficient represents solid academic mastery for 8th graders. Students reaching this level have demonstrated competency over challenging subject matter, including subject matter knowledge, application of such knowledge to real-world situations, and analytical skills appropriate to the subject matter. Based only on disabled students who were assessed.

Average Science Score for Public School Fourth Graders in 2005

National Average Score = 149*

ALPHA ORDER

RANK	STATE	AVERAGE SCORE
38	Alabama	142
NA	Alaska**	NA
42	Arizona	139
35	Arkansas	147
43	California	137
15	Colorado	155
15	Connecticut	155
21	Delaware	152
26	Florida	150
32	Georgia	148
38	Hawaii	142
15	Idaho	155
32	Illinois	148
21	Indiana	152
NA	Iowa**	NA
NA	Kansas**	NA
8	Kentucky	158
37	Louisiana	143
3	Maine	160
30	Maryland	149
3	Massachusetts	160
21	Michigan	152
14	Minnesota	156
44	Mississippi	133
8	Missouri	158
3	Montana	160
NA	Nebraska**	NA
41	Nevada	140
1	New Hampshire	161
19	New Jersey	154
40	New Mexico	141
NA	New York**	NA
30	North Carolina	149
3	North Dakota	160
12	Ohio	157
26	Oklahoma	150
24	Oregon	151
NA	Pennsylvania**	NA
36	Rhode Island	146
32	South Carolina	148
8	South Dakota	158
26	Tennessee	150
26	Texas	150
15	Utah	155
3	Vermont	160
1	Virginia	161
20	Washington	153
24	West Virginia	151
8	Wisconsin	158
12	Wyoming	157

RANK ORDER

RANK	STATE	AVERAGE SCORE
1	New Hampshire	161
1	Virginia	161
3	Maine	160
3	Massachusetts	160
3	Montana	160
3	North Dakota	160
3	Vermont	160
8	Kentucky	158
8	Missouri	158
8	South Dakota	158
8	Wisconsin	158
12	Ohio	157
12	Wyoming	157
14	Minnesota	156
15	Colorado	155
15	Connecticut	155
15	Idaho	155
15	Utah	155
19	New Jersey	154
20	Washington	153
21	Delaware	152
21	Indiana	152
21	Michigan	152
24	Oregon	151
24	West Virginia	151
26	Florida	150
26	Oklahoma	150
26	Tennessee	150
26	Texas	150
30	Maryland	149
30	North Carolina	149
32	Georgia	148
32	Illinois	148
32	South Carolina	148
35	Arkansas	147
36	Rhode Island	146
37	Louisiana	143
38	Alabama	142
38	Hawaii	142
40	New Mexico	141
41	Nevada	140
42	Arizona	139
43	California	137
44	Mississippi	133
NA	Alaska**	NA
NA	Iowa**	NA
NA	Kansas**	NA
NA	Nebraska**	NA
NA	New York**	NA
NA	Pennsylvania**	NA
	District of Columbia**	NA

Source: U.S. Department of Education, National Center for Education Statistics
   "The Nation's Report Card: Science 2005" (http://nces.ed.gov/nationsreportcard/)
*These scores are from the National Assessment of Educational Progress (NAEP). Scale ranges from 0 to 300.
**Not available.

Average Science Score for Public School Fourth Grade Males in 2005

National Average Score = 151*

<table>
<tr><td colspan="3">ALPHA ORDER</td><td colspan="3">RANK ORDER</td></tr>
<tr><td>RANK</td><td>STATE</td><td>AVERAGE SCORE</td><td>RANK</td><td>STATE</td><td>AVERAGE SCORE</td></tr>
<tr><td>38</td><td>Alabama</td><td>143</td><td>1</td><td>New Hampshire</td><td>163</td></tr>
<tr><td>NA</td><td>Alaska**</td><td>NA</td><td>2</td><td>North Dakota</td><td>163</td></tr>
<tr><td>42</td><td>Arizona</td><td>140</td><td>3</td><td>Montana</td><td>162</td></tr>
<tr><td>35</td><td>Arkansas</td><td>148</td><td>4</td><td>Maine</td><td>162</td></tr>
<tr><td>43</td><td>California</td><td>138</td><td>5</td><td>Vermont</td><td>162</td></tr>
<tr><td>17</td><td>Colorado</td><td>157</td><td>6</td><td>Virginia</td><td>162</td></tr>
<tr><td>18</td><td>Connecticut</td><td>156</td><td>7</td><td>Massachusetts</td><td>162</td></tr>
<tr><td>23</td><td>Delaware</td><td>153</td><td>8</td><td>South Dakota</td><td>161</td></tr>
<tr><td>29</td><td>Florida</td><td>151</td><td>9</td><td>Wyoming</td><td>161</td></tr>
<tr><td>33</td><td>Georgia</td><td>148</td><td>10</td><td>Missouri</td><td>160</td></tr>
<tr><td>39</td><td>Hawaii</td><td>142</td><td>11</td><td>Wisconsin</td><td>159</td></tr>
<tr><td>16</td><td>Idaho</td><td>157</td><td>12</td><td>Kentucky</td><td>159</td></tr>
<tr><td>34</td><td>Illinois</td><td>148</td><td>13</td><td>Ohio</td><td>159</td></tr>
<tr><td>22</td><td>Indiana</td><td>153</td><td>14</td><td>Minnesota</td><td>158</td></tr>
<tr><td>NA</td><td>Iowa**</td><td>NA</td><td>15</td><td>Utah</td><td>158</td></tr>
<tr><td>NA</td><td>Kansas**</td><td>NA</td><td>16</td><td>Idaho</td><td>157</td></tr>
<tr><td>12</td><td>Kentucky</td><td>159</td><td>17</td><td>Colorado</td><td>157</td></tr>
<tr><td>37</td><td>Louisiana</td><td>145</td><td>18</td><td>Connecticut</td><td>156</td></tr>
<tr><td>4</td><td>Maine</td><td>162</td><td>19</td><td>New Jersey</td><td>155</td></tr>
<tr><td>32</td><td>Maryland</td><td>148</td><td>20</td><td>Washington</td><td>155</td></tr>
<tr><td>7</td><td>Massachusetts</td><td>162</td><td>21</td><td>Michigan</td><td>154</td></tr>
<tr><td>21</td><td>Michigan</td><td>154</td><td>22</td><td>Indiana</td><td>153</td></tr>
<tr><td>14</td><td>Minnesota</td><td>158</td><td>23</td><td>Delaware</td><td>153</td></tr>
<tr><td>44</td><td>Mississippi</td><td>134</td><td>24</td><td>West Virginia</td><td>153</td></tr>
<tr><td>10</td><td>Missouri</td><td>160</td><td>25</td><td>Oregon</td><td>152</td></tr>
<tr><td>3</td><td>Montana</td><td>162</td><td>26</td><td>Tennessee</td><td>152</td></tr>
<tr><td>NA</td><td>Nebraska**</td><td>NA</td><td>27</td><td>Texas</td><td>152</td></tr>
<tr><td>41</td><td>Nevada</td><td>141</td><td>28</td><td>Oklahoma</td><td>151</td></tr>
<tr><td>1</td><td>New Hampshire</td><td>163</td><td>29</td><td>Florida</td><td>151</td></tr>
<tr><td>19</td><td>New Jersey</td><td>155</td><td>30</td><td>North Carolina</td><td>151</td></tr>
<tr><td>40</td><td>New Mexico</td><td>142</td><td>31</td><td>South Carolina</td><td>150</td></tr>
<tr><td>NA</td><td>New York**</td><td>NA</td><td>32</td><td>Maryland</td><td>148</td></tr>
<tr><td>30</td><td>North Carolina</td><td>151</td><td>33</td><td>Georgia</td><td>148</td></tr>
<tr><td>2</td><td>North Dakota</td><td>163</td><td>34</td><td>Illinois</td><td>148</td></tr>
<tr><td>13</td><td>Ohio</td><td>159</td><td>35</td><td>Arkansas</td><td>148</td></tr>
<tr><td>28</td><td>Oklahoma</td><td>151</td><td>36</td><td>Rhode Island</td><td>148</td></tr>
<tr><td>25</td><td>Oregon</td><td>152</td><td>37</td><td>Louisiana</td><td>145</td></tr>
<tr><td>NA</td><td>Pennsylvania**</td><td>NA</td><td>38</td><td>Alabama</td><td>143</td></tr>
<tr><td>36</td><td>Rhode Island</td><td>148</td><td>39</td><td>Hawaii</td><td>142</td></tr>
<tr><td>31</td><td>South Carolina</td><td>150</td><td>40</td><td>New Mexico</td><td>142</td></tr>
<tr><td>8</td><td>South Dakota</td><td>161</td><td>41</td><td>Nevada</td><td>141</td></tr>
<tr><td>26</td><td>Tennessee</td><td>152</td><td>42</td><td>Arizona</td><td>140</td></tr>
<tr><td>27</td><td>Texas</td><td>152</td><td>43</td><td>California</td><td>138</td></tr>
<tr><td>15</td><td>Utah</td><td>158</td><td>44</td><td>Mississippi</td><td>134</td></tr>
<tr><td>5</td><td>Vermont</td><td>162</td><td>NA</td><td>Alaska**</td><td>NA</td></tr>
<tr><td>6</td><td>Virginia</td><td>162</td><td>NA</td><td>Iowa**</td><td>NA</td></tr>
<tr><td>20</td><td>Washington</td><td>155</td><td>NA</td><td>Kansas**</td><td>NA</td></tr>
<tr><td>24</td><td>West Virginia</td><td>153</td><td>NA</td><td>Nebraska**</td><td>NA</td></tr>
<tr><td>11</td><td>Wisconsin</td><td>159</td><td>NA</td><td>New York**</td><td>NA</td></tr>
<tr><td>9</td><td>Wyoming</td><td>161</td><td>NA</td><td>Pennsylvania**</td><td>NA</td></tr>
<tr><td></td><td></td><td></td><td></td><td>District of Columbia**</td><td>NA</td></tr>
</table>

Source: U.S. Department of Education, National Center for Education Statistics
   "The Nation's Report Card: Science 2005" (http://nces.ed.gov/nationsreportcard/)
*These scores are from the National Assessment of Educational Progress (NAEP). Scale ranges from 0 to 300.
**Not available.

Average Science Score for Public School Fourth Grade Females in 2005

National Average Score = 147*

ALPHA ORDER

RANK	STATE	AVERAGE SCORE
37	Alabama	142
NA	Alaska**	NA
41	Arizona	138
34	Arkansas	146
43	California	135
15	Colorado	153
18	Connecticut	153
20	Delaware	151
26	Florida	149
32	Georgia	147
38	Hawaii	142
19	Idaho	152
31	Illinois	147
22	Indiana	150
NA	Iowa**	NA
NA	Kansas**	NA
8	Kentucky	156
39	Louisiana	140
4	Maine	157
27	Maryland	149
3	Massachusetts	158
23	Michigan	149
12	Minnesota	155
44	Mississippi	132
10	Missouri	156
7	Montana	157
NA	Nebraska**	NA
42	Nevada	138
2	New Hampshire	159
17	New Jersey	153
40	New Mexico	139
NA	New York**	NA
35	North Carolina	146
5	North Dakota	157
13	Ohio	154
29	Oklahoma	148
24	Oregon	149
NA	Pennsylvania**	NA
36	Rhode Island	145
33	South Carolina	147
11	South Dakota	155
28	Tennessee	149
30	Texas	147
16	Utah	153
6	Vermont	157
1	Virginia	160
21	Washington	151
25	West Virginia	149
9	Wisconsin	156
14	Wyoming	154

RANK ORDER

RANK	STATE	AVERAGE SCORE
1	Virginia	160
2	New Hampshire	159
3	Massachusetts	158
4	Maine	157
5	North Dakota	157
6	Vermont	157
7	Montana	157
8	Kentucky	156
9	Wisconsin	156
10	Missouri	156
11	South Dakota	155
12	Minnesota	155
13	Ohio	154
14	Wyoming	154
15	Colorado	153
16	Utah	153
17	New Jersey	153
18	Connecticut	153
19	Idaho	152
20	Delaware	151
21	Washington	151
22	Indiana	150
23	Michigan	149
24	Oregon	149
25	West Virginia	149
26	Florida	149
27	Maryland	149
28	Tennessee	149
29	Oklahoma	148
30	Texas	147
31	Illinois	147
32	Georgia	147
33	South Carolina	147
34	Arkansas	146
35	North Carolina	146
36	Rhode Island	145
37	Alabama	142
38	Hawaii	142
39	Louisiana	140
40	New Mexico	139
41	Arizona	138
42	Nevada	138
43	California	135
44	Mississippi	132
NA	Alaska**	NA
NA	Iowa**	NA
NA	Kansas**	NA
NA	Nebraska**	NA
NA	New York**	NA
NA	Pennsylvania**	NA
	District of Columbia**	NA

Source: U.S. Department of Education, National Center for Education Statistics
   "The Nation's Report Card: Science 2005" (http://nces.ed.gov/nationsreportcard/)
*These scores are from the National Assessment of Educational Progress (NAEP). Scale ranges from 0 to 300.
**Not available.

Average Science Score for Public School Fourth Graders
Eligible for Free or Reduced Price Lunch Program in 2005
National Average Score = 135*

ALPHA ORDER				RANK ORDER		
RANK	STATE	AVERAGE SCORE		RANK	STATE	AVERAGE SCORE
38	Alabama	129		1	Kentucky	151
NA	Alaska**	NA		1	Maine	151
41	Arizona	127		3	North Dakota	150
27	Arkansas	136		4	Montana	149
44	California	123		4	New Hampshire	149
20	Colorado	139		6	South Dakota	148
35	Connecticut	132		6	Wyoming	148
15	Delaware	141		8	Missouri	147
20	Florida	139		8	Vermont	147
29	Georgia	135		10	Idaho	145
36	Hawaii	131		10	Virginia	145
10	Idaho	145		12	Utah	144
37	Illinois	130		12	West Virginia	144
20	Indiana	139		14	Wisconsin	143
NA	Iowa**	NA		15	Delaware	141
NA	Kansas**	NA		15	Minnesota	141
1	Kentucky	151		15	Oklahoma	141
29	Louisiana	135		18	Massachusetts	140
1	Maine	151		18	Washington	140
38	Maryland	129		20	Colorado	139
18	Massachusetts	140		20	Florida	139
32	Michigan	134		20	Indiana	139
15	Minnesota	141		20	Ohio	139
43	Mississippi	125		20	Texas	139
8	Missouri	147		25	Oregon	138
4	Montana	149		25	Tennessee	138
NA	Nebraska**	NA		27	Arkansas	136
41	Nevada	127		27	South Carolina	136
4	New Hampshire	149		29	Georgia	135
29	New Jersey	135		29	Louisiana	135
34	New Mexico	133		29	New Jersey	135
NA	New York**	NA		32	Michigan	134
32	North Carolina	134		32	North Carolina	134
3	North Dakota	150		34	New Mexico	133
20	Ohio	139		35	Connecticut	132
15	Oklahoma	141		36	Hawaii	131
25	Oregon	138		37	Illinois	130
NA	Pennsylvania**	NA		38	Alabama	129
38	Rhode Island	129		38	Maryland	129
27	South Carolina	136		38	Rhode Island	129
6	South Dakota	148		41	Arizona	127
25	Tennessee	138		41	Nevada	127
20	Texas	139		43	Mississippi	125
12	Utah	144		44	California	123
8	Vermont	147		NA	Alaska**	NA
10	Virginia	145		NA	Iowa**	NA
18	Washington	140		NA	Kansas**	NA
12	West Virginia	144		NA	Nebraska**	NA
14	Wisconsin	143		NA	New York**	NA
6	Wyoming	148		NA	Pennsylvania**	NA
					District of Columbia**	NA

Source: U.S. Department of Education, National Center for Education Statistics
    "The Nation's Report Card: Science 2005" (http://nces.ed.gov/nationsreportcard/)
*These scores are from the National Assessment of Educational Progress (NAEP). Scale ranges from 0 to 300.
**Not available.

Percent of Public School Fourth Graders
Proficient or Better in Science in 2005
National Percent = 27%*

ALPHA ORDER

RANK	STATE	PERCENT
37	Alabama	21
NA	Alaska**	NA
40	Arizona	18
34	Arkansas	24
42	California	17
16	Colorado	32
13	Connecticut	33
22	Delaware	27
26	Florida	26
29	Georgia	25
39	Hawaii	19
20	Idaho	29
22	Illinois	27
22	Indiana	27
NA	Iowa**	NA
NA	Kansas**	NA
6	Kentucky	36
38	Louisiana	20
6	Maine	36
22	Maryland	27
2	Massachusetts	38
19	Michigan	30
13	Minnesota	33
44	Mississippi	12
6	Missouri	36
4	Montana	37
NA	Nebraska**	NA
42	Nevada	17
4	New Hampshire	37
16	New Jersey	32
40	New Mexico	18
NA	New York**	NA
29	North Carolina	25
6	North Dakota	36
10	Ohio	35
29	Oklahoma	25
26	Oregon	26
NA	Pennsylvania**	NA
36	Rhode Island	23
29	South Carolina	25
10	South Dakota	35
26	Tennessee	26
29	Texas	25
13	Utah	33
2	Vermont	38
1	Virginia	40
21	Washington	28
34	West Virginia	24
10	Wisconsin	35
16	Wyoming	32

RANK ORDER

RANK	STATE	PERCENT
1	Virginia	40
2	Massachusetts	38
2	Vermont	38
4	Montana	37
4	New Hampshire	37
6	Kentucky	36
6	Maine	36
6	Missouri	36
6	North Dakota	36
10	Ohio	35
10	South Dakota	35
10	Wisconsin	35
13	Connecticut	33
13	Minnesota	33
13	Utah	33
16	Colorado	32
16	New Jersey	32
16	Wyoming	32
19	Michigan	30
20	Idaho	29
21	Washington	28
22	Delaware	27
22	Illinois	27
22	Indiana	27
22	Maryland	27
26	Florida	26
26	Oregon	26
26	Tennessee	26
29	Georgia	25
29	North Carolina	25
29	Oklahoma	25
29	South Carolina	25
29	Texas	25
34	Arkansas	24
34	West Virginia	24
36	Rhode Island	23
37	Alabama	21
38	Louisiana	20
39	Hawaii	19
40	Arizona	18
40	New Mexico	18
42	California	17
42	Nevada	17
44	Mississippi	12
NA	Alaska**	NA
NA	Iowa**	NA
NA	Kansas**	NA
NA	Nebraska**	NA
NA	New York**	NA
NA	Pennsylvania**	NA
	District of Columbia**	NA

Source: U.S. Department of Education, National Center for Education Statistics
"The Nation's Report Card: Science 2005" (http://nces.ed.gov/nationsreportcard/)
*There are four achievement levels: Below Basic, Basic, Proficient, and Advanced. Proficient represents solid academic mastery for 4th graders. Students reaching this level have demonstrated competency over challenging subject matter, including subject matter knowledge, application of such knowledge to real-world situations, and analytical skills appropriate to the subject matter. **Not available.

Percent of Public School Fourth Grade Males
Proficient or Better in Science in 2005
National Percent = 31%*

ALPHA ORDER

RANK ORDER

RANK	STATE	PERCENT		RANK	STATE	PERCENT
38	Alabama	22		1	North Dakota	42
NA	Alaska**	NA		1	Virginia	42
39	Arizona	20		3	New Hampshire	41
35	Arkansas	26		3	Vermont	41
40	California	19		5	Maine	40
16	Colorado	35		5	Massachusetts	40
16	Connecticut	35		5	Montana	40
22	Delaware	29		5	South Dakota	40
27	Florida	28		9	Missouri	39
32	Georgia	27		9	Ohio	39
40	Hawaii	19		11	Kentucky	38
18	Idaho	34		11	Wisconsin	38
27	Illinois	28		11	Wyoming	38
22	Indiana	29		14	Minnesota	37
NA	Iowa**	NA		15	Utah	36
NA	Kansas**	NA		16	Colorado	35
11	Kentucky	38		16	Connecticut	35
37	Louisiana	24		18	Idaho	34
5	Maine	40		18	Michigan	34
27	Maryland	28		20	New Jersey	33
5	Massachusetts	40		21	Washington	32
18	Michigan	34		22	Delaware	29
14	Minnesota	37		22	Indiana	29
44	Mississippi	15		22	North Carolina	29
9	Missouri	39		22	Oregon	29
5	Montana	40		22	Tennessee	29
NA	Nebraska**	NA		27	Florida	28
40	Nevada	19		27	Illinois	28
3	New Hampshire	41		27	Maryland	28
20	New Jersey	33		27	Oklahoma	28
40	New Mexico	19		27	Texas	28
NA	New York**	NA		32	Georgia	27
22	North Carolina	29		32	South Carolina	27
1	North Dakota	42		32	West Virginia	27
9	Ohio	39		35	Arkansas	26
27	Oklahoma	28		36	Rhode Island	25
22	Oregon	29		37	Louisiana	24
NA	Pennsylvania**	NA		38	Alabama	22
36	Rhode Island	25		39	Arizona	20
32	South Carolina	27		40	California	19
5	South Dakota	40		40	Hawaii	19
22	Tennessee	29		40	Nevada	19
27	Texas	28		40	New Mexico	19
15	Utah	36		44	Mississippi	15
3	Vermont	41		NA	Alaska**	NA
1	Virginia	42		NA	Iowa**	NA
21	Washington	32		NA	Kansas**	NA
32	West Virginia	27		NA	Nebraska**	NA
11	Wisconsin	38		NA	New York**	NA
11	Wyoming	38		NA	Pennsylvania**	NA
					District of Columbia**	NA

Source: U.S. Department of Education, National Center for Education Statistics
     "The Nation's Report Card: Science 2005" (http://nces.ed.gov/nationsreportcard/)
*There are four achievement levels: Below Basic, Basic, Proficient, and Advanced. Proficient represents solid academic mastery for 4th graders. Students reaching this level have demonstrated competency over challenging subject matter, including subject matter knowledge, application of such knowledge to real-world situations, and analytical skills appropriate to the subject matter. **Not available.

Percent of Public School Fourth Grade Females
Proficient or Better in Science in 2005
National Percent = 26%*

ALPHA ORDER

RANK	STATE	PERCENT
37	Alabama	19
NA	Alaska**	NA
41	Arizona	15
31	Arkansas	22
41	California	15
16	Colorado	29
10	Connecticut	30
25	Delaware	24
28	Florida	23
28	Georgia	23
38	Hawaii	18
21	Idaho	25
21	Illinois	25
21	Indiana	25
NA	Iowa**	NA
NA	Kansas**	NA
4	Kentucky	33
39	Louisiana	17
8	Maine	32
19	Maryland	26
2	Massachusetts	36
19	Michigan	26
10	Minnesota	30
44	Mississippi	10
4	Missouri	33
4	Montana	33
NA	Nebraska**	NA
41	Nevada	15
4	New Hampshire	33
10	New Jersey	30
39	New Mexico	17
NA	New York**	NA
34	North Carolina	21
10	North Dakota	30
10	Ohio	30
31	Oklahoma	22
25	Oregon	24
NA	Pennsylvania**	NA
34	Rhode Island	21
28	South Carolina	23
10	South Dakota	30
25	Tennessee	24
31	Texas	22
16	Utah	29
3	Vermont	34
1	Virginia	38
21	Washington	25
36	West Virginia	20
8	Wisconsin	32
18	Wyoming	27

RANK ORDER

RANK	STATE	PERCENT
1	Virginia	38
2	Massachusetts	36
3	Vermont	34
4	Kentucky	33
4	Missouri	33
4	Montana	33
4	New Hampshire	33
8	Maine	32
8	Wisconsin	32
10	Connecticut	30
10	Minnesota	30
10	New Jersey	30
10	North Dakota	30
10	Ohio	30
10	South Dakota	30
16	Colorado	29
16	Utah	29
18	Wyoming	27
19	Maryland	26
19	Michigan	26
21	Idaho	25
21	Illinois	25
21	Indiana	25
21	Washington	25
25	Delaware	24
25	Oregon	24
25	Tennessee	24
28	Florida	23
28	Georgia	23
28	South Carolina	23
31	Arkansas	22
31	Oklahoma	22
31	Texas	22
34	North Carolina	21
34	Rhode Island	21
36	West Virginia	20
37	Alabama	19
38	Hawaii	18
39	Louisiana	17
39	New Mexico	17
41	Arizona	15
41	California	15
41	Nevada	15
44	Mississippi	10
NA	Alaska**	NA
NA	Iowa**	NA
NA	Kansas**	NA
NA	Nebraska**	NA
NA	New York**	NA
NA	Pennsylvania**	NA
	District of Columbia**	NA

Source: U.S. Department of Education, National Center for Education Statistics
"The Nation's Report Card: Science 2005" (http://nces.ed.gov/nationsreportcard/)
*There are four achievement levels: Below Basic, Basic, Proficient, and Advanced. Proficient represents solid academic mastery for 4th graders. Students reaching this level have demonstrated competency over challenging subject matter, including subject matter knowledge, application of such knowledge to real-world situations, and analytical skills appropriate to the subject matter. **Not available.

Percent of Public School Fourth Graders Eligible for
Free or Reduced Price Lunch Program Proficient or Better in Science in 2005
National Percent = 12%*

ALPHA ORDER

RANK	STATE	PERCENT
39	Alabama	8
NA	Alaska**	NA
41	Arizona	7
17	Arkansas	14
43	California	6
21	Colorado	13
36	Connecticut	9
21	Delaware	13
21	Florida	13
28	Georgia	12
36	Hawaii	9
11	Idaho	18
33	Illinois	10
21	Indiana	13
NA	Iowa**	NA
NA	Kansas**	NA
1	Kentucky	26
28	Louisiana	12
2	Maine	23
41	Maryland	7
17	Massachusetts	14
28	Michigan	12
14	Minnesota	15
43	Mississippi	6
6	Missouri	21
3	Montana	22
NA	Nebraska**	NA
39	Nevada	8
6	New Hampshire	21
31	New Jersey	11
33	New Mexico	10
NA	New York**	NA
33	North Carolina	10
3	North Dakota	22
14	Ohio	15
17	Oklahoma	14
21	Oregon	13
NA	Pennsylvania**	NA
36	Rhode Island	9
31	South Carolina	11
3	South Dakota	22
21	Tennessee	13
21	Texas	13
8	Utah	19
8	Vermont	19
13	Virginia	17
17	Washington	14
14	West Virginia	15
11	Wisconsin	18
8	Wyoming	19

RANK ORDER

RANK	STATE	PERCENT
1	Kentucky	26
2	Maine	23
3	Montana	22
3	North Dakota	22
3	South Dakota	22
6	Missouri	21
6	New Hampshire	21
8	Utah	19
8	Vermont	19
8	Wyoming	19
11	Idaho	18
11	Wisconsin	18
13	Virginia	17
14	Minnesota	15
14	Ohio	15
14	West Virginia	15
17	Arkansas	14
17	Massachusetts	14
17	Oklahoma	14
17	Washington	14
21	Colorado	13
21	Delaware	13
21	Florida	13
21	Indiana	13
21	Oregon	13
21	Tennessee	13
21	Texas	13
28	Georgia	12
28	Louisiana	12
28	Michigan	12
31	New Jersey	11
31	South Carolina	11
33	Illinois	10
33	New Mexico	10
33	North Carolina	10
36	Connecticut	9
36	Hawaii	9
36	Rhode Island	9
39	Alabama	8
39	Nevada	8
41	Arizona	7
41	Maryland	7
43	California	6
43	Mississippi	6
NA	Alaska**	NA
NA	Iowa**	NA
NA	Kansas**	NA
NA	Nebraska**	NA
NA	New York**	NA
NA	Pennsylvania**	NA
	District of Columbia**	NA

Source: U.S. Department of Education, National Center for Education Statistics
   "The Nation's Report Card: Science 2005" (http://nces.ed.gov/nationsreportcard/)
*There are four achievement levels: Below Basic, Basic, Proficient, and Advanced. Proficient represents solid academic
mastery for 4th graders. Students reaching this level have demonstrated competency over challenging subject matter, including
subject matter knowledge, application of such knowledge to real-world situations, and analytical skills appropriate to the subject
matter. **Not available.

Average Science Score for Public School Eighth Graders in 2005

National Average Score = 147*

ALPHA ORDER

RANK	STATE	AVERAGE SCORE
38	Alabama	138
NA	Alaska**	NA
37	Arizona	140
32	Arkansas	144
42	California	136
12	Colorado	155
22	Connecticut	152
22	Delaware	152
36	Florida	141
32	Georgia	144
42	Hawaii	136
8	Idaho	158
25	Illinois	148
24	Indiana	150
NA	Iowa**	NA
NA	Kansas**	NA
19	Kentucky	153
38	Louisiana	138
8	Maine	158
29	Maryland	145
5	Massachusetts	161
12	Michigan	155
8	Minnesota	158
44	Mississippi	132
16	Missouri	154
2	Montana	162
NA	Nebraska**	NA
38	Nevada	138
2	New Hampshire	162
19	New Jersey	153
38	New Mexico	138
NA	New York**	NA
32	North Carolina	144
1	North Dakota	163
12	Ohio	155
26	Oklahoma	147
19	Oregon	153
NA	Pennsylvania**	NA
28	Rhode Island	146
29	South Carolina	145
5	South Dakota	161
29	Tennessee	145
35	Texas	143
16	Utah	154
2	Vermont	162
12	Virginia	155
16	Washington	154
26	West Virginia	147
8	Wisconsin	158
7	Wyoming	159

RANK ORDER

RANK	STATE	AVERAGE SCORE
1	North Dakota	163
2	Montana	162
2	New Hampshire	162
2	Vermont	162
5	Massachusetts	161
5	South Dakota	161
7	Wyoming	159
8	Idaho	158
8	Maine	158
8	Minnesota	158
8	Wisconsin	158
12	Colorado	155
12	Michigan	155
12	Ohio	155
12	Virginia	155
16	Missouri	154
16	Utah	154
16	Washington	154
19	Kentucky	153
19	New Jersey	153
19	Oregon	153
22	Connecticut	152
22	Delaware	152
24	Indiana	150
25	Illinois	148
26	Oklahoma	147
26	West Virginia	147
28	Rhode Island	146
29	Maryland	145
29	South Carolina	145
29	Tennessee	145
32	Arkansas	144
32	Georgia	144
32	North Carolina	144
35	Texas	143
36	Florida	141
37	Arizona	140
38	Alabama	138
38	Louisiana	138
38	Nevada	138
38	New Mexico	138
42	California	136
42	Hawaii	136
44	Mississippi	132
NA	Alaska**	NA
NA	Iowa**	NA
NA	Kansas**	NA
NA	Nebraska**	NA
NA	New York**	NA
NA	Pennsylvania**	NA
	District of Columbia**	NA

Source: U.S. Department of Education, National Center for Education Statistics
   "The Nation's Report Card: Science 2005" (http://nces.ed.gov/nationsreportcard/)
*These scores are from the National Assessment of Educational Progress (NAEP). Scale ranges from 0 to 300.
**Not available.

Average Science Score for Public School Eighth Grade Males in 2005

National Average Score = 149*

<table>
<tr><td colspan="3">ALPHA ORDER</td><td colspan="3">RANK ORDER</td></tr>
<tr><td>RANK</td><td>STATE</td><td>AVERAGE SCORE</td><td>RANK</td><td>STATE</td><td>AVERAGE SCORE</td></tr>
<tr><td>41</td><td>Alabama</td><td>138</td><td>1</td><td>North Dakota</td><td>165</td></tr>
<tr><td>NA</td><td>Alaska**</td><td>NA</td><td>2</td><td>South Dakota</td><td>164</td></tr>
<tr><td>38</td><td>Arizona</td><td>141</td><td>3</td><td>Vermont</td><td>163</td></tr>
<tr><td>30</td><td>Arkansas</td><td>146</td><td>4</td><td>New Hampshire</td><td>163</td></tr>
<tr><td>43</td><td>California</td><td>138</td><td>5</td><td>Montana</td><td>162</td></tr>
<tr><td>12</td><td>Colorado</td><td>158</td><td>6</td><td>Massachusetts</td><td>162</td></tr>
<tr><td>24</td><td>Connecticut</td><td>153</td><td>7</td><td>Wyoming</td><td>161</td></tr>
<tr><td>23</td><td>Delaware</td><td>154</td><td>8</td><td>Idaho</td><td>161</td></tr>
<tr><td>36</td><td>Florida</td><td>142</td><td>9</td><td>Minnesota</td><td>161</td></tr>
<tr><td>32</td><td>Georgia</td><td>145</td><td>10</td><td>Wisconsin</td><td>160</td></tr>
<tr><td>42</td><td>Hawaii</td><td>138</td><td>11</td><td>Maine</td><td>159</td></tr>
<tr><td>8</td><td>Idaho</td><td>161</td><td>12</td><td>Colorado</td><td>158</td></tr>
<tr><td>25</td><td>Illinois</td><td>150</td><td>13</td><td>Virginia</td><td>157</td></tr>
<tr><td>22</td><td>Indiana</td><td>154</td><td>14</td><td>Ohio</td><td>157</td></tr>
<tr><td>NA</td><td>Iowa**</td><td>NA</td><td>15</td><td>Missouri</td><td>157</td></tr>
<tr><td>NA</td><td>Kansas**</td><td>NA</td><td>16</td><td>New Jersey</td><td>157</td></tr>
<tr><td>21</td><td>Kentucky</td><td>154</td><td>17</td><td>Michigan</td><td>156</td></tr>
<tr><td>39</td><td>Louisiana</td><td>141</td><td>18</td><td>Washington</td><td>155</td></tr>
<tr><td>11</td><td>Maine</td><td>159</td><td>19</td><td>Utah</td><td>155</td></tr>
<tr><td>34</td><td>Maryland</td><td>145</td><td>20</td><td>Oregon</td><td>155</td></tr>
<tr><td>6</td><td>Massachusetts</td><td>162</td><td>21</td><td>Kentucky</td><td>154</td></tr>
<tr><td>17</td><td>Michigan</td><td>156</td><td>22</td><td>Indiana</td><td>154</td></tr>
<tr><td>9</td><td>Minnesota</td><td>161</td><td>23</td><td>Delaware</td><td>154</td></tr>
<tr><td>44</td><td>Mississippi</td><td>135</td><td>24</td><td>Connecticut</td><td>153</td></tr>
<tr><td>15</td><td>Missouri</td><td>157</td><td>25</td><td>Illinois</td><td>150</td></tr>
<tr><td>5</td><td>Montana</td><td>162</td><td>26</td><td>West Virginia</td><td>150</td></tr>
<tr><td>NA</td><td>Nebraska**</td><td>NA</td><td>27</td><td>Oklahoma</td><td>149</td></tr>
<tr><td>40</td><td>Nevada</td><td>139</td><td>28</td><td>Rhode Island</td><td>149</td></tr>
<tr><td>4</td><td>New Hampshire</td><td>163</td><td>29</td><td>South Carolina</td><td>146</td></tr>
<tr><td>16</td><td>New Jersey</td><td>157</td><td>30</td><td>Arkansas</td><td>146</td></tr>
<tr><td>37</td><td>New Mexico</td><td>141</td><td>31</td><td>Tennessee</td><td>146</td></tr>
<tr><td>NA</td><td>New York**</td><td>NA</td><td>32</td><td>Georgia</td><td>145</td></tr>
<tr><td>35</td><td>North Carolina</td><td>145</td><td>33</td><td>Texas</td><td>145</td></tr>
<tr><td>1</td><td>North Dakota</td><td>165</td><td>34</td><td>Maryland</td><td>145</td></tr>
<tr><td>14</td><td>Ohio</td><td>157</td><td>35</td><td>North Carolina</td><td>145</td></tr>
<tr><td>27</td><td>Oklahoma</td><td>149</td><td>36</td><td>Florida</td><td>142</td></tr>
<tr><td>20</td><td>Oregon</td><td>155</td><td>37</td><td>New Mexico</td><td>141</td></tr>
<tr><td>NA</td><td>Pennsylvania**</td><td>NA</td><td>38</td><td>Arizona</td><td>141</td></tr>
<tr><td>28</td><td>Rhode Island</td><td>149</td><td>39</td><td>Louisiana</td><td>141</td></tr>
<tr><td>29</td><td>South Carolina</td><td>146</td><td>40</td><td>Nevada</td><td>139</td></tr>
<tr><td>2</td><td>South Dakota</td><td>164</td><td>41</td><td>Alabama</td><td>138</td></tr>
<tr><td>31</td><td>Tennessee</td><td>146</td><td>42</td><td>Hawaii</td><td>138</td></tr>
<tr><td>33</td><td>Texas</td><td>145</td><td>43</td><td>California</td><td>138</td></tr>
<tr><td>19</td><td>Utah</td><td>155</td><td>44</td><td>Mississippi</td><td>135</td></tr>
<tr><td>3</td><td>Vermont</td><td>163</td><td>NA</td><td>Alaska**</td><td>NA</td></tr>
<tr><td>13</td><td>Virginia</td><td>157</td><td>NA</td><td>Iowa**</td><td>NA</td></tr>
<tr><td>18</td><td>Washington</td><td>155</td><td>NA</td><td>Kansas**</td><td>NA</td></tr>
<tr><td>26</td><td>West Virginia</td><td>150</td><td>NA</td><td>Nebraska**</td><td>NA</td></tr>
<tr><td>10</td><td>Wisconsin</td><td>160</td><td>NA</td><td>New York**</td><td>NA</td></tr>
<tr><td>7</td><td>Wyoming</td><td>161</td><td>NA</td><td>Pennsylvania**</td><td>NA</td></tr>
<tr><td></td><td></td><td></td><td></td><td>District of Columbia**</td><td>NA</td></tr>
</table>

Source: U.S. Department of Education, National Center for Education Statistics
"The Nation's Report Card: Science 2005" (http://nces.ed.gov/nationsreportcard/)
*These scores are from the National Assessment of Educational Progress (NAEP). Scale ranges from 0 to 300.
**Not available.

Average Science Score for Public School Eighth Grade Females in 2005

National Average Score = 145*

ALPHA ORDER

RANK	STATE	AVERAGE SCORE
39	Alabama	137
NA	Alaska**	NA
37	Arizona	139
33	Arkansas	142
43	California	135
16	Colorado	152
21	Connecticut	151
23	Delaware	150
36	Florida	140
34	Georgia	142
42	Hawaii	135
12	Idaho	154
25	Illinois	146
24	Indiana	147
NA	Iowa**	NA
NA	Kansas**	NA
20	Kentucky	151
40	Louisiana	136
8	Maine	156
28	Maryland	144
5	Massachusetts	160
13	Michigan	154
10	Minnesota	155
44	Mississippi	130
19	Missouri	151
2	Montana	161
NA	Nebraska**	NA
38	Nevada	138
4	New Hampshire	161
22	New Jersey	150
41	New Mexico	135
NA	New York**	NA
32	North Carolina	143
1	North Dakota	161
11	Ohio	154
27	Oklahoma	144
18	Oregon	152
NA	Pennsylvania**	NA
30	Rhode Island	144
31	South Carolina	144
6	South Dakota	158
29	Tennessee	144
35	Texas	141
17	Utah	152
3	Vermont	161
14	Virginia	153
15	Washington	153
26	West Virginia	144
9	Wisconsin	156
7	Wyoming	157

RANK ORDER

RANK	STATE	AVERAGE SCORE
1	North Dakota	161
2	Montana	161
3	Vermont	161
4	New Hampshire	161
5	Massachusetts	160
6	South Dakota	158
7	Wyoming	157
8	Maine	156
9	Wisconsin	156
10	Minnesota	155
11	Ohio	154
12	Idaho	154
13	Michigan	154
14	Virginia	153
15	Washington	153
16	Colorado	152
17	Utah	152
18	Oregon	152
19	Missouri	151
20	Kentucky	151
21	Connecticut	151
22	New Jersey	150
23	Delaware	150
24	Indiana	147
25	Illinois	146
26	West Virginia	144
27	Oklahoma	144
28	Maryland	144
29	Tennessee	144
30	Rhode Island	144
31	South Carolina	144
32	North Carolina	143
33	Arkansas	142
34	Georgia	142
35	Texas	141
36	Florida	140
37	Arizona	139
38	Nevada	138
39	Alabama	137
40	Louisiana	136
41	New Mexico	135
42	Hawaii	135
43	California	135
44	Mississippi	130
NA	Alaska**	NA
NA	Iowa**	NA
NA	Kansas**	NA
NA	Nebraska**	NA
NA	New York**	NA
NA	Pennsylvania**	NA
	District of Columbia**	NA

Source: U.S. Department of Education, National Center for Education Statistics
"The Nation's Report Card: Science 2005" (http://nces.ed.gov/nationsreportcard/)
*These scores are from the National Assessment of Educational Progress (NAEP). Scale ranges from 0 to 300.
**Not available.

Average Science Score for Public School Eighth Graders Eligible for Free or Reduced Price Lunch Program in 2005
National Average Score = 130*

ALPHA ORDER				RANK ORDER		
RANK	STATE	AVERAGE SCORE		RANK	STATE	AVERAGE SCORE
41	Alabama	123		1	North Dakota	151
NA	Alaska**	NA		2	Maine	150
38	Arizona	124		2	Vermont	150
25	Arkansas	131		4	Montana	149
43	California	121		4	New Hampshire	149
22	Colorado	135		4	South Dakota	149
34	Connecticut	127		7	Wyoming	148
20	Delaware	136		8	Idaho	147
32	Florida	128		9	Kentucky	145
34	Georgia	127		10	Massachusetts	142
38	Hawaii	124		10	Utah	142
8	Idaho	147		12	Oregon	141
32	Illinois	128		13	Michigan	140
22	Indiana	135		13	Missouri	140
NA	Iowa**	NA		13	Washington	140
NA	Kansas**	NA		16	Minnesota	139
9	Kentucky	145		17	Oklahoma	137
34	Louisiana	127		17	West Virginia	137
2	Maine	150		17	Wisconsin	137
42	Maryland	122		20	Delaware	136
10	Massachusetts	142		20	Virginia	136
13	Michigan	140		22	Colorado	135
16	Minnesota	139		22	Indiana	135
43	Mississippi	121		24	Ohio	134
13	Missouri	140		25	Arkansas	131
4	Montana	149		25	New Jersey	131
NA	Nebraska**	NA		25	South Carolina	131
38	Nevada	124		25	Tennessee	131
4	New Hampshire	149		29	New Mexico	129
25	New Jersey	131		29	North Carolina	129
29	New Mexico	129		29	Texas	129
NA	New York**	NA		32	Florida	128
29	North Carolina	129		32	Illinois	128
1	North Dakota	151		34	Connecticut	127
24	Ohio	134		34	Georgia	127
17	Oklahoma	137		34	Louisiana	127
12	Oregon	141		34	Rhode Island	127
NA	Pennsylvania**	NA		38	Arizona	124
34	Rhode Island	127		38	Hawaii	124
25	South Carolina	131		38	Nevada	124
4	South Dakota	149		41	Alabama	123
25	Tennessee	131		42	Maryland	122
29	Texas	129		43	California	121
10	Utah	142		43	Mississippi	121
2	Vermont	150		NA	Alaska**	NA
20	Virginia	136		NA	Iowa**	NA
13	Washington	140		NA	Kansas**	NA
17	West Virginia	137		NA	Nebraska**	NA
17	Wisconsin	137		NA	New York**	NA
7	Wyoming	148		NA	Pennsylvania**	NA
					District of Columbia**	NA

Source: U.S. Department of Education, National Center for Education Statistics
"The Nation's Report Card: Science 2005" (http://nces.ed.gov/nationsreportcard/)
*These scores are from the National Assessment of Educational Progress (NAEP). Scale ranges from 0 to 300.
**Not available.

Percent of Public School Eighth Graders
Proficient or Better in Science in 2005
National Percent = 27%*

ALPHA ORDER

RANK	STATE	PERCENT
38	Alabama	19
NA	Alaska**	NA
37	Arizona	20
31	Arkansas	23
41	California	18
11	Colorado	35
16	Connecticut	33
23	Delaware	29
36	Florida	21
28	Georgia	25
43	Hawaii	15
10	Idaho	36
25	Illinois	27
23	Indiana	29
NA	Iowa**	NA
NA	Kansas**	NA
22	Kentucky	31
38	Louisiana	19
15	Maine	34
26	Maryland	26
3	Massachusetts	41
11	Michigan	35
7	Minnesota	39
44	Mississippi	14
16	Missouri	33
2	Montana	42
NA	Nebraska**	NA
38	Nevada	19
3	New Hampshire	41
16	New Jersey	33
41	New Mexico	18
NA	New York**	NA
35	North Carolina	22
1	North Dakota	43
11	Ohio	35
28	Oklahoma	25
21	Oregon	32
NA	Pennsylvania**	NA
26	Rhode Island	26
31	South Carolina	23
3	South Dakota	41
28	Tennessee	25
31	Texas	23
16	Utah	33
3	Vermont	41
11	Virginia	35
16	Washington	33
31	West Virginia	23
7	Wisconsin	39
9	Wyoming	37

RANK ORDER

RANK	STATE	PERCENT
1	North Dakota	43
2	Montana	42
3	Massachusetts	41
3	New Hampshire	41
3	South Dakota	41
3	Vermont	41
7	Minnesota	39
7	Wisconsin	39
9	Wyoming	37
10	Idaho	36
11	Colorado	35
11	Michigan	35
11	Ohio	35
11	Virginia	35
15	Maine	34
16	Connecticut	33
16	Missouri	33
16	New Jersey	33
16	Utah	33
16	Washington	33
21	Oregon	32
22	Kentucky	31
23	Delaware	29
23	Indiana	29
25	Illinois	27
26	Maryland	26
26	Rhode Island	26
28	Georgia	25
28	Oklahoma	25
28	Tennessee	25
31	Arkansas	23
31	South Carolina	23
31	Texas	23
31	West Virginia	23
35	North Carolina	22
36	Florida	21
37	Arizona	20
38	Alabama	19
38	Louisiana	19
38	Nevada	19
41	California	18
41	New Mexico	18
43	Hawaii	15
44	Mississippi	14
NA	Alaska**	NA
NA	Iowa**	NA
NA	Kansas**	NA
NA	Nebraska**	NA
NA	New York**	NA
NA	Pennsylvania**	NA
	District of Columbia**	NA

Source: U.S. Department of Education, National Center for Education Statistics
   "The Nation's Report Card: Science 2005" (http://nces.ed.gov/nationsreportcard/)
*There are four achievement levels: Below Basic, Basic, Proficient, and Advanced. Proficient represents solid academic mastery for 8th graders. Students reaching this level have demonstrated competency over challenging subject matter, including subject matter knowledge, application of such knowledge to real-world situations, and analytical skills appropriate to the subject matter. **Not available.

Percent of Public School Eighth Grade Males
Proficient or Better in Science in 2005
National Percent = 32%*

ALPHA ORDER

RANK	STATE	PERCENT
38	Alabama	21
NA	Alaska**	NA
38	Arizona	21
30	Arkansas	27
42	California	19
11	Colorado	38
21	Connecticut	34
24	Delaware	32
36	Florida	24
28	Georgia	28
43	Hawaii	17
6	Idaho	42
25	Illinois	31
22	Indiana	33
NA	Iowa**	NA
NA	Kansas**	NA
22	Kentucky	33
37	Louisiana	23
14	Maine	37
30	Maryland	27
6	Massachusetts	42
14	Michigan	37
3	Minnesota	43
44	Mississippi	16
14	Missouri	37
3	Montana	43
NA	Nebraska**	NA
41	Nevada	20
3	New Hampshire	43
11	New Jersey	38
38	New Mexico	21
NA	New York**	NA
34	North Carolina	25
1	North Dakota	46
11	Ohio	38
26	Oklahoma	30
18	Oregon	36
NA	Pennsylvania**	NA
27	Rhode Island	29
34	South Carolina	25
2	South Dakota	45
28	Tennessee	28
33	Texas	26
18	Utah	36
6	Vermont	42
14	Virginia	37
18	Washington	36
30	West Virginia	27
6	Wisconsin	42
10	Wyoming	40

RANK ORDER

RANK	STATE	PERCENT
1	North Dakota	46
2	South Dakota	45
3	Minnesota	43
3	Montana	43
3	New Hampshire	43
6	Idaho	42
6	Massachusetts	42
6	Vermont	42
6	Wisconsin	42
10	Wyoming	40
11	Colorado	38
11	New Jersey	38
11	Ohio	38
14	Maine	37
14	Michigan	37
14	Missouri	37
14	Virginia	37
18	Oregon	36
18	Utah	36
18	Washington	36
21	Connecticut	34
22	Indiana	33
22	Kentucky	33
24	Delaware	32
25	Illinois	31
26	Oklahoma	30
27	Rhode Island	29
28	Georgia	28
28	Tennessee	28
30	Arkansas	27
30	Maryland	27
30	West Virginia	27
33	Texas	26
34	North Carolina	25
34	South Carolina	25
36	Florida	24
37	Louisiana	23
38	Alabama	21
38	Arizona	21
38	New Mexico	21
41	Nevada	20
42	California	19
43	Hawaii	17
44	Mississippi	16
NA	Alaska**	NA
NA	Iowa**	NA
NA	Kansas**	NA
NA	Nebraska**	NA
NA	New York**	NA
NA	Pennsylvania**	NA
	District of Columbia**	NA

Source: U.S. Department of Education, National Center for Education Statistics
   "The Nation's Report Card: Science 2005" (http://nces.ed.gov/nationsreportcard/)
*There are four achievement levels: Below Basic, Basic, Proficient, and Advanced. Proficient represents solid academic mastery for 8th graders. Students reaching this level have demonstrated competency over challenging subject matter, including subject matter knowledge, application of such knowledge to real-world situations, and analytical skills appropriate to the subject matter. **Not available.

Percent of Public School Eighth Grade Females
Proficient or Better in Science in 2005
National Percent = 26%*

ALPHA ORDER

RANK	STATE	PERCENT
39	Alabama	17
NA	Alaska**	NA
36	Arizona	19
31	Arkansas	20
39	California	17
15	Colorado	31
11	Connecticut	32
23	Delaware	26
36	Florida	19
27	Georgia	23
43	Hawaii	13
15	Idaho	31
25	Illinois	24
24	Indiana	25
NA	Iowa**	NA
NA	Kansas**	NA
21	Kentucky	28
41	Louisiana	16
11	Maine	32
25	Maryland	24
3	Massachusetts	39
11	Michigan	32
7	Minnesota	36
44	Mississippi	12
19	Missouri	29
1	Montana	40
NA	Nebraska**	NA
38	Nevada	18
5	New Hampshire	38
21	New Jersey	28
42	New Mexico	15
NA	New York**	NA
31	North Carolina	20
1	North Dakota	40
9	Ohio	33
30	Oklahoma	21
19	Oregon	29
NA	Pennsylvania**	NA
27	Rhode Island	23
31	South Carolina	20
6	South Dakota	37
29	Tennessee	22
31	Texas	20
17	Utah	30
3	Vermont	39
11	Virginia	32
17	Washington	30
31	West Virginia	20
8	Wisconsin	35
9	Wyoming	33

RANK ORDER

RANK	STATE	PERCENT
1	Montana	40
1	North Dakota	40
3	Massachusetts	39
3	Vermont	39
5	New Hampshire	38
6	South Dakota	37
7	Minnesota	36
8	Wisconsin	35
9	Ohio	33
9	Wyoming	33
11	Connecticut	32
11	Maine	32
11	Michigan	32
11	Virginia	32
15	Colorado	31
15	Idaho	31
17	Utah	30
17	Washington	30
19	Missouri	29
19	Oregon	29
21	Kentucky	28
21	New Jersey	28
23	Delaware	26
24	Indiana	25
25	Illinois	24
25	Maryland	24
27	Georgia	23
27	Rhode Island	23
29	Tennessee	22
30	Oklahoma	21
31	Arkansas	20
31	North Carolina	20
31	South Carolina	20
31	Texas	20
31	West Virginia	20
36	Arizona	19
36	Florida	19
38	Nevada	18
39	Alabama	17
39	California	17
41	Louisiana	16
42	New Mexico	15
43	Hawaii	13
44	Mississippi	12
NA	Alaska**	NA
NA	Iowa**	NA
NA	Kansas**	NA
NA	Nebraska**	NA
NA	New York**	NA
NA	Pennsylvania**	NA

District of Columbia**   NA

Source: U.S. Department of Education, National Center for Education Statistics
   "The Nation's Report Card: Science 2005" (http://nces.ed.gov/nationsreportcard/)
*There are four achievement levels: Below Basic, Basic, Proficient, and Advanced. Proficient represents solid academic
mastery for 8th graders. Students reaching this level have demonstrated competency over challenging subject matter, including
subject matter knowledge, application of such knowledge to real-world situations, and analytical skills appropriate to the subject
matter. **Not available.

Percent of Public School Eighth Graders Eligible for
Free or Reduced Price Lunch Program Proficient or Better in Science in 2005
National Percent = 12%*

ALPHA ORDER

RANK	STATE	PERCENT
38	Alabama	8
NA	Alaska**	NA
41	Arizona	7
20	Arkansas	13
41	California	7
25	Colorado	12
34	Connecticut	9
25	Delaware	12
25	Florida	12
29	Georgia	10
41	Hawaii	7
7	Idaho	24
34	Illinois	9
19	Indiana	15
NA	Iowa**	NA
NA	Kansas**	NA
10	Kentucky	21
29	Louisiana	10
6	Maine	25
38	Maryland	8
14	Massachusetts	18
12	Michigan	19
11	Minnesota	20
44	Mississippi	6
14	Missouri	18
3	Montana	26
NA	Nebraska**	NA
38	Nevada	8
3	New Hampshire	26
28	New Jersey	11
29	New Mexico	10
NA	New York**	NA
29	North Carolina	10
1	North Dakota	27
20	Ohio	13
18	Oklahoma	16
12	Oregon	19
NA	Pennsylvania**	NA
34	Rhode Island	9
34	South Carolina	9
1	South Dakota	27
20	Tennessee	13
29	Texas	10
8	Utah	22
3	Vermont	26
20	Virginia	13
14	Washington	18
20	West Virginia	13
14	Wisconsin	18
8	Wyoming	22

RANK ORDER

RANK	STATE	PERCENT
1	North Dakota	27
1	South Dakota	27
3	Montana	26
3	New Hampshire	26
3	Vermont	26
6	Maine	25
7	Idaho	24
8	Utah	22
8	Wyoming	22
10	Kentucky	21
11	Minnesota	20
12	Michigan	19
12	Oregon	19
14	Massachusetts	18
14	Missouri	18
14	Washington	18
14	Wisconsin	18
18	Oklahoma	16
19	Indiana	15
20	Arkansas	13
20	Ohio	13
20	Tennessee	13
20	Virginia	13
20	West Virginia	13
25	Colorado	12
25	Delaware	12
25	Florida	12
28	New Jersey	11
29	Georgia	10
29	Louisiana	10
29	New Mexico	10
29	North Carolina	10
29	Texas	10
34	Connecticut	9
34	Illinois	9
34	Rhode Island	9
34	South Carolina	9
38	Alabama	8
38	Maryland	8
38	Nevada	8
41	Arizona	7
41	California	7
41	Hawaii	7
44	Mississippi	6
NA	Alaska**	NA
NA	Iowa**	NA
NA	Kansas**	NA
NA	Nebraska**	NA
NA	New York**	NA
NA	Pennsylvania**	NA
	District of Columbia**	NA

Source: U.S. Department of Education, National Center for Education Statistics
"The Nation's Report Card: Science 2005" (http://nces.ed.gov/nationsreportcard/)
*There are four achievement levels: Below Basic, Basic, Proficient, and Advanced. Proficient represents solid academic mastery for 8th graders. Students reaching this level have demonstrated competency over challenging subject matter, including subject matter knowledge, application of such knowledge to real-world situations, and analytical skills appropriate to the subject matter. **Not available.

Average Writing Score for Public School Fourth Graders in 2002

National Average Score = 153*

<table>
<tr><th colspan="3">ALPHA ORDER</th><th colspan="3">RANK ORDER</th></tr>
<tr><th>RANK</th><th>STATE</th><th>AVERAGE SCORE</th><th>RANK</th><th>STATE</th><th>AVERAGE SCORE</th></tr>
<tr><td>42</td><td>Alabama</td><td>140</td><td>1</td><td>Connecticut</td><td>174</td></tr>
<tr><td>NA</td><td>Alaska**</td><td>NA</td><td>2</td><td>Massachusetts</td><td>170</td></tr>
<tr><td>42</td><td>Arizona</td><td>140</td><td>3</td><td>Delaware</td><td>163</td></tr>
<tr><td>34</td><td>Arkansas</td><td>145</td><td>3</td><td>New York</td><td>163</td></tr>
<tr><td>33</td><td>California</td><td>146</td><td>5</td><td>North Carolina</td><td>159</td></tr>
<tr><td>NA</td><td>Colorado**</td><td>NA</td><td>6</td><td>Florida</td><td>158</td></tr>
<tr><td>1</td><td>Connecticut</td><td>174</td><td>6</td><td>Maine</td><td>158</td></tr>
<tr><td>3</td><td>Delaware</td><td>163</td><td>6</td><td>Vermont</td><td>158</td></tr>
<tr><td>6</td><td>Florida</td><td>158</td><td>6</td><td>Washington</td><td>158</td></tr>
<tr><td>25</td><td>Georgia</td><td>149</td><td>10</td><td>Maryland</td><td>157</td></tr>
<tr><td>25</td><td>Hawaii</td><td>149</td><td>10</td><td>Ohio</td><td>157</td></tr>
<tr><td>22</td><td>Idaho</td><td>150</td><td>10</td><td>Rhode Island</td><td>157</td></tr>
<tr><td>NA</td><td>Illinois**</td><td>NA</td><td>10</td><td>Virginia</td><td>157</td></tr>
<tr><td>17</td><td>Indiana</td><td>154</td><td>14</td><td>Minnesota</td><td>156</td></tr>
<tr><td>16</td><td>Iowa</td><td>155</td><td>14</td><td>Pennsylvania</td><td>156</td></tr>
<tr><td>25</td><td>Kansas</td><td>149</td><td>16</td><td>Iowa</td><td>155</td></tr>
<tr><td>17</td><td>Kentucky</td><td>154</td><td>17</td><td>Indiana</td><td>154</td></tr>
<tr><td>38</td><td>Louisiana</td><td>142</td><td>17</td><td>Kentucky</td><td>154</td></tr>
<tr><td>6</td><td>Maine</td><td>158</td><td>17</td><td>Nebraska</td><td>154</td></tr>
<tr><td>10</td><td>Maryland</td><td>157</td><td>17</td><td>Texas</td><td>154</td></tr>
<tr><td>2</td><td>Massachusetts</td><td>170</td><td>21</td><td>Missouri</td><td>151</td></tr>
<tr><td>31</td><td>Michigan</td><td>147</td><td>22</td><td>Idaho</td><td>150</td></tr>
<tr><td>14</td><td>Minnesota</td><td>156</td><td>22</td><td>North Dakota</td><td>150</td></tr>
<tr><td>41</td><td>Mississippi</td><td>141</td><td>22</td><td>Wyoming</td><td>150</td></tr>
<tr><td>21</td><td>Missouri</td><td>151</td><td>25</td><td>Georgia</td><td>149</td></tr>
<tr><td>25</td><td>Montana</td><td>149</td><td>25</td><td>Hawaii</td><td>149</td></tr>
<tr><td>17</td><td>Nebraska</td><td>154</td><td>25</td><td>Kansas</td><td>149</td></tr>
<tr><td>34</td><td>Nevada</td><td>145</td><td>25</td><td>Montana</td><td>149</td></tr>
<tr><td>NA</td><td>New Hampshire**</td><td>NA</td><td>25</td><td>Oregon</td><td>149</td></tr>
<tr><td>NA</td><td>New Jersey**</td><td>NA</td><td>25</td><td>Tennessee</td><td>149</td></tr>
<tr><td>38</td><td>New Mexico</td><td>142</td><td>31</td><td>Michigan</td><td>147</td></tr>
<tr><td>3</td><td>New York</td><td>163</td><td>31</td><td>West Virginia</td><td>147</td></tr>
<tr><td>5</td><td>North Carolina</td><td>159</td><td>33</td><td>California</td><td>146</td></tr>
<tr><td>22</td><td>North Dakota</td><td>150</td><td>34</td><td>Arkansas</td><td>145</td></tr>
<tr><td>10</td><td>Ohio</td><td>157</td><td>34</td><td>Nevada</td><td>145</td></tr>
<tr><td>38</td><td>Oklahoma</td><td>142</td><td>34</td><td>South Carolina</td><td>145</td></tr>
<tr><td>25</td><td>Oregon</td><td>149</td><td>34</td><td>Utah</td><td>145</td></tr>
<tr><td>14</td><td>Pennsylvania</td><td>156</td><td>38</td><td>Louisiana</td><td>142</td></tr>
<tr><td>10</td><td>Rhode Island</td><td>157</td><td>38</td><td>New Mexico</td><td>142</td></tr>
<tr><td>34</td><td>South Carolina</td><td>145</td><td>38</td><td>Oklahoma</td><td>142</td></tr>
<tr><td>NA</td><td>South Dakota**</td><td>NA</td><td>41</td><td>Mississippi</td><td>141</td></tr>
<tr><td>25</td><td>Tennessee</td><td>149</td><td>42</td><td>Alabama</td><td>140</td></tr>
<tr><td>17</td><td>Texas</td><td>154</td><td>42</td><td>Arizona</td><td>140</td></tr>
<tr><td>34</td><td>Utah</td><td>145</td><td>NA</td><td>Alaska**</td><td>NA</td></tr>
<tr><td>6</td><td>Vermont</td><td>158</td><td>NA</td><td>Colorado**</td><td>NA</td></tr>
<tr><td>10</td><td>Virginia</td><td>157</td><td>NA</td><td>Illinois**</td><td>NA</td></tr>
<tr><td>6</td><td>Washington</td><td>158</td><td>NA</td><td>New Hampshire**</td><td>NA</td></tr>
<tr><td>31</td><td>West Virginia</td><td>147</td><td>NA</td><td>New Jersey**</td><td>NA</td></tr>
<tr><td>NA</td><td>Wisconsin**</td><td>NA</td><td>NA</td><td>South Dakota**</td><td>NA</td></tr>
<tr><td>22</td><td>Wyoming</td><td>150</td><td>NA</td><td>Wisconsin**</td><td>NA</td></tr>
</table>

District of Columbia   135

Source: U.S. Department of Education, National Center for Education Statistics
  "The Nation's Report Card: Writing 2002" (http://nces.ed.gov/nationsreportcard/)
*These scores are from the National Assessment of Educational Progress (NAEP). Scale ranges from 0 to 300.
**Not available.

Average Writing Score for Public School Fourth Grade Males in 2002

National Average Score = 144*

ALPHA ORDER

ALPHA ORDER			RANK ORDER		
RANK	STATE	AVERAGE SCORE	RANK	STATE	AVERAGE SCORE
43	Alabama	130	1	Connecticut	166
NA	Alaska**	NA	2	Massachusetts	162
42	Arizona	132	3	New York	156
34	Arkansas	136	4	Delaware	154
34	California	136	5	North Carolina	151
NA	Colorado**	NA	5	Washington	151
1	Connecticut	166	7	Ohio	150
4	Delaware	154	7	Rhode Island	150
9	Florida	149	9	Florida	149
24	Georgia	141	9	Virginia	149
24	Hawaii	141	11	Maryland	148
21	Idaho	142	11	Pennsylvania	148
NA	Illinois**	NA	13	Maine	147
17	Indiana	144	13	Minnesota	147
17	Iowa	144	13	Vermont	147
24	Kansas	141	16	Texas	145
17	Kentucky	144	17	Indiana	144
32	Louisiana	137	17	Iowa	144
13	Maine	147	17	Kentucky	144
11	Maryland	148	17	Nebraska	144
2	Massachusetts	162	21	Idaho	142
31	Michigan	138	21	North Dakota	142
13	Minnesota	147	21	Wyoming	142
40	Mississippi	134	24	Georgia	141
24	Missouri	141	24	Hawaii	141
24	Montana	141	24	Kansas	141
17	Nebraska	144	24	Missouri	141
37	Nevada	135	24	Montana	141
NA	New Hampshire**	NA	29	Tennessee	140
NA	New Jersey**	NA	30	Oregon	139
40	New Mexico	134	31	Michigan	138
3	New York	156	32	Louisiana	137
5	North Carolina	151	32	West Virginia	137
21	North Dakota	142	34	Arkansas	136
7	Ohio	150	34	California	136
37	Oklahoma	135	34	South Carolina	136
30	Oregon	139	37	Nevada	135
11	Pennsylvania	148	37	Oklahoma	135
7	Rhode Island	150	37	Utah	135
34	South Carolina	136	40	Mississippi	134
NA	South Dakota**	NA	40	New Mexico	134
29	Tennessee	140	42	Arizona	132
16	Texas	145	43	Alabama	130
37	Utah	135	NA	Alaska**	NA
13	Vermont	147	NA	Colorado**	NA
9	Virginia	149	NA	Illinois**	NA
5	Washington	151	NA	New Hampshire**	NA
32	West Virginia	137	NA	New Jersey**	NA
NA	Wisconsin**	NA	NA	South Dakota**	NA
21	Wyoming	142	NA	Wisconsin**	NA
				District of Columbia	127

Source: U.S. Department of Education, National Center for Education Statistics
    "The Nation's Report Card: Writing 2002" (http://nces.ed.gov/nationsreportcard/)
*These scores are from the National Assessment of Educational Progress (NAEP). Scale ranges from 0 to 300.
**Not available.

Average Writing Score for Public School Fourth Grade Females in 2002

National Average Score = 162*

ALPHA ORDER

RANK	STATE	AVERAGE SCORE
38	Alabama	151
NA	Alaska**	NA
42	Arizona	148
36	Arkansas	154
29	California	157
NA	Colorado**	NA
1	Connecticut	184
3	Delaware	172
7	Florida	168
24	Georgia	158
24	Hawaii	158
22	Idaho	159
NA	Illinois**	NA
19	Indiana	163
9	Iowa	166
31	Kansas	156
12	Kentucky	165
43	Louisiana	147
5	Maine	169
12	Maryland	165
2	Massachusetts	178
31	Michigan	156
12	Minnesota	165
41	Mississippi	149
21	Missouri	160
29	Montana	157
16	Nebraska	164
35	Nevada	155
NA	New Hampshire**	NA
NA	New Jersey**	NA
38	New Mexico	151
4	New York	170
8	North Carolina	167
24	North Dakota	158
16	Ohio	164
40	Oklahoma	150
24	Oregon	158
16	Pennsylvania	164
9	Rhode Island	166
36	South Carolina	154
NA	South Dakota**	NA
24	Tennessee	158
19	Texas	163
31	Utah	156
5	Vermont	169
12	Virginia	165
9	Washington	166
31	West Virginia	156
NA	Wisconsin**	NA
22	Wyoming	159

RANK ORDER

RANK	STATE	AVERAGE SCORE
1	Connecticut	184
2	Massachusetts	178
3	Delaware	172
4	New York	170
5	Maine	169
5	Vermont	169
7	Florida	168
8	North Carolina	167
9	Iowa	166
9	Rhode Island	166
9	Washington	166
12	Kentucky	165
12	Maryland	165
12	Minnesota	165
12	Virginia	165
16	Nebraska	164
16	Ohio	164
16	Pennsylvania	164
19	Indiana	163
19	Texas	163
21	Missouri	160
22	Idaho	159
22	Wyoming	159
24	Georgia	158
24	Hawaii	158
24	North Dakota	158
24	Oregon	158
24	Tennessee	158
29	California	157
29	Montana	157
31	Kansas	156
31	Michigan	156
31	Utah	156
31	West Virginia	156
35	Nevada	155
36	Arkansas	154
36	South Carolina	154
38	Alabama	151
38	New Mexico	151
40	Oklahoma	150
41	Mississippi	149
42	Arizona	148
43	Louisiana	147
NA	Alaska**	NA
NA	Colorado**	NA
NA	Illinois**	NA
NA	New Hampshire**	NA
NA	New Jersey**	NA
NA	South Dakota**	NA
NA	Wisconsin**	NA

	District of Columbia	143

Source: U.S. Department of Education, National Center for Education Statistics
   "The Nation's Report Card: Writing 2002" (http://nces.ed.gov/nationsreportcard/)
*These scores are from the National Assessment of Educational Progress (NAEP). Scale ranges from 0 to 300.
**Not available.

Average Writing Score for Public School Fourth Graders Eligible for Free or Reduced Price Lunch Program in 2002
National Average Score = 141*

ALPHA ORDER				RANK ORDER		
RANK	STATE	AVERAGE SCORE		RANK	STATE	AVERAGE SCORE
42	Alabama	130		1	Connecticut	154
NA	Alaska**	NA		2	Massachusetts	151
43	Arizona	129		3	New York	150
30	Arkansas	137		4	Delaware	149
40	California	134		4	Florida	149
NA	Colorado**	NA		6	Minnesota	147
1	Connecticut	154		6	Texas	147
4	Delaware	149		8	North Carolina	146
4	Florida	149		9	Maryland	145
28	Georgia	138		10	Kentucky	144
24	Hawaii	139		10	Wyoming	144
21	Idaho	140		12	Nebraska	143
NA	Illinois**	NA		12	Ohio	143
19	Indiana	141		12	Vermont	143
16	Iowa	142		12	Washington	143
30	Kansas	137		16	Iowa	142
10	Kentucky	144		16	Maine	142
38	Louisiana	135		16	North Dakota	142
16	Maine	142		19	Indiana	141
9	Maryland	145		19	Rhode Island	141
2	Massachusetts	151		21	Idaho	140
40	Michigan	134		21	Virginia	140
6	Minnesota	147		21	West Virginia	140
38	Mississippi	135		24	Hawaii	139
24	Missouri	139		24	Missouri	139
24	Montana	139		24	Montana	139
12	Nebraska	143		24	Tennessee	139
33	Nevada	136		28	Georgia	138
NA	New Hampshire**	NA		28	Oregon	138
NA	New Jersey**	NA		30	Arkansas	137
33	New Mexico	136		30	Kansas	137
3	New York	150		30	Pennsylvania	137
8	North Carolina	146		33	Nevada	136
16	North Dakota	142		33	New Mexico	136
12	Ohio	143		33	Oklahoma	136
33	Oklahoma	136		33	South Carolina	136
28	Oregon	138		33	Utah	136
30	Pennsylvania	137		38	Louisiana	135
19	Rhode Island	141		38	Mississippi	135
33	South Carolina	136		40	California	134
NA	South Dakota**	NA		40	Michigan	134
24	Tennessee	139		42	Alabama	130
6	Texas	147		43	Arizona	129
33	Utah	136		NA	Alaska**	NA
12	Vermont	143		NA	Colorado**	NA
21	Virginia	140		NA	Illinois**	NA
12	Washington	143		NA	New Hampshire**	NA
21	West Virginia	140		NA	New Jersey**	NA
NA	Wisconsin**	NA		NA	South Dakota**	NA
10	Wyoming	144		NA	Wisconsin**	NA
					District of Columbia	131

Source: U.S. Department of Education, National Center for Education Statistics
"The Nation's Report Card: Writing 2002" (http://nces.ed.gov/nationsreportcard/)
*These scores are from the National Assessment of Educational Progress (NAEP). Scale ranges from 0 to 300.
**Not available.

Percent of Public School Fourth Graders
Proficient or Better in Writing in 2002
National Percent = 27%*

ALPHA ORDER

RANK	STATE	PERCENT
40	Alabama	15
NA	Alaska**	NA
40	Arizona	15
33	Arkansas	19
21	California	23
NA	Colorado**	NA
1	Connecticut	49
4	Delaware	35
5	Florida	33
21	Georgia	23
25	Hawaii	22
25	Idaho	22
NA	Illinois**	NA
20	Indiana	26
17	Iowa	27
30	Kansas	21
17	Kentucky	27
42	Louisiana	14
6	Maine	32
9	Maryland	30
2	Massachusetts	44
33	Michigan	19
12	Minnesota	29
43	Mississippi	13
25	Missouri	22
25	Montana	22
17	Nebraska	27
36	Nevada	18
NA	New Hampshire**	NA
NA	New Jersey**	NA
36	New Mexico	18
3	New York	37
6	North Carolina	32
31	North Dakota	20
16	Ohio	28
39	Oklahoma	16
25	Oregon	22
12	Pennsylvania	29
9	Rhode Island	30
38	South Carolina	17
NA	South Dakota**	NA
21	Tennessee	23
12	Texas	29
31	Utah	20
6	Vermont	32
12	Virginia	29
9	Washington	30
33	West Virginia	19
NA	Wisconsin**	NA
21	Wyoming	23

RANK ORDER

RANK	STATE	PERCENT
1	Connecticut	49
2	Massachusetts	44
3	New York	37
4	Delaware	35
5	Florida	33
6	Maine	32
6	North Carolina	32
6	Vermont	32
9	Maryland	30
9	Rhode Island	30
9	Washington	30
12	Minnesota	29
12	Pennsylvania	29
12	Texas	29
12	Virginia	29
16	Ohio	28
17	Iowa	27
17	Kentucky	27
17	Nebraska	27
20	Indiana	26
21	California	23
21	Georgia	23
21	Tennessee	23
21	Wyoming	23
25	Hawaii	22
25	Idaho	22
25	Missouri	22
25	Montana	22
25	Oregon	22
30	Kansas	21
31	North Dakota	20
31	Utah	20
33	Arkansas	19
33	Michigan	19
33	West Virginia	19
36	Nevada	18
36	New Mexico	18
38	South Carolina	17
39	Oklahoma	16
40	Alabama	15
40	Arizona	15
42	Louisiana	14
43	Mississippi	13
NA	Alaska**	NA
NA	Colorado**	NA
NA	Illinois**	NA
NA	New Hampshire**	NA
NA	New Jersey**	NA
NA	South Dakota**	NA
NA	Wisconsin**	NA
	District of Columbia	11

Source: U.S. Department of Education, National Center for Education Statistics
"The Nation's Report Card: Writing 2002" (http://nces.ed.gov/nationsreportcard/)
*There are four achievement levels: Below Basic, Basic, Proficient, and Advanced. Proficient represents solid academic
mastery for 4th graders. Students reaching this level have demonstrated competency over challenging subject matter, including
subject matter knowledge, application of such knowledge to real-world situations, and analytical skills appropriate to the subject
matter. **Not available.

Percent of Public School Fourth Grade Males
Proficient or Better in Writing in 2002
National Percent = 18%*

ALPHA ORDER

RANK	STATE	PERCENT
42	Alabama	8
NA	Alaska**	NA
41	Arizona	9
37	Arkansas	10
24	California	14
NA	Colorado**	NA
1	Connecticut	39
4	Delaware	25
6	Florida	23
18	Georgia	16
21	Hawaii	15
24	Idaho	14
NA	Illinois**	NA
18	Indiana	16
24	Iowa	14
24	Kansas	14
17	Kentucky	17
31	Louisiana	11
13	Maine	20
10	Maryland	21
2	Massachusetts	34
31	Michigan	11
16	Minnesota	18
42	Mississippi	8
30	Missouri	12
29	Montana	13
18	Nebraska	16
37	Nevada	10
NA	New Hampshire**	NA
NA	New Jersey**	NA
31	New Mexico	11
3	New York	30
4	North Carolina	25
31	North Dakota	11
13	Ohio	20
31	Oklahoma	11
21	Oregon	15
13	Pennsylvania	20
7	Rhode Island	22
37	South Carolina	10
NA	South Dakota**	NA
24	Tennessee	14
10	Texas	21
31	Utah	11
10	Vermont	21
7	Virginia	22
7	Washington	22
37	West Virginia	10
NA	Wisconsin**	NA
21	Wyoming	15

RANK ORDER

RANK	STATE	PERCENT
1	Connecticut	39
2	Massachusetts	34
3	New York	30
4	Delaware	25
4	North Carolina	25
6	Florida	23
7	Rhode Island	22
7	Virginia	22
7	Washington	22
10	Maryland	21
10	Texas	21
10	Vermont	21
13	Maine	20
13	Ohio	20
13	Pennsylvania	20
16	Minnesota	18
17	Kentucky	17
18	Georgia	16
18	Indiana	16
18	Nebraska	16
21	Hawaii	15
21	Oregon	15
21	Wyoming	15
24	California	14
24	Idaho	14
24	Iowa	14
24	Kansas	14
24	Tennessee	14
29	Montana	13
30	Missouri	12
31	Louisiana	11
31	Michigan	11
31	New Mexico	11
31	North Dakota	11
31	Oklahoma	11
31	Utah	11
37	Arkansas	10
37	Nevada	10
37	South Carolina	10
37	West Virginia	10
41	Arizona	9
42	Alabama	8
42	Mississippi	8
NA	Alaska**	NA
NA	Colorado**	NA
NA	Illinois**	NA
NA	New Hampshire**	NA
NA	New Jersey**	NA
NA	South Dakota**	NA
NA	Wisconsin**	NA
	District of Columbia	7

Source: U.S. Department of Education, National Center for Education Statistics
"The Nation's Report Card: Writing 2002" (http://nces.ed.gov/nationsreportcard/)
*There are four achievement levels: Below Basic, Basic, Proficient, and Advanced. Proficient represents solid academic mastery for 4th graders. Students reaching this level have demonstrated competency over challenging subject matter, including subject matter knowledge, application of such knowledge to real-world situations, and analytical skills appropriate to the subject matter. **Not available.

Percent of Public School Fourth Grade Females
Proficient or Better in Writing in 2002
National Percent = 35%*

ALPHA ORDER

RANK	STATE	PERCENT
39	Alabama	23
NA	Alaska**	NA
40	Arizona	22
35	Arkansas	27
21	California	32
NA	Colorado**	NA
1	Connecticut	60
3	Delaware	46
6	Florida	43
26	Georgia	30
29	Hawaii	29
21	Idaho	32
NA	Illinois**	NA
19	Indiana	35
8	Iowa	40
31	Kansas	28
15	Kentucky	37
43	Louisiana	17
4	Maine	44
13	Maryland	38
2	Massachusetts	54
31	Michigan	28
10	Minnesota	39
42	Mississippi	18
23	Missouri	31
26	Montana	30
13	Nebraska	38
36	Nevada	25
NA	New Hampshire**	NA
NA	New Jersey**	NA
38	New Mexico	24
4	New York	44
8	North Carolina	40
31	North Dakota	28
19	Ohio	35
40	Oklahoma	22
26	Oregon	30
15	Pennsylvania	37
10	Rhode Island	39
36	South Carolina	25
NA	South Dakota**	NA
23	Tennessee	31
15	Texas	37
29	Utah	29
7	Vermont	42
15	Virginia	37
10	Washington	39
31	West Virginia	28
NA	Wisconsin**	NA
23	Wyoming	31

RANK ORDER

RANK	STATE	PERCENT
1	Connecticut	60
2	Massachusetts	54
3	Delaware	46
4	Maine	44
4	New York	44
6	Florida	43
7	Vermont	42
8	Iowa	40
8	North Carolina	40
10	Minnesota	39
10	Rhode Island	39
10	Washington	39
13	Maryland	38
13	Nebraska	38
15	Kentucky	37
15	Pennsylvania	37
15	Texas	37
15	Virginia	37
19	Indiana	35
19	Ohio	35
21	California	32
21	Idaho	32
23	Missouri	31
23	Tennessee	31
23	Wyoming	31
26	Georgia	30
26	Montana	30
26	Oregon	30
29	Hawaii	29
29	Utah	29
31	Kansas	28
31	Michigan	28
31	North Dakota	28
31	West Virginia	28
35	Arkansas	27
36	Nevada	25
36	South Carolina	25
38	New Mexico	24
39	Alabama	23
40	Arizona	22
40	Oklahoma	22
42	Mississippi	18
43	Louisiana	17
NA	Alaska**	NA
NA	Colorado**	NA
NA	Illinois**	NA
NA	New Hampshire**	NA
NA	New Jersey**	NA
NA	South Dakota**	NA
NA	Wisconsin**	NA

District of Columbia — 15

Source: U.S. Department of Education, National Center for Education Statistics
    "The Nation's Report Card: Writing 2002" (http://nces.ed.gov/nationsreportcard/)
*There are four achievement levels: Below Basic, Basic, Proficient, and Advanced. Proficient represents solid academic
mastery for 4th graders. Students reaching this level have demonstrated competency over challenging subject matter, including
subject matter knowledge, application of such knowledge to real-world situations, and analytical skills appropriate to the subject
matter. **Not available.

Percent of Public School Fourth Graders Eligible for Free or Reduced Price Lunch Proficient or Better in Writing in 2002
National Percent = 15%*

ALPHA ORDER				RANK ORDER		
RANK	STATE	PERCENT		RANK	STATE	PERCENT
42	Alabama	7		1	Connecticut	27
NA	Alaska**	NA		2	Florida	24
42	Arizona	7		3	New York	23
28	Arkansas	12		4	Massachusetts	22
28	California	12		4	Minnesota	22
NA	Colorado**	NA		4	Texas	22
1	Connecticut	27		7	Delaware	20
7	Delaware	20		7	North Carolina	20
2	Florida	24		9	Maine	18
17	Georgia	14		9	Maryland	18
16	Hawaii	15		9	Wyoming	18
25	Idaho	13		12	Kentucky	17
NA	Illinois**	NA		12	Nebraska	17
17	Indiana	14		14	Vermont	16
17	Iowa	14		14	Washington	16
33	Kansas	11		16	Hawaii	15
12	Kentucky	17		17	Georgia	14
39	Louisiana	9		17	Indiana	14
9	Maine	18		17	Iowa	14
9	Maryland	18		17	Montana	14
4	Massachusetts	22		17	North Dakota	14
40	Michigan	8		17	Ohio	14
4	Minnesota	22		17	Rhode Island	14
40	Mississippi	8		17	Tennessee	14
33	Missouri	11		25	Idaho	13
17	Montana	14		25	Oregon	13
12	Nebraska	17		25	Utah	13
33	Nevada	11		28	Arkansas	12
NA	New Hampshire**	NA		28	California	12
NA	New Jersey**	NA		28	New Mexico	12
28	New Mexico	12		28	Virginia	12
3	New York	23		28	West Virginia	12
7	North Carolina	20		33	Kansas	11
17	North Dakota	14		33	Missouri	11
17	Ohio	14		33	Nevada	11
33	Oklahoma	11		33	Oklahoma	11
25	Oregon	13		37	Pennsylvania	10
37	Pennsylvania	10		37	South Carolina	10
17	Rhode Island	14		39	Louisiana	9
37	South Carolina	10		40	Michigan	8
NA	South Dakota**	NA		40	Mississippi	8
17	Tennessee	14		42	Alabama	7
4	Texas	22		42	Arizona	7
25	Utah	13		NA	Alaska**	NA
14	Vermont	16		NA	Colorado**	NA
28	Virginia	12		NA	Illinois**	NA
14	Washington	16		NA	New Hampshire**	NA
28	West Virginia	12		NA	New Jersey**	NA
NA	Wisconsin**	NA		NA	South Dakota**	NA
9	Wyoming	18		NA	Wisconsin**	NA
					District of Columbia	7

Source: U.S. Department of Education, National Center for Education Statistics
  "The Nation's Report Card: Writing 2002" (http://nces.ed.gov/nationsreportcard/)
*There are four achievement levels: Below Basic, Basic, Proficient, and Advanced. Proficient represents solid academic mastery for 4th graders. Students reaching this level have demonstrated competency over challenging subject matter, including subject matter knowledge, application of such knowledge to real-world situations, and analytical skills appropriate to the subject matter. **Not available.

Average Writing Score for Public School Eighth Graders in 2007

National Average Score = 154*

ALPHA ORDER

RANK	STATE	AVERAGE SCORE
36	Alabama	148
NA	Alaska**	NA
36	Arizona	148
32	Arkansas	151
36	California	148
5	Colorado	161
2	Connecticut	172
10	Delaware	158
10	Florida	158
27	Georgia	153
42	Hawaii	144
23	Idaho	154
7	Illinois	160
21	Indiana	155
21	Iowa	155
17	Kansas	156
32	Kentucky	151
40	Louisiana	147
5	Maine	161
NA	Maryland**	NA
3	Massachusetts	167
32	Michigan	151
17	Minnesota	156
45	Mississippi	142
27	Missouri	153
15	Montana	157
NA	Nebraska**	NA
43	Nevada	143
7	New Hampshire	160
1	New Jersey	175
43	New Mexico	143
23	New York	154
27	North Carolina	153
23	North Dakota	154
17	Ohio	156
27	Oklahoma	153
NA	Oregon**	NA
9	Pennsylvania	159
23	Rhode Island	154
36	South Carolina	148
NA	South Dakota**	NA
17	Tennessee	156
32	Texas	151
31	Utah	152
4	Vermont	162
15	Virginia	157
10	Washington	158
41	West Virginia	146
10	Wisconsin	158
10	Wyoming	158

RANK ORDER

RANK	STATE	AVERAGE SCORE
1	New Jersey	175
2	Connecticut	172
3	Massachusetts	167
4	Vermont	162
5	Colorado	161
5	Maine	161
7	Illinois	160
7	New Hampshire	160
9	Pennsylvania	159
10	Delaware	158
10	Florida	158
10	Washington	158
10	Wisconsin	158
10	Wyoming	158
15	Montana	157
15	Virginia	157
17	Kansas	156
17	Minnesota	156
17	Ohio	156
17	Tennessee	156
21	Indiana	155
21	Iowa	155
23	Idaho	154
23	New York	154
23	North Dakota	154
23	Rhode Island	154
27	Georgia	153
27	Missouri	153
27	North Carolina	153
27	Oklahoma	153
31	Utah	152
32	Arkansas	151
32	Kentucky	151
32	Michigan	151
32	Texas	151
36	Alabama	148
36	Arizona	148
36	California	148
36	South Carolina	148
40	Louisiana	147
41	West Virginia	146
42	Hawaii	144
43	Nevada	143
43	New Mexico	143
45	Mississippi	142
NA	Alaska**	NA
NA	Maryland**	NA
NA	Nebraska**	NA
NA	Oregon**	NA
NA	South Dakota**	NA

District of Columbia**   NA

Source: U.S. Department of Education, National Center for Education Statistics
   "The Nation's Report Card: Writing 2007" (http://nces.ed.gov/nationsreportcard/)
*These scores are from the National Assessment of Educational Progress (NAEP). Scale ranges from 0 to 300.
**Not available.

Average Writing Score for Public School Eighth Grade Males in 2007

National Average Score = 144*

<table>
<tr><td colspan="3">ALPHA ORDER</td><td colspan="3">RANK ORDER</td></tr>
<tr><td>RANK</td><td>STATE</td><td>AVERAGE SCORE</td><td>RANK</td><td>STATE</td><td>AVERAGE SCORE</td></tr>
<tr><td>38</td><td>Alabama</td><td>138</td><td>1</td><td>New Jersey</td><td>168</td></tr>
<tr><td>NA</td><td>Alaska**</td><td>NA</td><td>2</td><td>Connecticut</td><td>163</td></tr>
<tr><td>35</td><td>Arizona</td><td>139</td><td>3</td><td>Massachusetts</td><td>157</td></tr>
<tr><td>35</td><td>Arkansas</td><td>139</td><td>4</td><td>Colorado</td><td>152</td></tr>
<tr><td>35</td><td>California</td><td>139</td><td>5</td><td>Delaware</td><td>151</td></tr>
<tr><td>4</td><td>Colorado</td><td>152</td><td>5</td><td>Pennsylvania</td><td>151</td></tr>
<tr><td>2</td><td>Connecticut</td><td>163</td><td>7</td><td>Illinois</td><td>150</td></tr>
<tr><td>5</td><td>Delaware</td><td>151</td><td>8</td><td>Maine</td><td>149</td></tr>
<tr><td>11</td><td>Florida</td><td>147</td><td>8</td><td>New Hampshire</td><td>149</td></tr>
<tr><td>23</td><td>Georgia</td><td>143</td><td>8</td><td>Vermont</td><td>149</td></tr>
<tr><td>41</td><td>Hawaii</td><td>134</td><td>11</td><td>Florida</td><td>147</td></tr>
<tr><td>23</td><td>Idaho</td><td>143</td><td>11</td><td>Ohio</td><td>147</td></tr>
<tr><td>7</td><td>Illinois</td><td>150</td><td>13</td><td>Tennessee</td><td>146</td></tr>
<tr><td>20</td><td>Indiana</td><td>144</td><td>13</td><td>Virginia</td><td>146</td></tr>
<tr><td>23</td><td>Iowa</td><td>143</td><td>13</td><td>Washington</td><td>146</td></tr>
<tr><td>20</td><td>Kansas</td><td>144</td><td>13</td><td>Wisconsin</td><td>146</td></tr>
<tr><td>29</td><td>Kentucky</td><td>142</td><td>13</td><td>Wyoming</td><td>146</td></tr>
<tr><td>38</td><td>Louisiana</td><td>138</td><td>18</td><td>Montana</td><td>145</td></tr>
<tr><td>8</td><td>Maine</td><td>149</td><td>18</td><td>New York</td><td>145</td></tr>
<tr><td>NA</td><td>Maryland**</td><td>NA</td><td>20</td><td>Indiana</td><td>144</td></tr>
<tr><td>3</td><td>Massachusetts</td><td>157</td><td>20</td><td>Kansas</td><td>144</td></tr>
<tr><td>33</td><td>Michigan</td><td>140</td><td>20</td><td>Minnesota</td><td>144</td></tr>
<tr><td>20</td><td>Minnesota</td><td>144</td><td>23</td><td>Georgia</td><td>143</td></tr>
<tr><td>44</td><td>Mississippi</td><td>132</td><td>23</td><td>Idaho</td><td>143</td></tr>
<tr><td>23</td><td>Missouri</td><td>143</td><td>23</td><td>Iowa</td><td>143</td></tr>
<tr><td>18</td><td>Montana</td><td>145</td><td>23</td><td>Missouri</td><td>143</td></tr>
<tr><td>NA</td><td>Nebraska**</td><td>NA</td><td>23</td><td>Oklahoma</td><td>143</td></tr>
<tr><td>45</td><td>Nevada</td><td>131</td><td>23</td><td>Rhode Island</td><td>143</td></tr>
<tr><td>8</td><td>New Hampshire</td><td>149</td><td>29</td><td>Kentucky</td><td>142</td></tr>
<tr><td>1</td><td>New Jersey</td><td>168</td><td>29</td><td>North Carolina</td><td>142</td></tr>
<tr><td>42</td><td>New Mexico</td><td>133</td><td>29</td><td>North Dakota</td><td>142</td></tr>
<tr><td>18</td><td>New York</td><td>145</td><td>29</td><td>Texas</td><td>142</td></tr>
<tr><td>29</td><td>North Carolina</td><td>142</td><td>33</td><td>Michigan</td><td>140</td></tr>
<tr><td>29</td><td>North Dakota</td><td>142</td><td>33</td><td>Utah</td><td>140</td></tr>
<tr><td>11</td><td>Ohio</td><td>147</td><td>35</td><td>Arizona</td><td>139</td></tr>
<tr><td>23</td><td>Oklahoma</td><td>143</td><td>35</td><td>Arkansas</td><td>139</td></tr>
<tr><td>NA</td><td>Oregon**</td><td>NA</td><td>35</td><td>California</td><td>139</td></tr>
<tr><td>5</td><td>Pennsylvania</td><td>151</td><td>38</td><td>Alabama</td><td>138</td></tr>
<tr><td>23</td><td>Rhode Island</td><td>143</td><td>38</td><td>Louisiana</td><td>138</td></tr>
<tr><td>40</td><td>South Carolina</td><td>137</td><td>40</td><td>South Carolina</td><td>137</td></tr>
<tr><td>NA</td><td>South Dakota**</td><td>NA</td><td>41</td><td>Hawaii</td><td>134</td></tr>
<tr><td>13</td><td>Tennessee</td><td>146</td><td>42</td><td>New Mexico</td><td>133</td></tr>
<tr><td>29</td><td>Texas</td><td>142</td><td>42</td><td>West Virginia</td><td>133</td></tr>
<tr><td>33</td><td>Utah</td><td>140</td><td>44</td><td>Mississippi</td><td>132</td></tr>
<tr><td>8</td><td>Vermont</td><td>149</td><td>45</td><td>Nevada</td><td>131</td></tr>
<tr><td>13</td><td>Virginia</td><td>146</td><td>NA</td><td>Alaska**</td><td>NA</td></tr>
<tr><td>13</td><td>Washington</td><td>146</td><td>NA</td><td>Maryland**</td><td>NA</td></tr>
<tr><td>42</td><td>West Virginia</td><td>133</td><td>NA</td><td>Nebraska**</td><td>NA</td></tr>
<tr><td>13</td><td>Wisconsin</td><td>146</td><td>NA</td><td>Oregon**</td><td>NA</td></tr>
<tr><td>13</td><td>Wyoming</td><td>146</td><td>NA</td><td>South Dakota**</td><td>NA</td></tr>
<tr><td></td><td></td><td></td><td></td><td>District of Columbia**</td><td>NA</td></tr>
</table>

Source: U.S. Department of Education, National Center for Education Statistics
   "The Nation's Report Card: Writing 2007" (http://nces.ed.gov/nationsreportcard/)
*These scores are from the National Assessment of Educational Progress (NAEP). Scale ranges from 0 to 300.
**Not available.

Average Writing Score for Public School Eighth Grade Females in 2007

National Average Score = 164*

ALPHA ORDER

RANK	STATE	AVERAGE SCORE
38	Alabama	157
NA	Alaska**	NA
38	Arizona	157
27	Arkansas	164
38	California	157
11	Colorado	169
2	Connecticut	181
21	Delaware	166
11	Florida	169
27	Georgia	164
43	Hawaii	155
18	Idaho	167
8	Illinois	170
24	Indiana	165
18	Iowa	167
14	Kansas	168
34	Kentucky	161
41	Louisiana	156
5	Maine	174
NA	Maryland**	NA
3	Massachusetts	178
32	Michigan	162
14	Minnesota	168
44	Mississippi	152
30	Missouri	163
11	Montana	169
NA	Nebraska**	NA
41	Nevada	156
6	New Hampshire	173
1	New Jersey	183
44	New Mexico	152
30	New York	163
27	North Carolina	164
21	North Dakota	166
21	Ohio	166
32	Oklahoma	162
NA	Oregon**	NA
14	Pennsylvania	168
24	Rhode Island	165
36	South Carolina	159
NA	South Dakota**	NA
18	Tennessee	167
35	Texas	160
24	Utah	165
4	Vermont	176
14	Virginia	168
8	Washington	170
36	West Virginia	159
8	Wisconsin	170
7	Wyoming	171

RANK ORDER

RANK	STATE	AVERAGE SCORE
1	New Jersey	183
2	Connecticut	181
3	Massachusetts	178
4	Vermont	176
5	Maine	174
6	New Hampshire	173
7	Wyoming	171
8	Illinois	170
8	Washington	170
8	Wisconsin	170
11	Colorado	169
11	Florida	169
11	Montana	169
14	Kansas	168
14	Minnesota	168
14	Pennsylvania	168
14	Virginia	168
18	Idaho	167
18	Iowa	167
18	Tennessee	167
21	Delaware	166
21	North Dakota	166
21	Ohio	166
24	Indiana	165
24	Rhode Island	165
24	Utah	165
27	Arkansas	164
27	Georgia	164
27	North Carolina	164
30	Missouri	163
30	New York	163
32	Michigan	162
32	Oklahoma	162
34	Kentucky	161
35	Texas	160
36	South Carolina	159
36	West Virginia	159
38	Alabama	157
38	Arizona	157
38	California	157
41	Louisiana	156
41	Nevada	156
43	Hawaii	155
44	Mississippi	152
44	New Mexico	152
NA	Alaska**	NA
NA	Maryland**	NA
NA	Nebraska**	NA
NA	Oregon**	NA
NA	South Dakota**	NA
	District of Columbia**	NA

Source: U.S. Department of Education, National Center for Education Statistics
"The Nation's Report Card: Writing 2007" (http://nces.ed.gov/nationsreportcard/)
*These scores are from the National Assessment of Educational Progress (NAEP). Scale ranges from 0 to 300.
**Not available.

Average Writing Score for Public School Eighth Graders
Eligible for Free or Reduced Lunch Program in 2007
National Average Score = 141*

ALPHA ORDER				RANK ORDER		
RANK	STATE	AVERAGE SCORE		RANK	STATE	AVERAGE SCORE
43	Alabama	135		1	New Jersey	155
NA	Alaska**	NA		2	Maine	150
39	Arizona	136		3	Connecticut	149
23	Arkansas	141		4	Delaware	146
39	California	136		4	Florida	146
16	Colorado	143		4	Massachusetts	146
3	Connecticut	149		4	Oklahoma	146
4	Delaware	146		4	Tennessee	146
4	Florida	146		9	New York	145
23	Georgia	141		9	North Dakota	145
44	Hawaii	132		9	Wyoming	145
12	Idaho	144		12	Idaho	144
19	Illinois	142		12	Pennsylvania	144
19	Indiana	142		12	Vermont	144
29	Iowa	140		12	Washington	144
19	Kansas	142		16	Colorado	143
23	Kentucky	141		16	Montana	143
29	Louisiana	140		16	New Hampshire	143
2	Maine	150		19	Illinois	142
NA	Maryland**	NA		19	Indiana	142
4	Massachusetts	146		19	Kansas	142
36	Michigan	137		19	Wisconsin	142
29	Minnesota	140		23	Arkansas	141
39	Mississippi	136		23	Georgia	141
23	Missouri	141		23	Kentucky	141
16	Montana	143		23	Missouri	141
NA	Nebraska**	NA		23	North Carolina	141
44	Nevada	132		23	Virginia	141
16	New Hampshire	143		29	Iowa	140
1	New Jersey	155		29	Louisiana	140
36	New Mexico	137		29	Minnesota	140
9	New York	145		29	Ohio	140
23	North Carolina	141		29	Texas	140
9	North Dakota	145		34	South Carolina	139
29	Ohio	140		34	Utah	139
4	Oklahoma	146		36	Michigan	137
NA	Oregon**	NA		36	New Mexico	137
12	Pennsylvania	144		36	West Virginia	137
39	Rhode Island	136		39	Arizona	136
34	South Carolina	139		39	California	136
NA	South Dakota**	NA		39	Mississippi	136
4	Tennessee	146		39	Rhode Island	136
29	Texas	140		43	Alabama	135
34	Utah	139		44	Hawaii	132
12	Vermont	144		44	Nevada	132
23	Virginia	141		NA	Alaska**	NA
12	Washington	144		NA	Maryland**	NA
36	West Virginia	137		NA	Nebraska**	NA
19	Wisconsin	142		NA	Oregon**	NA
9	Wyoming	145		NA	South Dakota**	NA
					District of Columbia**	NA

Source: U.S. Department of Education, National Center for Education Statistics
    "The Nation's Report Card: Writing 2007" (http://nces.ed.gov/nationsreportcard/)
*These scores are from the National Assessment of Educational Progress (NAEP). Scale ranges from 0 to 300.
**Not available.

Percent of Public School Eighth Graders
Proficient or Better in Writing in 2007
National Percent = 31%*

ALPHA ORDER

RANK	STATE	PERCENT
37	Alabama	24
NA	Alaska**	NA
38	Arizona	23
29	Arkansas	27
36	California	25
6	Colorado	38
2	Connecticut	53
13	Delaware	34
9	Florida	36
26	Georgia	29
42	Hawaii	20
26	Idaho	29
8	Illinois	37
24	Indiana	30
17	Iowa	32
15	Kansas	33
32	Kentucky	26
43	Louisiana	17
6	Maine	38
NA	Maryland**	NA
3	Massachusetts	46
29	Michigan	27
17	Minnesota	32
45	Mississippi	15
32	Missouri	26
15	Montana	33
NA	Nebraska**	NA
41	Nevada	21
5	New Hampshire	39
1	New Jersey	56
43	New Mexico	17
21	New York	31
26	North Carolina	29
29	North Dakota	27
17	Ohio	32
32	Oklahoma	26
NA	Oregon**	NA
9	Pennsylvania	36
17	Rhode Island	32
38	South Carolina	23
NA	South Dakota**	NA
24	Tennessee	30
32	Texas	26
21	Utah	31
4	Vermont	40
21	Virginia	31
12	Washington	35
40	West Virginia	22
9	Wisconsin	36
13	Wyoming	34

RANK ORDER

RANK	STATE	PERCENT
1	New Jersey	56
2	Connecticut	53
3	Massachusetts	46
4	Vermont	40
5	New Hampshire	39
6	Colorado	38
6	Maine	38
8	Illinois	37
9	Florida	36
9	Pennsylvania	36
9	Wisconsin	36
12	Washington	35
13	Delaware	34
13	Wyoming	34
15	Kansas	33
15	Montana	33
17	Iowa	32
17	Minnesota	32
17	Ohio	32
17	Rhode Island	32
21	New York	31
21	Utah	31
21	Virginia	31
24	Indiana	30
24	Tennessee	30
26	Georgia	29
26	Idaho	29
26	North Carolina	29
29	Arkansas	27
29	Michigan	27
29	North Dakota	27
32	Kentucky	26
32	Missouri	26
32	Oklahoma	26
32	Texas	26
36	California	25
37	Alabama	24
38	Arizona	23
38	South Carolina	23
40	West Virginia	22
41	Nevada	21
42	Hawaii	20
43	Louisiana	17
43	New Mexico	17
45	Mississippi	15
NA	Alaska**	NA
NA	Maryland**	NA
NA	Nebraska**	NA
NA	Oregon**	NA
NA	South Dakota**	NA

	District of Columbia**	NA

Source: U.S. Department of Education, National Center for Education Statistics
   "The Nation's Report Card: Writing 2007" (http://nces.ed.gov/nationsreportcard/)
*There are four achievement levels: Below Basic, Basic, Proficient, and Advanced. Proficient represents solid academic
mastery for 8th graders. Students reaching this level have demonstrated competency over challenging subject matter, including
subject matter knowledge, application of such knowledge to real-world situations, and analytical skills appropriate to the subject
matter. **Not available.

Percent of Public School Eighth Grade Males
Proficient or Better in Writing in 2007
National Percent = 20%*

ALPHA ORDER

RANK	STATE	PERCENT
33	Alabama	15
NA	Alaska**	NA
37	Arizona	13
35	Arkansas	14
27	California	17
4	Colorado	28
2	Connecticut	42
9	Delaware	24
9	Florida	24
27	Georgia	17
39	Hawaii	12
22	Idaho	18
5	Illinois	27
27	Indiana	17
27	Iowa	17
15	Kansas	21
31	Kentucky	16
43	Louisiana	9
9	Maine	24
NA	Maryland**	NA
3	Massachusetts	32
35	Michigan	14
22	Minnesota	18
45	Mississippi	6
33	Missouri	15
19	Montana	19
NA	Nebraska**	NA
41	Nevada	11
7	New Hampshire	26
1	New Jersey	47
43	New Mexico	9
13	New York	22
22	North Carolina	18
37	North Dakota	13
15	Ohio	21
31	Oklahoma	16
NA	Oregon**	NA
7	Pennsylvania	26
17	Rhode Island	20
39	South Carolina	12
NA	South Dakota**	NA
19	Tennessee	19
22	Texas	18
22	Utah	18
5	Vermont	27
19	Virginia	19
12	Washington	23
41	West Virginia	11
13	Wisconsin	22
17	Wyoming	20

RANK ORDER

RANK	STATE	PERCENT
1	New Jersey	47
2	Connecticut	42
3	Massachusetts	32
4	Colorado	28
5	Illinois	27
5	Vermont	27
7	New Hampshire	26
7	Pennsylvania	26
9	Delaware	24
9	Florida	24
9	Maine	24
12	Washington	23
13	New York	22
13	Wisconsin	22
15	Kansas	21
15	Ohio	21
17	Rhode Island	20
17	Wyoming	20
19	Montana	19
19	Tennessee	19
19	Virginia	19
22	Idaho	18
22	Minnesota	18
22	North Carolina	18
22	Texas	18
22	Utah	18
27	California	17
27	Georgia	17
27	Indiana	17
27	Iowa	17
31	Kentucky	16
31	Oklahoma	16
33	Alabama	15
33	Missouri	15
35	Arkansas	14
35	Michigan	14
37	Arizona	13
37	North Dakota	13
39	Hawaii	12
39	South Carolina	12
41	Nevada	11
41	West Virginia	11
43	Louisiana	9
43	New Mexico	9
45	Mississippi	6
NA	Alaska**	NA
NA	Maryland**	NA
NA	Nebraska**	NA
NA	Oregon**	NA
NA	South Dakota**	NA

District of Columbia**   NA

Source: U.S. Department of Education, National Center for Education Statistics
    "The Nation's Report Card: Writing 2007" (http://nces.ed.gov/nationsreportcard/)
*There are four achievement levels: Below Basic, Basic, Proficient, and Advanced. Proficient represents solid academic mastery for 8th graders. Students reaching this level have demonstrated competency over challenging subject matter, including subject matter knowledge, application of such knowledge to real-world situations, and analytical skills appropriate to the subject matter. **Not available.

Percent of Public School Eighth Grade Females
Proficient or Better in Writing in 2007
National Percent = 41%*

ALPHA ORDER

ALPHA ORDER

RANK	STATE	PERCENT
36	Alabama	33
NA	Alaska**	NA
39	Arizona	32
28	Arkansas	40
36	California	33
9	Colorado	49
2	Connecticut	63
21	Delaware	43
10	Florida	48
28	Georgia	40
42	Hawaii	29
23	Idaho	42
10	Illinois	48
23	Indiana	42
13	Iowa	47
16	Kansas	46
34	Kentucky	36
43	Louisiana	26
5	Maine	53
NA	Maryland**	NA
3	Massachusetts	60
31	Michigan	39
16	Minnesota	46
45	Mississippi	23
32	Missouri	38
13	Montana	47
NA	Nebraska**	NA
41	Nevada	31
5	New Hampshire	53
1	New Jersey	65
44	New Mexico	25
26	New York	41
28	North Carolina	40
26	North Dakota	41
21	Ohio	43
33	Oklahoma	37
NA	Oregon**	NA
13	Pennsylvania	47
18	Rhode Island	45
39	South Carolina	32
NA	South Dakota**	NA
23	Tennessee	42
34	Texas	36
19	Utah	44
4	Vermont	56
19	Virginia	44
10	Washington	48
36	West Virginia	33
7	Wisconsin	50
7	Wyoming	50

RANK ORDER

RANK	STATE	PERCENT
1	New Jersey	65
2	Connecticut	63
3	Massachusetts	60
4	Vermont	56
5	Maine	53
5	New Hampshire	53
7	Wisconsin	50
7	Wyoming	50
9	Colorado	49
10	Florida	48
10	Illinois	48
10	Washington	48
13	Iowa	47
13	Montana	47
13	Pennsylvania	47
16	Kansas	46
16	Minnesota	46
18	Rhode Island	45
19	Utah	44
19	Virginia	44
21	Delaware	43
21	Ohio	43
23	Idaho	42
23	Indiana	42
23	Tennessee	42
26	New York	41
26	North Dakota	41
28	Arkansas	40
28	Georgia	40
28	North Carolina	40
31	Michigan	39
32	Missouri	38
33	Oklahoma	37
34	Kentucky	36
34	Texas	36
36	Alabama	33
36	California	33
36	West Virginia	33
39	Arizona	32
39	South Carolina	32
41	Nevada	31
42	Hawaii	29
43	Louisiana	26
44	New Mexico	25
45	Mississippi	23
NA	Alaska**	NA
NA	Maryland**	NA
NA	Nebraska**	NA
NA	Oregon**	NA
NA	South Dakota**	NA
	District of Columbia**	NA

Source: U.S. Department of Education, National Center for Education Statistics
"The Nation's Report Card: Writing 2007" (http://nces.ed.gov/nationsreportcard/)
*There are four achievement levels: Below Basic, Basic, Proficient, and Advanced. Proficient represents solid academic mastery for 8th graders. Students reaching this level have demonstrated competency over challenging subject matter, including subject matter knowledge, application of such knowledge to real-world situations, and analytical skills appropriate to the subject matter. **Not available.

Percent of Public School Eighth Graders Eligible for
Free or Reduced Price Lunch Proficient or Better in Writing in 2007
National Percent = 17%*

ALPHA ORDER

RANK	STATE	PERCENT
39	Alabama	12
NA	Alaska**	NA
43	Arizona	10
23	Arkansas	17
35	California	13
17	Colorado	18
2	Connecticut	28
17	Delaware	18
4	Florida	23
26	Georgia	16
42	Hawaii	11
17	Idaho	18
23	Illinois	17
23	Indiana	17
17	Iowa	18
17	Kansas	18
26	Kentucky	16
43	Louisiana	10
3	Maine	26
NA	Maryland**	NA
7	Massachusetts	21
33	Michigan	14
26	Minnesota	16
45	Mississippi	9
35	Missouri	13
9	Montana	20
NA	Nebraska**	NA
39	Nevada	12
9	New Hampshire	20
1	New Jersey	33
39	New Mexico	12
6	New York	22
26	North Carolina	16
13	North Dakota	19
30	Ohio	15
13	Oklahoma	19
NA	Oregon**	NA
13	Pennsylvania	19
30	Rhode Island	15
35	South Carolina	13
NA	South Dakota**	NA
13	Tennessee	19
30	Texas	15
17	Utah	18
4	Vermont	23
35	Virginia	13
9	Washington	20
33	West Virginia	14
9	Wisconsin	20
7	Wyoming	21

RANK ORDER

RANK	STATE	PERCENT
1	New Jersey	33
2	Connecticut	28
3	Maine	26
4	Florida	23
4	Vermont	23
6	New York	22
7	Massachusetts	21
7	Wyoming	21
9	Montana	20
9	New Hampshire	20
9	Washington	20
9	Wisconsin	20
13	North Dakota	19
13	Oklahoma	19
13	Pennsylvania	19
13	Tennessee	19
17	Colorado	18
17	Delaware	18
17	Idaho	18
17	Iowa	18
17	Kansas	18
17	Utah	18
23	Arkansas	17
23	Illinois	17
23	Indiana	17
26	Georgia	16
26	Kentucky	16
26	Minnesota	16
26	North Carolina	16
30	Ohio	15
30	Rhode Island	15
30	Texas	15
33	Michigan	14
33	West Virginia	14
35	California	13
35	Missouri	13
35	South Carolina	13
35	Virginia	13
39	Alabama	12
39	Nevada	12
39	New Mexico	12
42	Hawaii	11
43	Arizona	10
43	Louisiana	10
45	Mississippi	9
NA	Alaska**	NA
NA	Maryland**	NA
NA	Nebraska**	NA
NA	Oregon**	NA
NA	South Dakota**	NA
	District of Columbia**	NA

Source: U.S. Department of Education, National Center for Education Statistics
"The Nation's Report Card: Writing 2007" (http://nces.ed.gov/nationsreportcard/)
*There are four achievement levels: Below Basic, Basic, Proficient, and Advanced. Proficient represents solid academic mastery for 8th graders. Students reaching this level have demonstrated competency over challenging subject matter, including subject matter knowledge, application of such knowledge to real-world situations, and analytical skills appropriate to the subject matter. **Not available.

IV. Safety and Discipline

Percent of Students Expelled from Public Elementary and Secondary Schools: 2004
National Percent = 0.22%

<table>
<tr><td colspan="3">ALPHA ORDER</td><td colspan="3">RANK ORDER</td></tr>
<tr><td>RANK</td><td>STATE</td><td>PERCENT</td><td>RANK</td><td>STATE</td><td>PERCENT</td></tr>
<tr><td>36</td><td>Alabama</td><td>0.10</td><td>1</td><td>Louisiana</td><td>0.85</td></tr>
<tr><td>17</td><td>Alaska</td><td>0.21</td><td>2</td><td>South Carolina</td><td>0.69</td></tr>
<tr><td>26</td><td>Arizona</td><td>0.15</td><td>3</td><td>Indiana</td><td>0.67</td></tr>
<tr><td>24</td><td>Arkansas</td><td>0.17</td><td>4</td><td>Oklahoma</td><td>0.52</td></tr>
<tr><td>9</td><td>California</td><td>0.30</td><td>5</td><td>Tennessee</td><td>0.44</td></tr>
<tr><td>11</td><td>Colorado</td><td>0.28</td><td>6</td><td>Oregon</td><td>0.40</td></tr>
<tr><td>16</td><td>Connecticut</td><td>0.22</td><td>7</td><td>Georgia</td><td>0.37</td></tr>
<tr><td>11</td><td>Delaware</td><td>0.28</td><td>8</td><td>Washington</td><td>0.35</td></tr>
<tr><td>46</td><td>Florida</td><td>0.03</td><td>9</td><td>California</td><td>0.30</td></tr>
<tr><td>7</td><td>Georgia</td><td>0.37</td><td>9</td><td>Nevada</td><td>0.30</td></tr>
<tr><td>NA</td><td>Hawaii*</td><td>NA</td><td>11</td><td>Colorado</td><td>0.28</td></tr>
<tr><td>17</td><td>Idaho</td><td>0.21</td><td>11</td><td>Delaware</td><td>0.28</td></tr>
<tr><td>30</td><td>Illinois</td><td>0.12</td><td>13</td><td>Ohio</td><td>0.27</td></tr>
<tr><td>3</td><td>Indiana</td><td>0.67</td><td>14</td><td>Mississippi</td><td>0.25</td></tr>
<tr><td>39</td><td>Iowa</td><td>0.08</td><td>15</td><td>Nebraska</td><td>0.23</td></tr>
<tr><td>27</td><td>Kansas</td><td>0.14</td><td>16</td><td>Connecticut</td><td>0.22</td></tr>
<tr><td>39</td><td>Kentucky</td><td>0.08</td><td>17</td><td>Alaska</td><td>0.21</td></tr>
<tr><td>1</td><td>Louisiana</td><td>0.85</td><td>17</td><td>Idaho</td><td>0.21</td></tr>
<tr><td>42</td><td>Maine</td><td>0.06</td><td>17</td><td>Maryland</td><td>0.21</td></tr>
<tr><td>17</td><td>Maryland</td><td>0.21</td><td>20</td><td>New Mexico</td><td>0.20</td></tr>
<tr><td>39</td><td>Massachusetts</td><td>0.08</td><td>20</td><td>Pennsylvania</td><td>0.20</td></tr>
<tr><td>30</td><td>Michigan</td><td>0.12</td><td>22</td><td>Texas</td><td>0.19</td></tr>
<tr><td>36</td><td>Minnesota</td><td>0.10</td><td>22</td><td>West Virginia</td><td>0.19</td></tr>
<tr><td>14</td><td>Mississippi</td><td>0.25</td><td>24</td><td>Arkansas</td><td>0.17</td></tr>
<tr><td>30</td><td>Missouri</td><td>0.12</td><td>24</td><td>Wisconsin</td><td>0.17</td></tr>
<tr><td>34</td><td>Montana</td><td>0.11</td><td>26</td><td>Arizona</td><td>0.15</td></tr>
<tr><td>15</td><td>Nebraska</td><td>0.23</td><td>27</td><td>Kansas</td><td>0.14</td></tr>
<tr><td>9</td><td>Nevada</td><td>0.30</td><td>27</td><td>New York</td><td>0.14</td></tr>
<tr><td>46</td><td>New Hampshire</td><td>0.03</td><td>27</td><td>North Carolina</td><td>0.14</td></tr>
<tr><td>46</td><td>New Jersey</td><td>0.03</td><td>30</td><td>Illinois</td><td>0.12</td></tr>
<tr><td>20</td><td>New Mexico</td><td>0.20</td><td>30</td><td>Michigan</td><td>0.12</td></tr>
<tr><td>27</td><td>New York</td><td>0.14</td><td>30</td><td>Missouri</td><td>0.12</td></tr>
<tr><td>27</td><td>North Carolina</td><td>0.14</td><td>30</td><td>Wyoming</td><td>0.12</td></tr>
<tr><td>44</td><td>North Dakota</td><td>0.04</td><td>34</td><td>Montana</td><td>0.11</td></tr>
<tr><td>13</td><td>Ohio</td><td>0.27</td><td>34</td><td>Virginia</td><td>0.11</td></tr>
<tr><td>4</td><td>Oklahoma</td><td>0.52</td><td>36</td><td>Alabama</td><td>0.10</td></tr>
<tr><td>6</td><td>Oregon</td><td>0.40</td><td>36</td><td>Minnesota</td><td>0.10</td></tr>
<tr><td>20</td><td>Pennsylvania</td><td>0.20</td><td>36</td><td>South Dakota</td><td>0.10</td></tr>
<tr><td>44</td><td>Rhode Island</td><td>0.04</td><td>39</td><td>Iowa</td><td>0.08</td></tr>
<tr><td>2</td><td>South Carolina</td><td>0.69</td><td>39</td><td>Kentucky</td><td>0.08</td></tr>
<tr><td>36</td><td>South Dakota</td><td>0.10</td><td>39</td><td>Massachusetts</td><td>0.08</td></tr>
<tr><td>5</td><td>Tennessee</td><td>0.44</td><td>42</td><td>Maine</td><td>0.06</td></tr>
<tr><td>22</td><td>Texas</td><td>0.19</td><td>43</td><td>Utah</td><td>0.05</td></tr>
<tr><td>43</td><td>Utah</td><td>0.05</td><td>44</td><td>North Dakota</td><td>0.04</td></tr>
<tr><td>49</td><td>Vermont</td><td>0.02</td><td>44</td><td>Rhode Island</td><td>0.04</td></tr>
<tr><td>34</td><td>Virginia</td><td>0.11</td><td>46</td><td>Florida</td><td>0.03</td></tr>
<tr><td>8</td><td>Washington</td><td>0.35</td><td>46</td><td>New Hampshire</td><td>0.03</td></tr>
<tr><td>22</td><td>West Virginia</td><td>0.19</td><td>46</td><td>New Jersey</td><td>0.03</td></tr>
<tr><td>24</td><td>Wisconsin</td><td>0.17</td><td>49</td><td>Vermont</td><td>0.02</td></tr>
<tr><td>30</td><td>Wyoming</td><td>0.12</td><td>NA</td><td>Hawaii*</td><td>NA</td></tr>
<tr><td></td><td></td><td></td><td></td><td>District of Columbia*</td><td>NA</td></tr>
</table>

Source: U.S. Department of Education, National Center for Education Statistics
"2007 Digest of Education Statistics" (http://nces.ed.gov/programs/digest/index.asp)
*Not available.

Percent of Students Suspended from Public Elementary and Secondary Schools: 2004
National Percent = 6.8%

ALPHA ORDER

RANK	STATE	PERCENT
8	Alabama	9.6
22	Alaska	6.2
33	Arizona	5.6
19	Arkansas	6.6
14	California	7.4
22	Colorado	6.2
20	Connecticut	6.5
5	Delaware	10.5
10	Florida	9.2
8	Georgia	9.6
47	Hawaii	3.5
46	Idaho	3.6
22	Illinois	6.2
12	Indiana	8.6
44	Iowa	3.7
30	Kansas	5.8
17	Kentucky	7.0
1	Louisiana	11.9
39	Maine	4.8
16	Maryland	7.2
32	Massachusetts	5.7
13	Michigan	7.7
41	Minnesota	4.0
6	Mississippi	10.1
26	Missouri	6.0
40	Montana	4.6
43	Nebraska	3.8
18	Nevada	6.9
28	New Hampshire	5.9
33	New Jersey	5.6
35	New Mexico	5.3
41	New York	4.0
3	North Carolina	11.1
50	North Dakota	1.7
25	Ohio	6.1
30	Oklahoma	5.8
28	Oregon	5.9
20	Pennsylvania	6.5
6	Rhode Island	10.1
2	South Carolina	11.8
48	South Dakota	2.6
11	Tennessee	8.8
36	Texas	5.2
48	Utah	2.6
36	Vermont	5.2
15	Virginia	7.3
26	Washington	6.0
4	West Virginia	10.7
38	Wisconsin	5.1
44	Wyoming	3.7

RANK ORDER

RANK	STATE	PERCENT
1	Louisiana	11.9
2	South Carolina	11.8
3	North Carolina	11.1
4	West Virginia	10.7
5	Delaware	10.5
6	Mississippi	10.1
6	Rhode Island	10.1
8	Alabama	9.6
8	Georgia	9.6
10	Florida	9.2
11	Tennessee	8.8
12	Indiana	8.6
13	Michigan	7.7
14	California	7.4
15	Virginia	7.3
16	Maryland	7.2
17	Kentucky	7.0
18	Nevada	6.9
19	Arkansas	6.6
20	Connecticut	6.5
20	Pennsylvania	6.5
22	Alaska	6.2
22	Colorado	6.2
22	Illinois	6.2
25	Ohio	6.1
26	Missouri	6.0
26	Washington	6.0
28	New Hampshire	5.9
28	Oregon	5.9
30	Kansas	5.8
30	Oklahoma	5.8
32	Massachusetts	5.7
33	Arizona	5.6
33	New Jersey	5.6
35	New Mexico	5.3
36	Texas	5.2
36	Vermont	5.2
38	Wisconsin	5.1
39	Maine	4.8
40	Montana	4.6
41	Minnesota	4.0
41	New York	4.0
43	Nebraska	3.8
44	Iowa	3.7
44	Wyoming	3.7
46	Idaho	3.6
47	Hawaii	3.5
48	South Dakota	2.6
48	Utah	2.6
50	North Dakota	1.7
	District of Columbia	3.7

Source: U.S. Department of Education, National Center for Education Statistics
"2007 Digest of Education Statistics" (http://nces.ed.gov/programs/digest/index.asp)

Percent of Public School Teachers Who Reported Being Threatened by a Student in the Past 12 Months: 2004
National Percent = 7.5%*

ALPHA ORDER

RANK	STATE	PERCENT
30	Alabama	6.1
8	Alaska	8.9
22	Arizona	6.9
44	Arkansas	4.8
30	California	6.1
48	Colorado	3.8
22	Connecticut	6.9
16	Delaware	7.7
2	Florida	11.2
27	Georgia	6.4
7	Hawaii	9.1
38	Idaho	5.4
13	Illinois	8.0
20	Indiana	7.2
42	Iowa	4.9
50	Kansas	3.7
14	Kentucky	7.9
4	Louisiana	9.9
40	Maine	5.2
1	Maryland	13.5
27	Massachusetts	6.4
6	Michigan	9.3
12	Minnesota	8.2
36	Mississippi	5.5
11	Missouri	8.3
30	Montana	6.1
18	Nebraska	7.5
19	Nevada	7.3
34	New Hampshire	5.8
47	New Jersey	4.3
15	New Mexico	7.8
3	New York	10.5
9	North Carolina	8.7
35	North Dakota	5.6
29	Ohio	6.2
30	Oklahoma	6.1
36	Oregon	5.5
5	Pennsylvania	9.5
46	Rhode Island	4.6
10	South Carolina	8.6
39	South Dakota	5.3
25	Tennessee	6.6
16	Texas	7.7
40	Utah	5.2
42	Vermont	4.9
26	Virginia	6.5
24	Washington	6.8
20	West Virginia	7.2
45	Wisconsin	4.7
48	Wyoming	3.8

RANK ORDER

RANK	STATE	PERCENT
1	Maryland	13.5
2	Florida	11.2
3	New York	10.5
4	Louisiana	9.9
5	Pennsylvania	9.5
6	Michigan	9.3
7	Hawaii	9.1
8	Alaska	8.9
9	North Carolina	8.7
10	South Carolina	8.6
11	Missouri	8.3
12	Minnesota	8.2
13	Illinois	8.0
14	Kentucky	7.9
15	New Mexico	7.8
16	Delaware	7.7
16	Texas	7.7
18	Nebraska	7.5
19	Nevada	7.3
20	Indiana	7.2
20	West Virginia	7.2
22	Arizona	6.9
22	Connecticut	6.9
24	Washington	6.8
25	Tennessee	6.6
26	Virginia	6.5
27	Georgia	6.4
27	Massachusetts	6.4
29	Ohio	6.2
30	Alabama	6.1
30	California	6.1
30	Montana	6.1
30	Oklahoma	6.1
34	New Hampshire	5.8
35	North Dakota	5.6
36	Mississippi	5.5
36	Oregon	5.5
38	Idaho	5.4
39	South Dakota	5.3
40	Maine	5.2
40	Utah	5.2
42	Iowa	4.9
42	Vermont	4.9
44	Arkansas	4.8
45	Wisconsin	4.7
46	Rhode Island	4.6
47	New Jersey	4.3
48	Colorado	3.8
48	Wyoming	3.8
50	Kansas	3.7

District of Columbia	18.0

Source: U.S. Department of Education, National Center for Education Statistics
   "Indicators of School Crime and Safety: 2006" (http://nces.ed.gov/pubsearch/pubsinfo.asp?pubid=2007003)
*For 2003-2004 school year.

Percent of Public School Teachers Who Reported Being Physically Attacked in the Past 12 Months: 2004
National Percent = 3.7%*

ALPHA ORDER

RANK	STATE	PERCENT
30	Alabama	2.7
4	Alaska	6.0
35	Arizona	2.6
30	Arkansas	2.7
43	California	2.0
46	Colorado	1.5
27	Connecticut	2.8
25	Delaware	3.1
2	Florida	6.5
10	Georgia	4.6
7	Hawaii	5.4
36	Idaho	2.5
40	Illinois	2.3
13	Indiana	4.1
38	Iowa	2.4
21	Kansas	3.3
30	Kentucky	2.7
30	Louisiana	2.7
21	Maine	3.3
2	Maryland	6.5
16	Massachusetts	3.9
8	Michigan	4.9
19	Minnesota	3.6
48	Mississippi	0.9
6	Missouri	5.5
45	Montana	1.9
13	Nebraska	4.1
18	Nevada	3.7
27	New Hampshire	2.8
43	New Jersey	2.0
5	New Mexico	5.8
1	New York	6.6
11	North Carolina	4.4
40	North Dakota	2.3
36	Ohio	2.5
26	Oklahoma	3.0
47	Oregon	1.4
8	Pennsylvania	4.9
38	Rhode Island	2.4
23	South Carolina	3.2
27	South Dakota	2.8
20	Tennessee	3.5
16	Texas	3.9
13	Utah	4.1
NA	Vermont**	NA
30	Virginia	2.7
12	Washington	4.2
23	West Virginia	3.2
40	Wisconsin	2.3
NA	Wyoming**	NA

RANK ORDER

RANK	STATE	PERCENT
1	New York	6.6
2	Florida	6.5
2	Maryland	6.5
4	Alaska	6.0
5	New Mexico	5.8
6	Missouri	5.5
7	Hawaii	5.4
8	Michigan	4.9
8	Pennsylvania	4.9
10	Georgia	4.6
11	North Carolina	4.4
12	Washington	4.2
13	Indiana	4.1
13	Nebraska	4.1
13	Utah	4.1
16	Massachusetts	3.9
16	Texas	3.9
18	Nevada	3.7
19	Minnesota	3.6
20	Tennessee	3.5
21	Kansas	3.3
21	Maine	3.3
23	South Carolina	3.2
23	West Virginia	3.2
25	Delaware	3.1
26	Oklahoma	3.0
27	Connecticut	2.8
27	New Hampshire	2.8
27	South Dakota	2.8
30	Alabama	2.7
30	Arkansas	2.7
30	Kentucky	2.7
30	Louisiana	2.7
30	Virginia	2.7
35	Arizona	2.6
36	Idaho	2.5
36	Ohio	2.5
38	Iowa	2.4
38	Rhode Island	2.4
40	Illinois	2.3
40	North Dakota	2.3
40	Wisconsin	2.3
43	California	2.0
43	New Jersey	2.0
45	Montana	1.9
46	Colorado	1.5
47	Oregon	1.4
48	Mississippi	0.9
NA	Vermont**	NA
NA	Wyoming**	NA
	District of Columbia	5.2

Source: U.S. Department of Education, National Center for Education Statistics
"Indicators of School Crime and Safety: 2006" (http://nces.ed.gov/pubsearch/pubsinfo.asp?pubid=2007003)
*For 2003-2004 school year.

Percent of High School Students Who Felt Too Unsafe to Go to School: 2007

National Percent = 5.5%*

ALPHA ORDER

RANK	STATE	PERCENT
NA	Alabama**	NA
23	Alaska	5.5
2	Arizona	8.1
6	Arkansas	7.4
NA	California**	NA
NA	Colorado**	NA
23	Connecticut	5.5
26	Delaware	5.3
12	Florida	6.7
18	Georgia	5.8
3	Hawaii	7.8
21	Idaho	5.7
32	Illinois	4.6
17	Indiana	5.9
30	Iowa	4.9
21	Kansas	5.7
26	Kentucky	5.3
NA	Louisiana**	NA
26	Maine	5.3
6	Maryland	7.4
31	Massachusetts	4.7
13	Michigan	6.5
NA	Minnesota**	NA
3	Mississippi	7.8
5	Missouri	7.5
34	Montana	4.2
NA	Nebraska**	NA
9	Nevada	7.0
33	New Hampshire	4.5
NA	New Jersey**	NA
1	New Mexico	9.0
13	New York	6.5
9	North Carolina	7.0
NA	North Dakota**	NA
38	Ohio	3.8
29	Oklahoma	5.1
NA	Oregon**	NA
NA	Pennsylvania**	NA
34	Rhode Island	4.2
18	South Carolina	5.8
36	South Dakota	4.0
8	Tennessee	7.3
18	Texas	5.8
25	Utah	5.4
37	Vermont	3.9
NA	Virginia**	NA
NA	Washington**	NA
11	West Virginia	6.8
15	Wisconsin	6.3
16	Wyoming	6.1

RANK ORDER

RANK	STATE	PERCENT
1	New Mexico	9.0
2	Arizona	8.1
3	Hawaii	7.8
3	Mississippi	7.8
5	Missouri	7.5
6	Arkansas	7.4
6	Maryland	7.4
8	Tennessee	7.3
9	Nevada	7.0
9	North Carolina	7.0
11	West Virginia	6.8
12	Florida	6.7
13	Michigan	6.5
13	New York	6.5
15	Wisconsin	6.3
16	Wyoming	6.1
17	Indiana	5.9
18	Georgia	5.8
18	South Carolina	5.8
18	Texas	5.8
21	Idaho	5.7
21	Kansas	5.7
23	Alaska	5.5
23	Connecticut	5.5
25	Utah	5.4
26	Delaware	5.3
26	Kentucky	5.3
26	Maine	5.3
29	Oklahoma	5.1
30	Iowa	4.9
31	Massachusetts	4.7
32	Illinois	4.6
33	New Hampshire	4.5
34	Montana	4.2
34	Rhode Island	4.2
36	South Dakota	4.0
37	Vermont	3.9
38	Ohio	3.8
NA	Alabama**	NA
NA	California**	NA
NA	Colorado**	NA
NA	Louisiana**	NA
NA	Minnesota**	NA
NA	Nebraska**	NA
NA	New Jersey**	NA
NA	North Dakota**	NA
NA	Oregon**	NA
NA	Pennsylvania**	NA
NA	Virginia**	NA
NA	Washington**	NA
	District of Columbia**	NA

Source: U.S. Department of Health and Human Services, Centers for Disease Control and Prevention
  "Youth Risk Behavior Surveillance--U.S., 2007" (http://www.cdc.gov/HealthyYouth/yrbs/)
*On at least one of the 30 days preceding the survey. National percent includes nonreporting states.
**Not available.

Percent of High School Students Who Carried a Weapon on School Property in 2007
National Percent = 5.9%*

ALPHA ORDER

ALPHA ORDER

RANK	STATE	PERCENT
NA	Alabama**	NA
7	Alaska	8.4
10	Arizona	7.0
13	Arkansas	6.8
NA	California**	NA
NA	Colorado**	NA
22	Connecticut	5.5
23	Delaware	5.4
20	Florida	5.6
24	Georgia	5.3
37	Hawaii	3.7
6	Idaho	8.9
37	Illinois	3.7
11	Indiana	6.9
35	Iowa	4.4
19	Kansas	5.7
8	Kentucky	8.0
NA	Louisiana**	NA
28	Maine	4.9
17	Maryland	5.9
25	Massachusetts	5.0
25	Michigan	5.0
NA	Minnesota**	NA
30	Mississippi	4.8
34	Missouri	4.6
2	Montana	9.7
NA	Nebraska**	NA
32	Nevada	4.7
18	New Hampshire	5.8
NA	New Jersey**	NA
4	New Mexico	9.3
32	New York	4.7
13	North Carolina	6.8
25	North Dakota	5.0
36	Ohio	4.1
5	Oklahoma	9.0
NA	Oregon**	NA
NA	Pennsylvania**	NA
28	Rhode Island	4.9
30	South Carolina	4.8
16	South Dakota	6.3
20	Tennessee	5.6
13	Texas	6.8
9	Utah	7.5
3	Vermont	9.6
NA	Virginia**	NA
NA	Washington**	NA
11	West Virginia	6.9
39	Wisconsin	3.6
1	Wyoming	11.4

RANK ORDER

RANK	STATE	PERCENT
1	Wyoming	11.4
2	Montana	9.7
3	Vermont	9.6
4	New Mexico	9.3
5	Oklahoma	9.0
6	Idaho	8.9
7	Alaska	8.4
8	Kentucky	8.0
9	Utah	7.5
10	Arizona	7.0
11	Indiana	6.9
11	West Virginia	6.9
13	Arkansas	6.8
13	North Carolina	6.8
13	Texas	6.8
16	South Dakota	6.3
17	Maryland	5.9
18	New Hampshire	5.8
19	Kansas	5.7
20	Florida	5.6
20	Tennessee	5.6
22	Connecticut	5.5
23	Delaware	5.4
24	Georgia	5.3
25	Massachusetts	5.0
25	Michigan	5.0
25	North Dakota	5.0
28	Maine	4.9
28	Rhode Island	4.9
30	Mississippi	4.8
30	South Carolina	4.8
32	Nevada	4.7
32	New York	4.7
34	Missouri	4.6
35	Iowa	4.4
36	Ohio	4.1
37	Hawaii	3.7
37	Illinois	3.7
39	Wisconsin	3.6
NA	Alabama**	NA
NA	California**	NA
NA	Colorado**	NA
NA	Louisiana**	NA
NA	Minnesota**	NA
NA	Nebraska**	NA
NA	New Jersey**	NA
NA	Oregon**	NA
NA	Pennsylvania**	NA
NA	Virginia**	NA
NA	Washington**	NA
	District of Columbia**	NA

Source: U.S. Department of Health and Human Services, Centers for Disease Control and Prevention
"Youth Risk Behavior Surveillance--U.S., 2007" (http://www.cdc.gov/HealthyYouth/yrbs/)
*Weapons include guns, knives, clubs, or other instrument. National percent includes nonreporting states.
**Not available.

Percent of High School Students Who Were Threatened or Injured With a Weapon on School Property in 2007
National Percent = 7.8%*

RANK	STATE	PERCENT
NA	Alabama**	NA
23	Alaska	7.7
2	Arizona	11.2
10	Arkansas	9.1
NA	California**	NA
NA	Colorado**	NA
23	Connecticut	7.7
36	Delaware	5.6
12	Florida	8.6
19	Georgia	8.1
33	Hawaii	6.4
3	Idaho	10.2
21	Illinois	7.8
7	Indiana	9.6
28	Iowa	7.1
12	Kansas	8.6
14	Kentucky	8.3
NA	Louisiana**	NA
31	Maine	6.8
7	Maryland	9.6
38	Massachusetts	5.3
19	Michigan	8.1
NA	Minnesota**	NA
14	Mississippi	8.3
9	Missouri	9.3
29	Montana	7.0
NA	Nebraska**	NA
21	Nevada	7.8
25	New Hampshire	7.3
NA	New Jersey**	NA
4	New Mexico	10.1
25	New York	7.3
32	North Carolina	6.6
39	North Dakota	5.2
14	Ohio	8.3
29	Oklahoma	7.0
NA	Oregon**	NA
NA	Pennsylvania**	NA
14	Rhode Island	8.3
5	South Carolina	9.8
35	South Dakota	5.9
25	Tennessee	7.3
11	Texas	8.7
1	Utah	11.4
34	Vermont	6.2
NA	Virginia**	NA
NA	Washington**	NA
6	West Virginia	9.7
36	Wisconsin	5.6
14	Wyoming	8.3

RANK	STATE	PERCENT
1	Utah	11.4
2	Arizona	11.2
3	Idaho	10.2
4	New Mexico	10.1
5	South Carolina	9.8
6	West Virginia	9.7
7	Indiana	9.6
7	Maryland	9.6
9	Missouri	9.3
10	Arkansas	9.1
11	Texas	8.7
12	Florida	8.6
12	Kansas	8.6
14	Kentucky	8.3
14	Mississippi	8.3
14	Ohio	8.3
14	Rhode Island	8.3
14	Wyoming	8.3
19	Georgia	8.1
19	Michigan	8.1
21	Illinois	7.8
21	Nevada	7.8
23	Alaska	7.7
23	Connecticut	7.7
25	New Hampshire	7.3
25	New York	7.3
25	Tennessee	7.3
28	Iowa	7.1
29	Montana	7.0
29	Oklahoma	7.0
31	Maine	6.8
32	North Carolina	6.6
33	Hawaii	6.4
34	Vermont	6.2
35	South Dakota	5.9
36	Delaware	5.6
36	Wisconsin	5.6
38	Massachusetts	5.3
39	North Dakota	5.2
NA	Alabama**	NA
NA	California**	NA
NA	Colorado**	NA
NA	Louisiana**	NA
NA	Minnesota**	NA
NA	Nebraska**	NA
NA	New Jersey**	NA
NA	Oregon**	NA
NA	Pennsylvania**	NA
NA	Virginia**	NA
NA	Washington**	NA
	District of Columbia**	NA

Source: U.S. Department of Health and Human Services, Centers for Disease Control and Prevention
 "Youth Risk Behavior Surveillance--U.S., 2007" (http://www.cdc.gov/HealthyYouth/yrbs/)
*One or more times during the 12 months preceding the survey. National percent includes nonreporting states.
**Not available.

Percent of High School Students Who Engaged in a Physical Fight on School Property in 2007
National Percent = 12.4%*

ALPHA ORDER

RANK	STATE	PERCENT
NA	Alabama**	NA
30	Alaska	10.4
19	Arizona	11.3
4	Arkansas	13.0
NA	California**	NA
NA	Colorado**	NA
28	Connecticut	10.5
28	Delaware	10.5
6	Florida	12.5
3	Georgia	13.1
39	Hawaii	7.0
9	Idaho	12.3
19	Illinois	11.3
15	Indiana	11.5
37	Iowa	9.1
25	Kansas	10.6
25	Kentucky	10.6
NA	Louisiana**	NA
32	Maine	10.1
7	Maryland	12.4
37	Massachusetts	9.1
17	Michigan	11.4
NA	Minnesota**	NA
12	Mississippi	11.9
24	Missouri	10.7
11	Montana	12.0
NA	Nebraska**	NA
19	Nevada	11.3
19	New Hampshire	11.3
NA	New Jersey**	NA
1	New Mexico	16.9
10	New York	12.2
30	North Carolina	10.4
33	North Dakota	9.6
35	Ohio	9.4
25	Oklahoma	10.6
NA	Oregon**	NA
NA	Pennsylvania**	NA
33	Rhode Island	9.6
23	South Carolina	10.8
36	South Dakota	9.3
7	Tennessee	12.4
2	Texas	13.9
13	Utah	11.6
15	Vermont	11.5
NA	Virginia**	NA
NA	Washington**	NA
5	West Virginia	12.9
17	Wisconsin	11.4
13	Wyoming	11.6

RANK ORDER

RANK	STATE	PERCENT
1	New Mexico	16.9
2	Texas	13.9
3	Georgia	13.1
4	Arkansas	13.0
5	West Virginia	12.9
6	Florida	12.5
7	Maryland	12.4
7	Tennessee	12.4
9	Idaho	12.3
10	New York	12.2
11	Montana	12.0
12	Mississippi	11.9
13	Utah	11.6
13	Wyoming	11.6
15	Indiana	11.5
15	Vermont	11.5
17	Michigan	11.4
17	Wisconsin	11.4
19	Arizona	11.3
19	Illinois	11.3
19	Nevada	11.3
19	New Hampshire	11.3
23	South Carolina	10.8
24	Missouri	10.7
25	Kansas	10.6
25	Kentucky	10.6
25	Oklahoma	10.6
28	Connecticut	10.5
28	Delaware	10.5
30	Alaska	10.4
30	North Carolina	10.4
32	Maine	10.1
33	North Dakota	9.6
33	Rhode Island	9.6
35	Ohio	9.4
36	South Dakota	9.3
37	Iowa	9.1
37	Massachusetts	9.1
39	Hawaii	7.0
NA	Alabama**	NA
NA	California**	NA
NA	Colorado**	NA
NA	Louisiana**	NA
NA	Minnesota**	NA
NA	Nebraska**	NA
NA	New Jersey**	NA
NA	Oregon**	NA
NA	Pennsylvania**	NA
NA	Virginia**	NA
NA	Washington**	NA
	District of Columbia**	NA

Source: U.S. Department of Health and Human Services, Centers for Disease Control and Prevention
   "Youth Risk Behavior Surveillance--U.S., 2007" (http://www.cdc.gov/HealthyYouth/yrbs/)
*One or more times during the 12 months preceding the survey. National percent includes nonreporting states.
**Not available.

Percent of High School Students Who Had Property Stolen or Deliberately Damaged on School Property: 2007
National Percent = 27.1%*

ALPHA ORDER

RANK	STATE	PERCENT
NA	Alabama**	NA
7	Alaska	29.8
8	Arizona	29.2
6	Arkansas	30.0
NA	California**	NA
NA	Colorado**	NA
13	Connecticut	28.3
34	Delaware	19.8
21	Florida	26.3
10	Georgia	28.6
13	Hawaii	28.3
2	Idaho	33.1
19	Illinois	26.6
8	Indiana	29.2
17	Iowa	27.5
24	Kansas	24.8
25	Kentucky	24.7
NA	Louisiana**	NA
32	Maine	22.1
3	Maryland	32.4
33	Massachusetts	21.2
5	Michigan	30.1
NA	Minnesota**	NA
26	Mississippi	24.0
13	Missouri	28.3
10	Montana	28.6
NA	Nebraska**	NA
NA	Nevada**	NA
23	New Hampshire	24.9
NA	New Jersey**	NA
NA	New Mexico**	NA
28	New York	23.6
18	North Carolina	26.9
NA	North Dakota**	NA
20	Ohio	26.4
31	Oklahoma	22.3
NA	Oregon**	NA
NA	Pennsylvania**	NA
NA	Rhode Island**	NA
12	South Carolina	28.5
26	South Dakota	24.0
22	Tennessee	25.8
4	Texas	30.4
1	Utah	34.0
30	Vermont	22.6
NA	Virginia**	NA
NA	Washington**	NA
29	West Virginia	23.4
NA	Wisconsin**	NA
16	Wyoming	27.9

RANK ORDER

RANK	STATE	PERCENT
1	Utah	34.0
2	Idaho	33.1
3	Maryland	32.4
4	Texas	30.4
5	Michigan	30.1
6	Arkansas	30.0
7	Alaska	29.8
8	Arizona	29.2
8	Indiana	29.2
10	Georgia	28.6
10	Montana	28.6
12	South Carolina	28.5
13	Connecticut	28.3
13	Hawaii	28.3
13	Missouri	28.3
16	Wyoming	27.9
17	Iowa	27.5
18	North Carolina	26.9
19	Illinois	26.6
20	Ohio	26.4
21	Florida	26.3
22	Tennessee	25.8
23	New Hampshire	24.9
24	Kansas	24.8
25	Kentucky	24.7
26	Mississippi	24.0
26	South Dakota	24.0
28	New York	23.6
29	West Virginia	23.4
30	Vermont	22.6
31	Oklahoma	22.3
32	Maine	22.1
33	Massachusetts	21.2
34	Delaware	19.8
NA	Alabama**	NA
NA	California**	NA
NA	Colorado**	NA
NA	Louisiana**	NA
NA	Minnesota**	NA
NA	Nebraska**	NA
NA	Nevada**	NA
NA	New Jersey**	NA
NA	New Mexico**	NA
NA	North Dakota**	NA
NA	Oregon**	NA
NA	Pennsylvania**	NA
NA	Rhode Island**	NA
NA	Virginia**	NA
NA	Washington**	NA
NA	Wisconsin**	NA
	District of Columbia**	NA

Source: U.S. Department of Health and Human Services, Centers for Disease Control and Prevention
  "Youth Risk Behavior Surveillance--U.S., 2007" (http://www.cdc.gov/HealthyYouth/yrbs/)
*National percent includes nonreporting states.
**Not available.

Percent of High School Students Who Smoke: 2007

National Percent = 20.0%*

RANK	STATE	PERCENT	RANK	STATE	PERCENT
NA	Alabama**	NA	1	West Virginia	27.6
29	Alaska	17.8	2	Kentucky	26.0
10	Arizona	22.2	3	Tennessee	25.5
16	Arkansas	20.7	4	South Dakota	24.7
NA	California**	NA	5	New Mexico	24.2
NA	Colorado**	NA	6	Missouri	23.8
12	Connecticut	21.1	7	Oklahoma	23.2
19	Delaware	20.2	8	Indiana	22.5
33	Florida	15.9	8	North Carolina	22.5
26	Georgia	18.6	10	Arizona	22.2
38	Hawaii	12.8	11	Ohio	21.6
20	Idaho	20.0	12	Connecticut	21.1
22	Illinois	19.9	12	North Dakota	21.1
8	Indiana	22.5	12	Texas	21.1
25	Iowa	18.9	15	Wyoming	20.8
17	Kansas	20.6	16	Arkansas	20.7
2	Kentucky	26.0	17	Kansas	20.6
NA	Louisiana**	NA	18	Wisconsin	20.5
35	Maine	14.0	19	Delaware	20.2
32	Maryland	16.8	20	Idaho	20.0
31	Massachusetts	17.7	20	Montana	20.0
28	Michigan	18.0	22	Illinois	19.9
NA	Minnesota**	NA	23	Mississippi	19.2
23	Mississippi	19.2	24	New Hampshire	19.0
6	Missouri	23.8	25	Iowa	18.9
20	Montana	20.0	26	Georgia	18.6
NA	Nebraska**	NA	27	Vermont	18.2
37	Nevada	13.6	28	Michigan	18.0
24	New Hampshire	19.0	29	Alaska	17.8
NA	New Jersey**	NA	29	South Carolina	17.8
5	New Mexico	24.2	31	Massachusetts	17.7
36	New York	13.8	32	Maryland	16.8
8	North Carolina	22.5	33	Florida	15.9
12	North Dakota	21.1	34	Rhode Island	15.1
11	Ohio	21.6	35	Maine	14.0
7	Oklahoma	23.2	36	New York	13.8
NA	Oregon**	NA	37	Nevada	13.6
NA	Pennsylvania**	NA	38	Hawaii	12.8
34	Rhode Island	15.1	39	Utah	7.9
29	South Carolina	17.8	NA	Alabama**	NA
4	South Dakota	24.7	NA	California**	NA
3	Tennessee	25.5	NA	Colorado**	NA
12	Texas	21.1	NA	Louisiana**	NA
39	Utah	7.9	NA	Minnesota**	NA
27	Vermont	18.2	NA	Nebraska**	NA
NA	Virginia**	NA	NA	New Jersey**	NA
NA	Washington**	NA	NA	Oregon**	NA
1	West Virginia	27.6	NA	Pennsylvania**	NA
18	Wisconsin	20.5	NA	Virginia**	NA
15	Wyoming	20.8	NA	Washington**	NA
				District of Columbia**	NA

Source: U.S. Department of Health and Human Services, Centers for Disease Control and Prevention
   "Youth Risk Behavior Surveillance--U.S., 2007" (http://www.cdc.gov/HealthyYouth/yrbs/)
*Smoked cigarettes on one or more of the 30 days preceding the survey. National percent includes nonreporting states.
**Not available.

Percent of High School Students Who Smoked Cigarettes on School Property: 2007
National Percent = 5.7%*

ALPHA ORDER

RANK	STATE	PERCENT
NA	Alabama**	NA
7	Alaska	7.5
26	Arizona	5.0
26	Arkansas	5.0
NA	California**	NA
NA	Colorado**	NA
NA	Connecticut**	NA
4	Delaware	8.0
23	Florida	5.5
24	Georgia	5.2
NA	Hawaii**	NA
20	Idaho	6.0
19	Illinois	6.1
12	Indiana	7.0
30	Iowa	4.6
13	Kansas	6.5
1	Kentucky	9.5
NA	Louisiana**	NA
32	Maine	3.5
14	Maryland	6.4
11	Massachusetts	7.3
20	Michigan	6.0
NA	Minnesota**	NA
31	Mississippi	4.0
5	Missouri	7.7
18	Montana	6.2
NA	Nebraska**	NA
26	Nevada	5.0
NA	New Hampshire**	NA
NA	New Jersey**	NA
7	New Mexico	7.5
26	New York	5.0
NA	North Carolina**	NA
16	North Dakota	6.3
NA	Ohio**	NA
22	Oklahoma	5.8
NA	Oregon**	NA
NA	Pennsylvania**	NA
10	Rhode Island	7.4
16	South Carolina	6.3
3	South Dakota	8.3
6	Tennessee	7.6
25	Texas	5.1
33	Utah	2.4
NA	Vermont**	NA
NA	Virginia**	NA
NA	Washington**	NA
2	West Virginia	8.8
14	Wisconsin	6.4
7	Wyoming	7.5

RANK ORDER

RANK	STATE	PERCENT
1	Kentucky	9.5
2	West Virginia	8.8
3	South Dakota	8.3
4	Delaware	8.0
5	Missouri	7.7
6	Tennessee	7.6
7	Alaska	7.5
7	New Mexico	7.5
7	Wyoming	7.5
10	Rhode Island	7.4
11	Massachusetts	7.3
12	Indiana	7.0
13	Kansas	6.5
14	Maryland	6.4
14	Wisconsin	6.4
16	North Dakota	6.3
16	South Carolina	6.3
18	Montana	6.2
19	Illinois	6.1
20	Idaho	6.0
20	Michigan	6.0
22	Oklahoma	5.8
23	Florida	5.5
24	Georgia	5.2
25	Texas	5.1
26	Arizona	5.0
26	Arkansas	5.0
26	Nevada	5.0
26	New York	5.0
30	Iowa	4.6
31	Mississippi	4.0
32	Maine	3.5
33	Utah	2.4
NA	Alabama**	NA
NA	California**	NA
NA	Colorado**	NA
NA	Connecticut**	NA
NA	Hawaii**	NA
NA	Louisiana**	NA
NA	Minnesota**	NA
NA	Nebraska**	NA
NA	New Hampshire**	NA
NA	New Jersey**	NA
NA	North Carolina**	NA
NA	Ohio**	NA
NA	Oregon**	NA
NA	Pennsylvania**	NA
NA	Vermont**	NA
NA	Virginia**	NA
NA	Washington**	NA
	District of Columbia**	NA

Source: U.S. Department of Health and Human Services, Centers for Disease Control and Prevention
"Youth Risk Behavior Surveillance--U.S., 2007" (http://www.cdc.gov/HealthyYouth/yrbs/)
*Smoked cigarettes on one or more of the 30 days preceding the survey on school property. National percent includes nonreporting states.
**Not available.

Percent of High School Students Who Drink Alcohol: 2007

National Percent = 44.7%*

ALPHA ORDER

RANK	STATE	PERCENT
NA	Alabama**	NA
31	Alaska	39.7
8	Arizona	45.6
27	Arkansas	42.2
NA	California**	NA
NA	Colorado**	NA
6	Connecticut	46.0
9	Delaware	45.2
26	Florida	42.3
33	Georgia	37.7
38	Hawaii	29.1
23	Idaho	42.5
14	Illinois	43.7
13	Indiana	43.9
28	Iowa	41.0
24	Kansas	42.4
29	Kentucky	40.6
NA	Louisiana**	NA
32	Maine	39.3
19	Maryland	42.9
4	Massachusetts	46.2
21	Michigan	42.8
NA	Minnesota**	NA
29	Mississippi	40.6
12	Missouri	44.4
3	Montana	46.5
NA	Nebraska**	NA
35	Nevada	37.0
10	New Hampshire	44.8
NA	New Jersey**	NA
17	New Mexico	43.2
14	New York	43.7
33	North Carolina	37.7
5	North Dakota	46.1
7	Ohio	45.7
18	Oklahoma	43.1
NA	Oregon**	NA
NA	Pennsylvania**	NA
19	Rhode Island	42.9
36	South Carolina	36.8
11	South Dakota	44.5
37	Tennessee	36.7
2	Texas	48.3
39	Utah	17.0
22	Vermont	42.6
NA	Virginia**	NA
NA	Washington**	NA
16	West Virginia	43.5
1	Wisconsin	48.9
24	Wyoming	42.4

RANK ORDER

RANK	STATE	PERCENT
1	Wisconsin	48.9
2	Texas	48.3
3	Montana	46.5
4	Massachusetts	46.2
5	North Dakota	46.1
6	Connecticut	46.0
7	Ohio	45.7
8	Arizona	45.6
9	Delaware	45.2
10	New Hampshire	44.8
11	South Dakota	44.5
12	Missouri	44.4
13	Indiana	43.9
14	Illinois	43.7
14	New York	43.7
16	West Virginia	43.5
17	New Mexico	43.2
18	Oklahoma	43.1
19	Maryland	42.9
19	Rhode Island	42.9
21	Michigan	42.8
22	Vermont	42.6
23	Idaho	42.5
24	Kansas	42.4
24	Wyoming	42.4
26	Florida	42.3
27	Arkansas	42.2
28	Iowa	41.0
29	Kentucky	40.6
29	Mississippi	40.6
31	Alaska	39.7
32	Maine	39.3
33	Georgia	37.7
33	North Carolina	37.7
35	Nevada	37.0
36	South Carolina	36.8
37	Tennessee	36.7
38	Hawaii	29.1
39	Utah	17.0
NA	Alabama**	NA
NA	California**	NA
NA	Colorado**	NA
NA	Louisiana**	NA
NA	Minnesota**	NA
NA	Nebraska**	NA
NA	New Jersey**	NA
NA	Oregon**	NA
NA	Pennsylvania**	NA
NA	Virginia**	NA
NA	Washington**	NA
	District of Columbia**	NA

Source: U.S. Department of Health and Human Services, Centers for Disease Control and Prevention
"Youth Risk Behavior Surveillance--U.S., 2007" (http://www.cdc.gov/HealthyYouth/yrbs/)
*Drank alcohol on one or more of the 30 days preceding the survey. National percent includes nonreporting states.
**Not available.

Percent of High School Students Who Drank Alcohol on School Property: 2007

National Percent = 4.1%*

<table>
<tr><td colspan="3">ALPHA ORDER</td><td colspan="3">RANK ORDER</td></tr>
<tr><th>RANK</th><th>STATE</th><th>PERCENT</th><th>RANK</th><th>STATE</th><th>PERCENT</th></tr>
<tr><td>NA</td><td>Alabama**</td><td>NA</td><td>1</td><td>New Mexico</td><td>8.7</td></tr>
<tr><td>31</td><td>Alaska</td><td>4.1</td><td>2</td><td>Wyoming</td><td>6.9</td></tr>
<tr><td>5</td><td>Arizona</td><td>6.0</td><td>3</td><td>Idaho</td><td>6.2</td></tr>
<tr><td>13</td><td>Arkansas</td><td>5.1</td><td>3</td><td>Maryland</td><td>6.2</td></tr>
<tr><td>NA</td><td>California**</td><td>NA</td><td>5</td><td>Arizona</td><td>6.0</td></tr>
<tr><td>NA</td><td>Colorado**</td><td>NA</td><td>5</td><td>Hawaii</td><td>6.0</td></tr>
<tr><td>8</td><td>Connecticut</td><td>5.6</td><td>7</td><td>Montana</td><td>5.7</td></tr>
<tr><td>27</td><td>Delaware</td><td>4.5</td><td>8</td><td>Connecticut</td><td>5.6</td></tr>
<tr><td>12</td><td>Florida</td><td>5.3</td><td>8</td><td>Maine</td><td>5.6</td></tr>
<tr><td>28</td><td>Georgia</td><td>4.4</td><td>10</td><td>Illinois</td><td>5.5</td></tr>
<tr><td>5</td><td>Hawaii</td><td>6.0</td><td>10</td><td>West Virginia</td><td>5.5</td></tr>
<tr><td>3</td><td>Idaho</td><td>6.2</td><td>12</td><td>Florida</td><td>5.3</td></tr>
<tr><td>10</td><td>Illinois</td><td>5.5</td><td>13</td><td>Arkansas</td><td>5.1</td></tr>
<tr><td>31</td><td>Indiana</td><td>4.1</td><td>13</td><td>Mississippi</td><td>5.1</td></tr>
<tr><td>36</td><td>Iowa</td><td>3.4</td><td>13</td><td>New Hampshire</td><td>5.1</td></tr>
<tr><td>19</td><td>Kansas</td><td>4.8</td><td>13</td><td>New York</td><td>5.1</td></tr>
<tr><td>21</td><td>Kentucky</td><td>4.7</td><td>17</td><td>Oklahoma</td><td>5.0</td></tr>
<tr><td>NA</td><td>Louisiana**</td><td>NA</td><td>18</td><td>Texas</td><td>4.9</td></tr>
<tr><td>8</td><td>Maine</td><td>5.6</td><td>19</td><td>Kansas</td><td>4.8</td></tr>
<tr><td>3</td><td>Maryland</td><td>6.2</td><td>19</td><td>Rhode Island</td><td>4.8</td></tr>
<tr><td>21</td><td>Massachusetts</td><td>4.7</td><td>21</td><td>Kentucky</td><td>4.7</td></tr>
<tr><td>34</td><td>Michigan</td><td>3.6</td><td>21</td><td>Massachusetts</td><td>4.7</td></tr>
<tr><td>NA</td><td>Minnesota**</td><td>NA</td><td>21</td><td>North Carolina</td><td>4.7</td></tr>
<tr><td>13</td><td>Mississippi</td><td>5.1</td><td>21</td><td>South Carolina</td><td>4.7</td></tr>
<tr><td>36</td><td>Missouri</td><td>3.4</td><td>21</td><td>Utah</td><td>4.7</td></tr>
<tr><td>7</td><td>Montana</td><td>5.7</td><td>26</td><td>Vermont</td><td>4.6</td></tr>
<tr><td>NA</td><td>Nebraska**</td><td>NA</td><td>27</td><td>Delaware</td><td>4.5</td></tr>
<tr><td>28</td><td>Nevada</td><td>4.4</td><td>28</td><td>Georgia</td><td>4.4</td></tr>
<tr><td>13</td><td>New Hampshire</td><td>5.1</td><td>28</td><td>Nevada</td><td>4.4</td></tr>
<tr><td>NA</td><td>New Jersey**</td><td>NA</td><td>28</td><td>North Dakota</td><td>4.4</td></tr>
<tr><td>1</td><td>New Mexico</td><td>8.7</td><td>31</td><td>Alaska</td><td>4.1</td></tr>
<tr><td>13</td><td>New York</td><td>5.1</td><td>31</td><td>Indiana</td><td>4.1</td></tr>
<tr><td>21</td><td>North Carolina</td><td>4.7</td><td>31</td><td>Tennessee</td><td>4.1</td></tr>
<tr><td>28</td><td>North Dakota</td><td>4.4</td><td>34</td><td>Michigan</td><td>3.6</td></tr>
<tr><td>38</td><td>Ohio</td><td>3.2</td><td>34</td><td>South Dakota</td><td>3.6</td></tr>
<tr><td>17</td><td>Oklahoma</td><td>5.0</td><td>36</td><td>Iowa</td><td>3.4</td></tr>
<tr><td>NA</td><td>Oregon**</td><td>NA</td><td>36</td><td>Missouri</td><td>3.4</td></tr>
<tr><td>NA</td><td>Pennsylvania**</td><td>NA</td><td>38</td><td>Ohio</td><td>3.2</td></tr>
<tr><td>19</td><td>Rhode Island</td><td>4.8</td><td>NA</td><td>Alabama**</td><td>NA</td></tr>
<tr><td>21</td><td>South Carolina</td><td>4.7</td><td>NA</td><td>California**</td><td>NA</td></tr>
<tr><td>34</td><td>South Dakota</td><td>3.6</td><td>NA</td><td>Colorado**</td><td>NA</td></tr>
<tr><td>31</td><td>Tennessee</td><td>4.1</td><td>NA</td><td>Louisiana**</td><td>NA</td></tr>
<tr><td>18</td><td>Texas</td><td>4.9</td><td>NA</td><td>Minnesota**</td><td>NA</td></tr>
<tr><td>21</td><td>Utah</td><td>4.7</td><td>NA</td><td>Nebraska**</td><td>NA</td></tr>
<tr><td>26</td><td>Vermont</td><td>4.6</td><td>NA</td><td>New Jersey**</td><td>NA</td></tr>
<tr><td>NA</td><td>Virginia**</td><td>NA</td><td>NA</td><td>Oregon**</td><td>NA</td></tr>
<tr><td>NA</td><td>Washington**</td><td>NA</td><td>NA</td><td>Pennsylvania**</td><td>NA</td></tr>
<tr><td>10</td><td>West Virginia</td><td>5.5</td><td>NA</td><td>Virginia**</td><td>NA</td></tr>
<tr><td>NA</td><td>Wisconsin**</td><td>NA</td><td>NA</td><td>Washington**</td><td>NA</td></tr>
<tr><td>2</td><td>Wyoming</td><td>6.9</td><td>NA</td><td>Wisconsin**</td><td>NA</td></tr>
<tr><td></td><td></td><td></td><td></td><td>District of Columbia**</td><td>NA</td></tr>
</table>

Source: U.S. Department of Health and Human Services, Centers for Disease Control and Prevention
"Youth Risk Behavior Surveillance--U.S., 2007" (http://www.cdc.gov/HealthyYouth/yrbs/)
*Drank alcohol on one or more of the 30 days preceding the survey on school property. National percent includes nonreporting states.
**Not available.

Percent of High School Students Who Use Marijuana: 2007

National Percent = 19.7%*

ALPHA ORDER

RANK	STATE	PERCENT
NA	Alabama**	NA
12	Alaska	20.5
9	Arizona	22.0
30	Arkansas	16.4
NA	California**	NA
NA	Colorado**	NA
6	Connecticut	23.2
1	Delaware	25.1
21	Florida	18.9
15	Georgia	19.6
33	Hawaii	15.7
26	Idaho	17.9
13	Illinois	20.3
21	Indiana	18.9
38	Iowa	11.5
35	Kansas	15.3
30	Kentucky	16.4
NA	Louisiana**	NA
9	Maine	22.0
16	Maryland	19.4
3	Massachusetts	24.6
25	Michigan	18.0
NA	Minnesota**	NA
29	Mississippi	16.7
20	Missouri	19.0
11	Montana	21.0
NA	Nebraska**	NA
34	Nevada	15.5
8	New Hampshire	22.9
NA	New Jersey**	NA
2	New Mexico	25.0
23	New York	18.6
19	North Carolina	19.1
36	North Dakota	14.8
27	Ohio	17.7
32	Oklahoma	15.9
NA	Oregon**	NA
NA	Pennsylvania**	NA
6	Rhode Island	23.2
23	South Carolina	18.6
27	South Dakota	17.7
16	Tennessee	19.4
18	Texas	19.3
39	Utah	8.7
4	Vermont	24.1
NA	Virginia**	NA
NA	Washington**	NA
5	West Virginia	23.5
13	Wisconsin	20.3
37	Wyoming	14.4

RANK ORDER

RANK	STATE	PERCENT
1	Delaware	25.1
2	New Mexico	25.0
3	Massachusetts	24.6
4	Vermont	24.1
5	West Virginia	23.5
6	Connecticut	23.2
6	Rhode Island	23.2
8	New Hampshire	22.9
9	Arizona	22.0
9	Maine	22.0
11	Montana	21.0
12	Alaska	20.5
13	Illinois	20.3
13	Wisconsin	20.3
15	Georgia	19.6
16	Maryland	19.4
16	Tennessee	19.4
18	Texas	19.3
19	North Carolina	19.1
20	Missouri	19.0
21	Florida	18.9
21	Indiana	18.9
23	New York	18.6
23	South Carolina	18.6
25	Michigan	18.0
26	Idaho	17.9
27	Ohio	17.7
27	South Dakota	17.7
29	Mississippi	16.7
30	Arkansas	16.4
30	Kentucky	16.4
32	Oklahoma	15.9
33	Hawaii	15.7
34	Nevada	15.5
35	Kansas	15.3
36	North Dakota	14.8
37	Wyoming	14.4
38	Iowa	11.5
39	Utah	8.7
NA	Alabama**	NA
NA	California**	NA
NA	Colorado**	NA
NA	Louisiana**	NA
NA	Minnesota**	NA
NA	Nebraska**	NA
NA	New Jersey**	NA
NA	Oregon**	NA
NA	Pennsylvania**	NA
NA	Virginia**	NA
NA	Washington**	NA
	District of Columbia**	NA

Source: U.S. Department of Health and Human Services, Centers for Disease Control and Prevention
"Youth Risk Behavior Surveillance--U.S., 2007" (http://www.cdc.gov/HealthyYouth/yrbs/)
*Used marijuana one or more times in the 30 days preceding the survey. National percent includes nonreporting states.
**Not available.

Percent of High School Students Who Used Marijuana on School Property: 2007
National Percent = 4.5%*

ALPHA ORDER

RANK	STATE	PERCENT
NA	Alabama**	NA
5	Alaska	5.9
4	Arizona	6.1
34	Arkansas	2.8
NA	California**	NA
NA	Colorado**	NA
5	Connecticut	5.9
9	Delaware	5.4
14	Florida	4.7
29	Georgia	3.6
8	Hawaii	5.7
14	Idaho	4.7
20	Illinois	4.2
21	Indiana	4.1
38	Iowa	2.5
26	Kansas	3.8
25	Kentucky	3.9
NA	Louisiana**	NA
10	Maine	5.2
14	Maryland	4.7
13	Massachusetts	4.8
24	Michigan	4.0
NA	Minnesota**	NA
35	Mississippi	2.7
29	Missouri	3.6
11	Montana	5.0
NA	Nebraska**	NA
29	Nevada	3.6
14	New Hampshire	4.7
NA	New Jersey**	NA
1	New Mexico	7.9
21	New York	4.1
19	North Carolina	4.3
35	North Dakota	2.7
28	Ohio	3.7
37	Oklahoma	2.6
NA	Oregon**	NA
NA	Pennsylvania**	NA
2	Rhode Island	6.5
33	South Carolina	3.3
11	South Dakota	5.0
21	Tennessee	4.1
29	Texas	3.6
26	Utah	3.8
3	Vermont	6.3
NA	Virginia**	NA
NA	Washington**	NA
7	West Virginia	5.8
NA	Wisconsin**	NA
14	Wyoming	4.7

RANK ORDER

RANK	STATE	PERCENT
1	New Mexico	7.9
2	Rhode Island	6.5
3	Vermont	6.3
4	Arizona	6.1
5	Alaska	5.9
5	Connecticut	5.9
7	West Virginia	5.8
8	Hawaii	5.7
9	Delaware	5.4
10	Maine	5.2
11	Montana	5.0
11	South Dakota	5.0
13	Massachusetts	4.8
14	Florida	4.7
14	Idaho	4.7
14	Maryland	4.7
14	New Hampshire	4.7
14	Wyoming	4.7
19	North Carolina	4.3
20	Illinois	4.2
21	Indiana	4.1
21	New York	4.1
21	Tennessee	4.1
24	Michigan	4.0
25	Kentucky	3.9
26	Kansas	3.8
26	Utah	3.8
28	Ohio	3.7
29	Georgia	3.6
29	Missouri	3.6
29	Nevada	3.6
29	Texas	3.6
33	South Carolina	3.3
34	Arkansas	2.8
35	Mississippi	2.7
35	North Dakota	2.7
37	Oklahoma	2.6
38	Iowa	2.5
NA	Alabama**	NA
NA	California**	NA
NA	Colorado**	NA
NA	Louisiana**	NA
NA	Minnesota**	NA
NA	Nebraska**	NA
NA	New Jersey**	NA
NA	Oregon**	NA
NA	Pennsylvania**	NA
NA	Virginia**	NA
NA	Washington**	NA
NA	Wisconsin**	NA
	District of Columbia**	NA

Source: U.S. Department of Health and Human Services, Centers for Disease Control and Prevention
"Youth Risk Behavior Surveillance--U.S., 2007" (http://www.cdc.gov/HealthyYouth/yrbs/)
*Used marijuana one or more times in the 30 days preceding the survey on school property. National percent includes nonreporting states.
**Not available.

Percent of High School Students Who Use Cocaine: 2007

National Percent = 3.3%*

ALPHA ORDER			RANK ORDER		
RANK	STATE	PERCENT	RANK	STATE	PERCENT
NA	Alabama**	NA	1	Arizona	6.6
24	Alaska	2.9	2	New Mexico	5.4
1	Arizona	6.6	2	Texas	5.4
19	Arkansas	3.3	4	Vermont	5.1
NA	California**	NA	5	West Virginia	5.0
NA	Colorado**	NA	6	Connecticut	4.4
6	Connecticut	4.4	7	Maine	4.3
27	Delaware	2.7	7	Utah	4.3
9	Florida	3.9	9	Florida	3.9
29	Georgia	2.6	9	Kansas	3.9
34	Hawaii	2.0	11	Idaho	3.8
11	Idaho	3.8	11	Indiana	3.8
20	Illinois	3.1	13	Ohio	3.7
11	Indiana	3.8	14	Wyoming	3.6
36	Iowa	1.7	15	Kentucky	3.4
9	Kansas	3.9	15	New Hampshire	3.4
15	Kentucky	3.4	15	Rhode Island	3.4
NA	Louisiana**	NA	15	South Dakota	3.4
7	Maine	4.3	19	Arkansas	3.3
29	Maryland	2.6	20	Illinois	3.1
NA	Massachusetts**	NA	20	South Carolina	3.1
31	Michigan	2.5	20	Wisconsin	3.1
NA	Minnesota**	NA	23	Oklahoma	3.0
27	Mississippi	2.7	24	Alaska	2.9
31	Missouri	2.5	24	Montana	2.9
24	Montana	2.9	24	Tennessee	2.9
NA	Nebraska**	NA	27	Delaware	2.7
33	Nevada	2.4	27	Mississippi	2.7
15	New Hampshire	3.4	29	Georgia	2.6
NA	New Jersey**	NA	29	Maryland	2.6
2	New Mexico	5.4	31	Michigan	2.5
NA	New York**	NA	31	Missouri	2.5
NA	North Carolina**	NA	33	Nevada	2.4
34	North Dakota	2.0	34	Hawaii	2.0
13	Ohio	3.7	34	North Dakota	2.0
23	Oklahoma	3.0	36	Iowa	1.7
NA	Oregon**	NA	NA	Alabama**	NA
NA	Pennsylvania**	NA	NA	California**	NA
15	Rhode Island	3.4	NA	Colorado**	NA
20	South Carolina	3.1	NA	Louisiana**	NA
15	South Dakota	3.4	NA	Massachusetts**	NA
24	Tennessee	2.9	NA	Minnesota**	NA
2	Texas	5.4	NA	Nebraska**	NA
7	Utah	4.3	NA	New Jersey**	NA
4	Vermont	5.1	NA	New York**	NA
NA	Virginia**	NA	NA	North Carolina**	NA
NA	Washington**	NA	NA	Oregon**	NA
5	West Virginia	5.0	NA	Pennsylvania**	NA
20	Wisconsin	3.1	NA	Virginia**	NA
14	Wyoming	3.6	NA	Washington**	NA
				District of Columbia**	NA

Source: U.S. Department of Health and Human Services, Centers for Disease Control and Prevention
    "Youth Risk Behavior Surveillance--U.S., 2007" (http://www.cdc.gov/HealthyYouth/yrbs/)
*Used cocaine one or more times in the 30 days preceding the survey. National percent includes nonreporting states.
**Not available.

Percent of High School Students Who Were Offered, Sold, or Given an Illegal Drug on School Property: 2007
National Percent = 22.3%*

ALPHA ORDER

RANK	STATE	PERCENT
NA	Alabama**	NA
20	Alaska	25.1
1	Arizona	37.1
11	Arkansas	28.1
NA	California**	NA
NA	Colorado**	NA
5	Connecticut	30.5
25	Delaware	22.9
34	Florida	19.0
3	Georgia	32.0
2	Hawaii	36.2
20	Idaho	25.1
30	Illinois	21.2
32	Indiana	20.5
39	Iowa	10.1
38	Kansas	15.0
14	Kentucky	27.0
NA	Louisiana**	NA
6	Maine	29.1
12	Maryland	27.4
13	Massachusetts	27.3
6	Michigan	29.1
NA	Minnesota**	NA
37	Mississippi	15.6
36	Missouri	17.8
22	Montana	24.9
NA	Nebraska**	NA
8	Nevada	28.8
27	New Hampshire	22.5
NA	New Jersey**	NA
4	New Mexico	31.3
16	New York	26.6
10	North Carolina	28.5
35	North Dakota	18.7
15	Ohio	26.7
33	Oklahoma	19.1
NA	Oregon**	NA
NA	Pennsylvania**	NA
19	Rhode Island	25.3
16	South Carolina	26.6
31	South Dakota	21.1
29	Tennessee	21.6
18	Texas	26.5
24	Utah	23.2
28	Vermont	22.0
NA	Virginia**	NA
NA	Washington**	NA
9	West Virginia	28.6
26	Wisconsin	22.7
23	Wyoming	24.7

RANK ORDER

RANK	STATE	PERCENT
1	Arizona	37.1
2	Hawaii	36.2
3	Georgia	32.0
4	New Mexico	31.3
5	Connecticut	30.5
6	Maine	29.1
6	Michigan	29.1
8	Nevada	28.8
9	West Virginia	28.6
10	North Carolina	28.5
11	Arkansas	28.1
12	Maryland	27.4
13	Massachusetts	27.3
14	Kentucky	27.0
15	Ohio	26.7
16	New York	26.6
16	South Carolina	26.6
18	Texas	26.5
19	Rhode Island	25.3
20	Alaska	25.1
20	Idaho	25.1
22	Montana	24.9
23	Wyoming	24.7
24	Utah	23.2
25	Delaware	22.9
26	Wisconsin	22.7
27	New Hampshire	22.5
28	Vermont	22.0
29	Tennessee	21.6
30	Illinois	21.2
31	South Dakota	21.1
32	Indiana	20.5
33	Oklahoma	19.1
34	Florida	19.0
35	North Dakota	18.7
36	Missouri	17.8
37	Mississippi	15.6
38	Kansas	15.0
39	Iowa	10.1
NA	Alabama**	NA
NA	California**	NA
NA	Colorado**	NA
NA	Louisiana**	NA
NA	Minnesota**	NA
NA	Nebraska**	NA
NA	New Jersey**	NA
NA	Oregon**	NA
NA	Pennsylvania**	NA
NA	Virginia**	NA
NA	Washington**	NA
	District of Columbia**	NA

Source: U.S. Department of Health and Human Services, Centers for Disease Control and Prevention
   "Youth Risk Behavior Surveillance--U.S., 2007" (http://www.cdc.gov/HealthyYouth/yrbs/)
*One or more times during the 12 months preceding the survey. National percent includes nonreporting states.
**Not available.

Percent of High School Students Who Have Ever Had Sexual Intercourse: 2007

National Percent = 47.8%*

ALPHA ORDER

RANK	STATE	PERCENT
NA	Alabama**	NA
21	Alaska	45.1
17	Arizona	46.1
3	Arkansas	54.9
NA	California**	NA
NA	Colorado**	NA
31	Connecticut	42.4
2	Delaware	59.3
13	Florida	49.5
NA	Georgia**	NA
34	Hawaii	36.2
33	Idaho	42.1
12	Illinois	50.1
14	Indiana	49.1
28	Iowa	43.3
22	Kansas	45.0
11	Kentucky	50.3
NA	Louisiana**	NA
20	Maine	45.4
NA	Maryland**	NA
26	Massachusetts	44.4
31	Michigan	42.4
NA	Minnesota**	NA
1	Mississippi	59.5
7	Missouri	52.1
18	Montana	45.7
NA	Nebraska**	NA
29	Nevada	42.8
23	New Hampshire	44.7
NA	New Jersey**	NA
NA	New Mexico**	NA
27	New York	43.6
7	North Carolina	52.1
30	North Dakota	42.6
25	Ohio	44.5
10	Oklahoma	50.9
NA	Oregon**	NA
NA	Pennsylvania**	NA
19	Rhode Island	45.5
9	South Carolina	51.5
16	South Dakota	46.5
4	Tennessee	54.4
6	Texas	52.9
NA	Utah**	NA
NA	Vermont**	NA
NA	Virginia**	NA
NA	Washington**	NA
5	West Virginia	53.7
24	Wisconsin	44.6
15	Wyoming	47.2

RANK ORDER

RANK	STATE	PERCENT
1	Mississippi	59.5
2	Delaware	59.3
3	Arkansas	54.9
4	Tennessee	54.4
5	West Virginia	53.7
6	Texas	52.9
7	Missouri	52.1
7	North Carolina	52.1
9	South Carolina	51.5
10	Oklahoma	50.9
11	Kentucky	50.3
12	Illinois	50.1
13	Florida	49.5
14	Indiana	49.1
15	Wyoming	47.2
16	South Dakota	46.5
17	Arizona	46.1
18	Montana	45.7
19	Rhode Island	45.5
20	Maine	45.4
21	Alaska	45.1
22	Kansas	45.0
23	New Hampshire	44.7
24	Wisconsin	44.6
25	Ohio	44.5
26	Massachusetts	44.4
27	New York	43.6
28	Iowa	43.3
29	Nevada	42.8
30	North Dakota	42.6
31	Connecticut	42.4
31	Michigan	42.4
33	Idaho	42.1
34	Hawaii	36.2
NA	Alabama**	NA
NA	California**	NA
NA	Colorado**	NA
NA	Georgia**	NA
NA	Louisiana**	NA
NA	Maryland**	NA
NA	Minnesota**	NA
NA	Nebraska**	NA
NA	New Jersey**	NA
NA	New Mexico**	NA
NA	Oregon**	NA
NA	Pennsylvania**	NA
NA	Utah**	NA
NA	Vermont**	NA
NA	Virginia**	NA
NA	Washington**	NA
	District of Columbia**	NA

Source: U.S. Department of Health and Human Services, Centers for Disease Control and Prevention
    "Youth Risk Behavior Surveillance--U.S., 2007" (http://www.cdc.gov/HealthyYouth/yrbs/)
*Have had sexual intercourse at least once during their life. National percent includes nonreporting states.
**Not available.

Percent of High School Students Sexually Active: 2007

National Percent = 35.0%*

ALPHA ORDER

ALPHA ORDER

RANK	STATE	PERCENT
NA	Alabama**	NA
32	Alaska	30.9
20	Arizona	33.6
6	Arkansas	39.7
NA	California**	NA
NA	Colorado**	NA
27	Connecticut	31.8
1	Delaware	45.3
13	Florida	36.4
NA	Georgia**	NA
35	Hawaii	23.6
NA	Idaho**	NA
9	Illinois	37.4
10	Indiana	37.0
20	Iowa	33.6
16	Kansas	34.4
11	Kentucky	36.5
NA	Louisiana**	NA
22	Maine	33.4
NA	Maryland**	NA
25	Massachusetts	32.7
34	Michigan	30.0
NA	Minnesota**	NA
2	Mississippi	42.3
4	Missouri	40.6
30	Montana	31.2
NA	Nebraska**	NA
33	Nevada	30.5
18	New Hampshire	34.1
NA	New Jersey**	NA
29	New Mexico	31.5
31	New York	31.1
8	North Carolina	37.5
28	North Dakota	31.6
15	Ohio	35.1
11	Oklahoma	36.5
NA	Oregon**	NA
NA	Pennsylvania**	NA
23	Rhode Island	33.1
14	South Carolina	35.9
16	South Dakota	34.4
5	Tennessee	40.3
7	Texas	38.7
NA	Utah**	NA
26	Vermont	31.9
NA	Virginia**	NA
NA	Washington**	NA
3	West Virginia	41.4
24	Wisconsin	32.9
19	Wyoming	33.7

RANK ORDER

RANK	STATE	PERCENT
1	Delaware	45.3
2	Mississippi	42.3
3	West Virginia	41.4
4	Missouri	40.6
5	Tennessee	40.3
6	Arkansas	39.7
7	Texas	38.7
8	North Carolina	37.5
9	Illinois	37.4
10	Indiana	37.0
11	Kentucky	36.5
11	Oklahoma	36.5
13	Florida	36.4
14	South Carolina	35.9
15	Ohio	35.1
16	Kansas	34.4
16	South Dakota	34.4
18	New Hampshire	34.1
19	Wyoming	33.7
20	Arizona	33.6
20	Iowa	33.6
22	Maine	33.4
23	Rhode Island	33.1
24	Wisconsin	32.9
25	Massachusetts	32.7
26	Vermont	31.9
27	Connecticut	31.8
28	North Dakota	31.6
29	New Mexico	31.5
30	Montana	31.2
31	New York	31.1
32	Alaska	30.9
33	Nevada	30.5
34	Michigan	30.0
35	Hawaii	23.6
NA	Alabama**	NA
NA	California**	NA
NA	Colorado**	NA
NA	Georgia**	NA
NA	Idaho**	NA
NA	Louisiana**	NA
NA	Maryland**	NA
NA	Minnesota**	NA
NA	Nebraska**	NA
NA	New Jersey**	NA
NA	Oregon**	NA
NA	Pennsylvania**	NA
NA	Utah**	NA
NA	Virginia**	NA
NA	Washington**	NA
	District of Columbia**	NA

Source: U.S. Department of Health and Human Services, Centers for Disease Control and Prevention
"Youth Risk Behavior Surveillance--U.S., 2007" (http://www.cdc.gov/HealthyYouth/yrbs/)
*Sexual intercourse during the 3 months preceding the survey. National percent includes nonreporting states.
**Not available.

Percent of Sexually Active High School Students Who Used Condoms: 2007

National Percent = 61.5%*

ALPHA ORDER

RANK	STATE	PERCENT
NA	Alabama**	NA
23	Alaska	60.8
33	Arizona	55.5
27	Arkansas	59.0
NA	California**	NA
NA	Colorado**	NA
16	Connecticut	62.7
1	Delaware	69.2
5	Florida	66.4
NA	Georgia**	NA
35	Hawaii	54.2
NA	Idaho**	NA
10	Illinois	64.8
31	Indiana	57.1
6	Iowa	66.1
8	Kansas	65.8
27	Kentucky	59.0
NA	Louisiana**	NA
29	Maine	58.9
NA	Maryland**	NA
20	Massachusetts	61.1
9	Michigan	65.0
NA	Minnesota**	NA
3	Mississippi	67.2
26	Missouri	59.3
13	Montana	63.3
NA	Nebraska**	NA
2	Nevada	69.1
11	New Hampshire	64.2
NA	New Jersey**	NA
34	New Mexico	55.2
4	New York	66.7
18	North Carolina	61.5
12	North Dakota	63.6
24	Ohio	60.1
25	Oklahoma	59.6
NA	Oregon**	NA
NA	Pennsylvania**	NA
7	Rhode Island	66.0
17	South Carolina	62.4
30	South Dakota	58.3
22	Tennessee	60.9
32	Texas	56.4
NA	Utah**	NA
15	Vermont	62.8
NA	Virginia**	NA
NA	Washington**	NA
21	West Virginia	61.0
19	Wisconsin	61.4
14	Wyoming	63.1

RANK ORDER

RANK	STATE	PERCENT
1	Delaware	69.2
2	Nevada	69.1
3	Mississippi	67.2
4	New York	66.7
5	Florida	66.4
6	Iowa	66.1
7	Rhode Island	66.0
8	Kansas	65.8
9	Michigan	65.0
10	Illinois	64.8
11	New Hampshire	64.2
12	North Dakota	63.6
13	Montana	63.3
14	Wyoming	63.1
15	Vermont	62.8
16	Connecticut	62.7
17	South Carolina	62.4
18	North Carolina	61.5
19	Wisconsin	61.4
20	Massachusetts	61.1
21	West Virginia	61.0
22	Tennessee	60.9
23	Alaska	60.8
24	Ohio	60.1
25	Oklahoma	59.6
26	Missouri	59.3
27	Arkansas	59.0
27	Kentucky	59.0
29	Maine	58.9
30	South Dakota	58.3
31	Indiana	57.1
32	Texas	56.4
33	Arizona	55.5
34	New Mexico	55.2
35	Hawaii	54.2
NA	Alabama**	NA
NA	California**	NA
NA	Colorado**	NA
NA	Georgia**	NA
NA	Idaho**	NA
NA	Louisiana**	NA
NA	Maryland**	NA
NA	Minnesota**	NA
NA	Nebraska**	NA
NA	New Jersey**	NA
NA	Oregon**	NA
NA	Pennsylvania**	NA
NA	Utah**	NA
NA	Virginia**	NA
NA	Washington**	NA
	District of Columbia**	NA

Source: U.S. Department of Health and Human Services, Centers for Disease Control and Prevention
  "Youth Risk Behavior Surveillance--U.S., 2007" (http://www.cdc.gov/HealthyYouth/yrbs/)
*Reported that they or their partner used a condom during last sexual intercourse. National percent includes nonreporting states.
**Not available.

Teenage Birth Rate in 2005

National Rate = 40.5 Live Births per 1,000 Women 15 to 19 Years Old*

ALPHA ORDER

RANK	STATE	RATE
11	Alabama	49.7
28	Alaska	37.3
5	Arizona	58.2
4	Arkansas	59.1
24	California	38.8
19	Colorado	42.6
47	Connecticut	23.3
15	Delaware	44.0
21	Florida	42.4
8	Georgia	52.7
29	Hawaii	36.2
26	Idaho	37.7
25	Illinois	38.6
17	Indiana	43.2
35	Iowa	32.6
22	Kansas	41.4
12	Kentucky	49.1
12	Louisiana	49.1
45	Maine	24.4
37	Maryland	31.8
48	Massachusetts	21.8
36	Michigan	32.5
44	Minnesota	26.1
3	Mississippi	60.5
20	Missouri	42.5
30	Montana	35.2
32	Nebraska	34.2
10	Nevada	50.1
50	New Hampshire	17.9
46	New Jersey	23.4
1	New Mexico	61.6
43	New York	26.5
14	North Carolina	48.5
42	North Dakota	29.7
23	Ohio	38.9
7	Oklahoma	54.2
34	Oregon	33.0
40	Pennsylvania	30.4
38	Rhode Island	31.4
9	South Carolina	51.0
27	South Dakota	37.5
6	Tennessee	54.9
1	Texas	61.6
33	Utah	33.4
49	Vermont	18.6
31	Virginia	34.4
39	Washington	31.1
16	West Virginia	43.4
41	Wisconsin	30.3
17	Wyoming	43.2

RANK ORDER

RANK	STATE	RATE
1	New Mexico	61.6
1	Texas	61.6
3	Mississippi	60.5
4	Arkansas	59.1
5	Arizona	58.2
6	Tennessee	54.9
7	Oklahoma	54.2
8	Georgia	52.7
9	South Carolina	51.0
10	Nevada	50.1
11	Alabama	49.7
12	Kentucky	49.1
12	Louisiana	49.1
14	North Carolina	48.5
15	Delaware	44.0
16	West Virginia	43.4
17	Indiana	43.2
17	Wyoming	43.2
19	Colorado	42.6
20	Missouri	42.5
21	Florida	42.4
22	Kansas	41.4
23	Ohio	38.9
24	California	38.8
25	Illinois	38.6
26	Idaho	37.7
27	South Dakota	37.5
28	Alaska	37.3
29	Hawaii	36.2
30	Montana	35.2
31	Virginia	34.4
32	Nebraska	34.2
33	Utah	33.4
34	Oregon	33.0
35	Iowa	32.6
36	Michigan	32.5
37	Maryland	31.8
38	Rhode Island	31.4
39	Washington	31.1
40	Pennsylvania	30.4
41	Wisconsin	30.3
42	North Dakota	29.7
43	New York	26.5
44	Minnesota	26.1
45	Maine	24.4
46	New Jersey	23.4
47	Connecticut	23.3
48	Massachusetts	21.8
49	Vermont	18.6
50	New Hampshire	17.9
	District of Columbia	63.4

Source: U.S. Department of Health and Human Services, National Center for Health Statistics
     "National Vital Statistics Reports" (Vol. 56, No. 6, December 5, 2007, http://www.cdc.gov/nchs/births.htm)
*Final data by state of residence.

Percent of Children Living in Poverty in 2006

National Percent = 17.9%*

ALPHA ORDER

RANK	STATE	PERCENT
8	Alabama	22.7
33	Alaska	14.7
15	Arizona	19.1
5	Arkansas	23.8
19	California	17.7
28	Colorado	15.3
47	Connecticut	10.7
28	Delaware	15.3
21	Florida	17.0
13	Georgia	19.7
47	Hawaii	10.7
34	Idaho	14.5
22	Illinois	16.8
20	Indiana	17.4
38	Iowa	13.2
30	Kansas	15.1
9	Kentucky	22.3
2	Louisiana	27.5
23	Maine	16.7
49	Maryland	9.3
41	Massachusetts	12.0
18	Michigan	17.8
42	Minnesota	11.8
1	Mississippi	29.2
17	Missouri	18.2
24	Montana	16.6
36	Nebraska	13.8
37	Nevada	13.4
50	New Hampshire	9.0
45	New Jersey	11.5
3	New Mexico	25.3
13	New York	19.7
12	North Carolina	19.8
39	North Dakota	12.4
16	Ohio	18.3
5	Oklahoma	23.8
26	Oregon	16.2
25	Pennsylvania	16.5
31	Rhode Island	14.9
11	South Carolina	21.7
27	South Dakota	16.1
9	Tennessee	22.3
7	Texas	23.5
44	Utah	11.6
39	Vermont	12.4
43	Virginia	11.7
32	Washington	14.8
4	West Virginia	24.6
35	Wisconsin	14.3
46	Wyoming	11.4

RANK ORDER

RANK	STATE	PERCENT
1	Mississippi	29.2
2	Louisiana	27.5
3	New Mexico	25.3
4	West Virginia	24.6
5	Arkansas	23.8
5	Oklahoma	23.8
7	Texas	23.5
8	Alabama	22.7
9	Kentucky	22.3
9	Tennessee	22.3
11	South Carolina	21.7
12	North Carolina	19.8
13	Georgia	19.7
13	New York	19.7
15	Arizona	19.1
16	Ohio	18.3
17	Missouri	18.2
18	Michigan	17.8
19	California	17.7
20	Indiana	17.4
21	Florida	17.0
22	Illinois	16.8
23	Maine	16.7
24	Montana	16.6
25	Pennsylvania	16.5
26	Oregon	16.2
27	South Dakota	16.1
28	Colorado	15.3
28	Delaware	15.3
30	Kansas	15.1
31	Rhode Island	14.9
32	Washington	14.8
33	Alaska	14.7
34	Idaho	14.5
35	Wisconsin	14.3
36	Nebraska	13.8
37	Nevada	13.4
38	Iowa	13.2
39	North Dakota	12.4
39	Vermont	12.4
41	Massachusetts	12.0
42	Minnesota	11.8
43	Virginia	11.7
44	Utah	11.6
45	New Jersey	11.5
46	Wyoming	11.4
47	Connecticut	10.7
47	Hawaii	10.7
49	Maryland	9.3
50	New Hampshire	9.0
	District of Columbia	32.1

Source: U.S. Bureau of the Census
   "2006 American Community Survey" (http://www.census.gov/acs/www/index.html)
*Children 17 and under living in families with incomes below the poverty level.

Rate of Child Abuse and Neglect in 2006

National Rate = 12.1 Abused Children per 1,000 Population Under 18*

ALPHA ORDER				RANK ORDER		
RANK	STATE	RATE		RANK	STATE	RATE
31	Alabama	8.4		1	Florida	33.5
6	Alaska	19.2		2	Massachusetts	25.0
48	Arizona	2.7		3	West Virginia	21.4
15	Arkansas	13.3		4	Iowa	20.5
28	California	9.4		5	Kentucky	19.8
29	Colorado	9.3		6	Alaska	19.2
20	Connecticut	12.4		7	Rhode Island	18.5
27	Delaware	9.5		8	New York	17.7
1	Florida	33.5		9	Utah	16.5
10	Georgia	16.2		10	Georgia	16.2
36	Hawaii	6.9		11	Oregon	15.1
44	Idaho	4.2		12	Ohio	15.0
30	Illinois	8.6		12	Oklahoma	15.0
15	Indiana	13.3		14	Nebraska	13.8
4	Iowa	20.5		15	Arkansas	13.3
45	Kansas	3.8		15	Indiana	13.3
5	Kentucky	19.8		15	Tennessee	13.3
22	Louisiana	11.4		18	North Carolina	13.2
19	Maine	12.6		19	Maine	12.6
NA	Maryland**	NA		20	Connecticut	12.4
2	Massachusetts	25.0		21	New Mexico	11.6
23	Michigan	11.0		22	Louisiana	11.4
40	Minnesota	6.1		23	Michigan	11.0
33	Mississippi	8.3		24	Texas	10.6
42	Missouri	5.0		25	South Carolina	10.4
34	Montana	8.1		26	North Dakota	9.9
14	Nebraska	13.8		27	Delaware	9.5
31	Nevada	8.4		28	California	9.4
47	New Hampshire	2.8		29	Colorado	9.3
41	New Jersey	5.6		30	Illinois	8.6
21	New Mexico	11.6		31	Alabama	8.4
8	New York	17.7		31	Nevada	8.4
18	North Carolina	13.2		33	Mississippi	8.3
26	North Dakota	9.9		34	Montana	8.1
12	Ohio	15.0		35	South Dakota	7.9
12	Oklahoma	15.0		36	Hawaii	6.9
11	Oregon	15.1		37	Vermont	6.5
49	Pennsylvania	1.5		37	Wisconsin	6.5
7	Rhode Island	18.5		37	Wyoming	6.5
25	South Carolina	10.4		40	Minnesota	6.1
35	South Dakota	7.9		41	New Jersey	5.6
15	Tennessee	13.3		42	Missouri	5.0
24	Texas	10.6		43	Washington	4.8
9	Utah	16.5		44	Idaho	4.2
37	Vermont	6.5		45	Kansas	3.8
45	Virginia	3.8		45	Virginia	3.8
43	Washington	4.8		47	New Hampshire	2.8
3	West Virginia	21.4		48	Arizona	2.7
37	Wisconsin	6.5		49	Pennsylvania	1.5
37	Wyoming	6.5		NA	Maryland**	NA
					District of Columbia	24.0

Source: U.S. Department of Health and Human Services, Children's Bureau
"Child Maltreatment 2006" (http://www.acf.hhs.gov/programs/cb/pubs/cm06/index.htm)
*State-substantiated or indicated incidents.
**Not available.

Reported Juvenile Arrest Rate in 2006

National Rate = 6,417.1 Reported Arrests per 100,000 Juvenile Population*

ALPHA ORDER

RANK	STATE	RATE
46	Alabama	2,825.4
39	Alaska	5,120.6
15	Arizona	7,552.2
38	Arkansas	5,279.1
36	California	5,365.9
8	Colorado	9,103.7
25	Connecticut	6,343.2
12	Delaware	8,006.1
21	Florida	6,594.3
22	Georgia	6,594.2
7	Hawaii	9,172.2
4	Idaho	9,662.3
NA	Illinois**	NA
23	Indiana	6,510.4
19	Iowa	7,187.1
40	Kansas	4,936.4
11	Kentucky	8,228.3
5	Louisiana	9,446.4
32	Maine	5,611.2
13	Maryland	7,840.4
44	Massachusetts	3,108.9
43	Michigan	4,023.9
NA	Minnesota**	NA
27	Mississippi	6,134.3
14	Missouri	7,712.6
NA	Montana**	NA
10	Nebraska	8,579.7
17	Nevada	7,456.8
18	New Hampshire	7,207.9
24	New Jersey	6,488.9
31	New Mexico	5,656.4
42	New York	4,682.2
28	North Carolina	6,131.2
3	North Dakota	11,102.4
29	Ohio	6,039.4
33	Oklahoma	5,589.6
16	Oregon	7,526.1
9	Pennsylvania	9,025.7
41	Rhode Island	4,845.4
35	South Carolina	5,475.6
37	South Dakota	5,314.7
20	Tennessee	6,625.7
26	Texas	6,289.4
6	Utah	9,241.8
45	Vermont	2,951.1
34	Virginia	5,516.0
30	Washington	5,984.3
47	West Virginia	1,623.4
1	Wisconsin	17,572.3
2	Wyoming	12,189.9

RANK ORDER

RANK	STATE	RATE
1	Wisconsin	17,572.3
2	Wyoming	12,189.9
3	North Dakota	11,102.4
4	Idaho	9,662.3
5	Louisiana	9,446.4
6	Utah	9,241.8
7	Hawaii	9,172.2
8	Colorado	9,103.7
9	Pennsylvania	9,025.7
10	Nebraska	8,579.7
11	Kentucky	8,228.3
12	Delaware	8,006.1
13	Maryland	7,840.4
14	Missouri	7,712.6
15	Arizona	7,552.2
16	Oregon	7,526.1
17	Nevada	7,456.8
18	New Hampshire	7,207.9
19	Iowa	7,187.1
20	Tennessee	6,625.7
21	Florida	6,594.3
22	Georgia	6,594.2
23	Indiana	6,510.4
24	New Jersey	6,488.9
25	Connecticut	6,343.2
26	Texas	6,289.4
27	Mississippi	6,134.3
28	North Carolina	6,131.2
29	Ohio	6,039.4
30	Washington	5,984.3
31	New Mexico	5,656.4
32	Maine	5,611.2
33	Oklahoma	5,589.6
34	Virginia	5,516.0
35	South Carolina	5,475.6
36	California	5,365.9
37	South Dakota	5,314.7
38	Arkansas	5,279.1
39	Alaska	5,120.6
40	Kansas	4,936.4
41	Rhode Island	4,845.4
42	New York	4,682.2
43	Michigan	4,023.9
44	Massachusetts	3,108.9
45	Vermont	2,951.1
46	Alabama	2,825.4
47	West Virginia	1,623.4
NA	Illinois**	NA
NA	Minnesota**	NA
NA	Montana**	NA
	District of Columbia**	NA

Source: CQ Press using data from Federal Bureau of Investigation
"Crime in the United States 2006" (Uniform Crime Reports, September 24, 2007, www.fbi.gov/ucr/cius2006/index.html)
*By law enforcement agencies submitting complete reports to the F.B.I. for 12 months in 2006. Arrests of youths 17 years and younger divided into population of 10 to 17 year olds.
**Not available.

Juveniles in Custody in 2006

National Total = 92,854 Juveniles*

ALPHA ORDER					RANK ORDER			
RANK	STATE	JUVENILES	% of USA		RANK	STATE	JUVENILES	% of USA
13	Alabama	1,752	1.9%		1	California	15,240	16.4%
41	Alaska	363	0.4%		2	Texas	8,247	8.9%
14	Arizona	1,737	1.9%		3	Florida	7,302	7.9%
33	Arkansas	813	0.9%		4	Pennsylvania	4,323	4.7%
1	California	15,240	16.4%		5	New York	4,197	4.5%
12	Colorado	2,034	2.2%		6	Ohio	4,149	4.5%
38	Connecticut	498	0.5%		7	Michigan	2,760	3.0%
44	Delaware	303	0.3%		8	Georgia	2,631	2.8%
3	Florida	7,302	7.9%		8	Illinois	2,631	2.8%
8	Georgia	2,631	2.8%		10	Indiana	2,616	2.8%
49	Hawaii	123	0.1%		11	Virginia	2,310	2.5%
37	Idaho	522	0.6%		12	Colorado	2,034	2.2%
8	Illinois	2,631	2.8%		13	Alabama	1,752	1.9%
10	Indiana	2,616	2.8%		14	Arizona	1,737	1.9%
27	Iowa	1,062	1.1%		15	New Jersey	1,704	1.8%
28	Kansas	1,053	1.1%		16	Minnesota	1,623	1.7%
23	Kentucky	1,242	1.3%		17	Washington	1,455	1.6%
24	Louisiana	1,200	1.3%		18	Tennessee	1,419	1.5%
47	Maine	210	0.2%		19	Wisconsin	1,347	1.5%
26	Maryland	1,104	1.2%		20	South Carolina	1,320	1.4%
25	Massachusetts	1,164	1.3%		21	Missouri	1,293	1.4%
7	Michigan	2,760	3.0%		22	Oregon	1,254	1.4%
16	Minnesota	1,623	1.7%		23	Kentucky	1,242	1.3%
40	Mississippi	444	0.5%		24	Louisiana	1,200	1.3%
21	Missouri	1,293	1.4%		25	Massachusetts	1,164	1.3%
45	Montana	243	0.3%		26	Maryland	1,104	1.2%
34	Nebraska	735	0.8%		27	Iowa	1,062	1.1%
31	Nevada	885	1.0%		28	Kansas	1,053	1.1%
48	New Hampshire	189	0.2%		29	North Carolina	1,029	1.1%
15	New Jersey	1,704	1.8%		30	Oklahoma	924	1.0%
39	New Mexico	471	0.5%		31	Nevada	885	1.0%
5	New York	4,197	4.5%		32	Utah	864	0.9%
29	North Carolina	1,029	1.1%		33	Arkansas	813	0.9%
46	North Dakota	240	0.3%		34	Nebraska	735	0.8%
6	Ohio	4,149	4.5%		35	South Dakota	597	0.6%
30	Oklahoma	924	1.0%		36	West Virginia	579	0.6%
22	Oregon	1,254	1.4%		37	Idaho	522	0.6%
4	Pennsylvania	4,323	4.7%		38	Connecticut	498	0.5%
42	Rhode Island	348	0.4%		39	New Mexico	471	0.5%
20	South Carolina	1,320	1.4%		40	Mississippi	444	0.5%
35	South Dakota	597	0.6%		41	Alaska	363	0.4%
18	Tennessee	1,419	1.5%		42	Rhode Island	348	0.4%
2	Texas	8,247	8.9%		43	Wyoming	315	0.3%
32	Utah	864	0.9%		44	Delaware	303	0.3%
50	Vermont	54	0.1%		45	Montana	243	0.3%
11	Virginia	2,310	2.5%		46	North Dakota	240	0.3%
17	Washington	1,455	1.6%		47	Maine	210	0.2%
36	West Virginia	579	0.6%		48	New Hampshire	189	0.2%
19	Wisconsin	1,347	1.5%		49	Hawaii	123	0.1%
43	Wyoming	315	0.3%		50	Vermont	54	0.1%
						District of Columbia	339	0.4%

Source: U.S. Department of Justice, Office of Juvenile Justice and Delinquency Prevention
   "Census of Juveniles in Residential Placement Databook" (http://ojjdp.ncjrs.org/ojstatbb/cjrp/)
*Youths age 10 to 15.

Rate of Juveniles in Custody in 2006

National Rate = 125 Juveniles in Custody per 100,000 10 to 15 Year Olds*

ALPHA ORDER

RANK	STATE	RATE
3	Alabama	201
14	Alaska	145
30	Arizona	117
28	Arkansas	120
29	California	119
10	Colorado	152
31	Connecticut	114
20	Delaware	135
8	Florida	165
14	Georgia	145
49	Hawaii	36
13	Idaho	146
45	Illinois	62
5	Indiana	183
9	Iowa	163
23	Kansas	131
25	Kentucky	127
11	Louisiana	149
50	Maine	33
41	Maryland	81
42	Massachusetts	77
18	Michigan	137
25	Minnesota	127
39	Mississippi	85
24	Missouri	128
35	Montana	104
6	Nebraska	169
12	Nevada	147
44	New Hampshire	67
46	New Jersey	50
48	New Mexico	47
21	New York	133
40	North Carolina	82
6	North Dakota	169
16	Ohio	143
35	Oklahoma	104
32	Oregon	111
17	Pennsylvania	138
43	Rhode Island	75
4	South Carolina	185
1	South Dakota	373
37	Tennessee	91
19	Texas	136
33	Utah	108
46	Vermont	50
34	Virginia	107
38	Washington	88
27	West Virginia	123
22	Wisconsin	132
2	Wyoming	334

RANK ORDER

RANK	STATE	RATE
1	South Dakota	373
2	Wyoming	334
3	Alabama	201
4	South Carolina	185
5	Indiana	183
6	Nebraska	169
6	North Dakota	169
8	Florida	165
9	Iowa	163
10	Colorado	152
11	Louisiana	149
12	Nevada	147
13	Idaho	146
14	Alaska	145
14	Georgia	145
16	Ohio	143
17	Pennsylvania	138
18	Michigan	137
19	Texas	136
20	Delaware	135
21	New York	133
22	Wisconsin	132
23	Kansas	131
24	Missouri	128
25	Kentucky	127
25	Minnesota	127
27	West Virginia	123
28	Arkansas	120
29	California	119
30	Arizona	117
31	Connecticut	114
32	Oregon	111
33	Utah	108
34	Virginia	107
35	Montana	104
35	Oklahoma	104
37	Tennessee	91
38	Washington	88
39	Mississippi	85
40	North Carolina	82
41	Maryland	81
42	Massachusetts	77
43	Rhode Island	75
44	New Hampshire	67
45	Illinois	62
46	New Jersey	50
46	Vermont	50
48	New Mexico	47
49	Hawaii	36
50	Maine	33
	District of Columbia	294

Source: U.S. Department of Justice, Office of Juvenile Justice and Delinquency Prevention
    "Census of Juveniles in Residential Placement Databook" (http://ojjdp.ncjrs.org/ojstatbb/cjrp/)
*Youths age 10 to 15.

Percent of High School Students Who Were Obese or Overweight: 2007

National Percent = 28.8%

<table>
<tr><td colspan="3">ALPHA ORDER</td><td colspan="3">RANK ORDER</td></tr>
<tr><th>RANK</th><th>STATE</th><th>PERCENT</th><th>RANK</th><th>STATE</th><th>PERCENT</th></tr>
<tr><td>NA</td><td>Alabama**</td><td>NA</td><td>1</td><td>Mississippi</td><td>35.8</td></tr>
<tr><td>18</td><td>Alaska</td><td>27.3</td><td>2</td><td>Tennessee</td><td>35.0</td></tr>
<tr><td>25</td><td>Arizona</td><td>25.9</td><td>3</td><td>Georgia</td><td>32.0</td></tr>
<tr><td>12</td><td>Arkansas</td><td>29.7</td><td>3</td><td>Kentucky</td><td>32.0</td></tr>
<tr><td>NA</td><td>California**</td><td>NA</td><td>5</td><td>West Virginia</td><td>31.7</td></tr>
<tr><td>NA</td><td>Colorado**</td><td>NA</td><td>6</td><td>South Carolina</td><td>31.5</td></tr>
<tr><td>28</td><td>Connecticut</td><td>25.6</td><td>6</td><td>Texas</td><td>31.5</td></tr>
<tr><td>8</td><td>Delaware</td><td>30.8</td><td>8</td><td>Delaware</td><td>30.8</td></tr>
<tr><td>21</td><td>Florida</td><td>26.4</td><td>9</td><td>Hawaii</td><td>29.9</td></tr>
<tr><td>3</td><td>Georgia</td><td>32.0</td><td>9</td><td>North Carolina</td><td>29.9</td></tr>
<tr><td>9</td><td>Hawaii</td><td>29.9</td><td>9</td><td>Oklahoma</td><td>29.9</td></tr>
<tr><td>37</td><td>Idaho</td><td>22.8</td><td>12</td><td>Arkansas</td><td>29.7</td></tr>
<tr><td>15</td><td>Illinois</td><td>28.6</td><td>13</td><td>Indiana</td><td>29.1</td></tr>
<tr><td>13</td><td>Indiana</td><td>29.1</td><td>14</td><td>Michigan</td><td>28.9</td></tr>
<tr><td>32</td><td>Iowa</td><td>24.8</td><td>15</td><td>Illinois</td><td>28.6</td></tr>
<tr><td>29</td><td>Kansas</td><td>25.5</td><td>16</td><td>Maryland</td><td>28.3</td></tr>
<tr><td>3</td><td>Kentucky</td><td>32.0</td><td>17</td><td>Ohio</td><td>27.4</td></tr>
<tr><td>NA</td><td>Louisiana**</td><td>NA</td><td>18</td><td>Alaska</td><td>27.3</td></tr>
<tr><td>25</td><td>Maine</td><td>25.9</td><td>19</td><td>New York</td><td>27.2</td></tr>
<tr><td>16</td><td>Maryland</td><td>28.3</td><td>20</td><td>Rhode Island</td><td>26.9</td></tr>
<tr><td>27</td><td>Massachusetts</td><td>25.7</td><td>21</td><td>Florida</td><td>26.4</td></tr>
<tr><td>14</td><td>Michigan</td><td>28.9</td><td>22</td><td>Missouri</td><td>26.3</td></tr>
<tr><td>NA</td><td>Minnesota**</td><td>NA</td><td>22</td><td>Vermont</td><td>26.3</td></tr>
<tr><td>1</td><td>Mississippi</td><td>35.8</td><td>24</td><td>New Hampshire</td><td>26.1</td></tr>
<tr><td>22</td><td>Missouri</td><td>26.3</td><td>25</td><td>Arizona</td><td>25.9</td></tr>
<tr><td>36</td><td>Montana</td><td>23.4</td><td>25</td><td>Maine</td><td>25.9</td></tr>
<tr><td>NA</td><td>Nebraska**</td><td>NA</td><td>27</td><td>Massachusetts</td><td>25.7</td></tr>
<tr><td>29</td><td>Nevada</td><td>25.5</td><td>28</td><td>Connecticut</td><td>25.6</td></tr>
<tr><td>24</td><td>New Hampshire</td><td>26.1</td><td>29</td><td>Kansas</td><td>25.5</td></tr>
<tr><td>NA</td><td>New Jersey**</td><td>NA</td><td>29</td><td>Nevada</td><td>25.5</td></tr>
<tr><td>33</td><td>New Mexico</td><td>24.4</td><td>31</td><td>Wisconsin</td><td>25.1</td></tr>
<tr><td>19</td><td>New York</td><td>27.2</td><td>32</td><td>Iowa</td><td>24.8</td></tr>
<tr><td>9</td><td>North Carolina</td><td>29.9</td><td>33</td><td>New Mexico</td><td>24.4</td></tr>
<tr><td>34</td><td>North Dakota</td><td>23.7</td><td>34</td><td>North Dakota</td><td>23.7</td></tr>
<tr><td>17</td><td>Ohio</td><td>27.4</td><td>35</td><td>South Dakota</td><td>23.6</td></tr>
<tr><td>9</td><td>Oklahoma</td><td>29.9</td><td>36</td><td>Montana</td><td>23.4</td></tr>
<tr><td>NA</td><td>Oregon**</td><td>NA</td><td>37</td><td>Idaho</td><td>22.8</td></tr>
<tr><td>NA</td><td>Pennsylvania**</td><td>NA</td><td>38</td><td>Wyoming</td><td>20.7</td></tr>
<tr><td>20</td><td>Rhode Island</td><td>26.9</td><td>39</td><td>Utah</td><td>20.4</td></tr>
<tr><td>6</td><td>South Carolina</td><td>31.5</td><td>NA</td><td>Alabama**</td><td>NA</td></tr>
<tr><td>35</td><td>South Dakota</td><td>23.6</td><td>NA</td><td>California**</td><td>NA</td></tr>
<tr><td>2</td><td>Tennessee</td><td>35.0</td><td>NA</td><td>Colorado**</td><td>NA</td></tr>
<tr><td>6</td><td>Texas</td><td>31.5</td><td>NA</td><td>Louisiana**</td><td>NA</td></tr>
<tr><td>39</td><td>Utah</td><td>20.4</td><td>NA</td><td>Minnesota**</td><td>NA</td></tr>
<tr><td>22</td><td>Vermont</td><td>26.3</td><td>NA</td><td>Nebraska**</td><td>NA</td></tr>
<tr><td>NA</td><td>Virginia**</td><td>NA</td><td>NA</td><td>New Jersey**</td><td>NA</td></tr>
<tr><td>NA</td><td>Washington**</td><td>NA</td><td>NA</td><td>Oregon**</td><td>NA</td></tr>
<tr><td>5</td><td>West Virginia</td><td>31.7</td><td>NA</td><td>Pennsylvania**</td><td>NA</td></tr>
<tr><td>31</td><td>Wisconsin</td><td>25.1</td><td>NA</td><td>Virginia**</td><td>NA</td></tr>
<tr><td>38</td><td>Wyoming</td><td>20.7</td><td>NA</td><td>Washington**</td><td>NA</td></tr>
<tr><td></td><td></td><td></td><td></td><td>District of Columbia**</td><td>NA</td></tr>
</table>

Source: CQ Press using data from U.S. Department of Health and Human Services, Centers for Disease Control and Prevention
   "Youth Risk Behavior Surveillance--U.S., 2007" (http://www.cdc.gov/HealthyYouth/yrbs/)
*Students who were equal to or greater than 85th percentile for body mass index, by age and sex, based on reference data.
National figure includes nonreporting states.
**Not available.

Percent of High School Students Who Have Attempted Suicide: 2007

National Percent = 6.9%*

ALPHA ORDER				RANK ORDER		
RANK	STATE	PERCENT		RANK	STATE	PERCENT
NA	Alabama**	NA		1	New Mexico	14.3
4	Alaska	10.7		2	North Carolina	13.3
21	Arizona	7.8		3	Hawaii	12.0
6	Arkansas	9.8		4	Alaska	10.7
NA	California**	NA		5	Wyoming	10.5
NA	Colorado**	NA		6	Arkansas	9.8
6	Connecticut	9.8		6	Connecticut	9.8
34	Delaware	6.2		8	Utah	9.6
36	Florida	5.7		9	Rhode Island	9.3
17	Georgia	7.9		10	Michigan	9.1
3	Hawaii	12.0		10	West Virginia	9.1
15	Idaho	8.4		12	Nevada	8.9
31	Illinois	6.8		13	North Dakota	8.8
29	Indiana	7.2		14	South Dakota	8.7
32	Iowa	6.7		15	Idaho	8.4
32	Kansas	6.7		15	Texas	8.4
22	Kentucky	7.6		17	Georgia	7.9
NA	Louisiana**	NA		17	Mississippi	7.9
38	Maine	4.8		17	Missouri	7.9
25	Maryland	7.5		17	Montana	7.9
22	Massachusetts	7.6		21	Arizona	7.8
10	Michigan	9.1		22	Kentucky	7.6
NA	Minnesota**	NA		22	Massachusetts	7.6
17	Mississippi	7.9		22	New York	7.6
17	Missouri	7.9		25	Maryland	7.5
17	Montana	7.9		25	South Carolina	7.5
NA	Nebraska**	NA		27	Tennessee	7.4
12	Nevada	8.9		28	Wisconsin	7.3
37	New Hampshire	5.5		29	Indiana	7.2
NA	New Jersey**	NA		29	Ohio	7.2
1	New Mexico	14.3		31	Illinois	6.8
22	New York	7.6		32	Iowa	6.7
2	North Carolina	13.3		32	Kansas	6.7
13	North Dakota	8.8		34	Delaware	6.2
29	Ohio	7.2		35	Oklahoma	5.9
35	Oklahoma	5.9		36	Florida	5.7
NA	Oregon**	NA		37	New Hampshire	5.5
NA	Pennsylvania**	NA		38	Maine	4.8
9	Rhode Island	9.3		38	Vermont	4.8
25	South Carolina	7.5		NA	Alabama**	NA
14	South Dakota	8.7		NA	California**	NA
27	Tennessee	7.4		NA	Colorado**	NA
15	Texas	8.4		NA	Louisiana**	NA
8	Utah	9.6		NA	Minnesota**	NA
38	Vermont	4.8		NA	Nebraska**	NA
NA	Virginia**	NA		NA	New Jersey**	NA
NA	Washington**	NA		NA	Oregon**	NA
10	West Virginia	9.1		NA	Pennsylvania**	NA
28	Wisconsin	7.3		NA	Virginia**	NA
5	Wyoming	10.5		NA	Washington**	NA
				NA	District of Columbia**	NA

Source: U.S. Department of Health and Human Services, Centers for Disease Control and Prevention
   "Youth Risk Behavior Surveillance--U.S., 2007" (http://www.cdc.gov/HealthyYouth/yrbs/)
*Percent who actually attempted suicide one or more times during the preceding 12 months. The national percent of students who attempted suicide and required treatment by a doctor or a nurse was 2.0 percent. National percent includes nonreporting states.
**Not available.

Percent of High School Students Who Played on One or More Sports Teams: 2007
National Percent = 56.3%*

ALPHA ORDER

RANK	STATE	PERCENT
NA	Alabama**	NA
4	Alaska	61.7
28	Arizona	46.0
24	Arkansas	51.1
NA	California**	NA
NA	Colorado**	NA
NA	Connecticut**	NA
18	Delaware	55.0
25	Florida	49.8
21	Georgia	51.9
NA	Hawaii**	NA
12	Idaho	57.6
10	Illinois	58.0
14	Indiana	57.0
2	Iowa	65.4
8	Kansas	59.4
27	Kentucky	48.6
NA	Louisiana**	NA
NA	Maine**	NA
19	Maryland	54.3
7	Massachusetts	59.5
NA	Michigan**	NA
NA	Minnesota**	NA
20	Mississippi	53.4
16	Missouri	56.5
6	Montana	59.6
NA	Nebraska**	NA
NA	Nevada**	NA
13	New Hampshire	57.1
NA	New Jersey**	NA
NA	New Mexico**	NA
17	New York	55.3
NA	North Carolina**	NA
NA	North Dakota**	NA
15	Ohio	56.7
9	Oklahoma	58.6
NA	Oregon**	NA
NA	Pennsylvania**	NA
NA	Rhode Island**	NA
26	South Carolina	49.7
3	South Dakota	63.1
21	Tennessee	51.9
11	Texas	57.7
1	Utah	67.1
NA	Vermont**	NA
NA	Virginia**	NA
NA	Washington**	NA
23	West Virginia	51.8
NA	Wisconsin**	NA
5	Wyoming	59.8

RANK ORDER

RANK	STATE	PERCENT
1	Utah	67.1
2	Iowa	65.4
3	South Dakota	63.1
4	Alaska	61.7
5	Wyoming	59.8
6	Montana	59.6
7	Massachusetts	59.5
8	Kansas	59.4
9	Oklahoma	58.6
10	Illinois	58.0
11	Texas	57.7
12	Idaho	57.6
13	New Hampshire	57.1
14	Indiana	57.0
15	Ohio	56.7
16	Missouri	56.5
17	New York	55.3
18	Delaware	55.0
19	Maryland	54.3
20	Mississippi	53.4
21	Georgia	51.9
21	Tennessee	51.9
23	West Virginia	51.8
24	Arkansas	51.1
25	Florida	49.8
26	South Carolina	49.7
27	Kentucky	48.6
28	Arizona	46.0
NA	Alabama**	NA
NA	California**	NA
NA	Colorado**	NA
NA	Connecticut**	NA
NA	Hawaii**	NA
NA	Louisiana**	NA
NA	Maine**	NA
NA	Michigan**	NA
NA	Minnesota**	NA
NA	Nebraska**	NA
NA	Nevada**	NA
NA	New Jersey**	NA
NA	New Mexico**	NA
NA	North Carolina**	NA
NA	North Dakota**	NA
NA	Oregon**	NA
NA	Pennsylvania**	NA
NA	Rhode Island**	NA
NA	Vermont**	NA
NA	Virginia**	NA
NA	Washington**	NA
NA	Wisconsin**	NA
	District of Columbia**	NA

Source: U.S. Department of Health and Human Services, Centers for Disease Control and Prevention
"Youth Risk Behavior Surveillance--U.S., 2007" (http://www.cdc.gov/HealthyYouth/yrbs/)
*National percent includes nonreporting states.
**Not available.

Percent of High School Students Not Participating in 60 or More Minutes of Physical Activity: 2007
National Percent = 24.9%*

ALPHA ORDER

RANK	STATE	PERCENT
NA	Alabama**	NA
18	Alaska	16.5
1	Arizona	26.7
8	Arkansas	19.4
NA	California**	NA
NA	Colorado**	NA
24	Connecticut	14.5
11	Delaware	18.3
7	Florida	20.4
9	Georgia	18.9
9	Hawaii	18.9
33	Idaho	13.1
23	Illinois	14.7
20	Indiana	15.9
38	Iowa	10.6
24	Kansas	14.5
4	Kentucky	22.4
NA	Louisiana**	NA
30	Maine	13.3
2	Maryland	26.6
16	Massachusetts	16.9
22	Michigan	15.0
NA	Minnesota**	NA
3	Mississippi	23.4
19	Missouri	16.2
30	Montana	13.3
NA	Nebraska**	NA
29	Nevada	13.4
36	New Hampshire	11.7
NA	New Jersey**	NA
13	New Mexico	17.2
14	New York	17.1
12	North Carolina	17.4
35	North Dakota	12.3
26	Ohio	14.4
28	Oklahoma	14.1
NA	Oregon**	NA
NA	Pennsylvania**	NA
30	Rhode Island	13.3
5	South Carolina	21.5
34	South Dakota	12.6
14	Tennessee	17.1
20	Texas	15.9
39	Utah	10.5
37	Vermont	11.4
NA	Virginia**	NA
NA	Washington**	NA
17	West Virginia	16.8
6	Wisconsin	21.4
27	Wyoming	14.3

RANK ORDER

RANK	STATE	PERCENT
1	Arizona	26.7
2	Maryland	26.6
3	Mississippi	23.4
4	Kentucky	22.4
5	South Carolina	21.5
6	Wisconsin	21.4
7	Florida	20.4
8	Arkansas	19.4
9	Georgia	18.9
9	Hawaii	18.9
11	Delaware	18.3
12	North Carolina	17.4
13	New Mexico	17.2
14	New York	17.1
14	Tennessee	17.1
16	Massachusetts	16.9
17	West Virginia	16.8
18	Alaska	16.5
19	Missouri	16.2
20	Indiana	15.9
20	Texas	15.9
22	Michigan	15.0
23	Illinois	14.7
24	Connecticut	14.5
24	Kansas	14.5
26	Ohio	14.4
27	Wyoming	14.3
28	Oklahoma	14.1
29	Nevada	13.4
30	Maine	13.3
30	Montana	13.3
30	Rhode Island	13.3
33	Idaho	13.1
34	South Dakota	12.6
35	North Dakota	12.3
36	New Hampshire	11.7
37	Vermont	11.4
38	Iowa	10.6
39	Utah	10.5
NA	Alabama**	NA
NA	California**	NA
NA	Colorado**	NA
NA	Louisiana**	NA
NA	Minnesota**	NA
NA	Nebraska**	NA
NA	New Jersey**	NA
NA	Oregon**	NA
NA	Pennsylvania**	NA
NA	Virginia**	NA
NA	Washington**	NA
	District of Columbia**	NA

Source: U.S. Department of Health and Human Services, Centers for Disease Control and Prevention "Youth Risk Behavior Surveillance--U.S., 2007" (http://www.cdc.gov/HealthyYouth/yrbs/)

*Did not participate in 60 or more minutes of any kind of physical activity that increased their heart rate and made them breathe hard some of the time on at least 1 day during the 7 days before the survey. National percent includes nonreporting states.
**Not available.

Percent of High School Students Who Watched
Three or More Hours of Television Daily: 2007
National Percent = 35.4%

<table>
<tr><td colspan="3">ALPHA ORDER</td><td colspan="3">RANK ORDER</td></tr>
<tr><td>RANK</td><td>STATE</td><td>PERCENT</td><td>RANK</td><td>STATE</td><td>PERCENT</td></tr>
<tr><td>NA</td><td>Alabama**</td><td>NA</td><td>1</td><td>Mississippi</td><td>47.4</td></tr>
<tr><td>34</td><td>Alaska</td><td>23.0</td><td>2</td><td>Georgia</td><td>43.1</td></tr>
<tr><td>23</td><td>Arizona</td><td>28.2</td><td>3</td><td>Maryland</td><td>41.9</td></tr>
<tr><td>13</td><td>Arkansas</td><td>34.3</td><td>4</td><td>Florida</td><td>40.2</td></tr>
<tr><td>NA</td><td>California**</td><td>NA</td><td>5</td><td>Delaware</td><td>39.0</td></tr>
<tr><td>NA</td><td>Colorado**</td><td>NA</td><td>6</td><td>South Carolina</td><td>38.6</td></tr>
<tr><td>19</td><td>Connecticut</td><td>30.1</td><td>7</td><td>Texas</td><td>38.5</td></tr>
<tr><td>5</td><td>Delaware</td><td>39.0</td><td>8</td><td>Tennessee</td><td>38.3</td></tr>
<tr><td>4</td><td>Florida</td><td>40.2</td><td>9</td><td>New York</td><td>35.3</td></tr>
<tr><td>2</td><td>Georgia</td><td>43.1</td><td>9</td><td>North Carolina</td><td>35.3</td></tr>
<tr><td>15</td><td>Hawaii</td><td>32.9</td><td>11</td><td>Nevada</td><td>35.1</td></tr>
<tr><td>36</td><td>Idaho</td><td>22.0</td><td>12</td><td>Illinois</td><td>35.0</td></tr>
<tr><td>12</td><td>Illinois</td><td>35.0</td><td>13</td><td>Arkansas</td><td>34.3</td></tr>
<tr><td>21</td><td>Indiana</td><td>28.7</td><td>14</td><td>Oklahoma</td><td>33.3</td></tr>
<tr><td>31</td><td>Iowa</td><td>24.9</td><td>15</td><td>Hawaii</td><td>32.9</td></tr>
<tr><td>27</td><td>Kansas</td><td>25.9</td><td>16</td><td>Michigan</td><td>32.6</td></tr>
<tr><td>25</td><td>Kentucky</td><td>27.4</td><td>17</td><td>Ohio</td><td>32.0</td></tr>
<tr><td>NA</td><td>Louisiana**</td><td>NA</td><td>17</td><td>West Virginia</td><td>32.0</td></tr>
<tr><td>33</td><td>Maine</td><td>23.6</td><td>19</td><td>Connecticut</td><td>30.1</td></tr>
<tr><td>3</td><td>Maryland</td><td>41.9</td><td>20</td><td>Missouri</td><td>29.6</td></tr>
<tr><td>22</td><td>Massachusetts</td><td>28.4</td><td>21</td><td>Indiana</td><td>28.7</td></tr>
<tr><td>16</td><td>Michigan</td><td>32.6</td><td>22</td><td>Massachusetts</td><td>28.4</td></tr>
<tr><td>NA</td><td>Minnesota**</td><td>NA</td><td>23</td><td>Arizona</td><td>28.2</td></tr>
<tr><td>1</td><td>Mississippi</td><td>47.4</td><td>24</td><td>New Mexico</td><td>27.9</td></tr>
<tr><td>20</td><td>Missouri</td><td>29.6</td><td>25</td><td>Kentucky</td><td>27.4</td></tr>
<tr><td>35</td><td>Montana</td><td>22.2</td><td>25</td><td>Rhode Island</td><td>27.4</td></tr>
<tr><td>NA</td><td>Nebraska**</td><td>NA</td><td>27</td><td>Kansas</td><td>25.9</td></tr>
<tr><td>11</td><td>Nevada</td><td>35.1</td><td>28</td><td>Wisconsin</td><td>25.4</td></tr>
<tr><td>29</td><td>New Hampshire</td><td>25.1</td><td>29</td><td>New Hampshire</td><td>25.1</td></tr>
<tr><td>NA</td><td>New Jersey**</td><td>NA</td><td>30</td><td>North Dakota</td><td>25.0</td></tr>
<tr><td>24</td><td>New Mexico</td><td>27.9</td><td>31</td><td>Iowa</td><td>24.9</td></tr>
<tr><td>9</td><td>New York</td><td>35.3</td><td>32</td><td>South Dakota</td><td>23.8</td></tr>
<tr><td>9</td><td>North Carolina</td><td>35.3</td><td>33</td><td>Maine</td><td>23.6</td></tr>
<tr><td>30</td><td>North Dakota</td><td>25.0</td><td>34</td><td>Alaska</td><td>23.0</td></tr>
<tr><td>17</td><td>Ohio</td><td>32.0</td><td>35</td><td>Montana</td><td>22.2</td></tr>
<tr><td>14</td><td>Oklahoma</td><td>33.3</td><td>36</td><td>Idaho</td><td>22.0</td></tr>
<tr><td>NA</td><td>Oregon**</td><td>NA</td><td>37</td><td>Wyoming</td><td>20.8</td></tr>
<tr><td>NA</td><td>Pennsylvania**</td><td>NA</td><td>38</td><td>Utah</td><td>18.2</td></tr>
<tr><td>25</td><td>Rhode Island</td><td>27.4</td><td>NA</td><td>Alabama**</td><td>NA</td></tr>
<tr><td>6</td><td>South Carolina</td><td>38.6</td><td>NA</td><td>California**</td><td>NA</td></tr>
<tr><td>32</td><td>South Dakota</td><td>23.8</td><td>NA</td><td>Colorado**</td><td>NA</td></tr>
<tr><td>8</td><td>Tennessee</td><td>38.3</td><td>NA</td><td>Louisiana**</td><td>NA</td></tr>
<tr><td>7</td><td>Texas</td><td>38.5</td><td>NA</td><td>Minnesota**</td><td>NA</td></tr>
<tr><td>38</td><td>Utah</td><td>18.2</td><td>NA</td><td>Nebraska**</td><td>NA</td></tr>
<tr><td>NA</td><td>Vermont**</td><td>NA</td><td>NA</td><td>New Jersey**</td><td>NA</td></tr>
<tr><td>NA</td><td>Virginia**</td><td>NA</td><td>NA</td><td>Oregon**</td><td>NA</td></tr>
<tr><td>NA</td><td>Washington**</td><td>NA</td><td>NA</td><td>Pennsylvania**</td><td>NA</td></tr>
<tr><td>17</td><td>West Virginia</td><td>32.0</td><td>NA</td><td>Vermont**</td><td>NA</td></tr>
<tr><td>28</td><td>Wisconsin</td><td>25.4</td><td>NA</td><td>Virginia**</td><td>NA</td></tr>
<tr><td>37</td><td>Wyoming</td><td>20.8</td><td>NA</td><td>Washington**</td><td>NA</td></tr>
<tr><td></td><td></td><td></td><td></td><td>District of Columbia**</td><td>NA</td></tr>
</table>

Source: U.S. Department of Health and Human Services, Centers for Disease Control and Prevention
"Youth Risk Behavior Surveillance--U.S., 2007" (http://www.cdc.gov/HealthyYouth/yrbs/)
*National figure includes nonreporting states.
**Not available.

Percent of Eighth Grade Students Who Use a Computer at Home: 2007

National Percent = 90%*

ALPHA ORDER				RANK ORDER		
RANK	STATE	PERCENT		RANK	STATE	PERCENT
39	Alabama	88		1	Connecticut	96
NA	Alaska**	NA		1	Massachusetts	96
43	Arizona	87		1	New Hampshire	96
48	Arkansas	84		4	Maryland	95
39	California	88		5	Maine	94
22	Colorado	91		5	Minnesota	94
1	Connecticut	96		5	New Jersey	94
22	Delaware	91		5	New York	94
16	Florida	92		5	Pennsylvania	94
34	Georgia	89		10	Iowa	93
34	Hawaii	89		10	North Dakota	93
16	Idaho	92		10	Utah	93
22	Illinois	91		10	Vermont	93
22	Indiana	91		10	Virginia	93
10	Iowa	93		10	Wisconsin	93
29	Kansas	90		16	Florida	92
39	Kentucky	88		16	Idaho	92
44	Louisiana	86		16	Michigan	92
5	Maine	94		16	Rhode Island	92
4	Maryland	95		16	Washington	92
1	Massachusetts	96		16	Wyoming	92
16	Michigan	92		22	Colorado	91
5	Minnesota	94		22	Delaware	91
47	Mississippi	85		22	Illinois	91
34	Missouri	89		22	Indiana	91
29	Montana	90		22	Nebraska	91
22	Nebraska	91		22	Ohio	91
29	Nevada	90		22	South Dakota	91
1	New Hampshire	96		29	Kansas	90
5	New Jersey	94		29	Montana	90
49	New Mexico	82		29	Nevada	90
5	New York	94		29	North Carolina	90
29	North Carolina	90		29	West Virginia	90
10	North Dakota	93		34	Georgia	89
22	Ohio	91		34	Hawaii	89
44	Oklahoma	86		34	Missouri	89
34	Oregon	89		34	Oregon	89
5	Pennsylvania	94		34	South Carolina	89
16	Rhode Island	92		39	Alabama	88
34	South Carolina	89		39	California	88
22	South Dakota	91		39	Kentucky	88
39	Tennessee	88		39	Tennessee	88
44	Texas	86		43	Arizona	87
10	Utah	93		44	Louisiana	86
10	Vermont	93		44	Oklahoma	86
10	Virginia	93		44	Texas	86
16	Washington	92		47	Mississippi	85
29	West Virginia	90		48	Arkansas	84
10	Wisconsin	93		49	New Mexico	82
16	Wyoming	92		NA	Alaska**	NA
					District of Columbia	82

Source: U.S. Department of Education, National Center for Education Statistics
    "The Nation's Report Card: Mathematics 2007" (http://nces.ed.gov/nationsreportcard/)
*Students were asked, "Is there a computer at home that you use?"
**Not available.

Percent of Fourth Grade Students Who Use a Computer at Home: 2007

National Percent = 86%*

ALPHA ORDER				RANK ORDER		
RANK	STATE	PERCENT		RANK	STATE	PERCENT
40	Alabama	83		1	Massachusetts	94
NA	Alaska**	NA		1	New Hampshire	94
45	Arizona	82		3	New Jersey	92
49	Arkansas	79		4	Connecticut	91
34	California	85		4	Maine	91
27	Colorado	86		4	Minnesota	91
4	Connecticut	91		4	Pennsylvania	91
17	Delaware	88		8	Maryland	90
14	Florida	89		8	New York	90
34	Georgia	85		8	North Dakota	90
27	Hawaii	86		8	Rhode Island	90
20	Idaho	87		8	Utah	90
27	Illinois	86		8	Vermont	90
27	Indiana	86		14	Florida	89
17	Iowa	88		14	Michigan	89
20	Kansas	87		14	Virginia	89
40	Kentucky	83		17	Delaware	88
40	Louisiana	83		17	Iowa	88
4	Maine	91		17	Wisconsin	88
8	Maryland	90		20	Idaho	87
1	Massachusetts	94		20	Kansas	87
14	Michigan	89		20	Missouri	87
4	Minnesota	91		20	Ohio	87
47	Mississippi	80		20	South Dakota	87
20	Missouri	87		20	Washington	87
34	Montana	85		20	Wyoming	87
27	Nebraska	86		27	Colorado	86
40	Nevada	83		27	Hawaii	86
1	New Hampshire	94		27	Illinois	86
3	New Jersey	92		27	Indiana	86
47	New Mexico	80		27	Nebraska	86
8	New York	90		27	Oregon	86
38	North Carolina	84		27	South Carolina	86
8	North Dakota	90		34	California	85
20	Ohio	87		34	Georgia	85
40	Oklahoma	83		34	Montana	85
27	Oregon	86		34	West Virginia	85
4	Pennsylvania	91		38	North Carolina	84
8	Rhode Island	90		38	Tennessee	84
27	South Carolina	86		40	Alabama	83
20	South Dakota	87		40	Kentucky	83
38	Tennessee	84		40	Louisiana	83
45	Texas	82		40	Nevada	83
8	Utah	90		40	Oklahoma	83
8	Vermont	90		45	Arizona	82
14	Virginia	89		45	Texas	82
20	Washington	87		47	Mississippi	80
34	West Virginia	85		47	New Mexico	80
17	Wisconsin	88		49	Arkansas	79
20	Wyoming	87		NA	Alaska**	NA
					District of Columbia	80

Source: U.S. Department of Education, National Center for Education Statistics
   "The Nation's Report Card: Mathematics 2007" (http://nces.ed.gov/nationsreportcard/)
*Students were asked, "Is there a computer at home that you use?"
**Not available.

Percent of Eighth Grade Students Who Talk About
Their Studies at Home Every Day: 2007
National Percent = 19%*

ALPHA ORDER

RANK	STATE	PERCENT
21	Alabama	19
NA	Alaska**	NA
21	Arizona	19
21	Arkansas	19
11	California	20
5	Colorado	21
21	Connecticut	19
5	Delaware	21
11	Florida	20
11	Georgia	20
49	Hawaii	15
3	Idaho	22
41	Illinois	17
43	Indiana	16
43	Iowa	16
21	Kansas	19
43	Kentucky	16
11	Louisiana	20
21	Maine	19
21	Maryland	19
35	Massachusetts	18
11	Michigan	20
21	Minnesota	19
21	Mississippi	19
11	Missouri	20
5	Montana	21
35	Nebraska	18
21	Nevada	19
43	New Hampshire	16
11	New Jersey	20
11	New Mexico	20
35	New York	18
5	North Carolina	21
43	North Dakota	16
43	Ohio	16
21	Oklahoma	19
5	Oregon	21
35	Pennsylvania	18
41	Rhode Island	17
5	South Carolina	21
21	South Dakota	19
35	Tennessee	18
11	Texas	20
2	Utah	23
3	Vermont	22
35	Virginia	18
11	Washington	20
21	West Virginia	19
21	Wisconsin	19
1	Wyoming	24

RANK ORDER

RANK	STATE	PERCENT
1	Wyoming	24
2	Utah	23
3	Idaho	22
3	Vermont	22
5	Colorado	21
5	Delaware	21
5	Montana	21
5	North Carolina	21
5	Oregon	21
5	South Carolina	21
11	California	20
11	Florida	20
11	Georgia	20
11	Louisiana	20
11	Michigan	20
11	Missouri	20
11	New Jersey	20
11	New Mexico	20
11	Texas	20
11	Washington	20
21	Alabama	19
21	Arizona	19
21	Arkansas	19
21	Connecticut	19
21	Kansas	19
21	Maine	19
21	Maryland	19
21	Minnesota	19
21	Mississippi	19
21	Nevada	19
21	Oklahoma	19
21	South Dakota	19
21	West Virginia	19
21	Wisconsin	19
35	Massachusetts	18
35	Nebraska	18
35	New York	18
35	Pennsylvania	18
35	Tennessee	18
35	Virginia	18
41	Illinois	17
41	Rhode Island	17
43	Indiana	16
43	Iowa	16
43	Kentucky	16
43	New Hampshire	16
43	North Dakota	16
43	Ohio	16
49	Hawaii	15
NA	Alaska**	NA
	District of Columbia	22

Source: U.S. Department of Education, National Center for Education Statistics
    "The Nation's Report Card: Mathematics 2007" (http://nces.ed.gov/nationsreportcard/)
*Percent of students who answered that they talked about their studies at home every day.
**Not available.

Percent of Fourth Grade Students Who Talk About Their Studies at Home Every Day: 2007
National Percent = 37%*

ALPHA ORDER

RANK	STATE	PERCENT
4	Alabama	38
NA	Alaska**	NA
2	Arizona	39
22	Arkansas	36
4	California	38
2	Colorado	39
33	Connecticut	35
4	Delaware	38
11	Florida	37
11	Georgia	37
49	Hawaii	32
11	Idaho	37
11	Illinois	37
42	Indiana	34
42	Iowa	34
33	Kansas	35
33	Kentucky	35
4	Louisiana	38
22	Maine	36
33	Maryland	35
45	Massachusetts	33
33	Michigan	35
42	Minnesota	34
4	Mississippi	38
11	Missouri	37
11	Montana	37
22	Nebraska	36
11	Nevada	37
33	New Hampshire	35
33	New Jersey	35
4	New Mexico	38
22	New York	36
11	North Carolina	37
45	North Dakota	33
33	Ohio	35
22	Oklahoma	36
11	Oregon	37
22	Pennsylvania	36
45	Rhode Island	33
22	South Carolina	36
22	South Dakota	36
22	Tennessee	36
4	Texas	38
11	Utah	37
22	Vermont	36
33	Virginia	35
11	Washington	37
45	West Virginia	33
22	Wisconsin	36
1	Wyoming	41

RANK ORDER

RANK	STATE	PERCENT
1	Wyoming	41
2	Arizona	39
2	Colorado	39
4	Alabama	38
4	California	38
4	Delaware	38
4	Louisiana	38
4	Mississippi	38
4	New Mexico	38
4	Texas	38
11	Florida	37
11	Georgia	37
11	Idaho	37
11	Illinois	37
11	Missouri	37
11	Montana	37
11	Nevada	37
11	North Carolina	37
11	Oregon	37
11	Utah	37
11	Washington	37
22	Arkansas	36
22	Maine	36
22	Nebraska	36
22	New York	36
22	Oklahoma	36
22	Pennsylvania	36
22	South Carolina	36
22	South Dakota	36
22	Tennessee	36
22	Vermont	36
22	Wisconsin	36
33	Connecticut	35
33	Kansas	35
33	Kentucky	35
33	Maryland	35
33	Michigan	35
33	New Hampshire	35
33	New Jersey	35
33	Ohio	35
33	Virginia	35
42	Indiana	34
42	Iowa	34
42	Minnesota	34
45	Massachusetts	33
45	North Dakota	33
45	Rhode Island	33
45	West Virginia	33
49	Hawaii	32
NA	Alaska**	NA
	District of Columbia	46

Source: U.S. Department of Education, National Center for Education Statistics
"The Nation's Report Card: Mathematics 2007" (http://nces.ed.gov/nationsreportcard/)
*Percent of students who answered that they talked about their studies at home every day.
**Not available.

V. Special Education

Total Federal Government Special Education Grants to States in 2008

National Total = $11,068,573,364*

ALPHA ORDER

RANK	STATE	GRANTS	% of USA
22	Alabama	$178,333,270	1.6%
45	Alaska	35,612,037	0.3%
23	Arizona	178,168,543	1.6%
32	Arkansas	111,882,711	1.0%
1	California	1,203,813,321	10.9%
26	Colorado	148,962,255	1.3%
28	Connecticut	131,190,828	1.2%
46	Delaware	32,915,981	0.3%
4	Florida	616,607,451	5.6%
11	Georgia	313,608,596	2.8%
43	Hawaii	38,919,867	0.4%
40	Idaho	53,738,443	0.5%
5	Illinois	498,680,342	4.5%
14	Indiana	251,799,927	2.3%
30	Iowa	119,956,116	1.1%
33	Kansas	105,826,164	1.0%
25	Kentucky	160,064,152	1.4%
21	Louisiana	186,284,322	1.7%
39	Maine	54,478,220	0.5%
19	Maryland	196,857,052	1.8%
12	Massachusetts	279,522,356	2.5%
8	Michigan	393,055,765	3.6%
20	Minnesota	187,716,218	1.7%
31	Mississippi	117,261,207	1.1%
16	Missouri	221,786,128	2.0%
44	Montana	36,283,292	0.3%
37	Nebraska	73,186,150	0.7%
38	Nevada	67,231,011	0.6%
41	New Hampshire	46,635,897	0.4%
9	New Jersey	354,725,385	3.2%
35	New Mexico	89,755,351	0.8%
3	New York	754,682,168	6.8%
10	North Carolina	315,735,766	2.9%
49	North Dakota	26,518,785	0.2%
6	Ohio	428,304,772	3.9%
27	Oklahoma	144,154,312	1.3%
29	Oregon	126,364,102	1.1%
7	Pennsylvania	419,699,480	3.8%
42	Rhode Island	43,205,910	0.4%
24	South Carolina	173,493,803	1.6%
47	South Dakota	32,086,247	0.3%
15	Tennessee	228,416,992	2.1%
2	Texas	938,576,795	8.5%
34	Utah	105,752,891	1.0%
50	Vermont	25,648,124	0.2%
13	Virginia	276,667,389	2.5%
17	Washington	218,396,927	2.0%
36	West Virginia	75,606,332	0.7%
18	Wisconsin	207,176,069	1.9%
48	Wyoming	27,058,853	0.2%

RANK ORDER

RANK	STATE	GRANTS	% of USA
1	California	$1,203,813,321	10.9%
2	Texas	938,576,795	8.5%
3	New York	754,682,168	6.8%
4	Florida	616,607,451	5.6%
5	Illinois	498,680,342	4.5%
6	Ohio	428,304,772	3.9%
7	Pennsylvania	419,699,480	3.8%
8	Michigan	393,055,765	3.6%
9	New Jersey	354,725,385	3.2%
10	North Carolina	315,735,766	2.9%
11	Georgia	313,608,596	2.8%
12	Massachusetts	279,522,356	2.5%
13	Virginia	276,667,389	2.5%
14	Indiana	251,799,927	2.3%
15	Tennessee	228,416,992	2.1%
16	Missouri	221,786,128	2.0%
17	Washington	218,396,927	2.0%
18	Wisconsin	207,176,069	1.9%
19	Maryland	196,857,052	1.8%
20	Minnesota	187,716,218	1.7%
21	Louisiana	186,284,322	1.7%
22	Alabama	178,333,270	1.6%
23	Arizona	178,168,543	1.6%
24	South Carolina	173,493,803	1.6%
25	Kentucky	160,064,152	1.4%
26	Colorado	148,962,255	1.3%
27	Oklahoma	144,154,312	1.3%
28	Connecticut	131,190,828	1.2%
29	Oregon	126,364,102	1.1%
30	Iowa	119,956,116	1.1%
31	Mississippi	117,261,207	1.1%
32	Arkansas	111,882,711	1.0%
33	Kansas	105,826,164	1.0%
34	Utah	105,752,891	1.0%
35	New Mexico	89,755,351	0.8%
36	West Virginia	75,606,332	0.7%
37	Nebraska	73,186,150	0.7%
38	Nevada	67,231,011	0.6%
39	Maine	54,478,220	0.5%
40	Idaho	53,738,443	0.5%
41	New Hampshire	46,635,897	0.4%
42	Rhode Island	43,205,910	0.4%
43	Hawaii	38,919,867	0.4%
44	Montana	36,283,292	0.3%
45	Alaska	35,612,037	0.3%
46	Delaware	32,915,981	0.3%
47	South Dakota	32,086,247	0.3%
48	Wyoming	27,058,853	0.2%
49	North Dakota	26,518,785	0.2%
50	Vermont	25,648,124	0.2%
	District of Columbia	16,169,289	0.1%

Source: CQ Press using data from U.S. Department of Education, Budget Office
    "FY 2001-2009 State Tables" (http://www.ed.gov/about/overview/budget/statetables/index.html)
*Estimates for fiscal year 2008 appropriation. Includes grants for special education of children with disabilities from birth through age 21. Does not include $253,037,487 in grants to U.S. territories and Indian tribe set-aside.

Per Capita Total Federal Government
Special Education Grants to States in 2008
National Per Capita = $36.70*

ALPHA ORDER				RANK ORDER		
RANK	**STATE**	**PER CAPITA**		**RANK**	**STATE**	**PER CAPITA**
25	Alabama	$38.53		1	Alaska	$52.10
1	Alaska	52.10		2	Wyoming	51.75
49	Arizona	28.11		3	New Mexico	45.56
19	Arkansas	39.47		4	Louisiana	43.39
45	California	32.93		5	Massachusetts	43.34
47	Colorado	30.64		6	West Virginia	41.72
31	Connecticut	37.46		7	North Dakota	41.45
27	Delaware	38.06		8	Maine	41.36
41	Florida	33.78		9	Vermont	41.28
46	Georgia	32.86		10	Nebraska	41.24
48	Hawaii	30.33		11	New Jersey	40.84
37	Idaho	35.84		11	Rhode Island	40.84
24	Illinois	38.80		13	South Dakota	40.30
18	Indiana	39.68		14	Mississippi	40.17
15	Iowa	40.15		15	Iowa	40.15
26	Kansas	38.12		16	Utah	39.98
29	Kentucky	37.74		17	Oklahoma	39.85
4	Louisiana	43.39		18	Indiana	39.68
8	Maine	41.36		19	Arkansas	39.47
39	Maryland	35.04		20	South Carolina	39.36
5	Massachusetts	43.34		21	Texas	39.26
23	Michigan	39.03		22	New York	39.11
35	Minnesota	36.12		23	Michigan	39.03
14	Mississippi	40.17		24	Illinois	38.80
30	Missouri	37.73		25	Alabama	38.53
28	Montana	37.88		26	Kansas	38.12
10	Nebraska	41.24		27	Delaware	38.06
50	Nevada	26.21		28	Montana	37.88
38	New Hampshire	35.44		29	Kentucky	37.74
11	New Jersey	40.84		30	Missouri	37.73
3	New Mexico	45.56		31	Connecticut	37.46
22	New York	39.11		32	Ohio	37.35
40	North Carolina	34.85		33	Tennessee	37.10
7	North Dakota	41.45		34	Wisconsin	36.98
32	Ohio	37.35		35	Minnesota	36.12
17	Oklahoma	39.85		36	Virginia	35.87
44	Oregon	33.72		37	Idaho	35.84
42	Pennsylvania	33.76		38	New Hampshire	35.44
11	Rhode Island	40.84		39	Maryland	35.04
20	South Carolina	39.36		40	North Carolina	34.85
13	South Dakota	40.30		41	Florida	33.78
33	Tennessee	37.10		42	Pennsylvania	33.76
21	Texas	39.26		42	Washington	33.76
16	Utah	39.98		44	Oregon	33.72
9	Vermont	41.28		45	California	32.93
36	Virginia	35.87		46	Georgia	32.86
42	Washington	33.76		47	Colorado	30.64
6	West Virginia	41.72		48	Hawaii	30.33
34	Wisconsin	36.98		49	Arizona	28.11
2	Wyoming	51.75		50	Nevada	26.21
					District of Columbia	27.49

Source: CQ Press using data from U.S. Department of Education, Budget Office
   "FY 2001-2009 State Tables" (http://www.ed.gov/about/overview/budget/statetables/index.html)
*Estimates for fiscal year 2008 appropriation. Includes grants for special education of children with disabilities from birth through age 21. Does not include grants or population in U.S. territories and Indian tribe set-aside. Per capita calculated using 2007 population estimates.

Percent Change in Federal Government
Special Education Grants to States: 2004 to 2008
National Percent Change = 8.3% Increase*

ALPHA ORDER

RANK	STATE	PERCENT CHANGE
21	Alabama	7.4
9	Alaska	12.2
1	Arizona	12.8
21	Arkansas	7.4
18	California	8.2
11	Colorado	11.1
36	Connecticut	7.3
5	Delaware	12.7
18	Florida	8.2
1	Georgia	12.8
21	Hawaii	7.4
16	Idaho	8.3
36	Illinois	7.3
36	Indiana	7.3
21	Iowa	7.4
36	Kansas	7.3
20	Kentucky	8.1
13	Louisiana	9.3
47	Maine	7.2
21	Maryland	7.4
36	Massachusetts	7.3
21	Michigan	7.4
36	Minnesota	7.3
36	Mississippi	7.3
21	Missouri	7.4
15	Montana	8.6
21	Nebraska	7.4
1	Nevada	12.8
21	New Hampshire	7.4
21	New Jersey	7.4
36	New Mexico	7.3
47	New York	7.2
10	North Carolina	11.7
1	North Dakota	12.8
21	Ohio	7.4
21	Oklahoma	7.4
21	Oregon	7.4
21	Pennsylvania	7.4
36	Rhode Island	7.3
36	South Carolina	7.3
8	South Dakota	12.6
21	Tennessee	7.4
12	Texas	9.4
14	Utah	8.7
5	Vermont	12.7
16	Virginia	8.3
36	Washington	7.3
47	West Virginia	7.2
47	Wisconsin	7.2
5	Wyoming	12.7

RANK ORDER

RANK	STATE	PERCENT CHANGE
1	Arizona	12.8
1	Georgia	12.8
1	Nevada	12.8
1	North Dakota	12.8
5	Delaware	12.7
5	Vermont	12.7
5	Wyoming	12.7
8	South Dakota	12.6
9	Alaska	12.2
10	North Carolina	11.7
11	Colorado	11.1
12	Texas	9.4
13	Louisiana	9.3
14	Utah	8.7
15	Montana	8.6
16	Idaho	8.3
16	Virginia	8.3
18	California	8.2
18	Florida	8.2
20	Kentucky	8.1
21	Alabama	7.4
21	Arkansas	7.4
21	Hawaii	7.4
21	Iowa	7.4
21	Maryland	7.4
21	Michigan	7.4
21	Missouri	7.4
21	Nebraska	7.4
21	New Hampshire	7.4
21	New Jersey	7.4
21	Ohio	7.4
21	Oklahoma	7.4
21	Oregon	7.4
21	Pennsylvania	7.4
21	Tennessee	7.4
36	Connecticut	7.3
36	Illinois	7.3
36	Indiana	7.3
36	Kansas	7.3
36	Massachusetts	7.3
36	Minnesota	7.3
36	Mississippi	7.3
36	New Mexico	7.3
36	Rhode Island	7.3
36	South Carolina	7.3
36	Washington	7.3
47	Maine	7.2
47	New York	7.2
47	West Virginia	7.2
47	Wisconsin	7.2

District of Columbia   13.1

Source: CQ Press using data from U.S. Department of Education, Budget Office
   "FY 2001-2009 State Tables" (http://www.ed.gov/about/overview/budget/statetables/index.html)
*Based on estimates for fiscal year 2008 appropriation. Includes grants for special education of children with disabilities from birth through age 21. Does not include grants to U.S. territories and Indian tribe set-aside.

Percent Change in Per Capita Federal Government
Special Education Grants to States: 2004 to 2008
National Percent Change = 5.2% Increase*

ALPHA ORDER

RANK	STATE	PERCENT CHANGE
37	Alabama	4.6
6	Alaska	8.6
47	Arizona	2.3
39	Arkansas	3.9
21	California	5.8
29	Colorado	5.3
15	Connecticut	6.7
8	Delaware	7.9
42	Florida	2.8
24	Georgia	5.5
35	Hawaii	4.9
49	Idaho	0.5
19	Illinois	5.9
31	Indiana	5.2
19	Iowa	5.9
24	Kansas	5.5
24	Kentucky	5.5
1	Louisiana	14.3
17	Maine	6.5
21	Maryland	5.8
11	Massachusetts	7.1
9	Michigan	7.7
33	Minnesota	5.0
18	Mississippi	6.1
33	Missouri	5.0
32	Montana	5.1
24	Nebraska	5.5
46	Nevada	2.5
23	New Hampshire	5.6
13	New Jersey	6.8
40	New Mexico	3.1
12	New York	7.0
29	North Carolina	5.3
2	North Dakota	12.3
10	Ohio	7.2
38	Oklahoma	4.4
43	Oregon	2.7
16	Pennsylvania	6.6
5	Rhode Island	8.8
47	South Carolina	2.3
4	South Dakota	9.5
40	Tennessee	3.1
43	Texas	2.7
50	Utah	(0.1)
2	Vermont	12.3
36	Virginia	4.8
43	Washington	2.7
13	West Virginia	6.8
28	Wisconsin	5.4
7	Wyoming	8.4

RANK ORDER

RANK	STATE	PERCENT CHANGE
1	Louisiana	14.3
2	North Dakota	12.3
2	Vermont	12.3
4	South Dakota	9.5
5	Rhode Island	8.8
6	Alaska	8.6
7	Wyoming	8.4
8	Delaware	7.9
9	Michigan	7.7
10	Ohio	7.2
11	Massachusetts	7.1
12	New York	7.0
13	New Jersey	6.8
13	West Virginia	6.8
15	Connecticut	6.7
16	Pennsylvania	6.6
17	Maine	6.5
18	Mississippi	6.1
19	Illinois	5.9
19	Iowa	5.9
21	California	5.8
21	Maryland	5.8
23	New Hampshire	5.6
24	Georgia	5.5
24	Kansas	5.5
24	Kentucky	5.5
24	Nebraska	5.5
28	Wisconsin	5.4
29	Colorado	5.3
29	North Carolina	5.3
31	Indiana	5.2
32	Montana	5.1
33	Minnesota	5.0
33	Missouri	5.0
35	Hawaii	4.9
36	Virginia	4.8
37	Alabama	4.6
38	Oklahoma	4.4
39	Arkansas	3.9
40	New Mexico	3.1
40	Tennessee	3.1
42	Florida	2.8
43	Oregon	2.7
43	Texas	2.7
43	Washington	2.7
46	Nevada	2.5
47	Arizona	2.3
47	South Carolina	2.3
49	Idaho	0.5
50	Utah	(0.1)

	District of Columbia	11.5

Source: CQ Press using data from U.S. Department of Education, Budget Office
   "FY 2001-2009 State Tables" (http://www.ed.gov/about/overview/budget/statetables/index.html)
*Based on estimates for fiscal year 2008 appropriation. Includes grants for special education of children with disabilities from birth through age 21. Does not include grants or population in U.S. territories and Indian tribe set-aside. Per capita for 2008 calculated using 2007 population estimates.

Federal Government Pre-School Special Education Grants to States in 2008

National Total = $374,099,280*

ALPHA ORDER

RANK	STATE	GRANTS	% of USA
24	Alabama	$5,506,029	1.5%
44	Alaska	1,241,975	0.3%
26	Arizona	5,259,801	1.4%
25	Arkansas	5,279,323	1.4%
1	California	37,840,710	10.2%
27	Colorado	4,871,136	1.3%
28	Connecticut	4,827,210	1.3%
45	Delaware	1,235,499	0.3%
4	Florida	18,170,242	4.9%
13	Georgia	9,637,532	2.6%
48	Hawaii	978,634	0.3%
40	Idaho	2,152,049	0.6%
5	Illinois	17,369,463	4.7%
16	Indiana	8,757,566	2.4%
31	Iowa	3,928,346	1.1%
29	Kansas	4,265,253	1.1%
11	Kentucky	10,051,610	2.7%
22	Louisiana	6,372,736	1.7%
37	Maine	2,473,552	0.7%
21	Maryland	6,566,015	1.8%
12	Massachusetts	9,735,466	2.6%
7	Michigan	12,355,632	3.3%
18	Minnesota	7,310,811	2.0%
30	Mississippi	4,160,483	1.1%
23	Missouri	5,900,044	1.6%
46	Montana	1,162,983	0.3%
38	Nebraska	2,220,152	0.6%
39	Nevada	2,205,315	0.6%
42	New Hampshire	1,533,160	0.4%
9	New Jersey	11,197,629	3.0%
36	New Mexico	3,137,318	0.8%
2	New York	33,216,002	9.0%
10	North Carolina	11,133,329	3.0%
50	North Dakota	794,614	0.2%
8	Ohio	12,321,462	3.3%
33	Oklahoma	3,580,349	1.0%
32	Oregon	3,794,137	1.0%
6	Pennsylvania	13,749,342	3.7%
41	Rhode Island	1,645,016	0.4%
19	South Carolina	7,027,486	1.9%
43	South Dakota	1,442,067	0.4%
20	Tennessee	6,775,233	1.8%
3	Texas	22,438,331	6.0%
34	Utah	3,504,241	0.9%
49	Vermont	845,111	0.2%
15	Virginia	8,983,286	2.4%
17	Washington	8,039,547	2.2%
35	West Virginia	3,428,679	0.9%
14	Wisconsin	9,322,204	2.5%
47	Wyoming	1,038,035	0.3%

RANK ORDER

RANK	STATE	GRANTS	% of USA
1	California	$37,840,710	10.2%
2	New York	33,216,002	9.0%
3	Texas	22,438,331	6.0%
4	Florida	18,170,242	4.9%
5	Illinois	17,369,463	4.7%
6	Pennsylvania	13,749,342	3.7%
7	Michigan	12,355,632	3.3%
8	Ohio	12,321,462	3.3%
9	New Jersey	11,197,629	3.0%
10	North Carolina	11,133,329	3.0%
11	Kentucky	10,051,610	2.7%
12	Massachusetts	9,735,466	2.6%
13	Georgia	9,637,532	2.6%
14	Wisconsin	9,322,204	2.5%
15	Virginia	8,983,286	2.4%
16	Indiana	8,757,566	2.4%
17	Washington	8,039,547	2.2%
18	Minnesota	7,310,811	2.0%
19	South Carolina	7,027,486	1.9%
20	Tennessee	6,775,233	1.8%
21	Maryland	6,566,015	1.8%
22	Louisiana	6,372,736	1.7%
23	Missouri	5,900,044	1.6%
24	Alabama	5,506,029	1.5%
25	Arkansas	5,279,323	1.4%
26	Arizona	5,259,801	1.4%
27	Colorado	4,871,136	1.3%
28	Connecticut	4,827,210	1.3%
29	Kansas	4,265,253	1.1%
30	Mississippi	4,160,483	1.1%
31	Iowa	3,928,346	1.1%
32	Oregon	3,794,137	1.0%
33	Oklahoma	3,580,349	1.0%
34	Utah	3,504,241	0.9%
35	West Virginia	3,428,679	0.9%
36	New Mexico	3,137,318	0.8%
37	Maine	2,473,552	0.7%
38	Nebraska	2,220,152	0.6%
39	Nevada	2,205,315	0.6%
40	Idaho	2,152,049	0.6%
41	Rhode Island	1,645,016	0.4%
42	New Hampshire	1,533,160	0.4%
43	South Dakota	1,442,067	0.4%
44	Alaska	1,241,975	0.3%
45	Delaware	1,235,499	0.3%
46	Montana	1,162,983	0.3%
47	Wyoming	1,038,035	0.3%
48	Hawaii	978,634	0.3%
49	Vermont	845,111	0.2%
50	North Dakota	794,614	0.2%
	District of Columbia	240,249	0.1%

Source: U.S. Department of Education, Budget Office
   "FY 2001-2009 State Tables" (http://www.ed.gov/about/overview/budget/statetables/index.html)
*Estimates for fiscal year 2008 appropriation. Grants for special education of children with disabilities ages 3 through 5. Does not include $3,251,552 in grants to Puerto Rico.

Per Capita Federal Government Pre-School Special Education Grants to States in 2008
National Per Capita = $1.23*

ALPHA ORDER

RANK	STATE	PER CAPITA
33	Alabama	$1.19
6	Alaska	1.82
49	Arizona	0.83
5	Arkansas	1.86
40	California	1.04
43	Colorado	1.00
20	Connecticut	1.38
17	Delaware	1.43
43	Florida	1.00
41	Georgia	1.01
50	Hawaii	0.76
16	Idaho	1.44
23	Illinois	1.35
20	Indiana	1.38
25	Iowa	1.31
13	Kansas	1.54
1	Kentucky	2.37
15	Louisiana	1.48
4	Maine	1.88
34	Maryland	1.17
14	Massachusetts	1.51
30	Michigan	1.23
19	Minnesota	1.41
17	Mississippi	1.43
43	Missouri	1.00
32	Montana	1.21
27	Nebraska	1.25
48	Nevada	0.86
34	New Hampshire	1.17
26	New Jersey	1.29
10	New Mexico	1.59
8	New York	1.72
30	North Carolina	1.23
28	North Dakota	1.24
39	Ohio	1.07
46	Oklahoma	0.99
41	Oregon	1.01
37	Pennsylvania	1.11
12	Rhode Island	1.56
10	South Carolina	1.59
7	South Dakota	1.81
38	Tennessee	1.10
47	Texas	0.94
24	Utah	1.32
22	Vermont	1.36
36	Virginia	1.16
28	Washington	1.24
3	West Virginia	1.89
9	Wisconsin	1.66
2	Wyoming	1.99

RANK ORDER

RANK	STATE	PER CAPITA
1	Kentucky	$2.37
2	Wyoming	1.99
3	West Virginia	1.89
4	Maine	1.88
5	Arkansas	1.86
6	Alaska	1.82
7	South Dakota	1.81
8	New York	1.72
9	Wisconsin	1.66
10	New Mexico	1.59
10	South Carolina	1.59
12	Rhode Island	1.56
13	Kansas	1.54
14	Massachusetts	1.51
15	Louisiana	1.48
16	Idaho	1.44
17	Delaware	1.43
17	Mississippi	1.43
19	Minnesota	1.41
20	Connecticut	1.38
20	Indiana	1.38
22	Vermont	1.36
23	Illinois	1.35
24	Utah	1.32
25	Iowa	1.31
26	New Jersey	1.29
27	Nebraska	1.25
28	North Dakota	1.24
28	Washington	1.24
30	Michigan	1.23
30	North Carolina	1.23
32	Montana	1.21
33	Alabama	1.19
34	Maryland	1.17
34	New Hampshire	1.17
36	Virginia	1.16
37	Pennsylvania	1.11
38	Tennessee	1.10
39	Ohio	1.07
40	California	1.04
41	Georgia	1.01
41	Oregon	1.01
43	Colorado	1.00
43	Florida	1.00
43	Missouri	1.00
46	Oklahoma	0.99
47	Texas	0.94
48	Nevada	0.86
49	Arizona	0.83
50	Hawaii	0.76
	District of Columbia	0.41

Source: CQ Press using data from U.S. Department of Education, Budget Office
   "FY 2001-2009 State Tables" (http://www.ed.gov/about/overview/budget/statetables/index.html)
*Estimates for fiscal year 2008 appropriation. Grants for special education of children with disabilities ages 3 through 5. Does not include grants or population in Puerto Rico. Per capita calculated using 2007 population estimates.

Federal Government Special Education Grants to States
for Youths Age 6 to 21 in 2008
National Total = $10,697,550,970*

ALPHA ORDER

RANK	STATE	GRANTS	% of USA
23	Alabama	$172,827,241	1.6%
45	Alaska	34,370,062	0.3%
22	Arizona	172,908,742	1.6%
32	Arkansas	106,603,388	1.0%
1	California	1,165,972,611	10.9%
26	Colorado	144,091,119	1.3%
28	Connecticut	126,363,618	1.2%
46	Delaware	31,680,482	0.3%
4	Florida	598,437,209	5.6%
11	Georgia	303,971,064	2.8%
43	Hawaii	37,941,233	0.4%
40	Idaho	51,586,394	0.5%
5	Illinois	481,310,879	4.5%
14	Indiana	243,042,361	2.3%
30	Iowa	116,027,770	1.1%
34	Kansas	101,560,911	0.9%
25	Kentucky	150,012,542	1.4%
21	Louisiana	179,911,586	1.7%
39	Maine	52,004,668	0.5%
19	Maryland	190,291,037	1.8%
12	Massachusetts	269,786,890	2.5%
8	Michigan	380,700,133	3.6%
20	Minnesota	180,405,407	1.7%
31	Mississippi	113,100,724	1.1%
16	Missouri	215,886,084	2.0%
44	Montana	35,120,309	0.3%
37	Nebraska	70,965,998	0.7%
38	Nevada	65,025,696	0.6%
41	New Hampshire	45,102,737	0.4%
9	New Jersey	343,527,756	3.2%
35	New Mexico	86,618,033	0.8%
3	New York	721,466,166	6.7%
10	North Carolina	304,602,437	2.8%
49	North Dakota	25,724,171	0.2%
6	Ohio	415,983,310	3.9%
27	Oklahoma	140,573,963	1.3%
29	Oregon	122,569,965	1.1%
7	Pennsylvania	405,950,138	3.8%
42	Rhode Island	41,560,894	0.4%
24	South Carolina	166,466,317	1.6%
47	South Dakota	30,644,180	0.3%
15	Tennessee	221,641,759	2.1%
2	Texas	916,138,464	8.6%
33	Utah	102,248,650	1.0%
50	Vermont	24,803,013	0.2%
13	Virginia	267,684,103	2.5%
17	Washington	210,357,380	2.0%
36	West Virginia	72,177,653	0.7%
18	Wisconsin	197,853,865	1.8%
48	Wyoming	26,020,818	0.2%

RANK ORDER

RANK	STATE	GRANTS	% of USA
1	California	$1,165,972,611	10.9%
2	Texas	916,138,464	8.6%
3	New York	721,466,166	6.7%
4	Florida	598,437,209	5.6%
5	Illinois	481,310,879	4.5%
6	Ohio	415,983,310	3.9%
7	Pennsylvania	405,950,138	3.8%
8	Michigan	380,700,133	3.6%
9	New Jersey	343,527,756	3.2%
10	North Carolina	304,602,437	2.8%
11	Georgia	303,971,064	2.8%
12	Massachusetts	269,786,890	2.5%
13	Virginia	267,684,103	2.5%
14	Indiana	243,042,361	2.3%
15	Tennessee	221,641,759	2.1%
16	Missouri	215,886,084	2.0%
17	Washington	210,357,380	2.0%
18	Wisconsin	197,853,865	1.8%
19	Maryland	190,291,037	1.8%
20	Minnesota	180,405,407	1.7%
21	Louisiana	179,911,586	1.7%
22	Arizona	172,908,742	1.6%
23	Alabama	172,827,241	1.6%
24	South Carolina	166,466,317	1.6%
25	Kentucky	150,012,542	1.4%
26	Colorado	144,091,119	1.3%
27	Oklahoma	140,573,963	1.3%
28	Connecticut	126,363,618	1.2%
29	Oregon	122,569,965	1.1%
30	Iowa	116,027,770	1.1%
31	Mississippi	113,100,724	1.1%
32	Arkansas	106,603,388	1.0%
33	Utah	102,248,650	1.0%
34	Kansas	101,560,911	0.9%
35	New Mexico	86,618,033	0.8%
36	West Virginia	72,177,653	0.7%
37	Nebraska	70,965,998	0.7%
38	Nevada	65,025,696	0.6%
39	Maine	52,004,668	0.5%
40	Idaho	51,586,394	0.5%
41	New Hampshire	45,102,737	0.4%
42	Rhode Island	41,560,894	0.4%
43	Hawaii	37,941,233	0.4%
44	Montana	35,120,309	0.3%
45	Alaska	34,370,062	0.3%
46	Delaware	31,680,482	0.3%
47	South Dakota	30,644,180	0.3%
48	Wyoming	26,020,818	0.2%
49	North Dakota	25,724,171	0.2%
50	Vermont	24,803,013	0.2%
	District of Columbia	15,929,040	0.1%

Source: U.S. Department of Education, Budget Office
   "FY 2001-2009 State Tables" (http://www.ed.gov/about/overview/budget/statetables/index.html)
*Estimates for fiscal year 2008 appropriation. Grants for special education of children with disabilities ages 6 through 21 years.
Does not include $249,960,601 in grants to U.S. territories and Indian tribe set-aside.

Per Capita Federal Government Special Education Grants to States for Youths Age 6 to 21 in 2008
National Per Capita = $35.47*

ALPHA ORDER

RANK	STATE	PER CAPITA
25	Alabama	$37.35
1	Alaska	50.29
49	Arizona	27.28
22	Arkansas	37.61
45	California	31.90
47	Colorado	29.64
31	Connecticut	36.08
28	Delaware	36.63
41	Florida	32.79
46	Georgia	31.85
48	Hawaii	29.56
37	Idaho	34.40
23	Illinois	37.45
19	Indiana	38.30
14	Iowa	38.83
29	Kansas	36.59
33	Kentucky	35.37
4	Louisiana	41.91
11	Maine	39.48
39	Maryland	33.87
5	Massachusetts	41.83
20	Michigan	37.80
35	Minnesota	34.71
15	Mississippi	38.75
26	Missouri	36.73
27	Montana	36.67
7	Nebraska	39.99
50	Nevada	25.35
38	New Hampshire	34.28
10	New Jersey	39.55
3	New Mexico	43.97
24	New York	37.39
40	North Carolina	33.62
6	North Dakota	40.21
30	Ohio	36.28
13	Oklahoma	38.86
42	Oregon	32.71
43	Pennsylvania	32.65
12	Rhode Island	39.29
21	South Carolina	37.77
17	South Dakota	38.49
32	Tennessee	36.00
18	Texas	38.33
16	Utah	38.65
8	Vermont	39.92
35	Virginia	34.71
44	Washington	32.52
9	West Virginia	39.83
34	Wisconsin	35.32
2	Wyoming	49.77

RANK ORDER

RANK	STATE	PER CAPITA
1	Alaska	$50.29
2	Wyoming	49.77
3	New Mexico	43.97
4	Louisiana	41.91
5	Massachusetts	41.83
6	North Dakota	40.21
7	Nebraska	39.99
8	Vermont	39.92
9	West Virginia	39.83
10	New Jersey	39.55
11	Maine	39.48
12	Rhode Island	39.29
13	Oklahoma	38.86
14	Iowa	38.83
15	Mississippi	38.75
16	Utah	38.65
17	South Dakota	38.49
18	Texas	38.33
19	Indiana	38.30
20	Michigan	37.80
21	South Carolina	37.77
22	Arkansas	37.61
23	Illinois	37.45
24	New York	37.39
25	Alabama	37.35
26	Missouri	36.73
27	Montana	36.67
28	Delaware	36.63
29	Kansas	36.59
30	Ohio	36.28
31	Connecticut	36.08
32	Tennessee	36.00
33	Kentucky	35.37
34	Wisconsin	35.32
35	Minnesota	34.71
35	Virginia	34.71
37	Idaho	34.40
38	New Hampshire	34.28
39	Maryland	33.87
40	North Carolina	33.62
41	Florida	32.79
42	Oregon	32.71
43	Pennsylvania	32.65
44	Washington	32.52
45	California	31.90
46	Georgia	31.85
47	Colorado	29.64
48	Hawaii	29.56
49	Arizona	27.28
50	Nevada	25.35
	District of Columbia	27.08

Source: CQ Press using data from U.S. Department of Education, Budget Office
   "FY 2001-2009 State Tables" (http://www.ed.gov/about/overview/budget/statetables/index.html)
*Estimates for fiscal year 2008 appropriation. Grants for special education of children with disabilities ages 6 through 21. Does not include grants or population in U.S. territories and Indian tribe set-aside. Per capita calculated using 2007 population estimates.

Federal Government Grants for Children Age 3 to 21
Served Under the Individuals with Disabilities Education Act (IDEA) in 2007
National Total = $10,915,537,584*

ALPHA ORDER

RANK	STATE	GRANTS	% of USA
22	Alabama	$176,085,539	1.6%
45	Alaska	34,815,500	0.3%
23	Arizona	173,208,753	1.6%
32	Arkansas	110,522,019	1.0%
1	California	1,188,852,930	10.9%
26	Colorado	146,949,854	1.3%
28	Connecticut	129,555,264	1.2%
46	Delaware	32,007,368	0.3%
4	Florida	608,811,968	5.6%
11	Georgia	304,864,006	2.8%
43	Hawaii	38,429,941	0.4%
40	Idaho	53,073,616	0.5%
5	Illinois	492,440,463	4.5%
14	Indiana	248,645,811	2.3%
30	Iowa	118,446,351	1.1%
33	Kansas	104,517,733	1.0%
25	Kentucky	158,190,906	1.4%
21	Louisiana	183,953,717	1.7%
39	Maine	53,812,816	0.5%
19	Maryland	194,386,913	1.8%
12	Massachusetts	276,021,384	2.5%
8	Michigan	388,106,144	3.6%
20	Minnesota	185,387,810	1.7%
31	Mississippi	115,796,178	1.1%
16	Missouri	218,974,530	2.0%
44	Montana	35,756,675	0.3%
37	Nebraska	72,260,971	0.7%
38	Nevada	65,365,691	0.6%
41	New Hampshire	46,049,113	0.4%
9	New Jersey	350,248,511	3.2%
35	New Mexico	88,631,511	0.8%
3	New York	745,433,945	6.8%
10	North Carolina	309,517,986	2.8%
49	North Dakota	25,785,114	0.2%
6	Ohio	422,899,881	3.9%
27	Oklahoma	142,324,703	1.3%
29	Oregon	124,772,966	1.1%
7	Pennsylvania	414,427,321	3.8%
42	Rhode Island	42,668,882	0.4%
24	South Carolina	171,349,759	1.6%
47	South Dakota	31,209,015	0.3%
15	Tennessee	225,528,597	2.1%
2	Texas	926,680,185	8.5%
34	Utah	103,619,332	0.9%
50	Vermont	24,941,508	0.2%
13	Virginia	273,182,997	2.5%
17	Washington	215,674,263	2.0%
36	West Virginia	74,682,745	0.7%
18	Wisconsin	204,643,113	1.9%
48	Wyoming	26,316,469	0.2%

RANK ORDER

RANK	STATE	GRANTS	% of USA
1	California	$1,188,852,930	10.9%
2	Texas	926,680,185	8.5%
3	New York	745,433,945	6.8%
4	Florida	608,811,968	5.6%
5	Illinois	492,440,463	4.5%
6	Ohio	422,899,881	3.9%
7	Pennsylvania	414,427,321	3.8%
8	Michigan	388,106,144	3.6%
9	New Jersey	350,248,511	3.2%
10	North Carolina	309,517,986	2.8%
11	Georgia	304,864,006	2.8%
12	Massachusetts	276,021,384	2.5%
13	Virginia	273,182,997	2.5%
14	Indiana	248,645,811	2.3%
15	Tennessee	225,528,597	2.1%
16	Missouri	218,974,530	2.0%
17	Washington	215,674,263	2.0%
18	Wisconsin	204,643,113	1.9%
19	Maryland	194,386,913	1.8%
20	Minnesota	185,387,810	1.7%
21	Louisiana	183,953,717	1.7%
22	Alabama	176,085,539	1.6%
23	Arizona	173,208,753	1.6%
24	South Carolina	171,349,759	1.6%
25	Kentucky	158,190,906	1.4%
26	Colorado	146,949,854	1.3%
27	Oklahoma	142,324,703	1.3%
28	Connecticut	129,555,264	1.2%
29	Oregon	124,772,966	1.1%
30	Iowa	118,446,351	1.1%
31	Mississippi	115,796,178	1.1%
32	Arkansas	110,522,019	1.0%
33	Kansas	104,517,733	1.0%
34	Utah	103,619,332	0.9%
35	New Mexico	88,631,511	0.8%
36	West Virginia	74,682,745	0.7%
37	Nebraska	72,260,971	0.7%
38	Nevada	65,365,691	0.6%
39	Maine	53,812,816	0.5%
40	Idaho	53,073,616	0.5%
41	New Hampshire	46,049,113	0.4%
42	Rhode Island	42,668,882	0.4%
43	Hawaii	38,429,941	0.4%
44	Montana	35,756,675	0.3%
45	Alaska	34,815,500	0.3%
46	Delaware	32,007,368	0.3%
47	South Dakota	31,209,015	0.3%
48	Wyoming	26,316,469	0.2%
49	North Dakota	25,785,114	0.2%
50	Vermont	24,941,508	0.2%
	District of Columbia	15,708,817	0.1%

Source: U.S. Department of Education, Office of Special Education Programs
    "Data Tables for OSEP State Reported Data" (https://www.ideadata.org/arc_toc8.asp)
*State grant awards under Individuals with Disabilities Education Act (IDEA) for fiscal year 2007. Includes part B, sections 611 and 619 (disabled children ages 3-21). National total does not include $226,595,110 in grants to U.S. territories and Bureau of Indian Affairs programs.

Federal Government Grants per Child Age 3 to 21
Served Under the Individuals with Disabilities Education Act (IDEA) in 2007
National Rate = $1,633 per Child Served*

ALPHA ORDER

RANK	STATE	PER CHILD
2	Alabama	$1,978
3	Alaska	1,960
49	Arizona	1,368
25	Arkansas	1,622
15	California	1,767
16	Colorado	1,759
8	Connecticut	1,874
23	Delaware	1,653
38	Florida	1,529
36	Georgia	1,549
12	Hawaii	1,821
9	Idaho	1,866
41	Illinois	1,507
48	Indiana	1,389
22	Iowa	1,659
33	Kansas	1,588
44	Kentucky	1,447
1	Louisiana	2,057
40	Maine	1,513
12	Maryland	1,821
21	Massachusetts	1,663
28	Michigan	1,604
34	Minnesota	1,572
19	Mississippi	1,713
36	Missouri	1,549
4	Montana	1,927
26	Nebraska	1,612
50	Nevada	1,355
43	New Hampshire	1,467
47	New Jersey	1,400
11	New Mexico	1,850
24	New York	1,649
27	North Carolina	1,608
10	North Dakota	1,865
35	Ohio	1,571
42	Oklahoma	1,485
29	Oregon	1,603
45	Pennsylvania	1,415
46	Rhode Island	1,411
31	South Carolina	1,596
18	South Dakota	1,751
6	Tennessee	1,875
6	Texas	1,875
20	Utah	1,694
14	Vermont	1,780
30	Virginia	1,599
17	Washington	1,754
39	West Virginia	1,522
32	Wisconsin	1,592
5	Wyoming	1,887

RANK ORDER

RANK	STATE	PER CHILD
1	Louisiana	$2,057
2	Alabama	1,978
3	Alaska	1,960
4	Montana	1,927
5	Wyoming	1,887
6	Tennessee	1,875
6	Texas	1,875
8	Connecticut	1,874
9	Idaho	1,866
10	North Dakota	1,865
11	New Mexico	1,850
12	Hawaii	1,821
12	Maryland	1,821
14	Vermont	1,780
15	California	1,767
16	Colorado	1,759
17	Washington	1,754
18	South Dakota	1,751
19	Mississippi	1,713
20	Utah	1,694
21	Massachusetts	1,663
22	Iowa	1,659
23	Delaware	1,653
24	New York	1,649
25	Arkansas	1,622
26	Nebraska	1,612
27	North Carolina	1,608
28	Michigan	1,604
29	Oregon	1,603
30	Virginia	1,599
31	South Carolina	1,596
32	Wisconsin	1,592
33	Kansas	1,588
34	Minnesota	1,572
35	Ohio	1,571
36	Georgia	1,549
36	Missouri	1,549
38	Florida	1,529
39	West Virginia	1,522
40	Maine	1,513
41	Illinois	1,507
42	Oklahoma	1,485
43	New Hampshire	1,467
44	Kentucky	1,447
45	Pennsylvania	1,415
46	Rhode Island	1,411
47	New Jersey	1,400
48	Indiana	1,389
49	Arizona	1,368
50	Nevada	1,355

	District of Columbia	1,414

Source: CQ Press using data from U.S. Department of Education, Office of Special Education Programs
  "Data Tables for OSEP State Reported Data" (https://www.ideadata.org/arc_toc8.asp)
*State grant awards under Individuals with Disabilities Education Act (IDEA) for fiscal year 2007. Includes part B, sections 611 and 619 (disabled children ages 3-21). National figure does not include grants or children in U.S. territories and Bureau of Indian Affairs programs. Calculated using figures for children served for school year 2006-2007.

Infants and Toddlers Receiving Early Intervention Services Under Individuals with Disabilities Education Act (IDEA) in 2007
National Total = 299,848 Children Aged Birth Through Two Years*

ALPHA ORDER					RANK ORDER			
RANK	STATE		CHILDREN	% of USA	RANK	STATE	CHILDREN	% of USA
35	Alabama		2,468	0.8%	1	California	34,343	11.5%
50	Alaska		595	0.2%	2	New York	30,988	10.3%
16	Arizona		5,299	1.8%	3	Texas	23,232	7.7%
26	Arkansas		3,217	1.1%	4	Illinois	16,613	5.5%
1	California		34,343	11.5%	5	Pennsylvania	14,957	5.0%
22	Colorado		3,951	1.3%	6	Massachusetts	14,878	5.0%
19	Connecticut		4,018	1.3%	7	Ohio	11,696	3.9%
46	Delaware		908	0.3%	8	Florida	11,468	3.8%
8	Florida		11,468	3.8%	9	Indiana	9,547	3.2%
15	Georgia		5,357	1.8%	10	New Jersey	9,310	3.1%
21	Hawaii		3,970	1.3%	11	Michigan	8,836	2.9%
37	Idaho		1,919	0.6%	12	North Carolina	7,500	2.5%
4	Illinois		16,613	5.5%	13	Maryland	6,717	2.2%
9	Indiana		9,547	3.2%	14	Wisconsin	5,494	1.8%
31	Iowa		2,932	1.0%	15	Georgia	5,357	1.8%
28	Kansas		3,117	1.0%	16	Arizona	5,299	1.8%
23	Kentucky		3,786	1.3%	17	Virginia	4,619	1.5%
36	Louisiana		2,325	0.8%	18	Washington	4,412	1.5%
43	Maine		1,023	0.3%	19	Connecticut	4,018	1.3%
13	Maryland		6,717	2.2%	20	Tennessee	4,014	1.3%
6	Massachusetts		14,878	5.0%	21	Hawaii	3,970	1.3%
11	Michigan		8,836	2.9%	22	Colorado	3,951	1.3%
24	Minnesota		3,578	1.2%	23	Kentucky	3,786	1.3%
40	Mississippi		1,546	0.5%	24	Minnesota	3,578	1.2%
27	Missouri		3,216	1.1%	25	South Carolina	3,381	1.1%
48	Montana		679	0.2%	26	Arkansas	3,217	1.1%
42	Nebraska		1,354	0.5%	27	Missouri	3,216	1.1%
41	Nevada		1,520	0.5%	28	Kansas	3,117	1.0%
39	New Hampshire		1,588	0.5%	29	New Mexico	3,077	1.0%
10	New Jersey		9,310	3.1%	30	Oklahoma	3,043	1.0%
29	New Mexico		3,077	1.0%	31	Iowa	2,932	1.0%
2	New York		30,988	10.3%	32	West Virginia	2,786	0.9%
12	North Carolina		7,500	2.5%	33	Utah	2,767	0.9%
47	North Dakota		757	0.3%	34	Oregon	2,482	0.8%
7	Ohio		11,696	3.9%	35	Alabama	2,468	0.8%
30	Oklahoma		3,043	1.0%	36	Louisiana	2,325	0.8%
34	Oregon		2,482	0.8%	37	Idaho	1,919	0.6%
5	Pennsylvania		14,957	5.0%	38	Rhode Island	1,646	0.5%
38	Rhode Island		1,646	0.5%	39	New Hampshire	1,588	0.5%
25	South Carolina		3,381	1.1%	40	Mississippi	1,546	0.5%
44	South Dakota		1,006	0.3%	41	Nevada	1,520	0.5%
20	Tennessee		4,014	1.3%	42	Nebraska	1,354	0.5%
3	Texas		23,232	7.7%	43	Maine	1,023	0.3%
33	Utah		2,767	0.9%	44	South Dakota	1,006	0.3%
48	Vermont		679	0.2%	45	Wyoming	926	0.3%
17	Virginia		4,619	1.5%	46	Delaware	908	0.3%
18	Washington		4,412	1.5%	47	North Dakota	757	0.3%
32	West Virginia		2,786	0.9%	48	Montana	679	0.2%
14	Wisconsin		5,494	1.8%	48	Vermont	679	0.2%
45	Wyoming		926	0.3%	50	Alaska	595	0.2%
						District of Columbia	308	0.1%

Source: U.S. Department of Education, Office of Special Education Programs
"Data Tables for OSEP State Reported Data" (https://www.ideadata.org/arc_toc8.asp)
*2006-2007 school year. IDEA authorizes funding to states and other organizations to support research, demonstrations, technical assistance, and other programs to ensure that the rights of infants, toddlers, children, and youth with disabilities and their parents are protected. National total does not include 4,662 recipients served in U.S. territories and Bureau of Indian Affairs programs.

Percent of Infants and Toddlers Receiving Early Intervention Services Under Individuals with Disabilities Education Act (IDEA) in 2007
National Percent = 2.4% of Children Aged Birth Through 2 Years*

ALPHA ORDER

RANK	STATE	PERCENT
45	Alabama	1.4
29	Alaska	2.0
36	Arizona	1.8
17	Arkansas	2.8
28	California	2.1
34	Colorado	1.9
11	Connecticut	3.4
20	Delaware	2.7
40	Florida	1.7
48	Georgia	1.3
1	Hawaii	7.5
17	Idaho	2.8
13	Illinois	3.1
7	Indiana	3.7
24	Iowa	2.5
20	Kansas	2.7
26	Kentucky	2.3
48	Louisiana	1.3
25	Maine	2.4
15	Maryland	3.0
2	Massachusetts	6.4
26	Michigan	2.3
40	Minnesota	1.7
50	Mississippi	1.2
45	Missouri	1.4
34	Montana	1.9
40	Nebraska	1.7
45	Nevada	1.4
8	New Hampshire	3.6
17	New Jersey	2.8
8	New Mexico	3.6
6	New York	4.2
29	North Carolina	2.0
13	North Dakota	3.1
22	Ohio	2.6
29	Oklahoma	2.0
36	Oregon	1.8
11	Pennsylvania	3.4
4	Rhode Island	4.4
29	South Carolina	2.0
15	South Dakota	3.0
40	Tennessee	1.7
29	Texas	2.0
36	Utah	1.8
10	Vermont	3.5
44	Virginia	1.5
36	Washington	1.8
4	West Virginia	4.4
22	Wisconsin	2.6
3	Wyoming	4.6

RANK ORDER

RANK	STATE	PERCENT
1	Hawaii	7.5
2	Massachusetts	6.4
3	Wyoming	4.6
4	Rhode Island	4.4
4	West Virginia	4.4
6	New York	4.2
7	Indiana	3.7
8	New Hampshire	3.6
8	New Mexico	3.6
10	Vermont	3.5
11	Connecticut	3.4
11	Pennsylvania	3.4
13	Illinois	3.1
13	North Dakota	3.1
15	Maryland	3.0
15	South Dakota	3.0
17	Arkansas	2.8
17	Idaho	2.8
17	New Jersey	2.8
20	Delaware	2.7
20	Kansas	2.7
22	Ohio	2.6
22	Wisconsin	2.6
24	Iowa	2.5
25	Maine	2.4
26	Kentucky	2.3
26	Michigan	2.3
28	California	2.1
29	Alaska	2.0
29	North Carolina	2.0
29	Oklahoma	2.0
29	South Carolina	2.0
29	Texas	2.0
34	Colorado	1.9
34	Montana	1.9
36	Arizona	1.8
36	Oregon	1.8
36	Utah	1.8
36	Washington	1.8
40	Florida	1.7
40	Minnesota	1.7
40	Nebraska	1.7
40	Tennessee	1.7
44	Virginia	1.5
45	Alabama	1.4
45	Missouri	1.4
45	Nevada	1.4
48	Georgia	1.3
48	Louisiana	1.3
50	Mississippi	1.2
	District of Columbia	1.4

Source: U.S. Department of Education, Office of Special Education Programs
  "Data Tables for OSEP State Reported Data" (https://www.ideadata.org/arc_toc8.asp)
*2006-2007 school year. IDEA authorizes funding to states and other organizations to support research, demonstrations, technical assistance, and other programs to ensure that the rights of infants, toddlers, children, and youth with disabilities and their parents are protected. National percent does not include recipients or population in U.S. territories.

Children Age 3 to 21 Served Under the
Individuals with Disabilities Education Act (IDEA) in 2007
National Total = 6,686,361 Children*

ALPHA ORDER

RANK	STATE	CHILDREN	% of USA
26	Alabama	89,013	1.3%
47	Alaska	17,760	0.3%
17	Arizona	126,654	1.9%
31	Arkansas	68,133	1.0%
1	California	672,737	10.1%
27	Colorado	83,559	1.2%
30	Connecticut	69,127	1.0%
44	Delaware	19,366	0.3%
4	Florida	398,289	6.0%
10	Georgia	196,810	2.9%
43	Hawaii	21,099	0.3%
42	Idaho	28,439	0.4%
5	Illinois	326,763	4.9%
12	Indiana	179,043	2.7%
29	Iowa	71,394	1.1%
33	Kansas	65,831	1.0%
21	Kentucky	109,354	1.6%
25	Louisiana	89,422	1.3%
39	Maine	35,564	0.5%
23	Maryland	106,739	1.6%
14	Massachusetts	165,959	2.5%
9	Michigan	241,941	3.6%
20	Minnesota	117,924	1.8%
32	Mississippi	67,590	1.0%
15	Missouri	141,406	2.1%
45	Montana	18,557	0.3%
38	Nebraska	44,833	0.7%
36	Nevada	48,230	0.7%
40	New Hampshire	31,399	0.5%
8	New Jersey	250,109	3.7%
37	New Mexico	47,917	0.7%
3	New York	451,929	6.8%
11	North Carolina	192,451	2.9%
50	North Dakota	13,825	0.2%
7	Ohio	269,133	4.0%
24	Oklahoma	95,860	1.4%
28	Oregon	77,832	1.2%
6	Pennsylvania	292,798	4.4%
41	Rhode Island	30,243	0.5%
22	South Carolina	107,353	1.6%
46	South Dakota	17,824	0.3%
19	Tennessee	120,263	1.8%
2	Texas	494,302	7.4%
34	Utah	61,166	0.9%
48	Vermont	14,010	0.2%
13	Virginia	170,794	2.6%
18	Washington	122,979	1.8%
35	West Virginia	49,054	0.7%
16	Wisconsin	128,526	1.9%
49	Wyoming	13,945	0.2%

RANK ORDER

RANK	STATE	CHILDREN	% of USA
1	California	672,737	10.1%
2	Texas	494,302	7.4%
3	New York	451,929	6.8%
4	Florida	398,289	6.0%
5	Illinois	326,763	4.9%
6	Pennsylvania	292,798	4.4%
7	Ohio	269,133	4.0%
8	New Jersey	250,109	3.7%
9	Michigan	241,941	3.6%
10	Georgia	196,810	2.9%
11	North Carolina	192,451	2.9%
12	Indiana	179,043	2.7%
13	Virginia	170,794	2.6%
14	Massachusetts	165,959	2.5%
15	Missouri	141,406	2.1%
16	Wisconsin	128,526	1.9%
17	Arizona	126,654	1.9%
18	Washington	122,979	1.8%
19	Tennessee	120,263	1.8%
20	Minnesota	117,924	1.8%
21	Kentucky	109,354	1.6%
22	South Carolina	107,353	1.6%
23	Maryland	106,739	1.6%
24	Oklahoma	95,860	1.4%
25	Louisiana	89,422	1.3%
26	Alabama	89,013	1.3%
27	Colorado	83,559	1.2%
28	Oregon	77,832	1.2%
29	Iowa	71,394	1.1%
30	Connecticut	69,127	1.0%
31	Arkansas	68,133	1.0%
32	Mississippi	67,590	1.0%
33	Kansas	65,831	1.0%
34	Utah	61,166	0.9%
35	West Virginia	49,054	0.7%
36	Nevada	48,230	0.7%
37	New Mexico	47,917	0.7%
38	Nebraska	44,833	0.7%
39	Maine	35,564	0.5%
40	New Hampshire	31,399	0.5%
41	Rhode Island	30,243	0.5%
42	Idaho	28,439	0.4%
43	Hawaii	21,099	0.3%
44	Delaware	19,366	0.3%
45	Montana	18,557	0.3%
46	South Dakota	17,824	0.3%
47	Alaska	17,760	0.3%
48	Vermont	14,010	0.2%
49	Wyoming	13,945	0.2%
50	North Dakota	13,825	0.2%
	District of Columbia	11,113	0.2%

Source: U.S. Department of Education, Office of Special Education Programs
   "Data Tables for OSEP State Reported Data" (https://www.ideadata.org/arc_toc8.asp)
*2006-2007 school year. IDEA authorizes funding to states and other organizations to support research, demonstrations, technical assistance, and other programs to ensure that the rights of infants, toddlers, children, and youth with disabilities and their parents are protected. National total does not include 109,913 children served in U.S. territories and Bureau of Indian Affairs programs.

Percent of All Children Age 3 to 21 Served Under the Individuals with Disabilities Education Act (IDEA) in 2007
National Percent = 8.6%*

ALPHA ORDER

RANK	STATE	PERCENT
44	Alabama	7.5
18	Alaska	9.3
40	Arizona	7.6
15	Arkansas	9.4
50	California	6.7
48	Colorado	6.9
37	Connecticut	7.7
27	Delaware	8.8
15	Florida	9.4
37	Georgia	7.7
49	Hawaii	6.8
47	Idaho	7.0
10	Illinois	9.6
5	Indiana	10.7
19	Iowa	9.2
27	Kansas	8.8
7	Kentucky	10.5
37	Louisiana	7.7
2	Maine	11.6
45	Maryland	7.4
8	Massachusetts	10.4
22	Michigan	9.1
27	Minnesota	8.8
33	Mississippi	8.4
15	Missouri	9.4
36	Montana	7.9
13	Nebraska	9.5
40	Nevada	7.6
10	New Hampshire	9.6
3	New Jersey	11.4
25	New Mexico	8.9
19	New York	9.2
32	North Carolina	8.5
34	North Dakota	8.2
22	Ohio	9.1
9	Oklahoma	10.2
30	Oregon	8.6
13	Pennsylvania	9.5
4	Rhode Island	11.1
10	South Carolina	9.6
30	South Dakota	8.6
35	Tennessee	8.0
45	Texas	7.4
40	Utah	7.6
19	Vermont	9.2
25	Virginia	8.9
40	Washington	7.6
1	West Virginia	11.7
24	Wisconsin	9.0
6	Wyoming	10.6

RANK ORDER

RANK	STATE	PERCENT
1	West Virginia	11.7
2	Maine	11.6
3	New Jersey	11.4
4	Rhode Island	11.1
5	Indiana	10.7
6	Wyoming	10.6
7	Kentucky	10.5
8	Massachusetts	10.4
9	Oklahoma	10.2
10	Illinois	9.6
10	New Hampshire	9.6
10	South Carolina	9.6
13	Nebraska	9.5
13	Pennsylvania	9.5
15	Arkansas	9.4
15	Florida	9.4
15	Missouri	9.4
18	Alaska	9.3
19	Iowa	9.2
19	New York	9.2
19	Vermont	9.2
22	Michigan	9.1
22	Ohio	9.1
24	Wisconsin	9.0
25	New Mexico	8.9
25	Virginia	8.9
27	Delaware	8.8
27	Kansas	8.8
27	Minnesota	8.8
30	Oregon	8.6
30	South Dakota	8.6
32	North Carolina	8.5
33	Mississippi	8.4
34	North Dakota	8.2
35	Tennessee	8.0
36	Montana	7.9
37	Connecticut	7.7
37	Georgia	7.7
37	Louisiana	7.7
40	Arizona	7.6
40	Nevada	7.6
40	Utah	7.6
40	Washington	7.6
44	Alabama	7.5
45	Maryland	7.4
45	Texas	7.4
47	Idaho	7.0
48	Colorado	6.9
49	Hawaii	6.8
50	California	6.7

District of Columbia   8.3

Source: CQ Press using data from U.S. Department of Education, Office of Special Education Programs
"Data Tables for OSEP State Reported Data" (https://www.ideadata.org/arc_toc8.asp)
*2006-2007 school year. IDEA authorizes funding to states and other organizations to support research, demonstrations, technical assistance, and other programs to ensure that the rights of infants, toddlers, children, and youth with disabilities and their parents are protected. National percent does not include children served in U.S. territories and Bureau of Indian Affairs programs.

Percent of All Children Age 3 to 5 Served Under the Individuals with Disabilities Education Act (IDEA) in 2007
National Percent = 5.8%*

ALPHA ORDER

RANK	STATE	PERCENT
48	Alabama	4.4
18	Alaska	6.8
44	Arizona	5.0
3	Arkansas	10.3
49	California	4.2
35	Colorado	5.4
37	Connecticut	5.3
22	Delaware	6.6
42	Florida	5.1
46	Georgia	4.9
47	Hawaii	4.8
28	Idaho	5.9
15	Illinois	7.0
12	Indiana	7.5
34	Iowa	5.5
7	Kansas	8.3
2	Kentucky	12.8
28	Louisiana	5.9
4	Maine	9.8
37	Maryland	5.3
21	Massachusetts	6.7
26	Michigan	6.2
16	Minnesota	6.9
18	Mississippi	6.8
18	Missouri	6.8
31	Montana	5.7
22	Nebraska	6.6
37	Nevada	5.3
24	New Hampshire	6.4
28	New Jersey	5.9
12	New Mexico	7.5
8	New York	8.2
33	North Carolina	5.6
16	North Dakota	6.9
37	Ohio	5.3
42	Oklahoma	5.1
27	Oregon	6.0
25	Pennsylvania	6.3
10	Rhode Island	8.1
8	South Carolina	8.2
6	South Dakota	8.6
44	Tennessee	5.0
50	Texas	3.5
37	Utah	5.3
10	Vermont	8.1
31	Virginia	5.7
35	Washington	5.4
5	West Virginia	9.6
12	Wisconsin	7.5
1	Wyoming	13.5

RANK ORDER

RANK	STATE	PERCENT
1	Wyoming	13.5
2	Kentucky	12.8
3	Arkansas	10.3
4	Maine	9.8
5	West Virginia	9.6
6	South Dakota	8.6
7	Kansas	8.3
8	New York	8.2
8	South Carolina	8.2
10	Rhode Island	8.1
10	Vermont	8.1
12	Indiana	7.5
12	New Mexico	7.5
12	Wisconsin	7.5
15	Illinois	7.0
16	Minnesota	6.9
16	North Dakota	6.9
18	Alaska	6.8
18	Mississippi	6.8
18	Missouri	6.8
21	Massachusetts	6.7
22	Delaware	6.6
22	Nebraska	6.6
24	New Hampshire	6.4
25	Pennsylvania	6.3
26	Michigan	6.2
27	Oregon	6.0
28	Idaho	5.9
28	Louisiana	5.9
28	New Jersey	5.9
31	Montana	5.7
31	Virginia	5.7
33	North Carolina	5.6
34	Iowa	5.5
35	Colorado	5.4
35	Washington	5.4
37	Connecticut	5.3
37	Maryland	5.3
37	Nevada	5.3
37	Ohio	5.3
37	Utah	5.3
42	Florida	5.1
42	Oklahoma	5.1
44	Arizona	5.0
44	Tennessee	5.0
46	Georgia	4.9
47	Hawaii	4.8
48	Alabama	4.4
49	California	4.2
50	Texas	3.5
	District of Columbia	3.8

Source: CQ Press using data from U.S. Department of Education, Office of Special Education Programs
"Data Tables for OSEP State Reported Data" (https://www.ideadata.org/arc_toc8.asp)
*2006-2007 school year. IDEA authorizes funding to states and other organizations to support research, demonstrations, technical assistance, and other programs to ensure that the rights of infants, toddlers, children, and youth with disabilities and their parents are protected. National percent does not include children served in U.S. territories and Bureau of Indian Affairs programs.

Percent of All Children Age 6 to 17 Served Under the Individuals with Disabilities Education Act (IDEA) in 2007
National Percent = 11.5%*

<table>
<tr><td colspan="3">ALPHA ORDER</td><td colspan="3">RANK ORDER</td></tr>
<tr><th>RANK</th><th>STATE</th><th>PERCENT</th><th>RANK</th><th>STATE</th><th>PERCENT</th></tr>
<tr><td>43</td><td>Alabama</td><td>10.1</td><td>1</td><td>Rhode Island</td><td>15.8</td></tr>
<tr><td>19</td><td>Alaska</td><td>12.3</td><td>2</td><td>New Jersey</td><td>15.4</td></tr>
<tr><td>40</td><td>Arizona</td><td>10.2</td><td>2</td><td>West Virginia</td><td>15.4</td></tr>
<tr><td>27</td><td>Arkansas</td><td>11.6</td><td>4</td><td>Maine</td><td>15.2</td></tr>
<tr><td>48</td><td>California</td><td>9.1</td><td>5</td><td>Massachusetts</td><td>14.5</td></tr>
<tr><td>50</td><td>Colorado</td><td>9.0</td><td>6</td><td>Indiana</td><td>14.2</td></tr>
<tr><td>40</td><td>Connecticut</td><td>10.2</td><td>6</td><td>Oklahoma</td><td>14.2</td></tr>
<tr><td>21</td><td>Delaware</td><td>12.1</td><td>8</td><td>Wyoming</td><td>13.1</td></tr>
<tr><td>10</td><td>Florida</td><td>12.9</td><td>9</td><td>Nebraska</td><td>13.0</td></tr>
<tr><td>37</td><td>Georgia</td><td>10.5</td><td>10</td><td>Florida</td><td>12.9</td></tr>
<tr><td>47</td><td>Hawaii</td><td>9.3</td><td>10</td><td>New Hampshire</td><td>12.9</td></tr>
<tr><td>48</td><td>Idaho</td><td>9.1</td><td>10</td><td>Pennsylvania</td><td>12.9</td></tr>
<tr><td>13</td><td>Illinois</td><td>12.8</td><td>13</td><td>Illinois</td><td>12.8</td></tr>
<tr><td>6</td><td>Indiana</td><td>14.2</td><td>13</td><td>Iowa</td><td>12.8</td></tr>
<tr><td>13</td><td>Iowa</td><td>12.8</td><td>15</td><td>Kentucky</td><td>12.7</td></tr>
<tr><td>28</td><td>Kansas</td><td>11.5</td><td>16</td><td>South Carolina</td><td>12.6</td></tr>
<tr><td>15</td><td>Kentucky</td><td>12.7</td><td>17</td><td>Missouri</td><td>12.5</td></tr>
<tr><td>40</td><td>Louisiana</td><td>10.2</td><td>18</td><td>Vermont</td><td>12.4</td></tr>
<tr><td>4</td><td>Maine</td><td>15.2</td><td>19</td><td>Alaska</td><td>12.3</td></tr>
<tr><td>45</td><td>Maryland</td><td>9.9</td><td>20</td><td>Ohio</td><td>12.2</td></tr>
<tr><td>5</td><td>Massachusetts</td><td>14.5</td><td>21</td><td>Delaware</td><td>12.1</td></tr>
<tr><td>23</td><td>Michigan</td><td>12.0</td><td>21</td><td>Virginia</td><td>12.1</td></tr>
<tr><td>28</td><td>Minnesota</td><td>11.5</td><td>23</td><td>Michigan</td><td>12.0</td></tr>
<tr><td>34</td><td>Mississippi</td><td>11.0</td><td>23</td><td>New York</td><td>12.0</td></tr>
<tr><td>17</td><td>Missouri</td><td>12.5</td><td>23</td><td>Wisconsin</td><td>12.0</td></tr>
<tr><td>35</td><td>Montana</td><td>10.6</td><td>26</td><td>North Dakota</td><td>11.8</td></tr>
<tr><td>9</td><td>Nebraska</td><td>13.0</td><td>27</td><td>Arkansas</td><td>11.6</td></tr>
<tr><td>46</td><td>Nevada</td><td>9.8</td><td>28</td><td>Kansas</td><td>11.5</td></tr>
<tr><td>10</td><td>New Hampshire</td><td>12.9</td><td>28</td><td>Minnesota</td><td>11.5</td></tr>
<tr><td>2</td><td>New Jersey</td><td>15.4</td><td>28</td><td>New Mexico</td><td>11.5</td></tr>
<tr><td>28</td><td>New Mexico</td><td>11.5</td><td>28</td><td>North Carolina</td><td>11.5</td></tr>
<tr><td>23</td><td>New York</td><td>12.0</td><td>32</td><td>Oregon</td><td>11.4</td></tr>
<tr><td>28</td><td>North Carolina</td><td>11.5</td><td>33</td><td>South Dakota</td><td>11.1</td></tr>
<tr><td>26</td><td>North Dakota</td><td>11.8</td><td>34</td><td>Mississippi</td><td>11.0</td></tr>
<tr><td>20</td><td>Ohio</td><td>12.2</td><td>35</td><td>Montana</td><td>10.6</td></tr>
<tr><td>6</td><td>Oklahoma</td><td>14.2</td><td>35</td><td>Tennessee</td><td>10.6</td></tr>
<tr><td>32</td><td>Oregon</td><td>11.4</td><td>37</td><td>Georgia</td><td>10.5</td></tr>
<tr><td>10</td><td>Pennsylvania</td><td>12.9</td><td>38</td><td>Texas</td><td>10.3</td></tr>
<tr><td>1</td><td>Rhode Island</td><td>15.8</td><td>38</td><td>Utah</td><td>10.3</td></tr>
<tr><td>16</td><td>South Carolina</td><td>12.6</td><td>40</td><td>Arizona</td><td>10.2</td></tr>
<tr><td>33</td><td>South Dakota</td><td>11.1</td><td>40</td><td>Connecticut</td><td>10.2</td></tr>
<tr><td>35</td><td>Tennessee</td><td>10.6</td><td>40</td><td>Louisiana</td><td>10.2</td></tr>
<tr><td>38</td><td>Texas</td><td>10.3</td><td>43</td><td>Alabama</td><td>10.1</td></tr>
<tr><td>38</td><td>Utah</td><td>10.3</td><td>43</td><td>Washington</td><td>10.1</td></tr>
<tr><td>18</td><td>Vermont</td><td>12.4</td><td>45</td><td>Maryland</td><td>9.9</td></tr>
<tr><td>21</td><td>Virginia</td><td>12.1</td><td>46</td><td>Nevada</td><td>9.8</td></tr>
<tr><td>43</td><td>Washington</td><td>10.1</td><td>47</td><td>Hawaii</td><td>9.3</td></tr>
<tr><td>2</td><td>West Virginia</td><td>15.4</td><td>48</td><td>California</td><td>9.1</td></tr>
<tr><td>23</td><td>Wisconsin</td><td>12.0</td><td>48</td><td>Idaho</td><td>9.1</td></tr>
<tr><td>8</td><td>Wyoming</td><td>13.1</td><td>50</td><td>Colorado</td><td>9.0</td></tr>
<tr><td colspan="3"></td><td colspan="2">District of Columbia</td><td>13.7</td></tr>
</table>

Source: CQ Press using data from U.S. Department of Education, Office of Special Education Programs
   "Data Tables for OSEP State Reported Data" (https://www.ideadata.org/arc_toc8.asp)
*2006-2007 school year. IDEA authorizes funding to states and other organizations to support research, demonstrations, technical assistance, and other programs to ensure that the rights of infants, toddlers, children, and youth with disabilities and their parents are protected. National percent does not include children served in U.S. territories and Bureau of Indian Affairs programs.

Percent of All Young Adults Age 18 to 21 Served Under the Individuals with Disabilities Education Act (IDEA) in 2007
National Percent = 1.9%*

ALPHA ORDER

RANK	STATE	PERCENT
19	Alabama	2.0
12	Alaska	2.1
33	Arizona	1.7
24	Arkansas	1.9
47	California	1.3
33	Colorado	1.7
6	Connecticut	2.2
33	Delaware	1.7
12	Florida	2.1
47	Georgia	1.3
50	Hawaii	0.9
49	Idaho	1.2
19	Illinois	2.0
3	Indiana	2.5
24	Iowa	1.9
29	Kansas	1.8
33	Kentucky	1.7
40	Louisiana	1.6
6	Maine	2.2
46	Maryland	1.4
19	Massachusetts	2.0
12	Michigan	2.1
5	Minnesota	2.3
29	Mississippi	1.8
6	Missouri	2.2
40	Montana	1.6
33	Nebraska	1.7
44	Nevada	1.5
12	New Hampshire	2.1
1	New Jersey	2.7
6	New Mexico	2.2
6	New York	2.2
33	North Carolina	1.7
40	North Dakota	1.6
2	Ohio	2.6
6	Oklahoma	2.2
19	Oregon	2.0
12	Pennsylvania	2.1
19	Rhode Island	2.0
12	South Carolina	2.1
40	South Dakota	1.6
29	Tennessee	1.8
29	Texas	1.8
44	Utah	1.5
24	Vermont	1.9
12	Virginia	2.1
33	Washington	1.7
3	West Virginia	2.5
24	Wisconsin	1.9
24	Wyoming	1.9

RANK ORDER

RANK	STATE	PERCENT
1	New Jersey	2.7
2	Ohio	2.6
3	Indiana	2.5
3	West Virginia	2.5
5	Minnesota	2.3
6	Connecticut	2.2
6	Maine	2.2
6	Missouri	2.2
6	New Mexico	2.2
6	New York	2.2
6	Oklahoma	2.2
12	Alaska	2.1
12	Florida	2.1
12	Michigan	2.1
12	New Hampshire	2.1
12	Pennsylvania	2.1
12	South Carolina	2.1
12	Virginia	2.1
19	Alabama	2.0
19	Illinois	2.0
19	Massachusetts	2.0
19	Oregon	2.0
19	Rhode Island	2.0
24	Arkansas	1.9
24	Iowa	1.9
24	Vermont	1.9
24	Wisconsin	1.9
24	Wyoming	1.9
29	Kansas	1.8
29	Mississippi	1.8
29	Tennessee	1.8
29	Texas	1.8
33	Arizona	1.7
33	Colorado	1.7
33	Delaware	1.7
33	Kentucky	1.7
33	Nebraska	1.7
33	North Carolina	1.7
33	Washington	1.7
40	Louisiana	1.6
40	Montana	1.6
40	North Dakota	1.6
40	South Dakota	1.6
44	Nevada	1.5
44	Utah	1.5
46	Maryland	1.4
47	California	1.3
47	Georgia	1.3
49	Idaho	1.2
50	Hawaii	0.9

	District of Columbia	0.9

Source: CQ Press using data from U.S. Department of Education, Office of Special Education Programs
"Data Tables for OSEP State Reported Data" (https://www.ideadata.org/arc_toc8.asp)
*2006-2007 school year. IDEA authorizes funding to states and other organizations to support research, demonstrations, technical assistance, and other programs to ensure that the rights of infants, toddlers, children, and youth with disabilities and their parents are protected. National percent does not include children served in U.S. territories and Bureau of Indian Affairs programs.

Percent of Children Age 6 to 17 Served Under the Individuals with Disabilities Education Act (IDEA) for Specific Learning Disabilities in 2007
National Percent = 5.1%*

ALPHA ORDER

RANK	STATE	PERCENT
27	Alabama	5.0
11	Alaska	5.9
18	Arizona	5.3
33	Arkansas	4.6
33	California	4.6
45	Colorado	3.7
43	Connecticut	3.8
6	Delaware	6.6
7	Florida	6.3
49	Georgia	3.3
33	Hawaii	4.6
43	Idaho	3.8
9	Illinois	6.2
14	Indiana	5.5
1	Iowa	7.3
28	Kansas	4.9
50	Kentucky	2.0
46	Louisiana	3.6
20	Maine	5.2
46	Maryland	3.6
7	Massachusetts	6.3
24	Michigan	5.1
46	Minnesota	3.6
24	Mississippi	5.1
33	Missouri	4.6
18	Montana	5.3
32	Nebraska	4.7
11	Nevada	5.9
11	New Hampshire	5.9
5	New Jersey	6.7
14	New Mexico	5.5
20	New York	5.2
39	North Carolina	4.2
39	North Dakota	4.2
24	Ohio	5.1
2	Oklahoma	7.2
31	Oregon	4.8
3	Pennsylvania	7.0
4	Rhode Island	6.9
9	South Carolina	6.2
28	South Dakota	4.9
37	Tennessee	4.5
20	Texas	5.2
16	Utah	5.4
39	Vermont	4.2
28	Virginia	4.9
42	Washington	4.1
20	West Virginia	5.2
37	Wisconsin	4.5
16	Wyoming	5.4

RANK ORDER

RANK	STATE	PERCENT
1	Iowa	7.3
2	Oklahoma	7.2
3	Pennsylvania	7.0
4	Rhode Island	6.9
5	New Jersey	6.7
6	Delaware	6.6
7	Florida	6.3
7	Massachusetts	6.3
9	Illinois	6.2
9	South Carolina	6.2
11	Alaska	5.9
11	Nevada	5.9
11	New Hampshire	5.9
14	Indiana	5.5
14	New Mexico	5.5
16	Utah	5.4
16	Wyoming	5.4
18	Arizona	5.3
18	Montana	5.3
20	Maine	5.2
20	New York	5.2
20	Texas	5.2
20	West Virginia	5.2
24	Michigan	5.1
24	Mississippi	5.1
24	Ohio	5.1
27	Alabama	5.0
28	Kansas	4.9
28	South Dakota	4.9
28	Virginia	4.9
31	Oregon	4.8
32	Nebraska	4.7
33	Arkansas	4.6
33	California	4.6
33	Hawaii	4.6
33	Missouri	4.6
37	Tennessee	4.5
37	Wisconsin	4.5
39	North Carolina	4.2
39	North Dakota	4.2
39	Vermont	4.2
42	Washington	4.1
43	Connecticut	3.8
43	Idaho	3.8
45	Colorado	3.7
46	Louisiana	3.6
46	Maryland	3.6
46	Minnesota	3.6
49	Georgia	3.3
50	Kentucky	2.0

District of Columbia   6.7

Source: U.S. Department of Education, Office of Special Education Programs
"Data Tables for OSEP State Reported Data" (https://www.ideadata.org/arc_toc8.asp)
*2006-2007 school year. IDEA authorizes funding to states and other organizations to support research, demonstrations, technical assistance, and other programs to ensure that the rights of infants, toddlers, children, and youth with disabilities and their parents are protected. National percent does not include children served in U.S. territories and Bureau of Indian Affairs programs.

Percent of Children Age 6 to 17 Served Under the Individuals with Disabilities Education Act (IDEA) for Speech Impairments in 2007
National Percent = 2.3%*

<table>
<tr><td colspan="3">ALPHA ORDER</td><td colspan="3">RANK ORDER</td></tr>
<tr><td>RANK</td><td>STATE</td><td>PERCENT</td><td>RANK</td><td>STATE</td><td>PERCENT</td></tr>
<tr><td>26</td><td>Alabama</td><td>2.1</td><td>1</td><td>Indiana</td><td>3.6</td></tr>
<tr><td>20</td><td>Alaska</td><td>2.4</td><td>2</td><td>Maine</td><td>3.5</td></tr>
<tr><td>32</td><td>Arizona</td><td>2.0</td><td>2</td><td>Missouri</td><td>3.5</td></tr>
<tr><td>13</td><td>Arkansas</td><td>2.6</td><td>2</td><td>Wyoming</td><td>3.5</td></tr>
<tr><td>26</td><td>California</td><td>2.1</td><td>5</td><td>Nebraska</td><td>3.4</td></tr>
<tr><td>32</td><td>Colorado</td><td>2.0</td><td>6</td><td>New Jersey</td><td>3.3</td></tr>
<tr><td>26</td><td>Connecticut</td><td>2.1</td><td>6</td><td>North Dakota</td><td>3.3</td></tr>
<tr><td>NA</td><td>Delaware**</td><td>NA</td><td>8</td><td>Rhode Island</td><td>3.1</td></tr>
<tr><td>9</td><td>Florida</td><td>3.0</td><td>9</td><td>Florida</td><td>3.0</td></tr>
<tr><td>24</td><td>Georgia</td><td>2.2</td><td>9</td><td>Kentucky</td><td>3.0</td></tr>
<tr><td>NA</td><td>Hawaii**</td><td>NA</td><td>9</td><td>Mississippi</td><td>3.0</td></tr>
<tr><td>39</td><td>Idaho</td><td>1.9</td><td>12</td><td>Oregon</td><td>2.7</td></tr>
<tr><td>17</td><td>Illinois</td><td>2.5</td><td>13</td><td>Arkansas</td><td>2.6</td></tr>
<tr><td>1</td><td>Indiana</td><td>3.6</td><td>13</td><td>Louisiana</td><td>2.6</td></tr>
<tr><td>44</td><td>Iowa</td><td>1.4</td><td>13</td><td>Michigan</td><td>2.6</td></tr>
<tr><td>32</td><td>Kansas</td><td>2.0</td><td>13</td><td>Tennessee</td><td>2.6</td></tr>
<tr><td>9</td><td>Kentucky</td><td>3.0</td><td>17</td><td>Illinois</td><td>2.5</td></tr>
<tr><td>13</td><td>Louisiana</td><td>2.6</td><td>17</td><td>New Mexico</td><td>2.5</td></tr>
<tr><td>2</td><td>Maine</td><td>3.5</td><td>17</td><td>New York</td><td>2.5</td></tr>
<tr><td>26</td><td>Maryland</td><td>2.1</td><td>20</td><td>Alaska</td><td>2.4</td></tr>
<tr><td>22</td><td>Massachusetts</td><td>2.3</td><td>20</td><td>Wisconsin</td><td>2.4</td></tr>
<tr><td>13</td><td>Michigan</td><td>2.6</td><td>22</td><td>Massachusetts</td><td>2.3</td></tr>
<tr><td>32</td><td>Minnesota</td><td>2.0</td><td>22</td><td>Montana</td><td>2.3</td></tr>
<tr><td>9</td><td>Mississippi</td><td>3.0</td><td>24</td><td>Georgia</td><td>2.2</td></tr>
<tr><td>2</td><td>Missouri</td><td>3.5</td><td>24</td><td>Utah</td><td>2.2</td></tr>
<tr><td>22</td><td>Montana</td><td>2.3</td><td>26</td><td>Alabama</td><td>2.1</td></tr>
<tr><td>5</td><td>Nebraska</td><td>3.4</td><td>26</td><td>California</td><td>2.1</td></tr>
<tr><td>NA</td><td>Nevada**</td><td>NA</td><td>26</td><td>Connecticut</td><td>2.1</td></tr>
<tr><td>26</td><td>New Hampshire</td><td>2.1</td><td>26</td><td>Maryland</td><td>2.1</td></tr>
<tr><td>6</td><td>New Jersey</td><td>3.3</td><td>26</td><td>New Hampshire</td><td>2.1</td></tr>
<tr><td>17</td><td>New Mexico</td><td>2.5</td><td>26</td><td>North Carolina</td><td>2.1</td></tr>
<tr><td>17</td><td>New York</td><td>2.5</td><td>32</td><td>Arizona</td><td>2.0</td></tr>
<tr><td>26</td><td>North Carolina</td><td>2.1</td><td>32</td><td>Colorado</td><td>2.0</td></tr>
<tr><td>6</td><td>North Dakota</td><td>3.3</td><td>32</td><td>Kansas</td><td>2.0</td></tr>
<tr><td>40</td><td>Ohio</td><td>1.8</td><td>32</td><td>Minnesota</td><td>2.0</td></tr>
<tr><td>32</td><td>Oklahoma</td><td>2.0</td><td>32</td><td>Oklahoma</td><td>2.0</td></tr>
<tr><td>12</td><td>Oregon</td><td>2.7</td><td>32</td><td>Pennsylvania</td><td>2.0</td></tr>
<tr><td>32</td><td>Pennsylvania</td><td>2.0</td><td>32</td><td>Virginia</td><td>2.0</td></tr>
<tr><td>8</td><td>Rhode Island</td><td>3.1</td><td>39</td><td>Idaho</td><td>1.9</td></tr>
<tr><td>NA</td><td>South Carolina**</td><td>NA</td><td>40</td><td>Ohio</td><td>1.8</td></tr>
<tr><td>NA</td><td>South Dakota**</td><td>NA</td><td>41</td><td>Vermont</td><td>1.7</td></tr>
<tr><td>13</td><td>Tennessee</td><td>2.6</td><td>42</td><td>Texas</td><td>1.6</td></tr>
<tr><td>42</td><td>Texas</td><td>1.6</td><td>42</td><td>Washington</td><td>1.6</td></tr>
<tr><td>24</td><td>Utah</td><td>2.2</td><td>44</td><td>Iowa</td><td>1.4</td></tr>
<tr><td>41</td><td>Vermont</td><td>1.7</td><td>NA</td><td>Delaware**</td><td>NA</td></tr>
<tr><td>32</td><td>Virginia</td><td>2.0</td><td>NA</td><td>Hawaii**</td><td>NA</td></tr>
<tr><td>42</td><td>Washington</td><td>1.6</td><td>NA</td><td>Nevada**</td><td>NA</td></tr>
<tr><td>NA</td><td>West Virginia**</td><td>NA</td><td>NA</td><td>South Carolina**</td><td>NA</td></tr>
<tr><td>20</td><td>Wisconsin</td><td>2.4</td><td>NA</td><td>South Dakota**</td><td>NA</td></tr>
<tr><td>2</td><td>Wyoming</td><td>3.5</td><td>NA</td><td>West Virginia**</td><td>NA</td></tr>
<tr><td></td><td></td><td></td><td></td><td>District of Columbia**</td><td>NA</td></tr>
</table>

Source: U.S. Department of Education, Office of Special Education Programs
"Data Tables for OSEP State Reported Data" (https://www.ideadata.org/arc_toc8.asp)
*2006-2007 school year. IDEA authorizes funding to states and other organizations to support research, demonstrations, technical assistance, and other programs to ensure that the rights of infants, toddlers, children, and youth with disabilities and their parents are protected. National percent does not include children served in U.S. territories and Bureau of Indian Affairs programs.
**Percent could not be calculated.

Percent of Children Age 6 to 17 Served Under the Individuals with Disabilities Education Act (IDEA) for Mental Retardation in 2007
National Percent = 0.9%*

<table>
<tr><td colspan="3">ALPHA ORDER</td><td colspan="3">RANK ORDER</td></tr>
<tr><td>RANK</td><td>STATE</td><td>PERCENT</td><td>RANK</td><td>STATE</td><td>PERCENT</td></tr>
<tr><td>22</td><td>Alabama</td><td>0.9</td><td>1</td><td>West Virginia</td><td>2.8</td></tr>
<tr><td>36</td><td>Alaska</td><td>0.5</td><td>2</td><td>Kentucky</td><td>2.4</td></tr>
<tr><td>29</td><td>Arizona</td><td>0.7</td><td>3</td><td>Iowa</td><td>2.1</td></tr>
<tr><td>4</td><td>Arkansas</td><td>1.8</td><td>4</td><td>Arkansas</td><td>1.8</td></tr>
<tr><td>36</td><td>California</td><td>0.5</td><td>4</td><td>Ohio</td><td>1.8</td></tr>
<tr><td>42</td><td>Colorado</td><td>0.4</td><td>6</td><td>Indiana</td><td>1.7</td></tr>
<tr><td>42</td><td>Connecticut</td><td>0.4</td><td>7</td><td>Nebraska</td><td>1.5</td></tr>
<tr><td>10</td><td>Delaware</td><td>1.3</td><td>7</td><td>North Carolina</td><td>1.5</td></tr>
<tr><td>13</td><td>Florida</td><td>1.1</td><td>9</td><td>South Carolina</td><td>1.4</td></tr>
<tr><td>10</td><td>Georgia</td><td>1.3</td><td>10</td><td>Delaware</td><td>1.3</td></tr>
<tr><td>29</td><td>Hawaii</td><td>0.7</td><td>10</td><td>Georgia</td><td>1.3</td></tr>
<tr><td>32</td><td>Idaho</td><td>0.6</td><td>12</td><td>Michigan</td><td>1.2</td></tr>
<tr><td>16</td><td>Illinois</td><td>1.0</td><td>13</td><td>Florida</td><td>1.1</td></tr>
<tr><td>6</td><td>Indiana</td><td>1.7</td><td>13</td><td>Missouri</td><td>1.1</td></tr>
<tr><td>3</td><td>Iowa</td><td>2.1</td><td>13</td><td>Pennsylvania</td><td>1.1</td></tr>
<tr><td>25</td><td>Kansas</td><td>0.8</td><td>16</td><td>Illinois</td><td>1.0</td></tr>
<tr><td>2</td><td>Kentucky</td><td>2.4</td><td>16</td><td>Louisiana</td><td>1.0</td></tr>
<tr><td>16</td><td>Louisiana</td><td>1.0</td><td>16</td><td>Massachusetts</td><td>1.0</td></tr>
<tr><td>42</td><td>Maine</td><td>0.4</td><td>16</td><td>Oklahoma</td><td>1.0</td></tr>
<tr><td>36</td><td>Maryland</td><td>0.5</td><td>16</td><td>Vermont</td><td>1.0</td></tr>
<tr><td>16</td><td>Massachusetts</td><td>1.0</td><td>16</td><td>Wisconsin</td><td>1.0</td></tr>
<tr><td>12</td><td>Michigan</td><td>1.2</td><td>22</td><td>Alabama</td><td>0.9</td></tr>
<tr><td>22</td><td>Minnesota</td><td>0.9</td><td>22</td><td>Minnesota</td><td>0.9</td></tr>
<tr><td>25</td><td>Mississippi</td><td>0.8</td><td>22</td><td>Tennessee</td><td>0.9</td></tr>
<tr><td>13</td><td>Missouri</td><td>1.1</td><td>25</td><td>Kansas</td><td>0.8</td></tr>
<tr><td>32</td><td>Montana</td><td>0.6</td><td>25</td><td>Mississippi</td><td>0.8</td></tr>
<tr><td>7</td><td>Nebraska</td><td>1.5</td><td>25</td><td>North Dakota</td><td>0.8</td></tr>
<tr><td>42</td><td>Nevada</td><td>0.4</td><td>25</td><td>Virginia</td><td>0.8</td></tr>
<tr><td>50</td><td>New Hampshire</td><td>0.3</td><td>29</td><td>Arizona</td><td>0.7</td></tr>
<tr><td>42</td><td>New Jersey</td><td>0.4</td><td>29</td><td>Hawaii</td><td>0.7</td></tr>
<tr><td>42</td><td>New Mexico</td><td>0.4</td><td>29</td><td>South Dakota</td><td>0.7</td></tr>
<tr><td>42</td><td>New York</td><td>0.4</td><td>32</td><td>Idaho</td><td>0.6</td></tr>
<tr><td>7</td><td>North Carolina</td><td>1.5</td><td>32</td><td>Montana</td><td>0.6</td></tr>
<tr><td>25</td><td>North Dakota</td><td>0.8</td><td>32</td><td>Oregon</td><td>0.6</td></tr>
<tr><td>4</td><td>Ohio</td><td>1.8</td><td>32</td><td>Rhode Island</td><td>0.6</td></tr>
<tr><td>16</td><td>Oklahoma</td><td>1.0</td><td>36</td><td>Alaska</td><td>0.5</td></tr>
<tr><td>32</td><td>Oregon</td><td>0.6</td><td>36</td><td>California</td><td>0.5</td></tr>
<tr><td>13</td><td>Pennsylvania</td><td>1.1</td><td>36</td><td>Maryland</td><td>0.5</td></tr>
<tr><td>32</td><td>Rhode Island</td><td>0.6</td><td>36</td><td>Texas</td><td>0.5</td></tr>
<tr><td>9</td><td>South Carolina</td><td>1.4</td><td>36</td><td>Utah</td><td>0.5</td></tr>
<tr><td>29</td><td>South Dakota</td><td>0.7</td><td>36</td><td>Wyoming</td><td>0.5</td></tr>
<tr><td>22</td><td>Tennessee</td><td>0.9</td><td>42</td><td>Colorado</td><td>0.4</td></tr>
<tr><td>36</td><td>Texas</td><td>0.5</td><td>42</td><td>Connecticut</td><td>0.4</td></tr>
<tr><td>36</td><td>Utah</td><td>0.5</td><td>42</td><td>Maine</td><td>0.4</td></tr>
<tr><td>16</td><td>Vermont</td><td>1.0</td><td>42</td><td>Nevada</td><td>0.4</td></tr>
<tr><td>25</td><td>Virginia</td><td>0.8</td><td>42</td><td>New Jersey</td><td>0.4</td></tr>
<tr><td>42</td><td>Washington</td><td>0.4</td><td>42</td><td>New Mexico</td><td>0.4</td></tr>
<tr><td>1</td><td>West Virginia</td><td>2.8</td><td>42</td><td>New York</td><td>0.4</td></tr>
<tr><td>16</td><td>Wisconsin</td><td>1.0</td><td>42</td><td>Washington</td><td>0.4</td></tr>
<tr><td>36</td><td>Wyoming</td><td>0.5</td><td>50</td><td>New Hampshire</td><td>0.3</td></tr>
<tr><td></td><td></td><td></td><td></td><td>District of Columbia</td><td>1.5</td></tr>
</table>

Source: U.S. Department of Education, Office of Special Education Programs
"Data Tables for OSEP State Reported Data" (https://www.ideadata.org/arc_toc8.asp)
*2006-2007 school year. IDEA authorizes funding to states and other organizations to support research, demonstrations, technical assistance, and other programs to ensure that the rights of infants, toddlers, children, and youth with disabilities and their parents are protected. National percent does not include children served in U.S. territories and Bureau of Indian Affairs programs.

Percent of Children Age 6 to 17 Served Under the Individuals with Disabilities Education Act (IDEA) for Emotional Disturbance in 2007
National Percent = 0.9%*

ALPHA ORDER

RANK	STATE	PERCENT
49	Alabama	0.2
35	Alaska	0.6
30	Arizona	0.7
49	Arkansas	0.2
44	California	0.4
16	Colorado	1.0
20	Connecticut	0.9
35	Delaware	0.6
10	Florida	1.2
6	Georgia	1.3
16	Hawaii	1.0
41	Idaho	0.5
10	Illinois	1.2
6	Indiana	1.3
6	Iowa	1.3
30	Kansas	0.7
24	Kentucky	0.8
44	Louisiana	0.4
5	Maine	1.4
20	Maryland	0.9
6	Massachusetts	1.3
16	Michigan	1.0
2	Minnesota	1.8
48	Mississippi	0.3
24	Missouri	0.8
35	Montana	0.6
30	Nebraska	0.7
41	Nevada	0.5
14	New Hampshire	1.1
24	New Jersey	0.8
30	New Mexico	0.7
10	New York	1.2
35	North Carolina	0.6
14	North Dakota	1.1
20	Ohio	0.9
24	Oklahoma	0.8
24	Oregon	0.8
10	Pennsylvania	1.2
4	Rhode Island	1.6
35	South Carolina	0.6
35	South Dakota	0.6
44	Tennessee	0.4
24	Texas	0.8
41	Utah	0.5
1	Vermont	2.1
20	Virginia	0.9
44	Washington	0.4
30	West Virginia	0.7
3	Wisconsin	1.7
16	Wyoming	1.0

RANK ORDER

RANK	STATE	PERCENT
1	Vermont	2.1
2	Minnesota	1.8
3	Wisconsin	1.7
4	Rhode Island	1.6
5	Maine	1.4
6	Georgia	1.3
6	Indiana	1.3
6	Iowa	1.3
6	Massachusetts	1.3
10	Florida	1.2
10	Illinois	1.2
10	New York	1.2
10	Pennsylvania	1.2
14	New Hampshire	1.1
14	North Dakota	1.1
16	Colorado	1.0
16	Hawaii	1.0
16	Michigan	1.0
16	Wyoming	1.0
20	Connecticut	0.9
20	Maryland	0.9
20	Ohio	0.9
20	Virginia	0.9
24	Kentucky	0.8
24	Missouri	0.8
24	New Jersey	0.8
24	Oklahoma	0.8
24	Oregon	0.8
24	Texas	0.8
30	Arizona	0.7
30	Kansas	0.7
30	Nebraska	0.7
30	New Mexico	0.7
30	West Virginia	0.7
35	Alaska	0.6
35	Delaware	0.6
35	Montana	0.6
35	North Carolina	0.6
35	South Carolina	0.6
35	South Dakota	0.6
41	Idaho	0.5
41	Nevada	0.5
41	Utah	0.5
44	California	0.4
44	Louisiana	0.4
44	Tennessee	0.4
44	Washington	0.4
48	Mississippi	0.3
49	Alabama	0.2
49	Arkansas	0.2

District of Columbia   2.1

Source: U.S. Department of Education, Office of Special Education Programs
"Data Tables for OSEP State Reported Data" (https://www.ideadata.org/arc_toc8.asp)
*2006-2007 school year. IDEA authorizes funding to states and other organizations to support research, demonstrations, technical assistance, and other programs to ensure that the rights of infants, toddlers, children, and youth with disabilities and their parents are protected. National percent does not include children served in U.S. territories and Bureau of Indian Affairs programs.

Special Education Students Who Graduated with a Diploma in 2006

National Total = 222,570 Students*

ALPHA ORDER

RANK	STATE	STUDENTS	% of USA
35	Alabama	1,438	0.6%
49	Alaska	423	0.2%
28	Arizona	2,263	1.0%
24	Arkansas	3,112	1.4%
2	California	19,880	8.9%
26	Colorado	2,447	1.1%
19	Connecticut	3,730	1.7%
46	Delaware	550	0.2%
7	Florida	9,533	4.3%
21	Georgia	3,460	1.6%
39	Hawaii	1,159	0.5%
40	Idaho	968	0.4%
1	Illinois	25,038	11.2%
15	Indiana	4,694	2.1%
20	Iowa	3,707	1.7%
25	Kansas	2,994	1.3%
23	Kentucky	3,142	1.4%
38	Louisiana	1,248	0.6%
34	Maine	1,544	0.7%
18	Maryland	3,816	1.7%
8	Massachusetts	6,819	3.1%
12	Michigan	5,578	2.5%
14	Minnesota	5,323	2.4%
42	Mississippi	767	0.3%
9	Missouri	6,281	2.8%
41	Montana	874	0.4%
31	Nebraska	1,764	0.8%
43	Nevada	596	0.3%
32	New Hampshire	1,673	0.8%
6	New Jersey	13,167	5.9%
36	New Mexico	1,398	0.6%
5	New York	13,413	6.0%
13	North Carolina	5,498	2.5%
45	North Dakota	562	0.3%
10	Ohio	5,880	2.6%
16	Oklahoma	4,493	2.0%
30	Oregon	1,997	0.9%
3	Pennsylvania	15,447	6.9%
37	Rhode Island	1,338	0.6%
33	South Carolina	1,648	0.7%
47	South Dakota	498	0.2%
22	Tennessee	3,182	1.4%
4	Texas	13,550	6.1%
27	Utah	2,301	1.0%
44	Vermont	593	0.3%
17	Virginia	4,144	1.9%
NA	Washington**	NA	NA
29	West Virginia	2,133	1.0%
11	Wisconsin	5,829	2.6%
48	Wyoming	453	0.2%

RANK ORDER

RANK	STATE	STUDENTS	% of USA
1	Illinois	25,038	11.2%
2	California	19,880	8.9%
3	Pennsylvania	15,447	6.9%
4	Texas	13,550	6.1%
5	New York	13,413	6.0%
6	New Jersey	13,167	5.9%
7	Florida	9,533	4.3%
8	Massachusetts	6,819	3.1%
9	Missouri	6,281	2.8%
10	Ohio	5,880	2.6%
11	Wisconsin	5,829	2.6%
12	Michigan	5,578	2.5%
13	North Carolina	5,498	2.5%
14	Minnesota	5,323	2.4%
15	Indiana	4,694	2.1%
16	Oklahoma	4,493	2.0%
17	Virginia	4,144	1.9%
18	Maryland	3,816	1.7%
19	Connecticut	3,730	1.7%
20	Iowa	3,707	1.7%
21	Georgia	3,460	1.6%
22	Tennessee	3,182	1.4%
23	Kentucky	3,142	1.4%
24	Arkansas	3,112	1.4%
25	Kansas	2,994	1.3%
26	Colorado	2,447	1.1%
27	Utah	2,301	1.0%
28	Arizona	2,263	1.0%
29	West Virginia	2,133	1.0%
30	Oregon	1,997	0.9%
31	Nebraska	1,764	0.8%
32	New Hampshire	1,673	0.8%
33	South Carolina	1,648	0.7%
34	Maine	1,544	0.7%
35	Alabama	1,438	0.6%
36	New Mexico	1,398	0.6%
37	Rhode Island	1,338	0.6%
38	Louisiana	1,248	0.6%
39	Hawaii	1,159	0.5%
40	Idaho	968	0.4%
41	Montana	874	0.4%
42	Mississippi	767	0.3%
43	Nevada	596	0.3%
44	Vermont	593	0.3%
45	North Dakota	562	0.3%
46	Delaware	550	0.2%
47	South Dakota	498	0.2%
48	Wyoming	453	0.2%
49	Alaska	423	0.2%
NA	Washington**	NA	NA
	District of Columbia	225	0.1%

Source: U.S. Department of Education, Office of Special Education Programs
"Data Tables for OSEP State Reported Data" (https://www.ideadata.org/arc_toc8.asp)
*2005-2006 school year. National total does not include 1,773 graduates served in U.S. territories and Bureau of Indian Affairs programs.
**Not available.

Special Education Students Who Dropped Out of School in 2006

National Total = 102,986 Students*

ALPHA ORDER

RANK	STATE	STUDENTS	% of USA
13	Alabama	2,169	2.1%
43	Alaska	379	0.4%
14	Arizona	2,082	2.0%
34	Arkansas	761	0.7%
1	California	10,829	10.5%
35	Colorado	754	0.7%
32	Connecticut	868	0.8%
46	Delaware	213	0.2%
4	Florida	6,649	6.5%
9	Georgia	3,596	3.5%
49	Hawaii	47	0.0%
38	Idaho	559	0.5%
3	Illinois	8,452	8.2%
8	Indiana	3,851	3.7%
26	Iowa	1,402	1.4%
29	Kansas	1,131	1.1%
28	Kentucky	1,369	1.3%
15	Louisiana	2,079	2.0%
36	Maine	698	0.7%
16	Maryland	1,942	1.9%
11	Massachusetts	2,518	2.4%
18	Michigan	1,935	1.9%
20	Minnesota	1,787	1.7%
37	Mississippi	649	0.6%
12	Missouri	2,490	2.4%
42	Montana	386	0.4%
40	Nebraska	459	0.4%
30	Nevada	1,026	1.0%
24	New Hampshire	1,500	1.5%
7	New Jersey	4,184	4.1%
41	New Mexico	453	0.4%
2	New York	8,829	8.6%
6	North Carolina	4,237	4.1%
48	North Dakota	162	0.2%
19	Ohio	1,840	1.8%
17	Oklahoma	1,940	1.9%
25	Oregon	1,474	1.4%
22	Pennsylvania	1,647	1.6%
39	Rhode Island	472	0.5%
10	South Carolina	2,521	2.4%
47	South Dakota	201	0.2%
27	Tennessee	1,374	1.3%
5	Texas	5,399	5.2%
33	Utah	834	0.8%
44	Vermont	271	0.3%
21	Virginia	1,778	1.7%
NA	Washington**	NA	NA
31	West Virginia	955	0.9%
23	Wisconsin	1,587	1.5%
45	Wyoming	248	0.2%

RANK ORDER

RANK	STATE	STUDENTS	% of USA
1	California	10,829	10.5%
2	New York	8,829	8.6%
3	Illinois	8,452	8.2%
4	Florida	6,649	6.5%
5	Texas	5,399	5.2%
6	North Carolina	4,237	4.1%
7	New Jersey	4,184	4.1%
8	Indiana	3,851	3.7%
9	Georgia	3,596	3.5%
10	South Carolina	2,521	2.4%
11	Massachusetts	2,518	2.4%
12	Missouri	2,490	2.4%
13	Alabama	2,169	2.1%
14	Arizona	2,082	2.0%
15	Louisiana	2,079	2.0%
16	Maryland	1,942	1.9%
17	Oklahoma	1,940	1.9%
18	Michigan	1,935	1.9%
19	Ohio	1,840	1.8%
20	Minnesota	1,787	1.7%
21	Virginia	1,778	1.7%
22	Pennsylvania	1,647	1.6%
23	Wisconsin	1,587	1.5%
24	New Hampshire	1,500	1.5%
25	Oregon	1,474	1.4%
26	Iowa	1,402	1.4%
27	Tennessee	1,374	1.3%
28	Kentucky	1,369	1.3%
29	Kansas	1,131	1.1%
30	Nevada	1,026	1.0%
31	West Virginia	955	0.9%
32	Connecticut	868	0.8%
33	Utah	834	0.8%
34	Arkansas	761	0.7%
35	Colorado	754	0.7%
36	Maine	698	0.7%
37	Mississippi	649	0.6%
38	Idaho	559	0.5%
39	Rhode Island	472	0.5%
40	Nebraska	459	0.4%
41	New Mexico	453	0.4%
42	Montana	386	0.4%
43	Alaska	379	0.4%
44	Vermont	271	0.3%
45	Wyoming	248	0.2%
46	Delaware	213	0.2%
47	South Dakota	201	0.2%
48	North Dakota	162	0.2%
49	Hawaii	47	0.0%
NA	Washington**	NA	NA
	District of Columbia**	NA	NA

Source: U.S. Department of Education, Office of Special Education Programs
   "Data Tables for OSEP State Reported Data" (https://www.ideadata.org/arc_toc8.asp)
*2005-2006 school year. "Dropped out" is defined as the total who were enrolled at some point in the reporting year, were not enrolled at the end of the reporting year and who did not graduate, receive a certificate, die, or reach maximum age. Drop outs includes runaways, GED recipients, expulsions, status unknown, and other exiters.
**Not available.

Public Elementary and Secondary School Students with Individual Educational Plans (IEPs) in 2006
Reporting States Total = 6,677,945 Students*

<table>
<tr><th colspan="4">ALPHA ORDER</th><th colspan="4">RANK ORDER</th></tr>
<tr><th>RANK</th><th>STATE</th><th>STUDENTS</th><th>% of USA</th><th>RANK</th><th>STATE</th><th>STUDENTS</th><th>% of USA</th></tr>
<tr><td>18</td><td>Alabama</td><td>124,732</td><td>1.9%</td><td>1</td><td>California</td><td>676,752</td><td>10.1%</td></tr>
<tr><td>45</td><td>Alaska</td><td>18,056</td><td>0.3%</td><td>2</td><td>Texas</td><td>511,939</td><td>7.7%</td></tr>
<tr><td>11</td><td>Arizona</td><td>196,514</td><td>2.9%</td><td>3</td><td>Florida</td><td>398,226</td><td>6.0%</td></tr>
<tr><td>34</td><td>Arkansas</td><td>58,400</td><td>0.9%</td><td>4</td><td>New Jersey</td><td>372,003</td><td>5.6%</td></tr>
<tr><td>1</td><td>California</td><td>676,752</td><td>10.1%</td><td>5</td><td>New York</td><td>371,430</td><td>5.6%</td></tr>
<tr><td>27</td><td>Colorado</td><td>78,487</td><td>1.2%</td><td>6</td><td>Illinois</td><td>322,534</td><td>4.8%</td></tr>
<tr><td>31</td><td>Connecticut</td><td>66,521</td><td>1.0%</td><td>7</td><td>Pennsylvania</td><td>267,682</td><td>4.0%</td></tr>
<tr><td>46</td><td>Delaware</td><td>17,726</td><td>0.3%</td><td>8</td><td>Ohio</td><td>266,557</td><td>4.0%</td></tr>
<tr><td>3</td><td>Florida</td><td>398,226</td><td>6.0%</td><td>9</td><td>Michigan</td><td>246,400</td><td>3.7%</td></tr>
<tr><td>10</td><td>Georgia</td><td>197,596</td><td>3.0%</td><td>10</td><td>Georgia</td><td>197,596</td><td>3.0%</td></tr>
<tr><td>42</td><td>Hawaii</td><td>21,964</td><td>0.3%</td><td>11</td><td>Arizona</td><td>196,514</td><td>2.9%</td></tr>
<tr><td>40</td><td>Idaho</td><td>28,786</td><td>0.4%</td><td>12</td><td>North Carolina</td><td>192,233</td><td>2.9%</td></tr>
<tr><td>6</td><td>Illinois</td><td>322,534</td><td>4.8%</td><td>13</td><td>Indiana</td><td>176,887</td><td>2.6%</td></tr>
<tr><td>13</td><td>Indiana</td><td>176,887</td><td>2.6%</td><td>14</td><td>Virginia</td><td>175,177</td><td>2.6%</td></tr>
<tr><td>28</td><td>Iowa</td><td>71,616</td><td>1.1%</td><td>15</td><td>Massachusetts</td><td>150,154</td><td>2.2%</td></tr>
<tr><td>32</td><td>Kansas</td><td>65,418</td><td>1.0%</td><td>16</td><td>Wisconsin</td><td>129,875</td><td>1.9%</td></tr>
<tr><td>23</td><td>Kentucky</td><td>108,596</td><td>1.6%</td><td>17</td><td>Tennessee</td><td>126,933</td><td>1.9%</td></tr>
<tr><td>25</td><td>Louisiana</td><td>85,167</td><td>1.3%</td><td>18</td><td>Alabama</td><td>124,732</td><td>1.9%</td></tr>
<tr><td>38</td><td>Maine</td><td>33,084</td><td>0.5%</td><td>19</td><td>Washington</td><td>124,050</td><td>1.9%</td></tr>
<tr><td>21</td><td>Maryland</td><td>110,040</td><td>1.6%</td><td>20</td><td>Minnesota</td><td>115,534</td><td>1.7%</td></tr>
<tr><td>15</td><td>Massachusetts</td><td>150,154</td><td>2.2%</td><td>21</td><td>Maryland</td><td>110,040</td><td>1.6%</td></tr>
<tr><td>9</td><td>Michigan</td><td>246,400</td><td>3.7%</td><td>22</td><td>South Carolina</td><td>109,694</td><td>1.6%</td></tr>
<tr><td>20</td><td>Minnesota</td><td>115,534</td><td>1.7%</td><td>23</td><td>Kentucky</td><td>108,596</td><td>1.6%</td></tr>
<tr><td>29</td><td>Mississippi</td><td>67,922</td><td>1.0%</td><td>24</td><td>Oklahoma</td><td>96,342</td><td>1.4%</td></tr>
<tr><td>NA</td><td>Missouri**</td><td>NA</td><td>NA</td><td>25</td><td>Louisiana</td><td>85,167</td><td>1.3%</td></tr>
<tr><td>43</td><td>Montana</td><td>19,174</td><td>0.3%</td><td>26</td><td>Oregon</td><td>78,530</td><td>1.2%</td></tr>
<tr><td>36</td><td>Nebraska</td><td>46,500</td><td>0.7%</td><td>27</td><td>Colorado</td><td>78,487</td><td>1.2%</td></tr>
<tr><td>37</td><td>Nevada</td><td>45,763</td><td>0.7%</td><td>28</td><td>Iowa</td><td>71,616</td><td>1.1%</td></tr>
<tr><td>39</td><td>New Hampshire</td><td>30,487</td><td>0.5%</td><td>29</td><td>Mississippi</td><td>67,922</td><td>1.0%</td></tr>
<tr><td>4</td><td>New Jersey</td><td>372,003</td><td>5.6%</td><td>30</td><td>Utah</td><td>67,022</td><td>1.0%</td></tr>
<tr><td>33</td><td>New Mexico</td><td>64,283</td><td>1.0%</td><td>31</td><td>Connecticut</td><td>66,521</td><td>1.0%</td></tr>
<tr><td>5</td><td>New York</td><td>371,430</td><td>5.6%</td><td>32</td><td>Kansas</td><td>65,418</td><td>1.0%</td></tr>
<tr><td>12</td><td>North Carolina</td><td>192,233</td><td>2.9%</td><td>33</td><td>New Mexico</td><td>64,283</td><td>1.0%</td></tr>
<tr><td>47</td><td>North Dakota</td><td>13,819</td><td>0.2%</td><td>34</td><td>Arkansas</td><td>58,400</td><td>0.9%</td></tr>
<tr><td>8</td><td>Ohio</td><td>266,557</td><td>4.0%</td><td>35</td><td>West Virginia</td><td>49,304</td><td>0.7%</td></tr>
<tr><td>24</td><td>Oklahoma</td><td>96,342</td><td>1.4%</td><td>36</td><td>Nebraska</td><td>46,500</td><td>0.7%</td></tr>
<tr><td>26</td><td>Oregon</td><td>78,530</td><td>1.2%</td><td>37</td><td>Nevada</td><td>45,763</td><td>0.7%</td></tr>
<tr><td>7</td><td>Pennsylvania</td><td>267,682</td><td>4.0%</td><td>38</td><td>Maine</td><td>33,084</td><td>0.5%</td></tr>
<tr><td>41</td><td>Rhode Island</td><td>27,646</td><td>0.4%</td><td>39</td><td>New Hampshire</td><td>30,487</td><td>0.5%</td></tr>
<tr><td>22</td><td>South Carolina</td><td>109,694</td><td>1.6%</td><td>40</td><td>Idaho</td><td>28,786</td><td>0.4%</td></tr>
<tr><td>44</td><td>South Dakota</td><td>18,405</td><td>0.3%</td><td>41</td><td>Rhode Island</td><td>27,646</td><td>0.4%</td></tr>
<tr><td>17</td><td>Tennessee</td><td>126,933</td><td>1.9%</td><td>42</td><td>Hawaii</td><td>21,964</td><td>0.3%</td></tr>
<tr><td>2</td><td>Texas</td><td>511,939</td><td>7.7%</td><td>43</td><td>Montana</td><td>19,174</td><td>0.3%</td></tr>
<tr><td>30</td><td>Utah</td><td>67,022</td><td>1.0%</td><td>44</td><td>South Dakota</td><td>18,405</td><td>0.3%</td></tr>
<tr><td>49</td><td>Vermont</td><td>10,915</td><td>0.2%</td><td>45</td><td>Alaska</td><td>18,056</td><td>0.3%</td></tr>
<tr><td>14</td><td>Virginia</td><td>175,177</td><td>2.6%</td><td>46</td><td>Delaware</td><td>17,726</td><td>0.3%</td></tr>
<tr><td>19</td><td>Washington</td><td>124,050</td><td>1.9%</td><td>47</td><td>North Dakota</td><td>13,819</td><td>0.2%</td></tr>
<tr><td>35</td><td>West Virginia</td><td>49,304</td><td>0.7%</td><td>48</td><td>Wyoming</td><td>11,681</td><td>0.2%</td></tr>
<tr><td>16</td><td>Wisconsin</td><td>129,875</td><td>1.9%</td><td>49</td><td>Vermont</td><td>10,915</td><td>0.2%</td></tr>
<tr><td>48</td><td>Wyoming</td><td>11,681</td><td>0.2%</td><td>NA</td><td>Missouri**</td><td>NA</td><td>NA</td></tr>
<tr><td></td><td></td><td></td><td></td><td></td><td>District of Columbia</td><td>13,389</td><td>0.2%</td></tr>
</table>

Source: U.S. Department of Education, National Center for Education Statistics
   "Common Core of Data (CCD) Database" (http://nces.ed.gov/ccd/)
*National total is for reporting states only. These plans are for students participating in various special education services. For school year 2005-2006.
**Not available.

Percent of Public Elementary and Secondary School Students with Individualized Education Plans (IEPs) in 2006
Reporting States Percent = 13.9%*

ALPHA ORDER

RANK	STATE	PERCENT
8	Alabama	16.8
31	Alaska	13.5
3	Arizona	18.0
40	Arkansas	12.3
48	California	10.7
49	Colorado	10.1
43	Connecticut	11.6
20	Delaware	14.7
16	Florida	14.9
39	Georgia	12.4
41	Hawaii	12.0
47	Idaho	11.0
13	Illinois	15.3
6	Indiana	17.1
17	Iowa	14.8
27	Kansas	14.0
10	Kentucky	16.0
37	Louisiana	13.0
7	Maine	16.9
38	Maryland	12.8
12	Massachusetts	15.4
25	Michigan	14.1
28	Minnesota	13.8
29	Mississippi	13.7
NA	Missouri**	NA
34	Montana	13.2
9	Nebraska	16.2
46	Nevada	11.1
17	New Hampshire	14.8
1	New Jersey	26.7
2	New Mexico	19.7
34	New York	13.2
30	North Carolina	13.6
25	North Dakota	14.1
23	Ohio	14.5
14	Oklahoma	15.2
21	Oregon	14.6
21	Pennsylvania	14.6
3	Rhode Island	18.0
11	South Carolina	15.6
15	South Dakota	15.1
33	Tennessee	13.3
44	Texas	11.3
34	Utah	13.2
44	Vermont	11.3
24	Virginia	14.4
41	Washington	12.0
5	West Virginia	17.6
17	Wisconsin	14.8
31	Wyoming	13.5

RANK ORDER

RANK	STATE	PERCENT
1	New Jersey	26.7
2	New Mexico	19.7
3	Arizona	18.0
3	Rhode Island	18.0
5	West Virginia	17.6
6	Indiana	17.1
7	Maine	16.9
8	Alabama	16.8
9	Nebraska	16.2
10	Kentucky	16.0
11	South Carolina	15.6
12	Massachusetts	15.4
13	Illinois	15.3
14	Oklahoma	15.2
15	South Dakota	15.1
16	Florida	14.9
17	Iowa	14.8
17	New Hampshire	14.8
17	Wisconsin	14.8
20	Delaware	14.7
21	Oregon	14.6
21	Pennsylvania	14.6
23	Ohio	14.5
24	Virginia	14.4
25	Michigan	14.1
25	North Dakota	14.1
27	Kansas	14.0
28	Minnesota	13.8
29	Mississippi	13.7
30	North Carolina	13.6
31	Alaska	13.5
31	Wyoming	13.5
33	Tennessee	13.3
34	Montana	13.2
34	New York	13.2
34	Utah	13.2
37	Louisiana	13.0
38	Maryland	12.8
39	Georgia	12.4
40	Arkansas	12.3
41	Hawaii	12.0
41	Washington	12.0
43	Connecticut	11.6
44	Texas	11.3
44	Vermont	11.3
46	Nevada	11.1
47	Idaho	11.0
48	California	10.7
49	Colorado	10.1
NA	Missouri**	NA

District of Columbia — 17.4

Source: CQ Press using data from U.S. Department of Education, National Center for Education Statistics "Common Core of Data (CCD) Database" (http://nces.ed.gov/ccd/)

*National percent is for reporting states only. These plans are for students participating in various special education services. For school year 2005-2006.

**Not available.

Public Elementary and Secondary School Students Receiving English Language Learner (ELL) Services in 2006
Reporting States Total = 4,223,115 Students*

ALPHA ORDER

RANK	STATE	STUDENTS	% of USA
32	Alabama	16,550	0.4%
26	Alaska	20,743	0.5%
5	Arizona	174,856	4.1%
27	Arkansas	20,709	0.5%
1	California	1,571,463	37.2%
6	Colorado	99,797	2.4%
24	Connecticut	29,789	0.7%
39	Delaware	5,919	0.1%
3	Florida	221,705	5.2%
7	Georgia	86,615	2.1%
30	Hawaii	18,106	0.4%
29	Idaho	18,184	0.4%
NA	Illinois**	NA	NA
16	Indiana	56,510	1.3%
33	Iowa	15,156	0.4%
25	Kansas	24,671	0.6%
36	Kentucky	10,138	0.2%
35	Louisiana	12,006	0.3%
41	Maine	3,353	0.1%
21	Maryland	31,416	0.7%
17	Massachusetts	51,618	1.2%
11	Michigan	65,419	1.5%
15	Minnesota	57,831	1.4%
43	Mississippi	2,859	0.1%
28	Missouri	18,745	0.4%
38	Montana	6,711	0.2%
31	Nebraska	17,449	0.4%
13	Nevada	63,856	1.5%
NA	New Hampshire**	NA	NA
18	New Jersey	50,515	1.2%
14	New Mexico	62,682	1.5%
4	New York	194,123	4.6%
9	North Carolina	73,634	1.7%
NA	North Dakota**	NA	NA
23	Ohio	29,804	0.7%
20	Oklahoma	47,381	1.1%
12	Oregon	64,676	1.5%
NA	Pennsylvania**	NA	NA
37	Rhode Island	7,468	0.2%
34	South Carolina	14,388	0.3%
40	South Dakota	5,110	0.1%
NA	Tennessee**	NA	NA
2	Texas	711,737	16.9%
19	Utah	49,973	1.2%
45	Vermont	1,775	0.0%
10	Virginia	72,420	1.7%
8	Washington	75,103	1.8%
44	West Virginia	1,944	0.0%
22	Wisconsin	30,130	0.7%
42	Wyoming	3,077	0.1%

RANK ORDER

RANK	STATE	STUDENTS	% of USA
1	California	1,571,463	37.2%
2	Texas	711,737	16.9%
3	Florida	221,705	5.2%
4	New York	194,123	4.6%
5	Arizona	174,856	4.1%
6	Colorado	99,797	2.4%
7	Georgia	86,615	2.1%
8	Washington	75,103	1.8%
9	North Carolina	73,634	1.7%
10	Virginia	72,420	1.7%
11	Michigan	65,419	1.5%
12	Oregon	64,676	1.5%
13	Nevada	63,856	1.5%
14	New Mexico	62,682	1.5%
15	Minnesota	57,831	1.4%
16	Indiana	56,510	1.3%
17	Massachusetts	51,618	1.2%
18	New Jersey	50,515	1.2%
19	Utah	49,973	1.2%
20	Oklahoma	47,381	1.1%
21	Maryland	31,416	0.7%
22	Wisconsin	30,130	0.7%
23	Ohio	29,804	0.7%
24	Connecticut	29,789	0.7%
25	Kansas	24,671	0.6%
26	Alaska	20,743	0.5%
27	Arkansas	20,709	0.5%
28	Missouri	18,745	0.4%
29	Idaho	18,184	0.4%
30	Hawaii	18,106	0.4%
31	Nebraska	17,449	0.4%
32	Alabama	16,550	0.4%
33	Iowa	15,156	0.4%
34	South Carolina	14,388	0.3%
35	Louisiana	12,006	0.3%
36	Kentucky	10,138	0.2%
37	Rhode Island	7,468	0.2%
38	Montana	6,711	0.2%
39	Delaware	5,919	0.1%
40	South Dakota	5,110	0.1%
41	Maine	3,353	0.1%
42	Wyoming	3,077	0.1%
43	Mississippi	2,859	0.1%
44	West Virginia	1,944	0.0%
45	Vermont	1,775	0.0%
NA	Illinois**	NA	NA
NA	New Hampshire**	NA	NA
NA	North Dakota**	NA	NA
NA	Pennsylvania**	NA	NA
NA	Tennessee**	NA	NA
	District of Columbia	5,001	0.1%

Source: U.S. Department of Education, National Center for Education Statistics
  "Common Core of Data (CCD) Database" (http://nces.ed.gov/ccd/)
*For school year 2005-2006. Total shown is for reporting states only.   Increasingly, English language learner (ELL) or English learner (EL) are used in place of Limited English proficient (LEP) as the term to identify those students who have insufficient English to succeed in English-only classrooms.
**Not available.

Percent of Public Elementary and Secondary School Students Receiving English Language Learner (ELL) Services in 2006
Reporting States Percent = 9.6%*

ALPHA ORDER

RANK	STATE	PERCENT
36	Alabama	2.2
5	Alaska	15.6
3	Arizona	16.0
28	Arkansas	4.4
1	California	24.9
7	Colorado	12.8
23	Connecticut	5.2
25	Delaware	4.9
11	Florida	8.3
20	Georgia	5.4
9	Hawaii	9.9
14	Idaho	6.9
NA	Illinois**	NA
19	Indiana	5.5
35	Iowa	3.1
21	Kansas	5.3
43	Kentucky	1.5
39	Louisiana	1.8
41	Maine	1.7
31	Maryland	3.7
21	Massachusetts	5.3
30	Michigan	3.8
14	Minnesota	6.9
45	Mississippi	0.6
38	Missouri	2.0
27	Montana	4.6
17	Nebraska	6.1
6	Nevada	15.5
NA	New Hampshire**	NA
32	New Jersey	3.6
2	New Mexico	19.2
14	New York	6.9
23	North Carolina	5.2
NA	North Dakota**	NA
42	Ohio	1.6
12	Oklahoma	7.5
8	Oregon	12.0
NA	Pennsylvania**	NA
25	Rhode Island	4.9
37	South Carolina	2.1
29	South Dakota	4.2
NA	Tennessee**	NA
4	Texas	15.7
10	Utah	9.8
39	Vermont	1.8
18	Virginia	6.0
13	Washington	7.3
44	West Virginia	0.7
34	Wisconsin	3.4
32	Wyoming	3.6

RANK ORDER

RANK	STATE	PERCENT
1	California	24.9
2	New Mexico	19.2
3	Arizona	16.0
4	Texas	15.7
5	Alaska	15.6
6	Nevada	15.5
7	Colorado	12.8
8	Oregon	12.0
9	Hawaii	9.9
10	Utah	9.8
11	Florida	8.3
12	Oklahoma	7.5
13	Washington	7.3
14	Idaho	6.9
14	Minnesota	6.9
14	New York	6.9
17	Nebraska	6.1
18	Virginia	6.0
19	Indiana	5.5
20	Georgia	5.4
21	Kansas	5.3
21	Massachusetts	5.3
23	Connecticut	5.2
23	North Carolina	5.2
25	Delaware	4.9
25	Rhode Island	4.9
27	Montana	4.6
28	Arkansas	4.4
29	South Dakota	4.2
30	Michigan	3.8
31	Maryland	3.7
32	New Jersey	3.6
32	Wyoming	3.6
34	Wisconsin	3.4
35	Iowa	3.1
36	Alabama	2.2
37	South Carolina	2.1
38	Missouri	2.0
39	Louisiana	1.8
39	Vermont	1.8
41	Maine	1.7
42	Ohio	1.6
43	Kentucky	1.5
44	West Virginia	0.7
45	Mississippi	0.6
NA	Illinois**	NA
NA	New Hampshire**	NA
NA	North Dakota**	NA
NA	Pennsylvania**	NA
NA	Tennessee**	NA

District of Columbia   6.5

Source: CQ Press using data from U.S. Department of Education, National Center for Education Statistics
   "Common Core of Data (CCD) Database" (http://nces.ed.gov/ccd/)
*For school year 2005-2006. National percent is for reporting states only. Increasingly, English language learner (ELL) or English learner (EL) are used in place of Limited English proficient (LEP) as the term to identify those students who have insufficient English to succeed in English-only classrooms.
**Not available.

Special Education Teachers in 2006

National Total = 467,405 Teachers*

ALPHA ORDER

RANK	STATE	TEACHERS	% of USA
23	Alabama	6,243	1.3%
46	Alaska	1,066	0.2%
17	Arizona	8,372	1.8%
31	Arkansas	4,445	1.0%
2	California	33,669	7.2%
29	Colorado	4,861	1.0%
28	Connecticut	4,937	1.1%
43	Delaware	1,535	0.3%
5	Florida	24,250	5.2%
11	Georgia	15,102	3.2%
40	Hawaii	2,289	0.5%
44	Idaho	1,457	0.3%
4	Illinois	24,469	5.2%
18	Indiana	8,246	1.8%
25	Iowa	6,039	1.3%
33	Kansas	4,266	0.9%
21	Kentucky	6,714	1.4%
20	Louisiana	7,111	1.5%
36	Maine	2,949	0.6%
19	Maryland	7,936	1.7%
7	Massachusetts	21,795	4.7%
12	Michigan	14,608	3.1%
15	Minnesota	8,686	1.9%
32	Mississippi	4,403	0.9%
14	Missouri	9,937	2.1%
48	Montana	927	0.2%
39	Nebraska	2,568	0.5%
38	Nevada	2,815	0.6%
41	New Hampshire	2,277	0.5%
8	New Jersey	21,537	4.6%
30	New Mexico	4,512	1.0%
1	New York	49,254	10.5%
13	North Carolina	12,125	2.6%
49	North Dakota	909	0.2%
9	Ohio	18,426	3.9%
27	Oklahoma	4,959	1.1%
34	Oregon	3,548	0.8%
6	Pennsylvania	22,431	4.8%
42	Rhode Island	2,181	0.5%
22	South Carolina	6,467	1.4%
47	South Dakota	996	0.2%
24	Tennessee	6,196	1.3%
3	Texas	31,674	6.8%
37	Utah	2,842	0.6%
45	Vermont	1,142	0.2%
10	Virginia	15,310	3.3%
26	Washington	5,821	1.2%
35	West Virginia	3,100	0.7%
16	Wisconsin	8,454	1.8%
50	Wyoming	873	0.2%

RANK ORDER

RANK	STATE	TEACHERS	% of USA
1	New York	49,254	10.5%
2	California	33,669	7.2%
3	Texas	31,674	6.8%
4	Illinois	24,469	5.2%
5	Florida	24,250	5.2%
6	Pennsylvania	22,431	4.8%
7	Massachusetts	21,795	4.7%
8	New Jersey	21,537	4.6%
9	Ohio	18,426	3.9%
10	Virginia	15,310	3.3%
11	Georgia	15,102	3.2%
12	Michigan	14,608	3.1%
13	North Carolina	12,125	2.6%
14	Missouri	9,937	2.1%
15	Minnesota	8,686	1.9%
16	Wisconsin	8,454	1.8%
17	Arizona	8,372	1.8%
18	Indiana	8,246	1.8%
19	Maryland	7,936	1.7%
20	Louisiana	7,111	1.5%
21	Kentucky	6,714	1.4%
22	South Carolina	6,467	1.4%
23	Alabama	6,243	1.3%
24	Tennessee	6,196	1.3%
25	Iowa	6,039	1.3%
26	Washington	5,821	1.2%
27	Oklahoma	4,959	1.1%
28	Connecticut	4,937	1.1%
29	Colorado	4,861	1.0%
30	New Mexico	4,512	1.0%
31	Arkansas	4,445	1.0%
32	Mississippi	4,403	0.9%
33	Kansas	4,266	0.9%
34	Oregon	3,548	0.8%
35	West Virginia	3,100	0.7%
36	Maine	2,949	0.6%
37	Utah	2,842	0.6%
38	Nevada	2,815	0.6%
39	Nebraska	2,568	0.5%
40	Hawaii	2,289	0.5%
41	New Hampshire	2,277	0.5%
42	Rhode Island	2,181	0.5%
43	Delaware	1,535	0.3%
44	Idaho	1,457	0.3%
45	Vermont	1,142	0.2%
46	Alaska	1,066	0.2%
47	South Dakota	996	0.2%
48	Montana	927	0.2%
49	North Dakota	909	0.2%
50	Wyoming	873	0.2%

District of Columbia 676 0.1%

Source: CQ Press using data from U.S. Department of Education, Office of Special Education Programs
"Data Tables for OSEP State Reported Data" (https://www.ideadata.org/arc_toc8.asp)
*Figures are full-time equivalent (FTE). Includes fully certified and not fully certified teachers of disabled children ages 3 to 21
for school year 2005-2006. National total does not include 5,973 teachers in U.S. territories and Bureau of Indian Affairs
programs.

Pre-School Special Education Teachers in 2006

National Total = 46,588 Teachers*

RANK	STATE	TEACHERS	% of USA		RANK	STATE	TEACHERS	% of USA
21	Alabama	686	1.5%		1	Massachusetts	11,317	24.3%
48	Alaska	83	0.2%		2	New York	5,342	11.5%
5	Arizona	1,820	3.9%		3	California	2,142	4.6%
23	Arkansas	631	1.4%		4	Florida	1,996	4.3%
3	California	2,142	4.6%		5	Arizona	1,820	3.9%
33	Colorado	286	0.6%		6	Pennsylvania	1,535	3.3%
50	Connecticut	24	0.1%		7	Virginia	1,382	3.0%
44	Delaware	100	0.2%		8	Ohio	1,323	2.8%
4	Florida	1,996	4.3%		9	Illinois	1,276	2.7%
19	Georgia	714	1.5%		10	Indiana	1,207	2.6%
36	Hawaii	253	0.5%		11	North Carolina	1,122	2.4%
39	Idaho	174	0.4%		12	New Jersey	1,090	2.3%
9	Illinois	1,276	2.7%		13	Texas	1,035	2.2%
10	Indiana	1,207	2.6%		14	Louisiana	945	2.0%
27	Iowa	435	0.9%		15	Tennessee	894	1.9%
26	Kansas	456	1.0%		16	Missouri	827	1.8%
30	Kentucky	326	0.7%		17	Michigan	813	1.7%
14	Louisiana	945	2.0%		18	South Carolina	724	1.6%
34	Maine	272	0.6%		19	Georgia	714	1.5%
25	Maryland	486	1.0%		20	Wisconsin	699	1.5%
1	Massachusetts	11,317	24.3%		21	Alabama	686	1.5%
17	Michigan	813	1.7%		22	Mississippi	633	1.4%
32	Minnesota	291	0.6%		23	Arkansas	631	1.4%
22	Mississippi	633	1.4%		24	Washington	561	1.2%
16	Missouri	827	1.8%		25	Maryland	486	1.0%
46	Montana	93	0.2%		26	Kansas	456	1.0%
35	Nebraska	267	0.6%		27	Iowa	435	0.9%
29	Nevada	348	0.7%		28	Oklahoma	427	0.9%
41	New Hampshire	146	0.3%		29	Nevada	348	0.7%
12	New Jersey	1,090	2.3%		30	Kentucky	326	0.7%
30	New Mexico	326	0.7%		30	New Mexico	326	0.7%
2	New York	5,342	11.5%		32	Minnesota	291	0.6%
11	North Carolina	1,122	2.4%		33	Colorado	286	0.6%
47	North Dakota	84	0.2%		34	Maine	272	0.6%
8	Ohio	1,323	2.8%		35	Nebraska	267	0.6%
28	Oklahoma	427	0.9%		36	Hawaii	253	0.5%
40	Oregon	170	0.4%		37	West Virginia	244	0.5%
6	Pennsylvania	1,535	3.3%		38	Utah	186	0.4%
45	Rhode Island	99	0.2%		39	Idaho	174	0.4%
18	South Carolina	724	1.6%		40	Oregon	170	0.4%
43	South Dakota	110	0.2%		41	New Hampshire	146	0.3%
15	Tennessee	894	1.9%		42	Vermont	111	0.2%
13	Texas	1,035	2.2%		43	South Dakota	110	0.2%
38	Utah	186	0.4%		44	Delaware	100	0.2%
42	Vermont	111	0.2%		45	Rhode Island	99	0.2%
7	Virginia	1,382	3.0%		46	Montana	93	0.2%
24	Washington	561	1.2%		47	North Dakota	84	0.2%
37	West Virginia	244	0.5%		48	Alaska	83	0.2%
20	Wisconsin	699	1.5%		49	Wyoming	72	0.2%
49	Wyoming	72	0.2%		50	Connecticut	24	0.1%
						District of Columbia	5	0.0%

ALPHA ORDER

RANK ORDER

Source: U.S. Department of Education, Office of Special Education Programs
   "Data Tables for OSEP State Reported Data" (https://www.ideadata.org/arc_toc8.asp)
*Figures are full-time equivalent (FTE). Includes fully certified and not fully certified teachers of disabled children ages 3 to 5
for school year 2005-2006. National total does not include 297 teachers in U.S. territories and Bureau of Indian Affairs programs.

Fully Certified Pre-School Special Education Teachers in 2006

National Total = 41,490 Teachers*

ALPHA ORDER

RANK	STATE	TEACHERS	% of USA
20	Alabama	652	1.6%
47	Alaska	82	0.2%
5	Arizona	1,505	3.6%
24	Arkansas	531	1.3%
4	California	1,908	4.6%
36	Colorado	215	0.5%
50	Connecticut	24	0.1%
45	Delaware	98	0.2%
3	Florida	1,945	4.7%
21	Georgia	605	1.5%
34	Hawaii	238	0.6%
40	Idaho	139	0.3%
9	Illinois	1,249	3.0%
10	Indiana	1,176	2.8%
27	Iowa	435	1.0%
26	Kansas	437	1.1%
30	Kentucky	299	0.7%
16	Louisiana	776	1.9%
32	Maine	272	0.7%
25	Maryland	444	1.1%
1	Massachusetts	10,351	24.9%
19	Michigan	693	1.7%
31	Minnesota	279	0.7%
22	Mississippi	595	1.4%
15	Missouri	814	2.0%
46	Montana	90	0.2%
33	Nebraska	262	0.6%
35	Nevada	222	0.5%
41	New Hampshire	114	0.3%
11	New Jersey	1,071	2.6%
29	New Mexico	307	0.7%
2	New York	3,564	8.6%
12	North Carolina	947	2.3%
48	North Dakota	74	0.2%
8	Ohio	1,294	3.1%
28	Oklahoma	419	1.0%
39	Oregon	160	0.4%
6	Pennsylvania	1,503	3.6%
44	Rhode Island	99	0.2%
17	South Carolina	705	1.7%
42	South Dakota	104	0.3%
13	Tennessee	875	2.1%
14	Texas	816	2.0%
38	Utah	161	0.4%
43	Vermont	102	0.2%
7	Virginia	1,329	3.2%
23	Washington	548	1.3%
37	West Virginia	212	0.5%
18	Wisconsin	694	1.7%
49	Wyoming	51	0.1%

RANK ORDER

RANK	STATE	TEACHERS	% of USA
1	Massachusetts	10,351	24.9%
2	New York	3,564	8.6%
3	Florida	1,945	4.7%
4	California	1,908	4.6%
5	Arizona	1,505	3.6%
6	Pennsylvania	1,503	3.6%
7	Virginia	1,329	3.2%
8	Ohio	1,294	3.1%
9	Illinois	1,249	3.0%
10	Indiana	1,176	2.8%
11	New Jersey	1,071	2.6%
12	North Carolina	947	2.3%
13	Tennessee	875	2.1%
14	Texas	816	2.0%
15	Missouri	814	2.0%
16	Louisiana	776	1.9%
17	South Carolina	705	1.7%
18	Wisconsin	694	1.7%
19	Michigan	693	1.7%
20	Alabama	652	1.6%
21	Georgia	605	1.5%
22	Mississippi	595	1.4%
23	Washington	548	1.3%
24	Arkansas	531	1.3%
25	Maryland	444	1.1%
26	Kansas	437	1.1%
27	Iowa	435	1.0%
28	Oklahoma	419	1.0%
29	New Mexico	307	0.7%
30	Kentucky	299	0.7%
31	Minnesota	279	0.7%
32	Maine	272	0.7%
33	Nebraska	262	0.6%
34	Hawaii	238	0.6%
35	Nevada	222	0.5%
36	Colorado	215	0.5%
37	West Virginia	212	0.5%
38	Utah	161	0.4%
39	Oregon	160	0.4%
40	Idaho	139	0.3%
41	New Hampshire	114	0.3%
42	South Dakota	104	0.3%
43	Vermont	102	0.2%
44	Rhode Island	99	0.2%
45	Delaware	98	0.2%
46	Montana	90	0.2%
47	Alaska	82	0.2%
48	North Dakota	74	0.2%
49	Wyoming	51	0.1%
50	Connecticut	24	0.1%
	District of Columbia	5	0.0%

Source: U.S. Department of Education, Office of Special Education Programs
"Data Tables for OSEP State Reported Data" (https://www.ideadata.org/arc_toc8.asp)
*Figures are full-time equivalent (FTE). Includes fully certified teachers of disabled children ages 3 to 5 for school year
2005-2006. National total does not include 221 teachers in U.S. territories and Bureau of Indian Affairs programs.

Percent of Pre-School Special Education Teachers Fully Certified in 2006

National Percent = 89.1%*

ALPHA ORDER

RANK	STATE	PERCENT
24	Alabama	95.0
6	Alaska	98.8
42	Arizona	82.7
41	Arkansas	84.2
34	California	89.1
47	Colorado	75.2
1	Connecticut	100.0
11	Delaware	98.0
17	Florida	97.4
39	Georgia	84.7
27	Hawaii	94.1
44	Idaho	79.9
12	Illinois	97.9
17	Indiana	97.4
1	Iowa	100.0
23	Kansas	95.8
31	Kentucky	91.7
43	Louisiana	82.1
1	Maine	100.0
33	Maryland	91.4
32	Massachusetts	91.5
38	Michigan	85.2
22	Minnesota	95.9
29	Mississippi	94.0
7	Missouri	98.4
20	Montana	96.8
9	Nebraska	98.1
50	Nevada	63.8
46	New Hampshire	78.1
8	New Jersey	98.3
26	New Mexico	94.2
49	New York	66.7
40	North Carolina	84.4
35	North Dakota	88.1
15	Ohio	97.8
9	Oklahoma	98.1
27	Oregon	94.1
12	Pennsylvania	97.9
1	Rhode Island	100.0
17	South Carolina	97.4
25	South Dakota	94.5
12	Tennessee	97.9
45	Texas	78.8
37	Utah	86.6
30	Vermont	91.9
21	Virginia	96.2
16	Washington	97.7
36	West Virginia	86.9
5	Wisconsin	99.3
48	Wyoming	70.8

RANK ORDER

RANK	STATE	PERCENT
1	Connecticut	100.0
1	Iowa	100.0
1	Maine	100.0
1	Rhode Island	100.0
5	Wisconsin	99.3
6	Alaska	98.8
7	Missouri	98.4
8	New Jersey	98.3
9	Nebraska	98.1
9	Oklahoma	98.1
11	Delaware	98.0
12	Illinois	97.9
12	Pennsylvania	97.9
12	Tennessee	97.9
15	Ohio	97.8
16	Washington	97.7
17	Florida	97.4
17	Indiana	97.4
17	South Carolina	97.4
20	Montana	96.8
21	Virginia	96.2
22	Minnesota	95.9
23	Kansas	95.8
24	Alabama	95.0
25	South Dakota	94.5
26	New Mexico	94.2
27	Hawaii	94.1
27	Oregon	94.1
29	Mississippi	94.0
30	Vermont	91.9
31	Kentucky	91.7
32	Massachusetts	91.5
33	Maryland	91.4
34	California	89.1
35	North Dakota	88.1
36	West Virginia	86.9
37	Utah	86.6
38	Michigan	85.2
39	Georgia	84.7
40	North Carolina	84.4
41	Arkansas	84.2
42	Arizona	82.7
43	Louisiana	82.1
44	Idaho	79.9
45	Texas	78.8
46	New Hampshire	78.1
47	Colorado	75.2
48	Wyoming	70.8
49	New York	66.7
50	Nevada	63.8

District of Columbia	100.0

Source: CQ Press using data from U.S. Department of Education, Office of Special Education Programs
"Data Tables for OSEP State Reported Data" (https://www.ideadata.org/arc_toc8.asp)
*Figures are based on full-time equivalent (FTE). Includes teachers of disabled children ages 3 to 5 for school year 2005-2006.
National percent does not include teachers in U.S. territories and Bureau of Indian Affairs programs.

Elementary and Secondary Special Education Teachers in 2006

National Total = 421,817 Teachers*

<table>
<tr><td colspan="4">ALPHA ORDER</td><td colspan="4">RANK ORDER</td></tr>
<tr><th>RANK</th><th>STATE</th><th>TEACHERS</th><th>% of USA</th><th>RANK</th><th>STATE</th><th>TEACHERS</th><th>% of USA</th></tr>
<tr><td>24</td><td>Alabama</td><td>5,557</td><td>1.3%</td><td>1</td><td>New York</td><td>43,912</td><td>10.4%</td></tr>
<tr><td>46</td><td>Alaska</td><td>983</td><td>0.2%</td><td>2</td><td>California</td><td>31,527</td><td>7.5%</td></tr>
<tr><td>19</td><td>Arizona</td><td>6,552</td><td>1.6%</td><td>3</td><td>Texas</td><td>30,639</td><td>7.3%</td></tr>
<tr><td>31</td><td>Arkansas</td><td>3,814</td><td>0.9%</td><td>4</td><td>Illinois</td><td>23,193</td><td>5.5%</td></tr>
<tr><td>2</td><td>California</td><td>31,527</td><td>7.5%</td><td>5</td><td>Florida</td><td>22,254</td><td>5.3%</td></tr>
<tr><td>28</td><td>Colorado</td><td>4,575</td><td>1.1%</td><td>6</td><td>Pennsylvania</td><td>20,896</td><td>5.0%</td></tr>
<tr><td>27</td><td>Connecticut</td><td>4,913</td><td>1.2%</td><td>7</td><td>New Jersey</td><td>20,447</td><td>4.9%</td></tr>
<tr><td>43</td><td>Delaware</td><td>1,435</td><td>0.3%</td><td>8</td><td>Ohio</td><td>17,103</td><td>4.1%</td></tr>
<tr><td>5</td><td>Florida</td><td>22,254</td><td>5.3%</td><td>9</td><td>Georgia</td><td>14,388</td><td>3.4%</td></tr>
<tr><td>9</td><td>Georgia</td><td>14,388</td><td>3.4%</td><td>10</td><td>Virginia</td><td>13,928</td><td>3.3%</td></tr>
<tr><td>42</td><td>Hawaii</td><td>2,036</td><td>0.5%</td><td>11</td><td>Michigan</td><td>13,795</td><td>3.3%</td></tr>
<tr><td>44</td><td>Idaho</td><td>1,283</td><td>0.3%</td><td>12</td><td>North Carolina</td><td>11,003</td><td>2.6%</td></tr>
<tr><td>4</td><td>Illinois</td><td>23,193</td><td>5.5%</td><td>13</td><td>Massachusetts</td><td>10,478</td><td>2.5%</td></tr>
<tr><td>18</td><td>Indiana</td><td>7,039</td><td>1.7%</td><td>14</td><td>Missouri</td><td>9,110</td><td>2.2%</td></tr>
<tr><td>23</td><td>Iowa</td><td>5,604</td><td>1.3%</td><td>15</td><td>Minnesota</td><td>8,395</td><td>2.0%</td></tr>
<tr><td>32</td><td>Kansas</td><td>3,810</td><td>0.9%</td><td>16</td><td>Wisconsin</td><td>7,755</td><td>1.8%</td></tr>
<tr><td>20</td><td>Kentucky</td><td>6,388</td><td>1.5%</td><td>17</td><td>Maryland</td><td>7,450</td><td>1.8%</td></tr>
<tr><td>21</td><td>Louisiana</td><td>6,166</td><td>1.5%</td><td>18</td><td>Indiana</td><td>7,039</td><td>1.7%</td></tr>
<tr><td>36</td><td>Maine</td><td>2,677</td><td>0.6%</td><td>19</td><td>Arizona</td><td>6,552</td><td>1.6%</td></tr>
<tr><td>17</td><td>Maryland</td><td>7,450</td><td>1.8%</td><td>20</td><td>Kentucky</td><td>6,388</td><td>1.5%</td></tr>
<tr><td>13</td><td>Massachusetts</td><td>10,478</td><td>2.5%</td><td>21</td><td>Louisiana</td><td>6,166</td><td>1.5%</td></tr>
<tr><td>11</td><td>Michigan</td><td>13,795</td><td>3.3%</td><td>22</td><td>South Carolina</td><td>5,743</td><td>1.4%</td></tr>
<tr><td>15</td><td>Minnesota</td><td>8,395</td><td>2.0%</td><td>23</td><td>Iowa</td><td>5,604</td><td>1.3%</td></tr>
<tr><td>33</td><td>Mississippi</td><td>3,770</td><td>0.9%</td><td>24</td><td>Alabama</td><td>5,557</td><td>1.3%</td></tr>
<tr><td>14</td><td>Missouri</td><td>9,110</td><td>2.2%</td><td>25</td><td>Tennessee</td><td>5,302</td><td>1.3%</td></tr>
<tr><td>48</td><td>Montana</td><td>834</td><td>0.2%</td><td>26</td><td>Washington</td><td>5,260</td><td>1.2%</td></tr>
<tr><td>39</td><td>Nebraska</td><td>2,301</td><td>0.5%</td><td>27</td><td>Connecticut</td><td>4,913</td><td>1.2%</td></tr>
<tr><td>38</td><td>Nevada</td><td>2,467</td><td>0.6%</td><td>28</td><td>Colorado</td><td>4,575</td><td>1.1%</td></tr>
<tr><td>40</td><td>New Hampshire</td><td>2,131</td><td>0.5%</td><td>29</td><td>Oklahoma</td><td>4,532</td><td>1.1%</td></tr>
<tr><td>7</td><td>New Jersey</td><td>20,447</td><td>4.9%</td><td>30</td><td>New Mexico</td><td>4,186</td><td>1.0%</td></tr>
<tr><td>30</td><td>New Mexico</td><td>4,186</td><td>1.0%</td><td>31</td><td>Arkansas</td><td>3,814</td><td>0.9%</td></tr>
<tr><td>1</td><td>New York</td><td>43,912</td><td>10.4%</td><td>32</td><td>Kansas</td><td>3,810</td><td>0.9%</td></tr>
<tr><td>12</td><td>North Carolina</td><td>11,003</td><td>2.6%</td><td>33</td><td>Mississippi</td><td>3,770</td><td>0.9%</td></tr>
<tr><td>49</td><td>North Dakota</td><td>825</td><td>0.2%</td><td>34</td><td>Oregon</td><td>3,378</td><td>0.8%</td></tr>
<tr><td>8</td><td>Ohio</td><td>17,103</td><td>4.1%</td><td>35</td><td>West Virginia</td><td>2,856</td><td>0.7%</td></tr>
<tr><td>29</td><td>Oklahoma</td><td>4,532</td><td>1.1%</td><td>36</td><td>Maine</td><td>2,677</td><td>0.6%</td></tr>
<tr><td>34</td><td>Oregon</td><td>3,378</td><td>0.8%</td><td>37</td><td>Utah</td><td>2,656</td><td>0.6%</td></tr>
<tr><td>6</td><td>Pennsylvania</td><td>20,896</td><td>5.0%</td><td>38</td><td>Nevada</td><td>2,467</td><td>0.6%</td></tr>
<tr><td>41</td><td>Rhode Island</td><td>2,082</td><td>0.5%</td><td>39</td><td>Nebraska</td><td>2,301</td><td>0.5%</td></tr>
<tr><td>22</td><td>South Carolina</td><td>5,743</td><td>1.4%</td><td>40</td><td>New Hampshire</td><td>2,131</td><td>0.5%</td></tr>
<tr><td>47</td><td>South Dakota</td><td>886</td><td>0.2%</td><td>41</td><td>Rhode Island</td><td>2,082</td><td>0.5%</td></tr>
<tr><td>25</td><td>Tennessee</td><td>5,302</td><td>1.3%</td><td>42</td><td>Hawaii</td><td>2,036</td><td>0.5%</td></tr>
<tr><td>3</td><td>Texas</td><td>30,639</td><td>7.3%</td><td>43</td><td>Delaware</td><td>1,435</td><td>0.3%</td></tr>
<tr><td>37</td><td>Utah</td><td>2,656</td><td>0.6%</td><td>44</td><td>Idaho</td><td>1,283</td><td>0.3%</td></tr>
<tr><td>45</td><td>Vermont</td><td>1,031</td><td>0.2%</td><td>45</td><td>Vermont</td><td>1,031</td><td>0.2%</td></tr>
<tr><td>10</td><td>Virginia</td><td>13,928</td><td>3.3%</td><td>46</td><td>Alaska</td><td>983</td><td>0.2%</td></tr>
<tr><td>26</td><td>Washington</td><td>5,260</td><td>1.2%</td><td>47</td><td>South Dakota</td><td>886</td><td>0.2%</td></tr>
<tr><td>35</td><td>West Virginia</td><td>2,856</td><td>0.7%</td><td>48</td><td>Montana</td><td>834</td><td>0.2%</td></tr>
<tr><td>16</td><td>Wisconsin</td><td>7,755</td><td>1.8%</td><td>49</td><td>North Dakota</td><td>825</td><td>0.2%</td></tr>
<tr><td>50</td><td>Wyoming</td><td>801</td><td>0.2%</td><td>50</td><td>Wyoming</td><td>801</td><td>0.2%</td></tr>
<tr><td></td><td></td><td></td><td></td><td></td><td>District of Columbia</td><td>671</td><td>0.2%</td></tr>
</table>

Source: U.S. Department of Education, Office of Special Education Programs
"Data Tables for OSEP State Reported Data" (https://www.ideadata.org/arc_toc8.asp)
*Figures are full-time equivalent (FTE). Includes fully certified and not fully certified teachers of disabled children ages 6 to 21 for school year 2005-2006. National total does not include 5,676 teachers in U.S. territories and Bureau of Indian Affairs programs.

Fully Certified Elementary and Secondary Special Education Teachers in 2006

National Total = 380,372 Teachers*

ALPHA ORDER

RANK	STATE	TEACHERS	% of USA
23	Alabama	5,293	1.4%
46	Alaska	978	0.3%
20	Arizona	5,751	1.5%
33	Arkansas	3,493	0.9%
2	California	27,495	7.2%
30	Colorado	3,767	1.0%
27	Connecticut	4,913	1.3%
43	Delaware	1,294	0.3%
5	Florida	21,078	5.5%
11	Georgia	11,470	3.0%
42	Hawaii	1,469	0.4%
44	Idaho	1,166	0.3%
4	Illinois	22,491	5.9%
18	Indiana	6,023	1.6%
21	Iowa	5,604	1.5%
32	Kansas	3,570	0.9%
19	Kentucky	5,801	1.5%
24	Louisiana	5,100	1.3%
35	Maine	2,503	0.7%
17	Maryland	6,063	1.6%
13	Massachusetts	9,521	2.5%
10	Michigan	11,968	3.1%
15	Minnesota	8,048	2.1%
31	Mississippi	3,735	1.0%
14	Missouri	8,924	2.3%
47	Montana	809	0.2%
38	Nebraska	2,265	0.6%
40	Nevada	1,972	0.5%
41	New Hampshire	1,726	0.5%
7	New Jersey	19,310	5.1%
29	New Mexico	3,965	1.0%
1	New York	38,226	10.0%
12	North Carolina	9,600	2.5%
48	North Dakota	792	0.2%
8	Ohio	16,752	4.4%
28	Oklahoma	4,465	1.2%
34	Oregon	3,216	0.8%
6	Pennsylvania	20,665	5.4%
39	Rhode Island	2,001	0.5%
22	South Carolina	5,460	1.4%
49	South Dakota	743	0.2%
26	Tennessee	5,030	1.3%
3	Texas	22,787	6.0%
36	Utah	2,430	0.6%
45	Vermont	984	0.3%
9	Virginia	13,267	3.5%
25	Washington	5,096	1.3%
37	West Virginia	2,421	0.6%
16	Wisconsin	7,660	2.0%
50	Wyoming	729	0.2%

RANK ORDER

RANK	STATE	TEACHERS	% of USA
1	New York	38,226	10.0%
2	California	27,495	7.2%
3	Texas	22,787	6.0%
4	Illinois	22,491	5.9%
5	Florida	21,078	5.5%
6	Pennsylvania	20,665	5.4%
7	New Jersey	19,310	5.1%
8	Ohio	16,752	4.4%
9	Virginia	13,267	3.5%
10	Michigan	11,968	3.1%
11	Georgia	11,470	3.0%
12	North Carolina	9,600	2.5%
13	Massachusetts	9,521	2.5%
14	Missouri	8,924	2.3%
15	Minnesota	8,048	2.1%
16	Wisconsin	7,660	2.0%
17	Maryland	6,063	1.6%
18	Indiana	6,023	1.6%
19	Kentucky	5,801	1.5%
20	Arizona	5,751	1.5%
21	Iowa	5,604	1.5%
22	South Carolina	5,460	1.4%
23	Alabama	5,293	1.4%
24	Louisiana	5,100	1.3%
25	Washington	5,096	1.3%
26	Tennessee	5,030	1.3%
27	Connecticut	4,913	1.3%
28	Oklahoma	4,465	1.2%
29	New Mexico	3,965	1.0%
30	Colorado	3,767	1.0%
31	Mississippi	3,735	1.0%
32	Kansas	3,570	0.9%
33	Arkansas	3,493	0.9%
34	Oregon	3,216	0.8%
35	Maine	2,503	0.7%
36	Utah	2,430	0.6%
37	West Virginia	2,421	0.6%
38	Nebraska	2,265	0.6%
39	Rhode Island	2,001	0.5%
40	Nevada	1,972	0.5%
41	New Hampshire	1,726	0.5%
42	Hawaii	1,469	0.4%
43	Delaware	1,294	0.3%
44	Idaho	1,166	0.3%
45	Vermont	984	0.3%
46	Alaska	978	0.3%
47	Montana	809	0.2%
48	North Dakota	792	0.2%
49	South Dakota	743	0.2%
50	Wyoming	729	0.2%
	District of Columbia	483	0.1%

Source: U.S. Department of Education, Office of Special Education Programs
  "Data Tables for OSEP State Reported Data" (https://www.ideadata.org/arc_toc8.asp)
*Figures are full-time equivalent (FTE). Includes fully certified teachers of disabled children ages 6 to 21 for school year 2005-2006. National total does not include 5,389 teachers in U.S. territories and Bureau of Indian Affairs programs.

Percent of Elementary and Secondary Special Education Teachers Fully Certified in 2006
National Percent = 90.4%*

RANK	STATE	PERCENT
19	Alabama	95.2
3	Alaska	99.5
35	Arizona	87.8
28	Arkansas	91.6
36	California	87.2
44	Colorado	82.3
1	Connecticut	100.0
34	Delaware	90.2
23	Florida	94.7
48	Georgia	79.7
50	Hawaii	72.2
31	Idaho	90.9
11	Illinois	97.0
40	Indiana	85.6
1	Iowa	100.0
26	Kansas	93.7
33	Kentucky	90.8
43	Louisiana	82.7
27	Maine	93.5
45	Maryland	81.4
31	Massachusetts	90.9
39	Michigan	86.8
16	Minnesota	95.9
4	Mississippi	99.1
9	Missouri	98.0
11	Montana	97.0
8	Nebraska	98.4
47	Nevada	79.9
46	New Hampshire	81.0
25	New Jersey	94.4
23	New Mexico	94.7
38	New York	87.1
36	North Carolina	87.2
15	North Dakota	96.0
10	Ohio	97.9
7	Oklahoma	98.5
19	Oregon	95.2
5	Pennsylvania	98.9
14	Rhode Island	96.1
21	South Carolina	95.1
42	South Dakota	83.9
22	Tennessee	94.9
49	Texas	74.4
29	Utah	91.5
17	Vermont	95.4
18	Virginia	95.3
13	Washington	96.9
41	West Virginia	84.8
6	Wisconsin	98.8
30	Wyoming	91.0

RANK	STATE	PERCENT
1	Connecticut	100.0
1	Iowa	100.0
3	Alaska	99.5
4	Mississippi	99.1
5	Pennsylvania	98.9
6	Wisconsin	98.8
7	Oklahoma	98.5
8	Nebraska	98.4
9	Missouri	98.0
10	Ohio	97.9
11	Illinois	97.0
11	Montana	97.0
13	Washington	96.9
14	Rhode Island	96.1
15	North Dakota	96.0
16	Minnesota	95.9
17	Vermont	95.4
18	Virginia	95.3
19	Alabama	95.2
19	Oregon	95.2
21	South Carolina	95.1
22	Tennessee	94.9
23	Florida	94.7
23	New Mexico	94.7
25	New Jersey	94.4
26	Kansas	93.7
27	Maine	93.5
28	Arkansas	91.6
29	Utah	91.5
30	Wyoming	91.0
31	Idaho	90.9
31	Massachusetts	90.9
33	Kentucky	90.8
34	Delaware	90.2
35	Arizona	87.8
36	California	87.2
36	North Carolina	87.2
38	New York	87.1
39	Michigan	86.8
40	Indiana	85.6
41	West Virginia	84.8
42	South Dakota	83.9
43	Louisiana	82.7
44	Colorado	82.3
45	Maryland	81.4
46	New Hampshire	81.0
47	Nevada	79.9
48	Georgia	79.7
49	Texas	74.4
50	Hawaii	72.2

	District of Columbia	72.0

Source: CQ Press using data from U.S. Department of Education, Office of Special Education Programs
"Data Tables for OSEP State Reported Data" (https://www.ideadata.org/arc_toc8.asp)
*Figures are based on full-time equivalent (FTE). Includes fully certified teachers of disabled children ages 6 to 21 for school year 2005-2006. National percent does not include teachers in U.S. territories and Bureau of Indian Affairs programs.

Special Education Pupil-Teacher Ratio in 2006

National Ratio = 15.9 Students per Fully Certified Teacher*

ALPHA ORDER				RANK ORDER		
RANK	STATE	RATIO		RANK	STATE	RATIO
31	Alabama	15.6		1	Indiana	24.7
25	Alaska	17.0		2	Utah	23.4
23	Arizona	17.2		3	California	23.0
26	Arkansas	16.7		4	Oregon	22.9
3	California	23.0		5	Idaho	22.2
10	Colorado	21.0		6	Washington	22.1
36	Connecticut	14.6		7	Nevada	21.8
40	Delaware	13.5		8	Texas	21.5
21	Florida	17.3		9	Montana	21.4
27	Georgia	16.4		10	Colorado	21.0
43	Hawaii	12.9		11	South Dakota	20.8
5	Idaho	22.2		12	Tennessee	20.3
39	Illinois	13.6		13	Oklahoma	19.8
1	Indiana	24.7		14	Michigan	19.2
46	Iowa	12.0		15	West Virginia	18.9
27	Kansas	16.4		16	North Carolina	18.3
19	Kentucky	17.8		17	Nebraska	17.9
33	Louisiana	15.4		17	South Carolina	17.9
41	Maine	13.2		19	Kentucky	17.8
24	Maryland	17.1		20	Wyoming	17.6
50	Massachusetts	8.2		21	Florida	17.3
14	Michigan	19.2		21	New Hampshire	17.3
38	Minnesota	14.0		23	Arizona	17.2
30	Mississippi	15.7		24	Maryland	17.1
35	Missouri	14.7		25	Alaska	17.0
9	Montana	21.4		26	Arkansas	16.7
17	Nebraska	17.9		27	Georgia	16.4
7	Nevada	21.8		27	Kansas	16.4
21	New Hampshire	17.3		29	North Dakota	16.0
45	New Jersey	12.2		30	Mississippi	15.7
48	New Mexico	11.8		31	Alabama	15.6
49	New York	10.7		31	Wisconsin	15.6
16	North Carolina	18.3		33	Louisiana	15.4
29	North Dakota	16.0		34	Ohio	14.8
34	Ohio	14.8		35	Missouri	14.7
13	Oklahoma	19.8		36	Connecticut	14.6
4	Oregon	22.9		36	Rhode Island	14.6
42	Pennsylvania	13.0		38	Minnesota	14.0
36	Rhode Island	14.6		39	Illinois	13.6
17	South Carolina	17.9		40	Delaware	13.5
11	South Dakota	20.8		41	Maine	13.2
12	Tennessee	20.3		42	Pennsylvania	13.0
8	Texas	21.5		43	Hawaii	12.9
2	Utah	23.4		44	Vermont	12.8
44	Vermont	12.8		45	New Jersey	12.2
46	Virginia	12.0		46	Iowa	12.0
6	Washington	22.1		46	Virginia	12.0
15	West Virginia	18.9		48	New Mexico	11.8
31	Wisconsin	15.6		49	New York	10.7
20	Wyoming	17.6		50	Massachusetts	8.2

	District of Columbia	24.1

Source: CQ Press using data from U.S. Department of Education, Office of Special Education Programs
"Data Tables for OSEP State Reported Data" (https://www.ideadata.org/arc_toc8.asp)
*Figures for teachers are full-time equivalent (FTE). Includes fully certified teachers of disabled children ages 3 to 21 for school year 2005-2006. National rate does not include teachers or students in U.S. territories and Bureau of Indian Affairs programs.

Special Education Staff in 2006

National Total = 1,159,095 Staff*

ALPHA ORDER

RANK	STATE	STAFF	% of USA
27	Alabama	14,073	1.2%
49	Alaska	2,727	0.2%
15	Arizona	23,591	2.0%
34	Arkansas	9,083	0.8%
2	California	103,828	9.0%
26	Colorado	14,868	1.3%
22	Connecticut	17,048	1.5%
46	Delaware	2,899	0.3%
5	Florida	56,803	4.9%
11	Georgia	32,922	2.8%
38	Hawaii	6,861	0.6%
43	Idaho	3,767	0.3%
4	Illinois	68,091	5.9%
17	Indiana	20,620	1.8%
24	Iowa	15,693	1.4%
23	Kansas	16,625	1.4%
25	Kentucky	15,269	1.3%
20	Louisiana	17,829	1.5%
35	Maine	8,138	0.7%
16	Maryland	20,834	1.8%
8	Massachusetts	42,153	3.6%
14	Michigan	25,266	2.2%
13	Minnesota	26,696	2.3%
36	Mississippi	8,043	0.7%
18	Missouri	19,981	1.7%
48	Montana	2,834	0.2%
44	Nebraska	3,432	0.3%
40	Nevada	6,521	0.6%
32	New Hampshire	10,741	0.9%
6	New Jersey	56,219	4.9%
33	New Mexico	9,500	0.8%
1	New York	139,444	12.0%
12	North Carolina	29,419	2.5%
47	North Dakota	2,847	0.2%
10	Ohio	33,414	2.9%
31	Oklahoma	11,184	1.0%
29	Oregon	12,274	1.1%
7	Pennsylvania	48,834	4.2%
41	Rhode Island	5,906	0.5%
30	South Carolina	11,666	1.0%
45	South Dakota	3,258	0.3%
28	Tennessee	13,799	1.2%
3	Texas	71,210	6.1%
37	Utah	7,810	0.7%
42	Vermont	5,108	0.4%
9	Virginia	33,548	2.9%
21	Washington	17,075	1.5%
39	West Virginia	6,664	0.6%
19	Wisconsin	18,990	1.6%
50	Wyoming	2,485	0.2%

RANK ORDER

RANK	STATE	STAFF	% of USA
1	New York	139,444	12.0%
2	California	103,828	9.0%
3	Texas	71,210	6.1%
4	Illinois	68,091	5.9%
5	Florida	56,803	4.9%
6	New Jersey	56,219	4.9%
7	Pennsylvania	48,834	4.2%
8	Massachusetts	42,153	3.6%
9	Virginia	33,548	2.9%
10	Ohio	33,414	2.9%
11	Georgia	32,922	2.8%
12	North Carolina	29,419	2.5%
13	Minnesota	26,696	2.3%
14	Michigan	25,266	2.2%
15	Arizona	23,591	2.0%
16	Maryland	20,834	1.8%
17	Indiana	20,620	1.8%
18	Missouri	19,981	1.7%
19	Wisconsin	18,990	1.6%
20	Louisiana	17,829	1.5%
21	Washington	17,075	1.5%
22	Connecticut	17,048	1.5%
23	Kansas	16,625	1.4%
24	Iowa	15,693	1.4%
25	Kentucky	15,269	1.3%
26	Colorado	14,868	1.3%
27	Alabama	14,073	1.2%
28	Tennessee	13,799	1.2%
29	Oregon	12,274	1.1%
30	South Carolina	11,666	1.0%
31	Oklahoma	11,184	1.0%
32	New Hampshire	10,741	0.9%
33	New Mexico	9,500	0.8%
34	Arkansas	9,083	0.8%
35	Maine	8,138	0.7%
36	Mississippi	8,043	0.7%
37	Utah	7,810	0.7%
38	Hawaii	6,861	0.6%
39	West Virginia	6,664	0.6%
40	Nevada	6,521	0.6%
41	Rhode Island	5,906	0.5%
42	Vermont	5,108	0.4%
43	Idaho	3,767	0.3%
44	Nebraska	3,432	0.3%
45	South Dakota	3,258	0.3%
46	Delaware	2,899	0.3%
47	North Dakota	2,847	0.2%
48	Montana	2,834	0.2%
49	Alaska	2,727	0.2%
50	Wyoming	2,485	0.2%
	District of Columbia	1,205	0.1%

Source: CQ Press using data from U.S. Department of Education, Office of Special Education Programs
"Data Tables for OSEP State Reported Data" (https://www.ideadata.org/arc_toc8.asp)
*Full-time equivalent (FTE) employed certified and not certified staff for disabled children ages 3 to 21 in 2005-2006. National total does not include staff in U.S. territories and Bureau of Indian Affairs programs. Includes teachers, social workers, occupational, recreation and physical therapists, aides, phys ed teachers, administrators, psychologists, diagnostic staff, audiologists, work study coord., vocational ed, counselors, rehab counselors, interpreters, speech pathologists, and other staff.

Special Education Pupil-Staff Ratio in 2006

National Ratio = 5.8 Students per Staff Person*

ALPHA ORDER			RANK ORDER		
RANK	STATE	RATIO	RANK	STATE	RATIO
21	Alabama	6.6	1	Nebraska	13.2
21	Alaska	6.6	2	Michigan	9.6
32	Arizona	5.3	3	South Carolina	9.4
12	Arkansas	7.4	4	Tennessee	8.7
24	California	6.5	5	Indiana	8.6
29	Colorado	5.6	5	Oklahoma	8.6
44	Connecticut	4.2	7	Mississippi	8.5
24	Delaware	6.5	8	Ohio	8.0
18	Florida	7.0	9	Idaho	7.7
27	Georgia	6.0	9	Utah	7.7
47	Hawaii	3.2	11	West Virginia	7.5
9	Idaho	7.7	12	Arkansas	7.4
39	Illinois	4.8	13	Nevada	7.3
5	Indiana	8.6	13	Washington	7.3
40	Iowa	4.6	15	Missouri	7.2
45	Kansas	3.9	16	Kentucky	7.1
16	Kentucky	7.1	16	Texas	7.1
37	Louisiana	5.1	18	Florida	7.0
41	Maine	4.5	19	Montana	6.8
32	Maryland	5.3	19	Wisconsin	6.8
45	Massachusetts	3.9	21	Alabama	6.6
2	Michigan	9.6	21	Alaska	6.6
42	Minnesota	4.4	21	North Carolina	6.6
7	Mississippi	8.5	24	California	6.5
15	Missouri	7.2	24	Delaware	6.5
19	Montana	6.8	26	Oregon	6.3
1	Nebraska	13.2	27	Georgia	6.0
13	Nevada	7.3	28	Pennsylvania	5.9
49	New Hampshire	3.0	29	Colorado	5.6
42	New Jersey	4.4	30	Wyoming	5.5
32	New Mexico	5.3	31	South Dakota	5.4
47	New York	3.2	32	Arizona	5.3
21	North Carolina	6.6	32	Maryland	5.3
38	North Dakota	4.9	32	New Mexico	5.3
8	Ohio	8.0	35	Rhode Island	5.2
5	Oklahoma	8.6	35	Virginia	5.2
26	Oregon	6.3	37	Louisiana	5.1
28	Pennsylvania	5.9	38	North Dakota	4.9
35	Rhode Island	5.2	39	Illinois	4.8
3	South Carolina	9.4	40	Iowa	4.6
31	South Dakota	5.4	41	Maine	4.5
4	Tennessee	8.7	42	Minnesota	4.4
16	Texas	7.1	42	New Jersey	4.4
9	Utah	7.7	44	Connecticut	4.2
50	Vermont	2.7	45	Kansas	3.9
35	Virginia	5.2	45	Massachusetts	3.9
13	Washington	7.3	47	Hawaii	3.2
11	West Virginia	7.5	47	New York	3.2
19	Wisconsin	6.8	49	New Hampshire	3.0
30	Wyoming	5.5	50	Vermont	2.7
				District of Columbia	9.7

Source: CQ Press using data from U.S. Department of Education, Office of Special Education Programs
"Data Tables for OSEP State Reported Data" (https://www.ideadata.org/arc_toc8.asp)
*Full-time equivalent (FTE) employed certified and not certified staff for disabled children ages 3 to 21 in 2005-2006. National rate does not include staff or students in U.S. territories and Bureau of Indian Affairs programs. Includes teachers, social workers, occupational, recreation and physical therapists, aides, phys ed teachers, administrators, psychologists, diagnostic staff, audiologists, work study coord., vocational ed, counselors, rehab counselors, interpreters, and other staff.

Average Annual Salary of Middle School Special Education Teachers: 2007

National Average = $51,610*

ALPHA ORDER

RANK	STATE	SALARY
36	Alabama	$42,740
5	Alaska	59,430
44	Arizona	40,350
30	Arkansas	43,780
4	California	60,140
24	Colorado	48,520
1	Connecticut	64,810
10	Delaware	53,770
16	Florida	50,590
18	Georgia	49,860
26	Hawaii	45,160
NA	Idaho**	NA
9	Illinois	54,730
23	Indiana	49,220
39	Iowa	41,500
46	Kansas	38,620
31	Kentucky	43,710
37	Louisiana	42,610
38	Maine	42,450
6	Maryland	58,290
8	Massachusetts	55,590
11	Michigan	53,680
19	Minnesota	49,730
35	Mississippi	42,820
33	Missouri	43,580
42	Montana	40,880
31	Nebraska	43,710
34	Nevada	42,990
21	New Hampshire	49,390
7	New Jersey	57,110
27	New Mexico	44,650
2	New York	62,820
43	North Carolina	40,440
NA	North Dakota**	NA
12	Ohio	53,350
45	Oklahoma	39,740
17	Oregon	50,520
13	Pennsylvania	53,290
3	Rhode Island	61,690
29	South Carolina	44,420
48	South Dakota	35,930
41	Tennessee	41,230
28	Texas	44,580
40	Utah	41,290
20	Vermont	49,500
14	Virginia	52,170
15	Washington	51,360
47	West Virginia	37,110
25	Wisconsin	46,240
21	Wyoming	49,390

RANK ORDER

RANK	STATE	SALARY
1	Connecticut	$64,810
2	New York	62,820
3	Rhode Island	61,690
4	California	60,140
5	Alaska	59,430
6	Maryland	58,290
7	New Jersey	57,110
8	Massachusetts	55,590
9	Illinois	54,730
10	Delaware	53,770
11	Michigan	53,680
12	Ohio	53,350
13	Pennsylvania	53,290
14	Virginia	52,170
15	Washington	51,360
16	Florida	50,590
17	Oregon	50,520
18	Georgia	49,860
19	Minnesota	49,730
20	Vermont	49,500
21	New Hampshire	49,390
21	Wyoming	49,390
23	Indiana	49,220
24	Colorado	48,520
25	Wisconsin	46,240
26	Hawaii	45,160
27	New Mexico	44,650
28	Texas	44,580
29	South Carolina	44,420
30	Arkansas	43,780
31	Kentucky	43,710
31	Nebraska	43,710
33	Missouri	43,580
34	Nevada	42,990
35	Mississippi	42,820
36	Alabama	42,740
37	Louisiana	42,610
38	Maine	42,450
39	Iowa	41,500
40	Utah	41,290
41	Tennessee	41,230
42	Montana	40,880
43	North Carolina	40,440
44	Arizona	40,350
45	Oklahoma	39,740
46	Kansas	38,620
47	West Virginia	37,110
48	South Dakota	35,930
NA	Idaho**	NA
NA	North Dakota**	NA
	District of Columbia	57,350

Source: U.S. Department of Labor, Bureau of Labor Statistics
   "National Occupational Employment and Wage Estimates" (http://www.bls.gov/oes/)
*As of May 2007.
**Not available.

Average Annual Salary of Preschool, Kindergarten, and Elementary Special Education Teachers: 2007
National Average = $51,230*

ALPHA ORDER			RANK ORDER		
RANK	STATE	SALARY	RANK	STATE	SALARY
35	Alabama	$42,910	1	New York	$63,190
4	Alaska	60,330	2	Connecticut	61,980
45	Arizona	38,740	3	Rhode Island	60,690
39	Arkansas	41,180	4	Alaska	60,330
5	California	59,690	5	California	59,690
20	Colorado	48,890	6	Virginia	56,890
2	Connecticut	61,980	7	New Jersey	56,780
18	Delaware	50,380	8	Maryland	56,250
13	Florida	52,160	9	Pennsylvania	54,500
19	Georgia	49,380	10	Michigan	54,400
31	Hawaii	43,650	11	Illinois	54,210
50	Idaho	35,050	12	Massachusetts	52,910
11	Illinois	54,210	13	Florida	52,160
23	Indiana	47,530	14	Oregon	51,730
34	Iowa	43,220	15	Washington	50,870
42	Kansas	40,770	16	Ohio	50,780
29	Kentucky	44,090	17	Minnesota	50,610
47	Louisiana	38,550	18	Delaware	50,380
33	Maine	43,410	19	Georgia	49,380
8	Maryland	56,250	20	Colorado	48,890
12	Massachusetts	52,910	21	Wisconsin	48,670
10	Michigan	54,400	22	Vermont	48,340
17	Minnesota	50,610	23	Indiana	47,530
36	Mississippi	42,370	24	New Hampshire	46,880
30	Missouri	43,790	25	Nevada	45,430
48	Montana	38,330	26	North Dakota	45,410
38	Nebraska	41,490	27	Wyoming	45,050
25	Nevada	45,430	28	Texas	44,820
24	New Hampshire	46,880	29	Kentucky	44,090
7	New Jersey	56,780	30	Missouri	43,790
37	New Mexico	42,260	31	Hawaii	43,650
1	New York	63,190	31	South Carolina	43,650
41	North Carolina	40,800	33	Maine	43,410
26	North Dakota	45,410	34	Iowa	43,220
16	Ohio	50,780	35	Alabama	42,910
45	Oklahoma	38,740	36	Mississippi	42,370
14	Oregon	51,730	37	New Mexico	42,260
9	Pennsylvania	54,500	38	Nebraska	41,490
3	Rhode Island	60,690	39	Arkansas	41,180
31	South Carolina	43,650	40	Utah	40,840
49	South Dakota	35,170	41	North Carolina	40,800
44	Tennessee	39,000	42	Kansas	40,770
28	Texas	44,820	43	West Virginia	39,170
40	Utah	40,840	44	Tennessee	39,000
22	Vermont	48,340	45	Arizona	38,740
6	Virginia	56,890	45	Oklahoma	38,740
15	Washington	50,870	47	Louisiana	38,550
43	West Virginia	39,170	48	Montana	38,330
21	Wisconsin	48,670	49	South Dakota	35,170
27	Wyoming	45,050	50	Idaho	35,050
				District of Columbia	49,870

Source: U.S. Department of Labor, Bureau of Labor Statistics
    "National Occupational Employment and Wage Estimates" (http://www.bls.gov/oes/)
*As of May 2007.

Average Annual Salary of Secondary School Special Education Teachers: 2007

National Average = $53,020*

<table>
<tr><td colspan="3">ALPHA ORDER</td><td colspan="3">RANK ORDER</td></tr>
<tr><td>RANK</td><td>STATE</td><td>SALARY</td><td>RANK</td><td>STATE</td><td>SALARY</td></tr>
<tr><td>35</td><td>Alabama</td><td>$43,450</td><td>1</td><td>New York</td><td>$66,970</td></tr>
<tr><td>8</td><td>Alaska</td><td>58,580</td><td>2</td><td>Rhode Island</td><td>65,860</td></tr>
<tr><td>38</td><td>Arizona</td><td>42,780</td><td>3</td><td>Connecticut</td><td>64,900</td></tr>
<tr><td>33</td><td>Arkansas</td><td>44,370</td><td>4</td><td>New Jersey</td><td>62,530</td></tr>
<tr><td>5</td><td>California</td><td>61,090</td><td>5</td><td>California</td><td>61,090</td></tr>
<tr><td>22</td><td>Colorado</td><td>49,640</td><td>6</td><td>Virginia</td><td>60,240</td></tr>
<tr><td>3</td><td>Connecticut</td><td>64,900</td><td>7</td><td>Illinois</td><td>60,110</td></tr>
<tr><td>11</td><td>Delaware</td><td>55,610</td><td>8</td><td>Alaska</td><td>58,580</td></tr>
<tr><td>17</td><td>Florida</td><td>51,350</td><td>9</td><td>Maryland</td><td>57,760</td></tr>
<tr><td>21</td><td>Georgia</td><td>50,390</td><td>10</td><td>Massachusetts</td><td>56,450</td></tr>
<tr><td>31</td><td>Hawaii</td><td>45,200</td><td>11</td><td>Delaware</td><td>55,610</td></tr>
<tr><td>50</td><td>Idaho</td><td>36,550</td><td>12</td><td>Pennsylvania</td><td>53,660</td></tr>
<tr><td>7</td><td>Illinois</td><td>60,110</td><td>13</td><td>Michigan</td><td>53,630</td></tr>
<tr><td>24</td><td>Indiana</td><td>48,290</td><td>14</td><td>Minnesota</td><td>52,630</td></tr>
<tr><td>46</td><td>Iowa</td><td>40,300</td><td>15</td><td>Washington</td><td>52,280</td></tr>
<tr><td>45</td><td>Kansas</td><td>40,440</td><td>16</td><td>Ohio</td><td>52,230</td></tr>
<tr><td>29</td><td>Kentucky</td><td>45,310</td><td>17</td><td>Florida</td><td>51,350</td></tr>
<tr><td>40</td><td>Louisiana</td><td>42,400</td><td>18</td><td>Oregon</td><td>50,980</td></tr>
<tr><td>37</td><td>Maine</td><td>42,820</td><td>19</td><td>Vermont</td><td>50,940</td></tr>
<tr><td>9</td><td>Maryland</td><td>57,760</td><td>20</td><td>Wisconsin</td><td>50,560</td></tr>
<tr><td>10</td><td>Massachusetts</td><td>56,450</td><td>21</td><td>Georgia</td><td>50,390</td></tr>
<tr><td>13</td><td>Michigan</td><td>53,630</td><td>22</td><td>Colorado</td><td>49,640</td></tr>
<tr><td>14</td><td>Minnesota</td><td>52,630</td><td>23</td><td>New Hampshire</td><td>48,370</td></tr>
<tr><td>36</td><td>Mississippi</td><td>43,000</td><td>24</td><td>Indiana</td><td>48,290</td></tr>
<tr><td>39</td><td>Missouri</td><td>42,490</td><td>25</td><td>Wyoming</td><td>48,090</td></tr>
<tr><td>48</td><td>Montana</td><td>37,470</td><td>26</td><td>New Mexico</td><td>46,730</td></tr>
<tr><td>34</td><td>Nebraska</td><td>43,550</td><td>27</td><td>Nevada</td><td>46,210</td></tr>
<tr><td>27</td><td>Nevada</td><td>46,210</td><td>28</td><td>South Carolina</td><td>45,350</td></tr>
<tr><td>23</td><td>New Hampshire</td><td>48,370</td><td>29</td><td>Kentucky</td><td>45,310</td></tr>
<tr><td>4</td><td>New Jersey</td><td>62,530</td><td>30</td><td>Texas</td><td>45,300</td></tr>
<tr><td>26</td><td>New Mexico</td><td>46,730</td><td>31</td><td>Hawaii</td><td>45,200</td></tr>
<tr><td>1</td><td>New York</td><td>66,970</td><td>32</td><td>North Dakota</td><td>44,420</td></tr>
<tr><td>43</td><td>North Carolina</td><td>41,310</td><td>33</td><td>Arkansas</td><td>44,370</td></tr>
<tr><td>32</td><td>North Dakota</td><td>44,420</td><td>34</td><td>Nebraska</td><td>43,550</td></tr>
<tr><td>16</td><td>Ohio</td><td>52,230</td><td>35</td><td>Alabama</td><td>43,450</td></tr>
<tr><td>44</td><td>Oklahoma</td><td>40,850</td><td>36</td><td>Mississippi</td><td>43,000</td></tr>
<tr><td>18</td><td>Oregon</td><td>50,980</td><td>37</td><td>Maine</td><td>42,820</td></tr>
<tr><td>12</td><td>Pennsylvania</td><td>53,660</td><td>38</td><td>Arizona</td><td>42,780</td></tr>
<tr><td>2</td><td>Rhode Island</td><td>65,860</td><td>39</td><td>Missouri</td><td>42,490</td></tr>
<tr><td>28</td><td>South Carolina</td><td>45,350</td><td>40</td><td>Louisiana</td><td>42,400</td></tr>
<tr><td>49</td><td>South Dakota</td><td>36,670</td><td>41</td><td>Tennessee</td><td>41,730</td></tr>
<tr><td>41</td><td>Tennessee</td><td>41,730</td><td>42</td><td>Utah</td><td>41,330</td></tr>
<tr><td>30</td><td>Texas</td><td>45,300</td><td>43</td><td>North Carolina</td><td>41,310</td></tr>
<tr><td>42</td><td>Utah</td><td>41,330</td><td>44</td><td>Oklahoma</td><td>40,850</td></tr>
<tr><td>19</td><td>Vermont</td><td>50,940</td><td>45</td><td>Kansas</td><td>40,440</td></tr>
<tr><td>6</td><td>Virginia</td><td>60,240</td><td>46</td><td>Iowa</td><td>40,300</td></tr>
<tr><td>15</td><td>Washington</td><td>52,280</td><td>47</td><td>West Virginia</td><td>38,760</td></tr>
<tr><td>47</td><td>West Virginia</td><td>38,760</td><td>48</td><td>Montana</td><td>37,470</td></tr>
<tr><td>20</td><td>Wisconsin</td><td>50,560</td><td>49</td><td>South Dakota</td><td>36,670</td></tr>
<tr><td>25</td><td>Wyoming</td><td>48,090</td><td>50</td><td>Idaho</td><td>36,550</td></tr>
<tr><td></td><td></td><td></td><td></td><td>District of Columbia</td><td>57,540</td></tr>
</table>

Source: U.S. Department of Labor, Bureau of Labor Statistics
"National Occupational Employment and Wage Estimates" (http://www.bls.gov/oes/)
*As of May 2007.

VI. Staff

Special Note for Staff Chapter

At the time that *Education State Rankings* went to print, the National Center for Education Statistics (NCES) was delayed in issuing updated staff and teacher data for the 2006–2007 school year. We have included statistics showing estimated numbers of elementary and secondary school teachers for 2006–2007 school year from the National Education Association on page 374. However, the NCES data, which provides specific breakdowns by grade level and job type, were not yet available from NCES.

Once the new statistics are available, they will be posted on NCES' Common Core of Data Web site: http://nces.ed.gov/ccd.

Estimated Public Elementary and Secondary School Teachers in 2007

National Total = 3,174,354 Teachers*

ALPHA ORDER

RANK	STATE	TEACHERS	% of USA
21	Alabama	49,985	1.6%
48	Alaska	8,017	0.3%
22	Arizona	47,087	1.5%
31	Arkansas	34,139	1.1%
2	California	304,152	9.6%
23	Colorado	46,959	1.5%
26	Connecticut	42,533	1.3%
47	Delaware	8,041	0.3%
4	Florida	167,775	5.3%
9	Georgia	112,861	3.6%
43	Hawaii	11,477	0.4%
42	Idaho	14,770	0.5%
5	Illinois	131,926	4.2%
16	Indiana	61,183	1.9%
29	Iowa	35,405	1.1%
30	Kansas	34,351	1.1%
28	Kentucky	41,331	1.3%
25	Louisiana	46,406	1.5%
39	Maine	16,395	0.5%
17	Maryland	59,322	1.9%
13	Massachusetts	73,176	2.3%
10	Michigan	109,946	3.5%
20	Minnesota	50,237	1.6%
32	Mississippi	33,494	1.1%
14	Missouri	66,840	2.1%
44	Montana	10,518	0.3%
37	Nebraska	21,293	0.7%
34	Nevada	22,133	0.7%
40	New Hampshire	15,800	0.5%
8	New Jersey	114,994	3.6%
36	New Mexico	21,667	0.7%
3	New York	229,257	7.2%
11	North Carolina	95,542	3.0%
49	North Dakota	7,569	0.2%
7	Ohio	119,250	3.8%
27	Oklahoma	42,183	1.3%
33	Oregon	29,336	0.9%
6	Pennsylvania	123,150	3.9%
41	Rhode Island	14,945	0.5%
24	South Carolina	46,951	1.5%
46	South Dakota	9,024	0.3%
15	Tennessee	61,824	1.9%
1	Texas	311,654	9.8%
35	Utah	21,786	0.7%
45	Vermont	9,035	0.3%
12	Virginia	93,553	2.9%
19	Washington	53,951	1.7%
38	West Virginia	19,881	0.6%
18	Wisconsin	59,291	1.9%
50	Wyoming	6,457	0.2%

RANK ORDER

RANK	STATE	TEACHERS	% of USA
1	Texas	311,654	9.8%
2	California	304,152	9.6%
3	New York	229,257	7.2%
4	Florida	167,775	5.3%
5	Illinois	131,926	4.2%
6	Pennsylvania	123,150	3.9%
7	Ohio	119,250	3.8%
8	New Jersey	114,994	3.6%
9	Georgia	112,861	3.6%
10	Michigan	109,946	3.5%
11	North Carolina	95,542	3.0%
12	Virginia	93,553	2.9%
13	Massachusetts	73,176	2.3%
14	Missouri	66,840	2.1%
15	Tennessee	61,824	1.9%
16	Indiana	61,183	1.9%
17	Maryland	59,322	1.9%
18	Wisconsin	59,291	1.9%
19	Washington	53,951	1.7%
20	Minnesota	50,237	1.6%
21	Alabama	49,985	1.6%
22	Arizona	47,087	1.5%
23	Colorado	46,959	1.5%
24	South Carolina	46,951	1.5%
25	Louisiana	46,406	1.5%
26	Connecticut	42,533	1.3%
27	Oklahoma	42,183	1.3%
28	Kentucky	41,331	1.3%
29	Iowa	35,405	1.1%
30	Kansas	34,351	1.1%
31	Arkansas	34,139	1.1%
32	Mississippi	33,494	1.1%
33	Oregon	29,336	0.9%
34	Nevada	22,133	0.7%
35	Utah	21,786	0.7%
36	New Mexico	21,667	0.7%
37	Nebraska	21,293	0.7%
38	West Virginia	19,881	0.6%
39	Maine	16,395	0.5%
40	New Hampshire	15,800	0.5%
41	Rhode Island	14,945	0.5%
42	Idaho	14,770	0.5%
43	Hawaii	11,477	0.4%
44	Montana	10,518	0.3%
45	Vermont	9,035	0.3%
46	South Dakota	9,024	0.3%
47	Delaware	8,041	0.3%
48	Alaska	8,017	0.3%
49	North Dakota	7,569	0.2%
50	Wyoming	6,457	0.2%
	District of Columbia	5,503	0.2%

Source: National Education Association, Washington, D.C.
   "Rankings & Estimates" (Copyright © 2007, NEA, used with permission, http://www.nea.org/edstats/index.html)
*Estimates for school year 2006-2007.

Public Elementary and Secondary School Teachers in 2006

National Total = 3,136,921 Teachers*

ALPHA ORDER

RANK	STATE	TEACHERS	% of USA
18	Alabama	57,757	1.8%
49	Alaska	7,912	0.3%
21	Arizona	51,376	1.6%
31	Arkansas	32,997	1.1%
1	California	309,128	9.9%
24	Colorado	45,841	1.5%
28	Connecticut	39,687	1.3%
48	Delaware	7,998	0.3%
4	Florida	158,962	5.1%
9	Georgia	108,535	3.5%
43	Hawaii	11,226	0.4%
41	Idaho	14,521	0.5%
5	Illinois	133,857	4.3%
15	Indiana	60,592	1.9%
29	Iowa	35,181	1.1%
30	Kansas	33,608	1.1%
26	Kentucky	42,413	1.4%
25	Louisiana	44,660	1.4%
39	Maine	16,684	0.5%
19	Maryland	56,685	1.8%
13	Massachusetts	73,596	2.3%
10	Michigan	99,838	3.2%
22	Minnesota	51,107	1.6%
32	Mississippi	31,433	1.0%
14	Missouri	67,076	2.1%
44	Montana	10,369	0.3%
37	Nebraska	21,359	0.7%
36	Nevada	21,744	0.7%
40	New Hampshire	15,536	0.5%
8	New Jersey	112,673	3.6%
35	New Mexico	22,021	0.7%
3	New York	218,989	7.0%
12	North Carolina	95,664	3.0%
47	North Dakota	8,003	0.3%
7	Ohio	117,982	3.8%
27	Oklahoma	41,833	1.3%
33	Oregon	28,256	0.9%
6	Pennsylvania	122,397	3.9%
42	Rhode Island	14,299	0.5%
23	South Carolina	48,212	1.5%
45	South Dakota	9,129	0.3%
17	Tennessee	59,596	1.9%
2	Texas	302,425	9.6%
34	Utah	22,993	0.7%
46	Vermont	8,851	0.3%
11	Virginia	96,158	3.1%
20	Washington	53,508	1.7%
38	West Virginia	19,940	0.6%
16	Wisconsin	60,127	1.9%
50	Wyoming	6,706	0.2%

RANK ORDER

RANK	STATE	TEACHERS	% of USA
1	California	309,128	9.9%
2	Texas	302,425	9.6%
3	New York	218,989	7.0%
4	Florida	158,962	5.1%
5	Illinois	133,857	4.3%
6	Pennsylvania	122,397	3.9%
7	Ohio	117,982	3.8%
8	New Jersey	112,673	3.6%
9	Georgia	108,535	3.5%
10	Michigan	99,838	3.2%
11	Virginia	96,158	3.1%
12	North Carolina	95,664	3.0%
13	Massachusetts	73,596	2.3%
14	Missouri	67,076	2.1%
15	Indiana	60,592	1.9%
16	Wisconsin	60,127	1.9%
17	Tennessee	59,596	1.9%
18	Alabama	57,757	1.8%
19	Maryland	56,685	1.8%
20	Washington	53,508	1.7%
21	Arizona	51,376	1.6%
22	Minnesota	51,107	1.6%
23	South Carolina	48,212	1.5%
24	Colorado	45,841	1.5%
25	Louisiana	44,660	1.4%
26	Kentucky	42,413	1.4%
27	Oklahoma	41,833	1.3%
28	Connecticut	39,687	1.3%
29	Iowa	35,181	1.1%
30	Kansas	33,608	1.1%
31	Arkansas	32,997	1.1%
32	Mississippi	31,433	1.0%
33	Oregon	28,256	0.9%
34	Utah	22,993	0.7%
35	New Mexico	22,021	0.7%
36	Nevada	21,744	0.7%
37	Nebraska	21,359	0.7%
38	West Virginia	19,940	0.6%
39	Maine	16,684	0.5%
40	New Hampshire	15,536	0.5%
41	Idaho	14,521	0.5%
42	Rhode Island	14,299	0.5%
43	Hawaii	11,226	0.4%
44	Montana	10,369	0.3%
45	South Dakota	9,129	0.3%
46	Vermont	8,851	0.3%
47	North Dakota	8,003	0.3%
48	Delaware	7,998	0.3%
49	Alaska	7,912	0.3%
50	Wyoming	6,706	0.2%
	District of Columbia	5,481	0.2%

Source: U.S. Department of Education, National Center for Education Statistics
"Common Core of Data (CCD) Database" (http://nces.ed.gov/ccd/)
*School year 2005-2006. Counts are full-time equivalent figures.

Percent Change in Number of Public Elementary and Secondary School Teachers: 1996 to 2006
National Percent Change = 20.7% Increase*

<table>
<tr><td colspan="3">ALPHA ORDER</td><td colspan="3">RANK ORDER</td></tr>
<tr><td>RANK</td><td>STATE</td><td>PERCENT CHANGE</td><td>RANK</td><td>STATE</td><td>PERCENT CHANGE</td></tr>
<tr><td>7</td><td>Alabama</td><td>31.1</td><td>1</td><td>Nevada</td><td>56.7</td></tr>
<tr><td>40</td><td>Alaska</td><td>7.2</td><td>2</td><td>Florida</td><td>38.3</td></tr>
<tr><td>5</td><td>Arizona</td><td>35.1</td><td>3</td><td>Georgia</td><td>36.6</td></tr>
<tr><td>14</td><td>Arkansas</td><td>24.8</td><td>4</td><td>Rhode Island</td><td>36.4</td></tr>
<tr><td>6</td><td>California</td><td>33.9</td><td>5</td><td>Arizona</td><td>35.1</td></tr>
<tr><td>10</td><td>Colorado</td><td>29.5</td><td>6</td><td>California</td><td>33.9</td></tr>
<tr><td>30</td><td>Connecticut</td><td>10.0</td><td>7</td><td>Alabama</td><td>31.1</td></tr>
<tr><td>15</td><td>Delaware</td><td>23.8</td><td>8</td><td>North Carolina</td><td>30.7</td></tr>
<tr><td>2</td><td>Florida</td><td>38.3</td><td>9</td><td>New Jersey</td><td>29.9</td></tr>
<tr><td>3</td><td>Georgia</td><td>36.6</td><td>10</td><td>Colorado</td><td>29.5</td></tr>
<tr><td>41</td><td>Hawaii</td><td>6.9</td><td>11</td><td>Virginia</td><td>28.7</td></tr>
<tr><td>27</td><td>Idaho</td><td>13.6</td><td>12</td><td>New Hampshire</td><td>25.8</td></tr>
<tr><td>20</td><td>Illinois</td><td>17.9</td><td>12</td><td>Texas</td><td>25.8</td></tr>
<tr><td>36</td><td>Indiana</td><td>8.5</td><td>14</td><td>Arkansas</td><td>24.8</td></tr>
<tr><td>34</td><td>Iowa</td><td>8.9</td><td>15</td><td>Delaware</td><td>23.8</td></tr>
<tr><td>32</td><td>Kansas</td><td>9.4</td><td>16</td><td>South Carolina</td><td>20.8</td></tr>
<tr><td>37</td><td>Kentucky</td><td>8.4</td><td>17</td><td>New York</td><td>20.6</td></tr>
<tr><td>48</td><td>Louisiana</td><td>(4.9)</td><td>18</td><td>Michigan</td><td>20.0</td></tr>
<tr><td>37</td><td>Maine</td><td>8.4</td><td>19</td><td>Maryland</td><td>18.5</td></tr>
<tr><td>19</td><td>Maryland</td><td>18.5</td><td>20</td><td>Illinois</td><td>17.9</td></tr>
<tr><td>21</td><td>Massachusetts</td><td>17.4</td><td>21</td><td>Massachusetts</td><td>17.4</td></tr>
<tr><td>18</td><td>Michigan</td><td>20.0</td><td>22</td><td>Pennsylvania</td><td>16.7</td></tr>
<tr><td>35</td><td>Minnesota</td><td>8.8</td><td>23</td><td>Missouri</td><td>15.7</td></tr>
<tr><td>37</td><td>Mississippi</td><td>8.4</td><td>24</td><td>Vermont</td><td>15.3</td></tr>
<tr><td>23</td><td>Missouri</td><td>15.7</td><td>25</td><td>Utah</td><td>14.7</td></tr>
<tr><td>46</td><td>Montana</td><td>2.9</td><td>26</td><td>Washington</td><td>14.1</td></tr>
<tr><td>43</td><td>Nebraska</td><td>6.6</td><td>27</td><td>Idaho</td><td>13.6</td></tr>
<tr><td>1</td><td>Nevada</td><td>56.7</td><td>28</td><td>New Mexico</td><td>13.5</td></tr>
<tr><td>12</td><td>New Hampshire</td><td>25.8</td><td>29</td><td>Tennessee</td><td>11.6</td></tr>
<tr><td>9</td><td>New Jersey</td><td>29.9</td><td>30</td><td>Connecticut</td><td>10.0</td></tr>
<tr><td>28</td><td>New Mexico</td><td>13.5</td><td>31</td><td>Ohio</td><td>9.9</td></tr>
<tr><td>17</td><td>New York</td><td>20.6</td><td>32</td><td>Kansas</td><td>9.4</td></tr>
<tr><td>8</td><td>North Carolina</td><td>30.7</td><td>33</td><td>Wisconsin</td><td>9.3</td></tr>
<tr><td>42</td><td>North Dakota</td><td>6.7</td><td>34</td><td>Iowa</td><td>8.9</td></tr>
<tr><td>31</td><td>Ohio</td><td>9.9</td><td>35</td><td>Minnesota</td><td>8.8</td></tr>
<tr><td>44</td><td>Oklahoma</td><td>6.3</td><td>36</td><td>Indiana</td><td>8.5</td></tr>
<tr><td>45</td><td>Oregon</td><td>5.9</td><td>37</td><td>Kentucky</td><td>8.4</td></tr>
<tr><td>22</td><td>Pennsylvania</td><td>16.7</td><td>37</td><td>Maine</td><td>8.4</td></tr>
<tr><td>4</td><td>Rhode Island</td><td>36.4</td><td>37</td><td>Mississippi</td><td>8.4</td></tr>
<tr><td>16</td><td>South Carolina</td><td>20.8</td><td>40</td><td>Alaska</td><td>7.2</td></tr>
<tr><td>49</td><td>South Dakota</td><td>(5.3)</td><td>41</td><td>Hawaii</td><td>6.9</td></tr>
<tr><td>29</td><td>Tennessee</td><td>11.6</td><td>42</td><td>North Dakota</td><td>6.7</td></tr>
<tr><td>12</td><td>Texas</td><td>25.8</td><td>43</td><td>Nebraska</td><td>6.6</td></tr>
<tr><td>25</td><td>Utah</td><td>14.7</td><td>44</td><td>Oklahoma</td><td>6.3</td></tr>
<tr><td>24</td><td>Vermont</td><td>15.3</td><td>45</td><td>Oregon</td><td>5.9</td></tr>
<tr><td>11</td><td>Virginia</td><td>28.7</td><td>46</td><td>Montana</td><td>2.9</td></tr>
<tr><td>26</td><td>Washington</td><td>14.1</td><td>47</td><td>Wyoming</td><td>(0.4)</td></tr>
<tr><td>50</td><td>West Virginia</td><td>(5.4)</td><td>48</td><td>Louisiana</td><td>(4.9)</td></tr>
<tr><td>33</td><td>Wisconsin</td><td>9.3</td><td>49</td><td>South Dakota</td><td>(5.3)</td></tr>
<tr><td>47</td><td>Wyoming</td><td>(0.4)</td><td>50</td><td>West Virginia</td><td>(5.4)</td></tr>
<tr><td></td><td></td><td></td><td></td><td>District of Columbia</td><td>3.3</td></tr>
</table>

Source: CQ Press using data from U.S. Department of Education, National Center for Education Statistics
  "Common Core of Data (CCD) Database" (http://nces.ed.gov/ccd/)
*School year 1995-1996 to 2005-2006. Counts are full-time equivalent figures.

Estimated Percent of Public Elementary and Secondary Teachers Who are Men: 2007
National Percent = 24.1%*

ALPHA ORDER

ALPHA ORDER

RANK ORDER

RANK	STATE	PERCENT
43	Alabama	20.7
3	Alaska	30.9
11	Arizona	27.5
50	Arkansas	16.8
10	California	27.8
23	Colorado	25.5
23	Connecticut	25.5
30	Delaware	23.9
40	Florida	21.6
44	Georgia	19.4
22	Hawaii	25.6
13	Idaho	27.3
36	Illinois	22.8
4	Indiana	30.5
19	Iowa	25.9
1	Kansas	33.3
41	Kentucky	21.3
49	Louisiana	17.6
17	Maine	26.4
35	Maryland	22.9
18	Massachusetts	26.0
27	Michigan	24.4
11	Minnesota	27.5
48	Mississippi	17.9
42	Missouri	21.2
8	Montana	28.4
25	Nebraska	25.3
26	Nevada	24.7
31	New Hampshire	23.7
29	New Jersey	24.0
20	New Mexico	25.7
34	New York	23.3
45	North Carolina	19.1
15	North Dakota	26.5
15	Ohio	26.5
38	Oklahoma	22.3
2	Oregon	31.6
7	Pennsylvania	28.5
39	Rhode Island	21.7
47	South Carolina	18.0
28	South Dakota	24.1
31	Tennessee	23.7
36	Texas	22.8
20	Utah	25.7
9	Vermont	27.9
46	Virginia	18.8
6	Washington	29.5
33	West Virginia	23.6
14	Wisconsin	27.2
5	Wyoming	30.0

RANK	STATE	PERCENT
1	Kansas	33.3
2	Oregon	31.6
3	Alaska	30.9
4	Indiana	30.5
5	Wyoming	30.0
6	Washington	29.5
7	Pennsylvania	28.5
8	Montana	28.4
9	Vermont	27.9
10	California	27.8
11	Arizona	27.5
11	Minnesota	27.5
13	Idaho	27.3
14	Wisconsin	27.2
15	North Dakota	26.5
15	Ohio	26.5
17	Maine	26.4
18	Massachusetts	26.0
19	Iowa	25.9
20	New Mexico	25.7
20	Utah	25.7
22	Hawaii	25.6
23	Colorado	25.5
23	Connecticut	25.5
25	Nebraska	25.3
26	Nevada	24.7
27	Michigan	24.4
28	South Dakota	24.1
29	New Jersey	24.0
30	Delaware	23.9
31	New Hampshire	23.7
31	Tennessee	23.7
33	West Virginia	23.6
34	New York	23.3
35	Maryland	22.9
36	Illinois	22.8
36	Texas	22.8
38	Oklahoma	22.3
39	Rhode Island	21.7
40	Florida	21.6
41	Kentucky	21.3
42	Missouri	21.2
43	Alabama	20.7
44	Georgia	19.4
45	North Carolina	19.1
46	Virginia	18.8
47	South Carolina	18.0
48	Mississippi	17.9
49	Louisiana	17.6
50	Arkansas	16.8

	District of Columbia	23.0

Source: CQ Press using data from National Education Association, Washington, D.C.
   "Rankings & Estimates" (Copyright © 2007, NEA, used with permission, http://www.nea.org/edstats/index.html)
*Estimates for school year 2006-2007.

Public School Pre-Kindergarten Teachers in 2006

National Total = 47,649 Teachers*

ALPHA ORDER

RANK	STATE	TEACHERS	% of USA
14	Alabama	918	1.9%
48	Alaska	44	0.1%
35	Arizona	243	0.5%
26	Arkansas	438	0.9%
1	California	8,850	18.6%
21	Colorado	659	1.4%
34	Connecticut	256	0.5%
46	Delaware	78	0.2%
5	Florida	1,754	3.7%
4	Georgia	2,495	5.2%
32	Hawaii	262	0.5%
41	Idaho	142	0.3%
9	Illinois	1,323	2.8%
25	Indiana	544	1.1%
17	Iowa	839	1.8%
27	Kansas	396	0.8%
20	Kentucky	736	1.5%
13	Louisiana	938	2.0%
33	Maine	260	0.5%
23	Maryland	608	1.3%
19	Massachusetts	759	1.6%
15	Michigan	890	1.9%
9	Minnesota	1,323	2.8%
30	Mississippi	305	0.6%
7	Missouri	1,683	3.5%
40	Montana	162	0.3%
29	Nebraska	322	0.7%
45	Nevada	80	0.2%
43	New Hampshire	139	0.3%
39	New Jersey	171	0.4%
28	New Mexico	357	0.7%
3	New York	2,749	5.8%
11	North Carolina	1,181	2.5%
41	North Dakota	142	0.3%
6	Ohio	1,698	3.6%
12	Oklahoma	1,087	2.3%
38	Oregon	176	0.4%
24	Pennsylvania	600	1.3%
36	Rhode Island	236	0.5%
18	South Carolina	785	1.6%
44	South Dakota	136	0.3%
22	Tennessee	640	1.3%
2	Texas	7,039	14.8%
37	Utah	210	0.4%
47	Vermont	77	0.2%
16	Virginia	875	1.8%
48	Washington	44	0.1%
31	West Virginia	290	0.6%
8	Wisconsin	1,382	2.9%
50	Wyoming	17	0.0%

RANK ORDER

RANK	STATE	TEACHERS	% of USA
1	California	8,850	18.6%
2	Texas	7,039	14.8%
3	New York	2,749	5.8%
4	Georgia	2,495	5.2%
5	Florida	1,754	3.7%
6	Ohio	1,698	3.6%
7	Missouri	1,683	3.5%
8	Wisconsin	1,382	2.9%
9	Illinois	1,323	2.8%
9	Minnesota	1,323	2.8%
11	North Carolina	1,181	2.5%
12	Oklahoma	1,087	2.3%
13	Louisiana	938	2.0%
14	Alabama	918	1.9%
15	Michigan	890	1.9%
16	Virginia	875	1.8%
17	Iowa	839	1.8%
18	South Carolina	785	1.6%
19	Massachusetts	759	1.6%
20	Kentucky	736	1.5%
21	Colorado	659	1.4%
22	Tennessee	640	1.3%
23	Maryland	608	1.3%
24	Pennsylvania	600	1.3%
25	Indiana	544	1.1%
26	Arkansas	438	0.9%
27	Kansas	396	0.8%
28	New Mexico	357	0.7%
29	Nebraska	322	0.7%
30	Mississippi	305	0.6%
31	West Virginia	290	0.6%
32	Hawaii	262	0.5%
33	Maine	260	0.5%
34	Connecticut	256	0.5%
35	Arizona	243	0.5%
36	Rhode Island	236	0.5%
37	Utah	210	0.4%
38	Oregon	176	0.4%
39	New Jersey	171	0.4%
40	Montana	162	0.3%
41	Idaho	142	0.3%
41	North Dakota	142	0.3%
43	New Hampshire	139	0.3%
44	South Dakota	136	0.3%
45	Nevada	80	0.2%
46	Delaware	78	0.2%
47	Vermont	77	0.2%
48	Alaska	44	0.1%
48	Washington	44	0.1%
50	Wyoming	17	0.0%
	District of Columbia	311	0.7%

Source: U.S. Department of Education, National Center for Education Statistics
   "Common Core of Data (CCD) Database" (http://nces.ed.gov/ccd/)
*School year 2005-2006. Counts are full-time equivalent figures.

Percent of Public School Teachers Who Teach Pre-Kindergarten: 2006

National Percent = 1.5% of Teachers*

ALPHA ORDER

RANK	STATE	PERCENT
14	Alabama	1.6
42	Alaska	0.6
45	Arizona	0.5
24	Arkansas	1.3
1	California	2.9
22	Colorado	1.4
42	Connecticut	0.6
31	Delaware	1.0
28	Florida	1.1
6	Georgia	2.3
6	Hawaii	2.3
31	Idaho	1.0
31	Illinois	1.0
36	Indiana	0.9
5	Iowa	2.4
26	Kansas	1.2
12	Kentucky	1.7
10	Louisiana	2.1
14	Maine	1.6
28	Maryland	1.1
31	Massachusetts	1.0
36	Michigan	0.9
2	Minnesota	2.6
31	Mississippi	1.0
4	Missouri	2.5
14	Montana	1.6
19	Nebraska	1.5
47	Nevada	0.4
36	New Hampshire	0.9
49	New Jersey	0.2
14	New Mexico	1.6
24	New York	1.3
26	North Carolina	1.2
11	North Dakota	1.8
22	Ohio	1.4
2	Oklahoma	2.6
42	Oregon	0.6
45	Pennsylvania	0.5
12	Rhode Island	1.7
14	South Carolina	1.6
19	South Dakota	1.5
28	Tennessee	1.1
6	Texas	2.3
36	Utah	0.9
36	Vermont	0.9
36	Virginia	0.9
50	Washington	0.1
19	West Virginia	1.5
6	Wisconsin	2.3
48	Wyoming	0.3

RANK ORDER

RANK	STATE	PERCENT
1	California	2.9
2	Minnesota	2.6
2	Oklahoma	2.6
4	Missouri	2.5
5	Iowa	2.4
6	Georgia	2.3
6	Hawaii	2.3
6	Texas	2.3
6	Wisconsin	2.3
10	Louisiana	2.1
11	North Dakota	1.8
12	Kentucky	1.7
12	Rhode Island	1.7
14	Alabama	1.6
14	Maine	1.6
14	Montana	1.6
14	New Mexico	1.6
14	South Carolina	1.6
19	Nebraska	1.5
19	South Dakota	1.5
19	West Virginia	1.5
22	Colorado	1.4
22	Ohio	1.4
24	Arkansas	1.3
24	New York	1.3
26	Kansas	1.2
26	North Carolina	1.2
28	Florida	1.1
28	Maryland	1.1
28	Tennessee	1.1
31	Delaware	1.0
31	Idaho	1.0
31	Illinois	1.0
31	Massachusetts	1.0
31	Mississippi	1.0
36	Indiana	0.9
36	Michigan	0.9
36	New Hampshire	0.9
36	Utah	0.9
36	Vermont	0.9
36	Virginia	0.9
42	Alaska	0.6
42	Connecticut	0.6
42	Oregon	0.6
45	Arizona	0.5
45	Pennsylvania	0.5
47	Nevada	0.4
48	Wyoming	0.3
49	New Jersey	0.2
50	Washington	0.1

District of Columbia	5.7

Source: CQ Press using data from U.S. Department of Education, National Center for Education Statistics
"Common Core of Data (CCD) Database" (http://nces.ed.gov/ccd/)
*School year 2005-2006. Counts are full-time equivalent figures.

Public School Kindergarten Teachers in 2006

National Total = 156,481 Teachers*

ALPHA ORDER

RANK	STATE	TEACHERS	% of USA
NA	Alabama**	NA	NA
42	Alaska	417	0.3%
19	Arizona	2,510	1.6%
26	Arkansas	1,951	1.2%
1	California	21,003	13.4%
17	Colorado	2,924	1.9%
28	Connecticut	1,741	1.1%
48	Delaware	291	0.2%
4	Florida	9,198	5.9%
5	Georgia	7,233	4.6%
40	Hawaii	536	0.3%
39	Idaho	541	0.3%
9	Illinois	4,211	2.7%
16	Indiana	2,946	1.9%
18	Iowa	2,523	1.6%
29	Kansas	1,440	0.9%
32	Kentucky	1,200	0.8%
22	Louisiana	2,377	1.5%
35	Maine	1,054	0.7%
20	Maryland	2,499	1.6%
15	Massachusetts	3,075	2.0%
NA	Michigan**	NA	NA
21	Minnesota	2,384	1.5%
27	Mississippi	1,916	1.2%
12	Missouri	4,037	2.6%
38	Montana	654	0.4%
31	Nebraska	1,305	0.8%
37	Nevada	732	0.5%
44	New Hampshire	405	0.3%
14	New Jersey	3,095	2.0%
30	New Mexico	1,399	0.9%
3	New York	12,235	7.8%
6	North Carolina	6,590	4.2%
46	North Dakota	322	0.2%
7	Ohio	5,309	3.4%
25	Oklahoma	1,956	1.2%
33	Oregon	1,187	0.8%
8	Pennsylvania	4,911	3.1%
43	Rhode Island	407	0.3%
23	South Carolina	2,282	1.5%
41	South Dakota	427	0.3%
11	Tennessee	4,080	2.6%
2	Texas	18,512	11.8%
36	Utah	1,020	0.7%
45	Vermont	344	0.2%
10	Virginia	4,119	2.6%
24	Washington	2,226	1.4%
34	West Virginia	1,082	0.7%
13	Wisconsin	3,292	2.1%
47	Wyoming	312	0.2%

RANK ORDER

RANK	STATE	TEACHERS	% of USA
1	California	21,003	13.4%
2	Texas	18,512	11.8%
3	New York	12,235	7.8%
4	Florida	9,198	5.9%
5	Georgia	7,233	4.6%
6	North Carolina	6,590	4.2%
7	Ohio	5,309	3.4%
8	Pennsylvania	4,911	3.1%
9	Illinois	4,211	2.7%
10	Virginia	4,119	2.6%
11	Tennessee	4,080	2.6%
12	Missouri	4,037	2.6%
13	Wisconsin	3,292	2.1%
14	New Jersey	3,095	2.0%
15	Massachusetts	3,075	2.0%
16	Indiana	2,946	1.9%
17	Colorado	2,924	1.9%
18	Iowa	2,523	1.6%
19	Arizona	2,510	1.6%
20	Maryland	2,499	1.6%
21	Minnesota	2,384	1.5%
22	Louisiana	2,377	1.5%
23	South Carolina	2,282	1.5%
24	Washington	2,226	1.4%
25	Oklahoma	1,956	1.2%
26	Arkansas	1,951	1.2%
27	Mississippi	1,916	1.2%
28	Connecticut	1,741	1.1%
29	Kansas	1,440	0.9%
30	New Mexico	1,399	0.9%
31	Nebraska	1,305	0.8%
32	Kentucky	1,200	0.8%
33	Oregon	1,187	0.8%
34	West Virginia	1,082	0.7%
35	Maine	1,054	0.7%
36	Utah	1,020	0.7%
37	Nevada	732	0.5%
38	Montana	654	0.4%
39	Idaho	541	0.3%
40	Hawaii	536	0.3%
41	South Dakota	427	0.3%
42	Alaska	417	0.3%
43	Rhode Island	407	0.3%
44	New Hampshire	405	0.3%
45	Vermont	344	0.2%
46	North Dakota	322	0.2%
47	Wyoming	312	0.2%
48	Delaware	291	0.2%
NA	Alabama**	NA	NA
NA	Michigan**	NA	NA
	District of Columbia	271	0.2%

Source: U.S. Department of Education, National Center for Education Statistics
   "Common Core of Data (CCD) Database" (http://nces.ed.gov/ccd/)
*School year 2005-2006. Counts are full-time equivalent figures. Total is for reporting states.
**Not available.

Percent of Public School Teachers Who Teach Kindergarten: 2006

National Percent = 5.2% of Teachers*

ALPHA ORDER

RANK	STATE	PERCENT
NA	Alabama**	NA
19	Alaska	5.3
21	Arizona	4.9
14	Arkansas	5.9
3	California	6.8
6	Colorado	6.4
30	Connecticut	4.4
42	Delaware	3.6
15	Florida	5.8
5	Georgia	6.7
23	Hawaii	4.8
41	Idaho	3.7
44	Illinois	3.1
21	Indiana	4.9
1	Iowa	7.2
33	Kansas	4.3
45	Kentucky	2.8
19	Louisiana	5.3
8	Maine	6.3
30	Maryland	4.4
35	Massachusetts	4.2
NA	Michigan**	NA
24	Minnesota	4.7
10	Mississippi	6.1
13	Missouri	6.0
8	Montana	6.3
10	Nebraska	6.1
43	Nevada	3.4
48	New Hampshire	2.6
47	New Jersey	2.7
6	New Mexico	6.4
16	New York	5.6
2	North Carolina	6.9
38	North Dakota	4.0
29	Ohio	4.5
24	Oklahoma	4.7
35	Oregon	4.2
38	Pennsylvania	4.0
45	Rhode Island	2.8
24	South Carolina	4.7
24	South Dakota	4.7
3	Tennessee	6.8
10	Texas	6.1
30	Utah	4.4
40	Vermont	3.9
33	Virginia	4.3
35	Washington	4.2
18	West Virginia	5.4
17	Wisconsin	5.5
24	Wyoming	4.7

RANK ORDER

RANK	STATE	PERCENT
1	Iowa	7.2
2	North Carolina	6.9
3	California	6.8
3	Tennessee	6.8
5	Georgia	6.7
6	Colorado	6.4
6	New Mexico	6.4
8	Maine	6.3
8	Montana	6.3
10	Mississippi	6.1
10	Nebraska	6.1
10	Texas	6.1
13	Missouri	6.0
14	Arkansas	5.9
15	Florida	5.8
16	New York	5.6
17	Wisconsin	5.5
18	West Virginia	5.4
19	Alaska	5.3
19	Louisiana	5.3
21	Arizona	4.9
21	Indiana	4.9
23	Hawaii	4.8
24	Minnesota	4.7
24	Oklahoma	4.7
24	South Carolina	4.7
24	South Dakota	4.7
24	Wyoming	4.7
29	Ohio	4.5
30	Connecticut	4.4
30	Maryland	4.4
30	Utah	4.4
33	Kansas	4.3
33	Virginia	4.3
35	Massachusetts	4.2
35	Oregon	4.2
35	Washington	4.2
38	North Dakota	4.0
38	Pennsylvania	4.0
40	Vermont	3.9
41	Idaho	3.7
42	Delaware	3.6
43	Nevada	3.4
44	Illinois	3.1
45	Kentucky	2.8
45	Rhode Island	2.8
47	New Jersey	2.7
48	New Hampshire	2.6
NA	Alabama**	NA
NA	Michigan**	NA

District of Columbia 4.9

Source: CQ Press using data from U.S. Department of Education, National Center for Education Statistics
   "Common Core of Data (CCD) Database" (http://nces.ed.gov/ccd/)
*School year 2005-2006. Counts are full-time equivalent figures. National percent is for reporting states.
**Not available.

Public School Elementary Teachers in 2006

National Total = 1,508,899 Teachers*

ALPHA ORDER

RANK	STATE	TEACHERS	% of USA
16	Alabama	31,430	2.1%
44	Alaska	5,147	0.3%
15	Arizona	33,918	2.2%
35	Arkansas	11,453	0.8%
1	California	184,176	12.2%
27	Colorado	19,630	1.3%
23	Connecticut	24,325	1.6%
48	Delaware	3,639	0.2%
6	Florida	59,549	3.9%
7	Georgia	55,742	3.7%
46	Hawaii	5,070	0.3%
41	Idaho	6,832	0.5%
5	Illinois	72,267	4.8%
21	Indiana	28,321	1.9%
28	Iowa	19,604	1.3%
31	Kansas	12,993	0.9%
25	Kentucky	22,471	1.5%
22	Louisiana	28,077	1.9%
39	Maine	9,829	0.7%
18	Maryland	29,914	2.0%
12	Massachusetts	37,028	2.5%
20	Michigan	28,963	1.9%
26	Minnesota	21,691	1.4%
32	Mississippi	12,766	0.8%
19	Missouri	29,176	1.9%
43	Montana	6,111	0.4%
33	Nebraska	12,172	0.8%
37	Nevada	10,105	0.7%
36	New Hampshire	10,121	0.7%
10	New Jersey	40,625	2.7%
30	New Mexico	13,456	0.9%
3	New York	92,817	6.2%
8	North Carolina	49,242	3.3%
47	North Dakota	4,357	0.3%
4	Ohio	73,203	4.9%
29	Oklahoma	17,243	1.1%
34	Oregon	11,974	0.8%
9	Pennsylvania	47,203	3.1%
42	Rhode Island	6,783	0.4%
17	South Carolina	30,445	2.0%
45	South Dakota	5,075	0.3%
11	Tennessee	37,111	2.5%
2	Texas	124,409	8.2%
38	Utah	9,965	0.7%
49	Vermont	2,944	0.2%
13	Virginia	36,044	2.4%
24	Washington	23,964	1.6%
40	West Virginia	8,480	0.6%
14	Wisconsin	35,848	2.4%
50	Wyoming	2,888	0.2%

RANK ORDER

RANK	STATE	TEACHERS	% of USA
1	California	184,176	12.2%
2	Texas	124,409	8.2%
3	New York	92,817	6.2%
4	Ohio	73,203	4.9%
5	Illinois	72,267	4.8%
6	Florida	59,549	3.9%
7	Georgia	55,742	3.7%
8	North Carolina	49,242	3.3%
9	Pennsylvania	47,203	3.1%
10	New Jersey	40,625	2.7%
11	Tennessee	37,111	2.5%
12	Massachusetts	37,028	2.5%
13	Virginia	36,044	2.4%
14	Wisconsin	35,848	2.4%
15	Arizona	33,918	2.2%
16	Alabama	31,430	2.1%
17	South Carolina	30,445	2.0%
18	Maryland	29,914	2.0%
19	Missouri	29,176	1.9%
20	Michigan	28,963	1.9%
21	Indiana	28,321	1.9%
22	Louisiana	28,077	1.9%
23	Connecticut	24,325	1.6%
24	Washington	23,964	1.6%
25	Kentucky	22,471	1.5%
26	Minnesota	21,691	1.4%
27	Colorado	19,630	1.3%
28	Iowa	19,604	1.3%
29	Oklahoma	17,243	1.1%
30	New Mexico	13,456	0.9%
31	Kansas	12,993	0.9%
32	Mississippi	12,766	0.8%
33	Nebraska	12,172	0.8%
34	Oregon	11,974	0.8%
35	Arkansas	11,453	0.8%
36	New Hampshire	10,121	0.7%
37	Nevada	10,105	0.7%
38	Utah	9,965	0.7%
39	Maine	9,829	0.7%
40	West Virginia	8,480	0.6%
41	Idaho	6,832	0.5%
42	Rhode Island	6,783	0.4%
43	Montana	6,111	0.4%
44	Alaska	5,147	0.3%
45	South Dakota	5,075	0.3%
46	Hawaii	5,070	0.3%
47	North Dakota	4,357	0.3%
48	Delaware	3,639	0.2%
49	Vermont	2,944	0.2%
50	Wyoming	2,888	0.2%
	District of Columbia	2,303	0.2%

Source: U.S. Department of Education, National Center for Education Statistics
    "Common Core of Data (CCD) Database" (http://nces.ed.gov/ccd/)
*School year 2005-2006. Counts are full-time equivalent figures.

Percent of Public School Teachers Who Teach Elementary Grades: 2006

National Percent = 48.7% of Teachers*

ALPHA ORDER

RANK	STATE	PERCENT
17	Alabama	54.4
2	Alaska	65.1
1	Arizona	66.0
48	Arkansas	34.7
10	California	59.6
35	Colorado	42.8
8	Connecticut	61.3
29	Delaware	45.5
45	Florida	37.5
23	Georgia	51.4
30	Hawaii	45.2
26	Idaho	47.0
19	Illinois	54.0
27	Indiana	46.7
15	Iowa	55.7
43	Kansas	38.7
20	Kentucky	53.0
5	Louisiana	62.9
12	Maine	58.9
21	Maryland	52.8
24	Massachusetts	50.3
NA	Michigan**	NA
37	Minnesota	42.4
42	Mississippi	40.6
32	Missouri	43.5
12	Montana	58.9
14	Nebraska	57.0
28	Nevada	46.5
2	New Hampshire	65.1
47	New Jersey	36.1
9	New Mexico	61.1
37	New York	42.4
22	North Carolina	51.5
17	North Dakota	54.4
7	Ohio	62.0
40	Oklahoma	41.2
37	Oregon	42.4
44	Pennsylvania	38.6
25	Rhode Island	47.4
4	South Carolina	63.1
16	South Dakota	55.6
6	Tennessee	62.3
41	Texas	41.1
33	Utah	43.3
49	Vermont	33.3
45	Virginia	37.5
31	Washington	44.8
36	West Virginia	42.5
10	Wisconsin	59.6
34	Wyoming	43.1

RANK ORDER

RANK	STATE	PERCENT
1	Arizona	66.0
2	Alaska	65.1
2	New Hampshire	65.1
4	South Carolina	63.1
5	Louisiana	62.9
6	Tennessee	62.3
7	Ohio	62.0
8	Connecticut	61.3
9	New Mexico	61.1
10	California	59.6
10	Wisconsin	59.6
12	Maine	58.9
12	Montana	58.9
14	Nebraska	57.0
15	Iowa	55.7
16	South Dakota	55.6
17	Alabama	54.4
17	North Dakota	54.4
19	Illinois	54.0
20	Kentucky	53.0
21	Maryland	52.8
22	North Carolina	51.5
23	Georgia	51.4
24	Massachusetts	50.3
25	Rhode Island	47.4
26	Idaho	47.0
27	Indiana	46.7
28	Nevada	46.5
29	Delaware	45.5
30	Hawaii	45.2
31	Washington	44.8
32	Missouri	43.5
33	Utah	43.3
34	Wyoming	43.1
35	Colorado	42.8
36	West Virginia	42.5
37	Minnesota	42.4
37	New York	42.4
37	Oregon	42.4
40	Oklahoma	41.2
41	Texas	41.1
42	Mississippi	40.6
43	Kansas	38.7
44	Pennsylvania	38.6
45	Florida	37.5
45	Virginia	37.5
47	New Jersey	36.1
48	Arkansas	34.7
49	Vermont	33.3
NA	Michigan**	NA

	District of Columbia	42.0

Source: CQ Press using data from U.S. Department of Education, National Center for Education Statistics
"Common Core of Data (CCD) Database" (http://nces.ed.gov/ccd/)
*School year 2005-2006. Counts are full-time equivalent figures. National percent is for reporting states.
**Not available.

Public Secondary School Teachers in 2006

National Total = 1,146,894 Teachers*

ALPHA ORDER

RANK	STATE	TEACHERS	% of USA
26	Alabama	14,409	1.3%
50	Alaska	2,304	0.2%
25	Arizona	14,705	1.3%
23	Arkansas	16,778	1.5%
2	California	83,953	7.3%
17	Colorado	22,628	2.0%
30	Connecticut	12,177	1.1%
44	Delaware	3,990	0.3%
5	Florida	62,190	5.4%
8	Georgia	43,065	3.8%
42	Hawaii	5,321	0.5%
37	Idaho	7,006	0.6%
10	Illinois	34,923	3.0%
13	Indiana	26,413	2.3%
29	Iowa	12,215	1.1%
24	Kansas	15,069	1.3%
32	Kentucky	9,811	0.9%
28	Louisiana	13,268	1.2%
41	Maine	5,541	0.5%
15	Maryland	23,664	2.1%
19	Massachusetts	20,253	1.8%
16	Michigan	22,816	2.0%
14	Minnesota	24,312	2.1%
31	Mississippi	12,035	1.0%
12	Missouri	32,180	2.8%
46	Montana	3,442	0.3%
36	Nebraska	7,560	0.7%
35	Nevada	7,710	0.7%
43	New Hampshire	4,871	0.4%
4	New Jersey	68,782	6.0%
39	New Mexico	6,809	0.6%
3	New York	75,348	6.6%
11	North Carolina	32,239	2.8%
48	North Dakota	3,182	0.3%
9	Ohio	37,772	3.3%
21	Oklahoma	16,931	1.5%
33	Oregon	9,510	0.8%
7	Pennsylvania	52,694	4.6%
38	Rhode Island	6,873	0.6%
27	South Carolina	13,848	1.2%
49	South Dakota	2,547	0.2%
22	Tennessee	16,822	1.5%
1	Texas	116,750	10.2%
34	Utah	9,455	0.8%
45	Vermont	3,542	0.3%
6	Virginia	55,120	4.8%
18	Washington	22,224	1.9%
40	West Virginia	6,737	0.6%
20	Wisconsin	19,391	1.7%
47	Wyoming	3,393	0.3%

RANK ORDER

RANK	STATE	TEACHERS	% of USA
1	Texas	116,750	10.2%
2	California	83,953	7.3%
3	New York	75,348	6.6%
4	New Jersey	68,782	6.0%
5	Florida	62,190	5.4%
6	Virginia	55,120	4.8%
7	Pennsylvania	52,694	4.6%
8	Georgia	43,065	3.8%
9	Ohio	37,772	3.3%
10	Illinois	34,923	3.0%
11	North Carolina	32,239	2.8%
12	Missouri	32,180	2.8%
13	Indiana	26,413	2.3%
14	Minnesota	24,312	2.1%
15	Maryland	23,664	2.1%
16	Michigan	22,816	2.0%
17	Colorado	22,628	2.0%
18	Washington	22,224	1.9%
19	Massachusetts	20,253	1.8%
20	Wisconsin	19,391	1.7%
21	Oklahoma	16,931	1.5%
22	Tennessee	16,822	1.5%
23	Arkansas	16,778	1.5%
24	Kansas	15,069	1.3%
25	Arizona	14,705	1.3%
26	Alabama	14,409	1.3%
27	South Carolina	13,848	1.2%
28	Louisiana	13,268	1.2%
29	Iowa	12,215	1.1%
30	Connecticut	12,177	1.1%
31	Mississippi	12,035	1.0%
32	Kentucky	9,811	0.9%
33	Oregon	9,510	0.8%
34	Utah	9,455	0.8%
35	Nevada	7,710	0.7%
36	Nebraska	7,560	0.7%
37	Idaho	7,006	0.6%
38	Rhode Island	6,873	0.6%
39	New Mexico	6,809	0.6%
40	West Virginia	6,737	0.6%
41	Maine	5,541	0.5%
42	Hawaii	5,321	0.5%
43	New Hampshire	4,871	0.4%
44	Delaware	3,990	0.3%
45	Vermont	3,542	0.3%
46	Montana	3,442	0.3%
47	Wyoming	3,393	0.3%
48	North Dakota	3,182	0.3%
49	South Dakota	2,547	0.2%
50	Alaska	2,304	0.2%
	District of Columbia	2,316	0.2%

Source: U.S. Department of Education, National Center for Education Statistics
    "Common Core of Data (CCD) Database" (http://nces.ed.gov/ccd/)
*School year 2005-2006. Counts are full-time equivalent figures.

Percent of Public School Teachers Who Teach Secondary Grades: 2006

National Percent = 37.0% of Teachers*

RANK	STATE	PERCENT
48	Alabama	24.9
40	Alaska	29.1
42	Arizona	28.6
3	Arkansas	50.8
46	California	27.2
6	Colorado	49.4
38	Connecticut	30.7
5	Delaware	49.9
22	Florida	39.1
21	Georgia	39.7
11	Hawaii	47.4
7	Idaho	48.2
47	Illinois	26.1
13	Indiana	43.6
27	Iowa	34.7
12	Kansas	44.8
49	Kentucky	23.1
39	Louisiana	29.7
32	Maine	33.2
15	Maryland	41.7
45	Massachusetts	27.5
NA	Michigan**	NA
10	Minnesota	47.6
24	Mississippi	38.3
9	Missouri	48.0
32	Montana	33.2
26	Nebraska	35.4
25	Nevada	35.5
36	New Hampshire	31.4
1	New Jersey	61.0
37	New Mexico	30.9
28	New York	34.4
30	North Carolina	33.7
20	North Dakota	39.8
35	Ohio	32.0
18	Oklahoma	40.5
30	Oregon	33.7
14	Pennsylvania	43.1
8	Rhode Island	48.1
41	South Carolina	28.7
44	South Dakota	27.9
43	Tennessee	28.2
23	Texas	38.6
17	Utah	41.1
19	Vermont	40.0
2	Virginia	57.3
16	Washington	41.5
29	West Virginia	33.8
34	Wisconsin	32.3
4	Wyoming	50.6

RANK	STATE	PERCENT
1	New Jersey	61.0
2	Virginia	57.3
3	Arkansas	50.8
4	Wyoming	50.6
5	Delaware	49.9
6	Colorado	49.4
7	Idaho	48.2
8	Rhode Island	48.1
9	Missouri	48.0
10	Minnesota	47.6
11	Hawaii	47.4
12	Kansas	44.8
13	Indiana	43.6
14	Pennsylvania	43.1
15	Maryland	41.7
16	Washington	41.5
17	Utah	41.1
18	Oklahoma	40.5
19	Vermont	40.0
20	North Dakota	39.8
21	Georgia	39.7
22	Florida	39.1
23	Texas	38.6
24	Mississippi	38.3
25	Nevada	35.5
26	Nebraska	35.4
27	Iowa	34.7
28	New York	34.4
29	West Virginia	33.8
30	North Carolina	33.7
30	Oregon	33.7
32	Maine	33.2
32	Montana	33.2
34	Wisconsin	32.3
35	Ohio	32.0
36	New Hampshire	31.4
37	New Mexico	30.9
38	Connecticut	30.7
39	Louisiana	29.7
40	Alaska	29.1
41	South Carolina	28.7
42	Arizona	28.6
43	Tennessee	28.2
44	South Dakota	27.9
45	Massachusetts	27.5
46	California	27.2
47	Illinois	26.1
48	Alabama	24.9
49	Kentucky	23.1
NA	Michigan**	NA
	District of Columbia	42.3

Source: CQ Press using data from U.S. Department of Education, National Center for Education Statistics
    "Common Core of Data (CCD) Database" (http://nces.ed.gov/ccd/)
*School year 2005-2006. Counts are full-time equivalent figures. National percent is for reporting states.
**Not available.

Public Elementary and Secondary School Teachers of Ungraded Classes in 2006
National Total = 224,828 Teachers*

ALPHA ORDER

RANK	STATE	TEACHERS	% of USA
30	Alabama	0	0.0%
30	Alaska	0	0.0%
30	Arizona	0	0.0%
18	Arkansas	2,377	1.1%
7	California	11,146	5.0%
30	Colorado	0	0.0%
23	Connecticut	1,188	0.5%
30	Delaware	0	0.0%
3	Florida	26,271	11.7%
30	Georgia	0	0.0%
29	Hawaii	37	0.0%
30	Idaho	0	0.0%
4	Illinois	21,133	9.4%
19	Indiana	2,368	1.1%
30	Iowa	0	0.0%
15	Kansas	3,710	1.7%
8	Kentucky	8,195	3.6%
30	Louisiana	0	0.0%
30	Maine	0	0.0%
30	Maryland	0	0.0%
6	Massachusetts	12,481	5.6%
10	Michigan	5,999	2.7%
22	Minnesota	1,397	0.6%
14	Mississippi	4,411	2.0%
30	Missouri	0	0.0%
30	Montana	0	0.0%
30	Nebraska	0	0.0%
17	Nevada	3,117	1.4%
30	New Hampshire	0	0.0%
30	New Jersey	0	0.0%
30	New Mexico	0	0.0%
1	New York	35,840	15.9%
9	North Carolina	6,412	2.9%
30	North Dakota	0	0.0%
30	Ohio	0	0.0%
13	Oklahoma	4,616	2.1%
11	Oregon	5,409	2.4%
5	Pennsylvania	16,989	7.6%
30	Rhode Island	0	0.0%
26	South Carolina	852	0.4%
24	South Dakota	944	0.4%
25	Tennessee	943	0.4%
2	Texas	35,715	15.9%
20	Utah	2,343	1.0%
21	Vermont	1,944	0.9%
30	Virginia	0	0.0%
12	Washington	5,050	2.2%
16	West Virginia	3,351	1.5%
27	Wisconsin	214	0.1%
28	Wyoming	96	0.0%

RANK ORDER

RANK	STATE	TEACHERS	% of USA
1	New York	35,840	15.9%
2	Texas	35,715	15.9%
3	Florida	26,271	11.7%
4	Illinois	21,133	9.4%
5	Pennsylvania	16,989	7.6%
6	Massachusetts	12,481	5.6%
7	California	11,146	5.0%
8	Kentucky	8,195	3.6%
9	North Carolina	6,412	2.9%
10	Michigan	5,999	2.7%
11	Oregon	5,409	2.4%
12	Washington	5,050	2.2%
13	Oklahoma	4,616	2.1%
14	Mississippi	4,411	2.0%
15	Kansas	3,710	1.7%
16	West Virginia	3,351	1.5%
17	Nevada	3,117	1.4%
18	Arkansas	2,377	1.1%
19	Indiana	2,368	1.1%
20	Utah	2,343	1.0%
21	Vermont	1,944	0.9%
22	Minnesota	1,397	0.6%
23	Connecticut	1,188	0.5%
24	South Dakota	944	0.4%
25	Tennessee	943	0.4%
26	South Carolina	852	0.4%
27	Wisconsin	214	0.1%
28	Wyoming	96	0.0%
29	Hawaii	37	0.0%
30	Alabama	0	0.0%
30	Alaska	0	0.0%
30	Arizona	0	0.0%
30	Colorado	0	0.0%
30	Delaware	0	0.0%
30	Georgia	0	0.0%
30	Idaho	0	0.0%
30	Iowa	0	0.0%
30	Louisiana	0	0.0%
30	Maine	0	0.0%
30	Maryland	0	0.0%
30	Missouri	0	0.0%
30	Montana	0	0.0%
30	Nebraska	0	0.0%
30	New Hampshire	0	0.0%
30	New Jersey	0	0.0%
30	New Mexico	0	0.0%
30	North Dakota	0	0.0%
30	Ohio	0	0.0%
30	Rhode Island	0	0.0%
30	Virginia	0	0.0%
	District of Columbia	280	0.1%

Source: U.S. Department of Education, National Center for Education Statistics
"Common Core of Data (CCD) Database" (http://nces.ed.gov/ccd/)
*School year 2005-2006. Counts are full-time equivalent figures. These are teachers who instruct classes or programs to which students are assigned without standard grade designation.

Percent of Public Elementary and Secondary Teachers Who Teach
Ungraded Classes: 2006
National Percent = 7.2% of Teachers*

ALPHA ORDER

RANK	STATE	PERCENT
29	Alabama	0.0
29	Alaska	0.0
29	Arizona	0.0
18	Arkansas	7.2
21	California	3.6
29	Colorado	0.0
22	Connecticut	3.0
29	Delaware	0.0
6	Florida	16.5
29	Georgia	0.0
28	Hawaii	0.3
29	Idaho	0.0
8	Illinois	15.8
20	Indiana	3.9
29	Iowa	0.0
13	Kansas	11.0
2	Kentucky	19.3
29	Louisiana	0.0
29	Maine	0.0
29	Maryland	0.0
4	Massachusetts	17.0
NA	Michigan**	NA
23	Minnesota	2.7
10	Mississippi	14.0
29	Missouri	0.0
29	Montana	0.0
29	Nebraska	0.0
9	Nevada	14.3
29	New Hampshire	0.0
29	New Jersey	0.0
29	New Mexico	0.0
7	New York	16.4
19	North Carolina	6.7
29	North Dakota	0.0
29	Ohio	0.0
13	Oklahoma	11.0
3	Oregon	19.1
11	Pennsylvania	13.9
29	Rhode Island	0.0
24	South Carolina	1.8
15	South Dakota	10.3
25	Tennessee	1.6
12	Texas	11.8
16	Utah	10.2
1	Vermont	22.0
29	Virginia	0.0
17	Washington	9.4
5	West Virginia	16.8
27	Wisconsin	0.4
26	Wyoming	1.4

RANK ORDER

RANK	STATE	PERCENT
1	Vermont	22.0
2	Kentucky	19.3
3	Oregon	19.1
4	Massachusetts	17.0
5	West Virginia	16.8
6	Florida	16.5
7	New York	16.4
8	Illinois	15.8
9	Nevada	14.3
10	Mississippi	14.0
11	Pennsylvania	13.9
12	Texas	11.8
13	Kansas	11.0
13	Oklahoma	11.0
15	South Dakota	10.3
16	Utah	10.2
17	Washington	9.4
18	Arkansas	7.2
19	North Carolina	6.7
20	Indiana	3.9
21	California	3.6
22	Connecticut	3.0
23	Minnesota	2.7
24	South Carolina	1.8
25	Tennessee	1.6
26	Wyoming	1.4
27	Wisconsin	0.4
28	Hawaii	0.3
29	Alabama	0.0
29	Alaska	0.0
29	Arizona	0.0
29	Colorado	0.0
29	Delaware	0.0
29	Georgia	0.0
29	Idaho	0.0
29	Iowa	0.0
29	Louisiana	0.0
29	Maine	0.0
29	Maryland	0.0
29	Missouri	0.0
29	Montana	0.0
29	Nebraska	0.0
29	New Hampshire	0.0
29	New Jersey	0.0
29	New Mexico	0.0
29	North Dakota	0.0
29	Ohio	0.0
29	Rhode Island	0.0
29	Virginia	0.0
NA	Michigan**	NA

District of Columbia   5.1

Source: CQ Press using data from U.S. Department of Education, National Center for Education Statistics
"Common Core of Data (CCD) Database" (http://nces.ed.gov/ccd/)
*School year 2005-2006. Counts are full-time equivalent figures. These are teachers who instruct classes or programs to which
students are assigned without standard grade designation. National percent is for reporting states.
**Not available.

National Board Certified Teachers as of 2007

National Total = 63,879 Teachers*

ALPHA ORDER

RANK	STATE	TEACHERS	% of USA
13	Alabama	1,331	2.1%
45	Alaska	93	0.1%
21	Arizona	454	0.7%
16	Arkansas	846	1.3%
4	California	3,878	6.1%
29	Colorado	336	0.5%
41	Connecticut	126	0.2%
24	Delaware	395	0.6%
2	Florida	10,859	17.0%
8	Georgia	2,454	3.8%
37	Hawaii	163	0.3%
27	Idaho	337	0.5%
7	Illinois	2,489	3.9%
40	Indiana	137	0.2%
18	Iowa	564	0.9%
34	Kansas	268	0.4%
12	Kentucky	1,377	2.2%
14	Louisiana	1,215	1.9%
43	Maine	118	0.2%
15	Maryland	1,060	1.7%
20	Massachusetts	456	0.7%
35	Michigan	242	0.4%
31	Minnesota	305	0.5%
6	Mississippi	2,685	4.2%
22	Missouri	413	0.6%
46	Montana	64	0.1%
47	Nebraska	61	0.1%
27	Nevada	337	0.5%
50	New Hampshire	16	0.0%
38	New Jersey	149	0.2%
30	New Mexico	312	0.5%
17	New York	784	1.2%
1	North Carolina	12,779	20.0%
49	North Dakota	27	0.0%
5	Ohio	2,762	4.3%
9	Oklahoma	1,992	3.1%
36	Oregon	219	0.3%
25	Pennsylvania	370	0.6%
32	Rhode Island	300	0.5%
3	South Carolina	5,737	9.0%
48	South Dakota	60	0.1%
33	Tennessee	288	0.5%
23	Texas	400	0.6%
42	Utah	125	0.2%
44	Vermont	102	0.2%
11	Virginia	1,434	2.2%
10	Washington	1,799	2.8%
26	West Virginia	360	0.6%
19	Wisconsin	516	0.8%
39	Wyoming	144	0.2%

RANK ORDER

RANK	STATE	TEACHERS	% of USA
1	North Carolina	12,779	20.0%
2	Florida	10,859	17.0%
3	South Carolina	5,737	9.0%
4	California	3,878	6.1%
5	Ohio	2,762	4.3%
6	Mississippi	2,685	4.2%
7	Illinois	2,489	3.9%
8	Georgia	2,454	3.8%
9	Oklahoma	1,992	3.1%
10	Washington	1,799	2.8%
11	Virginia	1,434	2.2%
12	Kentucky	1,377	2.2%
13	Alabama	1,331	2.1%
14	Louisiana	1,215	1.9%
15	Maryland	1,060	1.7%
16	Arkansas	846	1.3%
17	New York	784	1.2%
18	Iowa	564	0.9%
19	Wisconsin	516	0.8%
20	Massachusetts	456	0.7%
21	Arizona	454	0.7%
22	Missouri	413	0.6%
23	Texas	400	0.6%
24	Delaware	395	0.6%
25	Pennsylvania	370	0.6%
26	West Virginia	360	0.6%
27	Idaho	337	0.5%
27	Nevada	337	0.5%
29	Colorado	336	0.5%
30	New Mexico	312	0.5%
31	Minnesota	305	0.5%
32	Rhode Island	300	0.5%
33	Tennessee	288	0.5%
34	Kansas	268	0.4%
35	Michigan	242	0.4%
36	Oregon	219	0.3%
37	Hawaii	163	0.3%
38	New Jersey	149	0.2%
39	Wyoming	144	0.2%
40	Indiana	137	0.2%
41	Connecticut	126	0.2%
42	Utah	125	0.2%
43	Maine	118	0.2%
44	Vermont	102	0.2%
45	Alaska	93	0.1%
46	Montana	64	0.1%
47	Nebraska	61	0.1%
48	South Dakota	60	0.1%
49	North Dakota	27	0.0%
50	New Hampshire	16	0.0%
	District of Columbia	24	0.0%

Source: National Board for Professional Teaching Standards
"NBCTs by State" (http://www.nbpts.org/resources/nbct_directory/nbcts_by_state)
*To be certified, teachers must demonstrate their knowledge and skills through a series of performance-based assessments that include student work samples, videotapes, and rigorous analyses of their classroom teaching and student learning. National total includes 117 teachers not shown by state.

Percent of Public Elementary and Secondary School Teachers with a Master's Degree or Higher in 2004
National Percent = 48.1%*

ALPHA ORDER

RANK	STATE	PERCENT
6	Alabama	60.6
32	Alaska	41.2
25	Arizona	49.2
36	Arkansas	38.4
29	California	43.1
14	Colorado	54.0
2	Connecticut	74.2
15	Delaware	53.5
38	Florida	36.7
18	Georgia	52.7
12	Hawaii	55.5
49	Idaho	27.0
15	Illinois	53.5
4	Indiana	61.9
40	Iowa	34.4
28	Kansas	44.5
3	Kentucky	70.6
42	Louisiana	34.0
41	Maine	34.3
9	Maryland	56.3
7	Massachusetts	60.2
12	Michigan	55.5
24	Minnesota	50.1
39	Mississippi	35.5
22	Missouri	50.8
43	Montana	33.6
34	Nebraska	39.5
11	Nevada	55.8
30	New Hampshire	42.5
31	New Jersey	42.2
33	New Mexico	41.0
1	New York	78.0
46	North Carolina	31.6
47	North Dakota	27.4
17	Ohio	52.8
44	Oklahoma	33.3
8	Oregon	58.0
23	Pennsylvania	50.3
20	Rhode Island	51.6
21	South Carolina	51.0
50	South Dakota	26.2
19	Tennessee	52.3
48	Texas	27.2
45	Utah	32.7
26	Vermont	45.4
34	Virginia	39.5
9	Washington	56.3
5	West Virginia	61.1
27	Wisconsin	45.1
37	Wyoming	37.2

RANK ORDER

RANK	STATE	PERCENT
1	New York	78.0
2	Connecticut	74.2
3	Kentucky	70.6
4	Indiana	61.9
5	West Virginia	61.1
6	Alabama	60.6
7	Massachusetts	60.2
8	Oregon	58.0
9	Maryland	56.3
9	Washington	56.3
11	Nevada	55.8
12	Hawaii	55.5
12	Michigan	55.5
14	Colorado	54.0
15	Delaware	53.5
15	Illinois	53.5
17	Ohio	52.8
18	Georgia	52.7
19	Tennessee	52.3
20	Rhode Island	51.6
21	South Carolina	51.0
22	Missouri	50.8
23	Pennsylvania	50.3
24	Minnesota	50.1
25	Arizona	49.2
26	Vermont	45.4
27	Wisconsin	45.1
28	Kansas	44.5
29	California	43.1
30	New Hampshire	42.5
31	New Jersey	42.2
32	Alaska	41.2
33	New Mexico	41.0
34	Nebraska	39.5
34	Virginia	39.5
36	Arkansas	38.4
37	Wyoming	37.2
38	Florida	36.7
39	Mississippi	35.5
40	Iowa	34.4
41	Maine	34.3
42	Louisiana	34.0
43	Montana	33.6
44	Oklahoma	33.3
45	Utah	32.7
46	North Carolina	31.6
47	North Dakota	27.4
48	Texas	27.2
49	Idaho	27.0
50	South Dakota	26.2

| | District of Columbia | 51.3 |

Source: CQ Press using data from U.S. Department of Education, National Center for Education Statistics "Schools and Staffing Survey (SASS)" (http://nces.ed.gov/surveys/sass/index.asp)
*For school year 2003-2004. Includes both full-time and part-time teachers.

Average Weekly Hours of Full-Time Elementary and Secondary Public School Teachers in 2004
National Average = 52.8 Hours*

ALPHA ORDER

RANK	STATE	HOURS
29	Alabama	52.4
1	Alaska	55.5
7	Arizona	54.4
41	Arkansas	51.5
25	California	53.1
6	Colorado	54.6
29	Connecticut	52.4
12	Delaware	53.8
20	Florida	53.4
12	Georgia	53.8
9	Hawaii	54.2
12	Idaho	53.8
34	Illinois	52.2
17	Indiana	53.6
27	Iowa	53.0
9	Kansas	54.2
37	Kentucky	51.9
41	Louisiana	51.5
37	Maine	51.9
3	Maryland	55.0
48	Massachusetts	50.2
39	Michigan	51.7
16	Minnesota	53.7
44	Mississippi	51.3
23	Missouri	53.2
23	Montana	53.2
5	Nebraska	54.7
25	Nevada	53.1
34	New Hampshire	52.2
49	New Jersey	50.1
46	New Mexico	51.1
43	New York	51.4
21	North Carolina	53.3
29	North Dakota	52.4
40	Ohio	51.6
34	Oklahoma	52.2
4	Oregon	54.9
32	Pennsylvania	52.3
50	Rhode Island	47.6
11	South Carolina	54.1
2	South Dakota	55.1
47	Tennessee	50.9
7	Texas	54.4
32	Utah	52.3
28	Vermont	52.6
12	Virginia	53.8
18	Washington	53.5
45	West Virginia	51.2
18	Wisconsin	53.5
21	Wyoming	53.3

RANK ORDER

RANK	STATE	HOURS
1	Alaska	55.5
2	South Dakota	55.1
3	Maryland	55.0
4	Oregon	54.9
5	Nebraska	54.7
6	Colorado	54.6
7	Arizona	54.4
7	Texas	54.4
9	Hawaii	54.2
9	Kansas	54.2
11	South Carolina	54.1
12	Delaware	53.8
12	Georgia	53.8
12	Idaho	53.8
12	Virginia	53.8
16	Minnesota	53.7
17	Indiana	53.6
18	Washington	53.5
18	Wisconsin	53.5
20	Florida	53.4
21	North Carolina	53.3
21	Wyoming	53.3
23	Missouri	53.2
23	Montana	53.2
25	California	53.1
25	Nevada	53.1
27	Iowa	53.0
28	Vermont	52.6
29	Alabama	52.4
29	Connecticut	52.4
29	North Dakota	52.4
32	Pennsylvania	52.3
32	Utah	52.3
34	Illinois	52.2
34	New Hampshire	52.2
34	Oklahoma	52.2
37	Kentucky	51.9
37	Maine	51.9
39	Michigan	51.7
40	Ohio	51.6
41	Arkansas	51.5
41	Louisiana	51.5
43	New York	51.4
44	Mississippi	51.3
45	West Virginia	51.2
46	New Mexico	51.1
47	Tennessee	50.9
48	Massachusetts	50.2
49	New Jersey	50.1
50	Rhode Island	47.6
	District of Columbia	50.8

Source: U.S. Department of Education, National Center for Education Statistics
   "Schools and Staffing Survey (SASS)" (http://nces.ed.gov/surveys/sass/index.asp)
*For school year 2003-2004. Includes hours spent on all teaching and other school-related activities during a typical full week.

Average Weekly Hours of Full-Time Elementary and Secondary Public School Principals in 2004
National Average = 59.0 Hours*

ALPHA ORDER

RANK	STATE	HOURS
11	Alabama	60.5
8	Alaska	60.8
32	Arizona	58.3
16	Arkansas	59.7
25	California	58.9
29	Colorado	58.5
7	Connecticut	61.0
1	Delaware	64.4
32	Florida	58.3
8	Georgia	60.8
2	Hawaii	63.9
43	Idaho	56.7
37	Illinois	58.0
21	Indiana	59.1
6	Iowa	61.4
36	Kansas	58.1
12	Kentucky	60.4
41	Louisiana	57.3
46	Maine	55.7
8	Maryland	60.8
13	Massachusetts	60.2
42	Michigan	56.8
34	Minnesota	58.2
17	Mississippi	59.6
28	Missouri	58.7
47	Montana	54.7
49	Nebraska	52.1
5	Nevada	62.7
19	New Hampshire	59.3
25	New Jersey	58.9
38	New Mexico	57.5
3	New York	63.5
14	North Carolina	60.1
44	North Dakota	56.4
25	Ohio	58.9
38	Oklahoma	57.5
30	Oregon	58.4
24	Pennsylvania	59.0
21	Rhode Island	59.1
4	South Carolina	63.2
45	South Dakota	55.8
34	Tennessee	58.2
21	Texas	59.1
48	Utah	53.6
18	Vermont	59.4
15	Virginia	60.0
20	Washington	59.2
30	West Virginia	58.4
40	Wisconsin	57.4
50	Wyoming	51.8

RANK ORDER

RANK	STATE	HOURS
1	Delaware	64.4
2	Hawaii	63.9
3	New York	63.5
4	South Carolina	63.2
5	Nevada	62.7
6	Iowa	61.4
7	Connecticut	61.0
8	Alaska	60.8
8	Georgia	60.8
8	Maryland	60.8
11	Alabama	60.5
12	Kentucky	60.4
13	Massachusetts	60.2
14	North Carolina	60.1
15	Virginia	60.0
16	Arkansas	59.7
17	Mississippi	59.6
18	Vermont	59.4
19	New Hampshire	59.3
20	Washington	59.2
21	Indiana	59.1
21	Rhode Island	59.1
21	Texas	59.1
24	Pennsylvania	59.0
25	California	58.9
25	New Jersey	58.9
25	Ohio	58.9
28	Missouri	58.7
29	Colorado	58.5
30	Oregon	58.4
30	West Virginia	58.4
32	Arizona	58.3
32	Florida	58.3
34	Minnesota	58.2
34	Tennessee	58.2
36	Kansas	58.1
37	Illinois	58.0
38	New Mexico	57.5
38	Oklahoma	57.5
40	Wisconsin	57.4
41	Louisiana	57.3
42	Michigan	56.8
43	Idaho	56.7
44	North Dakota	56.4
45	South Dakota	55.8
46	Maine	55.7
47	Montana	54.7
48	Utah	53.6
49	Nebraska	52.1
50	Wyoming	51.8

	District of Columbia	64.5

Source: U.S. Department of Education, National Center for Education Statistics
"Schools and Staffing Survey (SASS)" (http://nces.ed.gov/surveys/sass/index.asp)
*For school year 2003-2004. Includes hours spent on all school-related activities during a typical full week.

Estimated Average Salary of Public School Teachers in 2007
(National Education Association)
National Average = $50,816*

ALPHA ORDER

RANK	STATE	SALARY
35	Alabama	$43,389
12	Alaska	54,658
25	Arizona	45,941
31	Arkansas	44,245
1	California	63,640
26	Colorado	45,833
2	Connecticut	60,822
11	Delaware	54,680
28	Florida	45,308
17	Georgia	49,905
14	Hawaii	51,922
39	Idaho	42,798
6	Illinois	58,246
22	Indiana	47,831
37	Iowa	43,130
36	Kansas	43,334
34	Kentucky	43,646
38	Louisiana	42,816
44	Maine	41,596
7	Maryland	56,927
4	Massachusetts	58,624
10	Michigan	54,895
18	Minnesota	49,634
48	Mississippi	40,182
43	Missouri	41,839
45	Montana	41,225
42	Nebraska	42,044
27	Nevada	45,342
23	New Hampshire	46,527
3	New Jersey	59,920
40	New Mexico	42,780
5	New York	58,537
24	North Carolina	46,410
49	North Dakota	38,822
13	Ohio	51,937
41	Oklahoma	42,379
15	Oregon	50,911
9	Pennsylvania	54,970
8	Rhode Island	55,956
32	South Carolina	44,133
50	South Dakota	35,378
33	Tennessee	43,816
29	Texas	44,897
46	Utah	40,566
19	Vermont	48,370
30	Virginia	44,727
21	Washington	47,882
47	West Virginia	40,531
20	Wisconsin	47,901
16	Wyoming	50,692

RANK ORDER

RANK	STATE	SALARY
1	California	$63,640
2	Connecticut	60,822
3	New Jersey	59,920
4	Massachusetts	58,624
5	New York	58,537
6	Illinois	58,246
7	Maryland	56,927
8	Rhode Island	55,956
9	Pennsylvania	54,970
10	Michigan	54,895
11	Delaware	54,680
12	Alaska	54,658
13	Ohio	51,937
14	Hawaii	51,922
15	Oregon	50,911
16	Wyoming	50,692
17	Georgia	49,905
18	Minnesota	49,634
19	Vermont	48,370
20	Wisconsin	47,901
21	Washington	47,882
22	Indiana	47,831
23	New Hampshire	46,527
24	North Carolina	46,410
25	Arizona	45,941
26	Colorado	45,833
27	Nevada	45,342
28	Florida	45,308
29	Texas	44,897
30	Virginia	44,727
31	Arkansas	44,245
32	South Carolina	44,133
33	Tennessee	43,816
34	Kentucky	43,646
35	Alabama	43,389
36	Kansas	43,334
37	Iowa	43,130
38	Louisiana	42,816
39	Idaho	42,798
40	New Mexico	42,780
41	Oklahoma	42,379
42	Nebraska	42,044
43	Missouri	41,839
44	Maine	41,596
45	Montana	41,225
46	Utah	40,566
47	West Virginia	40,531
48	Mississippi	40,182
49	North Dakota	38,822
50	South Dakota	35,378

| | District of Columbia | 59,000 |

Source: National Education Association, Washington, D.C.
"Rankings & Estimates" (Copyright © 2007, NEA, used with permission, http://www.nea.org/edstats/index.html)
*Estimates for school year 2006-2007 for classroom teachers.

Average Teacher Salary as a Percent of Average Annual Pay of All Workers in 2006
National Percent = 117.4% of Average Annual Pay*

ALPHA ORDER

RANK	STATE	PERCENT
34	Alabama	115.6
11	Alaska	129.6
39	Arizona	113.2
2	Arkansas	134.3
17	California	127.7
48	Colorado	103.7
45	Connecticut	109.6
31	Delaware	117.7
35	Florida	115.1
25	Georgia	121.6
3	Hawaii	133.9
13	Idaho	128.8
14	Illinois	128.1
9	Indiana	130.1
19	Iowa	122.7
30	Kansas	118.8
20	Kentucky	122.5
39	Louisiana	113.2
24	Maine	121.8
27	Maryland	120.5
44	Massachusetts	109.7
10	Michigan	130.0
32	Minnesota	116.3
12	Mississippi	129.4
42	Missouri	110.8
7	Montana	132.5
23	Nebraska	121.9
41	Nevada	112.0
46	New Hampshire	108.1
38	New Jersey	114.3
22	New Mexico	122.1
47	New York	104.4
26	North Carolina	120.6
21	North Dakota	122.3
5	Ohio	132.6
29	Oklahoma	119.3
5	Oregon	132.6
8	Pennsylvania	131.8
1	Rhode Island	136.8
18	South Carolina	127.1
33	South Dakota	115.7
36	Tennessee	114.9
49	Texas	102.0
37	Utah	114.7
4	Vermont	133.6
50	Virginia	100.5
43	Washington	109.8
28	West Virginia	120.4
16	Wisconsin	128.0
14	Wyoming	128.1

RANK ORDER

RANK	STATE	PERCENT
1	Rhode Island	136.8
2	Arkansas	134.3
3	Hawaii	133.9
4	Vermont	133.6
5	Ohio	132.6
5	Oregon	132.6
7	Montana	132.5
8	Pennsylvania	131.8
9	Indiana	130.1
10	Michigan	130.0
11	Alaska	129.6
12	Mississippi	129.4
13	Idaho	128.8
14	Illinois	128.1
14	Wyoming	128.1
16	Wisconsin	128.0
17	California	127.7
18	South Carolina	127.1
19	Iowa	122.7
20	Kentucky	122.5
21	North Dakota	122.3
22	New Mexico	122.1
23	Nebraska	121.9
24	Maine	121.8
25	Georgia	121.6
26	North Carolina	120.6
27	Maryland	120.5
28	West Virginia	120.4
29	Oklahoma	119.3
30	Kansas	118.8
31	Delaware	117.7
32	Minnesota	116.3
33	South Dakota	115.7
34	Alabama	115.6
35	Florida	115.1
36	Tennessee	114.9
37	Utah	114.7
38	New Jersey	114.3
39	Arizona	113.2
39	Louisiana	113.2
41	Nevada	112.0
42	Missouri	110.8
43	Washington	109.8
44	Massachusetts	109.7
45	Connecticut	109.6
46	New Hampshire	108.1
47	New York	104.4
48	Colorado	103.7
49	Texas	102.0
50	Virginia	100.5

| | District of Columbia | 84.1 |

Source: CQ Press using data from National Education Association, Washington, D.C.
"Rankings & Estimates" (Copyright © 2007, NEA, used with permission, http://www.nea.org/edstats/index.html) and
"Quarterly Census of Employment and Wages" (http://www.bls.gov/cew/home.htm)
*Average of public elementary and secondary teacher salary for school years 2005-2006 and estimated 2006-2007 compared to each state's 2006 average annual pay for all workers covered by federal unemployment.

Average Annual Salary of Preschool Teachers in 2007

National Average = $25,800*

ALPHA ORDER

RANK	STATE	SALARY
44	Alabama	$21,630
12	Alaska	28,440
38	Arizona	22,550
31	Arkansas	23,600
9	California	28,660
20	Colorado	25,310
8	Connecticut	29,080
25	Delaware	24,650
19	Florida	25,350
40	Georgia	21,960
13	Hawaii	27,760
48	Idaho	20,040
11	Illinois	28,500
28	Indiana	24,070
43	Iowa	21,690
29	Kansas	23,960
23	Kentucky	24,940
50	Louisiana	18,760
15	Maine	26,950
7	Maryland	29,290
6	Massachusetts	29,510
2	Michigan	32,950
3	Minnesota	30,350
44	Mississippi	21,630
24	Missouri	24,710
47	Montana	20,570
39	Nebraska	22,540
35	Nevada	23,110
18	New Hampshire	26,160
1	New Jersey	33,330
21	New Mexico	25,250
4	New York	30,020
46	North Carolina	21,170
36	North Dakota	23,000
42	Ohio	21,730
41	Oklahoma	21,850
27	Oregon	24,340
30	Pennsylvania	23,660
5	Rhode Island	29,950
22	South Carolina	25,030
17	South Dakota	26,520
49	Tennessee	20,000
37	Texas	22,940
32	Utah	23,340
10	Vermont	28,640
16	Virginia	26,920
14	Washington	27,200
33	West Virginia	23,200
33	Wisconsin	23,200
26	Wyoming	24,550

RANK ORDER

RANK	STATE	SALARY
1	New Jersey	$33,330
2	Michigan	32,950
3	Minnesota	30,350
4	New York	30,020
5	Rhode Island	29,950
6	Massachusetts	29,510
7	Maryland	29,290
8	Connecticut	29,080
9	California	28,660
10	Vermont	28,640
11	Illinois	28,500
12	Alaska	28,440
13	Hawaii	27,760
14	Washington	27,200
15	Maine	26,950
16	Virginia	26,920
17	South Dakota	26,520
18	New Hampshire	26,160
19	Florida	25,350
20	Colorado	25,310
21	New Mexico	25,250
22	South Carolina	25,030
23	Kentucky	24,940
24	Missouri	24,710
25	Delaware	24,650
26	Wyoming	24,550
27	Oregon	24,340
28	Indiana	24,070
29	Kansas	23,960
30	Pennsylvania	23,660
31	Arkansas	23,600
32	Utah	23,340
33	West Virginia	23,200
33	Wisconsin	23,200
35	Nevada	23,110
36	North Dakota	23,000
37	Texas	22,940
38	Arizona	22,550
39	Nebraska	22,540
40	Georgia	21,960
41	Oklahoma	21,850
42	Ohio	21,730
43	Iowa	21,690
44	Alabama	21,630
44	Mississippi	21,630
46	North Carolina	21,170
47	Montana	20,570
48	Idaho	20,040
49	Tennessee	20,000
50	Louisiana	18,760
	District of Columbia	31,830

Source: U.S. Department of Labor, Bureau of Labor Statistics
"National Occupational Employment and Wage Estimates" (http://www.bls.gov/oes/)
*As of May 2007. Does not include special education pre-school teachers.

Average Annual Salary of Kindergarten Teachers in 2007

National Average = $47,750*

ALPHA ORDER			RANK ORDER		
RANK	STATE	SALARY	RANK	STATE	SALARY
33	Alabama	$40,540	1	Rhode Island	$62,600
6	Alaska	54,620	2	New York	62,320
44	Arizona	37,660	3	Connecticut	58,010
34	Arkansas	40,360	4	New Jersey	56,850
7	California	53,770	5	Virginia	54,790
23	Colorado	44,000	6	Alaska	54,620
3	Connecticut	58,010	7	California	53,770
16	Delaware	47,150	8	Michigan	53,320
11	Florida	49,530	9	Maryland	50,790
22	Georgia	44,070	10	Massachusetts	50,140
42	Hawaii	38,040	11	Florida	49,530
50	Idaho	28,190	12	Ohio	49,430
30	Illinois	41,990	13	Pennsylvania	49,310
17	Indiana	45,400	14	Washington	47,630
43	Iowa	37,860	15	Minnesota	47,440
37	Kansas	39,580	16	Delaware	47,150
27	Kentucky	42,600	17	Indiana	45,400
36	Louisiana	39,850	18	New Mexico	44,790
24	Maine	43,440	19	Vermont	44,740
9	Maryland	50,790	20	Wyoming	44,660
10	Massachusetts	50,140	21	Wisconsin	44,540
8	Michigan	53,320	22	Georgia	44,070
15	Minnesota	47,440	23	Colorado	44,000
45	Mississippi	36,590	24	Maine	43,440
31	Missouri	41,050	25	Texas	43,180
48	Montana	35,580	26	South Carolina	42,750
28	Nebraska	42,350	27	Kentucky	42,600
38	Nevada	38,650	28	Nebraska	42,350
39	New Hampshire	38,190	29	West Virginia	42,010
4	New Jersey	56,850	30	Illinois	41,990
18	New Mexico	44,790	31	Missouri	41,050
2	New York	62,320	32	Oregon	40,570
40	North Carolina	38,080	33	Alabama	40,540
41	North Dakota	38,070	34	Arkansas	40,360
12	Ohio	49,430	35	Tennessee	40,150
46	Oklahoma	36,020	36	Louisiana	39,850
32	Oregon	40,570	37	Kansas	39,580
13	Pennsylvania	49,310	38	Nevada	38,650
1	Rhode Island	62,600	39	New Hampshire	38,190
26	South Carolina	42,750	40	North Carolina	38,080
49	South Dakota	34,610	41	North Dakota	38,070
35	Tennessee	40,150	42	Hawaii	38,040
25	Texas	43,180	43	Iowa	37,860
47	Utah	35,830	44	Arizona	37,660
19	Vermont	44,740	45	Mississippi	36,590
5	Virginia	54,790	46	Oklahoma	36,020
14	Washington	47,630	47	Utah	35,830
29	West Virginia	42,010	48	Montana	35,580
21	Wisconsin	44,540	49	South Dakota	34,610
20	Wyoming	44,660	50	Idaho	28,190
				District of Columbia	36,400

Source: U.S. Department of Labor, Bureau of Labor Statistics
"National Occupational Employment and Wage Estimates" (http://www.bls.gov/oes/)
*As of May 2007.

Average Annual Salary of Elementary School Teachers in 2007

National Average = $50,040*

ALPHA ORDER

RANK	STATE	SALARY
37	Alabama	$41,610
5	Alaska	58,470
46	Arizona	37,230
41	Arkansas	39,880
4	California	58,850
26	Colorado	46,130
3	Connecticut	61,530
16	Delaware	49,450
15	Florida	49,920
22	Georgia	48,000
27	Hawaii	45,420
23	Idaho	46,930
10	Illinois	54,760
24	Indiana	46,520
46	Iowa	37,230
45	Kansas	38,220
32	Kentucky	43,850
39	Louisiana	40,960
31	Maine	44,090
9	Maryland	54,930
7	Massachusetts	56,620
8	Michigan	56,170
19	Minnesota	48,650
43	Mississippi	39,490
36	Missouri	42,020
49	Montana	36,550
35	Nebraska	42,230
44	Nevada	39,390
21	New Hampshire	48,010
6	New Jersey	57,980
28	New Mexico	45,130
2	New York	62,490
42	North Carolina	39,670
38	North Dakota	41,110
12	Ohio	51,880
48	Oklahoma	36,870
20	Oregon	48,460
14	Pennsylvania	50,410
1	Rhode Island	64,130
33	South Carolina	42,950
50	South Dakota	35,370
34	Tennessee	42,780
29	Texas	44,220
30	Utah	44,200
25	Vermont	46,470
11	Virginia	54,190
13	Washington	51,370
40	West Virginia	40,860
17	Wisconsin	49,000
18	Wyoming	48,960

RANK ORDER

RANK	STATE	SALARY
1	Rhode Island	$64,130
2	New York	62,490
3	Connecticut	61,530
4	California	58,850
5	Alaska	58,470
6	New Jersey	57,980
7	Massachusetts	56,620
8	Michigan	56,170
9	Maryland	54,930
10	Illinois	54,760
11	Virginia	54,190
12	Ohio	51,880
13	Washington	51,370
14	Pennsylvania	50,410
15	Florida	49,920
16	Delaware	49,450
17	Wisconsin	49,000
18	Wyoming	48,960
19	Minnesota	48,650
20	Oregon	48,460
21	New Hampshire	48,010
22	Georgia	48,000
23	Idaho	46,930
24	Indiana	46,520
25	Vermont	46,470
26	Colorado	46,130
27	Hawaii	45,420
28	New Mexico	45,130
29	Texas	44,220
30	Utah	44,200
31	Maine	44,090
32	Kentucky	43,850
33	South Carolina	42,950
34	Tennessee	42,780
35	Nebraska	42,230
36	Missouri	42,020
37	Alabama	41,610
38	North Dakota	41,110
39	Louisiana	40,960
40	West Virginia	40,860
41	Arkansas	39,880
42	North Carolina	39,670
43	Mississippi	39,490
44	Nevada	39,390
45	Kansas	38,220
46	Arizona	37,230
46	Iowa	37,230
48	Oklahoma	36,870
49	Montana	36,550
50	South Dakota	35,370
	District of Columbia	55,200

Source: U.S. Department of Labor, Bureau of Labor Statistics
"National Occupational Employment and Wage Estimates" (http://www.bls.gov/oes/)
*As of May 2007.

Average Annual Salary of Middle School Teachers in 2007

National Average = $50,630*

ALPHA ORDER			RANK ORDER		
RANK	**STATE**	**SALARY**	**RANK**	**STATE**	**SALARY**
35	Alabama	$43,290	1	New York	$64,140
6	Alaska	56,570	2	Connecticut	63,320
42	Arizona	39,750	3	California	60,820
38	Arkansas	41,400	4	Rhode Island	59,640
3	California	60,820	5	New Jersey	59,120
27	Colorado	46,460	6	Alaska	56,570
2	Connecticut	63,320	7	Michigan	56,330
14	Delaware	52,360	8	Massachusetts	55,330
16	Florida	50,630	9	Maryland	54,110
21	Georgia	48,620	10	Virginia	53,560
20	Hawaii	48,860	11	Ohio	53,290
44	Idaho	39,220	12	Pennsylvania	52,660
13	Illinois	52,630	13	Illinois	52,630
17	Indiana	49,440	14	Delaware	52,360
43	Iowa	39,580	15	Washington	52,230
46	Kansas	38,170	16	Florida	50,630
30	Kentucky	44,590	17	Indiana	49,440
39	Louisiana	40,580	18	Oregon	49,290
31	Maine	44,190	19	Wyoming	49,210
9	Maryland	54,110	20	Hawaii	48,860
8	Massachusetts	55,330	21	Georgia	48,620
7	Michigan	56,330	22	Wisconsin	48,430
28	Minnesota	46,320	23	Vermont	48,110
40	Mississippi	40,270	24	New Hampshire	48,010
33	Missouri	43,690	25	New Mexico	47,120
49	Montana	36,130	26	Utah	46,470
34	Nebraska	43,430	27	Colorado	46,460
32	Nevada	43,860	28	Minnesota	46,320
24	New Hampshire	48,010	29	Texas	45,180
5	New Jersey	59,120	30	Kentucky	44,590
25	New Mexico	47,120	31	Maine	44,190
1	New York	64,140	32	Nevada	43,860
45	North Carolina	39,060	33	Missouri	43,690
NA	North Dakota**	NA	34	Nebraska	43,430
11	Ohio	53,290	35	Alabama	43,290
48	Oklahoma	36,840	36	South Carolina	42,850
18	Oregon	49,290	37	Tennessee	42,810
12	Pennsylvania	52,660	38	Arkansas	41,400
4	Rhode Island	59,640	39	Louisiana	40,580
36	South Carolina	42,850	40	Mississippi	40,270
47	South Dakota	37,810	41	West Virginia	39,920
37	Tennessee	42,810	42	Arizona	39,750
29	Texas	45,180	43	Iowa	39,580
26	Utah	46,470	44	Idaho	39,220
23	Vermont	48,110	45	North Carolina	39,060
10	Virginia	53,560	46	Kansas	38,170
15	Washington	52,230	47	South Dakota	37,810
41	West Virginia	39,920	48	Oklahoma	36,840
22	Wisconsin	48,430	49	Montana	36,130
19	Wyoming	49,210	NA	North Dakota**	NA
				District of Columbia	52,920

Source: U.S. Department of Labor, Bureau of Labor Statistics
   "National Occupational Employment and Wage Estimates" (http://www.bls.gov/oes/)
*As of May 2007.
**Not available.

Average Annual Salary of Secondary School Teachers in 2007

National Average = $52,450*

ALPHA ORDER

RANK	STATE	SALARY
36	Alabama	$43,610
10	Alaska	56,160
45	Arizona	40,110
37	Arkansas	43,530
4	California	61,970
29	Colorado	47,040
3	Connecticut	63,290
12	Delaware	54,270
15	Florida	52,520
23	Georgia	48,630
16	Hawaii	52,330
24	Idaho	48,150
2	Illinois	63,640
25	Indiana	47,880
47	Iowa	38,200
46	Kansas	38,600
30	Kentucky	46,210
39	Louisiana	41,960
38	Maine	43,130
7	Maryland	56,850
8	Massachusetts	56,790
11	Michigan	54,560
21	Minnesota	48,700
42	Mississippi	40,760
35	Missouri	43,670
49	Montana	37,890
40	Nebraska	41,930
32	Nevada	44,750
19	New Hampshire	48,940
5	New Jersey	61,640
28	New Mexico	47,360
1	New York	64,020
41	North Carolina	41,520
44	North Dakota	40,130
14	Ohio	53,420
48	Oklahoma	37,960
20	Oregon	48,730
17	Pennsylvania	51,840
6	Rhode Island	60,640
33	South Carolina	44,670
50	South Dakota	36,300
34	Tennessee	43,960
31	Texas	46,110
22	Utah	48,690
18	Vermont	48,970
9	Virginia	56,740
13	Washington	54,050
43	West Virginia	40,270
26	Wisconsin	47,670
27	Wyoming	47,460

RANK ORDER

RANK	STATE	SALARY
1	New York	$64,020
2	Illinois	63,640
3	Connecticut	63,290
4	California	61,970
5	New Jersey	61,640
6	Rhode Island	60,640
7	Maryland	56,850
8	Massachusetts	56,790
9	Virginia	56,740
10	Alaska	56,160
11	Michigan	54,560
12	Delaware	54,270
13	Washington	54,050
14	Ohio	53,420
15	Florida	52,520
16	Hawaii	52,330
17	Pennsylvania	51,840
18	Vermont	48,970
19	New Hampshire	48,940
20	Oregon	48,730
21	Minnesota	48,700
22	Utah	48,690
23	Georgia	48,630
24	Idaho	48,150
25	Indiana	47,880
26	Wisconsin	47,670
27	Wyoming	47,460
28	New Mexico	47,360
29	Colorado	47,040
30	Kentucky	46,210
31	Texas	46,110
32	Nevada	44,750
33	South Carolina	44,670
34	Tennessee	43,960
35	Missouri	43,670
36	Alabama	43,610
37	Arkansas	43,530
38	Maine	43,130
39	Louisiana	41,960
40	Nebraska	41,930
41	North Carolina	41,520
42	Mississippi	40,760
43	West Virginia	40,270
44	North Dakota	40,130
45	Arizona	40,110
46	Kansas	38,600
47	Iowa	38,200
48	Oklahoma	37,960
49	Montana	37,890
50	South Dakota	36,300

District of Columbia	48,350

Source: U.S. Department of Labor, Bureau of Labor Statistics
   "National Occupational Employment and Wage Estimates" (http://www.bls.gov/oes/)
*As of May 2007.

Average Annual Salary of Elementary and Secondary School Administrators in 2007
National Average = $82,120*

ALPHA ORDER

RANK	STATE	SALARY
38	Alabama	$68,970
11	Alaska	87,870
32	Arizona	72,150
41	Arkansas	68,000
5	California	96,750
22	Colorado	76,950
1	Connecticut	104,770
3	Delaware	98,220
16	Florida	82,480
20	Georgia	78,730
23	Hawaii	74,640
24	Idaho	74,250
6	Illinois	95,990
30	Indiana	73,120
28	Iowa	73,480
42	Kansas	67,970
31	Kentucky	72,670
47	Louisiana	61,030
45	Maine	64,910
7	Maryland	88,650
13	Massachusetts	87,680
12	Michigan	87,790
14	Minnesota	85,730
43	Mississippi	67,740
27	Missouri	73,500
46	Montana	64,150
26	Nebraska	74,030
21	Nevada	77,000
33	New Hampshire	71,950
2	New Jersey	99,740
36	New Mexico	70,590
4	New York	97,290
44	North Carolina	66,060
37	North Dakota	70,050
8	Ohio	88,550
48	Oklahoma	60,710
18	Oregon	80,820
15	Pennsylvania	83,880
9	Rhode Island	88,470
34	South Carolina	70,940
49	South Dakota	60,210
39	Tennessee	68,120
40	Texas	68,110
25	Utah	74,110
35	Vermont	70,720
19	Virginia	79,570
10	Washington	87,890
50	West Virginia	57,750
17	Wisconsin	81,430
29	Wyoming	73,190

RANK ORDER

RANK	STATE	SALARY
1	Connecticut	$104,770
2	New Jersey	99,740
3	Delaware	98,220
4	New York	97,290
5	California	96,750
6	Illinois	95,990
7	Maryland	88,650
8	Ohio	88,550
9	Rhode Island	88,470
10	Washington	87,890
11	Alaska	87,870
12	Michigan	87,790
13	Massachusetts	87,680
14	Minnesota	85,730
15	Pennsylvania	83,880
16	Florida	82,480
17	Wisconsin	81,430
18	Oregon	80,820
19	Virginia	79,570
20	Georgia	78,730
21	Nevada	77,000
22	Colorado	76,950
23	Hawaii	74,640
24	Idaho	74,250
25	Utah	74,110
26	Nebraska	74,030
27	Missouri	73,500
28	Iowa	73,480
29	Wyoming	73,190
30	Indiana	73,120
31	Kentucky	72,670
32	Arizona	72,150
33	New Hampshire	71,950
34	South Carolina	70,940
35	Vermont	70,720
36	New Mexico	70,590
37	North Dakota	70,050
38	Alabama	68,970
39	Tennessee	68,120
40	Texas	68,110
41	Arkansas	68,000
42	Kansas	67,970
43	Mississippi	67,740
44	North Carolina	66,060
45	Maine	64,910
46	Montana	64,150
47	Louisiana	61,030
48	Oklahoma	60,710
49	South Dakota	60,210
50	West Virginia	57,750
	District of Columbia	88,830

Source: U.S. Department of Labor, Bureau of Labor Statistics
"National Occupational Employment and Wage Estimates" (http://www.bls.gov/oes/)
*As of May 2007.

Staff Employed by Public Elementary and Secondary School Systems in 2006

National Total = 6,122,358 Staff*

ALPHA ORDER

RANK	STATE	STAFF	% of USA
21	Alabama	103,775	1.7%
47	Alaska	17,930	0.3%
22	Arizona	100,162	1.6%
28	Arkansas	70,673	1.2%
2	California	579,024	9.5%
24	Colorado	93,148	1.5%
26	Connecticut	84,669	1.4%
48	Delaware	15,473	0.3%
4	Florida	314,219	5.1%
8	Georgia	218,965	3.6%
43	Hawaii	21,059	0.3%
41	Idaho	26,018	0.4%
5	Illinois	264,700	4.3%
14	Indiana	133,096	2.2%
29	Iowa	69,080	1.1%
32	Kansas	65,537	1.1%
23	Kentucky	97,937	1.6%
25	Louisiana	92,612	1.5%
38	Maine	35,249	0.6%
18	Maryland	111,215	1.8%
13	Massachusetts	139,522	2.3%
10	Michigan	206,533	3.4%
20	Minnesota	104,489	1.7%
30	Mississippi	67,659	1.1%
15	Missouri	128,794	2.1%
44	Montana	19,515	0.3%
36	Nebraska	41,166	0.7%
39	Nevada	32,346	0.5%
40	New Hampshire	32,022	0.5%
9	New Jersey	216,778	3.5%
34	New Mexico	47,940	0.8%
3	New York	373,504	6.1%
12	North Carolina	182,107	3.0%
49	North Dakota	15,128	0.2%
7	Ohio	238,977	3.9%
27	Oklahoma	81,857	1.3%
33	Oregon	60,088	1.0%
6	Pennsylvania	240,409	3.9%
42	Rhode Island	24,560	0.4%
31	South Carolina	67,453	1.1%
46	South Dakota	19,018	0.3%
16	Tennessee	114,171	1.9%
1	Texas	620,624	10.1%
35	Utah	45,821	0.7%
45	Vermont	19,024	0.3%
11	Virginia	183,853	3.0%
17	Washington	113,845	1.9%
37	West Virginia	38,152	0.6%
19	Wisconsin	105,564	1.7%
50	Wyoming	14,526	0.2%

RANK ORDER

RANK	STATE	STAFF	% of USA
1	Texas	620,624	10.1%
2	California	579,024	9.5%
3	New York	373,504	6.1%
4	Florida	314,219	5.1%
5	Illinois	264,700	4.3%
6	Pennsylvania	240,409	3.9%
7	Ohio	238,977	3.9%
8	Georgia	218,965	3.6%
9	New Jersey	216,778	3.5%
10	Michigan	206,533	3.4%
11	Virginia	183,853	3.0%
12	North Carolina	182,107	3.0%
13	Massachusetts	139,522	2.3%
14	Indiana	133,096	2.2%
15	Missouri	128,794	2.1%
16	Tennessee	114,171	1.9%
17	Washington	113,845	1.9%
18	Maryland	111,215	1.8%
19	Wisconsin	105,564	1.7%
20	Minnesota	104,489	1.7%
21	Alabama	103,775	1.7%
22	Arizona	100,162	1.6%
23	Kentucky	97,937	1.6%
24	Colorado	93,148	1.5%
25	Louisiana	92,612	1.5%
26	Connecticut	84,669	1.4%
27	Oklahoma	81,857	1.3%
28	Arkansas	70,673	1.2%
29	Iowa	69,080	1.1%
30	Mississippi	67,659	1.1%
31	South Carolina	67,453	1.1%
32	Kansas	65,537	1.1%
33	Oregon	60,088	1.0%
34	New Mexico	47,940	0.8%
35	Utah	45,821	0.7%
36	Nebraska	41,166	0.7%
37	West Virginia	38,152	0.6%
38	Maine	35,249	0.6%
39	Nevada	32,346	0.5%
40	New Hampshire	32,022	0.5%
41	Idaho	26,018	0.4%
42	Rhode Island	24,560	0.4%
43	Hawaii	21,059	0.3%
44	Montana	19,515	0.3%
45	Vermont	19,024	0.3%
46	South Dakota	19,018	0.3%
47	Alaska	17,930	0.3%
48	Delaware	15,473	0.3%
49	North Dakota	15,128	0.2%
50	Wyoming	14,526	0.2%
	District of Columbia	12,372	0.2%

Source: U.S. Department of Education, National Center for Education Statistics
"Public Elementary and Secondary School Student Enrollment, High School Completions and Staff"
(http://nces.ed.gov/pubsearch/pubsinfo.asp?pubid=2007352)
*School year 2005-2006. Counts are full-time equivalent figures. Staff includes teachers, administrators, support staff, aides, counselors, and coordinators.

Percent of Public Elementary and Secondary School Staff
Who are School District Administrators: 2006
National Percent = 1.1%*

ALPHA ORDER

RANK ORDER

RANK	STATE	PERCENT		RANK	STATE	PERCENT
50	Alabama	0.2		1	Ohio	3.3
3	Alaska	2.4		2	North Dakota	3.2
44	Arizona	0.5		3	Alaska	2.4
26	Arkansas	0.9		3	South Dakota	2.4
44	California	0.5		5	Wyoming	2.2
20	Colorado	1.2		6	Delaware	2.1
11	Connecticut	1.6		7	Minnesota	2.0
6	Delaware	2.1		8	Kansas	1.9
42	Florida	0.6		8	Maine	1.9
24	Georgia	1.0		10	New Hampshire	1.7
24	Hawaii	1.0		11	Connecticut	1.6
44	Idaho	0.5		11	Michigan	1.6
14	Illinois	1.4		13	Mississippi	1.5
32	Indiana	0.8		14	Illinois	1.4
14	Iowa	1.4		14	Iowa	1.4
8	Kansas	1.9		14	Nebraska	1.4
26	Kentucky	0.9		14	New Mexico	1.4
48	Louisiana	0.3		18	Oregon	1.3
8	Maine	1.9		18	Texas	1.3
32	Maryland	0.8		20	Colorado	1.2
20	Massachusetts	1.2		20	Massachusetts	1.2
11	Michigan	1.6		20	West Virginia	1.2
7	Minnesota	2.0		23	Missouri	1.1
13	Mississippi	1.5		24	Georgia	1.0
23	Missouri	1.1		24	Hawaii	1.0
32	Montana	0.8		26	Arkansas	0.9
14	Nebraska	1.4		26	Kentucky	0.9
32	Nevada	0.8		26	North Carolina	0.9
10	New Hampshire	1.7		26	Utah	0.9
40	New Jersey	0.7		26	Virginia	0.9
14	New Mexico	1.4		26	Wisconsin	0.9
32	New York	0.8		32	Indiana	0.8
26	North Carolina	0.9		32	Maryland	0.8
2	North Dakota	3.2		32	Montana	0.8
1	Ohio	3.3		32	Nevada	0.8
32	Oklahoma	0.8		32	New York	0.8
18	Oregon	1.3		32	Oklahoma	0.8
32	Pennsylvania	0.8		32	Pennsylvania	0.8
42	Rhode Island	0.6		32	Washington	0.8
47	South Carolina	0.4		40	New Jersey	0.7
3	South Dakota	2.4		40	Vermont	0.7
48	Tennessee	0.3		42	Florida	0.6
18	Texas	1.3		42	Rhode Island	0.6
26	Utah	0.9		44	Arizona	0.5
40	Vermont	0.7		44	California	0.5
26	Virginia	0.9		44	Idaho	0.5
32	Washington	0.8		47	South Carolina	0.4
20	West Virginia	1.2		48	Louisiana	0.3
26	Wisconsin	0.9		48	Tennessee	0.3
5	Wyoming	2.2		50	Alabama	0.2

District of Columbia   1.1

Source: CQ Press using data from U.S. Department of Education, National Center for Education Statistics
"Public Elementary and Secondary School Student Enrollment, High School Completions and Staff"
(http://nces.ed.gov/pubsearch/pubsinfo.asp?pubid=2007352)
*School year 2005-2006. Percents are based on full-time equivalent figures. Includes superintendents, assistant superintendents, and other school district administrators.

Percent of Public Elementary and Secondary School Staff
Who are School Administrators: 2006
National Percent = 2.8%*

<table>
<tr><td colspan="3">ALPHA ORDER</td><td colspan="3">RANK ORDER</td></tr>
<tr><th>RANK</th><th>STATE</th><th>PERCENT</th><th>RANK</th><th>STATE</th><th>PERCENT</th></tr>
<tr><td>9</td><td>Alabama</td><td>2.9</td><td>1</td><td>Rhode Island</td><td>5.7</td></tr>
<tr><td>4</td><td>Alaska</td><td>4.3</td><td>2</td><td>Texas</td><td>5.1</td></tr>
<tr><td>36</td><td>Arizona</td><td>2.3</td><td>3</td><td>South Carolina</td><td>5.0</td></tr>
<tr><td>31</td><td>Arkansas</td><td>2.4</td><td>4</td><td>Alaska</td><td>4.3</td></tr>
<tr><td>31</td><td>California</td><td>2.4</td><td>5</td><td>Iowa</td><td>3.2</td></tr>
<tr><td>14</td><td>Colorado</td><td>2.7</td><td>6</td><td>Maryland</td><td>3.1</td></tr>
<tr><td>14</td><td>Connecticut</td><td>2.7</td><td>6</td><td>Tennessee</td><td>3.1</td></tr>
<tr><td>26</td><td>Delaware</td><td>2.5</td><td>8</td><td>Nevada</td><td>3.0</td></tr>
<tr><td>36</td><td>Florida</td><td>2.3</td><td>9</td><td>Alabama</td><td>2.9</td></tr>
<tr><td>9</td><td>Georgia</td><td>2.9</td><td>9</td><td>Georgia</td><td>2.9</td></tr>
<tr><td>36</td><td>Hawaii</td><td>2.3</td><td>9</td><td>Oregon</td><td>2.9</td></tr>
<tr><td>14</td><td>Idaho</td><td>2.7</td><td>12</td><td>Louisiana</td><td>2.8</td></tr>
<tr><td>26</td><td>Illinois</td><td>2.5</td><td>12</td><td>Massachusetts</td><td>2.8</td></tr>
<tr><td>36</td><td>Indiana</td><td>2.3</td><td>14</td><td>Colorado</td><td>2.7</td></tr>
<tr><td>5</td><td>Iowa</td><td>3.2</td><td>14</td><td>Connecticut</td><td>2.7</td></tr>
<tr><td>14</td><td>Kansas</td><td>2.7</td><td>14</td><td>Idaho</td><td>2.7</td></tr>
<tr><td>36</td><td>Kentucky</td><td>2.3</td><td>14</td><td>Kansas</td><td>2.7</td></tr>
<tr><td>12</td><td>Louisiana</td><td>2.8</td><td>14</td><td>Maine</td><td>2.7</td></tr>
<tr><td>14</td><td>Maine</td><td>2.7</td><td>14</td><td>Mississippi</td><td>2.7</td></tr>
<tr><td>6</td><td>Maryland</td><td>3.1</td><td>14</td><td>Montana</td><td>2.7</td></tr>
<tr><td>12</td><td>Massachusetts</td><td>2.8</td><td>14</td><td>North Carolina</td><td>2.7</td></tr>
<tr><td>26</td><td>Michigan</td><td>2.5</td><td>14</td><td>Oklahoma</td><td>2.7</td></tr>
<tr><td>48</td><td>Minnesota</td><td>1.9</td><td>14</td><td>West Virginia</td><td>2.7</td></tr>
<tr><td>14</td><td>Mississippi</td><td>2.7</td><td>24</td><td>New Mexico</td><td>2.6</td></tr>
<tr><td>31</td><td>Missouri</td><td>2.4</td><td>24</td><td>North Dakota</td><td>2.6</td></tr>
<tr><td>14</td><td>Montana</td><td>2.7</td><td>26</td><td>Delaware</td><td>2.5</td></tr>
<tr><td>26</td><td>Nebraska</td><td>2.5</td><td>26</td><td>Illinois</td><td>2.5</td></tr>
<tr><td>8</td><td>Nevada</td><td>3.0</td><td>26</td><td>Michigan</td><td>2.5</td></tr>
<tr><td>50</td><td>New Hampshire</td><td>1.7</td><td>26</td><td>Nebraska</td><td>2.5</td></tr>
<tr><td>48</td><td>New Jersey</td><td>1.9</td><td>26</td><td>Washington</td><td>2.5</td></tr>
<tr><td>24</td><td>New Mexico</td><td>2.6</td><td>31</td><td>Arkansas</td><td>2.4</td></tr>
<tr><td>31</td><td>New York</td><td>2.4</td><td>31</td><td>California</td><td>2.4</td></tr>
<tr><td>14</td><td>North Carolina</td><td>2.7</td><td>31</td><td>Missouri</td><td>2.4</td></tr>
<tr><td>24</td><td>North Dakota</td><td>2.6</td><td>31</td><td>New York</td><td>2.4</td></tr>
<tr><td>46</td><td>Ohio</td><td>2.0</td><td>31</td><td>Utah</td><td>2.4</td></tr>
<tr><td>14</td><td>Oklahoma</td><td>2.7</td><td>36</td><td>Arizona</td><td>2.3</td></tr>
<tr><td>9</td><td>Oregon</td><td>2.9</td><td>36</td><td>Florida</td><td>2.3</td></tr>
<tr><td>46</td><td>Pennsylvania</td><td>2.0</td><td>36</td><td>Hawaii</td><td>2.3</td></tr>
<tr><td>1</td><td>Rhode Island</td><td>5.7</td><td>36</td><td>Indiana</td><td>2.3</td></tr>
<tr><td>3</td><td>South Carolina</td><td>5.0</td><td>36</td><td>Kentucky</td><td>2.3</td></tr>
<tr><td>45</td><td>South Dakota</td><td>2.1</td><td>36</td><td>Vermont</td><td>2.3</td></tr>
<tr><td>6</td><td>Tennessee</td><td>3.1</td><td>36</td><td>Virginia</td><td>2.3</td></tr>
<tr><td>2</td><td>Texas</td><td>5.1</td><td>36</td><td>Wisconsin</td><td>2.3</td></tr>
<tr><td>31</td><td>Utah</td><td>2.4</td><td>36</td><td>Wyoming</td><td>2.3</td></tr>
<tr><td>36</td><td>Vermont</td><td>2.3</td><td>45</td><td>South Dakota</td><td>2.1</td></tr>
<tr><td>36</td><td>Virginia</td><td>2.3</td><td>46</td><td>Ohio</td><td>2.0</td></tr>
<tr><td>26</td><td>Washington</td><td>2.5</td><td>46</td><td>Pennsylvania</td><td>2.0</td></tr>
<tr><td>14</td><td>West Virginia</td><td>2.7</td><td>48</td><td>Minnesota</td><td>1.9</td></tr>
<tr><td>36</td><td>Wisconsin</td><td>2.3</td><td>48</td><td>New Jersey</td><td>1.9</td></tr>
<tr><td>36</td><td>Wyoming</td><td>2.3</td><td>50</td><td>New Hampshire</td><td>1.7</td></tr>
<tr><td></td><td></td><td></td><td></td><td>District of Columbia</td><td>3.3</td></tr>
</table>

Source: CQ Press using data from U.S. Department of Education, National Center for Education Statistics
    "Public Elementary and Secondary School Student Enrollment, High School Completions and Staff"
        (http://nces.ed.gov/pubsearch/pubsinfo.asp?pubid=2007352)

*School year 2005-2006. Percents are based on full-time equivalent figures. Composed mostly of principals and assistant principals. Does not include school district administrators.

Percent of Public Elementary and Secondary School Staff
Who are Administrative Support Staff: 2006
National Percent = 7.0%*

ALPHA ORDER

RANK	STATE	PERCENT
7	Alabama	8.0
1	Alaska	13.2
22	Arizona	6.4
44	Arkansas	4.6
4	California	9.5
12	Colorado	7.3
36	Connecticut	5.4
42	Delaware	4.9
3	Florida	9.8
40	Georgia	5.0
15	Hawaii	7.0
37	Idaho	5.3
21	Illinois	6.7
29	Indiana	5.9
30	Iowa	5.8
45	Kansas	4.5
6	Kentucky	8.3
30	Louisiana	5.8
30	Maine	5.8
43	Maryland	4.7
11	Massachusetts	7.4
18	Michigan	6.9
26	Minnesota	6.1
26	Mississippi	6.1
20	Missouri	6.8
23	Montana	6.3
40	Nebraska	5.0
12	Nevada	7.3
48	New Hampshire	3.9
18	New Jersey	6.9
10	New Mexico	7.6
24	New York	6.2
33	North Carolina	5.7
50	North Dakota	3.1
2	Ohio	12.5
7	Oklahoma	8.0
7	Oregon	8.0
15	Pennsylvania	7.0
49	Rhode Island	3.4
5	South Carolina	8.8
47	South Dakota	4.1
37	Tennessee	5.3
39	Texas	5.2
24	Utah	6.2
34	Vermont	5.6
12	Virginia	7.3
46	Washington	4.3
34	West Virginia	5.6
26	Wisconsin	6.1
15	Wyoming	7.0

RANK ORDER

RANK	STATE	PERCENT
1	Alaska	13.2
2	Ohio	12.5
3	Florida	9.8
4	California	9.5
5	South Carolina	8.8
6	Kentucky	8.3
7	Alabama	8.0
7	Oklahoma	8.0
7	Oregon	8.0
10	New Mexico	7.6
11	Massachusetts	7.4
12	Colorado	7.3
12	Nevada	7.3
12	Virginia	7.3
15	Hawaii	7.0
15	Pennsylvania	7.0
15	Wyoming	7.0
18	Michigan	6.9
18	New Jersey	6.9
20	Missouri	6.8
21	Illinois	6.7
22	Arizona	6.4
23	Montana	6.3
24	New York	6.2
24	Utah	6.2
26	Minnesota	6.1
26	Mississippi	6.1
26	Wisconsin	6.1
29	Indiana	5.9
30	Iowa	5.8
30	Louisiana	5.8
30	Maine	5.8
33	North Carolina	5.7
34	Vermont	5.6
34	West Virginia	5.6
36	Connecticut	5.4
37	Idaho	5.3
37	Tennessee	5.3
39	Texas	5.2
40	Georgia	5.0
40	Nebraska	5.0
42	Delaware	4.9
43	Maryland	4.7
44	Arkansas	4.6
45	Kansas	4.5
46	Washington	4.3
47	South Dakota	4.1
48	New Hampshire	3.9
49	Rhode Island	3.4
50	North Dakota	3.1

	District of Columbia	8.9

Source: CQ Press using data from U.S. Department of Education, National Center for Education Statistics
"Public Elementary and Secondary School Student Enrollment, High School Completions and Staff"
(http://nces.ed.gov/pubsearch/pubsinfo.asp?pubid=2007352)

*School year 2005-2006. Percents are based on full-time equivalent figures. Includes secretarial and other clerical staff and persons whose activities are concerned with support of the teaching and administrative duties of the office of the principal or department chairpersons or central office administrators.

Percent of Public Elementary and Secondary School Staff
Who are Teachers: 2006
National Percent = 51.2%*

ALPHA ORDER

RANK	STATE	PERCENT
7	Alabama	55.7
49	Alaska	44.1
21	Arizona	51.3
43	Arkansas	46.7
8	California	53.4
32	Colorado	49.2
42	Connecticut	46.9
20	Delaware	51.7
27	Florida	50.6
30	Georgia	49.6
9	Hawaii	53.3
6	Idaho	55.8
27	Illinois	50.6
48	Indiana	45.5
25	Iowa	50.9
21	Kansas	51.3
50	Kentucky	43.3
37	Louisiana	48.2
39	Maine	47.3
24	Maryland	51.0
12	Massachusetts	52.7
36	Michigan	48.3
33	Minnesota	48.9
44	Mississippi	46.5
17	Missouri	52.1
10	Montana	53.1
19	Nebraska	51.9
2	Nevada	67.2
35	New Hampshire	48.5
18	New Jersey	52.0
47	New Mexico	45.9
3	New York	58.6
13	North Carolina	52.5
11	North Dakota	52.9
31	Ohio	49.4
23	Oklahoma	51.1
40	Oregon	47.0
25	Pennsylvania	50.9
4	Rhode Island	58.2
1	South Carolina	71.5
38	South Dakota	48.0
16	Tennessee	52.2
34	Texas	48.7
29	Utah	50.2
44	Vermont	46.5
14	Virginia	52.3
40	Washington	47.0
14	West Virginia	52.3
5	Wisconsin	57.0
46	Wyoming	46.2

RANK ORDER

RANK	STATE	PERCENT
1	South Carolina	71.5
2	Nevada	67.2
3	New York	58.6
4	Rhode Island	58.2
5	Wisconsin	57.0
6	Idaho	55.8
7	Alabama	55.7
8	California	53.4
9	Hawaii	53.3
10	Montana	53.1
11	North Dakota	52.9
12	Massachusetts	52.7
13	North Carolina	52.5
14	Virginia	52.3
14	West Virginia	52.3
16	Tennessee	52.2
17	Missouri	52.1
18	New Jersey	52.0
19	Nebraska	51.9
20	Delaware	51.7
21	Arizona	51.3
21	Kansas	51.3
23	Oklahoma	51.1
24	Maryland	51.0
25	Iowa	50.9
25	Pennsylvania	50.9
27	Florida	50.6
27	Illinois	50.6
29	Utah	50.2
30	Georgia	49.6
31	Ohio	49.4
32	Colorado	49.2
33	Minnesota	48.9
34	Texas	48.7
35	New Hampshire	48.5
36	Michigan	48.3
37	Louisiana	48.2
38	South Dakota	48.0
39	Maine	47.3
40	Oregon	47.0
40	Washington	47.0
42	Connecticut	46.9
43	Arkansas	46.7
44	Mississippi	46.5
44	Vermont	46.5
46	Wyoming	46.2
47	New Mexico	45.9
48	Indiana	45.5
49	Alaska	44.1
50	Kentucky	43.3

	District of Columbia	44.3

Source: CQ Press using data from U.S. Department of Education, National Center for Education Statistics
"Public Elementary and Secondary School Student Enrollment, High School Completions and Staff"
(http://nces.ed.gov/pubsearch/pubsinfo.asp?pubid=2007352)
*School year 2005-2006. Counts are full-time equivalent figures.

Percent of Public Elementary and Secondary School Staff
Who are Guidance Counselors: 2006
National Percent = 1.7%*

ALPHA ORDER

RANK	STATE	PERCENT
28	Alabama	1.7
37	Alaska	1.5
44	Arizona	1.4
13	Arkansas	2.0
47	California	1.2
37	Colorado	1.5
28	Connecticut	1.7
18	Delaware	1.8
18	Florida	1.8
34	Georgia	1.6
2	Hawaii	3.2
8	Idaho	2.3
47	Illinois	1.2
44	Indiana	1.4
28	Iowa	1.7
28	Kansas	1.7
37	Kentucky	1.5
2	Louisiana	3.2
18	Maine	1.8
12	Maryland	2.1
37	Massachusetts	1.5
46	Michigan	1.3
50	Minnesota	1.0
37	Mississippi	1.5
13	Missouri	2.0
10	Montana	2.2
16	Nebraska	1.9
7	Nevada	2.5
5	New Hampshire	2.6
49	New Jersey	1.1
34	New Mexico	1.6
18	New York	1.8
13	North Carolina	2.0
18	North Dakota	1.8
34	Ohio	1.6
16	Oklahoma	1.9
10	Oregon	2.2
18	Pennsylvania	1.8
1	Rhode Island	10.3
5	South Carolina	2.6
28	South Dakota	1.7
18	Tennessee	1.8
28	Texas	1.7
37	Utah	1.5
8	Vermont	2.3
37	Virginia	1.5
18	Washington	1.8
18	West Virginia	1.8
18	Wisconsin	1.8
4	Wyoming	2.7

RANK ORDER

RANK	STATE	PERCENT
1	Rhode Island	10.3
2	Hawaii	3.2
2	Louisiana	3.2
4	Wyoming	2.7
5	New Hampshire	2.6
5	South Carolina	2.6
7	Nevada	2.5
8	Idaho	2.3
8	Vermont	2.3
10	Montana	2.2
10	Oregon	2.2
12	Maryland	2.1
13	Arkansas	2.0
13	Missouri	2.0
13	North Carolina	2.0
16	Nebraska	1.9
16	Oklahoma	1.9
18	Delaware	1.8
18	Florida	1.8
18	Maine	1.8
18	New York	1.8
18	North Dakota	1.8
18	Pennsylvania	1.8
18	Tennessee	1.8
18	Washington	1.8
18	West Virginia	1.8
18	Wisconsin	1.8
28	Alabama	1.7
28	Connecticut	1.7
28	Iowa	1.7
28	Kansas	1.7
28	South Dakota	1.7
28	Texas	1.7
34	Georgia	1.6
34	New Mexico	1.6
34	Ohio	1.6
37	Alaska	1.5
37	Colorado	1.5
37	Kentucky	1.5
37	Massachusetts	1.5
37	Mississippi	1.5
37	Utah	1.5
37	Virginia	1.5
44	Arizona	1.4
44	Indiana	1.4
46	Michigan	1.3
47	California	1.2
47	Illinois	1.2
49	New Jersey	1.1
50	Minnesota	1.0

| District of Columbia | | 0.8 |

Source: CQ Press using data from U.S. Department of Education, National Center for Education Statistics
"Public Elementary and Secondary School Student Enrollment, High School Completions and Staff"
(http://nces.ed.gov/pubsearch/pubsinfo.asp?pubid=2007352)
*School year 2005-2006. Counts are full-time equivalent figures.

Percent of Public Elementary and Secondary School Staff
Who are Librarians: 2006
National Percent = 0.9%*

ALPHA ORDER

RANK	STATE	PERCENT
3	Alabama	1.4
23	Alaska	1.0
34	Arizona	0.8
3	Arkansas	1.4
50	California	0.2
28	Colorado	0.9
23	Connecticut	1.0
28	Delaware	0.9
28	Florida	0.9
23	Georgia	1.0
3	Hawaii	1.4
46	Idaho	0.6
34	Illinois	0.8
40	Indiana	0.7
34	Iowa	0.8
3	Kansas	1.4
18	Kentucky	1.1
15	Louisiana	1.2
40	Maine	0.7
18	Maryland	1.1
40	Massachusetts	0.7
46	Michigan	0.6
34	Minnesota	0.8
3	Mississippi	1.4
9	Missouri	1.3
1	Montana	1.9
9	Nebraska	1.3
18	Nevada	1.1
23	New Hampshire	1.0
40	New Jersey	0.7
46	New Mexico	0.6
28	New York	0.9
9	North Carolina	1.3
9	North Dakota	1.3
40	Ohio	0.7
9	Oklahoma	1.3
40	Oregon	0.7
28	Pennsylvania	0.9
9	Rhode Island	1.3
2	South Carolina	1.7
34	South Dakota	0.8
3	Tennessee	1.4
34	Texas	0.8
46	Utah	0.6
15	Vermont	1.2
18	Virginia	1.1
18	Washington	1.1
23	West Virginia	1.0
15	Wisconsin	1.2
28	Wyoming	0.9

RANK ORDER

RANK	STATE	PERCENT
1	Montana	1.9
2	South Carolina	1.7
3	Alabama	1.4
3	Arkansas	1.4
3	Hawaii	1.4
3	Kansas	1.4
3	Mississippi	1.4
3	Tennessee	1.4
9	Missouri	1.3
9	Nebraska	1.3
9	North Carolina	1.3
9	North Dakota	1.3
9	Oklahoma	1.3
9	Rhode Island	1.3
15	Louisiana	1.2
15	Vermont	1.2
15	Wisconsin	1.2
18	Kentucky	1.1
18	Maryland	1.1
18	Nevada	1.1
18	Virginia	1.1
18	Washington	1.1
23	Alaska	1.0
23	Connecticut	1.0
23	Georgia	1.0
23	New Hampshire	1.0
23	West Virginia	1.0
28	Colorado	0.9
28	Delaware	0.9
28	Florida	0.9
28	New York	0.9
28	Pennsylvania	0.9
28	Wyoming	0.9
34	Arizona	0.8
34	Illinois	0.8
34	Iowa	0.8
34	Minnesota	0.8
34	South Dakota	0.8
34	Texas	0.8
40	Indiana	0.7
40	Maine	0.7
40	Massachusetts	0.7
40	New Jersey	0.7
40	Ohio	0.7
40	Oregon	0.7
46	Idaho	0.6
46	Michigan	0.6
46	New Mexico	0.6
46	Utah	0.6
50	California	0.2

District of Columbia   0.3

Source: CQ Press using data from U.S. Department of Education, National Center for Education Statistics
"Public Elementary and Secondary School Student Enrollment, High School Completions and Staff"
(http://nces.ed.gov/pubsearch/pubsinfo.asp?pubid=2007352)
*School year 2005-2006. Counts are full-time equivalent figures.

Percent of Public Elementary and Secondary School Staff
Who are Instructional Aides: 2006
National Percent = 11.4%*

<table>
<tr><td colspan="3">ALPHA ORDER</td><td colspan="3">RANK ORDER</td></tr>
<tr><td>RANK</td><td>STATE</td><td>PERCENT</td><td>RANK</td><td>STATE</td><td>PERCENT</td></tr>
<tr><td>49</td><td>Alabama</td><td>6.5</td><td>1</td><td>Vermont</td><td>22.4</td></tr>
<tr><td>18</td><td>Alaska</td><td>12.5</td><td>2</td><td>New Hampshire</td><td>21.0</td></tr>
<tr><td>11</td><td>Arizona</td><td>14.5</td><td>3</td><td>South Dakota</td><td>18.0</td></tr>
<tr><td>34</td><td>Arkansas</td><td>10.4</td><td>4</td><td>Maine</td><td>17.2</td></tr>
<tr><td>25</td><td>California</td><td>11.6</td><td>5</td><td>Oregon</td><td>16.3</td></tr>
<tr><td>29</td><td>Colorado</td><td>11.3</td><td>6</td><td>Utah</td><td>15.9</td></tr>
<tr><td>10</td><td>Connecticut</td><td>14.7</td><td>7</td><td>North Carolina</td><td>15.8</td></tr>
<tr><td>32</td><td>Delaware</td><td>11.0</td><td>8</td><td>Indiana</td><td>14.9</td></tr>
<tr><td>45</td><td>Florida</td><td>9.3</td><td>9</td><td>Massachusetts</td><td>14.8</td></tr>
<tr><td>24</td><td>Georgia</td><td>11.7</td><td>10</td><td>Connecticut</td><td>14.7</td></tr>
<tr><td>36</td><td>Hawaii</td><td>10.2</td><td>11</td><td>Arizona</td><td>14.5</td></tr>
<tr><td>33</td><td>Idaho</td><td>10.9</td><td>11</td><td>Minnesota</td><td>14.5</td></tr>
<tr><td>16</td><td>Illinois</td><td>13.2</td><td>13</td><td>Kentucky</td><td>14.4</td></tr>
<tr><td>8</td><td>Indiana</td><td>14.9</td><td>14</td><td>Wyoming</td><td>14.2</td></tr>
<tr><td>15</td><td>Iowa</td><td>14.1</td><td>15</td><td>Iowa</td><td>14.1</td></tr>
<tr><td>27</td><td>Kansas</td><td>11.4</td><td>16</td><td>Illinois</td><td>13.2</td></tr>
<tr><td>13</td><td>Kentucky</td><td>14.4</td><td>17</td><td>Mississippi</td><td>12.8</td></tr>
<tr><td>31</td><td>Louisiana</td><td>11.1</td><td>18</td><td>Alaska</td><td>12.5</td></tr>
<tr><td>4</td><td>Maine</td><td>17.2</td><td>19</td><td>North Dakota</td><td>12.4</td></tr>
<tr><td>44</td><td>Maryland</td><td>9.5</td><td>20</td><td>Michigan</td><td>12.2</td></tr>
<tr><td>9</td><td>Massachusetts</td><td>14.8</td><td>20</td><td>New Jersey</td><td>12.2</td></tr>
<tr><td>20</td><td>Michigan</td><td>12.2</td><td>22</td><td>Tennessee</td><td>11.9</td></tr>
<tr><td>11</td><td>Minnesota</td><td>14.5</td><td>23</td><td>Nevada</td><td>11.8</td></tr>
<tr><td>17</td><td>Mississippi</td><td>12.8</td><td>24</td><td>Georgia</td><td>11.7</td></tr>
<tr><td>42</td><td>Missouri</td><td>9.6</td><td>25</td><td>California</td><td>11.6</td></tr>
<tr><td>38</td><td>Montana</td><td>10.1</td><td>26</td><td>Nebraska</td><td>11.5</td></tr>
<tr><td>26</td><td>Nebraska</td><td>11.5</td><td>27</td><td>Kansas</td><td>11.4</td></tr>
<tr><td>23</td><td>Nevada</td><td>11.8</td><td>27</td><td>New Mexico</td><td>11.4</td></tr>
<tr><td>2</td><td>New Hampshire</td><td>21.0</td><td>29</td><td>Colorado</td><td>11.3</td></tr>
<tr><td>20</td><td>New Jersey</td><td>12.2</td><td>30</td><td>Pennsylvania</td><td>11.2</td></tr>
<tr><td>27</td><td>New Mexico</td><td>11.4</td><td>31</td><td>Louisiana</td><td>11.1</td></tr>
<tr><td>41</td><td>New York</td><td>9.7</td><td>32</td><td>Delaware</td><td>11.0</td></tr>
<tr><td>7</td><td>North Carolina</td><td>15.8</td><td>33</td><td>Idaho</td><td>10.9</td></tr>
<tr><td>19</td><td>North Dakota</td><td>12.4</td><td>34</td><td>Arkansas</td><td>10.4</td></tr>
<tr><td>48</td><td>Ohio</td><td>7.4</td><td>34</td><td>Rhode Island</td><td>10.4</td></tr>
<tr><td>42</td><td>Oklahoma</td><td>9.6</td><td>36</td><td>Hawaii</td><td>10.2</td></tr>
<tr><td>5</td><td>Oregon</td><td>16.3</td><td>36</td><td>Virginia</td><td>10.2</td></tr>
<tr><td>30</td><td>Pennsylvania</td><td>11.2</td><td>38</td><td>Montana</td><td>10.1</td></tr>
<tr><td>34</td><td>Rhode Island</td><td>10.4</td><td>39</td><td>Texas</td><td>9.9</td></tr>
<tr><td>50</td><td>South Carolina</td><td>5.4</td><td>40</td><td>Wisconsin</td><td>9.8</td></tr>
<tr><td>3</td><td>South Dakota</td><td>18.0</td><td>41</td><td>New York</td><td>9.7</td></tr>
<tr><td>22</td><td>Tennessee</td><td>11.9</td><td>42</td><td>Missouri</td><td>9.6</td></tr>
<tr><td>39</td><td>Texas</td><td>9.9</td><td>42</td><td>Oklahoma</td><td>9.6</td></tr>
<tr><td>6</td><td>Utah</td><td>15.9</td><td>44</td><td>Maryland</td><td>9.5</td></tr>
<tr><td>1</td><td>Vermont</td><td>22.4</td><td>45</td><td>Florida</td><td>9.3</td></tr>
<tr><td>36</td><td>Virginia</td><td>10.2</td><td>46</td><td>Washington</td><td>9.0</td></tr>
<tr><td>46</td><td>Washington</td><td>9.0</td><td>47</td><td>West Virginia</td><td>8.6</td></tr>
<tr><td>47</td><td>West Virginia</td><td>8.6</td><td>48</td><td>Ohio</td><td>7.4</td></tr>
<tr><td>40</td><td>Wisconsin</td><td>9.8</td><td>49</td><td>Alabama</td><td>6.5</td></tr>
<tr><td>14</td><td>Wyoming</td><td>14.2</td><td>50</td><td>South Carolina</td><td>5.4</td></tr>
<tr><td></td><td></td><td></td><td></td><td>District of Columbia</td><td>11.1</td></tr>
</table>

Source: CQ Press using data from U.S. Department of Education, National Center for Education Statistics
    "Public Elementary and Secondary School Student Enrollment, High School Completions and Staff"
    (http://nces.ed.gov/pubsearch/pubsinfo.asp?pubid=2007352)
*School year 2005-2006. Percents are based on full-time equivalent figures. Aides directly assist teachers in providing instruction to students.

Percent of Public Elementary and Secondary School Staff
Who are Instructional Coordinators and Supervisors: 2006
National Percent = 0.8%*

ALPHA ORDER

RANK	STATE	PERCENT
19	Alabama	1.0
19	Alaska	1.0
47	Arizona	0.2
19	Arkansas	1.0
15	California	1.1
5	Colorado	1.7
40	Connecticut	0.5
4	Delaware	1.8
47	Florida	0.2
45	Georgia	0.3
1	Hawaii	2.7
19	Idaho	1.0
40	Illinois	0.5
10	Indiana	1.3
31	Iowa	0.7
47	Kansas	0.2
26	Kentucky	0.9
3	Louisiana	1.9
19	Maine	1.0
11	Maryland	1.2
31	Massachusetts	0.7
8	Michigan	1.6
9	Minnesota	1.5
15	Mississippi	1.1
31	Missouri	0.7
26	Montana	0.9
11	Nebraska	1.2
31	Nevada	0.7
35	New Hampshire	0.6
11	New Jersey	1.2
40	New Mexico	0.5
35	New York	0.6
35	North Carolina	0.6
29	North Dakota	0.8
47	Ohio	0.2
35	Oklahoma	0.6
19	Oregon	1.0
35	Pennsylvania	0.6
29	Rhode Island	0.8
15	South Carolina	1.1
2	South Dakota	2.0
43	Tennessee	0.4
45	Texas	0.3
5	Utah	1.7
5	Vermont	1.7
26	Virginia	0.9
43	Washington	0.4
19	West Virginia	1.0
11	Wisconsin	1.2
15	Wyoming	1.1

RANK ORDER

RANK	STATE	PERCENT
1	Hawaii	2.7
2	South Dakota	2.0
3	Louisiana	1.9
4	Delaware	1.8
5	Colorado	1.7
5	Utah	1.7
5	Vermont	1.7
8	Michigan	1.6
9	Minnesota	1.5
10	Indiana	1.3
11	Maryland	1.2
11	Nebraska	1.2
11	New Jersey	1.2
11	Wisconsin	1.2
15	California	1.1
15	Mississippi	1.1
15	South Carolina	1.1
15	Wyoming	1.1
19	Alabama	1.0
19	Alaska	1.0
19	Arkansas	1.0
19	Idaho	1.0
19	Maine	1.0
19	Oregon	1.0
19	West Virginia	1.0
26	Kentucky	0.9
26	Montana	0.9
26	Virginia	0.9
29	North Dakota	0.8
29	Rhode Island	0.8
31	Iowa	0.7
31	Massachusetts	0.7
31	Missouri	0.7
31	Nevada	0.7
35	New Hampshire	0.6
35	New York	0.6
35	North Carolina	0.6
35	Oklahoma	0.6
35	Pennsylvania	0.6
40	Connecticut	0.5
40	Illinois	0.5
40	New Mexico	0.5
43	Tennessee	0.4
43	Washington	0.4
45	Georgia	0.3
45	Texas	0.3
47	Arizona	0.2
47	Florida	0.2
47	Kansas	0.2
47	Ohio	0.2

District of Columbia	0.9

Source: CQ Press using data from U.S. Department of Education, National Center for Education Statistics
   "Public Elementary and Secondary School Student Enrollment, High School Completions and Staff"
      (http://nces.ed.gov/pubsearch/pubsinfo.asp?pubid=2007352)
*School year 2005-2006. Percents are based on full-time equivalent figures. Coordinators oversee functions such as curriculum development and in-service training.

Percent of Public Elementary and Secondary School Staff
Who are Student and Other Support Staff: 2006
National Percent = 23.2%*

ALPHA ORDER

RANK	STATE	PERCENT
30	Alabama	22.6
39	Alaska	20.0
29	Arizona	22.7
2	Arkansas	30.5
39	California	20.0
17	Colorado	24.3
11	Connecticut	25.6
25	Delaware	23.3
16	Florida	24.6
7	Georgia	26.9
44	Hawaii	18.8
36	Idaho	20.9
27	Illinois	23.0
5	Indiana	27.2
34	Iowa	21.5
14	Kansas	24.8
4	Kentucky	27.3
12	Louisiana	25.4
33	Maine	21.6
8	Maryland	26.6
46	Massachusetts	18.3
13	Michigan	24.9
22	Minnesota	23.4
9	Mississippi	26.5
18	Missouri	24.0
31	Montana	21.9
26	Nebraska	23.2
49	Nevada	5.7
42	New Hampshire	19.0
22	New Jersey	23.4
3	New Mexico	28.4
42	New York	19.0
45	North Carolina	18.5
31	North Dakota	21.9
28	Ohio	22.9
18	Oklahoma	24.0
38	Oregon	20.6
15	Pennsylvania	24.7
48	Rhode Island	9.3
50	South Carolina	3.6
35	South Dakota	21.0
20	Tennessee	23.6
6	Texas	27.1
37	Utah	20.7
47	Vermont	17.3
20	Virginia	23.6
1	Washington	33.2
10	West Virginia	25.8
41	Wisconsin	19.7
22	Wyoming	23.4

RANK ORDER

RANK	STATE	PERCENT
1	Washington	33.2
2	Arkansas	30.5
3	New Mexico	28.4
4	Kentucky	27.3
5	Indiana	27.2
6	Texas	27.1
7	Georgia	26.9
8	Maryland	26.6
9	Mississippi	26.5
10	West Virginia	25.8
11	Connecticut	25.6
12	Louisiana	25.4
13	Michigan	24.9
14	Kansas	24.8
15	Pennsylvania	24.7
16	Florida	24.6
17	Colorado	24.3
18	Missouri	24.0
18	Oklahoma	24.0
20	Tennessee	23.6
20	Virginia	23.6
22	Minnesota	23.4
22	New Jersey	23.4
22	Wyoming	23.4
25	Delaware	23.3
26	Nebraska	23.2
27	Illinois	23.0
28	Ohio	22.9
29	Arizona	22.7
30	Alabama	22.6
31	Montana	21.9
31	North Dakota	21.9
33	Maine	21.6
34	Iowa	21.5
35	South Dakota	21.0
36	Idaho	20.9
37	Utah	20.7
38	Oregon	20.6
39	Alaska	20.0
39	California	20.0
41	Wisconsin	19.7
42	New Hampshire	19.0
42	New York	19.0
44	Hawaii	18.8
45	North Carolina	18.5
46	Massachusetts	18.3
47	Vermont	17.3
48	Rhode Island	9.3
49	Nevada	5.7
50	South Carolina	3.6

District of Columbia — 29.3

Source: CQ Press using data from U.S. Department of Education, National Center for Education Statistics
"Public Elementary and Secondary School Student Enrollment, High School Completions and Staff"
(http://nces.ed.gov/pubsearch/pubsinfo.asp?pubid=2007352)

*School year 2005-2006. Percents are based on full-time equivalent figures. Includes library support staff, student support services staff, and all other support staff.

Private Elementary and Secondary School Teachers in 2006

National Total = 435,485 Teachers*

RANK	STATE	TEACHERS	% of USA		RANK	STATE	TEACHERS	% of USA
23	Alabama	6,583	1.5%		1	California	47,913	11.0%
48	Alaska	574	0.1%		2	New York	40,368	9.3%
30	Arizona	3,850	0.9%		3	Florida	28,414	6.5%
36	Arkansas	2,426	0.6%		4	Pennsylvania	23,303	5.4%
1	California	47,913	11.0%		5	Texas	21,888	5.0%
26	Colorado	4,643	1.1%		6	Illinois	19,158	4.4%
21	Connecticut	7,254	1.7%		7	New Jersey	18,492	4.2%
38	Delaware	2,198	0.5%		8	Ohio	16,432	3.8%
3	Florida	28,414	6.5%		9	Massachusetts	14,794	3.4%
12	Georgia	12,236	2.8%		10	Maryland	13,856	3.2%
35	Hawaii	2,506	0.6%		11	Virginia	12,890	3.0%
46	Idaho	933	0.2%		12	Georgia	12,236	2.8%
6	Illinois	19,158	4.4%		13	Michigan	10,519	2.4%
18	Indiana	8,902	2.0%		14	Missouri	10,478	2.4%
28	Iowa	4,311	1.0%		15	Wisconsin	10,088	2.3%
31	Kansas	3,445	0.8%		16	North Carolina	9,677	2.2%
24	Kentucky	5,256	1.2%		17	Louisiana	8,942	2.1%
17	Louisiana	8,942	2.1%		18	Indiana	8,902	2.0%
39	Maine	1,983	0.5%		19	Tennessee	8,901	2.0%
10	Maryland	13,856	3.2%		20	Washington	7,600	1.7%
9	Massachusetts	14,794	3.4%		21	Connecticut	7,254	1.7%
13	Michigan	10,519	2.4%		22	Minnesota	6,883	1.6%
22	Minnesota	6,883	1.6%		23	Alabama	6,583	1.5%
27	Mississippi	4,376	1.0%		24	Kentucky	5,256	1.2%
14	Missouri	10,478	2.4%		25	South Carolina	4,948	1.1%
41	Montana**	1,962	0.5%		26	Colorado	4,643	1.1%
33	Nebraska	2,806	0.6%		27	Mississippi	4,376	1.0%
44	Nevada	1,423	0.3%		28	Iowa	4,311	1.0%
37	New Hampshire	2,378	0.5%		29	Oregon	4,100	0.9%
7	New Jersey	18,492	4.2%		30	Arizona	3,850	0.9%
40	New Mexico	1,972	0.5%		31	Kansas	3,445	0.8%
2	New York	40,368	9.3%		32	Oklahoma	3,007	0.7%
16	North Carolina	9,677	2.2%		33	Nebraska	2,806	0.6%
49	North Dakota	514	0.1%		34	Rhode Island	2,562	0.6%
8	Ohio	16,432	3.8%		35	Hawaii	2,506	0.6%
32	Oklahoma	3,007	0.7%		36	Arkansas	2,426	0.6%
29	Oregon	4,100	0.9%		37	New Hampshire	2,378	0.5%
4	Pennsylvania	23,303	5.4%		38	Delaware	2,198	0.5%
34	Rhode Island	2,562	0.6%		39	Maine	1,983	0.5%
25	South Carolina	4,948	1.1%		40	New Mexico	1,972	0.5%
47	South Dakota	920	0.2%		41	Montana**	1,962	0.5%
19	Tennessee	8,901	2.0%		42	Utah	1,530	0.4%
5	Texas	21,888	5.0%		43	Vermont	1,465	0.3%
42	Utah	1,530	0.4%		44	Nevada	1,423	0.3%
43	Vermont	1,465	0.3%		45	West Virginia	1,371	0.3%
11	Virginia	12,890	3.0%		46	Idaho	933	0.2%
20	Washington	7,600	1.7%		47	South Dakota	920	0.2%
45	West Virginia	1,371	0.3%		48	Alaska	574	0.1%
15	Wisconsin	10,088	2.3%		49	North Dakota	514	0.1%
50	Wyoming	204	0.0%		50	Wyoming	204	0.0%
						District of Columbia	2,253	0.5%

Source: U.S. Department of Education, Institute of Education Sciences
"Characteristics of Private Schools in the United States" (http://nces.ed.gov/pubs2008/2008315.pdf)
*For school year 2005-2006. Figures are full-time equivalent (FTE) teachers.
**Interpret data for these states with caution.

VII. Students

Special Note for Students Chapter
At the time that *Education State Rankings* went to print, the National Center for Education Statistics (NCES) was delayed in issuing updated enrollment data for the 2006–2007 school year. Projected enrollment numbers for 2006–2007 are shown on page 414, however, more specific breakdowns of that data (i.e., by sex, race, type of school, and program) were not yet available.

Once the new statistics are available, they will be posted on NCES' Common Core of Data Web site: http://nces.ed.gov/ccd.

Estimated Percent of School-Age Population in Public Schools in 2007

National Percent = 92.8%*

ALPHA ORDER

RANK	STATE	PERCENT
40	Alabama	90.2
1	Alaska	100.8
23	Arizona	92.8
14	Arkansas	93.9
8	California	96.1
21	Colorado	92.9
9	Connecticut	94.4
50	Delaware	83.1
14	Florida	93.9
38	Georgia	90.3
24	Hawaii	92.5
26	Idaho	92.0
27	Illinois	91.9
38	Indiana	90.3
11	Iowa	94.3
17	Kansas	93.8
9	Kentucky	94.4
24	Louisiana	92.5
21	Maine	92.9
44	Maryland	88.4
29	Massachusetts	91.8
7	Michigan	96.3
20	Minnesota	93.0
34	Mississippi	90.8
45	Missouri	88.3
36	Montana	90.4
31	Nebraska	91.4
35	Nevada	90.7
27	New Hampshire	91.9
19	New Jersey	93.2
30	New Mexico	91.5
48	New York	87.6
36	North Carolina	90.4
11	North Dakota	94.3
33	Ohio	91.1
3	Oklahoma	99.0
47	Oregon	88.1
43	Pennsylvania	88.5
42	Rhode Island	89.7
18	South Carolina	93.4
49	South Dakota	86.2
40	Tennessee	90.2
4	Texas	98.5
6	Utah	96.6
5	Vermont	97.1
13	Virginia	94.0
32	Washington	91.2
2	West Virginia	99.3
45	Wisconsin	88.3
14	Wyoming	93.9

RANK ORDER

RANK	STATE	PERCENT
1	Alaska	100.8
2	West Virginia	99.3
3	Oklahoma	99.0
4	Texas	98.5
5	Vermont	97.1
6	Utah	96.6
7	Michigan	96.3
8	California	96.1
9	Connecticut	94.4
9	Kentucky	94.4
11	Iowa	94.3
11	North Dakota	94.3
13	Virginia	94.0
14	Arkansas	93.9
14	Florida	93.9
14	Wyoming	93.9
17	Kansas	93.8
18	South Carolina	93.4
19	New Jersey	93.2
20	Minnesota	93.0
21	Colorado	92.9
21	Maine	92.9
23	Arizona	92.8
24	Hawaii	92.5
24	Louisiana	92.5
26	Idaho	92.0
27	Illinois	91.9
27	New Hampshire	91.9
29	Massachusetts	91.8
30	New Mexico	91.5
31	Nebraska	91.4
32	Washington	91.2
33	Ohio	91.1
34	Mississippi	90.8
35	Nevada	90.7
36	Montana	90.4
36	North Carolina	90.4
38	Georgia	90.3
38	Indiana	90.3
40	Alabama	90.2
40	Tennessee	90.2
42	Rhode Island	89.7
43	Pennsylvania	88.5
44	Maryland	88.4
45	Missouri	88.3
45	Wisconsin	88.3
47	Oregon	88.1
48	New York	87.6
49	South Dakota	86.2
50	Delaware	83.1

District of Columbia	98.1

Source: CQ Press using data from U.S. Department of Education, National Center for Education Statistics
   "Common Core of Data (CCD) Database" (http://nces.ed.gov/ccd/)
*Estimate based on 2007 Census population estimates for 5 to 17 year olds compared to estimated 2006-2007 school year
public school student membership. Student membership figures include counts for pre-kindergarten programs. Figures higher
than 100 percent reflect using different sources for population and for student membership.

Projected Enrollment in Public Elementary and Secondary Schools in 2007

National Total = 49,370,000 Students*

ALPHA ORDER

RANK	STATE	ENROLLMENT	% of USA
23	Alabama	735,000	1.5%
45	Alaska	132,000	0.3%
13	Arizona	1,086,000	2.2%
33	Arkansas	471,000	1.0%
1	California	6,462,000	13.1%
22	Colorado	783,000	1.6%
28	Connecticut	575,000	1.2%
46	Delaware	122,000	0.2%
4	Florida	2,719,000	5.5%
9	Georgia	1,620,000	3.3%
42	Hawaii	184,000	0.4%
39	Idaho	266,000	0.5%
5	Illinois	2,121,000	4.3%
14	Indiana	1,038,000	2.1%
32	Iowa	486,000	1.0%
34	Kansas	469,000	0.9%
26	Kentucky	685,000	1.4%
24	Louisiana	723,000	1.5%
41	Maine	194,000	0.4%
19	Maryland	868,000	1.8%
16	Massachusetts	969,000	2.0%
8	Michigan	1,747,000	3.5%
21	Minnesota	843,000	1.7%
31	Mississippi	499,000	1.0%
18	Missouri	911,000	1.8%
44	Montana	145,000	0.3%
37	Nebraska	289,000	0.6%
35	Nevada	422,000	0.9%
40	New Hampshire	205,000	0.4%
11	New Jersey	1,404,000	2.8%
36	New Mexico	325,000	0.7%
3	New York	2,818,000	5.7%
10	North Carolina	1,429,000	2.9%
48	North Dakota	97,000	0.2%
6	Ohio	1,836,000	3.7%
27	Oklahoma	632,000	1.3%
29	Oregon	552,000	1.1%
7	Pennsylvania	1,820,000	3.7%
43	Rhode Island	154,000	0.3%
25	South Carolina	713,000	1.4%
47	South Dakota	121,000	0.2%
17	Tennessee	958,000	1.9%
2	Texas	4,566,000	9.2%
30	Utah	542,000	1.1%
49	Vermont	96,000	0.2%
12	Virginia	1,229,000	2.5%
15	Washington	1,015,000	2.1%
38	West Virginia	281,000	0.6%
20	Wisconsin	852,000	1.7%
50	Wyoming	84,000	0.2%

RANK ORDER

RANK	STATE	ENROLLMENT	% of USA
1	California	6,462,000	13.1%
2	Texas	4,566,000	9.2%
3	New York	2,818,000	5.7%
4	Florida	2,719,000	5.5%
5	Illinois	2,121,000	4.3%
6	Ohio	1,836,000	3.7%
7	Pennsylvania	1,820,000	3.7%
8	Michigan	1,747,000	3.5%
9	Georgia	1,620,000	3.3%
10	North Carolina	1,429,000	2.9%
11	New Jersey	1,404,000	2.8%
12	Virginia	1,229,000	2.5%
13	Arizona	1,086,000	2.2%
14	Indiana	1,038,000	2.1%
15	Washington	1,015,000	2.1%
16	Massachusetts	969,000	2.0%
17	Tennessee	958,000	1.9%
18	Missouri	911,000	1.8%
19	Maryland	868,000	1.8%
20	Wisconsin	852,000	1.7%
21	Minnesota	843,000	1.7%
22	Colorado	783,000	1.6%
23	Alabama	735,000	1.5%
24	Louisiana	723,000	1.5%
25	South Carolina	713,000	1.4%
26	Kentucky	685,000	1.4%
27	Oklahoma	632,000	1.3%
28	Connecticut	575,000	1.2%
29	Oregon	552,000	1.1%
30	Utah	542,000	1.1%
31	Mississippi	499,000	1.0%
32	Iowa	486,000	1.0%
33	Arkansas	471,000	1.0%
34	Kansas	469,000	0.9%
35	Nevada	422,000	0.9%
36	New Mexico	325,000	0.7%
37	Nebraska	289,000	0.6%
38	West Virginia	281,000	0.6%
39	Idaho	266,000	0.5%
40	New Hampshire	205,000	0.4%
41	Maine	194,000	0.4%
42	Hawaii	184,000	0.4%
43	Rhode Island	154,000	0.3%
44	Montana	145,000	0.3%
45	Alaska	132,000	0.3%
46	Delaware	122,000	0.2%
47	South Dakota	121,000	0.2%
48	North Dakota	97,000	0.2%
49	Vermont	96,000	0.2%
50	Wyoming	84,000	0.2%
	District of Columbia	76,000	0.2%

Source: U.S. Department of Education, National Center for Education Statistics
   "Digest of Education Statistics 2007 (http://nces.ed.gov/programs/digest/index.asp)
*For school year 2006-2007.

Enrollment in Public Elementary and Secondary Schools in 2006

National Total = 49,113,474 Students*

ALPHA ORDER

RANK	STATE	STUDENTS	% of USA
23	Alabama	741,758	1.5%
45	Alaska	133,288	0.3%
13	Arizona	1,094,454	2.2%
33	Arkansas	474,206	1.0%
1	California	6,437,202	13.1%
22	Colorado	779,826	1.6%
28	Connecticut	575,059	1.2%
47	Delaware	120,937	0.2%
4	Florida	2,675,024	5.4%
9	Georgia	1,598,461	3.3%
42	Hawaii	182,818	0.4%
39	Idaho	261,982	0.5%
5	Illinois	2,111,706	4.3%
14	Indiana	1,035,074	2.1%
32	Iowa	483,482	1.0%
34	Kansas	467,285	1.0%
25	Kentucky	679,878	1.4%
26	Louisiana	654,526	1.3%
41	Maine	195,498	0.4%
20	Maryland	860,020	1.8%
16	Massachusetts	971,909	2.0%
8	Michigan	1,741,845	3.5%
21	Minnesota	839,243	1.7%
31	Mississippi	494,954	1.0%
18	Missouri	917,705	1.9%
44	Montana	145,416	0.3%
37	Nebraska	286,646	0.6%
35	Nevada	412,395	0.8%
40	New Hampshire	205,767	0.4%
11	New Jersey	1,395,602	2.8%
36	New Mexico	326,758	0.7%
3	New York	2,815,581	5.7%
10	North Carolina	1,416,436	2.9%
48	North Dakota	98,283	0.2%
6	Ohio	1,839,683	3.7%
27	Oklahoma	634,739	1.3%
29	Oregon	552,194	1.1%
7	Pennsylvania	1,830,684	3.7%
43	Rhode Island	153,422	0.3%
24	South Carolina	701,544	1.4%
46	South Dakota	122,012	0.2%
17	Tennessee	953,928	1.9%
2	Texas	4,525,394	9.2%
30	Utah	508,430	1.0%
49	Vermont	96,638	0.2%
12	Virginia	1,214,472	2.5%
15	Washington	1,031,985	2.1%
38	West Virginia	280,866	0.6%
19	Wisconsin	875,174	1.8%
50	Wyoming	84,409	0.2%

RANK ORDER

RANK	STATE	STUDENTS	% of USA
1	California	6,437,202	13.1%
2	Texas	4,525,394	9.2%
3	New York	2,815,581	5.7%
4	Florida	2,675,024	5.4%
5	Illinois	2,111,706	4.3%
6	Ohio	1,839,683	3.7%
7	Pennsylvania	1,830,684	3.7%
8	Michigan	1,741,845	3.5%
9	Georgia	1,598,461	3.3%
10	North Carolina	1,416,436	2.9%
11	New Jersey	1,395,602	2.8%
12	Virginia	1,214,472	2.5%
13	Arizona	1,094,454	2.2%
14	Indiana	1,035,074	2.1%
15	Washington	1,031,985	2.1%
16	Massachusetts	971,909	2.0%
17	Tennessee	953,928	1.9%
18	Missouri	917,705	1.9%
19	Wisconsin	875,174	1.8%
20	Maryland	860,020	1.8%
21	Minnesota	839,243	1.7%
22	Colorado	779,826	1.6%
23	Alabama	741,758	1.5%
24	South Carolina	701,544	1.4%
25	Kentucky	679,878	1.4%
26	Louisiana	654,526	1.3%
27	Oklahoma	634,739	1.3%
28	Connecticut	575,059	1.2%
29	Oregon	552,194	1.1%
30	Utah	508,430	1.0%
31	Mississippi	494,954	1.0%
32	Iowa	483,482	1.0%
33	Arkansas	474,206	1.0%
34	Kansas	467,285	1.0%
35	Nevada	412,395	0.8%
36	New Mexico	326,758	0.7%
37	Nebraska	286,646	0.6%
38	West Virginia	280,866	0.6%
39	Idaho	261,982	0.5%
40	New Hampshire	205,767	0.4%
41	Maine	195,498	0.4%
42	Hawaii	182,818	0.4%
43	Rhode Island	153,422	0.3%
44	Montana	145,416	0.3%
45	Alaska	133,288	0.3%
46	South Dakota	122,012	0.2%
47	Delaware	120,937	0.2%
48	North Dakota	98,283	0.2%
49	Vermont	96,638	0.2%
50	Wyoming	84,409	0.2%
	District of Columbia	76,876	0.2%

Source: U.S. Department of Education, National Center for Education Statistics
   "Common Core of Data (CCD) Database" (http://nces.ed.gov/ccd/)
*For school year 2005-2006.

Percent Change in Enrollment in Public
Elementary and Secondary Schools: 1997 to 2007
National Percent Change = 8.2% Increase*

ALPHA ORDER

RANK ORDER

RANK	STATE	PERCENT CHANGE	RANK	STATE	PERCENT CHANGE
38	Alabama	(1.7)	1	Nevada	49.6
29	Alaska	1.6	2	Arizona	35.9
2	Arizona	35.9	3	Florida	21.3
25	Arkansas	3.0	4	Georgia	20.3
9	California	13.6	5	Texas	19.2
7	Colorado	16.3	6	North Carolina	18.1
14	Connecticut	9.1	7	Colorado	16.3
12	Delaware	10.4	8	New Jersey	14.3
3	Florida	21.3	9	California	13.6
4	Georgia	20.3	10	Utah	12.5
39	Hawaii	(1.9)	11	Virginia	12.1
15	Idaho	8.5	12	Delaware	10.4
16	Illinois	7.5	13	South Carolina	9.2
19	Indiana	5.6	14	Connecticut	9.1
42	Iowa	(3.4)	15	Idaho	8.5
32	Kansas	0.6	16	Illinois	7.5
20	Kentucky	4.4	17	Maryland	6.0
44	Louisiana	(8.9)	18	Tennessee	5.9
45	Maine	(9.2)	19	Indiana	5.6
17	Maryland	6.0	20	Kentucky	4.4
22	Massachusetts	3.8	21	Washington	4.2
23	Michigan	3.6	22	Massachusetts	3.8
33	Minnesota	(0.5)	23	Michigan	3.6
36	Mississippi	(1.0)	24	New Hampshire	3.4
30	Missouri	1.2	25	Arkansas	3.0
47	Montana	(11.9)	26	Oregon	2.6
36	Nebraska	(1.0)	27	Oklahoma	1.8
1	Nevada	49.6	27	Rhode Island	1.8
24	New Hampshire	3.4	29	Alaska	1.6
8	New Jersey	14.3	30	Missouri	1.2
40	New Mexico	(2.3)	31	Pennsylvania	0.9
35	New York	(0.9)	32	Kansas	0.6
6	North Carolina	18.1	33	Minnesota	(0.5)
50	North Dakota	(19.2)	33	Ohio	(0.5)
33	Ohio	(0.5)	35	New York	(0.9)
27	Oklahoma	1.8	36	Mississippi	(1.0)
26	Oregon	2.6	36	Nebraska	(1.0)
31	Pennsylvania	0.9	38	Alabama	(1.7)
27	Rhode Island	1.8	39	Hawaii	(1.9)
13	South Carolina	9.2	40	New Mexico	(2.3)
49	South Dakota	(15.6)	41	Wisconsin	(3.1)
18	Tennessee	5.9	42	Iowa	(3.4)
5	Texas	19.2	43	West Virginia	(7.6)
10	Utah	12.5	44	Louisiana	(8.9)
46	Vermont	(9.7)	45	Maine	(9.2)
11	Virginia	12.1	46	Vermont	(9.7)
21	Washington	4.2	47	Montana	(11.9)
43	West Virginia	(7.6)	48	Wyoming	(15.2)
41	Wisconsin	(3.1)	49	South Dakota	(15.6)
48	Wyoming	(15.2)	50	North Dakota	(19.2)

District of Columbia   (3.4)

Source: CQ Press using data from U.S. Department of Education, National Center for Education Statistics
"Digest of Education Statistics 2007 (http://nces.ed.gov/programs/digest/index.asp)
*Projected data for school years 2006-2007 and final data for school year 1996-1997.

Male Public Elementary and Secondary School Students: 2006

National Total = 24,974,591 Male Students*

ALPHA ORDER				RANK ORDER			
RANK	STATE	MALES	% of USA	RANK	STATE	MALES	% of USA
23	Alabama	380,688	1.5%	1	California	3,178,956	12.7%
45	Alaska	68,849	0.3%	2	Texas	2,323,824	9.3%
13	Arizona	563,258	2.3%	3	New York	1,458,601	5.8%
33	Arkansas	242,800	1.0%	4	Florida	1,374,746	5.5%
1	California	3,178,956	12.7%	5	Illinois	1,065,371	4.3%
22	Colorado	399,755	1.6%	6	Pennsylvania	939,497	3.8%
28	Connecticut	296,085	1.2%	7	Ohio	919,574	3.7%
47	Delaware	62,602	0.3%	8	Michigan	877,174	3.5%
4	Florida	1,374,746	5.5%	9	Georgia	797,493	3.2%
9	Georgia	797,493	3.2%	10	North Carolina	722,541	2.9%
42	Hawaii	95,936	0.4%	11	New Jersey	719,208	2.9%
39	Idaho	135,432	0.5%	12	Virginia	614,120	2.5%
5	Illinois	1,065,371	4.3%	13	Arizona	563,258	2.3%
14	Indiana	531,817	2.1%	14	Indiana	531,817	2.1%
32	Iowa	247,056	1.0%	15	Washington	525,963	2.1%
34	Kansas	234,895	0.9%	16	Massachusetts	492,295	2.0%
26	Kentucky	332,697	1.3%	17	Tennessee	491,436	2.0%
25	Louisiana	334,333	1.3%	18	Missouri	471,358	1.9%
41	Maine	100,899	0.4%	19	Wisconsin	450,786	1.8%
20	Maryland	440,801	1.8%	20	Maryland	440,801	1.8%
16	Massachusetts	492,295	2.0%	21	Minnesota	432,538	1.7%
8	Michigan	877,174	3.5%	22	Colorado	399,755	1.6%
21	Minnesota	432,538	1.7%	23	Alabama	380,688	1.5%
31	Mississippi	252,248	1.0%	24	South Carolina	357,710	1.4%
18	Missouri	471,358	1.9%	25	Louisiana	334,333	1.3%
44	Montana	75,282	0.3%	26	Kentucky	332,697	1.3%
37	Nebraska	147,737	0.6%	27	Oklahoma	327,101	1.3%
35	Nevada	212,567	0.9%	28	Connecticut	296,085	1.2%
40	New Hampshire	106,113	0.4%	29	Oregon	274,314	1.1%
11	New Jersey	719,208	2.9%	30	Utah	261,477	1.0%
36	New Mexico	167,805	0.7%	31	Mississippi	252,248	1.0%
3	New York	1,458,601	5.8%	32	Iowa	247,056	1.0%
10	North Carolina	722,541	2.9%	33	Arkansas	242,800	1.0%
48	North Dakota	50,855	0.2%	34	Kansas	234,895	0.9%
7	Ohio	919,574	3.7%	35	Nevada	212,567	0.9%
27	Oklahoma	327,101	1.3%	36	New Mexico	167,805	0.7%
29	Oregon	274,314	1.1%	37	Nebraska	147,737	0.6%
6	Pennsylvania	939,497	3.8%	38	West Virginia	144,905	0.6%
43	Rhode Island	78,270	0.3%	39	Idaho	135,432	0.5%
24	South Carolina	357,710	1.4%	40	New Hampshire	106,113	0.4%
46	South Dakota	63,246	0.3%	41	Maine	100,899	0.4%
17	Tennessee	491,436	2.0%	42	Hawaii	95,936	0.4%
2	Texas	2,323,824	9.3%	43	Rhode Island	78,270	0.3%
30	Utah	261,477	1.0%	44	Montana	75,282	0.3%
49	Vermont	49,861	0.2%	45	Alaska	68,849	0.3%
12	Virginia	614,120	2.5%	46	South Dakota	63,246	0.3%
15	Washington	525,963	2.1%	47	Delaware	62,602	0.3%
38	West Virginia	144,905	0.6%	48	North Dakota	50,855	0.2%
19	Wisconsin	450,786	1.8%	49	Vermont	49,861	0.2%
50	Wyoming	43,739	0.2%	50	Wyoming	43,739	0.2%
					District of Columbia	37,977	0.2%

Source: U.S. Department of Education, National Center for Education Statistics
   "Common Core of Data (CCD) Database" (http://nces.ed.gov/ccd/)
*For school year 2005-2006.

Percent of Public Elementary and Secondary School Students Who are Male: 2006
National Percent = 51.4% Male*

ALPHA ORDER

RANK	STATE	PERCENT
16	Alabama	51.5
8	Alaska	51.7
16	Arizona	51.5
45	Arkansas	51.2
30	California	51.4
42	Colorado	51.3
16	Connecticut	51.5
3	Delaware	51.8
30	Florida	51.4
47	Georgia	51.1
2	Hawaii	51.9
8	Idaho	51.7
30	Illinois	51.4
30	Indiana	51.4
30	Iowa	51.4
8	Kansas	51.7
3	Kentucky	51.8
47	Louisiana	51.1
12	Maine	51.6
42	Maryland	51.3
30	Massachusetts	51.4
16	Michigan	51.5
16	Minnesota	51.5
49	Mississippi	51.0
16	Missouri	51.5
3	Montana	51.8
16	Nebraska	51.5
16	Nevada	51.5
12	New Hampshire	51.6
16	New Jersey	51.5
30	New Mexico	51.4
30	New York	51.4
49	North Carolina	51.0
8	North Dakota	51.7
30	Ohio	51.4
16	Oklahoma	51.5
42	Oregon	51.3
30	Pennsylvania	51.4
12	Rhode Island	51.6
45	South Carolina	51.2
3	South Dakota	51.8
16	Tennessee	51.5
30	Texas	51.4
30	Utah	51.4
1	Vermont	52.0
16	Virginia	51.5
16	Washington	51.5
12	West Virginia	51.6
16	Wisconsin	51.5
3	Wyoming	51.8

RANK ORDER

RANK	STATE	PERCENT
1	Vermont	52.0
2	Hawaii	51.9
3	Delaware	51.8
3	Kentucky	51.8
3	Montana	51.8
3	South Dakota	51.8
3	Wyoming	51.8
8	Alaska	51.7
8	Idaho	51.7
8	Kansas	51.7
8	North Dakota	51.7
12	Maine	51.6
12	New Hampshire	51.6
12	Rhode Island	51.6
12	West Virginia	51.6
16	Alabama	51.5
16	Arizona	51.5
16	Connecticut	51.5
16	Michigan	51.5
16	Minnesota	51.5
16	Missouri	51.5
16	Nebraska	51.5
16	Nevada	51.5
16	New Jersey	51.5
16	Oklahoma	51.5
16	Tennessee	51.5
16	Virginia	51.5
16	Washington	51.5
16	Wisconsin	51.5
30	California	51.4
30	Florida	51.4
30	Illinois	51.4
30	Indiana	51.4
30	Iowa	51.4
30	Massachusetts	51.4
30	New Mexico	51.4
30	New York	51.4
30	Ohio	51.4
30	Pennsylvania	51.4
30	Texas	51.4
30	Utah	51.4
42	Colorado	51.3
42	Maryland	51.3
42	Oregon	51.3
45	Arkansas	51.2
45	South Carolina	51.2
47	Georgia	51.1
47	Louisiana	51.1
49	Mississippi	51.0
49	North Carolina	51.0
	District of Columbia	49.4

Source: CQ Press using data from U.S. Department of Education, National Center for Education Statistics "Common Core of Data (CCD) Database" (http://nces.ed.gov/ccd/)
*For school year 2005-2006. Based on enrollment where gender is known.

Female Public Elementary and Secondary School Students: 2006

National Total = 23,610,388 Female Students*

ALPHA ORDER

ALPHA ORDER

RANK	STATE	FEMALES	% of USA
23	Alabama	358,764	1.5%
45	Alaska	64,443	0.3%
13	Arizona	531,196	2.2%
33	Arkansas	231,406	1.0%
1	California	3,008,826	12.7%
22	Colorado	380,071	1.6%
28	Connecticut	278,973	1.2%
47	Delaware	58,335	0.2%
4	Florida	1,300,278	5.5%
9	Georgia	761,885	3.2%
42	Hawaii	88,989	0.4%
39	Idaho	126,337	0.5%
5	Illinois	1,008,619	4.3%
14	Indiana	502,905	2.1%
32	Iowa	234,043	1.0%
34	Kansas	219,081	0.9%
26	Kentucky	308,988	1.3%
25	Louisiana	320,064	1.4%
41	Maine	94,599	0.4%
20	Maryland	419,219	1.8%
16	Massachusetts	464,709	2.0%
8	Michigan	826,225	3.5%
21	Minnesota	406,546	1.7%
31	Mississippi	242,706	1.0%
18	Missouri	444,492	1.9%
44	Montana	70,134	0.3%
37	Nebraska	138,909	0.6%
35	Nevada	199,840	0.8%
40	New Hampshire	99,654	0.4%
11	New Jersey	676,394	2.9%
36	New Mexico	158,953	0.7%
3	New York	1,376,757	5.8%
10	North Carolina	693,895	2.9%
48	North Dakota	47,429	0.2%
7	Ohio	868,826	3.7%
27	Oklahoma	307,638	1.3%
29	Oregon	260,506	1.1%
6	Pennsylvania	888,790	3.8%
43	Rhode Island	73,420	0.3%
24	South Carolina	340,638	1.4%
46	South Dakota	58,762	0.2%
17	Tennessee	462,341	2.0%
2	Texas	2,200,049	9.3%
30	Utah	246,781	1.0%
49	Vermont	45,961	0.2%
12	Virginia	579,017	2.5%
15	Washington	494,348	2.1%
38	West Virginia	135,798	0.6%
19	Wisconsin	424,280	1.8%
50	Wyoming	40,670	0.2%

RANK ORDER

RANK	STATE	FEMALES	% of USA
1	California	3,008,826	12.7%
2	Texas	2,200,049	9.3%
3	New York	1,376,757	5.8%
4	Florida	1,300,278	5.5%
5	Illinois	1,008,619	4.3%
6	Pennsylvania	888,790	3.8%
7	Ohio	868,826	3.7%
8	Michigan	826,225	3.5%
9	Georgia	761,885	3.2%
10	North Carolina	693,895	2.9%
11	New Jersey	676,394	2.9%
12	Virginia	579,017	2.5%
13	Arizona	531,196	2.2%
14	Indiana	502,905	2.1%
15	Washington	494,348	2.1%
16	Massachusetts	464,709	2.0%
17	Tennessee	462,341	2.0%
18	Missouri	444,492	1.9%
19	Wisconsin	424,280	1.8%
20	Maryland	419,219	1.8%
21	Minnesota	406,546	1.7%
22	Colorado	380,071	1.6%
23	Alabama	358,764	1.5%
24	South Carolina	340,638	1.4%
25	Louisiana	320,064	1.4%
26	Kentucky	308,988	1.3%
27	Oklahoma	307,638	1.3%
28	Connecticut	278,973	1.2%
29	Oregon	260,506	1.1%
30	Utah	246,781	1.0%
31	Mississippi	242,706	1.0%
32	Iowa	234,043	1.0%
33	Arkansas	231,406	1.0%
34	Kansas	219,081	0.9%
35	Nevada	199,840	0.8%
36	New Mexico	158,953	0.7%
37	Nebraska	138,909	0.6%
38	West Virginia	135,798	0.6%
39	Idaho	126,337	0.5%
40	New Hampshire	99,654	0.4%
41	Maine	94,599	0.4%
42	Hawaii	88,989	0.4%
43	Rhode Island	73,420	0.3%
44	Montana	70,134	0.3%
45	Alaska	64,443	0.3%
46	South Dakota	58,762	0.2%
47	Delaware	58,335	0.2%
48	North Dakota	47,429	0.2%
49	Vermont	45,961	0.2%
50	Wyoming	40,670	0.2%
	District of Columbia	38,899	0.2%

Source: U.S. Department of Education, National Center for Education Statistics
   "Common Core of Data (CCD) Database" (http://nces.ed.gov/ccd/)
*For school year 2005-2006.

Percent of Public Elementary and Secondary School Students Who are Female: 2006
National Percent = 48.6% Female*

ALPHA ORDER

RANK	STATE	PERCENT
22	Alabama	48.5
40	Alaska	48.3
22	Arizona	48.5
5	Arkansas	48.8
10	California	48.6
7	Colorado	48.7
22	Connecticut	48.5
44	Delaware	48.2
10	Florida	48.6
3	Georgia	48.9
49	Hawaii	48.1
40	Idaho	48.3
10	Illinois	48.6
10	Indiana	48.6
10	Iowa	48.6
40	Kansas	48.3
44	Kentucky	48.2
3	Louisiana	48.9
36	Maine	48.4
7	Maryland	48.7
10	Massachusetts	48.6
22	Michigan	48.5
22	Minnesota	48.5
1	Mississippi	49.0
22	Missouri	48.5
44	Montana	48.2
22	Nebraska	48.5
22	Nevada	48.5
36	New Hampshire	48.4
22	New Jersey	48.5
10	New Mexico	48.6
10	New York	48.6
1	North Carolina	49.0
40	North Dakota	48.3
10	Ohio	48.6
22	Oklahoma	48.5
7	Oregon	48.7
10	Pennsylvania	48.6
36	Rhode Island	48.4
5	South Carolina	48.8
44	South Dakota	48.2
22	Tennessee	48.5
10	Texas	48.6
10	Utah	48.6
50	Vermont	48.0
22	Virginia	48.5
22	Washington	48.5
36	West Virginia	48.4
22	Wisconsin	48.5
44	Wyoming	48.2

RANK ORDER

RANK	STATE	PERCENT
1	Mississippi	49.0
1	North Carolina	49.0
3	Georgia	48.9
3	Louisiana	48.9
5	Arkansas	48.8
5	South Carolina	48.8
7	Colorado	48.7
7	Maryland	48.7
7	Oregon	48.7
10	California	48.6
10	Florida	48.6
10	Illinois	48.6
10	Indiana	48.6
10	Iowa	48.6
10	Massachusetts	48.6
10	New Mexico	48.6
10	New York	48.6
10	Ohio	48.6
10	Pennsylvania	48.6
10	Texas	48.6
10	Utah	48.6
22	Alabama	48.5
22	Arizona	48.5
22	Connecticut	48.5
22	Michigan	48.5
22	Minnesota	48.5
22	Missouri	48.5
22	Nebraska	48.5
22	Nevada	48.5
22	New Jersey	48.5
22	Oklahoma	48.5
22	Tennessee	48.5
22	Virginia	48.5
22	Washington	48.5
22	Wisconsin	48.5
36	Maine	48.4
36	New Hampshire	48.4
36	Rhode Island	48.4
36	West Virginia	48.4
40	Alaska	48.3
40	Idaho	48.3
40	Kansas	48.3
40	North Dakota	48.3
44	Delaware	48.2
44	Kentucky	48.2
44	Montana	48.2
44	South Dakota	48.2
44	Wyoming	48.2
49	Hawaii	48.1
50	Vermont	48.0

| | District of Columbia | 50.6 |

Source: CQ Press using data from U.S. Department of Education, National Center for Education Statistics
   "Common Core of Data (CCD) Database" (http://nces.ed.gov/ccd/)
*For school year 2005-2006. Based on enrollment where gender is known.

Pupil-Teacher Ratio in Public Elementary and Secondary Schools in 2006

National Ratio = 15.7 Pupils per Teacher*

ALPHA ORDER				RANK ORDER		
RANK	STATE	PERCENT		RANK	STATE	PERCENT
43	Alabama	12.8		1	Utah	22.1
11	Alaska	16.8		2	Arizona	21.3
2	Arizona	21.3		3	California	20.8
32	Arkansas	14.4		4	Oregon	19.5
3	California	20.8		5	Washington	19.3
10	Colorado	17.0		6	Nevada	19.0
31	Connecticut	14.5		7	Idaho	18.0
22	Delaware	15.1		8	Michigan	17.4
11	Florida	16.8		9	Indiana	17.1
27	Georgia	14.7		10	Colorado	17.0
14	Hawaii	16.3		11	Alaska	16.8
7	Idaho	18.0		11	Florida	16.8
17	Illinois	15.8		13	Minnesota	16.4
9	Indiana	17.1		14	Hawaii	16.3
36	Iowa	13.7		15	Kentucky	16.0
35	Kansas	13.9		15	Tennessee	16.0
15	Kentucky	16.0		17	Illinois	15.8
27	Louisiana	14.7		18	Mississippi	15.7
48	Maine	11.7		19	Ohio	15.6
20	Maryland	15.2		20	Maryland	15.2
40	Massachusetts	13.2		20	Oklahoma	15.2
8	Michigan	17.4		22	Delaware	15.1
13	Minnesota	16.4		23	Pennsylvania	15.0
18	Mississippi	15.7		23	Texas	15.0
36	Missouri	13.7		25	New Mexico	14.8
34	Montana	14.0		25	North Carolina	14.8
38	Nebraska	13.4		27	Georgia	14.7
6	Nevada	19.0		27	Louisiana	14.7
40	New Hampshire	13.2		29	South Carolina	14.6
46	New Jersey	12.4		29	Wisconsin	14.6
25	New Mexico	14.8		31	Connecticut	14.5
42	New York	12.9		32	Arkansas	14.4
25	North Carolina	14.8		33	West Virginia	14.1
47	North Dakota	12.3		34	Montana	14.0
19	Ohio	15.6		35	Kansas	13.9
20	Oklahoma	15.2		36	Iowa	13.7
4	Oregon	19.5		36	Missouri	13.7
23	Pennsylvania	15.0		38	Nebraska	13.4
50	Rhode Island	10.7		38	South Dakota	13.4
29	South Carolina	14.6		40	Massachusetts	13.2
38	South Dakota	13.4		40	New Hampshire	13.2
15	Tennessee	16.0		42	New York	12.9
23	Texas	15.0		43	Alabama	12.8
1	Utah	22.1		44	Virginia	12.6
49	Vermont	10.9		44	Wyoming	12.6
44	Virginia	12.6		46	New Jersey	12.4
5	Washington	19.3		47	North Dakota	12.3
33	West Virginia	14.1		48	Maine	11.7
29	Wisconsin	14.6		49	Vermont	10.9
44	Wyoming	12.6		50	Rhode Island	10.7
					District of Columbia	14.0

Source: U.S. Department of Education, National Center for Education Statistics
"Public Elementary and Secondary School Student Enrollment, High School Completions and Staff"
(http://nces.ed.gov/pubs2007/2007352.pdf)
*For school year 2005-2006. Based on full-time equivalency counts of teachers. National ratio calculated by editors.

Public Kindergarten Pupil-Teacher Ratio in 2006

National Ratio = 17.3 Students per Teacher*

ALPHA ORDER

RANK	STATE	RATIO
NA	Alabama**	NA
19	Alaska	23.8
7	Arizona	33.3
35	Arkansas	19.5
28	California	21.8
33	Colorado	20.3
20	Connecticut	23.7
10	Delaware	29.2
27	Florida	22.1
40	Georgia	17.8
11	Hawaii	26.6
4	Idaho	36.9
5	Illinois	35.1
13	Indiana	25.6
47	Iowa	14.8
18	Kansas	24.1
1	Kentucky	41.9
24	Louisiana	22.3
48	Maine	13.1
23	Maryland	22.8
25	Massachusetts	22.2
NA	Michigan**	NA
16	Minnesota	25.0
30	Mississippi	21.1
43	Missouri	16.9
45	Montana	15.7
44	Nebraska	16.8
3	Nevada	41.0
13	New Hampshire	25.6
9	New Jersey	30.1
39	New Mexico	18.0
46	New York	15.5
41	North Carolina	17.7
32	North Dakota	20.4
13	Ohio	25.6
17	Oklahoma	24.9
6	Oregon	33.5
12	Pennsylvania	25.9
21	Rhode Island	23.5
22	South Carolina	23.1
25	South Dakota	22.2
37	Tennessee	18.7
36	Texas	18.9
2	Utah	41.5
42	Vermont	17.6
29	Virginia	21.7
8	Washington	32.6
34	West Virginia	19.8
38	Wisconsin	18.3
31	Wyoming	20.5

RANK ORDER

RANK	STATE	RATIO
1	Kentucky	41.9
2	Utah	41.5
3	Nevada	41.0
4	Idaho	36.9
5	Illinois	35.1
6	Oregon	33.5
7	Arizona	33.3
8	Washington	32.6
9	New Jersey	30.1
10	Delaware	29.2
11	Hawaii	26.6
12	Pennsylvania	25.9
13	Indiana	25.6
13	New Hampshire	25.6
13	Ohio	25.6
16	Minnesota	25.0
17	Oklahoma	24.9
18	Kansas	24.1
19	Alaska	23.8
20	Connecticut	23.7
21	Rhode Island	23.5
22	South Carolina	23.1
23	Maryland	22.8
24	Louisiana	22.3
25	Massachusetts	22.2
25	South Dakota	22.2
27	Florida	22.1
28	California	21.8
29	Virginia	21.7
30	Mississippi	21.1
31	Wyoming	20.5
32	North Dakota	20.4
33	Colorado	20.3
34	West Virginia	19.8
35	Arkansas	19.5
36	Texas	18.9
37	Tennessee	18.7
38	Wisconsin	18.3
39	New Mexico	18.0
40	Georgia	17.8
41	North Carolina	17.7
42	Vermont	17.6
43	Missouri	16.9
44	Nebraska	16.8
45	Montana	15.7
46	New York	15.5
47	Iowa	14.8
48	Maine	13.1
NA	Alabama**	NA
NA	Michigan**	NA
	District of Columbia	20.5

Source: U.S. Department of Education, National Center for Education Statistics
  "Public Elementary and Secondary School Student Enrollment, High School Completions and Staff"
  (http://nces.ed.gov/pubs2007/2007352.pdf)
*For school year 2005-2006. Ratios are based on full-time equivalent counts.
**Not available.

Public Elementary School Pupil-Teacher Ratio in 2006

National Ratio = 19.4 Students per Teacher*

ALPHA ORDER

RANK	STATE	RATIO
36	Alabama	14.8
34	Alaska	15.4
22	Arizona	19.0
6	Arkansas	25.0
17	California	20.9
8	Colorado	23.8
41	Connecticut	14.2
18	Delaware	20.7
3	Florida	27.3
26	Georgia	17.6
13	Hawaii	22.0
9	Idaho	23.4
29	Illinois	17.4
11	Indiana	22.5
39	Iowa	14.4
16	Kansas	21.0
26	Kentucky	17.6
38	Louisiana	14.5
49	Maine	12.0
31	Maryland	17.0
32	Massachusetts	15.7
NA	Michigan**	NA
12	Minnesota	22.4
7	Mississippi	24.1
23	Missouri	18.8
41	Montana	14.2
44	Nebraska	13.7
4	Nevada	25.9
48	New Hampshire	12.4
20	New Jersey	19.9
37	New Mexico	14.7
28	New York	17.5
25	North Carolina	17.8
47	North Dakota	13.3
35	Ohio	15.0
15	Oklahoma	21.6
2	Oregon	28.2
10	Pennsylvania	23.1
44	Rhode Island	13.7
43	South Carolina	13.9
39	South Dakota	14.4
33	Tennessee	15.5
14	Texas	21.8
1	Utah	31.2
24	Vermont	18.5
19	Virginia	20.3
5	Washington	25.6
21	West Virginia	19.6
44	Wisconsin	13.7
29	Wyoming	17.4

RANK ORDER

RANK	STATE	RATIO
1	Utah	31.2
2	Oregon	28.2
3	Florida	27.3
4	Nevada	25.9
5	Washington	25.6
6	Arkansas	25.0
7	Mississippi	24.1
8	Colorado	23.8
9	Idaho	23.4
10	Pennsylvania	23.1
11	Indiana	22.5
12	Minnesota	22.4
13	Hawaii	22.0
14	Texas	21.8
15	Oklahoma	21.6
16	Kansas	21.0
17	California	20.9
18	Delaware	20.7
19	Virginia	20.3
20	New Jersey	19.9
21	West Virginia	19.6
22	Arizona	19.0
23	Missouri	18.8
24	Vermont	18.5
25	North Carolina	17.8
26	Georgia	17.6
26	Kentucky	17.6
28	New York	17.5
29	Illinois	17.4
29	Wyoming	17.4
31	Maryland	17.0
32	Massachusetts	15.7
33	Tennessee	15.5
34	Alaska	15.4
35	Ohio	15.0
36	Alabama	14.8
37	New Mexico	14.7
38	Louisiana	14.5
39	Iowa	14.4
39	South Dakota	14.4
41	Connecticut	14.2
41	Montana	14.2
43	South Carolina	13.9
44	Nebraska	13.7
44	Rhode Island	13.7
44	Wisconsin	13.7
47	North Dakota	13.3
48	New Hampshire	12.4
49	Maine	12.0
NA	Michigan**	NA

	District of Columbia	17.9

Source: U.S. Department of Education, National Center for Education Statistics
"Public Elementary and Secondary School Student Enrollment, High School Completions and Staff"
(http://nces.ed.gov/pubs2007/2007352.pdf)
*For school year 2005-2006. Ratios are based on full-time equivalent counts. Includes grades 1-8.
**Not available.

Public Secondary School Pupil-Teacher Ratio in 2006

National Ratio = 12.9 Students per Teacher*

ALPHA ORDER

RANK	STATE	RATIO
15	Alabama	14.7
5	Alaska	18.3
1	Arizona	24.1
46	Arkansas	8.2
3	California	23.3
41	Colorado	10.2
18	Connecticut	14.4
43	Delaware	9.1
23	Florida	12.9
37	Georgia	10.5
38	Hawaii	10.4
32	Idaho	11.3
6	Illinois	18.1
28	Indiana	11.8
23	Iowa	12.9
42	Kansas	9.4
4	Kentucky	19.5
22	Louisiana	13.0
34	Maine	11.2
30	Maryland	11.5
17	Massachusetts	14.6
2	Michigan	23.6
29	Minnesota	11.6
35	Mississippi	11.0
45	Missouri	8.8
20	Montana	13.8
27	Nebraska	12.1
11	Nevada	15.1
20	New Hampshire	13.8
50	New Jersey	5.9
19	New Mexico	14.3
32	New York	11.3
25	North Carolina	12.8
40	North Dakota	10.3
10	Ohio	15.3
38	Oklahoma	10.4
6	Oregon	18.1
31	Pennsylvania	11.4
48	Rhode Island	7.2
15	South Carolina	14.7
11	South Dakota	15.1
8	Tennessee	16.5
36	Texas	10.8
9	Utah	15.9
44	Vermont	9.0
49	Virginia	6.8
13	Washington	15.0
26	West Virginia	12.4
13	Wisconsin	15.0
47	Wyoming	8.0

RANK ORDER

RANK	STATE	RATIO
1	Arizona	24.1
2	Michigan	23.6
3	California	23.3
4	Kentucky	19.5
5	Alaska	18.3
6	Illinois	18.1
6	Oregon	18.1
8	Tennessee	16.5
9	Utah	15.9
10	Ohio	15.3
11	Nevada	15.1
11	South Dakota	15.1
13	Washington	15.0
13	Wisconsin	15.0
15	Alabama	14.7
15	South Carolina	14.7
17	Massachusetts	14.6
18	Connecticut	14.4
19	New Mexico	14.3
20	Montana	13.8
20	New Hampshire	13.8
22	Louisiana	13.0
23	Florida	12.9
23	Iowa	12.9
25	North Carolina	12.8
26	West Virginia	12.4
27	Nebraska	12.1
28	Indiana	11.8
29	Minnesota	11.6
30	Maryland	11.5
31	Pennsylvania	11.4
32	Idaho	11.3
32	New York	11.3
34	Maine	11.2
35	Mississippi	11.0
36	Texas	10.8
37	Georgia	10.5
38	Hawaii	10.4
38	Oklahoma	10.4
40	North Dakota	10.3
41	Colorado	10.2
42	Kansas	9.4
43	Delaware	9.1
44	Vermont	9.0
45	Missouri	8.8
46	Arkansas	8.2
47	Wyoming	8.0
48	Rhode Island	7.2
49	Virginia	6.8
50	New Jersey	5.9
	District of Columbia	8.1

Source: U.S. Department of Education, National Center for Education Statistics
   "Public Elementary and Secondary School Student Enrollment, High School Completions and Staff"
   (http://nces.ed.gov/pubs2007/2007352.pdf)
*For school year 2005-2006. Ratios are based on full-time equivalent counts. Includes grades 9-12.

Pupil-Staff Ratio in Public Elementary and Secondary Schools in 2006

National Ratio = 8.0 Students per Staff*

ALPHA ORDER

RANK	STATE	RATIO
31	Alabama	7.1
26	Alaska	7.4
4	Arizona	10.9
41	Arkansas	6.7
2	California	11.1
11	Colorado	8.4
39	Connecticut	6.8
17	Delaware	7.8
10	Florida	8.5
28	Georgia	7.3
9	Hawaii	8.7
6	Idaho	10.1
15	Illinois	8.0
17	Indiana	7.8
35	Iowa	7.0
31	Kansas	7.1
38	Kentucky	6.9
31	Louisiana	7.1
49	Maine	5.5
21	Maryland	7.7
35	Massachusetts	7.0
11	Michigan	8.4
15	Minnesota	8.0
28	Mississippi	7.3
31	Missouri	7.1
24	Montana	7.5
35	Nebraska	7.0
1	Nevada	12.7
44	New Hampshire	6.4
44	New Jersey	6.4
39	New Mexico	6.8
24	New York	7.5
17	North Carolina	7.8
43	North Dakota	6.5
21	Ohio	7.7
17	Oklahoma	7.8
7	Oregon	9.2
23	Pennsylvania	7.6
47	Rhode Island	6.2
5	South Carolina	10.4
44	South Dakota	6.4
11	Tennessee	8.4
28	Texas	7.3
2	Utah	11.1
50	Vermont	5.1
42	Virginia	6.6
8	Washington	9.1
26	West Virginia	7.4
14	Wisconsin	8.3
48	Wyoming	5.8

RANK ORDER

RANK	STATE	RATIO
1	Nevada	12.7
2	California	11.1
2	Utah	11.1
4	Arizona	10.9
5	South Carolina	10.4
6	Idaho	10.1
7	Oregon	9.2
8	Washington	9.1
9	Hawaii	8.7
10	Florida	8.5
11	Colorado	8.4
11	Michigan	8.4
11	Tennessee	8.4
14	Wisconsin	8.3
15	Illinois	8.0
15	Minnesota	8.0
17	Delaware	7.8
17	Indiana	7.8
17	North Carolina	7.8
17	Oklahoma	7.8
21	Maryland	7.7
21	Ohio	7.7
23	Pennsylvania	7.6
24	Montana	7.5
24	New York	7.5
26	Alaska	7.4
26	West Virginia	7.4
28	Georgia	7.3
28	Mississippi	7.3
28	Texas	7.3
31	Alabama	7.1
31	Kansas	7.1
31	Louisiana	7.1
31	Missouri	7.1
35	Iowa	7.0
35	Massachusetts	7.0
35	Nebraska	7.0
38	Kentucky	6.9
39	Connecticut	6.8
39	New Mexico	6.8
41	Arkansas	6.7
42	Virginia	6.6
43	North Dakota	6.5
44	New Hampshire	6.4
44	New Jersey	6.4
44	South Dakota	6.4
47	Rhode Island	6.2
48	Wyoming	5.8
49	Maine	5.5
50	Vermont	5.1
	District of Columbia	6.2

Source: CQ Press using data from U.S. Department of Education, National Center for Education Statistics
"Public Elementary and Secondary School Student Enrollment, High School Completions and Staff"
(http://nces.ed.gov/pubs2007/2007352.pdf)
*For school year 2005-2006. Ratios are based on full-time equivalent counts. Includes grades K-12. Includes administration, instructional, and all support staff.

Pupil-Administrative Staff Ratio in Public Elementary and Secondary Schools in 2006
National Ratio = 209.4 Students per Staff*

ALPHA ORDER

RANK	STATE	RATIO
16	Alabama	227.7
49	Alaska	111.1
1	Arizona	396.0
28	Arkansas	202.0
2	California	383.1
19	Colorado	218.0
40	Connecticut	156.2
37	Delaware	172.0
6	Florida	291.0
33	Georgia	186.1
9	Hawaii	259.3
5	Idaho	308.2
27	Illinois	203.6
11	Indiana	255.3
42	Iowa	152.4
41	Kansas	155.6
20	Kentucky	217.0
15	Louisiana	228.5
46	Maine	121.1
29	Maryland	200.0
36	Massachusetts	176.3
24	Michigan	209.2
25	Minnesota	207.4
35	Mississippi	177.1
26	Missouri	206.1
23	Montana	209.5
34	Nebraska	178.5
4	Nevada	329.4
31	New Hampshire	189.1
12	New Jersey	254.2
38	New Mexico	171.5
14	New York	238.9
21	North Carolina	212.2
48	North Dakota	112.5
43	Ohio	146.0
17	Oklahoma	225.6
18	Oregon	219.3
8	Pennsylvania	273.7
50	Rhode Island	99.4
30	South Carolina	191.1
44	South Dakota	143.4
13	Tennessee	249.2
47	Texas	113.8
3	Utah	345.2
39	Vermont	165.2
22	Virginia	211.9
7	Washington	275.0
32	West Virginia	187.6
10	Wisconsin	258.9
45	Wyoming	129.9

RANK ORDER

RANK	STATE	RATIO
1	Arizona	396.0
2	California	383.1
3	Utah	345.2
4	Nevada	329.4
5	Idaho	308.2
6	Florida	291.0
7	Washington	275.0
8	Pennsylvania	273.7
9	Hawaii	259.3
10	Wisconsin	258.9
11	Indiana	255.3
12	New Jersey	254.2
13	Tennessee	249.2
14	New York	238.9
15	Louisiana	228.5
16	Alabama	227.7
17	Oklahoma	225.6
18	Oregon	219.3
19	Colorado	218.0
20	Kentucky	217.0
21	North Carolina	212.2
22	Virginia	211.9
23	Montana	209.5
24	Michigan	209.2
25	Minnesota	207.4
26	Missouri	206.1
27	Illinois	203.6
28	Arkansas	202.0
29	Maryland	200.0
30	South Carolina	191.1
31	New Hampshire	189.1
32	West Virginia	187.6
33	Georgia	186.1
34	Nebraska	178.5
35	Mississippi	177.1
36	Massachusetts	176.3
37	Delaware	172.0
38	New Mexico	171.5
39	Vermont	165.2
40	Connecticut	156.2
41	Kansas	155.6
42	Iowa	152.4
43	Ohio	146.0
44	South Dakota	143.4
45	Wyoming	129.9
46	Maine	121.1
47	Texas	113.8
48	North Dakota	112.5
49	Alaska	111.1
50	Rhode Island	99.4
	District of Columbia	143.2

Source: U.S. Department of Education, National Center for Education Statistics
  "Public Elementary and Secondary School Student Enrollment, High School Completions and Staff"
    (http://nces.ed.gov/pubs2007/2007352.pdf)
*For school year 2005-2006. Ratios are based on full-time equivalent counts. Includes grades K-12.

Average Daily Attendance in Public Elementary and Secondary Schools in 2006

National Total = 45,484,979 Students*

ALPHA ORDER

RANK	STATE	STUDENTS	% of USA
23	Alabama	711,030	1.6%
45	Alaska	115,739	0.3%
13	Arizona	974,052	2.1%
34	Arkansas	397,264	0.9%
1	California	6,068,819	13.3%
22	Colorado	724,029	1.6%
28	Connecticut	554,472	1.2%
47	Delaware	113,986	0.3%
4	Florida	2,494,778	5.5%
9	Georgia	1,486,568	3.3%
42	Hawaii	168,809	0.4%
39	Idaho	246,717	0.5%
5	Illinois	1,905,638	4.2%
15	Indiana	953,192	2.1%
31	Iowa	453,387	1.0%
33	Kansas	406,957	0.9%
27	Kentucky	589,967	1.3%
25	Louisiana	647,836	1.4%
41	Maine	183,827	0.4%
20	Maryland	800,553	1.8%
16	Massachusetts	913,111	2.0%
8	Michigan	1,590,720	3.5%
21	Minnesota	780,233	1.7%
30	Mississippi	475,056	1.0%
18	Missouri	828,385	1.8%
44	Montana	126,380	0.3%
38	Nebraska	264,323	0.6%
35	Nevada	387,739	0.9%
40	New Hampshire	188,836	0.4%
10	New Jersey	1,358,562	3.0%
36	New Mexico	294,173	0.6%
3	New York	2,619,083	5.8%
11	North Carolina	1,294,132	2.8%
48	North Dakota	89,644	0.2%
7	Ohio	1,651,725	3.6%
26	Oklahoma	591,486	1.3%
29	Oregon	491,252	1.1%
6	Pennsylvania	1,701,962	3.7%
43	Rhode Island	152,909	0.3%
24	South Carolina	648,145	1.4%
46	South Dakota	114,555	0.3%
17	Tennessee	879,908	1.9%
2	Texas	4,209,672	9.3%
32	Utah	445,550	1.0%
49	Vermont	79,543	0.2%
12	Virginia	1,125,451	2.5%
14	Washington	960,463	2.1%
37	West Virginia	273,780	0.6%
19	Wisconsin	817,232	1.8%
50	Wyoming	77,757	0.2%

RANK ORDER

RANK	STATE	STUDENTS	% of USA
1	California	6,068,819	13.3%
2	Texas	4,209,672	9.3%
3	New York	2,619,083	5.8%
4	Florida	2,494,778	5.5%
5	Illinois	1,905,638	4.2%
6	Pennsylvania	1,701,962	3.7%
7	Ohio	1,651,725	3.6%
8	Michigan	1,590,720	3.5%
9	Georgia	1,486,568	3.3%
10	New Jersey	1,358,562	3.0%
11	North Carolina	1,294,132	2.8%
12	Virginia	1,125,451	2.5%
13	Arizona	974,052	2.1%
14	Washington	960,463	2.1%
15	Indiana	953,192	2.1%
16	Massachusetts	913,111	2.0%
17	Tennessee	879,908	1.9%
18	Missouri	828,385	1.8%
19	Wisconsin	817,232	1.8%
20	Maryland	800,553	1.8%
21	Minnesota	780,233	1.7%
22	Colorado	724,029	1.6%
23	Alabama	711,030	1.6%
24	South Carolina	648,145	1.4%
25	Louisiana	647,836	1.4%
26	Oklahoma	591,486	1.3%
27	Kentucky	589,967	1.3%
28	Connecticut	554,472	1.2%
29	Oregon	491,252	1.1%
30	Mississippi	475,056	1.0%
31	Iowa	453,387	1.0%
32	Utah	445,550	1.0%
33	Kansas	406,957	0.9%
34	Arkansas	397,264	0.9%
35	Nevada	387,739	0.9%
36	New Mexico	294,173	0.6%
37	West Virginia	273,780	0.6%
38	Nebraska	264,323	0.6%
39	Idaho	246,717	0.5%
40	New Hampshire	188,836	0.4%
41	Maine	183,827	0.4%
42	Hawaii	168,809	0.4%
43	Rhode Island	152,909	0.3%
44	Montana	126,380	0.3%
45	Alaska	115,739	0.3%
46	South Dakota	114,555	0.3%
47	Delaware	113,986	0.3%
48	North Dakota	89,644	0.2%
49	Vermont	79,543	0.2%
50	Wyoming	77,757	0.2%
	District of Columbia	55,593	0.1%

Source: National Education Association, Washington, D.C.
    "Rankings & Estimates" (Copyright © 2007, NEA, used with permission, http://www.nea.org/edstats/index.html)
*Estimates for school year 2005-2006.

Average Daily Attendance as a Percent of Fall Enrollment in Public Elementary and Secondary Schools in 2006
National Percent = 93.3%*

ALPHA ORDER

RANK	STATE	PERCENT
5	Alabama	96.3
49	Alaska	86.7
4	Arizona	96.4
46	Arkansas	87.7
6	California	96.2
30	Colorado	92.7
8	Connecticut	96.1
11	Delaware	94.3
18	Florida	93.5
25	Georgia	93.0
33	Hawaii	92.4
12	Idaho	94.2
42	Illinois	90.3
36	Indiana	92.1
15	Iowa	93.8
47	Kansas	87.1
38	Kentucky	91.9
1	Louisiana	99.0
34	Maine	92.3
24	Maryland	93.1
13	Massachusetts	94.0
41	Michigan	91.3
19	Minnesota	93.4
6	Mississippi	96.2
37	Missouri	92.0
48	Montana	86.9
31	Nebraska	92.6
15	Nevada	93.8
38	New Hampshire	91.9
3	New Jersey	97.4
43	New Mexico	90.0
25	New York	93.0
13	North Carolina	94.0
34	North Dakota	92.3
44	Ohio	88.7
23	Oklahoma	93.2
45	Oregon	87.8
25	Pennsylvania	93.0
10	Rhode Island	94.8
19	South Carolina	93.4
9	South Dakota	94.9
17	Tennessee	93.6
19	Texas	93.4
38	Utah	91.9
50	Vermont	84.1
31	Virginia	92.6
28	Washington	92.9
2	West Virginia	97.9
19	Wisconsin	93.4
28	Wyoming	92.9

RANK ORDER

RANK	STATE	PERCENT
1	Louisiana	99.0
2	West Virginia	97.9
3	New Jersey	97.4
4	Arizona	96.4
5	Alabama	96.3
6	California	96.2
6	Mississippi	96.2
8	Connecticut	96.1
9	South Dakota	94.9
10	Rhode Island	94.8
11	Delaware	94.3
12	Idaho	94.2
13	Massachusetts	94.0
13	North Carolina	94.0
15	Iowa	93.8
15	Nevada	93.8
17	Tennessee	93.6
18	Florida	93.5
19	Minnesota	93.4
19	South Carolina	93.4
19	Texas	93.4
19	Wisconsin	93.4
23	Oklahoma	93.2
24	Maryland	93.1
25	Georgia	93.0
25	New York	93.0
25	Pennsylvania	93.0
28	Washington	92.9
28	Wyoming	92.9
30	Colorado	92.7
31	Nebraska	92.6
31	Virginia	92.6
33	Hawaii	92.4
34	Maine	92.3
34	North Dakota	92.3
36	Indiana	92.1
37	Missouri	92.0
38	Kentucky	91.9
38	New Hampshire	91.9
38	Utah	91.9
41	Michigan	91.3
42	Illinois	90.3
43	New Mexico	90.0
44	Ohio	88.7
45	Oregon	87.8
46	Arkansas	87.7
47	Kansas	87.1
48	Montana	86.9
49	Alaska	86.7
50	Vermont	84.1

District of Columbia	90.4

Source: National Education Association, Washington, D.C.
"Rankings & Estimates" (Copyright © 2007, NEA, used with permission, http://www.nea.org/edstats/index.html)
*Estimates for school year 2005-2006.

Students in Average Daily Attendance per Teacher in Public Elementary and Secondary Schools in 2006
National Average = 14.6 Students*

ALPHA ORDER			RANK ORDER		
RANK	STATE	STUDENTS	RANK	STATE	STUDENTS
21	Alabama	14.3	1	Arizona	21.0
18	Alaska	14.5	2	California	20.2
1	Arizona	21.0	3	Utah	19.6
44	Arkansas	11.9	4	Nevada	17.9
2	California	20.2	4	Washington	17.9
8	Colorado	15.8	6	Oregon	17.4
33	Connecticut	12.9	7	Idaho	17.0
15	Delaware	14.7	8	Colorado	15.8
11	Florida	15.3	8	Indiana	15.8
26	Georgia	13.8	10	Michigan	15.4
13	Hawaii	14.8	11	Florida	15.3
7	Idaho	17.0	12	Minnesota	15.2
20	Illinois	14.4	13	Hawaii	14.8
8	Indiana	15.8	13	Mississippi	14.8
33	Iowa	12.9	15	Delaware	14.7
36	Kansas	12.6	15	Louisiana	14.7
17	Kentucky	14.6	17	Kentucky	14.6
15	Louisiana	14.7	18	Alaska	14.5
47	Maine	11.5	18	Tennessee	14.5
23	Maryland	13.9	20	Illinois	14.4
39	Massachusetts	12.4	21	Alabama	14.3
10	Michigan	15.4	22	Oklahoma	14.2
12	Minnesota	15.2	23	Maryland	13.9
13	Mississippi	14.8	23	Pennsylvania	13.9
38	Missouri	12.5	23	Texas	13.9
41	Montana	12.2	26	Georgia	13.8
36	Nebraska	12.6	26	Ohio	13.8
4	Nevada	17.9	26	West Virginia	13.8
41	New Hampshire	12.2	29	North Carolina	13.7
41	New Jersey	12.2	29	South Carolina	13.7
32	New Mexico	13.4	29	Wisconsin	13.7
48	New York	11.4	32	New Mexico	13.4
29	North Carolina	13.7	33	Connecticut	12.9
45	North Dakota	11.8	33	Iowa	12.9
26	Ohio	13.8	35	South Dakota	12.8
22	Oklahoma	14.2	36	Kansas	12.6
6	Oregon	17.4	36	Nebraska	12.6
23	Pennsylvania	13.9	38	Missouri	12.5
49	Rhode Island	10.5	39	Massachusetts	12.4
29	South Carolina	13.7	40	Virginia	12.3
35	South Dakota	12.8	41	Montana	12.2
18	Tennessee	14.5	41	New Hampshire	12.2
23	Texas	13.9	41	New Jersey	12.2
3	Utah	19.6	44	Arkansas	11.9
50	Vermont	8.8	45	North Dakota	11.8
40	Virginia	12.3	46	Wyoming	11.7
4	Washington	17.9	47	Maine	11.5
26	West Virginia	13.8	48	New York	11.4
29	Wisconsin	13.7	49	Rhode Island	10.5
46	Wyoming	11.7	50	Vermont	8.8

District of Columbia   11.2

Source: National Education Association, Washington, D.C.
"Rankings & Estimates" (Copyright © 2007, NEA, used with permission, http://www.nea.org/edstats/index.html)
*For school year 2005-2006.

Students Attending Regular Public Elementary and Secondary Schools in 2006

National Total = 47,957,375 Students*

ALPHA ORDER

RANK	STATE	STUDENTS	% of USA
23	Alabama	738,986	1.5%
46	Alaska	120,646	0.3%
14	Arizona	1,018,457	2.1%
33	Arkansas	473,256	1.0%
1	California	6,124,988	12.8%
22	Colorado	766,018	1.6%
28	Connecticut	558,749	1.2%
47	Delaware	112,253	0.2%
4	Florida	2,614,228	5.5%
9	Georgia	1,591,307	3.3%
42	Hawaii	184,598	0.4%
39	Idaho	257,032	0.5%
5	Illinois	2,076,435	4.3%
13	Indiana	1,030,592	2.1%
32	Iowa	476,177	1.0%
34	Kansas	466,266	1.0%
27	Kentucky	634,264	1.3%
25	Louisiana	639,218	1.3%
41	Maine	195,420	0.4%
20	Maryland	834,319	1.7%
17	Massachusetts	936,126	2.0%
8	Michigan	1,660,823	3.5%
21	Minnesota	808,648	1.7%
31	Mississippi	494,954	1.0%
18	Missouri	911,879	1.9%
44	Montana	145,259	0.3%
37	Nebraska	284,833	0.6%
35	Nevada	407,601	0.8%
40	New Hampshire	205,767	0.4%
11	New Jersey	1,363,174	2.8%
36	New Mexico	320,200	0.7%
3	New York	2,739,709	5.7%
10	North Carolina	1,408,664	2.9%
48	North Dakota	98,284	0.2%
6	Ohio	1,834,479	3.8%
26	Oklahoma	634,739	1.3%
29	Oregon	531,481	1.1%
7	Pennsylvania	1,794,967	3.7%
43	Rhode Island	147,610	0.3%
24	South Carolina	695,826	1.5%
45	South Dakota	120,971	0.3%
16	Tennessee	947,277	2.0%
2	Texas	4,451,130	9.3%
30	Utah	497,873	1.0%
49	Vermont	94,645	0.2%
12	Virginia	1,210,963	2.5%
15	Washington	991,469	2.1%
38	West Virginia	279,434	0.6%
19	Wisconsin	870,745	1.8%
50	Wyoming	83,029	0.2%

RANK ORDER

RANK	STATE	STUDENTS	% of USA
1	California	6,124,988	12.8%
2	Texas	4,451,130	9.3%
3	New York	2,739,709	5.7%
4	Florida	2,614,228	5.5%
5	Illinois	2,076,435	4.3%
6	Ohio	1,834,479	3.8%
7	Pennsylvania	1,794,967	3.7%
8	Michigan	1,660,823	3.5%
9	Georgia	1,591,307	3.3%
10	North Carolina	1,408,664	2.9%
11	New Jersey	1,363,174	2.8%
12	Virginia	1,210,963	2.5%
13	Indiana	1,030,592	2.1%
14	Arizona	1,018,457	2.1%
15	Washington	991,469	2.1%
16	Tennessee	947,277	2.0%
17	Massachusetts	936,126	2.0%
18	Missouri	911,879	1.9%
19	Wisconsin	870,745	1.8%
20	Maryland	834,319	1.7%
21	Minnesota	808,648	1.7%
22	Colorado	766,018	1.6%
23	Alabama	738,986	1.5%
24	South Carolina	695,826	1.5%
25	Louisiana	639,218	1.3%
26	Oklahoma	634,739	1.3%
27	Kentucky	634,264	1.3%
28	Connecticut	558,749	1.2%
29	Oregon	531,481	1.1%
30	Utah	497,873	1.0%
31	Mississippi	494,954	1.0%
32	Iowa	476,177	1.0%
33	Arkansas	473,256	1.0%
34	Kansas	466,266	1.0%
35	Nevada	407,601	0.8%
36	New Mexico	320,200	0.7%
37	Nebraska	284,833	0.6%
38	West Virginia	279,434	0.6%
39	Idaho	257,032	0.5%
40	New Hampshire	205,767	0.4%
41	Maine	195,420	0.4%
42	Hawaii	184,598	0.4%
43	Rhode Island	147,610	0.3%
44	Montana	145,259	0.3%
45	South Dakota	120,971	0.3%
46	Alaska	120,646	0.3%
47	Delaware	112,253	0.2%
48	North Dakota	98,284	0.2%
49	Vermont	94,645	0.2%
50	Wyoming	83,029	0.2%
	District of Columbia	71,607	0.1%

Source: U.S. Department of Education, National Center for Education Statistics
"Numbers and Types of Public Elementary and Secondary Schools"
(http://nces.ed.gov/pubs2007/2007354rev.pdf)
*For school year 2005-2006. Does not include special education, vocational education, or alternative education schools.
However, many regular schools include these programs.

Percent of Students Attending Regular
Public Elementary and Secondary Schools in 2006
National Percent = 98.0%*

ALPHA ORDER

RANK	STATE	PERCENT
11	Alabama	99.7
50	Alaska	90.5
48	Arizona	93.1
9	Arkansas	99.8
41	California	97.0
30	Colorado	98.2
40	Connecticut	97.2
49	Delaware	92.8
36	Florida	97.7
13	Georgia	99.6
9	Hawaii	99.8
30	Idaho	98.2
29	Illinois	98.3
13	Indiana	99.6
24	Iowa	99.0
1	Kansas	100.0
25	Kentucky	98.8
36	Louisiana	97.7
1	Maine	100.0
41	Maryland	97.0
46	Massachusetts	96.3
41	Michigan	97.0
45	Minnesota	96.4
1	Mississippi	100.0
13	Missouri	99.6
7	Montana	99.9
19	Nebraska	99.4
25	Nevada	98.8
1	New Hampshire	100.0
36	New Jersey	97.7
33	New Mexico	98.0
44	New York	96.5
16	North Carolina	99.5
1	North Dakota	100.0
7	Ohio	99.9
1	Oklahoma	100.0
19	Oregon	99.4
30	Pennsylvania	98.2
39	Rhode Island	97.3
22	South Carolina	99.2
22	South Dakota	99.2
21	Tennessee	99.3
27	Texas	98.4
34	Utah	97.9
34	Vermont	97.9
11	Virginia	99.7
47	Washington	96.1
16	West Virginia	99.5
16	Wisconsin	99.5
27	Wyoming	98.4

RANK ORDER

RANK	STATE	PERCENT
1	Kansas	100.0
1	Maine	100.0
1	Mississippi	100.0
1	New Hampshire	100.0
1	North Dakota	100.0
1	Oklahoma	100.0
7	Montana	99.9
7	Ohio	99.9
9	Arkansas	99.8
9	Hawaii	99.8
11	Alabama	99.7
11	Virginia	99.7
13	Georgia	99.6
13	Indiana	99.6
13	Missouri	99.6
16	North Carolina	99.5
16	West Virginia	99.5
16	Wisconsin	99.5
19	Nebraska	99.4
19	Oregon	99.4
21	Tennessee	99.3
22	South Carolina	99.2
22	South Dakota	99.2
24	Iowa	99.0
25	Kentucky	98.8
25	Nevada	98.8
27	Texas	98.4
27	Wyoming	98.4
29	Illinois	98.3
30	Colorado	98.2
30	Idaho	98.2
30	Pennsylvania	98.2
33	New Mexico	98.0
34	Utah	97.9
34	Vermont	97.9
36	Florida	97.7
36	Louisiana	97.7
36	New Jersey	97.7
39	Rhode Island	97.3
40	Connecticut	97.2
41	California	97.0
41	Maryland	97.0
41	Michigan	97.0
44	New York	96.5
45	Minnesota	96.4
46	Massachusetts	96.3
47	Washington	96.1
48	Arizona	93.1
49	Delaware	92.8
50	Alaska	90.5

District of Columbia   93.1

Source: CQ Press using data from U.S. Department of Education, National Center for Education Statistics
"Numbers and Types of Public Elementary and Secondary Schools"
(http://nces.ed.gov/pubs2007/2007354rev.pdf)
*For school year 2005-2006. Does not include special education, vocational education, or alternative education schools.
However, many regular schools include these programs.

Students Attending Public Elementary and Secondary
Title I Eligible Schools in 2006
National Total = 25,586,061 Students*

ALPHA ORDER

RANK	STATE	STUDENTS	% of USA
19	Alabama	411,887	1.6%
48	Alaska	45,104	0.2%
10	Arizona	564,669	2.2%
27	Arkansas	318,023	1.2%
1	California	3,661,772	14.3%
23	Colorado	359,238	1.4%
29	Connecticut	241,176	0.9%
47	Delaware	53,995	0.2%
8	Florida	934,059	3.7%
9	Georgia	734,274	2.9%
36	Hawaii	121,882	0.5%
33	Idaho	177,849	0.7%
6	Illinois	1,148,106	4.5%
7	Indiana	994,087	3.9%
32	Iowa	179,815	0.7%
31	Kansas	183,723	0.7%
21	Kentucky	388,732	1.5%
22	Louisiana	377,562	1.5%
35	Maine	124,688	0.5%
34	Maryland	172,726	0.7%
15	Massachusetts	493,684	1.9%
16	Michigan	449,481	1.8%
26	Minnesota	322,201	1.3%
25	Mississippi	324,597	1.3%
20	Missouri	391,169	1.5%
37	Montana	115,269	0.5%
40	Nebraska	98,949	0.4%
42	Nevada	67,861	0.3%
41	New Hampshire	78,092	0.3%
NA	New Jersey**	NA	NA
30	New Mexico	193,336	0.8%
3	New York	1,801,257	7.0%
13	North Carolina	528,164	2.1%
45	North Dakota	54,266	0.2%
4	Ohio	1,172,522	4.6%
18	Oklahoma	417,446	1.6%
11	Oregon	534,507	2.1%
5	Pennsylvania	1,158,285	4.5%
43	Rhode Island	59,620	0.2%
28	South Carolina	258,922	1.0%
44	South Dakota	54,970	0.2%
17	Tennessee	432,259	1.7%
2	Texas	2,927,787	11.4%
39	Utah	99,808	0.4%
46	Vermont	54,139	0.2%
24	Virginia	332,628	1.3%
12	Washington	532,727	2.1%
38	West Virginia	102,878	0.4%
14	Wisconsin	509,676	2.0%
49	Wyoming	40,389	0.2%

RANK ORDER

RANK	STATE	STUDENTS	% of USA
1	California	3,661,772	14.3%
2	Texas	2,927,787	11.4%
3	New York	1,801,257	7.0%
4	Ohio	1,172,522	4.6%
5	Pennsylvania	1,158,285	4.5%
6	Illinois	1,148,106	4.5%
7	Indiana	994,087	3.9%
8	Florida	934,059	3.7%
9	Georgia	734,274	2.9%
10	Arizona	564,669	2.2%
11	Oregon	534,507	2.1%
12	Washington	532,727	2.1%
13	North Carolina	528,164	2.1%
14	Wisconsin	509,676	2.0%
15	Massachusetts	493,684	1.9%
16	Michigan	449,481	1.8%
17	Tennessee	432,259	1.7%
18	Oklahoma	417,446	1.6%
19	Alabama	411,887	1.6%
20	Missouri	391,169	1.5%
21	Kentucky	388,732	1.5%
22	Louisiana	377,562	1.5%
23	Colorado	359,238	1.4%
24	Virginia	332,628	1.3%
25	Mississippi	324,597	1.3%
26	Minnesota	322,201	1.3%
27	Arkansas	318,023	1.2%
28	South Carolina	258,922	1.0%
29	Connecticut	241,176	0.9%
30	New Mexico	193,336	0.8%
31	Kansas	183,723	0.7%
32	Iowa	179,815	0.7%
33	Idaho	177,849	0.7%
34	Maryland	172,726	0.7%
35	Maine	124,688	0.5%
36	Hawaii	121,882	0.5%
37	Montana	115,269	0.5%
38	West Virginia	102,878	0.4%
39	Utah	99,808	0.4%
40	Nebraska	98,949	0.4%
41	New Hampshire	78,092	0.3%
42	Nevada	67,861	0.3%
43	Rhode Island	59,620	0.2%
44	South Dakota	54,970	0.2%
45	North Dakota	54,266	0.2%
46	Vermont	54,139	0.2%
47	Delaware	53,995	0.2%
48	Alaska	45,104	0.2%
49	Wyoming	40,389	0.2%
NA	New Jersey**	NA	NA
	District of Columbia	65,688	0.3%

Source: U.S. Department of Education, National Center for Education Statistics
"Numbers and Types of Public Elementary and Secondary Schools"
(http://nces.ed.gov/pubs2007/2007354rev.pdf)
*Estimate for school year 2005-2006. National total is only for reporting states. Title I schools are eligible for Title I federal funding to assist disadvantaged students. Includes schools with and without school-wide Title I programs.
**Not available.

Percent of Students Attending Public Elementary and Secondary Title I Eligible Schools in 2006
National Percent = 52.3%*

ALPHA ORDER

RANK	STATE	PERCENT
20	Alabama	55.5
44	Alaska	33.8
23	Arizona	51.6
5	Arkansas	67.1
17	California	58.0
27	Colorado	46.1
33	Connecticut	41.9
31	Delaware	44.6
42	Florida	34.9
28	Georgia	45.9
6	Hawaii	65.9
4	Idaho	67.9
22	Illinois	54.4
2	Indiana	96.1
38	Iowa	37.4
34	Kansas	39.4
14	Kentucky	60.6
18	Louisiana	57.7
10	Maine	63.8
47	Maryland	20.1
25	Massachusetts	50.8
46	Michigan	26.3
36	Minnesota	38.4
8	Mississippi	65.6
32	Missouri	42.7
3	Montana	79.3
43	Nebraska	34.5
49	Nevada	16.5
37	New Hampshire	38.0
NA	New Jersey**	NA
15	New Mexico	59.2
12	New York	63.5
39	North Carolina	37.3
21	North Dakota	55.2
10	Ohio	63.8
7	Oklahoma	65.8
1	Oregon	99.9
13	Pennsylvania	63.4
35	Rhode Island	39.3
40	South Carolina	36.9
30	South Dakota	45.1
29	Tennessee	45.3
9	Texas	64.7
48	Utah	19.6
19	Vermont	56.0
45	Virginia	27.4
23	Washington	51.6
41	West Virginia	36.7
16	Wisconsin	58.2
26	Wyoming	47.8

RANK ORDER

RANK	STATE	PERCENT
1	Oregon	99.9
2	Indiana	96.1
3	Montana	79.3
4	Idaho	67.9
5	Arkansas	67.1
6	Hawaii	65.9
7	Oklahoma	65.8
8	Mississippi	65.6
9	Texas	64.7
10	Maine	63.8
10	Ohio	63.8
12	New York	63.5
13	Pennsylvania	63.4
14	Kentucky	60.6
15	New Mexico	59.2
16	Wisconsin	58.2
17	California	58.0
18	Louisiana	57.7
19	Vermont	56.0
20	Alabama	55.5
21	North Dakota	55.2
22	Illinois	54.4
23	Arizona	51.6
23	Washington	51.6
25	Massachusetts	50.8
26	Wyoming	47.8
27	Colorado	46.1
28	Georgia	45.9
29	Tennessee	45.3
30	South Dakota	45.1
31	Delaware	44.6
32	Missouri	42.7
33	Connecticut	41.9
34	Kansas	39.4
35	Rhode Island	39.3
36	Minnesota	38.4
37	New Hampshire	38.0
38	Iowa	37.4
39	North Carolina	37.3
40	South Carolina	36.9
41	West Virginia	36.7
42	Florida	34.9
43	Nebraska	34.5
44	Alaska	33.8
45	Virginia	27.4
46	Michigan	26.3
47	Maryland	20.1
48	Utah	19.6
49	Nevada	16.5
NA	New Jersey**	NA
	District of Columbia	85.4

Source: CQ Press using data from U.S. Department of Education, National Center for Education Statistics
"Numbers and Types of Public Elementary and Secondary Schools"
(http://nces.ed.gov/pubs2007/2007354rev.pdf)
*Estimate for school year 2005-2006. National percent is only for reporting states. Title I schools are eligible for Title I federal funding to assist disadvantaged students. Includes schools with and without school-wide Title I programs.
**Not available.

Students Attending Title I School-Wide
Public Elementary and Secondary Schools in 2006
National Total = 15,296,618 Students*

ALPHA ORDER

RANK	STATE	STUDENTS	% of USA
14	Alabama	334,601	2.2%
44	Alaska	23,318	0.2%
11	Arizona	359,276	2.3%
20	Arkansas	217,423	1.4%
2	California	2,394,321	15.7%
26	Colorado	140,594	0.9%
34	Connecticut	71,350	0.5%
39	Delaware	36,025	0.2%
3	Florida	913,380	6.0%
5	Georgia	598,716	3.9%
29	Hawaii	99,110	0.6%
40	Idaho	31,843	0.2%
6	Illinois	523,696	3.4%
35	Indiana	70,747	0.5%
38	Iowa	41,512	0.3%
30	Kansas	91,578	0.6%
12	Kentucky	339,015	2.2%
15	Louisiana	333,719	2.2%
49	Maine	8,737	0.1%
24	Maryland	144,846	0.9%
22	Massachusetts	213,540	1.4%
7	Michigan	449,481	2.9%
31	Minnesota	82,670	0.5%
17	Mississippi	305,072	2.0%
25	Missouri	144,598	0.9%
42	Montana	28,749	0.2%
37	Nebraska	50,436	0.3%
36	Nevada	67,861	0.4%
47	New Hampshire	11,603	0.1%
NA	New Jersey**	NA	NA
23	New Mexico	154,642	1.0%
4	New York	900,421	5.9%
8	North Carolina	421,259	2.8%
48	North Dakota	11,202	0.1%
9	Ohio	397,369	2.6%
18	Oklahoma	292,681	1.9%
28	Oregon	115,146	0.8%
13	Pennsylvania	337,377	2.2%
41	Rhode Island	29,322	0.2%
19	South Carolina	241,020	1.6%
45	South Dakota	21,410	0.1%
10	Tennessee	368,029	2.4%
1	Texas	2,733,703	17.9%
32	Utah	79,085	0.5%
43	Vermont	25,401	0.2%
16	Virginia	332,628	2.2%
21	Washington	217,110	1.4%
33	West Virginia	73,527	0.5%
27	Wisconsin	136,536	0.9%
46	Wyoming	14,532	0.1%

RANK ORDER

RANK	STATE	STUDENTS	% of USA
1	Texas	2,733,703	17.9%
2	California	2,394,321	15.7%
3	Florida	913,380	6.0%
4	New York	900,421	5.9%
5	Georgia	598,716	3.9%
6	Illinois	523,696	3.4%
7	Michigan	449,481	2.9%
8	North Carolina	421,259	2.8%
9	Ohio	397,369	2.6%
10	Tennessee	368,029	2.4%
11	Arizona	359,276	2.3%
12	Kentucky	339,015	2.2%
13	Pennsylvania	337,377	2.2%
14	Alabama	334,601	2.2%
15	Louisiana	333,719	2.2%
16	Virginia	332,628	2.2%
17	Mississippi	305,072	2.0%
18	Oklahoma	292,681	1.9%
19	South Carolina	241,020	1.6%
20	Arkansas	217,423	1.4%
21	Washington	217,110	1.4%
22	Massachusetts	213,540	1.4%
23	New Mexico	154,642	1.0%
24	Maryland	144,846	0.9%
25	Missouri	144,598	0.9%
26	Colorado	140,594	0.9%
27	Wisconsin	136,536	0.9%
28	Oregon	115,146	0.8%
29	Hawaii	99,110	0.6%
30	Kansas	91,578	0.6%
31	Minnesota	82,670	0.5%
32	Utah	79,085	0.5%
33	West Virginia	73,527	0.5%
34	Connecticut	71,350	0.5%
35	Indiana	70,747	0.5%
36	Nevada	67,861	0.4%
37	Nebraska	50,436	0.3%
38	Iowa	41,512	0.3%
39	Delaware	36,025	0.2%
40	Idaho	31,843	0.2%
41	Rhode Island	29,322	0.2%
42	Montana	28,749	0.2%
43	Vermont	25,401	0.2%
44	Alaska	23,318	0.2%
45	South Dakota	21,410	0.1%
46	Wyoming	14,532	0.1%
47	New Hampshire	11,603	0.1%
48	North Dakota	11,202	0.1%
49	Maine	8,737	0.1%
NA	New Jersey**	NA	NA
	District of Columbia	62,498	0.4%

Source: U.S. Department of Education, National Center for Education Statistics
"Numbers and Types of Public Elementary and Secondary Schools"
(http://nces.ed.gov/pubs2007/2007354rev.pdf)

*Estimate for school year 2005-2006. National total is only for reporting states. Title I school-wide schools are those in which all of the pupils enrolled are eligible for Title I federal funding, which assists disadvantaged students.
**Not available.

Percent of Students Attending Title I School-Wide
Public Elementary and Secondary Schools in 2006
National Percent = 31.3%*

ALPHA ORDER

RANK	STATE	PERCENT
9	Alabama	45.1
34	Alaska	17.5
15	Arizona	32.8
8	Arkansas	45.8
11	California	37.9
32	Colorado	18.0
42	Connecticut	12.4
17	Delaware	29.8
14	Florida	34.1
12	Georgia	37.5
3	Hawaii	53.6
43	Idaho	12.2
23	Illinois	24.8
47	Indiana	6.8
46	Iowa	8.6
29	Kansas	19.6
4	Kentucky	52.8
5	Louisiana	51.0
49	Maine	4.5
37	Maryland	16.8
24	Massachusetts	22.0
20	Michigan	26.3
45	Minnesota	9.9
1	Mississippi	61.6
39	Missouri	15.8
28	Montana	19.8
33	Nebraska	17.6
38	Nevada	16.5
48	New Hampshire	5.6
NA	New Jersey**	NA
6	New Mexico	47.3
16	New York	31.7
18	North Carolina	29.7
44	North Dakota	11.4
25	Ohio	21.6
7	Oklahoma	46.1
26	Oregon	21.5
31	Pennsylvania	18.5
30	Rhode Island	19.3
13	South Carolina	34.4
34	South Dakota	17.5
10	Tennessee	38.6
2	Texas	60.4
40	Utah	15.6
20	Vermont	26.3
19	Virginia	27.4
27	Washington	21.0
22	West Virginia	26.2
40	Wisconsin	15.6
36	Wyoming	17.2

RANK ORDER

RANK	STATE	PERCENT
1	Mississippi	61.6
2	Texas	60.4
3	Hawaii	53.6
4	Kentucky	52.8
5	Louisiana	51.0
6	New Mexico	47.3
7	Oklahoma	46.1
8	Arkansas	45.8
9	Alabama	45.1
10	Tennessee	38.6
11	California	37.9
12	Georgia	37.5
13	South Carolina	34.4
14	Florida	34.1
15	Arizona	32.8
16	New York	31.7
17	Delaware	29.8
18	North Carolina	29.7
19	Virginia	27.4
20	Michigan	26.3
20	Vermont	26.3
22	West Virginia	26.2
23	Illinois	24.8
24	Massachusetts	22.0
25	Ohio	21.6
26	Oregon	21.5
27	Washington	21.0
28	Montana	19.8
29	Kansas	19.6
30	Rhode Island	19.3
31	Pennsylvania	18.5
32	Colorado	18.0
33	Nebraska	17.6
34	Alaska	17.5
34	South Dakota	17.5
36	Wyoming	17.2
37	Maryland	16.8
38	Nevada	16.5
39	Missouri	15.8
40	Utah	15.6
40	Wisconsin	15.6
42	Connecticut	12.4
43	Idaho	12.2
44	North Dakota	11.4
45	Minnesota	9.9
46	Iowa	8.6
47	Indiana	6.8
48	New Hampshire	5.6
49	Maine	4.5
NA	New Jersey**	NA

District of Columbia	81.3

Source: CQ Press using data from U.S. Department of Education, National Center for Education Statistics
"Numbers and Types of Public Elementary and Secondary Schools"
(http://nces.ed.gov/pubs2007/2007354rev.pdf)

*Estimate for school year 2005-2006. National percent is only for reporting states. Title I school-wide schools are those in which all of the pupils enrolled are eligible for Title I federal funding, which assists disadvantaged students.
**Not available.

Public Elementary and Secondary School Students
Eligible for Free or Reduced-Price Meals in 2006
Reporting States Total = 20,335,672 Students*

ALPHA ORDER

RANK	STATE	STUDENTS	% of USA
14	Alabama	383,219	1.9%
45	Alaska	41,872	0.2%
11	Arizona	492,450	2.4%
29	Arkansas	250,641	1.2%
1	California	3,063,776	15.1%
26	Colorado	258,264	1.3%
36	Connecticut	152,669	0.8%
44	Delaware	43,682	0.2%
4	Florida	1,224,228	6.0%
5	Georgia	795,394	3.9%
40	Hawaii	74,926	0.4%
39	Idaho	99,093	0.5%
6	Illinois	785,715	3.9%
18	Indiana	373,433	1.8%
35	Iowa	154,416	0.8%
32	Kansas	180,919	0.9%
23	Kentucky	336,287	1.7%
13	Louisiana	400,596	2.0%
41	Maine	65,993	0.3%
25	Maryland	272,069	1.3%
24	Massachusetts	274,515	1.3%
7	Michigan	609,951	3.0%
28	Minnesota	253,938	1.2%
22	Mississippi	344,107	1.7%
20	Missouri	358,428	1.8%
43	Montana	50,172	0.2%
38	Nebraska	99,387	0.5%
33	Nevada	170,437	0.8%
47	New Hampshire	35,087	0.2%
17	New Jersey	373,946	1.8%
31	New Mexico	181,916	0.9%
3	New York	1,260,933	6.2%
8	North Carolina	603,316	3.0%
48	North Dakota	29,064	0.1%
9	Ohio	597,517	2.9%
21	Oklahoma	346,070	1.7%
30	Oregon	230,884	1.1%
10	Pennsylvania	574,951	2.8%
42	Rhode Island	53,521	0.3%
19	South Carolina	361,567	1.8%
46	South Dakota	39,059	0.2%
12	Tennessee	449,622	2.2%
2	Texas	2,181,697	10.7%
34	Utah	164,255	0.8%
50	Vermont	25,487	0.1%
15	Virginia	377,725	1.9%
16	Washington	376,198	1.8%
37	West Virginia	137,878	0.7%
27	Wisconsin	256,645	1.3%
49	Wyoming	26,707	0.1%

RANK ORDER

RANK	STATE	STUDENTS	% of USA
1	California	3,063,776	15.1%
2	Texas	2,181,697	10.7%
3	New York	1,260,933	6.2%
4	Florida	1,224,228	6.0%
5	Georgia	795,394	3.9%
6	Illinois	785,715	3.9%
7	Michigan	609,951	3.0%
8	North Carolina	603,316	3.0%
9	Ohio	597,517	2.9%
10	Pennsylvania	574,951	2.8%
11	Arizona	492,450	2.4%
12	Tennessee	449,622	2.2%
13	Louisiana	400,596	2.0%
14	Alabama	383,219	1.9%
15	Virginia	377,725	1.9%
16	Washington	376,198	1.8%
17	New Jersey	373,946	1.8%
18	Indiana	373,433	1.8%
19	South Carolina	361,567	1.8%
20	Missouri	358,428	1.8%
21	Oklahoma	346,070	1.7%
22	Mississippi	344,107	1.7%
23	Kentucky	336,287	1.7%
24	Massachusetts	274,515	1.3%
25	Maryland	272,069	1.3%
26	Colorado	258,264	1.3%
27	Wisconsin	256,645	1.3%
28	Minnesota	253,938	1.2%
29	Arkansas	250,641	1.2%
30	Oregon	230,884	1.1%
31	New Mexico	181,916	0.9%
32	Kansas	180,919	0.9%
33	Nevada	170,437	0.8%
34	Utah	164,255	0.8%
35	Iowa	154,416	0.8%
36	Connecticut	152,669	0.8%
37	West Virginia	137,878	0.7%
38	Nebraska	99,387	0.5%
39	Idaho	99,093	0.5%
40	Hawaii	74,926	0.4%
41	Maine	65,993	0.3%
42	Rhode Island	53,521	0.3%
43	Montana	50,172	0.2%
44	Delaware	43,682	0.2%
45	Alaska	41,872	0.2%
46	South Dakota	39,059	0.2%
47	New Hampshire	35,087	0.2%
48	North Dakota	29,064	0.1%
49	Wyoming	26,707	0.1%
50	Vermont	25,487	0.1%
	District of Columbia	41,050	0.2%

Source: U.S. Department of Education, National Center for Education Statistics
"Common Core of Data (CCD) Database" (http://nces.ed.gov/ccd/)
*For school year 2005-2006.

Percent of Public Elementary and Secondary School Students Eligible for Free or Reduced-Price Meals in 2006
Reporting States Percent = 41.6%*

ALPHA ORDER				RANK ORDER		
RANK	STATE	PERCENT		RANK	STATE	PERCENT
7	Alabama	51.7		1	Mississippi	69.5
40	Alaska	31.4		2	Louisiana	61.2
15	Arizona	45.0		3	New Mexico	55.7
5	Arkansas	52.9		4	Oklahoma	54.5
11	California	48.5		5	Arkansas	52.9
33	Colorado	33.1		6	Kentucky	52.4
48	Connecticut	26.5		7	Alabama	51.7
26	Delaware	36.1		8	South Carolina	51.5
14	Florida	45.8		9	Georgia	49.8
9	Georgia	49.8		10	West Virginia	49.1
20	Hawaii	40.5		11	California	48.5
23	Idaho	37.8		12	Texas	48.2
24	Illinois	37.2		13	Tennessee	47.1
26	Indiana	36.1		14	Florida	45.8
36	Iowa	32.1		15	Arizona	45.0
22	Kansas	38.8		16	New York	44.4
6	Kentucky	52.4		17	Oregon	43.2
2	Louisiana	61.2		18	North Carolina	42.6
32	Maine	33.8		19	Nevada	41.3
38	Maryland	31.6		20	Hawaii	40.5
46	Massachusetts	28.2		21	Missouri	39.1
28	Michigan	35.6		22	Kansas	38.8
43	Minnesota	30.3		23	Idaho	37.8
1	Mississippi	69.5		24	Illinois	37.2
21	Missouri	39.1		25	Washington	36.5
31	Montana	34.5		26	Delaware	36.1
30	Nebraska	34.7		26	Indiana	36.1
19	Nevada	41.3		28	Michigan	35.6
50	New Hampshire	17.1		29	Rhode Island	35.3
47	New Jersey	26.8		30	Nebraska	34.7
3	New Mexico	55.7		31	Montana	34.5
16	New York	44.4		32	Maine	33.8
18	North Carolina	42.6		33	Colorado	33.1
44	North Dakota	29.6		34	Ohio	32.5
34	Ohio	32.5		35	Utah	32.3
4	Oklahoma	54.5		36	Iowa	32.1
17	Oregon	43.2		37	South Dakota	32.0
40	Pennsylvania	31.4		38	Maryland	31.6
29	Rhode Island	35.3		38	Wyoming	31.6
8	South Carolina	51.5		40	Alaska	31.4
37	South Dakota	32.0		40	Pennsylvania	31.4
13	Tennessee	47.1		42	Virginia	31.1
12	Texas	48.2		43	Minnesota	30.3
35	Utah	32.3		44	North Dakota	29.6
49	Vermont	26.4		45	Wisconsin	29.3
42	Virginia	31.1		46	Massachusetts	28.2
25	Washington	36.5		47	New Jersey	26.8
10	West Virginia	49.1		48	Connecticut	26.5
45	Wisconsin	29.3		49	Vermont	26.4
38	Wyoming	31.6		50	New Hampshire	17.1

District of Columbia	53.4

Source: CQ Press using data from U.S. Department of Education, National Center for Education Statistics
"Common Core of Data (CCD) Database" (http://nces.ed.gov/ccd/)
*For school year 2005-2006.

Students Attending Public Elementary and Secondary Magnet Schools in 2006

National Total = 2,103,013 Students*

ALPHA ORDER

RANK	STATE	STUDENTS	% of USA
14	Alabama	19,043	0.9%
22	Alaska	4,409	0.2%
10	Arizona	33,845	1.6%
20	Arkansas	7,104	0.3%
1	California	626,679	29.8%
23	Colorado	3,384	0.2%
17	Connecticut	15,527	0.7%
26	Delaware	1,188	0.1%
NA	Florida**	NA	NA
7	Georgia	59,176	2.8%
NA	Hawaii**	NA	NA
NA	Idaho**	NA	NA
2	Illinois	243,904	11.6%
18	Indiana	13,178	0.6%
NA	Iowa**	NA	NA
19	Kansas	10,480	0.5%
9	Kentucky	39,067	1.9%
8	Louisiana	39,451	1.9%
29	Maine	105	0.0%
NA	Maryland**	NA	NA
27	Massachusetts	1,175	0.1%
3	Michigan	182,281	8.7%
11	Minnesota	29,707	1.4%
21	Mississippi	4,658	0.2%
13	Missouri	19,206	0.9%
NA	Montana**	NA	NA
NA	Nebraska**	NA	NA
NA	Nevada**	NA	NA
NA	New Hampshire**	NA	NA
NA	New Jersey**	NA	NA
28	New Mexico	134	0.0%
5	New York	112,985	5.4%
6	North Carolina	106,453	5.1%
NA	North Dakota**	NA	NA
NA	Ohio**	NA	NA
NA	Oklahoma**	NA	NA
NA	Oregon**	NA	NA
12	Pennsylvania	26,705	1.3%
NA	Rhode Island**	NA	NA
15	South Carolina	18,864	0.9%
NA	South Dakota**	NA	NA
16	Tennessee	16,592	0.8%
NA	Texas**	NA	NA
24	Utah	2,653	0.1%
NA	Vermont**	NA	NA
4	Virginia	149,182	7.1%
NA	Washington**	NA	NA
NA	West Virginia**	NA	NA
25	Wisconsin	1,829	0.1%
NA	Wyoming**	NA	NA

RANK ORDER

RANK	STATE	STUDENTS	% of USA
1	California	626,679	29.8%
2	Illinois	243,904	11.6%
3	Michigan	182,281	8.7%
4	Virginia	149,182	7.1%
5	New York	112,985	5.4%
6	North Carolina	106,453	5.1%
7	Georgia	59,176	2.8%
8	Louisiana	39,451	1.9%
9	Kentucky	39,067	1.9%
10	Arizona	33,845	1.6%
11	Minnesota	29,707	1.4%
12	Pennsylvania	26,705	1.3%
13	Missouri	19,206	0.9%
14	Alabama	19,043	0.9%
15	South Carolina	18,864	0.9%
16	Tennessee	16,592	0.8%
17	Connecticut	15,527	0.7%
18	Indiana	13,178	0.6%
19	Kansas	10,480	0.5%
20	Arkansas	7,104	0.3%
21	Mississippi	4,658	0.2%
22	Alaska	4,409	0.2%
23	Colorado	3,384	0.2%
24	Utah	2,653	0.1%
25	Wisconsin	1,829	0.1%
26	Delaware	1,188	0.1%
27	Massachusetts	1,175	0.1%
28	New Mexico	134	0.0%
29	Maine	105	0.0%
NA	Florida**	NA	NA
NA	Hawaii**	NA	NA
NA	Idaho**	NA	NA
NA	Iowa**	NA	NA
NA	Maryland**	NA	NA
NA	Montana**	NA	NA
NA	Nebraska**	NA	NA
NA	Nevada**	NA	NA
NA	New Hampshire**	NA	NA
NA	New Jersey**	NA	NA
NA	North Dakota**	NA	NA
NA	Ohio**	NA	NA
NA	Oklahoma**	NA	NA
NA	Oregon**	NA	NA
NA	Rhode Island**	NA	NA
NA	South Dakota**	NA	NA
NA	Texas**	NA	NA
NA	Vermont**	NA	NA
NA	Washington**	NA	NA
NA	West Virginia**	NA	NA
NA	Wyoming**	NA	NA
	District of Columbia	1,149	0.1%

Source: U.S. Department of Education, National Center for Education Statistics
    "Numbers and Types of Public Elementary and Secondary Schools" (http://nces.ed.gov/pubs2007/2007354rev.pdf)
*For school year 2005-2006.
**Either no magnet schools designated or not available.

Percent of Students Attending Public Elementary and Secondary Magnet Schools in 2006
Reporting States Percent = 4.3%*

ALPHA ORDER				RANK ORDER		
RANK	STATE	PERCENT		RANK	STATE	PERCENT
15	Alabama	2.6		1	Virginia	12.3
11	Alaska	3.3		2	Illinois	11.6
12	Arizona	3.1		3	Michigan	10.7
19	Arkansas	1.5		4	California	9.9
4	California	9.9		5	North Carolina	7.5
25	Colorado	0.4		6	Kentucky	6.1
13	Connecticut	2.7		7	Louisiana	6.0
22	Delaware	1.0		8	New York	4.0
NA	Florida**	NA		9	Georgia	3.7
9	Georgia	3.7		10	Minnesota	3.5
NA	Hawaii**	NA		11	Alaska	3.3
NA	Idaho**	NA		12	Arizona	3.1
2	Illinois	11.6		13	Connecticut	2.7
21	Indiana	1.3		13	South Carolina	2.7
NA	Iowa**	NA		15	Alabama	2.6
16	Kansas	2.2		16	Kansas	2.2
6	Kentucky	6.1		17	Missouri	2.1
7	Louisiana	6.0		18	Tennessee	1.7
27	Maine	0.1		19	Arkansas	1.5
NA	Maryland**	NA		19	Pennsylvania	1.5
27	Massachusetts	0.1		21	Indiana	1.3
3	Michigan	10.7		22	Delaware	1.0
10	Minnesota	3.5		23	Mississippi	0.9
23	Mississippi	0.9		24	Utah	0.5
17	Missouri	2.1		25	Colorado	0.4
NA	Montana**	NA		26	Wisconsin	0.2
NA	Nebraska**	NA		27	Maine	0.1
NA	Nevada**	NA		27	Massachusetts	0.1
NA	New Hampshire**	NA		29	New Mexico	0.0
NA	New Jersey**	NA		NA	Florida**	NA
29	New Mexico	0.0		NA	Hawaii**	NA
8	New York	4.0		NA	Idaho**	NA
5	North Carolina	7.5		NA	Iowa**	NA
NA	North Dakota**	NA		NA	Maryland**	NA
NA	Ohio**	NA		NA	Montana**	NA
NA	Oklahoma**	NA		NA	Nebraska**	NA
NA	Oregon**	NA		NA	Nevada**	NA
19	Pennsylvania	1.5		NA	New Hampshire**	NA
NA	Rhode Island**	NA		NA	New Jersey**	NA
13	South Carolina	2.7		NA	North Dakota**	NA
NA	South Dakota**	NA		NA	Ohio**	NA
18	Tennessee	1.7		NA	Oklahoma**	NA
NA	Texas**	NA		NA	Oregon**	NA
24	Utah	0.5		NA	Rhode Island**	NA
NA	Vermont**	NA		NA	South Dakota**	NA
1	Virginia	12.3		NA	Texas**	NA
NA	Washington**	NA		NA	Vermont**	NA
NA	West Virginia**	NA		NA	Washington**	NA
26	Wisconsin	0.2		NA	West Virginia**	NA
NA	Wyoming**	NA		NA	Wyoming**	NA

District of Columbia	1.5

Source: CQ Press using data from U.S. Department of Education, National Center for Education Statistics
   "Numbers and Types of Public Elementary and Secondary Schools" (http://nces.ed.gov/pubs2007/2007354rev.pdf)
*For school year 2005-2006.
**Either no magnet schools designated or not available.

Students Attending Public Elementary and Secondary Charter Schools in 2006

National Total = 1,012,906 Students*

ALPHA ORDER					RANK ORDER			
RANK	STATE	STUDENTS	% of USA		RANK	STATE	STUDENTS	% of USA
NA	Alabama**	NA	NA		1	California	195,876	19.3%
27	Alaska	4,660	0.5%		2	Florida	92,335	9.1%
4	Arizona	90,597	8.9%		3	Michigan	91,384	9.0%
30	Arkansas	4,006	0.4%		4	Arizona	90,597	8.9%
1	California	195,876	19.3%		5	Texas	70,895	7.0%
8	Colorado	44,254	4.4%		6	Ohio	68,679	6.8%
32	Connecticut	2,927	0.3%		7	Pennsylvania	55,630	5.5%
23	Delaware	6,566	0.6%		8	Colorado	44,254	4.4%
2	Florida	92,335	9.1%		9	Wisconsin	27,450	2.7%
11	Georgia	26,440	2.6%		10	North Carolina	27,441	2.7%
24	Hawaii	6,498	0.6%		11	Georgia	26,440	2.6%
21	Idaho	8,003	0.8%		12	Massachusetts	21,958	2.2%
15	Illinois	16,968	1.7%		13	New York	21,539	2.1%
22	Indiana	7,409	0.7%		14	Minnesota	20,603	2.0%
36	Iowa	520	0.1%		15	Illinois	16,968	1.7%
34	Kansas	1,914	0.2%		16	New Jersey	14,937	1.5%
NA	Kentucky**	NA	NA		17	Utah	11,439	1.1%
20	Louisiana	8,315	0.8%		18	Missouri	10,972	1.1%
NA	Maine**	NA	NA		19	New Mexico	8,595	0.8%
31	Maryland	3,363	0.3%		20	Louisiana	8,315	0.8%
12	Massachusetts	21,958	2.2%		21	Idaho	8,003	0.8%
3	Michigan	91,384	9.0%		22	Indiana	7,409	0.7%
14	Minnesota	20,603	2.0%		23	Delaware	6,566	0.6%
37	Mississippi	374	0.0%		24	Hawaii	6,498	0.6%
18	Missouri	10,972	1.1%		25	Oregon	5,192	0.5%
NA	Montana**	NA	NA		26	Nevada	4,818	0.5%
NA	Nebraska**	NA	NA		27	Alaska	4,660	0.5%
26	Nevada	4,818	0.5%		28	South Carolina	4,104	0.4%
40	New Hampshire	200	0.0%		29	Oklahoma	4,081	0.4%
16	New Jersey	14,937	1.5%		30	Arkansas	4,006	0.4%
19	New Mexico	8,595	0.8%		31	Maryland	3,363	0.3%
13	New York	21,539	2.1%		32	Connecticut	2,927	0.3%
10	North Carolina	27,441	2.7%		33	Rhode Island	2,571	0.3%
NA	North Dakota**	NA	NA		34	Kansas	1,914	0.2%
6	Ohio	68,679	6.8%		35	Tennessee	1,685	0.2%
29	Oklahoma	4,081	0.4%		36	Iowa	520	0.1%
25	Oregon	5,192	0.5%		37	Mississippi	374	0.0%
7	Pennsylvania	55,630	5.5%		38	Wyoming	238	0.0%
33	Rhode Island	2,571	0.3%		39	Virginia	210	0.0%
28	South Carolina	4,104	0.4%		40	New Hampshire	200	0.0%
NA	South Dakota**	NA	NA		NA	Alabama**	NA	NA
35	Tennessee	1,685	0.2%		NA	Kentucky**	NA	NA
5	Texas	70,895	7.0%		NA	Maine**	NA	NA
17	Utah	11,439	1.1%		NA	Montana**	NA	NA
NA	Vermont**	NA	NA		NA	Nebraska**	NA	NA
39	Virginia	210	0.0%		NA	North Dakota**	NA	NA
NA	Washington**	NA	NA		NA	South Dakota**	NA	NA
NA	West Virginia**	NA	NA		NA	Vermont**	NA	NA
9	Wisconsin	27,450	2.7%		NA	Washington**	NA	NA
38	Wyoming	238	0.0%		NA	West Virginia**	NA	NA
						District of Columbia	17,260	1.7%

Source: U.S. Department of Education, National Center for Education Statistics
"Numbers and Types of Public Elementary and Secondary Schools" (http://nces.ed.gov/pubs2007/2007354rev.pdf)
*For school year 2005-2006. Charter schools provide free public elementary/secondary education under a charter granted by the state legislature or other appropriate authority.
**Either no charter school law or not available.

Percent of Students Attending Public Elementary and Secondary Charter Schools in 2006
Reporting States Percent = 2.1%*

ALPHA ORDER

RANK	STATE	PERCENT
NA	Alabama**	NA
6	Alaska	3.5
1	Arizona	8.3
26	Arkansas	0.8
9	California	3.1
2	Colorado	5.7
32	Connecticut	0.5
3	Delaware	5.4
6	Florida	3.5
18	Georgia	1.7
6	Hawaii	3.5
9	Idaho	3.1
26	Illinois	0.8
29	Indiana	0.7
37	Iowa	0.1
33	Kansas	0.4
NA	Kentucky**	NA
21	Louisiana	1.3
NA	Maine**	NA
33	Maryland	0.4
15	Massachusetts	2.3
4	Michigan	5.3
14	Minnesota	2.5
37	Mississippi	0.1
22	Missouri	1.2
NA	Montana**	NA
NA	Nebraska**	NA
22	Nevada	1.2
37	New Hampshire	0.1
24	New Jersey	1.1
13	New Mexico	2.6
26	New York	0.8
17	North Carolina	1.9
NA	North Dakota**	NA
5	Ohio	3.7
30	Oklahoma	0.6
25	Oregon	1.0
12	Pennsylvania	3.0
18	Rhode Island	1.7
30	South Carolina	0.6
NA	South Dakota**	NA
36	Tennessee	0.2
20	Texas	1.6
16	Utah	2.2
NA	Vermont**	NA
40	Virginia	0.0
NA	Washington**	NA
NA	West Virginia**	NA
9	Wisconsin	3.1
35	Wyoming	0.3

RANK ORDER

RANK	STATE	PERCENT
1	Arizona	8.3
2	Colorado	5.7
3	Delaware	5.4
4	Michigan	5.3
5	Ohio	3.7
6	Alaska	3.5
6	Florida	3.5
6	Hawaii	3.5
9	California	3.1
9	Idaho	3.1
9	Wisconsin	3.1
12	Pennsylvania	3.0
13	New Mexico	2.6
14	Minnesota	2.5
15	Massachusetts	2.3
16	Utah	2.2
17	North Carolina	1.9
18	Georgia	1.7
18	Rhode Island	1.7
20	Texas	1.6
21	Louisiana	1.3
22	Missouri	1.2
22	Nevada	1.2
24	New Jersey	1.1
25	Oregon	1.0
26	Arkansas	0.8
26	Illinois	0.8
26	New York	0.8
29	Indiana	0.7
30	Oklahoma	0.6
30	South Carolina	0.6
32	Connecticut	0.5
33	Kansas	0.4
33	Maryland	0.4
35	Wyoming	0.3
36	Tennessee	0.2
37	Iowa	0.1
37	Mississippi	0.1
37	New Hampshire	0.1
40	Virginia	0.0
NA	Alabama**	NA
NA	Kentucky**	NA
NA	Maine**	NA
NA	Montana**	NA
NA	Nebraska**	NA
NA	North Dakota**	NA
NA	South Dakota**	NA
NA	Vermont**	NA
NA	Washington**	NA
NA	West Virginia**	NA

District of Columbia	22.5

Source: CQ Press using data from U.S. Department of Education, National Center for Education Statistics
    "Numbers and Types of Public Elementary and Secondary Schools" (http://nces.ed.gov/pubs2007/2007354rev.pdf)
*For school year 2005-2006. Charter schools provide free public elementary/secondary education under a charter granted by the state legislature or other appropriate authority.
**Either no charter school law or not available.

Students Attending Public Elementary and Secondary Special Education Schools in 2006
National Total = 222,497 Students*

ALPHA ORDER

RANK	STATE	STUDENTS	% of USA
25	Alabama	846	0.4%
29	Alaska	528	0.2%
28	Arizona	539	0.2%
33	Arkansas	216	0.1%
2	California	28,606	12.9%
27	Colorado	605	0.3%
12	Connecticut	3,359	1.5%
20	Delaware	1,606	0.7%
6	Florida	14,598	6.6%
22	Georgia	1,280	0.6%
38	Hawaii	125	0.1%
36	Idaho	142	0.1%
3	Illinois	27,036	12.2%
19	Indiana	1,677	0.8%
24	Iowa	950	0.4%
44	Kansas	0	0.0%
31	Kentucky	390	0.2%
21	Louisiana	1,297	0.6%
41	Maine	78	0.0%
9	Maryland	6,703	3.0%
37	Massachusetts	136	0.1%
4	Michigan	19,765	8.9%
7	Minnesota	12,453	5.6%
44	Mississippi	0	0.0%
17	Missouri	1,740	0.8%
42	Montana	66	0.0%
15	Nebraska	1,813	0.8%
34	Nevada	168	0.1%
44	New Hampshire	0	0.0%
8	New Jersey	9,750	4.4%
23	New Mexico	1,127	0.5%
1	New York	46,970	21.1%
13	North Carolina	2,376	1.1%
44	North Dakota	0	0.0%
18	Ohio	1,705	0.8%
44	Oklahoma	0	0.0%
43	Oregon	42	0.0%
5	Pennsylvania	16,565	7.4%
35	Rhode Island	166	0.1%
26	South Carolina	810	0.4%
40	South Dakota	90	0.0%
16	Tennessee	1,807	0.8%
44	Texas	0	0.0%
11	Utah	4,091	1.8%
14	Vermont	1,954	0.9%
30	Virginia	403	0.2%
10	Washington	4,294	1.9%
32	West Virginia	249	0.1%
39	Wisconsin	100	0.0%
44	Wyoming	0	0.0%

RANK ORDER

RANK	STATE	STUDENTS	% of USA
1	New York	46,970	21.1%
2	California	28,606	12.9%
3	Illinois	27,036	12.2%
4	Michigan	19,765	8.9%
5	Pennsylvania	16,565	7.4%
6	Florida	14,598	6.6%
7	Minnesota	12,453	5.6%
8	New Jersey	9,750	4.4%
9	Maryland	6,703	3.0%
10	Washington	4,294	1.9%
11	Utah	4,091	1.8%
12	Connecticut	3,359	1.5%
13	North Carolina	2,376	1.1%
14	Vermont	1,954	0.9%
15	Nebraska	1,813	0.8%
16	Tennessee	1,807	0.8%
17	Missouri	1,740	0.8%
18	Ohio	1,705	0.8%
19	Indiana	1,677	0.8%
20	Delaware	1,606	0.7%
21	Louisiana	1,297	0.6%
22	Georgia	1,280	0.6%
23	New Mexico	1,127	0.5%
24	Iowa	950	0.4%
25	Alabama	846	0.4%
26	South Carolina	810	0.4%
27	Colorado	605	0.3%
28	Arizona	539	0.2%
29	Alaska	528	0.2%
30	Virginia	403	0.2%
31	Kentucky	390	0.2%
32	West Virginia	249	0.1%
33	Arkansas	216	0.1%
34	Nevada	168	0.1%
35	Rhode Island	166	0.1%
36	Idaho	142	0.1%
37	Massachusetts	136	0.1%
38	Hawaii	125	0.1%
39	Wisconsin	100	0.0%
40	South Dakota	90	0.0%
41	Maine	78	0.0%
42	Montana	66	0.0%
43	Oregon	42	0.0%
44	Kansas	0	0.0%
44	Mississippi	0	0.0%
44	New Hampshire	0	0.0%
44	North Dakota	0	0.0%
44	Oklahoma	0	0.0%
44	Texas	0	0.0%
44	Wyoming	0	0.0%
	District of Columbia	3,276	1.5%

Source: U.S. Department of Education, National Center for Education Statistics
"Numbers and Types of Public Elementary and Secondary Schools" (http://nces.ed.gov/pubs2007/2007354rev.pdf)
*For school year 2005-2006.

Percent of Students Attending Public Elementary and Secondary Special Education Schools in 2006
National Percent = 0.5%*

ALPHA ORDER

RANK	STATE	PERCENT
24	Alabama	0.1
15	Alaska	0.4
35	Arizona	0.0
35	Arkansas	0.0
13	California	0.5
24	Colorado	0.1
11	Connecticut	0.6
4	Delaware	1.3
13	Florida	0.5
24	Georgia	0.1
24	Hawaii	0.1
24	Idaho	0.1
4	Illinois	1.3
18	Indiana	0.2
18	Iowa	0.2
35	Kansas	0.0
24	Kentucky	0.1
18	Louisiana	0.2
35	Maine	0.0
8	Maryland	0.8
35	Massachusetts	0.0
6	Michigan	1.2
3	Minnesota	1.5
35	Mississippi	0.0
18	Missouri	0.2
35	Montana	0.0
11	Nebraska	0.6
35	Nevada	0.0
35	New Hampshire	0.0
10	New Jersey	0.7
17	New Mexico	0.3
2	New York	1.7
18	North Carolina	0.2
35	North Dakota	0.0
24	Ohio	0.1
35	Oklahoma	0.0
35	Oregon	0.0
7	Pennsylvania	0.9
24	Rhode Island	0.1
24	South Carolina	0.1
24	South Dakota	0.1
18	Tennessee	0.2
35	Texas	0.0
8	Utah	0.8
1	Vermont	2.0
35	Virginia	0.0
15	Washington	0.4
24	West Virginia	0.1
35	Wisconsin	0.0
35	Wyoming	0.0

RANK ORDER

RANK	STATE	PERCENT
1	Vermont	2.0
2	New York	1.7
3	Minnesota	1.5
4	Delaware	1.3
4	Illinois	1.3
6	Michigan	1.2
7	Pennsylvania	0.9
8	Maryland	0.8
8	Utah	0.8
10	New Jersey	0.7
11	Connecticut	0.6
11	Nebraska	0.6
13	California	0.5
13	Florida	0.5
15	Alaska	0.4
15	Washington	0.4
17	New Mexico	0.3
18	Indiana	0.2
18	Iowa	0.2
18	Louisiana	0.2
18	Missouri	0.2
18	North Carolina	0.2
18	Tennessee	0.2
24	Alabama	0.1
24	Colorado	0.1
24	Georgia	0.1
24	Hawaii	0.1
24	Idaho	0.1
24	Kentucky	0.1
24	Ohio	0.1
24	Rhode Island	0.1
24	South Carolina	0.1
24	South Dakota	0.1
24	West Virginia	0.1
35	Arizona	0.0
35	Arkansas	0.0
35	Kansas	0.0
35	Maine	0.0
35	Massachusetts	0.0
35	Mississippi	0.0
35	Montana	0.0
35	Nevada	0.0
35	New Hampshire	0.0
35	North Dakota	0.0
35	Oklahoma	0.0
35	Oregon	0.0
35	Texas	0.0
35	Virginia	0.0
35	Wisconsin	0.0
35	Wyoming	0.0

District of Columbia	4.3

Source: CQ Press using data from U.S. Department of Education, National Center for Education Statistics
   "Numbers and Types of Public Elementary and Secondary Schools" (http://nces.ed.gov/pubs2007/2007354rev.pdf)
*For school year 2005-2006.

Students Attending Public Elementary and Secondary
Vocational Education Schools in 2006
National Total = 217,621 Students*

ALPHA ORDER

RANK	STATE	STUDENTS	% of USA
23	Alabama	51	0.0%
19	Alaska	320	0.1%
1	Arizona	63,137	29.0%
26	Arkansas	0	0.0%
26	California	0	0.0%
16	Colorado	668	0.3%
6	Connecticut	10,325	4.7%
8	Delaware	5,764	2.6%
11	Florida	2,332	1.1%
26	Georgia	0	0.0%
26	Hawaii	0	0.0%
26	Idaho	0	0.0%
26	Illinois	0	0.0%
26	Indiana	0	0.0%
26	Iowa	0	0.0%
26	Kansas	0	0.0%
26	Kentucky	0	0.0%
26	Louisiana	0	0.0%
26	Maine	0	0.0%
7	Maryland	8,570	3.9%
3	Massachusetts	33,527	15.4%
13	Michigan	1,882	0.9%
24	Minnesota	5	0.0%
26	Mississippi	0	0.0%
26	Missouri	0	0.0%
26	Montana	0	0.0%
26	Nebraska	0	0.0%
22	Nevada	68	0.0%
26	New Hampshire	0	0.0%
4	New Jersey	22,678	10.4%
17	New Mexico	491	0.2%
2	New York	40,091	18.4%
20	North Carolina	260	0.1%
26	North Dakota	0	0.0%
15	Ohio	736	0.3%
26	Oklahoma	0	0.0%
26	Oregon	0	0.0%
5	Pennsylvania	15,855	7.3%
14	Rhode Island	1,749	0.8%
10	South Carolina	2,928	1.3%
26	South Dakota	0	0.0%
9	Tennessee	3,154	1.4%
26	Texas	0	0.0%
21	Utah	112	0.1%
26	Vermont	0	0.0%
26	Virginia	0	0.0%
12	Washington	2,301	1.1%
25	West Virginia	4	0.0%
18	Wisconsin	330	0.2%
26	Wyoming	0	0.0%

RANK ORDER

RANK	STATE	STUDENTS	% of USA
1	Arizona	63,137	29.0%
2	New York	40,091	18.4%
3	Massachusetts	33,527	15.4%
4	New Jersey	22,678	10.4%
5	Pennsylvania	15,855	7.3%
6	Connecticut	10,325	4.7%
7	Maryland	8,570	3.9%
8	Delaware	5,764	2.6%
9	Tennessee	3,154	1.4%
10	South Carolina	2,928	1.3%
11	Florida	2,332	1.1%
12	Washington	2,301	1.1%
13	Michigan	1,882	0.9%
14	Rhode Island	1,749	0.8%
15	Ohio	736	0.3%
16	Colorado	668	0.3%
17	New Mexico	491	0.2%
18	Wisconsin	330	0.2%
19	Alaska	320	0.1%
20	North Carolina	260	0.1%
21	Utah	112	0.1%
22	Nevada	68	0.0%
23	Alabama	51	0.0%
24	Minnesota	5	0.0%
25	West Virginia	4	0.0%
26	Arkansas	0	0.0%
26	California	0	0.0%
26	Georgia	0	0.0%
26	Hawaii	0	0.0%
26	Idaho	0	0.0%
26	Illinois	0	0.0%
26	Indiana	0	0.0%
26	Iowa	0	0.0%
26	Kansas	0	0.0%
26	Kentucky	0	0.0%
26	Louisiana	0	0.0%
26	Maine	0	0.0%
26	Mississippi	0	0.0%
26	Missouri	0	0.0%
26	Montana	0	0.0%
26	Nebraska	0	0.0%
26	New Hampshire	0	0.0%
26	North Dakota	0	0.0%
26	Oklahoma	0	0.0%
26	Oregon	0	0.0%
26	South Dakota	0	0.0%
26	Texas	0	0.0%
26	Vermont	0	0.0%
26	Virginia	0	0.0%
26	Wyoming	0	0.0%
	District of Columbia	283	0.1%

Source: U.S. Department of Education, National Center for Education Statistics
   "Numbers and Types of Public Elementary and Secondary Schools" (http://nces.ed.gov/pubs2007/2007354rev.pdf)
*For school year 2005-2006.

Percent of Students Attending Public Elementary and Secondary Vocational Education Schools in 2006
National Percent = 0.4%*

ALPHA ORDER

RANK ORDER

RANK	STATE	PERCENT	RANK	STATE	PERCENT
18	Alabama	0.0	1	Arizona	5.8
12	Alaska	0.2	2	Delaware	4.8
1	Arizona	5.8	3	Massachusetts	3.4
18	Arkansas	0.0	4	Connecticut	1.8
18	California	0.0	5	New Jersey	1.6
15	Colorado	0.1	6	New York	1.4
4	Connecticut	1.8	7	Rhode Island	1.2
2	Delaware	4.8	8	Maryland	1.0
15	Florida	0.1	9	Pennsylvania	0.9
18	Georgia	0.0	10	South Carolina	0.4
18	Hawaii	0.0	11	Tennessee	0.3
18	Idaho	0.0	12	Alaska	0.2
18	Illinois	0.0	12	New Mexico	0.2
18	Indiana	0.0	12	Washington	0.2
18	Iowa	0.0	15	Colorado	0.1
18	Kansas	0.0	15	Florida	0.1
18	Kentucky	0.0	15	Michigan	0.1
18	Louisiana	0.0	18	Alabama	0.0
18	Maine	0.0	18	Arkansas	0.0
8	Maryland	1.0	18	California	0.0
3	Massachusetts	3.4	18	Georgia	0.0
15	Michigan	0.1	18	Hawaii	0.0
18	Minnesota	0.0	18	Idaho	0.0
18	Mississippi	0.0	18	Illinois	0.0
18	Missouri	0.0	18	Indiana	0.0
18	Montana	0.0	18	Iowa	0.0
18	Nebraska	0.0	18	Kansas	0.0
18	Nevada	0.0	18	Kentucky	0.0
18	New Hampshire	0.0	18	Louisiana	0.0
5	New Jersey	1.6	18	Maine	0.0
12	New Mexico	0.2	18	Minnesota	0.0
6	New York	1.4	18	Mississippi	0.0
18	North Carolina	0.0	18	Missouri	0.0
18	North Dakota	0.0	18	Montana	0.0
18	Ohio	0.0	18	Nebraska	0.0
18	Oklahoma	0.0	18	Nevada	0.0
18	Oregon	0.0	18	New Hampshire	0.0
9	Pennsylvania	0.9	18	North Carolina	0.0
7	Rhode Island	1.2	18	North Dakota	0.0
10	South Carolina	0.4	18	Ohio	0.0
18	South Dakota	0.0	18	Oklahoma	0.0
11	Tennessee	0.3	18	Oregon	0.0
18	Texas	0.0	18	South Dakota	0.0
18	Utah	0.0	18	Texas	0.0
18	Vermont	0.0	18	Utah	0.0
18	Virginia	0.0	18	Vermont	0.0
12	Washington	0.2	18	Virginia	0.0
18	West Virginia	0.0	18	West Virginia	0.0
18	Wisconsin	0.0	18	Wisconsin	0.0
18	Wyoming	0.0	18	Wyoming	0.0

	District of Columbia	0.4

Source: CQ Press using data from U.S. Department of Education, National Center for Education Statistics
"Numbers and Types of Public Elementary and Secondary Schools" (http://nces.ed.gov/pubs2007/2007354rev.pdf)
*For school year 2005-2006.

Students Attending Public Elementary and Secondary Alternative Education Schools in 2006
National Total = 514,592 Students*

ALPHA ORDER

RANK	STATE	STUDENTS	% of USA
31	Alabama	1,664	0.3%
10	Alaska	11,798	2.3%
9	Arizona	12,321	2.4%
38	Arkansas	734	0.1%
1	California	158,509	30.8%
8	Colorado	12,535	2.4%
25	Connecticut	2,625	0.5%
34	Delaware	1,314	0.3%
3	Florida	43,866	8.5%
16	Georgia	5,874	1.1%
39	Hawaii	202	0.0%
19	Idaho	4,670	0.9%
13	Illinois	8,235	1.6%
26	Indiana	2,513	0.5%
21	Iowa	3,972	0.8%
43	Kansas	0	0.0%
14	Kentucky	7,031	1.4%
7	Louisiana	13,882	2.7%
43	Maine	0	0.0%
12	Maryland	10,428	2.0%
29	Massachusetts	2,120	0.4%
5	Michigan	29,074	5.6%
6	Minnesota	17,978	3.5%
43	Mississippi	0	0.0%
27	Missouri	2,231	0.4%
40	Montana	91	0.0%
43	Nebraska	0	0.0%
20	Nevada	4,570	0.9%
43	New Hampshire	0	0.0%
43	New Jersey	0	0.0%
18	New Mexico	4,940	1.0%
11	New York	11,439	2.2%
17	North Carolina	5,136	1.0%
43	North Dakota	0	0.0%
41	Ohio	71	0.0%
43	Oklahoma	0	0.0%
23	Oregon	3,300	0.6%
37	Pennsylvania	900	0.2%
28	Rhode Island	2,165	0.4%
30	South Carolina	1,980	0.4%
36	South Dakota	947	0.2%
32	Tennessee	1,560	0.3%
2	Texas	72,743	14.1%
15	Utah	6,354	1.2%
42	Vermont	39	0.0%
24	Virginia	2,863	0.6%
4	Washington	33,921	6.6%
35	West Virginia	1,016	0.2%
22	Wisconsin	3,891	0.8%
33	Wyoming	1,380	0.3%

RANK ORDER

RANK	STATE	STUDENTS	% of USA
1	California	158,509	30.8%
2	Texas	72,743	14.1%
3	Florida	43,866	8.5%
4	Washington	33,921	6.6%
5	Michigan	29,074	5.6%
6	Minnesota	17,978	3.5%
7	Louisiana	13,882	2.7%
8	Colorado	12,535	2.4%
9	Arizona	12,321	2.4%
10	Alaska	11,798	2.3%
11	New York	11,439	2.2%
12	Maryland	10,428	2.0%
13	Illinois	8,235	1.6%
14	Kentucky	7,031	1.4%
15	Utah	6,354	1.2%
16	Georgia	5,874	1.1%
17	North Carolina	5,136	1.0%
18	New Mexico	4,940	1.0%
19	Idaho	4,670	0.9%
20	Nevada	4,570	0.9%
21	Iowa	3,972	0.8%
22	Wisconsin	3,891	0.8%
23	Oregon	3,300	0.6%
24	Virginia	2,863	0.6%
25	Connecticut	2,625	0.5%
26	Indiana	2,513	0.5%
27	Missouri	2,231	0.4%
28	Rhode Island	2,165	0.4%
29	Massachusetts	2,120	0.4%
30	South Carolina	1,980	0.4%
31	Alabama	1,664	0.3%
32	Tennessee	1,560	0.3%
33	Wyoming	1,380	0.3%
34	Delaware	1,314	0.3%
35	West Virginia	1,016	0.2%
36	South Dakota	947	0.2%
37	Pennsylvania	900	0.2%
38	Arkansas	734	0.1%
39	Hawaii	202	0.0%
40	Montana	91	0.0%
41	Ohio	71	0.0%
42	Vermont	39	0.0%
43	Kansas	0	0.0%
43	Maine	0	0.0%
43	Mississippi	0	0.0%
43	Nebraska	0	0.0%
43	New Hampshire	0	0.0%
43	New Jersey	0	0.0%
43	North Dakota	0	0.0%
43	Oklahoma	0	0.0%
	District of Columbia	1,710	0.3%

Source: U.S. Department of Education, National Center for Education Statistics
  "Numbers and Types of Public Elementary and Secondary Schools" (http://nces.ed.gov/pubs2007/2007354rev.pdf)
*For school year 2005-2006.

Percent of Students Attending Public Elementary and Secondary Alternative Education Schools in 2006
National Percent = 1.1%*

ALPHA ORDER

RANK	STATE	PERCENT
31	Alabama	0.2
1	Alaska	8.9
16	Arizona	1.1
31	Arkansas	0.2
3	California	2.5
8	Colorado	1.6
23	Connecticut	0.5
16	Delaware	1.1
8	Florida	1.6
24	Georgia	0.4
38	Hawaii	0.1
6	Idaho	1.8
24	Illinois	0.4
31	Indiana	0.2
20	Iowa	0.8
40	Kansas	0.0
16	Kentucky	1.1
4	Louisiana	2.1
40	Maine	0.0
14	Maryland	1.2
31	Massachusetts	0.2
7	Michigan	1.7
4	Minnesota	2.1
40	Mississippi	0.0
31	Missouri	0.2
38	Montana	0.1
40	Nebraska	0.0
16	Nevada	1.1
40	New Hampshire	0.0
40	New Jersey	0.0
12	New Mexico	1.5
24	New York	0.4
24	North Carolina	0.4
40	North Dakota	0.0
40	Ohio	0.0
40	Oklahoma	0.0
22	Oregon	0.6
40	Pennsylvania	0.0
13	Rhode Island	1.4
30	South Carolina	0.3
20	South Dakota	0.8
31	Tennessee	0.2
8	Texas	1.6
14	Utah	1.2
40	Vermont	0.0
31	Virginia	0.2
2	Washington	3.3
24	West Virginia	0.4
24	Wisconsin	0.4
8	Wyoming	1.6

RANK ORDER

RANK	STATE	PERCENT
1	Alaska	8.9
2	Washington	3.3
3	California	2.5
4	Louisiana	2.1
4	Minnesota	2.1
6	Idaho	1.8
7	Michigan	1.7
8	Colorado	1.6
8	Florida	1.6
8	Texas	1.6
8	Wyoming	1.6
12	New Mexico	1.5
13	Rhode Island	1.4
14	Maryland	1.2
14	Utah	1.2
16	Arizona	1.1
16	Delaware	1.1
16	Kentucky	1.1
16	Nevada	1.1
20	Iowa	0.8
20	South Dakota	0.8
22	Oregon	0.6
23	Connecticut	0.5
24	Georgia	0.4
24	Illinois	0.4
24	New York	0.4
24	North Carolina	0.4
24	West Virginia	0.4
24	Wisconsin	0.4
30	South Carolina	0.3
31	Alabama	0.2
31	Arkansas	0.2
31	Indiana	0.2
31	Massachusetts	0.2
31	Missouri	0.2
31	Tennessee	0.2
31	Virginia	0.2
38	Hawaii	0.1
38	Montana	0.1
40	Kansas	0.0
40	Maine	0.0
40	Mississippi	0.0
40	Nebraska	0.0
40	New Hampshire	0.0
40	New Jersey	0.0
40	North Dakota	0.0
40	Ohio	0.0
40	Oklahoma	0.0
40	Pennsylvania	0.0
40	Vermont	0.0

District of Columbia   2.2

Source: CQ Press using data from U.S. Department of Education, National Center for Education Statistics
"Numbers and Types of Public Elementary and Secondary Schools" (http://nces.ed.gov/pubs2007/2007354rev.pdf)
*For school year 2005-2006.

Minority Students Enrolled in Public Elementary and Secondary Schools in 2006
National Total = 20,854,734 Students*

<table>
<tr><th colspan="4">ALPHA ORDER</th><th colspan="4">RANK ORDER</th></tr>
<tr><th>RANK</th><th>STATE</th><th>STUDENTS</th><th>% of USA</th><th>RANK</th><th>STATE</th><th>STUDENTS</th><th>% of USA</th></tr>
<tr><td>18</td><td>Alabama</td><td>300,315</td><td>1.4%</td><td>1</td><td>California</td><td>4,272,333</td><td>20.5%</td></tr>
<tr><td>39</td><td>Alaska</td><td>56,437</td><td>0.3%</td><td>2</td><td>Texas</td><td>2,873,143</td><td>13.8%</td></tr>
<tr><td>9</td><td>Arizona</td><td>578,168</td><td>2.8%</td><td>3</td><td>Florida</td><td>1,347,018</td><td>6.5%</td></tr>
<tr><td>31</td><td>Arkansas</td><td>150,923</td><td>0.7%</td><td>4</td><td>New York</td><td>1,332,919</td><td>6.4%</td></tr>
<tr><td>1</td><td>California</td><td>4,272,333</td><td>20.5%</td><td>5</td><td>Illinois</td><td>904,489</td><td>4.3%</td></tr>
<tr><td>19</td><td>Colorado</td><td>292,232</td><td>1.4%</td><td>6</td><td>Georgia</td><td>792,882</td><td>3.8%</td></tr>
<tr><td>29</td><td>Connecticut</td><td>190,004</td><td>0.9%</td><td>7</td><td>North Carolina</td><td>615,059</td><td>2.9%</td></tr>
<tr><td>40</td><td>Delaware</td><td>54,295</td><td>0.3%</td><td>8</td><td>New Jersey</td><td>607,230</td><td>2.9%</td></tr>
<tr><td>3</td><td>Florida</td><td>1,347,018</td><td>6.5%</td><td>9</td><td>Arizona</td><td>578,168</td><td>2.8%</td></tr>
<tr><td>6</td><td>Georgia</td><td>792,882</td><td>3.8%</td><td>10</td><td>Michigan</td><td>487,266</td><td>2.3%</td></tr>
<tr><td>32</td><td>Hawaii</td><td>146,704</td><td>0.7%</td><td>11</td><td>Virginia</td><td>479,686</td><td>2.3%</td></tr>
<tr><td>42</td><td>Idaho</td><td>44,541</td><td>0.2%</td><td>12</td><td>Pennsylvania</td><td>462,170</td><td>2.2%</td></tr>
<tr><td>5</td><td>Illinois</td><td>904,489</td><td>4.3%</td><td>13</td><td>Maryland</td><td>442,024</td><td>2.1%</td></tr>
<tr><td>27</td><td>Indiana</td><td>203,506</td><td>1.0%</td><td>14</td><td>Ohio</td><td>376,585</td><td>1.8%</td></tr>
<tr><td>37</td><td>Iowa</td><td>65,028</td><td>0.3%</td><td>15</td><td>South Carolina</td><td>320,935</td><td>1.5%</td></tr>
<tr><td>34</td><td>Kansas</td><td>111,820</td><td>0.5%</td><td>16</td><td>Louisiana</td><td>317,673</td><td>1.5%</td></tr>
<tr><td>36</td><td>Kentucky</td><td>88,073</td><td>0.4%</td><td>17</td><td>Washington</td><td>307,812</td><td>1.5%</td></tr>
<tr><td>16</td><td>Louisiana</td><td>317,673</td><td>1.5%</td><td>18</td><td>Alabama</td><td>300,315</td><td>1.4%</td></tr>
<tr><td>49</td><td>Maine</td><td>9,553</td><td>0.0%</td><td>19</td><td>Colorado</td><td>292,232</td><td>1.4%</td></tr>
<tr><td>13</td><td>Maryland</td><td>442,024</td><td>2.1%</td><td>20</td><td>Tennessee</td><td>291,363</td><td>1.4%</td></tr>
<tr><td>23</td><td>Massachusetts</td><td>253,535</td><td>1.2%</td><td>21</td><td>Mississippi</td><td>264,926</td><td>1.3%</td></tr>
<tr><td>10</td><td>Michigan</td><td>487,266</td><td>2.3%</td><td>22</td><td>Oklahoma</td><td>256,209</td><td>1.2%</td></tr>
<tr><td>30</td><td>Minnesota</td><td>182,259</td><td>0.9%</td><td>23</td><td>Massachusetts</td><td>253,535</td><td>1.2%</td></tr>
<tr><td>21</td><td>Mississippi</td><td>264,926</td><td>1.3%</td><td>24</td><td>New Mexico</td><td>225,147</td><td>1.1%</td></tr>
<tr><td>26</td><td>Missouri</td><td>214,390</td><td>1.0%</td><td>25</td><td>Nevada</td><td>221,062</td><td>1.1%</td></tr>
<tr><td>43</td><td>Montana</td><td>22,870</td><td>0.1%</td><td>26</td><td>Missouri</td><td>214,390</td><td>1.0%</td></tr>
<tr><td>38</td><td>Nebraska</td><td>64,553</td><td>0.3%</td><td>27</td><td>Indiana</td><td>203,506</td><td>1.0%</td></tr>
<tr><td>25</td><td>Nevada</td><td>221,062</td><td>1.1%</td><td>28</td><td>Wisconsin</td><td>194,414</td><td>0.9%</td></tr>
<tr><td>46</td><td>New Hampshire</td><td>13,851</td><td>0.1%</td><td>29</td><td>Connecticut</td><td>190,004</td><td>0.9%</td></tr>
<tr><td>8</td><td>New Jersey</td><td>607,230</td><td>2.9%</td><td>30</td><td>Minnesota</td><td>182,259</td><td>0.9%</td></tr>
<tr><td>24</td><td>New Mexico</td><td>225,147</td><td>1.1%</td><td>31</td><td>Arkansas</td><td>150,923</td><td>0.7%</td></tr>
<tr><td>4</td><td>New York</td><td>1,332,919</td><td>6.4%</td><td>32</td><td>Hawaii</td><td>146,704</td><td>0.7%</td></tr>
<tr><td>7</td><td>North Carolina</td><td>615,059</td><td>2.9%</td><td>33</td><td>Oregon</td><td>141,855</td><td>0.7%</td></tr>
<tr><td>48</td><td>North Dakota</td><td>12,610</td><td>0.1%</td><td>34</td><td>Kansas</td><td>111,820</td><td>0.5%</td></tr>
<tr><td>14</td><td>Ohio</td><td>376,585</td><td>1.8%</td><td>35</td><td>Utah</td><td>92,573</td><td>0.4%</td></tr>
<tr><td>22</td><td>Oklahoma</td><td>256,209</td><td>1.2%</td><td>36</td><td>Kentucky</td><td>88,073</td><td>0.4%</td></tr>
<tr><td>33</td><td>Oregon</td><td>141,855</td><td>0.7%</td><td>37</td><td>Iowa</td><td>65,028</td><td>0.3%</td></tr>
<tr><td>12</td><td>Pennsylvania</td><td>462,170</td><td>2.2%</td><td>38</td><td>Nebraska</td><td>64,553</td><td>0.3%</td></tr>
<tr><td>41</td><td>Rhode Island</td><td>45,444</td><td>0.2%</td><td>39</td><td>Alaska</td><td>56,437</td><td>0.3%</td></tr>
<tr><td>15</td><td>South Carolina</td><td>320,935</td><td>1.5%</td><td>40</td><td>Delaware</td><td>54,295</td><td>0.3%</td></tr>
<tr><td>44</td><td>South Dakota</td><td>18,336</td><td>0.1%</td><td>41</td><td>Rhode Island</td><td>45,444</td><td>0.2%</td></tr>
<tr><td>20</td><td>Tennessee</td><td>291,363</td><td>1.4%</td><td>42</td><td>Idaho</td><td>44,541</td><td>0.2%</td></tr>
<tr><td>2</td><td>Texas</td><td>2,873,143</td><td>13.8%</td><td>43</td><td>Montana</td><td>22,870</td><td>0.1%</td></tr>
<tr><td>35</td><td>Utah</td><td>92,573</td><td>0.4%</td><td>44</td><td>South Dakota</td><td>18,336</td><td>0.1%</td></tr>
<tr><td>50</td><td>Vermont</td><td>4,294</td><td>0.0%</td><td>45</td><td>West Virginia</td><td>18,091</td><td>0.1%</td></tr>
<tr><td>11</td><td>Virginia</td><td>479,686</td><td>2.3%</td><td>46</td><td>New Hampshire</td><td>13,851</td><td>0.1%</td></tr>
<tr><td>17</td><td>Washington</td><td>307,812</td><td>1.5%</td><td>47</td><td>Wyoming</td><td>12,737</td><td>0.1%</td></tr>
<tr><td>45</td><td>West Virginia</td><td>18,091</td><td>0.1%</td><td>48</td><td>North Dakota</td><td>12,610</td><td>0.1%</td></tr>
<tr><td>28</td><td>Wisconsin</td><td>194,414</td><td>0.9%</td><td>49</td><td>Maine</td><td>9,553</td><td>0.0%</td></tr>
<tr><td>47</td><td>Wyoming</td><td>12,737</td><td>0.1%</td><td>50</td><td>Vermont</td><td>4,294</td><td>0.0%</td></tr>
<tr><td></td><td></td><td></td><td></td><td></td><td>District of Columbia</td><td>73,392</td><td>0.4%</td></tr>
</table>

Source: CQ Press using data from U.S. Department of Education, National Center for Education Statistics
"Public Elementary and Secondary School Student Enrollment, High School Completions and Staff"
(http://nces.ed.gov/pubs2007/2007352.pdf)
*For school year 2005-2006. Minority includes all groups except non-Hispanic white.

Percent of Public Elementary and Secondary Students
Who are Minorities in 2006
National Percent = 42.9%

ALPHA ORDER

RANK	STATE	PERCENT
19	Alabama	40.6
18	Alaska	42.3
7	Arizona	52.8
24	Arkansas	31.8
2	California	69.0
22	Colorado	37.5
23	Connecticut	33.0
14	Delaware	44.9
10	Florida	50.4
9	Georgia	50.8
1	Hawaii	80.2
40	Idaho	17.0
15	Illinois	43.6
38	Indiana	19.7
45	Iowa	13.4
32	Kansas	24.6
44	Kentucky	13.7
11	Louisiana	48.5
49	Maine	4.9
8	Maryland	51.4
29	Massachusetts	26.5
28	Michigan	28.1
36	Minnesota	21.7
6	Mississippi	53.5
33	Missouri	23.4
41	Montana	15.7
34	Nebraska	22.5
5	Nevada	53.6
47	New Hampshire	6.7
16	New Jersey	43.5
3	New Mexico	68.9
12	New York	47.3
17	North Carolina	43.4
46	North Dakota	12.8
37	Ohio	21.0
20	Oklahoma	40.4
30	Oregon	26.4
31	Pennsylvania	25.2
27	Rhode Island	29.6
13	South Carolina	46.0
43	South Dakota	15.0
25	Tennessee	30.5
4	Texas	63.5
39	Utah	18.2
50	Vermont	4.5
21	Virginia	40.2
26	Washington	30.2
48	West Virginia	6.4
35	Wisconsin	22.2
42	Wyoming	15.1

RANK ORDER

RANK	STATE	PERCENT
1	Hawaii	80.2
2	California	69.0
3	New Mexico	68.9
4	Texas	63.5
5	Nevada	53.6
6	Mississippi	53.5
7	Arizona	52.8
8	Maryland	51.4
9	Georgia	50.8
10	Florida	50.4
11	Louisiana	48.5
12	New York	47.3
13	South Carolina	46.0
14	Delaware	44.9
15	Illinois	43.6
16	New Jersey	43.5
17	North Carolina	43.4
18	Alaska	42.3
19	Alabama	40.6
20	Oklahoma	40.4
21	Virginia	40.2
22	Colorado	37.5
23	Connecticut	33.0
24	Arkansas	31.8
25	Tennessee	30.5
26	Washington	30.2
27	Rhode Island	29.6
28	Michigan	28.1
29	Massachusetts	26.5
30	Oregon	26.4
31	Pennsylvania	25.2
32	Kansas	24.6
33	Missouri	23.4
34	Nebraska	22.5
35	Wisconsin	22.2
36	Minnesota	21.7
37	Ohio	21.0
38	Indiana	19.7
39	Utah	18.2
40	Idaho	17.0
41	Montana	15.7
42	Wyoming	15.1
43	South Dakota	15.0
44	Kentucky	13.7
45	Iowa	13.4
46	North Dakota	12.8
47	New Hampshire	6.7
48	West Virginia	6.4
49	Maine	4.9
50	Vermont	4.5

District of Columbia   95.5

Source: CQ Press using data from U.S. Department of Education, National Center for Education Statistics
"Public Elementary and Secondary School Student Enrollment, High School Completions and Staff"
(http://nces.ed.gov/pubs2007/2007352.pdf)
*For school year 2005-2006. Minority includes all groups except non-Hispanic white.

Percent of Public Elementary and Secondary Students Who Are White: 2006

National Percent = 57.1%*

ALPHA ORDER

RANK	STATE	PERCENT
32	Alabama	59.4
33	Alaska	57.7
44	Arizona	47.2
27	Arkansas	68.2
49	California	31.0
29	Colorado	62.5
28	Connecticut	67.0
37	Delaware	55.1
41	Florida	49.6
42	Georgia	49.2
50	Hawaii	19.8
11	Idaho	83.0
36	Illinois	56.4
13	Indiana	80.3
6	Iowa	86.6
19	Kansas	75.4
7	Kentucky	86.3
40	Louisiana	51.5
2	Maine	95.1
43	Maryland	48.6
22	Massachusetts	73.5
23	Michigan	71.9
15	Minnesota	78.3
45	Mississippi	46.5
18	Missouri	76.6
10	Montana	84.3
17	Nebraska	77.5
46	Nevada	46.4
4	New Hampshire	93.3
35	New Jersey	56.5
48	New Mexico	31.1
39	New York	52.7
34	North Carolina	56.6
5	North Dakota	87.2
14	Ohio	79.0
31	Oklahoma	59.6
21	Oregon	73.6
20	Pennsylvania	74.8
24	Rhode Island	70.4
38	South Carolina	54.0
8	South Dakota	85.0
26	Tennessee	69.5
47	Texas	36.5
12	Utah	81.8
1	Vermont	95.5
30	Virginia	59.8
25	Washington	69.8
3	West Virginia	93.6
16	Wisconsin	77.8
9	Wyoming	84.9

RANK ORDER

RANK	STATE	PERCENT
1	Vermont	95.5
2	Maine	95.1
3	West Virginia	93.6
4	New Hampshire	93.3
5	North Dakota	87.2
6	Iowa	86.6
7	Kentucky	86.3
8	South Dakota	85.0
9	Wyoming	84.9
10	Montana	84.3
11	Idaho	83.0
12	Utah	81.8
13	Indiana	80.3
14	Ohio	79.0
15	Minnesota	78.3
16	Wisconsin	77.8
17	Nebraska	77.5
18	Missouri	76.6
19	Kansas	75.4
20	Pennsylvania	74.8
21	Oregon	73.6
22	Massachusetts	73.5
23	Michigan	71.9
24	Rhode Island	70.4
25	Washington	69.8
26	Tennessee	69.5
27	Arkansas	68.2
28	Connecticut	67.0
29	Colorado	62.5
30	Virginia	59.8
31	Oklahoma	59.6
32	Alabama	59.4
33	Alaska	57.7
34	North Carolina	56.6
35	New Jersey	56.5
36	Illinois	56.4
37	Delaware	55.1
38	South Carolina	54.0
39	New York	52.7
40	Louisiana	51.5
41	Florida	49.6
42	Georgia	49.2
43	Maryland	48.6
44	Arizona	47.2
45	Mississippi	46.5
46	Nevada	46.4
47	Texas	36.5
48	New Mexico	31.1
49	California	31.0
50	Hawaii	19.8

District of Columbia — 4.5

Source: CQ Press using data from U.S. Department of Education, National Center for Education Statistics
"Public Elementary and Secondary School Student Enrollment, High School Completions and Staff"
(http://nces.ed.gov/pubs2007/2007352.pdf)
*For school year 2005-2006. Excludes white Hispanics.

Percent of Public Elementary and Secondary Students Who Are Black: 2006

National Percent = 17.2%*

ALPHA ORDER

RANK	STATE	PERCENT
6	Alabama	36.0
38	Alaska	4.6
35	Arizona	5.2
12	Arkansas	23.0
31	California	8.0
33	Colorado	6.0
21	Connecticut	13.7
7	Delaware	32.5
11	Florida	23.9
4	Georgia	39.2
41	Hawaii	2.4
49	Idaho	1.0
13	Illinois	20.6
22	Indiana	12.5
36	Iowa	5.1
27	Kansas	8.6
25	Kentucky	10.6
2	Louisiana	44.4
42	Maine	2.0
5	Maryland	38.1
30	Massachusetts	8.4
14	Michigan	20.3
29	Minnesota	8.5
1	Mississippi	51.2
16	Missouri	18.2
50	Montana	0.9
32	Nebraska	7.6
23	Nevada	11.1
43	New Hampshire	1.7
17	New Jersey	17.6
40	New Mexico	2.5
15	New York	19.8
8	North Carolina	31.5
45	North Dakota	1.5
18	Ohio	17.1
24	Oklahoma	10.9
39	Oregon	3.2
19	Pennsylvania	16.2
27	Rhode Island	8.6
3	South Carolina	40.3
44	South Dakota	1.6
10	Tennessee	25.1
20	Texas	14.7
48	Utah	1.3
45	Vermont	1.5
9	Virginia	27.0
34	Washington	5.7
37	West Virginia	5.0
26	Wisconsin	10.5
45	Wyoming	1.5

RANK ORDER

RANK	STATE	PERCENT
1	Mississippi	51.2
2	Louisiana	44.4
3	South Carolina	40.3
4	Georgia	39.2
5	Maryland	38.1
6	Alabama	36.0
7	Delaware	32.5
8	North Carolina	31.5
9	Virginia	27.0
10	Tennessee	25.1
11	Florida	23.9
12	Arkansas	23.0
13	Illinois	20.6
14	Michigan	20.3
15	New York	19.8
16	Missouri	18.2
17	New Jersey	17.6
18	Ohio	17.1
19	Pennsylvania	16.2
20	Texas	14.7
21	Connecticut	13.7
22	Indiana	12.5
23	Nevada	11.1
24	Oklahoma	10.9
25	Kentucky	10.6
26	Wisconsin	10.5
27	Kansas	8.6
27	Rhode Island	8.6
29	Minnesota	8.5
30	Massachusetts	8.4
31	California	8.0
32	Nebraska	7.6
33	Colorado	6.0
34	Washington	5.7
35	Arizona	5.2
36	Iowa	5.1
37	West Virginia	5.0
38	Alaska	4.6
39	Oregon	3.2
40	New Mexico	2.5
41	Hawaii	2.4
42	Maine	2.0
43	New Hampshire	1.7
44	South Dakota	1.6
45	North Dakota	1.5
45	Vermont	1.5
45	Wyoming	1.5
48	Utah	1.3
49	Idaho	1.0
50	Montana	0.9

	District of Columbia	83.3

Source: CQ Press using data from U.S. Department of Education, National Center for Education Statistics
   "Public Elementary and Secondary School Student Enrollment, High School Completions and Staff"
      (http://nces.ed.gov/pubs2007/2007352.pdf)
*For school year 2005-2006. Excludes black Hispanics.

Percent of Public Elementary and Secondary Students Who Are Hispanic: 2006

National Percent = 19.8%*

<table>
<tr><td colspan="3">ALPHA ORDER</td><td colspan="3">RANK ORDER</td></tr>
<tr><th>RANK</th><th>STATE</th><th>PERCENT</th><th>RANK</th><th>STATE</th><th>PERCENT</th></tr>
<tr><td>39</td><td>Alabama</td><td>2.8</td><td>1</td><td>New Mexico</td><td>54.0</td></tr>
<tr><td>35</td><td>Alaska</td><td>4.2</td><td>2</td><td>California</td><td>48.5</td></tr>
<tr><td>4</td><td>Arizona</td><td>39.0</td><td>3</td><td>Texas</td><td>45.3</td></tr>
<tr><td>27</td><td>Arkansas</td><td>6.8</td><td>4</td><td>Arizona</td><td>39.0</td></tr>
<tr><td>2</td><td>California</td><td>48.5</td><td>5</td><td>Nevada</td><td>33.6</td></tr>
<tr><td>6</td><td>Colorado</td><td>27.1</td><td>6</td><td>Colorado</td><td>27.1</td></tr>
<tr><td>13</td><td>Connecticut</td><td>15.4</td><td>7</td><td>Florida</td><td>23.9</td></tr>
<tr><td>20</td><td>Delaware</td><td>9.2</td><td>8</td><td>New York</td><td>20.1</td></tr>
<tr><td>7</td><td>Florida</td><td>23.9</td><td>9</td><td>Illinois</td><td>19.0</td></tr>
<tr><td>23</td><td>Georgia</td><td>8.7</td><td>10</td><td>New Jersey</td><td>18.2</td></tr>
<tr><td>33</td><td>Hawaii</td><td>4.5</td><td>11</td><td>Rhode Island</td><td>17.3</td></tr>
<tr><td>16</td><td>Idaho</td><td>12.8</td><td>12</td><td>Oregon</td><td>15.9</td></tr>
<tr><td>9</td><td>Illinois</td><td>19.0</td><td>13</td><td>Connecticut</td><td>15.4</td></tr>
<tr><td>31</td><td>Indiana</td><td>5.7</td><td>14</td><td>Washington</td><td>13.6</td></tr>
<tr><td>30</td><td>Iowa</td><td>5.8</td><td>15</td><td>Massachusetts</td><td>13.1</td></tr>
<tr><td>18</td><td>Kansas</td><td>12.1</td><td>16</td><td>Idaho</td><td>12.8</td></tr>
<tr><td>43</td><td>Kentucky</td><td>2.1</td><td>17</td><td>Utah</td><td>12.3</td></tr>
<tr><td>43</td><td>Louisiana</td><td>2.1</td><td>18</td><td>Kansas</td><td>12.1</td></tr>
<tr><td>49</td><td>Maine</td><td>0.9</td><td>19</td><td>Nebraska</td><td>11.5</td></tr>
<tr><td>26</td><td>Maryland</td><td>7.6</td><td>20</td><td>Delaware</td><td>9.2</td></tr>
<tr><td>15</td><td>Massachusetts</td><td>13.1</td><td>21</td><td>Wyoming</td><td>9.0</td></tr>
<tr><td>34</td><td>Michigan</td><td>4.4</td><td>22</td><td>Oklahoma</td><td>8.9</td></tr>
<tr><td>32</td><td>Minnesota</td><td>5.4</td><td>23</td><td>Georgia</td><td>8.7</td></tr>
<tr><td>47</td><td>Mississippi</td><td>1.4</td><td>24</td><td>North Carolina</td><td>8.4</td></tr>
<tr><td>38</td><td>Missouri</td><td>3.2</td><td>25</td><td>Virginia</td><td>7.7</td></tr>
<tr><td>41</td><td>Montana</td><td>2.4</td><td>26</td><td>Maryland</td><td>7.6</td></tr>
<tr><td>19</td><td>Nebraska</td><td>11.5</td><td>27</td><td>Arkansas</td><td>6.8</td></tr>
<tr><td>5</td><td>Nevada</td><td>33.6</td><td>28</td><td>Wisconsin</td><td>6.7</td></tr>
<tr><td>39</td><td>New Hampshire</td><td>2.8</td><td>29</td><td>Pennsylvania</td><td>6.4</td></tr>
<tr><td>10</td><td>New Jersey</td><td>18.2</td><td>30</td><td>Iowa</td><td>5.8</td></tr>
<tr><td>1</td><td>New Mexico</td><td>54.0</td><td>31</td><td>Indiana</td><td>5.7</td></tr>
<tr><td>8</td><td>New York</td><td>20.1</td><td>32</td><td>Minnesota</td><td>5.4</td></tr>
<tr><td>24</td><td>North Carolina</td><td>8.4</td><td>33</td><td>Hawaii</td><td>4.5</td></tr>
<tr><td>46</td><td>North Dakota</td><td>1.7</td><td>34</td><td>Michigan</td><td>4.4</td></tr>
<tr><td>41</td><td>Ohio</td><td>2.4</td><td>35</td><td>Alaska</td><td>4.2</td></tr>
<tr><td>22</td><td>Oklahoma</td><td>8.9</td><td>36</td><td>South Carolina</td><td>4.0</td></tr>
<tr><td>12</td><td>Oregon</td><td>15.9</td><td>37</td><td>Tennessee</td><td>3.8</td></tr>
<tr><td>29</td><td>Pennsylvania</td><td>6.4</td><td>38</td><td>Missouri</td><td>3.2</td></tr>
<tr><td>11</td><td>Rhode Island</td><td>17.3</td><td>39</td><td>Alabama</td><td>2.8</td></tr>
<tr><td>36</td><td>South Carolina</td><td>4.0</td><td>39</td><td>New Hampshire</td><td>2.8</td></tr>
<tr><td>45</td><td>South Dakota</td><td>2.0</td><td>41</td><td>Montana</td><td>2.4</td></tr>
<tr><td>37</td><td>Tennessee</td><td>3.8</td><td>41</td><td>Ohio</td><td>2.4</td></tr>
<tr><td>3</td><td>Texas</td><td>45.3</td><td>43</td><td>Kentucky</td><td>2.1</td></tr>
<tr><td>17</td><td>Utah</td><td>12.3</td><td>43</td><td>Louisiana</td><td>2.1</td></tr>
<tr><td>48</td><td>Vermont</td><td>1.0</td><td>45</td><td>South Dakota</td><td>2.0</td></tr>
<tr><td>25</td><td>Virginia</td><td>7.7</td><td>46</td><td>North Dakota</td><td>1.7</td></tr>
<tr><td>14</td><td>Washington</td><td>13.6</td><td>47</td><td>Mississippi</td><td>1.4</td></tr>
<tr><td>50</td><td>West Virginia</td><td>0.7</td><td>48</td><td>Vermont</td><td>1.0</td></tr>
<tr><td>28</td><td>Wisconsin</td><td>6.7</td><td>49</td><td>Maine</td><td>0.9</td></tr>
<tr><td>21</td><td>Wyoming</td><td>9.0</td><td>50</td><td>West Virginia</td><td>0.7</td></tr>
</table>

District of Columbia   10.6

Source: CQ Press using data from U.S. Department of Education, National Center for Education Statistics
"Public Elementary and Secondary School Student Enrollment, High School Completions and Staff"
(http://nces.ed.gov/pubs2007/2007352.pdf)
*For school year 2005-2006. Hispanic is an ethnic designation, not a race. People of any race can be Hispanic.

Percent of Public Elementary and Secondary Students Who Are Asian: 2006

National Percent = 4.6%*

RANK	STATE	PERCENT
45	Alabama	1.0
6	Alaska	6.9
22	Arizona	2.5
35	Arkansas	1.4
2	California	11.7
16	Colorado	3.3
14	Connecticut	3.6
20	Delaware	2.8
26	Florida	2.2
20	Georgia	2.8
1	Hawaii	72.8
32	Idaho	1.6
13	Illinois	3.8
42	Indiana	1.2
28	Iowa	1.9
24	Kansas	2.4
47	Kentucky	0.9
39	Louisiana	1.3
35	Maine	1.4
9	Maryland	5.2
12	Massachusetts	4.7
24	Michigan	2.4
8	Minnesota	5.7
49	Mississippi	0.8
32	Missouri	1.6
43	Montana	1.1
30	Nebraska	1.8
5	Nevada	7.3
28	New Hampshire	1.9
4	New Jersey	7.5
39	New Mexico	1.3
6	New York	6.9
27	North Carolina	2.1
47	North Dakota	0.9
35	Ohio	1.4
31	Oklahoma	1.7
11	Oregon	4.9
22	Pennsylvania	2.5
17	Rhode Island	3.1
39	South Carolina	1.3
45	South Dakota	1.0
35	Tennessee	1.4
17	Texas	3.1
17	Utah	3.1
32	Vermont	1.6
9	Virginia	5.2
3	Washington	8.1
50	West Virginia	0.6
14	Wisconsin	3.6
43	Wyoming	1.1

RANK	STATE	PERCENT
1	Hawaii	72.8
2	California	11.7
3	Washington	8.1
4	New Jersey	7.5
5	Nevada	7.3
6	Alaska	6.9
6	New York	6.9
8	Minnesota	5.7
9	Maryland	5.2
9	Virginia	5.2
11	Oregon	4.9
12	Massachusetts	4.7
13	Illinois	3.8
14	Connecticut	3.6
14	Wisconsin	3.6
16	Colorado	3.3
17	Rhode Island	3.1
17	Texas	3.1
17	Utah	3.1
20	Delaware	2.8
20	Georgia	2.8
22	Arizona	2.5
22	Pennsylvania	2.5
24	Kansas	2.4
24	Michigan	2.4
26	Florida	2.2
27	North Carolina	2.1
28	Iowa	1.9
28	New Hampshire	1.9
30	Nebraska	1.8
31	Oklahoma	1.7
32	Idaho	1.6
32	Missouri	1.6
32	Vermont	1.6
35	Arkansas	1.4
35	Maine	1.4
35	Ohio	1.4
35	Tennessee	1.4
39	Louisiana	1.3
39	New Mexico	1.3
39	South Carolina	1.3
42	Indiana	1.2
43	Montana	1.1
43	Wyoming	1.1
45	Alabama	1.0
45	South Dakota	1.0
47	Kentucky	0.9
47	North Dakota	0.9
49	Mississippi	0.8
50	West Virginia	0.6

District of Columbia	1.4

Source: CQ Press using data from U.S. Department of Education, National Center for Education Statistics
   "Public Elementary and Secondary School Student Enrollment, High School Completions and Staff"
   (http://nces.ed.gov/pubs2007/2007352.pdf)
*For school year 2005-2006. Includes Pacific Islander.

Percent of Public Elementary and Secondary Students
Who Are American Indian: 2006
National Percent = 1.2%*

ALPHA ORDER

RANK	STATE	PERCENT
21	Alabama	0.8
1	Alaska	26.6
7	Arizona	6.2
24	Arkansas	0.7
21	California	0.8
19	Colorado	1.2
30	Connecticut	0.4
34	Delaware	0.3
34	Florida	0.3
47	Georgia	0.1
25	Hawaii	0.6
13	Idaho	1.6
42	Illinois	0.2
34	Indiana	0.3
25	Iowa	0.6
15	Kansas	1.5
42	Kentucky	0.2
21	Louisiana	0.8
28	Maine	0.5
30	Maryland	0.4
34	Massachusetts	0.3
20	Michigan	1.0
11	Minnesota	2.1
42	Mississippi	0.2
30	Missouri	0.4
3	Montana	11.3
12	Nebraska	1.7
13	Nevada	1.6
34	New Hampshire	0.3
42	New Jersey	0.2
4	New Mexico	11.1
28	New York	0.5
18	North Carolina	1.4
6	North Dakota	8.6
47	Ohio	0.1
2	Oklahoma	18.9
10	Oregon	2.4
47	Pennsylvania	0.1
25	Rhode Island	0.6
34	South Carolina	0.3
5	South Dakota	10.5
42	Tennessee	0.2
34	Texas	0.3
15	Utah	1.5
30	Vermont	0.4
34	Virginia	0.3
9	Washington	2.7
47	West Virginia	0.1
15	Wisconsin	1.5
8	Wyoming	3.5

RANK ORDER

RANK	STATE	PERCENT
1	Alaska	26.6
2	Oklahoma	18.9
3	Montana	11.3
4	New Mexico	11.1
5	South Dakota	10.5
6	North Dakota	8.6
7	Arizona	6.2
8	Wyoming	3.5
9	Washington	2.7
10	Oregon	2.4
11	Minnesota	2.1
12	Nebraska	1.7
13	Idaho	1.6
13	Nevada	1.6
15	Kansas	1.5
15	Utah	1.5
15	Wisconsin	1.5
18	North Carolina	1.4
19	Colorado	1.2
20	Michigan	1.0
21	Alabama	0.8
21	California	0.8
21	Louisiana	0.8
24	Arkansas	0.7
25	Hawaii	0.6
25	Iowa	0.6
25	Rhode Island	0.6
28	Maine	0.5
28	New York	0.5
30	Connecticut	0.4
30	Maryland	0.4
30	Missouri	0.4
30	Vermont	0.4
34	Delaware	0.3
34	Florida	0.3
34	Indiana	0.3
34	Massachusetts	0.3
34	New Hampshire	0.3
34	South Carolina	0.3
34	Texas	0.3
34	Virginia	0.3
42	Illinois	0.2
42	Kentucky	0.2
42	Mississippi	0.2
42	New Jersey	0.2
42	Tennessee	0.2
47	Georgia	0.1
47	Ohio	0.1
47	Pennsylvania	0.1
47	West Virginia	0.1

District of Columbia — 0.1

Source: CQ Press using data from U.S. Department of Education, National Center for Education Statistics
"Public Elementary and Secondary School Student Enrollment, High School Completions and Staff"
(http://nces.ed.gov/pubs2007/2007352.pdf)
*For school year 2005-2006. Includes Alaska Native.

Children Enrolled in State Funded Pre-Kindergarten Programs in 2007

National Total = 1,008,597 Children*

ALPHA ORDER

RANK	STATE	CHILDREN	% of USA
36	Alabama	1,062	0.1%
39	Alaska	0	0.0%
27	Arizona	5,076	0.5%
20	Arkansas	12,216	1.2%
4	California	82,572	8.2%
21	Colorado	11,868	1.2%
23	Connecticut	8,532	0.8%
38	Delaware	843	0.1%
2	Florida	124,390	12.3%
6	Georgia	74,155	7.4%
39	Hawaii	0	0.0%
39	Idaho	0	0.0%
5	Illinois	79,819	7.9%
39	Indiana	0	0.0%
34	Iowa	2,033	0.2%
25	Kansas	5,971	0.6%
13	Kentucky	21,623	2.1%
16	Louisiana	14,543	1.4%
32	Maine	2,263	0.2%
9	Maryland	25,674	2.5%
15	Massachusetts	15,200	1.5%
11	Michigan	21,801	2.2%
33	Minnesota	2,109	0.2%
39	Mississippi	0	0.0%
28	Missouri	4,972	0.5%
39	Montana	0	0.0%
35	Nebraska	1,473	0.1%
37	Nevada	939	0.1%
39	New Hampshire	0	0.0%
7	New Jersey	45,499	4.5%
31	New Mexico	2,739	0.3%
3	New York	84,660	8.4%
14	North Carolina	17,961	1.8%
39	North Dakota	0	0.0%
24	Ohio	6,849	0.7%
8	Oklahoma	34,375	3.4%
30	Oregon	3,438	0.3%
17	Pennsylvania	13,584	1.3%
39	Rhode Island	0	0.0%
12	South Carolina	21,716	2.2%
39	South Dakota	0	0.0%
18	Tennessee	13,046	1.3%
1	Texas	187,238	18.6%
39	Utah	0	0.0%
29	Vermont	3,936	0.4%
19	Virginia	12,501	1.2%
26	Washington	5,834	0.6%
22	West Virginia	10,659	1.1%
10	Wisconsin	25,428	2.5%
39	Wyoming	0	0.0%

RANK ORDER

RANK	STATE	CHILDREN	% of USA
1	Texas	187,238	18.6%
2	Florida	124,390	12.3%
3	New York	84,660	8.4%
4	California	82,572	8.2%
5	Illinois	79,819	7.9%
6	Georgia	74,155	7.4%
7	New Jersey	45,499	4.5%
8	Oklahoma	34,375	3.4%
9	Maryland	25,674	2.5%
10	Wisconsin	25,428	2.5%
11	Michigan	21,801	2.2%
12	South Carolina	21,716	2.2%
13	Kentucky	21,623	2.1%
14	North Carolina	17,961	1.8%
15	Massachusetts	15,200	1.5%
16	Louisiana	14,543	1.4%
17	Pennsylvania	13,584	1.3%
18	Tennessee	13,046	1.3%
19	Virginia	12,501	1.2%
20	Arkansas	12,216	1.2%
21	Colorado	11,868	1.2%
22	West Virginia	10,659	1.1%
23	Connecticut	8,532	0.8%
24	Ohio	6,849	0.7%
25	Kansas	5,971	0.6%
26	Washington	5,834	0.6%
27	Arizona	5,076	0.5%
28	Missouri	4,972	0.5%
29	Vermont	3,936	0.4%
30	Oregon	3,438	0.3%
31	New Mexico	2,739	0.3%
32	Maine	2,263	0.2%
33	Minnesota	2,109	0.2%
34	Iowa	2,033	0.2%
35	Nebraska	1,473	0.1%
36	Alabama	1,062	0.1%
37	Nevada	939	0.1%
38	Delaware	843	0.1%
39	Alaska	0	0.0%
39	Hawaii	0	0.0%
39	Idaho	0	0.0%
39	Indiana	0	0.0%
39	Mississippi	0	0.0%
39	Montana	0	0.0%
39	New Hampshire	0	0.0%
39	North Dakota	0	0.0%
39	Rhode Island	0	0.0%
39	South Dakota	0	0.0%
39	Utah	0	0.0%
39	Wyoming	0	0.0%
	District of Columbia**	NA	NA

Source: Rutgers, The State University of New Jersey, National Institute for Early Education Research
   "The State of Preschool: 2007 State Preschool Yearbook" (http://nieer.org/yearbook/)
*Children age 3 and 4 for school year 2006-2007.
**Not available.

Percent of Children Enrolled in State Funded
Pre-Kindergarten Programs in 2007
National Percent = 12.5%*

RANK	STATE	PERCENT
38	Alabama	0.9
39	Alaska	0.0
33	Arizona	2.7
14	Arkansas	16.1
22	California	7.9
18	Colorado	8.8
16	Connecticut	10.0
28	Delaware	3.7
3	Florida	28.3
4	Georgia	26.6
39	Hawaii	0.0
39	Idaho	0.0
7	Illinois	22.6
39	Indiana	0.0
33	Iowa	2.7
23	Kansas	7.8
9	Kentucky	19.9
15	Louisiana	12.3
21	Maine	8.1
12	Maryland	17.6
17	Massachusetts	9.8
19	Michigan	8.5
36	Minnesota	1.6
39	Mississippi	0.0
31	Missouri	3.3
39	Montana	0.0
32	Nebraska	3.0
37	Nevada	1.3
39	New Hampshire	0.0
8	New Jersey	20.1
26	New Mexico	4.9
13	New York	17.5
24	North Carolina	7.4
39	North Dakota	0.0
35	Ohio	2.3
1	Oklahoma	34.2
28	Oregon	3.7
27	Pennsylvania	4.7
39	Rhode Island	0.0
10	South Carolina	19.3
39	South Dakota	0.0
20	Tennessee	8.3
6	Texas	24.7
39	Utah	0.0
2	Vermont	30.1
25	Virginia	6.3
30	Washington	3.6
5	West Virginia	25.5
11	Wisconsin	18.4
39	Wyoming	0.0

RANK	STATE	PERCENT
1	Oklahoma	34.2
2	Vermont	30.1
3	Florida	28.3
4	Georgia	26.6
5	West Virginia	25.5
6	Texas	24.7
7	Illinois	22.6
8	New Jersey	20.1
9	Kentucky	19.9
10	South Carolina	19.3
11	Wisconsin	18.4
12	Maryland	17.6
13	New York	17.5
14	Arkansas	16.1
15	Louisiana	12.3
16	Connecticut	10.0
17	Massachusetts	9.8
18	Colorado	8.8
19	Michigan	8.5
20	Tennessee	8.3
21	Maine	8.1
22	California	7.9
23	Kansas	7.8
24	North Carolina	7.4
25	Virginia	6.3
26	New Mexico	4.9
27	Pennsylvania	4.7
28	Delaware	3.7
28	Oregon	3.7
30	Washington	3.6
31	Missouri	3.3
32	Nebraska	3.0
33	Arizona	2.7
33	Iowa	2.7
35	Ohio	2.3
36	Minnesota	1.6
37	Nevada	1.3
38	Alabama	0.9
39	Alaska	0.0
39	Hawaii	0.0
39	Idaho	0.0
39	Indiana	0.0
39	Mississippi	0.0
39	Montana	0.0
39	New Hampshire	0.0
39	North Dakota	0.0
39	Rhode Island	0.0
39	South Dakota	0.0
39	Utah	0.0
39	Wyoming	0.0
	District of Columbia**	NA

Source: Rutgers, The State University of New Jersey, National Institute for Early Education Research
"The State of Preschool: 2007 State Preschool Yearbook" (http://nieer.org/yearbook/)
*Children age 3 and 4 for school year 2006-2007.
**Not available.

Head Start Program Enrollment in 2007

National Total = 908,412 Children*

ALPHA ORDER					RANK ORDER			

RANK	STATE	CHILDREN	% of USA		RANK	STATE	CHILDREN	% of USA
15	Alabama	16,374	1.8%		1	California	98,353	10.8%
49	Alaska	1,583	0.2%		2	Texas	67,630	7.4%
22	Arizona	13,175	1.5%		3	New York	48,818	5.4%
26	Arkansas	10,778	1.2%		4	Illinois	39,640	4.4%
1	California	98,353	10.8%		5	Ohio	37,940	4.2%
29	Colorado	9,820	1.1%		6	Florida	35,457	3.9%
35	Connecticut	7,076	0.8%		7	Pennsylvania	35,362	3.9%
46	Delaware	2,071	0.2%		8	Michigan	35,067	3.9%
6	Florida	35,457	3.9%		9	Mississippi	26,657	2.9%
10	Georgia	23,436	2.6%		10	Georgia	23,436	2.6%
40	Hawaii	3,049	0.3%		11	Louisiana	21,592	2.4%
41	Idaho	2,943	0.3%		12	North Carolina	18,963	2.1%
4	Illinois	39,640	4.4%		13	Missouri	17,456	1.9%
18	Indiana	14,213	1.6%		14	Tennessee	16,397	1.8%
32	Iowa	7,710	0.8%		15	Alabama	16,374	1.8%
31	Kansas	8,178	0.9%		16	Kentucky	16,070	1.8%
16	Kentucky	16,070	1.8%		17	New Jersey	14,854	1.6%
11	Louisiana	21,592	2.4%		18	Indiana	14,213	1.6%
38	Maine	3,871	0.4%		19	Wisconsin	13,538	1.5%
27	Maryland	10,347	1.1%		20	Virginia	13,518	1.5%
23	Massachusetts	12,807	1.4%		21	Oklahoma	13,474	1.5%
8	Michigan	35,067	3.9%		22	Arizona	13,175	1.5%
28	Minnesota	10,332	1.1%		23	Massachusetts	12,807	1.4%
9	Mississippi	26,657	2.9%		24	South Carolina	12,248	1.3%
13	Missouri	17,456	1.9%		25	Washington	11,278	1.2%
42	Montana	2,919	0.3%		26	Arkansas	10,778	1.2%
37	Nebraska	5,080	0.6%		27	Maryland	10,347	1.1%
44	Nevada	2,754	0.3%		28	Minnesota	10,332	1.1%
48	New Hampshire	1,632	0.2%		29	Colorado	9,820	1.1%
17	New Jersey	14,854	1.6%		30	Oregon	8,814	1.0%
34	New Mexico	7,279	0.8%		31	Kansas	8,178	0.9%
3	New York	48,818	5.4%		32	Iowa	7,710	0.8%
12	North Carolina	18,963	2.1%		33	West Virginia	7,682	0.8%
45	North Dakota	2,353	0.3%		34	New Mexico	7,279	0.8%
5	Ohio	37,940	4.2%		35	Connecticut	7,076	0.8%
21	Oklahoma	13,474	1.5%		36	Utah	5,400	0.6%
30	Oregon	8,814	1.0%		37	Nebraska	5,080	0.6%
7	Pennsylvania	35,362	3.9%		38	Maine	3,871	0.4%
39	Rhode Island	3,104	0.3%		39	Rhode Island	3,104	0.3%
24	South Carolina	12,248	1.3%		40	Hawaii	3,049	0.3%
43	South Dakota	2,827	0.3%		41	Idaho	2,943	0.3%
14	Tennessee	16,397	1.8%		42	Montana	2,919	0.3%
2	Texas	67,630	7.4%		43	South Dakota	2,827	0.3%
36	Utah	5,400	0.6%		44	Nevada	2,754	0.3%
50	Vermont	1,552	0.2%		45	North Dakota	2,353	0.3%
20	Virginia	13,518	1.5%		46	Delaware	2,071	0.2%
25	Washington	11,278	1.2%		47	Wyoming	1,840	0.2%
33	West Virginia	7,682	0.8%		48	New Hampshire	1,632	0.2%
19	Wisconsin	13,538	1.5%		49	Alaska	1,583	0.2%
47	Wyoming	1,840	0.2%		50	Vermont	1,552	0.2%
						District of Columbia	3,403	0.4%

Source: U.S. Department of Health and Human Services, Administration for Children and Families
    "Head Start Fact Sheet" (http://www.acf.hhs.gov/programs/ohs/about/fy2008.html)
*For fiscal year 2007. National total includes 59,013 enrollees in Migrant and Native American programs and 40,685 enrollees in U.S. territories.

Private Elementary and Secondary School Enrollment in 2006

National Total = 5,057,520 Students*

ALPHA ORDER

RANK	STATE	ENROLLMENT	% of USA
22	Alabama	77,204	1.5%
49	Alaska	5,890	0.1%
28	Arizona	50,013	1.0%
34	Arkansas	30,876	0.6%
1	California	614,861	12.2%
29	Colorado	49,515	1.0%
24	Connecticut	66,022	1.3%
38	Delaware	24,869	0.5%
3	Florida	323,302	6.4%
12	Georgia	126,425	2.5%
36	Hawaii	29,721	0.6%
45	Idaho	11,140	0.2%
5	Illinois	261,751	5.2%
17	Indiana	116,816	2.3%
25	Iowa	54,147	1.1%
31	Kansas	41,968	0.8%
23	Kentucky	67,262	1.3%
14	Louisiana	124,810	2.5%
42	Maine	18,670	0.4%
9	Maryland	143,316	2.8%
11	Massachusetts	130,998	2.6%
10	Michigan	141,615	2.8%
21	Minnesota	90,811	1.8%
27	Mississippi	50,496	1.0%
15	Missouri	122,890	2.4%
33	Montana**	32,259	0.6%
32	Nebraska	38,239	0.8%
41	Nevada	19,879	0.4%
39	New Hampshire	21,711	0.4%
8	New Jersey	196,541	3.9%
40	New Mexico	21,130	0.4%
2	New York	447,627	8.9%
18	North Carolina	102,333	2.0%
48	North Dakota	6,279	0.1%
7	Ohio	222,738	4.4%
35	Oklahoma	29,899	0.6%
30	Oregon	49,117	1.0%
4	Pennsylvania	284,944	5.6%
37	Rhode Island	25,976	0.5%
26	South Carolina	52,070	1.0%
46	South Dakota	10,961	0.2%
20	Tennessee	91,794	1.8%
6	Texas	228,979	4.5%
43	Utah	16,269	0.3%
47	Vermont	10,295	0.2%
16	Virginia	120,241	2.4%
19	Washington	93,695	1.9%
44	West Virginia	14,290	0.3%
13	Wisconsin	125,050	2.5%
50	Wyoming	1,677	0.0%

RANK ORDER

RANK	STATE	ENROLLMENT	% of USA
1	California	614,861	12.2%
2	New York	447,627	8.9%
3	Florida	323,302	6.4%
4	Pennsylvania	284,944	5.6%
5	Illinois	261,751	5.2%
6	Texas	228,979	4.5%
7	Ohio	222,738	4.4%
8	New Jersey	196,541	3.9%
9	Maryland	143,316	2.8%
10	Michigan	141,615	2.8%
11	Massachusetts	130,998	2.6%
12	Georgia	126,425	2.5%
13	Wisconsin	125,050	2.5%
14	Louisiana	124,810	2.5%
15	Missouri	122,890	2.4%
16	Virginia	120,241	2.4%
17	Indiana	116,816	2.3%
18	North Carolina	102,333	2.0%
19	Washington	93,695	1.9%
20	Tennessee	91,794	1.8%
21	Minnesota	90,811	1.8%
22	Alabama	77,204	1.5%
23	Kentucky	67,262	1.3%
24	Connecticut	66,022	1.3%
25	Iowa	54,147	1.1%
26	South Carolina	52,070	1.0%
27	Mississippi	50,496	1.0%
28	Arizona	50,013	1.0%
29	Colorado	49,515	1.0%
30	Oregon	49,117	1.0%
31	Kansas	41,968	0.8%
32	Nebraska	38,239	0.8%
33	Montana**	32,259	0.6%
34	Arkansas	30,876	0.6%
35	Oklahoma	29,899	0.6%
36	Hawaii	29,721	0.6%
37	Rhode Island	25,976	0.5%
38	Delaware	24,869	0.5%
39	New Hampshire	21,711	0.4%
40	New Mexico	21,130	0.4%
41	Nevada	19,879	0.4%
42	Maine	18,670	0.4%
43	Utah	16,269	0.3%
44	West Virginia	14,290	0.3%
45	Idaho	11,140	0.2%
46	South Dakota	10,961	0.2%
47	Vermont	10,295	0.2%
48	North Dakota	6,279	0.1%
49	Alaska	5,890	0.1%
50	Wyoming	1,677	0.0%
	District of Columbia	18,138	0.4%

Source: U.S. Department of Education, Institute of Education Sciences
"Characteristics of Private Schools in the United States" (http://nces.ed.gov/pubs2008/2008315.pdf)
*For school year 2005-2006.
**Interpret data for these states with caution.

Glossary

Achievement levels: Performance standards that provide a context for interpreting student performance on the National Assessment of Educational Progress (NAEP) student assessments, based on recommendations from panels of educators and members of the public. The levels, which include Basic, Proficient, and Advanced, measure what students should know at each grade assessed.

ACT: American College Testing Program. Founded in 1959, this is a national college entrance-testing program administered by ACT Inc., an independent, not-for-profit organization. Students are assessed in English, math, reading, and science. There is an optional writing test. The ACT score range is 1 to 36.

Adequate Yearly Progress (AYP): A statewide accountability system mandated by the No Child Left Behind Act of 2001 which requires each state to ensure that all schools and districts make progress in reading, math, graduation rates (for high schools) and attendance rates (for junior high/middle schools.)

Administrative support staff: Comprised of (1) school district staff who provide direct support to superintendents, assistant superintendents, and other local agency administrators; and (2) school building support staff who work to support the teaching and administrative duties of the office of the principal or department chairpersons.

Advanced: One of the three NAEP achievement levels, denoting superior performance at each grade assessed.

Advanced Placement (A.P.) courses: A course designed to prepare students for the Advanced Placement subject assessments administered by The College Board.

Alternative education schools: Schools that provide nontraditional education and address the needs of students that typically cannot be met in the regular school setting.

Averaged freshman graduation rate: A measurement of the percentage of high school students who graduate on time. The rate uses enrollment data for a freshman class and the number of diplomas awarded four years later. The incoming freshman class is estimated by summing the enrollment in eighth grade in one year, ninth grade for the next year, and tenth grade for the year after and then dividing by three. The averaged freshman graduation rate is considered an interim step in the process to develop a more comprehensive and accurate assessment of how many students graduate from high school.

Basic: One of the three National Assessment of Educational Progress (NAEP) achievement levels, denoting partial mastery of prerequisite knowledge and skills that are fundamental for proficient work at each grade assessed.

Board certified teachers: Teachers who have demonstrated their knowledge and skills through a series of performance-based assessments that include student work samples, videotapes, and rigorous analyses of their classroom teaching and student learning.

Capital outlay: Direct expenditure for construction of buildings, roads, and other improvements undertaken either on a contractual basis by private contractors or through a government's own staff (i.e., force account); for purchases of equipment, land, and existing structures; and for payments on capital leases. Includes amounts for additions, replacements, and major alterations to fixed works and structures. However, expenditure for maintenance and repairs to such works and structures is classified as current spending.

Charter schools: Schools that provide free public elementary/secondary education under a charter granted by the state legislature or other appropriate authority.

Child nutrition programs: Payments by the Department of Agriculture for the National School Lunch, Special Milk, School Breakfast, and Ala Carte programs. Excludes the value of donated commodities.

Class size: Number of students taught by a teacher in a self-contained classroom, or average number of students per class taught by a teacher who provides departmentalized instruction.

Common Core of Data: A group of surveys administered by the National Center for Education Statistics that acquire and maintain public elementary and secondary education data from the 50 states, District of Columbia, and outlying areas.

Compensatory program revenue: Revenue for "at risk" or other economically disadvantaged students including migratory children. Also includes monies from state programs directed toward the attainment of basic skills and categorical education excellence and quality education programs that provide more than staff enhancements such as materials, resource centers, and equipment.

Current expenditures: Direct expenditures for salaries, employee benefits, purchased professional and technical services, purchased property and other services, and supplies. It includes gross school system expenditure for instruction, support services, and non-instructional functions. It excludes expenditure for debt service, capital outlay, and reimbursement to other governments (including other school systems).

Dropout rate: The high school dropout rate shown in *Education State Rankings* is an "event" dropout rate. It measures the proportion of students who leave school each year without completing a high school program. This annual measure of recent dropout occurrences provides important information about how effective educators are in keeping students enrolled in school.

Elementary teachers: The full-time equivalent count of the number of teachers in a state who are of general level instruction classified by state and local practice as elementary and composed of any span of grades not above grade 8. Excludes pre-kindergarten and kindergarten teachers.

Employee benefit expenditures: Amounts paid by a school system for fringe benefits. These amounts are not included in salaries and wages paid directly to employees. Includes contributions on behalf of employees for retirement coverage, social security, group health and life insurance, tuition reimbursement, workers's compensation, and unemployment compensation.

Federal aid direct: Aid from project grants for programs such as Impact Aid, Indian Education, Bilingual Education, Head Start, Follow Through, Magnet Schools, Dropout Demonstration Assistance, and Gifted and Talented.

Federal aid distributed by state governments: Aid from formula grants distributed through state government agencies. Includes revenue from programs such as child nutrition, Title I, special education, vocational, and other federal aid distributed by state governments.

Formula assistance: Revenue from general non-categorical state assistance programs such as foundation, minimum or basic formula support, apportionment, equalization, flat or block grants, and state public school fund distributions. This category also includes revenue dedicated from major state taxes, such as income and sales taxes.

Free or reduced-price meal eligibility: Number of students in a school who are eligible to receive free or reduced price meals under the National School Lunch Act.

General administration expenditures: Spending for board of education and executive administration (office of the superintendent) services.

Graduates: High school students who received diplomas during the previous school year and subsequent summer school. A diploma recognizes that the recipient has successfully completed a state's prescribed course of studies at the secondary school level.

Graduation rate: The graduation rates shown in *Education State Rankings* compare numbers of public high school graduates with 9th grade enrollment four years prior. These are basic completion ratios that exclude ungraded pupils and are not adjusted for interstate migration or students switching to private schools. They should be viewed as estimates. The U.S. Department of Education has begun to issue averaged freshman graduation rates (see definition above) as an interim step in the process to develop a more comprehensive and accurate assessment of how many students graduate from high school.

Head Start: The federal government's preschool program for disadvantaged children. Its goal is to increase school readiness of young children in low income families.

High schools: Schools with a low grade of 7 to 12 and must extend through grade 12.

Highly Qualified Teachers: Under the No Child Left Behind Act, highly qualified teachers must hold a bachelor's degree, demonstrate competence in his or her academic subject, obtain full state certification or pass the state licensure exam, and hold a license to teach.

IDEA: The Individuals with Disabilities Education Act. Originally passed in 1975 as the Education for All Handicapped Children Act, the IDEA supports states and localities in protecting the rights of, meeting the individual needs of, and improving the educational results for infants, toddlers, children, and youth with disabilities and their families.

IEP: Individualized Education Programs as defined by the Individuals with Disabilities Education Act (IDEA)—Part B. Each public school student who receives special education and related services must have an IEP. Each IEP is designed specifically for that student. It provides a plan for teachers, parents, school administrators, related services personnel, and students (where appropriate) to improve educational results for children with disabilities.

Instruction expenditures: Includes payments from all funds for salaries, employee benefits (paid by school system only if under "current operation" or paid by both school and state if under "current spending"), supplies, materials, and contractual services. It excludes capital outlay, debt service, and inter-fund transfers. Instruction covers regular, special, and vocational programs offered in both the regular school year and summer school. It excludes instructional, student, and other support activities, as well as adult education, community services, and student enterprise activities.

Instructional aides: The full-time equivalent count in a state for the number of staff members assigned to assist a teachers in activities requiring minor decisions regarding students, and in such activities as monitoring, conducting rote exercises, operating equipment and clerking and includes only paid staff.

Instructional coordinators and supervisors: The full-time equivalent count in a state for the number of staff supervising instructional programs at the school or district of sub-district level.

Instructional staff support expenditures: Spending for supervision of instruction service improvements, curriculum development, instructional staff training, and media, library, audiovisual, television, and computer-assisted instruction services.

Kindergarten teachers: The full-time equivalent count of the number of teachers in a state who teach a group or class that is part of a public school program and is taught during the year preceding the first grade.

Librarians: The full-time equivalent count in a state of professional staff members and supervisors who are assigned specific duties and school time for professional library and media service activities.

Limited English proficiency students: Students served in appropriate programs of language assistance (English as a Second Language, High Intensity Language Training, bilingual education). Does not include students enrolled in programs to learn a language other than English. Students may be referred to as English Language Learners (ELL).

Magnet schools: Schools that are designed to attract students of different racial/ethnic backgrounds for the purpose of reducing racial isolation, or to provide an academic or social focus on a specific theme (ex. performing arts.)

Membership count: Annual headcount of students enrolled in school on October 1st.

Middle schools: Schools with a low grade of 4 to 7 and a high grade ranging from 4 to 9. (A 4th grade center is a middle school.)

NAEP: National Assessment of Educational Progress. Since 1969, this program, administered by the U.S. Department of Education's National Center for Education Statistics, has assessed students on their knowledge of reading, mathematics, science, writing, U.S. history, civics, geography, and the arts.

No Child Left Behind: The federal government's reauthorization of the Elementary and Secondary Education Act. Passed in 2001, the law aims at bringing reform and greater accountability to public elementary and secondary education in the United States.

Operation and maintenance of facilities expenditures: Spending for building services (heating, electricity, air conditioning, property insurance), care and upkeep of grounds and equipment, non-student transportation vehicle operation and maintenance, and security services.

Other high school completer: Student who has received a certificate of attendance or other certificate of completion in lieu of a diploma.

"Other" schools: Schools that have grade configurations other than those of primary, middle, and high school. Ungraded schools are included.

Parent government contributions: Tax receipts and other amounts appropriated by a parent government and transferred to its dependent school system. Excludes intergovernmental revenue, current charges, and miscellaneous general revenue.

Pre-kindergarten teachers: The full-time equivalent count of the number of teachers in a state who teach a group or class that is part of a public school program and is taught during the year or years preceding kindergarten.

Primary schools: Schools with a low grade of pre-kindergarten through grade 3 and a high grade of up to 8.

Proficient: One of the three NAEP achievement levels, representing solid academic performance for each grade assessed. Students reaching this level have demonstrated competency over challenging subject matter, including subject-matter knowledge, application of such knowledge to real-world situations, and analytical skills appropriate to the subject matter.

Property taxes: Taxes conditioned on ownership of property and measured by its value. Includes general property taxes relating to property as a whole, taxed at a single rate or at classified rates according to the class of property. Property refers to real property (e.g., land and structures), as well as personal property. Personal property can be either tangible (e.g., automobiles and boats) or intangible (e.g., bank accounts and stocks and bonds).

Public schools: Schools that provide education services to students, have an assigned administrator, receive public funds as their primary support, and are operated by an education agency.

Pupil support service expenditures: Spending for attendance record keeping, social work, student accounting, counseling, student appraisal, record maintenance, and placement services. This category also includes medical, dental, nursing, psychological, and speech services.

Pupil–teacher ratio: The total number of students divided by the number of full-time equivalent teachers in schools.

Pupil transportation service expenditures: Spending for the transportation of public school students including vehicle operation, monitoring riders, and vehicle servicing and maintenance.

Race/Ethnicity categories: Student race and ethnicity categories are American Indian/Alaskan Native; Asian/Pacific Islander; Black, not Hispanic; Hispanic and White, not Hispanic. They are mutually exclusive. "Minority" students include all categories but White, not Hispanic.

Regular school districts: Agencies responsible for providing free public education for school-age children residing within their jurisdiction. This category excludes local supervisory unions that provide management services for a group of associated school districts, although it includes the "component" districts that receive these services.

Regular schools: Schools that do not focus primarily on special, vocational, or alternative education, although they may offer these programs in addition to the regular curriculum.

Revenue: All amounts of money received by a school system from external sources net of refunds and other correcting transactions other than from issuance of debt, liquidation of investments, or as agency and private trust transactions. Note that revenue excludes noncash transactions, such as receipt of services, commodities, or other "receipts in-kind."

Salaries and wages: Amounts paid for compensation of school system officers and employees. Consists of gross compensation before deductions for withheld taxes, retirement contributions, or other purposes.

SAT: Formerly known as the Scholastic Aptitude Test, the SAT is a national college entrance exam that assesses student reasoning based on knowledge and skills developed by the student in school coursework. The SAT assesses students in reading and mathematics and, as of March of 2005, includes a writing assessment. Each subject area is scored separately on a scale from 200 to 800. The SAT is administered by The College Board, a not-for-profit membership organization founded in 1900.

School administration expenditures: Spending for the office of principal services.

School administrators: The full-time equivalent count in a state of staff members whose activities are concerned with directing and managing the operation of a particular school.

School district administrators: The full-time equivalent count in a state of local education agency superintendents, deputy and assistant superintendents, and other persons with district-wide responsibilities such as business managers and administrative assistants.

Secondary school teachers: The full-time equivalent count of the number of teachers in a state who are of general level instruc-

tion classified by state and local practice as secondary and composed of any span of grades beginning with the next grade following the elementary grades and ending with or below grade 12.

Special education programs: Revenue for the education of physically and mentally disabled students.

Special education schools: Schools that focus primarily on special education, with materials and instructional approaches adapted to meet students' needs.

Support services expenditures: Spending for general administration, instructional staff support, operation and maintenance of plant, pupil support services, pupil transportation services, school administration, other support services and nonspecified support services. Excluded is spending for capital outlay, debt service, and interfund transfers.

Support staff: Comprised of library, student support services, and all other support staff. Library support staff oversee library or media services such as preparing, caring for, and making available to members of the instructional staff the equipment, films, filmstrips, transparencies, tapes, TV programs, and similar materials. Student support services staff provide noninstructional services to students.

Talented/gifted program: Programs designed for students with specifically identified talents or exceptional academic achievement.

Title I schools: Schools designated as eligible for programs authorized by Title I of Public Law 107-110, the Elementary and Secondary Education Act of 2002. This federally-funded program provides educational services, such as remedial reading or mathematics, to children who live in areas with high concentrations of low-income families.

Title I school-wide schools: Schools in which all students enrolled are designated as eligible for programs authorized by Title I of Public Law 107-110, the Elementary and Secondary Education Act of 2002. This federally-funded program provides educational services, such as remedial reading or mathematics, to children who live in areas with high concentrations of low-income families.

Transportation programs: Payments for various state transportation aid programs, such as those that compensate the school system for part of its transportation expense and those that provide reimbursement for transportation salaries or school bus purchase.

Ungraded students: Students who are assigned to programs or classes without standard grade designation. States are requested to report teachers of ungraded classes even if all students are assigned a grade level of record. In many states, ungraded students are special education students.

Vocational education schools: Schools that focus primarily on vocational, technical, or career education and provide education or training in at least one semi-skilled or technical occupation.

Sources

ACT, Inc.
500 ACT Drive, PO Box 168
Iowa City IA 52243-0168
319-337-1000
Internet: www.act.org

Administration for Children and Families
370 L'Enfant Promenade, SW
Washington DC 20201
202-401-9215
Internet: www.acf.hhs.gov

Budget Office
U.S. Department of Education
400 Maryland Avenue, SW
Washington DC 20202
800-USA-LEARN
Internet: www.ed.gov/about/overview/budget/index.html

Bureau of Labor Statistics
2 Massachusetts Avenue, NE
Washington DC 20212
202-691-5200
Internet: www.bls.gov

Bureau of the Census
Governments Division
Elementary and Secondary Education Statistics Branch
GOVS, CENHQ, Room 6K060
Washington DC 20233
800-622-6193
Internet: www.census.gov

Centers for Disease Control and Prevention
Youth Risk Behavior Surveillance System
1600 Clifton Road
Atlanta GA 30333
800-311-3435
Internet: www.cdc.gov/HealthyYouth/yrbs

College Board
45 Columbus Avenue
New York NY 10023-6992
212-713-8000
Internet: www.collegeboard.com

Federal Bureau of Investigation
Criminal Justice Information Services Division
1000 Custer Hollow Road
Clarksburg WV 26306
304-625-4995
Internet: www.fbi.gov

Head Start Bureau
Administration for Children and Families
370 L'Enfant Promenade, SW
Washington DC 20201
866-763-6481
Internet: www.acf.hhs.gov/programs/hsb/

National Board for Professional Teaching Standards
1525 Wilson Blvd.
Arlington VA 22209
800-228-3224
Internet: www.nbpts.org

National Center for Education Statistics
U.S. Department of Education
1990 K Street, NW
Washington DC 20006
202-502-7300
Internet: http://nces.ed.gov

National Education Association
1201 16th Street, NW
Washington DC 20036
202-833-4000
Internet: www.nea.org

National Institute for Early Education Research
Rutgers University
120 Albany Street, Suite 500
New Brunswick, NJ 08901
732-932-4350
Internet: www.nieer.org

National Library of Education
U.S. Department of Education
400 Maryland Ave, SW
Washington DC 20202
800-424-1616
Internet: www.ed.gov/NLE (case sensitive)

Office of Juvenile Justice and Delinquency Prevention
810 Seventh Street, NW
Washington DC 20531
202-307-5911
Internet: http://ojjdp.ncjrs.org

Special Education and Rehabilitative Services
U.S. Department of Education
400 Maryland Ave, SW
Washington DC 20202
800-872-5327 or 202-245-7868
Internet: www.ed.gov/about/offices/list/osers/index.html

Index